Lecture Notes in Computer Science   13537

Editors
Shiqi Yu (iD)
Southern University of Science
and Technology
Shenzhen, China

Pong C. Yuen (iD)
Hong Kong Baptist University
Hong Kong, China

Tieniu Tan
Institute of Automation
Chinese Academy of Sciences
Beijing, China

Jianhuang Lai
Sun Yat-sen University
Guangzhou, China

Zhaoxiang Zhang
Institute of Automation
Chinese Academy of Sciences
Beijing, China

Junwei Han
Northwestern Polytechnical University
Xi'an, China

Yike Guo
Hong Kong Baptist University
Hong Kong, China

Jianguo Zhang (iD)
Southern University of Science
and Technology
Shenzhen, China

ISSN 0302-9743   ISSN 1611-3349 (electronic)
Lecture Notes in Computer Science
ISBN 978-3-031-18915-9   ISBN 978-3-031-18916-6 (eBook)
https://doi.org/10.1007/978-3-031-18916-6

Preface

Welcome to the proceedings of the 5th Chinese Conference on Pattern Recognition and Computer Vision (PRCV 2022) held in Shenzhen, China!

PRCV was established to further boost the impact of the Chinese community in pattern recognition and computer vision, which are two core areas of artificial intelligence, and further improve the quality of academic communication. Accordingly, PRCV is co-sponsored by four major academic societies of China: the China Society of Image and Graphics (CSIG), the Chinese Association for Artificial Intelligence (CAAI), the China Computer Federation (CCF), and the Chinese Association of Automation (CAA).

PRCV aims at providing an interactive communication platform for researchers from academia and from industry. It promotes not only academic exchange but also communication between academia and industry. In order to keep track of the frontier of academic trends and share the latest research achievements, innovative ideas, and scientific methods, international and local leading experts and professors are invited to deliver keynote speeches, introducing the latest advances in theories and methods in the fields of pattern recognition and computer vision.

PRCV 2022 was hosted by the Southern University of Science and Technology and Shenzhen Polytechnic. We received 564 full submissions. Each submission was reviewed by at least three reviewers selected from the Program Committee and other qualified researchers. Based on the reviewers' reports, 233 papers were finally accepted for presentation at the conference, comprising 40 oral presentations and 193 posters. The acceptance rate was 41%. The conference took place during November 4–7, 2022, and the proceedings are published in this volume in Springer's Lecture Notes in Computer Science (LNCS) series.

We are grateful to the keynote speakers, Alan Yuille from Johns Hopkins University, USA, Kyoung Mu Lee from the Korea National Open University, South Korea, Zhengyou Zhang from the Tencent AI Lab, China, Yaonan Wang from Hunan University, China, Wen Gao from the Pengcheng Laboratory and Peking University, China, Hong Qiao from the Institute of Automation, Chinese Academy of Sciences, China, and Muming Poo from the Institute of Neuroscience, Chinese Academy of Sciences, China.

We give sincere thanks to the authors of all submitted papers, the Program Committee members and the reviewers, and the Organizing Committee. Without their contributions, this conference would not have been possible. Special thanks also go to all of the sponsors.

October 2022

Tieniu Tan
Yike Guo
Jianhuang Lai
Jianguo Zhang
Shiqi Yu
Zhaoxiang Zhang
Pong C. Yuen
Junwei Han

Organization

Steering Committee Chair

Tieniu Tan — Institute of Automation, Chinese Academy of Sciences, China

Steering Committee

Xilin Chen — Institute of Computing Technology, Chinese Academy of Sciences, China

Chenglin Liu — Institute of Automation, Chinese Academy of Sciences, China

Yong Rui — Lenovo, China

Hongbing Zha — Peking University, China

Nanning Zheng — Xi'an Jiaotong University, China

Jie Zhou — Tsinghua University, China

Steering Committee Secretariat

Liang Wang — Institute of Automation, Chinese Academy of Sciences, China

General Chairs

Tieniu Tan — Institute of Automation, Chinese Academy of Sciences, China

Yike Guo — Hong Kong Baptist University, Hong Kong, China

Jianhuang Lai — Sun Yat-sen University, China

Jianguo Zhang — Southern University of Science and Technology, China

Program Chairs

Shiqi Yu — Southern University of Science and Technology, China

Zhaoxiang Zhang — Institute of Automation, Chinese Academy of Sciences, China

Pong C. Yuen — Hong Kong Baptist University, Hong Kong, China

Junwei Han — Northwest Polytechnic University, China

Organizing Committee Chairs

Jinfeng Yang	Shenzhen Polytechnic, China
Guangming Lu	Harbin Institute of Technology, Shenzhen, China
Baoyuan Wu	The Chinese University of Hong Kong, Shenzhen, China
Feng Zheng	Northwest Polytechnic University, China

Sponsorship Chairs

Liqiang Nie	Harbin Institute of Technology, Shenzhen, China
Yu Qiao	Shenzhen Institute of Advanced Technology, Chinese Academy of Sciences, China
Zhenan Sun	Institute of Automation, Chinese Academy of Sciences, China
Xiaochun Cao	Sun Yat-sen University, China

Publicity Chairs

Weishi Zheng	Sun Yat-sen University, China
Wei Jia	Hefei University of Technology, China
Lifang Wu	Beijing University of Technology, China
Junping Zhang	Fudan University, China

Local Arrangement Chairs

Yujiu Yang	Tsinghua Shenzhen International Graduate School, China
Yanjie Wei	Shenzhen Institute of Advanced Technology, Chinese Academy of Sciences, China

International Liaison Chairs

Jingyi Yu	ShanghaiTech University, China
Qifeng Liu	Shenzhen Polytechnic, China
Song Guo	Hong Kong Polytechnic University, Hong Kong, China

Competition Chairs

Wangmeng Zuo	Harbin Institute of Technology, China
Di Huang	Beihang University, China
Bin Fan	University of Science and Technology Beijing, China

Tutorial Chairs

Jiwen Lu	Tsinghua University, China
Ran He	Institute of Automation, Chinese Academy of Sciences, China
Xi Li	Zhejiang University, China
Jiaying Liu	Peking University, China

Special Session Chairs

Jing Dong	Institute of Automation, Chinese Academy of Sciences, China
Zhouchen Lin	Peking University, China
Xin Geng	Southeast University, China
Yong Xia	Northwest Polytechnic University, China

Doctoral Forum Chairs

Tianzhu Zhang	University of Science and Technology of China, China
Shanshan Zhang	Nanjing University of Science and Technology, China
Changdong Wang	Sun Yat-sen University, China

Publication Chairs

Kui Jia	South China University of Technology, China
Yang Cong	Institute of Automation, Chinese Academy of Sciences, China
Cewu Lu	Shanghai Jiao Tong University, China

Registration Chairs

Weihong Deng	Beijing University of Posts and Telecommunications, China
Wenxiong Kang	South China University of Technology, China
Xiaohu Yan	Shenzhen Polytechnic, China

Exhibition Chairs

Hongmin Liu	University of Science and Technology Beijing, China
Rui Huang	The Chinese University of Hong Kong, Shenzhen, China

| Kai Lei | Peking University Shenzhen Graduate School, China |
| Zechao Li | Nanjing University of Science and Technology, China |

Finance Chairs

| Xu Wang | Shenzhen Polytechnic, China |
| Li Liu | Southern University of Science and Technology, China |

Website Chairs

Zhaofeng He	Beijing University of Posts and Telecommunications, China
Mengyuan Liu	Sun Yat-sen University, China
Hanyang Peng	Pengcheng Laboratory, China

Program Committee

Yuntao Chen	TuSimple, China
Gong Cheng	Northwest Polytechnic University, China
Runmin Cong	Beijing Jiaotong University, China
Bin Fan	University of Science and Technology Beijing, China
Chen Gong	Nanjing University of Science and Technology, China
Fuyuan Hu	Suzhou University of Science and Technology, China
Huaibo Huang	Institute of Automation, Chinese Academy of Sciences, China
Sheng Huang	Chongqing University, China
Du Huynh	University of Western Australia, Australia
Sen Jia	Shenzhen University, China
Baiying Lei	Shenzhen University, China
Changsheng Li	Beijing Institute of Technology, China
Haibo Liu	Harbin Engineering University, China
Chao Ma	Shanghai Jiao Tong University, China
Vishal M. Patel	Johns Hopkins University, USA
Hanyang Peng	Pengcheng Laboratory, China
Manivannan Siyamalan	University of Jaffna, Sri Lanka
Anwaar Ulhaq	Charles Sturt University, Australia
Changdong Wang	Sun Yat-sen University, China

Contents – Part IV

Image Processing and Low-Level Vision

Video Deraining via Temporal Discrepancy Learning

Yirui Fan[1], Long Ma[1], and Risheng Liu[2(✉)]

[1] School of Software Technology, Dalian University of Technology, Liaoning, China
{yrfan,longma}@mail.dlut.edu.cn
[2] International School of Information Science and Engineering,
Dalian University of Technology, Liaoning, China
rsliu@dlut.edu.cn

Abstract. Learning-based video deraining has attracted much attention and shown superior performance. However, existing methods mostly depict the temporal correspondence between the consecutive frames implicitly, leading to insufficient temporal exploration so that performing badly in unseen real-world scenarios. To settle these issues, we develop a novel Temporal Discrepancy Learning (TDL) framework to provide interpretability in modeling temporal correspondence and improve robustness in real-world scenarios. To be specific, we define a new explicit spatio-temporal video deraining model by reformulating the task from a set representation perspective. The model describes the intuitive correspondences between different frames in terms of rain regions. Inspired by this model, we further construct a TDL, that firstly learns the temporal correlation under temporal discrepancy sequences and attention mechanism, then recovers the clear frame by performing a spatial-aware ensemble deraining process. Performance evaluations on various scenarios verify our excellence compared with advanced video deraining networks.

Keywords: Video deraining · Discrepancy learning · Temporal correlation

1 Introduction

The rain streaks will block the object and blur the image, which greatly affects the visual processing performance of the algorithm on subsequent tasks like image segmentation, object detection and image fusion [11]. Over the past few decades, many methods have been proposed to eliminate the effect of rain on images and video quality. In the following, we will briefly retrospect existing techniques and conclude our main contributions to clearly describe our innovation (Fig. 1).

S. Yu et al. (Eds.): PRCV 2022, LNCS 13537, pp. 3–14, 2022.
https://doi.org/10.1007/978-3-031-18916-6_1

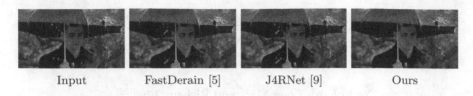

Input   FastDerain [5]   J4RNet [9]   Ours

Fig. 1. Visual comparison on a real-world example among state-of-the-art video deraining approaches. By comparison, our work realizes the best performances which have fewer rain streaks and clearer background.

1.1   Related Work

Image Deraining. In the earlier study, the removal of rain is based primarily on physical characteristics. Li *et al.* [14] used the gaussian model to encode the prior information. By using these simple patch-based priors, their model can accommodate multiple orientations and scales of the rain streaks. In addition to this, Luo *et al.* [13] also proposed a dictionary learning-based algorithm for single image deraining. Nevertheless, there is still over smooth because of excessive rain removal. Then, the emergence of deep learning and its application in other fields [10,15] has promoted the development of the field of rain removal. Yang *et al.* [23] proposed a deep combined rain detection and removal method to remove rain streaks and accumulated rain. Zhang *et al.* [26] proposed a density-aware multi-stream CNN which can efficiently remove the corresponding rain streaks guided by the estimated density label. Yang *et al.* [22] also developed a perception-generated antagonistic network. Wang *et al.* [18] proposed a semi-automatic method to generate a high-quality clean image from real rain images.

Video Deraining. The temporal information from the video sequence provides other possibilities for rain removal. In [2] utilized the intensity changement at a pixel as falling to simply utilize the temporal information. Besides, Li *et al.* [8] used multiple convolutional filters convolved on the sparse feature maps to deliver the former characteristic and represent different scales of rain streaks. The paper in [21] stochastically encoded rain streaks and background as patch-based mixtures of Gaussian. Jiang *et al.* [5] and Ren *et al.* [17] respectively utilized directional gradient priors and matrix decomposition realized the rain removal in the video. In terms of network-based methods, Chen *et al.* [1] proposed a spatial-temporal content alignment algorithm at superpixel levels to complete deraining. Yang *et al.* [9] developed a multi-task deep learning architecture to handle rain streak accumulation. And SLDNet [24] developed a self-learned rain streak removal method, which does not require the ground truth images in the training process. And [25] proposed a new semi-supervised video deraining method, in which a dynamic rain generator is employed to fit the rain layer.

1.2   Our Contributions

In order to break down the black-box property for temporal exploitation in video deraining and make full use of temporal information to complete deraining task, we establish an explicit spatial-temporal video deraining model. We further derived a temporal discrepancy learning framework based on this model and conducted extensive experiments to verify our superiority and effectiveness. In brief, our contributions can be concluded as:

- We propose a new model for video deraining by explicitly characterizing the latent correspondences between different frames in terms of rain regions. This model can definitely point out how to utilize temporal correlation for completing the video deraining and recovering the current frame.
- Inspired by our proposed model, we design an end-to-end video deraining network, which automatically learns temporal correlation on newly-introduced discrepancy sequences under the self-and mutual-attention mechanisms.
- Extensive experiments are conducted on various scenarios to show our superiority against recently-proposed state-of-the-art approaches. A series of analyses are performed to verify our effectiveness.

2 Explicit Spatial-Temporal Video Deraining Model

Generally, deraining can be formulated as a layer decomposition problem [6], where a rain streak layer is superimposed on a background layer containing the true scene content. But the model couldn't present the temporal correlation between different frames. In order to clearly describe the temporal correlation and the correspondence between different frames, we reformulate the video deraining task from a set representation perspective. This model can also be written as,

$$\pi(\mathbf{Y}_t) = \pi_r(\mathbf{Y}_t) \cup \pi_b(\mathbf{Y}_t), \pi_r(\mathbf{Y}_t) \cap \pi_b(\mathbf{Y}_t) = \varnothing, \qquad (1)$$

where $\pi(\mathbf{Y}_t)$, $\pi_b(\mathbf{Y}_t)$ and $\pi_r(\mathbf{Y}_t)$ are the pixel location sets of the rainy frame, the rain-free layer and the rain layer, respectively. As shown in Fig. 2, we further explain the temporal correlation from the neighbor frames. The adjacent frames in the video sequence overlap not only in the background information but also in the rain streaks. Therefore, $\pi_r(\mathbf{Y}_t)$ can be further expressed by rain layer for adjacent frames $\pi_r(\mathbf{Y}_{adj})$ as,

$$\pi_r(\mathbf{Y}_t) = \left(\pi_r(\mathbf{Y}_t) \cap \pi_r(\mathbf{Y}_{adj})\right) \cup \bar{\pi}_r(\mathbf{Y}_t), \qquad (2)$$

where $\cap$ expresses the overlap of the rain pixel location between the current frame and the adjacent frame, $\bar{\pi}_r(\mathbf{Y}_t)$ is the location of the current rain streaks from the adjacent frame. It should be noted that the overlap and special description here includes both the concept of position and the concept of intensity, that is, not a relationship between 0 and 1, but a specific magnitude.

In this way, we successfully establish a new video deraining model, which explicitly describes how to exploit the temporal correlation to pave the way for the subsequent mission of deraining by simple subtraction. However, during the discussion of the above model, we do not take into account the background image of the video frame. In the real-world scenario, the background elements are constantly moving, which will bring about the movement of the background pixel. So we need to carry out certain processing which will be described below.

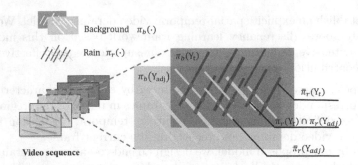

Fig. 2. Illustration of the explicit spatial-temporal video deraining model. It shows the schematic diagram for this model. As for two adjacent frames, their rain streaks have overlapping parts (the red regions) and their unique parts (the residual yellow and purple regions). (Color figure online)

3 Temporal Discrepancy Learning

As shown in Fig. 3, the overall pipeline of our TDL method mainly contains four key modules, i.e., flow-based alignment, temporal discrepancy subtraction, attention-driven temporal correlation learning, spatial-aware ensemble deraining. The four parts receive the video rainframe, and then form the final result of deraining under mutual cooperation. In the following, we will make an elaborate description of these modules and the loss function.

3.1 Flow-Based Alignment Module

First of all, to eliminate the effect of background movement in adjacent frames, we define three rain input frames as $[\mathbf{Y}_{t-1}, \mathbf{Y}_t, \mathbf{Y}_{t+1}]$. Subsequently, we feed them into a flow estimation network to align adjacent frames with the current frame to reduce errors that may be introduced in subsequent subtraction. The flow-based alignment process mainly used the trained SPyNet whose architecture can be seen in [16]. To better adapt to the rain scenario to complete the task of deraining, the network parameters of SPyNet also participate in the learning procedure. And the following part of the article describes of the rain relationships are all based on $\bar{\mathbf{Y}}_{t+i}$ which denotes frames has be aligned.

3.2 Temporal Discrepancy Subtraction

Actually, Eq. (2) can be extended to the general case of more adjacent frames. Here we provide an example when input three adjacent frames, we can subtract the frames after alignment, according the overlapping parts and the special parts of the rain in adjacent frames, and finally we would get the initial rain streaks extracted without overlap rain streaks,

$$\mathbf{T}_{t+i} = \left| \bar{\mathbf{Y}}_t - \bar{\mathbf{Y}}_{t+i} \right|, \quad i \in \{-1, 1\}. \tag{3}$$

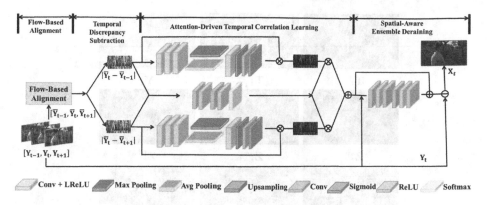

Fig. 3. Flow chart of our proposed TDL, which contains four modules. The input of the network is defined as three adjacent frames. Flow-based alignment aligns these inputs for better extracting temporal information. The temporal discrepancy subtraction and the attention-driven temporal correlation learning module estimate the rain streaks of the current frame and also remove the unwanted background information introduced by the motion. Finally, the spatial-aware ensemble network would integrate all intermediate results to generate the desired clear frame.

After this step, we encounter the other problem. Although the alignment has been completed, the resulting rain streaks of this step still have additional rain streaks and background information and need further fine process.

3.3 Attention-Driven Temporal Correlation Learning

The attention-driven temporal correlation learning also can play the important role mentioned above. It distinguishes rain areas that belong to different frames and superfluous background pieces of information by learning from discrepancy with the ground truth images. The formulation is denoted as,

$$
\begin{cases}
\mathbf{Z}_{t+i}^{se} = \mathbf{T}_{t+i} \otimes \mathcal{A}_{\mathbf{s}}\Big(\mathbf{T}_{t+i}\Big), \\
(\boldsymbol{\omega}_{t-1}, \boldsymbol{\omega}_{t+1}) = \mathcal{A}_{\mathbf{m}}\Big(\mathbf{T}_{t-1}, \mathbf{T}_{t+1}\Big), \\
\mathbf{Z}_t^{td} = \sum_i \boldsymbol{\omega}_{t+i} \otimes \mathbf{Z}_{t+i}^{se},
\end{cases}
\tag{4}
$$

where $\mathcal{A}_{\mathbf{s}}$ represents the self-attention. After the element-wise multiplication with the input, the target result $\mathbf{Z}_{t+i}^{se}$ can be received. With this section, we can remove most of the background information and additional rain lines from the rain chart. We modified the architecture of self-attention is based on the spatial attention form in [19], and the detailed architecture and implementation can be found in Fig. 3. Obviously, different self-attention networks get different results when processing adjacent frames. Therefore, we need to further process the intermediate results from different attention networks. To avoid placing

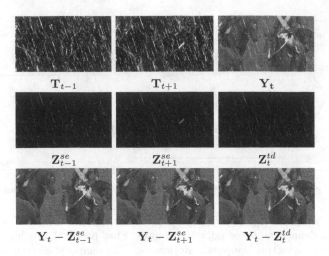

Fig. 4. Renderings of attention-driven temporal correlation learning. The first and second columns represent the results of different self-attention networks respectively. The third column represents the deraining results after mutual-attention network.

the entire training burden on the attention network, the acquisition of training results becomes more difficult and less accurate. So we introduced a weight learning mechanism $\mathcal{A}_m$ which is named mutual-attention. Its structure is mainly composed of the convolutional neural network, activation function, and softmax function, so as to calculate the probability weight ω_{t+i} of each self-attention network. This weight will carry out a weighted synthesis of the results of different self-attention networks for different inputs to obtain a more perfect result $\mathbf{Z}_t^{td}$. And the effect of the network's processing power is shown in Fig. 4. Obviously, the weighted results have better visual effect than before.

3.4 Spatial-Aware Ensemble Deraining

For video deraining, how to use the current frame itself spatial information is also a challenge. We also define the following spatial-aware ensemble deraining,

$$\mathbf{Z}_t^{sae} = \mathcal{M}_{sae}\left(\mathbf{Y}_t, \mathbf{Z}_t^{td}\right) \oplus \mathbf{Z}_t^{td}, \tag{5}$$

where $\mathcal{M}_{sae}\left(\cdot\right)$ is the spatial-aware ensemble deraining, $\mathbf{Z}_t^{sae}$ denotes the rain streaks of the current frame after ensemble deraining. Through this module, we can remove the rain streaks that cannot be covered by the adjacent frames. At the same time, we can also reconstruct the background in further detail. As for the network architecture of this module, we build two residual blocks (Conv+ReLU+Conv). And the result $\mathbf{X}_t$ will be got by subtracting $\mathbf{Z}_t^{sae}$ from the input current rain frame $\mathbf{Y}_t$.

3.5 Training Loss

Our network is a gradual deraining which guided by comparison with ground truth using L1-norm and the SSIM [20] loss as the loss function, so the training loss can be formulated as follows,

$$
\begin{cases}
\mathcal{L}_{\text{TDL}} = \lambda_\alpha \mathcal{L}_\text{T} + \lambda_\beta \mathcal{L}_{\text{S1}} + \lambda_\gamma \mathcal{L}_{\text{S2}}, \\
\mathcal{L}_\text{T} = \lambda \sum_i \left\| \mathbf{X}_t^{gt} - \mathbf{X}_{t+i}^{se} \right\|_1 + \left\| \mathbf{X}_t^{gt} - \mathbf{X}_t^{td} \right\|_1, \\
\mathcal{L}_{\text{S1}} = \left\| \mathbf{X}_t^{gt} - (\mathbf{Y}_t - \mathbf{Z}_t^{sae}) \right\|_1, \\
\mathcal{L}_{\text{S2}} = 1 - \text{SSIM}\left(\mathbf{X}_t^{gt}, \mathbf{Y}_t - \mathbf{Z}_t^{sae} \right),
\end{cases}
\tag{6}
$$

where λ_α, λ_β and λ_γ is the weighting parameters to balance each term. The loss function $\mathcal{L}_\text{T}$, $\mathcal{L}_{\text{S1}}$ and $\mathcal{L}_{\text{S1}}$ respectively represents the modules that utilize the temporal and spatial information. The difference between $\mathcal{L}_{\text{S1}}$ and $\mathcal{L}_{\text{S2}}$ lies in the calculation method of loss, respectively L1-norm and the SSIM loss. Combine the two to get a more comprehensive rain-removing effect, so as to improve the comprehensive performance. λ is also the weighting parameters. This is also one of the settings that balance the role of each self-attention network with that of other networks. Where $\mathbf{X}_{t+i}^{se}$ expression $\left(\mathbf{Y}_t - \mathbf{Z}_{t+i}^{se} \right)$, $\mathbf{X}_t^{td}$ expression $\left(\mathbf{Y}_t - \mathbf{Z}_t^{td} \right)$, that means the intermediate result from the initial rain frame minus the intermediate rain maps.

4 Experimental Results

4.1 Implementation Details

Parameter Settings. In our learning process, we use ADAM optimizer [7] with parameters $\beta_1 = 0.9$, $\beta_2 = 0.999$, and weight decay is set to be 10^{-4}. The epoch was 300, the batch size was 1. learning rate was 0.0005. The learning rate is initialized to be 10^{-4}. During the training, we use slightly different loss function parameter settings to achieve the optimal effects when we deal with different dataset. In RSLight25 and RSComplex25 datasets, the parameters λ_α and λ_β are setted as 1. And the parameter λ_γ is 0 in the Eq. 6. And for the NTURain dataset that move fast in the background, the parameter λ_β is setted as 1 and λ_γ is 0. And the parameter λ in the Eq. 6 always is 0.5.

Compared Methods. We compared our proposed TDL with two well-known single image deraining methods JORDER [23] and SPANet [18], three traditional video deraining methods including MS-CSC [8], SE [21], DIP [4] and Fast-DeRain [5], four deep learning video deraining methods including SpacCNN [1], J4RNet [9] and the latest job S2VD [25].

Benchmarks Description and Metrics. We tested the performance on synthetic testing video sequences from RSLight25 and RSComplex25 benchmarks [9] which contain rain video sequences with light and heavy rain streaks, respectively. At the same time, in order to test the experimental effect of our method

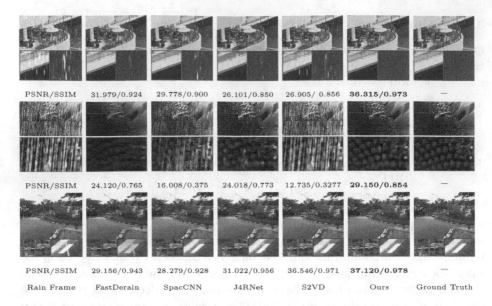

| PSNR/SSIM | 31.979/0.924 | 29.778/0.900 | 26.101/0.850 | 26.905/ 0.856 | **36.315/0.973** | — |

| PSNR/SSIM | 24.120/0.765 | 16.008/0.375 | 24.018/0.773 | 12.735/0.3277 | **29.150/0.854** | — |

| PSNR/SSIM | 29.156/0.943 | 28.279/0.928 | 31.022/0.956 | 36.546/0.971 | **37.120/0.978** | — |
| Rain Frame | FastDerain | SpacCNN | J4RNet | S2VD | Ours | Ground Truth |

Fig. 5. Visual comparison on the synthetic datasets. The top and bottom rows represent the results in RSLight25, RSComplex25 and NTURain benchmark, respectively.

Table 1. Quantitative results on multiple video deraining benchmarks.

Dataset	Metrics	JORDER	SPANet	MS-CSC	SE	DIP	FastDeRain	SpacCNN	J4RNet	S2VD	Ours
RSLight25	PSNR	31.03	27.39	24.44	25.44	28.07	29.20	31.670	30.53	26.22	**34.79**
	SSIM	0.91	0.88	0.73	0.76	0.85	0.88	0.900	0.91	0.83	**0.96**
RSComplex25	PSNR	19.99	18.19	16.57	18.83	17.90	24.74	21.26	23.61	17.61	**28.76**
	SSIM	0.61	0.58	0.48	0.59	0.53	0.74	0.59	0.75	0.54	**0.87**
NTURain	PSNR	32.39	31.66	26.20	25.42	30.76	29.51	33.02	31.02	36.04	**37.37**
	SSIM	0.94	0.94	0.76	0.76	0.90	0.93	0.95	0.94	0.96	**0.97**

in scenes with large background movement to deal with different situations, we also carried out the experiments on NTURain [1] datasets. And we used the widely-adopted Peak Signal-to-Noise Ratio (PSNR) [3] and Structure Similarity Index Measure (SSIM) [20] to evaluate the quantitative performance among state-of-the-art approaches. Additionally, we also evaluated the average running time on RSLight25 benchmark.

4.2 Comparison with State-of-the-Arts

Synthetic Datasets. Table 1 reported the quantitative results compared with state-of-the-art deraining methods. We can easily see that our TDL method obtains numerical scores and significant improvement in SSIM and PSNR indicators on RSLight25, RSComplex25 benchmarks. And We also obtain the consistent best numerical scores on *NTURain* benchmark. In terms of visual effect,

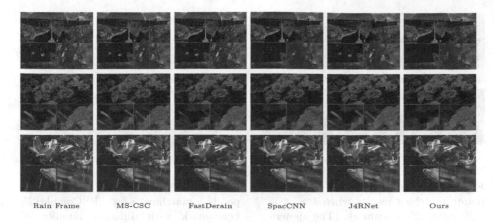

Fig. 6. Visual comparison on real-world scenarios.

Table 2. Comparing running time on the RSComplex25 benchmark.

Method	DIP	SE	FastDeRain	SpacCNN	J4RNet	Ours
Time (s)	4.57	19.74	0.67	4.47	9.62	**0.15**

as shown in Fig. 5, most of the work failed to remove the whole rain streaks. A large amount of rain streaks remain can be seen in the result(e.g. S2VD). And some works (e.g. FastDerain) deviated in color and detail. Compared with other works, our TDL has advantages in rain removal and detail retention.

Real-World Scenarios. We considered two different real-world scenarios to evaluate these methods. Figure 6 showed the visual effect comparison on the real-world rain video from the website "mixkit.co". Some early deraining works (e.g. MS-CSC) reserved many conspicuous rain streaks. Some recently proposed approaches indeed removed most of the rain streaks, but some nonnegligible rain streaks still existed. At the same time, some methods (e.g. SpacCNN) have defects in the restoration of details, resulting in the absence of part of the picture affecting the visual effect while our algorithm obtained a better visual expression.

Running Time. Running speed is of high value in the evaluation of video rain-removal methods, which is convenient for us to apply in some immediate video tasks. An increase in speed means an increase in overall mission performance efficiency. So we also evaluated the average running time on the RSLight25 benchmark. As shown in Table 2, our proposed TDL achieved the absolute optimal speed of other video-based deraining methods.

4.3 Local Keypoints Matching

To further verify the effect of our experiment on more high-level tasks like robotics and automation, we carried out a series of experiments contrapose local

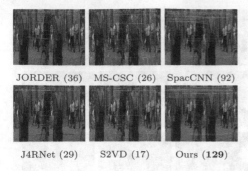

JORDER (36)   MS-CSC (26)   SpacCNN (92)

J4RNet (29)   S2VD (17)   Ours (**129**)

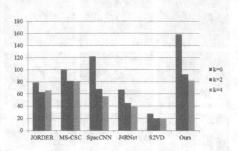

Fig. 7. Visual comparison of local keypoints matching results when $k = 4$ in RSComplex25 benchmark. (The numerical scores are in parentheses.)

Fig. 8. Numerical scores of local keypoints matching on RSComplex25 benchmark with different number of intervals.

Table 3. Ablation study on RSComplex25 benchmark.

Methods	S_a	S_b	S_c	S_d	TDL
FBA	✓	✓	✓	✓	✓
TDS	✓	✗	✓	✓	✓
ATC − S	✓	✓	✗	✓	✓
ATC − M	✓	✓	✗	✗	✓
SAE	✗	✓	✓	✓	✓
PSNR	26.98	26.62	27.12	26.97	**28.27**
SSIM	0.80	0.76	0.81	0.84	**0.87**

keypoints matching problem which is of great significance for visual matching and localization. In the case of autopilot, the key points taken from the video can be used as coordinates on a map. In this way, it can tell the position direction of the vehicle driving in real-time and accurately, and make follow-up instructions. Specifically, we used the scale-invariant feature transform method [12] to detect key points for feature matching. In order to test the stability of our algorithm, we conducted tests on two datasets respectively. And the different results caused by the different number of frames matching the two frame intervals k are recorded.

The Fig. 7 shows the contrast specific visual representations among state-of-the-art deraining approaches. Since our TDL method has a better effect of removing rain streaks and more accurate restoration of details and colors, more key points in the image are matched out. Some deraining works (e.g. S2VD) although the number of matches is enough, the incorrect match of rain pixels exists caused by incomplete removal of rain, which generates a lot of false matches. And the Fig. 8 reported the numerical scores of the matching result on RSComplex25 benchmark. k represents the interval number of matched frames. As we can see, no matter how the interval frames change, our rain removal effect is stable. Thus it can be seen that the completion of rain has great help to improve the matching quality. Our work can achieve a good rain removal effect to avoid mismatching and improve overall performance.

4.4 Ablation Study

In this part, we made some analytical experiments to reflect the necessity of our TDL. In our designed network architecture, there exist four key modules including the flow-based alignment (FBA), temporal discrepancy subtraction (TDS), attention-driven temporal correlation learning (ATC), and spatial-aware ensemble deraining (SAE). And the attention-driven temporal correlation learning is consisting of self-attention (ATC-S) and mutual-attention (ATC-M). If removing the module will bring a series of problems such as rain streaks residue and blurred images. Table 3 reported the quantitative results of the ablation study, our TDL kept the best quantitative scores.

5   Conclusion and Future Works

In this work, we propose a new model to express the temporal correspondence between frames from a position set representation perspective to explicitly exploit the temporal information of adjacent frames. We develop a temporal discrepancy learning framework to assist the rain removal and detailed background recovery, based on our proposed model. Extensive experiments are conducted on various scenarios to show our superiority against recently-proposed state-of-the-art approaches. In the future, we will keep on exploring how to better exploit the temporal and spatial information for video deraining. On the other hand, we also will make an extension of our algorithm for other related video tasks.

Acknowledgement. This work is partially supported by the National Natural Science Foundation of China (Nos. 61922019, 61733002, and 62027826), and the Fundamental Research Funds for the Central Universities.

References

1. Chen, J., Tan, C., Hou, J., Chau, L., Li, H.: Robust video content alignment and compensation for rain removal in a CNN framework. In: CVPR, pp. 6286–6295 (2018)
2. Garg, K., Nayar, S.K.: Detection and removal of rain from videos. In: CVPR, vol. 1, p. 1. IEEE (2004)
3. HuynhThu, Q., Ghanbari, M.: Scope of validity of PSNR in image/video quality assessment. Electron. Lett. **44**(13), 800–801 (2008)
4. Jiang, T., Huang, T., Zhao, X., Deng, L., Wang, Y.: A novel tensor-based video rain streaks removal approach via utilizing discriminatively intrinsic priors. In: CVPR, pp. 4057–4066 (2017)
5. Jiang, T., Huang, T., Zhao, X., Deng, L., Wang, Y.: FastDerain: a novel video rain streak removal method using directional gradient priors. TIP **28**(4), 2089–2102 (2018)

6. Kim, J., Lee, C., Sim, J., Kim, C.: Single-image deraining using an adaptive non-local means filter. In: ICIP, pp. 914–917 (2013)
7. Kingma, D., Ba, J.: Adam: a method for stochastic optimization. In: ICLR (2014)
8. Li, M., Xie, Q., Zhao, Q., Wei, W., Gu, S., Tao, J., Meng, D.: Video rain streak removal by multiscale convolutional sparse coding. In: CVPR, pp. 6644–6653 (2018)
9. Liu, J., Yang, W., Yang, S., Guo, Z.: Erase or fill? Deep joint recurrent rain removal and reconstruction in videos. In: CVPR, pp. 3233–3242 (2018)
10. Liu, R., Gao, J., Zhang, J., Meng, D., Lin, Z.: Investigating bi-level optimization for learning and vision from a unified perspective: a survey and beyond. TPAMI. 1 (2021). https://doi.org/10.1109/TPAMI.2021.3132674
11. Liu, R., Liu, J., Jiang, Z., Fan, X., Luo, Z.: A bilevel integrated model with data-driven layer ensemble for multi-modality image fusion. TIP **30**, 1261–1274 (2021). https://doi.org/10.1109/TIP.2020.3043125
12. Lowe, D.G.: Distinctive image features from scale-invariant keypoints. IJCV **60**(2), 91–110 (2004)
13. Luo, Y., Xu, Y., Ji, H.: Removing rain from a single image via discriminative sparse coding. In: ICCV, pp. 3397–3405 (2015)
14. Luo, Y., Xu, Y., Ji, H.: Rain streak removal using layer priors. In: CVPR, pp. 2736–2744 (2016)
15. Ma, L., Liu, R., Zhang, J., Fan, X., Luo, Z.: Learning deep context-sensitive decomposition for low-light image enhancement. TNNLS. 1–15 (2021). https://doi.org/10.1109/TNNLS.2021.3071245
16. Ranjan, A., Black, M.J.: Optical flow estimation using a spatial pyramid network. In: CVPR, pp. 4161–4170 (2017)
17. Ren, W., Tian, J., Han, Z., Chan, A., Tang, Y.: Video desnowing and deraining based on matrix decomposition. In: CVPR, pp. 4210–4219 (2017)
18. Wang, T., Yang, X., Xu, K., Chen, S., Zhang, Q., Lau, R.W.: Spatial attentive single-image deraining with a high quality real rain dataset. In: CVPR, pp. 12270–12279 (2019)
19. Wang, X., Chan, K.C., Yu, K., Dong, C., Change Loy, C.: EDVR: video restoration with enhanced deformable convolutional networks. In: CVPR Workshops (2019)
20. Wang, Z., Bovik, A.C., Sheikh, H.R., Simoncelli, E.P.: Image quality assessment: from error visibility to structural similarity. TIP **13**(4), 600–612 (2004)
21. Wei, W., Yi, L., Xie, Q., Zhao, Q., Meng, D., Xu, Z.: Should we encode rain streaks in video as deterministic or stochastic? In: ICCV, pp. 2516–2525 (2017)
22. Yang, W., Tan, R.T., Feng, J., Guo, Z., Yan, S., Liu, J.: Joint rain detection and removal from a single image with contextualized deep networks. TPAMI **42**(6), 1377–1393 (2020)
23. Yang, W., Tan, R.T., Feng, J., Liu, J., Guo, Z., Yan, S.: Deep joint rain detection and removal from a single image. In: CVPR, pp. 1357–1366 (2017)
24. Yang, W., Tan, R.T., Wang, S., Liu, J.: Self-learning video rain streak removal: when cyclic consistency meets temporal correspondence. In: CVPR, pp. 1717–1726 (2020)
25. Yue, Z., Xie, J., Zhao, Q., Meng, D.: Semi-supervised video deraining with dynamic rain generator. arXiv preprint arXiv:2103.07939 (2021)
26. Zhang, H., Patel, V.M.: Density-aware single image de-raining using a multi-stream dense network. In: CVPR, pp. 695–704 (2018)

Multi-priors Guided Dehazing Network Based on Knowledge Distillation

Nian Wang, Zhigao Cui$^{(\boxtimes)}$, Aihua Li, Yanzhao Su, and Yunwei Lan

Xi'an Research Institute of High-tech, Xi'an 710025, China
`cuizg10@126.com`

Abstract. Single image dehazing is a key prerequisite of high-level computer vision tasks since degraded images seriously affect the recognition ability of computers. Traditional prior-based methods conduct favorable dehazing effect but tend to cause artifacts and color distortions due to inaccurate parameter estimations. By contrast, recent learning-based methods can provide better color fidelity via the supervised training of synthetic images. But unfortunately, these methods always acquire under-dehazed results due to the domain differences between synthetic hazy images and their real-world ones. To combine the merits of these two categories, we propose a multi-priors guided dehazing network (MGDNet) based on knowledge distillation. Specifically, we adopt the dehazed images of dark channel prior and non-local dehazing prior as fake ground truths, and use them to pretrain two teacher networks. Then we build a student network based on encoder-decoder structure, and set up both feature-level and pixel-level knowledge distillation losses to guide the training process of the student network. Experimental results on some real-world datasets widely used in recent works demonstrate that our MGDNet can generate visually appealing images with more discriminative textures and vivid color when compared with the state-of-the-arts.

Keywords: Single image dehazing · Knowledge distillation · Multi-priors guiding

1 Introduction

Particles in the atmosphere absorb and scatter the reflected lights of object and result in poor image visibility, which hinders the performance of high-level computer vision tasks [1]. Hence, as a key prerequisite, single image dehazing has been widely studied in the latest decade, which can be roughly divided into model-based methods and model-free methods [2].

Traditional model-based methods estimate the unknown atmospheric light and transmission maps by the statistical rules of haze-free images, which include dark channel prior (DCP) [3], color-lines prior (CLP) [4], color attenuation prior (CAP) [5], and non-local dehazing (NLD) [6]. These methods achieve favorable dehazing effect and generalization ability, but tend to cause some color distortion and artifacts since unilateral hypothesis cannot maintain the accuracy of parameter estimations in various scenes.

To this end, recent model-based methods utilize convolutional neural networks (CNNs) to estimate the atmospheric light and transmission maps respectively [7, 8] or simultaneously [9, 10]. These learning-based methods estimate parameters by data driving rather than man-made priors, and thus acquire more visually pleasing images. However, the atmospheric scattering model is just an ideal model, which influences the convergence of networks and restricts the final dehazing performance [11].

More recently, learning-based methods [12–16] tend to avoid the atmospheric scattering model and adopt an end-to-end training strategy (directly building the mapping between hazy images and haze-free images) to acquire high quality results. However, due to the huge differences between the features of hazy images and their haze-free ones, model-free methods always expand the network depths and scales to enhance feature extraction ability, which results in large computational consumption. Moreover, these methods fail to dehaze when applied to real scenes, mainly because networks trained on synthetic dataset cannot fit in uneven haze distribution and complex illumination existing in real scenes. To this end, some works [17–19] start to combine prior-based methods and model-free methods to reduce the differences between synthetic domain and real domain, which achieve better dehazing effect when applied to real-world images.

In this paper, we propose a multi-priors guided dehazing network (MGDNet) based on knowledge distillation. Different from a recent work [20], we pretrain two teacher networks by minimizing the losses between hazy images and supervised images (dehazed images of dark channel prior and non-local dehazing), and then teach a student network to learn their features by minimizing both feature-level and pixel-level distillation loss. Considering that the supervisions of teacher networks contain some color distortion, we utilize discrete wavelet transform (DWT) to get the high-frequency and low-frequency of the outputs of teacher networks and only use the high-frequency part to build the pixel-level distillation loss.

Comparative experiments on some real-world hazy images show that our MGDNet performs favorably against the state-of-the-arts, which validates that guiding with the partially correct teacher networks (the supervisions are dehazed images of DCP and NLD rather than ground truths) can effectively improve the dehazing ability in real scenes. In addition, these added negative information from teacher networks can be refined by the training process and the student network finally acquire dehazed images with more vivid color.

2 Related Work

2.1 Model-Based Methods

Model-based methods estimate the atmospheric light and transmission maps, and then restore dehazed images by atmospheric scattering model. Early model-based methods, also called prior-based methods, adopt statistical assumptions concluded from haze-free images to estimate the atmospheric light and transmission maps. For example, dark channel prior (DCP) [3] assumes clear RGB images have low intensity in at least one channel, and quickly acquires these two parameters based on the theory. Color-lines prior (CLP) [4] constructs a local formation model to recover the transmission map based on the lines offset. In addition, Color attenuation prior (CAP) [5] builds a linear relationship among color, haze concentration and scene depth to estimate the atmospheric light and transmission maps. Differently, another method NLD [6] estimates the transmission map by hundreds of distinct colors. Above prior-based methods dehaze favorably and have strong generalization in real scenes but tend to cause artifacts, halos and color distortion since unilateral assumption cannot estimate accurate atmospheric light and transmission maps in various scenes. To this end, recent model-based methods tend to estimate the atmospheric light and transmission maps by convolutional neural networks (CNNs). For example, some works estimate transmission maps by stacked CNN [7] or multiscale CNN [8]. Moreover, to avoid the cumulative error of two times estimation, AOD-Net [9] sets a linear equation to combine the atmospheric light and transmission map into a parameter $K(x)$. Another method DCPDN [10] embeds the atmospheric scattering model into CNN, which directly acquires dehazed images by the joint estimation of atmospheric light and transmission maps. However, the atmospheric scattering model, as a simplified mathematical model, cannot completely replace the formation process of haze. Hence, model-based methods cannot acquire high quality results and still suffer from some color and illumination changes.

2.2 Model-Free Methods

Model-free methods, also called end-to-end methods, directly establish the mapping between hazy images and clear images instead of using atmospheric scattering model. Due to the huge gap between the features of hazy images and clear images, model-free methods often increase network depths and scales to enhance the feature extraction ability. For example, FFA [12] and DuRN [13] build a deep network based on residual blocks, and directly recover dehazed images by merging features from convolutional layers in different depths. GFN [14] utilizes white balance (WB), contrast enhancing (CE), and gamma correction (GC) to derive three subimages of the hazy input, and directly recovers dehazed images by using learned confidence maps to fuse these three subimages. Moreover, EPDN [15] acquires high contrast results by the adversarial training between a multiscale generator and discriminator. MSBDN [16] adopts back-projection feedback to connect non-adjacent layers, which reduces the loss of spatial information during sampling and improves the resolution of restored results. However, due to lacking of the knowledge to real-world haze, above networks conduct poor dehazing performance in real scenes. To this end, DANet [17] builds a bidirectional translation network to solve the domain adaptation problem, and acquires visually pleasing results on both synthetic and real scenes. RefineDNet [18] embeds DCP in CNN-based method, and adopts an adversarial training between unpaired real-world images to improve dehazing effect in both synthetic and real scenes. PSD [19] uses multiple prior losses to guide the training process, which acquires high contrast results in real scenes but tend to overenhance images. Differently, KDDN [20] pretrains a reconstruction network of clear images, and adopts the intermediate features to guide the training process of a dehazing network.

3 Proposed Method

As shown in Fig. 1, considering that dark channel prior (DCP) and non-local dehazing (NLD) dehaze favorably in real scenes, we dehaze images by these two prior-based methods and use them as fake ground truths to pretrain two teacher networks. During the training process of student network, we use the features of teacher networks to guide the student network, and make it achieve favorable dehazing effect in real scenes.

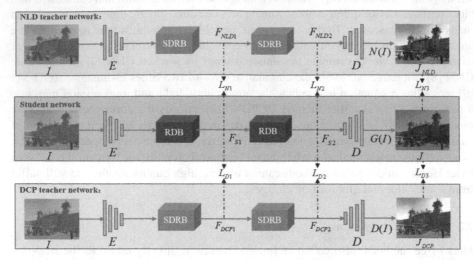

Fig. 1. The architecture of the proposed MGDNet

3.1 Teacher Networks

The DCP and NLD teacher networks have the same architecture, which are based on classic encoder-decoder architecture. As shown in Fig. 1, we first extract features on four scales by an encoder E containing four convolutions. The first convolution preliminarily extracts features of hazy inputs and change the shape from $256 \times 256 \times 3$ to $256 \times 256 \times 64$, and the following three convolutions sequentially adjust the shape of features to $128 \times 128 \times 128$, $64 \times 64 \times 256$ and $32 \times 32 \times 512$, respectively. Moreover, considering paper [21] has shown that applying dilated convolutions into bottleneck layers of encoder-decoder structure can effectively alleviate the generation of artifacts. Hence, we design smoothed dilated residual block (SDRB) and add two SDRBs in the bottleneck layers of these two teacher networks. After that, a decoder D, consists of four deconvolutions, unsamples features to the shape of the corresponding layer in the encoder E, and finally outputs the dehazed images.

As shown in Fig. 2(a), the SDRB consists of two smoothed dilated convolutions (SDC) [22] and a residual connection [23], and each SDC contains a ShareSepConv, a 3×3 convolution and a ReLU function. The ShareSepConv (Separable and Shared Convolution) performs as a preprocessing module, which builds a connection between non-adjacent regions and solves the spatial discontinuity caused by the expansion of receptive field. The theories and details of ShareSepConv can be seen in paper [22]. The 3×3 convolution sets the dilation as 2 to expand the receptive fields, and enhances the perception ability to global features. Finally, the ReLU function improves network nonlinearity and the residual connection after two SDCs enhances feature flow.

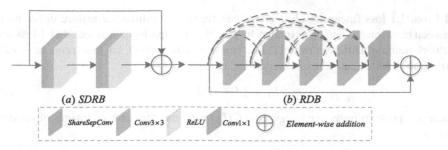

Fig. 2. The structure of SDRB and RDB.

3.2 Student Networks

The student network is a dehazing network trained by synthetic hazy images, which has the similar structures to the teacher networks. As shown in Fig. 1, the student network is still based on a encoder-decoder structure but two residual dense blocks (RDBs) are applied to the bottleneck layers. RDB [24] combines the advantages of residual connection and densely connected network [25], which extracts structures effectively and helps the feature backpropagation. As shown in Fig. 2 (b), these two RDBs contain four 3×3 convolutions and one 1×1 convolution. All 3×3 convolutions are densely connected to avoid the loss of structure information extracted by shallower layers, and then the 1×1 convolution merges these abundant features to provide clear texture perception.

3.3 Overall Loss Function

Recent research [26] has shown that the combination of pixel-wise loss and feature-wise loss can effectively accelerate network training. Hence, for the training of MGDNet, the overall loss function contains L1 loss, perceptual loss, and distillation loss, which can be expressed as Eq. (1):

$$L_{loss} = L_1 + L_{per} + \lambda L_{diss} \tag{1}$$

where L_1, L_{per} and L_{diss} denotes the L1 loss, perceptual loss and distillation loss, respectively. λ is a trade-off coefficient to balance the effect of learning-based method and prior-based method. As shown in Fig. 3, our method can effectively improve the dehazing effect while maintain the color fidelity when setting λ as 1.

Hazy image $\lambda=0.1$ $\lambda=10$ $\lambda=1$

Fig. 3. The results when setting different λ.

L1 Loss. L1 loss (mean absolute error) can rapidly minimize the feature differences between hazy images and clear images by per-pixel comparison, thus we add L1 loss for network training. Different from L2 loss (mean squared error), L1 loss trains networks more stably, which can be expressed as Eq. (2):

$$L_1 = \|J - G(I)\|_1 \tag{2}$$

where J represents haze-free images and $G(I)$ represents the dehazed images of student network.

Perceptual Loss. Perceptual loss [27] compares two images by perceptual and semantic differences, which effectively helps the network restore more vivid images. In this paper, we pretrain VGG19 network on the ImageNet and extract the features of the convolutions in number $2, 7, 15, 21$, and 28 (the last convolution of each scale) to calculate loss, which can be expressed as Eq. (3):

$$L_{per} = \sum_{i=1}^{5} \frac{1}{C_i H_i W_i} \|\Phi_i(J) - \Phi_i(G(I))\|_1 \tag{3}$$

where J presents clear images and $G(I)$ represents dehazed images generated by student network. $\Phi_i(J)$ and $\Phi_i(G(I))$ respectively represent the five scales perceptual features of the dehazed images and clear images extracted from the trained VGG19 network. C_i, H_i, and W_i represent the number of channels, height, and width of feature maps.

Distillation Loss. As shown in Fig. 1, to make the trained student network conduct strong generalization ability to real scenes, we pretrain two teacher networks by minimize the L1 loss between $N(I)$ $(D(I))$ and the dehazed images of NLD (DCP) (named as J_{NLD} (J_{DCP})), respectively. Then we adopt the pretrained networks to optimize the training of student network by both of feature-level losses $(L_{N1}, L_{D1}, L_{N2}, L_{D2})$ and pixel-level distillation losses (L_{N3}, L_{D3}). For feature-level guiding, we output the features after each SDRB (RDB) in the teacher networks (student network) by an extra 3×3 convolution. For pixel-level guiding, considering that the supervisions (dehazed images of NLD and DCP) contain some negative information such as color and illumination distortion, we adopt discrete wavelet transform (DWT) in paper [28] to distinct the high-frequency and low-frequency parts of the outputs of teacher networks, and only the high-frequency images are sent to guide the training process of student network. Hence, the whole distillation loss can be expressed as Eq. (4):

$$\begin{aligned} L_{diss} &= \|F_{NLD1} - F_{S1}\|_1 + \|F_{DCP1} - F_{S1}\|_1 + \|F_{NLD2} - F_{S2}\|_1 + \|F_{DCP2} - F_{S2}\|_1 \\ &+ \|DWT_h(N(I)) - DWT_h(G(I))\|_1 + \|DWT_h(D(I)) - DWT_h(G(I))\|_1 \end{aligned} \tag{4}$$

where F_{DCP1}, F_{DCP2} and F_{NLD1}, F_{NLD2} denote the features extracted from each SDRB of DCP teacher network and NLD teacher network, respectively. F_{S1} and F_{S2} denote the features extracted from each RDB of student network. $DWT_h(\cdot)$ is a high pass DWT, which extracts the structures and textures of input images for pixel-level guiding and makes the student network $G(\cdot)$ avoid the negative low-frequency information (color and illumination distortion) from dehazed images $N(I)$ and $D(I)$.

4 Experiments

In this section, we conduct some experiments on real-world images to show that the proposed MGDNet performs better than some state-of-the-arts. These methods include DCP [3], NLD [6], DANet [17], RefineDNet [18], PSD [19] and KDDN [20]. All these methods are learning-based methods except DCP and NLD, which are two prior-based methods. Moreover, DANet, RefineDNet and PSD are prior-combined methods, and KDDN is a dehazing network using knowledge distillation similar to our MGDNet.

4.1 Dataset

To effectively train our MGDNet, we adopt the Indoor Training Set (ITS) in Realistic Single Image Dehazing (RESIDE) [29], which is a synthetic indoor training set containing 13990 hazy images and the corresponding haze-free images. We test the MGDNet and all comparative methods on IHAZE [30] and OHAZE [31] to verify the dehazing performance, which contains 5 indoor and outdoor paired testing images, respectively. Moreover, some real-world images in [17] and [32] are also adopted to further verify the generalization of MGDNet in real scenes.

4.2 Implementation Details

The proposed MGDNet is trained and tested in the PyTorch framework. During the training, we randomly crop local regions (256 × 256) of input paired images, and randomly flip or rotate them to enhance the diversity of training dataset. The training batch size is set to 4, and we train the MGDNet 30 epochs. To accelerate the training process, we use the Adam optimizer [33] and adopt a default value for the attenuation coefficient β_1 and β_2 being 0.9 and 0.999 respectively. Moreover, we set the initial learning rate to 0.0002, and decrease it to half every five epochs. All the experiments are implemented on a PC with two RTX 2080Ti GPUs.

4.3 Comparisons with State-of-the-Art Methods

Results on IHAZE and OHAZE. The comparison results are shown in Table 1, where the values are the average PSNR and SSIM of five indoor and outdoor testing images of IHAZE [30] and OHAZE [31], respectively. For IHAZE, the proposed MGDNet achieves the second-best performance of image dehazing in terms of both PSNR and SSIM. For OHAZE, the proposed MGDNet also achieves the second-best PSNR, and enhance SSIM by 0.02 when compared with second-best method DANet. These data show the DANet and our MGDNet conduct better dehazing effect on these two datasets. Also, we notice that prior-based methods DCP and NLD perform poorly in terms of both PSNR and SSIM, which shows the generated artifacts and color changes seriously reduce the quality of the dehazed images.

Table 1. Comparison of the state-of-the-art dehazing methods on IHAZE and OHAZE. Number in red and bule represent the best and second-best results, respectively.

Method		DCP	NLD	DANet	KDDN	PSD	RefineDNet	Ours
IHAZE	PSNR	12.49	13.57	16.23	13.42	13.67	15.9	16.02
	SSIM	0.58	0.59	0.72	0.62	0.63	0.75	0.73
OHAZE	PSNR	14.95	15.24	18.32	16.28	15.72	17.26	18.07
	SSIM	0.67	0.69	0.74	0.71	0.68	0.71	0.76

Results on Natural Hazy Images. Considering that hazy images acquired by haze machine may not completely verify the dehazing ability in real scenes, we further test all these methods on some real-world images in [17] and [33]. As shown in Fig. 4, prior-based methods DCP and NLD dehaze favorably but tent to cause color distortion and artifacts, which shows these methods have excellent generalization ability in real scenes. By contrast, learning-based methods tend to acquire under-dehazed results due to lacking of the knowledge to real-world hazy images. KDDN fails to dehaze in these scenes and a large amount of residual haze degrades the visibility of the generated results. More importantly, DANet cannot remove haze thoroughly and leads to obvious color changes although it shows favorable performance in IHAZE and OHAZE, which verifies this method cannot fit in natural scenes. The results of PSD suffer from severe color and illumination distortion, and some local regions have residual haze. Moreover, RefineDNet dehazes effectively in these scenes and acquires visually pleasing results. However, the results still contain some residual haze in local regions especially when applied to images with colorful textures. Better than above methods, the proposed MGDNet recovers high quality results with discriminative structures and vivid color, which shows it has strong dehazing effect in real scenes by the guiding of DCP and NLD methods. Moreover, compared to the dehazed images of DCP and NLD, we also notice that the results of MGDNet alleviate color distortion and artifacts by the training of synthetic images.

4.4 Ablation Study

To demonstrate the effectiveness of each module, we conduct an ablation study by the combination of four factors: DCP teacher network (DCP), NLD teacher network (NLD), pixel-wise distillation loss (PDL), discrete wavelet transform (DWT). We construct the following variants with different component combinations: (1) Student: only the student network is used; (2) Student+DCP: only the DCP teacher network is used to guide the student network by feature-wise distillation loss. (3) Student + NLD: only.

the NLD teacher network is used to guide the student network by feature-wise distillation losses. (4) Student+DCP+NLD: both the DCP and NLD teacher networks are used to guide the student network by feature-wise distillation losses. (5) Student+DCP+NLD+PDL: two teacher networks guide the student network by both feature-wise distillation losses and pixel-wise distillation losses (6) Student+DCP+NLD+PDL+DWT (Ours): a DWT module is applied before pixel-wise guiding, and only the high-frequency parts of DCP and NLD teacher networks are used

Fig. 4. Comparison of the state-of-the-art dehazing methods on the real-world images.

to guide the student network during pixel-wise comparison. The results are shown in Table 2, it demonstrates that the proposed MGDNet achieves the best performance of image dehazing in terms of PSNR and SSIM. Moreover, adding DCP teacher network, we can improve PSNR from 19.68 dB to 20.32 dB and enhance SSIM by 0.01. And adding NLD teacher network, we can also improve the metrics by 0.56 dB and 0.007. These results show that the combination of prior-based methods improves the performance in outdoor scenes although the network is only trained by indoor images, and the DCP is more efficient than the NLD for our method. Moreover, adding both of DCP teacher network and NLD teacher network also provides with a little gain, which means that combining with multiple priors further improve the generalization ability since unilateral prior cannot hold in various scenes. Additionally, we have also noticed that the addition of PDL drops the performance. It shows that directly using pixel-wise distillation losses may degrade final results since prior-based dehazing images always contain some negative information such as color shifts and artifacts. Fortunately, with the help of DWT, the network can alleviate the distortions in the outputs of teacher networks and further improves the metrics to 20.49 dB and 0.904, respectively.

Table 2. Comparison of variants with different components on the outdoor dataset of SOTS.

Method	PSNR	SSIM
Student	19.68	0.882
Student+DCP	20.32	0.892
Student+NLD	20.24	0.889
Student+DCP+NLD	20.34	0.902
Student+DCP+NLD+PDL	20.24	0.897
Ours	20.49	0.904

5   Conclusion

In this paper, we propose a multi-priors guided dehazing network (MGDNet) based on knowledge distillation, which combines the complementary merits of prior-based dehazing methods and learning-based dehazing methods. Specifically, we pretrain two teacher networks to efficiently use the partially correct features of dark channel prior (DCP) and non-local dehazing (NLD) dehazed results by both of feature-level and pixel-level distillation losses. Moreover, we adopt a high-pass discrete wavelet transform (DWT) before pixel-level guiding to alleviate the negative information of prior dehazed images such as color shifts and artifacts. And the added features of two teacher networks can be refined during the supervised training of student network. Experiments on real-world images demonstrate that the proposed MGDN achieves favorable dehazing effect by both of the quantitative and qualitative comparisons.

References

1. Ancuti, C.O., Ancuti, C.: Single image dehazing by multi-scale fusion. IEEE Trans. Image Process. **2**(8), 3271–3282 (2013)
2. Wang, N., Cui, Z., Su, Y., He, C., Li, A.: Multiscale supervision-guided context aggregation network for single image dehazing. IEEE Signal Process Lett. **29**, 70–74 (2022)
3. He, K., Sun, J., Tang, X.: Single image haze removal using dark channel prior. IEEE Trans. Pattern Anal. Mach. Intell. **33**(12), 2341–2353 (2011)
4. Fattal, R.: Dehazing using color-lines. ACM Trans. Graph. **34**(1), 1–14 (2014)
5. Zhu, Q., Mai, J., Shao, L.: A fast single image haze removal algorithm using color attenuation prior. IEEE Trans. Image Process. **24**(11), 3522–3533 (2015)
6. Berman, D., Treibitz, T., Avidan, S.: Non-local image dehazing. In: Computer Society Conference on Computer Vision and Pattern Recognition (CVPR), LAS Vegas , pp. 1674–1682. IEEE (2016)
7. Cai, B., Xu, X., Jia, K., Qing, C., Tao, D.: DehazeNet: an end-to-end system for single image haze removal. IEEE Trans. Image Process. **25**(11), 5187–5198 (2016)
8. Ren, W., Liu, S., Zhang, H., Pan, J., Cao, X., Yang, MH.: Single image dehazing via multi-scale convolutional neural networks. In: Leibe, B., Matas, J., Sebe, N., Welling, M. (eds.) ECCV 2016. LNCS, vol. 9906, pp. 154–169. Springer, Cham (2016). https://doi.org/10.1007/978-3-319-46475-6_10
9. Li, B., Peng, X., Wang, Z., Xu, J., Feng, D.: AOD-Net: all-in-one dehazing network. In: IEEE International Conference on Computer Vision (ICCV), Venice, pp. 4770–4778. IEEE (2017)
10. Zhang, H., Pattel, V. M.: Densely connected pyramid dehazing network. In: Computer Society Conference on Computer Vision and Pattern Recognition (CVPR), Salt Lake City, pp. 3194–3203. IEEE (2018)
11. Liu, X., Ma, Y., Shi, Z, Chen, J.: GridDehazeNet: attention-based multi-scale network for image dehazing. In: IEEE International Conference on Computer Vision (ICCV), Seoul, Korea, pp. 7313–7322. IEEE (2019)
12. Qin, X., Wang, Z., Bai, Y., Xie, X. Jia, H.: FFA-Net: feature fusion attention network for single image dehazing. In: IEEE Conference on Computer Vision and Pattern Recognition (CVPR), Long Beach, CA, pp. 1–8. IEEE (2019)
13. Liu, X., Suganuma, M., Sun, Z., Okatani, T.: Dual residual networks leveraging the potential of paired operations for image restoration. In: IEEE Conference on Computer Vision and Pattern Recognition (CVPR), Long Beach, CA, pp. 7000–7009. IEEE (2019)
14. Ren, W., et al.: Gated fusion network for single image dehazing. In: Computer Society Conference on Computer Vision and Pattern Recognition (CVPR), Salt Lake City, pp. 3253–3261. IEEE (2018)
15. Qu Y, Chen Y, Huang J, Xie, Y.: Enhanced Pix2pix dehazing network. In: IEEE Conference on Computer Vision and Pattern Recognition (CVPR), Long Beach, CA , pp. 8152–8160. IEEE (2019)
16. Dong H, et al.: Multi-scale boosted dehazing network with dense feature fusion. In: IEEE Conference on Computer Vision and Pattern Recognition (CVPR), Seattle, WA, pp. 2154–2164. IEEE (2020)
17. Shao, Y., Li, L., Ren, W., Gao, C., Sang, N.: Domain adaptation for image dehazing. In: IEEE Conference on Computer Vision and Pattern Recognition (CVPR), Seattle, WA, pp. 2144–2155. IEEE (2020)
18. Zhao, S., Zhang, L., Shen, Y., Zhou, Y.: RefineDNet: a weakly supervised refinement framework for single image dehazing. IEEE Trans. Image Process. **30**(1), 3391–3404 (2021)
19. Chen, Z., Wang, Y., Yang, Y., Liu, D.: PSD: principled synthetic-to-real dehazing guided by physical priors. In: IEEE Conference on Computer Vision and Pattern Recognition (CVPR), pp. 7176–7185 (2021)

20. Hong, M., Xie, Y., Li, C., Qu, Y.: Distilling image dehazing with heterogeneous task imitation. In: IEEE Conference on Computer Vision and Pattern Recognition (CVPR), Seattle, WA, pp. 3459–3468. IEEE (2020)
21. Chen, D., et al.: Gated context aggregation network for image dehazing and deraining. In: IEEE Winter Conference on Applications of Computer Vision (WACV), Hilton Waikoloa Village, Hawaii, pp. 1375–1383 (2019)
22. Wang, Z., Ji, S.: Smoothed dilated convolutions for improved dense prediction. In: WIREs Data Mining and Knowledge Discovery, vol. 35, no. 2, pp. 2468–2495 (2021)
23. He, K., Zhang, X., Ren, S., Sun, J.: Deep residual learning for image recognition. In: IEEE Conference on Computer Vision and Pattern Recognition (CVPR), Las Vegas, NV, pp. 770–778, IEEE (2016)
24. Zhang, Y., Tian, Y., Kong, Y., Zhong, B., Fu, Y.: Residual dense network for image super-resolution. In: IEEE Conference on Computer Vision and Pattern Recognition (CVPR), Salt Lake City, UT, pp. 2472–2481. IEEE (2018)
25. Huang, G., Liu, Z., Laurens, V., Weinberger, K. Q.: Densely connected convolutional networks. In: IEEE Conference on Computer Vision and Pattern Recognition (CVPR), LAS Vegas , pp. 2261–2269 (2016)
26. Zhao, H., Gallo, O., Frosio, I., Kautz, J.: Loss functions for image restoration with neural networks. IEEE Trans. Comput. Imaging 3(1), 47–57 (2017)
27. Johnson, J., Alahi, A., Fei-Fei, L.: Perceptual losses for real-time style transfer and super-resolution. In: Leibe, B., Matas, J., Sebe, N., Welling, M. (eds.) ECCV 2016. LNCS, vol. 9906, pp. 694–711. Springer, Cham (2016). https://doi.org/10.1007/978-3-319-46475-6_43
28. Fu, M. Liu, H., Yu, Y., Chen, J., Wang, K.: DW-GAN: a discrete wavelet transform GAN for nonhomogeneous dehazing. In: IEEE Conference on Computer Vision and Pattern Recognition Workshops (CVPRW), pp. 203–212 (2021)
29. Li, B., et al.: Benchmarking single-image dehazing and beyond. IEEE Trans. Image Process. 28(1), 492–505 (2019)
30. Ancuti, C.O., Ancuti, C., Timofte, R., Vleeschouwer, C.D.: I-HAZE: a dehazing benchmark with real hazy and haze-free indoor images. In: IEEE Computer Vision and Pattern Recognition (CVPR), Salt Lake City, pp. 746–754. IEEE (2018)
31. Ancuti, C.O., Ancuti, C., Timofte, R., Vleeschouwer, C.D.: O-HAZE: a dehazing benchmark with real hazy and haze-free outdoor images. In: IEEE Computer Vision and Pattern Recognition (CVPR), Salt Lake City, pp. 754–762. IEEE (2018)
32. Fattal, R.: Single image dehazing. ACM Trans. Graph. 27(3), 1–9 (2008)
33. Kingma, D., Ba, J.: Adam: a method for stochastic optimization. In: 3rd International Conference on Learning Representations (ICLR), San Diego, CA, USA (2015)

DLMP-Net: A Dynamic Yet Lightweight Multi-pyramid Network for Crowd Density Estimation

Qi Chen[1,2], Tao Lei[1,2(✉)], Xinzhe Geng[1,2], Hulin Liu[1,2], Yangyi Gao[1,2],
Weiqiang Zhao[3], and Asoke Nandi[4]

[1] Shaanxi Joint Laboratory of Artificial Intelligence, Shannxi University of Science
and Technology, Xi'an 710021, China
`leitao@sust.edu.cn`
[2] School of Electronic Information and Artificial Intelligence, Shannxi University
of Science and Technology, Xi'an 710021, China
[3] CETC Northwest Group Co., Ltd., Xi'an 710065, China
[4] Brunel University London, Uxbeidge, Middlesex UB8 3PH, UK

Abstract. The current deep neural networks used for crowd density estimation face two main problems. First, due to different surveillance distance from the camera, densely populated regions are characterized by dramatic scale change, thus using vanilla convolution kernels for feature extraction will inevitably miss discriminative information and reduce the accuracy of crowd density estimation results. Second, popular networks for crowd density estimation still depend on complex encoders with a large number of parameters, and adopt fixed convolutional kernels to extract image features at different spatial positions, resulting in spatial-invariance and computation-heavy. To remedy the above problems, in this paper, we propose a Dynamic yet Lightweight Multi-Pyramid Network (DLMP-Net) for crowd density estimation. The proposed DLMP-Net mainly makes two contributions. First, we design a shuffle-pyramid feature extraction and fusion module (SPFFM), which employs multi-dilated convolution to extract and fuse various scale features. In addition, we add group and channel shuffle operation to reduce the model complexity and improve the efficiency of feature fusion. Second, we introduce a Dynamic Bottleneck Block (DBB), which predicts exclusive kernels pixel by pixel and channel by channel dynamically conditioned on an input, boosting the model performance while decreasing the number of parameters. Experiments are conducted on five datasets: ShanghaiTech dataset, UCF_CC_50 dataset, UCF_QRNF dataset, GCC dataset and NWPU dataset and the ablation studies are performed on ShanghaiTech dataset. The final results show that the proposed DLMP-Net can effectively overcome the problems mentioned above and provides high crowd counting accuracy with smaller model size than state-of-the-art networks.

Keywords: Crowd density estimation · Feature fusion · Dynamic bottleneck block

© The Author(s), under exclusive license to Springer Nature Switzerland AG 2022
S. Yu et al. (Eds.): PRCV 2022, LNCS 13537, pp. 27–39, 2022.
https://doi.org/10.1007/978-3-031-18916-6_3

1   Introduction

In crowd analysis, crowd density estimation is an important branch which can predict the density maps of congested scenes. This development follows the demand of real-life applications since the same number of people could have completely different crowd distributions, thus just counting the number in a crowd is not enough. The density map can help us obtain more accurate and comprehensive information and is essential for making correct decisions in high-risk environments such as violence and stampede. The recent development of crowd density estimation relies on CNN-based methods because of the high accuracy they have achieved in image classification, semantic segmentation and object detection. Though many compelling CNN-based models [1,2,4,6–8] have been proposed, it is still challenging to achieve high-precision crowd counting results in complex crowd scenarios in [2–5,10].

Due to different surveillance distances from the camera, people in images or across scenes usually exhibit various scales and distributions. To tackle these problems, previous methods mainly use multi-column network such as [1,2,4,7] or multi-dilated decoders such as [6,8] to extract image multi-scale features. Though these methods have achieved success, they still have limitations. On the one hand, multi-column (usually three columns) network usually introduces more redundant information leading to low efficiency. Especially for the scene that is over-crowded or over-sparse, roughly dividing head size into three levels is equivocal for the targets at the edge of the boundary. On the other hand, prevailing density estimation models based on multi-dilated convolution just simply uses one or two different dilation rate convolutions, which will not fully meet the requirement of scale variation.

Typical backbones for crowd density estimation are VGG or ResNet. Based on these backbones, dozens of crowd density estimation methods have been proposed and they have achieved some success, but there is still much big promotion space. The fundamental assumption in the design of these classic network layers is the same and static convolution kernels shared by all images in a dataset, which ignores the content diversity and introduces high memory consumption. To increase the content-adaptive capacity of a model, many groundbreaking dynamic filters [18,19,21,22] have been proposed. Even though they attain accuracy gains, they are either compute-intensive or memory-intensive, leading to a difficulty of model deployment on low-resource devices. To facilitate model deployment, brilliant model compression approach channel pruning [17] is reported to reduce the computation and storage cost, but improper application of this method may lead to performance drops. Thus, how to design a crowd density estimation network that can balance model accuracy and model size is a challenge. In this paper, we propose a dynamic yet lightweight multi-pyramid network (DLMP-Net) for crowd density estimation. It mainly consists of two parts: a ResNet backbone based on dynamic bottleneck block and a shuffle-pyramid feature fusion module. The architecture of the proposed network can be seen in Fig. 1. Unlike the most previous networks that use VGG16 as the backbone, we employ a ResNet101 backbone as the encoder for its stronger representation power. We substitute all original bottleneck blocks with the proposed dynamic bottleneck block (DBB) in ResNwt101 to obtain content-diversity information. Then, a shuffle-pyramid feature fusion module (SPFFM) is designed for feature fusion to solve effectively the scale variation problem.

In general, the contributions of our work are twofold:

1) We present SPFFM to improve the feature fusion effectiveness and efficiency for crowd density estimation under complex scenes. The proposed SPFFM uses multi-dilated kernels and shuffled parallel group convolution to enlarge the receptive field and simultaneously improve the model inference speed.

2) We present DBB to achieve dynamic feature extraction depending on the inputs for crowd density estimation. The proposed DDB adjusts the convolution kernels dynamically conditioned on an input, which can attain richer semantic information requiring fewer parameters.

2   Related Work

For crowd density estimation, the challenge of scale change is one of the most important factors that affects model accuracy. To remedy this issue, MCNN [1] employs a multi-column convolutional neural network that utilizes multi-size filters to extract features for different receptive fields. Switch-CNN [2] further adds a density level classifier in front of the MCNN columns and allocates image patches with different density levels to corresponding branches to generate density maps. Analogously, CP-CNN [11] captures multi-scale information by using different CNN networks instead of multi-column structure to combine global and local context priors. To achieve better feature fusion, MBTTBF [20] presents a multi-level bottom-top and top-bottom fusion network to combine multiple shallow and deep features. Contrary to above multi-columns network structures, CSRNet [6] is a representative single-column density estimation network which utilizes six dilated convolution layers to expand the field of view. To go a step further, SFCN [7] adds a spatial encoder to the top of the FCN backbone, so as to improve the accuracy of population density map estimation. Though these works have achieved accuracy improvement by using different strategies of multi-scale feature fusion, they suffer from the increase of model complexity and parameters to some extent.

Therefore, lightweight networks become very popular in practical applications and model compression offers reduced computation cost. Channel pruning [17] as a typical model compression approach aims to remove the useless channels for easier acceleration in practice. Furthermore, other compact models such as Xception [12] and MobileNets [14] utilize lightweight convolutions to reduce the number of parameters. ShuffleNets [16] introduce channel shuffle operation to improve the information flow exchange between groups. Although these model compression approaches can effectively reduce the number of parameters, they usually sacrifice the model accuracy. In contrast to model compression approaches, dynamic convolution can effectively improve model accuracy. One of the early dynamic filters CondConv [18] predicts coefficients to combine several expert filters and learns specialized convolutional kernels for different inputs. DynamicConv [19] follows the idea of CondConv [18] but involves sum-to-one constraint and temperature annealing for efficient joint optimization. Albeit these approaches have improved model accuracy, the combined filters require a large number of parameters. For better parameter-accuracy tradeoff, the latest dynamic filter DDF [21] decouples dynamic filters into spatial and channel ones, which attains content-adaption but is lightweight even compared with the standard convolutions. Involution [22] breaks through existing inductive biases of convolution and also achieves superior performance while reducing the model size and computation load. These two latest dynamic filters raise the curtain of dynamic yet lightweight network design.

3   Proposed Solution

The architecture of the proposed DLMP-Net is illustrated in Fig. 1. Inspired by the idea in [4], we choose ResNet101 as the backbone for its flexible architecture and stronger feature extraction ability. In order to ensure the consistency and fairness with other crowd density estimation networks, we only use the first three layers of the ResNet101 and change the stride of the third layer from 2 to 1 to preserve the scale of the final density maps. This is because if we continue to stack more convolutional layers and pooling layers, the output size would be further shrunken and it is hard to generate high-quality density maps [6]. In particular, we use the proposed DBB to replace the traditional bottleneck blocks in the ResNet101 to achieve dynamic feature extraction depending on the inputs. For the encoding stage, we propose a shuffle-pyramid feature fusion module (SPFFM) to enlarge the receptive field of the extracted feature maps, which outputs high-quality density maps and simultaneously improves the inference speed of our model.

3.1   Shuffle-Pyramid Feature Fusion Module

In crowd density estimation tasks, standard convolution has two main defects. One is that it usually has a fixed receptive filed thus cannot efficiently extract multi-scale features in crowd images. The other is that stacking different scales of standard convolution kernels increases of the number of parameters. To solve the above problems, we design SPFFM to capture multi-scale features in crowd scenes. Specifically, we first divide input feature maps into multiple blocks, and then in each divided block, we perform group convolution and different rates of dilated convolutions. The structure of SPFFM is shown in Fig. 1.

In each layer of SPFFM, the number of groups G follows a sequential increment by 2^n ($G = 2^0, 2^1, 2^2, 2^3$) in a pyramid-shape and the dilation rate r increases by 1 (r = 1, 2, 3 and 4) also following the sequential increment of groups in a pyramid-shape. For example, in the first layer, we assume that the channels of the input feature maps are K; We divide the input feature maps into four blocks, and each block contains C1, C2, C3, C4 channels respectively, thus

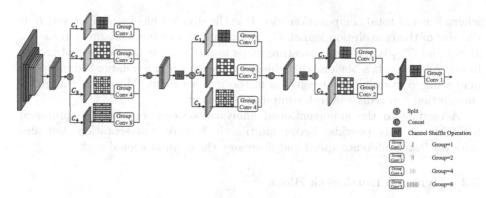

Fig. 1. The pipeline of the proposed DLMP-Net. We use ResNet101-DBB as the backbone. The shuffle-pyramid feature fusion module is used to extract multi-scale features. The detailed SPFFM is illustrated above.

apparently C1 + C2 + C3 + C4 = K. The first block contains C1 channels and the dilation rate and group number are 1 and 2^0, respectively. The second block contains C2 channels and the dilation rate and group number are 2 and 2^1, respectively. The third block and the last block continually follow the pyramid-shape increment as defined above. The second layer is divided into three blocks, the third layer is divided into two blocks and for the last layer, there is only one block in which we use standard convolution with G=1. Moreover, we introduce a channel shuffle operation before each division to improve the feature extraction efficiency and accuracy, since group convolution can reduce the amount of calculation. But between different groups, there is no connection and information exchanges. Channel shuffle operation can realize direct communication between different groups and prevents same feature maps between different layers from being divided into the same block.

According to the principle of SPFFM, the input feature maps are defined as I and the output feature maps are defined as O, then

$$O_i(I) = \begin{cases} Gconv(I, B_i, G_i, d_i), & i = 1 \\ Sf(Gconv(O_1(I), B_i, G_i, d_i)), & i = 2 \\ \vdots \\ Sf(Gconv(O_{N-1}(I), B_i, G_i, d_i)), & i = N \end{cases} \tag{1}$$

where $Gconv(I, B_i, G_i, d_i)$ represents the group dilated convolution, B_i is the number of blocks, G_i is the number of groups, d_i is the dilation rate, and N is the number of layers. It is worth noting that B_i, G_i, d_i and N are hyperparameters. The Sf denotes the channel shuffle operation. The overall computational cost of SPFFM is

$$F(B, G, K, C_{in}, C_{out}) = \sum_{i=1}^{B} \left(\frac{K_i \times C_{in}^i \times C_{out}^i \times H \times W}{G_i} \right), \tag{2}$$

where F is the total computation cost, B is the divided blocks number and K is the size of the convolution kernel. C_{in}^i is the number of input features in the i_{th} group and C_{out}^i is the output feature maps number. G_i is the number of groups in the i_{th} block. It's obvious that dilated convolution can enlarge the receptive field while containing the resolution of the feature maps. Moreover, the group convolution can reduce overall computational load.

According to the aforementioned analysis, we can see that the proposed SPFFM not only provides better multi-scale feature representation, but also achieves faster inference speed and decreases the computational cost.

3.2 Dynamic Bottleneck Block

The deep CNNs based on vanilla convolution usually apply the same convolution kernels to all pixels in an crowd image, inevitably leading to sub-optimal feature learning. To address the above problem, we propose a dynamic bottleneck block, namely DBB, which adjusts the convolution kernels dynamically conditioned on an input.

In DBB, a spatial filter and a channel filter are respectively predicted depending on the input features through their corresponding filter prediction branches, then the two filters are pixel-wise multiplied to obtain a new filter as shown in Fig. 2. The new filter is finally used in image feature extraction. This operation can be written as:

$$V'_{(r,i)} = \sum_{p_n \in R} \left\{ D_i^{spatial} \cdot (p_i - p_j) \cdot D_r^{channel} \cdot (p_i - p_j) \cdot V_{(r,j)} \right\} \qquad (3)$$

where $V'_{(r,i)}$ is the value at i_{th} pixel and r_{th} channel of output feature. $V_{(r,j)}$ is the value at j_{th} pixel and r_{th} channel the input feature. $D_i^{spatial}$ is the spatial dynamic filter at i_{th} pixel; $D_r^{channel}$ is the channel dynamic filter at r_{th} channel.

In practical applications, we usually consider DBB as a block and apply it to a backbone. For the prediction branch of spatial filter, the channel number is changed into K^2 only by 1×1 convolution, and the K^2 (which is reshaped as $K \times K$ later) corresponding to each pixel is what we want as a spatial filter. For the prediction branch of channel filter, a structure similar to SE attention operation [15] is adopted. Firstly, input feature maps are directly squeezed into a $C \times 1 \times 1$ tensor through global average pooling, and this tensor is considered to have global information. Then through a gate mechanism composed of two layers of fully connection (excitation layers), $C \times 1 \times 1$ is reshaped into $C \times K^2$, that is, each channel C_i corresponds to an attention value $(K^2)_i$. Then we combine the predicted spatial and channel filters by pixel-wise multiplication to obtain a new filter. Thus, the final filter is exclusive pixel by pixel and channel by channel. As the generated filter values might be extremely large or small for some input samples, the Filter Normalization is introduced to maintain the stability of the training process. Due to the limited space, we do not make the detailed explanation. We compared the performance of traditional ResNet101 and ResNet101-DBB in crowd density estimation, as shown in Fig. 3, our ResNet101-DDB is more sensitive on both sparse and crowded regions.

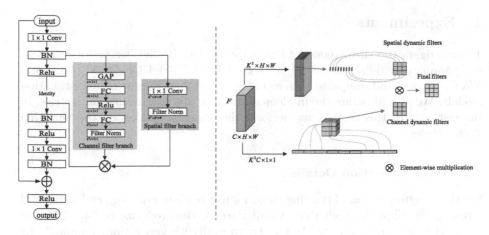

Fig. 2. The proposed Dynamic Bottleneck Block (DBB) and the detailed spatial/channel filter prediction branches.

Here we have a brief discussion about the parameter comparison between spatial/channel filters prediction branches in DDB and vanilla convolution. We assume n as the number of pixels, c as the channel numbers (for simplicity, both input channel and output channel numbers are c), k as the filter size and σ as the squeeze ratio in excitation layer. For prediction branch of spatial filter, the channel number is changed from c into k^2 only by 1×1 convolution and thus it contains ck^2 parameters; For prediction branch of channel filter, in the squeeze layer, it contains σc^2 parameters. In the excitation layer, the channel number is changed from σc into $k^2 c$, so it contains $\sigma c^2 k^2$ parameters. In total, the prediction branches contain $(ck^2 + \sigma c^2 + \sigma c^2 k^2)$ parameters. Considering that the values of k, c and σ, are usually set to 3, 256 and 0.2, the number of parameters for the prediction branches in DBB can be much lower even than a vanilla convolution layer.

Fig. 3. The heat map comparison between ResNet101 and proposed ResNet101-DBB in the same crowd scene from GCC dataset.

4   Experiments

To investigate the effectiveness of the proposed DLMP-Net, we performed it on five popular crowd datasets: ShanghaiTech, UCF_CC_50, UCF-QRNF, GCC and NWPU-Crowd and compared with recent seven state-of-the-art crowd estimation models. We also illustrate the implementation details and evaluation metrics. In the last part of this section, we perform the ablation studies on the Shanghai Tech dataset.

4.1   Implementation Details

For data augmentation of training data, we use random cropping and horizontal flipping. For ShanghaiTech Part A and Part B, the crop size is 256×256 and 512×512 for other datasets. As for the groundtruth generation, we adopt the same strategy in [1], which utilizes Gaussian kernels to blur and smooth the head annotations. It is defined as:

$$F_i^{Groundtruth} = \sum_{x_i \in p} G_{\sigma^2}(x) \times \theta(x - x_i) \tag{4}$$

where the pixel position in the image is defined as x and the position of the i_{th} head on the annotation map θ is defined as x_i. $G_{\sigma^2}(x)$ is the Gaussian kernel and σ is the deviation of Gaussian distribution. We set the Gaussian kernel size to 15 and σ to 4 for all datasets for fair comparison. The backbone is pretrained on the ImageNet dataset [9] and we use the Adam algorithm with a learning rate 1×10^{-5} for optimization. Our DLMP-Net is implemented on an eight NVIDIA RTX 3090 GPU (24 GB).

4.2   Evaluation Metrics

For crowd density estimation, we use two evaluation metrics namely mean absolute error (MAE) and mean squared error (MSE).

$$MAE = \frac{1}{N} \sum_{i=1}^{N} \left| Y_i - \widehat{Y_i} \right| \tag{5}$$

$$MSE = \sqrt{\frac{1}{N} \sum_{i=1}^{N} \left| Y_i - \widehat{Y_i} \right|^2} \tag{6}$$

where N is the samples number and Y_i is the groundtruth crowd counting result of the ith image. $\widehat{Y_i}$ is the predicted count of the ith image. We sum up the predicted density map to obtain the counting result. To measure the quality of the predicted density map, we choose the pixel-wise mean square error (MSE) loss as the objective function. During the optimization process, the model parameter β is defined as follows:

$$Loss\,(\beta) = \frac{1}{2Z} \sum_{i=1}^{Z} ||S_i^{GT} - \hat{S}_i^{PRE}||_2^2 \tag{7}$$

where batch size is Z and the groundtruth density map of the input image is S_i^{GT}. The estimated density map is $\hat{S}_i^{PRE}$.

4.3   Main Comparison

We compared our method with seven state-of-the-art methods on five popular datasets comprehensively. The overall comparison results demonstrate that our DLMP-Net can provide good prediction results for various complex scenarios.

ShanghaiTech Dataset. In ShanghaiTech Part A, 300 and 183 images are used for training and testing, respectively. The ShanghaiTech Part B includes 716 images, in which 400 images are used for training and 316 images are used for testing. It can be seen in Table 1 that our DLMP-Net obtains MAE/MSE of 59.2/90.7 as the best performance.

UCF_CC_50 Dataset. UCF_CC_50 dataset includes 50 images with different perspectives and resolutions, and we follow the 5-fold cross-validation method in [13]. In the experiments, four groups are used for training and the last one group is used for testing. As shown in Table 1, Our DLMP-Net still reached the smallest values of MAE/MSE of 183.7/268.5. Notably, the overall MSE/MAE values are much higher in all approaches compared with others datasets because UCF_CC_50 dataset contains imbalanced samples and small number of images.

UCF_QRNF Dataset. The images are divided into the training set with 1,201 images and the test set with 334 images, respectively. As shown in Table 1, our DLMP-Net attains optimal MAE/MSE values of 99.1/169.7, especially the MAE value is less than 100, which shows our stronger feature extraction ability.

GCC Dataset. GCC consists of 15,212 images and we randomly divided 75% images for training and rest 25% for testing. Table 1 shows the comparison between our DLMP-Net and seven other state-of-the-art approaches. Our DLMP-Net attains the smallest values of MAE/MAE, namely 25.3/73.2, especially the MSE value achieves a tremendous drop from nearly 80 to 66.2.

NWPU-Crowd Dataset. The NWPU-Crowd dataset is a large-scale and challenging dataset that contains 5,109 images and 2,133,238 labeled instances. Table 1 shows that the value of MAE for DLMP-Net is 87.7, with an improvement of 7.3 over SFCN[†] [7]. The value of MSE provided a slight reduction of

Table 1. Experimental results of DLMP-Net with other seven state-of-the-art methods on five main stream datasets. The best values are in bold.

Methods	ShanghaiTechA		ShanghaiTechB		UCF_CC_50		UCF_QRNF		GCC(RS)		NWPU-crowd	
	MAE(↓)	MSE(↓)	MAE(↓)	MSE(↓)	MAE(↓)	MSE(↓)	MAE(↓)	MSE(↓)	MAE(↓)	MSE(↓)	MAE(↓)	MSE(↓)
CSRNet (2018)	68.2	115.0	10.6	16.0	266.1	397.5	121.3	208.0	38.5	86.6	103.0	433.8
SCAR (2018)	66.3	114.1	9.5	15.2	259.0	374.0	-	-	31.7	76.8	-	-
SFCN (2019)	67.0	104.5	8.4	13.6	266.4	397.6	135.1	239.8	36.1	81.0	106.2	615.8
SFCN† (2019)	64.8	107.5	7.6	13.0	245.3	375.8	114.5	193.6	28.8	71.2	95.0	597.4
CAN (2019)	62.3	100.0	7.8	12.2	212.2	243.7	107.0	183.0	-	-	-	-
PSCC+DCL (2020)	65.0	108.0	8.1	13.3	-	-	108.0	182.0	31.3	83.3	-	-
HYCNN (2020)	60.2	94.5	7.5	12.7	184.4	270.1	100.8	185.3	-	-	-	-
Our DLMP-Net	**59.2**	**90.7**	**7.1**	**11.3**	**183.7**	**268.5**	**99.1**	**169.7**	**25.3**	**73.2**	**87.7**	**431.6**

2.2 compared with CSRNet [6], this is because crowd scenes in NWPU-Crowd have a various distribution. Figure 4 further shows the quantitative counting results and comparative estimated density maps on the NWPU-Crowd dataset using SCAR [8], SFCN† [7], and our DLMP-Net. It is clear that the proposed DLMP-Net can provide better counting results and high quality density maps for various complex scenarios.

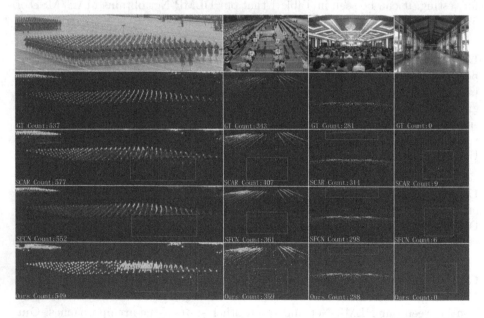

Fig. 4. The density estimation results comparison between SCAR, SFCN and DLMP-Net on NWPU dataset

4.4 Ablation Studies

To demonstrate the effectiveness of our DLMP-Net, we perform ablation experiments on ShanghaiTech dataset and the results are presented in Table 2. For all ablation studies, we adopt ResNet101 as the basic component and combine three different types of SPFFM with or without DDB to further investigate the effectiveness. Specifically, SPFFM (A) utilizes vanilla convolution with the kernel size 3×3, SPFFM(B) utilizes dilated convolution with fixed dilation rate r = 2 and SPFFM (Ours) is the proposed method with the dilation rate r =(1, 2, 3 and 4). It can be seen that without DBB, all model sizes increase 8.5M and using vanilla convolution for feature fusion has the worst performance. Compared with vanilla convolution and fixed-rate dilated convolution, SPFFM (ours) has tremendously improvements of 24.6/55.2 (MAE/MSE) over SPFFM(A) and 10 /20.6 (MAE/MSE) over SPFFM(B) on ShanghaiTechA even without adding DBB. On ShanghaiTechB, SPFFM (ours) also achieves the best results. In the last three ablation experiments, we combined DBB with three different types of SPFFM. The experimental results show that we can obtain more accurate and efficient models by adding DBB. SPFFM (ours) + DBB greatly improves 20.2/45.3 (MAE/MSE) over SPFFM(A)+DBB and 8.6/24.2 (MAE/MSE) over SPFFM(B)+DBB on ShanghaiTechA. Significant improvements can also be seen on ShanghaiTechB.

Table 2. Comparison of the model size and MAE/MSE on ShanghaiTech dataset for different SPFFM types and DBB. The best values are in bold.

backbone	SPFFM structure			DBB	Parameters (M)	ShanghaiTechA		ShanghaiTechB	
	SPFFM (A)	SPFFM (B)	SPFFM (Ours)			MAE($\downarrow$)	MSE ($\downarrow$)	MAE ($\downarrow$)	MSE ($\downarrow$)
	✓				33.27	87.2	157.0	28.4	48.4
		✓			33.27	72.6	122.4	12.2	17.6
ResNet101			✓		33.27	62.6	101.8	7.7	12.9
	✓			✓	24.77	79.7	136.0	15.1	21.8
		✓		✓	24.77	67.8	104.9	10.2	16.5
Our DLMP-Net			✓	✓	**24.77**	**59.2**	**90.7**	**7.1**	**11.3**

5 Conclusion

In this paper, we present a dynamic yet lightweight multi-pyramid network (DLMP-Net) for crowd density estimation. DLMP-Net is superior to the current models due to the design of a shuffle-pyramid feature extraction and fusion module (SPFFM) and a dynamic bottleneck block (DBB) which can replace the standard bottleneck blocks in ResNet backbone. SPFFM employs multi-dilated convolution to extract and fuse various scale features. In addition, we add group and channel shuffle operation to reduce the model complexity and improve the efficiency of feature fusion. DBB predicts exclusive kernels pixel by pixel and channel by channel dynamically conditioned on the input, boosting the model performance while decreasing the number of parameters. Extensive experiments demonstrate that the proposed DLMP-Net has better performance for crowd counting and density estimation in different congested images. In future work, we will further investigate the improved dynamic filters and explore how to form a fully dynamic crowd density estimation network.

Acknowledgements. This work was supported in part by Natural Science Basic Research Program of Shaanxi (Program No. 2022JQ-634).

References

1. Zhang, Y., Zhou, D., Chen S., Gao, S., Ma, Y.: Single-image crowd counting via multi-column convolutional neural network. In: 2016 IEEE Conference on Computer Vision and Pattern Recognition (CVPR), pp. 589–597. IEEE, Las Vegas (2016)
2. Sam, D.B., Surya, S., Babu R.V.: Switching convolutional neural network for crowd counting. In: 2017 IEEE Conference on Computer Vision and Pattern Recognition (CVPR), pp. 5744–5752. IEEE, Hawaii (2017)
3. Wang, Q., Gao, J., Lin, W., Li, X.: A large-scale benchmark for crowd counting and localization. IEEE Trans. Pattern Anal. Mach. Intell. **1**(3), 7 (2020)
4. Wang, Q., Gao, J., Lin, W., Yuan, Y.: Learning from synthetic data for crowd counting in the wild. In: 2019 IEEE Conference on Computer Vision and Pattern Recognition (CVPR), pp. 8198–8207. IEEE, Los Angeles (2019)
5. Idrees, H., et al.: Composition loss for counting, density map estimation and localization in dense crowds. In: Ferrari, V., Hebert, M., Sminchisescu, C., Weiss, Y. (eds.) ECCV 2018. LNCS, vol. 11206, pp. 544–559. Springer, Cham (2018). https://doi.org/10.1007/978-3-030-01216-8_33
6. Li, Y., Zhang, X., Chen, D.: CSRNet: dilated convolutional neural networks for understanding the highly congested scenes. In: 2018 IEEE Conference on Computer Vision and Pattern Recognition (CVPR), pp. 1091–1100. IEEE, Salt Lack City (2018)
7. Liu, W., Salzmann, M., Fua, P.: Context-aware crowd counting. In: 2019 IEEE Conference on Computer Vision and Pattern Recognition (CVPR), pp. 5099–5108. IEEE, Los Angeles (2019)
8. Gao, J., Wang, Q., Yuan, Y.: SCAR: spatial-channel-wise attention regression networks for crowd counting. Neurocomputing **363**, 1–8 (2019)
9. Deng, J., Dong, W., Socher, R.: Imagenet: a large-scale hierarchical image database. In: 2009 IEEE Conference on Computer Vision and Pattern Recognition (CVPR), pp. 248–255. IEEE, Miami (2009)
10. Idrees, H., Saleemi, I., Seibert, C., Shah, M.: Multi-source multi-scale counting in extremely dense crowd images. In: 2013 IEEE Conference on Computer Vision and Pattern Recognition (CVPR), pp. 2547–2554. IEEE, Portland (2013)
11. Sindagi, V.A., Patel, V.M.: Generating high quality crowd density maps using contextual pyramid CNNs. In: 2017 IEEE International Conference on Computer Vision (ICCV), pp. 1861–1870, IEEE, Venice (2017)
12. Chollet, F.: Xception: Deep learning with depthwise separable convolutions. In 2017 IEEE Conference on Computer Vision and Pattern Recognition (CVPR), pp. 1251–1258. IEEE, Hawaii (2017)
13. Lei, T., Zhang, D., Wang, R., Li, S., Zhang, Z., Nandi, A.K.: MFP-Net: multi-scale feature pyramid network for crowd counting. IET. Image Process. **15**(14), 3522–3533 (2021)

14. Howard, A.G., Zhu, M., Chen, B., Kalenichenko, D., Wang, W., Weyand, T.: MobileNets: efficient convolutional neural networks for mobile vision applications. arXiv:1704.04861. (2017)
15. Hu, J., Shen, L., Sun, G.: Squeeze-and-excitation networks. In: 2018 IEEE Conference on Computer Vision and Pattern Recognition (CVPR), pp. 7132–7141. IEEE, Salt Lack City (2018)
16. Ma, N., Zhang, X., Zheng, H.-T., Sun, J.: ShuffleNet V2: practical guidelines for efficient CNN architecture design. In: Ferrari, V., Hebert, M., Sminchisescu, C., Weiss, Y. (eds.) Computer Vision – ECCV 2018. LNCS, vol. 11218, pp. 122–138. Springer, Cham (2018). https://doi.org/10.1007/978-3-030-01264-9_8
17. Wen, W., Wu, C., Wang, Y., Chen, Y., Li, H.: Learning structured sparsity in deep neural networks. In: Advances in Neural Information Processing Systems (NIPS), vol. 29 (2016)
18. Yang, B., Bender, G., Le, Q.V., Ngiam, J.: Condconv: conditionally parameterized convolutions for efficient inference. Adv. Neural Inf. Process. Syst. (NeurIPS) **32**, 1–12 (2019)
19. Chen, Y., Dai, X., Liu, M., Chen, D., Yuan, L., Liu, Z.: Dynamic convolution: attention over convolution kernels. In: 2020 IEEE Conference on Computer Vision and Pattern Recognition (CVPR), pp. 11030–11039. IEEE, Seattle (2020)
20. Sindagi, V.A., Patel, V.M.: Multi-level bottom-top and top-bottom feature fusion for crowd counting. In: 2019 International Conference on Computer Vision, pp. 1002–1012, IEEE, Los Angeles (2019)
21. Zhou, J., Jampani, V., Pi, Z., Liu, Q., Yang, M.H.: Decoupled dynamic filter networks. In:2021 IEEE Conference on Computer Vision and Pattern Recognition (CVPR), pp. 6647–6656. IEEE, Online (2021)
22. Li, D., Hu, J., Wang, C., Li, X., She, Q., Zhu, L.: Involution: inverting the inherence of convolution for visual recognition. In:2021 IEEE Conference on Computer Vision and Pattern Recognition (CVPR), pp. 12321–12330. IEEE, Online (2021)

CHENet: Image to Image Chinese Handwriting Eraser

Biao Wang, Jiayi Li[✉], Xin Jin, and Qiong Yuan

Beijing Electronic Science and Technology Institute, Beijing, China
675773306@qq.com

Abstract. Erasing Chinese handwritten words in images has many applications in our daily life. It can hide the private information in the archive images (home address, identity information), delete the signature information in the contract images, and clear the handwriting in the test paper to reuse it. However, the existing research mainly focuses on scene text removal. To fill this gap and facilitate this research direction, we propose a novel model called CHENet (Chinese Handwriting Eraser Network) that can automatically remove Chinese handwriting located on the images. In particular, we design two modules: CAB (Convolution Attention Block) and CAP (Chain Attention Pooling) that can improve the ability of the CHENet. Also, for information protection, we collect images with Chinese handwritten words from the archive, contract, and exam papers, and build the CH-dataset that consists of 1623 scrupulously annotated images. Qualitative and quantitative evaluations show that our CHENet can solve this task well.

Keywords: Text removal · Chinese handwriting removal · End-to-end network · Attention network

1 Introduction

The text removal task has drawn the attention of researchers due to its use value for privacy protection. However, recent researches focus more on scene text removal task, which aims to remove the text in a scene image. Scene text is the information carrier and contains a considerable amount of personal, private, or sensitive information, such as an address, ID number, telephone number, and license plate number.

But there is little attention paid to another sub-topic of the Text removal task: handwritten text removal. As shown in Fig. 1. Handwritten text is one of the most important media for information transmission. It can be seen everywhere, especially in test papers, archives and contracts. Recently, information security has been gradually emphasized especially in handwritten messages. The disclosure of the images containing confidential information will cause irreparable losses to individuals, companies, and government agencies. Therefore, removing handwritten words from the image is conducive to protecting private information. However, handwritten words are diverse. This paper mainly focuses on Chinese handwritten words.

© The Author(s), under exclusive license to Springer Nature Switzerland AG 2022
S. Yu et al. (Eds.): PRCV 2022, LNCS 13537, pp. 40–51, 2022.
https://doi.org/10.1007/978-3-031-18916-6_4

Fig. 1. The task of Chinese handwriting removal.

We have made a lot of attempts. Our first attempt is an end-to-end encoding decoding convolutional neural network. Then we convert the encoding and decoding architecture to Unet-like [12] architecture. We find that the attention mechanism can capture and distinguish information from background regions and handwriting regions well. So we design the Convolution Attention Block (CAB), which combines the spatial and channel attention mechanism to get the low-level features maps. Also, we design the Chain Attention Pooling module to fuse high-level semantic information and low-level feature maps, to generate the resulting image with the invasive background. Based on these two modules, we propose the CHENet, which can erase the Chinese handwriting area while retaining the background information. Recently, many methods of scene text removal have built comprehensive real-world datasets, such as SCUT-EnsText [8], MLT-2019 [11], ArTs [2]. But for the task of Chinese handwriting removal, we need to collect and annotate images first. Although there are many images with Chinese handwriting, we mainly collect files, contracts, and test paper images. Then we carefully erase the text and fill the text region with a visually plausible background. Finally, our CH-dataset contains 1623 carefully annotated paired images (original and ground truths).

The main contributions of our paper can be summarized as:

- We propose the CHENet, which can automatically remove Chinese handwriting located on the images for purpose of personal private information protection.
- We design the Convolution Attention Block, which can effectively capture the semantic features of images, and the Chain Attention Pooling module, which replaces long-range skip connections and can obtain background information from a wide range of areas.
- We construct CH-dataset, which contains 1623 images with high-quality annotations for the Chinese handwriting removal task.

2   Related Work

2.1   Text Removal

Khodadadi *et al.* [7] estimate the background and text color in the candidate blocks using the color histogram measured in different sub-blocks of the candidate text blocks. Modha *et al.* [9] combine the inpainting techniques with the techniques of text-finding using a simple morphological algorithm. But afore-mentioned methods are traditional non-learning methods based on hand-crafted text-detection and inpainting algorithms which lack of generality.

Recently, due to the powerful learning capacity of deep neural networks, a variety of approaches have shown great achievements in the task of text removal. ST Eraser [10] is the first to use the convolutional neural network (CNN) for the task of scene text removal. EnsNet [18] is the first to propose an end-to-end framework based on the conditional GAN. Compared with the ST Eraser, it removes the scene text on the whole images with four carefully designed loss functions. MTRNet [14] is a conditional adversarial generative network (cGAN) with an auxiliary mask. They not only relieve the cGAN of overcoming text detection challenges such as scene complexity, illumination and blurring, but also focus the network on the task of text inpainting. MTRNet++ [13] is a one-stage mask-based text inpainting network. It has a novel architecture that includes mask-refine, coarse-inpainting and fine-inpainting branches, and attention blocks. Compared to MTRNet, it can remove text under very coarse masks. TSDNet [1] is a novel "end-to-end" framework based on a text stroke detection network and a text removal generation network. EraseNet [8] is a novel GAN-based model that can automatically remove text located on the natural images with an additional segmentation head to help more accurately erase the text regions. The model is a two-stage network that consists of a coarse-erasure sub-network and a refinement sub-network.

2.2 Handwriting Recognition

In this section, we will introduce the methods of handwriting recognition. Although the task of handwriting recognition is not suitable for handwriting removal, some methods of scene text removal are to detect the text in the image first, and then remove them. Kang et al. [5] propose a generative method for handwritten text-line images, which is conditioned on both visual appearance and textual content and use the generated samples to boost Handwritten Text Recognition performance. Gao et al. [3] propose a network that use the separable convolution and data augmentation techniques to improve the expression ability of the dataset and the generalization capabilities of the model. Zhu et al. [19] propose a method based on generative adversarial networks (GANs) of Chinese character handwriting-to-printing font conversion is proposed herein, where Chinese handwriting-to-printing font conversion is represented as a font style conversion and regarded as the optimal state of normalization of handwritten Chinese characters. Kass et al. [6] proposes an attention-based sequence-to-sequence model for handwritten word recognition and explores transfer learning for data-efficient training of HTR systems.

3 Chinese Handwriting Dataset

For the purpose of information protection, we collect images with Chinese handwritten words from the following three perspectives:

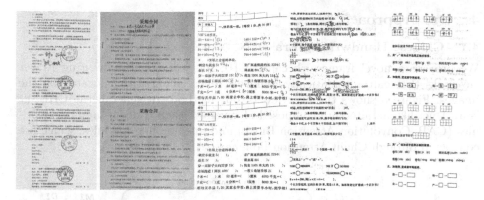

Fig. 2. Some examples of our collected dataset. First line is the original images, second line is the ground-truths.

- Contract: it often involves some confidential information: company or organization information, date and time information, etc.
- Archive: it often contains users' personal privacy information: name, home address, work unit, family members, etc.
- Test paper: it contains a large number of handwritten Chinese words.

Some examples are shown in Fig. 2. We collect these images from the Internet and also take some manually. We mainly use the copy stamp and image repair functions from PS (PhotoShop). The copy stamp function can copy the pixels in one part of the picture to the specified region, the image repair function selects one region of an image and can automatically restore this region according to the surrounding texture.

In summary, as shown in Table 1, the CH-dataset contains a total of 1623 images with diverse Chinese handwritten words. It is split into a training set and a testing set (randomly select approximately 80% of images for training and the remainder for testing.)

Table 1. Quantity statistics of our collected dataset.

	Contract	Archive	TestPaper	Total
Train	314	362	747	1423
Test	50	50	100	200
Total	364	412	847	1623

4   Our Approach

4.1   Chinese Handwriting Eraser Network

We propose a novel framework called CHENet (Chinese Handwriting Eraser Network) that can automatically remove Chinese handwriting located on the images. Figure 3 shows the overview of our method. In general, the CHENet is an Unet-like architecture composed of several designed down-sampling modules (CAB, Convolution Attention Block) and up-sampling modules, which are connected through Chain Attention Pooling (CAP) modules

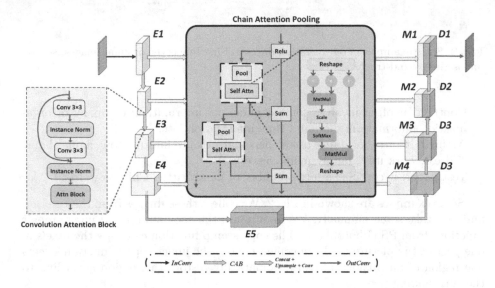

Fig. 3. The overview of our CHENet. The CHENet is the end-to-end network and we add the Convolution Attention Block and Chain Attention Pooling block to it. These designed modules can better capture the low-level features and high-level semantic features and combine them well.

Following the illustration in Fig. 4 up bottom, we start from the Inconv (just the convolution operation) and use four Convolution Attention Blocks to get the low-level features maps E_1, E_2, E_3, E_4, E_5. The output feature maps $E_1 - E_4$ then go through the Chain Attention Pooling modules to get the $M_1 - M_4$. In the next stage, similar to the original Unet, we use up-sampling operation and concat operation to fuse the high-level features $D_1 - D_4$ and low-level features M_1, M_2, M_3, M_4, E_5.

The entire CHENet can be efficiently trained end-to-end. It is significant to note that we introduce the Chain Attention Pooling module between the encoder and decoder which replaces the long-range skip connections.

Convolution Attention Block. We change the UNET original convolution operation and add spatial attention and channel attention mechanism. As shown in Fig. 4. We have mainly implemented three minor changes for the CAB module.

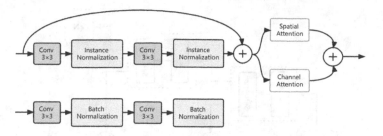

Fig. 4. The comparison of the original Unet Convolution Block and the Convolution Attention Block. Below: the original Unet Down-sampling Block which consists of several convolution layers and Batch Norm layers. Above: the Convolution Attention Block. we have mainly implemented three minor changes. 1) residual shortcut connections; 2) Instance Normalization instead of Batch Normalization; 3) Channel Attention Module (CAM) and Spartial Attention Module (SAM).

1) We add the residual module of ResNet [4] to our Convolution Attention Block. We use shortcut connections to prevent network degradation.
2) We replace BN (Batch Normalization) with IN (Instance Normalization) [15]. The application of IN can not only accelerate the convergence of the model, but also maintain the independence between each image instance. Because the image generation mainly depends on a single source image instance, it is not suitable to normalize the whole batch.
3) Inspired by previous work CBAM [17], we add Channel Attention Module (CAM) and Spartial Attention Module (SAM) to our convolution blocks. Because CBAM [17] is a lightweight and general module, it can be integrated into any CNN architecture seamlessly with negligible overheads and is end-to-end trainable along with base CNNs.

Chain Attention Pooling. We believe that the potential limitation of using Unet-like model is the skip connection. So we modify encoder-decoder with the attention module.

Not each skip connection setting is effective due to the issue of incompatible feature sets of encoder and decoder stage. Therefore, we design the Chain Attention Pooling (CAP) module between the encoder and decoder to better integrate the features of them. As shown in Fig. 5. The proposed Chain Attention Pooling module can obtain background information from a wide range of areas. As depicted in Fig. 5, the output feature map of the encoder will go through the Chain Attention Pooling module. It is able to efficiently pool features with multiple window sizes and fuse them together. Note that, the CAP is built as a chain of multiple attention blocks, each consisting of one max-pooling layer and self-attention [16] layer. Self attention is better at capturing the internal correlation of features. We use its long dependence modeling advantage to fuse the

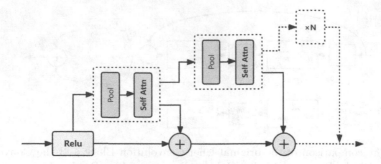

Fig. 5. The detail of the Chain Attention Pooling module. It is built as a chain of multiple attention blocks, each consisting of one max-pooling layer and self-attention layer. One attention block takes the output of the previous attention block as input.

features of multi-scale encoder. One attention block takes the output of the previous attention block as input. Therefore, the current attention block is able to reuse the result from the previous operation and thus access the features from a large region without using a large window.

4.2 Training Loss

ℓ_1 **loss** We minimize the ℓ_1 loss of the synthesized image $\hat{I}_{trg}$ and of the ground truth target I_{trg}. The reconstruction ℓ_1 loss is written as

$$L_{\ell_1} = \| \hat{I}_{trg} - I_{trg} \|_1 \tag{1}$$

Perceptual Loss. The perceptual loss calculates ℓ_1 distance between activation maps of a pre-trained network of the synthesized image $\hat{I}_{trg}$ and of the ground truth target I_{trg}. It can be written as

$$L_{perc} = \Sigma \| \phi(\hat{I}_{trg}) - \phi(I_{trg}) \|_1 \tag{2}$$

where ϕ is the activation map of the middle layer of a pre-trained network. In our network, we use the VGG16 model, and calculate the output feature maps of the middle layers, and then compare the difference to get the loss.

Style Loss. The style loss calculates the statistic error between the activation maps. It can be written as

$$L_{style} = \Sigma \| G^{\phi}(\hat{I}_{trg}) - G^{\phi}(I_{trg}) \|_1 \tag{3}$$

Mask Loss. Mask loss mainly focuses on the distance between the generated image and the real image compared with the source image. it can be written as

$$L_{mask} = \| Dice((I_{src} - \hat{I}_{trg}) - (I_{src} - I_{trg})) \|_1 \tag{4}$$

We calculate the mask between $\hat{I}_{trg}$ and I_{src} and the mask between I_{src} and I_{trg}.

Adversarial Loss. We also design the Multiscale Patch Discriminator. So we calculate the adversarial loss by:

$$L_{adv} = \Sigma \parallel D(\hat{I}_{trg}) \parallel_1 \tag{5}$$

where D is the designed Multiscale Patch Discriminator.

Therefore, our final loss is:

$$L_{total} = \ell_1 + L_{perc} + L_{style} + L_{mask} + L_{adv} \tag{6}$$

5 Experiments

Fig. 6. The outputs of our CHENet. The first line is the input images, the second line is the output images. It shows that our method generate more realistic images which already have no Chinese handwriting.

5.1 Network Implementation and Training Details

We implement our model with PyTorch. We use ADAM optimizer with a learning rate of 0.0001 and beta parameters $(0.5, 0.9)$. These parameters are the same for CHENet and discriminator. We set the training epoch to 100 and the batch size to 1. When resize the image, if the $image - width > image - height$, we set the image-width to 1024, then resize the image to maintain the aspect ratio, and if the $image - height > image - width$, we set the image-width to 1024, then resize the image to maintain the aspect ratio.

Table 2. Quantitative comparison with the state-of-the-art methods.

Model	PSNR	SSIM
EnsNet [18]	15.3126	0.6742
EraseNet [8]	16.3828	0.7241
Quark	17.1458	0.7621
Ours	**17.4638**	**0.7941**

5.2 Comparison with State-of-the-Art Methods

Figure 6 shows that our method generate more realistic images which already have no Chinese handwritten words. Note that none of the previous approaches address exactly our task, so we cannot compare our approach with previous work using their datasets. In the following section, we will discuss and analyse their results, but before that we briefly introduce their implementation details and the quantitative evaluation metrics.

- **EnsNet** [18]. We reimplement the EnsNet for the visual comparisons, because there is no available public EnsNet trained model. We ensure that we train the EnsNet on our collected dataset with the same settings.
- **EraseNet** [8]. EraseNet is a two-stage network, we use the same setting of the original paper to train it with our collected dataset.
- **Quark application.** In fact, some software has implemented the function of Chinese handwritten words removal, such as Quark browser. We will compare the results with it.

We report the peak signal-to-noise ratio (PSNR), structural similarity index measure (SSIM). Actually, PSNR/SSIM often do not correlate well with perceived quality, particularly for synthesis tasks. So, we report these metrics only for completeness.

source   EnsNet   EraserNet   Quark   Ours

Fig. 7. The qualitative comparisons with several state-of-the-art models.

We report the quantitative evaluation in Table 2. And as shown in Fig. 7, our proposed method has achieved good synthetic results in removal effect and background retention. Compared with EnsNet and EraseNet, our method has better removal effect and can effectively remove Chinese handwritten words from the images. But the EnsNet and EraserNet are not directly designed for this Chinese handwriting removal task. So we compare our method with Quark application which is a mature commercial browser app that integrates the function of removing handwritten words. As we can see in Fig. 7, although quark effectively erases the Chinese handwritten words in the image, it does not fully retain the background information. For example, the non hand writing area is changed, and some details are erased. Note that, in test cases, the QR code information of the image generated by quark has been unrecognized, but ours is not missing.

5.3   Ablation Study

In this section, we study the effect of different components of our CHENet. The corresponding results are reported in Table 3 (Fig. 8).

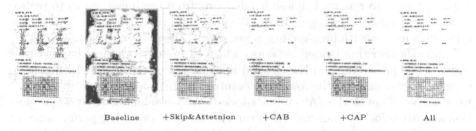

Baseline   +Skip&Attetnion   +CAB   +CAP   All

Fig. 8. Ablation study. Starting from the baseline architecture, we prove the effectiveness by adding the designed component.

+ **Baseline:** For baseline model, we use end-to-end encoder-decoder as the generator. From the visual results, we find such baseline model shows massive artifacts and does not work well on handwriting removal.

+ **Unet-like Architecture and Patch Discriminator.** In this work, we add the long-range skip connections between the encoder and the decoder. In addition, using generative advantageous networks, we design the Multiscale Patch Discriminator. It first downsample the results to the multiscale resolution, then pass to the PatchGAN discriminator. Comparing the "Baseline" in Table 3, it shows that our propose discriminator can improve the performance of the baseline model.

+ **Convolution Attention Block.** The CAB (Convolution Attention Block) module is added into the baseline model to prove the effectiveness of the feature capture. As shown in Table 3, baseline model with CAB obtains much higher PSNR, SSIM.

+ **Chain Attention Pooling.** The CAP (Chain Attention Pooling) module is added into the baseline model to replace the long-range skip connections. As shown in Table 3, when combining the CAB and CAP, the performance can be further improved.

Table 3. Ablation study.

Model configuration	PSNR	SSIM
A. baseline	10.1083	0.5132
B. + skip connection and multiscale discriminator	12.7826	0.5834
C. + attention	14.3124	0.6158
D. + CAB (Convolution Attention Block)	15.1267	0.6847
E. + CAP (Chain Attention Pooling)	**17.4638**	**0.7941**

6   Conclusion

In this work, we focus on the task of Chinese handwriting removal. Different from the common scene text removal task, the purpose of Chinese handwriting removal task is to remove Chinese handwriting from the image, so as to realize privacy protection and image editing. We first build the CH-dataset which contains 1623 images with high-quality annotations. Then, we propose the CHENet (Chinese Handwriting Eraser Network) which can remove Chinese handwritten words while preserving the background information of the image. In detail, in order to better capture the low-level features and high-level semantic features, we designed Convolution Attention Block (CAB) combining residual connection and attention mechanism, which can effectively improve the performance of the model. In order to effectively combine the low-level features and high-level semantic features and obtain more background information at the same time, we designed Chain Attention Pooling (CAP) module to original long-range skip connection operation. Qualitative and quantitative evaluations demonstrate that our CHENet can handle this task well.

But Chinese handwriting removal is a challenging task in the field of computer vision. Many issues have not been well addressed. Therefore, it remains an open research problem and deserves more attention and further investigation.

Acknowledgement. We thank the ACs and reviewers. This work is partially supported by the National Natural Science Foundation of China (62072014 & 62106118), the Beijing Natural Science Foundation (L192040), the Open Fund Project of the State Key Laboratory of Complex System Management and Control (2022111), the Project of Philosophy and Social Science Research, Ministry of Education of China (20YJC760115).

References

1. Bian, X., Wang, C., Quan, W., Ye, J., Zhang, X., Yan, D.-M.: Scene text removal via cascaded text stroke detection and erasing. Comput. Visual Media **8**(2), 273–287 (2021). https://doi.org/10.1007/s41095-021-0242-8
2. Chng, C.K., et al.: ICDAR 2019 robust reading challenge on arbitrary-shaped text-RRC-art. In: 2019 International Conference on Document Analysis and Recognition (ICDAR), pp. 1571–1576. IEEE (2019)

3. Gao, H., Ergu, D., Cai, Y., Liu, F., Ma, B.: A robust cross-ethnic digital hand-writing recognition method based on deep learning - sciencedirect (2022)
4. He, K., Zhang, X., Ren, S., Sun, J.: Deep residual learning for image recognition. IEEE (2016)
5. Kang, L., Riba, P., Rusiñol, M., Fornés, A., Villegas, M.: Content and style aware generation of text-line images for handwriting recognition. IEEE Trans. Pattern Anal. Mach. Intell. (2022)
6. Kass, D., Vats, E.: AttentionHTR: handwritten text recognition based on attention encoder-decoder networks. arXiv e-prints (2022)
7. Khodadadi, M., Behrad, A.: Text localization, extraction and inpainting in color images. In: 20th Iranian Conference on Electrical Engineering (ICEE2012), pp. 1035–1040. IEEE (2012)
8. Liu, C., Liu, Y., Jin, L., Zhang, S., Luo, C., Wang, Y.: EraseNet: end-to-end text removal in the wild. IEEE Trans. Image Process. **29**, 8760–8775 (2020)
9. Modha, U., Dave, P.: Image inpainting-automatic detection and removal of text from images. Int. J. Eng. Res. App. (IJERA), ISSN, pp. 2248–9622 (2014)
10. Nakamura, T., Zhu, A., Yanai, K., Uchida, S.: Scene text eraser. In: 2017 14th IAPR International Conference on Document Analysis and Recognition (ICDAR), vol. 01, pp. 832–837 (2017). https://doi.org/10.1109/ICDAR.2017.141
11. Nayef, N., et al.: ICDAR 2019 robust reading challenge on multi-lingual scene text detection and recognition-RRC-MLT-2019. In: 2019 International Conference on Document Analysis and Recognition (ICDAR), pp. 1582–1587. IEEE (2019)
12. Ronneberger, O., Fischer, P., Brox, T.: U-net: convolutional networks for biomed-ical image segmentation. In: Navab, N., Hornegger, J., Wells, W.M., Frangi, A.F. (eds.) MICCAI 2015. LNCS, vol. 9351, pp. 234–241. Springer, Cham (2015). https://doi.org/10.1007/978-3-319-24574-4_28
13. Tursun, O., Denman, S., Zeng, R., Sivapalan, S., Sridharan, S., Fookes, C.: Mtr-net++: one-stage mask-based scene text eraser. Comput. Vis. Image Underst. **201**, 103066 (2020)
14. Tursun, O., Zeng, R., Denman, S., Sivapalan, S., Sridharan, S., Fookes, C.: MTR-Net: a generic scene text eraser. In: Proceedings-15th IAPR International Confer-ence on Document Analysis and Recognition, ICDAR 2019, pp. 39–44. Institute of Electrical and Electronics Engineers (IEEE) (2019)
15. Ulyanov, D., Vedaldi, A., Lempitsky, V.: Instance normalization: the missing ingre-dient for fast stylization (2016)
16. Vaswani, A., et al.: Attention is all you need. Adv. Neural Inf. Process. Syst. **30**, 1–9 (2017)
17. Woo, S., Park, J., Lee, J.-Y., Kweon, I.S.: CBAM: convolutional block attention module. In: Ferrari, V., Hebert, M., Sminchisescu, C., Weiss, Y. (eds.) ECCV 2018. LNCS, vol. 11211, pp. 3–19. Springer, Cham (2018). https://doi.org/10.1007/978-3-030-01234-2_1
18. Zhang, S., Liu, Y., Jin, L., Huang, Y., Lai, S.: EnsNet: ensconce text in the wild. In: Proceedings of the AAAI Conference on Artificial Intelligence, vol. 33, pp. 801–808 (2019)
19. Zhu, Y., Zhang, H., Huang, X., Liu, Z.: Visual normalization of handwritten Chi-nese characters based on generative adversarial networks. Int. J. Pattern Recogn. Artif. Intell. **36**(03), 2253002 (2022)

Identification Method for Rice Pests with Small Sample Size Problems Combining Deep Learning and Metric Learning

Gensheng Hu[1] , Xin Tang[1], Weihui Zeng[1,2]([✉]) , Dong Liang[1], and Xiaowei Yang[1]

[1] National Engineering Research Center for Agro-Ecological Big Data Analysis & Application, Anhui University, 230601 Hefei, China
whzeng@ahu.edu.cn

[2] Guo Chuang Software Co., Ltd., University of Science and Technology of China, Hefei 230088, China

Abstract. To achieve accurate identification of rice pests with small sample size problems under complex backgrounds, we proposed a rice pest identification method combining deep learning and metric learning. To overcome the effect of the complex background of the rice pest image, we used the U-Net network which can well retain target information and has a good segmentation effect on rice pests with small sample size problems to remove the background. We also improved the backbone network of VGG16 to extract a more effective feature for identification. Finally, we introduced metric learning to project the feature vector of the pest image to a new feature space for similarity matching and solve the lower accuracy caused by the small sample size. Experimental results showed that the accuracy of the proposed method is better than that of SVM, kNN, AlexNet, VGGNet and Mobilenet. Thus, our method could accurately identify rice pests with small sample size problems under complex rice backgrounds.

Keywords: Pest identification · Small sample size problems · Deep learning · Metric learning · Machine learning

1 Introduction

Rice is among the main economic crops in China. The rice cultivation area and yield in China are at the global forefront. However, serious losses occur due to insect pest infestation, which causes poor growth of rice, insufficient grains, and even death of the whole plant. These problems affect the normal growth of rice and reduce its quality and yield. Thus, accurate identification of rice pests is conducive to pest control and prevention. At present, crop pests are mainly identified by experts [1], but manual methods are expensive and inefficient. With the advancements in artificial intelligence technology, automatic identification of rice pests using artificial intelligence is of great significance to the development of precision and smart agriculture.

© The Author(s), under exclusive license to Springer Nature Switzerland AG 2022
S. Yu et al. (Eds.): PRCV 2022, LNCS 13537, pp. 52–65, 2022.
https://doi.org/10.1007/978-3-031-18916-6_5

Machine learning methods have been used to identify pests in images. Liu et al. studied the automatic identification and counting of wheat aphids under a background of simple wheat field; they extracted the histogram of oriented gradients features of wheat aphid images, trained with a support vector machine, and showed a mean identification rate of 86.81% [2]. Xie et al. used advanced multitasking sparse representation and multi-kernel learning technology to identify farm pest images and demonstrated higher identification accuracy than earlier support vector machines and neural network methods [3]. Larios et al. proposed an image classification method based on Haar random forest to extract image features and combined them with spatial matching kernel SVM; a low mean error was achieved in the identification of aquatic stonefly larvae [4]. These traditional machine learning-based methods mainly demonstrated the global features of pest image but ignored the relative spatial information of the pest itself. Obtaining accurate identification of crop pests with different attitudes and backgrounds remains a challenge.

In recent years, the more popular deep learning methods can extract the features of the target directly through the data itself, thereby avoiding the complicated manual design process [5]. They have been successfully applied to pedestrian recognition [6], vehicle detection [7], video classification [8], and agriculture [9]. Compared with traditional machine learning methods, using deep learning improves the accuracy of crop pest identification. Ding and Taylor used sliding windows to obtain detection regions and five-layer convolutional neural networks to determine whether these regions contained moths; they proved that deep learning convolutional neural networks have higher recall rates than LogReg algorithm [10]. Amanda et al. used transfer learning to train a deep learning convolutional neural network to identify three diseases and two types of pests, and achieved high identification accuracy [11]. Shen et al. used Faster R-CNN and Inception network to detect and classify pests, and showed that these methods can effectively detect and identify pests under grain storage conditions [12]. Liu et al. proposed an end-to-end pest detection and classification method based on deep learning network, PestNet. The average accuracy of the proposed PestNet for 16 types of pest detection was 75.46% [13]. AlexNet, GoogLeNet, and VGGNet have also been used for crop pest identification [14–16]. Deep learning methods require a large number of training samples, and the identification accuracies of the above methods may be insufficient because of insufficient samples and complex backgrounds.

In this paper, common rice pests were used as the main research object, and a rice pest identification method was proposed based on deep and metric learnings to identify rice pests with small sample size problems under complex backgrounds. U-Net [17] network was used to segment the pests in the image and reduce the influence of the rice background in the pest image on subsequent identification. The pest images after image segmentation were used to train the feature extraction network improved by the VGG16 network and extract the segmented pest features. Finally, metric learning was used to improve the accuracy of identifying rice pests with small sample size problems.

2 Materials and Methods

2.1 Rice Pest Image Acquisition

The images of rice pests in a farmland environment used in this paper were collected by Xie et al. [3][1] and were mainly captured with a color digital camera at a resolution of 1280 × 960. A small portion of the images was obtained from the Internet. We selected five kinds of rice pests, namely, *Chilo suppressalis, Cletus punctiger, Cnaphalocrocis medinalis, Eysarcoris guttiger,* and *Nephotettix bipunctatus,* corresponding to a, b, c, d, and e in Fig. 1 and Table 1.

For the convenience of the subsequent experiment, we cropped and resized the images to 224 × 224. A part of the processing results is shown in Fig. 1. The processed images were randomly divided into training and test sets. Given that training a deep learning model requires a large number of training samples, the insufficient number of samples may lead to model overfitting and reduces the identification accuracy. To augment the sample, the rice pest images we used in the training samples were rotated to 90, 180, and 270° and flipped left and right and up and down. The numbers of original and augmented training samples and test samples are shown in Table 1.

a) Chilo suppressalis   b) Cletus punctiger   c) Cnaphalocrocis medinalis   d) Eysarcoris guttiger   e) Nephotettix bipunctatus

Fig. 1. Cropped and resized images of rice pests.

Table 1. Species and quantities of rice pests.

Name	a	b	c	d	e	Total
Number of original training samples	38	40	36	45	45	204
Number of augmented training samples	228	240	216	270	270	1224
Number of test samples	10	10	10	10	10	50

---

[1] http://www2.ahu.edu.cn/pchen/web/insectRecognition.htm.

2.2   Pest Image Background Removal

The rice pest images used in this paper were taken from the farmland environment. The images contained complex backgrounds, such as rice ears, branches, and leaves. Without background segmentation, these complex backgrounds participate in feature extraction and identification of pest images. They may also affect pest identification. Segmenting the pest from these complex backgrounds may benefit pest identification. Given the small number of pest samples, we chose the U-Net network, which is advantageous for segmentation of images with small sample size problems, to segment the pest image and optimize it by filtering the maximum connected region.

The U-Net network is composed of two parts, namely, a contracting path and an expanding path. The contracting path is mainly used to capture context information in the image, whereas the expanding path can accurately localize the part that needs to be segmented in the image. U-Net was improved through FCN, but it did not simply encode and decode the image. To achieve accurate localization, the features extracted by U-Net on the contracting path were combined with the new feature map during the upsampling process, and some important feature information of the previous subsampling process was retained to the greatest extent. No fully connected layer was retained in the structure to make the network structure run more efficiently, which greatly reduced the parameters required by the network. The special U-shaped structure could well retain all the information in the image. Compared with the general neural network's classifier, which directly depends on the features of the last layer of the network, the structure of U-Net in the decoding stage could be sufficiently combined with the simpler features of the shallow layer, thereby increasing the amount of information in the samples. Even if the sample dataset inputted was small, it was not easy to overfit. Thus, this structure had a good segmentation effect on rice pests with small sample size problems.

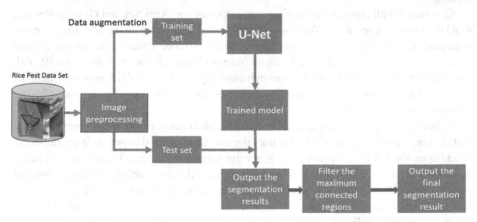

Fig. 2. Flow chart of rice pest image segmentation.

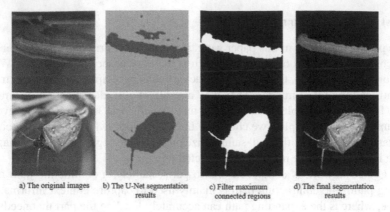

a) The original images   b) The U-Net segmentation   c) Filter maximum   d) The final segmentation
                                  results   connected regions   results

Fig. 3. Segmentation results of rice pests.

The segmentation process of the rice pest images via the U-Net network is shown in Fig. 2, and the partial segmentation results are shown in Fig. 3.

2.3 Feature Extraction

On the one hand, traditional image identification methods are based on manually designed features; they rely on the knowledge of experts and cannot summarize image features well [18]. Their performance seriously affects the overall result. Designing features manually is a complex and time-consuming process that needs to be changed when a problem or dataset changes. On the other hand, deep learning methods do not need to extract features manually. They can locate important features automatically through training.

Compared with other deep learning networks, such as AlexNet and GoogLeNet, the VGG16 network uses a smaller convolution kernel and has a more non-linear transformation than a single convolution layer, which is more suitable for image feature extraction of rice pests with small sample size problems in the present paper [9, 19]. The VGG16 [20] network has 13 convolutional layers. The VGG16 network includes five maximum pooling and three fully-connected layers. The latter is followed by the softmax classification layer.

Training a good model from scratch was difficult because of the small number of rice pest training samples in this study. We used the fine-tune method to pre-train the network. In addition, the fully-connected layer generates more parameters. Therefore, two fully-connected layers were used in this study to replace the three original fully-connected layers. The number of neurons in the first layer was 4096, whereas that in the second fully-connected layer was 5, which was the number of pest species we needed to identify. The fourth maximum pooling layer of the network was modified to be the average pooling layer. Average pooling can retain more global information about the image [21]. For the pest images that were segmented out, the effective use of average pooling can retain more global information about the rice pests. Finally, the softmax classification layer was removed. These operations could reduce network parameters effectively and improve model accuracy and efficiency while keeping the feature extraction capabilities of the

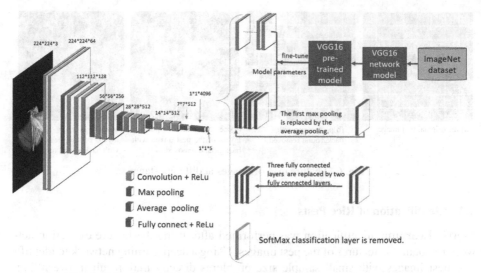

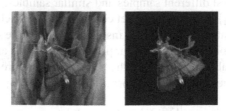

Fig. 4. Schematics of the improved rice pest feature extraction network.

network as much as possible. The improved network for extracting the features of rice pests is shown in Fig. 4.

The visualizations of the feature extraction of the rice pest image by the improved network are shown in Fig. 5, Fig. 6, and Fig. 7. Figure 5 shows the original rice pest image and the one with backgrounds removed. Figure 6 (a) and Fig. 6 (b) show the feature map of the original rice pest image and that of the rice pest image with backgrounds removed. The convolution layer could extract a part of the features of rice pests. However, for the rice pest image with complex backgrounds, the extracted features also contained complex backgrounds and could not effectively extract the pest feature. After the background was removed, the extracted features were mainly pest features without background information. Figure 6 (c) and Fig. 6 (d) show the feature map output from the maximum and average pooling layers of the pest image with backgrounds removed. After improving the pooling layer, the feature extraction network could extract features such as edge and back textures of the pest image more clearly.

Fig. 5. Original pest image and pest image with backgrounds removed.

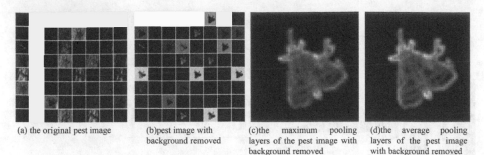

| (a) the original pest image | (b)pest image with background removed | (c)the maximum pooling layers of the pest image with background removed | (d)the average pooling layers of the pest image with background removed |

Fig. 6. Feature map of images at different stages.

2.4 Identification of Rice Pests

Metric Learning. Identification was performed after using the feature extraction network to obtain the features of the pest images. Using a deep learning network to identify rice pest images with small sample size problems directly may result in overfitting. Although the samples were augmented in this experiment, the total sample number was still insufficient. We chose distance metric learning to identify the rice pests which is one of the most basic methods of similarity metric learning. The feature vector of the pest image in metric learning was projected to a new feature space through feature mapping, and similarity matching operations were performed in the new feature space. The pest images were matched according to the corresponding similarity matching principle to identify the rice pests. Metric learning can solve the problem of low identification accuracy of machine learning methods when the sample size is insufficient.

LMNN algorithm was first proposed at the 2005 Neural Information Processing Systems Conference [22]. The main process of this algorithm is to first learn a linear transformation and then project and transform the original features to maximize the Euclidean distance among different samples in the new feature space.

For an input sample x_i, similar and different samples existed in its k-nearest neighborhood. After the original feature space was projected by a Mahalanobis matrix M, the distribution of similar samples was more compact in the new feature space on the right, whereas the distribution among different samples became more discrete. For the input sample, only similar samples existed in the k-nearest neighborhood, and a large gap was found between the nearest different samples and similar samples.

Suppose $X = \{x_i, y_i\}_{i=1}^{N}$ is a training set consisting of N labeled samples, where x_i is the d-dimensional feature vector of the instance and y_i is the category label of the sample. The LMNN algorithm learns a linear projection matrix L and carries out a linear projection of the original feature x. Then, the transformed feature vector is L_x, and the Euclidean distance of the two feature vectors after the linear projection is as follows:

$$d(x_i, x_j) = \left\| L(x_i, x_j) \right\|_2 \tag{1}$$

Suppose the Mahalanobis matrix $M = L^T L$, M must be a positive semidefinite matrix. The Mahalanobis distance formula can be written as

$$d(x_i, x_j) = \sqrt{(x_i - x_j)^T M (x_i - x_j)} \tag{2}$$

For any input sample, the LMNN algorithm requires that the distances of its k similar neighbors are as close as possible. The following equation was used to minimize the average distance among similar samples:

$$\min \sum\nolimits_{x_i, x_j \in X, y_i = y_j} d(x_i, x_j) \tag{3}$$

The intervals of different samples should also be maximized. For a sample x_i, the interval is at least one unit closer to the distance between it and any similar samples than the distance between it and any different samples. x_j represents a similar sample of x_i, and x_l is a different sample of x_i

$$\forall_{x_i, x_j, x_l \in X, y_i = y_j, y_i \neq y_l} d(x_i, x_j) + 1$$
$$\leq d(x_i, x_l) \tag{4}$$

Therefore, after introducing slack variable ξ, the final optimization objective function is

$$\min \left(\sum_{x_i x_j \in X, y_i = y_j} d(x_i, x_j) + \sum_{i,j,l} \xi_{ijl} \right)$$
$$\text{s.t.} \forall_{x_i, x_j, x_l \in X, y_i = y_j, y_i \neq y_l} \begin{cases} d(x_i, x_j) + 1 \leq d(x_i, x_l) + \xi_{ijl} \\ \xi_{ijl} \geq 0 \end{cases} \tag{5}$$

The LMNN algorithm minimizes the distance among similar samples and maximizes the distance among different samples. In this paper, we extracted the features of the small sample dataset of rice pests and obtained a relatively accurate identification result via metric learning.

Steps and Processes of Identification. The main steps for identifying rice pests with small sample size problems are as follows (as shown in Fig. 7):

Step1. The images of the rice pest were selected, cropped, and resized. They were randomly divided into training and test sets, and the samples were augmented in the training set.

Step2. The U-Net network was used to remove the background of the rice pest image and optimize it by filtering the maximum connected region to obtain rice pest images with no background.

Step3. The VGG16 network was pre-trained with ImageNet dataset to obtain the initial parameters of the model.

Step4. We changed the fourth maximum pooling layer of the VGG16 network to the average pooling layer and three fully-connected layers to two fully-connected layers. The pest images with no background were inputted into the improved feature extraction network to extract the features.

Step5. The extracted rice pest features were inputted into the LMNN metric learning model to identify rice pests.

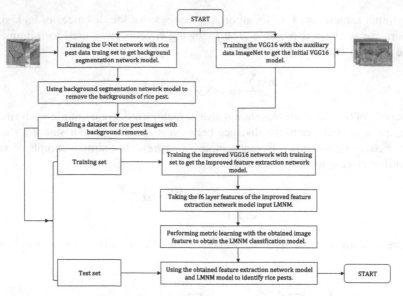

Fig. 7. Flow chart of rice pest identification.

3 Experimental Results and Analysis

3.1 Background Removal

The U-Net network was used to remove the rice background from the rice pest image and retain the rice pest. Optimization was performed by screening the maximum connected region.

Figure 8 compares the results of k-means [23], GrabCut [24], FCN [24], U-Net, and the proposed background removal method. As shown in Fig. 8, k-means and GrabCut cannot segment the pest well from the rice background in images with complex backgrounds. The U-Net model was improved via the FCN structure. Compared with FCN, the U-Net network was more meticulous in segmenting pest details, such as antennas and feet. The U-Net network was used as the main way to segment pest images with small sample size problems and filter the maximum connected region for optimization. This network can segment pests accurately under complex rice backgrounds and successfully filter out the extra-fine fragments extracted by the U-Net. The proposed method was superior to k-means, GrabCut, and FCN methods in removing the background of rice pests with small sample size problems.

3.2 Data Augmentation

We augmented the rice pest images in the training samples to improve the accuracy of rice pest identification. Augmenting the training samples can increase their diversity, avoid overfitting, and improve the performance of the model. The number of training samples after augmentation is shown in Table 1. We compared the accuracy of the following:

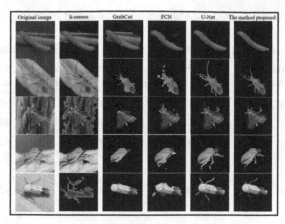

Fig. 8. Comparison of several pest segmentation methods.

the traditional machine learning method, SVM; the deep learning network, VGG16; and the proposed method of identifying rice pests with and without data augmentation (see Table 2). The identification results for each type of rice pests are shown in Fig. 9. When the improved feature extraction network was used, the loss value area tended to be stable after the network was trained 1500 times. Thus, we selected the 2000th iteration result as the feature extraction model.

Table 2 and Fig. 9 demonstrate the following:

(1) When identifying rice pests, the identification accuracies of the deep convolutional network VGG16 and the proposed method were higher than that of the SVM with or without background.

(2) Before the augmentation of data, the accuracy of rice pest identification after background removal by all identification networks was higher than that of pest identification without background removal. After data augmentation, the accuracy of pest identification before background removal by VGG16 with transfer learning was higher than that after background removal. However, for SVM and the proposed method, the accuracies of rice pest identification after background removal were higher than those before background removal. These findings showed that the background of rice pests influences their identification. Whether the background needs to be removed depends on the experimental results of different datasets and networks.

(3) Before removing the background, the proposed method demonstrated a lower pest identification rate after data augmentation than before data augmentation. The reason may be because for metric learning when the background is not removed, data augmentation makes rice background and rice pest information increase simultaneously, thereby making it difficult for metric learning to identify rice pests. The accuracies of the other methods in identifying pests after data augmentation were higher than before data augmentation. Therefore, we augmented the data after background removal to process the dataset. The proposed method showed the highest identification accuracy of 92% among other methods.

Table 2. Accuracy of rice pest identification before and after augmentation.

	Before background removal		After background removal	
	Before data augmentation	After data augmentation	Before data augmentation	After data augmentation
SVM	42%	54%	56%	62%
VGG16	42%	68%	66%	84%
VGG16 (Transfer learning)	72%	88%	76%	86%
Proposed method	84%	80%	86%	92%

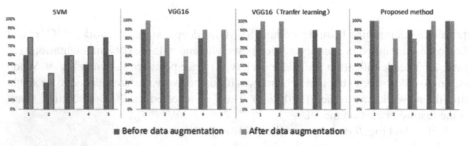

■ Before data augmentation   ■ After data augmentation

1.Chilo suppressalis 2.Cletus punctiger 3.Cnaphalocrocis medinalis 4.Eysarcoris guttiger 5.Nephotettix bipunctatus

Fig. 9. Identification accuracies for each type of rice pests by different methods before and after data augmentation. The abscissa and ordinate represent the pest species and identification accuracy, respectively.

(4) When subdivided into each type of rice pests, the accuracy of identifying each type after data augmentation was generally higher than before augmentation, as shown in Fig. 9. Thus, data augmentation has a positive effect on the identification of rice pests.

3.3 Comparison of Different Rice Pest Identification Methods

VGG16 was used as the backbone network in the image feature extraction stage, and the average pooling layer was used to replace one of the maximum pooling layers. To determine the pooling layer combination that achieved the most accurate rice pest identification, we performed the following. After data augmentation and background removal, we set up different pooling layer combinations in the feature extraction network of the proposed model and used metric learning to identify the extracted rice pest features.

Table 3. Comparison experiments of different pooling layer combinations during feature extraction.

Combination of different pooling layers	5 MAX	4MAX + AVG	2MAX + AVG + 2MAX	MAX + AVG + 3MAX	2MAX + AVG + MAX + AVG	2(AVG + MAX) + AVG	3MAX + AVG + MAX
Rice pest identification accuracy	88%	90%	88%	86%	86%	84%	92%

As shown in Table 3, the proposed pooling layer combination achieved the most accurate rice pest identification.

After data augmentation and background removal, we compared the proposed method with two traditional machine learning methods, SVM and kNN, and deep learning networks such as AlexNet, VGGNet, GoogleNet, and Mobilenet (as shown in Table 4). AlexNet and the lightweight deep learning network, Mobilenet, showed low identification accuracy at only 56% and 54%, respectively. By contrast, VGG16, Inception V1, Inception V2, and Inception V3 demonstrated significantly higher identification accuracies than kNN and SVM. After data augmentation and the removal of the background of the rice pests with small sample size problems, the identification accuracy of the proposed method was 92%, which was better than that obtained using SVM, kNN, AlexNet, VGGNet, GoogLeNet, and Mobilenet. Therefore, the proposed method can identify rice pests more accurately than traditional machine learning methods and deep learning networks.

Table 4. Comparison experiments on rice pest identification.

Method	kNN	SVM	Mobilenet	AlexNet	InceptionV1	InceptionV2	InceptionV3	VGG16	**Our method**
Accuracy	34%	62%	54%	56%	84%	74%	84%	86%	**92%**

4 Conclusion

A method that combines deep and metric learnings to identify rice pests with small sample size problems was proposed. The U-Net network was used to segment the background of the pest dataset with small sample size problems under complex rice backgrounds. The maximum connected region was selected for optimization. The VGG16 network was improved to obtain a new network for extracting the features of rice pests. Finally, the metric learning method was used to identify the rice pests. The experimental results showed that whether the background of rice pests needs to be removed depends on the dataset and network. At the same time, we augmented the training samples of rice pests, thereby considerably improving the accuracy of rice pest identification. AlexNet and the lightweight deep learning network, Mobilenet, showed low accuracies for identifying rice pests with small sample size problems. By contrast, the identification accuracies of deep learning networks such as VGG16, Inception V1, Inception V2, and Inception V3 are higher than those of the two traditional machine learning methods, namely, kNN and SVM. The proposed method combining deep and metric learnings exhibited the highest identification accuracy and performance among the above networks. In future work, we plan to improve the structure of the background segmentation and feature extraction networks or the identification algorithm to further optimize the network structure of the proposed model and collect more morphological images of rice pests to improve the accuracy and efficiency of rice pest identification.

Acknowledgments. This work was supported in part by Natural Science Foundation of Anhui Province, China, under Grant No. 2108085MC95, and the University Natural Science Research Project of Anhui Province under Grant Nos. KJ2020ZD03 and KJ2020A0039, and the open research fund of the National Engineering Research Center for Agro-Ecological Big Data Analysis & Application, Anhui University, under Grant No. AE202004.

References

1. Deng, L., Wang, Y., Han, Z., Yu, R.: Research on insect pest image detection and recognition based on bio-inspired methods. Biosyst. Eng. **169**, 139–148 (2018)
2. Liu, T., Chen, W., Wu, W., Sun, C., Guo, W., Zhu, X.: Detection of aphids in wheat fields using a computer vision technique. Biosyst. Eng. **141**, 82–93 (2016)
3. Xie, C., et al.: Automatic classification for field crop insects via multiple-task sparse representation and multiple-kernel learning. Comput. Electron. Agric. **119**, 123–132 (2015)
4. Larios, N., Soran, B., Shapiro, L.G., Martínez-Muñoz, G., Lin, J., Dietterich, T.G.: Haar random forest features and SVM spatial matching kernel for stonefly species identification. In: 2010 20th International Conference on Pattern Recognition, pp. 2624–2627. IEEE (2010)
5. Sermanet, P., Eigen, D., Zhang, X., Mathieu, M., Fergus, R., LeCun, Y.: OverFeat: integrated recognition, localization and detection using convolutional networks. arXiv preprint arXiv: 1312.6229 (2013)
6. Xiao, T., Li, S., Wang, B., Lin, L., Wang, X.: Joint detection and identification feature learning for person search. In: Proceedings of the IEEE Conference on Computer Vision and Pattern Recognition, pp. 3415–3424 (2017)
7. Chen, X., Xiang, S., Liu, C.L., Pan, C.H.: Vehicle detection in satellite images by hybrid deep convolutional neural networks. IEEE Geosci. Remote Sens. Lett. **11**(10), 1797–1801 (2014)
8. Yue-Hei Ng, J., Hausknecht, M., Vijayanarasimhan, S., Vinyals, O., Monga, R., Toderici, G.: Beyond short snippets: deep networks for video classification. In: Proceedings of the IEEE Conference on Computer Vision and Pattern Recognition, pp. 4694–4702 (2015)
9. Hu, G., Wu, H., Zhang, Y., Wan, M.: A low shot learning method for tea leaf's disease identification. Comput. Electron. Agric. **163**, 104852 (2019)
10. Ding, W., Taylor, G.: Automatic moth detection from trap images for pest management. Comput. Electron. Agric. **123**, 17–28 (2016)
11. Ramcharan, A., Baranowski, K., McCloskey, P., Ahmed, B., Legg, J., Hughes, D.P.: Deep learning for image-based cassava disease detection. Front. Plant Sci. **8**, 1852 (2017)
12. Shen, Y., Zhou, H., Li, J., Jian, F., Jayas, D.S.: Detection of stored-grain insects using deep learning. Comput. Electron. Agric. **145**, 319–325 (2018)

13. Liu, L., et al.: PestNet: an end-to-end deep learning approach for large-scale multi-class pest detection and classification. IEEE Access **7**, 45301–45312 (2019)
14. Mohanty, S.P., Hughes, D.P., Salathé, M.: Using deep learning for image-based plant disease detection. Front. Plant Sci. **7**, 1419 (2016)
15. Brahimi, M., Boukhalfa, K., Moussaoui, A.: Deep learning for tomato diseases: classification and symptoms visualization. Appl. Artif. Intell. **31**(4), 299–315 (2017)
16. Lu, J., Hu, J., Zhao, G., Mei, F., Zhang, C.: An in-field automatic wheat disease diagnosis system. Comput. Electron. Agric. **142**, 369–379 (2017)
17. Ronneberger, O., Fischer, P., Brox, T.: U-Net: convolutional networks for biomedical image segmentation. In: Navab, N., Hornegger, J., Wells, W., Frangi, A. (eds.) MICCAI 2015. LNCS, vol. 9351, pp. 234–241. Springer, Cham (2015). https://doi.org/10.1007/978-3-319-24574-4_28
18. Kamilaris, A., Prenafeta-Boldú, F.X.: Deep learning in agriculture: a survey. Comput. Electron. Agric. **147**, 70–90 (2018)
19. Sainath, T.N.: Deep convolutional neural networks for LVCSR. In: IEEE International Conference on Acoustics, Speech and Signal Processing, vol. 8614, p. 8618 (2013)
20. Simonyan, K., Zisserman, A.: Very deep convolutional networks for large-scale image recognition. arXiv preprint arXiv:1409.1556 (2014)
21. Boureau, Y.L., Bach, F., LeCun, Y., Ponce, J.: Learning mid-level features for recognition. In: 2010 IEEE Computer Society Conference on Computer Vision and Pattern Recognition, pp. 2559–2566. IEEE (2010)
22. Weinberger, K.Q., Saul, L.K.: Distance metric learning for large margin nearest neighbor classification. J. Mach. Learn. Res. **10**(2) (2009)
23. MacQueen, J.: Classification and analysis of multivariate observations. In: 5th Berkeley Symposium on Mathematical Statistics and Probability, pp. 281–297 (1967)
24. Rother, C., Kolmogorov, V., Blake, A.: "GrabCut" interactive foreground extraction using iterated graph cuts. ACM Trans. Graph. (TOG) **23**(3), 309–314 (2004)
25. Long, J., Shelhamer, E., Darrell, T.: Fully convolutional networks for semantic segmentation. In: Proceedings of the IEEE Conference on Computer Vision and Pattern Recognition, pp. 3431–3440 (2015)

Boundary-Aware Polyp Segmentation Network

Lu Lu, Xitong Zhou, Shuhan Chen$^{(\boxtimes)}$, Zuyu Chen, Jinhao Yu, Haonan Tang, and Xuelong Hu

Yangzhou University, YangZhou 225000, China
shchen@yzu.edu.cn

Abstract. Colorectal cancer (CRC) caused by polyps has a high mortality rate worldwide. Accurately segmenting the polyp from colonoscopy images is important for the clinical treatment of CRC. The traditional method of polyp segmentation involves the physician manually marking the location of the polyp, resulting in unreliable segmentation results. The complex structure of polyps, the low contrast with mucosal tissue, and the fact that polyp boundary is usually hidden in the background make the task of polyp segmentation extremely challenging. To address these issues, we propose a boundary-aware polyp segmentation network. Specifically, we first propose an attention-aware location module to accurately identify the primary location of polyp. In order to improve the missing polyp portion in the initial region prediction and to mine the polyp boundary hidden in the background, we propose a residual pyramid convolution. Further, we propose a boundary-guided refinement module for more accurate segmentation in order to use the boundary information provided from residual pyramid convolution for constrained polyp region prediction. Extensive experiments show that our proposed network has advantages over existing state-of-the-art methods on five challenging polyp datasets.

Keywords: Polyp segmentation · Contextual attention · Boundary guidance · Residual pyramid convolution

1 Introduction

In recent years, the incidence and mortality rate of colorectal cancer (CRC) has been increasing. Colonoscopy is the primary way to detect colorectal polyp lesions, and removing colorectal polyps before they develop into CRC is an effective way for patients to recover. Therefore, accurate segmentation of polyps from the colonoscopy images is critical for clinical treatment. However, polyps have a complex structure with different sizes, shapes and textures. Moreover, polyps have low contrast with the surrounding mucosal tissue, making it difficult to precisely segment polyps from indeterminate regions and ambiguous backgrounds. Thus, for the clinical treatment of CRC, an autonomous polyp segmentation

© The Author(s), under exclusive license to Springer Nature Switzerland AG 2022
S. Yu et al. (Eds.): PRCV 2022, LNCS 13537, pp. 66–77, 2022.
https://doi.org/10.1007/978-3-031-18916-6_6

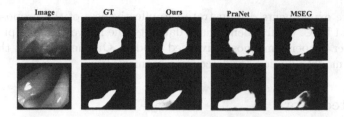

Fig. 1. Visual comparison. It can be seen that the boundary segmentation of our method is accurate, while the existing method has ambiguous boundary localization, which leads to wrong segmentation. From left to right: input image, ground truth (GT), our method, PraNet [7], MSEG [12].

technique that can accurately identify the location and precisely segment the boundary is critical [16].

Most traditional polyp segmentation methods are based on low-level features such as texture or iterative clustering superpixels, which often have high false detection rates and missed detection rates [19,27]. With the development of deep learning in the field of medical images, polyp segmentation methods based on U-Net structures [24] have been proposed. Despite the fact that existing approaches have considerably improved the accuracy and generalization of polyp segmentation techniques, satisfactory results for polyp boundary segmentation have yet to be achieved, as shown in Fig. 1. Since these methods only focus on local details of polyps, they do not consider the relationship between polyp region and boundary, they are not highly adaptable to the multi-scale features of polyps. To address the problems in the above polyp segmentation task, in this paper we propose a boundary-aware polyp segmentation network. We found the fact that the physician looking at the polyp image would first locate the primary region of the polyp, and then look for details of the polyp until the polyp was completely separated from the background. Inspired by that fact, we first proposed an attention-aware location module (ALM) to capture the primary region of polyps. After obtaining the primary region of the polyps, we further proposed the boundary-guided refinement module (BRM) to accurately segment the polyps from the background. The main contributions of this paper are summarised as follows:

1) We propose ALM to accomplish the initial region recognition of polyps. A position attention module (PAM) is introduced in the ALM to collect semantic information of polyps and inter-pixel contextual relationships from high-level features.
2) We propose a residual pyramid convolution (RPC) to complement the missing polyp portion in the initial region recognition and to mine the hidden boundaries. Further, we propose BRM, which utilizes the boundary information in the RPC to correct the initial region prediction results for more accurate segmentation.

3) Extensive experiments demonstrate the effectiveness of the proposed ALM, BRM and RPC. On five benchmark datasets, the network model proposed in this paper outperforms most advanced models. Our network has the advantages of model simplicity and accurate segmentation.

2 Related Work

2.1 Polyp Segmentation

Early methods of polyp segmentation required manual segmentation modeling by the physician based on experience, and these models often had low discriminatory power and were highly influenced by human factors. Thanks to the development of deep learning, for the boundary segmentation problem of polyps, Akbari et al. [1] proposed a polyp segmentation method based on full convolutional neural network. Many medical image segmentation networks have been derived from the U-Net structure. Zhou et al. [34] proposed a polyp segmentation method based on nested and skip connections for U-Net++. Jha et al. [16] proposed a ResUNet++ semantic segmentation network based on Spatial Pyramid Pooling. All of these methods have achieved good results in the polyp segmentation task. However, these methods do not take into account the mutual constraint relationship between the polyp region and the boundary, which is essential for accurate segmentation of the polyp boundary. To this end, Murugesan et al. [22] proposed the Psi-Net polyp segmentation model, which focuses on both region and boundary features of polyps. Fan et al. [7] proposed a PraNet polyp segmentation model based on parallel decoders and attention mechanisms. However, these methods are not well adapted to the multi-scale features of polyps and cannot be accurately segmented for polyps with variable shapes. Our proposed method adopts BRM to capture the multi-scale features of polyps and refine the boundary details, which can better perform the task of polyp segmentation.

2.2 Self-attention Mechanism

The self-attention module is one of the most widely used attention modules [17,18,25]. Recently, many researchers have applied self-attention modules to image segmentation tasks [9,11,13] and achieved very good results. Zhang et al. [33] proposed a self-attention generative adversarial network to model attention-driven remote dependencies for image generation tasks. Wang et al. [29] employed a self-attention module to study the effectiveness of nonlocal operations on video and images in the space-time dimension. Unlike previous work, we introduce an extension of self-attention into the polyp segmentation task. We embed a positional attention module [9] in our proposed ALM to model rich contextual dependencies in high-level features and enhance its representation capability. We also design a RPC using the reverse attention module [3] to enhance the adaptability of the network to multi-scale features, and capture the boundary features of polyps.

2.3   Boundary-Aware Methods

Originally designed for the saliency object detection task, boundary-guided methods have been gradually applied to polyp image segmentation tasks as well. High-quality saliency maps are often inseparable from accurate boundary prediction. Qin et al. [23] proposed a network consisting of a densely supervised encoder-decoder that accurately predicts object boundaries by refinement operations with residual modules. Wu et al. [30] proposed a novel stacked cross-refinement network that accurately predicts object boundaries by stacking cross-refinement units simultaneously refine multi-level features. However, the segmentation results do not achieve the expected results when the boundary guidance is directly employed in the polyp segmentation task. Therefore, we propose a boundary guidance mechanism in BRM to better guide the region prediction using boundary prediction.

3   Proposed Framework

3.1   Overview

We designed a boundary-aware polyp segmentation network. The network contains an ALM for identifying the initial region and three BRMs for completing the missing polyp portion and refining the boundary information. Our network structure is shown in Fig. 2, and each component will be described in detail in the following subsections.

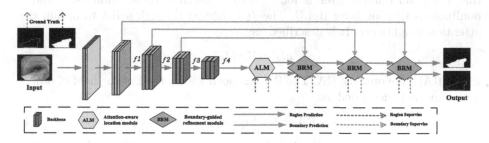

Fig. 2. The overall structure of the proposed boundary-aware polyp segmentation network includes an ALM and three BRMs.

3.2   Residual Pyramid Convolution

In clinical practice, different degrees of polyp lesions can result in colorectal polyps of different sizes and shapes. Moreover, early polyps have low contrast with the surrounding mucosal tissue. Therefore, we propose RPC and embed it in BRM to enhance the multi-scale representation capability of the network. Specifically, we employ reverse attention blocks (RA) [3] to erase the current prediction region to gradually discover complementary object regions and details.

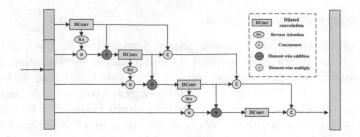

Fig. 3. Illustration of the proposed RPC.

Instead of the common 3×3 convolution, we employed dilated convolution [32] with different dilation rates to further improve the ability to extract multi-scale features. The RPC structure is shown in Fig. 3.

Given a side output feature T of backbone network with channel number C, it is uniformly divided into d sub-feature groups in the channel dimension. It is described as:

$$[T_1, ..., T_k, ..., T_d] = \text{Split}(T), k \in [1, d], \tag{1}$$

where T_k denotes the kth sub-feature group, containing $w = C/d$ channels. The first sub-feature group T_k is then fed into a convolutional layer with dilation rate i for learning, and the output feature f_k. It is described as:

$$f_k = \text{DConv}_i(T_k), \tag{2}$$

where $\text{DConv}_i(\cdot)$ denotes the dilated convolution layer with dilation rate i. Note that each convolution layer is followed by a batch normalization layer and a nonlinear activation layer ReLU. The f_k is passed through a RA to obtain the attention weights at_k. It is described as:

$$at_k = \text{RA}(f_k), \tag{3}$$

where $\text{RA}(\cdot)$ denotes the RA. The RA has been widely used in the field of object detection. It is described as:

$$\text{RA} = 1 - \text{Sigmoid}(f_k), \tag{4}$$

where $\text{Sigmoid}(\cdot)$ denotes the sigmoid activation function. Then the attention weights at_k are fed into the second sub-feature group T_{k+1}, the attented output could be computed by their element-wise multiplication. It is described as:

$$A_{k,k+1} = at_k \cdot T_{k+1}. \tag{5}$$

Then, the output feature f_k and the attented output $A_{k,k+1}$ are element-wise summed and fed into another dilated convolution layer with a dilation rate of $i + 1$ to output feature f_{k+1}. Finally, the f_{k+1} is then connected to the output feature f_k. This operation is repeated several times until the last sub-feature group is completed, recovering the original number of channels C. Each sub-feature group corresponds to a different number of channels and is combined with RA to further discover complementary detail of objects at different scales.

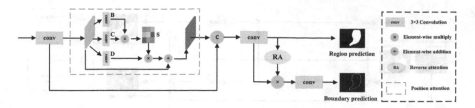

Fig. 4. Illustration of the proposed ALM. The input features are first passed through a PAM, and then the learning of regions and boundaries is performed separately.

3.3   Attention-Aware Location Module

We designed an ALM to identify the primary region of polyps, as shown in Fig. 4. Inspired by Fu et al. [9], we apply PAM to the proposed ALM, adaptively combining the local features of polyps with global dependencies. The input feature T is first fed into the PAM to capture the contextual relationship between any two pixels. It is described as:

$$x^i = \text{PAM}(\text{Convs}(T^i)), \qquad (6)$$

where i denotes the number of side output stages of the backbone network and $i = 4$ in ALM. Convs$(\cdot)$ denotes the 3×3 convolution layer. PAM$(\cdot)$ denotes the PAM, and its specific process is as follows: after the input feature T enters the PAM, it first passes through three convolution layers to obtain three feature mappings B, C, and D, respectively. It is described as:

$$\begin{cases} B = \text{Convs}\,(T^i) \\ C = \text{Convs}\,(T^i) \,. \\ D = \text{Convs}\,(T^i) \end{cases} \qquad (7)$$

Then, the feature map B are multiplied with the feature map C to obtain the spatial attention map S. It is described as:

$$S = B \times C. \qquad (8)$$

where the "$\times$" indicates the element-wise multiply. Finally, D is multiplied by S and reshape to its original shape, and then added to the input feature T to obtain the final output feature x^i. It is described as:

$$x^i = D \times S + \text{Convs}(T^i). \qquad (9)$$

Further, we concatenate feature x^i with the input feature T^i. Then it is fed into several convolution layers to learn the regional features. Finally the main location map M_R^i of polyps is obtained. It is described as:

$$M_R^i = \text{Convs}\,(\,\text{Cat}(x^i, T^i)), \qquad (10)$$

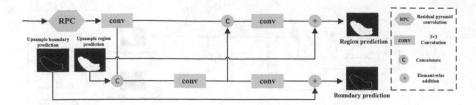

Fig. 5. Illustration of the proposed BRM. Input features are divided into region branches and boundary branches for learning after RPC.

where $\mathrm{Cat}(\cdot)$ denotes the concatenate operation. Finally, we employ the RA to obtain the attention weight at^i. It is described as:

$$at^i = \mathrm{RA}(M_R^i). \tag{11}$$

This attention weight at^i is then multiplied with the region map M_R^i by element-wise to obtain the initial polyp boundary map M_B^i. It is described as:

$$M_B^i = \mathrm{Convs}(at^i \cdot M_R^i). \tag{12}$$

3.4 Boundary-Guided Refinement Module

After passing the ALM we have obtained the primary region of the polyp, and need to further capture the missing portion and refine boundary information. We embed RPC into BRM to improve the ability to capture multi-scale features, and introduce a boundary-guided strategy to constrain regional learning using the feature obtained in RPC. The proposed BRM is shown in Fig. 5. Specifically, we first feed the input features T into the RPC to capture the multi-scale features. It is described as:

$$x^i = \mathrm{Conv}(\mathrm{RPC}(T^i)). \tag{13}$$

Then, we will divide into region branch and boundary branch for feature learning. In the boundary branch, we concatenate the upsampled depth region prediction with the input feature x^i and feed it into the 3×3 convolution layer. It is described as:

$$x_B^i = \mathrm{Conv}(\mathrm{Cat}(\mathrm{Up}\left(M_R^{i+1}, x^i\right), x^i)), \tag{14}$$

where i denotes the number of side output stages of the backbone network, and $i = [1, 2, 3]$ in BRM, M_R^{i+1} denotes the depth region prediction, $\mathrm{Up}\,(a, b)$ denotes bilinear interpolation operation that upsamples a to the same size as b. Further, we feed feature x_B^i into the region branch and concatenated with the input feature x^i. The region branch is restricted to perform feature learning inside the boundary. Then, it is summed by element-wise the upsampled depth region prediction to obtain the final region map M_R^i. It is described as:

$$M_R^i = \mathrm{Convs}(\mathrm{Cat}(x_B^i, x^i)) + \mathrm{Up}\left(M_R^{i+1}, x^i\right). \tag{15}$$

Finally, we add the learned boundary features x_B^i with the upsampled deep boundary predictions by element-wise to obtain the final boundary map M_B^i. It is described as:

$$M_B^i = \text{Convs}(x_B^i) + \text{Up}\left(M_B^{i+1}, x_B^i\right). \tag{16}$$

Note that we use M_R^1 as the final output of the model.

4   Experiments

4.1   Datasets

We conducted extensive experiments on five challenging polyp segmentation datasets: Endosece [28], CVC-ClinicDB [2], CVC-ColonDB [27], ETIS-LaribPolypDB [26], and Kvasir [14]. Among them, CVC-ClinicDB, CVC-ColonDB, ETIS-LaribPolypDB are frame databases extracted from colonoscopy videos, which contain 612, 380 and 196 polyp images, respectively. Kvasir is a new and challenging dataset containing 1000 polyp images.

4.2   Evaluation Metrics

We employ four widely employed metrics to evaluate our model and existing advanced polyp segmentation models: F-measure (F_β) [20], S-measure $(S\alpha)$ [5], E-measure $(E\varphi)$ [6], and MAE (M). F_β is the weighted summed average of precision and recall with non-negative weights β, and we set β^2 to 0.3. $S\alpha$ is the structural metric of both region-aware and object-aware, where α is set to 0.5. $E\varphi$ is used to capture image level statistics and local pixel matching information.

4.3   Implementation Details

We built our network using the Pytorch framework and examined it on a PC with an NVIDIA 2080ti GPU and an Intel i9-9900K CPU running at 4.0 GHz. In order to reduce the risk of overfitting and enhance the generalization ability of the model, we applied data enhancement strategies such as random flip and multi-scale input images. Only CVC-ClinicDB and Kvasir were used for the training datasets, of which 80% was used for training, 10% for validation, and 10% for testing [15]. The backbone network of our model is Res2Net-50 [10], and the training learning rate is set dynamically, with the maximum learning rate set to 0.005 for the backbone network and 0.05 for the other parts. The batchsize is set to 16, and the size of the input image is set to 352 × 352. We employ both weighted intersection over union loss (IOU) [21] and weighted binary cross entropy loss (BCE) [4] as a joint loss to deeply supervise the predicted results for each side output. In particular, our model takes only 40 epochs to train, converges in about 10 h, and it tests at about 28 FPS in real time.

4.4   Comparisons with SOTAs

Quantitative Evaluation. For a fair comparison, we employ the results given in the paper or the results obtained using the provided pre-trained model. We compared our model with 6 advanced polyp segmentation models: U-Net [24], U-Net++ [34], SFA [8], PraNet [7], DCRNet [31], and MSEG [12]. Table 1 shows the detailed quantitative results of the above methods on five publicly available polyp datasets. It is clear to see that our model achieves better performance on almost all metrics. In particular, for the testing datasets Endosece-CVC300 and ETIS-LaribPolypDB show a strong generalization ability. We observed that the images in the CVC-ColonDB dataset were blurred compared to other datasets, thus we speculate that this is the reason why they did not achieve optimal performance. We will put more effort into this in the future to solve this challenging case.

Table 1. Quantitative results. The best two results are highlighted in **bold**, *italic* respectively. ↑ and ↓ indicate higher and lower is better performance.

Methods	CVC300				CVC-ClinicDB				CVC-ColonDB				ETIS				Kvasir			
	$S\alpha\uparrow$	$E\varphi\uparrow$	$F_\beta\uparrow$	$M\downarrow$	$S\alpha\uparrow$	$E\varphi\uparrow$	$F_\beta\uparrow$	$M\downarrow$	$S\alpha\uparrow$	$E\varphi\uparrow$	$F_\beta\uparrow$	$M\downarrow$	$S\alpha\uparrow$	$E\varphi\uparrow$	$F_\beta\uparrow$	$M\downarrow\downarrow$	$S\alpha\uparrow$	$E\varphi\uparrow$	$F_\beta\uparrow$	$M\downarrow$
15' U-Net [24]	0.843	0.847	0.684	0.022	0.889	0.913	0.811	0.019	0.712	0.696	0.498	0.061	0.684	0.643	0.366	0.036	0.858	0.881	0.794	0.055
18' U-Net++ [34]	0.839	0.834	0.687	0.018	0.873	0.891	0.785	0.022	0.691	0.68	0.467	0.064	0.683	0.629	0.39	0.035	0.862	0.886	0.808	0.048
19' SFA [8]	0.64	0.644	0.61	0.065	0.793	0.84	0.647	0.042	0.634	0.675	0.379	0.094	0.557	0.531	0.231	0.109	0.782	0.834	0.67	0.075
20' PraNet [7]	*0.925*	*0.95*	0.843	0.01	0.936	0.963	0.896	0.009	0.819	0.847	0.696	0.045	0.794	0.808	0.6	0.031	*0.915*	*0.944*	*0.885*	0.03
21' DCRNet [31]	0.921	0.943	0.83	0.01	0.933	*0.964*	0.89	0.01	0.821	0.84	0.684	0.052	0.736	0.742	0.506	0.096	0.911	0.933	0.868	0.035
21' MSEG [12]	0.924	0.948	*0.852*	*0.009*	*0.938*	0.961	*0.907*	**0.007**	**0.834**	**0.859**	*0.724*	**0.038**	*0.828*	*0.854*	*0.671*	*0.015*	0.912	*0.942*	*0.885*	*0.028*
Ours	**0.945**	**0.972**	**0.895**	**0.006**	**0.94**	**0.966**	**0.916**	*0.009*	*0.833*	*0.852*	**0.752**	*0.042*	**0.846**	**0.869**	**0.73**	**0.014**	**0.918**	0.941	**0.909**	**0.027**

Qualitative Comparison. Figure 6 shows the visual comparison results. We selected challenging images with different sizes and textures for comparison. It can be seen that our model can accurately segment polyps from the background in different scenes. As shown in the first row of Fig. 6, the boundary segmentation results of our method are closer to the ground truth label and can be well adapted to the variable shape of polyps. As we can see from the third row of Fig. 6, our method is more accurate in locating polyps and there is no false detection of parts that are extremely similar to polyps.

4.5   Ablation Analysis

We will verify the effectiveness of ALM, BRM and RPC to gain insight into the proposed network. The experimental setups in this section are all the same as in Section 4.2. We replace the modules to be verified with common 3 × 3 convolutions. The experimental results are shown in Table 2. In the proposed network, we remove ALM (Baseline+BRM) and BRM (Baseline+ALM) respectively to verify their effectiveness. It can be seen from Table 2 that the performance of the model decreases significantly, especially on the ETIS-LaribPolypDB, where the removal of ALM and the removal of BRM decreases $E\varphi$ from 0.869 to 0.841 and 0.794, respectively. In addition, we remove the RPC in the BRM of the proposed network to verify its effectiveness. The results are shown in the last two rows of Table 2, where it can be seen that the performance of the model also decreases significantly, indicating that RPC plays a positive effect on the network.

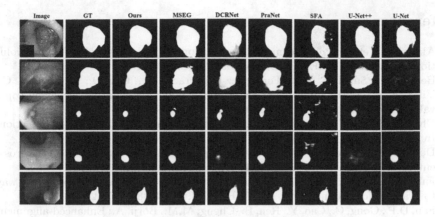

Fig. 6. Visual comparisons with SOTAs

Table 2. Results of ablation experiments. The last two rows of the table show the results of ablation experiments for RPC.

Settings		CVC-ColonDB				ETIS				Kvasir			
		$S\alpha\uparrow$	$E\varphi\uparrow$	$F_\beta\uparrow$	$M\downarrow$	$S\alpha\uparrow$	$E\varphi\uparrow$	$F_\beta\uparrow$	$M\downarrow$	$S\alpha\uparrow$	$E\varphi\uparrow$	$F_\beta\uparrow$	$M\downarrow$
Baseline		0.789	0.787	0.681	0.044	0.79	0.796	0.652	0.015	0.894	0.93	0.887	0.034
Baseline+ALM		0.813	0.84	0.699	0.05	0.819	0.841	0.655	0.028	0.909	0.948	0.88	0.028
Baselinee+BRM		0.796	0.805	0.698	0.046	0.801	0.794	0.657	0.017	0.904	0.931	0.893	0.034
Baseline+ALM+BRM		**0.833**	**0.852**	**0.752**	**0.042**	**0.846**	**0.869**	**0.73**	**0.014**	**0.918**	**0.941**	**0.909**	**0.027**
RPC	✗	0.824	0.851	0.733	0.041	0.804	0.825	0.627	0.025	0.908	0.932	0.897	0.036
	✓	**0.833**	**0.852**	**0.752**	**0.042**	**0.846**	**0.869**	**0.73**	**0.014**	**0.918**	**0.941**	**0.909**	**0.027**

5   Conclusion

We propose a boundary-aware polyp segmentation network that consists of ALM and BRM. The ALM can aggregate contextual features at a high level to accurately identify the primary location of polyps. The RPC is embedded in the BRM to refine the missing polyp portions and boundary details in the initial prediction. The BRM can effectively utilize the features obtained in the RPC for boundary guidance and further constrain the learning of regional features to achieve more accurate segmentation. Extensive experiments have shown that our network outperforms existing polyp segmentation methods on all five widely used datasets. In addition, our proposed network is simpler and more efficient compared to previous works.

Acknowledgement. This work is partially supported by the Natural Science Foundation of China (No. 61802336), and Yangzhou University"Qinglan Project".

References

1. Akbari, M., et al.: Polyp segmentation in colonoscopy images using fully convolutional network. In: IEEE EMBC, pp. 69–72. IEEE (2018)
2. Bernal, J., Sánchez, F.J., Fernández-Esparrach, G., Gil, D., Rodríguez, C., Vilariño, F.: WM-DOVA maps for accurate polyp highlighting in colonoscopy: validation vs. saliency maps from physicians. CMIG **43**, 99–111 (2015)
3. Chen, S., Tan, X., Wang, B., Hu, X.: Reverse attention for salient object detection. In: ECCV, pp. 234–250 (2018)
4. De Boer, P.T., Kroese, D.P., Mannor, S., Rubinstein, R.Y.: A tutorial on the cross-entropy method. Ann. Oper. Res. **134**(1), 19–67 (2005)
5. Fan, D.P., Cheng, M.M., Liu, Y., Li, T., Borji, A.: Structure-measure: a new way to evaluate foreground maps. In: IEEE ICCV, pp. 4548–4557 (2017)
6. Fan, D.P., Gong, C., Cao, Y., Ren, B., Cheng, M.M., Borji, A.: Enhanced-alignment measure for binary foreground map evaluation. arXiv preprint arXiv:1805.10421 (2018)
7. Fan, D.-P., et al.: PraNet: parallel reverse attention network for polyp segmentation. In: Martel, A.L., et al. (eds.) MICCAI 2020. LNCS, vol. 12266, pp. 263–273. Springer, Cham (2020). https://doi.org/10.1007/978-3-030-59725-2_26
8. Fang, Y., Chen, C., Yuan, Y., Tong, K.: Selective feature aggregation network with area-boundary constraints for polyp segmentation. In: Shen, D., et al. (eds.) MICCAI 2019. LNCS, vol. 11764, pp. 302–310. Springer, Cham (2019). https://doi.org/10.1007/978-3-030-32239-7_34
9. Fu, J., et al.: Dual attention network for scene segmentation. In: IEEE CVPR, pp. 3146–3154 (2019)
10. Gao, S.H., Cheng, M.M., Zhao, K., Zhang, X.Y., Yang, M.H., Torr, P.: Res2Net: a new multi-scale backbone architecture. IEEE Trans. Pattern Anal. Mach. Intell. **43**(2), 652–662 (2019)
11. Hou, Q., Zhang, L., Cheng, M.M., Feng, J.: Strip pooling: rethinking spatial pooling for scene parsing. In: IEEE CVPR, pp. 4003–4012 (2020)
12. Huang, C.H., Wu, H.Y., Lin, Y.L.: HarDNet-MSEG: a simple encoder-decoder polyp segmentation neural network that achieves over 0.9 mean dice and 86 FPS. arXiv preprint arXiv:2101.07172 (2021)
13. Huang, Z., Wang, X., Huang, L., Huang, C., Wei, Y., Liu, W.: CCNet: Criss-cross attention for semantic segmentation. In: IEEE ICCV, pp. 603–612 (2019)
14. Jha, D., et al.: Kvasir-SEG: a segmented polyp dataset. In: Ro, Y.M., et al. (eds.) MMM 2020. LNCS, vol. 11962, pp. 451–462. Springer, Cham (2020). https://doi.org/10.1007/978-3-030-37734-2_37
15. Jha, D., et al.: Resunet++: an advanced architecture for medical image segmentation. In: IEEE ISM, pp. 225–2255. IEEE (2019)
16. Jia, X., Xing, X., Yuan, Y., Xing, L., Meng, M.Q.H.: Wireless capsule endoscopy: a new tool for cancer screening in the colon with deep-learning-based polyp recognition. Proc. IEEE **108**(1), 178–197 (2019)
17. Lin, G., Shen, C., Van Den Hengel, A., Reid, I.: Efficient piecewise training of deep structured models for semantic segmentation. In: IEEE CVPR, pp. 3194–3203 (2016)
18. Lin, Z., et al.: A structured self-attentive sentence embedding. arXiv preprint arXiv:1703.03130 (2017)
19. Mamonov, A.V., Figueiredo, I.N., Figueiredo, P.N., Tsai, Y.H.R.: Automated polyp detection in colon capsule endoscopy. IEEE TMI **33**(7), 1488–1502 (2014)

20. Margolin, R., Zelnik-Manor, L., Tal, A.: How to evaluate foreground maps? In: CVPR, pp. 248–255 (2014)
21. Máttyus, G., Luo, W., Urtasun, R.: Deeproadmapper: extracting road topology from aerial images. In: IEEE ICCV, pp. 3438–3446 (2017)
22. Murugesan, B., Sarveswaran, K., Shankaranarayana, S.M., Ram, K., Joseph, J., Sivaprakasam, M.: Psi-net: shape and boundary aware joint multi-task deep network for medical image segmentation. In: IEEE EMBC, pp. 7223–7226. IEEE (2019)
23. Qin, X., Zhang, Z., Huang, C., Gao, C., Dehghan, M., Jagersand, M.: Basnet: boundary-aware salient object detection. In: IEEE CVPR, pp. 7479–7489 (2019)
24. Ronneberger, O., Fischer, P., Brox, T.: U-Net: convolutional networks for biomedical image segmentation. In: Navab, N., Hornegger, J., Wells, W.M., Frangi, A.F. (eds.) MICCAI 2015. LNCS, vol. 9351, pp. 234–241. Springer, Cham (2015). https://doi.org/10.1007/978-3-319-24574-4_28
25. Shen, T., Zhou, T., Long, G., Jiang, J., Pan, S., Zhang, C.: DiSAN: directional self-attention network for RNN/CNN-free language understanding. In: AAAI Conference on Artificial Intelligence, vol. 32 (2018)
26. Silva, J., Histace, A., Romain, O., Dray, X., Granado, B.: Toward embedded detection of polyps in WCE images for early diagnosis of colorectal cancer. IJCARS 9(2), 283–293 (2014)
27. Tajbakhsh, N., Gurudu, S.R., Liang, J.: Automated polyp detection in colonoscopy videos using shape and context information. IEEE TMI 35(2), 630–644 (2015)
28. Vázquez, D., et al.: A benchmark for endoluminal scene segmentation of colonoscopy images. J. Healthc. Eng. 2017 (2017)
29. Wang, X., Girshick, R., Gupta, A., He, K.: Non-local neural networks. In: IEEE CVPR, pp. 7794–7803 (2018)
30. Wu, Z., Su, L., Huang, Q.: Stacked cross refinement network for edge-aware salient object detection. In: IEEE ICCV, pp. 7264–7273 (2019)
31. Yin, Z., Liang, K., Ma, Z., Guo, J.: Duplex contextual relation network for polyp segmentation. arXiv preprint arXiv:2103.06725 (2021)
32. Yu, F., Koltun, V.: Multi-scale context aggregation by dilated convolutions. arXiv preprint arXiv:1511.07122 (2015)
33. Zhang, H., Goodfellow, I., Metaxas, D., Odena, A.: Self-attention generative adversarial networks. In: ICML, pp. 7354–7363. PMLR (2019)
34. Zhou, Z., Rahman Siddiquee, M.M., Tajbakhsh, N., Liang, J.: UNet++: a nested U-Net architecture for medical image segmentation. In: Stoyanov, D., et al. (eds.) DLMIA/ML-CDS -2018. LNCS, vol. 11045, pp. 3–11. Springer, Cham (2018). https://doi.org/10.1007/978-3-030-00889-5_1

SUDANet: A Siamese UNet with Dense Attention Mechanism for Remote Sensing Image Change Detection

Chengzhe Sun[1], Chun Du[1], Jiangjiang Wu[1], and Hao Chen[1,2]([✉])

[1] National University of Defense Technology, Changsha 410000, China
hchen@nudt.edu.cn
[2] Key Laboratory of Natural Resources Monitoring and Natural Resources, Changsha 410000, China

Abstract. Change detection is one of the main applications of remote sensing images. Pixel-to-pixel change detection using deep learning has been a hot research spot. However, the current approach are not effective enough to fuse deep semantic features and raw spatial information, and the network does not have the ability to perform long-distance information aggregation due to the limitation of the convolutional kernel size. In this manuscript, we propose a Siamese UNet with a dense attention mechanism, named SUDANet to do change detection for remote sensing images. SUDANet add a channel attention mechanism and a self-attention mechanism to the dense skip connection between encoder and decoder which enable the model to fuse feature information in channel dimensions and spatial dimensions. Graph attention module is also added at the end of the encoder, enabling the model to perform correlation analysis and long-distance aggregation of deep semantic features. The experimental results on LEVIR dataset show that our method outperforms the state-of-the-art change detection methods.

Keywords: Change detection · Deep learning · Attention mechanism · Remote sensing (RS) images

1 Introduction

The remote sensing change detection (CD) task aims to detect semantic changes of our interest from remote sensing images of the same area at different time phases [1]. Change detection plays an important role in ecosystem monitoring [2], land resources and land use mapping [3], damage assessment [4], and urban expansion monitoring [5] to provide a basis for relevant analysis and decision making.

In recent years, deep learning (DL) has developed rapidly, especially deep convolutional neural networks(CNNs) have made a series of significant advances in the field of image processing. In remote sensing image processing, deep learning has been widely used in problems such as image registration [6], road extraction [7], and image to map translation [8,9] and has shown excellent performance. Solving CD tasks using deep learning is also a current research hotspot,

S. Yu et al. (Eds.): PRCV 2022, LNCS 13537, pp. 78–88, 2022.
https://doi.org/10.1007/978-3-031-18916-6_7

and most deep learning networks for CD tasks are based on CNNs. Among them, UNet based on fully convolutional networks has become one of the standard frameworks for change detection tasks [10] and has many extensions. UNet is a symmetric encoder-decoder structure that captures contextual information to extract features in the downsampling part and reconstructs the image and outputs the final change map in the upsampling part [11]. UNet adds skip connections between the encoder and decoder, allowing the network to better fuse deep semantic information and shallow spatial information, improving the accuracy of change detection. Jaturapitpornchai et al. [12] implemented new building detection for SAR images using UNet. Peng et al. [13] proposed a UNet++ network for VHR image change detection tasks with dense hop connections to make information transfer in UNet is more compact and improves the accuracy of CD. Daudt et al. [14] used Siamese network as the encoder part of UNet for the CD task whose input is dual time phase remote sensing image and achieved satisfactory results. However, although UNet is able to fuse coarse-grained spatial information and deep semantic information, it is difficult to effectively fuse the information due to the semantic gap between these information. Therefore, attention mechanisms are applied to CD tasks to solve such problems.

The attention mechanism originates from the human visual system and has been a research hotspot in the field of image processing, enabling the network to fuse different features more effectively, which has a significant effect on the accuracy improvement of image processing problems. Chen et al. [15] proposed a spatio-temporal attention mechanism to model spatio-temporal relationships by introducing a self-attention mechanism in the model, which enables the model to capture spatio-temporal dependencies at different scales. Zhang et al. [16] improved the boundary completeness and internal compactness of objects in the output change map by adding channel attention mechanism(CAM) and spatial attention mechanism(SAM) to the decoder part of the UNet. Fang et al. [17] proposed an Ensemble Channel Attention Module (ECAM) to fuse multiple outputs of Nested UNet and extract the most representative features at different semantic levels for the final classification. In addition, the graph attention mechanism (GAT) has been introduced into the field of remote sensing in recent years due to its powerful long-range feature representation and information aggregation capabilities [18].

Inspired by the above work, we propose a model that combines the dense attention mechanism, Siamese structure and Nested UNet to solve the CD task for RS image, called SUDANet. By adding a dense attention mechanism (DAM) [19] to the skip connection between the encoder and decoder, we enable the model to overcome the semantic gap and effectively aggregate channel information and spatial information. In addition, we include a graph attention mechanism (GAT) module in the model which can extract long-range information and enable the model to mine and exploit the relationships between features.

The main contributions of this manuscript are as follows:

1) An end-to-end SUDANet with dense attention mechanism(DAM) is proposed for remote sensing image change detection task based on Siamese network and

Nested UNet. Dense attention mechanism can effectively solve the semantic gap problem when aggregating information.

2) The use of graph attention mechanism allows the model to have the ability to fuse long-range information and better exploit the features.

3) Through a series of comparative experiments on a widely used benchmark dataset, our method outperforms the state-of-the-art methods in F1-score, Kappa and IoU.

2   Methodology

2.1   SUDANet Architecture

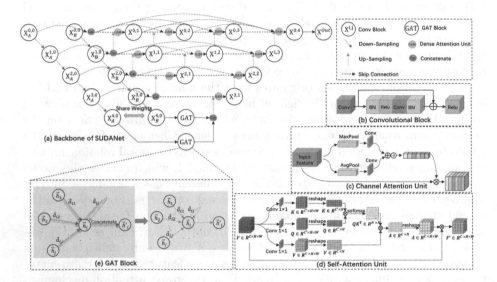

Fig. 1. Illustration of SUDANet. (a) The backbone of SUDANet.(b) Illustration of the convolution block. (c) Channel attention unit in dense attention mechanism(DAM), the output goes to the self-attention unit (d) Self-attention unit in DAM, the input comes from the channel attention unit. (e) GAT block, including a multi-headed graph attention unit and a single-headed graph attention unit.

The backbone of SUDANet is Nested UNet, as shown in Fig. 1(a), where the downward and upward arrows indicate down-sampling and up-sampling respectively, the dashed line indicates the skip connection, cat represents the concatenation in the channel dimension, and $x^{i,j}$ represents the convolution block. Nested UNet enables better aggregation of features with different semantic scales by adding more dense skip connections between encoder and decoder. To fit the characteristics of the change detection task, we design the encoder part of the Nested UNet as a Siamese structure. The dual-temporal remote sensing images enter SUDANet from two branches of the Siamese network, which are sharing weights. After entering the network, the images are processed in each convolutional block cell for convolutional operation as shown in Fig. 1(b). Each convolutional block consists of a combination of convolution, batch normalization and activation functions, and a shortcut connection is used to ensure the integrity of the information transfer. To solve the semantic gap problem of dense skip connection in aggregating multi-scale semantic information, we add a dense attention mechanism (DAM) after features are skip connected. Each DAM unit consists of two parts: channel attention unit and self-attention unit, as shown in Fig. 1(c) and Fig. 1(d), respectively. Dense attention mechanism (DAM) can filter multi-scale features in channel and space, allowing features to be efficiently aggregated and preventing information confusion. In addition, to make the network capable of long-distance information aggregation, we add a GAT block at the end of the encoder, as shown in Fig. 1(e). The GAT block further aggregates the features extracted from the two full convolutional network branches in the encoder by mining the correlation between the features. Our GAT block consists of a multi-head GAT unit and a single-head GAT unit.

2.2 Dense Attention Mechanism

Dense attention mechanism is used when features with different semantic information are fused. DAM includes channel attention mechanism and self-attention mechanism.

As shown in Fig. 1(c), in the channel attention mechanism, the input features are pooled and convolved to obtain attention weights which are applied to the input features. In this process, the network learns the importance of different channels through training and assigns weights to enhance the channels that are useful for the task and suppress the channels that are useless. This process can be represented by the following equation.

$$F'_{cam} = \sigma \left(Conv_{1 \times 1} \left(MaxPool \left(F_{cam} \right) \right) + Conv_{1 \times 1} \left(AvgPool \left(F_{cam} \right) \right) \right) \otimes F_{cam} \tag{1}$$

where F_{cam} and F'_{cam} represent the input features and output features of the channel attention mechanism respectively, and σ is the sigmoid function.

After the features go through the channel attention, the output will enter the self-attention mechanism as shown in Fig. 1(d). In the self-attention unit, the features are convolved and reshaped to obtain query, key and value, and the correlation of each element is calculated and acted on the input features by multiplying them, as represented by the following equation.

$$Key = Reshape \left(Conv_{1 \times 1} \left(F_{sam} \right) \right) \tag{2}$$

$$Query = Reshape \left(Conv_{1 \times 1} \left(F_{sam} \right) \right) \tag{3}$$

$$Value = Reshape \left(Conv_{1 \times 1} \left(F_{sam} \right) \right) \tag{4}$$

$$A = Value \otimes Softmax(Query \otimes Key) \tag{5}$$

$$F'_{sam} = F_{sam} \otimes Reshape(A) \tag{6}$$

where F_{sam} and F'_{sam} represent the input features and output features of the self-attention mechanism, respectively, and A represents the attention coefficient. Dense attention mechanism (DAM) combines the channel attention mechanism and the self-attention mechanism, which makes the features consider both the channel discrepancy and the spatial correlation in the fusion process, and can effectively suppress the semantic gap.

2.3 GAT Block

Since CNN is limited by the size of convolutional kernel, it cannot fuse the long-distance feature information. We introduce the graph attention module at the end of the Encoder part of SUDANet to solve this problem, as shown in Fig. 1(e). We use the features extracted as nodes, which denoted by $\{h_1, h_2, h_3, ...h_N\}$ and N denotes the number of features, to construct the graph. The correlation between nodes can be learned through the graph attention mechanism to obtain the attention coefficients, and assign weights to each node during feature fusion. The attention coefficient a_{ij} of node i to neighbor node j can be calculated by the following equation.

$$e_{ij} = LeakyReLU(a^T[\mathbf{W}h_i||\mathbf{W}h_j]) \tag{7}$$

$$a_{ij} = Softmax_j(e_{ij}) = \frac{exp(e_{ij})}{\sum_{k \in N_i} exp(e_{ik})} \tag{8}$$

where a and $\mathbf{W}$ are trainable parameters, and we can achieve automatic attention allocation by neural network training. $||$ denotes concatenation. Then by weighting we can get the new feature value h'_i of node i, which fuses the features of its neighbor nodes.

$$h'_i = \sum_{j \in N_i} a_{ij} \mathbf{W} h_j \tag{9}$$

The first GAT layer we use in the model is a GAT with multi-head attention, which can improve the generalization of the attention mechanism. Using K sets of attention layers that are independent of each other, their results are concatenated. The formula for computing h'_i using the multi-head attention mechanism is as follows:

$$h'_i = ||_{k=1}^K \sum_{j \in N_i} a_{ij}^k \mathbf{W}^k h_j \tag{10}$$

Note that in order to make the feature information and spatial context information extracted by encoder correspond to the same position of the dual-temporal remote sensing image pair, the GAT networks in both branches share the weights.

2.4 Loss Function

For the change detection task where the number of unchanged pixels is much larger than the number of changed pixels, we use a combination of cross-entropy loss L_{ce} and dice loss L_{dice} as the loss function, defined as follows.

$$L_{hybrid} = L_{ce} + L_{dice} \qquad (11)$$

Let the label be Y and the change image $\hat{Y} = \hat{y}_k, k = 1, 2, \ldots, H \times W$, where H is the height of the image, W is the width of the image, and $\hat{y}_k$ is the pixel value of the kth pixel of the image. Let c be 0 or 1, representing the change or not of the kth pixel in the label. The cross-entropy loss is calculated as follows.

$$L_{ce} = \frac{1}{H \times W} \sum_{k=1}^{H \times W} log \left(\frac{exp\left(\hat{y}_{kc}\right)}{\sum_{l=0}^{1} exp\left(\hat{y}_{kl}\right)} \right) \qquad (12)$$

In addition, the dice losses are calculated as follows:

$$L_{dice} = 1 - \frac{2 \cdot Y \cdot softmax\left(\hat{Y}\right)}{Y + softmax\left(\hat{Y}\right)} \qquad (13)$$

3 Dataset and Evaluation Metrics

The dataset we use in our experiments is the LEVIR-CD dataset, which consists of 637 very high resolution (0.5 m/pixel) Remote Sensing image pairs. The images in this dataset are from 20 different areas in several cities in Texas, USA, and focus on building-related changes, covering various types of buildings such as villa houses, high-rise apartments, small garages and large warehouses, with each image size of 1024×1024 pixels. Due to the limited memory of GPU, we crop the images to 256×256 pixels and finally get 7120 images as the training set and 1024 images as the validation set.

To effectively evaluate the change detection effectiveness of various methods, we used F1-Score, Overall accuracy (OA), Kappa coefficient (Kappa) and Intersection-over-Union (IoU) as evaluation metrics, and they are defined as follows:

$$F1 = \frac{2 \times P \times R}{P + R} \qquad (14)$$

$$OA = \frac{TP + TN}{TP + TN + FP + FN} \qquad (15)$$

$$Kappa = \frac{OA - PRE}{1 - PRE} \qquad (16)$$

$$IoU = \frac{TP}{TP + FP + FN} \qquad (17)$$

Let TP denote the number of true positives, FP denote the number of false positives, TN denote the number of true negatives, and FN denote the number of false negatives, we can calculate P, R and PRE as follows:

$$P = \frac{TP}{TP + FP} \tag{18}$$

$$R = \frac{TP}{TP + FN} \tag{19}$$

$$PRE = \frac{(TP + FN) \times (TP + FP) + (TN + FP) \times (TN + FN)}{(TP + TN + FP + FN)^2} \tag{20}$$

4 Experimental Results and Analysis

4.1 Training Details

Our change detection approach is implemented via Pytorch on a deep learning server powered by $2 \times$ GeForce GTX 2080Ti GPU, 256 GB RAM, 2×10 GB VRAM. The optimizer used in the experiments for SUDANet is AdamW, and the learning rate is set to 0.001. The number of iterations is 2000, and the batch size is set to 8.

4.2 Comparative Experiments

In this paper, several representative deep learning methods in the field of change detection are selected for comparison. FC-Diff, FC-Conc [14] is a combination of siamese network and UNet. DSIFN [16] uses pre-trained vgg16 as an encoder, incorporating a dual attention mechanism and a multi-scale deep monitoring strategy. SNUNet-ECAM [17] is a combination of Nested UNet and Siamese network, while adding an ensemble channel attention module. BIT [20] is the latest result of Transformer applied to change detection tasks.

Table 1. Performance comparison on LEVIR-CD data set.

Model	F1-score	OA	Kappa	IoU
FC-Diff	0.8232	0.9862	0.816	0.6995
FC-Conc	0.8545	0.988	0.8482	0.7549
DSIFN	0.8966	0.9915	0.8922	0.8126
SNUNet-ECAM	0.895	0.9914	0.8905	0.81
BITCD	0.8954	0.9913	0.8909	0.8106
SUDANet	**0.9102**	**0.9925**	**0.9063**	**0.8353**

We present the evaluation results of each method in Table 1. The quantitative results in Table 1 show that our method outperforms the other methods for remote sensing change detection in complex scenes, with F1-score, Kappa, and IoU outperforming the best results of the comparison methods by 1.36%, 1.41%, and 2.27%, respectively. Figure 2 presents the change detection results for each method. From the results in rows 1 to 3, we can see that when the changes are similar to the surrounding environment, other methods will miss the detection, while our method can still detect the results stably. From the results in rows 4 and 5, we can see that our model is also more effective than other methods for change detection of small targets. This is due to the application of the dense attention mechanism that suppresses the semantic gap and enhances the semantic information of changes.

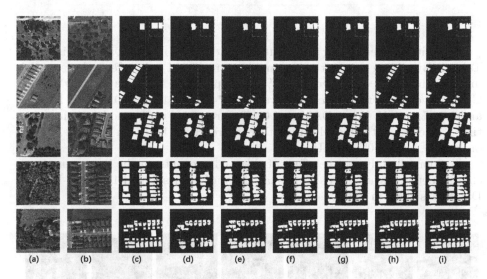

Fig. 2. Visualization results on LEVIR data set. (a) Image T_1. (b) Image $T2$. (c) Ground truth. (d) FC-Diff (e) FC-Conc. (f) DSIFN. (g) SNUNet-ECAM. (h) BIT. (i) SUDANet.

4.3 Ablation Experiments

In order to examine the effect of the various components of the model, we conducted ablation experiments on the model. By removing the components of the model, we obtained the following three sub-models.

SUDANet-noDG: The framework model of SUDANet is obtained after removing the dense attention mechanism and the graph attention module from SUDANet. It is composed of a siamese network and Nested UNet. It should be noted that the feature extraction results of the two branches in the encoder part at each level are first concatenated before entering decoder.

SUDANet-noDAM: Obtained by removing the dense attention mechanism from SUDANet.

SUDANet-noGAT: Obtained by removing the graph attention module from SUDANet.

Table 2. Ablation results On LEVIR-CD Data Set.

Model	F1-score	OA	Kappa	IoU
SUDANet-noDG	0.8952	0.9913	0.8907	0.8103
SUDANet-noDAM	0.9023	0.9918	0.8980	0.8220
SUDANet-noGAT	0.9026	0.9919	0.8983	0.8225
SUDANet	**0.9102**	**0.9925**	**0.9063**	**0.8353**

Quantitative results for each submodel on the LEVIR DataSet listed in Table 2. By adding dense attention mechanism (DAM), the effect of the model improves by 0.71% on F1-score, 0.73% on Kappa, and 1.17% on IoU. By adding GAT, the effect of the model improves by 0.74% on F1-score, 0.76% on Kappa, and 1.22% on IoU. When DAM and GAT were added to the model at the same time, the effect of the model was further improved by 1.50% on F1-score, 1.56% on Kappa, and 2.50% on IoU.

To more directly see the effect of these components on the improvement of change detection accuracy, the visual effect of each submodel on the LEVIR DataSet is given in Fig. 3.

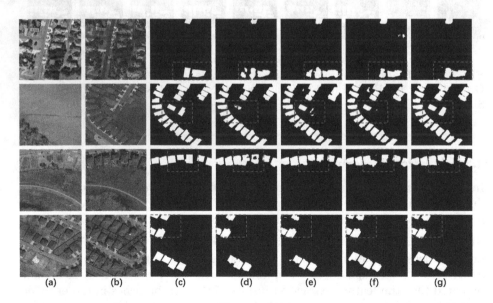

(a)   (b)   (c)   (d)   (e)   (f)   (g)

Fig. 3. Visualization results on LEVIR data set. (a) Image T_1. (b) Image $T2$. (c) Ground truth. (d) SUDANet-noDG. (e) SUDANet-noGAT. (f) SUDANet-noDAM. (g) SUDANet.

It can be seen that the addition of dense attention mechanism improves the shape integrity and smoothness of the object in change detection by suppressing the redundant information of features in channels and space. The addition of GAT gives the model the ability to aggregate long-distance information, which reduces false alarm and missed alarm errors in change detection. SUDANet combines the advantages of both of them and achieves the best performance in change detection on LEVIR DataSet.

5 Conclusion

In this manuscript, we propose a Siamese UNet with dense attention mechanism for change detection task of remote sensing images, i.e., SUDANet. SUDANet overcomes the semantic gap by adding a channel attention mechanism and a self-attention mechanism to the dense skip connection between encoder and decoder, which can filter the features in the channel and spatial dimensions when they are skip connected. SUDANet also adds a GAT at the end of the encoder. The graph attention module enables the model to mine the relevance of deep semantic features and aggregate long-distance information, further improving the performance of the model on change detection tasks. The experimental results on the LEVIR dataset show that SUDANet takes the best results compared with other methods. The change image results show that SUDANet can still detect change objects when other methods miss small targets or change objects that are similar to the background.

References

1. Shao, R., Du, C., Chen, H., Li, J.: SUNet: change detection for heterogeneous remote sensing images from satellite and UAV using a dual-channel fully convolution network. Remote Sens. **13**(18), 3750 (2021)
2. Willis, K.S.: Remote sensing change detection for ecological monitoring in united states protected areas. Biol. Cons. **182**, 233–242 (2015)
3. Madasa, A., Orimoloye, I.R., Ololade, O.O.: Application of geospatial indices for mapping land cover/use change detection in a mining area. J. Afr. Earth Sci. **175**, 104108 (2021)
4. Huang, F., Chen, L., Yin, K., Huang, J., Gui, L.: Object-oriented change detection and damage assessment using high-resolution remote sensing images, Tangjiao landslide, three gorges reservoir, china. Environ. Earth Sci. **77**(5), 1–19 (2018)
5. Ji, S., Shen, Y., Lu, M., Zhang, Y.: Building instance change detection from large-scale aerial images using convolutional neural networks and simulated samples. Remote Sens. **11**(11), 1343 (2019)
6. Xu, Y., Li, J., Du, C., Chen, H.: NBR-Net: a non-rigid bi-directional registration network for multi-temporal remote sensing images. IEEE Trans. Geosci. Remote Sens. **60**, 1–15 (2022)
7. Xu, Y., Chen, H., Du, C., Li, J.: MSACon: mining spatial attention-based contextual information for road extraction. IEEE Trans. Geosci. Remote Sens. **60**, 1–17 (2021)

8. Song, J., Li, J., Chen, H., Wu, J.: MapGen-GAN: a fast translator for remote sensing image to map via unsupervised adversarial learning. IEEE J. Sel. Top. Appl. Earth Obs. Remote Sens. **14**, 2341–2357 (2021)

9. Song, J., Li, J., Chen, H., Wu, J.: RSMT: a remote sensing image-to-map translation model via adversarial deep transfer learning. Remote Sens. **14**(4), 919 (2022)

10. Khelifi, L., Mignotte, M.: Deep learning for change detection in remote sensing images: comprehensive review and meta-analysis. IEEE Access **8**, 126385–126400 (2020)

11. Alexakis, E.B., Armenakis, C.: Evaluation of UNet and UNet++ architectures in high resolution image change detection applications. Int. Arch. Photogramm. Remote Sens. Spat. Inf. Sci. **43**, 1507–1514 (2020)

12. Jaturapitpornchai, R., Matsuoka, M., Kanemoto, N., Kuzuoka, S., Ito, R., Nakamura, R.: Newly built construction detection in SAR images using deep learning. Remote Sens. **11**(12), 1444 (2019)

13. Peng, D., Zhang, Y., Guan, H.: End-to-end change detection for high resolution satellite images using improved UNet++. Remote Sens. **11**(11), 1382 (2019)

14. Daudt, R.C., Le Saux, B., Boulch, A.: Fully convolutional siamese networks for change detection. In: 2018 25th IEEE International Conference on Image Processing (ICIP), pp. 4063–4067. IEEE (2018)

15. Chen, H., Shi, Z.: A spatial-temporal attention-based method and a new dataset for remote sensing image change detection. Remote Sens. **12**(10), 1662 (2020)

16. Zhang, C., et al.: A deeply supervised image fusion network for change detection in high resolution bi-temporal remote sensing images. ISPRS J. Photogramm. Remote. Sens. **166**, 183–200 (2020)

17. Fang, S., Li, K., Shao, J., Li, Z.: SNUNet-CD: a densely connected Siamese network for change detection of VHR images. IEEE Geosci. Remote Sens. Lett. **19**, 1–5 (2021)

18. Zi, W., Xiong, W., Chen, H., Li, J., Jing, N.: SGA-Net: self-constructing graph attention neural network for semantic segmentation of remote sensing images. Remote Sens. **13**(21), 4201 (2021)

19. Peng, D., Bruzzone, L., Zhang, Y., Guan, H., Ding, H., Huang, X.: SemiCDNet: a semisupervised convolutional neural network for change detection in high resolution remote-sensing images. IEEE Trans. Geosci. Remote Sens. **59**(7), 5891–5906 (2020)

20. Chen, H., Qi, Z., Shi, Z.: Efficient transformer based method for remote sensing image change detection. arXiv e-prints pp. arXiv-2103 (2021)

A Local-Global Self-attention Interaction Network for RGB-D Cross-Modal Person Re-identification

Chuanlei Zhu, Xiaohong Li$^{(\boxtimes)}$, Meibin Qi, Yimin Liu, and Long Zhang

Hefei University of Technology, Anhui 230009, China
`jsjlxh@hfut.edu.cn, yiminliu@mail.hfut.edu.cn`

Abstract. RGB-D cross-modal person re-identification (Re-ID) task aims to match the person images between the RGB and depth modalities. This task is rather challenging for the tremendous discrepancy between these two modalities in addition to common issues such as lighting conditions, human posture, camera angle, etc. Nowadays only few types of research focus on this task, and existing Re-ID methods tend to learn homogeneous structural relationships in an image, which have limited discriminability and weak robustness to noisy images. In this paper, we propose A Local-Global Interaction Network dedicated to processing cross-modal problems. The network can constrain the center distance between two modals, and improve the intra-class cross-modality similarity. Besides, it can also learn the local and global features of different modalities to enrich the features extracted from different modes. We validate the effectiveness of our approach on public benchmark datasets. Experimental results demonstrate our method outperforms other state-of-the-arts in terms of visual quality and quantitative measurement.

Keywords: Cross-modal person re-identification · Global self-attention · Intra-class cross-modality similarity

1 Introduction

Person re-identification (Re-ID) is designed to retrieve the same person from multiple non-overlapping cameras deployed in different perspectives [1]. It has attracted widespread attention in the computer vision community because it plays a vital role in intelligent video surveillance and criminal investigation application. Existing works [4–6] mainly focus on RGB-based person Re-ID. With the introduction of deep learning technology [7], it has made exciting progress and achieved high precision [8]. But RGB-based person Re-ID cannot work under dark conditions. To solve this issue, considering that the Microsoft Kinect camera can work well ignoring the variance of illumination, RGB-D dual-modal person Re-ID [9] is proposed, which aims at achieving cross-modal Re-ID in RGB and depth images. Compared with the RGB-based person Re-ID, the matching of

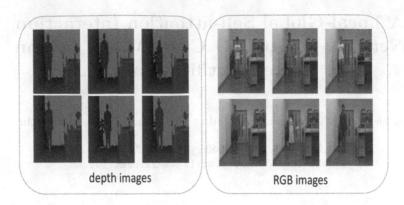

Fig. 1. Examples of depth images and RGB images from the RobotPKU dataset.

RGB-D person Re-ID is much more difficult, due to the tremendous discrepancy between RGB images and depth images, as shown in Fig. 1.

Most person Re-ID [20, 22] works pay attention to part-level feature learning while ignoring the importance of global features. Besides, existing cross-modality person Re-ID studies mainly focus on enlarging inter-class differences of features to solve the problem of cross-modal images matching difficulty. However, few studies note the importance of the intra-class cross-modality similarity. To tackle the above issues, we construct A Local-Global Self-attention Interaction Network (LGSIN). We introduce a mechanism of combining local and global self-attention. Its purpose is to make up for the defect that Convolutional Neural Network (CNN) only extracts local deep features and ignores global features. Our method takes global features into account. Besides, the architecture introduces an improved method combining Hetero-Center (HC) [16] with Cross-Entropy (CE) [17] loss to improve the similarity of intra-class cross-modality. To sum up, the main contributions of this paper can be summarized as follows:

(1) We design A Local-Global Self-attention Interaction Network(LGSIN), where local and global self-attention mechanisms are introduced into the cross-modal network innovatively for training.
(2) We propose a novel loss function mechanism to constrain the center distance between the two modalities and improve the similarity of intra-class cross-modal features.
(3) We perform in-depth experiments to analyze our method. Moreover, our method achieves the effect of the state-of-the-art on the BIWI and RobotPKU datasets.

2   Related Work

2.1   RGB-Infrared (IR) Cross-Modal Person Re-ID

Infrared (IR) images refer to the images captured by the infrared camera. These images can be used as supplements to RGB images because they are not easily affected by illumination changes. The RGB-IR cross-modal person Re-ID task aims to match the visible and infrared images of a person under different cameras. CMGN [24] introduced a fine-grained network to enable the network to learn the common features of different modalities. Work [21] aimed to narrow the modal gap by exploiting the concept of pixel alignment. Ye et al. [23] proposed global feature learning to alleviate the modality discrepancy. Li et al. [25] generated a new X-modality to connect the visible and infrared images to make cross-modal images easier to match.

2.2 RGB-D Person Re-ID

In recent years, depth images have been widely used in the field of computer vision. Compared with the RGB images, the depth images are more robust to illumination changes. The characteristic of the depth images is that it has nothing to do with light and color. The features of depth images can remain unchanged under extremely poor illumination conditions. Therefore, the depth image can be used as a supplement to the RGB image and applied to the person Re-ID task, and the RGB-D cross-modal person Re-ID is proposed. Recently, only few works [10–12] paid attention to RGB-D dual-modal person Re-ID. Some researchers [10, 11] focused on fusing the information of RGB images and depth images to form the complementarity between these two modalities and achieve the person Re-ID task. To improve the accuracy of pedestrian recognition, Pala et al. [11] extracted the human metric features from the depth images and fuse them with the appearance features extracted from the RGB images. Mogelmose et al. [10] merged the RGB features, the depth features, and the infrared features to achieve better recognition results. For all we know, work [12] was the first paper that proposes a deep network for the RGB-D cross-modal person Re-ID. Its purpose is to reduce the gap between these two modes to improve the accuracy of the cross-modal recognition. Considering the long-term application prospect of RGB-D person Re-ID, this paper concentrate on this task. Concretely, this paper proposes a local-global self-attention interaction network for RGB-D cross-modal person Re-ID. Moreover, it exploits two branches to extract local and global information. Besides, it can reduce the tremendous discrepancy between these two modalities, which is beneficial in promoting recognition accuracy.

3 Method

Figure 2 provides an overview of our proposed A Local-Global Self-attention Interaction Network (LGSIN) method. This network inputs images of two modes, including RGB images and depth images, which have already been processed by using the method in work [13]. The LGSIN mainly consists of three parts, containing the base branch, the residual swin transformer branch, and the loss function. The remaining contents in this section are organized as follows: The base branch is introduced in Sect. 3.1. The residual swin transformer branch is explained in Sect. 3.2. Finally, we introduce the loss functions of the whole network in Sect. 3.3.

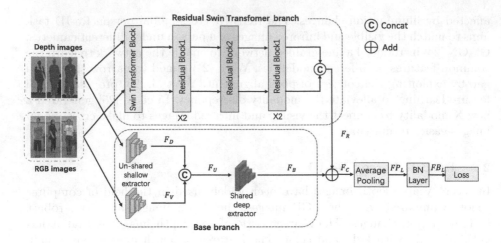

Fig. 2. The proposed A Local-Global Self-attention Interaction Network (LGSIN) learning framework for RGB-D Re-ID. It inputs RGB images and depth images of two modes. This network consists of two branches: the base branch and the residual swin transformer branch.

3.1 Base Branch

RGB images and depth images are fed into the base branch of the network. This branch exploits the un-shared shallow extractor to extract the modal-specific features from the input images. The un-shared shallow extractor is composed of the front part of ResNet [14], including its initial convolution layer and max pool layer. This part is not shared when extracting two modal features.

Then, the feature maps extracted from the un-shared shallow extractor will be sent to the shared deep extractor to extract deeper representations. This element is used to obtain the common features of these two modal images, which is beneficial to narrow the gap between input images. This part is shared when extracting two modal features. The shared deep extractor is composed of the latter of ResNet [14], including Stage 1, Stage 2, Stage 3, and Stage 4. The output features of the shared deep extractor are denoted as F_B.

These deep features F_B extracted from ResNet and global features F_R extracted from the residual swin transformer branch are fed into the average pool layer to conduct one-level down-sampling of the overall feature information, contributing to reducing parameter dimension. The feature maps treated from the average pooling layer are denoted as FP_L, and we send the feature FP_L into Triplet loss [15] and Hetero-Center (HC) loss [16]. Then, the feature is input into the batch normalization (BN) layer to capture the feature FB_L, which is subsequently fed into the Softmax loss function [17] for the learning supervision of the network. These losses are introduced in Sect. 3.3.

3.2 Residual Swin Transformer Branch

In this part, just like the base branch, RGB images and depth images are input into the local-global self-attention branch of the network. Considering that Convolutional Neural Network (CNN) extracts local deep features and ignores global features, this element is aiming to make up for the defect of the Convolutional Neural Network (CNN), and take global features into account to achieve excellent recognition results. This branch mainly consists of two parts, including the swin transformer unit and residual block unit. The swin transformer unit is a mechanism combining local and global self-attention, and the residual block unit saves the shallow features extracted from the swin transformer unit. These will be introduced as follows.

Swin Transformer Unit. For the setting of the swin transformer unit, referring to the structure of the swin transformer [18], which is an improvement on the original Transformer layer [19], the main differences are the calculation method of multi-head self-attention and the shifted window mechanism. We split the network, and only apply the patch partition and stage 1 of it, as shown in Fig. 3.

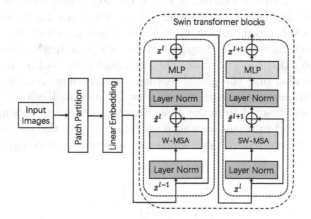

Fig. 3. An overview of the swin transformer unit. It is composed of three parts, including patch partition, linear embedding and swin transformer block. MLP in the figure refers to the multi-layer perceptron.

For one thing, RGB images and depth images are sent into the patch partition module to do blocking processing, and the feature map is flatted on the channel dimension. Subsequently, to adjust the dimension of the input feature matrix, the feature map processed by patch partition input into the linear embedding module. After the above processing, Swin Transformer Block is used to do post-processing, which mainly contains two parts, including Windows Multi-Head

Self-Attention (W-MSA) and Shifted Windows Multi-Head Self-Attention (SW-MSA). W-MSA is an improvement made based on the original Transformer layer [24]. Firstly, this module reshapes an input of size $H \times W \times C$ to $\frac{HW}{M^2} \times M^2 \times C$ feature by partitioning the input into non-overlapping $M \times M$ local windows, and then self-attention is performed separately within each window. For each window feature $X \in \mathbb{R}^{M^2 \times C}$, computing the self-attention feature [19] as:

$$Q = XW^Q, K = XW^K, V = XW^V \tag{1}$$

$$\text{Attention}(Q, K, V) = \text{Softmax}(QK^T/\sqrt{d} + B)V \tag{2}$$

where W^Q, W^K, W^V are trainable weight matrices with different windows and B is the learnable relative positional encoding. Since W-MSA only calculates the self-attention within each window, it is impossible to transfer information between windows. Based on this, further improvements are made and Shifted Windows Multi-Head Self-Attention (SW-MSA) is proposed. SW-MSA is a global attention mechanism. Unlike W-MSA, SW-MSA plays a role in enhancing the receptive field, which solves the problem of information exchange between different windows.

Residual Block Unit. As shown in Fig. 4, the top is Residual Block1 and the lower is the Residual Block2. For designing the residual block unit, we refer to the structure of ResNet and modify it on its basis. When we set up this module, we retain the characteristics of the deep feature extraction of ResNet and make some improvements on this basis to make the extracted deep feature more obvious. In addition, we also take the global features into account, aiming to make up for the shortcomings of ignoring the shallow features in ResNet. We save the shallow features extracted from the swin transformer unit in this module, such as some background information and scene information, the account of this is also part of the image recognition, which can achieve better recognition results.

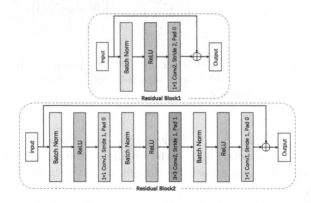

Fig. 4. An overview of the residual block unit.

3.3   Loss Function

Losses in the network consist of three parts, including $\mathcal{L}_{HC}$, $\mathcal{L}_{tri}$ and $\mathcal{L}_{id}$. In this branch, the initial purpose is to hope that the features from the shared deep extractor can be as similar as possible and reduce the tremendous discrepancy between the two modalities. To achieve this, we introduced Hetero-Center loss (HC), and it first split the feature F_C into two parts, including RGB image features and depth image features. We divide each feature map into six parts in the second dimension to save computing costs, and then feed them to the Hetero-Center (HC) loss $\mathcal{L}_{HC}$ to constrain the distance between RGB and depth images. $\mathcal{L}_{HC}$ is utilized to close the center distance between two modals instead of the distance of two modals to improve the intra-class cross-modality similarity. The $\mathcal{L}_{HC}$ is obtained with Eq. 3.

$$\mathcal{L}_{HC} = \sum_{i=1}^{T} \left[\|c_{i,1} - c_{i,2}\|_2^2 \right] \tag{3}$$

where $c_{i,1} = \frac{1}{M} \sum_{j=1}^{M} x_{i,1,j}$, $c_{i,2} = \frac{1}{N} \sum_{j=1}^{N} x_{i,2,j}$ are the centers of feature distribution of RGB modality and depth modality in the ith class. T is the total number of classes, M and N are the numbers of RGB images and depth images in the ith class. $x_{i,1,j}$ denotes the jth RGB image and $x_{i,2,j}$ denotes depth image in the ith class.

Subsequently, the feature FP_L is fed into the cross-modal Triplet loss, which is recorded as $\mathcal{L}_{tri}$, its input is a triplet set $<a, p, n>$, where the 'a' is the anchor given in one image modal, the 'p' is the positive sample of the same modal as 'a' and 'n' is the negative sample from the other image modality. The $\mathcal{L}_{tri}$ is computed as follows:

$$\mathcal{L}_{tri} = \max(d(a,p) - d(a,n) + \beta, 0) \tag{4}$$

where β is the margin of the Triplet loss, $d(a,p)$ is the feature distance between cross-modal positive pairs and $d(a,n)$ is the feature distance between cross-modal negative pairs. The final optimization objective is to shorten the distance between a and p and enlarge the distance between a and n. This loss optimizes the triple-wise relations between different human images across two modes.

After that, the feature FB_L is input into the Softmax function to compute a cross-entropy between the class probabilities and ground-truth identities, which is recorded as $\mathcal{L}_{id}$ and expressed in terms of Eq. 5.

$$\mathcal{L}_{id} = -\sum_{i=1}^{T} y_i' \log(y_i) \tag{5}$$

where the T is the total number of classes, the y_i is the forecasting result and the y_i' is the ground truth. Therefore, minimizing this loss is equivalent to maximizing the possibility of being assigned to the ground-truth category.

In summary, the loss function of whole networks L_{total} is gained by the following formula:

$$\mathcal{L}_{total} = \mathcal{L}_{tri} + \mathcal{L}_{id} + \lambda\mathcal{L}_{HC} \qquad (6)$$

where λ is a hyperparameter to balance corresponding terms, which is regarded as the weight of HC loss in the overall loss. The $\mathcal{L}_{tri}$ and $\mathcal{L}_{id}$ are basic losses, the purpose of adding λ is to balance the weight of different losses.

4   Experiments

4.1   Datasets and Evaluation Protocol

BIWI RGBD-ID Dataset [27]: This dataset captures the long-term depth and RGB video sequences in pairs with a Microsoft Kinect camera. The same people with distinct clothes is regarded as a separate individual. Specifically, it contains 78 instances with 22,038 images in RGB and depth modals. For the fair evaluation on the BIWI dataset, we randomly select 32 instances for training, 8 individuals for validation, and 38 persons for testing.

RobotPKU Dataset [26]: The RobotPKU dataset is captured via a Microsoft Kinect camera. It is composed of 90 pedestrians with 16,512 images in RGB and depth modes. There is a slight time delay between the depth and RGB images. Some images only contain local parts of persons of the RobotPKU dataset compared to the BIWI dataset. Those images pose a greater challenge to the cross-modal person Re-ID task. We randomly divide the RobotPKU dataset into 40 persons for training, 10 people for validation, and the remaining 40 individuals for testing.

Evaluation Protocol: For the cross-modal Re-ID task, there are two testing modes, including RGB-D and D-RGB. In RGB-D testing mode, the query is given in the RGB image modal while the gallery is provided in the depth modal. The other D-RGB testing mode is just the opposite, that is, the query is given in the depth modal while the gallery is provided in the RGB modal. For both of the testing modes, the Mean Average Precision (mAP) is applied for the performance evaluation. We measure the result with Rank-1, Rank-5, Rank-10 of Cumulative Matching Characteristics (CMC) and the mean Average Precision (mAP) to verify the performance of the network on cross-modal Re-ID tasks in this paper.

4.2   Implementation Details

We resize the input images to 288×144 uniformly. In the residual swin transformer branch, the M is set to 7. The β of the loss $\mathcal{L}_{tri}$ equals to 0.3, and the λ of the loss $\mathcal{L}_{total}$ is 0.1. The network is trained with 32 image pairs per batch for 80 epochs. A stochastic gradient descent optimizer is adopted to train the network. We apply a warm-up learning strategy to set the learning rate. Specifically, in the first 10 epochs, the learning rate increases linearly from 0 to 0.1. In the 10th and 20th epochs, it equals to 0.1. After that, the learning rate is set to 0.01 from the 20th to the 50th epochs. At last, it is set to 0.001 in the latter epochs. The ResNet network is pre-trained on the ImageNet [28]. The whole network is trained on a single Nvidia GTX 1080 Ti. The residual swin transformer branch and the loss function are only applied during the training phase.

4.3   State-of-the-Art Comparison

Results on RobotPKU Dataset: We first present a comparison between our LGSIN and the current state-of-arts on the RobotPKU dataset. The results of two testing modes are shown in Table 1. The methods for comparison include LOMO+Euclidean [29], LOMO+XQDA [29], WHOS+Euclidean [30], WHOS+XQDA [30], cross-modal distillation network [12] and HRN [13].

As shown in Table 1, in the RGB-D testing mode, our approach achieves the Rank-1 matching rate of 34.2% and mAP 24.0%, which exceeds all previous methods. It shows a significant improvement over the second-best HRN, with an 11.1% increase in Rank-1 accuracy and an 6.7% increase in mAP. As some images in the RobotPKU dataset only contain local parts of persons, the cross-modal person Re-ID on this dataset is more challenging compared to BIWI dataset. However, our method still exceeds the existing methods on this dataset, which demonstrates the effectiveness of our approach to hard sample.

The results of the D-RGB testing case are also listed in Table 1. Our method achieves 28.5% Rank-1 matching rate and 26.4% mAP, which far outperforms to all compared methods. The performances of our method are preferable in both RGB-D and D-RGB testing cases, which show that our proposed LGSIN owns significant generalization for different sample styles.

Table 1. Comparisons with the state-of-the-art on RobotPKU dataset. The RGB-D testing mode is adopted in the comparisons.

Testing mode	RGB-D		D-RGB	
Method	Rank-1	mAP	Rank-1	mAP
LOMO+Euclidean [29]	3.6	3.9	3.7	4.9
LOMO+XQDA [29]	12.9	10.1	12.3	12.3
WHOS+Euclidean [30]	3.6	3.9	3.5	5.4
WHOS+XQDA [30]	10.0	8.2	9.8	9.8
Cross-modal distillation network [12]	17.5 ± 2.2	17.1 ± 1.9	19.5 ± 2.0	19.8 ± 2.1
HRN [13]	23.1	17.3	25.7	23.5
Ours	**34.2**	**24.0**	**28.5**	**26.4**

Results on BIWI Dataset: The comparison results on BIWI dataset are shown in Table 2 and Table 3. Our method is superior to the methods for comparison, including traditional methods LOMO+Euclidean [29], LOMO+XQDA [29], Corr.Dict. [3], LSSCDL [3] and ICMDL [2], deep learning method cross-modal distillation network [12] and HRN [13].

As displayed in Table 2, for the RGB-D testing case, our method achieves the Rank-1 matching rate of 51.4%, which outperforms all compared methods. Compared to the best HRN, the Rank-1 matching rate of our method is higher than this method by 7.5%. Moreover, the mAP metric of our method is also superior to the existing methods. It can achieve 33.6% mAP, which is better than the HRN by 2.7%.

As shown in Table 2, in the D-RGB testing mode, our method achieves performances with Rank-1 matching rate of 47.8% and mAP 40.8%. It can be found from the table that the Rank-1 of our method is higher than HRN, but the mAP is lower than it. It may be because that the dataset is too small and there are fewer pedestrian images in some perspectives, resulting in unretrievable, so the mAP is lower. Our method is less robust to the change of pedestrian perspective, which is the future direction of this paper.

Table 2. Comparisons with the state-of-the-art on BIWI dataset. The RGB-D testing mode is adopted in the comparisons.

Testing mode	RGB-D		D-RGB	
Method	Rank-1	mAP	Rank-1	mAP
LOMO+Euclidean [29]	3.2	3.7	5.1	5.6
LOMO+XQDA [29]	13.7	12.9	16.3	15.9
Corr.Dict. [3]	12.1	-	11.3	-
LSSCDL [3]	9.5	-	7.4	-
ICMDL [2]	-	-	7.1	17.5
Cross-modal distillation network [12]	26.9 ± 1.8	27.3 ± 1.7	29.2 ± 2.3	30.5 ± 2.0
HRN [13]	43.9	30.9	47.1	**44.6**
Ours	**51.4**	**33.6**	**47.8**	40.8

4.4   Ablation Study

To demonstrate the effectiveness of the LGSIN, we show an ablation analysis on the residual swin transformer branch and loss function. The results are shown in Table 3.

Table 3. Comparisons with the state-of-the-art on RobotPKU dataset. The RGB-D testing mode is adopted in the comparisons. 'w/o' denotes 'without'.

Method	Rank-1	Rank-5	Rank-10	mAP
w/o Hetero-Center loss	31.6	71.7	89.4	19.7
w/o Residual Swin Transformer branch	32.1	72.7	86.9	21.6
w/o Residual Block unit	28.5	66.4	83.3	15.9
Ours	**34.2**	**76.3**	**90.9**	**24.0**

The Effectiveness of the Hetero-Center Loss: We can observe from Table 3 that the method removing the Hetero-Center (HC) loss deteriorates the performance of Rank-1 and mAP compared to our method with these two parts. The Hetero-Center (HC) loss is utilized to close the center distance between two modals to solve the tremendous discrepancy between RGB images and depth images. The results in Table 3 indicate that this element is material for the RGB-D cross-modal person Re-ID task.

The Effectiveness of the Residual Swin Transformer Branch: We remove the residual swin transformer branch from the proposed LGSIN to analyze the contribution to the cross-modal person Re-ID task, as shown in Table 3. We observe that the method without residual swin transformer branch has less performance than our method with this branch. Besides, we do some experiments on removing the residual block unit and find the accuracy of cross-modal identification decreases. The residual swin transformer branch is applied to save the global features of input images, such as some background information and scene information, and enriches these extracted features. This component contributes to boosting performance of the network, which is certificated in the experiments. It indicates that this branch is also essential for the RGB-D cross-modal person Re-ID task.

Features Visualization: As shown in Fig. 5, we can observe from it that our proposed method extracts the common pedestrian contour features of two modes. RGB images contain rich color and texture information, while depth images include scene depth information. Our approach uses depth image as the assistant of RGB image to extract pedestrian pose features effectively. Besides, person and background information are distinguished, which is beneficial to person Re-ID task.

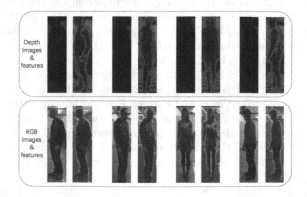

Fig. 5. The feature visualizations of both depth and RGB images. In one image pair, the left image shows the input image and the right one displays its feature visualization.

5 Conclusion

In this paper, in order to solve the problem of identification between different modals, we put forward a local-global self-attention interaction network for the RGB-D cross-modal person re-identification task. On the one hand, it proposes a novel loss function mechanism to constrain the center distance between the two modalities and improve the similarity of intra-class cross-modal features. On the other hand, this paper introduces a residual swin transformer branch to capture the local and global features to enrich the extracted features. Our experiments on public datasets can strongly demonstrate that our approach has superior performances than the state-of-the-art. And we have proved the effectiveness of each component in this method through experiments.

Acknowledgements. This work was supported by Hefei Municipal Natural Science Foundation under Grant No. 2021050. This work was also supported by The National Natural Science Foundation of China under Grant No. 62172137.

References

1. Gong, S., Cristani, M., Loy, C.C., Hospedales, T.M.: The re-identification challenge. In: Gong, S., Cristani, M., Yan, S., Loy, C.C. (eds.) Person Re-Identification. ACVPR, pp. 1–20. Springer, London (2014). https://doi.org/10.1007/978-1-4471-6296-4_1
2. Zhang, P., Xu, J., Wu, Q., Huang, Y., Zhang, J.: Top-push constrained modality-adaptive dictionary learning for cross-modality person re-identification. IEEE Trans. Circuits Syst. Video Technol. **30**(12), 4554–4566 (2019)
3. Zhuo, J., Zhu, J., Lai, J., Xie, X.: Person re-identification on heterogeneous camera network. In: Yang, J., et al. (eds.) CCCV 2017. CCIS, vol. 773, pp. 280–291. Springer, Singapore (2017). https://doi.org/10.1007/978-981-10-7305-2_25
4. Liao, S., Hu, Y., Zhu, X., Li, S.Z.: Person re-identification by local maximal occurrence representation and metric learning. In: Proceedings of the IEEE Conference on Computer Vision and Pattern Recognition, pp. 2197–2206 (2015)
5. Zheng, L., Shen, L., Tian, L., Wang, S., Wang, J., Tian, Q.: Scalable person re-identification: a benchmark. In: Proceedings of the IEEE International Conference on Computer Vision, pp. 1116–1124 (2015)
6. Lv, J., Chen, W., Li, Q., et al.: Unsupervised cross-dataset person re-identification by transfer learning of spatial-temporal patterns. In: Proceedings of the IEEE Conference on Computer Vision and Pattern Recognition, pp. 7948–7956 (2018)
7. Wu, D., Zheng, S.J., Zhang, X.P., et al.: Deep learning-based methods for person re-identification: a comprehensive review. Neurocomputing **337**, 354–371 (2019)
8. Wu, L., Wang, Y., Gao, J.B., et al.: Where-and-when to look: deep Siamese attention networks for video-based person re-identification. IEEE Trans. Multimedia **21**(6), 1412–1424 (2019)
9. Ye, M., Lan, X.Y., Li, J.W., et al.: Hierarchical discriminative learning for visible thermal person re-identification. In: Proceedings of the AAAI Conference on Artificial Intelligence, vol. 32, no. 1, pp. 7501–7508 (2018)
10. Mogelmose, A., Bahnsen, C., Moeslund, T., Clapés, A., Escalera, S.: Tri-modal person re-identification with RGB, depth and thermal features. In: Proceedings of the IEEE Conference on Computer Vision and Pattern Recognition Workshops, pp. 301–307 (2013)

11. Pala, F., Satta, R., Fumera, G., Roli, F.: Multimodal person reidentification using RGB-D cameras. IEEE Trans. Circuits Syst. Video Technol. **26**(4), 788–799 (2015)
12. Hafner, F.M., Bhuiyan, A., Kooij, J.F., Granger, E.: RGB-depth cross-modal person re-identification. In: 2019 16th IEEE International Conference on Advanced Video and Signal Based Surveillance (AVSS), pp. 1–8. IEEE (2019)
13. Wu, J., Jiang, J., Qi, M., et al.: An end-to-end heterogeneous restraint network for RGB-D cross-modal person re-identification. ACM Trans. Multimedia Comput. Commun. Appl. **18**(4), 1–22 (2022)
14. He, K., Zhang, X., Ren, S., et al.: Deep residual learning for image recognition. In: Proceedings of the IEEE Conference on Computer Vision and Pattern Recognition, pp. 770–778 (2016)
15. Hermans, A., Beyer, L., Leibe, B.: In defense of the triplet loss for person re-identification. arXiv preprint arXiv:1703.07737 (2017)
16. Zhu, Y., Yang, Z., Wang, L., et al.: Hetero-center loss for cross-modality person re-identification. Neurocomputing **386**(2020), 97–109 (2020)
17. Liu, W., Wen, Y., Yu, Z., et al.: Large-margin softmax loss for convolutional neural networks. In: ICML, vol. 2, no. 3, p. 7 (2016)
18. Liu, Z., Lin, Y., Cao, Y., et al.: Swin transformer: hierarchical vision transformer using shifted windows. In: Proceedings of the IEEE/CVF International Conference on Computer Vision, pp. 10012–10022 (2021)
19. Vaswani, A., Shazeer, N., Parmar, N., et al.: Attention is all you need. In: Advances in Neural Information Processing Systems, vol. 30 (2017)
20. Sun, Y., Xu, Q., Li, Y., et al.: Perceive where to focus: learning visibility-aware part-level features for partial person re-identification. In: Proceedings of the IEEE/CVF Conference on Computer Vision and Pattern Recognition, pp. 393–402 (2019)
21. Ye, M., Shen, J., Shao, L.: Visible-infrared person re-identification via homogeneous augmented tri-modal learning. IEEE Trans. Inf. Forensics Secur. **16**, 728–739 (2020)
22. Wang, G., Yang, S., Liu, H., et al.: High-order information matters: learning relation and topology for occluded person re-identification. In: Proceedings of the IEEE/CVF Conference on Computer Vision and Pattern Recognition, pp. 6449–6458 (2020)
23. Ye, M., Shen, J., Crandall, D.J., Shao, L., Luo, J.: Dynamic dual-attentive aggregation learning for visible-infrared person re-identification. In: Vedaldi, A., Bischof, H., Brox, T., Frahm, J.-M. (eds.) ECCV 2020. LNCS, vol. 12362, pp. 229–247. Springer, Cham (2020). https://doi.org/10.1007/978-3-030-58520-4_14
24. Jiang, J., Jin, K., Qi, M., et al.: A cross-modal multi-granularity attention network for RGB-IR person re-identification. Neurocomputing **406**, 59–67 (2020)
25. Li, D., Wei, X., Hong, X., et al.: Infrared-visible cross-modal person re-identification with an x modality. In: Proceedings of the AAAI Conference on Artificial Intelligence, vol. 34, no. 4, pp. 4610–4617 (2020)
26. Liu, H., Hu, L., Ma, L.: Online RGB-D person re-identification based on metric model update. CAAI Trans. Intell. Technol. **2**(1), 48–55 (2017)
27. Munaro, M., Fossati, A., Basso, A., Menegatti, E., Van Gool, L.: One-shot person re-identification with a consumer depth camera. In: Gong, S., Cristani, M., Yan, S., Loy, C.C. (eds.) Person Re-Identification. ACVPR, pp. 161–181. Springer, London (2014). https://doi.org/10.1007/978-1-4471-6296-4_8
28. Deng, J., Dong, W., Socher, R.: Imagenet: a large-scale hierarchical image database. In: IEEE Conference on Computer Vision and Pattern Recognition, pp. 248–255. IEEE (2009)

29. Liao, S., Hu, Y., Zhu, X., et al.: Person re-identification by local maximal occurrence representation and metric learning. In: Proceedings of the IEEE Conference on Computer Vision and Pattern Recognition, pp. 2197–2206 (2015)
30. Lisanti, G., Masi, I., Bagdanov, A.D., et al.: Person re-identification by iterative re-weighted sparse ranking. IEEE Trans. Pattern Anal. Mach. Intell. **37**(8), 1629–1642 (2014)

A RAW Burst Super-Resolution Method with Enhanced Denoising

Qian Zheng[1], Ruipeng Gang[2(✉)], Yuntian Cao[1], Chenghua Li[3], Ji Fang[2], Chenming Liu[2], and Yizhen Cao[1]

[1] Communication University of China, Beijing 100024, China
[2] Academy of Broadcasting Science, NRTA, Beijing 100866, China
gangruipeng@abs.ac.cn
[3] Institute of Automation, Chinese Academy of Science, Beijing 100190, China

Abstract. Deep learning-based burst super-resolution (SR) approaches are extensively studied in recent years, prevailing in the synthetic datasets and the real datasets. However, the existing networks rarely pay attention to the enhanced denoising problem in raw domain and they are not sufficient to restore complex texture relationships between frames. In this paper, we propose a new framework named A RAW Burst Super-Resolution Method with Enhanced Denoising (EDRBSR), which solves the BurstSR problem by jointly denoising structure and reconstruction enhancement structure. We adopt a Denoising Network to further improve the performance of noise-free SR images. Also, we propose a Reconstruction Network to enhance spatial feature representation and eliminate the influence of spatial noise. In addition, we introduce a new pipeline to compensate for lost information. Experimental results demonstrate that our method over the existing state-of-the-art in both synthetic datasets and real datasets. Furthermore, our approach takes the 5th place in synthetic track of the NTIRE 2022 Burst Super-Resolution Challenge.

Keywords: Burst super-resolution · Denoise · Reconstruction

1 Introduction

As a fundamental problem in Computer Vision field, the Super-Resolution (SR) task aims to generate a higher resolution output from a single or multiple low-resolution (LR) images by adding missing high-frequency details. In recent years, the Multi-Frame Super-Resolution (MFSR) problem achieves impressive SR performance. Since the burst images contain sub-pixel shifts due to handholding camera, MFSR can be leveraged to improve the burst image resolution. Instead of taking a single picture, burst mode captures multiple photos of a scene in quick succession. Additionally, if burst images are captured with different exposure settings, they can be combined to perform HDR imaging. Nonetheless,

---

Q. Zheng and R. Gang—Equal contribution.

S. Yu et al. (Eds.): PRCV 2022, LNCS 13537, pp. 103–116, 2022.
https://doi.org/10.1007/978-3-031-18916-6_9

the Burst Super-Resolution (BurstSR) problem received limited attention. As demonstrated in [8,14,15], RAW bursts are usually noisy and misaligned. The noise in raw domain contains the shot noise modeled by Poisson noise and read noise modeled by Gaussian noise. To recovering highquality images better, we need a more efficient architecture to address these challenges.

The NTIRE 2022 Challenge on Burst Super-Resolution aims to propose more effective solutions to solve the BurstSR problem. The challenge consists of two tracks. In both tracks, the methods provide a burst sequence of 14 images, where each image contains the RAW sensor data from a bayer filter (RGGB) mosaic. The task is to perform joint denoising, demosaicking and super-resolution to generate a clean RGB image with 4 times higher resolution. Track 1 evaluates on synthetically generated data to improve its fidelity score. The input bursts are generated from RGB images using a synthetic data generation pipeline:

$$b_i = B_i \left(P_{inverse} \left(x_{sRGB} \right) \right) \quad i = 1, \ldots, N \tag{1}$$

$$burst = F_{noise} \left(F_{mosaick} \left(b_1, \ldots, b_N \right)_{\downarrow s} \right) \tag{2}$$

where $P_{inverse}$ is an inverse camera pipeline. B_i donates random translations and rotations. $F_{mosaick}$ and F_{noise} are mosaick and noise operations. $\downarrow s$ means s times bilinear downsample. And Track 2 evaluates on real-world bursts from mobile camera to improve visual perception. This challenge promotes more research on BurstSR. Some existing BurstSR methods [4,5,22] can perform joint denoising, demosaicking and SR. These methods have the following steps: feature extraction, alignment, fusion and HR image reconstruction. However, they do not have a dedicated denoising enhanced module to efficiently aggregate noise-free information. Due to their poor reconstruction modules, they are not sufficient to restore complex texture relationships between frames.

To solve the above problems, we propose a framework called A RAW Burst Super-Resolution Method with Enhanced Denoising (EDRBSR), as shown in Fig. 1. Our network can enhance the effectiveness of denoising and reconstruction on both synthetic bursts task and real-world bursts task. The main components of EDRBSR are a Denoising Network, a Reconstruction Network and a Align and Fusion module. According to our study, noise-free information is crucial for the reconstruction of burst SR. So we use a Denoising Network to generate compensation for the denoising information lost by the network. Unlike previous works, our method emphasizes on channel feature fusion during reconstruction. We introduce a Reconstruction Network, which is a combined solution for channel attention and spatial attention. It can eliminate the influence of spatial noise. In addition, we introduce a new pipeline for lost information compensation operation to use the RAW and noise-free information from the network. For better fidelity score performance on synthetic bursts, we apply two training strategies, which are combined a loss function and a Test Time Augmentation (TTA) [25] data enhancement strategy. For a better subjective effect on real-world bursts, we adopt a perceptual loss and a post-processing strategy in order to enhance details and sharpen edges.

By the improvements mentioned above, our method can recover richer texture details and give people a better sensory experience than other methods. The main contributions are summarized as follows:

- We introduce a Denoising Network to enhance the effectiveness of extracting denoising feature and improve the performance of noise-free SR images. And we apply a lost information compensation operation to complement the RAW information lost and noise-free information lost by the network.
- Unlike previous works, our method pays more attention to channel feature fusion during reconstruction. We introduce a Reconstruction Network to enhance the channel feature representation and eliminate the influence of spatial noise.
- Extensive experiments show that our method achieves superior performance to prior art on both synthetic datasets and realworld datasets.

2   Related Work

Single Image Super-Resolution. Single Image Super-Resolution (SISR) is an important research topic with a variety of proposed methods, for example based on traditional sparse coding [10], the frequency domain [20], locally linear embedding [7] and interpolation techniques [11]. Deep SISR is first proposed by SRCNN which is an end-to-end network with fewer layers. In consequence, various improved methods are proposed. These methods not only focus on the improvement of the network structure [13], but also the optimization of the loss function [12,17], such as VGG loss and GAN loss.

Burst Super-Resolution. Unlike SISR methods, the BurstSR method aims to merge multiple burst images in a short period of time to reconstruct a higher resolution output. The first MFSR method is purposed by Tsai and Huang [27], which is a frequency domain-based method. In recent, deep learning-based methods are proposed to focus on multi-frame motion compensation, feature fusion and reconstruction. Wronski [30] utilizes a kernel regression technique for fusion. DeepSUM [23] assumed only translation motion between frames and utilizes 3D convolution for fusion and reconstruction. MAFFSRN [24] extracts features using multiple attention mechanisms, and fuses them using channel shuffle, aiming to minimize the computation cost and maximize the network performance. Also, a few recent works try to address this issue by learning real world degradation models. DBSR [5] introduces a new dataset BurstSR and proposes a network which can adaptively combine information. EBSR [22] proposes a cascaded residual structure which improves performance of features alignment.

Denoising Methods. Image denoising can help RAW BurstSR tasks generate more aesthetically pleasing results. Classic denoising approaches typically rely on the use of sparse image priors, such as nonlocal mean (NLM) and sparse coding. The recent proposed public raw image denoising benchmark dataset [1,2] assisted CNN-based methods [6,16] to achieve better results. But the cost of these methods is large, which increases the risk of network structure. PDRID [29] proposed a lightweight denoising network that uses separable-conv structure [9] in all encoder and decoder stages to reduce computational cost. Inspired by this work, we use a U-Net-like denoising network to process RAW images.

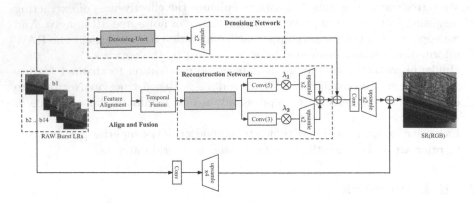

Fig. 1. An overview of the EDRBSR network. The network contains a denoising network, a reconstruction network, and a align and fusion.

3   Proposed Method

3.1   Overview

In this section, we describe the details of EDRBSR and the loss function. An overview of our architecture is shown in Fig. 1. Let $\{b_i\}_{i=1}^{N}$, $b_i \in R^{4 \times \frac{H}{2} \times \frac{W}{2}}$ be the input bursts which are 4-channels 'RGGB' RAW images and $I_{HR} \in R^{3 \times Hs \times Ws}$ be the ground truth HR image (RGB). Given the upscaling factor s, the overall burst super resolution problem can be formulated as

$$b_i = (T_i \circ I_{HR})_{\downarrow s} + \eta_i \quad for \ i = 1, ..., N \tag{3}$$

where T_i is a transformation representing the scene motion, i.e., translation and rotation. $\circ$ is the warping operator and $\downarrow$ denotes downsampling. η_i represents some additive noise. Note that, we denote the first frame as the reference frame and other frames as neighboring frames.

The goal of EDRBSR is to generate a noise-free HR RGB image from 14 LR RAW burst images. In the synthetic BurstSR task, the input LR bursts are generated from RGB images using a synthetic data generation pipeline, as we describe in Sect. 1. One challenge is that the synthetic inputs are corrupted by random noise that is difficult to eliminate. So we apply a Denoising Network which is calculated from the reference frame:

$$F_{denoise} = f_{denoise}\left(Conv\left(b_1\right)\right) \tag{4}$$

where $F_{denoise}$ donates the noise-free feature, and $f_{denoise}$ donates our Denoising Network. Another challenge is to align and fuse neighbor frames and reconstruct the spatial information. So we align other neighboring features to the reference features, using a Feature Alignment module. And a Temporal Fusion module is adopted for fusing align features. The Align and Fusion can be formulated as

$$F_{AF} = f_{fusion}\left(f_{align}\left(b_1, b_i\right)\right) \tag{5}$$

where f_{fusion} and f_{align} donate Feature Alignment module and Temporal Fusion module respectively. F_{AF} donates the output feature of the Align and Fusion. To pay more attention to channel feature expression, the fused features are reconstructed through the Reconstruction Network. In order to realize the operation of lost information compensation, we add denoising features and raw features to the corresponding ×2 and ×4 reconstructed high-resolution features. The operation can be formulated as

$$I_{SR} = Up_{\times 2}\left(f_{rec}\left(F_{AF}\right) + F_{denoise}\right) + Up_{\times 4}\left(Conv\left(b_1\right)\right) \tag{6}$$

where Up donates Pixelshuffle operation. f_{rec} donates the Reconstruction Network. I_{SR} donates the output super resolution image. So far, the EDRBSR network can output a denoised 4x super-resolution image. The details are described in Sect. 3.2. Section 3.3 introduces two loss functions.

3.2 Network Structure

Denoising Network

To extract noise-free features and reconstruct high-quality images, we consider the burst SR denoising operation in the RAW domain. As shown in Fig. 1, the Denoising Network adds a reference-frame based lightweight Denoising-Unet module, and supervised training with synthesized raw noisy-clean image pairs. The Denoising-Unet module is inspired by PDRID [29], which uses separable-conv structure [9] in all encoder and decoder stages to reduce computational cost. However, PDRID is inefficient in RAW SR tasks since it does not consider HR images outputs. Therefore, we involve a PDRID module with a 2x up-sampling module to simultaneously achieve the function of removing noise and acquiring reconstructed HR images:

$$F_{denoise} = Up_{\times 2}\left(f_{Unet}\left(b_1\right)\right) \tag{7}$$

where f_{Unet} donates the Denoising-Unet module. $Up_{\times 2}$ donates 2x up-sampling module. After processing, we can obtain denoised clean features to supplement the network with more noise-free information. The effectiveness of the module is proved on Sect. 4.2.

Align and Fusion

In order to achieve an effective fusion of multiple frames, the information needs to be aligned. We address this problem by aligning other neighboring features to the reference feature, using a Feature Alignment module inspired by FEPCD [22]. Combining the efficacy of FEPCD and the Denoising Network, the noise of

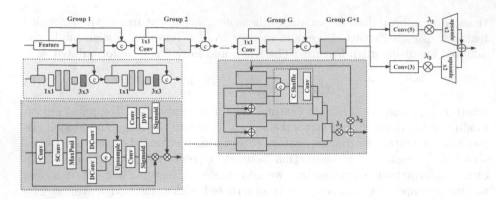

Fig. 2. An overview of the Reconstruction Network. 'C Shuffle' refers to channel shuffle. 'SConv' means strided convolution. 'DConv' means dilated convolution and 'DW' means depth-wise convolution. The content in the corresponding dotted box shows the detailed structure of the corresponding color module.

the outputs can be well eliminated. To fuse the aligned feature maps, we use the Temporal Fusion module introduced in [22] to generate fused features and measure the similarity between every two pixels in multi-frame features.

Reconstruction Network

Unlike previous works, our method pays more attention to channel feature fusion during reconstruction. The initial part of Reconstruction Network is composed of G groups simple residual blocks and $G + 1th$ group channel feature fusion block, as shown in Fig. 2. In order to enhance spatial feature representation and eliminate the influence of spatial noise, we add two special structures in this module. By taking the inspiration from ShuffleNet [32], we introduce a channel shuffle to mix the information between concatenated channels in the $G + 1th$ group. [21] proposed a combined solution for channel attention and spatial attention. We modify it by introducing dilated convolutions with different filter sizes to increase spatial filter sizes. The process can be formulated as

$$x_{rec} = f^{G+1} \left(f^G \left(\ldots f^1 \left(x_{fuse} \right) \right) \right) \tag{8}$$

where f^{G+1} denotes the nth group step. x_{fuse} is the output of the Temporal Fusion module. x_{rec} is the output of the $G + 1$ groups residual blocks.

At the end of the reconstruction Network, we apply an adaptive residual learning approach to output features, which includes convolutional layers with different filter sizes to extract multi-scale features. We assign two trainable weights λ to distinguish feature importance. The process can be formulated as

$$x_{rn} = f_{up} \left(\lambda_1 f_5 \left(x_{rec} \right) \right) + f_{up} \left(\lambda_2 f_3 \left(x_{rec} \right) \right) \tag{9}$$

where f_{up} denotes the pixel-shuffle layer, and f_3 and f_5 are convolution kernel sizes of 3 and 5 respectively. x_{rn} represents the output of the Reconstruction Network. The effectiveness of this network is proved on Sect. 4.2.

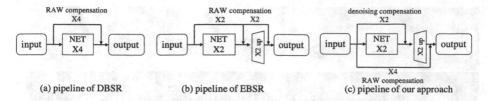

Fig. 3. Illustration of the lost information compensation operation and comparison with other pipelines.

Lost Information Compensation Operation

As shown in Fig. 3, we introduce a new pipeline for lost information compensation operation. In previous works, [5] was upscaled ×4 with bilinear interpolation directly to compensate for the loss of network information. [22] added two consecutive pixelshuffle (×2) layers, which may lead to loss of RAW information during superposition computation. Taking above works into consideration, we use a pixelshuffle (×4) RAW layer and a pixelshuffle (×2) denoising layer to compensate for the RAW information lost and noise-free information lost by the network. So far, the EDRBSR network can output a SR RGB image with 4x up-scaling factor.

3.3 Loss Function

For better PSNR metric performance on synthetic bursts, our network is trained with a combined loss, which is composed by reconstruction loss L_{rec} and denoising loss L_{den}. The L_{rec} can help us to achieve powerful Super-Resolution. The L_{den} is designed to remove image noise. We find that such combined loss is more suitable for this task than a single loss. Our loss function is formulated as

$$L = L_{rec} + \lambda L_{den},$$
$$L_{rec} = \left\| R\left(\sum_{i=1}^{n} I_i\right) - O_{HR} \right\|_1, \tag{10}$$
$$L_{den} = \|S(I_1) - O_{DHR}\|_1$$

where R is EDRBSR model. S is Denoising-Unet module. I_1 is the reference frame. n is the number of input burst frames, i.e. 14. O_{HR} is HR ground truth in the sRGB domain. O_{DHR} is the noise free ground truth, as described in Sect. 4.1.

For a better subjective effect on real bursts, the network is trained by both reconstruction loss L_{rec} and perceptual loss L_{per}. We define the two loss functions that measure high-level perceptual and semantic differences between images. The perceptual loss makes the use of a pretrained loss network ϕ [26]. The loss function is formulated as

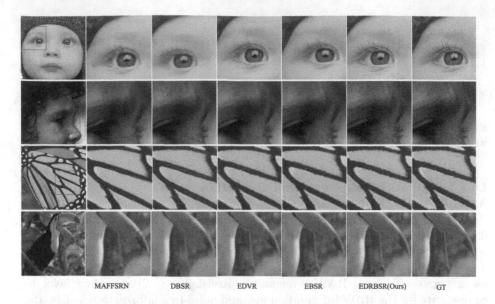

MAFFSRN   DBSR   EDVR   EBSR   EDRBSR(Ours)   GT

Fig. 4. Qualitative results of a comparison between our method and other existing methods on the synthetic dataset.

$$L = L_{rec} + \lambda L_{per},$$

$$L_{per} = \frac{1}{C_j H_j W_j} \left\| \phi_j \left(O_{HR} \right) - \phi_j \left(R \left(\sum_{i=1}^{n} I_i \right) \right) \right\|_2^2,$$

$$L_{rec} = \left\| R \left(\sum_{i=1}^{n} I_i \right) - O_{HR} \right\|_1 \tag{11}$$

where $\phi_j(x)$ is the activations of the jth layer when processing x. $C_j \times H_j \times W_j$ is the shape of feature map. I is the input RAW LR frames.

4   Experiment

4.1   Dataset and Implementation Details

Training Datasets. Our method is trained on two datasets provided by the NTIRE 2022 Burst Super-Resolution Challenge. The synthetic track employ the synthetic RAW burst dataset (Zurich RAW to RGB dataset [19]). The dataset provide 4X SR images as ground truth for training the whole network. As described in Sect. 1, before noise added to bursts, we choose the noise-free RAW images as ground truth for training the Denoising-Unet module:

$$burst_{denoise} = F_{mosaick} \left(b_1, \ldots, b_N \right)_{\downarrow s} \tag{12}$$

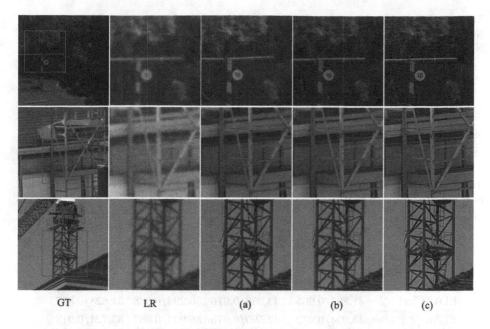

GT   LR   (a)   (b)   (c)

Fig. 5. Ablation studies of our loss function and post-processing strategy on the real-world BurstSR dataset. (a) The network is trained without the perceptual loss. (b) Not use post-processing strategy to generate the results. (c) Ours network.

Where $burst_{denoise}$ donates the noise-free RAW images. The real track employs the real-world BurstSR dataset [5]. For each burst, a high-resolution RGB image captured using a DSLR is provided. We use a pre-processed version of the dataset containing 160×160 crops to fine-tune the pretrained model from the synthetic track.

Training Settings. We use Adam optimizer and set exponential decay rates as 0.9 and 0.999. On the synthetic track, the initial learning rate is set to 2×10^{-4} and then reduced to half in 100 epochs and 150 epoch. We train 400 epoch in total. The model of the real track is fine-tuned from the synthetic track pretrained model using the BurstSR training dataset. The learning rate is set to 5×10^{-5}. We use PyTorch framework with 4 NVIDIA 2080Ti GPUs.

Testing Description. For better PSNR metric performance on synthetic bursts, we use Test Time Augmentation (TTA) data enhancement strategy during testing time. The transposed burst image and the original burst image are passed through the network respectively. The output is the average of two outputs. We find that using original burst and transposed burst are better than both original with transposed burst and shuffled burst. In other words, shuffled burst has negative effects in this task. For a better subjective effect on real-world bursts, we use a post-processing strategy to process the output RGB images. We choose an edge-enhanced 2D filter to join the network in order to enhance details and sharpen edges.

Table 1. The table shows the effectiveness of Denoising Network and Reconstruction Network. NoReconstruct means EDRBSR without the Reconstruction Network, and Nodenoise means EDRBSR without the Denoising Network.

	RAW2rgb [19] PSNR/SSIM	Set5 [3] PSNR/SSIM	Set14 [31] PSNR/SSIM	Urban100 [18] PSNR/SSIM
NoReconstruct	42.478/0.968	43.432/0.976	37.281/0.940	33.098/0.900
Nodenoise	42.840/0.969	43.304/0.976	37.176/0.941	33.451/0.906
EDRBSR	43.261/0.973	44.481/0.977	38.424/0.949	34.148/0.915

Table 2. The table shows a comparison between our model and other SR models. The best one is marked in red.

	RAW2rgb [19] PSNR/SSIM	Set5 [3] PSNR/SSIM	Set14 [31] PSNR/SSIM	Urban100 [18] PSNR/SSIM
MAFFSRN [24]	37.031/0.923	39.358/0.957	32.291/0.867	29.384/0.801
DBSR [5]	39.031/0.940	40.537/0.960	34.343/0.904	30.032/0.824
EDVR [28]	41.897/0.965	43.256/0.976	36.294/0.928	31.828/0.897
EBSR [22]	43.094/0.972	42.590/0.976	36.933/0.937	33.724/0.913
Ours	43.261/0.973	44.481/0.977	38.424/0.949	34.148/0.915

4.2   Ablation Studies

In this section, we conduct ablation studies to demonstrate the effectiveness of the main components of EDRBSR, our loss function and post-processing strategy.

Effectiveness of Key Modules. We examine the effectiveness of the Denoising Network and the Reconstruction Network by removing then respectively. The results are shown in Table 1. It can be proved that these tow networks are the key point to the improvement of PSNR metric.

Loss Function and Post-processing Strategy. We study the contribution of the perceptual loss by comparing the training results of the two formulas with and without this loss function. The effectiveness of the Post-Processing strategy is verified by removing it or not. The results are shown in Fig. 5. It can be seen that the combined loss function of adding the perceptual loss improves images visual perception, which makes the image with more detailed texture information. And Post-Processing strategy improves the performance of SR images, especially the text edge contrast.

4.3   Comparisons with Existing Methods

In this section, we conduct comparative experiments to demonstrate the effectiveness of our network in terms of quantitative metrics and qualitative results.

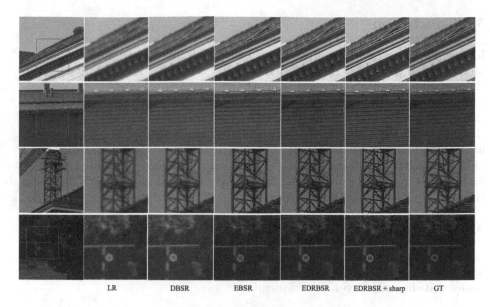

LR   DBSR   EBSR   EDRBSR   EDRBSR + sharp   GT

Fig. 6. Qualitative results of a comparison between our method and other existing methods on the real-world BurstSR dataset. EDRBSR represents our network. EDRBSR+sharp represents EDRBSR network with post-processing strategy.

We compare with state-of-the-art RAW BurstSR methods, i.e. DBSR, EBSR in both synthetic datasets and real datasets. We modify the video SR method EDVR [28] to use the first LR RAW image as reference. We implement SISR method MAFFSRN [24] by directly concatenating multiple images on the channel axis. All these methods are trained using the same training dataset, and they are evaluated on standard benchmarks, such as Zurich RAW to RGB [19], Set5 [3] Set14 [31] Urban100 [18]. The input bursts are generated from RGB images using a synthetic data generation pipeline, as we describe in Sect. 1.

As shown in Table 2, we compare the PSNR and SSIM metrics of different models, which are evaluated on the synthetic datasets. Our method significantly outperforms previous methods. As shown in Fig. 4, we present our qualitative results on the synthetic dataset. It can be seen that the eyelashes are accurately reconstructed by our method, whereas other methods show blurry results. To get the advantage of our method on sensory effects, we present our qualitative results on real-world bursts in Fig. 6. Our method reconstructs text and stripe texture much better than others. Overall, our method shows improved results comparing with existing methods, both on sythetic bursts and real-world bursts.

5 Conclusion

In this paper, we propose a framework named A RAW Burst Super-Resolution Method with Enhanced Denoising (EDRBSR), which is designed to solve the BurstSR problem in the synthetic datasets and the real-world datasets. We consider that the difficulties of restoring SR images lie in the effective denoising and channel feature reconstruction of RAW bursts. Experimental results demonstrate that the Denoising Network and the Reconstruction Network can solve these difficulties and improve results in both quantitative metrics and qualitative results. Our approach demonstrates superior performance to the existing state-of-the-art on BurstSR tasks. And it takes the 5th place in synthetic track of NTIRE 2022 Burst Super-Resolution Challenge.

Acknowledgement. This paper is funded by the "Video Super-Resolution Algorithm Design and Software Development for Face Blur Problem" (JBKY20220210) and "Research and Simulation Experiment of Lightweight Sports Event Remote Production System" (ZZLX-2020-001) projects of the Academy of Broadcasting Science, National Radio and Television Administration.

References

1. Abdelhamed, A., Lin, S., Brown, M.S.: A high-quality denoising dataset for smartphone cameras. In: Proceedings of the IEEE Conference on Computer Vision and Pattern Recognition, pp. 1692–1700 (2018)
2. Anaya, J., Barbu, A.: Renoir-a dataset for real low-light image noise reduction. J. Vis. Commun. Image Represent. **51**, 144–154 (2018)
3. Bevilacqua, M., Roumy, A., Guillemot, C., Alberi-Morel, M.L.: Low-complexity single-image super-resolution based on nonnegative neighbor embedding (2012)
4. Bhat, G., Danelljan, M., Timofte, R.: NTIRE 2021 challenge on burst super-resolution: methods and results. In: Proceedings of the IEEE/CVF Conference on Computer Vision and Pattern Recognition, pp. 613–626 (2021)
5. Bhat, G., Danelljan, M., Van Gool, L., Timofte, R.: Deep burst super-resolution. In: Proceedings of the IEEE/CVF Conference on Computer Vision and Pattern Recognition, pp. 9209–9218 (2021)
6. Burger, H.C., Schuler, C.J., Harmeling, S.: Image denoising: can plain neural networks compete with BM3D? In: 2012 IEEE Conference on Computer Vision and Pattern Recognition, pp. 2392–2399. IEEE (2012)
7. Chang, H., Yeung, D.Y., Xiong, Y.: Super-resolution through neighbor embedding. In: Proceedings of the 2004 IEEE Computer Society Conference on Computer Vision and Pattern Recognition, CVPR 2004, vol. 1, pp. I-I. IEEE (2004)
8. Chen, C., Chen, Q., Do, M.N., Koltun, V.: Seeing motion in the dark. In: Proceedings of the IEEE/CVF International Conference on Computer Vision, pp. 3185–3194 (2019)
9. Chollet, F.: Xception: deep learning with depthwise separable convolutions. In: Proceedings of the IEEE Conference on Computer Vision and Pattern Recognition, pp. 1251–1258 (2017)
10. Dai, D., Timofte, R., Van Gool, L.: Jointly optimized regressors for image super-resolution. Comput. Graph. Forum **34**, 95–104 (2015)

11. Dai, S., Han, M., Xu, W., Wu, Y., Gong, Y.: Soft edge smoothness prior for alpha channel super resolution. In: 2007 IEEE Conference on Computer Vision and Pattern Recognition, pp. 1–8. IEEE (2007)
12. Deudon, M., et al.: HighRes-net: recursive fusion for multi-frame super-resolution of satellite imagery (2020)
13. Farsiu, S., Elad, M., Milanfar, P.: Multiframe demosaicing and super-resolution of color images. IEEE Trans. Image Process. **15**(1), 141–159 (2006)
14. Foi, A., Trimeche, M., Katkovnik, V., Egiazarian, K.: Practical poissonian-gaussian noise modeling and fitting for single-image raw-data. IEEE Trans. Image Process. **17**(10), 1737–1754 (2008)
15. Fu, J., et al.: Dual attention network for scene segmentation. In: Proceedings of the IEEE/CVF Conference on Computer Vision and Pattern Recognition, pp. 3146–3154 (2019)
16. Gharbi, M., Chaurasia, G., Paris, S., Durand, F.: Deep joint demosaicking and denoising. ACM Trans. Graph. (ToG) **35**(6), 1–12 (2016)
17. Hardie, R.C.: High-resolution image reconstruction from a sequence of rotated and translated frames and its application to an infrared imaging system. Opt. Eng. **37**(1), 247–260 (1998)
18. Huang, J.B., Singh, A., Ahuja, N.: Single image super-resolution from transformed self-exemplars. In: Proceedings of the IEEE Conference on Computer Vision and Pattern Recognition, pp. 5197–5206 (2015)
19. Ignatov, A., et al.: AIM 2019 challenge on raw to RGB mapping: methods and results. In: 2019 IEEE/CVF International Conference on Computer Vision Workshop (ICCVW), pp. 3584–3590. IEEE (2019)
20. Ji, H., Fermüller, C.: Wavelet-based super-resolution reconstruction: theory and algorithm. In: Leonardis, A., Bischof, H., Pinz, A. (eds.) ECCV 2006. LNCS, vol. 3954, pp. 295–307. Springer, Heidelberg (2006). https://doi.org/10.1007/11744085_23
21. Liu, J., Zhang, W., Tang, Y., Tang, J., Wu, G.: Residual feature aggregation network for image super-resolution. In: Proceedings of the IEEE/CVF Conference on Computer Vision and Pattern Recognition, pp. 2359–2368 (2020)
22. Luo, Z., et al.: EBSR: feature enhanced burst super-resolution with deformable alignment. In: Proceedings of the IEEE/CVF Conference on Computer Vision and Pattern Recognition, pp. 471–478 (2021)
23. Molini, A.B., Valsesia, D., Fracastoro, G., Magli, E.: DeepSUM: deep neural network for super-resolution of unregistered multitemporal images. IEEE Trans. Geosci. Remote Sens. **58**(5), 3644–3656 (2019)
24. Muqeet, A., Hwang, J., Yang, S., Kang, J.H., Kim, Y., Bae, S.-H.: Multi-attention based ultra lightweight image super-resolution. In: Bartoli, A., Fusiello, A. (eds.) ECCV 2020. LNCS, vol. 12537, pp. 103–118. Springer, Cham (2020). https://doi.org/10.1007/978-3-030-67070-2_6
25. Shanmugam, D., Blalock, D., Balakrishnan, G., Guttag, J.: When and why test-time augmentation works. arXiv e-prints pp. arXiv-2011 (2020)
26. Simonyan, K., Zisserman, A.: Very deep convolutional networks for large-scale image recognition. arXiv preprint arXiv:1409.1556 (2014)
27. Tsai, R.: Multiframe image restoration and registration. Adv. Comput. Vis. Image Process. **1**, 317–339 (1984)
28. Wang, X., Chan, K.C., Yu, K., Dong, C., Change Loy, C.: EDVR: video restoration with enhanced deformable convolutional networks. In: Proceedings of the IEEE/CVF Conference on Computer Vision and Pattern Recognition Workshops (2019)

29. Wang, Y., Huang, H., Xu, Q., Liu, J., Liu, Y., Wang, J.: Practical deep raw image denoising on mobile devices. In: Vedaldi, A., Bischof, H., Brox, T., Frahm, J.-M. (eds.) ECCV 2020. LNCS, vol. 12351, pp. 1–16. Springer, Cham (2020). https://doi.org/10.1007/978-3-030-58539-6_1
30. Wronski, B., et al.: Handheld multi-frame super-resolution. ACM Trans. Graph. (TOG) 38(4), 1–18 (2019)
31. Zeyde, R., Elad, M., Protter, M.: On single image scale-up using sparse-representations. In: Boissonnat, J.-D., et al. (eds.) Curves and Surfaces 2010. LNCS, vol. 6920, pp. 711–730. Springer, Heidelberg (2012). https://doi.org/10.1007/978-3-642-27413-8_47
32. Zhang, X., Zhou, X., Lin, M., Sun, J.: Shufflenet: an extremely efficient convolutional neural network for mobile devices. In: Proceedings of the IEEE Conference on Computer Vision and Pattern Recognition, pp. 6848–6856 (2018)

Unpaired and Self-supervised Optical Coherence Tomography Angiography Super-Resolution

Chaofan Zeng[1], Songtao Yuan[2], and Qiang Chen[1]([✉])

[1] School of Computer Science and Engineering, Nanjing University of Science and Technology, Nanjing 210094, China
chen2qiang@njust.edu.cn
[2] Department of Ophthalmology, The First Affiliated Hospital With Nanjing Medical University, Nanjing 210094, China

Abstract. Optical coherence tomography angiography (OCTA) is usually used to observe the blood flow information of retina and choroid. It is meaningful for clinicians to observe more microvascular details by enhancing the resolution of OCTA images, which is conducive to the diagnosis of diseases. However, due to the limitation of imaging equipment, when the resolution of OCTA is improved, the field of view (FOV) will be reduced. In the existing methods to enhance the resolution of OCTA, paired training data from the same eye are generally required, but paired data are usually difficult to be obtained, and the resolution of enhanced images is difficult to exceed that of original high resolution (3×3 mm^2) OCTA images. Therefore, to improve the resolution of low resolution (6×6 mm^2) OCTA images, this paper proposes an unpaired and self-supervised OCTA super-resolution (USOSR) method by down sampling and enhancing the original 3×3 mm^2 OCTA images. Experimental results demonstrate that the enhanced 6×6 mm^2 OCTA images have significantly stronger contrast, sharper edges and higher information entropy than the original images.

Keywords: OCTA · Super-resolution · Unpaired · Self-supervised

1 Introduction

Optical coherence tomography angiography (OCTA) is a new non-invasive fundus imaging technology. It can recognize the three-dimensional blood flow movement information of retina and choroid through scanning. In recent years, it has gradually become an effective tool for the diagnosis of fundus related diseases. Different from optical coherence tomography (OCT) that emphasizes the structural information of retinal layer and common color fundus photography (CFP), OCTA can visualize the blood flow information of retina and choroid well (Fig. 1), which is considered to be the best fundus imaging technology of retinal vascular system [1]. The capillary level microvascular details can

Supplementary Information The online version contains supplementary material available at https://doi.org/10.1007/978-3-031-18916-6_10.

be observed through OCTA, especially the microvascular systems distributed at different depths around the central fovea of macula can be imaged with relatively high resolution. Observing and quantifying these microvascular morphological structures is helpful for clinicians to diagnose ophthalmic diseases, which makes OCTA play an important role in retinal diagnosis [2, 3], and even neurodegenerative diseases [4].

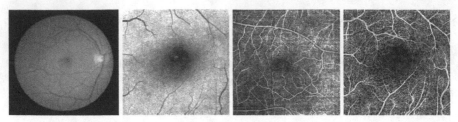

Fig. 1. From left to right are CFP, OCT, OCTA with 6×6 mm^2 and 3×3 mm^2 FOV.

For the diagnosis of retinal diseases, it is necessary to improve the resolution of OCTA images and expand the field of view (FOV) (Fig. 1). However, when we expand the FOV, due to the limitation of the scanning speed of the OCTA system and the difficulty for people to keep blinking for a long time, the number of A-lines contained in each B-scan is difficult to change significantly, which means that the resolution of the OCTA image will decrease with the decrease of sampling density. In other words, the resolution of OCTA image and the FOV cannot be increased at the same time.

Therefore, to solve the above problems, this paper proposes a deep learning based method to enhance the resolution of OCTA image. Image super-resolution (SR) is an important branch of image enhancement, which aims to recover high-resolution (HR) images from corresponding low-resolution (LR) images [5]. Recently, the deep learning based methods are widely used for image SR [6–9]. In the OCTA SR algorithms, the HR angiogram reconstruction network uses the paired image training network to enhance the resolution of OCTA images [10]. Although there is unsupervised learning using cyclic consensus against network architecture, unregistered data from the same eye are still used in the training data [11]. However, these methods require paired training data, which is very difficult for many applications, especially in medicine.

To avoid the need for paired training data, the self-supervised super-resolution method is more widely used [12]. These methods obtain paired training data by down sampling the original image. For example, SRGAN enhances the resolution of natural images by generative adversarial networks [13]. DRRN uses a ResBlock as the recursive unit for 25 recursions and obtains even better performance than 17-ResBlock [14]. MemNet is composed of a 6-recursive ResBlock where the outputs of every recursion are concatenated, and go through an extra 1×1 convolution for memorizing and forgetting [15].

However, the methods mentioned above still have certain limitations. The SR networks can only learn the mapping from LR to HR, which makes the resolution of LR image cannot exceed the original HR image after enhancement. Such resolution is not high enough for OCTA image, because the resolution of original 3×3 mm^2 OCTA image is not very high (Fig. 1). In addition, among the current SR methods for OCTA images, there is no method suitable for unpaired images. In order to address these issues, this paper proposes an unpaired and self-supervised OCTA super-resolution method (USOSR) based on deep learning to enhance the resolution of en face OCTA images.

The main contributions of this work can be summarized as follows:

- We present a self-supervised super-resolution method for OCTA images, which uses unpaired LR (6×6 mm^2) and HR (3×3 mm^2) en face OCTA images.
- To improve the resolution of 6×6 mm^2 OCTA images further, we enhance the resolution of original 3×3 mm^2 OCTA images, which are taken as the ultra high resolution (UHR) ground truth.
- Experiments show that the proposed method can obtain significantly higher resolution OCTA images, which is useful for the clinical diagnosis.

2   Methods

This paper uses USOSR to enhance the resolution of 6×6 mm^2 OCTA image. In order to use unpaired 6×6 mm^2 OCTA images and 3×3 mm^2 OCTA images, we adopt a self-supervised super-resolution method. Because the paired image quality used for training will affect the performance of the trained deep neural network. Therefore, while reducing the quality of 3×3 mm^2 OCTA image to obtain paired data, we also use the plug-and-play super-resolution method [16] to enhance the resolution of original 3×3 mm^2 OCTA images for training, so that the low-resolution image can be transformed into a higher resolution image. In the following, we will describe the details of our proposed USOSR.

2.1   Data

Two sets of OCTA images from Optovue device are used, whose imaging ranges are 3×3 mm^2 and 6×6 mm^2 centered on the fovea, respectively. Each eye corresponds to three types of projection images, OCTA full-projection, OCTA maximum-projection between internal limiting membrane (ILM) and outer plexiform layer (OPL), and OCTA maximum-projection between OPL and Bruch's membrane (BM). These images are all from the OCTA-500 dataset [17].

6×6 mm^2 OCTA images with the size of 400×400 from 300 different eyes are called low resolution images (LR 6×6 mm^2), used only for testing.

3×3 mm^2 OCTA images with the size of 304×304 from 200 different eyes are called high resolution images (HR 3×3 mm^2). We also generated low resolution images (LR 3×3 mm^2) and ultra high resolution images (UHR 3×3 mm^2) from the original HR 3×3 mm^2. The paired 3×3 mm^2 images from 160 eyes are used for training, and the images of the remaining 40 eyes are used for testing.

For the images of the training dataset, we increase the robustness of deep neural network through data augmentation, including vertical flipping, horizontal flipping, 90-degree rotation and transposition.

2.2 Framework

Images will lose information in the process of down sampling. In this paper, the quality of HR 3×3 mm^2 is reduced by down sampling to obtain LR 3×3 mm^2, which can simulate LR 6×6 mm^2 in visual effect and data distribution.

The performance of SR network will also be affected by the resolution of the ground truth during training. In order to further enhance the resolution of LR images, we use a plug-and-play super-resolution method to enhance the resolution of HR 3×3 mm^2 for obtaining UHR 3×3 mm^2 ground truth. LR 3×3 mm^2 and UHR 3×3 mm^2 are used as paired images for the training of SR network, so that the images can be transformed from LR to UHR (Fig. 2). Before inputting LR 3×3 mm^2 into the network, we first use bilinear interpolation to make its size same as UHR 3×3 mm^2 to ensure the equal size

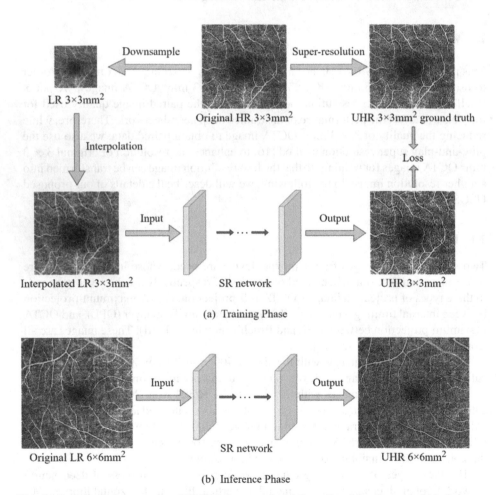

Fig. 2. Overview of our proposed USOSR framework. (a) Overall training Process. (b) Inference using the trained super-resolution model. The super-resolution network generates UHR 6×6 mm^2 images directly from original 6×6 mm^2 images without additional operation.

of input and output images of SR network. Perhaps one question is that why we do not directly use the plug-and-play method to enhance the resolution of LR 6×6 mm^2. The reason is that the resolution of LR 6×6 mm^2 is too low to directly use the plug-and-play method to enhance the resolution.

2.3 Loss Function

In this paper, we use the mean square error (MSE) to minimize the pixel level difference and the structural similarity (SSIM) to minimize the overall difference.

$$L_{MSE} = \frac{1}{w \times h} \sum_{i=1}^{w} \sum_{j=1}^{h} (H(i,j) - G(i,j))^2 \tag{1}$$

$$L_{SSIM} = \frac{2\mu_H\mu_G + C_1}{\mu_H^2 + \mu_G^2 + C_1} \cdot \frac{2\sigma_{HG} + C_2}{\sigma_H^2 + \sigma_G^2 + C_2} \tag{2}$$

$$L = L_{MSE} + (1 - L_{SSIM}) \tag{3}$$

where w and h refer to the width and height of the image, H refers to the output of SR network, G refers to the ground truth, μ_H and μ_G are the mean pixel values, σ_H and σ_G are the standard deviations, and σ_{HG} is the covariance. The constants $C_1 = 0.01$ and $C_2 = 0.03$ are taken from the literature [18]. L_{MSE}, L_{SSIM}, L denote the MSE loss, the SSIM loss and the overall loss, respectively.

2.4 Model Training

The experiment in this paper is based on the deep learning framework PyTorch. The training of the model is carried out on NVIDIA GeForce RTX 3090 GPU. This paper uses four different SR network architectures, and uses Adam optimizer [19] to train the deep neural network from scratch. The initial learning rate is 0.001 and the batch size depends on the SR network. In the training of the network, the convergence speed of the loss curve is very fast. It takes no more than 6 h to converge after 40000 iterations.

3 Experimental Results and Analysis

3.1 Evaluation Metrics

Due to our LR 6×6 mm^2 has no paired ground truth, so we cannot use SSIM and peak signal to noise ratio (PSNR). We use Brenner gradient [20], contrast [21], Vollath [22] and entropy [23] as quantitative indicators. The larger the value of these indicators, the higher the image resolution.

- **Brenner gradient.** It calculates the square of the grayscale difference between two adjacent pixels of the image. The larger this intensity changes, the sharper the edges. The function is defined as follows:

$$B(f) = \sum_{y} \sum_{x} |f(x+2,y) - f(x,y)|^2 \tag{4}$$

– **Contrast.** HR images have greater grayscale difference than LR images. It calculates the global contrast of the image. The function is defined as follows:

$$C(f) = \sqrt{\frac{1}{w \times h} \times \sum_{y} \sum_{x} (f(x, y) - \mu)^2}$$ (5)

– **Vollath.** The vollath function can evaluate the sharpness of the images. This function is defined as follows:

$$V(f) = \sum_{y} \sum_{x} f(x, y) \times f(x + 1, y) - w \times h \times \mu^2$$ (6)

– **Entropy.** The entropy function based on statistical features is an important index to measure the richness of image information. According to Shannon's information theory, when the entropy is maximum, the amount of information is the most. Therefore, the higher entropy, the higher the image resolution. The amount of information of an image f is measured by the information entropy:

$$E(f) = -\sum_{i=0}^{L-1} P_i \, ln(P_i)$$ (7)

Here $f(x, y)$ represents the grayscale of the pixel (x, y) corresponding to image f, w and h are the width and height of the image respectively, and μ is its mean value. Where P_i is the probability of pixels with grayscale i in the image, and L is the total number of grayscales.

3.2 Performance on 6 × 6 mm^2 Images

In order to verify that USOSR can improve the quality of LR images, we evaluated its performance on 6×6 mm^2 images. Our input and output are original LR 6×6 mm^2 and UHR 6×6 mm^2 images, and there is no ground truth. We compared the performance of USOSR with four different SR networks, namely deep recursive residual network (DRRN) [14], very deep super-resolution (VDSR) [24], high-resolution angiogram reconstruction network (HARNet) [10], memory network (MemNet) [15]. Figure 3(C) shows that USOSR with VDSR performs not good, and the reason is that

Table 1. The quantitative results of USOSR on original LR 6×6 mm^2

	Brenner	Contrast	Vollath	Entropy
LR 6 × 6 mm^2	7151.07	49.95	4163.75	4.078
USOSR-DRRN	28990.73	75.43	7157.39	5.098
USOSR-VDSR	6031.78	49.09	4190.44	5.133
USOSR-MemNet	23402.16	64.97	3352.65	5.169
USOSR-HARNet	20143.02	68.39	6686.65	5.196

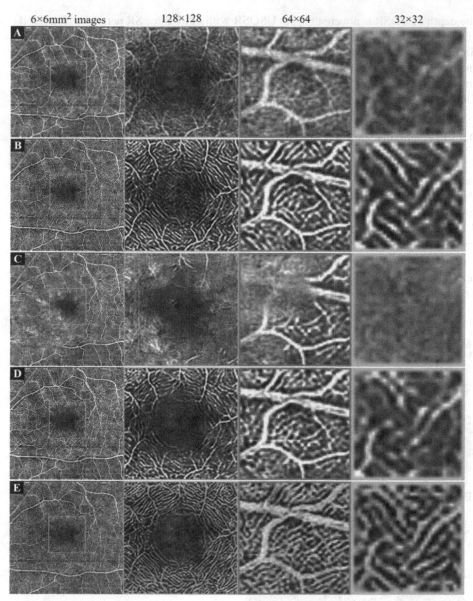

Fig. 3. Super-resolution results for LR 6 × 6 mm² images. Original LR 6 × 6 mm² (A), the super-resolution results of USOSR by using four different SR networks (DRRN (B), VDSR (C), HARNet (D), MemNet (E)). The second, third and fourth columns are the magnified views of the front boxes.

the depth of VDSR is not enough, but USOSR with other three SR networks (Figs. 3(B) (D) (E)) performs well, and UHR 6×6 mm^2 images have very clear capillary structure. Table 1 demonstrates that the enhanced images have significant improvement on edge intensity, contrast and information entropy compared with the original 6×6 mm^2 images. Therefore, our method is applicable on general LR images, and the enhanced UHR images will have much higher quality.

3.3 Performance on 3×3 mm^2 Images

Since the SR network is trained on 3×3 mm^2 images, we also evaluated its performance on 3×3 mm^2 images. Our input is the interpolated LR 3×3 mm^2 images from test dataset, and output is UHR 3×3 mm^2. Figure 4 demonstrates that LR 3×3 mm^2 images have been significantly enhanced into UHR 3×3 mm^2, and the resolution of UHR 3×3 mm^2 is closer to UHR ground truth than HR 3×3 mm^2. The quantitative results in Table 2 show that the enhanced images have stronger contrast, sharper edges and higher information entropy than LR and HR 3×3 mm^2. Therefore, our method is applicable to LR images, and the enhanced UHR images will have higher quality than original HR images.

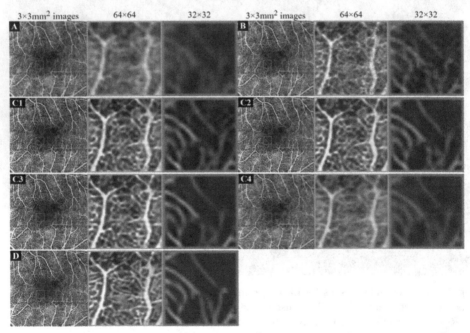

Fig. 4. Super-resolution results for LR 3×3 mm^2 images. Interpolated LR 3×3 mm^2 (A), original HR 3×3 mm^2 (B), the super-resolution results of USOSR by using four different SR networks (DRRN (C1), VDSR(C2), HARNet (C3), MemNet (C4)), UHR 3×3 mm^2 ground truth (D).

Table 2. The quantitative results of USOSR on LR 3×3 mm^2 images

	Brenner	Contrast	Vollath	Entropy
LR 3×3 mm^2	1063.45	37.30	2022.02	4.980
HR 3×3 mm^2	4351.59	51.45	2551.89	4.734
USOSR-DRRN	5176.65	54.94	3340.45	5.247
USOSR-VDSR	5566.80	55.26	3397.68	5.205
USOSR-MemNet	2199.47	41.13	2331.96	5.060
USOSR-HARNet	5920.81	58.12	3613.40	5.217
UHR ground truth	6612.75	58.01	3176.26	5.216

4 Conclusions

In this paper, we propose an unpaired and self-supervised super-resolution method based on deep learning, namely USOSR, which can enhance the resolution of OCTA en face images without reducing the field of view. Our method does not require paired 6×6 mm^2 and 3×3 mm^2 OCTA images, only 3×3 mm^2 images used for self-supervised learning. To improve the resolution of 6×6 mm^2 OCTA images further, we enhance the resolution of original 3×3 mm^2 OCTA images, which are taken as ground truth. Then we use the trained SR network to enhance LR images, and experiments show that the proposed method can obtain significantly higher resolution OCTA images with clear microvascular details, which is useful for the clinical diagnosis.

Acknowledgment. This study was supported by National Natural Science Foundation of China (62172223, 61671242), and the Fundamental Research Funds for the Central Universities (30921013105).

References

1. Or, C., Sabrosa, A.S., Sorour, O., Arya, M., Waheed, N.: Use of OCTA, FA, and ultra-widefield imaging in quantifying retinal ischemia: a review. Asia Pac. J. Ophthalmol. **7**(1), 46–51 (2018)
2. Waheed, N.K., Moult, E.M., Fujimoto, J.G., Rosenfeld, P.J.: Optical coherence tomography angiography of dry age-related macular degeneration. OCT Angiogr. Retin. Macular Dis. **56**, 91–100 (2016)
3. Huang, D., Jia, Y., Rispoli, M., Tan, O., Lumbroso, B.: OCT angiography of time course of choroidal neovascularization in response to anti-angiogenic treatment. Retina **35**(11), 2260 (2015)
4. O'Bryhim, B.E., Apte, R.S., Kung, N., Coble, D., Van Stavern, G.P.: Association of pre-clinical Alzheimer disease with optical coherence tomographic angiography findings. JAMA Ophthalmol. **136**(11), 1242–1248 (2018)
5. Liu, Y., Qiao, Y., Hao, Y., Wang, F., Rashid, S.F.: Single image super resolution techniques based on deep learning: status, applications and future directions. J. Image Graph. **9**(3) (2021)

6. Timofte, R., Agustsson, E., Van Gool, L., Yang, M.H., Zhang, L.: Ntire 2017 challenge on single image super-resolution: methods and results. In: Proceedings of the IEEE Conference on Computer Vision and Pattern Recognition Workshops, pp. 114–125 (2017)
7. Blau, Y., Mechrez, R., Timofte, R., Michaeli, T., Zelnik-Manor, L.: The 2018 PIRM challenge on perceptual image super-resolution. In: Leal-Taixé, L., Roth, S. (eds.) ECCV 2018. LNCS, vol. 11133, pp. 334–355. Springer, Cham (2019). https://doi.org/10.1007/978-3-030-11021-5_21
8. Mahapatra, D., Bozorgtabar, B., Hewavitharanage, S., Garnavi, R.: Image super resolution using generative adversarial networks and local saliency maps for retinal image analysis. In: Descoteaux, M., Maier-Hein, L., Franz, A., Jannin, P., Collins, D., Duchesne, S. (eds.) MICCAI 2017. LNCS, vol. 10435, pp. 382–390. Springer, Cham (2017). https://doi.org/10.1007/978-3-319-66179-7_44
9. Du, J., et al.: Super-resolution reconstruction of single anisotropic 3D MR images using residual convolutional neural network. Neurocomputing **392**, 209–220 (2020)
10. Gao, M., Guo, Y., Hormel, T.T., Sun, J., Hwang, T.S., Jia, Y.: Reconstruction of high-resolution 6×6-mm OCT angiograms using deep learning. Biomed. Opt. Express **11**(7), 3585–3600 (2020)
11. Zhou, T., et al.: Digital resolution enhancement in low transverse sampling optical coherence tomography angiography using deep learning. OSA Contin. **3**(6), 1664–1678 (2020)
12. Zhao, C., Dewey, B.E., Pham, D.L., Calabresi, P.A., Reich, D.S., Prince, J.L.: SMORE: a self-supervised anti-aliasing and super-resolution algorithm for MRI using deep learning. IEEE Trans. Med. Imaging **40**(3), 805–817 (2020)
13. Ledig, C., et al.: Photo-realistic single image super-resolution using a generative adversarial network. In: Proceedings of the IEEE Conference on Computer Vision and Pattern Recognition, pp. 4681–4690 (2017)
14. Tai, Y., Yang, J., Liu, X.: Image super-resolution via deep recursive residual network. In: Proceedings of the IEEE Conference on Computer Vision and Pattern Recognition, pp. 3147–3155 (2017)
15. Tai, Y., Yang, J., Liu, X., Xu, C.: MemNet: a persistent memory network for image restoration. In: Proceedings of the IEEE International Conference on Computer Vision, pp. 4539–4547 (2017)
16. Zhang, K., Li, Y., Zuo, W., Zhang, L., Van Gool, L., Timofte, R.: Plug-and-play image restoration with deep denoiser prior. IEEE Trans. Pattern Anal. Mach. Intell. (2021)
17. Li, M., et al.: IPN-V2 and octa-500: methodology and dataset for retinal image segmentation. arXiv preprint arXiv:2012.07261 (2020)
18. Wang, Z., Bovik, A.C., Sheikh, H.R., Simoncelli, E.P.: Image quality assessment: from error visibility to structural similarity. IEEE Trans. Image Process. **13**(4), 600–612 (2004)
19. Kingma, D.P., Ba, J.: Adam: a method for stochastic optimization. arXiv preprint arXiv:1412.6980 (2014)
20. Brenner, J.F., Dew, B.S., Horton, J.B., King, T., Neurath, P.W., Selles, W.D.: An automated microscope for cytologic research a preliminary evaluation. J. Histochem. Cytochem. **24**(1), 100–111 (1976)
21. Peli, E.: Contrast in complex images. JOSA A **7**(10), 2032–2040 (1990)
22. Vollath, D.: The influence of the scene parameters and of noise on the behaviour of automatic focusing algorithms. J. Microsc. **151**(2), 133–146 (1988)
23. Rényi, A.: On measures of entropy and information. In: Proceedings of the Fourth Berkeley Symposium on Mathematical Statistics and Probability, Volume 1: Contributions to the Theory of Statistics, vol. 4, pp. 547–562. University of California Press (1961)
24. Kim, J., Lee, J. K., Lee, K.M.: Accurate image super-resolution using very deep convolutional networks. In: Proceedings of the IEEE Conference on Computer Vision and Pattern Recognition, pp. 1646–1654 (2016)

Multi-feature Fusion Network for Single Image Dehazing

Jie Luo, Tong Chang, and Qirong Bo[✉]

Northwestern University, Xi'an, Shaanxi, China
boqirong@nwu.edu.cn

Abstract. Existing image dehazing methods consider the learning-based methods as the mainstream. Most of them are trained on synthetic dataset, and may not be able to efficiently transfer to real outdoor scenes. In order to further improve the dehazing effect of the model in real outdoor scenes, this paper proposes an end-to-end Multi-Feature Fusion Network for Single Image Dehazing (MFFN). The proposed network combines the prior-based methods and learning-based methods. This paper first uses the method of supporting backpropagation in order to directly extract the dark channel prior and color attenuation prior features. It then designs a Multi-Feature Adaptive Fusion Module (MFAFM) which can adaptively fuse and enhance the two prior features. Finally, the prior features are added to the decoding stage of the backbone network in a multi-scale manner. The experimental results on the synthetic dataset and real-world dataset demonstrate that the proposed model performs favorably against the state-of-the-art dehazing algorithms.

Keywords: Single Image Dehazing · Prior-based methods · Learning-based methods

1 Introduction

In haze weather, the increase of suspended particles in the air absorbs and scatters light, which results in poor visibility, reduced contrast and color distortion of the taken images. This process can be modeled as [1, 2]:

$$I(x) = J(x)t(x) + A(1 - t(x)) \tag{1}$$

where I(x) denotes the hazy image, J(x) is the corresponding clear image, t(x) represents the transmission map, A is the global atmospheric light, and x represents the pixel location. Image dehazing aims at making the image clear. That is, given I(x), in order to get J(x), we focus on the solution of t(x) and A.

Supported by Yulin science and technology plan project CXY-2020-07.

The commonly used dehazing methods can be divided into two categories: the prior-based methods [3–6] and learning-based methods [7–13]. The prior is generally based on data statistics, which is often very efficient in real outdoor scenes. However, it still has limitations. For instance, dark channel prior will fail in the sky region. The learning-based methods can estimate t(x) or A using a neural network [7, 8], and then synthesize a clear image according to Eq. (2). However, it will cause error superposition, and increase the final error. Therefore, the recent methods for the estimation of clear images directly from hazy images using a neural network [9–13] are the mainstream.

However, these methods lead to some problems. More precisely, training such a neural network requires a large number of hazy/clear image pairs, and it is very difficult to obtain such data. Therefore, the currently used training images are generally synthetic images, while the hazy images are formed by hazing real and clear images according to Eq. (3). As the neural network is trained on synthetic dataset, the effect of dehazing in real scenes is often not satisfactory (see Fig. 1). Although NTIRE has organized several dehazing challenges and introduced several small-scale real-world datasets, these datasets are rare and incomplete. Several studies have been proposed to solve this problem [22, 23]. In fact, we believe that, in order to improve the effect of the model in real scenes, we should extract as many real image features as possible from the hazy images that are suitable for dehazing tasks, especially the prior features. This is due to the fact that the prior features are very efficient in real outdoor scenes. However, they have some limitations. In addition, deep learning is versatile. However, it relies too much on the training set. Therefore, this paper uses the fusion of prior features and deep learning features to further improve the performance of the network in complex real outdoor scenes.

| (a) | (b) | (c) | (d) |

Fig. 1. Dehazing results on synthetic and real images using FFA-Net [13]. (a) synthetic hazy image, (b) dehazed image for (a), (c) real hazy image, (d) dehazed image for (c).

An end-to-end Multi-Feature Fusion Network for Single Image Dehazing (MFFN) is proposed. Note that the proposed network is based on our previous study [14]. The baseline is a global feature fusion attention network based on encoder-decoder architecture, which can extract global context information and fully fuse it. Through experiments, two prior features are selected for extraction then fused into the network: the Dark Channel Prior (DCP) [3] and color attenuation prior (CAP) [15]. According to the definition of two priors, a simple and direct extraction method is designed using tensor calculation and maxpooling, in order to make the extraction process support back-propagation. The Multi-Feature Adaptive Fusion Module (MFAFM) is proposed to selectively fuse the two prior features using the attention mechanism, and enhance the features using residual connections. Finally, the fusion of two scales is performed in the decoder stage of the baseline.

The experiments show that the proposed algorithm has higher performance than other state-of-the-art dehazing algorithms. The contributions of this paper include:

By combining the advantages of the prior-based methods and learning-based methods, the proposed MFFN fuses the two prior features and deep learning features. This model has a better performance in real outdoor scenes.

DCP and CAP are directly and efficiently extracted, while supporting backpropagation in order to make the model end-to-end.

The MFAFM is proposed to select the effective feature from the two prior features for fusion, so as to avoid excessive features that affect the network performance.

2   Proposed Method

In this section, the proposed MFFN is detailed. The latter consists of three parts: extraction of two prior features, MFAFM and basic network (see Fig. 2).

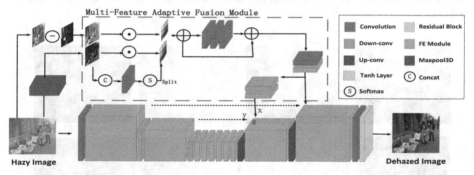

Fig. 2. The architecture of the Multi-Feature Fusion Network for Single Image Dehazing (MFFN).

2.1   Extraction of Two Prior Features

Dark Channel Prior. He et al. [3] made statistics of a large number of outdoor hazy-free images and determined a rule: in most of the local areas of the outdoor hazy-free image, there are some pixels that have very low values (approaching 0) in at least one color channel. It is referred to as the dark channel prior, expressed as:

$$J^{dark}(x) = \min_{y \in \Omega(x)} (\min_{c \in \{r,g,b\}} J^c(y)) \tag{4}$$

The input of the neural network is the hazy image. Due to the presence of haze, the white area in the image increases, which makes the dark channel value of the image not approaching 0. Therefore, the DCP feature map, obtained from the hazy image

I(x), can represent the concentration and hazy area to a certain extent. In this paper, three-dimensional maxpooling is used to perform DCP feature map extraction:

$$I^{dark}(x) = 1 - \max pool3D(1 - I(x)) \tag{5}$$

The obtained result is shown in Fig. 3 (b). It can be seen that, in the near non-hazy area, Idark(x) is almost all black, and it is possible to clearly distinguish between the hazy area and the non-hazy area. Due to the dark channel value of each local area (of 7 ◊ 7 size) is the same, it lacks detailed information.

Color Attenuation Prior. Hu et al. [15] found that the difference between brightness and saturation is positively correlated with the haze density, using statistics of outdoor hazy images. The CAP feature map is directly computed as:

$$sv(x) = HSV(I(x))_v - HSV(I(x))_s \tag{6}$$

The hazy image is converted to the HSV format. The value of the s channel minus that of the v channel is then used as the color attenuation prior feature map (sv(x)). It can be seen from Fig. 3(c) that sv(x) has a larger pixel value in the area where the hazy density is greater, and it contains lot of detailed information due to the direct extraction method.

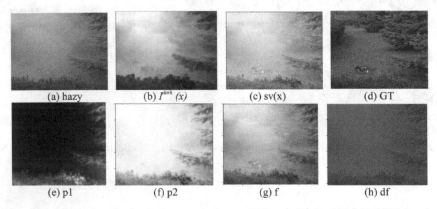

Fig. 3. Results of prior feature extraction, and intermediate results of MFSFM.

2.2 Multi-feature Adaptive Fusion Module

The two priors are based on statistics of real outdoor images. Therefore, their addition will allow the model to capture features that are more suitable for real outdoor scenes. In this paper, the extraction of prior feature maps is straightforward. The most primitive prior features can then be extracted. However, these two types of prior feature maps have some shortcomings. More precisely, the DCP feature map will be invalid in the white or sky area, and the CAP feature map will also show white color in the close-range hazy-free area. The direct introduction of these features to the network will affect the performance of the network. Therefore, this paper designs the MFAFM (see Fig. 2) using the attention mechanism to adaptively and selectively fusion the two prior feature maps, in order to obtain the most efficient features:

$$p1, p2 = split(soft \max(conv(concat(I^{dark}(x), sv(x))))) \tag{7}$$

$$f = (p1 \otimes I^{dark}(x)) \oplus (p2 \otimes sv(x)) \tag{8}$$

$$df = f \oplus conv(conv(conv(f))) \tag{9}$$

The two prior feature maps are first concatenated. A 2-channel attention feature is then obtained using a 3×3 convolution and softmax function. Afterwards, the feature map of each channel is treated as an attention map of a prior feature map. The corresponding multiplication and addition are then performed to obtain the fusion feature f, which is gone and added using three convolutions. Finally, the residual connection is used to enhance the feature of f, and therefore the enhanced feature ef is obtained.

In Fig. 3, p1 and p2 represent the attention maps of $I^{dark}(x)$ and sv(x), respectively. It can be seen that for $I^{dark}(x)$, the close-range non-hazy area is mainly reserved, while for sv(x), the hazy area and the detailed information of the close-range area are reserved. In f, the recovery effect is better in the close-range non-hazy area. In addition, a certain dehazing effect is achieved in the hazy area. Moreover, e f removes more haze while retaining the detailed features. Finally, e f will be fused to the two scales of the decoder.

2.3 Baseline

The baseline in this paper is a global feature fusion attention network [14], based on the encoder-decoder architecture. The Feature Enhancement (FE) module is its main module. Figure 4 presents the FE module of the decoder, where x is the information passed by the layer skip connection, y represents the prior features, and z is the information to be up-sampled after decoding. The Global Feature Fusion Attention (GFFA) module is the core of the FE module (see Fig. 5). It can extract the global context features, and fully integrate them with the prior features using the multi-scale and attention mechanism, as well as the residual connection of the FE module, in order to enhance the features. Note that the Mean Square Error (MSE) and perceptual loss are used as the loss function.

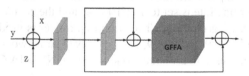

Fig. 4. Architecture of the Feature Enhancement (FE) module [14].

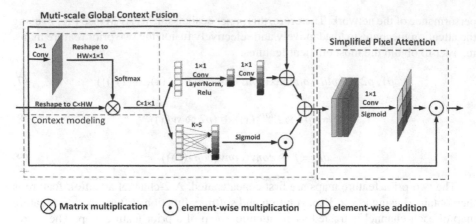

Fig. 5. The architecture of the Global Feature Fusion Attention (GFFA) module [14], including the Muti-scale Global Context Fusion (MGCF) block (red box) and Simplified Pixel Attention (SPA) block (black box). (Color figure online)

3   Experiments

3.1   Datasets

Synthetic Dataset. The synthetic RESIDE [16] dataset contains indoor and outdoor images. The dataset used by MSBDN [17] after data enhancement, is considered as training set. The Outdoor Training Set (OTS) is used as the test set, which contains 500 pairs of outdoor synthetic images.

Real-World Dataset. The O-HAZE dataset [18] from NTIRE2018 Dehazing Challenge and NH-HAZE dataset [19, 20] from NTIRE2020 Dehazing Challenge are used. O-HAZE contains 45 pairs of outdoor hazy and haze-free images, while the first 40 images are used to train the models and the last 5 images are used to test. NH-HAZE contains 55 pairs of outdoor hazy and haze-free images, while the first 50 images are used to train the models and the last 5 images are used to test.

3.2   Implementation Details

A 256×256 patch is cropped from the image and used as input, while the batch-size is set to 8. The initial learning rate is set to $1 \times 10 - 4$, and the cosine annealing strategy [25] is used to adjust the learning rate. The Adam optimizer is used, where $\beta 1$ and $\beta 2$ have the default values of 0.9 and 0.999, respectively. The network is trained for 1×106 iterations. PyTorch is used to train the models with an NVIDIA GTX2080 SUPPER GPU.

3.3   Comparison with the State-of-the-Art Methods

In order to more accurately evaluate the proposed MFFN, quantitative and qualitative comparisons with the state-of-the-art methods are conducted on the synthetic dataset and real-world dataset, respectively. The involved state-of-the-art methods include DCP [3], MSCNN [7], AOD-Net [10], DCPDN [8], GFN [9], GCA-Net [21], GDN [12], FFA [13], MSBDN [17] and MSTN [22].

The comparison results on the three datasets, are presented in Table 1. It can be seen that the proposed model has the highest PSNR and SSIM on the OTS and O-HAZE datasets, where the PSNR values are 0.48 dB and 0.49 dB higher than the sub-optimal models, respectively. On the NH-HAZE dataset, the SSIM of the proposed method is only lower than that of MSTN, but the PSNR is much higher than MSTN.

Table 1. Quantitative evaluation (PSNR/SSIM) with some state-of-the-art methods using there datasets

Methods	OTS	O-HAZE	NH-HAZE
DCP	19.13/0.815	16.78/0.653	10.57/0.520
MSCNN	19.48/0.839	17.56/0.650	13.42/0.489
AOD-Net	20.29/0.877	15.03/0.539	15.41/0.569
DCPDN	19.93/0.845	18.97/0.664	17.42/0.610
GFN Text follows	21.55/0.844	18.16/0.671	15.17/0.520
GCA-Net	28.13/0.945	16.28/0.645	17.58/0.594
GDN	30.86/0.982	18.92/0.672	15.23/0.560
FFA-Net	33.57/0.984	21.62/0.738	19.45/0.612
MSBDN	32.21/0.979	24.36/0.749	18.80/0.590
MSTN	32.61/0.981	-	18.42/**0.630**
Ours	**34.05/0.985**	**24.85/0.762**	**19.59**/0.615

Figure 6 and Fig. 7 present the qualitative comparison results. It can be seen that DCP has clear color distortion, AOD-Net and DCPDN have poor dehazing effects, some areas of FFA-Net are not completely dehazed, and MSBND has insufficient recovery of detailed features. The proposed model has the best performance, and it is efficient for color and details restoration, even in the case of hazy GT images. This proves that the proposed model has a strong dehazing ability, and is suitable for real outdoor environments.

3.4 Ablation Study

Table 2 presents the results of the ablation experiments, performed on the O-HAZE real-world dataset. Both the fusion of $sv(x)$ and $I^{dark}(x)$ are beneficial to the network. Even if MFAFM is not used, the two prior features can be directly added to the decoder, which can highly improve the network performance. This proves the effectiveness of the prior features when dealing with real-world datasets. Furthermore, MFAFM can well fuse the two prior features and further improve the performance of the model.

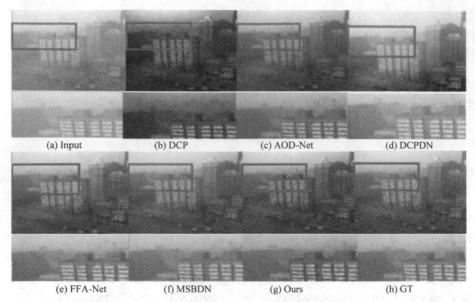

(a) Input   (b) DCP   (c) AOD-Net   (d) DCPDN

(e) FFA-Net   (f) MSBDN   (g) Ours   (h) GT

Fig. 6. Qualitative evaluation with some state-of-the-art methods using the OTS synthetic dataset. The bottom row is an enlarged version of the red box area on the top row. (Color figure online)

(a) Input   (b) DCP   (c) AOD-Net   (d) DCPDN   (e) FFA-Net   (f) MSBDN   (g) Ours   (h) GT

Fig. 7. Qualitative evaluation with some state-of-the-art methods on the O-HAZE and NH-HAZE real-world datasets.

In order to verify whether the fusion of the two prior features is beneficial for the model trained on the synthetic dataset to better transfer to the real scene, the model is trained for $2*10^5$ iterations on the RESIDE synthetic dataset, and then directly tested on the OTS and O-HAZE datasets. The obtained results are presented in Table 3, where the prior feature fusion uses MFAFM. The color attenuation prior is not applicable on the synthetic dataset. However, the two prior features are applicable to real scenes, which can improve the transfer ability of the model and allow it to directly transfer to real-world images. Finally, when using MFAFM for multi-feature fusion, only a very small number of parameters (0.07M) is increased, which verifies the operating efficiency of the model.

Table 2. Comparison of different types of networks on the O-HAZE

Baseline	✓	✓	✓	✓	✓
MFAFM		✓	✓		✓
sv(x)			✓	✓	✓
Idark(x)		✓		✓	✓
PSNR	24.57	24.73	24,75	24.79	**24.85**
SSIM	0.756	0.760	0.753	0.759	**0.762**

Table 3. Comparison of the transfer ability and parameters of different models

Methods	OTS	O-HAZE	Params
Baseline	30.98/0.975	19.39/0.677	8.49253M
+sv(x)	30.82/0.975	19.49/0.679	8.56696M
+$I^{dark}(x)$	**31.12/0.977**	19.47/0.680	8.56696M
+sv(x) + $I^{dark}(x)$	31.06/0.976	**19.61/0.682**	8.56699M

4 Conclusion

This paper proposed an end-to-end Multi-Feature Fusion Network for Single Image Dehazing (MFFN). By combining dark channel prior, color attenuation prior and deep learning, the neural network has a stronger dehazing capacity. A very simple and effective prior feature extraction method is first used. A Multi-Feature Selective Fusion Module (MFSFM) is then designed. It combines the advantages and discards the disadvantages of the two prior features, in order to perform feature enhancement. The experimental results on synthetic and real-world datasets have shown that the proposed MFFN achieved better results than those obtained by the state-of-the-art methods, which proves its effectiveness for real outdoor scenes.

References

1. Narasimhan, S.G., Nayar, S.K.: Vision and the atmosphere. Int. J. Comput. Vis. 48(3), 233–254 (2002)
2. Cantor, A.: Optics of the atmosphere–scattering by molecules and particles. IEEE J. Quantum Electron., 698–699 (1978)
3. He, K., Sun, J., Tang, X.: Single image haze removal using dark channel prior. IEEE Trans. Pattern Anal. Mach. Intell. 33(12), 2341–2353 (2011)
4. Liu, Q., Gao, X., He, L., Lu, W.: Single image dehazing with depth aware non-local total variation regularization. IEEE Trans. Image Process, 27, 5178–5191 (2018)
5. Fattal, R.: Dehazing using color-lines. ACM Trans. Graph. 34(1), Article no. 13 (2014)
6. Meng, G., Wang, Y., Duan, J., Xiang, S., Pan, C.: Efficient image dehazing with boundary constraint and contextual regularization. In: Proceeding IEEE International Conference Computer Vision, pp. 617–624 (2013)

7. Ren, W., Liu, S., Zhang, H., Pan, J., Cao, X., Yang, MH.: Single image dehazing via multi-scale convolutional neural networks. In: Leibe, B., Matas, J., Sebe, N., Welling, M. (eds.) ECCV 2016. LNCS, vol. 9906, pp. 154–169. Springer, Cham (2016). https://doi.org/10.1007/978-3-319-46475-6_10

8. Zhang, H., Patel, V.M.: Densely connected pyramid dehazing network. In: Proceeding IEEE Conference Computer Vision Pattern Recognition, pp. 3194–3203 (2018)

9. Ren, W. et al.: Gated fusion network for single image dehazing. In: Proceeding IEEE/CVF Conference Computer Vision Pattern Recognition, pp. 3253–3261 (2018)

10. Li, B., Peng, X., Wang, Z., Xu, J., Feng D.: AOD-Net: all-in-one dehazing network. In: Proceeding IEEE International Conference Computer Vision, pp. 4780–4788 (2017)

11. Qu, Y., Chen, Y., Huang, J., Xie, Y.: Enhanced Pix2pix dehazing network. In: Proceeding IEEE/CVF Conference Computer Vision Pattern Recognition, pp. 8152–8160 (2019)

12. Liu, X., Ma, Y., Shi, Z., Chen, J.: GridDehazeNet: attention-based multi-scale network for image dehazing. In: Proceeding IEEE International Conference Computer Vision, pp. 7313–7322 (2019)

13. Qin, X., Wang, Z., Bai, Y., Xie, X., Jia, H.: FFA-Net: feature fusion attention network for single image dehazing. In: Proceeding AAAI Conference Artificial Intelligence, pp. 11908–11915 (2020)

14. Luo, J., Bu, Q., Zhang, L., Feng, J.: Global feature fusion attention network for single image dehazing. In: IEEE International Conference on Multimedia & Expo Workshops, pp. 1–6 (2021)

15. Zhu, Q., Mai, J., Shao, L.: A fast single image haze removal algorithm using color attenuation prior. IEEE Trans. Image Process. **24**(11), 3522–3533 (2015)

16. Li, B., et al.: Benchmarking single-image dehazing and beyond. IEEE Trans. Image Process. **28**(1), 492–505 (2019)

17. Dong, H., Pan, J., Xiang, L., Hu, Z., Zhang, X.: Multi-scale boosted dehazing network with dense feature fusion. In: Proceeding IEEE/CVF Conference Computer Vision Pattern Recognition (2020)

18. Ancuti, C.O., Ancuti, C., De Vleeschouwer, C., Timofte, R.: O-HAZE: a dehazing benchmark with real hazy and haze-free outdoor images. In: Proceeding Conference Computer Vision Pattern Recognition Workshops, pp. 88–97 (2018)

19. Ancuti, C.O., Ancuti, C., Timofte, R.: NH-HAZE: an image dehazing benchmark with non-homogeneous hazy and haze-free images. In: Proceeding IEEE/CVF Conference Computer Vision Pattern Recognition (2020)

20. Ancuti, C.O., Ancuti, C., Vasluianu, F.-A., Timofte, R.: Ntire 2020 challenge on nonhomogeneous dehazing. In: Proceeding Conference Computer Vision Pattern Recognition Workshops (2020)

21. Chen, D., et al.: Gated context aggregation network for image dehazing and deraining. In: IEEE Winter Conference on Applications of Computer Vision, pp. 1375–1383 (2019)

22. Yi, Q., Li, J., Fang, F., Jiang, A., Zhang, G.: Efficient and accurate multi-scale topological network for single image dehazing. IEEE Trans. Multimedia (2021)

23. Li, L., Dong, Y., Ren, W., Pan, J., Gao, C., Sang, N.: Semi-supervised image dehazing. IEEE Trans. Image Process. **29**, 2766–2779 (2019)

24. Shao, Y., Li, L., Ren, W., Gao, C., Sang, N.: Domain adaptation for image dehazing. In: Proceeding IEEE/CVF Conference Computer Vision Pattern Recognition, pp. 2805–2814 (2020)

25. He, T., Zhang, Z., Zhang, H., Zhang, Z., Xie, J., Li, M.: Bag of tricks for image classification with convolutional neural networks. In: Proceeding IEEE/CVF Conference Computer Vision Pattern Recognition, pp. 558–567 (2019)

LAGAN: Landmark Aided Text to Face Sketch Generation

Wentao Chao, Liang Chang$^{(\boxtimes)}$, Fangfang Xi, and Fuqing Duan

Beijing Normal University, Beijing, China
{changliang,fqduan}@bnu.edu.cn, chaowentao@mail.bnu.edu.cn

Abstract. Face sketch is a concise representation of the human face, and it has a variety of applications in criminal investigation, biometrics, and social entertainment. It is well known that facial attribute is an underlying representation of the facial description. However, generating vivid face sketches, especially sketches with rich details, from given facial attributes text is still a challenging task as the text information is limited. Existing work synthetic face sketch is not realistic, especially the facial areas are not natural enough, even distorted. We aim to relieve the situation by introducing face prior knowledge, such as landmarks. This paper proposes a method, called LAGAN, that Landmark Aided Text to Face Sketch Generation. Specifically, we design a novel scale translation-invariant similarity loss based on the facial landmarks. It can measure the mutual similarity between real sketch and synthetic sketch and also measure the self similarity based on the symmetry of face attributes. Further to counter data deficiency, we construct a novel facial attribute text to sketch dataset called TextCUFSF with CUFSF face sketch dataset. Each sketch has 4 manual annotations. Qualitative and quantitative experiments demonstrate the effectiveness of our proposed method for sketch synthesis with attribute text. The code and data are available: https://github.com/chaowentao/LAGAN.

Keywords: Face sketch · Text to sketch · Generative adversarial nets

1 Introduction

Face sketches play an important role in forensic investigation and biometrics [23,33]. Face sketches drawn according to the witness' depictions provide an important reference for forensic investigation, especially when the face photos of the suspect are not available. However, sketching by well-trained and skilled artists is labor-intensive. So, it is desired to generate face sketches from face attribute depictions.

The existing face sketch synthesis [8,23,33,43,45] mostly focuses on generating face sketches based on photos. Wang *et al.* [32] give a comprehensive survey on face hallucination and sketch synthesis. Various photo-sketch synthesis methods have been proposed, including the traditional methods of subspace representation [27], sparse representation [2], and Markov random field [33]. Recent

© The Author(s), under exclusive license to Springer Nature Switzerland AG 2022
S. Yu et al. (Eds.): PRCV 2022, LNCS 13537, pp. 137–151, 2022.
https://doi.org/10.1007/978-3-031-18916-6_12

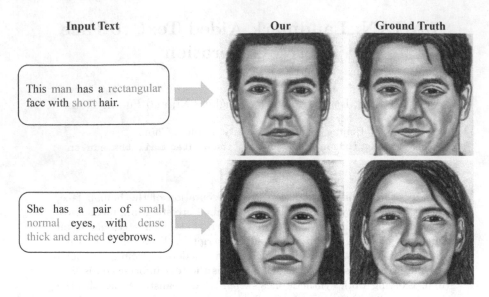

Input Text   **Our**   **Ground Truth**

This man has a rectangular face with short hair.

She has a pair of small normal eyes, with dense thick and arched eyebrows.

Fig. 1. Illustration of face sketches synthesis from face attribute text. From left to right: input text, face sketches with our LAGAN and Ground Truth.

work of face sketch synthesis is mainly built upon deep neural network or variable autoencoder (VAE) [9]. However, in a real scenario, even a single photo may not be available for sketch synthesis.

Recently, great progress has been made on synthesizing natural images form text [7,13,17,18,28,39,41,42]. These works generally use generate natural images with text descriptions, and can not meet the requirement of face sketch synthesis with rich facial features, because these methods overlook the key details of face structure and textures. The main difficulties of face sketch synthesis from attribute text lie in two aspects: 1) Face sketch contains rich detail information, and it is necessary to recover more facial details in the face sketch synthesis task from attribute text compared to previous work on synthesizing natural images from the text; 2) No text-to-face sketch database is available. Due to the ambiguity and diversity of sketches, an important component of the database, i.e. the attributes for sketches, is not easy to collect; Moreover, existing sketch databases are relatively smaller compared with the off-the-shelf image and graph databases, such as ImageNet [4] and ShapeNet [1].

Face landmarks are important feature points of each part of the face, usually contour points and corners, including eyebrows, eyes, nose, mouth, face contour. Considering geometric constraints inherent in human faces, we propose a method that landmark aided text to face sketch generation, named LAGAN. In order to measure the similarity of landmarks, we propose a new similarity loss, which is invariant of scale and translation. Then, the mutual similarity of landmark between real sketch and the synthetic sketch is weighed by similarity loss. Considering the symmetry of the face, we also measure the self similarity of landmark between synthetic sketch and synthetic sketch flipped horizontally. In order to address the data deficiency issue, we built a text-to-sketch dataset named TextCUFSF. It contains 1,139 sketches, and then we annotate manually each sketch with 4 facial attribute text. Benefiting from our dataset, our LAGAN can successfully generate face sketches with rich details. Some examples are shown in Fig. 1.

Our contribution lies in the following aspects: 1) We propose the text to face sketch generation method aided by facial landmarks. Given an attribute text, our method can generate a high-quality sketch corresponding to the attribute text; 2) We propose a novel similarity loss for facial landmarks, which is used to measure the mutual similarity and self similarity; 3) We construct a new facial attribute text to the sketch dataset named TextCUFSF based on the CUFSF face sketch dataset.

2 Related Work

Attribute to Image Synthesis. Attribute-to-image aims to generate synthetic images based on attribute descriptions. Attribute2Image [37] develops a layered generative model with disentangled latent variables, which conditioned image generation from visual attributes using VAE. Attribute2Sketch2Face [5], which is based on a combination of a deep conditional variational autoencoder and generative adversarial networks. Han *et al.* [8] present a deep multi-task learning approach to jointly estimate multiple heterogeneous attributes from a single face image.

Text to Natural Image Synthesis. Prior art methods to generate images using text include [7,13,17,18,28,41,42]. These methods generate images using text as input. Reed *et al.* [17] used conditional GAN to generate low-resolution natural images of 64 × 64 pixels with a text description. The subsequent work GAWWN [18] can generate higher resolution images of 128 × 128 pixels with additional annotations, such as the bounding box or part of the key points. StackGAN [42] is mostly related to our problem, which uses two stacked GAN networks to get the high-resolution natural images of 256 × 256 pixels using text as input. StackGAN++ [41] exploits multiple generators and discriminators of a tree structure. Yuan *et al.* [39] propose symmetrical distillation networks to address the problem of heterogeneous and homogeneous gaps in the text-to-image synthesis task. Gorti *et al.* [7] introduce a text-to-image translation GAN and image-to-text translation GAN by enforcing cycle consistency. AttnGAN [36] designs the attention module to fusing the feature of text and images. ControlGAN [12] further leverages the spatial and channel-wise attention module to generate better images. These methods [12,36,41,42] area cascaded in multiple stages to gradually improve the resolution of synthetic images, while some recent methods [13,28] can directly synthesize the high-resolution images. DF-GAN [28] designs the new deep fusion block to fuse the information of text and image. SSA-GAN [13] introduces the semantic mask to guide the process of text and image. Compared to text to natural image synthesis, face sketch generation from attribute text is more challenging due to the fact that more appearance details are in face sketches. These methods use different GAN models to synthesize natural images from text and overlook the structured priors of the output. Compared to text to natural image synthesis, face sketch generation from attribute text is more challenging due to the key details of face structure and texture.

Face Photo-to-Sketch and Sketch-to-Photo Synthesis. These methods aim to synthesize face sketches using face photos, which is called "Face photo-sketch synthesis" [30,31,33]. Wang *et al.* [32] gives a comprehensive survey on face hallucination and sketch synthesis. Various photo-sketch synthesis methods have been proposed, including the traditional methods of subspace representation [27], sparse representation [2], and Markov random field [33]. Recent work of face sketch synthesis is mainly built upon a deep neural network or variable autoencoder (VAE) [9]. Concerning photo synthesis from a given sketch, Sangkloy *et al.* [20] propose a deep adversarial image synthesis architecture, named Scribbler. It is conditioned on sketched boundaries and sparse color strokes to generate realistic photos, including face photos. The feed-forward architecture is fast and interactive. Wang *et al.* [43] propose a photo-face sketch synthesis framework consisting of a coarse stage and a refine stage. In the coarse stage, a coarse face sketch is synthesized. In the refine stage, a probabilistic graphic model starts by erasing the noise of the coarse synthesized sketches and then obtains the details on the facial components. DualGAN [38] enables both sketch-to-photo and photo-to-sketch generation from unlabeled data. Compared to photo-to-sketch and sketch-to-photo synthesis, attribute text to sketch synthesis addressed in this work is more challenging due to the large domain difference between a sketch and attribute text.

Generative Adversarial Networks and its Applications. Generative Adversarial Networks (GAN) [6] shows promising performance for generating photo-realistic images. Various GANs have been proposed to manipulate face images. On face image editing, Choi *et al.* [3] propose StarGAN, which performs image-to-image conversion on multiple domains by utilizing a mask vector method to control all available domain labels and is effective in facial attribute transfer as well as facial expression synthesis tasks. Shen *et al.* [21] address the problem of face attribute manipulation by modifying a face image according to a given attribute value. On face image synthesis, M-AAE [24] combines the VAE and GAN to generate photo-realistic images. Face recognition loss, cycle consistency loss, and facial mask loss are integrated with the network. G2-GAN [22] employs facial landmarks as a controllable condition to guide facial texture synthesis under specific expressions.

In this work, we propose a method to generate face sketches with face attribute text. Considering the geometry of face, we also define the mutual similarity and self similarity based on the face landmarks.

3   TextCUFSF Dataset

Sketch Dataset. We build our text-sketch dataset named TextCUFSF based the CUFSF [33,44] dataset. CUFSF includes 1,139 photos from the FERET dataset and detailed face sketches drawn by an artist. The main reason that we use CUFSF for annotation is that CUFSF is one of the largest public sketch datasets with a wide range. We selected 1,000 pairs of sketches as train sets and the rest as test sets. We align the face sketches using face landmarks such as eye centers and nose points, which are extracted with the SDM method [35].

Face Attributes. We design our facial attribute set inspired by a seminal criminal appearance study [10,29]. In criminal appearance studies, facial appearance characteristics can be divided into eleven categories, namely hairstyle, head shape, wrinkles, eyebrows, eyes, nose, ears, mouth, beard, hat, and other features. We choose eight key features from them and add gender, and glasses features (refer to Table 1 for details). We do not take features such as expressions and wrinkles into consideration, since they are difficult to accurately characterize the face sketches. Then, we choose representative words for each feature based on the theory in criminal appearance studies.

Table 1. Face attribute description.

Face components	Attribute description
Face	Diamond, heart, triangle, round, inverted triangle, oval, square, rectangular
Eyebrows	Dense, sparse, thick, thin, flat, arched, up, down
Eyes	Big, normal, short, wide, narrow
Hair	Long, medium, short
Nose	Big, medium, small
Mouth	Thick, thin, wide, narrow
Ears	Small, normal, big
Glasses	Has, hasn't
Beard	Has, hasn't
Gender	Man, woman

Specifically, the face has eight types. The eyebrow is characterized according to density, thickness and shape. The nose is characterized according to the height and the size of the nostrils. The lip is characterized in terms of the thickness and width. The ear is represented by the size. Beard and glasses are taken into account as well.

Face Attribute Text Annotation. We invite 50 annotators to annotate the 1,139 sketches in the CUSFS dataset. Each sketch has 4 captions, as shown in Fig. 2. In order to enforce the quality of data annotation, we prepare well-annotated attribute sketch pairs for the qualification tests. The qualification tests are pre-conducted for every annotator using three different sketches, and those who pass the tests are qualified for the annotation. For the annotated results, we then manually review and correct them to ensure the annotation accuracy.

This man has a rectangular face with medium hair.
He has a pair of small normal eyes,with dense thick and flat eyebrows.
His mouth is thick and narrow, with a big long nose and his ears are small.
He hasn't glasses and hasn't beard.

Fig. 2. Examples of face sketches and face attribute text. From left to right: face attribute text, faces sketches drawn by artists.

4   Method

In this section, we propose the LAGAN network to generate the sketch from our TextCUFSF dataset. Our method can synthesize the 256 × 256 high-resolution face sketches based on the given attribute text. Firstly, we introduce the pipeline of our LAGAN. Then, the loss functions used are described. Finally, we present the experimental implementation details.

4.1   Network Structure

Figure 3(a) shows the structure of our LAGAN. Inspired by AttnGAN [36], we adopt a similar multi-stage mode to synthesize face sketches. For the sake of presentation, some intermediate results are not presented. We first convert the input facial attribute text to text embedding through a text encoder, then use a face sketch synthesis model with various loss functions for sketch synthesis. Finally, we use a discriminator to distinguish between true and false synthetic sketches and true and false matches between attribute text and sketches.

Generator. We can encode the attribute text t into a sentence embedding s and word embedding w by text encoder, which is a pre-trained bidirectional LSTM. The sentence embedding s is augmented by Conditioning augmentation (CA) [42] module. Augmented sentence embedding s and random noise (e.g. Gaussian Distribution) z are concatenated and through FC layers as input to the attention module [12]. Specifically, the function of the attention module calculates the spatial and channel-wise correlation between image features and word embedding. After three attention modules, we can obtain the final synthesized face sketches $\hat{I}$ of 256 × 256 pixels.

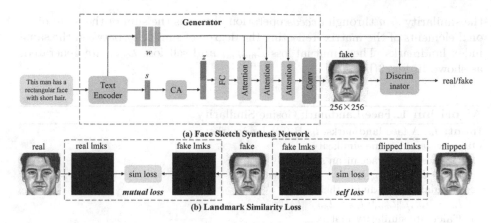

Fig. 3. The pipeline of our LAGAN. (a) Face Sketch Synthesis Network. It consists of a generator and a discriminator. The input of the generator is the facial attribute text and random Gaussian noises, the output is the synthesized face sketches of 256×256. The function of the discriminator is used in both distinguishing between the real and false synthesized sketch as well as the true and false matching of attribute text and sketch. (b) Landmark Similarity Loss. We show schematic diagrams of mutual loss and self Loss.

Discriminator. The input of the discriminator has two parts that text embedding and face sketches. Further, we extract the image feature $\hat{\eta}$ of the synthesized face sketch $\hat{I}$ by GoogleNet-based [25] image encoder. The discriminator is designed to compute the word-level text-sketch correlation between word embedding w and image feature $\hat{\eta}$, and also to distinguish the quality of synthetic sketches, real or false.

4.2 Loss Functions

In this section, we introduce landmark similarity loss and the GAN loss, then summarize the total generator loss and discriminator loss.

Landmark Similarity Loss. We find previous methods [12,13,28,36,42] are mainly text-to-image task, such as generate birds and flowers. Such objects' structures compared with face sketches are simpler and the information in the text is limited. When we apply these methods in face sketches, synthesized results are not satisfactory, which are not natural and some facial areas are not reasonable, even distorted. So we aim to add face prior knowledge to relieve these problems, such as facing landmark constrain. Based on Riemannian distance, we design a novel invariant landmark similarity loss. The specific operation process is shown in Algorithm 1. Specifically, the algorithm input are two lists of 2D face landmarks, e.g. l_a and l_b. The main steps of the algorithm are to subtract l_{ma}, l_{mb} and regularize the mean values of each landmark l_{na}, l_{nb}, then generate the similarity matrix m_{ab}, calculate the trace of the matrix t_{ab}, and finally obtain the similarity sim through $arccos$ operation. Trace is the sum of the main diagonal elements of the matrix, reflecting the degree of similarity between the same index landmarks. Then, mutual loss $\mathcal{L}_{mutual}$ and self loss $\mathcal{L}_{self}$ are generated, as shown in Fig. 3(b).

Algorithm 1. Face Landmark Cosine Similarity

Input: l_a: A face landmarks; l_b: B face landmarks;
Output: sim: cosine similarity;
 1: De-mean, subtract mean separately
    $l_{ma} = l_a - mean(l_a)$; $l_{mb} = l_b - mean(l_b)$;
 2: Normalization, divide their norm
    $l_{na} = l_{ma}/\|l_{ma}\|$; $l_{nb} = l_{mb}/\|l_{mb}\|$;
 3: Calculate similarity matrix
    $m_{ab} = l_{na}^T \times l_{nb}$;
 4: Calculate absolute value of matrix trace
    $t_{ab} = |trace(m_{ab})|$;
 5: Calculate cosine similarity
    $sim = 1 - arccos(min(t_{ab}, 1))$;

Mutual Loss. In order to obtain realistic facial areas corresponding to the given attribute text, the mutual loss $\mathcal{L}_{mutual}$ is proposed to calculate the similarity between the landmarks of real sketches I and synthesized face sketches $\hat{I}$. We use the portion of landmarks, which show the area of attribute text, e.g. face, eyes, or mouth. The loss function of $\mathcal{L}_{mutual}$ is as follows:

$$\mathcal{L}_{mutual} = similarity\left(I, \hat{I}\right) \tag{1}$$

Self Loss. We also find the symmetry of face prior knowledge. Specifically, areas of the left face attribute are similar to the right. Therefore, self loss $\mathcal{L}_{self}$ is used to calculate the similarity synthesized sketches $\hat{I}$ and corresponding flipped synthesized sketches $\hat{I}_{flip}$. add symmetry constraints. When calculating self loss, all facial landmarks are considered. The loss $\mathcal{L}_{self}$ can be defined as follows:

$$\mathcal{L}_{self} = similarity\left(I, \hat{I}_{flip}\right) \tag{2}$$

GAN Loss Our method is based on conditional generative adversarial network (CGAN) [15], which learns a mapping $y = G(c, z)$ from input c and random noise vector z to y. The goal of discriminator D is to correctly distinguish between the real sketches and the synthesized sketches by generator G, while the goal of generator G is to generate synthesized sketches that can fool the discriminator D. The objective function of GAN in this work is:

$$\min_G \max_D V(D, G) = \mathbb{E}_{I \sim p_{data}}[D(I, t)] + \mathbb{E}_{z \sim p_z}[1 - D(G(z, t), t)] \tag{3}$$

where I is a real face sketch from the true data distribution p_{data}, z is a noise vector sampled from distribution p_z, and t is a given facial attribute text.

The loss function of D is as follows:

$$\mathcal{L}_{GAN}(D) = \mathbb{E}_{I \sim p_{data}}[D(I, t)] + \mathbb{E}_{z \sim p_z}[1 - D(G(z, t), t)] \qquad (4)$$

The loss function of G is as follows:

$$\mathcal{L}_{GAN}(G) = \mathbb{E}_{z \sim p_z}[1 - D(G(z, t), t)] \qquad (5)$$

Generator Loss. Inspired by these work [12,36], we also use perceptual loss and DAMSM loss. So the total loss of the generator $\mathcal{L}_G$ contains GAN loss, mutual loss, self loss, perceptual loss and DAMSM loss, which is defined as the follows:

$$\mathcal{L}_G = \mathcal{L}_{GAN}(G) + \lambda_1 \mathcal{L}_{DAMSM} + \lambda_2 \mathcal{L}_{per} + \lambda_3 \mathcal{L}_{mutual} + \lambda_4 \mathcal{L}_{self} \qquad (6)$$

Discriminator Loss. The objective function of discriminators $\mathcal{L}_D$ is mainly the GAN loss defined as Eq. (4).

$$\mathcal{L}_D = \mathcal{L}_{GAN}(D) \qquad (7)$$

4.3   Implementation Details

The structure of the model is shown in Fig. 3. Our experiments are performed on our TextCUFSF dataset, with 1,000 pairs of text sketches for training and 100 pairs for testing. We use a horizontal flip for data augmentation. The dimension of the encoded text attribute is 100. In our experiment, hyperparameters are set as: $\lambda_1 = 5$, $\lambda_1 = 1$, $\lambda_3 = 100$ and $\lambda_4 = 100$. Dlib module is employed to extract 68 facial landmarks. Our LAGAN is implemented by Pytorch and trained with a learning rate of 0.002. We set 600 epochs for training, with a batchsize of 8. The generator and discriminator have trained alternatively. The training time is about 15 h on a 1080 Ti GPU.

5   Experiments

In order to evaluate our method, we conduct comparison experiments with two related state-of-the-art methods and ablation study on the TextCUFSF dataset.

5.1   Evaluation Metrics

In this work, we mainly use two standard measures, i.e. FID (Fréchet Inception Distance) [14] and SSIM (Structure Similarity Index Measure) [34] for performance evaluations.

FID. FID (Fréchet Inception Distance) [14] can capture the similarity of generated images to real ones, it has better performance than the Inception Score [19].

It is consistent with human visual system, and is often used to evaluate the quality of results from GAN [11,16,40]. FID is calculated by the Fréchet distance between two Gaussian's fitted to the feature representations of the Inception network.

SSIM. SSIM (Structure Similarity Index Measure) [34] indicates the local structural similarity between the image segmentation result and the reference image. It is widely used to evaluate the similarities between synthesized face sketches and real face sketches [26].

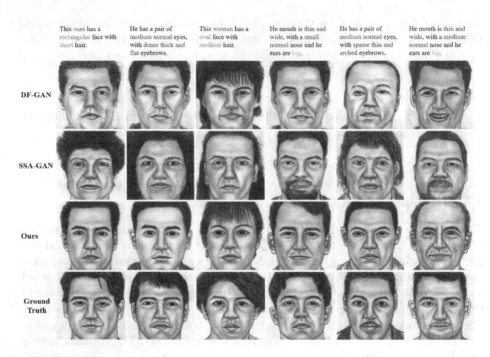

Fig. 4. Example of synthesized face sketches by DF-GAN [28], SSA-GAN [13], our method given face attribute description text and ground truth. The resolution of face sketches is 256 × 256.

5.2 Comparison with the State-of-the-Art Methods

We compare our results with the state-of-the-art methods of DF-GAN [28] and SSA-GAN [13] on our TextCUFSF dataset. As shown in Fig. 4, all the three models can produce the face sketches of 256 × 256 pixels. In terms of quality, some of the results of DF-GAN are ambiguous and coarse, such as the areas of face shape, ears, and eyes on the first, third, and fifth sketches in Fig. 4, respectively. The quality of sketches generated by SSA-GAN is better, while some attributes are not complete, such as the beard area. Our method can generate high-resolution sketches with complete facial areas. Considering the consistency, SSA-GAN is not well consistent with the input attribute text, such as gender attribute. DF-GAN is more consistent with the input attribute text than SSA-GAN, while some attributes are of low quality. Our method can achieve the best synthesized sketches that are more consistent and high-quality with the input attribute text.

In addition to two standard evaluation indicators, we also compare the MS (Mutual Similarity) and SS (Self Similarity) to validate the similarity of face landmarks. Table 2 illustrates the quantitative evaluations. Our LAGAN performs best in all evaluation metrics. The FID of our method is 29.60, which is 19.16 higher than DF-GAN, and 15.83 higher than SSA-GAN. The PSNR and MSSIM of our method are 13.01% and 32.81% higher than StackGAN, respectively. Our method also achieved 0.03–0.05 improvement in SSIM index compared with two other methods. We also observe that our method can achieve best result when calculating the similarity of face landmarks.

Table 2. Quantitative comparison of our LAGAN with state-of-the-art methods, including FID, SSIM, MS (Mutual Similarity), SS (Self Similarity) , MR (Match Rank) and QR (Quality Rank).

Method	FID↓	SSIM ↑	MS ↑	SS ↑	MR ↓	QR ↓
DF-GAN [28]	48.76	0.3005	0.88	0.88	2.80	2.78
SSA-GAN [13]	45.43	0.2745	0.89	0.91	1.98	1.86
Ours	**29.60**	**0.3311**	**0.93**	**0.94**	**1.22**	**1.36**

User Study. Although the above metrics correlate well with human perception on visual quality [19], it cannot be used to measure the matching of sketch with attribute text and the quality of sketch. We design user study for matching and quality evaluations. The matching evaluation aims to rank the consistence between the synthesized sketch and input attribute text, 1 represents the highest priority, and 3 represents the lowest priority. The quality evaluation is similar to the matching evaluation except without providing the text description. We randomly invited 48 people to perform user study of matching and quality evaluations. Table 2 shows the MR (Match Rank) and QR (Quality Rank) results, our method gets the highest priority. The consistency and quality of the sketch synthesized by our method are more recognized by people.

Ablation Study. Firstly, We analyze the effect of face landmark similarity on the performance of sketch synthesis. The quantitative evaluation for our LAGAN with different combinations of loss functions are shown in Table 3. We observe that our model combined with mutual loss and self loss can get the lowest value of FID and comparable results of SSIM. Then, we carry out detailed experiments to

Table 3. Comparison using different combinations of loss functions and different hyper-parameters with the our LAGAN.

Mutual loss	Self loss	FID↓	SSIM ↑
		34.13	0.3108
	✓	36.78	**0.3321**
✓		35.97	0.3315
✓	✓	**29.60**	0.3311
$\lambda_3 = 1$	$\lambda_4 = 1$	31.26	0.3293
$\lambda_3 = 10$	$\lambda_4 = 10$	38.57	0.3356
$\lambda_3 = 10$	$\lambda_4 = 100$	33.79	0.3262
$\lambda_3 = 100$	$\lambda_4 = 10$	32.22	**0.3372**
$\lambda_3 = 100$	$\lambda_4 = 100$	**29.60**	0.3311
$\lambda_3 = 300$	$\lambda_4 = 300$	32.26	0.3365
$\lambda_3 = 1000$	$\lambda_4 = 1000$	33.85	0.3363

find the optimal hyper-parameters of mutual loss and self loss. When $\lambda_3 = 100$ and $\lambda_4 = 100$, our LAGAN can achieve better performance. Finally, we also compare the results of DF-GAN and SSA-GAN with our face landmark similarity loss. Table 4 shows that SSIM have been improved in different models using our loss, which validate the generalization ability of our loss.

Table 4. The performance of face landmark similarity loss on different models

Model	Mutual loss	Self loss	SSIM↑
DF-GAN [28]			0.3005
	✓	✓	**0.3240**(+0.02)
SSA-GAN [13]			0.2745
	✓	✓	**0.2855**(+0.01)
LAGAN			0.3108
	✓	✓	**0.3311**(+0.02)

6   Conclusion

In this work, we provide a LAGAN method to generate face sketches based on attribute text. We also design a novel landmark similarity loss, which is invariant of scale and translation. Based on the similarity loss, we further measure the mutual similarity and self similarity. We construct the first attribute text to face sketch dataset, called TextCUFSF. Qualitative and quantitative experiments show that our method can obtain high-quality synthesized face sketches from attribute text. Our method also has some limitations regarding beard and glasses attributes, we analyze the reason due to the training samples of the related attributes are too few. By collecting more samples, this situation can be alleviated. In the future, we intend to support text-based sketch editing for interactive, dynamic synthesis of high-quality sketches to meet artist expectations.

Acknowledgement. This work was supported by the National Key Research and Development Program of China under grant No. 2019YFC1521104, Natural Science Foundation of China (61772050, 62172247).

References

1. Chang, A.X., et al.: ShapeNet: an information-rich 3D model repository. arXiv preprint arXiv:1512.03012 (2015)
2. Chang, L., Zhou, M., Han, Y., Deng, X.: Face sketch synthesis via sparse representation. In: ICPR, pp. 2146–2149 (2010)
3. Choi, Y., Choi, M., Kim, M., Ha, J.W., Kim, S., Choo, J.: StarGAN: unified generative adversarial networks for multi-domain image-to-image translation. In: CVPR, pp. 8789–8797 (2018)
4. Deng, J., Dong, W., Socher, R., Li, L.J., Li, K., Fei-Fei, L.: ImageNet: a large-scale hierarchical image database. In: CVPR, pp. 248–255 (2009)
5. Di, X., Patel, V.M.: Face synthesis from visual attributes via sketch using conditional vaes and gans. arXiv preprint arXiv:1801.00077 (2017)
6. Goodfellow, I.J., et al.: Generative adversarial nets. In: NeurIPS, pp. 2672–2680 (2014)
7. Gorti, S.K., Ma, J.: Text-to-image-to-text translation using cycle consistent adversarial networks. arXiv preprint arXiv:1808.04538 (2018)
8. Han, H., Jain, A.K., Wang, F., Shan, S., Chen, X.: Heterogeneous face attribute estimation: a deep multi-task learning approach. TPAMI **40**(11), 2597–2609 (2017)
9. Kingma, D.P., Welling, M.: Auto-encoding variational bayes. arXiv preprint arXiv:1312.6114 (2013)
10. Klare, B.F., Klum, S., Klontz, J.C., Taborsky, E., Akgul, T., Jain, A.K.: Suspect identification based on descriptive facial attributes. In: IJCB, pp. 1–8 (2014)
11. Kurach, K., Lucic, M., Zhai, X., Michalski, M., Gelly, S.: The GAN landscape: losses, architectures, regularization, and normalization (2018). CoRR abs/1807.04720
12. Li, B., Qi, X., Lukasiewicz, T., Torr, P.H.: Controllable text-to-image generation. In: NeurIPS, pp. 2065–2075 (2019)
13. Liao, W., Hu, K., Yang, M.Y., Rosenhahn, B.: Text to image generation with semantic-spatial aware GAN. arXiv preprint arXiv:2104.00567 (2021)
14. Lucic, M., Kurach, K., Michalski, M., Gelly, S., Bousquet, O.: Are gans created equal? a large-scale study. arXiv preprint arXiv:1711.10337 (2017)
15. Mirza, M., Osindero, S.: Conditional generative adversarial nets. arXiv preprint arXiv:1411.1784 (2014)
16. Miyato, T., Kataoka, T., Koyama, M., Yoshida, Y.: Spectral normalization for generative adversarial networks. arXiv preprint arXiv:1802.05957 (2018)
17. Reed, S., Akata, Z., Yan, X., Logeswaran, L., Schiele, B., Lee, H.: Generative adversarial text to image synthesis. In: ICML, pp. 1060–1069 (2016)

18. Reed, S.E., Akata, Z., Mohan, S., Tenka, S., Schiele, B., Lee, H.: Learning what and where to draw. In: NeurIPS, pp. 217–225 (2016)
19. Salimans, T., Goodfellow, I., Zaremba, W., Cheung, V., Radford, A., Chen, X.: Improved techniques for training GANs. In: NeurIPS, pp. 2234–2242 (2016)
20. Sangkloy, P., Lu, J., Fang, C., Yu, F., Hays, J.: Scribbler: controlling deep image synthesis with sketch and color. In: CVPR, pp. 6836–6845 (2017)
21. Shen, W., Liu, R.: Learning residual images for face attribute manipulation. In: CVPR, pp. 1225–1233 (2017)
22. Song, L., Lu, Z., He, R., Sun, Z., Tan, T.: Geometry guided adversarial facial expression synthesis. arXiv preprint arXiv:1712.03474 (2017)
23. Song, Y., Bao, L., Yang, Q., Yang, M.-H.: Real-time exemplar-based face sketch synthesis. In: Fleet, D., Pajdla, T., Schiele, B., Tuytelaars, T. (eds.) ECCV 2014. LNCS, vol. 8694, pp. 800–813. Springer, Cham (2014). https://doi.org/10.1007/978-3-319-10599-4_51
24. Sun, R., Huang, C., Shi, J., Ma, L.: Mask-aware photorealistic face attribute manipulation. arXiv preprint arXiv:1804.08882 (2018)
25. Szegedy, C., et al.: Going deeper with convolutions. In: CVPR, pp. 1–9 (2015)
26. Tan, Y., Tang, L., Wang, X.: An improved criminisi inpainting algorithm based on sketch image. J. Comput. Theor. Nanosci. **14**(8), 3851–3860 (2017)
27. Tang, X., Wang, X.: Face sketch recognition. TCSVT **14**(1), 50–57 (2004)
28. Tao, M., et al.: DF-GAN: a simple and effective baseline for text-to-image synthesis. arXiv preprint arXiv:2008.05865 (2020)
29. Tome, P., Vera-Rodriguez, R., Fierrez, J., Ortega-Garcia, J.: Facial soft biometric features for forensic face recognition. Forensic Sci. Int. **257**, 271–284 (2015)
30. Wang, N., Gao, X., Sun, L., Li, J.: Bayesian face sketch synthesis. TIP **26**(3), 1264–1274 (2017)
31. Wang, N., Li, J., Sun, L., Song, B., Gao, X.: Training-free synthesized face sketch recognition using image quality assessment metrics. arXiv preprint arXiv:1603.07823 (2016)
32. Wang, N., Tao, D., Gao, X., Li, X., Li, J.: A comprehensive survey to face hallucination. IJCV **106**(1), 9–30 (2014)
33. Wang, X., Tang, X.: Face photo-sketch synthesis and recognition. TPAMI **31**(11), 1955–1967 (2008)
34. Wang, Z., Bovik, A.C., Sheikh, H.R., Simoncelli, E.P.: Image quality assessment: from error visibility to structural similarity. TIP **13**(4), 600–612 (2004)
35. Xiong, X., Torre, F.D.L.: Supervised descent method and its applications to face alignment. In: CVPR, pp. 532–539 (2013)
36. Xu, T., et al.: Attngan: fine-grained text to image generation with attentional generative adversarial networks. In: CVPR, pp. 1316–1324 (2018)
37. Yan, X., Yang, J., Sohn, K., Lee, H.: Attribute2Image: conditional image generation from visual attributes. In: Leibe, B., Matas, J., Sebe, N., Welling, M. (eds.) ECCV 2016. LNCS, vol. 9908, pp. 776–791. Springer, Cham (2016). https://doi.org/10.1007/978-3-319-46493-0_47
38. Yi, Z., Zhang, H., Tan, P., Gong, M.: Dualgan: unsupervised dual learning for image-to-image translation. In: ICCV, pp. 2868–2876 (2017)
39. Yuan, M., Peng, Y.: Text-to-image synthesis via symmetrical distillation networks. arXiv preprint arXiv:1808.06801 (2018)
40. Zhang, H., Goodfellow, I., Metaxas, D., Odena, A.: Self-attention generative adversarial networks. In: ICML, pp. 7354–7363. PMLR (2019)
41. Zhang, H., et al.: StackGAN++: realistic image synthesis with stacked generative adversarial networks. arXiv preprint arXiv:1710.10916 (2017)

42. Zhang, H., et al.: StackGAN: text to photo-realistic image synthesis with stacked generative adversarial networks. In: ICCV, pp. 5907–5915 (2017)
43. Zhang, M., Wang, N., Li, Y., Wang, R., Gao, X.: Face sketch synthesis from coarse to fine. In: AAAI, pp. 7558–7565 (2018)
44. Zhang, W., Wang, X., Tang, X.: Coupled information-theoretic encoding for face photo-sketch recognition. In: CVPR, pp. 513–520. IEEE (2011)
45. Zou, C., et al.: SketchyScene: richly-annotated scene sketches. In: Ferrari, V., Hebert, M., Sminchisescu, C., Weiss, Y. (eds.) ECCV 2018. LNCS, vol. 11219, pp. 438–454. Springer, Cham (2018). https://doi.org/10.1007/978-3-030-01267-0_26

DMF-CL: Dense Multi-scale Feature Contrastive Learning for Semantic Segmentation of Remote-Sensing Images

Mengxing Song[1], Bicao Li[1,2(✉)], Pingjun Wei[1], Zhuhong Shao[3], Jing Wang[1], and Jie Huang[1]

[1] School of Electronic and Information Engineering, Zhongyuan University of Technology, Zhengzhou 450007, China
lbc@zut.edu.cn
[2] School of Computer and Artificial Intelligence, Zhengzhou University, Zhengzhou 450001, China
[3] College of Information Engineering, Capital Normal University, Beijing 100048, China

Abstract. Recently, many segmentation methods based on supervised deep learning have been widely used in remote sensing images. However, these approaches often require a large number of labeled samples, which is difficult to obtain them for remote sensing images. Self-supervision is a new learning paradigm, and can solve the problem of lack of labeled samples. In this method, a large number of unlabeled samples are employed for pre-training, and then a few of labeled samples are leveraged for downstream tasks. Contrast learning is a typical self-supervised learning method. Inspired, we propose a Dense Multi-scale Feature Contrastive Learning Network (DMF-CLNet), which is divided into global and local feature extraction parts. Firstly, in the global part, instead of traditional ASPP, DenseASPP can obtain more context information of remote sensing images in a dense way without increasing parameters. Secondly, in the global and local parts, Coordinate Attention (CA) modules are introduced respectively to improve the overall performance of the segmentation model. Thirdly, in the global and local parts, the perceptual loss is calculated to extract deeper features. Two remote sensing image segmentation datasets are evaluated. The experimental results show that our model is superior to the current self-supervised contrastive learning methods and ImageNet pre-training techniques.

Keywords: Coordinate attention · Contrast learning · DenseASPP · Perceptual loss

1 Introduction

With the rapid development of science and technology, it is easy to acquire remote sensing images. Remote sensing images are extensively used in numerous fields, such as urban planning [1], environmental protection and other fields [2], and extracting information from remote sensing images is the basic task of these applications. Semantic segmentation of images is a pixel-level image analysis technology [3], and it is also one popular research direction in the field of remote sensing images [4]. At present, the semantic segmentation methods of remote sensing images are mainly divided into two categories. One is the traditional image segmentation method based on the handcrafted features, and the other is the image segmentation method based on the deep learning method.

Traditional segmentation methods of remote sensing images are mostly machine learning methods based on handcrafted features [5], such as support vector machines [6], random forests [7], and artificial neural networks [8]. However, since AlexNet [9] won the ILSVR competition, deep learning methods have gradually become well known. Because deep learning can obtain the deep features of the images, so it is widely used in computer vision task. Image segmentation is one of the computer vision tasks. Because the supervised semantic segmentation methods of deep learning depend on lots of pixel level labeled images [10], and obtaining the pixel level labeled images is difficult, the supervised segmentation methods of remote sensing images are more expensive.

Recently, remote sensing image segmentation based on self-supervised learning methods has attracted more and more attention [11]. Firstly, a large number of unmarked datasets are used to obtain their own supervision information, and the constructed super-vision information is utilized for network training. After that, it is transferred to down-stream tasks (such as image classification, etc.), which can be perfectly comparable to the effect of supervised learning model. Among them, contrastive learning is a new learning paradigm of self-supervised learning.

Due to the continuous change of time and space, the content of remote sensing images is different [12]. Remote-sensing images not only cover a large area, but also are high-resolution images. Therefore, the general image segmentation network is not suitable to remote sensing images. In order to solve the problem, firstly, in the pre-training stage, data enhancement methods are used to enhance the consistency of the image. Secondly, inspired by GLCNet network [13], this paper proposes a new contrastive learning method which is exploited to train a large number of unmarked remote sensing images by introducing DenseASPP [14] module and coordinated attention block [15], the region of interest can be captured without increasing the size of the model, and the feature map covering a wide range can be generated and covered in a dense manner. Finally, the perceptual loss [16] function is added in the training stage to help the network extract deeper features and improve the segmentation accuracy. The specific contributions are as follows:

1. This paper proposes a new contrastive learning network by introducing DenseASPP. DenseASPP can obtain more context information of remote sensing images in a dense way without increasing parameters.
2. A coordinated attention block is added in the global and local modules to encode the channel relationship and long-term dependence.
3. In the training process, the feature maps are fed into the vgg19 network to calculate the perception loss. Therefore, deeper semantic information of remote sensing images can be obtained.

2 Methodology

2.1 Networks Architecture

In this section, DenseASPP is firstly employed to generate the feature map with wider coverage and obtain more plentiful information; secondly, the coordination attention module can accurately capture the region of interest. The overall network structure is shown in Fig. 1. Where, CABlock represents coordinate attention block, patch 1 and patch 2 are local samples of the image, respectively. The two parts are described as follows, respectively.

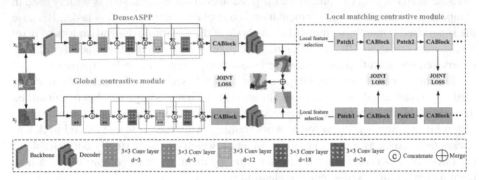

Fig. 1. Overall framework of the network.

DenseASPP. The usage of the dilated convolution can balance the tradeoff between the dimension of feature map and the size of the receptive field [2]. Compared with the traditional convolution, the dilated convolution can enlarge receptive field without increasing parameters [2]. Traditional ASPP [17] concatenates the dilated feature maps with different dilated rates to generate the final feature map. Although multi-scale features can be generated, the expanded feature map can only obtain a single scale information as a result of feature map with the same receptive field, which is not enough for remote sensing images [18]. Inversely, DenseASPP can connect different expansion convolutions closely, and the neuron coding of each intermediate feature map can obtain multi-scale feature information. In this way, DenseASPP can not only generate a feature map with large coverage [14], but also cover the feature map in a densely connected way. The formula of ASPP is as follows:

$$y = H_{3,6}(x) + H_{3,12}(x) + H_{3,18}(x) + H_{3,24}(x) \tag{1}$$

y represents the output signal, $H_{3,6}(x)$, $H_{3,12}(x)$, $H_{3,18}(x)$, $H_{3,24}(x)$ representing dilated convolution with the dilated rate of 6, 12, 18, 24 respectively, where the convolution kernel size is 3×3. Thus, formula 2 of DenseASPP is obtained as follows:

$$y_{[l]} = H_{K,d_l}\left(\left[y_{[l-1]}, y_{[l-2]}, \cdots\cdots, y_{[0]}\right]\right) \tag{2}$$

$y_{[l]}$ represents the output signal, and $[\cdots\cdots]$ represents the splicing operation of cascading style. d_l represents the expansion rate of different layers, K is the size of the filter, and H represents a dilated convolution.

This change can obtain denser feature pyramids and larger receptive fields [14]. The denser feature pyramid has better scale diversity of DenseASPP compared with ASPP [18]. Compared with the traditional ASPP, the four subbranches do not share information in the feed-forward process [14]. DenseASPP shares information in a densely connected way. In the feed-forward stage, layers with different expansion rates are connected together, where perceive more context information by generating a large filter [14]. The structure of DenseASPP is shown in the left component of Fig. 1.

Coordinate Attention. The last few years, attention mechanisms have been extensively used in image segmentation. Among them, the classical approaches consist of SENet [19] and CBAM [20], the former simply compresses the feature map and constructs the interdependence between channels, the emergence of CBAM [20] promotes this idea. In addition, nonlocal or self-attention networks focus on constructing spatial or channel attention to construct dependencies, such as ALNet [21], CGNet [22], SCNet [23] and CCNet [24]. Different from the above methods, CA can capture location information, and it is leveraged to encode channel relationships and long-term dependencies [15]. The structure of CA is shown in Fig. 2. Firstly, the embedding of local information is coordinated [15]. Specifically, given the input feature map, the pooling kernel of size (H, 1) or (1, W) is used to encode each channel along the horizontal and vertical coordinates, respectively. The formula is given as follows:

$$A_c^h = \frac{1}{H} \sum_{0 \leq i \leq w} x_c(H, i), A_c^w = \frac{1}{W} \sum_{0 \leq i \leq H} x_c(j, W) \tag{3}$$

where, A_c^h represents the output of the second channel c of height H, A_c^w represents the output of the second channel c of width W, x_c represents the input, H and W represent the height and width of the feature respectively. This transformation can obtain a pair of direction aware feature maps, so that the attention module can capture the chronic dependence of one spatial direction and save the precise location information of the other spatial direction [15], which facilitate the network to accurately locate the region of interest.

Secondly, generate coordinate attention [15]. Specifically, the above transformation is spliced, and then the convolution function F_l is applied for the transformation. The specific formula is as follows:

$$f = \delta\left(F_l\left(\left[A_c^h, A_c^w\right]\right)\right) \tag{4}$$

where, [.,.] represents the splicing operation. δ represents the nonlinear activation function, and f is the intermediate characteristic mapping of the spatial information in the horizontal and vertical directions.

Then, another two convolution operations are used to transform f^h and f^w into tensors with the same size of channels [14]. The formula is defined as follows:

$$g^h = \delta\left(F_h\left(f^h\right)\right), \; g^w = \delta\left(F_w\left(f^w\right)\right) \tag{5}$$

δ is the activation function. The final output y_c of coordinated attention can be written as formula (6):

$$y_c(i,j) = x_c(i,j) \times g^h(i) \times g^w(j) \tag{6}$$

It can be seen that the coordinated attention module can not only capture cross-channel information, but also capture direction perception and position sensitive information, to prompt the model to locate and identify the region of interest more accurately [25]. Secondly, this module is more flexible and can be easily inserted into the mobile network.

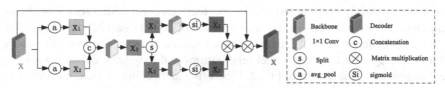

Fig. 2. Overall structure of coordinate attention network

2.2 Loss Function

The loss function of traditional contrastive learning methods hopes that the similarity between positive samples is higher and the similarity of negative samples is lower [13]. N samples are expanded to 2N samples by using the data enhancement methods. A pair of samples expanded from the same sample are positive samples, and the other $2 \times (N - 1)$ samples are negative samples [13]. Therefore, the contrastive loss (L_C) function is defined as:

$$L_C = \frac{1}{2N} \sum_{k=1}^{N} (\varepsilon(x_i, x_j) + \varepsilon(x_j, x_i)) \tag{7}$$

$$\varepsilon(x_i, x_j) = - \log \frac{\exp(sim(z_i, z_j)/\tau)}{\sum_{x \in \Lambda^-} \exp((sim(z_i, g(f(x)))/\tau)}$$

Among them, *sim* represents similarity between two feature vectors x_i and x_j, Λ^- represents $2 \times (N - 1)$ negative samples other than positive samples, and τ represents temperature parameters.

In this paper, cross entropy is used as the calculation of loss function. According to reference [16], the probability of the truth value of each sample is only considered by cross entropy and the likelihood function of these truth values is maximized. The authors reported that the information of other wrong categories may be lost, and the scattered characteristics is learned. Therefore, to address the above problems, a perceptual loss based on vgg19 network is added. Perceptual loss constrains the image at the depth feature level. The depth features are extracted by vgg19. By penalizing the difference of depth features, the generated feature map can preserve high semantic feature information [16]. The formula is as follows:

$$L_V = \frac{1}{C \times H \times W} \left\| \varphi(z_i) - \varphi(z_j) \right\|_2^2 \qquad (8)$$

where, C represents the number of channels of the feature map, with H and W representing the height and width, respectively. φ denotes the image passing through the vgg19 network, and $\|\cdot\|_2^2$ represent the square of the L2 norm. Therefore, the total loss function can be calculated as:

$$L = L_C + L_V \qquad (9)$$

And, the total loss function is show in Fig. 3.

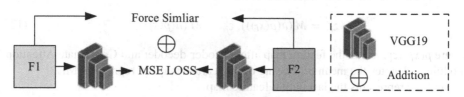

Fig. 3. Joint loss

2.3 Contrastive Learning

In this paper, the purpose of global contrastive learning is to compare different enhanced versions of one sample with other samples, it is similar to the existing instance contrast learning method [13]. The global contrastive module only extracts features through the encoder. DenseASPP is a part of the encoder, followed by CA module and MLP (Multi-Layer Perceptron). MLP has been proved in SimCLR [26] to allow the encoder to retain more potentially useful information for downstream tasks. Therefore, the extracted feature vector is defined as:

$$z_i^G = M\left(u(e(x_i))\right),\ z_j^G = M\left(u(e(x_j))\right) \qquad (10)$$

where e represents encoder and CA module, u represents the mean processing of the feature map, M are present MLP, and z_i^G, z_j^G the last output feature map.

Thus, the loss function of global style contrastive module is given as follows:

$$L_G = \frac{1}{2N} \sum_{k=1}^{N} \left(\varepsilon(x_i, x_j) + \varepsilon(x_j, x_i) \right) + \frac{1}{C \times H \times W} \left\| \varphi\left(z_i^G\right) - \varphi\left(z_j^G\right) \right\|_2^2$$

$$\varepsilon(x_i, x_j) = -\log \frac{\exp(sim(z_i^G, z_j^G)/\tau)}{\sum_{x \in \Lambda^-} \exp((sim(z_i^G, M\left(u(e(x))\right))/\tau)} \qquad (11)$$

Firstly, for remote sensing images datasets, the land cover categories in a single image are rich [13], if global image features are only extracted, local information may be lost. Secondly, the instance-wise contrastive learning methods is not optimum for the semantic segmentation task that needs pixel level features. So, use a local matching contrast learning module to learn the representation of local regions, which is beneficial to pixel level semantic segmentation. For different enhancement samples, random clipping, flipping and other methods will lead to the position mismatch of samples. Therefore, an index label is needed to record the pixel position [13], to select the same local samples. The local matching contrastive loss updates a complete semantic segmentation encoder-decoder network by forcing the feature representations of matching local regions to be similar and the feature representations of different local regions to be dissimilar. In the global contrastive module, the $e(x_i)$ and $e(x_j)$ are obtained from a pair of positive samples (x_i, x_j) from the encoder segmentation network. However, in the local matching comparison module, the $d(e(x_i))$ and $d(e(x_j))$ are obtained a pair of positive samples (x_i, x_j) from the encoder-coder segmentation network, followed by CA module and MLP. In this paper, the $p(x_i)$ and $p(x_j)$ represent $d(e(x_i))$ and $d(e(x_j))$, respectively. The extracted feature vector is:

$$z_i^U = M(u(p(x_i))), z_j^U = M(u(p(x_j)))$$ (12)

where $p(x_i)$ represents the feature map after encoder-decoder and Coordinate Attention module, u denotes the mean processing of the feature map, M represents MLP, and z, z represents the last output feature map.

Thus, we can get the loss function of the local matching contrastive module as follows:

$$L_U = \frac{1}{2N} \sum_{k=1}^{N} (\varepsilon(x_i, x_j) + \varepsilon(x_j, x_i)) + \frac{1}{C \times H \times W} \left\| \varphi\left(z_i^U\right) - \varphi\left(z_j^U\right) \right\|_2^2$$

$$\varepsilon(x_i, x_j) = -\log \frac{\exp(sim(z_i^U, z_j^U)/\tau)}{\sum_{x \in \Lambda^-} \exp((sim(z_i^U, M(u(p(x)))/\tau))}$$ (13)

3 Experiment Results

3.1 Data Description

ISPRS Potsdam Dataset. The dataset contains 38 high-resolution remote sensing images with a size of 6000 × 6000 and includes six classes, namely vehicles, buildings, trees, impervious water surface, low plants, and unknown elements [26]. 24 images are randomly selected and cut into 13824 images with a resolution of 256 × 256 for the training of contrastive learning. In order to evaluate the performance of contrast learning, 1% of these images are randomly selected as the training set of remote sensing image segmentation [13]. In addition, the remaining 14 images are randomly cropped into 256 × 256 images, a total of 1500. The details of the datasets are described in Table 1.

Deep Globe Land Cover Classification Dataset (DGLC): The dataset contains 803 images with a size of 2448 × 2448 [27]. 730 images are randomly selected from these images as the training data set of contrastive learning, and the remaining 73 images are used as the training set of remote sensing image segmentation [13]. The picture needs to be randomly cropped to a size of 512 × 512. The elaborate description is shown in Table 1.

3.2 Experimental Results

Due to the continuous change of time and space, it is difficult to obtain a large number of multi-resolutions, multi seasonal, multi spectral marker samples. Secondly, in order to learn the general spatial invariance characteristics of the model, data enhancement methods such as random shear, interpolation are used in this paper. Specifically: for a given image sample x, it is expanded by the methods of data enhancement to generate x_i and x_j respectively. In this paper, i represents random clipping, and j denotes random clipping, random scaling, interpolation, etc.

Table 1. Description of two datasets in our experiments

Datasets	Potsdam	DGLC
Ground resolution	0.05 m	0.5 m
Spectral bands	NIR, RGB	RGB
Crop size	256 × 256	512 × 512
Amount of self-supervised data	13824	18248
Default amount of fine-tuning data	138	182
Amount of testing data	1500	1825

3.3 Evaluation Metrics

Overall Accuracy (OA): In the image segmentation task, it is defined as the ratio of the sum of correctly predicted pixels to the sum of total pixels [28]. Among them, the number of correctly predicted pixels is distributed along the diagonal of a confusion matrix, and the sum of total pixels is the summation of pixels of the image label [29]. The computational formula is as follows:

$$OA = \frac{TP}{N} \qquad (14)$$

Kappa Coefficient: It is an indicator of statistical moderate quantity consistency. For image segmentation, consistency is exploited to assess whether the predicted mask of the model is consistent with the label [30]. The definition of Kappa coefficient is given as follows:

$$k = \frac{OA - p_e}{1 - p_e}, p_e = \frac{a_1 \times b_1 + a_2 \times b_2 + \ldots a_c \times b_c}{N \times N} \tag{15}$$

where, a_c represents the correct number of pixels in class c, and b_c denotes the total number of pixels in class c.

3.4 Experimental Results

In this section, the performance of our proposed network for remote sensing image semantic segmentation on data sets with limited labels is evaluated. In addition, a comparison with the current self-supervised contrastive learning methods and ImageNet pre-training methods [13] is conducted. Among them, random baseline represents the model without including pre-training, which directly trains specific semantic segmentation tasks.

The experimental results show that the proposed method is much better than random baseline. The experimental results of Potsdam dataset and DGLC dataset are tabulated in Table 2, and the visualization results are displayed in Fig. 4.

Table 2. Experimental results

Pretext task	Potsdam	DGLC
	Kappa OA	Kappa OA
Radom baseline	58.27 67.39	51.47 71.70
ImageNet_Supervised_Baseline	67.65 74.83	65.64 79.17
Jigsaw	60.99 69.68	44.05 68.88
Inpainting	63.62 71.70	43.82 67.78
MoCov2	59.81 68.73	54.02 72.93
SimCLR	65.62 73.21	67.33 79.77
DMF-CL	**71.92 78.35**	**68.13 81.12**

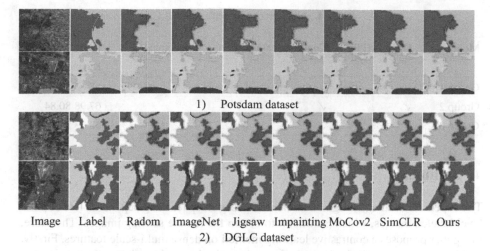

1)   Potsdam dataset

Image   Label   Radom   ImageNet   Jigsaw   Impainting   MoCov2   SimCLR   Ours

2)   DGLC dataset

Fig. 4. Examples of visualization results on two datasets.

3.5 Ablation Experiments

In order to intuitively assess the impact of different modules in our model, three groups of experiments are designed for ablation experiments. The tests of group 1, 2 and 3 demonstrate the segmentation results of three models. In this paper, we conducted ablation experiments on Potsdam dataset and DGLC dataset, respectively. The quantitative results are illustrated in Table 3 and Table 4.

DenseASPP in the coding part can improve the ability of the network to capture multi-scale context information. It can be obviously observed that the values of kappa and OA metrics are improved. In the second group of experiments, coordinate attention module is added on the basis of the first group. Due to its flexible characteristics, the coordination attention module can be inserted into any position of the backbone network, which improves the performance of the model to a certain extent. In the third group of experiments, the addition of perceptual loss makes the network obtain deeper characteristics in the training stage.

Table 3. Ablation experiments on Potsdam.

Model	DenseASPP	Coordinate attention	Perceptual loss	Potsdam
				Kappa OA
Group 1	✓			68.56 75.54
Group 2	✓	✓		70.34 77.25
Group 3	✓	✓	✓	71.92 78.35

Table 4. Ablation experiments on DGLC.

Model	DenseASPP	Coordinate attention	Perceptual loss	DGLC	
				Kappa	OA
Group 1	✓			67.63	80.34
Group 2	✓	✓		67.98	80.84
Group 3	✓	✓	✓	68.13	81.12

4 Summary

The supervised semantic segmentation methods of deep learning depend on lots of pixel level labeled images, which is difficult to obtain for remote sensing images. Therefore, this paper proposes a contrastive learning method on dense multi-scale features. Firstly, in the pre-training stage, the data enhancement method is used to enhance the consistency of remote sensing images; secondly, DenseASPP is selected as a part of the segmented network encoder, and the dense connection mode makes the network get more context information; Adding CA module in the global and local parts helps the network obtain the region of interest and improve the network performance; finally, in the training, the addition of perceptual loss improves the network performance.

Acknowledgement. This research was supported by the National Natural Science Foundation of China (No. 61901537), Research Funds for Overseas Students in Henan Province, China Postdoctoral Science Foundation (No. 2020M672274), Science and Technology Guiding Project of China National Textile and Apparel Council (No. 2019059), Postdoctoral Research Sponsorship in Henan Province (No. 19030018), Program of Young backbone teachers in Zhongyuan University of Technology (No. 2019XQG04), Training Program of Young Master's Supervisor in Zhongyuan University of Technology (No. SD202207).

References

1. Zhang, J., Feng, L., Yao, F.: Improved maize cultivated area estimation over a large scale combining MODIS–EVI time series data and crop phenological information. ISPRS J. Photogramm. Remote Sens. **94**, 102–113 (2014)
2. Chen, L.-C., Zhu, Y., Papandreou, G., Schroff, F., Adam, H.: Encoder-decoder with atrous separable convolution for semantic image segmentation. In: Ferrari, V., Hebert, M., Sminchisescu, C., Weiss, Y. (eds.) ECCV 2018. LNCS, vol. 11211, pp. 833–851. Springer, Cham (2018). https://doi.org/10.1007/978-3-030-01234-2_49
3. Sargent, I., Zhang, C., Atkinson, P.M.: Joint deep learning for land cover and land use classification (2020). https://doi.org/10.17635/Lancaster/thesis/42
4. Sulla-Menashe, D., Gray, J.M., Abercrombie, S.P., Friedl, M.A.: Hierarchical mapping of annual global land cover 2001 to present: the MODIS collection 6 land cover product. Remote Sens. Environ. **222**, 183–194 (2019)

5. Nan, L., Hong, H., Tao, F.: A novel texture-preceded segmentation algorithm for high-resolution imagery. IEEE Trans. Geosc. Remote Sens. **48**(7), 2818–2828 (2010)
6. Huang, X., Zhang, L.: An SVM ensemble approach combining spectral, structural, and semantic features for the classification of high-resolution remotely sensed imagery. IEEE Trans. Geosci. Remote Sens. **51**(1), 257–272 (2013)
7. Du, S., Zhang, F., Zhang, X.: Semantic classification of urban buildings combining VHR image and GIS data: an improved random forest approach. ISPRS J. Photogramm. Remote Sens. **105**, 107–119 (2015)
8. Li, Z., Duan, W.: Classification of hyperspectral image based on double-branch dual-attention mechanism network. Remote Sens. **12**(3), 582 (2020)
9. Alom, M.Z., Taha, T.M., Yakopcic, C., Westberg, S., Asari, V.K.: The history began from AlexNet: a comprehensive survey on deep learning approaches (2018)
10. Shorten, C., Khoshgoftaar, T.M.: A survey on image data augmentation for deep learning. J. Big Data **6**(1), 1–48 (2019). https://doi.org/10.1186/s40537-019-0197-0
11. Supervised, S., Welling, B.M., Zemel, R.S.: Self Supervised (2008)
12. Jing, L., Tian, Y.: Self-supervised visual feature learning with deep neural networks: a survey. IEEE Trans. Pattern Anal. Mach. Intell. **PP**(99), 1 (2020)
13. Li, H., et al.: Global and local contrastive self-supervised learning for semantic segmentation of HR remote sensing images. IEEE Trans. Geosci. Remote Sens. **60**, 1–14 (2022)
14. Yang, M., Yu, K., Chi, Z., Li, Z., Yang, K.: DenseASPP for semantic segmentation in street scenes CVPR (2018)
15. Hou, Q., Zhou, D., Feng, J.: Coordinate attention for efficient mobile network design (2021)
16. Johnson, J., Alahi, A., Fei-Fei, L.: Perceptual losses for real-time style transfer and super-resolution. In: Leibe, B., Matas, J., Sebe, N., Welling, M. (eds.) ECCV 2016. LNCS, vol. 9906, pp. 694–711. Springer, Cham (2016). https://doi.org/10.1007/978-3-319-46475-6_43
17. Frid-Adar, M., Ben-Cohen, A., Amer, R., Greenspan, H.: Improving the segmentation of anatomical structures in chest radiographs using U-Net with an ImageNet pre-trained encoder. arXiv (2018)
18. Ma, X., Li, R., Lu, Z., Wei, W.: Mining constraints in role-based access control. Math. Comput. Model. **55**(1–2), 87–96 (2012)
19. Jie, H., Li, S., Gang, S., Albanie, S.: Squeeze-and-excitation networks. IEEE Trans. Pattern Anal. Mach. Intell. **PP**(99) (2012)
20. Woo, S., Park, J., Lee, J.-Y., Kweon, I.S.: CBAM: convolutional block attention module. In: Ferrari, V., Hebert, M., Sminchisescu, C., Weiss, Y. (eds.) ECCV 2018. LNCS, vol. 11211, pp. 3–19. Springer, Cham (2018). https://doi.org/10.1007/978-3-030-01234-2_1
21. Hu, Z., Xu, M., Bai, S., Huang, T., Bai, X.: Asymmetric non-local neural networks for semantic segmentation. IEEE (2019)
22. Cao, Y., Xu, J., Lin, S., Wei, F., Hu, H.: GCNet: non-local networks meet squeeze-excitation networks and beyond. arXiv (2019)
23. Li, X., Wang, W., Hu, X., Yang, J.: Selective kernel networks. IEEE (2020)
24. Huang, Z., Wang, X., Huang, L., Huang, C., Wei, Y., Liu, W.: CCNet: criss-cross attention for semantic segmentation. In: International Conference on Computer Vision (2018)
25. Fw, A., Fi, D.B.: Deep learning on edge: extracting field boundaries from satellite images with a convolutional neural network. Remote Sens. Environ. **245**, 111741 (2020)
26. Chen, T., Kornblith, S., Norouzi, M., Hinton, G.: A simple framework for contrastive learning of visual representations (2020)
27. Ding, L., Zhang, J., Bruzzone, L.: Semantic segmentation of large-size VHR remote sensing images using a two-stage multiscale training architecture. IEEE Trans. Geosci. Remote Sens. **PP**(99), 1–10 (2020)

28. Demir, I., Koperski, K., Lindenbaum, D., Pang, G., Huang, J., Basu, S.: DeepGlobe 2018: a challenge to parse the earth through satellite images. IEEE (2018)
29. Doersch, C., Gupta, A., Efros, A.A.: Unsupervised visual representation learning by context prediction. IEEE Computer Society (2015)
30. Pathak, D., Krahenbuhl, P., Donahue, J., Darrell, T., Efros, A.A.: Context encoders: feature learning by inpainting. In: 2016 IEEE Conference on Computer Vision and Pattern Recognition (CVPR) (2016)

Image Derain Method for Generative Adversarial Network Based on Wavelet High Frequency Feature Fusion

Jiao Li⬤, Hao Feng⬤, Zhennan Deng⬤, Xintong Cui⬤, Hongxia Deng(✉)⬤,
and Haifang Li

Taiyuan University of Technology, Jinzhong 030600, Shanxi, China
denghongxia@tyut.edu.cn

Abstract. Photos taken on rainy days can be affected by rain streaks that reduce the sharpness of the image. Due to insufficient attention on feature extraction of rain streaks area, the removal effect of noise area needs to be improved. Wavelet transform is used to separate the high frequency information of the image, convolution is used to extract the high frequency features of the image, and the features of the original image with rain streaks extracted by the network are superimposed and fused. High frequency information graph represents the location of image noise. By incorporating high frequency features, the network can further learn the features of the rain stripes region. Feature fusion is introduced into the generative network, and the generative network guided by the attention distribution map considers global information more on the precondition of paying attention to the rain stripes region, so as to improve the clarity of the image after removing the rain fringes. The comparison experiment of wavelet high frequency feature fusion generative adversarial network and other methods is completed. The evaluation metrics are peak signal-to-noise ratio (PSNR) and structure similarity (SSIM), which verify the superiority of the proposed method compared with other methods.

Keywords: Derain · Generative adversarial network · Wavelet transform · Feature fusion · Self-attention

1 Introduction

With the rapid development of computer hardware and software, artificial intelligence-related software and systems emerge one after another and are applied in a wide range of fields, such as driving, finance and economics, medical treatment, image recognition and so on. Image processing usually appears as preprocessing, so it is an important branch of artificial intelligence and computer recognition field. Different kinds of noise are often encountered in the process of image processing, including noise, haze, rain stripes and so on. The image acquisition will be affected by different weather, and the image clarity will be reduced due to the attachment of rain stripes in cloudy and rainy days, which will ultimately affect the research results. Since the rain fringes area blocks the background information of the image and reduces the image quality, it is necessary to extract the

© The Author(s), under exclusive license to Springer Nature Switzerland AG 2022
S. Yu et al. (Eds.): PRCV 2022, LNCS 13537, pp. 165–178, 2022.
https://doi.org/10.1007/978-3-031-18916-6_14

features of the rain fringes area, and then guide the network to remove the rain fringes and restore the clarity of the image. To solve the above problems, this paper proposes a generative adversarial network (GAN) [1] based on wavelet high frequency feature fusion.

Many corresponding methods have been proposed in terms of image derain including removing the rain contained in the video frame [2–4] and the rain stripes attached to the image. Image derain methods also includes traditional methods [5–9] and deep learning methods [10–14]. Compared with generative adversarial network, the sharpness, contrast and structure of images restored by traditional methods need to be improved, so this paper chooses generative adversarial network as the infrastructure.

Image derain methods based on deep learning: D. Eigen et al. [11] proposed a method to remove local rainwater and dirt artifacts from a single image. The dataset of this method was used to train a special form of convolutional neural network and they finally effectively removed dust and rain under outdoor test conditions. Wenhan Yang et al. [12] proposed a method to remove image rain stripes by introducing three losses through special cyclic iteration on three convolution channels. The effect of deep learning methods on removing image rain fringes need to be improved. Image derain methods based on generative adversarial network: In 2017, Rui Qian et al. [13] proposed attention generative adversarial network to realize image derain, and added attention-cycling network to generate attention distribution map to guide the network to detect and remove rain stripes area. C. Ledig et al. [14] proposed SRGAN, a generative adversarial network for image super-resolution (SR). It was aimed at the problem of how to restore finer texture details in super-resolution with large magnification coefficients. The work focused on minimizing the mean square reconstruction error, and proposed a perceptual loss function consisting of adversarial loss and content loss. It was the first framework capable of inferring photorealistic natural images for 4 × magnification factor. These methods do not pay enough attention to feature extraction of rain stripes area when removing rain stripes. Therefore, this paper integrates high frequency features extracted by wavelet transform and features extracted from original rain stripes images by network, and finally realizes the removal of rain stripes in image.

2   Wavelet High Frequency Feature Fusion Generative Adversarial Network

2.1   Network Framework

The network framework of this paper is based on generative adversarial network, which consists of a generative network and a discriminative network, and the two confront each other to make the network work. In this paper, the role of the generative network is to remove the rain streaks in the image, and the role of the discriminant network is to judge whether the image comes from the output of the generative network or a clear image, until the output probability of the discriminant network is 0.5, that is, the discriminant network cannot discriminate the real source of the image. At this point the network reaches an equilibrium state and training stops.

Rui Qian et al. [13] proposed attention generative adversarial network in 2017 to realize image derain. Specifically, he added an attention-recurrent network to the generative network to generate an attention map to guide the network to detect and remove raindrop regions. Figure 1 shows the overall architecture of the network in this paper. Three improvements are proposed on Qian's existing network (marked in the figure):

1. A feature fusion module is introduced at the front of the autoencoder structure of the generative adversarial network to make it easier for the network to extract the features of the image rain streak area, and then remove the rain streak.
2. A self-attention layer [15] is added to the autoencoder structure to improve the global dependencies of images.
3. A multiscale discriminator [16] is introduced to better distinguish the difference between the generated derained and clear images.

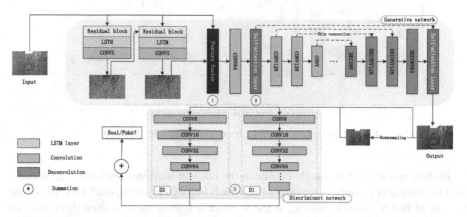

Fig. 1. Generative adversarial network based on wavelet high frequency feature fusion.

The autoencoder [17] on the right side of the generative network contains 16 Conv-Relu blocks and jump connections, as well as 2 self-attention layers, and the number of discriminators used to discriminant network is 2.

2.2 Wavelet Transform and Discriminant Network

Wavelet transform [18] is a method to analyze signals in time domain and frequency domain. Its principle is to reflect or highlight some corresponding features by changing waveform. Because the short-time Fourier transform has some disadvantages, including localization and the window remains unchanged when the frequency changes. But the time-frequency window provided by wavelet transform can change with the change of frequency, so the wavelet transform can analyze the time domain and frequency domain of the signal. Based on the characteristics of wavelet transform, we can know that the feature can be highlighted by wavelet transform. The problem studied in this paper is to remove the rain stripes from the image, which is a kind of image noise. Before removing the rain stripes, the area where the rain stripes are located needs to be highlighted. Based on the understanding of the characteristics of the image, the low-frequency information of the image represents the area where the color transition is moderated, that is, the background area of the image. The high-frequency information represents the area where the color transition is more intense, that is, the area where the rain stripes (noise) exist on the image. Therefore, in this paper, the wavelet transform of the image is used to separate the low frequency and high frequency information of the image, and the high frequency features are integrated into the network structure to remove the rain stripes more effectively.

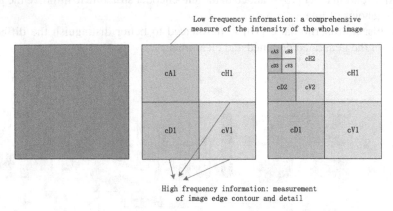

Fig. 2. Three-order wavelet transform principle of image.

Orthogonal wavelet is usually chosen as the basis of wavelet transform. The wavelet used in this paper is Dobesy wavelet [19], which belongs to orthogonal wavelet. In the process of fast wavelet transform, if the wavelet length is limited, then there are two sequences, which both represent the corresponding coefficients. One is used in front of the high-pass filter, the other is the low-pass filter. Since the filters have different lengths, dobesy wavelets have different representations according to their lengths. This paper uses DB2 wavelets. When Dobesy wavelet is used, N value is usually in the range of 2 to 20.

Figure 2 shows the structure of the three-order wavelet transform of the image. In the figure, cA is the low-frequency information decomposed by wavelet transform at each level, and the rest are high-frequency information. Where cD represents horizontal information, cH represents longitudinal information, and cV represents high-frequency information in the diagonal direction. The three-order wavelet transform of the image will gradually narrow down the final high-frequency information graphic. Figure 2 mainly introduces the reasons for high-frequency information graphic narrowing, which provides the basis for the position introduced by the feature fusion module in this paper.

After each image goes through the three-order wavelet transform, 9 high-frequency information graphs are generated, as shown in Fig. 3.

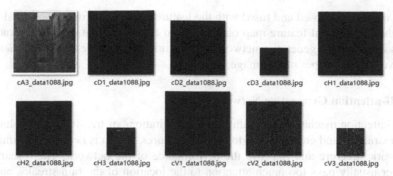

cA3_data1088.jpg   cD1_data1088.jpg   cD2_data1088.jpg   cD3_data1088.jpg   cH1_data1088.jpg

cH2_data1088.jpg   cH3_data1088.jpg   cV1_data1088.jpg   cV2_data1088.jpg   cV3_data1088.jpg

Fig. 3. Wavelet transform results of images.

2.3 Feature Fusion Module

One of the innovations of this paper is to introduce feature fusion in the generative network of the generative adversarial network. The main idea is to fuse the high-frequency
features obtained by wavelet transform with the features extracted from images without
wavelet transform. As the characteristics of the wavelet transform introduced above,
the generative adversarial network that introduces feature fusion is easier to extract the
features of the image rain stripes area, and then remove the rain stripes.

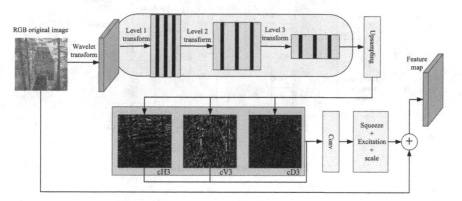

Fig. 4. The structure of feature fusion module.

Figure 4 shows the specific structure diagram of feature fusion designed in this paper.
After the original RGB image with rain stripes is input, the high-frequency information
graph is obtained through the three-order wavelet transform of the image. Since the
image wavelet transform will reduce the size of the image, the upsampling process of
the image is used to restore the size of the image, and the high-frequency information
graph of the same size is obtained. Next, the high frequency features of the image
are extracted by convolution. The SE module [20] added here aims to make the high-
frequency feature representation of the image clearer, so that the location of rain stripes
can be highlighted in the learning process of the network. Finally, the high frequency

features are superimposed and fused with the features extracted from the original RGB image, that is, the final feature map obtained from the whole feature fusion structure, which is input into the generative network of the original generative adversarial network to remove the rain stripes of the image.

2.4 Self-attention Generative Network

The self-attention mechanism can alleviate the limitations of traditional convolutional feature extraction and enhance the globality of features, which is beneficial to improve the network structure and improve the performance of the network. The research in this paper usually pays too much attention to the location of the rain streaks, and the overall information of the original image and the interdependence between features are therefore ignored. The use of self-attention mechanism can solve the above problems. In this paper, a self-attention layer is added to the generative network, and the feature stacking details are added on the basis of the original self-attention layer [15], as shown in Fig. 5.

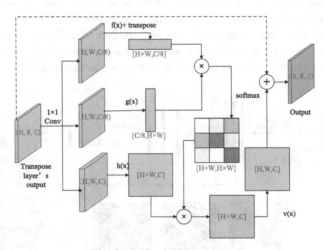

Fig. 5. Self-attention structure.

The image features of the previous hidden layer $x \in R^{C \times N}$ are first transformed into two feature spaces f, g to compute attention, where $f(x) \rightarrow W_f x$, $g(x) \rightarrow W_g x$.

$$\beta_{j,i} = \frac{\exp(S_{ij})}{\sum_{i=1}^{N} \exp(S_{ij})}, \ where \ S_{ij} = f(x_i)^T g(x_j) \tag{1}$$

where $\beta_{j,i}$ represents the attention of the model to the ith position when synthesizing the jth region. C is the number of channels, and N is the number of hidden element locations in the upper layer. The output of the original attention layer is $o = (o_1, o_2, \ldots, o_j, \ldots, o_N) \in R^{C \times N}$:

$$o_j = v\left(\sum_{i=1}^{N} \beta_{j,i} h(x_i)\right), \ where \ h(x_i) = W_h x_i, \ v(x_i) = W_v x_i \tag{2}$$

In the above formula, $W_g \in R^{\overline{C} \times C}$, $W_f \in R^{\overline{C} \times C}$, $W_h \in R^{\overline{C} \times C}$, $W_v \in R^{C \times \overline{C}}$ are the weight matrix to be learned, which are obtained by 1×1 convolution. And here $\overline{C}$ is taken as $C/8$.

Here, we add this feature map o to the feature map output by the previous convolutional layer to get the output of the self-attention layer, which is the input of the next convolutional layer.

Self-attention layers achieve structures with long-term dependencies through special convolution, mapping, normalization, and other designs to boost image global dependencies and generate sharper images.

2.5 Loss

Multiscale loss and perceptual loss are included in this paper. For multiscale loss, features are extracted from different decoder layers to form outputs of different sizes, and losses under different resolutions are evaluated. In this way, more context information can be obtained at different scales.

$$L_M (\{S\} \cdot \{T\}) = \sum_{i=1}^{M} \lambda_i L_{MSE}(S_i, T_i) \tag{3}$$

where M is the number of selected decoder layers, $L_{MSE}()$ is the mean square error, $S_i \in \{S\}$ is the ith output feature extracted from the decoder layer, $T_i \in \{T\}$ is the real feature with the same scale as S_i, and λ_i is the weight of different scales.

Perceptual loss measures the overall difference between the feature output by the autoencoder and the corresponding sharp image. These functions can be extracted from a trained CNN.

$$L_p = (O, T) = L_{MSE}(VGG(O), VGG(T)) \tag{4}$$

where VGG is a pre-trained CNN model that can generate features for a given input image, O represents the image generated after the generation network has processed: $O = g(I)$, and I is the input noise of the generative adversarial network here, T is a real image that is not affected by rain streaks.

The loss of generative network in this paper can be written as:

$$L_G = 10^{-2} L_{GAN}(O) + L_{ATT}(\{A\}, M) + L_M (\{S\}, \{T\}) + L_P(O, T) \tag{5}$$

where $A \in \{A\}$ is the attention map generated by the attention-recurrent network, L_{ATT} is the attention loss, M is the binary mask, $L_{GAN}(O) = \log(1 - D(O))$, and $D()$ is the discriminative probability generated by the discriminative network.

3 Experiments and Results

3.1 Dataset

The dataset used in this paper comes from the common rain streaks dataset, including the sparse rain streaks dataset and the dense rain streaks dataset, as shown in Fig. 6. Each dataset includes 4400 pairs of images with rain streaks and ground truth. Among them, there are 4000 pairs of training sets and 400 pairs of test sets.

Fig. 6. Sample rain streaks dataset. The left one is a image with dense rain streaks, the middle one is a image with sparse rain streaks, and the right one is a clear picture without rain streaks.

3.2 Evaluation Metrics

PSNR (Peak Signal to Noise Ratio) is the most common and widely used objective evaluation metric of image. The higher the value of PSNR is, the better the image quality is.

$$MSE = \frac{1}{mn} \sum_{i=0}^{m-1} \sum_{j=0}^{n-1} [I(i,j) - K(i,j)]^2 \tag{6}$$

$$PSNR = 10 \cdot \log_{10}(\frac{MAX_I^2}{MSE}) \tag{7}$$

In the formula, MSE is the mean square error of the current image I and K, and m and n are the height and width of the image respectively. MAX_I represents the maximum value of the image point color. If each sample point is represented by 8 bits, the maximum is 255. PSNR is an image quality assessment based on error sensitivity.

SSIM (Structural Similarity) is a fully referenced image quality evaluation index. It compares brightness, contrast and structure between images. Given two images X and Y, the SSIM of the two images can be calculated as follows:

$$SSIM(x,y) = \frac{(2\mu_x\mu_y + c_1)(2\sigma_{xy} + c_2)}{(\mu_x^2 + \mu_y^2 + c_1)(\sigma_x^2 + \sigma_y^2 + c_2)} \tag{8}$$

where μ_x is the average value of x and μ_y is the average value of y. σ_x^2 is the variance of x, σ_y^2 is the variance of y, and σ_{xy} is the covariance of x and y. $c_1 = (k_1L)^2$ and $c_2 = (k_2L)^2$ are constants used to maintain stability. L is the dynamic range of pixel values. $k_1 = 0.01$, $k_2 = 0.03$.

The value range of SSIM is $[-1, 1]$. The larger the value, the smaller the distortion.

3.3 Experimental Environment

The experiment designed in this paper has certain requirements for the experimental environment during operation. Due to the complex structure, large amount of data and number of parameters of wavelet high frequency feature fusion generative adversarial network, experiments must rely on GPU environment to run. The whole experiment code framework based on tensorflow1.12.0, language is python3.6. The version requirements that include some dependent packages are as follows: opencv_python3.4.1.15, glog0.3.1, numpy1.15.4, scikit_image0.14.1, easydict1.9, mat-plotlib3.0.2, scikit-image0.14.1, pyqt5 5.15.2, pillow8.1.0.

3.4 Parameter Settings

The number of iterations of the network will affect the experimental effect of the final network. Therefore, in this paper, the number of iterations is selected as 80, 100 and 120 thousand times respectively in the process of training the network, as shown in Fig. 7. It can be seen that when choose 100 thousand times, the PSNR value is the highest, so 100 thousand iteration times are selected.

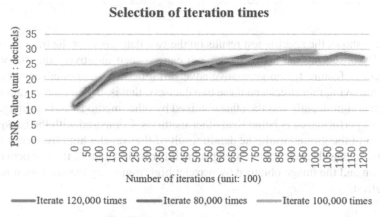

Fig. 7. Selection of iteration times.

3.5 Comparision Experiment

Table 1 shows the quantitative results. In the experiment, we compare the wavelet high frequency feature fusion generative adversarial network with other existing methods on different datasets, i.e. rain stripes (dense) and rain stripes (sparse). The left column is the method, and the right columns are the display of the evaluation metrics value of the derain result of this method in the rain stripes sparse and dense datasets. Other derain methods include Eigen [11], F-S GAN [21], R-IPM CA [22], AttGAN [13] and EfDeRain [23]. As shown in Table 1, PSNR and SSIM metrics values of ground truths and corresponding rain-free images obtained by each method were compared. It can be seen that in the rain stripes (sparse) and rain stripes (dense) datasets, the PSNR and SSIM values obtained by the wavelet high-frequency features generative adversarial network are nearly 2, 0.25 and 3, 0.26 higher than those obtained by other methods, respectively. Although the PSNR value obtained by the EfDeRain method is higher in the case of sparse rain streaks, the performance of the EfDeRain is not as good as our method from the subsequent visual effects (Fig. 8). It shows that the high-frequency feature fusion method proposed in this paper has advantages in removing rain streaks.

Table 1. Quantitative results of removing rain stripes by different methods. The best results have been **boldfaced**.

	PSNR (dB) Rain streaks (sparse)	SSIM Rain streaks (sparse)	PSNR (dB) Rain streaks (dense)	SSIM Rain streaks (dense)
Eigen	25.69	0.6524	25.94	0.6354
EfDeRain	**28.41**	0.8322	26.86	0.7998
F-S GAN	24.21	0.7785	24.51	0.7756
R-IPM CA	21.66	0.8695	21.04	0.8562
AttGAN	27.11	0.8762	26.95	0.8701
Ours	27.85	**0.8995**	**27.79**	**0.8986**

Figure 8 shows the specific test results on the two datasets after the training of each network. By observing the above pictures, it can be seen intuitively that the wavelet high frequency feature fusion generative adversarial network shows advantages in the results of removing rain streaks on these two datasets, that is, the amount of rain streaks attachment is significantly less than that obtained by other methods, and the image color and contrast performance is better than other methods. Compared with the background information of the ground truth, the derain result of the wavelet high frequency feature fusion network has the least loss of background information, that is, the gap between the ground truth and the image obtained by wavelet high frequency feature fusion network is the smallest.

3.6 Ablation Experiments

Table 2 shows the quantitative results of the ablation experiment. AttGAN is the baseline method before the change. Att + MS means that only attention module is added to the original network model, and Att + FF means only feature fusion module is added. It can be seen that the network model with attention module and feature fusion module performs best.

Figure 9 is the qualitative results of ablation experiments. By observing the images in the fourth and fifth columns of the table, it can be seen that the self-attention multiscale generative adversarial network with feature fusion module has a better effect on removing rain streaks. The images generated by the baseline method have white blur residues, while the images generated by the network without the feature fusion module sharpen the background obviously, which is less natural than our method.

Figure 10 shows a self-comparison diagram of loss values. The left figure (a) shows the loss value of the generative adversarial network without feature fusion, and the right figure (b) shows the loss value of the wavelet high frequency feature fusion generative adversarial network. As can be seen, the loss value on the right converges faster and is closer to 0.

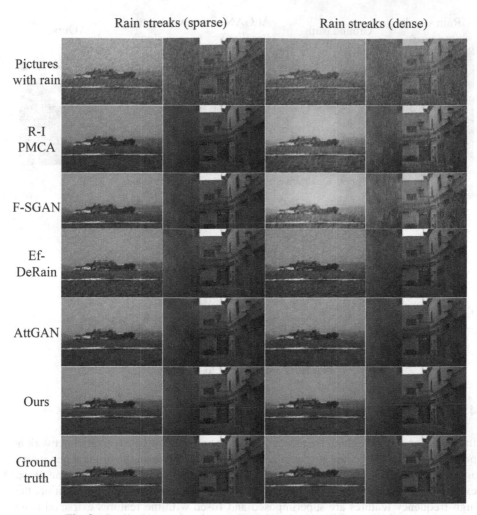

Fig. 8. Qualitative results of removing rain stripes by different methods.

Table 2. Quantitative results of ablation experiments. The best results have been **boldfaced.**

	PSNR (dB) Rain streaks (sparse)	SSIM Rain streaks (sparse)	PSNR (dB) Rain streaks (dense)	SSIM Rain streaks (dense)
AttGAN (Baseline)	27.11	0.8762	26.95	0.8701
Att + MS	27.25	0.8951	27.61	0.8894
Att + FF	26.63	0.8834	26.32	0.8754
Ours	**27.85**	**0.8995**	**27.79**	**0.8986**

Rain streaks (dense)　Ground truth　AttGAN (Baseline)　w/o Feature fusion　Ours

Fig. 9. Qualitative results of ablation experiments.

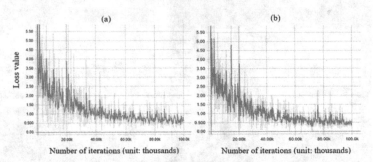

Fig. 10. Comparison of loss values.

4 Conclusion

In this paper, a wavelet high frequency feature fusion generative adversarial network is proposed to remove the rain stripes attached to images. Based on the original generative adversarial network framework, we add feature fusion module to generative network, extract high frequency features of the image by wavelet transform and convolution, the high frequency features are superimposed and fused with the features extracted from the original RGB image, and self-attention and multiscale modules are added to realize derain on the datasets with inconsistent intensity of two rain streaks, and the advantages are confirmed.

Acknowledgements. This research was supported by the 2022 Open Project Fund of the State Key Laboratory of CAD&CG of Zhejiang University (A2221), the Shanxi Provincial Central and Local Science and Technology Development Fund (YDZJSX2021C005), and the Science Foundation Grant (201901D111091).

References

1. Goodfellow, I.J.: Generative adversarial nets. In: Proceedings of the Advances in Neural Information Processing Systems 27 (NIPS 2014), pp. 2672–2680. Montreal, Quebec, Canada (2014)

2. Brewer, N., Liu, N.: Using the shape characteristics of rain to identify and remove rain from video. In: da Vitoria Lobo, N., Kasparis, T., Roli, F., Kwok, J.T., Georgiopoulos, M., Anagnostopoulos, G.C., Loog, M. (eds.) SSPR /SPR 2008. LNCS, vol. 5342, pp. 451–458. Springer, Heidelberg (2008). https://doi.org/10.1007/978-3-540-89689-0_49
3. Santhaseelan, V.: Utilizing local phase information to remove rain from video. Int. J. Comput. Vision 112(1), 71–89 (2015)
4. Zhou, Y., Shimada, N.: Using motion compensation and matrix completion algorithm to remove rain streaks and snow for video sequences. In: Palaiahnakote, S., Sanniti di Baja, G., Wang, L., Yan, W.Q. (eds.) ACPR 2019. LNCS, vol. 12046, pp. 91–104. Springer, Cham (2020). https://doi.org/10.1007/978-3-030-41404-7_7
5. Garg, K.: Vision and rain. Int. J. Comput. 75(1), 3–27 (2007)
6. Kang, L.W.: Automatic single-image-based rain streaks removal via image decomposition. IEEE Trans. Image Process. 21(4), 1742–1755 (2011)
7. Kim, J.: Single-image deraining using an adaptive nonlocal means filter. In: Proceedings of the 2013 IEEE International Conference on Image Processing, pp. 914–917. IEEE, Melbourne, Australia (2013)
8. Chen, Y.L.: A generalized low-rank appearance model for spatio-temporally cor-related rain streaks. In: Proceedings of the IEEE International Conference on Computer Vision, pp. 1968–1975. IEEE, Sydney, Australia (2013)
9. Huang, D.A.: Self-learning based image decomposition with applications to single image denoising. IEEE Trans. Multimedia 16(1), 83–93 (2013)
10. Fu, X.: A deep network architecture for single-image rain removal. IEEE Trans. Image Process. 26(6), 2944–2956 (2017)
11. Eigen, D.: Restoring an image taken through a window covered with dirt or rain. In: Proceedings of the IEEE International Conference on Computer Vision, pp. 633–640. IEEE, Sydney, Australia (2013)
12. Yang, W.: Deep joint rain detection and removal from a single image. In: Proceedings of the IEEE Conference on Computer Vision and Pattern Recognition, pp. 1357–1366. IEEE, Honolulu, HI (2017)
13. Qian, R.: Attentive generative adversarial network for raindrop removal from a single image. In: Proceedings of the IEEE Conference on Computer Vision and Pattern Recognition, pp. 2482–2491. IEEE, Salt Lake City, UT (2018)
14. Ledig, C.: Photo-realistic single image super-resolution using a generative ad-versarial network. In: Proceedings of the IEEE Conference on Computer Vision and Pattern Recognition, pp. 4681–4690. IEEE, Honolulu, HI (2017)
15. Zhang, H.: Self-attention generative adversarial networks. In: International Conference on Machine Learning, pp. 7354–7363. Long Beach, CA (2019)
16. Jun, H.: A Research on Segmentation of Prostate MRI Image Based on Generative Adversarial Networks. Hefei University of Technology, Hefei (2019)
17. Zhu, S., Xu, G., Cheng, Y., Han, X., Wang, Z.: BDGAN: image blind denoising using generative adversarial networks. In: Lin, Z., Wang, L., Yang, J., Shi, G., Tan, T., Zheng, N., Chen, X., Zhang, Y. (eds.) PRCV 2019. LNCS, vol. 11858, pp. 241–252. Springer, Cham (2019). https://doi.org/10.1007/978-3-030-31723-2_21
18. 邵学广.: 小波变换与分析化学信号处理. 化学进展 12(003), 233–244 (2000)
19. Lina, J.M.: Complex daubechies wavelets. Appl. Comput. Harmon. Anal. 2(3), 219–229 (1995)
20. Hu, J.: Squeeze-and-excitation networks. IEEE Trans. Pattern Anal. Mach. Intell. 8(42), 2011–2023 (2020)
21. Xiang, P.: Single-image de-raining with feature-supervised generative advesarial network. IEEE Signal Process. Lett. 26(5), 650–654 (2019)

22. Li, R.: Heavy rain image restoration: Integrating physics model and conditional adversarial learning. In: Proceedings of the IEEE/CVF Conference on Computer Vision and Pattern Recognition, pp. 1633–1642. Long Beach, CA (2019)
23. Guo, Q., Sun, J.: EfficientDeRain: learning pixel-wise dilation filtering for high-efficiency single-image deraining. In: Proceedings of the 35th AAAI Conference on Artificial Intelligence/33rd Conference on Innovative Applications of Artificial Intelligence/11th Symposium on Educational Advances in Artificial Intelligence, pp. 1487–1495. AAAI Conference on Artificial Intelligence, ELECTR NETWORK (2021)

GPU-Accelerated Infrared Patch-Image Model for Small Target Detection

Xuying Hao[1,2,3], Yujia Liu[1,2,3], Fei Song[1,2,4], Tao Lei[1(✉)], Yi Cui[1], and Yunjing Zhang[1]

[1] Institute of Optics and Electronics, Chinese Academy of Science, Chengdu, China
taoleiyan@ioe.an.cn
[2] University of Chinese Academy of Sciences, Beijing, China
[3] School of Electronic, Electrical and Communication Engineering, University of Chinese Academy of Sciences, Beijing, China
[4] School of Information and Communication Engineering, University of Electronic Science and Technology of China, Chengdu, China

Abstract. Infrared small target detection plays a significant role in precision guidance and infrared warning systems. Although existing methods based on infrared patch-image (IPI) model have achieved good detection results, most algorithms provide high detection accuracy but with low real-time performance, which limits their use in practical applications. In this paper, we presents a GPU based parallel implementation to focus on real-time performance of the small target detection by using IPI model and various optimization strategies. The parallel implementation is first analysed in details. Then, the speed of the method is tested on the embedded GPU Jetson AGX Xavier. Finally, the running time of the traditional algorithm on the CPU is compared. Experiments show a speedup of $20\times$ over CPU implementation for images with a resolution of 1024×1024 pixels, which has great potential for real-time applications. Our acceleration strategy is also useful for other infrared image-patch based small target detection algorithms.

Keywords: Infrared small target detection · GPU · Parallel implementation · IPI · Optimization strategies

1 Introduction

Infrared small target detection has always been a trendy and challenging point in the fields of military early warning, pattern recognition and image processing [1]. Small targets of infrared images are often overwhelmed due to a low signal-to-noise ratio and complex background clutter. Therefore, there is a greater challenge to the effectiveness of detection technology for small infrared targets [2].

The current detection technologies for small infrared targets can be divided into two categories: single-frame spatial image and sequence based methods [3]. Detection methods based on sequence require more prior information and usually rely on single-frame spatial detection methods, so it is of great significance to the research of single-frame spatial image detection. Traditional single-frame spatial detection often uses background suppression filtering algorithms, such as maximum mean filter [4],

S. Yu et al. (Eds.): PRCV 2022, LNCS 13537, pp. 179–188, 2022.
https://doi.org/10.1007/978-3-031-18916-6_15

high-pass filter [5], median filter [6], and Top-hat filter [7]. These methods have good suppression effect on the background when the target signal-to-noise ratio is high, but when the target brightness is lower than the background peak brightness, the false alarm rate will be high and the detection performance will be deteriorated.

In recent years, the low-rank matrix recovery (LRMR) algorithm has gradually developed, and some scholars have applied it to the field of target detection. Since the algorithm is more robust to data with outliers and sparse noise [8], it achieves better detection results. Methods based on LRMR exploit the non-local autocorrelation properties of infrared background images [9]. Under this assumption, Gao et al. [10] proposed an Infrared Patch Image (IPI) model using the sliding window in infrared images, and firstly proposed to transform the problem of small target detection into a low-rank sparse matrix recovery problem. As the lowrank and sparse assumptions fit the most scenes well, the IPI model achieves excellent performance. Inspired by the IPI model, more and more algorithms have been proposed. Dai [11] proposed weighted infrared patch-image (WIPI) model by weighted each column during construction. Then he constructed non-negative IPI model via partial sum minimization of singular values (NIPPS) [12]. Further, some non-convex optimization methods are proposed. For example, Zhang [13] proposed to use the l2 norm to constrain the background clutter, and Zhang [14] introduced the lp norm to constrain the sparse target. In addition, Dai [15] introduced the tensor model on the basis of the IPI model and proposed the reweighted infrared patch-tensor (RIPT) model. The partial sum of the tensor nuclear norm (PSTNN) is proposed by Zhang [16].

The proposal of the IPI model based on low-rank and sparse recovery have achieved excellent results in the infrared small target detection. Since constructing and reconstructing patch images and matrix factorization in the IPI model is very time-consuming, most of these methods obtain high detection accuracy but with low real-time performance, which limits their use in practical applications. In addition, traditional CPU-based serial processing methods cannot process complex algorithms in real time. Therefore, it is of great significance to pay attention to the realization of IPI on GPU-based parallel systems.

In this paper, we propose a GPU based parallel implementation for accelerating the IPI model of infrared small target detection. More specifically, for fast processing of the entire image, multi-threaded parallelism is first adopted to build patch-image. Simultaneously, robust principal component analysis (RPCA) is accelerated by buffer reuse and optimization of iteration termination conditions. Moreover, the filtering is optimized after reconstruction from patch images in parallel. We implement the parallel algorithm on the embedded GPU Jetson AGX Xavier and also evaluate our method with images of different resolutions. The rest of this paper is organized as follows. In Sect. 2, IPI Model based low-rank and sparse recovery is introduced. The proposed parallel implementation scheme is described in Sect. 3. Experimental results and discussion are presented in Sect. 4. We conclude this article in Sect. 5.

2 IPI Model

2.1 Patch Image

Figure 1 shows the process of constructing patch-image from an infrared image using a sliding window and reconstructing an image from the patch-image. Each column of the block image corresponds to a sliding window in the traditional image, and the size of the sliding window and the sliding step determine the size of the block image. Since each pixel of the traditional image may be related to several patches, the processed image needs to be reconstructed. The 1D filter [10] is chosen to reconstruct the separated image pixels. It is defined as follows:

$$v = f(x) \tag{1}$$

where $v \in R^{m \times n}$ is the gray value after reconstruction. x is the gray value interrelated with v. f can choose median($\cdot$), mean($\cdot$), max($\cdot$), min($\cdot$) etc.

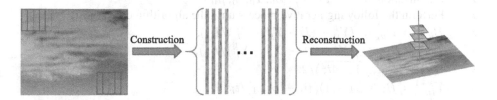

Fig. 1. Construction patch-image and reconstruction from patch-image.

2.2 Formulation of Small Target Detection and Solution

The IPI model transforms the traditional infrared image model into a patch-image model. Image matrix $D \in R^{m \times n}$ is decomposed into low-rank matrix $B \in R^{m \times n}$ and sparse matrix $T \in R^{m \times n}$ and $N \in R^{m \times n}$:

$$D = B + T + N \tag{2}$$

The small target detection task is essentially the process of separating and obtaining the sparse component T. IPI proposed that under the condition of matrix low rank constraint, the convex optimization problem is expressed as follows:

$$min_{B,T} rank(B) + \lambda \|T\|_0, s.t. \|D - B - T\|_F \leq \delta \tag{3}$$

where: $\|T\|_0$ means finding the 0 norm of matrix T, λ is usually a constant greater than 0, which is taken generally $\lambda = 1/\sqrt{max(m, n)}$.

Since Eq. 3 is a non-deterministic polynomial (NP) hard problem, the objective function needs relaxation when solving. Since the envelope of the matrix rank is the kernel norm and the convex hull of the matrix 0 norm is the matrix 1 norm, the relaxation of the objective function is as follows:

$$min_{B,T} \|B\|_* + \lambda \|T\|_1, s.t. \|D - B - T\|_F \leq \delta \tag{4}$$

The algorithms for solving Eq. 4 include accelerated proximal gradient (APG), exact augmented Lagrange multipliers (EALM), and inexact augmented multipliers (IALM) [18]. In this paper, the APG algorithm with better convergence is used as the specific execution algorithm of RPCA. The APG algorithm relaxes the equality constraints of Eq. 4 into the objective function, and obtains the following Lagrangian function:

$$L(B, T, \mu) = \mu(\|A\|_* + \lambda\|E\|_1) + \|D - B - T\|_F^2/2 \tag{5}$$

where μ is relaxation factor. The iterative algorithm for solving Eq. 5 is shown in Algorithm 1.

Algorithm 1: Accelerated Proximal Gradient

    input   : Observation matrix D, parameter λ, η, $\widetilde{\mu}$

    output : (B_k, T_k)

1   Initialization: $k = 0$, Y_B^0, Y_T^0, B_0, T_0, t_0, μ_0;

2   Perform the following iterative process until the algorithm converges:;

3      $B_{k+1} = D_{\mu_k/L_f}(Y_B^k + (D - Y_B^k - Y_T^k)/L_f)$;

4      $T_{k+1} = S_{\lambda\mu_k/L_f}(Y_T^k + (D - Y_B^k - Y_T^k)/L_f)$;

5      $t_{k+1} = (1 + \sqrt{1 + 4t_k^2})/2$;

6      $Y_B^{k+1} = B_k + (t_k - 1)(B_k - B_{k+1})/t_{k+1}$;

7      $Y_T^{k+1} = B_k + (t_k - 1)(B_k - B_{k+1})/t_{k+1}$;

8      $\mu_{k+1} = max(\eta\mu_k, \widetilde{\mu})$;

---

3   GPU Parallel Implementation

3.1   Parallel Implementation for Constructing the Patch-Image (PICPI)

In the IPI algorithm, construction and reconstruction are time-consuming parts. Since the processing of the sliding window is independent of each other, these two parts are suitable for parallel processing. Figure 2 shows the method of parallel processing. Each thread can process the current sliding window independently at the same time, pulling it into a column vector to form a patch-image.

In this scheme, the number of sliding windows in the x-direction is set to the block's x-direction value. Parameters related to the thread block and grid are adjusted according to the image size. For example, for a 200×150 size image, the block is set to (16, 11) and the grid size is set to (1, 1). In each thread, pixels covered in the sliding window are pulled into a column vector. Constant parameters such as sliding step and the size of the image and window would be accessed at each time. As GPU handles multiple threads simultaneously, the constant parameters would be repeatedly accessed. Therefore, the optimization of memory access is very crucial. In our method, we store

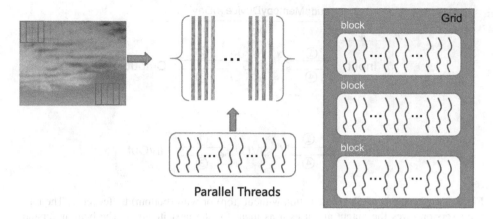

Fig. 2. Parallel threads construct patch-image.

constant parameters in shared memory to reduce the visit times of memory from GPU. The thread needs to determine the initial position of the processed window, and the thread number corresponds to the window sequence number, which is the column the number of the patch-image.

3.2 RPCA Iterative Solution (RPCAIS)

The time-consuming of the iterative solution process of RPCA mainly comes from two aspects, one is the time-consuming caused by multiple iterations, and the other is the time-consuming caused by the data transmission in the iterative process constantly accessing the memory. So we use two means to speed up this part. First, reduce the number of iterations by changing the iteration termination condition, and then use buffer reuse to reduce memory accesses.

Inspired by [17], we add a condition to the iteration termination condition of the IPI algorithm: compare the number of non-zero elements in the current target image with the previous iteration, if the number of non-zero elements added is not greater than 1, the iteration stop. Each input of the iterative process is based on the solution result of the previous iteration. This process requires constant access to memory to access the intermediate results. The principle of buffer reuse is to change the position of input and output in each iteration, and avoid using buffers to save input and output. Figure 3 illustrates this process. In addition, each step in the iterative solution of the APG algorithm involves singular value decomposition (SVD) calculations. We use the cusolver function in the optimized cublas library for SVD. Further, we use multi-threaded parallel computing for matrix addition, subtraction and multiplication in the iterative process, which greatly reduces the time of matrix operations.

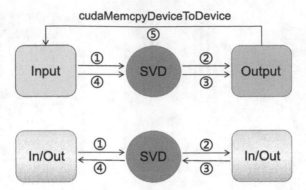

Fig. 3. Two iterations of SVD calculation without (top) or with (bottom) buffer reuse. The top-level version saves the output and uses it as input for the next iteration. The bottom version transforms the input and output locations to avoid using a buffer to access the result.

3.3   Parallel Implementation for Reconstructing the Patch-Image (PIRPI)

We use two kernels to complete the acceleration of refactoring. The first kernel performs the reconstruction process at the patch-image position, and the second kernel performs the filtering. The thread and grid settings of the first kernel are the same as the construction process in Sect. 3.1. Each thread restores a column in patch-image to the corresponding patch of the traditional image, the GPU can process the reconstruction process of each column simultaneously. The pixel position of the traditional image covered by the current column is determined by finding the starting position of the corresponding patch, and then the patch is restored to a large matrix. The height of the large matrix is set to the size of the traditional image, and the width is set to the number of sliding windows. The corresponding valid positions in the large matrix store the pixel information of the traditional image, and the invalid positions are initialized with NaN.

The second kernel thread block is set to $(32, 32)$, the grid size is set to $(1, (imgsize - 0.1)/1024 + 1)$, where $imgsize$ denotes size of an image, each thread processes a row in the large matrix to calculate the filtered pixel value. To reduce unnecessary computations, we determine where threads start by finding the first column in the large matrix that stores valid information, and where threads end by determining the maximum number of overlapping patches. In this way, each thread only needs to count and calculate the positions in the matrix that contain valid information. The proposed method is shown in the Fig. 4.

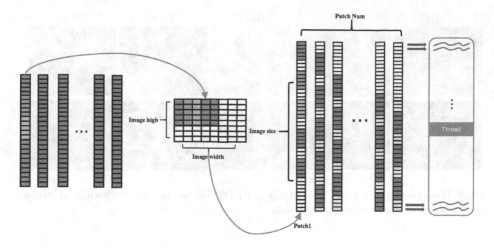

Fig. 4. Parallel filtering. Filter the section where valid information is stored.

4   Experimental Results and Analysis

To test the speed-up effect of this method, we test the running time of the algorithm on the embedded GPU Jetson AGX Xavier and compare it with the traditional IPI algorithm implemented in matlab on the CPU. The CPU is an i7-8750 processor. The Jetson AGX Xavier is our actual target for industrial applications. The Jetson AGX Xavier has 512 cores, twice as many as the Jetson TX2. To ensure the accuracy of the measurement time, we take the average of 10 experimental execution times. All processes on the GPU are computed on 32-bit precision floating point numbers in order to guarantee algorithmic precision. We test the algorithm time on datasets with resolutions ranging from 200×150 to 1024×1024, including data from different backgrounds such as sea and sky. Figure 5 shows some of the data and detection results used in the experiment. We compare the intermediate results of the three parts in the algorithm with the traditional algorithm to ensure that the results of the GPU-accelerated algorithm are consistent with the traditional algorithm. In order to shorten the time-consuming of the algorithm, we set the sliding window of images with a resolution smaller than 320×256 to 50×50 and the step size to 10. For images larger than this resolution, the sliding window size is set to 100×100, and the step size is set to 30×30.

During the entire acceleration process, we output and compare the intermediate results to ensure that the accuracy of the GPU-based IPI is consistent with the original algorithm. To evaluate the speedup of our method at each part of the IPI algorithm, we separately time the three parts mentioned above. The first part: constructing the patch image, the second part: RPCA iterative solution, the third part: reconstruction and filtering. As shown in Table 1, our method has obvious advantages in the first and third

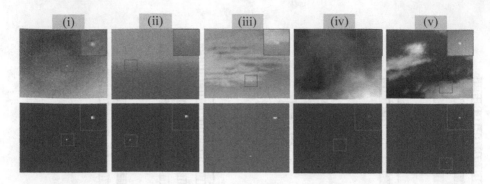

Fig. 5. Illustrations of five group infrared images (i)–(v). The first row denotes traditional images and the second row denotes detection results.

parts, and the reconstruction part can achieve a speedup close to two orders of magnitude. This also shows that the part of constructing and reconstructing patch-image in the IPI algorithm is very suitable for parallel acceleration of GPU. For the second stage, our method can also speed up at least close to three times, which is mainly due to the reduction of the number of accesses to global memory during the iteration process through buffer reuse, and the use of high-performance functions in cublas and npp libraries. The algorithm has been optimized. In Fig. 6, we see that our algorithm becomes more dominant as the image resolution increases. We can notice that the execution time by CPU for the larger image dimension (1024×1024) is around twenty times higher than the GPU.

Table 1. The average running time (s) of different resolution (pixels) images

Methods	Platforms	200×150	320×256	640×512	1000×750	1024×1024
PICPI	CPU	0.0053	0.0108	0.4112	0.0321	0.0684
	GPU	**0.0011**	**0.0033**	**0.0022**	**0.0085**	**0.0095**
RPCAI	CPU	1.2814	13.335	15.7048	45.2045	109.5898
	GPU	**0.5404**	**4.9593**	**3.3305**	**5.1699**	**5.8723**
PIRPI	CPU	0.2920	0.7767	2.2409	5.1706	7.0958
	GPU	**0.0016**	**0.0286**	**0.0438**	**0.0121**	**0.0134**

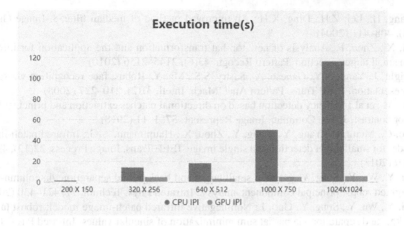

Fig. 6. Total execution time at different resolution (pixels).

5   Conclusion

In this paper, we introduce a GPU based parallel implementation for accelerating the IPI model of infrared small target detection. In order to process quickly the whole image, multi-threaded parallelism is first applied to construct patch-image in parallel. Meanwhile, two strategies (i.e., buffer reuse and optimizing iterative conditions) are adopted to accelerate the iterative solution process of RPCA. The reconstructed image from patch-image and optimized filtering are performed in parallel to obtain the final detection results. In our experiments, we compare the running time of IPI under CPU and GPU on images of different resolutions, which proves that our method greatly reduces the running time. Our method has important implications for a series of algorithms proposed based on the patch model, and greatly improves the practicability of low-rank sparse decomposition-based small object detection methods.

References

1. Schwering, P.B., Bezuidenhout, D.F., Gunter, W. H., le Roux, F.P., Sieberhagen, R.H.: IRST infrared background analysis of bay environments. In: Infrared Technology and Applications XXXIV, vol. 6940, pp. 467–478. SPIE (2008)
2. Zhang, C., He, Y., Tang, Q., Chen, Z., Mu, T.: Infrared small target detection via interpatch correlation enhancement and joint local visual saliency prior. IEEE Trans. Geosci. Remote Sens. **60**, 1–14 (2021)
3. Wang, G., Tao, B., Kong, X., Peng, Z.: Infrared small target detection using nonoverlapping patch spatial-temporal tensor factorization with capped nuclear norm regularization. IEEE Trans. Geosci. Remote Sens. **60**, 1–17 (2021)
4. Deshpande, S.D., Er, M.H., Venkateswarlu, R., Chan, P.: Max-mean and max-median filters for detection of small targets. In: Signal and Data Processing of Small Targets 1999, vol. 3809, pp. 74–83. SPIE (1999)
5. Wang, P., Tian, J., Gao, C.Q.: Infrared small target detection using directional highpass filters based on LS-SVM. Electron. Lett. **45**(3), 156–158 (2009)

6. Zhang, H., Lei, Z.H., Ding, X.H.: An improved method of median filter. J. Image Graph. **9**(4), 408–411 (2004)
7. Bai, X., Zhou, F.: Analysis of new top-hat transformation and the application for infrared dim small target detection. Pattern Recogn. **43**(6), 2145–2156 (2010)
8. Wright, J., Yang, A.Y., Ganesh, A., Sastry, S.S., Ma, Y.: Robust face recognition via sparse representation. IEEE Trans. Pattern Anal. Mach. Intell. **31**(2), 210–227 (2008)
9. Jian, M., et al.: Saliency detection based on directional patches extraction and principal local color contrast. J. Vis. Commun. Image Represent. **57**, 1–11 (2018)
10. Gao, C., Meng, D., Yang, Y., Wang, Y., Zhou, X., Hauptmann, A.G.: Infrared patch-image model for small target detection in a single image. IEEE Trans. Image Process. **22**(12), 4996–5009 (2013)
11. Dai, Y., Wu, Y., Song, Y.: Infrared small target and background separation via column-wise weighted robust principal component analysis. Infrared Phys. Technol. **77**, 421–430 (2016)
12. Dai, Y., Wu, Y., Song, Y., Guo, J.: Non-negative infrared patch-image model: robust target-background separation via partial sum minimization of singular values. Infrared Phys. Technol. **81**, 182–194 (2017)
13. Zhang, L., Peng, L., Zhang, T., Cao, S., Peng, Z.: Infrared small target detection via non-convex rank approximation minimization joint l 2, 1 norm. Remote Sens. **10**(11), 1821 (2018)
14. Zhang, T., Wu, H., Liu, Y., Peng, L., Yang, C., Peng, Z.: Infrared small target detection based on non-convex optimization with LP-norm constraint. Remote Sens. **11**(5), 559 (2019)
15. Dai, Y., Wu, Y.: Reweighted infrared patch-tensor model with both nonlocal and local priors for single-frame small target detection. IEEE J. Sel. Top. Appl. Earth Observ. Remote Sens. **10**(8), 3752–3767 (2017)
16. Zhang, L., Peng, Z.: Infrared small target detection based on partial sum of the tensor nuclear norm. Remote Sens. **11**(4), 382 (2019)
17. Zhang, T., Peng, Z., Wu, H., He, Y., Li, C., Yang, C.: Infrared small target detection via self-regularized weighted sparse model. Neurocomputing **420**, 124–148 (2021)

Hyperspectral and Multispectral Image Fusion Based on Unsupervised Feature Mixing and Reconstruction Network

Rui Zhang[1], Peng Fu[1,2]($\boxtimes$), Leilei Geng[3], and Quansen Sun[1]

[1] School of Computer Science and Engineering, Nanjing University of Science and Technology, Nanjing 210094, China
{ruizhang,fupeng,sunquansen}@njust.edu.cn
[2] Jiangsu Key Laboratory of Spectral Imaging and Intelligent Sense, Nanjing University of Science and Technology, Nanjing 210094, China
[3] School of Computer Science and Technology, Shandong University of Finance and Economics, Jinan 250014, China
gengleilei@sdufe.edu.cn

Abstract. Hyperspectral image (HSI) usually has rich spectral information and multispectral image (MSI) has higher spatial resolution. Thus, the fusion of HSI and MSI can achieve information complementarity and increase the reliability of information. Deep learning has been widely applied in the field of HSI/MSI fusion. In order to obtain a HSI with high spatial resolution without sufficient training data, in this paper, we propose a novel unsupervised HSI-MSI fusion network named UFMRS-net. Our model consists of three parts. First, two encoder networks are adopted to obtain the preliminary fusion feature. Second, multiscale preliminary fusion features are fed into the feature mixing and reconstruction module, which is designed to enhance the communication across different levels of backbone features. Finally a spatial attention network is devised to extract tiny textures and enhance the spatial structure. Experimental results compared with some state-of-the-art methods illustrate that our method is outstanding in both visual and numerical results.

Keywords: Hyperspectral image · Multispectral image · Image fusion · Unsupervised learning

1 Introduction

Different remote sensing image sensors can obtain rich remote sensing images and various information about ground objects. For example, panchromatic images have rich spatial information, MSI has rich spatial information and partial spectral information, while HSI has rich spectral information and partial spatial information. Due to its abundant spectral information, HSI is widely used in the fields of ground object classification [8, 14], target detection and so on [11, 18].

To obtain a high-resolution HSI (HR-HSI), an economical solution is to fuse a low-resolution HSI (LR-HSI) and a high-resolution MSI (HR-MSI) of the same scene. At present, in the field of hyperspectral image and multispectral image fusion (HSI/MSI fusion), there are mainly the following four methods: fusion method based on panchromatic (PAN) sharpening, fusion method based on matrix decomposition, fusion method based on tensor representation and fusion method based on deep learning [5].

In the first category, Aiazzi et al. [1] proposed a component substitution fusion method that took the spectral response function (SRF) as part of the model. In the second category, the most classical method based on matrix decomposition is called coupled nonnegative matrix decomposition (CNMF) [22], which has been improved by many researchers later. Bieniarz et al. [3] employed sparse regularization and Lanaras et al. proposed an effective projected gradient solver in [10]. Besides, dictionary learning and sparse coding techniques were adopted in [2, 6]. Various kinds of tensor factorization strategies are also studied, such as Tucker decomposition adopted by Dian et al. [4], coupled sparse tensor factorization by Kanatsoulis et al. [9]. Although conventional methods are widely studied, they usually need to solve complex optimization problems. Moreover, these methods often need reliable prior knowledge and the fusion quality is easily affected by initial parameters.

Recent years, the development of deep learning technology has made remarkable achievements in various fields. Compared with traditional methods, methods based on deep learning do not need cumbersome hand-crafted priors. The supervised methods are commonly used. For example, the PanNet [20] proposed the method which firstly concatenates the features of upsampled observed HSI with observed MSI in high-pass domain and then input them into the CNN. In [19], Xie et al. designed a network that integrates the observation models and image prior knowledge into a single network architecture. Zhou et al. [23] proposed an encoder sub-network to encode the LR-HSI into a latent image and used a pyramid fusion sub-network to enhance the local information of the latent image. However, to achieve a good performance of deep learning method, abundant training data is needed. Due to the limited amount of remote sensing images obtained from remote sensors, unsupervised methods have recently become a trend. Qu et al. [15] developed an unsupervised HSI-SR net with Dirichlet distribution-induced layer embedded, which results in a multi-stage alternating optimization. Li et al. [12] proposed a novel unsupervised HSI-MSI fusion network with the ability of degradations adaptive learning. Attention mechanisms enable networks to ignore irrelevant features and focus on important features. Yao et al. [21] propose a novel unsupervised model including an effective cross-attention module which models the physically mixing properties in HSI into the networks to transfer the spatial information of MSI to HSI and preserve the high spectral resolution itself simultaneously in a coupled fashion. According to the deep image prior (DIP) algorithm, a guided deep decoder (GDD) network was proposed in [16] which can be applied for image denoising and image fusion without training, and Liu et al. [13] proposed an unsupervised multiattention guided network.

Although unsupervised methods make up for the problem of data shortage, these methods do not extract enough semantic features and detailed information. The spectral and spatial information from MSI and HSI is not fully mixed. In order to improve the fusion effect under unsupervised networks, we propose a new unsupervised HSI/MSI

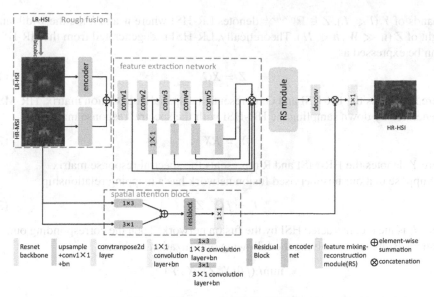

Fig. 1. Structure of the UFMRS-net

fusion method to get high spatial resolution HSI. The contributions of this paper are briefly summarized as follows:

1. We propose a novel unsupervised HSI/MSI fusion model, called UFMRS-net. Specifically, UFMRS-net extracts deep spatial-spectral fused information from the preliminary fusion feature to transfer the spatial information to HSI preserving the high spectral information.
2. We design an effective feature fusion module. Different levels of backbone features are fused and reconstructed in a novel way. The result achieves full complementarity of effective spectral information and spatial information.
3. We devise an effective spatial-attention module to recover the high frequency details of HSI, guiding the generation of output HSI with full semantic information.

2 Proposed Method

2.1 Problem Formulation

Let $X \in \mathbb{R}^{W \times H \times L}$ denote HR-HSI and W, H, and L denote the width, height, and the count of bands, separately. $Y \in \mathbb{R}^{W \times H \times l}$ denotes HR-MSI where l denotes the count

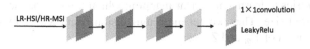

Fig. 2. Structure of encoder net

of bands of Y ($l \ll L$). $Z \in \mathbb{R}^{w \times h \times L}$ denotes LR-HSI where w and h are the width and height of Z ($w \ll W$, $h \ll H$). Theoretically, LR-HSI is degenerated from the HR-HSI. It can be expressed as

$$Z = XG \tag{1}$$

where Z denotes the LR-HSI and G represents the spatial degradation matrix. HR-MSI is generated by down sampling the HR-HSI with the spectral response matrix as

$$Y = RX \tag{2}$$

where Y denotes the HR-MSI and R represents the spectral response matrix.

Suppose that our unsupervised fusion network has a mapping relationship:

$$F = f(Y, Z) \tag{3}$$

where F is the reconstructed HSI by the fusion network. Then the corresponding output X can be estimated by solving the following optimization problem:

$$\min_{\theta} L(f\theta(Y, Z), X, Y) \tag{4}$$

where θ represents the network parameters.

2.2 Network Architecture

Our network structure is shown in Fig. 1, which consists of a rough fusion network, a feature extraction network, a feature mixing-reconstruction network, and a spatial attention branch. The rough fusion network extracts preliminary features of LR-HSI and HR-MSI. The feature extraction network obtains multiscale refine features. Then, multiscale features are fully mixed and reconstructed by the feature mixing-reconstruction network. The spatial attention branch recovers the high frequency details of HSI.

Rough Fusion Network. The rough fusion network is composed of two encoder nets as shown in Fig. 2. This encoder net is like that of autoencoder network except for that the final depth of channels is transformed to 64 for further semantic extraction by Resnet. All the convolution kernel sizes are set to be 1×1. Because the two-dimensional convolution layer which has a kernel size of 1 is equivalent to the full connection layer when applied to the spectral vector, all the full connection layers in the traditional automatic encoder network are replaced by the convolution layer [7]. The LR-HSI is up-scaled to the same size with the HR-HSI by bicubic interpolation before feeding it into the encoder nets. LR-HSI and HR-MSI are transformed as:

$$Y_{en} = f_{enY}(Y) \tag{5}$$

$$Z_{en} = f_{enZ}(Z) \tag{6}$$

where the $f_{en}()$ tries to learn a nonlinear mapping which transforms the input HSI and MSI to the desired size. Then we get the rough fusion result X_{rough} by element-wise summation operation of Y_{en} and Z_{en} as:

$$X_{rough} = Y_{en} + Z_{en}. \tag{7}$$

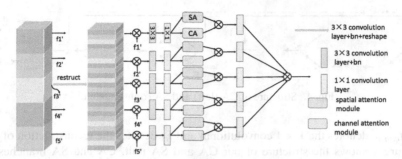

Fig. 3. Structure of RS module

Feature Extraction and Feature Mixing-Reconstruction Networks. To obtain a HR-HSI, X_{rough} will be sent to the later finer network for further processing. First is the feature extraction network as shown in Fig. 1. It is composed of pyramid layers of the ResNet50 backbone. We first extract multi-scale backbone features $f1$ to $f5$ and then upsample them to the same spatial resolution as $f1$. Moreover, five 1×1 convolution units are applied on five feature maps so that they have the same channel depth (64). After above steps, we get five new feature maps f_1' to $f5'$ with the same shape which will be concatenated as f in with 320 (64×5) channels. For every feature map, we have

$$f_1 = f_{conv1}(X_{rough}) \tag{8}$$

$$f_1' = f_{upsample+conv}(f_1) \tag{9}$$

$$\vdots$$

$$f_5 = f_{conv5}(f_5) \tag{10}$$

$$f_5' = f_{upsample+conv}(f_5) \tag{11}$$

$$f_{in} = f_1' \otimes f_2' \otimes f_3' \otimes f_4' \otimes f_5' \tag{12}$$

where f_{conv} represents the convolution of ResNet backbone, $f_{upsample+conv}$ denotes the process of upsample and 1×1 convolution layer and $\otimes$ represents the operation of concatenation.

The feature mixing-reconstruction network is shown in Fig. 3. We divide the input feature f_{in} into five layers according to different sources, then divide each layer into five equal parts, and extract one equal part from each layer to form a new 64 channels feature map. Then according to the previous division order each new formed feature map is concatenated with the former feature layer, that is, a feature map of 64×2 channels is obtained. After the reshape-transpose-reshape process of the feature maps, we generate the final enhanced features (f_1'' to f_5''). Take f_1'' as an example

$$f_1'' = f_{convfli}(f_{rs}(f_{in}) \otimes f_1') \tag{13}$$

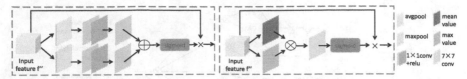

Fig. 4. Structure of CA (left) and SA (right) module

where $f_{convfli}$ denotes the 1×1 convolutional and f_{rs} denotes the reconstruction of f_{in}.

Figure 4 shows the structure of our CA and SA unit. CA and SA branches are channel-wise and spatial-wise attention blocks, respectively. Given the feature f_1'', after CA block, we can get the spatial-wise feature f_{CA}:

$$f_{CA} = f_1'' * sigmoid\left(conv_{1\times1}\left(relu\left(conv_{1\times1}\left(avgpool\left(f_1''\right)\right)\right)\right)\right.$$
$$\left. + conv_{1\times1}\left(relu\left(conv_{1\times1}\left(maxpool\left(f_1''\right)\right)\right)\right)\right). \tag{14}$$

Similarly, after SA block, f_{SA} can be computed as

$$f_{SA} = f_1'' * sigmoid\left(conv_{7\times7}\left(avgpool(f_1'') \otimes maxpool(f_1'')\right)\right) \tag{15}$$

where $conv_{1\times1}$ denotes the convolutional layer with kernel size 1, $conv_{7\times7}$ denotes the convolutional layer with kernel size 7 and $*$ denotes the dot product operation. f_{CA} and f_{SA} will be concatenated and fed into a convolutional layer with kernel size 1 as

$$f'''_1 = conv_{1\times1}(f_{SA} \otimes f_{CA}). \tag{16}$$

The depth of channels for f'''_1 is $128(64 \times 2)$.

Finally, according to the above steps, reconstructed features f'''_1 to f'''_5 are concatenated as the final output of our feature extraction and mixing-reconstruction networks. The depth of channels for the output is $128(64 \times 2)$ which can be described as

$$f_{out} = f'''_1 \otimes f'''_2 \otimes f'''_3 \otimes f'''_4 \otimes f'''_5. \tag{17}$$

Spatial Attention Branch. To recover the high frequency details, such as tiny textures, we design a spatial attention block as shown in Fig. 1. We use HR-MSI as the input of this branch. We first extract low-level features along the horizontal and vertical directions which can maximize the use of spatial information from the input by two 1×3 and 3×1 convolution layers. These low-level features are then fed into a residual block for feature refinement. The output of the spatial attention branch can be described as

$$f_{sa-out} = conv_{1\times1}(Resbolck(conv_{1\times3}(Y) \otimes conv_{3\times1}(Y))). \tag{18}$$

By concatenating f_{sa-out} with the output from the main branch, and passing through a convolution layer, we get the final output image that not only has high spatial resolution, but also retains the spectral information to the greatest extent. This process is represented as

$$\tilde{X} = conv_{hsi}(f_{sa-out} \otimes deconv(f_{out})) \tag{19}$$

where *deconv* denotes a convtranpose2d layer which makes the feature f_{out} the same spatial shape with f_{sa-out}, *conv*$_{hsi}$ denotes a 1×1 convolutional layer that transforms the depth of channels to the same with our desired HR-HSI and $\tilde{X}$ represents the estimated HSI.

2.3   Network Training

Loss Function. Let $X \in \mathbb{R}^{W \times H \times L}$ denote the ground truth HR-HSI, $Y \in \mathbb{R}^{W \times H \times l}$ denotes HR-MSI, $Z \in \mathbb{R}^{w \times h \times L}$ denotes LR-HSI and $\tilde{X} \in \mathbb{R}^{W \times H \times L}$ represents the estimated HSI. The loss function can be defined as

$$\mathcal{L}\left(X, Y, \tilde{X}\right) = \|R\tilde{X} - Y\|_F^2 + \lambda \|\tilde{X} - X\|_F^2 \tag{20}$$

where $\| \cdot \|_F$ is the Frobenius norm, R is the matrix of spectral response function(SRF), and the balance term λ is set to 0.1. The loss function is designed to encourage the spectral similarity and promote the spatial similarity.

Implementation. The proposed method is implemented with pytorch framework running on a NVIDIA GeForce RTX 2080 Ti GPU. We choose Adam optimizer to minimize our loss with a learning rate of 0.001.

3   Experiments

3.1   Datasets and Evaluation Metrics

Datasets. We choose two widely used datasets, including the University of Houston and Washington DC to verify the effectiveness of our proposed method. The University of Houston data covers the spectral range 380–1050 nm with 48 bands. We selected 46 bands consisting of 320×320 pixels for use as experimental data. The Washington DC data has a spectral range of 400–2500 nm including 210 bands. After removing 19 noise bands, we selected 191 bands covering 304×304 pixels for use. All the datasets are used as ground truth. To estimate LR-HSI we use a Gaussian filter to blur the ground truth, then the downsampling operation is performed on the blurred image. The HR-MSI is generated by downsampling the HSI with the spectral response matrix. Specifically, the blue-green-red bands of the Landsat 8 SRF was used for Houston and the blue to SWIR2 part of the Landsat 8 SRF was used for Washington DC.

Evaluation Metrics. Five widely used quality measures are used to evaluate the performance of the fusion results: peak SNR (PSNR), spectral angle mapper (SAM), relative global dimension error (ERGAS), correlation coefficient (CC) and root-mean-square error (RMSE).

3.2 Comparative Experiments

Compared Methods. In this paper, seven state-of-the-art (SOTA) methods in HSI/MSI fusion tasks are compared with our proposed method: traditional method GSA [1], FUSE [17] from Bayesian representation, CNMF [22] based on matrix factorization, tensor-based approach STEREO [9], dictionary learning-based approach NSSR [6], and unsupervised methods uSDN [15] and CUCaNet [21].

Table 1. Quantitative performance comparison with the investigated methods on the Washington DC. The best results are shown in bold.

Methods	PSNR	ERGAS	RMSE	SAM	CC
GSA	39.775	1.2753	0.019709	4.9432	0.97253
FUSE	36.8567	1.2449	0.019406	4.0138	0.96957
CNMF	33.9958	1.2454	0.018142	4.5077	0.95268
NSSR	33.8758	1.8456	0.027685	6.5658	0.9035
STEREO	35.7469	1.923	0.030484	7.6162	0.92246
uSDN	31.6967	2.1741	0.038043	9.8444	0.86629
CUCaNet	35.789	1.3574	0.016317	3.301	0.95139
UFMRS-net	**42.4566**	**0.31965**	**0.003264**	**1.0075**	**0.98391**

Table 2. Quantitative performance comparison with the investigated methods on the University of Houston. The best results are shown in bold.

Methods	PSNR	ERGAS	RMSE	SAM	CC
GSA	36.1889	1.2556	0.019843	3.4666	0.97905
FUSE	33.5127	1.4683	0.023043	3.8707	0.97102
CNMF	34.3297	1.0195	**0.016171**	2.6773	0.98708
NSSR	33.8487	1.3419	0.02123	3.4864	0.9758
STEREO	35.3496	2.4075	0.037255	7.2024	0.92951
uSDN	29.1759	1.9487	0.030407	5.2673	0.95513
CUCaNet	35.2907	1.1854	0.018584	2.8712	0.98111
UFMRS-net	**38.2587**	**0.65884**	0.019451	**1.9287**	**0.99449**

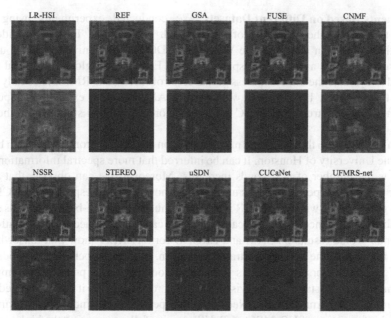

Fig. 5. Visual results and error maps on the Washington DC. First row: LR-HSI, reference and RGB images of the reconstructed HS. Second row: The corresponding error maps.

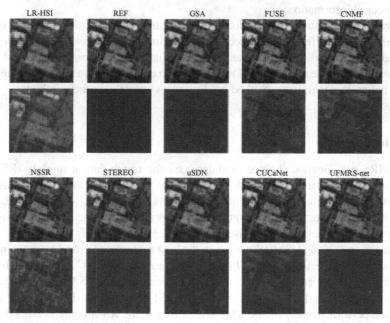

Fig. 6. Visual results and error maps on the University of Houston. First row: LR-HSI, reference and RGB images of the reconstructed HS. Second row: The corresponding error maps.

Experiments Based on Different Datasets. We conducted experiments using two datasets to evaluate the generality of our method. Table 1 and Table 2 provide the quantitative evaluation results of the Washington DC and the University of Houston, respectively. PSNR is a measure of spatial quality. ERGAS is a global statistical measure used to evaluate the dimensionless global error of fused data. RMSE is usually used to show the similarity between the two images. SAM is used to evaluate the spectral consistency of reconstructed HSI. CC is used to score the content similarity of the two images.

It can be seen from the tables that most metrics on the Washington DC perform better than on the University of Houston. It can be inferred that more spectral information will be used as the number of HSI bands increases. Moreover, we can observe that apart from our method, the performance is unstable for most methods, especially that CNMF achieves great RMSE while the PSNR is not up to much. Bayesian-based methods show more stable performance which indicates that they can maintain accurate estimation of coefficients. Worse results on SAM and ERGAS for STEREO show that tensor-based methods may cause the loss of spectral information. In the unsupervised methods, the result of uSDN is worse than others because it does not use a priori downsampling matrix and the multi-stage unsupervised training process makes it easily trapped into local minima. Furthermore, CUCaNet has better performance, indicating it transfers the spatial information of HR-MSI to LR-HSI successfully preserving the high spectral resolution. Remarkably, our method has much better performance in most indicators which proves that our method is outstanding in capturing and effectively preserving spatial-spectral information.

Figures 5, 6 show the visual results of the reconstructed HSI. Due to the difficulty to visually discern the differences of fused results, we display the corresponding error maps compared with ground truth for better visual evaluation. Traditional methods such as CNMF and NSSR have obvious local reconstruction errors while unsupervised methods perform better. In general, our method produces less error than other methods.

3.3 Ablation Study

Our UFMRS-net consists of three modules, i.e., the rough fusion module (RF), the feature mixing-reconstruction module (RS) and the spatial attention module (SA). To investigate the performance of different components in networks, we perform ablation analysis on the Washington DC dataset. Table 3 shows details of the quantitative results, in which CNMF is adopted as the baseline method.

As shown in Table 3, UFMRS-net shows the best performance. And by reducing any block, the network performance will be degraded to some extent. After removing the SA block, the indicators become worse which indicates that the SA block can capture more spatial details and transfer information to HSI. In addition, the network without RS module performs worse than CNMF which means the RS module is crucial in the whole network and supports to fuse more effective spatial and spectral information. Overall, the combination of all the three modules can outperform CNMF in all metrics demonstrating the effectiveness of our whole network architecture.

Table 3. Ablation study on the Washington DC dataset by our UFMRS-net with different modules and a baseline CNMF.

Methods	Module			Metric				
	RF	RS	SA	PSNR	ERGAS	RMSE	SAM	CC
CNMF	-	-	-	33.9958	1.2454	0.018142	4.5077	0.95268
UFMRS-net	✓	✗	✗	24.7099	3.2012	0.045086	12.9322	0.67409
UFMRS-net	✓	✗	✓	29.9895	1.6208	0.014647	4.3886	0.81771
UFMRS-net	✓	✓	✗	36.7658	0.68657	0.00684	2.0617	0.96055
UFMRS-net	✓	✓	✓	**42.4566**	**0.31965**	**0.003264**	**1.0075**	**0.98391**

4   Conclusions

In this paper, an unsupervised method for HSI and MSI fusion is proposed. In this method, the fusion is divided into two steps. Firstly, HSI and MSI are preliminarily fused through two encoder nets. Then, the preliminary fusion feature is fed into the feature mixing and reconstruction module to obtain fully fused spatial and spectral information. At the same time, the final fusion result is obtained by using the detailed information leading by a spatial attention branch. The experimental results show that our method makes full use of the spatial details and spectral features of HSI and MSI. Compared with other HSI/MSI fusion methods, our method obtains the best image fusion results.

Acknowledgement. This work was in part supported by the National Natural Science Foundation of China under Grant no. 61801222, in part supported by the Fundamental Research Funds for the Central Universities under Grant no. 30919011230, in part supported by the Fundamental Research Funds for the Central Universities under Grant no. JSGP202204, and in part supported by the Natural Science Foundation of Shandong Province, under Grant No. ZR2021MF039.

References

1. Aiazzi, B., Baronti, S., Selva, M.: Improving component substitution pansharpening through multivariate regression of ms + pan data. IEEE Trans. Geosci. Remote Sens. **45**(10), 3230–3239 (2007)
2. Akhtar, N., Shafait, F., Mian, A.: Sparse spatio-spectral representation for hyperspectral image super-resolution. In: Fleet, D., Pajdla, T., Schiele, B., Tuytelaars, T. (eds.) ECCV 2014. LNCS, vol. 8695, pp. 63–78. Springer, Cham (2014). https://doi.org/10.1007/978-3-319-10584-0_5
3. Bieniarz, J., Cerra, D., Avbelj, J., M¨uller, R., Reinartz, P.: Hyperspectral image resolution enhancement based on spectral unmixing and information fusion (2011)
4. Dian, R., Li, S., Fang, L.: Learning a low tensor-train rank representation for hyperspectral image super-resolution. IEEE Trans. Neural Networks Learn. Syst. **30**(9), 2672–2683 (2019)
5. Dian, R., Li, S., Sun, B., Guo, A.: Recent advances and new guidelines on hyperspectral and multispectral image fusion. Information Fusion **69**, 40–51 (2021)
6. Dong, W., et al.: Hyperspectral image super-resolution via non-negative structured sparse representation. IEEE Trans. Image Process. **25**(5), 2337–2352 (2016)

7. He, K., Zhang, X., Ren, S., Sun, J.: Deep residual learning for image recognition. In: Proceedings of the IEEE Conference on Computer Vision and Pattern Recognition, pp. 770–778 (2016)
8. Hong, D., Wu, X., Ghamisi, P., Chanussot, J., Yokoya, N., Zhu, X.X.: Invariant attribute profiles: a spatial-frequency joint feature extractor for hyperspectral image classification. IEEE Trans. Geosci. Remote Sens. **58**(6), 3791–3808 (2020)
9. Kanatsoulis, C.I., Fu, X., Sidiropoulos, N.D., Ma, W.K.: Hyperspectral superresolution: a coupled tensor factorization approach. IEEE Trans. Signal Process. **66**(24), 6503–6517 (2018)
10. Lanaras, C., Baltsavias, E., Schindler, K.: Hyperspectral super-resolution by coupled spectral unmixing. In: Proceedings of the IEEE International Conference on Computer Vision, pp. 3586–3594 (2015)
11. Li, C., Gao, L., Wu, Y., Zhang, B., Plaza, J., Plaza, A.: A real-time unsupervised background extraction-based target detection method for hyperspectral imagery. J. Real-Time Image Proc. **15**(3), 597–615 (2017). https://doi.org/10.1007/s11554-017-0742-z
12. Li, J., Zheng, K., Yao, J., Gao, L., Hong, D.: Deep unsupervised blind hyperspectral and multispectral data fusion. IEEE Geosci. Remote Sens. Lett. **19**, 1–5 (2022)
13. Liu, S., Miao, S., Su, J., Li, B., Hu, W., Zhang, Y.D.: Umag-net: a new unsupervised multiattention-guided network for hyperspectral and multispectral image fusion. IEEE J. Sel. Top. Appl. Earth Obs. Remote Sens. **14**, 7373–7385 (2021)
14. Mei, S., Ji, J., Bi, Q., Hou, J., Wei, L.: Integrating spectral and spatial information into deep convolutional neural networks for hyperspectral classification. In: Proceedings of the IGARSS 2016 - 2016 IEEE International Geoscience and Remote Sensing Symposium (2016)
15. Qu, Y., Qi, H., Kwan, C.: Unsupervised sparse dirichlet-net for hyperspectral image super-resolution. In: Proceedings of the IEEE Conference on Computer Vision and Pattern Recognition, pp. 2511–2520 (2018)
16. Uezato, T., Hong, D., Yokoya, N., He, W.: Guided deep decoder: unsupervised image pair fusion. In: Vedaldi, A., Bischof, H., Brox, T., Frahm, J.-M. (eds.) ECCV 2020. LNCS, vol. 12351, pp. 87–102. Springer, Cham (2020). https://doi.org/10.1007/978-3-030-58539-6_6
17. Wei, Q., Dobigeon, N., Tourneret, J.Y.: Fast fusion of multi-band images based on solving a sylvester equation. IEEE Trans. Image Process. **24**(11), 4109–4121 (2015)
18. Wu, X., Hong, D., Tian, J., Chanussot, J., Li, W., Tao, R.: Orsim detector: a novel object detection framework in optical remote sensing imagery using spatial frequency channel features. IEEE Trans. Geosci. Remote Sens. **57**(7), 5146–5158 (2019)
19. Xie, Q., Zhou, M., Zhao, Q., Meng, D., Zuo, W., Xu, Z.: Multispectral and hyperspectral image fusion by ms/hs fusion net. In: Proceedings of the IEEE/CVF Conference on Computer Vision and Pattern Recognition, pp. 1585–1594 (2019)
20. Yang, J., Fu, X., Hu, Y., Huang, Y., Ding, X., Paisley, J.: Pannet: a deep network architecture for pan-sharpening. In: Proceedings of the IEEE International Conference on Computer Vision, pp. 5449–5457 (2017)
21. Yao, J., Hong, D., Chanussot, J., Meng, D., Zhu, X., Xu, Z.: Cross-attention in coupled unmixing nets for unsupervised hyperspectral super-resolution. In: Vedaldi, A., Bischof, H., Brox, T., Frahm, J.-M. (eds.) ECCV 2020. LNCS, vol. 12374, pp. 208–224. Springer, Cham (2020). https://doi.org/10.1007/978-3-030-58526-6_13
22. Yokoya, N., Yairi, T., Iwasaki, A.: Coupled nonnegative matrix factorization unmixing for hyperspectral and multispectral data fusion. IEEE Trans. Geosci. Remote Sens. **50**(2), 528–537 (2011)
23. Zhou, F., Hang, R., Liu, Q., Yuan, X.: Pyramid fully convolutional network for hyperspectral and multispectral image fusion. IEEE J. Sel. Top. Appl. Earth Obs. Remote Sens. **12**(5), 1549–1558 (2019)

Information Adversarial Disentanglement for Face Swapping

Tingting Chen[1,2], Yang Yu[1,2], Rongrong Ni[1,2(✉)], and Yao Zhao[1,2]

[1] Institute of Information Science, Beijing Jiaotong University, Beijing 100044, China
rrni@bjtu.edu.cn
[2] Beijing Key Laboratory of Advanced Information Science and Network Technology, Beijing 100044, China

Abstract. Face swapping can provide data support for face forgery detection, which is a very significant topic in forensics. It is the task of converting the source identity to the target face while preserving target attributes, thus disentangling identity and identity-unrelated (i.e., attribute) features is still a challenging task. In this work, we focus on intra-class (i.e. identities) and inter-class (i.e. identity and attribute) relationships to comprehensively decouple identity and attribute features in an adversarial way for face swapping. The whole network includes Identity-Attribute Adversary (IAA) module, Identity Reconstruction (IR) module and Re-Feeding module. Specifically, for the inter-class relationship, we first propose the IAA module to initially extract independent identity and attribute features. Besides, the Re-Feeding module re-disentangles the generated images and reconstructs original images to further confirm the complete disentanglement of the inter-class information. Finally, for the intra-class relationship, we adopt the IR module based on the same identity image pairs to learn the consistent identity feature without being influenced by attributes. Extensive experiments and comparisons to the existing state-of-the-art face swapping methods demonstrate the effectiveness of our framework.

Keywords: Face forgery detection · Face swapping feature disentanglement · Identity-attribute adversary · Identity reconstruction

1 Introduction

The purpose of face forgery detection is to identify whether a given face has been modified, which is significant in social security. At present, most methods [1–5] are data-driven, thus better face-swapping methods are needed to promote the development of forgery detection algorithms.

The goal of face swapping is to exchange identities while maintaining the attribute information of the target face (e.g., pose, expression, illumination etc.).

This work was supported in part by the National Key R&D Program of China (No. 2021ZD0112100), National NSF of China (No. U1936212, No. 62120106009), and Beijing NSF (No. 4222014).

S. Yu et al. (Eds.): PRCV 2022, LNCS 13537, pp. 201–212, 2022.
https://doi.org/10.1007/978-3-031-18916-6_17

| Source | Target | Generated | Source | Target | Generated |

(a)   (b)

Fig. 1. Two examples of incomplete decoupling. In (a), the result comes with the smile and skin color of the source image, which should be discarded in the swapping stage. In (b), the eyes should have been closed, but became inconsistent due to the influence of the source image. (Color figure online)

Some early learning-based methods (e.g., Deepfakes [6] and FaceSwap [7]) are proposed to perform the task of face swapping, but generated faces have poor visual quality. With the development of Generative Adversarial Networks (GAN) in the field of image generation, GAN-based works [8–11] are proposed to generate more realistic swapping faces. However, the identity and attribute information are expressed by facial features (e.g., nose, mouth), thus the two kinds of information are highly correlated and difficult to disentangle. There are some examples of incomplete decoupling shown in Fig. 1. Specifically, Fig. 1(a) is the swapping face with the smile and skin color of the source image, which carries the attributes that should be discarded in the source identity feature. Figure 1(b) has inconsistent eyes due to the introduction of the source's open eyes. These methods do not disentangle the identity and attribute information completely in the extraction phase, which will inevitably bring the coupled information (i.e., source's attributes and target's identity) that need to be discarded into the fusion process, leading to low fidelity results. Therefore, more independent identity and attribute features need to be extracted for face swapping.

In this paper, we propose a novel framework to extract the more independent identity and attribute feature based on the adversarial feature disentanglement. The most recent work [12] attempts to adopt the information bottleneck principle to purify face identity information, thereby realizing the disentanglement of face identity and attribute information. Compared to this work, we focus on intra-class (i.e. identities) and inter-class (i.e. identity and attribute) relationships, and further reduce the correlation between identity and attribute features in an adversarial way. To be more precise, for the inter-class relationship, we first design the Identity-Attribute Adversary (IAA) module to disentangle the source identity and target attribute for generating identity-changing face images. Then, to confirm that the identity and attribute are completely decoupled, the Re-Feeding module is introduced to perform image-level and feature-level supervision by re-disentangling the generated images to reconstruct original images. Finally, for the intra-class relationship, pairs of images with the same identity are constructed to ensure that identity information is not affected by attribute information, facilitating the decoupling of identity and attribute features. Experiments demonstrate that our method can generate higher fidelity swapping faces.

The main contributions of the paper are summarized as follows. 1) We propose a feature disentanglement framework to better disentangle the identity and attribute feature in an adversarial way to achieve face swapping. 2) For the interclass relationship, we propose the Identity-Attribute Adversary (IAA) module to learn independent identity and attribute features. To further confirm the complete disentanglement of identity and attribute information, we introduce the Re-Feeding module which re-disentangles the swapping face images to provide the supervise at image-level and feature-level. 3) For the intra-class relationship, we design the Identity Reconstruction (IR) module to learn the consistent identity features.

2   Related Works

2.1   Face Swapping

Face swapping has been developing rapidly. The earliest work [22] simply replaces the pixels in the inner face area to achieve face swapping, which can only be achieved when the source and target images have the similar angle and lighting, and the generated faces cannot keep the target expression well. 3D-based methods are proposed to solve these problems. Face2Face [23] uses 3D Morphable Models (3DMM) to simultaneously estimate the expressions of source and target images to achieve expression transfer. These methods make the source faces reenact the expression and pose of the target faces through 3D fitting, resulting in unnatural lighting and textures. Recently, GAN-based methods have made great progress in face swapping. RSGAN [9] processes the face and hair appearance in the latent space, and then achieves face swapping by replacing the latent space representation of the face. IPGAN [10] uses an identity encoder and an attribute encoder to decouple face identity and attribute into vectors to synthesize faces outside the training set. In order to maintain identity and attribute consistency, FaceShifter [11] uses the attention mechanism to adjust the effective area of identity embedding and attribute embedding in the fusion stage. However, these methods do not completely disentangle the identity information and attribute information in the extraction stage, and therefore the coupled information will be brought into the fusion process which makes the swapping faces with the strange identities or inconsistent attributes.

Recently, some works attempt to solve this problem. The work of [24] disentangles the face identity via latent space mapping for the entire head generation. In [13], a hierarchical representation face encoder is leveraged for feature extracting, which represents attribute and identity information with low-level and high-level features, respectively. InfoSwap [12] uses the principle of information bottleneck to purify the face identity information and compress irrelevant attribute information. Unlike these methods, we extract independent identity and attribute features in an adversarial manner.

3   Methods

3.1   Overview

In this section, the architecture of our proposed feature disentanglement framework is shown in Fig. 2. The network is divided into Identity-Attribute Adversary (IAA) module, Re-Feeding module and Identity Reconstruction (IR) module. In order to learn independent identity and attribute features, we construct paired training data with the same identity. Firstly, for inter-class, the IAA module disentangles two images with different identities and generates identity-changing images. Then, we propose the re-feeding strategy which re-disentangles the generated images to supervise the disentangling process effectively. In addition, for intra-class, the IR module disentangles two images with the same identity and reconstructs the attribute images to make identity and attribute more independent.

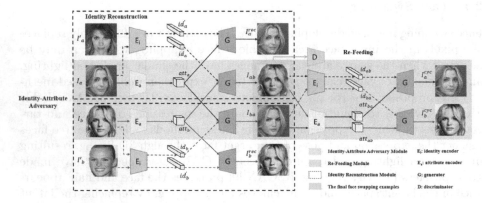

Fig. 2. The proposed framework for face swapping. The whole network consists of three parts. For inter-class, the identity encoder E_i and attribute encoder E_a encode two images with different identities and the generator G generates the identity-changing face images. The discriminator D is used to distinguish the original images (I_a, I_b) from the generated images (I_{ab}, I_{ba}) in the Identity-Attribute Adversary module (IAA in grey). Then the encoders re-disentangle the identity-changing images and generate the original images back in the Re-Feeding module (in blue). Finally, for intra-class, E_i and E_a encode two images with the same identity and then G reconstructs the images provided attribute information in Identity Reconstruction (IR) module. For viewing convenience, the black line represents the flow of information about identity a, and the red line represents the flow of information about identity b. Solid lines represent attribute information, dotted lines represent identity information. (Color figure online)

3.2   Identity-Attribute Adversary

In this section, we encourage encoders to learn independent identity and attribute information. Specifically, we first train the encoder E_i and E_a to extract the identity and attribute features separately. Then, the identity and attribute features are fused to generate the new images across different identities:

$$I_{ab} = G(id_a, att_b) \tag{1}$$

$$I_{ba} = G(id_b, att_a) \tag{2}$$

Although two encoders are trained to extract different features, the generator G will ignore identity features and tend to rely on attribute features with more spatial information to a large extent. To avoid introducing identity information in the target attribute, we propose a new decorrelation loss to learn the independent attribute and identity features based on the distance covariance [21]. Motivated by the conclusion that the distance covariance of two random variables is zero if and only if they are independent, we first compute the Euclidean distance matrices for identity features $a_{i,j}$ and attribute features $b_{i,j}$, respectively.

$$a_{i,j} = ||id_i - id_j||_2, \quad i,j = 1,2,\ldots,n, \tag{3}$$

$$b_{i,j} = ||att_i - att_j||_2, \quad i,j = 1,2,\ldots,n \tag{4}$$

Then take all doubly centered distances.

$$A_{i,j} = a_{i,j} - \bar{a}_{i\cdot} - \bar{a}_{\cdot j} + \bar{a}_{\cdot\cdot} \tag{5}$$

$$B_{i,j} = b_{i,j} - \bar{b}_{i\cdot} - \bar{b}_{\cdot j} + \bar{b}_{\cdot\cdot} \tag{6}$$

where $\bar{a}_{i\cdot}$ is the mean value of the ith row, $\bar{a}_{\cdot j}$ is the mean value of the jth column, and $\bar{a}_{\cdot\cdot}$ is the mean value of the distance matrix A. The notation is similar for the b values. Finally, we regard the squared sample distance covariance which calculates the average of the products $A_{i,j}B_{i,j}$ as our decorrelation loss.

$$L_{decor} = \frac{1}{N^2} \sum_{i=1}^{N} \sum_{j=1}^{N} A_{i,j}B_{i,j} \tag{7}$$

In order to preserve the identity of the source face while maintaining a certain distance from the target identity, the identity contrastive loss is formulated as:

$$L_{id} = 1 - cos(id_{ij}, id_i) + [cos(id_{ij}, id_j) - cos(id_i, id_j)]^2 \tag{8}$$

where i, j come from different identities, id_{ij} represents the identity feature of the face swapping image that generates from source identity i and target identity j.

To make the generated swapping faces realistic, we use the discriminator to discriminate the real images I_b, I_a with the generated images I_{ab}, I_{ba}:

$$\min_{G} \max_{D} L_{adv}(G, D) \tag{9}$$

$$L_{adv}^{ba} = E_{(I_a, I_{ba})}(log(D(I_a)) + log(1 - D(I_{ba}))) \tag{10}$$

$$L_{adv}^{ab} = E_{(I_b, I_{ab})}(log(D(I_b)) + log(1 - D(I_{ab}))) \tag{11}$$

The total adversarial loss is formulated as:

$$L_{adv} = L_{adv}^{ba} + L_{adv}^{ab} \tag{12}$$

3.3 Re-Feeding Module

To further supervise the decoupling process, as for identity, the pre-trained face recognition network can be used to measure identity similarity, while attributes involve many aspects (e.g., pose, expression, illumination), which are difficult to supervise fully and accurately. Therefore, we design a re-feeding strategy to solve this issue.

The whole strategy includes supervision at the feature-level and pixel-level. We assume that the generated results maintain consistent identity and attribute such that the following conditions are satisfied: 1) The generated image and the target image are two images with the same attribute and different identities, which can be extracted the same attribute information through the attribute encoder E_a; 2) The re-swapping images can restore the original images. To achieve the goal, we re-disentangle the generated face swapping images to reconstruct the original images:

$$I_a^{cyc} = G(E_i(I_{ab}), E_a(I_{ba})) \tag{13}$$

$$I_b^{cyc} = G(E_i(I_{ba}), E_a(I_{ab})) \tag{14}$$

Then, we define a feature-level reconstruction loss between the disentangled and re-disentangled attribute features from original target images and the adversarial identities-changing images to confirm the complete disentanglement of attribute features. The feature-level reconstruction loss is defined as:

$$L_{rec}^{fea} = ||att_{ba} - att_a||_1 + ||att_{ab} - att_b||_1 \tag{15}$$

In addition, the image-level reconstruction loss is used between the reconstruction images and the original images to indirectly supervise the identities-changing images maintaining the corresponding attribute and identity information:

$$L_{cyc}^{img} = ||I_a - I_a^{cyc}||_1 + ||I_b - I_b^{cyc}||_1 \tag{16}$$

3.4 Identity Reconstruction

In addition to focusing on inter-class relationships, we further focus on intra-class relationships. Concretely, to further decouple identity and attribute information, we construct a pair of images with the same identity and different attributes to encourage the identity encoder to ignore the variation of attributes and extract the consistent identity feature which can make identity information independent of attribute information. Specifically, we use E_i, E_a to extract identity and attribute features from two images I' and I with the same identity. Then the generator integrates these two features to reconstruct the target image that provides the attribute feature. We adopt the attribute image as the supervision information to guide the identity encoder to disentangle the same identity information from different attributes. Therefore, we define a reconstruction loss L_{rec}^{img} between the reconstructed images and the target images:

$$L_{rec}^{img} = ||I - G(E_i(I'), E_a(I))||_1 \tag{17}$$

	Source	Target	FaceSwap	DeepFakes	FaceShifter	InfoSwap	Ours

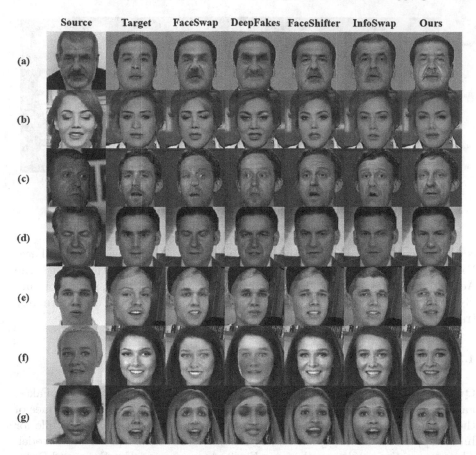

Fig. 3. Qualitative comparison results.

Therefore, the total loss L of the model is formulated as:

$$L = \lambda_{rec}^{img}(L_{rec}^{img} + L_{cyc}^{img}) + \lambda_{rec}^{fea}L_{rec}^{fea} + \lambda_{id}L_{id} + \lambda_{decor}L_{decor} + \lambda_{adv}L_{adv} \quad (18)$$

where $\lambda_{rec}^{img} = 5$ and $\lambda_{rec}^{fea} = \lambda_{id} = \lambda_{decor} = \lambda_{adv} = 1$.

4 Experiments

4.1 Datasets and Implement Details

During training, we take the pre-trained face recognition model [14] as the initial identity encoder. The attribute encoder uses residual blocks to obtain 3-dimensional attribute features including spatial information. As for the generator, the attribute feature is inserted into the generator in a feedforward manner to generate the spatial attributes, such as pose and expression, and the identity is embedded into the generator using weight demodulation [15]. The model

Fig. 4. More results on CelebA-HQ and VGGFace2-HQ.

is trained on CelebA-HQ [16] and VGGFace2-HQ [17], and evaluated on Face-Forensics++ (FF++) [18]. All images are resized to 256×256 for input. The Adam optimizer is adopted. The initial learning rate for encoder, generator, and discriminator is 0.002. The encoder and generator as a whole are alternately trained with the discriminator.

4.2   Comparison with Previous Methods

Qualitative Comparison: Firstly, we compare our results with DeepFakes, FaceSwap, FaceShifter and InfoSwap. In the experiments, we extract frames of the same index in FF++ for DeepFakes, FaceSwap and FaceShifter. While for InfoSwap, the results are generated by the official codes and pre-trained model. The comparative results are shown in Fig. 3. As we can see, FaceSwap and Deep-Fakes have obvious artifacts, because they only synthesize the inner face area and blend it into the target face which leads to the inconsistency between inner and outer face regions. Faceshifter is capable of keeping the identity consistent with the source face but fails to maintain the attribute of the target image and the generated faces look unnatural. In row (b), the generated faces are expected to keep the mouth slightly closed while Faceshifter fails. Simultaneously, the swapping face has two overlapping eyebrows making the face weird in row (g). Benefiting from the full decoupling of identity and attribute information in the extraction stage, our method can be free from the interference of eye closure of the source faces in row (b) and row (d). Besides, we can preserve the identity better than InfoSwap, for instance, we can accurately restore plump cheeks and nasolabial folds of the source face in row (b) and row (d). There are more results on CelebA-HQ and VGGFace2-HQ in Fig. 4. Our method can generate high fidelity face swapping results even when there are large differences in pose (column h), age (column e), and gender (column a) between the source and target images. Faced with occlusions on the source face, we can still extract accurate identity information while maintaining target attributes in column (d).

Table 1. Comparison with SOTA methods.

Method	ID retrieval ↑	Pose ↓	Expression ↓
Deepfakes [6]	85.18	0.9614	0.1806
FaceSwap [7]	67.51	0.4815	**0.0506**
FaceShifter [11]	97.50	0.5015	0.0508
InfoSwap [12]	99.62	0.4475	0.0714
Ours	**99.73**	**0.4471**	0.0768

Quantitative Comparison: We further use three quantitative metrics to evaluate the ability of our method in preserving source identity and target attributes. Specifically, for Deepfakes, FaceSwap and FaceShifter, we sample ten frames from each manipulated video, producing a test set of 10000 images, like the setting in [12]. For InfoSwap and our method, the test set is generated using the same source-target image pairs. We use the other face recognition model [19] to extract the identity embeddings and adopt the cosine similarity to find the nearest source face in the original video frames. ID retrieval in Table 1 is the average retrieval rate, checking whether the nearest face belongs to the correct source, which is used to measure the preservation of source identity. Then we use a 3D face alignment model [20] to estimate the pose and expression parameters and calculate the l_2 distance between swapped faces and the target faces as pose and expression error in Table 1, measuring the preservation of target attributes. As shown in Table 1, our method can achieve the highest ID retrieval score while comparable to InfoSwap in terms of expression and pose preservation.

Table 2. Ablation results of the parts of our framework on FF++.

Model	ID retrieval ↑	Pose ↓	Expression ↓
w/o decorrelation loss	95.41	0.6965	0.1046
w pearson loss	98.64	0.5063	0.0860
w/o Re-Feeding module	96.88	0.5988	0.0969
w/o IR module	97.48	0.4957	0.0874
Final model	**99.73**	**0.4471**	**0.0768**

4.3 Ablation Study

To evaluate the effectiveness of the key component of our framework, we perform the ablation experiments on the FF++. The results are shown in Table 2.

Firstly, in order to analyze the effectiveness of our decorrelation loss, we remove this loss in the IAA module. From the results in the first row of Table 2, the performance of maintaining source identity and target attributes drops, and then we replace this loss with another loss which minimizes the Pearson correlation coefficients between attribute and identity features to reduce the correlation

Fig. 5. Visualization of attribute information.

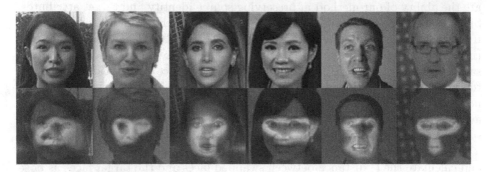

Fig. 6. Visualization of identity information.

between these two types of information. The results are presented in the second row of Table 2. The performance of our framework still drops, which verifies the effectiveness of the decorrelation loss to facilitate the disentanglement of identity and attribute features. Then, to verify the superiority of the re-feeding strategy, we test the framework without the Re-Feeding module. It can be seen that the image-level supervision can effectively confirm whether identity and attribute features are disentangled. Finally, to study the effectiveness of the IR module, we evaluate the performance without the IR module. The training process is unstable and the identity retrieval rate significantly drops. We also employ the same image in place of the image pair of the same identity. The results shown in Table 2 reveal that extracting consistent identity information from different attributes to reconstruct images enables attribute and identity features to be more independent.

To further illustrate the information contained in attribute features, we visualize the information extracted by attribute encoders in Fig. 5. It can be seen that attribute features focus more on pose, expression, lighting and so on. As for identity information, Fig. 6 is the heatmaps of our identity features, indicating that the identity encoder pays more attention to the facial region related to identity.

5 Conclusion

In this paper, we propose a novel adversarial feature disentanglement network to focus on intra-class and inter-class relationships, and further fully disentangle the identity and attribute feature for face swapping. Firstly, for the inter-class relationship, we adopt the Identity-Attribute Adversary (IAA) module to initially extract independent identity and attribute features. Then, the Re-Feeding module re-disentangles the generated images and reconstructs the original images to further confirm the complete disentanglement of the two types of information. Finally, for the intra-class relationship, the Identity Reconstruction (IR) module based on the same identity is designed to extract similar identity information which is not affected by attribute information, making the disentanglement of identity and attribute information more completely. Extensive experiments demonstrate the proposed framework outperforms the previous face swapping methods.

References

1. Afchar, D., Nozick, V., Yamagishi, J., Echizen, I.: MesoNet: a compact facial video forgery detection network. In: 2018 IEEE International Workshop on Information Forensics and Security, pp. 1–7 (2018)
2. Dang, H., Liu, F., Stehouwer, J., Liu, X., Jain, A.K.: On the detection of digital face manipulation. In: Proceedings of the IEEE/CVF Conference on Computer Vision and Pattern recognition, pp. 5781–5790 (2020)
3. Zhao, H., Zhou, W., Chen, D., Wei, T., Zhang, W., Yu, N.: Multi-attentional deepfake detection. In: Proceedings of the IEEE/CVF Conference on Computer Vision and Pattern Recognition, pp. 2185–2194 (2021)
4. Chai, L., Bau, D., Lim, S.-N., Isola, P.: What makes fake images detectable? understanding properties that generalize. In: Vedaldi, A., Bischof, H., Brox, T., Frahm, J.-M. (eds.) ECCV 2020. LNCS, vol. 12371, pp. 103–120. Springer, Cham (2020). https://doi.org/10.1007/978-3-030-58574-7_7
5. Yu, Y., Ni, R., Li, W., Zhao, Y.: Detection of AI-manipulated fake faces via mining generalized features. ACM Trans. Multimed. Comput. Commun. Appl. (TOMM) **18**(4), 1–23 (2022)
6. Deepfakes. https://github.com/deepfakes/faceswap. Accessed 10 May 2022
7. Korshunova, I., Shi, W., Dambre, J., Theis, L.: Fast face-swap using convolutional neural networks. In: Proceedings of the IEEE International Conference on Computer Vision, pp. 3677–3685 (2017)
8. Natsume, R., Yatagawa, T., Morishima, S.: FSNet: an identity-aware generative model for image-based face swapping. In: Jawahar, C.V., Li, H., Mori, G., Schindler, K. (eds.) ACCV 2018. LNCS, vol. 11366, pp. 117–132. Springer, Cham (2019). https://doi.org/10.1007/978-3-030-20876-9_8
9. Natsume, R., Yatagawa, T., Morishima, S.: RSGAN: face swapping and editing using face and hair representation in latent spaces. arXiv preprint arXiv:1804.03447. (2018)
10. Bao, J., Chen, D., Wen, F., Li, H., Hua, G.: Towards open-set identity preserving face synthesis. In: Proceedings of the IEEE Conference on Computer Vision and Pattern Recognition, pp. 6713–6722 (2018)

11. Li, L., Bao, J., Yang, H., Chen, D., Wen, F.: FaceShifter: towards high fidelity and occlusion aware face swapping. arXiv preprint arXiv:1912.13457 (2019)
12. Gao, G., Huang, H., Fu, C., Li, Z., He, R.: Information bottleneck disentanglement for identity swapping. In: Proceedings of the IEEE/CVF Conference on Computer Vision and Pattern Recognition, pp. 3404–3413 (2021)
13. Zhu, Y., Li, Q., Wang, J., Xu, C. Z., Sun, Z.: One shot face swapping on megapixels. In: Proceedings of the IEEE/CVF Conference on Computer Vision and Pattern Recognition, pp. 4834–4844 (2021)
14. He, K., Zhang, X., Ren, S., Sun, J.: Deep residual learning for image recognition. In: Proceedings of the IEEE Conference on Computer Vision and Pattern Recognition, pp. 770–778 (2016)
15. Karras, T., Laine, S., Aittala, M., Hellsten, J., Lehtinen, J., Aila, T.: Analyzing and improving the image quality of StyleGAN. In: Proceedings of the IEEE/CVF Conference on Computer Vision and Pattern Recognition, pp. 8110–8119 (2020)
16. Karras, T., Aila, T., Laine, S., Lehtinen, J.: Progressive growing of GANs for improved quality, stability, and variation. arXiv preprint arXiv:1710.10196 (2017)
17. VGGFace2-HQ. https://github.com/NNNNAI/VGGFace2-HQ. Accessed 10 May 2022
18. Rossler, A., Cozzolino, D., Verdoliva, L., Riess, C., Thies, J., Nießner, M.: Face-Forensics++: learning to detect manipulated facial images. In: Proceedings of the IEEE/CVF International Conference on Computer Vision, pp. 1–11 (2019)
19. Wang, H., et al.: CosFace: large margin cosine loss for deep face recognition. In: Proceedings of the IEEE Conference on Computer Vision and Pattern Recognition, pp. 5265–5274 (2018)
20. Guo, J., Zhu, X., Yang, Y., Yang, F., Lei, Z., Li, S.Z.: Towards fast, accurate and stable 3D dense face alignment. In: Vedaldi, A., Bischof, H., Brox, T., Frahm, J.-M. (eds.) ECCV 2020. LNCS, vol. 12364, pp. 152–168. Springer, Cham (2020). https://doi.org/10.1007/978-3-030-58529-7_10
21. Székely, G.J., Rizzo, M.L.: Brownian distance covariance. Ann. Appl. Stat. 3(4), 1236–1265 (2009)
22. Bitouk, D., Kumar, N., Dhillon, S., Belhumeur, P., Nayar, S.K.: Face swapping: automatically replacing faces in photographs. In: ACM SIGGRAPH 2008 papers, pp. 1–8 (2008)
23. Thies, J., Zollhofer, M., Stamminger, M., Theobalt, C., Nießner, M.: Face2Face: real-time face capture and reenactment of RGB videos. In: Proceedings of the IEEE Conference on Computer Vision and Pattern Recognition, pp. 2387–2395 (2016)
24. Nitzan, Y., Bermano, A., Li, Y., Cohen-Or, D.: Face identity disentanglement via latent space mapping. arXiv preprint arXiv:2005.07728 (2020)

A Dense Prediction ViT Network for Single Image Bokeh Rendering

Zhifeng Wang[ID] and Aiwen Jiang[✉][ID]

School of Computer and Information Engineering, Jiangxi Normal University, No. 99, Ziyang Avenue, Nanchang 330022, Jiangxi, China
jiangaiwen@jxnu.edu.cn

Abstract. Rendering bokeh effects has become a research hotspot in the field of computational photography. Its essence is to focus on foreground area of interest, and blur other background areas for vision aesthetic requirements. Witness of the great success of vision transformer on dense prediction tasks, in this paper, we further expand the ability of transformer on new task and propose a dense prediction ViT structure for single bokeh image rendering. We leverage vision transformers as the backbone networks and operates on "bag-of-words" representations of image at high levels. Image-like feature representations of different resolutions are aggregated to obtain the final dense prediction. The proposed network has been compared with several state-of-the-art methods on a public large-scale bokeh dataset- the "EBB!" Dataset. The experiment results demonstrate that the proposed network can achieve new state-of-the-art performances on SSIM, LPIPS and MOS criterions. Its predicted bokeh effects are more in line with popular perception. Related source codes and pre-trained models of the proposed model will be available soon on https://github.com/zfw-cv/BEViT.

Keywords: Bokeh rendering · Vision transformers · Dense prediction · Vision tokens

1 Introduction

Bokeh effect is a kind of "blurring quality". It generally refers to "the soft out of focus background effect obtained when fast shooting an object with a lens of large aperture". In practice, images with visual pleasing bokeh effect are often produced through professional DLSR cameras, as shown in the Fig. 1. However, they are often unattainable for low-cost mobile cameras with compact optics and tiny sensors [23]. In order to balance the aesthetic requirements of photo quality and the cost of expensive high-end SLR cameras, bokeh effect has to be simulated computationally. Therefore, synthetic bokeh effect rendering has emerged as an attractive machine learning technology [1–3] for engineering applications on imaging systems.

From the aspect of modeling strategies, many of mainstream methods heavily relied on prior knowledge, such as the estimation of scene depth [20] for

S. Yu et al. (Eds.): PRCV 2022, LNCS 13537, pp. 213–222, 2022.
https://doi.org/10.1007/978-3-031-18916-6_18

Fig. 1. The examples of image with bokeh effects which highlights object of interest in focus.

rendering. One of the main solutions was to capture depth information with dual-cameras. For example, Busam et al. [7] proposed a method based on stereo vision, which uses high-quality depth information for refocusing and rendering. However, in cases of monocular camera or post-processing already captured images, the dual-camera strategy is unapplicable. Therefore, pre-trained depth estimation models were instead employed as an alternate strategy. Typically, Dutta et al. [16] performed convolutions of different sizes by means of Gaussian blur kernels, and then perform weighted summation. Ligun et al. [10] proposed a deep neural network to synthesize a lens blur and guided upsampling module, and render to generate a bokeh effect. Purohit et al. proposed the DDDF [4], which was guided by pre-trained salient-region segmentation and depth-estimation modules to distinguish between large foreground and background regions and their relative depth.

Depth estimation inevitably increases the computation burden unaffordable on small mobile cameras. Moreover, the robustness and applicability of the prior knowledge like the depth affects final results in the pros and the cons. Though incorporating prior knowledge to simulate realistic bokeh blur has potentials to improve visual effect, however, when the prior information estimated does not work, unexpected out-of-focus blurriness conversely deteriorates the quality of ultimate synthetic image.

In order to solve the above problems, researchers recently consider bokeh synthetic as a kind of image translation task and achieve impressive success. Ignatov et al. [5] proposed a multi-scale end-to-end PyNet structure for image rendering. Dutta et al. [9] proposed a deep multi-scale hierarchical network (DMSHN) for bokeh effect rendering. Their model synthesized bokeh effect by exploiting multi-scale input images at different processing levels. Each lower level acts in the residual manner by contributing its residual image to the higher level.

In these mainstream bokeh rendering strategies, CNNs have dominated the tasks. Recently, the Vision Transformer (ViT) [11] architecture has shown superiorities over traditional CNNs, since the transformers can offer parallel processing and global view in a single layer. Pioneering applications of ViT were to directly employ vanilla Transformer architectures. Specifically, Dosovitskiy et al. [24] split an image into non-overlapping patches, taking these image patches as input tokens of the Transformer after a linear patch projection layer.

Witness of the great success of vision transformer with vanilla structure, various variants have emerged in an endless stream [22]. Among them, Swin Transformer [12] introduced a hierarchical feature expression method, and achieved excellent performance in the field of object detection and semantic segmentation. Rene Ranftl et al. [14] designed a dense prediction transformer to provide fine-grained and globally coherent predictions. Moreover, in many low-level dense prediction practices, such as the recursive transformer [13] for single-image deraining, self-attention structure with residual connections based on recursive local windows was employed.

Following these strategies, in this paper, we further expand the ability of transformer on new dense prediction task and propose a dense prediction ViT structure for single bokeh image rendering. The contributions are summarized as followings:

- The proposed network is a new attempt of vision transformer in the field of bokeh rendering. The evaluations have been performed on a large public dataset "EBB!". Compared with the current mainstream algorithm models, the proposed method has greater advantages on SSIM and LPIPS performance.
- Image-like feature representation in the dense prediction ViT structure enables the proposed model to obtain global receptive field at each resolutions, which is easier to maintain foreground details and render bokeh effects more aesthetically pleasingly and more realistically.

2   Model

The proposed network is in encoder-decoder structure, as shown in Fig. 2. We leverage vision transformers as the backbone networks, and show how to predict out-of-focus bokeh through the representation generated by the encoder. In the following sub-sections, we describe the proposed network in details.

2.1   Encoder

Similar to traditional transformers [11], vision transformer operates on "bag-of-words" representations of image at high levels. Firstly, the image is divided into non-overlap patches in grid. The patch is of size 16×16. Each a patch is similarly taken as a "token", which is flattened and linearly mapped to feature vector. To keep the spatial positions of these patches, the patch embedding and its corresponding position embedding are concatenated as the patch representation.

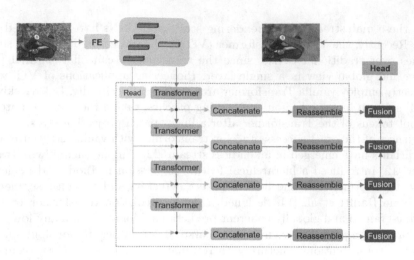

Fig. 2. The architecture of the proposed ViT structure for single image bokeh rendering

Following the applying way of transformer in NLP, a special token is additionally added into token set. The special token is not grounded in the input image and serves as the global image representation. Therefore, a image of size $W \times H$ is represented by a set $t = \{t_0, t_1, ..., t_N\}$, where $N = \frac{WH}{p^2}$ and t_0 is the special token.

The input token set is transformed using L transformer layers into new representations. Since there is a one-to-one relationship between tokens and image patches, the encoder can maintain the spatial resolution of the initial embedding at each stage.

2.2 Decoder

The decoder is similar to the convolutional decoder in the DPT model [14]. The main purpose is to convert a series of tokens into image-like feature representations of different resolutions, and then aggregate these features to obtain the final dense prediction. The basic steps include reassemble modules and fusion modules. Their module details are shown in Fig. 3.

The reassemble process include three stages, as defined in Eq. 1.

$$Reassemble_s^{\hat{D}}(t) = (Resample_s \circ Concatenate \circ Read(t)) \qquad (1)$$

where s represents the output size ratio of the restored representation relative to the input image, and $\hat{D}$ represents the feature dimension of the output.

At the first "Read" stage $R^{N+1 \times D} \rightarrow R^{N \times D}$, N+1 tokens are mapped to N tokens that is amenable to spatial concatenation into an image-like representation through the projection as defined in Eq. 2. It is to handle the token that potentially still can be useful to capture and distribute global information.

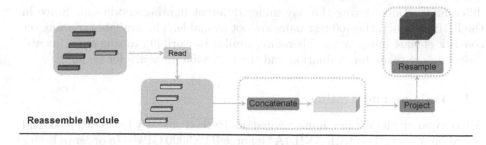

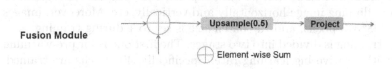

Fig. 3. Details of reassemble module and fusion module. Above: Overview of the Reassemble. Tokens are reassembled into different feature maps in four different stages with a resolution of $\frac{1}{s}$ of the input image. Bottom: Overview of the Fusion blocks. This part upsamples each stage, where feature fusion is performed using residual convolutional units [8].

$$Read_{proj}(t) = mlp(cat(t_1, t_0)), ..., mlp(cat(t_N, t_0)) \tag{2}$$

At the second "Concatenation" stage, the resulting N tokens are reshaped into an image-like representation by placing them according to their spatial positions of the initial patches. Similar to the feature reorganization in [14], features of four different stages at different resolutions are selected. Specifically, features from deeper layers of the transformer are selected for lower resolution, whereas features from early layers are assembled at higher resolution. In this paper, we select tokens from $\{3, 6, 9, 12\}^{th}$ layers.

At the third "Resample" stage $R^{\frac{W}{p} \times \frac{H}{p} \times D} \rightarrow R^{\frac{W}{s} \times \frac{H}{s} \times \hat{D}}$, 1×1 convolutions are employed to project the input representation to $\hat{D}$, followed by a padded 3×3 convolutions before spatial downsampling (if $s > q$) and upsampling (if $s \leq q$) operations, respectively. The final feature dimension is $\hat{D} = 256$.

Finally, in the fusion module, the extracted feature maps from consecutive stages are combined with residual connections, and progressively upsampling by a factor of two at each fusion stage. Therefore, the final output after all fusion processes has half the resolution of the input image. Output head with one deconvolutional layer is attached to produce the bokeh effect predictions at the same resolution as the input image.

3 Experiments

3.1 Dataset

All experiments are performed on the "Everything is Better with Bokeh (EBB!)" dataset [16]. It contains 5094 pairs of bokeh and bokeh-free images taken at different locations during the day under different lighting conditions. Since in the EBB! Dataset, the 400 test pairs are not available. The available training set consists of 4694 image pairs. Therefore, similar to work [9], during experiments, 294 pairs are taken for evaluation and the rest 4400 pairs are for training.

3.2   Training and Testing

All compared models are implemented in Python and PyTorch, trained and tested on workstations with NVIDIA GeForce RTX3090 GPUs. In order to better apply to the transformer structure, we have expanded the dataset through affine transformation, flipping image horizontally and vertically, etc. Moreover, images are scaled to 768*512 pixels, and the batch size is set to 1 during training.

The whole training is divided into two stages. The first one is for pre-warming the network with relative big learning rate. Specifically, 40 epochs are trained, and the learning rate is set to 1e-5. Then, at the second stage, learning rate is adjusted to a smaller one, such as 2e-6. The outputs of the first stage are taken as input of the proposed model, and 60 epochs are further trained with small learning rates. In this case, it facilitates quick generation of bokeh results and reduces model training time.

For comprehensively parameters learning, training losses both on global and component levels are considered.

In the first training stage, for facilitating global implementation, L_1 loss is implemented, as shown in Eq. 3. The $Loss_B$ loss benefits pixel-wise reconstruction of synthesized bokeh image.

$$Loss_B = |\hat{I}_b - GT|_1 \tag{3}$$

In the second training stage, $Loss_C$ loss, composed of L_1 loss and $SSIM$ loss are employed, shown in Eq. 4. It can be a good measure of the similarity between the reconstructed image and the original image.

$$Loss_C = Loss_B + SSIM(\hat{I}_b, GT) \tag{4}$$

3.3   Evaluation Metrics

Peak Signal-to-Noise Ratio (PSNR) [17], Structural Similarity (SSIM) [18] and Perceptual Image Patch Similarity Index (LPIPS) [19] are employed as performance evaluation metrics. The PSNR and SSIM emphasize objective evaluation of image pixel quality. The LPIPS is more concerned with perceptual judgment of image quality.

Since the evaluation of bokeh effects is subjective, we pay more attention to the essential needs of the bokeh rendering task. The goal is to generate a bokeh image with aesthetic effects that is in line with public aesthetics, not solely in the pursuit of excellence on objective performance metrics. Therefore, a user study with MOS (Mean Opinion Scores) metric [2] is conducted to rank perceptual qualities of the predicted images. Specifically, we recruited 30 people with some photography knowledge to participate in the evaluation. Participants were asked to compare the original images from the Canon by choosing between 1–5 levels (5 of comparable perceived quality, 4 of slightly poorer, 3 of markedly poorer, and 1 of a completely damaged image). The expressed preferences were then averaged according to each test image, and then the final MOS was obtained according to each method.

3.4 Results

To demonstrate the effectiveness of the proposed strategy, we compare it with some current state-of-the-art methods. The experiment results are shown in Table 1. The experiment results show that, in most aspects, our model has surpassed the current international mainstream algorithms, achieving state-of-the-art performance.

Table 1. The comparisons with state-of-the-art methods on "EBB!" Bokeh Dataset. ↑ means the higher the value, the better the performance. ↓ means the smaller the value, the better the performance.

Method	PSNR↑	SSIM↑	LPIPS↓	MOS↑
SKN [1]	24.66	0.8521	0.3323	4.1
Stacked DMSHN [9]	24.72	0.8793	0.2271	4.3
DDDF [4]	24.14	0.8713	0.2482	3.4
BGGAN [15]	24.39	0.8645	0.2467	3.8
PyNet [5]	24.93	0.8788	0.2219	4.2
DBSI [16]	23.45	0.8657	0.2463	3.5
Ours	24.57	0.8880	0.1985	4.4

For better understanding the advantages of the proposed strategy on bokeh rendering, samples of visual comparisons are demonstrated in Fig. 4 and Fig. 5.

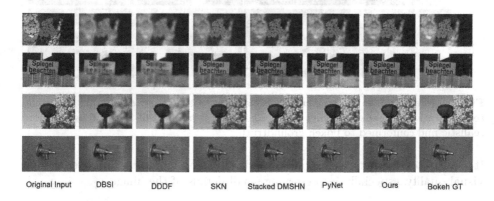

Original Input   DBSI   DDDF   SKN   Stacked DMSHN   PyNet   Ours   Bokeh GT

Fig. 4. Samples of visual comparisons between the proposed network and some representative state-of-the-art methods. The images predicted by our method have more realistic effects.

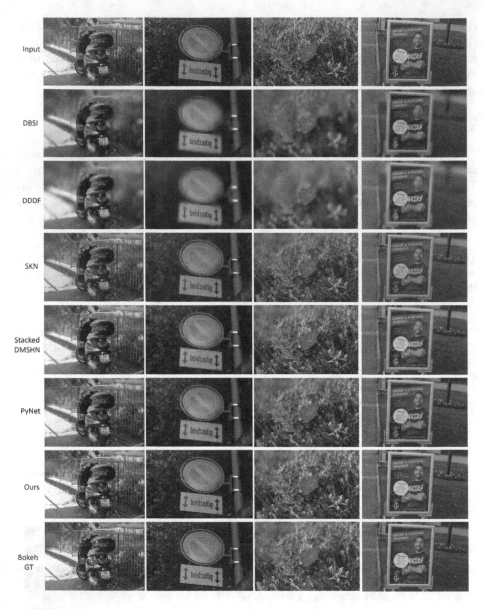

Fig. 5. More examples of visual comparisons between the proposed network and some representative state-of-the-art methods. The in-focus and out-of-focus areas are more realistic and conformed to bokeh groundtruth.

It is easy to see that the proposed method has a significant improvement on visual quality, especially in preserving small details of the image.

4   Conclusion

In this paper, a new attempt of applying vision transformer (ViT) on bokeh rendering task has been conducted. Image-like feature representation in the dense prediction ViT structure enables the proposed model to obtain global receptive field at each resolutions, maintaining foreground details and background blurring. The proposed network is experimented on an existing public large-scale bokeh dataset "EBB!". Compared with state-of-the-art methods, its bokeh predictions are more in line with popular perception and achieve new state-of-the-art performances on SSIM, LPIPS and MOS criterions.

Acknowledgement. This work is supported by National Natural Science Foundation of China under Grand No. 61966018.

References

1. Ignatov, A., Patel, J., Timofte, R., et al.: Aim 2019 challenge on bokeh effect synthesis: methods and results. In: 2019 IEEE/CVF International Conference on Computer Vision Workshop (ICCVW), pp. 3591–3598. IEEE (2019)
2. Ignatov, A., et al.: AIM 2020 challenge on rendering realistic Bokeh. In: Bartoli, A., Fusiello, A. (eds.) ECCV 2020. LNCS, vol. 12537, pp. 213–228. Springer, Cham (2020). https://doi.org/10.1007/978-3-030-67070-2_13
3. Wang, Z., Jiang, A., Zhang, C., et al.: Self-supervised multi-scale pyramid fusion networks for realistic bokeh effect rendering. J. Vis. Commun. Image Represen. **87**, 103580 (2022)
4. Purohit, K., Suin, M., Kandula, P., et al.: Depth-guided dense dynamic filtering network for bokeh effect rendering. In: 2019 IEEE/CVF International Conference on Computer Vision Workshop (ICCVW), pp. 3417–3426. IEEE (2019)
5. Ignatov, A., Patel, J., Timofte, R.: Rendering natural camera bokeh effect with deep learning. In: Proceedings of the IEEE/CVF Conference on Computer Vision and Pattern Recognition Workshops, pp. 418–419 (2020)
6. Long, J., Shelhamer, E., Darrell, T.: Fully convolutional networks for semantic segmentation. In: Proceedings of the IEEE Conference on Computer Vision and Pattern Recognition, pp. 3431–3440 (2015)
7. Busam, B., Hog, M., McDonagh, S., et al.: Sterefo: efficient image refocusing with stereo vision. In: Proceedings of the IEEE/CVF International Conference on Computer Vision Workshops (2019)
8. Lin, G., Milan, A., Shen, C., et al.: Refinenet: multi-path refinement networks for high-resolution semantic segmentation. In: Proceedings of the IEEE Conference on Computer Vision and Pattern Recognition, pp. 1925–1934 (2017)
9. Dutta, S., Das, S.D., Shah, N.A., et al.: Stacked deep multi-scale hierarchical network for fast Bokeh effect rendering from a single image. In: Proceedings of the IEEE/CVF Conference on Computer Vision and Pattern Recognition, pp. 2398–2407 (2021)
10. Wang, L., Shen, X., Zhang, J., et al.: DeepLens: shallow depth of field from a single image. arXiv preprint arXiv:1810.08100 (2018)
11. Vaswani, A., Shazeer, N., Parmar, N., et al.: Attention is all you need. In: Advances in Neural Information Processing Systems, vol. 30 (2017)

12. Liu, Z., Lin, Y., Cao, Y., et al.: Swin transformer: hierarchical vision transformer using shifted windows. In: Proceedings of the IEEE/CVF International Conference on Computer Vision, vol. 10012–10022 (2021)
13. Liang, Y., Anwar, S., Liu, Y.: DRT: A Lightweight Single Image Deraining Recursive Transformer. arXiv preprint arXiv:2204.11385 (2022)
14. Ranftl, R., Bochkovskiy, A., Koltun, V.: Vision transformers for dense prediction. In: Proceedings of the IEEE/CVF International Conference on Computer Vision, pp. 12179–12188 (2021)
15. Qian, M., et al.: BGGAN: Bokeh-glass generative adversarial network for rendering realistic bokeh. In: Bartoli, A., Fusiello, A. (eds.) ECCV 2020. LNCS, vol. 12537, pp. 229–244. Springer, Cham (2020). https://doi.org/10.1007/978-3-030-67070-2_14
16. Dutta, S.: Depth-aware blending of smoothed images for bokeh effect generation. J. Vis. Commun. Image Represent. **77**, 103089 (2021)
17. Paul, E.S., Anitha, J.: Chapter 5 - analysis of transform-based com-pression techniques for mri and ct images. In: Hemanth, D.J., Gupta, D., Emilia Balas, V. (eds.) Intelligent Data Analysis for Biomedical Applications. Intelligent Data-Centric Systems, pp. 103–120. Academic Press (2019)
18. Wang, Z., Bovik, A.C., Sheikh, H.R., et al.: Image quality assessment: from error visibility to structural similarity. IEEE Trans. Image Process. **13**(4), 600–612 (2004)
19. Zhang, R., Isola, P., Efros, A.A, et al.: The unreasonable effectiveness of deep features as a perceptual metric. In: Proceedings of the IEEE Conference on Computer Vision and Pattern Recognition, pp. 586–595 (2018)
20. Li, Z., Snavely, N.: Megadepth: learning single-view depth prediction from internet photos. In: Proceedings of the IEEE Conference on Computer Vision and Pattern Recognition, pp. 2041–2050 (2018)
21. He, K., Zhang, X., Ren, S., et al.: Deep residual learning for image recognition. In: Proceedings of the IEEE Conference on Computer Vision and Pattern Recognition, pp. 770–778 (2016)
22. Chen, H., Wang, Y., Guo, T., et al.: Pre-trained image processing transformer. In: Proceedings of the IEEE/CVF Conference on Computer Vision and Pattern Recognition, pp. 12299–12310 (2021)
23. Xu, X., et al.: Rendering portraitures from monocular camera and beyond. In: Ferrari, V., Hebert, M., Sminchisescu, C., Weiss, Y. (eds.) ECCV 2018. LNCS, vol. 11213, pp. 36–51. Springer, Cham (2018). https://doi.org/10.1007/978-3-030-01240-3_3
24. Dosovitskiy, A., Beyer, L., Kolesnikov, A., et al.: An image is worth 16x16 words: transformers for image recognition at scale. In: International Conference on Learning Representations (2021)

Multi-scale Coarse-to-Fine Network for Demoiréing

Chenming Liu[1,2], Jinjing Li[1], Ruipeng Gang[2(✉)], Shuang Feng[1], and Mengqi Chang[1]

[1] Communication University of China, Beijing, China
[2] Academy of Broadcasting Science, NRTA, Beijing, China
gangruipeng@abs.ac.cn

Abstract. Demoiréing is a multi-level image restoration task involving texture and color restoration. However, the moiré pattern in documents is difficult to remove, and the blurred font also appears. In this paper, we propose a multi-scale coarse-to-fine neural network to solve this problem. First, a multi-scale dense network structure is adopted to capture the moiré pattern from different resolution features, in which a spatial attention module is utilized that has remarkable performance in capturing moiré pattern. Second, a lightweight deblurring network is taken to remove the blur in documents for further optimziation. Through ablation experiments, the effectiveness of our method is demonstrated. The network proposed in this paper takes the third place in the document demoiréing track of the 2022 Baidu.com AI Competition.

Keywords: Image restoration · Demoiréing · Deep learning

1 Introduction

Digital documents are very common in our daily life, taking pictures through mobile devices is an easy way to save information. But the moiré pattern will appear when we scan electronic screens, because of the color filter array of the camera interferes. This phenomenon reduces the visual quality severely. So it is necessary to remove the moiré pattern from the picture in the later stages of shooting.

With the development of deep learning, Convolutional Neural Networks (CNN)-based models have made great progress in image restoration. In image restoration tasks such as color enhancement, denoising, and super-resolution, the complex mapping relationship between input images and real images can be better fitted by CNN-based methods. However, unlike other image restoration, moiré patterns have a mixture of low and high frequency information with different variation in frequency, shape, and color. As shown in Fig. 1, it is difficult to remove the moiré patterns in documents. Some works [4,19,26] try to

---

Jinjing Li—Equal contribution.

© The Author(s), under exclusive license to Springer Nature Switzerland AG 2022
S. Yu et al. (Eds.): PRCV 2022, LNCS 13537, pp. 223–235, 2022.
https://doi.org/10.1007/978-3-031-18916-6_19

design different deep learning networks for dmoiréing. DMCNN [19] proposes a multi-scale CNN with multi-resolution branches to process moiré patterns and sums the outputs of different scales to obtain the final output image. MMDM [4] improves DMCNN by introducing an adaptive instance normalization method based on dynamic feature encoders. MBCNN [26] proposes a multi-scale learnable band-pass filter to learn the frequency of an image after moiré removal, while applying a two-step tone mapping strategy to recover color. Considering that it is difficult to distinguish moiré stripes from the real image content in RGB space, WDNet [14] takes the input images into a wavelet transform, then inputs it into the double branch network, and finally through utilize a wavelet inverse transform to obtain a moiré-removed RGB image. In this paper, we propose a multi-scale coarse-to-fine network. There are two key points in our method: first, a multi-scale encoder is used to encode the input images, which can better capture the moiré patterns in different scales. Second, a coarse-to-fine structure is used to further optimize the results of multi-scale network. Our contributions are as follows:

- In the first stage, we apply a multi-scale network which can remove the moiré patterns and a spatial attention module to improve the ability to capture moiré pattern.
- To optimize visual quality of font deblurring, we apply a lightweight deblurring network to cascade with the first-stage network. By introducing the second-stage network, the details of the image become clearer.
- The network model proposed in this paper takes the third place in the document demoiréing track of 2022 Baidu.com AI competition.

2   Related Work

Image restoration is one of the most important tasks in computer vision. It is divided into many different subtasks, such as image denoising [23] and super-resolution [10], which focus on high-frequency details. In contrast, color enhancement focuses on low-frequency information of images. According to the characteristics of moiré generation, demoiréing task need to focus on both low-frequency and high-frequency. Therefore, it is more difficult to remove moiré from an image than other tasks.

Image Restoration. Dong et al. [3] firstly propose an end-to-end convolutional neural networks for image super-resolution. Several subsequent works [13,24] further improve these models by increasing network depth, introducing skip connections [18] and residual networks. Later, deeper network models [12,20] are also proposed. DRCN [12] employs recurrent network learning with parameter sharing. Tai et al. [20] introduce recurrent residual learning networks and proposes a network memory module. EDVR [21] proposes a pyramidal, cascaded alignment module and extract features using a time-space attention module, which proves the effectiveness of multi-scale information in image restoration. In addition, several studies focus their attention on multi-scale convolutional neural networks. Mao et al. [5] propose a multi-scale auto-encoder based on skip connections. Cavigelli et al. [2] introduce a multi-supervised network for reducing compression artifacts. These methods also inspire us to use multi-scale information for demoiréing.

Frequency Domain Learning. Several studies [6,9,27] have recently appeared for the frequency domain. Liu et al. [15] replace the traditional image zoom-in and zoom-out operations by introducing wavelet transform. Guo et al. [6] introduce convolution-based window sampling, discrete cosine transform (DCT) to construct a network model in the DCT domain. These methods prove that CNN is effective in frequency domain. Zheng et al. [27] introduce implicit DCT to extend DCT domain learning to color image compression, reducing artifacts in images. Jiang et al. [9] demonstrate that the quality of model-generated images can be significantly improved by reducing the gap between frequency domains. WDNet [14] feeds the input images into a two-branch network by wavelet transform. These methods inspire us to process moiré pattern in the frequency domain.

Image Demoiréing. Sun et al. [19] first introduce a CNN for image deblurring (DMCNN) and create a moiré dataset based on ImageNet [17] for training and testing. MBCNN [26] proposes a multi-scale learnable bandpass filter to learn the frequency of an image after moiré removal, while applying a two-step tone-mapping strategy to restore the color. In previous works, demoiréing was achieved by training a complete network, and we decompose this task into two steps: demoiréing and deblurring.

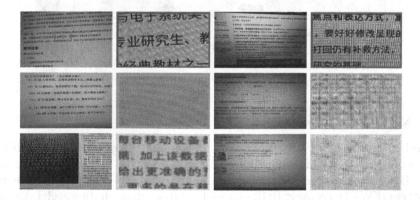

Fig. 1. Moire texture of different scales, frequencies, and colors. The proportions of moiré is different in the first row images. In the second row, because of the frequency difference, the first moiré looks like a wave and the second one looks like a grid. In the third row, the color of the moiré patterns is different.

3   Proposed Method

In this paper, we first input the RGB image in a weight fixed WaveletSRNet [8] to obtain wavelet domain features. The wavelet transform scale is setted to 2. The RGB image is transformed into 48 channels, and the spatial size of input image ($H \times W \times 3$) is reduced to ($(H/4) \times (W/4) \times 48$). This process is formulated as:

$$f_w = \mathcal{W}(I_{moire}; \delta) \tag{1}$$

where I_{moire} is a RGB image with moiré pattern, $\mathcal{W}$ is the weight fixed Wavelet-SRNet with the parameters δ. f_w is the results of WaveletSRNet. After wavelet transformation, the feature f_w inputs to the multi-scale dense network for demoiréing. We define this process as:

$$f_{clean} = \mathcal{D}(f_w; \gamma) \tag{2}$$

where $\mathcal{D}$ is the multi-scale dense network, γ is the model parameters. f_{clean} is the results features of $\mathcal{D}$, which with the same spatial size as f_w. We define the inverse process as $\mathcal{W}^{-1}$, the demoiréing RGB image could be restored from f_{clean} by using $\mathcal{W}^{-1}$. After the demoiréing stage, we find it is difficult to obtain satisfied demoiréing and deblurred image with the single stage network. This inspires us to use a coarse-to-fine method to optimize the results of demoiréing network. The main structure of our model is shown in Fig. 2. We define the deblurring network as $\mathcal{F}$, and the final results can be formulated as:

$$I_{clean} = \mathcal{F}(\mathcal{W}^{-1}(f_{clean}; \delta); \theta) \tag{3}$$

where I_{clean} is the clean RGB image.

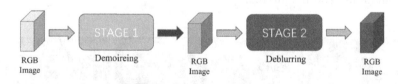

Fig. 2. Our coarse-to-fine demoiréing network structure.

3.1   Multi-scale Demoiréing

Several works use UNet structure as the backbone [19,26], which can learn rich representations by fusing different resolutions features. In this work, we also adopt UNet structure for demoiréing. In the first stage, we adopt 2D fast wavelet transform (FWT) to convert RGB images to wavelet domain. In wavelet domain, moiré pattern can be easily captured [14].

As shown in Fig. 3, the RGB image first is wavelet transformed into a tensor, then two residual modules are adopted for feature extraction, and the input features are mapped to a tensor of 64 channels. In order to extract moiré features in

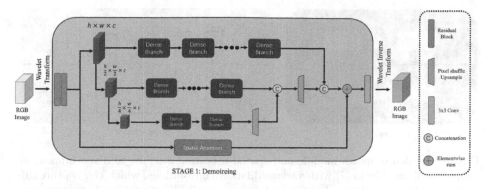

Fig. 3. The structure of multi-scale dense network. After wavelet transformation and two residual blocks, the feature size is ($h \times w \times c$). We use two convolution with *stride* = 2 to output multi-scale features, which will be the input to different dense branchs. The pixel shuffle upsample is adopted to resize the features to the same size for concatenation. A spatial attention module is used as the skip connection.

different scales, a convolutional layer with a stride of 2 is used as a downsampling layer. After downsampling from top of the main branch, the features as input to the same thickening module. In this paper, we introduce a spatial attention module as the global skip connection. Finally, the features are converted into a 48-channel tensor by convolution of 3×3, and then recovered into RGB images by wavelet inverse transform.

The dense module is adopted to alleviate the gradient vanishing problem. It also reduces the number of network parameters. In low-level tasks of vision, dense blocks can be used for haze removal, denoising, and super-resolution.

As shown in Fig. 4, our dense branch uses two dense blocks as the main structure [14], which alleviates the gradient disappearance and enhances the transmission of features. The structure of spatial attention module [21] is shown in Fig. 4, which enables the model to apply the appropriate attention to the features in spatial and better recovery details in later.

3.2 Deblurring Module

The moiré in original images can be obviously removed by stage 1 network, but due to the complex calculation, the clear texture details start to become blurred. In order to recover the texture details, the results of stage 1 are deblurred by the debulring module.

The network structure of the deblurring model in stage 2 is shown in Fig. 5. The stage 2 is an optimization of stage 1, in order to minimize the increase of inference time, PAN(Pixel Attention Networks) [25] is adopted in bachbone, which is a lightweight network for super-resolution, that only calculates the attention map of features through a layer of sigmoid instead of overly complex

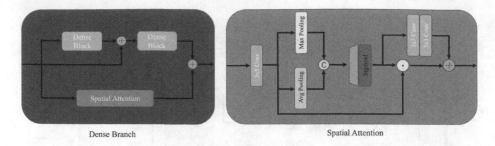

Dense Branch   Spatial Attention

Fig. 4. The dense branch module and spatial attention module. In dense branch, we adopt two dense blocks [7] with variant dilation convolutions, which can capture different moiré scale patterns. A spatial attention module [21] is used for skip connection. In spatial attention module, we use two kind pooling layers to extract spatial features. After concatenation, a sigmoid layer is used to obtain the attention map.

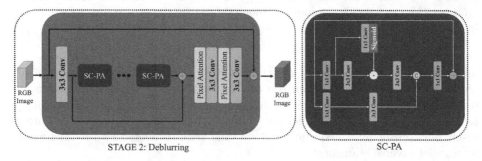

STAGE 2: Deblurring   SC-PA

Fig. 5. The structure of our deblurring network.

attention mechanism. As listed in Table 1, the parameters, operations and runtime of stage 2 (PAN) is less than stage 1 model.

Table 1. The details of model size and runtime in different stages.

	Params (M)	Flops (G)	Runtime (ms)
Stage 1	14.4	10.89	527
Stage 2	0.39	1.58	236

The structure of SC-PA is also shown in Fig. 5. As can be seen, 1×1 convolution is adopted to reduce computation. It brings less computational effort to the total process that only one layer of sigmoid is used in SC-PA.

4   Experiments

4.1   Training Datasets and Details

Training Datasets. We use the dataset provided by the 2022 Baidu.com AI Competition for experiments [1]. It includes 10,00 pairs of training images, 200 pairs of validation images and 200 pairs of test images. All the images are obtained from real scenes and then processed accordingly through technical means to generate usable desensitized data.

Training Details. As for the demoiréing model in stage 1, we use two residual blocks for feature extraction. The number of Dense Branch modules for each different scale branchs is set to 7, 5, and 4 respectively. The base channel size in each Dense Branch is set to 64. The learning rate is initialized to be 2×10^{-4}, and halved after each 1/4 of the total epochs. We use 128×128 patches which were randomly cropped from the images, and the batch size set to 16. When the 128×128 patches trained model converged, we re-group the training data into 256×256 patches for fine-tuning the model. Then, we use 512×512 patches for fine-tuning our model to converge, the learning rate was set to 1e-4, the batch size was set to 4. The training data is flipped randomly in horizontal rotations. Our model is trained with Adam optimizer by setting $\beta_1 = 0.9$ and $\beta_2 = 0.999$.

Considering the limitation of the competition time, we use the RGB image results of the demoiréing model to train the deblurring model. And we used the same training strategy as we did in demoiréing stage. We only adopt L1 penalty function as the final loss. Because of competition restrictions, we implement our models with the PaddlePaddle framework and train them by using 1 NVIDIA RTX3090 GPU.

4.2   Comparisons with Other Models

In this section, we compare our network with other 4 models on test dataset of the 2022 Baidu.com AI Competition, including VDSR [11], U-Net [16], WDNet [14] and MBCNN [26]. The quantitative results can be seen in Table 2. As shown in Table 2, our method achieves better than other methods.

Table 2. Comparison of our method and other methods.

	VDSR	U-Net	WDNet	MBCNN	Ours
PSNR (dB)	20.23	24.31	25.30	26.73	31.45
SSIM	0.8064	0.8279	0.7944	0.9443	0.9649

Some qualitative comparisons shows in Fig. 6. Our method can recover more details, and the results much cleaner.

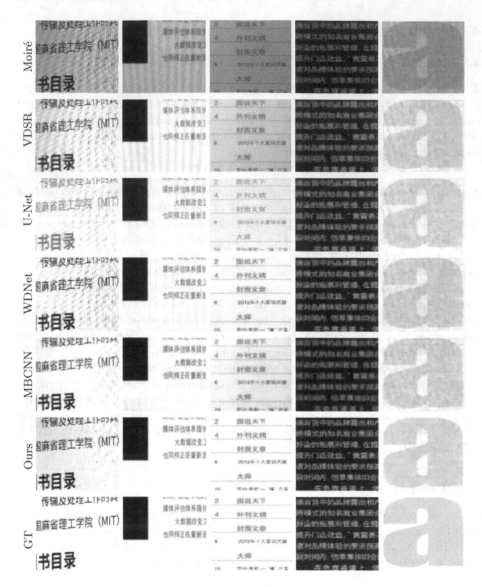

Fig. 6. Qualitative comparison of our network with other methods.

5   Ablation Experiments

In this section, we perform ablation experiments on multi-scale coarse-to-fine network to prove the effectiveness of the proposed module.

Muiti-scale Demoiréing Network. The baseline model is a single-branch which does not use downsampling and upsampling, and the training strategy remains the same as 4.1. Visual results are presented in Fig. 7. Single column means that the only one kind spatial feature size is adopted. It can be seen that using muiti-scale can successfully remove moiré pattern. As shown in Table 3, muiti-scale Demoiréing Network also performes better than the baseline model of single branch in PSNR and SSIM on testB dataset.

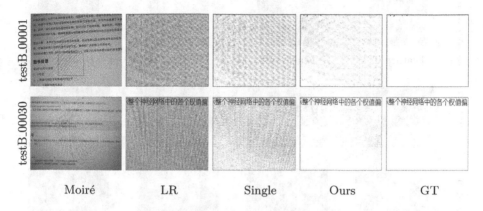

Fig. 7. Ablation study on muiti-scale demoiréing network

Spatial Attention. We also investigate the contribution of our spatial attention. We removed all the spatial attention modules from our complete model. And some results produced by two different variants are shown in Fig. 8. Several features is visualized. With the spatial attention, the moiré pattern is more obvious in different feature maps. This means the spatial attention can learn and capture moiré patterns (Fig. 9).

Coarse-to-fine Structure. To vertify the effectiveness of our coarse-to-fine structure, the PAN deblurring network is used. The experimental results can be seen in Table 3. With coarse-to-fine structure, complete model is 1.39 dB and 0.057 higher than that without coarse-to-fine in PSNR and SSIM respectively. Qualitative experiments are shown in Fig. 6.

Table 3. Quantitative comparison of different modules.

	w/o multi-scale	w/o spatial attention	w/o coarse-to-fine	Ours
PSNR(dB)/SSIM	28.20/0.8683	26.81/0.8518	29.47/0.8991	31.45/0.9649

6 2022 Baidu.com AI Competition

There are challenges on demoiréing and text removal in 2022 Baidu.com AI Competition. Although we are allowed to use additional dataset for training,

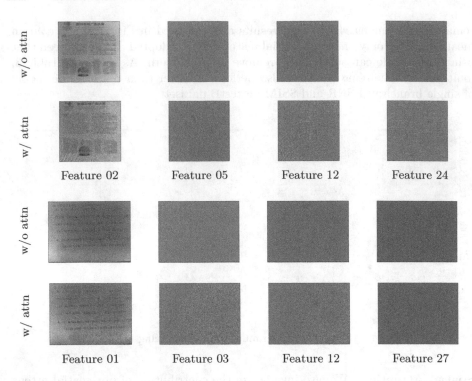

Fig. 8. Ablation study on w/o spatial attention module

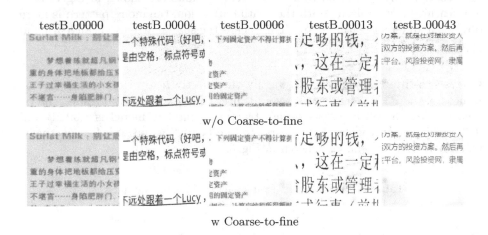

Fig. 9. Ablation study on w/o coarse-to-fine method.

there are some differences between the distribution of the other datasets and the one used in the competition, which can lead to a degradation of performance after direct training. Additionally, the evaluation metrics used in the competition were PSNR and MSSSIM [22], and the weight coefficients are 0.5 respectively. We test our model on the test dataset B. The results are shown in Table 4.

Table 4. Results for 2022 Baidu.com AI competition on demoiréing challenge.

Method	MSSSIM	PSNR (dB)	Score
1st	0.98589	33.36587	0.65977
2nd	0.98222	32.85817	0.65540
ours	0.98189	31.33234	0.64761
4th	0.97898	31.51529	0.64707
5th	0.97722	31.28724	0.64505

7 Conclusion

In this paper, we propose an image demoiréing network, which transforms image into wavelet domain and has multi-scale feature encoding ability. The proposed three key modules (Multi-Scale, Spatial-Attention, and Cascade-Structure) of our model is proved to be highly effective for image restoration tasks. Later, we will do further study in the effect of multi-scale of other image restoration tasks.

Acknowledgement. This paper is supported by "Design and Software Development of Video Super-resolution Algorithm for Face Blur" (JBKY20220210) and "Research and Simulation Experiment of Remote Production System for Lightweight Sports Events" (ZZLX-2020–001) of China National Radio and Television Research Institute.

References

1. Baidu: AIstudio Competition. https://www.aistudio.baidu.com/aistudio/competition/detail/128/0/datasets (2022). Accessed 1 January 2022
2. Cavigelli, L., Hager, P., Benini, L.: CAS-CNN: a deep convolutional neural network for image compression artifact suppression. In: 2017 International Joint Conference on Neural Networks (IJCNN), pp. 752–759 (2017). https://doi.org/10.1109/IJCNN.2017.7965927
3. Chao, D., Chen, C.L., He, K., Tang, X.: Learning a deep convolutional network for image super-resolution. In: ECCV (2014)
4. Cheng, X., Fu, Z., Yang, J.: Multi-scale dynamic feature encoding network for image demoireing (2019)
5. Dong, J., Mao, X.J., Shen, C., Yang, Y.B.: Learning deep representations using convolutional auto-encoders with symmetric skip connections (2016)
6. Guo, J., Chao, H.: Building dual-domain representations for compression artifacts reduction. In: Leibe, B., Matas, J., Sebe, N., Welling, M. (eds.) ECCV 2016. LNCS, vol. 9905, pp. 628–644. Springer, Cham (2016). https://doi.org/10.1007/978-3-319-46448-0_38

7. Huang, G., Liu, Z., Van Der Maaten, L., Weinberger, K.Q.: Densely connected convolutional networks. In: Proceedings of the IEEE Conference on Computer Vision and Pattern Recognition, pp. 4700–4708 (2017)
8. Huang, H., He, R., Sun, Z., Tan, T.: Wavelet-SRNet: a wavelet-based CNN for multi-scale face super resolution. In: IEEE International Conference on Computer Vision, pp. 1689–1697 (2017)
9. Jiang, L., Dai, B., Wu, W., Loy, C.C.: Focal frequency loss for image reconstruction and synthesis (2020)
10. Kim, J., Lee, J.K., Lee, K.M.: Accurate image super-resolution using very deep convolutional networks. In: 2016 IEEE Conference on Computer Vision and Pattern Recognition (CVPR), pp. 1646–1654 (2016). https://doi.org/10.1109/CVPR.2016.182
11. Kim, J., Lee, J.K., Lee, K.M.: Accurate image super-resolution using very deep convolutional networks. In: Proceedings of the IEEE Conference on Computer Vision and Pattern Recognition, pp. 1646–1654 (2016)
12. Kim, J., Lee, J.K., Lee, K.M.: Deeply-recursive convolutional network for image super-resolution. In: 2016 IEEE Conference on Computer Vision and Pattern Recognition (CVPR), pp. 1637–1645 (2016). https://doi.org/10.1109/CVPR.2016.181
13. Lai, W.S., Huang, J.B., Ahuja, N., Yang, M.H.: Fast and accurate image super-resolution with deep laplacian pyramid networks. IEEE Trans. Patt. Anal. Mach. Intell. **41**(11), 2599–2613 (2019). https://doi.org/10.1109/TPAMI.2018.2865304
14. Liu, L., Liu, J., Yuan, S., Slabaugh, G., Tian, Q.: Wavelet-based dual-branch network for image demoireing (2020)
15. Liu, P., Zhang, H., Zhang, K., Lin, L., Zuo, W.: Multi-level wavelet-CNN for image restoration. In: 2018 IEEE/CVF Conference on Computer Vision and Pattern Recognition Workshops (CVPRW), pp. 886–88609 (2018). https://doi.org/10.1109/CVPRW.2018.00121
16. Ronneberger, O., Fischer, P., Brox, T.: U-Net: convolutional networks for biomedical image segmentation. In: Navab, N., Hornegger, J., Wells, W.M., Frangi, A.F. (eds.) MICCAI 2015. LNCS, vol. 9351, pp. 234–241. Springer, Cham (2015). https://doi.org/10.1007/978-3-319-24574-4_28
17. Russakovsky, O., et al.: ImageNet large scale visual recognition challenge. Int. J. Comput. Vis. **115**(3), 211–252 (2015)
18. Shelhamer, E., Long, J., Darrell, T.: Fully convolutional networks for semantic segmentation. IEEE Trans. Patt. Anal. Mach. Intell. **39**(4), 640–651 (2016)
19. Sun, Y., Yu, Y., Wang, W.: Moiré photo restoration using multiresolution convolutional neural networks. IEEE Trans. Image Process. **27**, 4160–4172 (2018)
20. Tai, Y., Yang, J., Liu, X.: Image super-resolution via deep recursive residual network. In: 2017 IEEE Conference on Computer Vision and Pattern Recognition (CVPR), pp. 2790–2798 (2017). https://doi.org/10.1109/CVPR.2017.298
21. Wang, X., Chan, K.C., Yu, K., Dong, C., Loy, C.C.: EDVR: video restoration with enhanced deformable convolutional networks. In: 2019 IEEE/CVF Conference on Computer Vision and Pattern Recognition Workshops (CVPRW), pp. 1954–1963 (2019). https://doi.org/10.1109/CVPRW.2019.00247
22. Wang, Z., Simoncelli, E., Bovik, A.: Multiscale structural similarity for image quality assessment. In: The Thrity-Seventh Asilomar Conference on Signals, Systems Computers, vol. 2, pp. 1398–1402 (2003). https://doi.org/10.1109/ACSSC.2003.1292216

23. Zhang, K., Zuo, W., Chen, Y., Meng, D., Zhang, L.: Beyond a gaussian denoiser: residual learning of deep CNN for image denoising. IEEE Trans. Image Process. **26**(7), 3142–3155 (2017). https://doi.org/10.1109/TIP.2017.2662206

24. Zhang, K., Zuo, W., Gu, S., Zhang, L.: Learning deep CNN denoiser prior for image restoration. In: 2017 IEEE Conference on Computer Vision and Pattern Recognition (CVPR), pp. 2808–2817 (2017). https://doi.org/10.1109/CVPR.2017. 300

25. Zhao, H., Kong, X., He, J., Qiao, Yu., Dong, C.: Efficient image super-resolution using pixel attention. In: Bartoli, A., Fusiello, A. (eds.) ECCV 2020. LNCS, vol. 12537, pp. 56–72. Springer, Cham (2020). https://doi.org/10.1007/978-3-030-67070-2_3

26. Zheng, B., Yuan, S., Slabaugh, G., Leonardis, A.: Image demoireing with learnable bandpass filters. IEEE (2020)

27. Zheng, B., Chen, Y., Tian, X., Zhou, F., Liu, X.: Implicit dual-domain convolutional network for robust color image compression artifact reduction. IEEE Trans. Circ. Syst. Video Technol. **30**(11), 3982–3994 (2020). https://doi.org/10.1109/TCSVT.2019.2931045

Learning Contextual Embedding Deep Networks for Accurate and Efficient Image Deraining

Zebin Chen[1,4,5], Guangguang Yang[2], Jun Chen[3], Xiaohua Xie[1,4,5(✉)],
and Jian-Huang Lai[1,4,5]

[1] School of Computer Science and Engineering, Sun Yat-sen University,
Guangzhou, China
stsljh@mail.sysu.edu.cn
[2] School of Electronic Information Engineering, Foshan University, Foshan, China
[3] School of Industrial Design and Ceramic Art, Foshan University, Foshan, China
chenj269@mail2.sysu.edu.cn
[4] Key Laboratory of Machine Intelligence and Advanced Computing,
Ministry of Education, Guangzhou, China
[5] Guangdong Province Key Laboratory of Information Security Technology,
Guangzhou, China
xiexiaoh6@mail.sysu.edu.cn

Abstract. The existing state-of-the-art deraining methods rely on a bulky network structure to accurately capture rain streaks, resulting in prohibitive memory consumption and computation cost. In addition, most of them destroy background details along with the process of rain removal. This paper presents a simple but effective network to address the above problems. Firstly, we developed a lightweight model, called Cross-Scale Contextual Embedding Network (CSCEN), to achieve the cross-scale embedding of rain streaks in different scale contexts. We also introduced a new deeply-supervised rain detection loss, making the training process of the intermediate layers be direct and transparent thus the transfer of rain information layer-by-layer would be under appropriate supervision. Qualitative and quantitative experiments show that the proposed network is superior to the advanced deraining methods and inherits better generalization in real-world rain removal.

Keywords: Image deraining · Lightweight structure · Cross-scale

1 Introduction

Blurred images with rain streaks can severely degrade the performance of advanced vision tasks, such as segmentation [1], tracking [2], pedestrian recognition [3]. Therefore, removing rain streaks from the image and recovering a clear background image is of importance to the reliable operation of the intelligent system in the real-world [4–7].

S. Yu et al. (Eds.): PRCV 2022, LNCS 13537, pp. 236–248, 2022.
https://doi.org/10.1007/978-3-031-18916-6_20

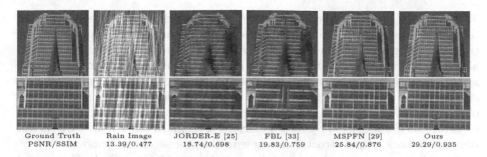

Ground Truth	Rain Image	JORDER-E [25]	FBL [33]	MSPFN [29]	Ours
PSNR/SSIM	13.39/0.477	18.74/0.698	19.83/0.759	25.84/0.876	29.29/0.935

Fig. 1. Visual comparison of CNNs-based deraining methods. Regions in red boxes show key differences. (Color figure online)

Early image deraining methods are mainly divided into filter- and sparse-based methods. Filter-based methods [8,9] regard the process of rain streaks removal as a signal separation problem, using the spatial information of neighboring pixels or relying on non-local mean smoothing. For instance, Xu et al. [8] proposed an algorithm based on guided filter to obtain a rain-free image using a linear transformation. To alleviate image blurring caused by the filtering process, many efforts have been devoted to designing sparse coding methods [10–12]. For instance, Luo et al. [11] took advantage of high discriminative coding to sparsely approximate the background layer and the local block of the rain layer on the dictionary. However, the traditional methods are not robust enough to scale variation. As a result, they cannot effectively deal with the changeable rain streaks.

Thanks to the development of deep learning, convolutional neural networks (CNNs) are now extensively applied to image deraining [13–15]. Different from traditional methods that only perform simple linear-mapping transformations, CNNs-based methods can learn abstract and complex mapping relationships from images by cascading a pile of convolutional and non-linear layers [16,17]. Such powerful non-linear modeling capability enables CNNs-based methods to overcome the shortcomings of traditional methods so that better results in rain removal could be achieved [18–20].

Contextual information and scale analysis are essential for CNNs to capture rain locations since the distinguishment of rain streaks characteristics are multi-directional and multi-scale [21–23]. Some CNNs-based methods [24–26] adopt the dilated convolution [27] for obtaining larger receptive fields together with the improvement of deraining quality through recurrent operation. In [25], Yang et al. developed a multi-task learning CNN, which can learn the position and intensity prediction of rain streaks. Further, Fu et al. [26] proposed a model based on graph convolutional networks (GCNs) [28] to extract and complement global context information for rain removal. However, these methods are prone to over-deraining, resulting in the restored image being blurred.

Recently, some works [29–33] have explored cross-scale representations of rain streaks and obtained multi-scale predictions by running a single network on multiple (scaled) input images. For example, Jiang et al. [29] explored a multi-scale collaborative representation of rain to characterize the target rain streaks.

Yang et al. [33] created a fractal frequency band network based on frequency band restoration and added a cross-scale self-supervision method to standardize the training. Although these methods can vastly improve the CNNs representation ability for varying scales rain streaks, it is prohibitive memory-consuming. What's worse, these methods can hardly distinguish the background structure from rain streaks within the context of different scales. As demonstrated in Fig. 1, previous methods have difficulty in distinguishing between rain streaks and background structure, so the predicted result is a mixture of them. In other words, CNNs will destroy the background structure along with the process of rain removal.

In this paper, a novel lightweight model, named Cross-Scale Contextual Embedding Network (CSCEN), has been proposed to address the above problems. CSCEN can accurately capture the location and intensity of rain streaks and then effectively recover clean background details. In particular, it is expected that the rain information could be supervised layer-by-layer in CNNs to promote the representation ability of the network for rain streaks. To this end, we first design a Cross-Scale Contextual Embedding Modules (CSCEM) to capture rain streaks with different scales from the context. It is worth highlighting that CSCEM explicitly models the scale correlation of rain streaks to represent its cross-scale context embedding appropriately. Second, a new loss function, called deeply-supervised rain detection (DSRD) loss, has been proposed to improve the learning performance of CSCEN. The critical component of DSRD loss is the rain deep supervision block (RDSB), which is only applied in the training phase and can be removed in the testing phase. In short, the main contributions of this work are summarized as follows:

- A novel model, called CSCEN, has been proposed for accurate and efficient image deraining. It has the advantage of being lightweight and easy implementation.
- DSRD loss has been introduced to improve the performance of the rain removal network. In addition, RDSB, which holds the merit of high removability, has been designed to propagate the rain supervised information layer-by-layer.
- Experimental results show that our model outperforms the state-of-the-art methods on synthetic and real-world datasets.

2   Proposed Method

Our model consists of two components, which are one main branch and multiple side outputs, respectively. The main branch is the core of deraining structure, while the side-output is used to realize the transfer of rain supervised information.

2.1   Cross-Scale Contextual Embedding Network

The CSCEN, as the main branch of the image deraining, is used to extract the cross-scale embedding features of rain streaks. The structure is shown in

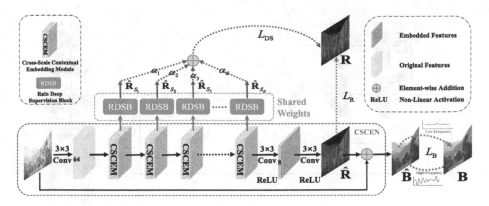

Fig. 2. The framework of the proposed method includes one main branch CSCEN and multiple side-output RDSB.

Fig. 2. Apparently, CSCEN contains one convolutional layer at the beginning, d CSCEM in the middle, and two convolutional layers at the end. The initial convolutional layer uses 3×3 convolution to realize the transformation from the image space to the feature space.

We design the critical module CSCEM for context embedding to explore the cross-scale response of rain features, whose structure is shown in Fig. 3(a). Given that rain streaks have various scales at different positions in the image space, we use dilated convolution [27] to capture multi-scale features of spatial changes. The convolution of three dilated factors (DF) expands the receptive field without increasing the parameters. It should be pointed out that feature map $\mathbf{F}_{DF=r}$ ($r = 1, 2, 3$) contains enough contextual information, which effectively reflects the spatial distribution of rain streaks. We concatenate different $\mathbf{F}_{DF=r}$ to form a cross-scale feature map $\mathbf{F}_{DF}$ and then use the Squeeze-and-Excitation (SE) operation [35] to explicitly model rain features at different scales. In this way, the feature correspondence among different channels of rain streaks through weights can be adaptively calibrated. Furthermore, we also use 1×1 convolution to achieve cross-channel information interaction, which reduces the channel dimension while refining the rain streak features. Finally, a parameter-free identity shortcut [34] is introduced into the module to reduce training complexity. As a result, our model can effectively capture the location and intensity of rain streaks without employing the recurrent strategy, which significantly reduces the number of parameters.

The widely used background loss L_{B} in main branch training is mean squared error (MSE). However, results generated from MSE tend to be over smooth. Motivated by [36], we regard the process of background restoration as the problem of mutual restriction between low-frequency (LF) and high-frequency (HF) information. In particular, the restoration result $\hat{\mathbf{B}}$ and natural background $\mathbf{B}$ should be consistent in both the LF and HF parts. LF is the overall contour of the image, and it is calculated using the L_1-norm. HF, measured by SSIM [37],

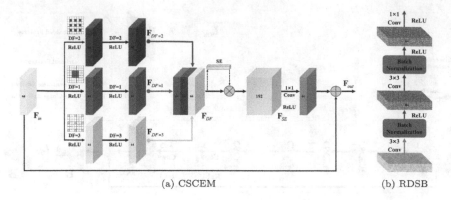

(a) CSCEM   (b) RDSB

Fig. 3. The detailed structure of CSCEM and RDSB.

is the edge and texture of the image. We use a hybrid loss to balance the contour restoration and details preservation:

$$L_{\mathrm{B}} = \left\| \hat{\mathbf{B}} - \mathbf{B} \right\|_1 + (1 - SSIM(\hat{\mathbf{B}}, \mathbf{B})) \tag{1}$$

The rain streaks show unique sparsity in the whole scene. Therefore, the L_1-norm can also be used to measure the distance between rain layers:

$$L_{\mathrm{R}} = \left\| \hat{\mathbf{R}} - \mathbf{R} \right\|_1 \tag{2}$$

where $\hat{\mathbf{R}}$ is the output of CSCEN, and $\mathbf{R}$ is the real rain layer.

2.2 Deeply-Supervised Rain Detection Loss

Since rain streaks belong to the high-frequency part of image, they are easily mixed with the background structure. In particular, shallow layers may not properly access rain pattern supervision information when the network becomes deeper. This results in the inability of the main branch to effective learning more robust and discriminative features. Therefore, we supervise each intermediate layer such that gradient flows propagation across layers is direct and transparent. For clarity, we first denote the collection of main branch layer parameters as $\mathcal{W}$. Then, let w be a set of rain detection auxiliary heads attached to the top of each intermediate layer of CSCEN. Theoretically, the optimization objective of the deeply-supervised learning scheme for rain streaks removal can be expressed as:

$$\underset{\mathcal{W},w}{\arg\min}\, L_{\mathrm{B}}(\mathcal{W}) + L_{\mathrm{R}}(\mathcal{W}) + \lambda L_{\mathrm{DS}}(\mathcal{W}; w) \tag{3}$$

where λ is used to control the influence of DSRD loss L_{DS}.

Generally, the proposed DSRD loss L_{DS} is implemented as the following formula:

$$L_{\mathrm{DS}}(\mathcal{W}; w) = \sum_{n=1}^{d} \alpha_n \ell_{side}(\mathcal{W}; w^{(n)}) \tag{4}$$

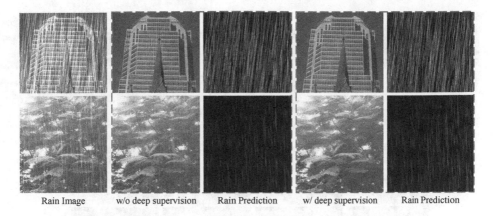

Rain Image   w/o deep supervision   Rain Prediction   w/ deep supervision   Rain Prediction

Fig. 4. Ablation study with respect to deep supervision.

Table 1. Quantitative evaluation of three synthetic datasets. The best and the second best results are **boldfaced** and underlined, respectively. [†] denotes the results from the original paper.

Methods	Datasets					
	Rain100L		Rain100H		Rain1400	
	PSNR	SSIM	PSNR	SSIM	PSNR	SSIM
Input	26.9	0.838	13.6	0.371	25.4	0.810
GMM [7]	29.0	0.867	15.3	0.449	27.8	0.859
SRNet[†] [22]	37.4	0.978	30.1	0.906	32.9	**0.949**
SPAIR[†] [6]	36.9	0.969	<u>31.0</u>	0.892	33.3	0.936
MPRNet [5]	36.4	0.965	30.4	0.890	**33.6**	<u>0.938</u>
GCN [26]	38.7	0.984	29.9	<u>0.907</u>	32.3	0.937
JORDER-E [25]	<u>39.5</u>	<u>0.985</u>	30.4	0.896	31.7	0.936
FBL [33]	35.4	0.968	27.0	0.839	29.9	0.911
MSPFN [29]	32.2	0.929	28.2	0.850	33.1	0.946
Ours	**40.4**	**0.987**	31.9	**0.917**	<u>33.5</u>	**0.949**

where α_n is the loss weight of each side-output, and $\sum_{n=1}^{d} \alpha_n = 1$. $\ell_{side}(\cdot)$ denotes the image-level L_1 loss for side-output $\hat{\mathbf{R}}_{S_n}$ and real rain layer $\mathbf{R}$. In particular, the weighting factor α_n are all initialized with $1/d$ in the training phase.

The cross-layer propagation of effective information relies on the RDSB, which structure is shown in Fig. 3(b). Due to the homology of rain streaks, the intrinsic properties of each side-output $\hat{\mathbf{R}}_{S_n}$ should be close to each other. Here, we use the consistency constraint, that is, sharing the weight $w^{(n)} \in [1, d]$ of the RDSB to force the rain streaks to have the same representation in multi-layer supervision. Deep supervision is introduced into CSCEN to realize layer-by-layer supervised learning, which assists in propagating adequate rain supervised infor-

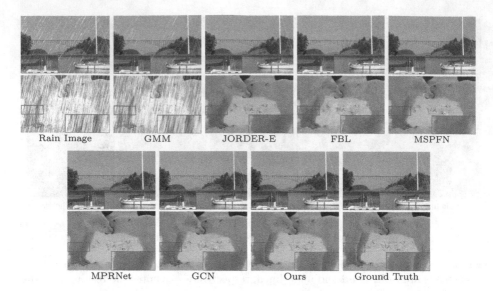

Fig. 5. Visual comparison of image deraining results by different methods. Our method effectively removes rain and generates pleasant images that are visually closer to the ground truth. Zooming-in is recommended for better visualization.

mation to lower layers with shortcuts. In addition, the RDSB is only used in the training phase and can be removed during the testing phase without additional computation cost. As shown in Fig. 4, deep supervision can improve the detection and prediction performance of CSCEN to distinguish the rain streaks from the background structure more accurately.

2.3   Training

The proposed method is trained using the PyTorch framework [39]. The initial learning rate is set to be 0.001, and it is reduced by a factor of 2 in every 100 epochs from the 150th epoch, with the training stage terminating at the 500th epoch. The number d of RDSB and regularization parameter λ in the loss function are set as 9 and 0.1, respectively.

3   Experiments and Analysis

3.1   Baselines and Datasets

The proposed method has been compared with eight representative methods to show its superiority. One of them is the model-based method [7], and the other seven are deep learning-based methods [5,6,22,25,26,29,33]. Three typical synthetic datasets [13,15] and a real-world rain image set are selected to implement the experiments. Rain100L and Rain100H are from [15], while Rain1400 is provided by [13]. The real-world rain image can be obtained from [38].

Rain Image   GMM   JORDER-E   MSPFN   Ours

Fig. 6. Visual comparison of different methods on real-world.

Table 2. Effect of λ on deraining performance.

CSCEN	w/ DSRD loss					w/o DSRD loss
λ	10^0	10^{-1}	10^{-2}	10^{-3}	10^{-4}	0
PSNR	31.35	**31.85**	31.03	31.18	31.13	30.96
SSIM	0.910	**0.917**	0.908	0.910	0.908	0.908

Table 3. Comparison of different background losses L_{B}.

MSE loss	L_1 loss	SSIM loss	PSNR	SSIM
✓	✗	✗	31.39	0.909
✗	✓	✗	31.60	0.915
✗	✗	✓	31.58	0.915
✓	✗	✓	31.42	0.910
✗	✓	✓	**31.85**	**0.917**

3.2 Comparison on Synthetic Datasets

The experiments on synthetic datasets are evaluated both qualitatively and quantitatively. As can be seen from Table 1, our model gives the best overall results on the three datasets. Visual comparison results from datasets are presented in Fig. 5. One can see that GMM only imposes a particular effect on dealing with light rain, but it still cannot thoroughly remove them. JORDER-E and FBL can remove rain marks under various conditions, but noticeable artifacts will be generated, and this is the main side effect. Rain removal effects from MPRNet and GCN are relatively better but sometimes destroy the background details (see the bottom row). As observed, our method holds a good balance between the deraining quality and details recovery.

3.3 Comparison on Real-World Datasets

The ability to remove rain in natural scenes can test the generalization of the model. We only compared the visual effects of deraining from the image since

Table 4. Ablation study with respect to L_R and L_{DS}.

Methods	PSNR	SSIM
Baseline (MSE)	31.25	0.909
w/o L_R & w/o L_{DS}	31.40 ($\uparrow$ 0.15)	0.913 ($\uparrow$ 0.004)
w/ L_R & w/o L_{DS}	30.96 ($\downarrow$ 0.29)	0.908 ($\downarrow$ 0.001)
w/o L_R & w/ L_{DS}	31.54 ($\uparrow$ 0.29)	0.914 ($\uparrow$ 0.005)
CSCEN	**31.85** ($\uparrow$ 0.60)	**0.917** ($\uparrow$ 0.008)

Table 5. PSNR and SSIM results using different d.

d	1	3	6	9	12
PSNR/SSIM	26.53/0.826	29.39/0.887	31.19/0.910	31.85/0.917	32.26/0.921
Params	0.25M	0.72M	1.44M	2.16M	2.88M

no ground truth is available. Figure 6 presents the visual comparison results. It can be seen that GMM will leave a small number of rain streaks in some regions. With regard to MSPFN, it fails to remove clean rain streaks in some cases, such as the region in the red box in the second image. The red boxes also show the situation after the deraining of JORDER-E. These artifacts are caused by the failure of the network in the real-world. In addition, JORDER-E also destroys the details when dealing with objects with similar brightness and orientation to rain streaks (the blue box in the second image in Fig. 6). Remarkably, our model can remove rain streaks and preserve the scene details in a better way, so its applicability is self-evident.

3.4   Ablation Study

In this section, the ablation study of the proposed method is carried out on Rain100H.

Effect of λ. As shown in Table 2, varying λ imposes a significant effect on the intensity of DSRD loss. In particular, DSRD loss is most conducive to network training when $\lambda = 0.1$. Compared to the case of $\lambda = 0$, PSNR and SSIM with $\lambda = 0.1$ have increased by 0.89 and 0.009, respectively.

Effect of L_B. Various combinations of background loss L_B are presented in Table 3. From the perspective of a single loss function, one can clearly note that MSE loss is the least helpful for training, followed by SSIM loss. Although the PSNR and SSIM from L_1 loss are the highest among all single loss functions, the improvement is tiny in comparison with the subsequent SSIM loss. Similarly, the combination of MSE loss and SSIM loss gives only a slight increase in the result of a single MSE loss. The last row of Table 3 is the adopted solution, which significantly improves deraining effect.

Table 6. The running time and parameters of different methods.

Methods	GMM	JORDER-E	MSPFN	Ours
Params. / Reduction	—	4.17M / -48.20%	15.82M / -86.35%	2.16M
PSNR / SSIM	15.3 / 0.449	30.4 / 0.896	28.2 / 0.850	31.9 / 0.917
Runtime (seconds)	259.72	0.37	10.21	0.32

Effect of L_{DS} and L_R. We set a baseline for which the training excludes L_{DS} and L_R, while MSE is used for the background loss L_B. The relevant results are shown in Table 4. It is worth noting that the performance has been reduced and even lower than the baseline after the introduction of L_R as the supervised information. It is counter intuitive to find that more supervised information cannot improve the performance but makes the network more difficult to learn. The last row in Table 4 is the complete result of CSCEN. Interestingly, one can observe that L_R and L_{DS} are mutual promotion. Comparison with baseline shows that PSNR and SSIM have increased by 1.92% and 0.88%, respectively.

Effect of d. Table 5 lists the results of different d. Apparently, the performance of CSCEN gradually improves with increasing d, and the number of parameters shows up approximately linear increase. When d is large, the gains of performance are relatively tiny. Increasing the depth of the network will eventually bring only limited improvements. Therefore, we set the default value of d as 9 to balance the quality and efficiency of deraining.

3.5 Model Complexity

Comparison of the parameters (in millions) and runtime (in seconds) of the proposed network with some methods has been studied. Rain100H was used to evaluate the average running time of each model. The comparison results are shown in Table 6. It is worth noting that the proposed network can properly handle the heavy rain, so increase of parameters multiplier caused by multi-stage recurrent processing of rain streaks can be steered away. For example, compared with the two-stage network (*i.e.*, JORDER-E), our PSNR is improved by 1.5 dB while the parameters have been reduced by about 48%. Comprehensive studies show that our network can achieve a good trade-off between performance and calculation.

4   Conclusion

This paper proposes a lightweight network with deep supervision to achieve single image deraining. A CSCEN to extract the cross-scale information of rain streaks has been designed. In addition, we introduced DSRD loss to achieve layer-by-layer supervised learning so that complete rain streaks can be captured. Comprehensive experiments show that the proposed method is superior to state-of-the-art methods regarding deraining performance and computational efficiency.

Acknowledgment. This work was supported by the National Natural Science Foundation of China under Grants 62072482 and 62002061, and in part by the Guangdong Natural Science Foundation under Grants 2021A1515011504, 2019A1515111208, and 2020A1515111107.

References

1. Mittal, S., Tatarchenko, M., Brox, T.: Semi-supervised semantic segmentation with high- and low-level consistency. IEEE Trans. Pattern Anal. Mach. Intell. **43**(4), 1369–1379 (2021)
2. Deng, C., He, S., Han, Y., Zhao, B.: Learning dynamic spatial-temporal regularization for UAV object tracking. IEEE Signal Process. Lett. **28**, 1230–1234 (2021)
3. Jiao, Y., Yao, H., Xu, C.: SAN: selective alignment network for cross-domain pedestrian detection. IEEE Trans. Image Process. **30**, 2155–2167 (2021)
4. Garg, K., Nayar, S.K.: Vision and rain. Int. J. Comput. Vis. **75**(1), 3–27 (2007)
5. Zamir, S.W., et al.: Multi-stage progressive image restoration. In: Proceedings IEEE Conference Computer Vision Pattern Recognition, pp. 14821–14831 (2021)
6. Purohit, K., Suin, M., Rajagopalan, A.N., Boddeti, V.N.: Spatially-adaptive image restoration using distortion-guided networks. In: Proceedings IEEE International Conference Computer Vision, pp. 2289–2299 (2021)
7. Li, Y., Tan, R.T., Guo, X., Lu, J., Brown, M.S.: Single image rain streak decomposition using layer priors. IEEE Trans. Image Process. **26**(8), 3874–3885 (2017)
8. Xu, J., Zhao, W., Liu, P., Tang, X: Removing rain and snow in a single image using guided filter. In: Proceedings IEEE International Conference Computer Science Automation Engineering, pp. 304–307 (2012)
9. Kim, J.-H., Lee, C., Sim, J.-Y., Kim, C.-S.: Single-image deraining using an adaptive nonlocal means filter. In: Proceedings IEEE International Conference Image Process, pp. 914–917 (2013)
10. Kang, L.-W., Lin, C.-W., Fu, Y.-H.: Automatic single-image-based rain streaks removal via image decomposition. IEEE Trans. Image Process. **21**(4), 1742–1755 (2012)
11. Luo, Y., Xu, Y., Ji, H.: Removing rain from a single image via discriminative sparse coding. In: Proceedings IEEE International Conference Computer Vision, pp. 3397–3405 (2015)
12. Gu, S., Meng, D., Zuo, W., Zhang, L.: Joint convolutional analysis and synthesis sparse representation for single image layer separation. In: Proceedings IEEE International Conference Computer Vision, pp. 1717–1725 (2017)
13. Fu, X., Huang, J., Zeng, D., Huang, Y., Ding, X., Paisley, J.: Removing rain from single images via a deep detail network. In: Proceedings IEEE International Conference Computer Vision Pattern Recognition, pp. 1715–1723 (2017)
14. Luo, W., Lai, J., Xie, X.: Weakly supervised learning for raindrop removal on a single image. IEEE Trans. Circuits Syst. Video Technol. **31**(5), 1673–1683 (2021)
15. Yang, W., Tan, R. T., Feng, J., Liu, J., Guo, Z., Yan, S.: Deep joint rain detection and removal from a single image. In: Proceedings IEEE International Conference Computer Vision Pattern Recognition, pp. 1357–1366 (2017)
16. Wang, H., Xie, Q., Zhao, Q., Meng, D.: A model-driven deep neural network for single image rain removal. In: Proceedings IEEE International Conference Computer Vision Pattern Recognition, pp. 3100–3109 (2020)

17. Li, S., et al.: A comprehensive benchmark analysis of single image deraining: current challenges and future perspectives. Int. J. Comput. Vis. **129**(4), 1301–1322 (2021)
18. Yang, W., Tan, R.T., Wang, S., Fang, Y., Liu, J.: Single image deraining: from model-based to data-driven and beyond. IEEE Trans. Pattern Anal. Mach. Intell. **43**(11), 4059–4077 (2021)
19. Ren, D., Zuo, W., Hu, Q., Zhu, P., Meng, D.: Progressive image deraining networks: a better and simpler baseline. In: Proceedings IEEE International Conference Computer Vision Pattern Recognition, pp. 3932–3941 (2019)
20. Deng, S., et al.: Detail-recovery image deraining via context aggregation networks. In: Proceedings IEEE International Conference Computer Vision Pattern Recognition, pp. 14548–14557 (2020)
21. Peng, L., Jiang, A., Yi, Q., Wang, M.: Cumulative rain density sensing network for single image derain. IEEE Signal Process. Lett. **27**, 406–410 (2020)
22. Wang, H., et al.: Structural residual learning for single image rain removal. Knowl. Based Syst. **213**, 106595 (2021)
23. Hu, X., Zhu, L., Wang, T., Fu, C.-W., Heng, P.-A.: Single-image real-time rain removal based on depth-guided non-local features. IEEE Trans. Image Process. **30**, 1759–1770 (2021)
24. Li, X., Wu, J., Lin, Z., Liu, H., Zha, H.: Recurrent squeeze-and-excitation context aggregation net for single image deraining. In: Proceedings European Conference Computer Vision, pp. 254–269 (2018)
25. Yang, W., Tan, R.T., Feng, J., Liu, J., Yan, S., Guo, Z.: Joint rain detection and removal from a single image with contextualized deep networks. IEEE Trans. Pattern Anal. Mach. Intell. **42**(6), 1377–1393 (2020)
26. Fu, X., Qi, Q., Zha, Z.-J., Ding, X., Wu, F., Paisley, J.: Successive graph convolutional network for image de-raining. Int. J. Comput. Vis. **129**(5), 1691–1711 (2021)
27. Yu, F., Koltun, V.: Multi-scale context aggregation by dilated convolutions. In: Proceedings International Conference Learning Represent (2016)
28. Kipf, T. N., Welling, M.: Semi-supervised classification with graph convolutional networks. In: Proceedings International Conference Learning Represent (2017)
29. Jiang, K., et al.: Multi-scale progressive fusion network for single image deraining. In: Proceedings IEEE Conference Computer Vision Pattern Recognition, pp. 8346–8355 (2020)
30. Yang, W., Wang, S., Liu, J.: Removing arbitrary-scale rain streaks via fractal band learning with self-supervision. IEEE Trans. Image Process. **29**, 6759–6772 (2020)
31. Jiang, N., Chen, W., Lin, L., Zhao, T.: Single image rain removal via multi-module deep grid network. Comput. Vis. Image Understand. **202**, 103106 (2021)
32. Wang, Q., Sun, G., Fan, H., Li, W., Tang, Y.: APAN: across-scale progressive attention network for single image deraining. IEEE Signal Process. Lett. **29**, 159–163 (2022)
33. Yang, W., Wang, S., Xu, D., Wang, X., Liu, J.: Towards scale-free rain streak removal via self-supervised fractal band learning. Proc. AAAI **34**(7), 12629–12636 (2020)
34. He, K., Zhang, X., Ren, S., Sun, J.: Deep residual learning for image recognition. In: Proceedings IEEE Conference Computer Vision Pattern Recognition, pp. 770–778 (2016)
35. Hu, J., Shen, L., Albanie, S., Sun, G., Wu, E.: Squeeze-and-excitation networks. IEEE Trans. Pattern Anal. Mach. Intell. **42**(8), 2011–2023 (2020)

36. Zhao, H., Gallo, O., Frosio, I., Kautz, J.: Loss functions for image restoration with neural networks. IEEE Trans. Comput. Imaging **3**(1), 47–57 (2017)
37. Wang, Z., Bovik, A.C., Sheikh, H.R., Simoncelli, E.P.: Image quality assessment: from error visibility to structural similarity. IEEE Trans. Image Process. **13**(4), 600–612 (2004)
38. Wei, W., Meng, D., Zhao, Q., Xu, Z., Wu, Y.: Semi-supervised transfer learning for image rain removal. In: Proceedings IEEE Conference Computer Vision Pattern Recognition, pp. 3877–3886 (2019)
39. Paszke, A. et al.: PyTorch: an imperative style, high-performance deep learning library. In: Proceedings Advanced Neural Information Processing System, pp. 8024–8035 (2019)

A Stage-Mutual-Affine Network for Single Remote Sensing Image Super-Resolution

Shu Tang[✉], Jianing Liu, Xianbo Xie, Shuli Yang, Wanling Zeng,
and Xinyi Wang

Chongqing Key Laboratory of Computer Network and Communications Technology,
Chongqing University of Posts and Telecommunications, Chongqing 400065, China
tangshu@cqupt.edu.cn

Abstract. The deep neural network (DNN) has made significant progress in the single remote sensing image super-resolution (SRSISR). The success of DNN-based SRSISR methods mainly stems from the use of the global information and the fusion of shallow features and the deep features, which fits the non-local self-similarity characteristic of the remote sensing image very well. However, for the fusion of different depth (level) features, most DNN-based SRSISR methods always use the simple skip-connection, e.g. the element-wise addition or concatenation, to transform the feature coming from preceding layers to later layers directly. To achieve sufficient complementation between different levels and capture more informative features, in this paper, we propose a stage-mutual-affine network (SMAN) for high-quality SRSISR. First, for the use of the global information, we construct a convolution-transformer dual-branch module (CTDM), in which we propose an adaptive multi-head attention (AMHA) strategy to dynamically rescale the head-wise features of the transformer for more effective global information extraction. Then, the global information is fused with the local structure information extracted by the convolution branch for more accurate recurrence information reconstruction. Second, a novel hierarchical feature aggregation module (HFAM) is proposed to effectively fuse shallow features and deep features by using a mutual affine convolution operation. The superiority of the proposed HFAM is that it achieves sufficient complementation and enhances the representational capacity of the network by extracting the global information and exploiting the interdependencies between different levels of features, effectively. Extensive experiments demonstrate the superior performance of our SMAN over the state-of-the-art methods in terms of both qualitative evaluation and quantitative metrics.

Keywords: Single remote sensing image super resolution ·
Transformer · Shallow features · Deep features · Mutual affine

Supplementary Information The online version contains supplementary material available at https://doi.org/10.1007/978-3-031-18916-6_21.

1   Introduction

Single remote sensing image super-resolution (SRSISR), which aims to reconstruct a high-resolution (HR) image based on the given low-resolution (LR) image, is a server ill-posed issue. To overcome this problem, most SRSISR methods are proposed and can be broadly classified into three categories, specifically are interpolation-based methods, learning-based methods and DNN-based methods.

The interpolation-based methods typically utilize bicubic interpolation to construct models, which are simply designed with the local information in an unsupervised manner, thus result in blurring of edges as well as other image details. Learning-based super-resolution algorithms can be further divided into two classes, specifically are neighborhood embedding-based algorithms [2] and sparse representation-based algorithms [20]. However, among these methods, only low-level features are introduced to models, such as image texture and details which may damage their capability.

With the advancement of DNN, a growing number of DNN-based methods are used for SRSISR in recent years. Compared with low-level features used by traditional methods, DNN can extract multi-level deep features effectively. Nevertheless, some researches [13,17] only consider the combination between features at different scales but ignores information at different levels, which may result in the loss of information such as details and textures. There are also some methods [4,5] that simply utilize element-wise addition or concatenation to transform the feature coming from preceding layers to later layers directly. However, some research has found that the frequency bands of feature maps from different layers are frequently different, therefore, treating feature maps which have different frequency information equally is not a good idea [21].

Aiming at the problems existing in the current methods, we propose a stage-mutual-affine network. The major contributions of this paper are introduced as follows:

1. In view of the obvious self-similarity in the remote sensing images (RSI), we propose a convolution-transformer dual-branch module (CTDM), which can extract and fuse the local and global features of the RSI effectively.
2. Inspired by channel attention in convolutional neural network, we design an adaptive multi-head attention (AMHA) module to dynamically rescale the head-wise features of the transformer for more effective global information extraction.
3. To get the most out of the hierarchical features, we design a novel hierarchical feature aggregation module (HFAM). By exploring the dependencies among the features extracted from each CTDM, affine transformation is used to effectively fuse the information from multiple levels and further improve the expression capability of SMAN.

2   Related Work

Some attempts [27,28] have been made to investigate the solution to super-resolution problems in recent years. Numerous DNN-based networks for SRSISR have been proposed in the literature. In this section, methods closely related to our work are briefly introduced.

2.1 Remote Sensing Image Super-Resolution

In the early years, Pan et al. [20] first introduced the dictionary based on sparse representation to reconstruct RSI. Hou et al. [8] provided a new insight to obtain better internal relationships, which constructed a dictionary model from global and local. Shao et al. [22] designed a sparse self-encoder to explore the relationships between the sparse representation coefficients of LR images and HR images, which is applicable to RSI with different spatial scales.

DNN has been extensively employed in the field of SRSISR since the emergence of deep learning. By incorporating the residual connection and network-in-network strategy into the process of SRSISR, Haut et al. [7] developed a deep compendium model. Pan et al. [19] designed back-projection blocks that consisted of up- and down-sampling to improve the reconstruction capability of the proposed model.

In addition, some researchers have addressed the SRSISR issue from the perspective of wavelet transform. In order to learn multiple frequency band features from different dimensions, Wang et al. [26] proposed a parallel shallow neural network. Zhang et al. [30] proposed a multi-scale attention model to learn different level features of RSI.

2.2 Attention Mechanism

With the deepening of network structure, the residual network presents significant challenges to learn correct training center owing to the tendency of ignoring the correlation between image space, structure and texture. In order to address this issue, DNN based on attention mechanism has become a promising and trending learning paradigm. Hu et al. focused on employing channel-wise relationships to improve the performance of classification and proposed a squeeze-and-excitation network [9]. Zhang et al. implemented adaptive adjustment of channel features by exploring relationship among channels via channel attention mechanism [31]. Dai et al. used second-order feature statistics to explore more powerful feature and proposed the second-order attention model [3].

3 The Proposed SMAN

3.1 Network Architecture

SMAN is made up of five parts: shallow feature extraction, deep feature extraction, upscale module, HFAM and reconstruction module (See Fig. 1). Let's denote I_{LR} and I_{SR} as the input and output of SMAN. Only three convolutional layers are utilized to get shallow feature F_{SF} from the I_{LR}. F_{SF} is then utilized to extract deep feature, resulting in features as

$$F_{CTDM}^n = H_{CTDM}^n(H_{CTDM}^{n-1}(\ldots(H_{CTDM}^1(F_{SF})))), \tag{1}$$

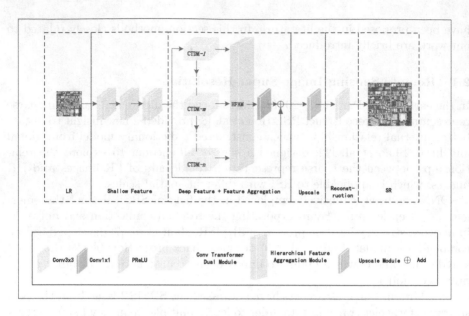

Fig. 1. Our proposed Stage-Mutual-Affine Network (SMAN).

where H_{CTDM}^n stands for n-th CTDM. Then HFAM is proposed to effectively fuse shallow features and deep features by using a mutual affine transformation (ATM) via

$$F_{ATM}^n = H_{ATM}^n(F_{CTDM}^n, \overline{F_{CTDM}^n}),$$ (2)

where F_{CTDM}^n and $\overline{F_{CTDM}^n}$ are the output of n-th CTDM and concatenation of splits that are complementary to F_{CTDM}^n, H_{ATM}^n and F_{ATM}^n represent the n-th ATM and the result of n-th ATM respectively. Furthermore, different features $F_{ATM}^1, F_{ATM}^2, \ldots, F_{ATM}^n$ are concatenated to generate the output of HFAM

$$F_{HFAM} = H_{Concat}(F_{ATM}^1, F_{ATM}^2, \ldots, F_{ATM}^n).$$ (3)

Then the sum of aggregation feature F_{HFAM} and F_{SF} is upscaled by the upscale module $H_\uparrow$ and the upscaled feature $F_\uparrow$ is obtained by

$$F_\uparrow = H_\uparrow(F_{HFAM} + F_{SF}).$$ (4)

Specifically, $H_\uparrow$ is performed using the Sub-pixel Convoluntion of ESPCN [23]. The upscaled feature is then mapped into super-resolution image via the reconstruction layer H_R composed by one convolutional layer

$$I_{SR} = H_R(F_\uparrow) = H_{SMAN}(I_{LR}),$$ (5)

where H_{SMAN} is the function of SMAN.

Then SMAN is optimized under the guidance of the loss function. To verify the effectiveness of SMAN, the Identical objective function as prior studies is adopted. For a given training set $\{I_{LR}^i, I_{HR}^i\}_{i=1}^N$, it contains N LR images and their HR images. More in detail, the aim of training SMAN is to minimize the L1 loss function, which is optimized by stochastic gradient descent algorithm and can be represented as

$$L(\Theta) = \frac{1}{N} \sum_{i=1}^{N} \|H_{SMAN}(I_{LR}^i) - I_{HR}^i\|_1, \tag{6}$$

where Θ is the parameters of the model.

3.2 Convolution-Transformer Dual-Branch Module

Aiming at the obvious self-similarity of RSI, we design a module which can maintain long range modelling capabilities without compromising local modelling capabilities. The whole process is shown in Fig. 2. F_{global} and F_{local} are the output of convolution-branch and transformer-branch respectively. To facilitates the information flow greatly, we concat the features extracted from the two branches and use a skip connection to obtain the output of CTDM, i.e. F.

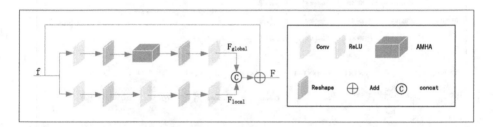

Fig. 2. The proposed convolution-transformer dual-branch module (CTDM).

3.3 Adaptive Multi-head Attention

In order to extract global features more effectively, an adaptive multi-head attention (AMHA) module (See Fig. 3) which replaces the plain multi-head attention is designed in transformer. Due to space limitations, only the differences from the original transformer are shown. For input feature $X \in R^{HW \times D}$, the query, key and value matrices Q, K and V are computed and reshaped as

$$K = H_R(XP_K), Q = H_R(XP_Q), V = H_R(XP_V), \tag{7}$$

where $K \in R^{N \times HW \times \frac{D}{N}}$, $Q \in R^{N \times \frac{D}{N} \times HW}$, $V \in R^{N \times HW \times \frac{D}{N}}$ and N is the number of heads in transformer. The attention matrix is thus computed by the self-attention mechanism as

$$Attention(Q, K, V) = H_{SoftMax}(QK)V, \tag{8}$$

and get the feature map

$$F_{AMHA} = Attention \odot V. \tag{9}$$

To fully capture head-wise dependencies from F_{AMHA}, global avgerage pooling, global maximum pooling, convolution, and nonlinear operation are all introduced to AMHA. Finally, the result can be obtained by the following form

$$Y = H_R(H_S(H_{C2}(H_{C1}(H_{GAP}(F_{AMHA}) + H_{GMP}(F_{AMHA})))) \odot F_{AMHA}). \tag{10}$$

In previous works, channel attention mechanism was used to process the features extracted by convolution, which led to the final result of local features. However, the proposed AMHA is based on transformer, and thanks to its Multi-head Self-attention, AMHA is able to obtain global information. Further, inspired by the channel attention mechanism, the global features extracted by each head are different and should be treated differently, so AMHA can obtain more effective global features by dynamically adjusting the features extracted by each head of the transformer.

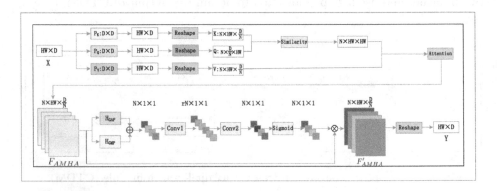

Fig. 3. The proposed adaptive multi-head attention (AMHA).

3.4   Hierarchical Feature Aggregation Module

HFAM, which contains n affine transformation module (ATM) is proposed to effectively fuse shallow features and deep features by using a mutual affine convolution operation. Let $F_{CTDM_n} \in R^{C \times H \times W}$ and $\overline{F_{CTDM_n}} \in R^{C(n-1) \times H \times W}$ which are complementary to F_{CTDM_n} are the input feature of the ATM. As shown in Fig. 4, $\overline{F_{CTDM_n}}$ is first passed into the ATM, which has a lightweight network to learn transformation parameters α_n and β_n. Then, α_n and β_n are used to scale and shift F_{CTDM_m}, respectively. The process is formulated as

$$F_n = \alpha_n + F_{CTDM_n} \odot \beta_n, \tag{11}$$

where $\odot$ denotes the element product. Finally, different features $F_1, F_2, ..., F_n$ are concatenated to genreate the output of HFAM, i.e. F_{HFAM}.

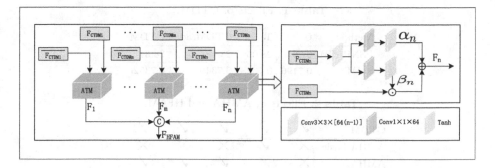

Fig. 4. The proposed hierarchical feature aggregation module (HFAM).

4   Experiment

The Datasets Used for Training. Following [11,12,24,25,29], 800 nature images from DIV2K dataset and 10000 remote sensing images from AID dataset are used to demonstrate the outstanding performance of SMAN against state-of-the-art algorithms.

Implementation Details. For training of ×4 and ×8 model, the batch size and the num of CTDMs are set to 2 and 6, respectively. And the Adam with $\beta_1 = 0.9$, $\beta_2 = 0.999$ and $\epsilon = 1e - 8$ is used as the optimizer to optimize the proposed network. The initial learning rate is set to 10^{-4} and the decay rate is set to 0.5.

4.1   Ablation Study

In this paper, three novel components are introduced to improve the SR capability of the model, specifically are CTDM, AMHA, and HFAM. In this part, the effectiveness of the three modules is verified. All ablation experiments are performed on Test14 which is derived from RSSCN7.

Evaluation of the CTDM. As shown in Table 1, three models including convolution (C), transformer (T) and CTDM_add are compared with CTDM. Among them, C and T mean only convolution or transformer respectively. CTDM-_add represents the addition of branches C and T. Compared with other models, CTDM makes full use of global and local information and achieves the best results.

Evaluation of the AMHA and HFAM. We further explore the effect of AMHA and HFAM (See Table 2). When we compare the results of first three columns, we find that model with AMHA performs better than that without AMHA and our AMHA is superior to the AMHA_basic which based on basic channel attention mechanism. Then all the output of CTDM for image reconstruction named HFAM_simple are simply concated. The performance was negatively affected when HFAM_simple was introduced, because the frequency bands

Table 1. Effects of CTDM.

Method	C	T	CTDM_add	CTDM
PSNR(dB)	27.91	28.05	28.18	28.31
SSIM	0.7196	0.7328	0.7340	0.7352

Table 2. Effects of AMHA and HFAM.

CTDM	✓	✓	✓	✓	✓
AMHA_basic	✗	✓	✗	✗	✗
AMHA	✗	✗	✓	✓	✓
HFAM_simple	✗	✗	✗	✓	✗
HFAM_novel	✗	✗	✗	✗	✓
PSNR(dB)	28.31	28.32	28.34	28.28	28.37
SSIM	0.7352	0.7354	0.7359	0.7347	0.7368

of feature maps from different layers are frequently different, therefore, treating feature maps which have different frequency information equally is not a good idea. Finally, novel HFAM (HFAM_novel) is used to improve PSNR by nearly 0.1 on the basis of HFAM_simple.

4.2 The Comparisons with the State-of-the-Art Methods

To verify the performance of our proposed SMAN, first, experiments on three RSI datasets are conducted, namely, WHURS19, RSSCN7, and UCMERCED. In addition, experiments on four natural image datasets including SET5, SET14, B100, and URBAN100 are further conducted.

On Remote Sensing Image Datasets. Due to space limitations, we present the average results of every approach on different datasets under ×4 and ×8 circumstances, which proves that our method outperforms other models in Table 3. The qualitative results are shown in Fig. 5–Fig. 6, in which positions that show clear contrasts among different approaches are marked out. Among them, LGC-NET [14], DCM [7], HSENET [13] and MHAN [29] are SOTA methods in the remote sensing SR field. We can see that only the proposed method can recover the correct and clear texture, whereas others have varying degrees of blurring. It convincingly demonstrates the consistent strength of the proposed SMAN in quantitative and qualitative comparisons.

On Nature Image Datasets. The performance of SMAN is further validated by employing four broadly used benchmark natural image datasets. The quantitative evaluation results are shown in Table 4 and Fig. 7 further shows the qualitative comparison of ×8 reconstructed results. It is interesting to note that Urban100 is a natural image test set on which the model performs well compared to other datasets, which proves that the proposed method works well for remote sensing images with significant self-similarity. For more experimental results, please refer to our supplementary material.

Table 3. Quantitative results on remote sensing image datasets.

Method	Scale	RSSCN7		WHURS19		UCMERCED	
		PSNR	SSIM	PSNR	SSIM	PSNR	SSIM
LGCNET [14]	×4	28.81	0.7291	30.64	0.8041	28.28	0.7628
DCM [7]	×4	29.05	0.7392	31.14	0.8171	28.80	0.7781
HSENET [13]	×4	29.17	0.7448	31.31	0.8229	29.05	0.7860
MHAN [29]	×4	29.26	0.7486	31.49	0.8279	29.23	0.7929
SRCNN [10]	×4	28.70	0.7240	30.51	0.7987	28.09	0.7548
RCAN [31]	×4	29.25	0.7481	31.45	0.8269	29.22	0.7925
SAN [3]	×4	29.24	0.7475	31.41	0.8260	29.19	0.7911
DRLN [1]	×4	29.22	0.7468	31.40	0.8252	29.16	0.7903
HAN [18]	×4	<u>29.28</u>	<u>0.7492</u>	<u>31.50</u>	**0.8280**	29.27	<u>0.7933</u>
NLSN [16]	×4	<u>29.28</u>	0.7488	31.45	0.8269	<u>29.29</u>	0.7931
Ours	×4	**29.34**	**0.7541**	**31.53**	**0.8280**	**29.49**	**0.7995**
LGCNET [14]	×8	26.12	0.5798	26.70	0.6350	24.29	0.5733
DCM [7]	×8	26.46	0.5960	26.72	0.6300	24.86	0.6008
HSENET [13]	×8	26.52	0.5999	27.33	0.6620	24.97	0.6070
MHAN [29]	×8	26.59	0.6049	27.48	0.6707	25.09	0.6152
SRCNN [10]	×8	26.06	0.5755	26.62	0.6293	24.18	0.5655
RCAN [31]	×8	26.60	0.6055	27.52	0.6725	25.09	0.6158
SAN [3]	×8	26.60	0.6050	27.50	0.6713	25.09	0.6146
DRLN [1]	×8	26.65	0.6024	27.39	0.6656	25.03	0.6109
HAN [18]	×8	<u>26.61</u>	0.6056	<u>27.52</u>	0.6723	25.11	0.6165
NLSN [16]	×8	<u>26.61</u>	<u>0.6064</u>	<u>27.52</u>	<u>0.6727</u>	<u>25.14</u>	<u>0.6180</u>
Ours	×8	**26.66**	**0.6092**	**27.57**	**0.6743**	**25.21**	**0.6217**

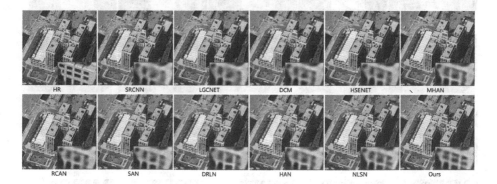

Fig. 5. Visual comparison for ×4 SR on remote sensing image datasets.

Table 4. Quantitative results for ×8 on natural image datasets.

Method	Param(M)	Set5		Set14		B100		Urban100	
		PSNR	SSIM	PSNR	SSIM	PSNR	SSIM	PSNR	SSIM
SRCNN [10]	0.07	24.94	0.6959	23.37	0.5848	24.14	0.5655	21.07	0.5422
EDSR [15]	45.45	26.79	0.7658	24.75	0.6340	24.70	0.5924	22.21	0.6041
RDN [32]	22.42	27.10	0.7797	24.90	0.6423	24.83	0.5988	22.56	0.6231
D-DBPN [6]	23.21	27.21	0.7840	25.13	0.6480	24.88	0.6010	22.73	0.6312
RCAN [31]	15.74	27.22	0.7843	<u>25.25</u>	**0.6506**	<u>24.96</u>	<u>0.6042</u>	<u>22.94</u>	<u>0.6423</u>
SAN [3]	15.63	26.74	0.7615	24.76	0.6325	24.69	0.5914	22.21	0.6023
HAN [18]	16.22	<u>27.24</u>	<u>0.7850</u>	**25.26**	<u>0.6502</u>	24.95	0.6040	22.92	0.6412
Ours	8.24	**27.30**	**0.7856**	<u>25.25</u>	0.6484	**24.99**	**0.6049**	**23.03**	**0.6425**

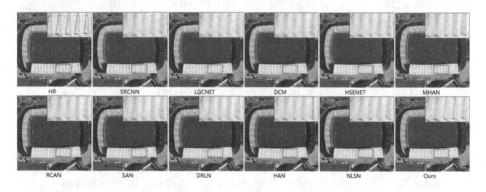

Fig. 6. Visual comparison for ×8 SR on remote sensing image datasets.

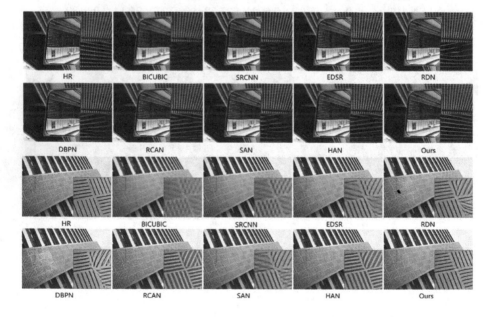

Fig. 7. Visual comparison for ×8 SR on natural image datasets.

5   Conclusion

In this paper, a stage-mutual-affine network (SMAN) for SRSISR. A convolution-transformer dual-branch module (CTDM) is firstly proposed to extract local and global features and thus result in a better representational capability. Different from existing transformer models, an adaptive multi-head attention (AMHA) module is designed to adjust the information extracted by different heads dynamically. Finally, a novel hierarchical feature aggregation module (HFAM) is proposed for effectively fusing shallow features and deep features by using a mutual affine convolution operation. Compared with the conventional channel concat, it can fully exploit the dependency between hierarchical features. Extensive experiments show that our method can obtain better reconstruction results than the state-of-the-art SRSISR methods in terms of both qualitative evaluation and quantitative metrics.

References

1. Anwar, S., Barnes, N.: Densely residual Laplacian super-resolution. IEEE Trans. Pattern Anal. Mach. Intell. **44**(3), 1192–1204 (2022)
2. Chang, H., Yeung, D.Y., Xiong, Y.: Super-resolution through neighbor embedding. In: Proceedings of the 2004 IEEE Computer Society Conference on Computer Vision and Pattern Recognition 2004. CVPR 2004, vol. 1, p. I (2004)
3. Dai, T., Cai, J., Zhang, Y., Xia, S.T., Zhang, L.: Second-order attention network for single image super-resolution. In: 2019 IEEE/CVF Conference on Computer Vision and Pattern Recognition (CVPR), pp. 11057–11066 (2019)
4. Dong, X., Sun, X., Jia, X., Xi, Z., Gao, L., Zhang, B.: Remote sensing image super-resolution using novel dense-sampling networks. IEEE Trans. Geosci. Remote Sens. **59**(2), 1618–1633 (2021)
5. Dong, X., Wang, L., Sun, X., Jia, X., Gao, L., Zhang, B.: Remote sensing image super-resolution using second-order multi-scale networks. IEEE Trans. Geosci. Remote Sens. **59**(4), 3473–3485 (2021)
6. Haris, M., Shakhnarovich, G., Ukita, N.: Deep back-projection networks for super-resolution. In: 2018 IEEE/CVF Conference on Computer Vision and Pattern Recognition, pp. 1664–1673 (2018)
7. Haut, J.M., Paoletti, M.E., Fernández-Beltran, R., Plaza, J., Plaza, A., Li, J.: Remote sensing single-image superresolution based on a deep compendium model. IEEE Geosci. Remote Sens. Lett. **16**(9), 1432–1436 (2019)
8. Hou, B., Zhou, K., Jiao, L.: Adaptive super-resolution for remote sensing images based on sparse representation with global joint dictionary model. IEEE Trans. Geosci. Remote Sens. **56**(4), 2312–2327 (2017)
9. Hu, J., Shen, L., Sun, G.: Squeeze-and-excitation networks. In: 2018 IEEE/CVF Conference on Computer Vision and Pattern Recognition, pp. 7132–7141 (2018)
10. Ji, X., Lu, Y., Guo, L.: Image super-resolution with deep convolutional neural network. In: 2016 IEEE First International Conference on Data Science in Cyberspace (DSC), pp. 626–630 (2016)
11. Jo, Y., Oh, S.W., Vajda, P., Kim, S.J.: Tackling the ill-posedness of super-resolution through adaptive target generation. In: Proceedings of the IEEE/CVF Conference on Computer Vision and Pattern Recognition, pp. 16236–16245 (2021)

12. Kong, X., Zhao, H., Qiao, Y., Dong, C.: ClassSR: a general framework to accelerate super-resolution networks by data characteristic. In: Proceedings of the IEEE/CVF Conference on Computer Vision and Pattern Recognition, pp. 12016–12025 (2021)
13. Lei, S., Shi, Z.: Hybrid-scale self-similarity exploitation for remote sensing image super-resolution. IEEE Trans. Geosci. Remote Sens. **60**, 1–10 (2022)
14. Lei, S., Shi, Z., Zou, Z.: Super-resolution for remote sensing images via local-global combined network. IEEE Geosci. Remote Sens. Lett. **14**(8), 1243–1247 (2017)
15. Lim, B., Son, S., Kim, H., Nah, S., Lee, K.M.: Enhanced deep residual networks for single image super-resolution. In: 2017 IEEE Conference on Computer Vision and Pattern Recognition Workshops (CVPRW), pp. 1132–1140 (2017)
16. Mei, Y., Fan, Y., Zhou, Y.: Image super-resolution with non-local sparse attention. In: 2021 IEEE/CVF Conference on Computer Vision and Pattern Recognition (CVPR), pp. 3516–3525 (2021)
17. Mei, Y., Fan, Y., Zhou, Y., Huang, L., Huang, T.S., Shi, H.: Image super-resolution with cross-scale non-local attention and exhaustive self-exemplars mining. In: 2020 IEEE/CVF Conference on Computer Vision and Pattern Recognition (CVPR), pp. 5689–5698 (2020)
18. Niu, B., et al.: Single image super-resolution via a holistic attention network. In: European Conference on Computer Vision, pp. 191–207. Springer (2020). https://doi.org/10.1007/978-3-030-58610-2_12
19. Pan, Z., Ma, W., Guo, J., Lei, B.: Super-resolution of single remote sensing image based on residual dense backprojection networks. IEEE Trans. Geosci. Remote Sens. **57**(10), 7918–7933 (2019)
20. Pan, Z., Yu, J., Huang, H., Hu, S., Zhang, A., Ma, H.: Super-resolution based on compressive sensing and structural self-similarity for remote sensing images. IEEE Trans. Geosci. Remote Sens. **51**(9), 4864–4876 (2013)
21. Qiu, Y., Wang, R., Tao, D., Cheng, J.: Embedded block residual network: a recursive restoration model for single-image super-resolution. In: 2019 IEEE/CVF International Conference on Computer Vision (ICCV), pp. 4179–4188 (2019)
22. Shao, Z., Wang, L., Wang, Z., Deng, J.: Remote sensing image super-resolution using sparse representation and coupled sparse autoencoder. IEEE J. Sel. Top. Appl. Earth Obser. Remote Sens. **12**(8), 2663–2674 (2019)
23. Shi, W., et al.: Real-time single image and video super-resolution using an efficient sub-pixel convolutional neural network. In: 2016 IEEE Conference on Computer Vision and Pattern Recognition (CVPR), pp. 1874–1883 (2016)
24. Song, D., Wang, Y., Chen, H., Xu, C., Xu, C., Tao, D.: AdderSR: towards energy efficient image super-resolution. In: 2021 IEEE/CVF Conference on Computer Vision and Pattern Recognition (CVPR), pp. 15643–15652 (2021)
25. Wang, L., et al.: Exploring sparsity in image super-resolution for efficient inference. In: Proceedings of the IEEE/CVF Conference on Computer Vision and Pattern Recognition, pp. 4917–4926 (2021)
26. Wang, T., Sun, W., Qi, H., Ren, P.: Aerial image super resolution via wavelet multiscale convolutional neural networks. IEEE Geosci. Remote Sens. Lett. **15**(5), 769–773 (2018)
27. Wen, W., Ren, W., Shi, Y., Nie, Y., Zhang, J., Cao, X.: Video super-resolution via a spatio-temporal alignment network. IEEE Trans. Image Process. **31**, 1761–1773 (2022)
28. Yan, Y., Ren, W., Hu, X., Li, K., Shen, H., Cao, X.: SRGAT: Single image super-resolution with graph attention network. IEEE Trans. Image Process. **30**, 4905–4918 (2021)

29. Zhang, D., Shao, J., Li, X., Shen, H.T.: Remote sensing image super-resolution via mixed high-order attention network. IEEE Trans. Geosci. Remote Sens. **59**(6), 5183–5196 (2021)
30. Zhang, S., Yuan, Q., Li, J., Sun, J., Zhang, X.: Scene-adaptive remote sensing image super-resolution using a multiscale attention network. IEEE Trans. Geosci. Remote Sens. **58**(7), 4764–4779 (2020)
31. Zhang, Y., Li, K., Li, K., Wang, L., Zhong, B., Fu, Y.: Image super-resolution using very deep residual channel attention networks. In: Proceedings of the European Conference on Computer Vision (ECCV), pp. 286–301 (2018)
32. Zhang, Y., Tian, Y., Kong, Y., Zhong, B., Fu, Y.: Residual dense network for image super-resolution. In: 2018 IEEE/CVF Conference on Computer Vision and Pattern Recognition, pp. 2472–2481 (2018)

Style-Based Attentive Network
for Real-World Face Hallucination

Mandi Luo[1,3] , Xin Ma[2] , Huaibo Huang[3] , and Ran He[3(✉)]

[1] School of Artificial Intelligence, University of Chinese Academy of Sciences,
Beijing, China
[2] Meituan, Beijing, China
`xin.ma@cripac.ia.ac.cn`
[3] Institute of Automation, Chinese Academy of Sciences, Beijing, China
`luomandi2019@ia.ac.cn, huaibo.huang@cripac.ia.ac.cn, rhe@nlpr.ia.ac.cn`

Abstract. Real-world face hallucination is a challenging image translation problem. There exist various unknown transformations in real-world
LR images that are hard to be modeled using traditional image degradation procedures. To address this issue, this paper proposes a novel
pipeline, which consists of a style Variational Autoencoder (styleVAE)
and an SR network incorporated with an attention mechanism. To get
real-world-like low-quality images paired with the HR images, we design
the styleVAE to transfer the complex nuisance factors in real-world LR
images to the generated LR images. We also use mutual information estimation (MI) to get better style information. In addition, both global and
local attention residual blocks are proposed to learn long-range dependencies and local texture details, respectively. It is worth noticing that
styleVAE is presented in a plug-and-play manner and thus can help to
improve the generalization and robustness of our SR method as well as
other SR methods. Extensive experiments demonstrate that our method
is effective and generalizable both quantitatively and qualitatively.

1 Introduction

Single image super-resolution (SISR) aims to infer a natural high-resolution (HR)
image from the low-resolution (LR) input. Recently, many deep learning based
super-resolution (SR) methods have been greatly developed and achieved promising results. These methods are mostly trained on paired LR and HR images,
while the LR images are usually obtained by performing a predefined degradation mode on the HR images, e.g., bicubic interpolation.

However, there is a huge difference between the LR images after bicubic interpolation and real-world LR images. There are various nuisance factors leading to
image quality degeneration, e.g., motion blur, lens aberration and sensor noise.
Moreover, these nuisance factors are usually unknown and mixed up with each
other, making the real-world SR task challenging. The LR generated manually
can only simulate limited patterns and methods trained on them inherently lack
the ability to deal with real-world SR issues.

M. Luo and X. Ma—Contributed equally to this work.

S. Yu et al. (Eds.): PRCV 2022, LNCS 13537, pp. 262–273, 2022.
https://doi.org/10.1007/978-3-031-18916-6_22

In order to solve this problem, we propose a generative network based on variational autoencoders (VAEs) to synthesize real-world-like LR images. The essential idea is derived from the separable property of image style and image content, which has been widely explored in image style transfer [7,14,18]. It means that one can change the style of an image while preserving its content. Based on these previous researches, we propose to consider the fore-mentioned nuisance factors as a special case of image styles. We then design styleVAE to transfer the complex nuisance factors in real-world LR images to generated LR images. In this manner, real-world-like LR images, as well as LR-HR pairs, are generated automatically. Furthermore, styleVAE is presented as a plug-and-play component and can also be applied to existing SR methods to improve their generalization and robustness.

In addition, we build an SR network for real-world super-resolution. Following the principle of global priority in human visual perception systems, our proposed SR network consists mainly of two modules. On the one hand, we develop a global attention residual block (GARB) to capture long-range dependency correlations, helping the SR network to focus on global topology information. On the other hand, we introduce a local attention residual block (LARB) for better feature learning, which is essential to infer high-frequency information in images.

In summary, we make the following contributions: (1) we propose to generate paired LR and HR images with a newly designed styleVAE by learning real-world degradation modes; (2) we propose an SR network with two kinds of attention modules for real-world super-resolution; (3) extensive experiments on real-world LR images demonstrate that styleVAE effectively facilitates SR methods and the proposed SR network achieves state-of-the-art results.

2   Related Work

Some previous methods make use of the specific static information of face images obtained by the face analysis technique. Zhu *et al.* [28] utilized the dense correspondence field estimation to help recovering textual details. Meanwhile, some other methods use face image prior knowledge obtained by CNN or GAN-based network. For example, Chen and Bulat [2,5] utilized facial geometric priors, such as parsing maps or face landmark heatmaps, to super-resolve LR face images. Moreover, some wavelet-based methods have also been proposed. Huang *et al.* [13] introduced a method combined with wavelet transformation to predict the corresponding wavelet coefficients.

3   Methodology

Figure 1 shows the overall architecture of our method that consists of two stages. In the first stage, styleVAE is proposed to generate real-world-like LR images. In the second stage, the generated LR images paired with the corresponding HR images are fed into the SR network.

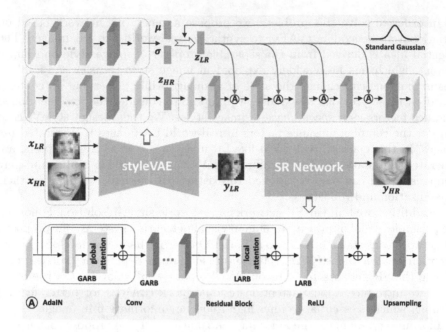

Fig. 1. Overall architecture the proposed network. StyleVAE takes unpaired LR and HR images as its inputs to generate real-world-like LR images. SR network takes paired real-world-like LR and HR images as its inputs. By simulating image degradation processes in reality through styleVAE, we can improve the performance of SR methods for real-world SISR.

3.1 Style Variational Autoencoder

We adopt Adaptive Instance Normal (AdaIN) to transfer nuisance factors in real-world LR images to generated LR images. There are two inference networks E_{LR} and E_{HR}, and one generator G in styleVAE. E_{LR} and E_{HR} project input real-world LR images and HR images into two latent spaces, representing style information and content information, respectively. The two latent codes produced by E_{LR} and E_{HR} are combined in a style transfer way (AdaIN) rather than concatenated directly. The style information y (i.e., Z_{LR}) controls AdaIN [7] operations after each residual block in the generator G.

Following VAE, we use the Kullback-Leibler (KL) divergence to regularize the latent space obtained by E_{LR}. The E_{LR} branch has two output variables, i.e., μ and σ. To a reparameterization trick, we have $Z_{LR} = \mu_{LR} + \sigma \odot \epsilon$, where $\epsilon \sim \mathcal{N}(0, I)$, $\odot$ means Hadamard product; μ and σ denote the mean and the standard deviation, respectively. Given N data samples, the posterior distribution $q_\phi(z|x_{LR})$ is constrained through Kullback-Leibler divergence:

$$\mathcal{L}_{kl} = KL(q_\phi(z|x_{LR})||p(z)) = \frac{1}{2N} \sum_{i=1}^{N} \sum_{j=1}^{M} (1 + log(\sigma_{ij}^2) - \mu_{ji}^2 - \sigma_{ij}^2), \quad (1)$$

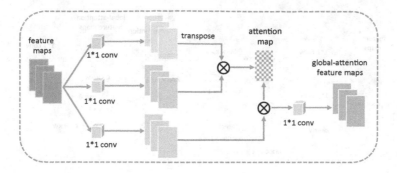

Fig. 2. The proposed GA module in GARB. The $\otimes$ denotes the matrix multiplication operation.

where $q_\phi(\cdot)$ is the inference network E_{LR}. The prior $p(z)$ is the standard multivariate Gaussian distribution. M is the dimension of z.

The generator $p_\theta(y_{LR}|z_{LR}, z_{HR})$ in styleVAE is required to generate LR images y_{LR} from the latent space z_{HR} and the learned distribution z_{LR}. Similar [13,14], we use a pre-trained VGG network [23] to calculate the following loss function:

$$\mathcal{L}_{style} = \alpha\mathcal{L}_c + \beta\mathcal{L}_s, \tag{2}$$

where α and β are the weights for the content loss and the style loss, respectively. Here we set α and β to 1 and 0.1, respectively. It defines at a specific layer J of the VGG network [23]:

$$\mathcal{L}_c = \left\|\phi^J(y_{LR}) - \phi^J(x_{HR})\right\|_F^2, \tag{3}$$

where y_{LR} and x_{HR} denote generated the LR images and the corresponding HR images, respectively. We resize the size of x_{HR} to match that of y_{LR}. Furthermore, $\mathcal{L}_s$ is defined by a weighted sum of the style loss at different layers of the pre-trained VGG network:

$$\mathcal{L}_s = \sum_i w_i \mathcal{L}_s^i(y_{LR}, x_{LR}), \tag{4}$$

where w_i is the trade-off factor for the style loss $\mathcal{L}_s^i$ at ith layer of the pre-trained VGG network. $\mathcal{L}_s^i$ is computed as the Euclidean distance between the Gram matrices of the feature maps for y_{LR} and x_{LR}.

Mutual Information Maximization. The purpose of the inference network E_{LR} is to extract the style information. To gain style representation better, the mutual information between real-world and generated LR images is required to be maximized as follows:

$$\mathcal{L}_{mi} = \sup_{\theta \in \Theta} \mathbb{E}_{p(x_{LR}, y_{LR})}[T_\theta] - log(\mathbb{E}_{p(x_{LR}) \otimes p(x_{HR})}[e^{T_\theta}]), \tag{5}$$

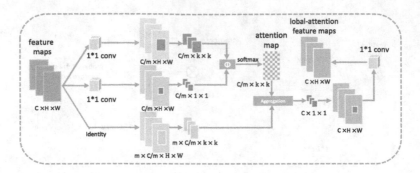

Fig. 3. The proposed LA module in LARB. Different from GA, it obtains the composability between a target pixel and a pixel from the visible scope of the target pixel instead of all pixels of images.

where T_θ denotes a static deep neural network parameterized by $\theta \in \Theta$. The inputs of the T_θ are empirically drawn from the joint distribution $p_{(x_{LR}, y_{LR})}$ and the product of the marginal $p_{x_{LR}} \otimes p_{y_{LR}}$.

According to all the loss functions mentioned above, the overall loss to optimize styleVAE is formulated as:

$$\mathcal{L}_{styleVAE} = \lambda_1 \mathcal{L}_{kl} + \lambda_2 \mathcal{L}_{style} + \lambda_3 \mathcal{L}_{mi}, \tag{6}$$

where λ_1, λ_2, and λ_3 are the trade-off factors.

3.2 Super-Resolution Network

Our proposed SR network mainly consists of global attention residual block (GARB) and local attention residual block (LARB).

Global Attention Residual Block. As shown in Fig. 2, we propose a global attention residual block to learn long-range dependencies by using the global attention (GA) module [25]. It maintains efficiency in calculation and statistics. There is a skip connection in GARB due to the success of residual blocks (RBs) [27] (See Fig. 1). The GA module is formulated as follows:

$$\beta_{j,i} = \frac{exp(s_{i,j})}{\sum_{i=1}^{N} exp(s_{i,j})}, \tag{7}$$

where $s_{i,j} = f(x_i)^T g(x_j)$ ($f(x) = W_f x$, $g(x) = W_g x$) represents that the feature maps of the former hidden layer are projected into two latent spaces to obtain the attention value. $\beta_{i,j}$ indicates the degree of attention that the ith position receives when generating the jth area. The output of the attention layer is defined as:

$$o_j = v(\sum_{i=1}^{N} \beta_{(j,i)} h(x_i)), \tag{8}$$

where $h(x_i) = W_h x_i$, $v(x_i) = W_v x_i$. The above W_f, W_g, W_h, W_v are implemented by a convolution layer with kernel size 1×1. We connect o_i and x_i in a residual way, so the final output is shown as below:

$$y_i = \lambda o_i + x_i, \tag{9}$$

where λ is a learnable scalar.

Local Attention Residual Block. As shown in Fig. 3, we also propose a local attention residual block (LARB) to capture local details through the local attention (LA) module [9]. The LA module forms local pixel pairs with a flexible bottom-up way, which efficiently deals with visual patterns with increasing size and complexity. We use a general method of relational modeling to calculate the LA module, which is defined as:

$$\omega(p^{'}, p) = softmax(\Phi(f_{\theta_q}(x_{p'}), f_{\theta_k}(x_p))), \tag{10}$$

where $\omega(p^{'}, p)$ obtains a representation at one pixel by computing the composability between it (target pixel $p^{'}$) and a pixel p in its visible position range. Transformation functions f_{θ_q} and f_{θ_k} are implemented by 1×1 convolution layer. The function Φ is chosen the squared difference:

$$\Phi(q_{p'}, k_p) = -(q_{p'} - k_p)^2. \tag{11}$$

4 Experiments

In this section, we firstly introduce the datasets and implementation in detail. Then we evaluate our proposed method from both qualitative and quantitative aspects.

4.1 Datasets and Implementation

Training Dataset. As illustrated in [3], we select the following four datasets to build the HR training dataset that contains 180k faces. The first is a subset of VGGFace2 [4] that contains images with 10 large poses for each identity (9k identities). The second is a subset of Celeb-A [22] that contains 60k faces. The third is the whole AFLW [17] that contains 25k faces used for facial landmark localization originally. The last is a subset of LS3D-W [1] that contains face images with various poses.

We also utilize the WIDER FACE [24] to build a real-world LR dataset. WIDER FACE is a face detection benchmark dataset that consists of more than 32k images affected by various noise and degradation types. We randomly select 90% images in the LR training dataset.

Testing Dataset. Another 10% images from WIDER FACE described in the latest section are selected as real-world LR testing dataset. We conduct experiments on it to verify the performance of our proposed method.

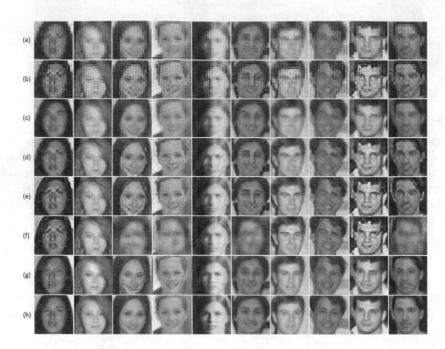

Fig. 4. Comparisons with the state-of-art methods (4×). (a) Input real-world LR images. (b) Results of SRCNN [6]. (c) Results of SRGAN [20]. (d) Results of VDSR [15]. (e) Results of EDSR [21]. (f) Results of RDN [27]. (g) Results of [3]'s method (h) Our results. Compared with other methods, our proposed pipeline reconstructs sharper SR images with better details.

Implementation Details. Our proposed styleVAE is trained on the unpaired training HR and LR images for 10 epochs. After that, the paired LR-HR dataset is created used to train the SR network with 50 epochs. We train our styleVAE and SR network through the ADAM algorithm [16] with $\beta_1 = 0.9$, $\beta_2 = 0.999$. The learning rate is initially set to 10^{-4} and remains unchanged during the training process. The weights λ_1, λ_2, and λ_3 are set as 0.01, 1, and 0.1, respectively. We use PyTorch to implement our models and train them on NVIDIA Titan Xp GPUs.

4.2   Experimental Results

Real-World Images. In this section, We conduct experiments on the testing dataset described in Sect. 4.1. In order to evaluate the performance of our proposed method, we compare with the following state-of-the-art methods both numerically and qualitatively: SRCNN [6], SRGAN [20], VDSR [15], EDSR [21], Bulat's method [3] and RDN [26]. We retrain all these compared methods for the sake of fairness on our HR training dataset with the default configurations described in their respective papers. Note that LR images are produced by applying a bicubic kernel to the corresponding HR images.

Table 1. Results of different SR methods. The second and third columns show PSNR and SSIM based performance on synthetic real-world-like LR images (Higher is better). The fourth column shows FID based performance on our testing dataset (Lower is better).

Method	PSNR	SSIM	FID
BICUBIC	21.19	0.5570	288.47
SRCNN [6]	19.57	0.4030	256.78
SRGAN [20]	20.36	0.5007	179.70
VDSR [15]	20.61	0.5584	144.29
EDSR [21]	20.44	0.5137	129.93
RDN [27]	18.18	0.4063	162.04
Bulat's [3]	22.76	0.6296	149.97
Ours	**24.16**	**0.7197**	**98.61**

Table 2. Results of experiments on deep plug-and-play SR in FID. (Lower is better).

Data Type	Scale	SRCNN	EDSR
BICUBIC	×4	256.78	129.93
styleVAE	×4	198.75	107.63

In numerical terms, we use Fréchet Inception Distance (FID) [8] to measure the quality of the generated images since there are no corresponding HR images. The quantitative results of different SR methods on our testing dataset are summarized in Table 1 (with the factor ×4). It clearly demonstrates that our proposed method is superior to other compared approaches and achieves the best performance on the testing dataset. We also discover that the performances of compared methods trained on bicubic-downsampled LR images are degraded when applied to real-world LR images. The main reason is that nuisance factors, e.g. motion blur, lens aberration and sensor noise, are not taken into synthetic LR images by bicubic interpolation. By training on real-world-like LR images, our method is superior to all compared methods, and the FID value is reduced by a maximum of 158.17.

In Fig. 4, we visually show the qualitative results the our testing dataset with ×4 scale. There are significant artifacts in HR images generated by shallower networks, e.g. SRCNN [6] and SRGAN [20]. Serious mesh phenomenons are found in reconstructed images by SRCNN. We also discover that generated images of VDSR [15], EDSR [21] and RDN [27] are usually distorted. On the contrary, SR images generated by our proposed method are more realistic than Bulat's method [3], since LR images produced by styleVAE exceedingly resemble real-world LR images.

Real-World-Like Images. In order to verify the performance of the proposed method on LR images with unknown degradation modes, we conduct experiment on synthetic real-world-like LR images obtained by styleVAE with ×4 scale. We utilize images from LFW [10–12,19] as the HR image inputs of styleVAE to generate real-world-like LR images. The second and third columns of Table 1 report PSNR and SSIM results of different SR methods. We find that the performances of compared methods are very limited, even lower than that of bicubic up-sampling directly. It also demonstrates that simulating real-world-like LR images is an effective way to improve performance when applied to real-world LR images.

Deep Plug-and-Play Super-Resolution. To further validate the effectiveness of styleVAE, we design two pipelines with the help of plug-and-play framework. We can simply plug styleVAE into SR networks to replace bicubic down-sampled LR images that are used in many previous SR methods. We choose two of the compared methods as the plugged SR networks: a shallower SR network SRCNN [6] and a deeper SR network EDSR. Thus there are four versions of SR networks: SRCNN-B and EDSR-B, trained on bicubic down-sampled LR images, SRCNN-S and EDSR-S, trained on LR images generated by styleVAE. The FID results on our testing dataset are reported in Table 2. As shown in Table 2, the FID values of SRCNN-B and EDSR-B (the second row of Table 2) are higher than those of EDSR-S and EDSR-S (the last row of the Table 2). By simulating real-world LR images using styleVAE, SRCNN gains an improvement of 58.3 (the third column of Table 2) and EDSR is improved by 22.3 (the last column of Table 2).

We also demonstrate the visual results in Fig. 5. As shown in Fig. 5, compared (a) with (b), SRCNN-S effectively eliminates the mesh phenomenon in the image generated by SRCNN-B. When training on LR images generated by styleVAE, EDSR-S produces more pleasing results (d) rather than distorted reconstructed images (c) by EDSR-B. Compared (b), (d) and (e), our proposed method is able to generate sharper images.

4.3   Ablation Studies

StyleVAE. In order to investigate the effectiveness of the mutual information estimation (MI) and Adaptive Instance Normalization (AdaIN) used in styleVAE, we train several other variants of styleVAE: remove MI or/and AdaIN. To evaluate the performance of these variants of styleVAE, we measure FID between LR images generated by these variants and real-world LR images from our testing dataset. FID results are provided in Table 3. When both AdaIN and MI are removed, the FID value is relatively high. After arbitrarily adding one of the two, the value of FID is decreased. For both MI and AdaIN used in styleVAE, the FID result is the lowest. We also evaluate how similar the synthetic LR images by bicubic down-sample and real-world LR images from WIDER FACE. The FID result is found as 31.20. These results faithfully indicate that AdaIN and MI are essential for styleVAE.

SR Network. Similar to the ablation investigation of styleVAE, we also train several variants of the proposed SR network: remove the GA or/and LA module(s) in the SR network. These several variants are trained on LR images

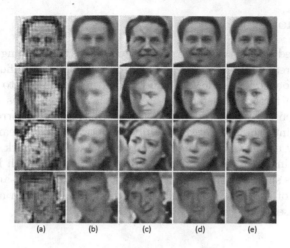

(a)   (b)   (c)   (d)   (e)

Fig. 5. Results of experiments on deep plug-and-play super-resolution. (a) Results of SRCNN-B. (b) Results of SRCNN-S. (c) Results of EDSR-B. (d) Results of EDSR-S. (e) Results of our method. This suggests that the performance of SR methods can be improved by training on LR images generated by styleVAE.

Table 3. Investigations of AdaIN and MI in styleVAE. We also evaluate how similar the synthetic LR images by bicubic down-sample and real-world LR images in WIDER FACE. The FID value between these is 31.20 (Lower is better). Results of experiments on deep plug-and-play SR in FID. (Lower is better).

AdaIN	×	×	✓	✓
MI	×	✓	×	✓
FID	26.6	25.78	24.63	18.77

produced by performing bicubic interpolation on corresponding HR images. In Table 4, when both the GA and LA modules are removed, the PSNR value on LFW (with upscale factor ×4) is the lowest. When the LA module is added, the PSNR value is increased by 0.1 dB. After adding the GA module, the performance reaches 30.27 dB. When both attention modules are added, the performance is the best, with a PSNR of 30.43 dB. These experimental results clearly demonstrate that these two attention modules are necessary for the proposed SR network and greatly improve its performance (Table 4).

Table 4. Ablation investigation on the effects of the GA and LA modules in SR network. The PSNR (dB) values are reported on LFW (higher is better).

GA	×	×	✓	✓
LA	×	✓	×	✓
PSNR	30.08	30.18	30.27	30.43

5   Conclusion

We have proposed a novel two-stage process to address the challenging problem of super-resolving real-world LR images. The proposed pipeline unifies a style-based Variational Autoencoder (styleVAE) and an SR network. Due to the participation of nuisance factors transfer and VAE, styleVAE generates real-world-like LR images. Then the generated LR images paired with the corresponding HR images are fed into the SR network. Our SR network firstly learns long-range dependencies by using GARB. Then the attention of SR network moves to local areas of images in which texture detail will be filled out through LARB. Extensive experiments show our superiority over existing state-of-the-art SR methods and the ability of styleVAE to facilitate method generalization and robustness to real-world cases.

References

1. Bulat, A., Tzimiropoulos, G.: How far are we from solving the 2D & 3D face alignment problem? (and a dataset of 230,000 3D facial landmarks). In: International Conference on Computer Vision (2017)
2. Bulat, A., Tzimiropoulos, G.: Super-FAN: integrated facial landmark localization and super-resolution of real-world low resolution faces in arbitrary poses with GANs. In: Proceedings of the IEEE Conference on Computer Vision and Pattern Recognition (CVPR) (2018)
3. Bulat, A., Yang, J., Tzimiropoulos, G.: To learn image super-resolution, use a GAN to learn how to do image degradation first. In: Proceedings of the European Conference on Computer Vision (ECCV) (2018)
4. Cao, Q., Shen, L., Xie, W., Parkhi, O.M., Zisserman, A.: VGGFace2: a dataset for recognising faces across pose and age. In: IEEE International Conference on Automatic Face & Gesture Recognition (FG) (2018)
5. Chen, Y., Tai, Y., Liu, X., Shen, C., Yang, J.: FSRNet: end-to-end learning face super-resolution with facial priors. In: Proceedings of the IEEE Conference on Computer Vision and Pattern Recognition (CVPR), pp. 2492–2501 (2018)
6. Dong, C., Loy, C.C., He, K., Tang, X.: Image super-resolution using deep convolutional networks. IEEE Trans. Patt. Anal. Mach. Intell. **38**, 295–307 (TPAMI) (2015)
7. Gatys, L.A., Ecker, A.S., Bethge, M.: Image style transfer using convolutional neural networks. In: Proceedings of the IEEE Conference on Computer Vision and Pattern Recognition (CVPR), pp. 2414–2423 (2016)
8. Heusel, M., Ramsauer, H., Unterthiner, T., Nessler, B., Hochreiter, S.: GANs trained by a two time-scale update rule converge to a local Nash equilibrium. In: Conference on Neural Information Processing Systems (NeurIPS) (2017)
9. Hu, H., Zhang, Z., Xie, Z., Lin, S.: Local relation networks for image recognition. arXiv preprint arXiv:1904.11491 (2019)
10. Huang, G.B., Jain, V., Learned-Miller, E.: Unsupervised joint alignment of complex images. In: Proceedings of the IEEE International Conference on Computer Vision (ICCV) (2007)
11. Huang, G.B., Mattar, M., Lee, H., Learned-Miller, E.: Learning to align from scratch. In: Conference on Neural Information Processing Systems (NeurIPS) (2012)

12. Huang, G.B., Ramesh, M., Berg, T., Learned-Miller, E.: Labeled faces in the wild: a database for studying face recognition in unconstrained environments. University of Massachusetts, Amherst, Technical report (2007)

13. Huang, H., He, R., Sun, Z., Tan, T.: Wavelet domain generative adversarial network for multi-scale face hallucination. Int. J. Comput. Vis. **127**(6–7), 763–784 (2019)

14. Huang, X., Belongie, S.: Arbitrary style transfer in real-time with adaptive instance normalization. In: Proceedings of the IEEE International Conference on Computer Vision (ICCV), pp. 1501–1510 (2017)

15. Kim, J., Lee, J.K., Mu Lee, K.: Accurate image super-resolution using very deep convolutional networks. In: Proceedings of the IEEE Conference on Computer Vision and Pattern Recognition (CVPR), pp. 1646–1654 (2016)

16. Kingma, D.P., Ba, J.: Adam: a method for stochastic optimization. arXiv preprint arXiv:1412.6980 (2014)

17. Koestinger, M., Wohlhart, P., Roth, P.M., Bischof, H.: Annotated facial landmarks in the wild: a large-scale, real-world database for facial landmark localization. In: IEEE International Conference on Computer Vision Workshops (ICCV workshops) (2011)

18. Kotovenko, D., Sanakoyeu, A., Lang, S., Ommer, B.: Content and style disentanglement for artistic style transfer. In: Proceedings of the IEEE International Conference on Computer Vision (ICCV) (2019)

19. Learned-Miller, G.B.H.E.: Labeled faces in the wild: Updates and new reporting procedures. University of Massachusetts, Amherst, Technical report (2014)

20. Ledig, C., et al.: Photo-realistic single image super-resolution using a generative adversarial network. In: Proceedings of the IEEE Conference on Computer Vision and Pattern Recognition (CVPR), pp. 4681–4690 (2017)

21. Lim, B., Son, S., Kim, H., Nah, S., Lee, K.M.: Enhanced deep residual networks for single image super-resolution. In: Proceedings of the IEEE Conference on Computer Vision and Pattern Recognition (CVPR) Workshops, July 2017

22. Liu, Z., Luo, P., Wang, X., Tang, X.: Deep learning face attributes in the wild. In: Proceedings of the IEEE International Conference on Computer Vision (ICCV), pp. 3730–3738 (2015)

23. Simonyan, K., Zisserman, A.: Very deep convolutional networks for large-scale image recognition. arXiv preprint arXiv:1409.1556 (2014)

24. Yang, S., Luo, P., Loy, C.C., Tang, X.: Wider face: a face detection benchmark. In: Proceedings of the IEEE Conference on Computer Vision and Pattern Recognition (CVPR), pp. 5525–5533 (2016)

25. Zhang, H., Goodfellow, I., Metaxas, D., Odena, A.: Self-attention generative adversarial networks. arXiv preprint arXiv:1805.08318 (2018)

26. Zhang, Y., Li, K., Li, K., Wang, L., Zhong, B., Fu, Y.: Image super-resolution using very deep residual channel attention networks. In: Proceedings of the European Conference on Computer Vision (ECCV), pp. 286–301 (2018)

27. Zhang, Y., Tian, Y., Kong, Y., Zhong, B., Fu, Y.: Residual dense network for image super-resolution. In: Proceedings of the IEEE Conference on Computer Vision and Pattern Recognition (CVPR), pp. 2472–2481 (2018)

28. Zhu, S., Liu, S., Loy, C.C., Tang, X.: Deep cascaded Bi-network for face hallucination. In: Leibe, B., Matas, J., Sebe, N., Welling, M. (eds.) ECCV 2016. LNCS, vol. 9909, pp. 614–630. Springer, Cham (2016). https://doi.org/10.1007/978-3-319-46454-1_37

Cascade Scale-Aware Distillation Network for Lightweight Remote Sensing Image Super-Resolution

Haowei Ji[1], Huijun Di[1(⊠)], Shunzhou Wang[1], and Qingxuan Shi[2]

[1] Beijing Laboratory of Intelligent Information Technology, School of Computer Science and Technology, Beijing Institute of Technology, Beijing 100081, China
ajon@bit.edu.cn

[2] School of Cyber Security and Computer, Hebei University, Baoding 071000, China

Abstract. Recently, convolution neural network based methods have dominated the remote sensing image super-resolution (RSISR). However, most of them own complex network structures and a large number of network parameters, which is not friendly to computational resources limited scenarios. Besides, scale variations of objects in the remote sensing image are still challenging for most methods to generate high-quality super-resolution results. To this end, we propose a scale-aware group convolution (SGC) for RSISR. Specifically, each SGC firstly uses group convolutions with different dilation rates for extracting multi-scale features. Then, a scale-aware feature guidance approach and enhancement approach are leveraged to enhance the representation ability of different scale features. Based on SGC, a cascaded scale-aware distillation network (CSDN) is designed, which is composed of multiple SGC based cascade scale-aware distillation blocks (CSDBs). The output of each CSDB will be fused via the backward feature fusion module for final image super-resolution reconstruction. Extensive experiments are performed on the commonly-used UC Merced dataset. Quantitative and qualitative experiment results demonstrate the effectiveness of our method.

Keywords: Remote sensing image super-resolution · Lightweight neural network · Multi-scale feature learning · Feature distillation

1 Introduction

Remote sensing image super-resolution (RSISR) aims to reconstruct the high-resolution image from the low-resolution image [6]. It can be used in many practical fields like agriculture [15], forestry [1] and meteorology [23], and has attracted considerable research interests.

With the development of deep learning, convolution neural networks have been widely used for RSISR. Current remote sensing image super-resolution

---

This work is supported by the Natural Science Foundation of Hebei Province (F2019201451).

S. Yu et al. (Eds.): PRCV 2022, LNCS 13537, pp. 274–286, 2022.
https://doi.org/10.1007/978-3-031-18916-6_23

networks can realize high-quality image reconstruction through the complex network models. For example, Haut *et al.* [7] propose a deep compendium model which adopts efficient feature extract modules (*i.e.*, residual unit [8] and network in network [17]) to learn low-resolution feature representations. Pan *et al.* [22] construct a residual dense backprojection network based on dense connection learning and backprojection mechanism. Although they achieve promising results, most of them own a huge amount of parameters and cost a lot of computation resources, which hinders their applications in scenarios with limited computing resources. To this end, we aim to develop a lightweight model for RSISR.

In recent years, the design of lightweight natural image super-resolution has made significant progress. Among them, the approach of compact lightweight network model design (*e.g.*, information distillation [11] and feature distillation [18]) dominates the lightweight image super-resolution [19]. However, different from natural images, remote sensing images usually contain similar objects with different scales. The approach of information distillation or feature distillation does not consider modeling the multi-scale information in the image. Therefore, the above methods can not achieve promising reconstruction results without any modifications.

Some researchers try to use image self-similarity to improve the performance of remote sensing image super-resolution reconstruction. For example, Lei *et al.* [13] develop a hybrid-scale self-similarity exploitation network (HSENet) which adopts non-local operation [25] to leverage the different scale features. However, HSENet also has a large number of parameters, which deviates from the original intention of the lightweight model design.

To this end, we propose a scale-aware group convolution (SGC) to extract multi-scale features in a lightweight manner. SGC is composed of three components: Multi-scale Feature Extraction (MFE), Large Scale Feature Guidance (LSG), and Scale-aware Feature Enhancement (SFE). MFE is designed to generate multi-scale features. LSG is responsible for learning complementary information between different scale features. SFE is developed to further enhance the extracted different scale features. Based on SGC, we construct a Cascaded Scale Distillation Block (CSDB) for efficient hierarchical feature extraction, and multiple CSDBs construct our Cascaded Scale Distillation Network (CSDN). We have performed extensive experiments on the UC Merced dataset [31]. Both the quantitative and qualitative results demonstrate the effectiveness of our method. The main contributions of our paper are two-fold:

- We propose a scale-aware group convolution (SGC) to extract multi-scale features in a lightweight manner.
- Based on SGC, we propose a cascade scale-aware distillation network (CSDN) which makes full use of the multi-scale feature extracted by SGC.

2   Related Work

2.1   Remote Sensing Image Super-Resolution Networks

With the renaissance of deep learning, many convolution neural network based RSISR methods are proposed. For instance, Lei et al. [14] proposed a local-global combined network, which learns multi-scale features by combining different hierarchical representations of the CNN model. Similarly, Dong et al. [5] obtained multi-scale features by aggregating the features learned at different depths of the network. Huan et al. [10] employed convolution layers with different dilation rates to extract multi-scale features. While Wang et al. [26] used convolution layers with different kernel sizes to obtain multi-scale features. And Lei et al. [13] proposed a long-range self-attention model, which can take advantage of the single and cross-scale feature similarities in the remote sensing images. Different from the above works, we develop a lightweight RSISR network termed CSDN with fewer parameters and multi-adds operations.

2.2   Lightweight Image Super-Resolution Networks

To decrease the number of network parameters and save computation costs, the design of lightweight image super-resolution networks has raised a lot of research interest. For example, Kim et al. [12] employed a recursive network to reduce the network parameters. Ahn et al. [2] adopted the group convolutions and parameter sharing strategy to decrease the parameters. Hui et al. [11] and Liu et al. [18] leveraged the lightweight information distillation modules to extract the efficient low-resolution features . Different from the above works, we develop a lightweight SGC layer, which can efficiently extract multi-scale features in a lightweight manner.

3   Proposed Method

Figure 1 illustrates the overview and components of CSDN. As seen, CSDN mainly consists of three parts: shallow feature extraction $\mathcal{F}_{feat}$, hierarchical feature extraction $\mathcal{F}_{hier}$, image reconstruction $\mathcal{F}_{rest}$. Given a low-resolution image $L \in \mathbb{R}^{H \times W \times 3}$, CSDN generates a super-resolved image as follows:

$$
\begin{aligned}
\text{shallow feature extraction} &: F = \mathcal{F}_{feat}(L) \in \mathbb{R}^{H \times W \times C}, \\
\text{hierarchical feature extraction} &: S = \mathcal{F}_{hier}(F) \in \mathbb{R}^{H \times W \times C}, \\
\text{image reconstruction} &: H = \mathcal{F}_{rest}(S) \in \mathbb{R}^{sH \times sW \times 3},
\end{aligned}
\tag{1}
$$

where s ($s>1$) denotes the upsample scale factor, F indicates the extracted shallow feature and S represents the hierarchical feature. We implement $\mathcal{F}_{feat}$ with a 3×3 convolution layer, and $\mathcal{F}_{rest}$ with a pixel-shuffle layer followed by a 1×1 convolution layer.

To obtain efficient multi-scale features in a lightweight manner, we mainly design a hierarchical feature extraction module $\mathcal{F}_{hier}$, which is composed of

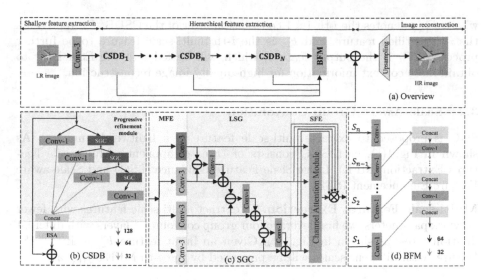

Fig. 1. Illustration of CSDN. (a) Overview. (b) Cascaded scale distillation block (CSDB). (c) Scale-aware group convolution (SGC). (d) Backward fusion module (BFM). $\oplus$ and $\ominus$ represent the element-wise summation and element-wise subtraction, respectively.

multiple proposed CSDBs (Fig. 1(b)). Specifically, each CSDB organizes SGC layers (Fig. 1(c)) and 1×1 convolution layers in an feature distillation manner following the work [18]. Finally, the output of each CSDB will be processed by the backward feature fusion module (Fig. 1(d)) [20] to obtain efficient hierarchical features for RSISR. Next, we will introduce them in details.

3.1 Cascaded Scale Distillation Block

As shown in Fig. 1(b), each CSDB is constructed by a progressive refinement module and an enhanced spatial attention layer (ESA). The progressive refinement module is implemented with 1×1 convolution layers and the SGCs. For each step, we employ the 1×1 convolution layer and SGC on the given features, respectively. The features processed by 1×1 convolution layer are used to generate the distillation features, and the features processed by SGC are used to extract multi-scale features and further fed to the next calculation unit. Given the input feature F_{in}, the above work process can be summarized as

$$
\begin{aligned}
F_{d_1}, F_{c_1} &= \mathcal{F}^1_{1 \times 1}(F_{in}), \mathcal{F}^1_{\text{SGC}}(F_{in}), \\
F_{d_2}, F_{c_2} &= \mathcal{F}^2_{1 \times 1}(F_{c_1}), \mathcal{F}^2_{\text{SGC}}(F_{c_1}), \\
F_{d_3}, F_{c_3} &= \mathcal{F}^3_{1 \times 1}(F_{c_2}), \mathcal{F}^3_{\text{SGC}}(F_{c_2}), \\
F_{d_4} &= \mathcal{F}^4_{1 \times 1}(F_{c_3}), \\
F_d &= Concat(F_{d_1}, F_{d_2}, F_{d_3}, F_{d_4}),
\end{aligned}
\tag{2}
$$

where $\mathcal{F}_{1\times 1}^i$ denotes the i-th 1×1 convolution layer of the CSDB, F_{d_i} represents the i-th distilled feature, and F_{c_i} is the i-th multi-scale feature to be further processed. F_d is the output feature, which will be fed into the ESA layer to obtain more context information for high-quality image reconstruction.

3.2   Scale-Aware Group Convolution

SGC is proposed to extract multi-scale feature in a lightweight manner. As shown in Fig. 1(c), each SGC consists of three components: Multi-scale Features Extraction (MFE), Large Scale Feature Guidance (LSG) and Scale-aware Feature Enhancement (SFE).

Multi-scale Features Extraction. To extract multi-scale features with fewer network parameters, we first leverage four group convolution layers with different dilation rates, as shown in Fig. 1(c). Given an input feature $F_{c_i} \in \mathbb{R}^{H \times W \times C}$, features with different scales will be processed by the j-th MFE $\mathcal{F}_{\mathrm{MFE}}^j$ as

$$F_{c_{i,j}} = \mathcal{F}_{\mathrm{MFE}}^j(F_{c_i}), \tag{3}$$

where $F_{c_{i,j}} \in \mathbb{R}^{H \times W \times C/4}$ denotes the j-th scale feature, and $j \in \{1, \cdots, 4\}$. The larger the value of j is, the larger the scale information represents.

Large Scale Feature Guidance. Although features with different scales are obtained, the extracted features are independent and do not interact with each other, which limits the representation ability for multi-scale learning. To this end, we develop a feature interaction method named LSG. The motivation of LSG is exploring the self-similarity of image content for high-resolution image reconstruction. Specifically, the large scale feature can be used to guide the small scale feature to learn to reconstruct image content, and this approach has been applied to natural image super-resolution [21] and remote sensing image super-resolution [13]. However, most self-similarity exploration approaches cost a large amount of computation resources, which deviates from the original intention of lightweight RSISR. Different from them, LSG is only implemented with three 1×1 convolution layers and parameter-free feature operations.

As shown in Fig. 1(c), given the large scale feature $F_{c_{i,j+1}}$ and the small scale feature $F_{c_{i,j}}$, the element-wise subtraction operation is leveraged to obtain the difference scale information. The extracted difference scale information will be processed by a 1×1 convolution layer to transform to the same feature space as small-scale features, and then perform element-by-element summation to achieve the purpose of enhancing small-scale feature information with large-scale feature information. The above descriptions can be summarized as follows:

$$\bar{F}_{c_{i,j}} = \mathcal{F}_{1\times 1}^j(F_{c_{i,j+1}} \ominus F_{c_{i,j}}) \oplus F_{c_{i,j}}, \tag{4}$$

where $\oplus$ and $\ominus$ represent the element-wise summation and element-wise subtraction, respectively. $\bar{F}_{c_{i,j}}$ represents the generated j-th scale feature, and $\bar{F}_{c_{i,4}}$ is equal to $F_{c_{i,4}}$.

Scale-Aware Feature Enhancement. Attention based models have achieved great successes in many computer vision tasks (*e.g.,* video object segmentation [32,35], semantic segmentation [16,33], human-object interaction detection [34,36], super-resolution [24,27,28], etc.) due to their powerful representative abilities. To better cope with the reconstruction of remote sensing objects at different scales, we use a weight-sharing channel attention module $\mathcal{F}_{ca}$ [9] to process features of different scales, obtain the attention weight of each scale, and use this weight to enhance the features of the corresponding scale as

$$
\begin{aligned}
A_{c_{i,j}} &= \mathcal{F}_{ca}(\bar{F}_{c_{i,j}}), \\
\hat{F}_{c_{i,j}} &= A_{c_{i,j}} \otimes \bar{F}_{c_{i,j}},
\end{aligned}
\tag{5}
$$

where $A_{c_{i,j}}$ denotes the attention weight for j-th scale feature $\bar{F}_{c_{i,j}}$. $\otimes$ represents the element-wise multiplication operation.

With the help of the channel attention module, SGC can adaptively adjust the weights of different scale features according to the image content, so as to obtain more efficient multi-scale features. We denote the output of SGC as

$$
F_{c_i} = Concat(\hat{F}_{c_{i,1}}, \hat{F}_{c_{i,2}}, \hat{F}_{c_{i,3}}, \hat{F}_{c_{i,4}}).
\tag{6}
$$

3.3 Hierarchical Feature Fusion

Efficiently aggregating hierarchical features is the key to improving the quality of image super-resolution results. To this end, following the literature [20], we use the BFM to aggregate the output features of each CSDB, as shown in Fig. 1 (d). We denote the output of the n-th CSDB as S_n, and the aggregation process is as

$$
H_n = \begin{cases} S_n & n = N, \\ \mathcal{F}_{1\times1}^n(Concat(S_n, H_{n+1})) & n = N-1, ..., 2, 1. \end{cases}
\tag{7}
$$

The feature H_1 adding the S_1 is fed into the upsampling layer to generate the final super-resolution image H.

4 Experiment

4.1 Dataset and Evaluation Metrics

We perform extensive experiments on UC Merced dataset to evaluate the effectiveness of CSDN. UC Merced dataset consists of 21 classes of remote-sensing scenes such as agricultural, airplane, baseball diamond, and so on. Each class contains 100 images with the spatial size 256×256. We equally divide UC Merced dataset into two parts. One part is for training and the other one is for testing. PSNR and SSIM are used to evaluate the network performance. All results are evaluated on the RGB channels. In addition, we also compare the number of network parameters (Params) and multi-adds (M-Adds) operations to evaluate the computation efficiency of different RSISR methods.

Table 1. Performance comparisons of different methods on UC Merced dataset.

Method	Scale	Params	M-Adds	PSNR/SSIM
Bicubic	×2	–	–	30.76/0.8789
SC [30]	×2	–	–	32.77/0.9166
SRCNN [3]	×2	69K	4.5G	32.84/0.9152
FSRCNN [4]	×2	17K	0.3G	33.18/0.9196
LGCNet [14]	×2	193K	12.7G	33.48/0.9235
DMCN [29]	×2	–	–	34.19/0.8941
DCM [7]	×2	1842K	30.2G	33.65/0.9274
HSENet [13]	×2	5286K	66.8G	**34.22/0.9327**
Ours	×2	301K	0.6G	33.62/0.9255
Bicubic	×3	–	–	27.46/0.7631
SC [30]	×3	–	–	28.26/0.7971
SRCNN [3]	×3	69K	4.5G	28.66/0.8038
FSRCNN [4]	×3	25K	0.2G	29.09/0.8167
LGCNet [14]	×3	193K	12.7G	29.28/0.8238
DMCN [29]	×3	–	–	29.86/0.7454
DCM [7]	×3	2258K	16.3G	29.52/0.8394
HSENet [13]	×3	5470K	30.8G	**30.00/0.8420**
Ours	×3	309K	0.6G	29.34/0.8294
Bicubic	×4	–	–	25.65/0.6725
SC [30]	×4	–	–	26.51/0.7152
SRCNN [3]	×4	69K	4.5G	26.78/0.7219
FSRCNN [4]	×4	35K	0.1G	26.93/0.7267
LGCNet [14]	×4	193K	12.7G	27.02/0.7333
DMCN [29]	×4	–	–	27.57/0.6150
DCM [7]	×4	2175K	13.0G	27.22/0.7528
HSENet [13]	×4	5433K	19.2G	**27.73/0.7623**
Ours	×4	321K	0.6G	27.39/0.7467

4.2   Implementation Details

CSDN is implemented with 6 CSDBs. We randomly crop image patches with the spatial size of 96 × 96, 144 × 144, and 192 × 192 from the high-resolution images, and leverage the Bicubic interpolation method to generate low-resolution images for ×2, ×3 and ×4 SR. The horizontal and random flipping strategies are used to augment the training data. We use Adam to optimize our network with batch size 16. The initial learning rate is set to $1e^{-4}$, and the learning rate will be half after every 400 epochs. We train our network for 1000 epochs. $L1$ loss is chosen as the network optimization function. All experiments are performed on a server equipped with a single NVIDIA RTX 2080Ti GPU card and implemented with the Pytorch framework.

4.3 Comparison with State-of-the-Arts

Quantitative Results. Table 1 reports the quantitative comparisons of different RSISR methods. As seen, CSDN achieves comparable or even superior results compared with DCM [7], with extreme fewer network parameters and multi-adds operations. Compared with the state-of-the-art method HSENet [13], we can achieve comparable PSNR value for ×3 and ×4 SR. Although CSDN does not outperform HSENet, the parameters and multi-add operations of CSDN are far less than HSENet. The above comparisons demonstrate the effectiveness of CSDN. We also compare the PSNR of each class of different methods. As shown in Table 2, we can see that CSDN has achieved comparable results to HSENet and DCM in some remote sensing scenes, but the number of parameters and computation are far less than the former two methods, which further shows that CSDN is an effective lightweight remote sensing image super-resolution network.

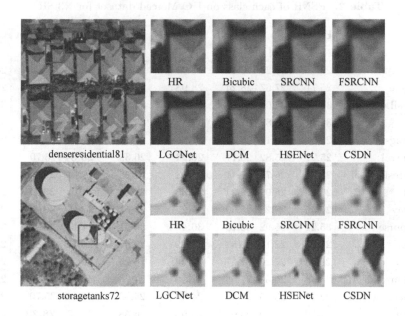

Fig. 2. Visualization results of different RSISR methods on UC Merced for ×4 SR.

Qualitative Results. Figure 2 presents visual results of different methods for ×4 SR. As seen, compared with other methods, CSDN can generate satisfactory visual results with clear edges and contours on scale-variation remote sensing scene, which further demonstrates the effectiveness of our method.

4.4 Ablation Studies

Number of CSDB. We explore the performance of CSDN with different numbers of CSDB. As shown in Table 3, we can see that with the increase of the number of CSDB, the performance also improves, and achieves the saturation performance when N is equal to 8. However, as seen, the performance of $N = 6$ is similar to $N = 8$ but with smaller parameters and multi-adds operations. Considering the trade-off between performance and computation efficiency, we set N to 6.

Impact of Multi-scale Feature Extraction. We explore the different settings of dilation rates in MFE, as shown in Table 4. As seen, with the increase of dilation rates, we can see that the performance also increases. CSDN achieves the best performance when the configuration is set to $\{d_1 = 1, d_2 = 1, d_3 = 2, d_4 = 4\}$. Considering the trade-off between the performance and computation resource cost, we set the default dilation rates as $\{d_1 = 1, d_2 = 1, d_3 = 2, d_4 = 3\}$, whose performance is similar to the best configuration results.

Table 2. PSNR of each class on UC Merced dataset for ×3 SR.

Class	Bicubic	SC [30]	SRCNN [3]	FSRCNN [4]	LGCNet [14]	DCM [7]	HSENet [13]	Ours
Agricultural	26.86	27.23	27.47	27.61	27.66	**29.06**	27.64	28.39
Airplane	26.71	27.67	28.24	28.98	29.12	**30.77**	30.09	29.26
Baseball diamond	33.33	34.06	34.33	34.64	34.72	33.76	**35.05**	34.70
Beach	36.14	36.87	37.00	37.21	37.37	36.38	**37.69**	37.41
Buildings	25.09	26.11	26.84	27.50	27.81	28.51	**28.95**	27.83
Chaparral	25.21	25.82	26.11	26.21	26.39	**26.81**	26.70	26.36
Denseresidential	25.76	26.75	27.41	28.02	28.25	28.79	**29.24**	28.27
Forest	27.53	28.09	28.24	28.35	28.44	28.16	**28.59**	28.40
Freeway	27.36	28.28	28.69	29.27	29.52	30.45	**30.63**	29.51
Golfcourse	35.21	35.92	36.15	36.43	36.51	34.43	**36.62**	36.23
Harbor	21.25	22.11	22.82	23.29	23.63	**26.55**	24.88	23.86
Intersection	26.48	27.20	27.67	28.06	28.29	**29.28**	29.21	28.30
Mediumresidential	25.68	26.54	27.06	27.58	27.76	27.21	**28.55**	27.74
Mobilehomepark	22.25	23.25	23.89	24.34	24.59	**26.05**	25.70	24.82
Overpass	24.59	25.30	25.65	26.53	26.58	27.77	**28.22**	27.17
Parkinglot	21.75	22.59	23.11	23.34	23.69	**24.95**	24.66	23.50
River	28.12	28.71	28.89	29.07	29.12	28.89	**29.22**	28.99
Runway	29.30	30.25	30.61	31.01	31.15	**32.53**	31.15	30.50
Sparseresidential	28.34	29.33	29.40	30.23	30.53	29.81	**31.64**	31.13
Storagetanks	29.97	30.86	31.33	31.92	32.17	29.02	**32.95**	32.31
Tenniscourt	29.75	30.62	30.98	31.34	31.58	30.76	**32.71**	31.63
AVG	27.46	28.23	28.66	29.09	29.28	29.52	**30.00**	29.34

Table 3. Performance comparisons of different numbers of CSDB.

#	Params	M-Adds	PSNR/SSIM
4	223K	0.4G	27.29/0.7428
6	321K	0.6G	27.39/0.7467
8	420K	0.8G	**27.40/0.7482**
10	474K	1.0G	27.39/0.7476

Table 4. Performance comparisons of different dilation rate settings of Multi-scale Feature Extraction.

Configurations	PSNR/SSIM
$d_1 = 1$, $d_2 = 1$, $d_3 = 1$, $d_4 = 1$	27.32/0.7453
$d_1 = 1$, $d_2 = 1$, $d_3 = 2$, $d_4 = 2$	27.37/0.7465
$d_1 = 1$, $d_2 = 1$, $d_3 = 2$, $d_4 = 3$	**27.39**/0.7467
$d_1 = 1$, $d_2 = 1$, $d_3 = 2$, $d_4 = 4$	**27.39/0.7471**
$d_1 = 1$, $d_2 = 2$, $d_3 = 3$, $d_4 = 4$	27.34/0.7457
$d_1 = 1$, $d_2 = 2$, $d_3 = 3$, $d_4 = 6$	27.32/0.7441

Table 5. Performance comparisons between dilated group convolution layer and standard group convolution layer.

Configurations	Params	M-Adds	PSNR/SSIM
$d_1 = 1$, $d_2 = 1$, $d_3 = 2$, $d_4 = 3$	**321K**	**0.6G**	**27.39**/0.7467
$k_1 = 3$, $k_2 = 3$, $k_3 = 5$, $k_4 = 7$	370K	0.7G	27.36/**0.7470**

Table 6. Ablation study of large scale feature guidance and scale-aware feature enhancement.

Variants	w/o LSG	w/o SFE	SGC
PSNR	27.33	27.36	**27.39**
SSIM	0.7450	**0.7472**	0.7467

Besides, we also use ordinary group convolution layers to replace the dilated group convolution layers. For fair comparisons, we use large convolution kernels to achieve the receptive field as dilated group convolution, *e.g.,* using the group convolution with kernel size 5 and dilate rate 3 to replace the group convolution with kernel size 3 and dilate rate 2. The new model variant is denoted as $\{k_1 = 3, k_2 = 3, k_3 = 5, k_4 = 7\}$. Table 5 reports the detailed comparisons. We can see that the model with ordinary group convolution layers does not perform better than CSDN but increases extra network parameters, which demonstrates the effectiveness of MFE.

Efficacy of Large Scale Feature Guidance. Table 6 reports the performance comparisons between SGC without using LSG (w/o LSG) and the full implementation of SGC. As seen, the performance drops in both PSNR and SSIM, demonstrating the effectiveness of the proposed LSG approach.

Effectiveness of Scale-Aware Feature Enhancement. Table 6 also reports the performance of SGC without using SFE (w/o SFE). As seen, full implementation of SGC also performs better than the variant without using SFE, demonstrating the importance of adaptive enhancement of different scale features.

5   Conclusion

In this paper, we propose a lightweight RSISR network termed as CSDN, which is constructed with multiple CSDBs for multi-scale hierarchical feature learning. The extracted hierarchical features are further aggregated via the BFM for final high-resolution image reconstruction. Extensive experiments are performed on UC Merced dataset. Our CSDN has smaller parameters while achieving satisfactory results compared to the other RSISR methods. In the future, we will explore the application of CSDN to other remote sensing image restoration tasks, such as remote sensing image denoising and remote sensing image deblurring.

References

1. Latif, Z.A., Zaqwan, H.M., Saufi, M., Adnan, N.A., Omar, H.: Deforestation and carbon loss estimation at tropical forest using multispectral remote sensing: case study of Besul Tambahan permanent forest reserve. In: IconSpace, pp. 348–351 (2015)
2. Ahn, N., Kang, B., Sohn, K.A.: Fast, accurate, and lightweight super-resolution with cascading residual network. In: ECCV, pp. 252–268 (2018)
3. Dong, C., Loy, C.C., He, K., Tang, X.: Learning a deep convolutional network for image super-resolution. In: ECCV, pp. 184–199 (2014)
4. Dong, C., Loy, C.C., Tang, X.: Accelerating the super-resolution convolutional neural network. In: ECCV, pp. 391–407 (2016)
5. Dong, X., Wang, L., Sun, X., Jia, X., Gao, L., Zhang, B.: Remote sensing image super-resolution using second-order multi-scale networks. IEEE T-GRS **59**(4), 3473–3485 (2020)
6. Haut, J.M., Fernandez-Beltran, R., Paoletti, M.E., Plaza, J., Plaza, A., Pla, F.: A new deep generative network for unsupervised remote sensing single-image super-resolution. IEEE T-GRS **56**(11), 6792–6810 (2018)
7. Haut, J.M., Paoletti, M.E., Fernández-Beltran, R., Plaza, J., Plaza, A., Li, J.: Remote sensing single-image superresolution based on a deep compendium model. IEEE GRSL **16**(9), 1432–1436 (2019)
8. He, K., Zhang, X., Ren, S., Sun, J.: Deep residual learning for image recognition. In: CVPR, pp. 770–778 (2016)
9. Hu, J., Shen, L., Sun, G.: Squeeze-and-excitation networks. In: CVPR, pp. 7132–7141 (2018)

10. Huan, H., et al.: End-to-end super-resolution for remote-sensing images using an improved multi-scale residual network. Remote Sens. **13**(4), 666 (2021)
11. Hui, Z., Gao, X., Yang, Y., Wang, X.: Lightweight image super-resolution with information multi-distillation network. In: ACM MM, pp. 2024–2032 (2019)
12. Kim, J., Lee, J.K., Lee, K.M.: Deeply-recursive convolutional network for image super-resolution. In: CVPR, pp. 1637–1645 (2016)
13. Lei, S., Shi, Z.: Hybrid-scale self-similarity exploitation for remote sensing image super-resolution. IEEE T-GRS **60**, 1–10 (2021)
14. Lei, S., Shi, Z., Zou, Z.: Super-resolution for remote sensing images via local-global combined network. IEEE GRSL **14**(8), 1243–1247 (2017)
15. Li, D., Liu, J., Zhou, Q., Wang, L., Huang, Q.: Study on information extraction of rape acreage based on TM remote sensing image. In: IGARSS, pp. 3323–3326 (2011)
16. Li, X., Zhou, T., Li, J., Zhou, Y., Zhang, Z.: Group-wise semantic mining for weakly supervised semantic segmentation. In: AAAI, vol. 35, pp. 1984–1992 (2021)
17. Lin, M., Chen, Q., Yan, S.: Network in network. arXiv preprint arXiv:1312.4400 (2013)
18. Liu, J., Tang, J., Wu, G.: Residual feature distillation network for lightweight image super-resolution. In: ECCV, pp. 41–55 (2020)
19. Lu, H., Lu, Y., Li, G., Sun, Y., Wang, S., Li, Y.: Scale-aware distillation network for lightweight image super-resolution. In: PRCV, pp. 128–139 (2021)
20. Luo, X., Xie, Y., Zhang, Y., Qu, Y., Li, C., Fu, Y.: LatticeNet: towards lightweight image super-resolution with lattice block. In: ECCV, pp. 272–289 (2020)
21. Mei, Y., Fan, Y., Zhou, Y., Huang, L., Huang, T.S., Shi, H.: Image super-resolution with cross-scale non-local attention and exhaustive self-exemplars mining. In: CVPR, pp. 5690–5699 (2020)
22. Pan, Z., Ma, W., Guo, J., Lei, B.: Super-resolution of single remote sensing image based on residual dense backprojection networks. IEEE T-GRS **57**(10), 7918–7933 (2019)
23. Tang, Z., Chen, Q., Wang, X.: Meteorological observation station's environment identification base on remote sensing image. In: AIMSEC, pp. 4056–4060 (2011)
24. Wang, S., Zhou, T., Lu, Y., Di, H.: Detail preserving transformer for light field image super-resolution. In: AAAI, vol. 36, pp. 2522–2530 (2022)
25. Wang, X., Girshick, R., Gupta, A., He, K.: Non-local neural networks. In: CVPR, pp. 7794–7803 (2018)
26. Wang, X., Wu, Y., Ming, Y., Lv, H.: Remote sensing imagery super resolution based on adaptive multi-scale feature fusion network. Sensors **20**(4), 1142 (2020)
27. Wang, Y., Lu, Y., Wang, S., Zhang, W., Wang, Z.: Local-global feature aggregation for light field image super-resolution. In: ICASSP, pp. 2160–2164 (2022)
28. Wang, Z., Lu, Y., Li, W., Wang, S., Wang, X., Chen, X.: Single image super-resolution with attention-based densely connected module. Neurocomputing **453**, 876–884 (2021)
29. Xu, W., Xu, G., Wang, Y., Sun, X., Lin, D., Wu, Y.: Deep memory connected neural network for optical remote sensing image restoration. Remote Sens. **10**(12), 1893 (2018)
30. Yang, J., Wright, J., Huang, T.S., Ma, Y.: Image super-resolution via sparse representation. IEEE TIP **19**(11), 2861–2873 (2010)
31. Yang, Y., Newsam, S.: Bag-of-visual-words and spatial extensions for land-use classification. In: Proceedings of the 18th SIGSPATIAL International Conference on Advances in Geographic Information Systems, pp. 270–279 (2010)

32. Zhou, T., Li, J., Wang, S., Tao, R., Shen, J.: MATNet: motion-attentive transition network for zero-shot video object segmentation. IEEE TIP **29**, 8326–8338 (2020)
33. Zhou, T., Li, L., Li, X., Feng, C.M., Li, J., Shao, L.: Group-wise learning for weakly supervised semantic segmentation. IEEE TIP **31**, 799–811 (2021)
34. Zhou, T., Qi, S., Wang, W., Shen, J., Zhu, S.C.: Cascaded parsing of human-object interaction recognition **44**(6), 2827–2840 (2021)
35. Zhou, T., Wang, S., Zhou, Y., Yao, Y., Li, J., Shao, L.: Motion-attentive transition for zero-shot video object segmentation. In: AAAI, vol. 34, pp. 13066–13073 (2020)
36. Zhou, T., Wang, W., Qi, S., Ling, H., Shen, J.: Cascaded human-object interaction recognition. In: CVPR, pp. 4263–4272 (2020)

Few-Shot Segmentation via Rich Prototype Generation and Recurrent Prediction Enhancement

Hongsheng Wang, Xiaoqi Zhao, Youwei Pang, and Jinqing Qi[✉]

Dalian University of Technology, Dalian, China
{wanghongsheng,zxq,lartpang}@mail.dlut.edu.cn, jinqing@dlut.edu.cn

Abstract. Prototype learning and decoder construction are the keys for few-shot segmentation. However, existing methods use only a single prototype generation mode, which can not cope with the intractable problem of objects with various scales. Moreover, the one-way forward propagation adopted by previous methods may cause information dilution from registered features during the decoding process. In this research, we propose a rich prototype generation module (RPGM) and a recurrent prediction enhancement module (RPEM) to reinforce the prototype learning paradigm and build a unified memory-augmented decoder for few-shot segmentation, respectively. Specifically, the RPGM combines superpixel and K-means clustering to generate rich prototype features with complementary scale relationships and adapt the scale gap between support and query images. The RPEM utilizes the recurrent mechanism to design a round-way propagation decoder. In this way, registered features can provide object-aware information continuously. Experiments show that our method consistently outperforms other competitors on two popular benchmarks PASCAL-5^i and COCO-20^i.

Keywords: Few-shot segmentation · Rich prototype · Recurrent prediction

1 Introduction

In recent years, with the use of deep neural networks and large-scale datasets, significant progress has been made in fully-supervised semantic segmentation [4, 6, 12, 14, 32]. However, the labor cost of acquiring a large number of labeled datasets is very expensive. To address this challenge, the few-shot segmentation task [20] has been proposed. It aims to segment a new object class with only one or a few annotated examples, which is agnostic to the network at the training phase. Most methods adopt the general structure as shown in Fig. 1. Prototype learning and decoder construction play an important role in few-shot segmentation. The prototype represents only object-related features and does not contain any background information. Some efforts [7, 17, 25, 26, 30] investigate different prototype feature generation mechanisms to provide an effective reference

© The Author(s), under exclusive license to Springer Nature Switzerland AG 2022
S. Yu et al. (Eds.): PRCV 2022, LNCS 13537, pp. 287–298, 2022.
https://doi.org/10.1007/978-3-031-18916-6_24

for query images. Both CANet [30] and PFENet [22] generate a single prototype by the masked average pooling operation to represent all features in the foreground of the support image. SCL [27] uses a self-guided mechanism to produce an auxiliary feature prototype. ASGNet [13] is proposed to split support features adaptively into several feature prototypes and select the most relevant prototype to match the query image. However, the aforementioned methods all adopt a single approach to construct prototype features and ignore complex scale differences between support images and query images, which may introduce scale-level interference for the subsequent similarity measure. The decoder can finish the feature aggregation and transfer them into the task-required mode. Nevertheless, many methods [13,16,22,27,29] focus on designing the feature enrichment module or applying the multi-scale structure (e.g. ASPP [5]) directly to aggregate the query features through a one-way forward propagation and obtain the final prediction results. This limitation not only makes the semantic information of the probability map generated by mid-level features insufficient, but also results in truly useful features not being adequately utilized due to information dilution.

In response to these challenges, we propose a rich prototype generation module (RPGM) and a recurrent prediction enhancement module (RPEM) to improve the performance for few-shot segmentation. The RPGM combines two clustering strategies, superpixel and K-means, to generate rich prototype features that are complete representations of the supporting feature information. Superpixel clustering can generate $N_s \in \{1, \ldots, N\}$ prototypes depending on the size of the image, while K-means clustering generates specific $N_k = N$ prototypes regardless of the image size. The RPEM is a round-way feedback propagation module based on the original forward propagation decoder and is motivated by the recurrent mechanism. Specifically, it is composed of a multi-scale iterative enhancement (MSIE) module and a query self-contrast enhancement (QSCE) module. The former produces multi-scale information for the registered features of each stage, while the latter performs the self-contrast operation on query prototype features and then corrects those registered features. In this way, object-aware information can be constantly obtained from the registered features. In addition, taking into account the parameter-free nature, the proposed RPEM can also be considered as a flexible post-processing technology by using it only during the inference phase.

Our main contributions can be summarized as follows:

- For few-shot segmentation, we design two simple yet effective improvement strategies from the perspectives of prototype learning and decoder construction.
- We put forward a rich prototype generation module, which generates complementary prototype features at two scales through two clustering algorithms with different characteristics.

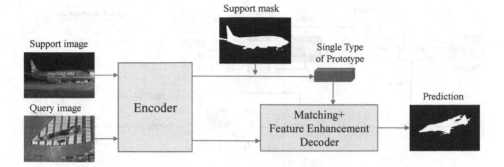

Fig. 1. A popular few-shot segmentation architecture.

- An more efficient semantic decoder is powered by the proposed novel recurrent prediction enhancement module, where multi-scale and discriminative information is adequately propagate to each decoder block.
- Extensive experiments on two benchmark datasets demonstrate that the proposed model outperforms other existing competitors under the same metrics.

2   Related Work

Semantic Segmentation is a fundamental computer vision task that aims to accurately predict the label of each pixel. Currently, the encoder-decoder architecture [1,6] is widely used. The encoder extracts high-level semantic features at low resolution, while the decoder progressively recovers the resolution of feature maps to obtain the segmentation mask. Besides, many semantic segmentation methods adopt the pyramid pooling structure [12,31,33] to capture semantic context from multiple perspectives. Although these methods achieve good performance, they rely on pixel-level annotation of all classes in the training phase and can not be generalized to those new classes with only a few number of labels.

Few-shot Learning is proposed to leverage limited prior knowledge to predict new classes. Current solutions are mainly based on meta-learning [3,9,19] and metric learning [18,23,28]. Meta-learning aims to obtain a model that can be quickly adapted to new tasks using previous experience, while metric learning models the similarity among objects to generate discriminative representations for new categories.

Few-shot Segmentation aims to segment query images containing new categories through utilizing useful information from a small number of labeled data. PL [7] is the first to introduce prototype learning into few-shot segmentation and obtains segmentation results by comparing support prototypes and query features. Prototype alignment regularization is used in PANet [25], which encourages mutual guidance between support and query images. PGNet [29] introduces a graph attention unit to explore the local similarity between support and query features. PPNet [16] moves away from the limitations of the overall

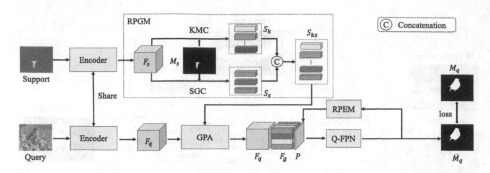

Fig. 2. The overall structure of our method with the rich prototype generation module (RPGM) and the recurrent prediction enhancement module (RPEM).

prototype and proposes partial perception prototypes that represent fine-grained features. In PFENet [22], a prior generated by advanced features of the support and query is utilized to guide the segmentation. Nevertheless, the above methods can not capture fully geometric information limited by employing a single prototype generation mode. Once there is a large size gap between the support and query objects, the similarity calculation between them will produce large errors and interfere with the decoder to generate the final prediction.

3   Problem Definition

In few-shot segmentation task, the categories in the training and test datasets are disjoint, models are trained on base classes C_{train} and tested on novel classes C_{test} in episodes ($C_{train} \cap C_{test} = \varnothing$). Each episode consists of a support set S and a query set Q belonging to the same class C. The support set S has K samples $S = \{S_1, S_2, \ldots, S_K\}$, and the i-th support sample S_i consists of a support image I_s and a pixel-wise annotation M_s with class C. Also, the query set Q consists simply of a query image I_q and the ground truth M_q indicating the object belonging to class C. The query-support pair $\{I_q, S\}$ forms the input branch of the network and the ground truth M_q of the query image is not available during training, but is used for the evaluation of the query image.

4   Proposed Approach

4.1   Overall Framework

Our network architecture shown in Fig. 2 uses a strong baseline ASGNet [13] to explore the effectiveness of each proposed component. First, we feed the support and query images into a shared encoder to extract features. And then, the support features are passed through the rich prototype generation module (RPGM) to produce two different representations of the prototype and are matched to the query features by the guided prototype allocation (GPA) module. Meanwhile, in the GPA module, the cosine similarity information of each support proto-type and the query features is accumulated to generate a probability map. Once the correspondence is established, the matched features will participate in the decoding phase. With the recurrent prediction enhancement module (RPEM), the decoder can continuously enhance the semantic information of the probability map and gradually restore a more accurate segmentation result.

4.2   Rich Prototype Generation

For generating a series of complementary prototypes, K-means clustering (KMC) [16] and superpixel-guided clustering (SGC) [13], two strategies with different scale-aware capabilities play a central role in the proposed rich prototype generation module (RPGM). The internal structure of the RPGM is shown in Fig. 2.

Specifically, we first apply KMC to compute a data partition $D = \{D_i\}_{i=1}^{N_k}$ and generate a set of prototypes $S_k = \{S_i\}_{i=1}^{N_k}$ by the average pooling as follows:

$$S_i = \frac{1}{|D_i|} \sum_{j \in D_i} F_s^j, \tag{1}$$

where $|D_i|$ and F_s^j represent the number of elements in D_i and the support feature indexed by D_i, respectively. In parallel, the collection of superpixel prototypes $S_s = \{S_r\}_{r=1}^{N_s}$ is produced from F_s in the SGC branch:

$$S_r = \frac{\sum_p A_{pr} \cdot F_s^p}{\sum_p A_{pr}}, \tag{2}$$

where A denotes the association mapping between each pixel p and all superpixels. The enhanced prototype S_{ks} with diverse representations is the combination of the two sets of feature prototypes:

$$S_{ks} = C(S_k, S_s), \tag{3}$$

where $C(\cdot, \cdot)$ is the channel-wise concatenation operation.

Then, we convey the integrated prototype S_{ks} and the query feature F_q to the GPA module for matching. In the GPA, the cosine similarity maps $\{B_i\}_{i=1}^{N_k+N_s}$ corresponding to each support prototype S_{ks}^i and the query features are fed into a two-branch structure. In the first branch, the index value of the most relevant prototype at each pixel location (x, y) is collected as the guide map g:

$$g^{x,y} = \underset{i \in \{0,...,N_k+N_s\}}{\arg \max} B_i^{x,y}. \tag{4}$$

Based on g, the corresponding prototypes are gathered to form the guide feature map F_g. In the second branch, all similarity maps are accumulated to obtain the probability map P:

$$P = \sum_{i=1}^{N_k+N_s} B_i. \tag{5}$$

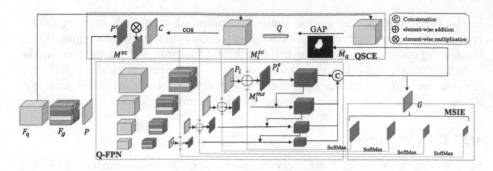

Fig. 3. Visual illustration of our proposed RPEM.

More details about the SGC and the GPA can be found in [13].

Finally, the query feature F_q, the guide feature F_g and the probability map P are fed into the Q-FPN for further enhancement of feature information. The Q-FPN is a module that provides multi-scale input to the decoder [22]. According to [22], the feature scales are chosen as $\{60, 30, 15, 8\}$.

4.3 Recurrent Prediction Enhancement

The recurrent mechanism has been applied to some segmentation methods [21, 30]. They rely heavily on the initial prediction to hard-compute correlations at the map-level by iterative operations and introduce more convolution parameters to optimize the prediction. Different from them, we pass the initial prediction information into the GPA module, and update the probability map through a recurrent mechanism to refine the prediction in a soft way. As shown in Fig. 3, we propose a recurrent prediction enhancement module (RPEM), including two parts: the multi-scale iterative enhancement (MSIE) and the query self-contrast enhancement (QSCE).

Multi-scale Iterative Enhancement (MSIE). The multi-scale operation can provide multi-level spatial information for features. The output feature G of the last layer is first processed with the adaptive average pooling operation to produce the feature set $\{G_i\}_{i=1}^v$ corresponding to v different spatial sizes. And we perform the softmax operation for each G_i to get a two-channel foreground-background probability map $M_i = \{M_i^c\}_{c=1}^2$. To further enhance the information representation, a min-max normalization is introduced to process the foreground map M_i^1, as described below:

$$M_i^1 = \frac{M_i^1 - \min(M_i^1)}{\max(M_i^1) - \min(M_i^1) + 10^{-7}}. \tag{6}$$

Finally, an affine transformation is applied to maintain interval consistency between M_i^1 and the probability map P_i:

$$M_i^{ms} = \alpha M_i^1 - \beta, \tag{7}$$

where α is set to 2 and β is set to 1. M_i^{ms} represents the additional information required by the probability map P_i.

Query Self-contrast Enhancement (QSCE). The pseudo mask $\widehat{M_q}$ is first generated from the two-channel map G by the argmax operation. The foreground and background are represented by 1 and 0, respectively. And the query prototype Q can be obtained by averaging the masked query feature F_q:

$$Q = \frac{\sum\limits_{i=1}^{hw} F_q(i) \odot \widehat{M_q}(i)}{\sum\limits_{i=1}^{hw} \widehat{M_q}(i)}, \tag{8}$$

where $\odot$ is the broadcast element-wise multiplication. The cosine distance between the query prototype and each query feature element is calculated as

$$C = \frac{Q \cdot F_q}{\|Q\| \cdot \|F_q\|}, \tag{9}$$

where C is the self-contrast similarity information of the query feature. Following Eq. (6), the value of initial probability map P is normalized to be between 0 and 1. By multiplying the normalized probability map P' with C, we can generate the complementary information M^{sc}:

$$M^{sc} = P' \cdot \frac{C+1}{2}, \tag{10}$$

where we convert the value on C to between 0 and 1 to ensure that the same range of values and the operation make sense. To maintain interval consistency, the same transformation is imposed on M^{sc} as Eq. (7). Similarly, we also perform a multi-scale operation on M^{sc} to obtain M_i^{sc}.

Finally, we accumulate the additional information M_i^{ms} and M_i^{sc} obtained by the MSIE and the QSCE together to the probability map P_i to generate a new enhanced probability map P_i^e as

$$P_i^e = P_i + M_i^{ms} + M_i^{sc}. \tag{11}$$

5 Experiments

5.1 Experimental Settings

We evaluate the performance of our method on PASCAL-5^i and COCO-20^i, two datasets that are frequently used to measure few-shot segmentation. PASCAL-5^i is composed of PASCAL VOC 2012 [8] and additional annotations of the SBD dataset [10], containing 20 categories. COCO-20^i is modified from the MSCOCO dataset [15] and consists of 80 categories. For each dataset, all categories are divided equally into four folds and our method is evaluated with reference to the setting in ASGNet [13]. Following [25], we use the widely adopted mean intersection over union (mIoU) as the evaluation metric.

Table 1. Comparison with state-of-the-art methods on PASCAL-5^i.

Backbone	Method	1-shot					5-shot				
		s-0	s-1	s-2	s-3	Mean	s-0	s-1	s-2	s-3	Mean
Res-50	CANet [30]	52.50	65.90	51.30	51.90	55.40	55.50	67.80	51.90	53.20	57.10
	PFENet [22]	61.70	69.50	55.40	56.30	60.80	63.10	70.70	55.80	57.90	61.90
	SCL [27]	**63.00**	**70.00**	56.50	**57.70**	**61.80**	64.50	70.90	57.30	58.70	62.90
	RePRI [2]	59.80	68.30	**62.10**	48.50	59.70	64.60	**71.40**	**71.10**	59.30	**66.60**
	ASGNet [13]	58.84	67.86	56.79	53.66	59.29	63.66	70.55	64.17	57.38	63.94
	Ours	60.95	68.16	59.87	55.12	61.03	**65.16**	70.71	69.51	**60.30**	66.42
Res-101	PFENet [22]	60.50	69.40	54.40	**55.90**	60.10	62.80	70.40	54.90	57.60	61.40
	RePRI [2]	59.60	68.60	**62.20**	47.20	59.40	**66.20**	71.40	67.00	57.70	65.60
	ASGNet [13]	59.84	67.43	55.59	54.39	59.31	64.55	71.32	64.24	57.33	64.36
	Ours	**60.80**	**69.83**	58.19	54.93	**60.94**	64.86	**72.72**	71.11	**59.99**	**67.17**

Table 2. Comparison with state-of-the-art methods on COCO-20^i.

Backbone	Method	1-shot					5-shot				
		s-0	s-1	s-2	s-3	Mean	s-0	s-1	s-2	s-3	Mean
Res-101	DAN [24]	–	–	–	–	24.20	–	–	–	–	29.60
	PFENet [22]	34.30	33.00	32.30	30.10	32.40	38.50	38.60	38.20	34.30	37.40
	SCL [27]	**36.40**	38.60	**37.50**	**35.40**	**37.00**	38.90	40.50	41.50	38.70	39.00
Res-50	RPMM [26]	29.53	36.82	28.94	27.02	30.58	33.82	41.96	32.99	33.33	35.52
	RePRI [2]	31.20	38.10	33.30	33.00	34.00	38.50	46.20	40.00	**43.60**	42.10
	ASGNet [13]	34.89	36.94	34.33	32.08	34.56	40.99	**48.28**	40.10	40.54	42.48
	Ours	36.21	**39.47**	33.97	34.07	35.93	**43.05**	47.91	**42.71**	41.24	**43.73**

5.2   Implementation Details

All experiments are conducted on the PyTorch framework. Our approach is built on ASGNet [13], and the backbone networks are ResNet-50 [11] and ResNet-101 [11]. The proposed model is trained at PASCAL-5^i for 200 epochs and at COCO-20^i for 50 epochs. Due to the limited computing resources, we choose a learning rate of 0.0025 and a batchsize of 4 for training on both datasets, but this does not prevent us from proving the effectiveness of our method. In this paper, we use the cross-entropy loss as supervision. Based on the experience of PPNet [16], we set the number of clusters N to 5 on each dataset, and please see ASGNet [13] for some other details. All of our experiments are conducted on an NVIDIA GTX 1080 GPU and an NVIDIA RTX 2080Ti GPU.

5.3   Results

In Table 1, we compare the proposed method with other state-of-the-art methods on PASCAL-5^i. Experiments show that our method significantly outperforms the baseline and achieves new state-of-the-art performance on the 5-shot setting. When using ResNet-101 as the backbone, our method improves 1.63 % and

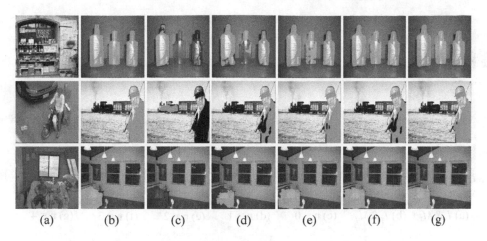

Fig. 4. Qualitative comparison of different components on PASCAL-5^i. (a) $I_s \& M_s$. (b) $I_q \& M_q$. (c) Baseline (ASGNet). (d) +RPGM. (e) +RPGM+MSIE. (f) +RPGM+QSCE. (g) +RPGM+RPEM.

Table 3. Ablation study of our RPGM and RPEM (MSIE and QSCE) on PASCAL-5^i.

Method	Res-50		Res-101	
	1-shot	5-shot	1-shot	5-shot
Baseline (ASGNet)	59.29	63.94	59.31	64.36
+RPGM	60.13	65.66	60.05	66.47
+RPGM+MSIE	60.51	**66.43**	60.73	67.13
+RPGM+QSCE	**61.07**	65.72	60.64	66.73
+RPGM+RPEM (MSIE+QSCE)	61.03	66.42	**60.94**	**67.17**

2.81 % over ASGNet in 1-shot and 5-shot segmentation, respectively. In Fig. 4, we show some representative results for all our setups. As can be seen from the first and third lines, our method can segment query images with different complexity very well even if the foreground of the support image is small. In Table 2, our method outperforms 1.37 % and 1.25 % in terms of mIoU over the baseline ASGNet under the 1-shot and 5-shot setting on COCO-20^i.

5.4 Ablation Study

In this subsection, we conduct extensive ablation studies on PASCAL-5^i to evaluate the effects of our proposed components.

Effects of RPGM and RPEM. The comparison shown in Table 3 validates the effectiveness of each proposed component. And the visualization in Fig. 4 also

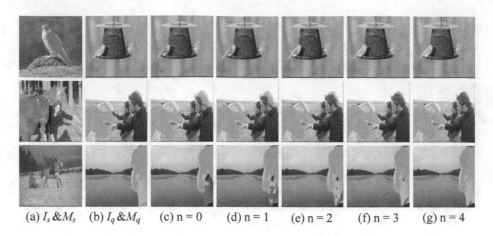

(a) $I_s \& M_s$ (b) $I_q \& M_q$ (c) n = 0   (d) n = 1   (e) n = 2   (f) n = 3   (g) n = 4

Fig. 5. Predictions from different iterations.

Table 4. Ablation study on the number of iterations n.

n iterations	s-0	s-1	s-2	s-3	Mean
0	60.06	68.16	58.43	53.88	60.13
2	**61.03**	**68.30**	59.47	54.89	60.92
4	60.95	68.16	**59.87**	**55.12**	**61.03**
6	60.34	67.58	59.86	54.87	60.66

reflects that these modules can brings consistent improvements across different samples. It can be seen that the RPGM can fully present the details of the supported images and the RPEM can refine the missing foreground in the query image segmentation.

Number of Recurrent Prediction Iterations. To explore the optimal number of iterations, we conduct several controlled experiments and results are summarized in Table 4. We observe that the model with the number of iterations "$n = 4$" achieves the best mean performance. In Fig. 5, we also show the prediction of each iteration. It can be intuitively seen that as the iteration proceeds, the missing foreground parts of the query image are increasingly filled in while the misclassified background parts are gradually removed.

6   Conclusion

In this paper, we propose the novel rich prototype generation module (RPGM) and the recurrent prediction enhancement module (RPEM) for few-shot segmentation. The RPGM generates rich prototypes that compensate for the loss of detail when only a single type of prototypes is available. The RPEM includes the multi-scale iterative enhancement (MSIE) and the query self-contrast enhancement (QSCE), which can be directly applied to gradually guide the probability map towards completeness and refine the segmentation map in the inference phase. Extensive experiments and ablation studies demonstrate the effectiveness of these proposed components, and our approach substantially improve the performance of the baseline on PASCAL-5^i and COCO-20^i datasets.

Acknowledgements. This work was supported by the National Natural Science Foundation of China #62176039.

References

1. Badrinarayanan, V., Kendall, A., Cipolla, R.: Segnet: a deep convolutional encoder-decoder architecture for image segmentation. IEEE TPAMI **39**, 2481–2495 (2017)
2. Boudiaf, M., Kervadec, H., Masud, Z.I., Piantanida, P., Ben Ayed, I., Dolz, J.: Few-shot segmentation without meta-learning: a good transductive inference is all you need? In: CVPR, pp. 13979–13988 (2021)
3. Cai, Q., Pan, Y., Yao, T., Yan, C., Mei, T.: Memory matching networks for one-shot image recognition. In: CVPR, pp. 4080–4088 (2018)
4. Chen, L.C., Papandreou, G., Kokkinos, I., Murphy, K., Yuille, A.L.: Deeplab: semantic image segmentation with deep convolutional nets, atrous convolution, and fully connected crfs. IEEE TPAMI **40**, 834–848 (2017)
5. Chen, L.C., Papandreou, G., Schroff, F., Adam, H.: Rethinking atrous convolution for semantic image segmentation. arXiv preprint arXiv:1706.05587 (2017)
6. Chen, L.C., Zhu, Y., Papandreou, G., Schroff, F., Adam, H.: Encoder-decoder with atrous separable convolution for semantic image segmentation. In: ECCV, pp. 801–818 (2018)
7. Dong, N., Xing, E.P.: Few-shot semantic segmentation with prototype learning. In: BMVC, no. 4 (2018)
8. Everingham, M., Van Gool, L., Williams, C.K., Winn, J., Zisserman, A.: The pascal visual object classes (voc) challenge. IJCV **88**, 303–338 (2010). https://doi.org/10.1007/s11263-009-0275-4
9. Finn, C., Abbeel, P., Levine, S.: Model-agnostic meta-learning for fast adaptation of deep networks. In: ICML, pp. 1126–1135 (2017)
10. Hariharan, B., Arbeláez, P., Bourdev, L., Maji, S., Malik, J.: Semantic contours from inverse detectors. In: ICCV, pp. 991–998 (2011)
11. He, K., Zhang, X., Ren, S., Sun, J.: Deep residual learning for image recognition. In: CVPR, pp. 770–778 (2016)
12. Huang, Z., Wang, X., Huang, L., Huang, C., Wei, Y., Liu, W.: Ccnet: criss-cross attention for semantic segmentation. In: ICCV, pp. 603–612 (2019)
13. Li, G., Jampani, V., Sevilla-Lara, L., Sun, D., Kim, J., Kim, J.: Adaptive prototype learning and allocation for few-shot segmentation. In: CVPR, pp. 8334–8343 (2021)
14. Li, X., et al.: Improving semantic segmentation via decoupled body and edge supervision. In: Vedaldi, A., Bischof, H., Brox, T., Frahm, J.-M. (eds.) ECCV 2020, Part XVII. LNCS, vol. 12362, pp. 435–452. Springer, Cham (2020). https://doi.org/10.1007/978-3-030-58520-4_26
15. Lin, T.Y., et al.: Microsoft coco: common objects in context. In: Fleet, D., Pajdla, T., Schiele, B., Tuytelaars, T. (eds.) ECCV 2014, Part V. LNCS, vol. 8693, pp. 740–755. Springer, Cham (2014). https://doi.org/10.1007/978-3-319-10602-1_48

16. Liu, Y., Zhang, X., Zhang, S., He, X.: Part-aware prototype network for few-shot semantic segmentation. In: Vedaldi, A., Bischof, H., Brox, T., Frahm, J.-M. (eds.) ECCV 2020, Part IX. LNCS, vol. 12354, pp. 142–158. Springer, Cham (2020). https://doi.org/10.1007/978-3-030-58545-7_9

17. Nguyen, K., Todorovic, S.: Feature weighting and boosting for few-shot segmentation. In: ICCV, pp. 622–631 (2019)

18. Qi, H., Brown, M., Lowe, D.G.: Low-shot learning with imprinted weights. In: CVPR, pp. 5822–5830 (2018)

19. Rusu, A.A., et al.: Meta-learning with latent embedding optimization. arXiv preprint arXiv:1807.05960 (2018)

20. Shaban, A., Bansal, S., Liu, Z., Essa, I., Boots, B.: One-shot learning for semantic segmentation. arXiv preprint arXiv:1709.03410 (2017)

21. Tang, H., Liu, X., Sun, S., Yan, X., Xie, X.: Recurrent mask refinement for few-shot medical image segmentation. In: ICCV, pp. 3918–3928 (2021)

22. Tian, Z., Zhao, H., Shu, M., Yang, Z., Li, R., Jia, J.: Prior guided feature enrichment network for few-shot segmentation. IEEE TPAMI **44**, 1050–1065 (2022)

23. Vinyals, O., Blundell, C., Lillicrap, T., kavukcuoglu, k., Wierstra, D.: Matching networks for one shot learning. In: NeurIPS (2016)

24. Wang, H., Zhang, X., Hu, Y., Yang, Y., Cao, X., Zhen, X.: Few-shot semantic segmentation with democratic attention networks. In: Vedaldi, A., Bischof, H., Brox, T., Frahm, J.-M. (eds.) ECCV 2020, Part XIII. LNCS, vol. 12358, pp. 730–746. Springer, Cham (2020). https://doi.org/10.1007/978-3-030-58601-0_43

25. Wang, K., Liew, J.H., Zou, Y., Zhou, D., Feng, J.: Panet: few-shot image semantic segmentation with prototype alignment. In: ICCV, pp. 9197–9206 (2019)

26. Yang, B., Liu, C., Li, B., Jiao, J., Ye, Q.: Prototype mixture models for few-shot semantic segmentation. In: Vedaldi, A., Bischof, H., Brox, T., Frahm, J.-M. (eds.) ECCV 2020, Part VIII. LNCS, vol. 12353, pp. 763–778. Springer, Cham (2020). https://doi.org/10.1007/978-3-030-58598-3_45

27. Zhang, B., Xiao, J., Qin, T.: Self-guided and cross-guided learning for few-shot segmentation. In: CVPR, pp. 8312–8321 (2021)

28. Zhang, C., Cai, Y., Lin, G., Shen, C.: Deepemd: few-shot image classification with differentiable earth mover's distance and structured classifiers. In: CVPR, pp. 12203–12213 (2020)

29. Zhang, C., Lin, G., Liu, F., Guo, J., Wu, Q., Yao, R.: Pyramid graph networks with connection attentions for region-based one-shot semantic segmentation. In: ICCV, pp. 9587–9595 (2019)

30. Zhang, C., Lin, G., Liu, F., Yao, R., Shen, C.: Canet: class-agnostic segmentation networks with iterative refinement and attentive few-shot learning. In: CVPR, pp. 5217–5226 (2019)

31. Zhang, H., et al.: Context encoding for semantic segmentation. In: CVPR, pp. 7151–7160 (2018)

32. Zhao, H., Shi, J., Qi, X., Wang, X., Jia, J.: Pyramid scene parsing network. In: CVPR, pp. 2881–2890 (2017)

33. Zhao, H., et al.: Psanet: point-wise spatial attention network for scene parsing. In: ECCV, pp. 267–283 (2018)

Object Detection, Segmentation and Tracking

TAFDet: A Task Awareness Focal Detector for Ship Detection in SAR Images

Yilong Lv[ID], Min Li[(✉)], Yujie He[ID], and Yu Song

Xi'an Institute of High Technology, Xi'an, China
504998692@qq.com, limin301908@163.com, ksy520131@163.com,
songyu888@yeah.net

Abstract. With the wide application of Synthetic Aperture Radar(SAR) radar in maritime surveillance, ship detection method has been developed rapidly. However, there is still a key problem that is the general parallel detection head network has task inconsistency between different tasks. In this work, we proposes a task awareness focal Detector (TAFDet) that alleviate the problem of task inconsistency, consisting of two sub-networks: task awareness attention(TAA-Subnet) and cross-task focal sub-network (CTF-Subnet). Firstly, we design TAA-Subnet that can use the standard backpropagation operation to transform the gradient signal into an attention map of different tasks. To select prominent attention features and obtain a task awareness mask, we proposed a mask generation module(MGM) in TAA-Subnet. Second, CTF-Subnet is designed to tune features in different tasks using task awareness mask, where a feature focal module (FFM) was proposed to enhance the features not paid attention to in the task. Experiments show that our method consistently improved state-of-the-art detectors on SSDD and HRSID datasets. Specifically, our TAFDet consistently surpasses the strong baseline by 0.4∼5.8 AP with different backbones on SSDD and HRSID datasets.

Keywords: Task awareness focal detector · Task awareness attention sub-network · Cross-task focal sub-network · SAR ship detection

1 Introduction

Synthetic aperture radar (SAR) is a high-resolution image radar. As an active microwave imaging sensor, its microwave imaging process has a certain penetration effect on ground objects and is less affected by the environment. Thus, SAR has been widely used in ship detection [1–6].

Traditional SAR image ship detection methods mainly infer the ships location and classification by observing the difference between the hull and background. There are three methods based on statistical features, threshold, and transformation. However, the traditional SAR ship detection method is not very reliable,

ⓒ The Author(s), under exclusive license to Springer Nature Switzerland AG 2022
S. Yu et al. (Eds.): PRCV 2022, LNCS 13537, pp. 301–314, 2022.
https://doi.org/10.1007/978-3-031-18916-6_25

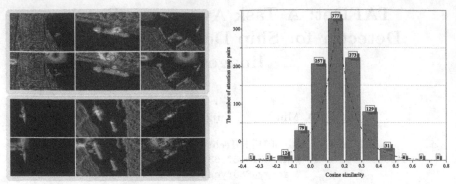

(a) Visualizations of attention maps for classification and localization.

(b) Cosine similarity of all pairs of attention.

Fig. 1. (a) Each gray box contains all the attention maps, among which the above is classified attention maps, and the following is regression attention maps. Among them, we can find that the highlighted parts in the two attention heat maps were not similar or even very different. (b) Its y-ordinate represents the total amount of attention pairs, equal to the number of images multiplied by the number of scales in feature pyramid. Cosine similarity ranges from 0 to 1, and the closer it gets to 1, the more similar it gets. The cosine similarity of the original network is mainly concentrated in 0.1–0.2, indicating that the attention maps of classification and regression are very different. (Color figure online)

and it is difficult to achieve accurate detection based on the difference between the hull and background.

Due to the significant improvement of GPU computing capability in recent years, object detection models based on deep learning have been booming. To explore the rules of these detection models, researchers divide general object detection models into backbone, bottleneck, and head network. Head network is a crucial structure of object detection task, which can classify and locate object according to input features. Early object detection models, such as Faster RCNN [7], YOLO [8], and SSD [9], share a head network for classification and regression tasks. With the development of models such as RetinaNet [10], FCOS [11], Fove-aBox [12], and IoU-Net [13], it is a trend to construct parallel classification and regression branches. However, the subsequent problem is that the two tasks are not directly related and supervise each other in the network structure, resulting in task inconsistencies between classification and regression.

To prove that the bifurcation between classification and regression does exist, Fig. 1(a) visualizes the attention map of the classification and regression branches based on the NAS-FCOS [14] algorithm. The redder the color is in the image, the more sensitive it is to the result. The bluer the color in the image, the vice versa. In addition, we calculated the cosine similarity between the attention maps of each input image in classification and regression features. According to the cosine similarity distribution on Fig. 1(b), there was a significant difference between the attention maps, which would limit the model to achieve the best performance to some extent.

To alleviate the problem of task inconsistency in the head network, this paper proposes a task awareness focal Detector(TAFDet), consisting of two sub-networks: task awareness attention(TAA-Subnet) and cross-task focal sub-network(CTF-Subnet). In the convolutional neural network, the feature gradient in the backpropagation encodes the sensitivity of the output to the exact position of the feature map. Therefore, this paper designed a TAA-Subnet that can use the standard backpropagation operation to transform the gradient signal into an attention map of different branches. In order to select prominent attention features and obtain a task awareness mask, we proposed a mask generation module(MGM) in the sub-network. Further, a CTF-Subnet is designed, added separately to the two branches. The role of a CTF-Subnet is to use task awareness mask to adjust the features in different tasks, which is implemented by a feature focal module(FFM), to enhance the features not paid attention to in the task. Our method is applied to the training and inference process of the network. Significantly, the model adds no additional training parameters and is simple and plug and play.

The Main Contributions of Our Work Can Be Summarized as Follows.

- We proposes a TAFDet that alleviate the problem of task inconsistency, consisting of two sub-networks: TAA-Subnet and CTF-Subnet.
- TAA-Subnet can use the standard backpropagation operation to transform the gradient signal into task awareness masks of different branches.
- CTF-Subnet uses task awareness masks to tune features in different tasks.
- We conducted extensive experiments on SSDD and HRSID datasets where our method performs favorably against state-of-the-art methods. Specifically, our TAFDet consistently surpasses the strong baseline by 0.4~5.8 AP with different backbones on SSDD and HRSID datasets.

2 Related Work

2.1 Detection Head Network

FCOS proposed a object detection method based on anchor-free, adding a Center-ness prediction branch to the conventional divide-and-rule structure. This branch will tend to produce higher scores for pixels near the object's center and vice versa. Based on the FCOS network, NAS-FCOS added the Neural Architecture Search and realized the improvement in detection performance. Considering the inconsistencies between classification and regression branches, IoU-Net innovatively added an IoU prediction branch, used this branch to predict regression scores, and finally used regression scores and classification scores to decide whether to retain predicted results jointly. Dynamic Head [15] proposes a dynamic detection head network and reconstructs the head network through various representations of the attention mechanism.

2.2 Attention Network

The attention mechanism is often used to make the network focus on local information. CBAM [16] proposes a lightweight attention module to add attention to
the two dimensions of space and channel. In the spatial domain, adding attention can make a vanilla network focus on local features in the space domain.
Adding channel attention can make the vanilla network focus on some special
channels. CBAM network has a simple structure and good flexibility. IAN [17]
network proposes a fine-grained attention mechanism that inverted attention.
Unlike focusing only on the central part of the object, the network pays more
attention to the complementary object part, feature channel, and context. This
method enables the network to learn more object regions by suppressing the
weight of the region of interest to improve the object detection performance.
Our method is similar to IAN's operation. But different from IAN, we need to
achieve the opposite goal. IAN occludes the network's attention to the object,
while our method only retains the network's attention by TAA-Subnet. The network's attention is divided into the attention of the classification task and the
regression task. Next, The two tasks use CTF-Subnet through the attention of
the different task to enhance consistency. However, no module in IAN enables
task consistency similar to CTF-Subnet.

2.3 Task Inconsistency

TOOD [18] found that the general parallel head network would cause misalignment between the two tasks and ultimately lead to inconsistent prediction
results. GFL [19] considers inconsistencies between classification and regression
tasks during the training and inference phases. Its solution is to combine the
classification and regression tasks into a unified whole and propose the QFL loss
function. PISA [20] believes that classification and positioning are interrelated.
In particular, well-placed samples need to be classified with high scores, so it
proposes a classification awareness regression loss. At the same time, it proves
that classification awareness regression loss can optimize both classification and
regression prediction in the training process.

3 Task Awareness Focal Detector

We use the general parallel detection head frame to illustrate our TAFDet. Its
network structure is shown in Fig. 2, which consists of TAA-Subnet and CTF-
Subnet. This section will show how our method can effectively enhance the
original network to overcome the lack of communication in classification and
regression.

3.1 Task Awareness Attention Sub-network

Attention Map Generation. We first master the attention of a single task.
Take classification task as an example, it is assumed that the input feature

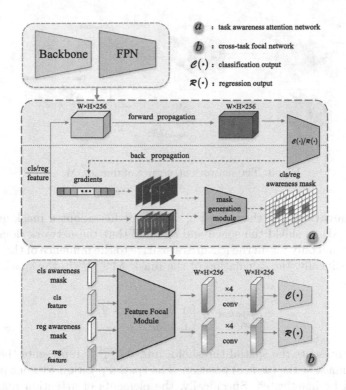

Fig. 2. The network structure of our TAFDet.

is expressed as $\mathcal{F}^{cls} \in \mathbb{R}^{W \times H}$, and the output classification score is $\mathcal{Y}^{cls} \in \mathbb{R}^{W \mathcal{H} \mathcal{K} \times \mathcal{N}}$, where $\mathcal{K}$ represents the number of preset anchors and $\mathcal{N}$ represents the number of categories of the dataset. Then, the attention on the classification branch is calculated as follows.

$$a_{w,h,c}^{cls} = f_{w,h,c}^{cls} \times \frac{\partial(\sum_{i}^{W \mathcal{H} \mathcal{K}} \max_{0<j<\mathcal{N}} y_{i,j}^{cls})}{\partial f_{w,h,c}^{cls}} \qquad (1)$$

where, $a_{w,h,c}^{cls}$ represents the attention value of coordinates (w, h, c) on the classification branch.

The process of regression branch is almost the same as that of classification. Suppose that the output of the regression branch is regression offset $\mathcal{Y}^{reg} \in \mathbb{R}^{W \mathcal{H} \mathcal{K} \times 4}$, the attention on the regression branch is calculated as follows.

$$a_{w,h,c}^{reg} = f_{w,h,c}^{reg} \times \frac{\partial(\sum_{i}^{W \mathcal{H} \mathcal{K}} \sum_{j}^{4} y_{i,j}^{reg})}{\partial f_{w,h,c}^{reg}} \qquad (2)$$

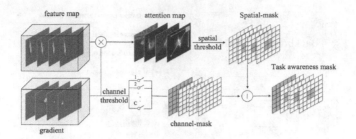

Fig. 3. The network structure of our MGM.

Mask Generation. As shown in Fig. 3, We further adopt a mask generation module(MGM) to shield the space and channel that the network does not pay attention to and only retain the features sensitive to the influence of the predicted output. Specifically, the calculation of the mask $\mathcal{M}^{spatial}$ in the spatial domain is as follows:

$$\mathcal{M}^{spatial}_{w,h,c} = \begin{cases} 1 & if\, a_{w,h,c} > \mathcal{T}_s \\ 0 & else \end{cases} \tag{3}$$

where $\mathcal{T}_s$ represents the spatial threshold, and $\mathcal{M}^{spatial}_{w,h,c}$ represents the value of the spatial mask at the (w, h, c) position. The spatial position without prominent feature will be inactivated. Specifically, the elements of attention map greater than $\mathcal{T}_s$ are reserved, and the remaining elements are set to 0.

For channels in which the average value of attention is small enough, we directly inactivate all pixels in the channel, finally leaving only the channel with a sufficiently sizeable average value, so a threshold $\mathcal{T}_c$ will be applied to control the opening or closing of the channel. Specifically, the calculation process of an mask $\mathcal{M}^{channel}$ in the channel domain is as follows:

$$\mathcal{M}^{channel}_{w,h,c} = \begin{cases} 1 & if\, \frac{1}{\mathcal{W}\mathcal{H}} \sum_{i}^{\mathcal{W}} \sum_{j}^{\mathcal{H}} a_{i,j,c} > \mathcal{T}_c \\ 0 & else \end{cases} \tag{4}$$

Finally, we combined the masks in the spatial domain and the channel domain into task awareness mask $\mathcal{M}$, and the calculation process was as follows:

$$\mathcal{M}_{w,h,c} = \begin{cases} \mathcal{M}^{spatial}_{w,h,c} & if\, \mathcal{M}^{channel}_{w,h,c} = 1 \\ 0 & else \end{cases} \tag{5}$$

The task awareness mask will follow the training and inference process to iterate and be used downstream of the network. The operation process in the inference process is the same as the training process.

3.2 Cross-Task Focal Sub-network

CTF-Subnet presents asymmetrical distribution based on classification and regression branches. We design a FFM with the structure as shown in the Fig. 4, which can use the mask to re-weight the input feature $\mathcal{F}$. Finally, the processed features are fed into the network for training. The whole process does not change the original network structure and training flow.

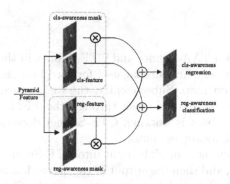

Fig. 4. The network structure of our FFM.

Feature Focal Module. Specifically, taking the classification branch as an example, the input classification feature, input regression feature, and regression awareness mask are $\mathcal{F}^{cls}$, $\mathcal{F}^{reg}$, $\mathcal{M}^{reg}$, respectively. Since the classification task lacks the attention of the regression task, the classification task should pay more attention to the feature information concerned the regression task. We cut the feature concerned by the regression task and paste it into the classification feature. The calculation process of a classification feature is as follows.

$$\hat{\mathcal{F}}^{cls} = \mathcal{F}^{reg} * \mathcal{M}^{reg} + \mathcal{F}^{cls} \tag{6}$$

The same goes for operations on regression branches, which's calculation process is as follows.

$$\hat{\mathcal{F}}^{reg} = \mathcal{F}^{cls} * \mathcal{M}^{cls} + \mathcal{F}^{reg} \tag{7}$$

3.3 Training and Inference Details

Our TAFDet includes a TAA-Subnet and CTF-Subnet in the training and inference process. TAA-Subnet first propagated forward and then propagated back to obtain the attention map. Subsequently, the task awareness attention map can generate the task awareness mask through the FFM. It should be noted that when the TAA-Subnet is working, CTF-Subnet does not start to flow and is waiting for the task awareness mask.

When the task awareness mask is input into CTF-Subnet, the network starts to propagate forward, and then the output of the network is used to construct the loss function. Finally, the model parameters are updated by backpropagation. Therefore, TAFDet method needs to carry out two forward propagation and backpropagation in the training process, but only the second backpropagation updates model parameters. In addition, TAFDet method performs two forward propagation and the first backpropagation during the inference without updating model parameters.

3.4 Detail

Our TAFDet includes a TAA-Subnet and CTF-Subnet in the training and inference process. TAA-Subnet first propagated forward and then propagated back to obtain the attention map. Subsequently, the task awareness attention map can generate the task awareness mask through the FFM. It should be noted that when the TAA-Subnet is working, CTF-Subnet does not start to flow and is waiting for the task awareness mask.

When the task awareness mask is input into CTF-Subnet, the network starts to propagate forward, and then the output of the network is used to construct the loss function. Finally, the model parameters are updated by backpropagation. Therefore, TAFDet method needs to carry out two forward propagation and backpropagation in the training process, but only the second backpropagation updates model parameters. In addition, TAFDet method performs two forward propagation and the first backpropagation during the inference without updating model parameters.

4 Experiment

4.1 Datasets

To evaluate the validity of the proposed method, we conducted extensive experiments on the SSDD and HRSID datasets.

SSDD. It is the first SAR ship dataset established in 2017. It has been widely used by many researchers since its publication and has become the baseline dataset for SAR ship detection. The label file settings of this dataset are the same as those of the mainstream PASCAL VOC dataset, so training of the algorithms is convenient.

HRSID. It is used for ship detection, semantic segmentation, and instance segmentation tasks in high-resolution SAR images. The dataset contains 5,604 high-resolution SAR images and 16,951 ship instances. Its label file settings are the same as those of the mainstream of the Microsoft common objects in context (COCO) dataset.

Table 1. Ablation study on the effectiveness of different masks and hyper-parameters.

Spatial	Channel	AP	AP_{50}	AP_{75}	AP_S	AP_M	AP_L
10^{-7}	✗	50.3	89.7	52.1	50.6	53.8	39.4
✗	10^{-6}	47.7	86.8	49.2	48.2	49.4	32.7
10^{-8}	10^{-7}	49.5	87.9	54.1	49.9	53.4	33.9
10^{-7}	10^{-7}	51.1	**90.5**	55.0	51.4	53.8	40.8
10^{-7}	10^{-6}	**51.8**	89.8	**58.6**	**52.0**	**54.7**	**42.1**
10^{-6}	10^{-6}	47.7	87.1	50.7	48.1	50.4	34.1
ATSS: std1	ATSS: std1	13.5	38.4	4.4	19.3	6.3	0
ATSS: std2	ATSS: std2	48.9	89.5	50.0	48.7	54.1	38.8

4.2 Implementation

Our experimental hardware platform includes Intel(R) Xeon(R) Silver 4110 CPU and 2 T V100 GPUs. In addition, most of our algorithm models are based on the MMDetection framework. The optimizer adopts the stochastic gradient descent method. The learning rate settings include 0.01, 0.005 and 0.001, momentum is 0.9, and weight attenuation is 0.0001.

In the single-stage methods, we will follow Fig. 2. First, we connect the TAA subnetwork behind the FPN network and obtain the task-aware mask by forward and backward propagation. Then, with the CTF subnetwork, the classification and regression features are reweighted by the task awareness mask to get task-consistent features.

In the two-stage methods, we improve the RPN. There are two convolutional layers in the RPN, which output the classification and regression features, respectively. We treat them as different task branches, and the following process is similar to the single-stage methods.

4.3 Ablation Study

The subsequent ablation study was based on the NAS-FCOS model with ResNet-50 and SSDD datasets.

Effectiveness of Different Masks. In this section, we will study the influence of the two masks on the experimental results, as shown in Table 1. It can be seen from the first two lines in the table that the AP of spatial and channel mask is 50.3% and 47.7% respectively, and the AP of the combination of the two is 51.8%. All data show that the spatial mask is better than the channel mask, but the effect alone is not as good as their combined effect. According to the experimental results, the SSDD dataset has only a single category, so the semantic information is lacking, and the feature representation capability in the channel domain is weak. On the contrary, the size and position of ship targets in the SSDD dataset are diversified, which makes spatial masks play an important role.

Table 2. Ablation study on the effectiveness of different branches.

Cls awareness	Reg awareness	AP	AP_{50}	AP_{75}	AP_S	AP_M	AP_L
		46.1	84.7	47.5	47.0	46.9	34.5
	✓	37.5	78.7	29.8	39.5	35.2	26.3
✓		48.6	**89.9**	48.1	47.9	**54.9**	35.3
✓	✓	**51.8**	89.8	**58.6**	**52.0**	54.7	**42.1**

On Hyper-parameters. Spatial threshold and channel threshold in TAFDet are two crucial hyperparameters, so the influence of threshold setting on experimental results will be explored in this section. We use two schemes, fixed threshold, and ATSS.

Fixed thresholds are a simple and widely used approach. We first perform numerical statistics on the gradient of features to purposefully set spatial and channel thresholds. According to statistics, the spatial values of features are mainly distributed in three orders of magnitude 10^{-6}-10^{-8}, while the values of channels are distributed in the range 10^{-6}-10^{-7}. Therefore, we set up four groups of setting schemes, and the results are shown in Table 1. According to Table 1, when the space threshold and channel threshold are 10^{-7} and 10^{-6}, respectively, the AP is 51.8%, which is superior to other schemes.

The idea of the ATSS method is to take the sum of mean value and standard deviation as the threshold value. In this section, we set two groups of parameters based on ATSS method, and the results are shown in Table 1. As shown in Table 1, when the sum of mean and standard deviation is used as the threshold, AP is 13.5%, showing a sharp decline. It may be because the threshold value is too low, and many background features are retained, leading to the decline of target feature representation ability. When the mean value and the sum of 2 standard deviations were used as the threshold, the AP was 48.9%, which recovered to normal but was still lower than 51.8%.

Effectiveness of Different Branches. In this section, we study the effects of classification and regression branches on detection performance. Therefore, we reconstructed the classification and regression branches, respectively, and the results are shown in the Table 2. It can be seen from Table 2 that the AP after classification features are re-weighted is 48.6%, higher than the AP46.1% of the original network, and the AP after regression features are re-weighted is 37.5%. This phenomenon is not difficult to understand because most current methods rely on classification scores for post-processing, so the improved classification features improve detection performance. The improved regression features did not match the corresponding classification scores, so the performance decreased.

4.4 Consistent Attention Map

Based on the same training conditions, we conducted simulation and found that the attention map of the NAS-FCOS algorithm on the classification and

Table 3. Comparing with state-of-the-art methods on SSDD and HRSID.

Method	Backbone	Datasets	AP	AP_{50}	AP_{75}	AP_S	AP_M	AP_L
YOLOV3	DarkNet53	SSDD	58.4	**95.7**	65.9	54.6	64.3	**61.8**
Dynamic RCNN	ResNet-50	SSDD	59.1	94.2	67.2	55.5	65.7	61.3
TOOD	ResNet-50	SSDD	53.7	92.7	55.9	50.2	61.1	43.1
ATSS	ResNet-50	SSDD	52.4	89.3	58.5	52.0	56.6	36.8
ATSS	ResNet-101	SSDD	58.4	95.0	65.8	54.2	**66.8**	52.0
ATSS+TAFDet(ours)	ResNet-50	SSDD	53.5(+1.1)	89.9(+0.6)	60.2(+1.7)	52.0(+0.0)	58.8(+2.2)	44.7(+7.9)
ATSS+TAFDet(ours)	ResNet-101	SSDD	58.8(+0.4)	95.6(+0.6)	67.0(+1.2)	54.8(+0.6)	66.7(-0.1)	58.8(+6.8)
NAS-FCOS	ResNet-50	SSDD	46.1	84.7	47.5	47.0	46.9	34.5
NAS-FCOS+TAFDet(ours)	ResNet-50	SSDD	51.8(+5.7)	89.8(+5.1)	58.6(+11.1)	52.0(+5.0)	54.7(+7.8)	42.1(+7.6)
FoveaBox	ResNet-50	SSDD	50.0	88.0	52.9	49.0	54.3	33.5
FoveaBox+TAFDet(ours)	ResNet-50	SSDD	55.8(+5.8)	93.3(+5.3)	62.9(+10.0)	53.7(+4.7)	61.8(+7.5)	52.4(+18.9)
Faster RCNN	ResNet-50	SSDD	58.1	93.8	65.5	54.9	63.8	53.6
Faster RCNN+TAFDet(ours)	ResNet-50	SSDD	**59.4(+1.3)**	94.9(+1.1)	**67.8(+2.3)**	**56.6(+1.7)**	64.6(+0.8)	60.0(+6.4)
YOLOV3	DarkNet53	HRSID	58.6	**88.8**	64.7	59.7	57.5	19.3
TOOD	ResNet-50	HRSID	53.3	80.3	58.8	54.0	55.5	14.3
ATSS	ResNet-50	HRSID	58.7	82.8	65.6	59.8	62.2	13.5
ATSS	ResNet-101	HRSID	57.9	82.5	64.1	58.6	62.4	15.9
ATSS+TAFDet(ours)	ResNet-50	HRSID	59.6(+1.2)	84.5(+1.7)	66.6(+1.0)	60.6(+0.8)	63.8(+1.6)	17.5(+4.0)
ATSS+TAFDet(ours)	ResNet-101	HRSID	**59.9(+2.0)**	85.3(+2.8)	**66.7(+2.6)**	**60.8(+2.2)**	**64.2(+1.8)**	**24.9(+9.0)**
foveaBox	ResNet-50	HRSID	50.2	76.5	55.3	51.0	56.9	18.8
foveaBox	ResNet-101	HRSID	50.4	76.2	55.9	51.3	58.2	6.7
foveaBox+TAFDet(ours)	ResNet-50	HRSID	55.1(+4.9)	80.6(+4.1)	60.7(+5.4)	56.2(+5.2)	58.5(+1.6)	20.5(+1.7)
foveaBox+TAFDet(ours)	ResNet-101	HRSID	55.3(+4.9)	81.2(+5.0)	61.0(+4.2)	56.1(+4.8)	58.5(+0.3)	24.8(+18.1)
nas-fcos	ResNet-50	HRSID	54.6	80.3	60.2	55.8	58.1	6.5
nas-fcos+TAFDet(ours)	ResNet-50	HRSID	56.8(+2.2)	83.3(+3.0)	62.4(+2.2)	57.8(+2.0)	61.4(+3.3)	9.1(+2.6)

positioning branches after optimization by our method is shown in Fig. 6. Compared with Fig. 6, it is found that the classification and regression attention tend to be more consistent, which indicates that the classification and regression branches tend to focus on the same object during inference so that the two branches cooperate more closely in the objecct detection.

4.5   Comparison with the State-of-the-Art

We implemented TAFDet based on a variety of methods. For SSDD and HRSID datasets, all results were produced by the official evaluation server. The performance of our method is shown in Table 3.

On SSDD datasets, our method significantly improves the performance of various methods. For ResNet-50 FoveaBox, TAFDet increased AP from 50.0 of the baseline to 55.8, which is a 5.8 improvement. In addition, for ResNet-50 NAS-FCOS, TAFDet increased AP from 46.1 of the baseline to 51.8, which is a 5.7 improvement. This shows that our TAFDet can alleviate the problem of task inconsistency.

In order to prove the robustness of our method, we conducted experiments on the HRSID datasets. For ATSS, TAFDet gets 1.2 higher AP with ResNet50 and achieves 59.6 AP. When using the more powerful backbone ResNet-101, TAFDet consistently gains over 2.0AP more than baselines. For FoveaBox, TAFDet's AP improved by 4.9 to 59.6 when ResNet-50 was used. The gain of TAFDet was consistently higher than 4.9 when the more powerful backbone RseNet-101 was

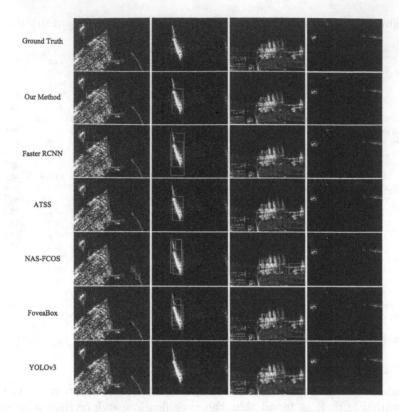

Fig. 5. Detection results by state-of-the Art methods. Our method makes detected boxes become more accurate.

Fig. 6. Visualizations of attention maps for classification and localization.

used. Meanwhile, TAFDet gains 2.2 higher AP for bounding box evaluation in NAS-FCOS framework. This verifies the robustness of our method.

Figure 5 shows some of the detection results on the SSDD dataset. In Fig. 5, the detection images of our method are compared with those of ResNet-50 Faster RCNN, ResNet-101 ATSS, ResNet-50 NAS-FCOS, ResNet-50 FoveaBox, and DarkNet-53 Yolov3. These results show that our method can handle image defects, such as small object, large object, occlusions.

5 Conclusion

Our TAFDet can improve the model based on parallel detection head network. TAFDet consists of two sub-networks. TAA-Subnet uses the standard back-propagation algorithm to transform the gradient signal into the task awareness masks of different tasks. CTF-Subnet uses task awareness masks to tune features in different tasks. significantly, the proposed method only contains some simple operations, such as pooling and threshold, without adding training parameters, so it does not add a burden to the network. As a result, TAFDet effectively compensates for task inconsistencies, and makes the network robust to image defects. It is desirable to explore TAFDet applications in all other computer vision tasks.

References

1. Du, L., Dai, H., Wang, Y., Xie, W., Wang, Z.: Target discrimination based on weakly supervised learning for high-resolution SAR images in complex scenes. IEEE Trans. Geosci. Remote Sens. **58**(1), 461–472 (2020)
2. Shahzad, M., Maurer, M., Fraundorfer, F., Wang, Y., Zhu, X.X.: Buildings detection in VHR SAR images using fully convolution neural networks. IEEE Trans. Geosci. Remote Sens. **57**(2), 1100–1116 (2019)
3. Huang, L., et al.: OpenSARShip: a dataset dedicated to Sentinel-1 ship interpretation. IEEE J. Sel. Topics Appl. Earth Observ. Remote Sens. **11**(1), 195–208 (2018)
4. Zhang, Z., Wang, H., Xu, F., Jin, Y.-Q.: Complex-valued convolutional neural network and its application in polarimetric SAR image classification. IEEE Trans. Geosci. Remote Sens. **55**(12), 7177–7188 (2017)
5. Yang, G., Li, H.-C., Yang, W., Fu, K., Sun, Y.-J., Emery, W.J.: Unsupervised change detection of SAR images based on variational multivariate Gaussian mixture model and Shannon entropy. IEEE Geosci. Remote Sens. Lett. **16**(5), 826–830 (2019)
6. Gierull, C.H.: Demystifying the capability of sublook correlation techniques for vessel detection in SAR imagery. IEEE Trans. Geosci. Remote Sens. **57**(4), 2031–2042 (2019)
7. Ren, S., He, K., Girshick, R., Sun, J.: Faster r-cnn: towards real-time target detection with region proposal networks. IEEE Trans. Pattern Anal. Mach. Intell. **39**(6), 1137–1149 (2017)
8. Redmon, J., Divvala, S., Girshick, R., Farhadi, A.: You only look once: unified, real-time object detection. In: Proceedings of IEEE Conference on Computer Vision and Pattern Recognition, pp. 779–788 (2016)
9. Liu, W., Anguelov, D., Erhan, D., Szegedy, C., Reed, S., Fu, C.-Y., Berg, A.C.: SSD: single shot multibox detector. In: Leibe, B., Matas, J., Sebe, N., Welling, M. (eds.) ECCV 2016. LNCS, vol. 9905, pp. 21–37. Springer, Cham (2016). https://doi.org/10.1007/978-3-319-46448-0_2
10. Lin, T., Goyal, P., Girshick, R., He, K., Dollar, P.: Focal loss for dense object detection. IEEE Trans. Pattern Anal. Mach. Intell. **42**(2), 318–327 (2020)
11. Tian, Z., Shen, C., Chen, H., He, T.: FCOS: fully convolutional one-stage object detection. In: Proceedings of IEEE/CVF International Conference on Computer Vision (2019)

12. Kong, T., et al.: FoveaBox: beyond anchor-based object detector (2019)
13. Jiang, B., et al.: Acquisition of localization confidence for accurate object detection (2018)
14. Wang, N., et al.: NAS-FCOS: fast neural architecture search for object detection. In: 2020 IEEE/CVF Conference on Computer Vision and Pattern Recognition (CVPR). IEEE (2020)
15. Dai, X., et al.: Dynamic head: Unifying object detection heads with attentions (2021)
16. Woo, S., Park, J., Lee, J.-Y., Kweon, I.S.: CBAM: convolutional block attention module. In: Ferrari, V., Hebert, M., Sminchisescu, C., Weiss, Y. (eds.) ECCV 2018. LNCS, vol. 11211, pp. 3–19. Springer, Cham (2018). https://doi.org/10.1007/978-3-030-01234-2_1
17. Huang, Z., Ke, W., Huang, D.: Improving object detection with inverted attention. arXiv:1903.12255 (2019)
18. Feng, C., et al.: TOOD: task-aligned one-stage object detection (2021)
19. Li, X., et al.: Generalized focal loss: learning qualified and distributed bounding boxes for dense objectdetection. arXiv preprint arXiv:2006.04388 (2020)
20. Cao, Y., Chen, K., Loy, C.C., Lin, D.: Prime sample attention in object detection. arXivpreprint arXiv:1904.04821 (2019)

MSDNet: Multi-scale Dense Networks for Salient Object Detection

Hui Zhang$^{(\boxtimes)}$, Xiao Zhao, Chen Yang, Yuechen Li, and Ruonan Wang

Shaanxi University of Science and Technology, Xi'an, China
201612040@sust.edu.cn

Abstract. Since the fully convolutional networks was proposed, it has made great progress in the salient object detection. However, this kind of network structure still has obvious problems of incomplete salient objects segmentation and redundant information. Therefore, this paper propose a novel network model named Multi-scale Dense Network (MSDNet) to solve the above problems. First, we designed a multi-receptive enhancement and supplementation module(MRES), which increases the discriminability of features through feature interaction under different receptive fields. Second, we design a network framework MSDNet that first uses dense feature interactions and a pyramid-shaped feature fusion structure to get enhanced features and better features fusion. Experimental results on five benchmark datasets demonstrate the proposed method against 11 state-of-the-art approaches, it can effectively improve the completeness of salient objects and suppress background information.

Keywords: Salient object detection · Multi-scales feature fusion · Fully convolutional network

1 Introduction

Salient object detection(SOD), which can simulate the attention mechanism of human vision to quickly detect the most attractive object from an image, which is called a salient object. At present, salient object detection algorithms have been applied to various tasks, such as object tracking, image retrieval and semantic segmentation [11]. Compared with other tasks in computer vision, the history of salient object detection is relatively short. Traditional models mainly rely on low-level features and are inspired by priors such as color contrast and background. Since 2015, with the continuous development of deep learning theory, various deep learning network models have been proposed one after another. Since these network models have a sufficiently deep network length, they can extract rich image details and deep semantic information. After that, the fully convolutional network(FCN) [11] became a more mainstream SOD architecture.

U-Net [16] is a classic network based on FCN which is divided into a top-down feature extraction process and a bottom-up feature recovery process. The feature extraction process is composed of a series of convolution operations and down-sampling operations. During this process, the receptive field of the feature map is

S. Yu et al. (Eds.): PRCV 2022, LNCS 13537, pp. 315–324, 2022.
https://doi.org/10.1007/978-3-031-18916-6_26

getting larger, and the feature size is getting smaller. Low-level features tend to have smaller receptive fields and more local detail information, and high-level features tend to have larger receptive fields and more global semantic information. For low-level features or features with small receptive fields, we need their rich detailed information to help us get a prediction map with clear boundary and local information. However, due to the lack of high-level semantic information, the distinction between salient objects and non-salient objects is weak, and it often transmits some information of non-salient objects, resulting in inaccurate final prediction results. Therefore, We want to design an effective multi-scale feature extraction method and a multi-layer feature interaction fusion structure to solve this problems. The main contribution of this paper can be concluded as follows:

We propoed MRES module can increase the interaction between different receptive field features and make the feature map more discriminative, then we design a dence feature interaction and a pyramid-shaped feature fusion structure get enhanced features and suppress background information.

2   Related Work

In order to overcome the shortcomings of insufficient semantic information of low-level features of FCN network and insufficient combination of global and local information, the direction of improvement mainly on deep semantic information enhancement and the combination of global and local features.

Liu [9] et al. proposed the PoolNet algorithm and designed a feature integration module FAM, which made full use of the pooling function to fuse the obtained high-level semantic features with the up-sampled features. Ma [13] et al. proposed a pyramid shrinkage decoding network structure PSD, which defines adjacent feature maps as similar feature maps and non-adjacent feature maps as mutually independent feature maps. Luo [12] et al. proposed that the NLDF network extracts and enhances local features from feature maps of different scales, obtains global features through pooling operations, then uses up-pooling to fully fuse global and local features. Feng [5] et al. proposed that the global perception module GPM can effectively utilize both global and local features by considering the neighbors of local pixels.

3   Proposed Method

In this paper, we propose an multi-scale dense network which use a multi-receptive enhancement and supplementation module and use dense feature interactions and an inverted pyramid-shaped feature fusion structure to deal with the incomplete sailent object segmentation and reduce redundant information. The overall network structure is shown in Fig. 1.

3.1   Network Overview

Our model uses ResNet-50 [6] as the backbone network. The specific execution process is: input a picture of size $H \times W$ to the network, and extract the 5-layer

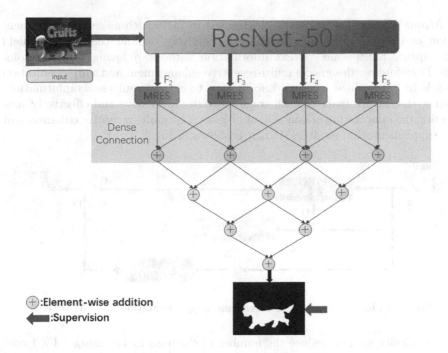

Fig. 1. MSDNet: multi-scale dense networks

feature map through ResNet-50, which are marked as $\{F_i \mid i = 1, 2, 3, 4, 5\}$. Since the feature maps in the first stage will greatly increase the computational cost, but only have a limited effect. So we only utilize the feature maps of the last four layers. Then, the feature maps of each layer are sent to the MRES module to obtain feature maps with effectively enhanced semantic information. The output of the MRES module is sent to the dense feature interaction and fusion structure to fully integrate and supplement high-level features and low-level features, and finally get prediction map.

3.2 Multi-receptive Enhancement and Supplementation Module

As we know, the larger the receptive field of a neuron, the larger the range of pictures it can touch, which means that it can contain more global and semantic-level features, and the smaller receptive field included more local and detailed information. In the backbone network, the size of the receptive field of each layer is limited in the process of feature extraction, so the features of each stage may have insufficient semantic information, which makes it difficult to make a correct judgment on whether a pixel at a certain position belongs to a salient object.

Atrous convolution has been widely used in tasks such as semantic segmentation and object detection, which can effectively expand the receptive field and capture multi-scale context information without reducing spatial resolution. Therefore, we designed a multi-receptive enhancement and supplementation module to fully utilize semantic information to extract multi-scale information, making the feature maps of each stage more discriminative and effectively suppressing the information of non-salient objects. The multi-receptive enhancement and supplementation module(MRES) is shown in Fig. 2.

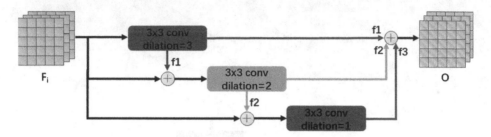

Fig. 2. Multi-receptive enhancement and supplementation module(MRES)

Specifically, we first reduce the number of channels to 128 using a 1×1 convolution on the input feature map. We apply the module to the feature maps of the last four stages. For the feature map $\{F_i \mid i = 2, 3, 4\}$, we use three atrous convolutions with dilation rates of 1, 2, and 3. For F_5, the three atrous convolutions with dilation ratios of 1, 3, and 5 are used. We put the output by 1×1 convolution first through the atrous convolution with the largest dilation rate. After its output is added to the original feature map, it goes through the atrous convolution with the second largest dilation rate. The output is then repeated added to the original feature map, then it goes through the atrous convolution with the minimum dilation rate, finally add the three outputs. The MRES can be formulized as:

$$f1 = Relu(bn(conv_{3 \times 3 - 3})(F_i)) \tag{1}$$

$$f2 = Relu(bn(conv_{3 \times 3 - 2})(F_i \oplus f1)) \tag{2}$$

$$f3 = Relu(bn(conv_{3 \times 3 - 1})(F_i \oplus f2)) \tag{3}$$

$$O = f1 \oplus f1 \oplus f2 \oplus f3 \tag{4}$$

where F_i denote the input feature of MRES, $conv_{3 \times 3 - 3}$ represent 3×3 convolution with dilation rate of 3, $\oplus$ denote the add operation, O is the output feature of MRES.

The advantage of MRES is that when extracting information at a smaller scale, the higher-level semantic information extracted at a large scale can be fully utilized, which is conducive to extracting more discriminative information at the current scale and generating more accurate and complete saliency objects.

3.3 Dense Connection and Pyramid-Shaped Feature Fusion Structure

After obtaining the feature maps enhanced by multi-scale information, we want to continue to exploit the relationship between feature maps of adjacent stages. The feature maps on the left side of the current feature map tend to have richer detailed information such as textures, borders, and the feature maps on the right have richer semantic information, the adjacent feature maps are more similar, and their combination can better extract common features, suppress non-sailent objects information. We proposed a relatively simple structure and a simple featrue fusion method, which uses the characteristics of higher similarity of adjacent features and can effectively avoid the downward transmission of information of non-salient objects and effectively enhance the representation ability of features. It can be seen in Fig. 1.

First, we use a series of dense connections to further optimize the feature of each layer. We just fuse each layer's feature map with its adjacent feature map using a simple add operation. Then to get the final saliency map, we need to fuse the four features to one feature. We adopt a pyramid-shaped feature fusion mechanism, which use add operation to fuse two adjacent features to one feature layer by layer. This structure can effectively use all features information to get more complete salient object.

4 Experiment

4.1 Implementation

We use DUTS-TR [18] as our training set and augment the data with flipping, cropping, etc. The training environment of our algorithm is PyTorch1.5.0 with cuda 10.2 and NVIDIA RTX 2080Ti with 11G memory. The parameters of the backbone ResNet-50 are pre-trained on the ImageNet dataset. The algorithm is trained for 50 epochs and the batch size is 16. The momentum is set to 0.9 and weight decay is set to 5e-4. The learning rate is set to 0.018.

4.2 Datasets and Evaluation Metrics

We use five widely used datasets as test datasets, namely ECSSD [17], PASCAL-S [8], DUT-OMRON [23], HKUIS [7] and DUTS [18].

ECSSD contains 1000 test images, most of which are natural images with complex scenes. PASCAL-S is a dataset for salient object detection consisting of a set of 850 images with multiple salient objects in the scene. DUT-OMRON is composed of 5,168 high-quality images manually selected from over 140,000 images which have one or more salient objects and relatively complex backgrounds. HKUIS dataset contains 4447 original images and corresponding ground truth images. DUTS contains 10,553 training images and 5,019 testing images. Both training and test sets contain very challenging saliency detection scenarios.

We use four metrics to evaluate our method, namely Mean F-measure (mF), mean absolute error (MAE) [1], S-measure [3] and E-measure [4].

After the binarized saliency prediction map is obtained, Precision and Recall can be calculated between the prediction map and the ground truth map. Mean F-measure is based on Precision or Recall cannot comprehensively evaluate the saliency images output by our model, so F-measure is proposed to obtain the weighted harmonic average of Precision and Recall. The F-measure is then calculated as follows.

$$F_\beta = \frac{\left(1 + \beta^2\right) \times Precision \times Recall}{\beta^2 \times Precision \times Recall} \tag{5}$$

β is set to 0.3. MAE is the average of the absolute error between the predicted map and the corresponding ground-truth.The MAE is calculated as follows.

$$MAE = \frac{1}{H \times W} \sum_{i=1}^{H} \sum_{j=1}^{W} |P(i,j) - G(i,j)| \tag{6}$$

H and W represent the height and width of the picture. $P(i,j), G(i,j)$ represent the pixel values of the predicted map and ground truth map at position (i,j), respectively.

The S-measure is widely used to measure the structural similarity between the ground truth and the predicted map. The E-measure is a widely used new metric that combines local pixel values with image-level averages to jointly capture image-level statistics and local pixel matching information.

4.3   Comparison with State-of-the-Arts

In this part, We compared ours proposed method with 11 state-of-the-arts which is strongly supervised, including R3Net [2], PICA-Net [10], PAGE [19], EG-Net [24], BASNet [15], PoolNet [9], CPD [22] F3Net [20], MINet [14], LDF [21] and CTD [25]. These methods have achieved good results in the task of salient object detection, and they also focus on how to effectively extract and fuse different features.

Quantitative Comparison. The comparision between the proposed MSDNet and other methods on mF, MAE, S-measure, and E-measure is shown in Table 1. It can been seen our proposed method can get better results in DUT-OMRON, HKU-IS and DUTS. Most metrics on the other two datasets are also higher than the other methods. This is due to the fact that our method can make full use of semantic information and better feature fusion structure.

Table 1. Quantitative comparison of our method with 11 state-of-the-arts over five widely used datasets. The higher mF, Smeasure, E-measure, and the lower MAE are better, the best results are bolded.

Model	Datasets																			
	ECSSD				PASCAL-S				DUT-OMRON				HKU-IS				DUTS			
	mF	MAE	S_β	E_ϵ	mF	MAE	S_β	E_ϵ	mF	MAE	S_β	E_ϵ	mF	MAE	S_β	E_ϵ	mF	MAE	S_β	E_ϵ
R3Net [2]	.916	.040	.913	.929	.795	.102	.802	.837	.751	.060	.813	.850	.890	.033	.890	.935	.790	.055	.836	.880
PICA-Net [10]	.857	.053	.894	.915	.785	.083	.835	.830	.710	.062	.832	.833	.872	.040	.905	.936	.744	.053	.874	.856
PAGE [19]	.910	.040	.915	.921	.810	.073	.836	.845	.735	.067	.825	.856	.880	.038	.910	.938	.779	.048	.857	.871
EG-Net [24]	.922	.040	.916	.926	.815	.077	**.855**	.846	.758	.054	.844	.865	.895	.033	.920	.946	.816	.040	.878	.886
BASNet [15]	.883	.038	.913	.924	.774	.078	.833	.847	.754	.058	.840	.867	.894	.033	.907	.943	.790	.045	.868	.870
PooLNet [9]	.920	.039	.923	.922	.820	.077	.846	.853	.748	.057	.836	.860	.897	.030	.918	.945	.810	.038	.887	.886
CPD [22]	.918	.038	.916	.924	.822	.074	.845	.847	.745	.057	.827	.865	.889	.033	.903	.946	.807	.044	.865	.888
F3Net [20]	.926	.038	.920	.925	.825	.074	.845	.850	.750	.055	.825	.867	.892	.035	.906	.946	.806	.045	.870	.884
MINet [14]	.925	.039	**.924**	.929	.844	.065	.848	.855	.756	.056	.835	.866	.907	.029	.918	.953	.828	.038	.885	.899
LDF [21]	.928	**.033**	.911	.924	.846	.067	.840	.853	.777	.053	.830	.871	.916	.030	.900	.920	.855	.036	.886	.903
CTD [25]	.926	.034	.915	.926	.845	.062	.845	.858	.783	.054	.830	**.875**	.918	.030	.915	.954	.882	**.034**	.887	.910
Ours	**.945**	.037	.917	**.931**	**.874**	**.060**	.849	**.860**	**.822**	.050	**.850**	**.875**	**.939**	**.029**	**.919**	**.956**	**.895**	.034	**.890**	**.911**

Visual Comparison. In order to better prove the superiority of ours proposed method and qualitatively analyse the performance of the model, we show some visualization results, as shown in Fig. 3. We selected some test images with relatively complex environments from different test datasets, Image and GT denote the original image and ground truth, respectively. Ours represent the performance of our proposed method, the other columns is the performance of other methods. From a visualization point of view, our method can generate salient objects more completely than other methods, such as the first three rows. From the last three rows it can be seen that our method can perform better segmentation on some low-contrast images.

4.4 Ablation Studies

In this part, we investigate the effctiveness of our proposed multi-receptive enhancement and supplementation module. All experiments are conducted on DUTS-TE, PASCAL-S and HKUIS datasets.

Multi-receptive Enhancement and Supplementation Module. We trained two models to verify the validity of the MRES module, one with the MRES module($\checkmark$) and one without($\times$), and the other configuration parameters of the model are the same. The experimental results is shown in Table 2. It can be seen from the table that after adding the MRES module, the indicators of each data set are improved. This shows that while expanding the receptive field, increasing the connection between different receptive field feature maps can effectively improve the performance of the model. With the help of the MRES module, the model is able to generate a more complete saliency map.

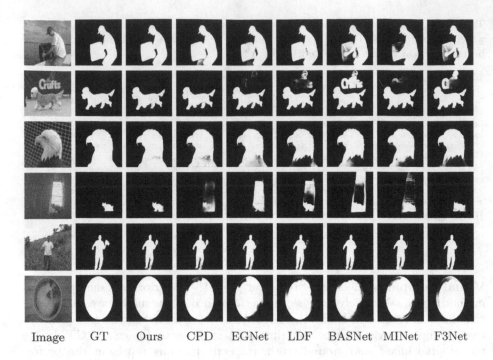

Image   GT   Ours   CPD   EGNet   LDF   BASNet   MINet   F3Net

Fig. 3. Visualization of comparative results. It can be seen that our method can accurately locates the salient objects and generates more completely saliency map.

Table 2. Performance comparison on DUTS, ECSSD, and HKUIS dataset.

	MRES	mF	MAE	S_β	E_ϵ
DUTS	×	.884	.038	.882	.898
	✓	**.895**	**.034**	**.890**	**.911**
ECSSD	×	.938	.040	.913	.922
	✓	**.945**	**.037**	**.917**	**.931**
HKUIS	×	.930	.033	.911	.950
	✓	**.939**	**.029**	**.919**	**.956**

5   Conclusion

In this paper, we propose a novel salient object detection model MSDNet. The MRES module can increase the interaction between different receptive field features and make the feature map more discriminative. Densely connected and pyramid-shaped feature fusion structure get enhanced features and suppress background information. Ablation analysis confirms the effectiveness of the proposed module. Experimental results on five datasets demonstrate the proposed method is more effective than the 11 state-of-the-arts.

References

1. Borji, A., Cheng, M.-M., Jiang, H., Li, J.: Salient object detection: a benchmark. IEEE Trans. Image Process. **24**(12), 5706–5722 (2015)
2. Deng, Z., et al.: R3net: recurrent residual refinement network for saliency detection. In: Proceedings of the 27th International Joint Conference on Artificial Intelligence, pp. 684–690. AAAI Press, Menlo Park (2018)
3. Fan, D.P., Cheng, M.M., Liu, Y., Li, T., Borji, A.: Structure-measure: a new way to evaluate foreground maps. In: Proceedings of the IEEE International Conference on Computer Vision, pp. 4548–4557 (2017)
4. Fan, D.P., Gong, C., Cao, Y., Ren, B., Cheng, M.M., Borji, A.: Enhanced-alignment measure for binary foreground map evaluation. arXiv preprint arXiv:1805.10421 (2018)
5. Feng, M., Lu, H., Ding, E.: Attentive feedback network for boundary-aware salient object detection. In Proceedings of the IEEE/CVF Conference on Computer Vision and Pattern Recognition, pp. 1623–1632 (2019)
6. He, K., Zhang, X., Ren, S., Sun, J.: Deep residual learning for image recognition. In: Proceedings of the IEEE Conference on Computer Vision and Pattern Recognition, pp. 770–778 (2016)
7. Li, G., Yu, Y.: Visual saliency based on multiscale deep features. In: Proceedings of the IEEE Conference on Computer Vision and Pattern Recognition, pp. 5455–5463 (2015)
8. Li, Y., Hou, X., Koch, C., Rehg, J.M., Yuille, A.L.: The secrets of salient object segmentation. In: Proceedings of the IEEE Conference on Computer Vision and Pattern Recognition, pp. 280–287 (2014)
9. Liu, J.J., Hou, Q., Cheng, M.M., Feng, J., Jiang, J.: A simple pooling-based design for real-time salient object detection. In: Proceedings of the IEEE/CVF Conference on Computer Vision and Pattern Recognition, pp. 3917–3926 (2019)
10. Liu, N., Han, J., Yang, M.H.: Picanet: learning pixel-wise contextual attention for saliency detection. In: Proceedings of the IEEE Conference on Computer Vision and Pattern Recognition, pp. 3089–3098 (2018)
11. Long, J., Shelhamer, E., Darrell, T.: Fully convolutional networks for semantic segmentation. In: Proceedings of the IEEE Conference on Computer Vision and Pattern Recognition, pp. 3431–3440 (2015)
12. Luo, Z., Mishra, A., Achkar, A., Eichel, J., Li, S., Jodoin, P.M.: Non-local deep features for salient object detection. In Proceedings of the IEEE Conference on Computer Vision and Pattern Recognition, pp. 6609–6617 (2017)
13. Ma, M., Xia, C., Li, J.: Pyramidal feature shrinking for salient object detection (2021)
14. Pang, Y., Zhao, X., Zhang, L., Lu, H.: Multi-scale interactive network for salient object detection. In: Proceedings of the IEEE/CVF Conference on Computer Vision and Pattern Recognition, pp. 9413–9422 (2020)
15. Qin, X., Zhang, Z., Huang, C., Gao, C., Dehghan, M., Jagersand, M.: Basnet: boundary-aware salient object detection. In: Proceedings of the IEEE/CVF Conference on Computer Vision and Pattern Recognition, pp. 7479–7489 (2019)
16. Ronneberger, O., Fischer, P., Brox, T.: U-Net: convolutional networks for biomedical image segmentation. In: Navab, N., Hornegger, J., Wells, W.M., Frangi, A.F. (eds.) MICCAI 2015. LNCS, vol. 9351, pp. 234–241. Springer, Cham (2015). https://doi.org/10.1007/978-3-319-24574-4_28

17. Shi, J., Yan, Q., Li, X., Jia, J.: Hierarchical image saliency detection on extended CSSD. IEEE Trans. Pattern Anal. Mach. Intell. **38**(4), 717–729 (2015)
18. Wang, L., et al.: Learning to detect salient objects with image-level supervision. In: Proceedings of the IEEE Conference on Computer Vision and Pattern Recognition, pp. 136–145 (2017)
19. Wang, W., Zhao, S., Shen, J., Hoi, S.C.H., Borji, A.: Salient object detection with pyramid attention and salient edges. In: Proceedings of the IEEE/CVF Conference on Computer Vision and Pattern Recognition, pp. 1448–1457 (2019)
20. Wei, J., Wang, S., Huang, Q.: F^{3}net: fusion, feedback and focus for salient object detection. In: Proceedings of the AAAI Conference on Artificial Intelligence, vol. 34, pp. 12321–12328 (2020)
21. Wei, J., Wang, S., Wu, Z., Su, C., Huang, Q., Tian, Q.: Label decoupling framework for salient object detection. In: Proceedings of the IEEE/CVF Conference on Computer Vision and Pattern Recognition, pp. 13025–13034 (2020)
22. Wu, Z., Su, L., Huang, Q.: Cascaded partial decoder for fast and accurate salient object detection. In: Proceedings of the IEEE/CVF Conference on Computer Vision and Pattern Recognition, pp. 3907–3916 (2019)
23. Yang, C., Zhang, L., Lu, H., Ruan, X., Yang, M-H.: Saliency detection via graph-based manifold ranking. In: Proceedings of the IEEE Conference on Computer Vision and Pattern Recognition, pp. 3166–3173 (2013)
24. Zhao, J.-X., Liu, J.-J., Fan, D.-P., Cao, Y., Yang, J., Cheng, M.-M.: Egnet: edge guidance network for salient object detection. In: Proceedings of the IEEE/CVF International Conference on Computer Vision, pp. 8779–8788 (2019)
25. Zhao, Z., Xia, C., Xie, C., Li, J.: Complementary trilateral decoder for fast and accurate salient object detection. In: Proceedings of the 29th ACM International Conference on Multimedia, pp. 4967–4975 (2021)

WaveSNet: Wavelet Integrated Deep Networks for Image Segmentation

Qiufu Li[1,2,3] (ID) and Linlin Shen[1,2,3](✉) (ID)

[1] CVI, College of Computer Science and Software Engineering, Shenzhen University, Shenzhen, China
{liqiufu, llshen}@szu.edu.cn
[2] Shenzhen Institute of Artificial Intelligence and Robotics for Society, Shenzhen, China
[3] Guangdong Key Laboratory of Intelligent Information Processing, Shenzhen University, Shenzhen 518060, China

Abstract. In deep networks, the lost data details significantly degrade the performances of image segmentation. In this paper, we propose to apply Discrete Wavelet Transform (DWT) to extract the data details during feature map downsampling, and adopt Inverse DWT (IDWT) with the extracted details during the up-sampling to recover the details. On the popular image segmentation networks, U-Net, SegNet, and DeepLabV3+, we design wavelet integrated deep networks for image segmentation (WaveSNets). Due to the effectiveness of the DWT/IDWT in processing data details, experimental results on CamVid, Pascal VOC, and Cityscapes show that our WaveSNets achieve better segmentation performances than their vanilla versions.

Keywords: Deep network · Wavelet transform · Image segmentation

1 Introduction

Due to the advantage of deep network in extracting high-level features, deep learning has achieved high performances in various tasks, particular in the computer vision. However, the current deep networks are not good at extracting and processing data details. While deep networks with more layers are able to fit more functions, the deeper networks are not always associated with better performances [11]. An important reason is that the details will be lost as the data flow through the layers. In particular, the lost data details significantly degrade the performacnes of the deep networks for the image segmentation. Various techniques, such as condition random field, àtrous convolution [3,4], PointRend [12], are introduced into the deep networks to improve the segmentation performance. However, these techniques do not explicitly process the data details.

Wavelets [6,15], well known as "mathematical microscope", are effective time-frequency analysis tools, which could be applied to decompose an image into the low-frequency component containing the image main information and the high-frequency components containing the details. In this paper, we rewrite Discrete Wavelet Transform (DWT) and Inverse DWT (IDWT) as the general network layers, which are applicable to various wavelets. One can flexibly design end-to-end architectures using them, and

S. Yu et al. (Eds.): PRCV 2022, LNCS 13537, pp. 325–337, 2022.
https://doi.org/10.1007/978-3-031-18916-6_27

directly process the data details in the deep networks. We design wavelet integrated deep networks for image segmentation, termed WaveSNets, by replacing the down-sampling with DWT and the up-sampling with IDWT in the U-Net [18], SegNet [1], and DeepLabv3+ [4]. When Haar, Cohen, and Daubechies wavelets are used, we evaluate WaveSNets using dataset CamVid [2], Pascal VOC [8], and Cityscapes [5]. The experimental results show that WaveSNets achieve better performances in semantic image segmentation than their vanilla versions, due to the effective segmentation for the fine and similar objects. In summary:

- We rewrite DWT and IDWT as general network layers, which are applicable to various wavelets and can be applied to design end-to-end deep networks for processing the data details during the network inference;
- We design WaveSNets using various network architectures, by replacing the down-sampling with DWT layer and up-sampling with IDWT layer;
- WaveSNets are evaluated on the dataset of CamVid, Pascal VOC, Cityscapes, and achieve better performance for semantic image segmentation.

2   Related Works

2.1   Sampling Operation

Down-sampling operations, such as max-pooling and strided-convolution, are used in the deep networks for local connectivity and weight sharing. These down-sampling operations usually ignore the classic sampling theorem [16], which result in aliasing among the data components in different frequency intervals. As a result, the data details presented by its high-frequency components are totally lost, and random noises showing up in the same components could be sampled into the low resolution data. In addition, the object basic structures presented by the low-frequency component will be broken. Anti-aliased CNNs [22] and WaveCNets [13] integrate the low-pass filtering with the down-sampling in the deep networks, which achieve increased classification accuracy and better noise-robustness. While these works extract robust features from the data's low-frequency component, they exclude the useful details contained in the high-frequency components.

Up-sampling operations, such as max-unpooling [1], deconvolution [18], and bilinear interpolation [3,4], are widely used in the deep networks for image-to-image translation tasks. These up-sampling operations are usually applied to gradually recover the data resolution, while the data details can not be recovered from them. The lost data details would significantly degrade the network performance for the image-to-image tasks, such as the image segmentation. Various techniques, including àtrous convolution [3,4], PointRend [12], etc., are introduced into the design of deep networks to capture the fine details for performance improvement of image segmentation. However, these techniques try to recover the data details from the detail-unrelated information.

2.2   Wavelet

Wavelets are powerful time-frequency analysis tools, which have been widely used in signal analysis, image processing, and pattern recognition. A wavelet is usually associated with scaling function and wavelet functions. The shifts and expansions of these functions compose stable basis for the signal space, with which the signal can be decomposed and reconstructed. The functions are closely related to the low-pass and high-pass filters of the wavelet. In practice, these filters are applied for the data decomposition and reconstruction. 2D Discrete Wavelet Transform (DWT) decompose the image into its low-frequency component and three high-frequency components. While the low-frequency component is a low resolution version of the image, keeping its main information, the high-frequency components save the original image's horizontal, vertical, and diagonal details, respectively. 2D Inverse DWT (IDWT) could reconstruct the image using the DWT output.

In the deep learning, while wavelets are widely applied as data preprocessing or postprocessing tools, wavelet transforms are also introduced into the design of deep networks by taking them as substitutes of sampling operations. Multi-level Wavelet CNN (MWCNN) [14] integrates Wavelet Package Transform (WPT) into the deep network for image restoration. MWCNN concatenates the low-frequency and high-frequency components of the input feature map, and processes them in a unified way. Convolutional-Wavelet Neural Network (CWNN) [7] applies the redundant dual-tree complex wavelet transform (DT-CWT) to suppress the noise and keep the object structures for extracting robust features from SAR images. Wavelet pooling proposed in [20] is designed using a two-level DWT. Its back-propagation performs a one-level DWT with a two-level IDWT, which does not follow the mathematical principle of gradient. Recently, the application of wavelet transform in image style transfer [21] is studied. In these works, the authors evaluate their methods using only one or two wavelets, because of the absence of the general wavelet transform layers; the data details presented by the high-frequency components are abandoned or processed together with the low-frequency component, which limits the detail restoration in the image-to-image translation tasks.

3   Our Method

Our method is to replace the sampling operations in the deep networks with wavelet transforms. We firstly introduce 2D Discrete Wavelet Transform (DWT) and Inverse DWT (IDWT).

3.1   Discrete Wavelet Transform

For a given 2D data $X \in \mathbb{R}^{m \times n}$, 2D DWT decomposes it into four components,

$$X_{c_0 c_1} = (\downarrow 2)(f_{c_0 c_1} * X), \quad c_0, c_1 \in \{l, h\}, \tag{1}$$

where f_{ll} is the low-pass filter and f_{lh}, f_{hl}, f_{hh} are the high-pass filters of the 2D orthogonal wavelet. X_{ll} is the low-frequency component of the original data, which is a low-resolution version containing the data main information; X_{lh}, X_{hl}, X_{hh} are three high-frequency components, which store the vertical, horizontal, and diagonal details of the data. 2D IDWT reconstruct the original data from these components,

$$X = \sum_{c_0, c_1 \in \{l, h\}} f_{c_0 c_1} * (\uparrow 2) X_{c_0 c_1}. \tag{2}$$

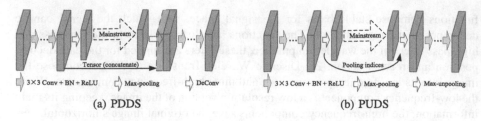

(a) PDDS   (b) PUDS

Fig. 1. The dual structures used in U-Net and SegNet.

The size of every component is $1/2$ size of the original 2D data in terms of the two dimensional direction, i.e.,

$$X_{c_0 c_1} \in \mathbb{R}^{\lfloor \frac{m}{2} \rfloor \times \lfloor \frac{n}{2} \rfloor}, \quad c_0, c_1 \in \{l, h\}. \tag{3}$$

Therefore, m, n are usually even numbers.

Generally, the filters of high-dimensional wavelet are tensor products of the two filters of 1D wavelet. For 2D wavelet, the four filters could be designed from

$$\mathrm{f}_{c_0 c_1} = \mathrm{f}_{c_1} \otimes \mathrm{f}_{c_0}, \quad c_0, c_1 \in \{l, h\}, \tag{4}$$

where $\otimes$ is the tensor product operation. For example, the low-pass and high-pass filters of 1D Haar wavelet are

$$\mathrm{f}_l^{\mathrm{H}} = \frac{1}{\sqrt{2}}(1, 1)^T, \quad \mathrm{f}_h^{\mathrm{H}} = \frac{1}{\sqrt{2}}(1, -1)^T. \tag{5}$$

Then, the filters of the corresponding 2D Haar wavelet are

$$\mathrm{f}_{ll}^{\mathrm{H}} = \mathrm{f}_l^{\mathrm{H}} \otimes \mathrm{f}_l^{\mathrm{H}} = \frac{1}{2}\begin{bmatrix} 1 & 1 \\ 1 & 1 \end{bmatrix}, \qquad \mathrm{f}_{hl}^{\mathrm{H}} = \mathrm{f}_l^{\mathrm{H}} \otimes \mathrm{f}_h^{\mathrm{H}} = \frac{1}{2}\begin{bmatrix} 1 & -1 \\ 1 & -1 \end{bmatrix} \tag{6}$$

$$\mathrm{f}_{lh}^{\mathrm{H}} = \mathrm{f}_h^{\mathrm{H}} \otimes \mathrm{f}_l^{\mathrm{H}} = \frac{1}{2}\begin{bmatrix} 1 & 1 \\ -1 & -1 \end{bmatrix}, \qquad \mathrm{f}_{hh}^{\mathrm{H}} = \mathrm{f}_h^{\mathrm{H}} \otimes \mathrm{f}_h^{\mathrm{H}} = \frac{1}{2}\begin{bmatrix} 1 & -1 \\ -1 & 1 \end{bmatrix} \tag{7}$$

Equations (1) and (2) present the forward propagations for 2D DWT and IDWT. It is onerous to deduce the gradient for the backward propagations from these equations. Fortunately, the modern deep learning framework PyTorch [17] could automatically deduce the gradients for the common tensor operations. We have rewrote 2D DWT and IDWT as network layers in PyTorch. In the layers, we do DWT and IDWT channel by channel for multi-channel data.

3.2   WaveSNet

We design wavelet integrated deep networks for image segmentation (WaveSNets), by replacing the down-sampling operations with 2D DWT and the up-sampling operations with 2D IDWT. We take U-Net, SegNet, and DeepLabv3+ as the basic architectures.

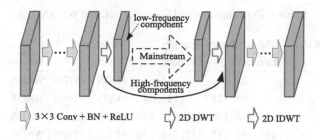

Fig. 2. The wavelet based dual structure (WADS).

WSegNets. SegNet and U-Net share a similar symmetrical encoder-decoder architecture, but differ in their sampling operations. We name the pair of connected down-sampling and up-sampling operations and the associated convolutional blocks as **dual structure**, where the convolutional blocks process the feature maps with the same size. Figure 1(a) and Fig. 1(b) show the dual structures used in U-Net and SegNet, which are named as PDDS (Pooling Deconvolution Dual Structure) and PUDS (Pooling-Unpooling Dual Structure), respectively. U-Net and SegNet consist of multiple nested dual structures. While they apply the max-pooling during their down-sampling, PDDS and PUDS use deconvolution and max-unpooling for the up-sampling, respectively. As Fig. 1(a) shows, PDDS copys and transmits the feature maps from encoder to decoder, concatenating them with the up-sampled features and extracting detailed information for the object boundaries restoration. However, the data tensor injected to the decoder might contain redundant information, which interferes with the segmentation results and introduces more convolutional paramters. PUDS transmits the pooling indices via the branch path for the upgrading of the feature map resolution in the decoder, while the lost data details can not be restored from the pooling indices.

To overcome the weaknesses of PDDS and PUDS, we adopt DWT for down-sampling and IDWT for up-sampling, and design WADS (WAvelet Dual Structure, Fig. 2). During its down-samping, WADS decomposes the feature map into low-frequency and high-requency components. Then, WADS injects the low-frequency component into the following layers in the deep networks to extract high-level features, and transmits the high-frequency components to the up-sampling layer for the recovering of the feature map resolution using IDWT. IDWT could also restore the data details from the high-frequency components during the up-sampling. We design wavelet integrated encoder-decoder networks using WADS, termed WSegNets, for imag segmentation.

Table 1 illustrates the configuration of WSegNets, together with that of U-Net and SegNet. In this paper, the U-Net consists of eight more convolutional layers than the original one [18]. In Table 1, the first column shows the input size, though these networks can process images with arbitrary size. Every number in the table corresponds to a convolutional layer followed by a Batch Normalization (BN) and Rectified Linear Unit (ReLU). While the number in the column "encoder" is the number of the input channels of the convolution, the number in the column "decoder" is the number of the output channels. The encoder of U-Net and SegNet consists of 13 convolutional layers

Table 1. Configurations of U-Net, SegNet, and WSegNet.

Data size	The number of channels		Networks		
	Encoder	Decoder	SegNet	U-Net	WSegNet
512×512	3, 64	64, 64	PUDS	PDDS	WADS
256×256	64, 128	128, 64	PUDS	PDDS	WADS
128×128	128, 256, 256	256, 256, 128	PUDS	PDDS	WADS
64×64	256, 512, 512	512, 512, 256	PUDS	PDDS	WADS
32×32	512, 512, 512	512, 512, 512	PUDS	PDDS	WADS

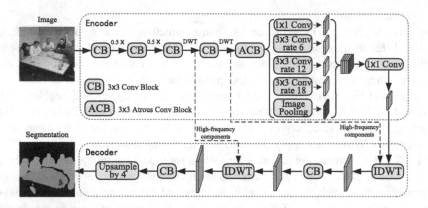

Fig. 3. WDeepLabv3+ structure.

corresponding to the first 13 layers in the VGG16bn [19]. A convolutional layer with kernel size of 1×1 converts the decoder output into the predicted segmentation result.

WDeepLabv3+.   DeepLabv3+ [4] employs an unbalanced encoder-decoder architecture. The encoder applys an àtrous convolutional version of CNN to alleviate the detailed information loss, and an Àtrous Spatial Pyramid Pooling (ASPP) to extract image multiscale representations. At the begin of the decoder, the encoder feature map is directly upsampled using a bilinear interpolation with factor of 4, and then concatenated with a low-level feature map transmitted from the encoder. DeepLabv3+ adopts a dual structure connecting its encoder and decoder, which differs with PDDS only on the up-sampling and suffers the same drawbacks.

We design WDeepLabv3+, a wavelet integrated version of DeepLabv3+, by applying two wavelet version of dual structures. As Fig. 3 shows, the encoder applys a wavelet integrated àtrous CNN followed by the ASPP, which output encoder feature map and two sets of high-frequency components. The encoder feature map is up-sampled by two IDWT, integrated with the detail information contained in the high-frequency components, while the two IDWT are connected with a convolutional block. The decoder then apply a few 3×3 convolutions to refine the feature map, followed by a bilinear interpolation to recover the resolution.

Table 2. WSegNet results on CamVid test set

	SegNet	U-Net	WSegNet									
			haar	ch2.2	ch3.3	ch4.4	ch5.5	db2	db3	db4	db5	db6
Sky	90.50	**91.52**	91.31	91.38	91.29	91.39	91.24	91.35	91.48	90.99	90.89	90.63
Building	77.80	**80.28**	79.90	79.27	78.82	79.37	78.65	79.48	79.60	78.52	78.58	77.84
Pole	9.14	27.97	27.99	**29.38**	27.90	28.96	27.26	27.91	28.38	28.04	26.66	25.96
Poad	92.69	93.71	93.69	93.47	93.47	93.77	93.78	93.72	**93.91**	92.57	92.12	92.11
Sidewalk	78.05	80.05	80.33	79.44	79.34	79.89	80.08	79.67	**80.58**	76.95	75.62	76.65
Tree	72.40	73.51	73.34	73.27	73.21	73.07	71.60	73.61	**73.68**	72.90	72.28	71.92
Symbol	37.61	43.07	44.44	42.68	40.42	43.57	42.33	**44.72**	44.01	41.06	41.72	39.69
Fence	19.92	27.50	**32.59**	24.62	25.59	28.40	28.85	25.52	29.60	26.90	24.15	29.00
Car	79.31	**85.04**	83.21	84.43	82.63	84.57	84.14	84.30	83.97	81.92	81.07	78.38
Walker	39.93	50.35	49.35	**50.98**	50.52	50.43	49.09	50.15	49.39	47.69	48.02	43.17
Bicyclist	39.48	44.45	50.38	47.94	48.69	47.93	**52.64**	51.15	47.73	46.08	43.53	38.96
mIoU	57.89	63.40	**64.23**	63.35	62.90	63.76	63.61	63.78	63.85	62.15	61.33	60.39
Global accuracy	91.04	92.19	92.08	92.04	91.98	92.10	91.73	92.06	**92.40**	91.60	91.30	91.14
Parameter ($\times 10^6$)	29.52	37.42	**29.52**									

4 Experiment

We evaluate the WaveSNets (WSegNet, WDeepLabv3+) on the image dataset of CamVid, Pascal VOC, and Cityscapes, in terms of mean intersection over union (mIoU).

4.1 WSegNet

CamVid. CamVid contains 701 road scene images (367, 101 and 233 for the training, validation and test respectively) with size of 360×480, which was used in [1] to quantify SegNet performance. Using the training set, we train SegNet, U-Net, and WSegNet when various wavelets are applied. The trainings are supervised by cross-entropy loss. We employ SGD solver, initial learning rate of 0.007 with "poly" policy and $power = 0.9$, momentum of 0.9 and weight decay of 0.0005. With a mini-batch size of 20, we train the networks 12 K iterations (about 654 epochs). The input image size is 352×480. For every image, we adopt random resizing between 0.75 and 2, random rotation between -20 and $20°$, random horizontal flipping and cropping with size of 352×480. We apply a pre-trained VGG16bn model for the encoder initialization and initialize the decoder using the technique proposed in [10]. We do not tune above hyper-parameters for a fair comparison.

Table 2 shows the mIoU and global accuracy on the CamVid test set, together with the parameter numbers of U-Net, SegNet, and WSegNet with various wavelets. In the table, "dbx" represents orthogonal Daubechies wavelet with approximation order x, and "chx.y" represents biorthogonal Cohen wavelet with approximation orders (x, y). Their low-pass and high-pass filters can be found in [6]. The length of these filters increase as the order increases. While Haar and Cohen wavelets are symmetric, Daubechies are not. The mIoU of WSegNet decreases from 63.78 % to 60.39 % as asymmetric wavelet

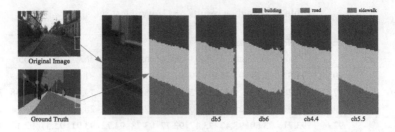

Fig. 4. Boundary comparison for images segmented by WSegNet with different wavelets.

varies from "db2" to "db6", while it varies from 63.35 % to 63.61 % as symmetric wavelet varies from "ch2.2" to "ch5.5". It seems that the performances among different asymmetric wavelets are much diverse than that among various symmetric wavelets. In the wavelet integrated deep networks, we truncate the DWT output to make them to be 1/2 size of input data. As a result, IDWT with asymmetric wavelet can not fully restore an image in the region near the image boundary, and the region width increases as the wavelet filter length increases. With symmetric wavelet, however, one can fully restore the image based on symmetric extension of the DWT output. Consequently, WSegNet with Cohen wavelets performs better than that with Daubechies ones near the image boundary. Figure 4 shows an example image, its manual annotation, a region consisting of "building", "road" and "sidewalk" and the segmentation results achieved using different wavelets. The region is located close to the image boundary and has been enlarged with colored segmentation results for better illustration. One can observe from the results of "db5" and "db6" that a long line of "sidewalk" pixels, located near the image boundary, are classified as "road". In comparison, the results of "ch4.4" and "ch5.5" match well with the ground truth.

In [1], the authors train the SegNet using an extended CamVid training set containing 3433 images, which achieved 60.10 % mIoU on the CamVid test set. We train SegNet, U-Net and WSegNet using only 367 CamVid training images. From Table 2, one can find WSegNet achieves the best mIoU (64.23 %) using Haar wavelet, and the best global accuracy (92.40 %) using "db3" wavelet. WSegNet is significantly superior to SegNet in terms of mIoU and the global accuracy, while they require the same amount of parameters (29.52×10^6). The segmentation performance of WSegNet is also better than that of U-Net, while it requires much less parameters than U-Net (37.42×10^6).

Table 2 also lists the IoUs for the 11 categories in the CamVid. Compared with U-Net and WSegNet, SegNet performs very poor on the fine objects, such as "pole", "symbol", and "fence", as that the max-pooling indices used in SegNet are not helpful for restoring the image details. While U-Net achieves comparable or even better IoUs on the easily identifiable objects, such as the "sky", "building", and "car", it does not discriminate well similar objects like"walker" and "bicyclist", or "building" and "fence". The feature maps of these two pairs of objects might look similar to the decoder of U-Net, as the data details are not separately provided. Table 3 shows the confusion matrices on these four categories. The proportion of "building" in the predicted "fence" decreases from 34.11 % to 30.16 %, as the network varies from SegNet to WPUNet, while that of "bicyclist" in the predicted "walker" decreases from 2.54 % to 1.90 %.

Table 3. Confusion matrices for the CamVid test set.

	SegNet		U-Net		WSegNet(haar)	
	Building	Fence	Building	Fence	Building	Fence
Building	88.01	1.30	89.91	1.19	90.22	1.08
Fence	34.11	29.12	30.64	40.16	30.16	44.65
	Walker	Bicyclist	Walker	Bicyclist	Walker	Bicyclist
Walker	53.30	2.54	66.83	1.95	68.74	1.90
Bicyclist	13.69	49.66	16.73	51.45	12.52	59.80

These results suggest that WSegNet is more powerful than SegNet and U-Net in distinguishing similar objects.

Pascal VOC and Cityscapes. The original Pascal VOC2012 semantic segmentation dataset contains 1464 and 1449 annotated images for training and validation, respectively, and contains 20 object categories and one background class. The images are with various sizes. We augment the training data to 10582 by extra annotations provided in [9]. We train SegNet, U-Net, and WSegNet with various wavelets on the extended training set 50 epochs with batch size of 16. During the training, we adopt random horizontal flipping, random Gaussian blurring, and cropping with size of 512×512. The other hyper-parameters are the same with that used in CamVid training. Table 4 presents the results on the validation set for the trained networks.

Cityscapes contains 2975 and 500 high quality annotated images for the training and validation, respectively. The images are with size of 1024×2048. We train the networks on the training set 80 epochs with batch size of 8 and initial learning rate of 0.01. During the training, we adopt random horizontal flipping, random resizing between 0.5 and 2, and random cropping with size of 768×768. Table 4 presents the results on the validation set.

From Tabel 4, one can find the segmentation performance of SegNet is significant inferior to that of U-Net and WSegNet. While WSegNet achieves better mIoU (63.95 % for Pascal VOC and 70.63 % for Cityscapes) and requires less parameters (29.52×10^6), the global accuracies of WSegNet on the two dataset are a little lower than that of U-Net. This result suggest that, compared with U-Net, WSegNet could more precisely classify the pixels at the "critical" locations.

Table 4. WSegNet results on Pascal VOC and Cityscapes *val* set.

		SegNet	U-Net	WSegNet					
				haar	ch2.2	ch3.3	ch4.4	ch5.5	db2
Pascal VOC	mIoU	61.33	63.64	**63.95**	63.50	63.46	63.48	63.62	63.48
	Global accuracy	90.14	**90.82**	90.79	90.72	90.72	90.73	90.76	90.75
Cityscapes	mIoU	65.75	70.05	70.09	69.86	69.73	70.13	**70.63**	70.37
	Global accuracy	94.65	**95.21**	95.20	95.18	95.09	95.17	95.15	95.20
Parameters ($\times 10^6$)		29.52	37.42	**29.52**					

Table 5. WDeepLabv3+ results on Pascal VOC *val* set.

	DeepLabv3+	WDeepLabv3+					
		haar	ch2.2	ch3.3	ch4.4	ch5.5	db2
Background	93.83	93.82	93.85	**93.94**	93.91	93.86	93.87
Aeroplane	92.29	93.14	92.50	91.56	**93.21**	92.73	92.41
Bike	41.42	43.08	42.19	42.21	**43.42**	42.59	42.84
Bird	91.47	90.47	**91.60**	90.34	91.24	90.81	90.73
Boat	75.39	**75.47**	72.04	75.19	74.20	72.40	72.90
Bottle	82.05	80.18	81.14	82.12	79.55	**82.23**	81.89
Bus	**93.64**	93.25	93.25	93.20	93.07	93.52	93.31
Car	89.30	90.36	90.00	**90.67**	88.79	86.31	87.11
cat	93.69	92.80	93.31	92.62	93.56	93.84	**93.97**
Chair	38.28	40.80	40.75	39.32	39.79	**43.27**	41.60
Cow	86.60	89.72	89.04	90.49	88.42	**92.04**	88.17
Table	61.37	63.24	62.67	65.49	64.93	**67.31**	65.58
Dog	**91.16**	90.24	91.04	89.54	89.97	90.38	90.65
Horse	86.60	88.86	88.88	90.23	89.00	**91.02**	89.19
Motorbike	88.47	87.94	87.89	**88.61**	88.36	87.30	87.58
Person	86.71	86.88	86.61	86.35	86.59	86.32	**86.96**
Plant	64.48	64.33	64.69	**68.45**	65.50	68.01	65.41
Sheep	83.04	87.45	86.50	87.43	85.70	**88.14**	85.95
Sofa	49.24	47.43	48.06	49.85	46.74	**51.94**	50.19
Train	85.49	84.18	83.88	85.47	83.88	85.16	**86.69**
Monitor	77.80	76.55	78.31	79.04	78.32	78.78	**79.11**
mIoU	78.68	79.06	78.96	79.62	78.96	**79.90**	79.34
Global accuracy	94.64	94.69	94.68	94.75	94.68	**94.77**	94.75
Parameter ($\times 10^6$)	**59.34**	60.22					

4.2 WDeepLabv3+

Taking ResNet101 as backbone, we build DeepLabv3+ and WDeepLabv3+, and train them on the Pascal VOC using the same training policy with that used in the training of WSegNet. Table 5 shows the segmentation results on the validation set.

We achieve 78.68% mIoU using DeepLabv3+ on the Pascal VOC validation set, which is comparable to that (78.85%) obtained by the inventors of this network [4]. With a few increase of parameter (0.88×10^6, 1.48 %), the segmentation performance of WDeepLabv3+ with various wavelet is always better than that of DeepLabv3+, in terms of mIoU and global accuracy. Using "ch5.5" wavelet, WDeepLabv3+ achieves the best performance, 79.90 % mIoU and 94.77 % global accuracy. From Table 5, one can find that the better performance of WDeepLabv3+ is mainly resulted from its better segmentation for the fine objects ("chair", "table", and "plant") and similar objects ("cow",

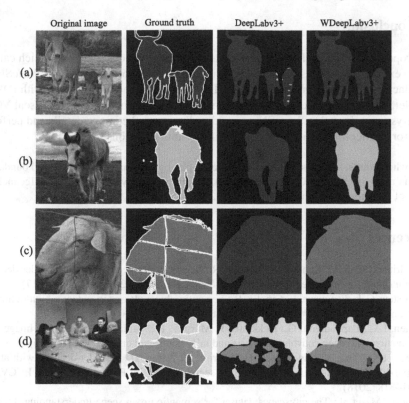

Fig. 5. Comparison of DeepLabv3+ and WDeepLabv3+ results.

"horse", and "sheep"). The above results justify the high efficiency of DWT/IDWT layers in processing data details.

Figure 5 shows four visual examples of segmentation results for DeepLabv3+ and WDeepLabv3+. The first and second columns present the original images and the segmentation ground truth, while the third and fourth columns show the segmentation results of DeepLabv3+ and WDeepLabv3+ with "ch5.5" wavelet, respectively. We show the segmentation results with colored pictures for better illustration. For the example image in Fig. 5(a), DeepLabv3+ falsely classifies the pixels in some detail regions on the cow and her calfs as "background" or "horse", i.e., the regions for the cow's left horn, the hind leg of the brown calf, and some fine regions on the two calfs. While WDeepLabv3+ correctly classifies the horse and the sheep in the Fig. 5(b) and Fig. 5(c), DeepLabv3+ classifies them as "cow" because of the similar object structures. In Fig. 5(d), the "table" segmented by WDeepLabv3+ is more complete than that segmented by DeepLabv3+. These results illustrate that WDeepLabv3+ performs better on the detail regions and the similar objects.

5   Conclusion

The proposed DWT and IDWT layers are applicable to various wavelets, which can be used to extract and process the data details in the deep networks. We design WaveSNets by replacing the down-sampling with DWT and replacing the up-sampling with IDWT, in U-Net, SegNet, and DeepLabv3+. Experimental results on the CamVid, Pascal VOC, and Cityscapes show that WaveSNets could well recover the image details and perform better for segmenting similar objects than their vanilla versions.

Acknowledgments. This research was supported in part by National Natural Science Foundation of China under grant no. 62006156 and 91959108, and in part by the Science and Technology Project of Guangdong Province under Grant 2022A1515012125.

References

1. Badrinarayanan, V., Kendall, A., Cipolla, R.: Segnet: a deep convolutional encoder-decoder architecture for image segmentation. IEEE Trans. PAMI **39**(12), 2481–2495 (2017)
2. Brostow, G.J., Fauqueur, J., Cipolla, R.: Semantic object classes in video: a high-definition ground truth database. Pattern Recogn. Lett. **30**(2), 88–97 (2009)
3. Chen, L.C., Papandreou, G., Kokkinos, I., Murphy, K., Yuille, A.L.: Semantic image segmentation with deep convolutional nets and fully connected crfs. In: ICLR (2015)
4. Chen, L.C., Zhu, Y., Papandreou, G., Schroff, F., Adam, H.: Encoder-decoder with atrous separable convolution for semantic image segmentation. In: Proceedings of the ECCV, pp. 801–818 (2018)
5. Cordts, M., et al.: The cityscapes dataset for semantic urban scene understanding. In: Proceedings of the IEEE conference on CVPR, pp. 3213–3223 (2016)
6. Daubechies, I.: Ten Lectures on Wavelets, vol. 61. SIAM (1992)
7. Duan, Y., Liu, F., Jiao, L., Zhao, P., Zhang, L.: SAR image segmentation based on convolutional-wavelet neural network and markov random field. Pattern Recogn. **64**, 255–267 (2017)
8. Everingham, M., Eslami, S.M.A., Van Gool, L., Williams, C.K.I., Winn, J., Zisserman, A.: The pascal visual object classes challenge: a retrospective. Int. J. Comput. Vis. **111**(1), 98–136 (2014). https://doi.org/10.1007/s11263-014-0733-5
9. Hariharan, B., Arbeláez, P., Bourdev, L., Maji, S., Malik, J.: Semantic contours from inverse detectors. In: 2011 International Conference on Computer Vision, pp. 991–998. IEEE (2011)
10. He, K., Zhang, X., Ren, S., Sun, J.: Delving deep into rectifiers: surpassing human-level performance on imagenet classification. In: Proceedings of the IEEE ICCV, pp. 1026–1034 (2015)
11. He, K., Zhang, X., Ren, S., Sun, J.: Deep residual learning for image recognition. In: Proceedings of the IEEE Conference on CVPR, pp. 770–778 (2016)
12. Kirillov, A., Wu, Y., He, K., Girshick, R.: Pointrend: image segmentation as rendering. In: Proceedings of the IEEE/CVF Conference on CVPR, pp. 9799–9808 (2020)
13. Li, Q., Shen, L., Guo, S., Lai, Z.: WaveCNet: wavelet integrated cnns to suppress aliasing effect for noise-robust image classification. IEEE TIP **30**, 7074–7089 (2021)
14. Liu, P., Zhang, H., Lian, W., Zuo, W.: Multi-level wavelet convolutional neural networks. IEEE Access **7**, 74973–74985 (2019)
15. Mallat, S.G.: A theory for multiresolution signal decomposition: the wavelet representation. IEEE Trans. PAMI **11**(7), 674–693 (1989)

16. Nyquist, H.: Certain topics in telegraph transmission theory. Trans. Am. Inst. Electr. Eng. **47**(2), 617–644 (1928)
17. Paszke, A., et al.: Automatic differentiation in pytorch (2017)
18. Ronneberger, O., Fischer, P., Brox, T.: U-Net: convolutional networks for biomedical image segmentation. In: Navab, N., Hornegger, J., Wells, W.M., Frangi, A.F. (eds.) MICCAI 2015, Part III. LNCS, vol. 9351, pp. 234–241. Springer, Cham (2015). https://doi.org/10.1007/978-3-319-24574-4_28
19. Simonyan, K., Zisserman, A.: Very deep convolutional networks for large-scale image recognition. arXiv preprint arXiv:1409.1556 (2014)
20. Williams, T., Li, R.: Wavelet pooling for convolutional neural networks. In: International Conference on Learning Representations (2018)
21. Yoo, J., Uh, Y., Chun, S., Kang, B., Ha, J.W.: Photorealistic style transfer via wavelet transforms. In: Proceedings of the IEEE/CVF ICCV, pp. 9036–9045 (2019)
22. Zhang, R.: Making convolutional networks shift-invariant again. In: International Conference on Machine Learning, pp. 7324–7334. PMLR (2019)

Infrared Object Detection Algorithm Based on Spatial Feature Enhancement

Hao Guo[✉], Zhiqiang Hou, Ying Sun, Juanjuan Li, and Sugang Ma

Shaanxi Key Laboratory of Network Data Analysis and Intelligent Processing, Xi'an University of Posts and Telecommunications, Xi'an 710121, China
HaoGuo@stu.xupt.edu.cn, {hzq,msg}@xupt.edu.cn

Abstract. Focusing on the problems of CenterNet in infrared images, such as feature loss and insufficient information utilization, an improved algorithm based on spatial feature enhancement is proposed. Firstly, a frequency-space enhancement module is used to enhance the details of the target region. Secondly, a module that can count global information is introduced into the backbone network to model the feature graph globally. Finally, in the case of no increase in computation and complexity, the residual mechanism is adopted to redesign the overall structure of the algorithm, which strengthens the feature interaction simply and efficiently. Experimental tests are carried out on the self-established infrared object detection dataset G-TIR and public infrared object detection dataset FLIR. The proposed algorithm improves the accuracy of the baseline by 8.4% and 15.3% respectively, and is better than many mainstream object detection algorithms in recent years. Meanwhile, the detection speed reaches 72 FPS, which balances the detection accuracy and speed well, then meet the real-time detection requirements.

Keywords: Object detection · Infrared images · Feature enhancement · Attention mechanism · Multi-feature fusion

1 Introduction

Object detection is an important research direction of computer vision. It is widely used in medical, military, monitoring system and other fields [1]. In recent years, deep learning technology has made great progress in object detection of visible images.

The object detection algorithm based on deep learning can be mainly divided into two-stage methods and one-stage methods in the field of visible images. In the two-stage algorithm category, R-CNN [2] uses selective search algorithm to generate candidate box regions, Fast R-CNN introduces regions of interest (RoIs) pooling to unify feature maps of different sizes, Faster R-CNN [3] proposes region proposal network (RPN) to replace selective search algorithm, so as to improve the quality and generation speed of candidate boxes, and also enable the algorithm to be trained end-to-end. In order to better balance detection accuracy and speed, one-stage object detection algorithms were subsequently proposed. For example, YOLO series [4–6] and SSD integrate candidate box generation and detection, greatly improving the detection speed. RetinaNet proposes focal loss

© The Author(s), under exclusive license to Springer Nature Switzerland AG 2022
S. Yu et al. (Eds.): PRCV 2022, LNCS 13537, pp. 338–350, 2022.
https://doi.org/10.1007/978-3-031-18916-6_28

to solve the imbalance between positive and negative samples, further improving the detection accuracy. In the field of thermal infrared (TIR) images, these algorithms do not necessarily perform well. Some of them in order to improve the detection performance, need to use the visible images corresponding to the infrared scene for feature fusion of different source, such datasets are scarce, then can significantly increase the storage and computational burden. Secondly, all of them are anchor-based object detection algorithms, only few anchors can overlap with the ground truth, which can cause positive and negative sample imbalance, thus slowing down the training process. Furthermore, there are many complex hyperparameters need to be designed, such as number, size and aspect ratio.

In this paper, to solve these problems, the anchor-free object detection algorithm CenterNet [7] as baseline is introduced into the field of infrared images for general object detection. The anchor-free mechanism significantly reduces the number of design parameters that need to be adjusted through heuristics, such as anchor clustering and grid perception, which can ultimately speed up encoding and decoding phases. But due to the particularity of targets in infrared images, such as lack of details, local blur, and small proportion of pixels, the precision of anchor-free algorithms may not be as accurate as anchor-based algorithms. Therefore, it is still a great challenge to use anchor-free object detection algorithm to detect targets in infrared images. To solve these problems, we introduce a spatial feature enhancement network (SFENet) based on CenterNet to detect targets in infrared images.

Our contributions are as follows: (a) A spatial feature enhancement module is designed to capture more precise details of the target, and enhance the features such as edges and contours of shallow layer targets; (b) The network structure of the algorithm is designed, a multi-head self-attention module is introduced into the residual network to learn the global information, and the feature maps of different stages of the network are used to jump backward to enhance the degree of feature fusion; (c) Create a general infrared target dataset G-TIR, and mark precise location of the target in every image.

2 Related Work

Chen et al. [8] design four convolution networks with different functions and fused multiple branch features to detect targets in TIR images. Liu et al. [9] analyse the characteristics of visible and infrared images to make full use of their complementary information for detection. Ghose et al. [10] use an attention mechanism for pedestrian detection in infrared images, which trains YOLOv3 for detection by fusing multi-spectral images. Wei et al. [11] use the attention mechanism to design a soft far network to detect small infrared targets, and Dai et al. [12] improve the SSD algorithm by adding residual branches to make network learn with robust features.

However, all of them are anchor-based algorithms, the detection process is complex and slow.Some of them need the visible light datasets of the corresponding scene, but SFENet only uses the TIR images for training and testing.

340   H. Guo et al.

3   Our Approach

3.1   Overview

As shown in Fig. 1, SFENet is mainly divided into three parts: feature extraction network (backbone), feature fusion network (neck) and prediction network (head).

The backbone network uses a lightweight residual network that can learn the global information and extract efficient features of TIR images, the architecture of the purple stage in Fig. 1 is different from that of the deep residual network (ResNet), we will discuss it in the subsequent section. The size of the last layer of feature is 512 × 16 × 16, and then add one 3 × 3 deformable convolutional (DCN) [13] layer before each up-convolution with channel 256, 128, 64, respectively, DCN can improve the ability of the network to model the target and reduce errors due to different shapes.

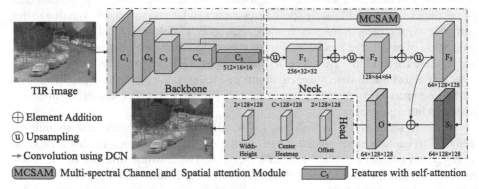

Fig. 1. The framework of the proposed spatial feature enhancement network.

Because the TIR images have one channel, its target information is insufficient. After a great number of convolution layers, the original information of the image is greatly lost, therefore, we add the layer features of backbone network to the corresponding upsampling features. The skip connections are relatively common in object detection algorithms [14], they always use 1 × 1 convolutions to keep features have same dimensions. But too many 1 × 1 convolutions may increase memory access and loss some original information. SFENet keeps the size of feature dimension consistent before and after skip connections, without adjusting channel and resolution. The addition operation here also does not increase the complexity of the algorithm compared to the concatenation operation. Last but not least, SFENet simply and efficiently strengthens the information exchange ability between backbone and neck network, so as to maintain certain features originality.

Let us denote C_x as output feature, where x denotes the stage of the backbone network. Within the neck network, we denote F_y as upsampling feature and y indicates that feature have been upsampled several times. S_1 and O denote enhanced feature and the feature that ultimately need to predict targets, respectively. Firstly, In order to further highlight the target location, feature C_2 is extracted, and then the multi-spectral channel and spatial attention module (MCSAM) based on information frequency is proposed to enhance spatial details of targets. The resolution of feature map of C_2 is 128×128 pixel, and target has obvious edge. Secondly, after using 7×7 convolutions and max pooling operation in first stage of the backbone network, then using 3×3 convolutions in second stage, so that feature C_2 already have some semantic information. Finally, we use MCSAM to enhance C_2 and get feature S_1, S_1 and F_3 have the same dimension, they can be fusion together by element addition naturally and get feature O, it contributes to the accurate calculation of the center point, width, height, and position offset of the target.

3.2 CenterNet

As shown in Fig. 2, let us denote $I \in R^{W \times H \times 1}$ be an input image of width W and height H. CenterNet produces a keypoint heat map, it can be written as:

$$\hat{Y} \in [0, 1]^{\frac{W}{R} \times \frac{H}{R} \times C} \tag{1}$$

where C is the number of keypoint types and R is the output stride, the value of R is 4 in the code. $\hat{Y}_{x,y,c} = 1$ corresponds to a target, while $\hat{Y}_{x,y,c} = 0$ is background. CenterNet splat ground truth onto a heat map $\hat{Y}$ using a Gaussian kernel, it defined as:

$$Y_{xyc} = \exp(-\frac{(x - \tilde{p}_x)^2 + (y - \tilde{p}_y)^2}{2\sigma_p^2}) \tag{2}$$

in which $\tilde{p} = \lfloor p/R \rfloor$, it is the location of targets after down sampling and p is the ground truth keypoint for class c, where σ_p is an object size-adaptive standard deviation.

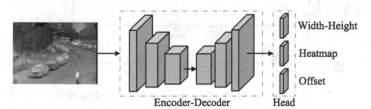

Fig. 2. The framework of CenterNet.

CenterNet has three loss functions for training, the first loss function is generates heat maps of the center point, it can be written as:

$$L_k = -\frac{1}{N} \sum_{xyc} \begin{cases} \left(1 - \hat{Y}_{xyc}\right)^\alpha \log\left(\hat{Y}_{xyc}\right), & \text{if } \hat{Y}_{xyc} = 1 \\ \left(1 - Y_{xyc}\right)^\beta \left(\hat{Y}_{xyc}\right)^\alpha \log\left(1 - \hat{Y}_{xyc}\right), & \text{otherwise} \end{cases} \tag{3}$$

where $\alpha = 2$ and $\beta = 4$, N is the number of keypoints in image I. The second loss function predicts a local offset, it defined as:

$$L_{off} = \frac{1}{N} \sum_{p} \hat{O}_{\tilde{p}} - \left(\frac{p}{R} - \tilde{p}\right) \tag{4}$$

in which $\widehat{O}$ is offset for each center point. The third loss function regresses to the object size, it defined as:

$$L_{size} = \frac{1}{N} \sum_{k=1}^{N} \left| \widehat{S}_{pk} - s_k \right| \tag{5}$$

where s_k is object size for each object k and $\widehat{S}$ is the predictions for all classes. The total loss for training can be written as:

$$L_{det} = L_k + \lambda_{size} L_{size} + \lambda_{off} L_{off} \tag{6}$$

in which $\lambda_{size} = 0.1$ and $\lambda_{off} = 1$.

3.3   MCSAM Network

In this section, we propose the MCSAM (Multi-spectral Channel and Spatial Attention Module) network. As shown in Fig. 3, it contains two branches, one is the frequency based channel attention mechanism (FcaNet) [15], the other gets max value of each channel.

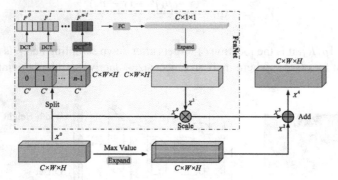

Fig. 3. The framework of the proposed MCSAM network.

Firstly, we split feature into n parts and denote C′ is C/n, the discrete cosine transform (DCT) can be written as:

$$D_{h,w}^{i,j} = \cos(\frac{\pi h}{H}(i + \frac{1}{2})) \cos(\frac{\pi w}{W}(j + \frac{1}{2})) \tag{7}$$

two-dimensional (2D) DCT is defined as:

$$f_{h,w}^{2d} = \sum_{i=0}^{H-1} \sum_{j=0}^{W-1} x_{i,j}^0 D_{h,w}^{i,j} \tag{8}$$

where cos is cosine function, H and W denote height and width of the input feature x^0, $h \in \{0, 1, \cdots, H-1\}$ and $w \in \{0, 1, \cdots, W-1\}$, the same as i and j respectively, in which f^{2d} is the 2D frequency spectrum. We use different spectrums to generate multi-spectral vector F^t, and denote $t \in \{0, 1, \cdots, n-1\}$. The result of the multi-spectral channel attention can be written as:

$$att = sigmoid\,(fc(concat(F^0, F^1, \cdots F^{n-1}))) \tag{9}$$

in which *sigmoid* is a activation function, *fc* is a fully connection layer and *concat* is the concatenation operation. We use expand module to change the dimensions of the feature, such as $C \times 1 \times 1$ to $C \times W \times H$. The other branch use max value of each channel to extract spatial details, the result of MCSAM can be written as:

$$mcsm = x^0 \cdot att(x^0) + max\_value_{channel}(x^0) \tag{10}$$

3.4 Our Backbone Network

As we known, convolution operation can effectively capture local information, while long-range dependencies needs to be modeled, so we introduce a multi-head self-attention (MHSA) [16] layer into the basic block of fifth stage of ResNet-18, as shown in Fig. 4, we call it SResNet.

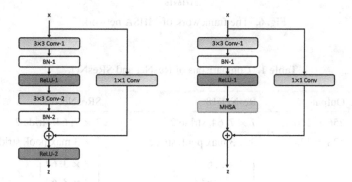

Fig. 4. The last basic block of ResNet (left) and SResNet (right) respectively.

The self-attention (SA) layer as shown in Fig. 5, we denote the size of input feature x is $128 \times 16 \times 16$, use three 1×1 pointwise convolutions and matrixes of linear transformation, such as W_Q, W_K, W_V, where q, k, r represent query, key and position encodings, then R_w and R_h represent the height and width of position encodings, respectively.

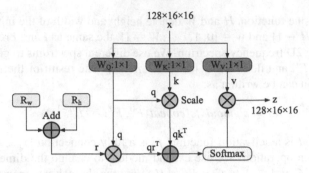

Fig. 5. The framework of self-attention layer.

As shown in Fig. 6, the size of input feature of MHSA is $512 \times 16 \times 16$, split it into four $128 \times 16 \times 16$ features and enter into SA layers to model long-range dependencies, then concatenate them.

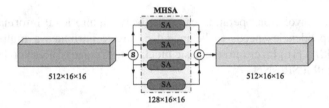

Fig. 6. The framework of MHSA network.

Table 1. Comparisons of ResNet and SResNet.

Stage	Output	ResNet-18	SResNet-18
C_1	256×256	7×7, 64, stride 2	7×7, 64, stride 2
C_2	128×128	3×3 max pool, stride 2	3×3 max pool, stride 2
		$\begin{bmatrix} 3 \times 3, 64 \\ 3 \times 3, 64 \end{bmatrix} \times 2$	$\begin{bmatrix} 3 \times 3, 64 \\ 3 \times 3, 64 \end{bmatrix} \times 2$
C_3	64×64	$\begin{bmatrix} 3 \times 3, 128 \\ 3 \times 3, 128 \end{bmatrix} \times 2$	$\begin{bmatrix} 3 \times 3, 128 \\ 3 \times 3, 128 \end{bmatrix} \times 2$
C_4	32×32	$\begin{bmatrix} 3 \times 3, 256 \\ 3 \times 3, 256 \end{bmatrix} \times 2$	$\begin{bmatrix} 3 \times 3, 256 \\ 3 \times 3, 256 \end{bmatrix} \times 2$
C_5	16×16	$\begin{bmatrix} 3 \times 3, 512 \\ 3 \times 3, 512 \end{bmatrix} \times 2$	$\begin{bmatrix} 3 \times 3, 512 \\ \text{MHSA}, 512 \end{bmatrix} \times 2$

Table 1 presents the details of different backbone network, since the resolution of the last layer is small, the amount of computation can be reduced. Therefore, the multi-head self-attention module is added in the fifth stage to replace the second spatial 3×3 convolution in the last stage to learn the global information about the targets.

4 Experiments

4.1 Implementation Details

Code environment: Ubuntu 16.04, Intel Core i5-8400 CPU, TITAN Xp GPU, PyTorch 1.8.0, Torchvision 0.9.0, CUDA 11.1, some experimental results of other algorithms are generated by mmdetection, which is a deep learning object detection toolbox.

Datasets: one is G-TIR and the other is FLIR [17], G-TIR has eight categories, such as car, person, kite, bicycle, motorcycle, ball, plant and umbrella, it divided by 8:2 and contains 4071 training images and 1018 testing images. FLIR is a popular benchmark dataset for object detection on infrared images, it has four categories, they are bicycle, dog, car and person, it has 6287 training images and 1572 testing images.

Training: the initial learning rate is 1.25e-4, ResNet-18 is used to pre-train the model on ImageNet to initialize the backbone network parameters, we train the whole network for 150 epochs with learning rate dropped $10 \times$ at 90 and 120 epochs. The batch size is 8, we use SGD optimizer and loss function is the same as CenterNet.

Evaluation: the algorithm is used to evaluate mAP and frames per second (FPS). The threshold of intersection over union (IoU) is 0.5, when IoU is greater than 0.5, the detection is successful. The mAP refers to the average sum of the precision of every categories, and FPS can effectively reflect the detection speed of the algorithm.

4.2 Performance with G-TIR

As shown in Table 2, many algorithms have the problem of high detection speed but low accuracy, such as ATSS [18] and CenterNet using ResNet-18 as the backbone network. However, when the accuracy is high, the detection speed is often too slow to meet the real-time requirements, such as CenterNet using Hourglass-104, FCOS [19] and Faster R-CNN. YOLOv3, YOLOv4, YOLOX-S and CenterNet based on DLA-34 achieve a good balance of accuracy and speed, but there is still a certain gap compared with our method. Red, green, and blue are the first, second, and third in precision, respectively. As shown in Fig. 7, SFENet is accurate and no errors, and the target on the heat map is more obvious.

Table 2. The results on G-TIR dataset.

Algorithm	Backbone	Resolution	mAP@0.5	FPS
Faster R- CNN(2015)	ResNet-50	1000×600	76.4	18
SSD(2016)	VGG-16	512×512	78.9	35
YOLOv3(2018)	DarkNet-53	416×416	80.2	50
FCOS(2019)	ResNet-101	1333×800	78.3	12
CenterNet(2019)	ResNet-18	512×512	74.7	100
	ResNet-101	512×512	75.3	30
	DLA-34	512×512	79.6	33
	Hourglass-104	512×512	80.3	6
YOLOv4(2020)	CSPDarkNet-53	416×416	80.7	53
ATSS(2020)	ResNet-50	1333×800	79.4	14
YOLOX-S(2021)	Modified CSP v5	640×640	82.3	53
Ours	SResNet-18	512×512	83.1	72

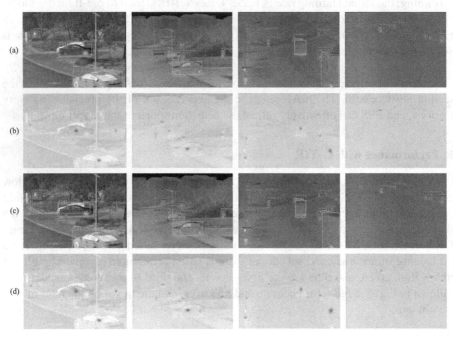

Fig. 7. (a) is the results of CenterNet, (b) is the heat maps of CenterNet, (c) is the results of SFENet, (d) is the heat maps of SFENet.

4.3   Performance with FLIR

As shown in Table 3, the mean average precision of SFENet is 84.8% on FLIR dataset, which is excellent ompared with most of the mainstream object detection algorithms, it

Table 3. The results on FLIR dataset.

Algorithm	Backbone	Resolution	mAP@0.5	FPS
Faster R-CNN(2015)	ResNet-50	1000×600	84.4	13.2
SSD(2016)	VGG-16	512×512	83.3	28
YOLOv3(2018)	DarkNet-53	416×416	82.6	50
FCOS(2019)	ResNet-101	1333×800	78.4	16
CenterNet(2019)	ResNet-18	512×512	69.5	100
	ResNet-101	512×512	72.2	30
	DLA-34	512×512	85.3	33
	Hourglass-104	512×512	84.0	6
YOLObile(2021)	CSPDarkNet-53	416×416	77.2	30.5
YOLOv4-tiny(2020)	CSPDarkNet-53	416×416	75.6	42.2
ATSS(2020)	ResNet-50	1333×800	84.1	14
Ours	SResNet-18	512×512	84.8	72

Fig. 8. (a) is the results of CenterNet, (b) is the heat maps of CenterNet, (c) is the results of SFENet, (d) is the heat maps of SFENet.

balances the speed and accuracy. We find that CenterNet using DLA-34 has the highest mAP, but FPS of our method is faster 2 × than it. As shown in Fig. 8, SFENet is more accurate when CenterNet used ResNet-18.

4.4 Ablation Study

Table 4. The results of only use MHSA in basic block

MHSA	BN-1	ReLU-1	MHSA	BN-2	ReLU-2	mAP@0.5 (G-TIR)	mAP@0.5 (FLIR)
✓			✓			80.94	82.72
✓	✓	✓	✓	✓	✓	79.22	82.82
✓	✓		✓	✓	✓	79.70	80.44
✓		✓	✓	✓	✓	80.65	81.96
✓			✓	✓	✓	79.13	82.26
✓	✓	✓	✓	✓		79.56	80.23
✓	✓	✓	✓		✓	80.67	82.92
✓	✓	✓	✓			80.05	84.28

As shown in Fig. 4 and Table 4, we use MHSA replace Conv-1 and Conv-2, and ✓□ represents use this component, observe the effect of BN and ReLU on the results; As shown in Table 5, we combine MHSA and Conv-1 or Conv-2; Finally, the best process is to replace Conv-2 with MHSA, not use BN-2 and ReLU-2, and this is the last basic block of SResNet. As shown in Table 6 and Fig. 9, they show changes in algorithm performance and comparison of different metrics.

Table 5. The results of use MHSA and 3 × 3 convolutions in basic block

MHSA	Conv-1 + BN-1 + ReLU-1	Conv-2 + BN-2 + ReLU-2	mAP@0.5 (G-TIR)	mAP@0.5 (FLIR)
	✓	✓	81.03	80.63
✓		✓	80.30	81.33
✓	✓		**83.11**	**84.81**

Table 6. Ablation for different parts

Baseline	Skip-connection	MCSAM	MHSA	mAP@0.5 (G-TIR)	mAP@0.5 (FLIR)
✓				74.7	79.2
✓	✓			78.2(+3.5)	80.2(+1.0)
✓	✓	✓		81.0(+2.8)	80.6(+0.4)
✓	✓	✓	✓	83.1(+2.1)	84.8(+4.2)

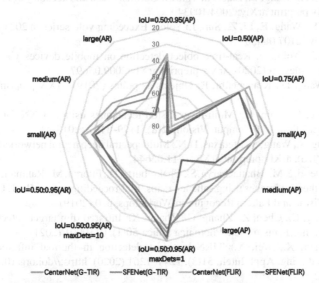

Fig. 9. It shows the performance of different algorithms under the COCO metric, AP and AR represent average precision and average recall, respectively. The 0.50:0.95 refers to IoU from 0.5 to 0.95, the mean value after AP and AR for all categories calculated under each 0.05 interval, maxDets refers to the maximum number of detection boxes allowed by one category on a picture, divide the target into small, medium and large according to the proportion of pixels.

5   Conclusion

In this paper, we introduce an anchor-free algorithm for object detection based on spatial feature enhancement for infrared images, which finally achieves remarkable results on G-TIR and FLIR datasets. Through the spatial feature enhancement module and global information modeling, the features of the region around the target can be highlighted to avoid excessive weakening or even loss caused by a large number of convolution operations. However, in the experimental process, if the target is too small, our detector may fail to detect it, and better fusion and regression strategies will be adopted in the future work to improve these problems.

References

1. Zhou, Y., Tuzel, O.: Voxelnet: end-to-end learning for point cloud based 3d object detection. In: Proceedings of the IEEE Conference on Computer Vision and Pattern Recognition, pp. 4490–4499 (2018)
2. Girshick, R., Donahue, J., Darrell, T., Malik, J.: Rich feature hierarchies for accurate object detection and semantic segmentation. In: Proceedings of the IEEE Conference on Computer Vision and Pattern Recognition, pp. 580–587 (2014)
3. Ren, S., He, K., Girshick, R., Sun, J.: Faster R-CNN: towards real-time object detection with region proposal networks. IEEE Trans. Pattern Anal. Mach. Intell. **39**(6), 1137–1149 (2016)
4. Bochkovskiy, A., Wang, C., Liao, H.: Yolov4: Optimal speed and accuracy of object detection (2020). arXiv preprint arXiv: 2004.10934
5. Ge, Z., Liu, S., Wang, F., Li, Z., Sun, J.: Yolox: Exceeding yolo series in 2021 (2021). arXiv preprint arXiv: 2107.08430
6. Cai, Y., et al.: Yolobile: Real-time object detection on mobile devices via compression-compilation co-design (2020). arXiv preprint arXiv:2009.05697
7. Zhou, X., Wang, D., Krähenbühl, P.: Objects as points (2019). arXiv preprint arXiv:1904.07850
8. Chen, Y., Xie, H., Shin, H.: Multi-layer fusion techniques using a CNN for multispectral pedestrian detection. IET Comput. Vision **12**(8), 1179–1187 (2018)
9. Liu, J., Zhang, S., Wang, S., Metaxas, D.N.: Multispectral deep neural networks for pedestrian detection (2016). arXiv preprint arXiv:1611.02644
10. Ghose, D., Desai, S.M., Bhattacharya, S., Chakraborty, D., Fiterau, M., Rahman, T.: Pedestrian detection in thermal images using saliency maps. In: Proceedings of the IEEE Conference on Computer Vision and Pattern Recognition Workshops, p. 0 (2019)
11. Wei, S., Wang, C., Chen, Z., Zhang, C., Zhang, X.: Infrared dim target detection based on human visual mechanism. Acta Photonica Sinica **50**(1), 0110001 (2021)
12. Dai, X., Yuan, X., Wei, X.: TIRNet: object detection in thermal infrared images for autonomous driving. Appl. Intell. **51**(3), 1244–1261 (2020). https://doi.org/10.1007/s10489-020-01882-2
13. Zhu, X., Hu, H., Lin, S., Dai, J.: Deformable convnets v2: more deformable, better results. In: Proceedings of the IEEE Conference on Computer Vision and Pattern Recognition, pp. 9308–9316 (2019)
14. Yi, J., Wu, P., Liu, B., Huang, Q., Qu, H., Metaxas, D.: Oriented object detection in aerial images with box boundary-aware vectors. In: Proceedings of the IEEE Winter Conference on Applications of Computer Vision, pp. 2150–2159 (2021)
15. Qin, Z., Zhang, P., Wu, F., Li, X.: Fcanet: frequency channel attention networks. In: Proceedings of the IEEE International Conference on Computer Vision, pp. 783–792 (2021)
16. Srinivas, A., Lin, T.Y., Parmar, N., Shlens, J., Abbeel, P., Vaswani, A.: Bottleneck transformers for visual recognition. In: Proceedings of the IEEE Conference on Computer Vision and Pattern Recognition, pp. 16519–16529 (2021)
17. FLIR Homepage. https://www.flir.cn/oem/adas/adas-dataset-form. Accessed 12 Apr 2022
18. Zhang, S., Chi, C., Yao, Y., Lei, Z., Li, S.Z.: Bridging the gap between anchor-based and anchor-free detection via adaptive training sample selection. In: Proceedings of the IEEE Conference on Computer Vision and Pattern Recognition, pp. 9759–9768 (2020)
19. Tian, Z., Shen, C., Chen, H.: Fcos: fully convolutional one-stage object detection. In: Proceedings of the IEEE International Conference on Computer Vision, pp. 9627–9636 (2019)

Object Detection Based on Embedding Internal and External Knowledge

Qian Liu and Xiaoyu Wu(✉)

Communication University of China, Beijing, China
{liuqian_19,wuxiaoyu}@cuc.edu.cn

Abstract. Object detection has great application value. It is frequently used in many fields such as industry, transportation, security, aerospace, etc. In the object detection task, the objects are inevitably occluded, blurred, etc. At the same time, the multi-object detection datasets inevitably have certain data bias and long-tailed distribution, which makes the model unable to extract complete visual features and seriously hinders the object detection. Therefore, we propose an object detection algorithm based on embedding internal and external knowledge (EIEK) into the detection network to enrich the feature representation and guide the model to get better detection performance. First, the basic object detection framework is built on Faster RCNN with Swin Transformer. And then, the internal and external knowledge embedding modules are presented to give the model spatial awareness and semantic understanding abilities. The experiments on multiple object detection datasets show the superiority of our EIEK and it achieves improvements of the mAP by 1.2%, 2.2%, and 3.1% on the PASCAL VOC 2007, MS COCO 2017, and ADE20k datasets, respectively.

Keywords: Object detection · Knowledge-aided vision · Internal knowledge mining · External knowledge transfer

1 Introduction

Object detection is a popular research direction in computer vision and digital image processing. It has been widely used in various fields, which can reduce the consumption of human resources and has important application value. At the same time, object detection is the basic algorithm for various computer vision tasks. For example, in the field of pan-identity recognition, object detection plays a crucial role in subsequent tasks such as face recognition and instance segmentation. And it also has important theoretical value.

In real scenes object detection, occlusions among different object areas exist in most cases, and the multi-object detection datasets also inevitably have long-tailed distribution, so the model can't detect precisely with the visual feature. Inspired by humans who can use various information to infer the object when its visual features are not obvious, the recent work [1] uses implicit and internal information of the image to guide the model, and [2] makes use of explicit human common sense to enrich the model. Although the method [3] adapts these two kinds of information considering their complementary, it

S. Yu et al. (Eds.): PRCV 2022, LNCS 13537, pp. 351–365, 2022.
https://doi.org/10.1007/978-3-031-18916-6_29

encodes the information using the local visual feature and fails when severe occlusion and blurring occur.

To address the above problems, we propose the internal and external knowledge embedding (EIEK) module for object detection to encode two kinds of knowledge and obtain global feature representation. The basic framework is based on the Faster RCNN [4] with Swin Transformer [5] and FPN [6], besides, the internal and external knowledge are added to the baseline model. As shown in Fig. 1, we use the nearby player and prior knowledge to help the model identify that the blurred area is a football. EIEK algorithm includes two knowledge embedding modules: one is the internal knowledge module that exploits the spatial position relationship of the image regions to improve the ability of space perception, and the other is the external knowledge module that embeds general information similar to human common sense into the model to improve the ability of semantic understanding.

Specifically, the internal knowledge module establishes the graph of regions firstly, then propagates the relative position relationship information of regions through graph convolution network, thereby establishing the model's perception of space. The external knowledge module establishes the graph of categories at the global level through external prior knowledge and uses the attention mechanism to perform external knowledge adaptive reasoning on a single image, thereby establishing the model's semantic understanding ability. The EIEK object detection model we built not only learns the visual features but also enables the model to have the ability of spatial perception and semantic understanding. Experimental results on three public datasets demonstrate that our proposed method is effective.

Fig. 1. Illustration of internal and external knowledge-aided detection. As shown on the left side, it is difficult to recognize football because of its fuzzy area, however with the help of the internal knowledge of player-football position and the external knowledge of the "players play football", it is easier to identify the area as a football.

2 Related Work

Object Detection. It can be classified into three types of algorithm for object detecion. First, the anchor-free algorithm, such as CornerNet [7] and CenterNet [8] implement object detection task through key points instead of anchors. Second, one-stage method, the most prominent one is YOLO [9], which has formed YOLOv4 [10] by replacing the feature extraction network and adopting a multi-branch structure. The third is the two-stage method, the most prominent one is RCNN [11], which has successively launched

Faster RCNN to improve its computational load and detection speed. On the basis of these frameworks, the improvement ideas of most algorithms [5, 12] are to improve the detection accuracy by extracting better feature representations of images, however, the visual features of objects are not always effective as shown in Fig. 1. Therefore, this paper adopts the idea of knowledge-aided vision to alleviate the excessive dependence of the model on visual features.

Knowledge-Aided Vision. One is to mine the intrinsic characteristics and attributes of images, which is a kind of self-supervision idea. DeepCluster [13] obtains image common features through image clustering, and Video jigsaw [14] divides images into grids to capture spatial associations between regions. The other is to guide vision through external prior knowledge. Universal RCNN [15] defines the target domain and the source domain and uses the rich object category relationship of the source domain to help the target domain obtain more semantic information. There are two difficulties in the method of knowledge-aided vision: one is how to effectively mine implicit internal knowledge, the other is how to construct more general external knowledge and use external knowledge more conveniently.

Graph Convolution Network. Topological graphs are usually composed of nodes and edges, which are generally expressed as $G < N, E >$, where N represents a graph node, and E represents an edge connecting the nodes in the graph. Similar to the convolution in the image, there is also a convolution operation in the graph structure, that is, the graph convolution network (GCN) [16]. The GCN can propagate the information between nodes to update the feature representation of the current node. The graph convolutional network has undergone continuous evolution in recent years, forming a series of improvements to GCN. For example, and DCNN [17] regards graph convolutions as a diffusion process, DGCN [18] introduces a dual graph convolutional architecture with two graph convolutional layers in parallel. This paper will also use the GCN method to propagate the information between graph nodes.

3 Our Proposed Method

3.1 The Overall Architecture

The Embedding Internal and External Knowledge (EIEK) object detection model proposed in this paper is shown in Fig. 2. Faster RCNN is used as the framework, and Swin Transformer superimposes the Feature Pyramid Network (FPN) as the backbone to get image feature f_{im}. And the internal and external knowledge embedding modules are added to assist object detection.

The Internal Knowledge Embedding Module (IKEM) gives the object detection model spatial awareness by mining the implicit spatial relationship between regions. IKEM builds a graph between regions. And the graph is named Internal Region Graph (IRG). IRG's nodes are represented by the features that include the high-level semantic information of the regions. IRG's edges establish a sparse graph structure by retaining the most relevant regional connections, and then sends the positional relationship of the paired proposals into the Gaussian kernel for learning, later updating it with graph convolution, and finally get the internal knowledge embedding $f_{internal}$.

The External Knowledge Embedding Module (EKEM) guides the object detection model by introducing common sense. EKEM builds the graph between categories. And the graph is named External Category Graph (ECG). ECG's nodes are represented by features that include high-level semantic information of categories, ECG's edges are extracted from the large knowledge base, and knowledge embeddings for each image are obtained through adaptive reasoning by attention, and finally get the external knowledge embedding $f_{external}$.

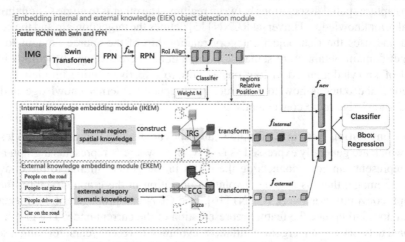

Fig. 2. The overview of the EIEK object detection model, internal and external knowledge are introduced into the model to enhance the detection together.

Finally, the output $f_{internal}$ and $f_{external}$ of IKEM and EKEM are concatenated to the original network feature f, so the new feature f_{new} is expressed as:

$$f_{new} = f \oplus f_{internal} \oplus f_{external} \qquad (1)$$

3.2   Internal Knowledge Embedding Module (IKEM)

Figure 3 shows the Internal Knowledge Embedding Module (IKEM) mines and uses the positional relationship between regions as a constraint to guide the object detection model. Here, internal knowledge refers to exploiting the hidden information of images without relying on additional annotation information. The property of internal knowledge makes it free of additional labor costs, which greatly reduces the model transfer costs.

IKEM constructs the Internal Region Graph (IRG) to encode internal knowledge. The IRG's nodes use the high-level semantic representation of the region, and the IRG's edges are obtained by calculating the similarity of the regions. Then, through GCN propagation of the positional relationship between regions, spatial perception is formed to assist object detection.

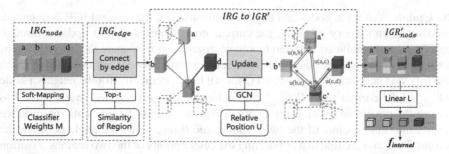

Fig. 3. An overview of the internal knowledge embedding module. IKEM constructs the implicit positional relationship between regions, and generates internal knowledge embedding.

IRG Node. The IRG's nodes need to be represented by the high-level semantics of the regions. If the nodes directly use the high-level visual feature, it will cause two problems: one is that object occlusion and blur lead to visual features that are not significant. Another is that region visual features can only exchange information local after being updated by GCN, however, the classifier of the object detection network is trained by the entire dataset, and its weight parameter M actually implies the global high-level semantic information of the categories. Therefore, we map the classifier weights to regions as nodes of the IRG. The mapping uses the classifier output probability matrix P, and then the P's probability value is smoothed by all category probabilities as soft-mapping. To sum up, the IRG_{node} are obtained by classifier weights soft-mapping to the regions.

$$IRG_{node} = PM \qquad (2)$$

where $IRG_{node} \in \mathbb{R}^{N \times D}$, $P \in \mathbb{R}^{N \times C}$, $M \in \mathbb{R}^{C \times D}$, and N and C is the number of regions and categories respectively, and D is the visual feature dimension.

IRG Edge. The edges of the IGR obtain the adjacency matrix of the regional relationship by calculating the similarity of the visual features of the regions.

$$f' = \{\beta(f_1), \beta(f_2), \ldots, \beta(f_N)\} \qquad (3)$$

$$IRG_{edge} = f'(f')^T \qquad (4)$$

where β consists of two fully connected layers with nonlinear activation function $ReLU$, and $f \in \mathbb{R}^{N \times D}$ is the region features. $IRG_{node} \in \mathbb{R}^{N \times N}$ is a dense adjacency matrix. Obviously, it causes problems: First, the fully-connected not only leads to a large amount of calculation in the subsequent graph reasoning, but also leads to insufficient differences between adjacent nodes therefore the information disseminated by graph reasoning is similar. The second is that fully connecting regional features will introduce a large amount of background noise. Therefore, the edges selected by Eq. (5) retain the maximum value to filter out the more relevant connections in the IRG.

$$e'_{ij} = \begin{cases} f'_i \left(f'_j\right)^T, & e_{ij} \in Top_t\left(e_{ij}\right) \\ 0, & e_{ij} \notin Top_t\left(e_{ij}\right) \end{cases} \quad e_{ij} \in IRG_{edge} \qquad (5)$$

IRG Update. After the nodes and edges are constructed, the original IGR is obtained. According to the theory of GCN, the current node features can be updated through graph reasoning combined with the topology structure to propagate the information of the neighbor nodes. We introduce positional relationships between regions into the graph reasoning via Gaussian Mixture Model (Monet)[19]. Specifically, for the neighbor node IRG_{node}^{j} of the current node IRG_{node}^{i}, the polar coordinate $u(i,j) = (\rho, \theta)$ is used to measure the positional relationship between regions, where ρ represents the distance between the center points of the two regions, and θ represents the angle between the horizontal line and the line that connecting the center points of the two regions. Position information is propagated through a set of Gaussian kernels $g_k(x)$ with learnable means x and covariances χ_k. Then after linear transformation L to get the final internal knowledge embedding $f_{internal}$.

$$g_k(x) = exp(-\frac{1}{2}\frac{(x - \chi_k)^T}{\sum_k (x - \chi_k)}) \tag{6}$$

$$IGR_{node}' = \sum_{j \in Neighbor(i)} g_k(u(i,j)) IRG_{node}^{j} e_{ij}' \tag{7}$$

$$f_{internal} = IGR_{node}' L \tag{8}$$

where $IGR_{node}' \in \mathbb{R}^{N \times D}, L \in \mathbb{R}^{D \times E}, f_{internal} \in \mathbb{R}^{N \times E}$. And N is the number of regions, D is the visual feature dimension, and E is the transform dimension.

3.3   External Knowledge Embedding Module (EKEM)

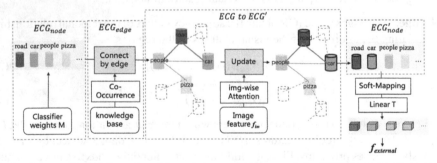

Fig. 4. An overview of the external knowledge embedding module. EKEM constructs semantic relationships between categories, and generates external knowledge embeddings.

Figure 4 illustrates the idea of the external knowledge embedding module. In this paper, external knowledge refers to extra information beyond the current dataset. Through external information, some prior knowledge can be introduced into the model, thereby correcting the errors and improving the accuracy of the model. The external knowledge can be summarized as various relationships between categories, such as verb relation (e.g. *eat, hold*) or preposition relation (e.g. *on, at*). This paper aims to establish a universal external knowledge similar to human common sense, so we encode external knowledge by collecting amounts of pairs of category information from the large knowledge base. Such external knowledge is highly portable and can be applied to various object detection datasets.

EKEM constructs the external category graph to encode external knowledge. The nodes of the ECG are represented by high-level semantic information of the categories, and the edges of the ECG are represented by extracting general category relationships from the large knowledge base. Finally, the attention mechanism is used to adaptively adjust each external knowledge embedding of the image enhances the model's semantic understanding of the category to help object detection.

ECG Node. The nodes of ECG need to be represented by the high-level semantics of the category. As mentioned in 3.2, the classifier weight M has high-level semantic information of the categories, and the global classifier weights can avoid spreading information locally, so the classifier weights M are selected as the ECG nodes.

$$ECG_{node} = M \qquad (9)$$

where $M \in \mathbb{R}^{C \times D}, ECG_{node} \in \mathbb{R}^{C \times D}$, and C is the number of categories, D is the visual feature dimension.

ECG Edge. Two categories can naturally establish their association through relationships like "on", "drive", etc. And co-occurrence probability largely characterizes the degree of association between two categories, so it can well characterize the relationships between the categories, which is beneficial to object detection, therefore we statistic the probability of categories co-occurring in the large knowledge base, and normalize it as the edges of ECG.

$$e_{ab} = Normalize\big(P_{co-occurring}(c_a, c_b)\big), e_{ab} \in E \qquad (10)$$

where c_a is category a, c_b is category b, and e_{ab} is the edge between them. $ECG_{edge} = E \in \mathbb{R}^{C \times C}$, C is the number of categories.

ECG Update. To sum up, the ECG contains the information of all category relationships in the dataset now. When analyzing each image, it can be found that all categories in the dataset do not appear in a single image. If the external knowledge we constructed is directly used, the categories that do not appear in the image are noise. So we adopt the attention mechanism to adaptively adjust the ECG. Through the operation similar to Squeeze-Excitation [20], the image feature f_{im} is dimensionally reduced by CNN and the global pool during *Squeeze* to obtain f_s, and *Excitation* uses the fully-connected layer (its weight is W_{f_s}), we get an image-wise attention weight α. Finally, the feature is adjusted with α.

$$\alpha = softmax(f_s W_{f_s} M^T) \qquad (11)$$

$$ECG'_{node} = \alpha \otimes M \qquad (12)$$

where $\alpha \in \mathbb{R}^C$, $ECG'_{node} \in \mathbb{R}^{C \times D}$. And C is the number of categories and D is the visual feature dimension.

ECG Mapping. ECG represents the relational information of categories and needs to be mapped from category semantic space to visual space to use. The classifier obtains the probability P of the visual feature corresponding to each category. P can be considered as a relationship between the region and the category learned by the network. Further analysis of its physical meaning shows that the higher the score, the higher the confidence that the region is a certain category. To avoid inaccurate classifiers, probability smoothing is also used on P as a soft-mapping method. And then after linear transformation T gets the external knowledge embedding $f_{external}$.

$$f_{external} = P(E(\alpha \otimes M))T \tag{13}$$

where $P \in \mathbb{R}^{N \times C}$, $T \in \mathbb{R}^{D \times E}$, $f_{external} \in \mathbb{R}^{N \times E}$, and N is the number of regions and D is the visual feature dimension, E is the transformed dimension.

3.4   Object Detection Loss Function

To sum up, the new feature f_{new} as shown in Eq. (1) embedded with internal and external knowledge will put into new classifier and regression to get better detection prediction. And the loss function uses the same as Faster RCNN.

$$Loss(p_i, t_i) = \sum_i L_{cls}(p_i, p_i^*) + \gamma \sum_i p_i^* L_{reg}(t_i, t_i^*) \tag{14}$$

where L_{cls} is the cross entropy loss and L_{reg} is the smooth L1 loss. And in it $p_i = W_{classifier}(f_{new})$, $t_i = W_{regression}(f_{new})$, and the $W_{classifier}$ and $W_{regression}$ are the weights of full connected layers of new classifier and regression respectively.

4   Experiment

4.1   Experiment Setup

Datasets. For the VOC dataset, we use about 10k images of VOC 2007 and 2012 TRAINVAL to train the network and use about 4.9k images for testing. For the COCO dataset, we use about 118k images for training and about 5k images for testing. For the ADE dataset, about 20.1k images are used for training, and 1k images are used for testing and converting the instance mask annotations of the ADE dataset into Bbox annotations.

Evaluation Metrics. COCO and ADE datasets use mean Average Precision (mAP) to evaluate and measure the mAP of the model under two Intersection-over-Union (IoU) thresholds of 0.5 and 0.75, as well as the mAP under small, medium, and big object scales. For the VOC dataset, the mAP evaluation metric with IoU = 0.5 is used.

Implement Details. The experiment uses 4 GPUs for training and a single GPU for testing. For the hyperparameters in the object detection network, most of the parameter settings in Faster RCNN are consistent with the original paper, where the scales in anchor generation are set to 8, ratios are set to [0.5, 1.0, 2.0], strides are set to [4, 8, 16, 32, 64]. After NMS, 256 candidate regions are extracted, in which the IoU threshold of positive samples is set to 0.7, and the IoU threshold of negative samples is set to 0.3. In terms of the backbone, the same parameter settings are consistent with the original paper, and the Swin Transformer Tiny with the simplest model structure and the fewest parameters are used for experiments. The Swin Transformer Blocks depths is [2, 2, 2, 6], the num_heads = [3, 6, 12, 24] of the multi-head attention mechanism of each layer, and the window size is set to 7. Most of the parameter settings in FPN are the same as the original. And the number of its input channels is [96, 192, 384, 768] corresponding to the feature dimension of the hierarchical feature map from Swin Transformer, and the number of output channels is set to 256.

Our external knowledge uses the region graph annotation information in the VG [33] dataset to construct a universal external knowledge graph. In order to extract common knowledge, we statistic the most frequently occurring 200 kinds of relationships of amounts categories on VG annotations. Then category synonymous matching is performed on each of the three datasets to establish ECG edges respectively.

4.2 Comparison with State-of-Art

The experimental results of the three datasets show that the method in this paper can improve the performance on different datasets, which proves that the internal and external knowledge embedding method has the advantages of the spatial perception ability and semantic understanding ability which improve the model's certain universality and robustness.

From Table 1, it shows that the EIEK method is effectively verified on multiple evaluations of the mainstream object detection dataset COCO. Table 1 also lists some large-scale object detection methods results of the ADE dataset. It can be seen that the EIEK method also has achieved the best accuracy significantly on the ADE dataset, which shows that the EIEK method can assist the detection effectively when the dataset has large categories. According to the comparison results of AP_s and AP_m, when the model detects objects with insignificant visual features such as a small pixel range, the dual assistance of IKEM and EKEM improve the detection accuracy significantly.

Table 2 lists the results of the VOC dataset in recent years. It shows that the EIEK model achieves the best performance. At the same time, it can be seen that the detection accuracy of the UP-DERT algorithm on the VOC dataset is not as competitive as on the COCO dataset, so it can be seen EIEK algorithm in this paper is more robust.

Table 1. Comparative experiment on COCO and ADE

Dataset	Method	mAP%	AP50%	AP75%	AP_s%	AP_m%	AP_1%
COCO	UP DETR [21]	42.8	63.0	45.3	20.8	47.1	**61.7**
	Deformable DETR [22]	43.8	62.6	47.7	26.4	47.1	58.0
	FCOS [23]	41.0	59.8	44.1	26.2	44.6	52.2
	TSP RCNN [24]	43.8	63.3	48.3	28.6	46.9	55.7
	Sparse RCNN [25]	42.8	61.2	45.7	26.7	44.6	57.6
	CornerNet [7]	40.6	56.4	43.2	19.1	42.8	54.3
	CenterNet [8]	42.1	61.1	45.9	24.1	45.5	52.8
	EIEK(ours)	**45.2**	**66.7**	**49.3**	**29.9**	**49.0**	58.7
ADE	CascadeRCNN [27]	9.1	16.8	8.9	3.5	7.1	15.3
	HKRM [3]	10.3	18.0	10.4	4.1	7.8	16.8
	Reasoning RCNN [2]	15.5	24.6	16.3	8.8	15.5	23.5
	SGRN [1]	14.0	23.1	14.8	8.1	13.7	21.4
	Universal-RCNN [15]	15.4	24.2	16.7	9.4	15.5	24.3
	AABO [28]	11.9	20.7	11.9	7.4	12.2	17.5
	AWEM [29]	10.5	18.2	10.5	4.3	8.1	16.9
	EIEK(ours)	**17.4**	**26.8**	**18.7**	**9.7**	**17.1**	**26.9**

Table 2. Comparative experiment on VOC dataset.

Dataset	Method	AP50 (%)
VOC	FCOS [23]	79.1
	Pseudo-IoU [26]	80.4
	UP-DERT [21]	78.7
	MG-Net [30]	81.5
	DTN [31]	82.7
	HarmonicDet [32]	83.0
	EIEK(ours)	**87.7**

4.3 Ablation Studies

Different Effects of IKEM and EKEM. In Table 3, the experimental results of IKEM and EKEM show that for different datasets, the EKEM improves the model accuracy slightly, which outperforms the IKEM. Moreover, when IKEM and EKEM are used together, the performance of the model improves more, which fully shows that IKEM and EKEM have complementarity.

Table 3. IKEM and EKEM ablation experiments on three datasets. Here, "w/o" means without, "w" means with, and '↑' means update.

Dataset	Classes	Backbone	IKEM	EKEM	AP(%)
COCO	80	ResNet101	w/o	w/o	38.4
			w	w/o	40.4(↑ 2.0)
			w/o	w	40.7(↑ 2.3)
			w	w	42.1(↑ 3.7)
		Swin Transformer Tiny	w/o	w/o	43.0
			w	w/o	44.0(↑ 1.0)
			w/o	w	44.5(↑ 1.5)
			w	w	45.2(↑ 2.2)
VOC	20	Swin Transformaer Tiny	w/o	w/o	86.5
			w	w/o	87.0(↑ 0.5)
			w/o	w	87.2(↑ 0.7)
			w	w	87.7(↑ 1.2)
ADE	455	Swin Transformaer Tiny	w/o	w/o	14.3
			w	w/o	15.8(↑ 1.5)
			w/o	w	16.5(↑ 2.2)
			w	w	17.4(↑ 3.1)

Effect on the Different Visual Features. It can also be seen from Table 3 that the experimental results on the COCO dataset show that both IKEM and EKEM can positively affect the performance of different backbones. It can be seen that the impact of EIEK on the ResNet, whose feature representation is insufficient, is greater than that on the Swin Transformer. Although the accuracy improvement of EIEK is not as large as that of the replacement feature extraction network, it still has a good auxiliary effect.

Effect on Different Datasets. In addition, Table 3 shows our model EIEK can improve its performance significantly on ADE compared with the other two datasets of COCO and VOC. The reason is that ADE with 455 classes has more serious long-tail problems which cause the model unable to learn enough good visual features of some categories. However, our detection model can be well guided by IKEM and EKEM and deal with the long-tail problem of ADE dataset effectively, which furtherly verifies the auxiliary role of the EIEK for the model with an insufficient visual feature.

Comparison of Parameters and Inference Speed. The first and second rows in the Table 4 give the results of the original Faster RCNN algorithm using two different backbones including the corresponding parameters, single image inference time with a single GPU, and mAP. It can be seen that the inference time of Faster RCNN with the smallest number of parameters is faster, but it is not competitive in the mAP. When the feature extractor in the Faster RCNN is replaced by the Swin Transformer, the model's parameters and inference time have increased, but the corresponding mAP has increased significantly, so the increased cost of these parameters and inference time is tolerable. In terms of inference time, the time delay of 0.13 s for a single image to complete the full-image object detection is also acceptable.

The last row in Table 4 lists our method's results. Comparing the second row, it can be seen that the addition of the embedded internal and external knowledge modules in this paper only slightly increases the parameters and the inference time, while the method brings the mAP gain impressively. In summary, although the method in this paper has increased the parameters and inference time, the mAP gain makes the proposed method still competitive.

Table 4. Comparison of model parameters and inference speed.

Method	Backbone	Parameters (M)	Times (ms)	mAP (%)
Faster RCNN	ResNet101	60.4	80.6	38.4
Faster RCNN	Swin-Tiny	86.0	131.2	43.0
EIEK-OD(Ours)	Swin-Tiny	90.3	156.3	**45.2**

4.4 Visualization on Three Datasets

Figure 5 and Fig. 6 show the comparison visualization results of the detection effect before and after embedding internal and external knowledge on the VOC, COCO, and ADE datasets. In addition, for the convenience of display and fair comparison, the object detection test results with Softmax scores of more than 0.7 are selected for drawing, and the comparison is made between the baseline (Faster RCNN with FPN) and EIEK.

It can be seen that our method which embeds internal and external knowledge can improve the detection performance effectively, mainly reflected in the following points:

First, it can detect objects that are hard to be detected, such as occlusion, blur, unclear lighting, etc. As shown in the Fig. 5, the method we proposed in this paper successfully detects the airplane and grass in the first image pair, and detects the dining table in the complex situation of being occluded by people and full of tableware in the second image pair. And it can be seen that in the last two image pairs for the densely appearing object arrangement, whether it is a wine bottle or a crowd, our method can detect more objects.

Second, the selections of the detection bounding box are more accurate. As shown in the Fig. 6, our method located objects more accurately, such as the floor with a dark light in the first image pair, two separate pieces of pizza on a plate in the second image pair, the bird on the tree in the third image pair, and building with lots windows in last image pair.

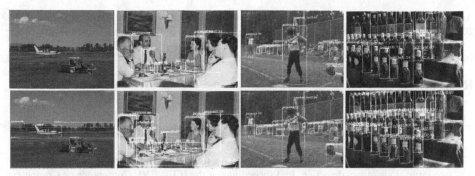

Fig. 5. The examples show our method's advantage of detecting more objects. And the first row is the detection result of the baseline, and the second row is the detection result of our method.

Fig. 6. The examples show our method's advantage of locating objects more accurate. And the first row is the detection result of the baseline, and the second row is the detection result of our method.

5   Conclusion

This paper proposes an object detection module that embedded internal and external knowledge to alleviate the detection problems such as object occlusion, blur, and dataset long-tail distribution. The main contributions of this paper can be summarized as follows: First, we rebuild the object detection framework and replace the feature extractor as Swin Transformer with FPN. Second, two modules are proposed to embed internal and external knowledge, which have the advantages of high flexibility and easy reuse. The internal knowledge embedding module uses the implicit positional relationship between regions to strengthen the model's ability to perceive spatial positions. The external knowledge embedding module encodes the categories relation information to assist the model semantic understanding. Compared with the baseline, our method's mAP has been improved by 1.2%, 2.2%, and 3.1% on the VOC, COCO, and ADE datasets, respectively.

Acknowledgments. This work is supported by National Key R&D Program of China (No. 2021YYF0900701) and National Natural Science Foundation of China (No. 61801441).

References

1. Xu, H., Jiang, C., Liang, X., et al.: Spatial-aware graph relation network for large-scale object detection. In: Proceedings of the IEEE/CVF Conference on Computer Vision and Pattern Recognition, pp. 9298–9307 (2019)
2. Xu, H., Jiang, C.H., Liang, X., et al.: Reasoning-rcnn: unifying adaptive global reasoning into large-scale object detection. In: Proceedings of the IEEE/CVF Conference on Computer Vision and Pattern Recognition, pp. 6419–6428 (2019)
3. Jiang, C., Xu, H., Liang, X., et al.: Hybrid knowledge routed modules for large-scale object detection. Adv. Neural Inf. Process. Syst. **31** (2018)
4. Ren, S., He, K., Girshick, R., et al.: Faster r-cnn: towards real-time object detection with region proposal networks. Adv. Neural Inf. Process. Syst. **28** (2015)
5. Liu, Z., Lin, Y., Cao, Y., et al.: Swin transformer: hierarchical vision transformer using shifted windows. In: Proceedings of the IEEE/CVF International Conference on Computer Vision, pp. 10012–10022 (2021)
6. Lin, T.Y., Dollár, P., Girshick, R., et al.: Feature pyramid networks for object detection. In: Proceedings of the IEEE Conference on Computer Vision and Pattern Recognition, pp. 2117–2125 (2017)
7. Law, H., Deng, J.: Cornernet: detecting objects as paired keypoints. In: Proceedings of the European Conference on Computer Vision (ECCV), pp. 734–750 (2018)
8. Duan, K., Bai, S., Xie, L., et al.: Centernet: keypoint triplets for object detection. In: Proceedings of the IEEE/CVF International Conference on Computer Vision, pp. 6569–6578 (2019)
9. Redmon, J., Divvala, S., Girshick, R., et al.: You only look once: unified, real-time object detection. In: Proceedings of the IEEE Conference on Computer Vision and Pattern Recognition, pp. 779–788 (2016)
10. Bochkovskiy, A., Wang, C.Y., Liao, H.Y.M.: Yolov4: optimal speed and accuracy of object detection (2020). arXiv preprint arXiv:2004.10934
11. Girshick, R., Donahue, J., Darrell, T., et al.: Rich feature hierarchies for accurate object detection and semantic segmentation. In: Proceedings of the IEEE Conference on Computer Vision and Pattern Recognition, pp. 580–587 (2014)
12. Beal, J., Kim, E., Tzeng, E., et al.: Toward transformer-based object detection (2020). arXiv preprint arXiv:2012.09958
13. Caron, M., Bojanowski, P., Joulin, A., et al.: Deep clustering for unsupervised learning of visual features. In: Proceedings of the European Conference on Computer Vision (ECCV), pp. 132–149 (2018)
14. Ahsan, U., Madhok, R., Essa, I.: Video jigsaw: unsupervised learning of spatiotemporal context for video action recognition. In: Proceedings of the 2019 IEEE Winter Conference on Applications of Computer Vision (WACV), pp. 179–189. IEEE (2019)
15. Xu, H., Fang, L., Liang, X., et al.: Universal-rcnn: universal object detector via transferable graph r-cnn. Proc. AAAI Conf. Artif. Intell. **34**(07), 12492–12499 (2020)
16. Scarselli, F., Gori, M., Tsoi, A.C., et al.: The graph neural network model. IEEE Trans. Neural Networks **20**(1), 61–80 (2008)
17. Atwood, J., Towsley, D.: Diffusion-convolutional neural networks. In: Proceedings of NIPS, pp. 1993–2001 (2016)

18. Zhuang, C., Ma, Q.: Dual graph convolutional networks for graph based semi-supervised classification. In: WWW, pp. 499–508 (2018)
19. Monti, F., Boscaini, D., Masci, J., et al.: Geometric deep learning on graphs and manifolds using mixture model cnns. In: Proceedings of the IEEE Conference on Computer Vision and Pattern Recognition, pp. 5115–5124 (2017)
20. Hu, J., Shen, L., Sun, G.: Squeeze-and-excitation networks. In: Proceedings of the IEEE Conference on Computer Vision and Pattern Recognition, pp. 7132–7141 (2018)
21. Dai, Z., Cai, B., Lin, Y., et al.: Up-detr: unsupervised pre-training for object detection with transformers. In: Proceedings of the IEEE/CVF Conference on Computer Vision and Pattern Recognition, pp. 1601–1610 (2021)
22. Zhu, X., Su, W., Lu, L., et al.: Deformable detr: deformable transformers for end-to-end object detection (2020). arXiv preprint arXiv:2010.04159
23. Tian, Z., Shen, C., Chen, H., et al.: Fcos: fully convolutional one-stage object detection. In: Proceedings of the IEEE/CVF International Conference on Computer Vision, pp. 9627–9636 (2019)
24. Sun, Z., Cao, S., Yang, Y., et al.: Rethinking transformer-based set prediction for object detection. In: Proceedings of the IEEE/CVF International Conference on Computer Vision, pp. 3611–3620 (2021)
25. Sun, P., Zhang, R., Jiang, Y., et al.: Sparse r-cnn: end-to-end object detection with learnable proposals. In: Proceedings of the IEEE/CVF Conference on Computer Vision and Pattern Recognition, pp. 14454–14463 (2021)
26. Li, J., Cheng, B., Feris, R., et al.: Pseudo-IoU: improving label assignment in anchor-free object detection. In: Proceedings of the IEEE/CVF Conference on Computer Vision and Pattern Recognition, pp. 2378–2387 (2021)
27. Cai, Z., Vasconcelos, N.,: Cascade r-cnn: delving into high quality object detection. In: Proceedings of the IEEE Conference on Computer Vision and Pattern Recognition, pp. 6154–6162 (2018)
28. Ma, W., Tian, T., Xu, H., Huang, Y., Li, Z.: Aabo: adaptive anchor box optimization for object detection via bayesian sub-sampling. In: Vedaldi, A., Bischof, H., Brox, T., Frahm, J.-M. (eds.) ECCV 2020. LNCS, vol. 12350, pp. 560–575. Springer, Cham (2020). https://doi.org/10.1007/978-3-030-58558-7_33
29. Zhang, Y., Wu, X., Zhu, R.: Adaptive word embedding module for semantic reasoning in large-scale detection. In: Proceedings of the 2020 25th International Conference on Pattern Recognition (ICPR), pp. 2103–2109. IEEE (2021)
30. Zhang, H., Fromont, E., Lefèvre, S., et al.: Localize to classify and classify to localize: mutual guidance in object detection. In: Proceedings of the Asian Conference on Computer Vision (2020)
31. Wu, S., Xu, Y., Zhang, B., et al.: Deformable template network (dtn) for object detection. IEEE Trans. Multimedia 24, 2058–2068 (2021)
32. Wang, K., Zhang, L.: Reconcile prediction consistency for balanced object detection. In: Proceedings of the IEEE/CVF International Conference on Computer Vision, pp. 3631–3640 (2021)
33. Krishna, R., Zhu, Y., Groth, O., et al.: Visual genome: connecting language and vision using crowdsourced dense image annotations. Int. J. Comput. Vision 123(1), 32–73 (2017)

ComLoss: A Novel Loss Towards More Compact Predictions for Pedestrian Detection

Xiaolin Song[✉], Jin Feng, Tianming Du, and Honggang Zhang

Beijing University of Posts and Telecommunications, Beijing, China
{sxlshirley,fengjin2012,dtm,zhhg}@bupt.edu.cn

Abstract. CNN-based detectors have achieved great success in pedestrian detection. However, poor localization of bounding boxes leads to high false positive detection errors to a large degree. This paper gives insight into reducing localization errors and better performing bounding box regression. We propose a novel loss named *ComLoss* to enforce predicted bounding boxes with the same designated target ground truth box to locate more *compactly* around the target, which minimizes the internal region distances of these predicted boxes to some extent. Evaluations on both CityPersons and Caltech dataset show the effectiveness of our method: (1) ComLoss yields an absolute 1.05% and 0.60% miss rate improvement on these two datasets respectively. (2) By adding ComLoss during training, our baseline detector achieves competitive results compared to state-of-the-arts on both datasets.

Keywords: Pedestrian detection · Convolutional neural networks · SSD · ComLoss

1 Introduction

Pedestrian detection, which aims to accurately locate pedestrian instances in an image, is a popular task in computer vision field due to its diverse applications. As the development of convolutional neural network (CNN), pedestrian detection witnessed a significant boost in the past few years.

In pedestrian detection, false positives and false negatives are two types of errors that detectors can do. According to [18], poor localization is an important source of high confidence false positive errors. Localization errors are defined as false detections overlapping with ground truth bounding boxes. Double detections (detections with high confidence scores targeting the same ground truth bounding boxes) and larger bounding-boxes are two typical localization errors. The false detection of adjacent pedestrians is another type of localization error in crowd scenes, where false bounding boxes usually cover body parts of two pedestrian instances. Localization errors have a bad influence on detection accuracy. Hence, object localization is an important part of detectors, which is generally

S. Yu et al. (Eds.): PRCV 2022, LNCS 13537, pp. 366–375, 2022.
https://doi.org/10.1007/978-3-031-18916-6_30

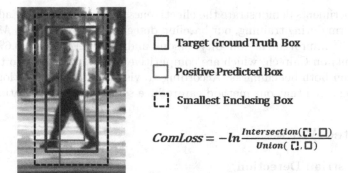

$$ComLoss = -ln\frac{Intersection(\square,\square)}{Union(\square,\square)}$$

Fig. 1. Illustration of our proposed ComLoss. The green solid boxes are positive predicted boxes designated to the blue solid ground truth target (For better visualization, here we take two predicted boxes for example.). The red dotted box is the smallest enclosing box of these positive predicted boxes. Our ComLoss narrows the gap between the smallest enclosing box and its corresponding ground truth box. (Color figure online)

considered as a bounding box regression problem. Bounding box regression technique is employed almost in all state-of-the-art pedestrian detectors to narrow the gap between default anchor boxes in [10] or proposals in [13] and ground truth bounding boxes. However, default anchor boxes or proposals are supposed to approach to the target ground truth boxes from all directions. Figure 1 presents a simple example for better illustration, where green solid boxes are two positive predicted bounding boxes designated to the blue solid ground truth target and red dotted box is the smallest box enclosing the two predicted boxes (denote as the smallest enclosing box). As seen in Fig. 1, the smallest enclosing box is too larger than ground truth box, which indicates that these two predicted boxes are not compact enough. One predicted box shifts to the left-top side and the other one shifts to the right-bottom side. These two primary predictions will be further processed by non-maximum suppression (NMS) in the detection framework. If the Intersection over Union (IoU) between them is smaller than the NMS threshold, the worse one of them cannot be suppressed by NMS and will be regarded as false detection in evaluations. As a result, localization errors occur and affect the detection accuracy significantly.

In this paper, we focus on reducing localization errors. For this purpose, we expect predicted bounding boxes designated to the same ground truth boxes to be more compact so that the NMS process will work better. Therefore, we design the ComLoss to minimize the internal distances of positive predicted bounding boxes with the same target. We use the Intersection over Union (IoU) between the smallest enclosing box of all positive predicted bounding boxes with the same target and the corresponding target ground truth box to represent the compactness degree of these predicted boxes and define $-\ln IoU$ as the value of ComLoss.

Our experiments demonstrate the effectiveness of our method. By adding our ComLoss term during training, our baseline detector achieves 15.28% MR^{-2} (an 1.05% MR^{-2} improvement) on CityPersons and 8.84% MR^{-2} (a 0.6% MR^{-2} improvement) on Caltech, which are competitive results compared to the state-of-the-arts on both benchmarks. According to visualization of detection results, it can be observed that our method can reduce some typical localization errors.

2   Related Work

2.1   Pedestrian Detection

Pedestrian detection is a sub-field of general object detection. In the last few years, this field is dominated by CNN-based methods. These methods can be generally classified into two categories: the Faster R-CNN [13] based two-stage pedestrian detector and the SSD [10] based single-stage detector. Two-stage methods generate rough region proposals at the first stage and then refine the results by a post-processing sub-network while single-stage methods directly regress predefined default anchor boxes. Single-stage detectors outperform two-stage ones in speed but are inferior in accuracy. Variations of [1,12,17,20–22,24] Faster R-CNN have shown top performance in accuracy on most standard benchmarks. RPN+BF [17] adapts the original RPN in Faster RCNN to pedestrian detection and uses a boosted forest as the downstream classifier. SDS-RCNN [1] proposes to jointly learn the task of pedestrian detection and semantic segmentation by adding semantic segmentation branches to both detection stages. OR-CNN [21] replaces the RoI pooling layer with a part occlusion-aware region of interest pooling unit to handle occlusion. FasterRCNN+ATT [20] proposes to employ channel-wise attention to handle various occlusion patterns. In contrast, less work has been done for pedestrian detection in the single-stage framework. GDFL [8] encodes scale-aware attention masks into feature maps of multi-layers of SSD [10] in order to make features more discriminative for pedestrian. ALFNet [11] proposes the asymptotic localization fitting strategy to regress the default anchor boxes step by step. In this paper, we give insight into error source and aim to reduce the most crucial localization errors by optimizing the bounding box regression process.

2.2   Object Localization

Object localization is a crucial part of detectors in general object detection field, which is generally considered as a bounding box regression problem that relocates an initial default box [10] or proposal [13] to its designated target ground truth box. In this literature, many kinds of bounding box regression losses have been proposed. In R-CNN [5], Euclidean distance is used to measure the difference between a proposal and its target. In Fast RCNN [4], the SmoothL1 loss is proposed to replace the Euclidean distance for bounding box regression to alleviate the sensitiveness to the outliers. However, all methods above optimize the coordinates of a bounding box as four independent variables, which results in many failure cases where some bounds are very close to the ground truth but the entire box is poor-aligned. To address this drawback, IoU Loss is proposed in [16] to directly maximize the Intersection over Union(IoU) between a predicted box and a ground-truth box. In terms of pedestrian detection, repulsion loss [15] is designed for detecting pedestrian in crowd scenes, which includes RepGT Loss and RepBox Loss. RepGT loss penalizes boxes for shifting to other ground truth targets while RepBox Loss keeps predicted boxes away from boxes with different targets. AggLoss in [21] uses the SmoothL1 loss to measure the difference between the average prediction of predictions with the same target and their target, describing the compactness degree of these predictions. However, the obtained low loss calculated with average boxes makes boxes with big error are hard to optimized.

3 Proposed Method

In this section, we introduce the proposed ComLoss in detail. We choose the Intersection over Union (IoU) as the distance metric and maximize the IoU between the smallest enclosing box of all positive predicted boxes with the same target and the corresponding target ground truth box. When using ComLoss, the detection framework is optimized by a multi-task loss function with three objectives:

$$L = L_{cls} + L_{loc} + \lambda_c L_{com}, \tag{1}$$

where the classification loss term with focal weight is the same one used in ALFNet [11], the localization loss term is the same SmoothL1 loss employed in Fater RCNN [13] and SSD [10].

3.1 ComLoss

In this part, all boxes are represented by their top-left and bottom-right corners, i.e. (x_1, y_1, x_2, y_2). Considering one ground truth box $B^g = (x_1^g, y_1^g, x_2^g, y_2^g)$ which allocated with more than one positive predicted bounding boxes, we set P={B_1^p, B_2^p, ..., B_N^p} to be the set of all positive bounding boxes designated to B^g, where N is the total number of these positive bounding boxes. The coordinates of B_i^p, for $\forall B_i^p \in P$, is $(x_1^{pi}, y_1^{pi}, x_2^{pi}, y_2^{pi})$. We denote the smallest enclosing box of $\forall B_i^p \in P$ as $B^c = (x_1^c, y_1^c, x_2^c, y_2^c)$. Firstly, we calculate the coordinates of B^c according to (2) and (3):

$$x_1^c = \min_{1 \le i \le N} (x_1^{pi}), \ y_1^c = \min_{1 \le i \le N} (y_1^{pi}) \tag{2}$$

$$x_2^c = \max_{1 \le i \le N} (x_2^{pi}), \ y_2^c = \max_{1 \le i \le N} (y_2^{pi}) \tag{3}$$

Algorithm 1. ComLoss.

Input: Ground-truth bounding boxes coordinate: $B^g = (x_1^g, y_1^g, x_2^g, y_2^g)$; Positive predicted bounding boxes designated to B^g set: P = $\{B_1^p, B_2^p, ..., B_N^p\}$; The coordinates of B_i^p, where $B_i^p \in P$: $B_i^p = (x_1^{pi}, y_1^{pi}, x_2^{pi}, y_2^{pi})$;

Output: L_{com};

1: Calculating the coordinates of smallest enclosing box B^c;
2: Calculating area of B^c: $A^c = (x_2^c - x_1^c) \times (y_2^c - y_1^c)$;
3: Calculating area of B^g: $A^g = (x_2^g - x_1^g) \times (y_2^g - y_1^g)$;
4: Calculating intersection I between B^c and B^g:
$$x_1^I = \max(x_1^c, x_1^g), x_2^I = \min(x_2^c, x_2^g)$$
$$y_1^I = \max(y_1^c, y_1^g), y_2^I = \min(y_2^c, y_2^g)$$
5: I=$\begin{cases} (x_2^I - x_1^I) \times (y_2^I - y_1^I), & if x_2^I > x_1^I, y_2^I > y_1^I \\ 0, & otherwise \end{cases}$
6: Calculating Union U between B^c and B^g: U=A^c+A^g-I;
7: Calculating IoU between B^c and B^g: $IoU = \frac{I}{U}$;
8: Calculating ComLoss: $L_{com} = -\ln IoU$;
9: **return** L_{com};

Then, we calculate the IoU of B^c and B^g. More detailed calculation process is presented in Algorithm 1. We define ComLoss as:

$$L_{com} = -\ln IoU(B^c, B^g) \tag{4}$$

We use $-\ln IoU$ as the final value of ComLoss because of its great performance in [16], which is a cross-entropy loss in essence with input of IoU. Since *min*, *max* and other linear functions in our algorithm can be back-propagating, every components have a well-behaved derivative.

3.2 Loss Stability

In this part, we discuss the stability of proposed ComLoss. The definition of the smallest enclosing box ensures that non-overlapping cases are impossible to occur, so the intersection I between B^c and B^g is always a positive value, i.e. $I > 0$. Also, the union U of B^c and B^g is always a positive value, i.e. $U > 0$ and union is always bigger than intersection, i.e. $U \geqslant I$. Therefore, the value of IoU is always bounded in $(0, 1]$ and the lower bound of $-\ln IoU$ is 0 when the value of IoU is 1. Since both B^c and B^g are rectangles with areas bigger than zero and always inside the image, the value of $-\ln IoU$ has a upper bound. Therefore, there is no abnormal case where ComLoss is unstable or undefined.

4   Experiments

In this section, we introduce the datasets used for experiment and some implementation details firstly. Then, we analyze the experiment results. Finally, the detector trained with ComLoss is compared with the state-of-the-art methods on both CityPersons and Caltech datasets.

4.1   Datasets

CityPersons. The CityPersons [19] dataset is a challenging large-scale pedestrian detection dataset, which is composed of a total of 5000 images and more than 35000 persons. The image size is 2048 × 1024. In our experiments, we use the train and validation sets for training and testing, which contain 2,975 and 500 images respectively.

Caltech. The Caltech dataset [3] is another challenging dataset in pedestrian detection, which consists of 10 h of 640 × 480 30 Hz video taken from vehicle driving through Los Angeles. The standard training and testing sets contain 42,782 images and 4,024 images, which sampled 10 Hz 1 Hz respectively.

4.2   Implementation Details

Our method is implemented based on PyTorch, with 2 GTX 1080Ti GPUs for training. The Adam solver is employed. The backbone network is pretrained on ImageNet [6]. To increase the diversity of training data, each training patch is augmented by several operations, i.e. random colour distortion, random horizontal flip and random crop.

   The baseline detector in our experiments is built based on the standard SSD [10] architecture with some modifications as done in [11]. The backbone network consists of the truncated ResNet50 [7] (before stage 5) and an extra 3 × 3 convolutional layer with a stride of 2. We choose the last layers of stage 3, 4, and 5 in ResNet-50 and the added convolutional layer as detection layers. Detection is performed on feature maps with sizes downsampled by 8, 16, 32, 64 w.r.t. the input image respectively. The default anchor boxes with width of {(16, 24), (32, 48), (64, 80), (128, 160)} pixels and a fixed aspect ratio of 0.41 are assigned to each detection layers, respectively.

   Our experiments follow the standard Caltech evaluation metric [3]: the log average Miss Rate over False Positive Per Image (FPPI) of 9 points ranging from 10^{-2} to 10^{0} (denote as MR^{-2}). We use the original image size without upsampling in evaluations. On both CityPersons and Caltech datasets, we evaluate our methods on three subsets with different occlusion levels: (1) Reasonable (R): $height \geqslant 50, visibility \geqslant 0.65$; (2) Heavy occlusion (HO): $height \geqslant 50, 0.20 \leqslant visibility \leqslant 0.65$; (3) $R+HO$: $height \geqslant 50, visibility \geqslant 0.20$.

4.3   Experiment Results

Sensitivity Analysis. We firstly study how to balance our ComLoss term and two other loss terms in Eq. (1) on the reasonable subset of CityPersons. We show results with different settings of λ_c in Table 1 and get the best MR^{-2} when the value of λ_c is 0.75. We also see that detection results are stable when the value of λ_c is in [0.25, 1.00], which indicates that ComLoss is not sensitive to hyper-parameter λ_c in this interval.

Table 1. The MR^{-2} of ComLoss with different λ_c on CityPersons validation set.

λ_c	0.25	0.50	0.75	1.00	1.25
MR^{-2}	15.51%	15.43%	15.28%	15.39%	16.21%

Table 2. Ablation study on CityPersons validation set and Caltech test set. Numbers refer to MR^{-2} (lower is better)

	CityPersons		Caltech	
	R	HO	R	HO
Baseline	16.33	49.00	9.44	40.81
Baseline+ComLoss	15.28	47.18	8.84	39.42

Effectiveness of ComLoss. We validate the effectiveness of our approach by performing the ablation study on both CityPersons and Caltech dataset. Table 2 summarizes our experiment results. On the validation set of CityPersons, we achieve 15.28% MR^{-2} on the reasonable subset by adding ComLoss term, which outperforms our baseline detector with an improvement of 1.05% MR^{-2}. On the standard test set of Caltech (see Table 4), it can be seen that the MR^{-2} decreases from 9.44% to 8.84% on the reasonable subset by using ComLoss during training. Also, it shows obvious improvements on the HO subsets of both datasets.

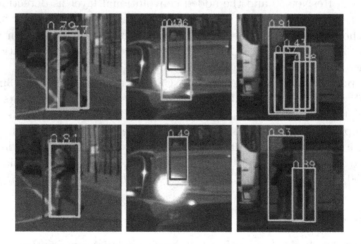

Fig. 2. The visualized comparison of predicted bounding boxes after NMS from baseline detector and baseline+ComLoss detector when NMS threshold is 0.5 and FPPI is 1.0. Three samples in top line are results from our baseline SSD based detector while the three samples in bottom line are ones from our baseline+ComLoss detector. The blue solid boxes represent ground truth annotations and the green solid boxes denote detection results. (Color figure online)

Visualization Results. We also show visualization results after NMS on CityPersons validation set in Fig. 2, where we can see that after using our Com-Loss for training, our baseline detector produces better predictions. The three samples in top line show three typical localization errors: double detections, larger bounding boxes and false detections of adjacent pedestrians. As seen in the bottom line, the errors have been corrected by adding our ComLoss.

4.4   Comparisons with State-of-the-Art Methods

As shown in Table 3 and Table 4, we compare our method with some state-of-the-arts on both CityPersons and Caltech under different occlusion levels. It can be observed that by adding ComLoss term, our detector outperforms all state-of-the-art methods listed on both datasets across all occlusion level. Noted that our proposed can be used in all anchor-based detectors. In this paper, we show the improvement to the SSD-based detector, and we also expect similar behaviour if applied to other detectors.

Table 3. Performance comparisons with state-of-the-art methods on the CityPersons validation set. Numbers refer to MR^{-2} (lower is better)

Method	R	HO	R+HO
FasterRCNN [20]	15.52	64.83	41.45
FasterRCNN+ATT(self) [20]	20.93	58.33	40.83
FasterRCNN+ATT(vbb) [20]	16.40	57.31	39.49
FasterRCNN+ATT(part) [20]	15.96	56.66	38.23
Ours	15.28	47.18	30.58

Table 4. Performance comparisons with state-of-the-art methods on the Caltech test set. Numbers refer to MR^{-2} (lower is better)

Method	R	HO	R+HO
DeepParts [14]	11.89	60.42	22.79
FasterRCNN+ATT(vbb) [20]	10.33	45.18	18.21
JL-TopS [23]	10.04	49.18	19.22
MS-CNN [2]	9.95	59.94	21.53
RPN+BF [17]	9.58	74.36	24.01
FasterRCNN [20]	9.18	57.58	20.03
Ours	8.84	39.42	17.19

5   Conclusion

In this paper, we design a new ComLoss in order to make predicted bounding boxes with the same designated targets locate more compactly and reduce localization errors in pedestrian detection by narrowing the gap between the smallest enclosing box of all positive predictions with the same target and the corresponding target ground truth box. The experimental results demonstrate that our method can effectively alleviate typical localization errors. By adding our ComLoss term during training, our detector achieves 15.28% MR^{-2} (1.05% MR^{-2} improvement over the baseline) on CityPersons and 8.84% MR^{-2} (0.6% MR^{-2} improvement over the baseline) on Caltech, which are competitive results compared to state-of-the-arts. The proposed ComLoss can be incorporated into other detectors like Faster RCNN [13] and FPN [9], which will be studied in the future.

References

1. Brazil, G., Yin, X., Liu, X.: Illuminating pedestrians via simultaneous detection & segmentation. In: The IEEE International Conference on Computer Vision (ICCV), October 2017
2. Cai, Z., Fan, Q., Feris, R.S., Vasconcelos, N.: A unified multi-scale deep convolutional neural network for fast object detection. In: Leibe, B., Matas, J., Sebe, N., Welling, M. (eds.) ECCV 2016. LNCS, vol. 9908, pp. 354–370. Springer, Cham (2016). https://doi.org/10.1007/978-3-319-46493-0_22
3. Dollár, P., Wojek, C., Schiele, B., Perona, P.: Pedestrian detection: a benchmark. In: CVPR, June 2009
4. Girshick, R.: Fast R-CNN. In: 2015 IEEE International Conference on Computer Vision (ICCV), pp. 1440–1448, December 2015. https://doi.org/10.1109/ICCV.2015.169
5. Girshick, R., Donahue, J., Darrell, T., Malik, J.: Rich feature hierarchies for accurate object detection and semantic segmentation. In: 2014 IEEE Conference on Computer Vision and Pattern Recognition, pp. 580–587, June 2014. https://doi.org/10.1109/CVPR.2014.81
6. He, K., Zhang, X., Ren, S., Sun, J.: Deep residual learning for image recognition. In: 2016 IEEE Conference on Computer Vision and Pattern Recognition (CVPR), pp. 770–778, June 2016. https://doi.org/10.1109/CVPR.2016.90
7. He, K., Zhang, X., Ren, S., Sun, J.: Deep residual learning for image recognition. In: CVPR (2016)
8. Lin, C., Lu, J., Wang, G., Zhou, J.: Graininess-aware deep feature learning for pedestrian detection. In: Ferrari, V., Hebert, M., Sminchisescu, C., Weiss, Y. (eds.) ECCV 2018. LNCS, vol. 11213, pp. 745–761. Springer, Cham (2018). https://doi.org/10.1007/978-3-030-01240-3_45
9. Lin, T., Dollár, P., Girshick, R., He, K., Hariharan, B., Belongie, S.: Feature pyramid networks for object detection. In: 2017 IEEE Conference on Computer Vision and Pattern Recognition (CVPR), pp. 936–944, July 2017. https://doi.org/10.1109/CVPR.2017.106
10. Liu, W., et al.: SSD: single shot MultiBox detector. In: Leibe, B., Matas, J., Sebe, N., Welling, M. (eds.) ECCV 2016. LNCS, vol. 9905, pp. 21–37. Springer, Cham (2016). https://doi.org/10.1007/978-3-319-46448-0_2

11. Liu, W., Liao, S., Hu, W., Liang, X., Chen, X.: Learning efficient single-stage pedestrian detectors by asymptotic localization fitting. In: Ferrari, V., Hebert, M., Sminchisescu, C., Weiss, Y. (eds.) Computer Vision – ECCV 2018. LNCS, vol. 11218, pp. 643–659. Springer, Cham (2018). https://doi.org/10.1007/978-3-030-01264-9_38

12. Pang, Y., Xie, J., Khan, M.H., Anwer, R.M., Khan, F.S., Shao, L.: Mask-guided attention network for occluded pedestrian detection. In: ICCV, October 2019

13. Ren, S., He, K., Girshick, R., Sun, J.: Faster R-CNN: Towards real-time object detection with region proposal networks. In: Cortes, C., Lawrence, N.D., Lee, D.D., Sugiyama, M., Garnett, R. (eds.) Advances in Neural Information Processing Systems, VOL. 28, pp. 91–99. Curran Associates, Inc. (2015). http://papers.nips.cc/paper/5638-faster-r-cnn-towards-real-time-object-detection-with-region-proposal-networks.pdf

14. Tian, Y., Luo, P., Wang, X., Tang, X.: Deep learning strong parts for pedestrian detection. In: 2015 IEEE International Conference on Computer Vision (ICCV), pp. 1904–1912, December 2015. https://doi.org/10.1109/ICCV.2015.221

15. Wang, X., Xiao, T., Jiang, Y., Shao, S., Sun, J., Shen, C.: Repulsion loss: detecting pedestrians in a crowd. In: The IEEE Conference on Computer Vision and Pattern Recognition (CVPR), June 2018

16. Yu, J., Jiang, Y., Wang, Z., Cao, Z., Huang, T.S.: Unitbox: an advanced object detection network. CoRR abs/1608.01471 (2016). http://arxiv.org/abs/1608.01471

17. Zhang, L., Lin, L., Liang, X., He, K.: Is faster R-CNN doing well for pedestrian detection? (2016)

18. Zhang, S., Benenson, R., Omran, M., Hosang, J., Schiele, B.: How far are we from solving pedestrian detection? In: The IEEE Conference on Computer Vision and Pattern Recognition (CVPR), June 2016

19. Zhang, S., Benenson, R., Schiele, B.: Citypersons: a diverse dataset for pedestrian detection. In: The IEEE Conference on Computer Vision and Pattern Recognition (CVPR), July 2017

20. Zhang, S., Yang, J., Schiele, B.: Occluded pedestrian detection through guided attention in CNNs. In: The IEEE Conference on Computer Vision and Pattern Recognition (CVPR), June 2018

21. Zhang, S., Wen, L., Bian, X., Lei, Z., Li, S.Z.: Occlusion-aware R-CNN: detecting pedestrians in a crowd. In: Ferrari, V., Hebert, M., Sminchisescu, C., Weiss, Y. (eds.) ECCV 2018. LNCS, vol. 11207, pp. 657–674. Springer, Cham (2018). https://doi.org/10.1007/978-3-030-01219-9_39

22. Zhou, C., Yang, M., Yuan, J.: Discriminative feature transformation for occluded pedestrian detection. In: ICCV, October 2019

23. Zhou, C., Yuan, J.: Multi-label learning of part detectors for heavily occluded pedestrian detection. In: Proceedings of the IEEE International Conference on Computer Vision, pp. 3486–3495 (2017)

24. Zhou, C., Yuan, J.: Bi-box regression for pedestrian detection and occlusion estimation. In: Ferrari, V., Hebert, M., Sminchisescu, C., Weiss, Y. (eds.) ECCV 2018. LNCS, vol. 11205, pp. 138–154. Springer, Cham (2018). https://doi.org/10.1007/978-3-030-01246-5_9

Remote Sensing Image Detection Based on Attention Mechanism and YOLOv5

Pengsen Ma[1,2] and Jin Che[1,2(✉)] [iD]

[1] School of Physics and Electronic-Electrical Engineering, Ningxia University,
Yinchuan 750021, Ningxia, China
1078371585@qq.com
[2] Key Laboratory of Intelligent Sensing for Desert Information, Ningxia University,
Yinchuan 750021, Ningxia, China

Abstract. Due to the lack of characteristic information of remote sensing small targets and the large interference of complex environments, the detection accuracy is not high and the detection performance is not good. Aiming at this problem, an improved Yolov5 algorithm based on attention mechanism is proposed, which firstly adds a prediction head suitable for small targets detection, and secondly uses mosaic data enhancement technology at the input to enrich the dataset, and at the end of the backbone network, the C3Transformer module is introduced to obtain global information; at the same time, the BiFPN feature fusion network is used in the neck network to better process the feature information, and some CBAM modules are integrated to focus on the acquisition of key feature information. Then it is compared with other network models on RSOD dataset and NWPU VHR-10 dataset. The results show that the size of the improved network model is only 17.8 MB, and compared with the original Yolov5, the detection accuracy on the two datasets is increased by 6.9% and 2.6% respectively.

Keywords: YOLOv5 · Remote sensing image · Small target detection · Attention mechanism · BiFPN

1 Introduction

Object detection is the foundation of computer vision tasks and is now applied in various fields, such as intelligent transportation, industrial automation, medicine, security, and autonomous driving. In particular, with the continuous development of deep learning, there are more and more theories and methods about object detection, but in general, object detection algorithms based on deep learning can be divided into single-stage object detection algorithms and two-stage object detection algorithm. Two-stage target detection algorithms, such as R-CNN [1], Fast R-CNN [2], etc. These algorithms first generate the target candidate area, and then the classifier is used to determine whether the candidate area contains the object to be detected and the category to which the object

S. Yu et al. (Eds.): PRCV 2022, LNCS 13537, pp. 376–388, 2022.
https://doi.org/10.1007/978-3-031-18916-6_31

belongs, and then the final predicted result is obtained by correcting the bounding box and using algorithms such as NMS, so the detection accuracy of this type of algorithm is high, but the detection speed is slow. The single-stage target detection algorithm directly predicts the coordinates and categories of the entire image, so the detection speed is fast and the real-time performance is good. The representative algorithms include SSD [3], YOLO [4–7] series.

Remote sensing images are widely used in various fields, including military reconnaissance, resource detection, and natural disaster monitoring. However, the detection process becomes more difficult due to the relatively small objects in remote sensing images, low resolution and inconspicuous features. Therefore, how to detect small targets more accurate is the work that many researchers are doing. For example, Ali [8] et al. proposed an improved Yolov4 model, which improves mAP results by 2% on the VisDrone dataset while maintaining the same speed as the original Yolov4 model; Liu [9] et al. proposed an improved Faster-RCNN algorithm and experimented on the RSOD dataset, and the mAP value reached 87.9%; Wu [10] et al. proposed an adaptive feature enhancement object detection network (YOLO-AFENet), which improved the average accuracy by 6.3% on the UAVDT dataset; Ye [11] et al. proposed an improved Yolov3 algorithm, which improved mAP by 1.63% on the NWPU VHR-10 dataset to 79.89%; Zhang [12] et al. proposed an improved Yolov3-based algorithm, which improved the recall rate and the average precision of target detection compared to the original algorithm; Chen [13] et al. proposed an improved feature fusion network, which achieved good accuracy and real-time performance on the dataset NWPU VHR-10; Feng [14] et al. proposed an improved YOLOv3 small target detection algorithm, which achieved a mAP value of 90.3% on the RSOD dataset. Nevertheless, the previous algorithms still have many shortcomings in the detection performance and practical application of small objects. New methods are urgently needed to inspire small object detection tasks, and it is expected that they can be applied to remote sensing image detection tasks.

In view of the existing problems, this paper proposes an improved YOLOv5 small target detection algorithm. First, a detection head is added to detect small targets to reduce the impact of large scale changes; at the same time, the input uses mosaic data enhancement technology to enrich data set. Second, in the backbone network part, the last C3 module is replaced by the C3Transformer module, focusing on the acquisition of global information. At the same time, the BiFPN structure is used in the Neck part to better process and to fuse features [13]. And the CBAM structure is integrated, so that the model can focus on useful target objects and ignore information outside the target. After that, experiments were carried out on the dataset RSOD and the dataset NWPU VHR-10, and higher detection accuracy was obtained. At the same time, the model size was only 17.8 MB, which is of great significance for the research on improving the detection accuracy of small targets and its implementation in practical applications.

2   Introduction to the YOLOv5 Model

Since the appearance of the YOLOv5 model, it has been applied to various detection tasks because of its excellent detection performance. The models are divided into yolov5s, yolov5m, yolov5l and yolov5x from small to large. In this experiment, considering the practicability and portability of the model, the YOLOv5s model is used as the baseline to improve the model.

The YOLOv5 model as a whole can be divided into four parts, including Input, BackBone, Neck network, and Prediction. Among them, the input end will perform mosaic data enhancement on the data, that is, randomly select four pictures around a center point for random splicing, random cropping, random scaling, random arrangement, and a variety of traditional data enhancement methods to enrich the data set. Adaptive anchor box calculation and adaptive image scaling are used to preprocess the image; secondly, feature extraction is performed in backbone. YOLOv5 consists of C3 module, Conv module and SPPF module in backbone. After several iterations of versions, the current backbone of YOLOv5 has not only improved its performance, but also improved its model portability; then uses the FPN+PAN structure in the Neck network to fuse and process multi-scale features; finally, CIoU is used as the loss function of the prediction frame, and NMS (Non-Maximum Suppression) is used to find the best position for object detection, so as to complete the prediction of the target object.

3   Network Model Improvements

3.1   Backbone Network Improvement

Because most of the dataset RSOD and dataset NWPU VHR-10 are small objects, a tiny object detection head is first introduced to better detect small objects in the dataset. Secondly, in order to improve the network's ability to control global information [15], a C3Tranformer module is introduced in the last feature extraction layer of the network. Which is a module with a transformer structure added to the original C3 module, which aims to improve the model's ability to extract small target features while reducing the complexity of the model. The structure diagram of the C3Transformer module [16] is shown in Fig. 1. In order to intuitively understand the role of C3Transformer in the backbone network, the feature map visualization result of an oiltank sample M in the RSOD dataset during the detection process was randomly selected, and its performance is shown in Fig. 2.

3.2   Using BiFPN Structure

With the proposal of FPN [17], various feature fusion strategies have emerged one after another, including PANet [18], NAS-FPN [19], ASFF [20], and BiFPN [21]. BiFPN is a weighted bidirectional feature pyramid network, which is designed to solve the problem that the contribution of different input features to output features is often different during multi-scale fusion. However, in this paper, the BiFPN structure without weights is applied to process the features of the extracted small targets. The structural diagram of BiFPN is shown in Fig. 3.

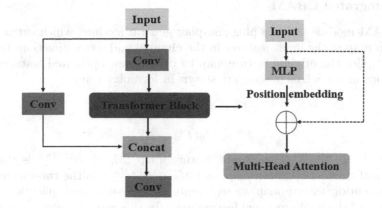

Fig. 1. C3Transformer structure diagram

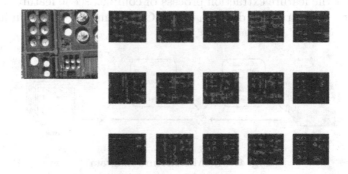

Fig. 2. Visualization of the feature map of C3Transformer module

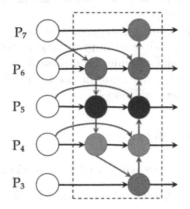

Fig. 3. BiFPN structure diagram

3.3 Integrated CBAM

The CBAM module [22] is a plug-and-play general module, which extracts the attention map of the input features in the channel and space directions in turn, and multiplies the original feature map to obtain new optimized features. The expressions of the whole process are shown in formulas 1 and 2.

$$F' = M_C(F) \otimes F \tag{1}$$

$$F'' = M_S(F') \otimes F' \tag{2}$$

where $F \in R^{C \times H \times W}$ is the input feature map, $M_c \in R^{C \times 1 \times 1}$ is the one-dimensional channel attention map, and $M_S \in R^{1 \times H \times W}$ is the two-dimensional spatial attention feature map. $\otimes$ represents element-wise multiplication. F'' is the output of the final processed feature map. In this way, the background noise can be suppressed in the rich information, and the key features can be highlighted, so as to accurately find the target object and locate its location, which is suitable for the feature extraction process of complex scene features and dense small targets. The structure diagram of the CBAM module is shown in Fig. 4.

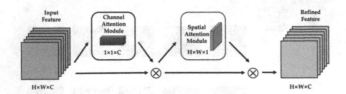

Fig. 4. CBAM structure diagram

In order to visually represent the work of CBAM, the feature map visualization results of the CBAM module of an oiltank sample M in the RSOD dataset is extracted, as shown in Fig. 5.

In summary, it is the whole strategy of the improved YOLOv5. Through these improvements, it is possible to improve the accuracy while ensuring the lightweight requirements, and provide a solution for the practical application of remote sensing small target detection in the future. Figure 6 is the structure diagram of the improved network model.

4 Experiments and Results

4.1 Experimental Configuration and Evaluation Indicators

This experiment uses the Pytorch deep learning framework, the hardware configuration is GeForce RTX 2080Ti, 11 GB video memory. The improved model in this paper and the corresponding experimental results are obtained in this configuration environment.

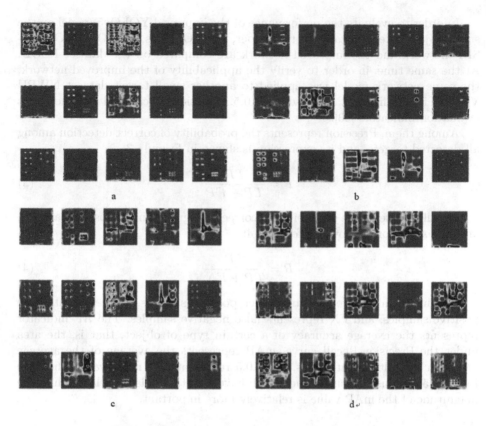

a   b

c   d

Fig. 5. CBAM feature map visualization results

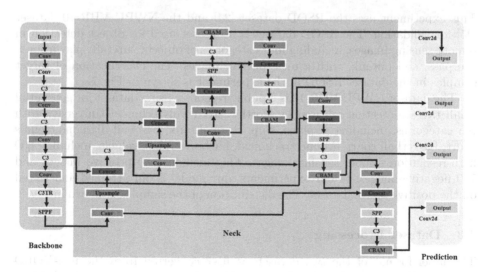

Fig. 6. Structure of Improved_YOLOv5

In order to evaluate the performance of the improved YOLOv5 model on the small object detection task. In this paper, the YOLOv5s, YOLOv3, YOLOv3-SPP network and the improved network are compared on the dataset RSOD. At the same time, in order to verify the applicability of the improved network, the same network model was applied to another small target dataset NWPU VHR-10 for verification. And use mAP_0.5, Precision, Recall and Parameters as evaluation indicators [23].

Among them, Precision represents the probability of correct detection among all detected targets, and its expression is shown in formula 3:

$$P = \frac{TP}{TP + FP} \tag{3}$$

Recall represents the probability of correct recognition in all positive samples, and its expression is shown in formula 4:

$$R = \frac{TP}{TP + FN} \tag{4}$$

Among them, TP represents correct positive samples, FP represents false positive samples, and FN represents false negative samples. The AP indicator represents the average accuracy of a certain type of object, that is, the area under the Precision-Recall curve. mAP represents the average of the average precision of multiple categories, mAP_0.5 represents the mAP value when the IoU is 0.5, because Precision and Recall have a certain balance relationship, the magnitude of the mAP value is relatively more important.

4.2   Experimental Datasets

This experiment uses the RSOD dataset [24] and the NWPU VHR-10 dataset [25] for validation. The RSOD dataset is a dataset used for object detection in remote sensing images, including four categories of objects: aircraft, playground, overpass, and oiltank, with a total of 976 images. The classification of target samples in the dataset RSOD in the experiment is shown in Fig. 7.

The dataset NWPU VHR-10 is a public remote sensing dataset for geospatial small target detection released by Northwestern Polytechnical University with ten categories, including airplane, ship, storage tank, baseball diamond, tennis court, basketball court, ground track field, harbor, bridge, vehicle, including 800 high-resolution remote sensing images. This includes 650 positive images and 150 negative images. In our experiments, our model is only trained and tested on the positive image dataset. The distribution of the samples is shown in Fig. 8.

4.3   Dataset Processing

The label format of the two datasets is first converted from the non-YOLO format to the label in the YOLO format. Then the two datasets are divided into training set and validation set according to the ratio of 8:2.

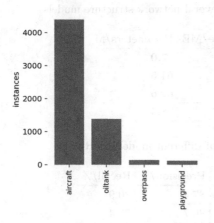

Fig. 7. Classification of RSOD   **Fig. 8.** Classification of NWPU VHR-10

4.4   Comparative Analysis of Experimental Results

This paper verifies the effectiveness of the improved network by comparing the improved YOLOv5 network with other algorithms. First of all, because the target detection task needs to have applicability, that is, it has the ability to embed and transplant. Therefore, Table 1 shows the comparison of parameters and model size under several network structures. It can be seen from Table 1 that the Yolov5 model is the smallest, and the number of parameters is only 7.0M, which is the smallest; the size of the Yolov3 model and the Yolov3-SPP model has exceeded 100 MB, which is not suitable for application in the actual scene, and it will be more difficult to embed; although the size of the Improved-Yolov5 model is slightly larger than that of Yolov5, it is only 17.8 MB. Relatively speaking, it is advantageous to embed it in some detection systems and to put into practical applications.

Secondly, Table 2 presents the performance indicators of different network structures on the dataset RSOD, including Precision, Recall, and mAP_0.5. It can be seen from Table 2 that the average accuracy of the improved Yolov5 model can reach 92.7%, which is 6.9% higher than the original Yolov5, and compared with the Yolov3 network model, the accuracy is 16.5% higher; compared with the Yolov3-SPP model, the accuracy is 4.4% improvement, but it is known from Table 1 that the Yolov3-SPP model is larger and is not suitable for practical applications. Therefore, it can be concluded from Table 1 and Table 2 that the improved network model can be used as a practical lightweight small target detection model.

In order to more clearly and intuitively see the detection capabilities of different network structures for different categories of RSOD dataset, Table 3 shows the AP values of different categories of RSOD dataset. It can be seen from Table 3 that the improved network model has advantages in oiltank, overpass and playground classes, and the average accuracy on aircraft targets also has better performance.

Table 1. Comparison of the sizes of several network structure models

Model	Model size/MB	Parameters/M
Yolov5s	**13.9**	**7.0**
Yolov3	117.9	61.5
Yolov3-SPP	119.9	62.6
Improved-Yolov5s	17.8	8.4

Table 2. Performance comparison of different models on RSOD

Model	mAP_0.5/%	Precision/%	Recall/%
Yolov5s	85.8	87.4	80.9
Yolov3	76.3	80.7	73.4
Yolov3-SPP	88.4	89.8	84.6
Liu [9]	87.9	–	–
Feng [14]	90.2	–	–
Improved-Yolov5s	**92.7**	**94.0**	**85.9**

Table 3. AP values of different categories in RSOD dataset

Model	Yolov5	Yolov3	Yolov3-SPP	Liu [9]	Feng [14]	Improved-Yolov5s
Aircraft	0.974	**0.980**	0.977	0.902	0.923	0.955
Oiltank	0.981	0.874	0.940	0.907	–	**0.982**
Overpass	0.594	0.356	0.754	0.750	–	**0.809**
Playground	0.881	0.840	0.863	0.955	–	**0.963**

In order to verify the universality of the improved model, the same comparative experiments are done on the NWPU VHR-10 dataset. Table 4 shows the performance of different network structures on this dataset. It can be seen that the improved network structure has a 2.6% improvement on the dataset NWPU VHR-10 compared to the original Yolov5 model. Compared with other networks, the average accuracy is also superior, which verifies the applicability of the network model.

4.5   Comparison of Ablation Experiments

In order to better verify the effectiveness of embedding C3Transformer module, using BiFPN feature fusion network and integrating CBAM module mentioned in the paper. In this paper, the above schemes are added to the dataset RSOD and the dataset NWPU VHR-10 respectively for experimental comparison. The results are shown in Table 5 and Table 6. It can be seen from the table that when the improvement points are added, the detection accuracy of the model

Table 4. Performance comparison of different models on NWPU VHR-10

Model	mAP_0.5/%	Precision/%	Recall/%
Yolov5s	82.8	91.4	**79.9**
Yolov3	79.2	94.4	73.4
Yolov3-SPP	77.6	**94.9**	72.9
Lu [26]	69.8	–	–
Ye [11]	79.9	–	–
Improved-Yolov5s	**85.4**	92.4	79.8

Table 5. Dataset RSOD ablation experiment comparison results

Model	mAP_0.5/%	Precision/%	Recall/%
Yolov5s	85.8	87.4	80.9
BiFPN	89.2	87.7	82.2
BiFPN+CBAM	89.6	86.2	82.8
BiFPN+CBAM+C3TR	**92.7**	**94.0**	**85.9**

Table 6. Dataset NWPU VHR-10 ablation experiment comparison results

Model	mAP_0.5/%	Precision/%	Recall/%
Yolov5s	82.8	91.4	79.9
BiFPN	84.2	87.7	**83.0**
BiFPN+CBAM	84.9	86.2	80.5
BiFPN+CBAM+C3TR	**85.4**	**92.4**	79.8

will be continuously improved. The main roles are the C3Transformer module that controls the global information in the backbone and the BiFPN feature fusion strategy in the Neck network.

4.6 Demonstration of Experimental Results

In order to more intuitively and clearly show the effectiveness of the improved network structure, two images were selected from the dataset RSOD and the dataset NWPU VHR-10 for detection. The detection results are shown in Figs. 9 and 10. From the detection results, it can be concluded that the improved network structure can better complete the task of remote sensing small target detection.

Fig. 9. Example of RSOD detection results in the dataset

Fig. 10. Example of detection results of NWPU VHR-10 dataset

5   Conclusion

This paper proposes an improved Yolov5 model. First, a detection head for small target detection is added to specifically improve the detection performance of small target objects. At the same time, in order to obtain the global information of the input data, the C3 Transformer module is used to replace the C3 module at the end of the backbone network. After that, the BiFPN feature fusion structure is used in feature fusion to make better use of the obtained features, and the CBAM module is integrated, so that the network can ignore the background noise, and it can focus on the key features of the target. The experimental results show that the improved network model has achieved good results on both public datasets. Compared with the original Yolov5 algorithm, the average accuracy has been improved to a certain extent. Moreover, compared with some popular network models, the improved algorithm also has certain advantages, which verifies the effectiveness of the model in the task of remote sensing small target detection.

References

1. Girshick, R., Donahue, J., Darrell, T., Malik, J.: Rich feature hierarchies for accurate object detection and semantic segmentation. In: Proceedings of the IEEE Conference on Computer Vision and Pattern Recognition, pp. 580–587. IEEE (2014)
2. Girshick, R.: Fast R-CNN. In: Proceedings of the IEEE International Conference on Computer Vision, pp. 1440–1448. IEEE (2015)

3. Liu, W., et al.: SSD: single shot MultiBox detector. In: Leibe, B., Matas, J., Sebe, N., Welling, M. (eds.) ECCV 2016. LNCS, vol. 9905, pp. 21–37. Springer, Cham (2016). https://doi.org/10.1007/978-3-319-46448-0_2

4. Redmon, J., Divvala, S., Girshick, R., Farhadi, A.: You only look once: unified, real-time object detection. In: Proceedings of the IEEE Conference on Computer Vision and Pattern Recognition, pp. 779–788. IEEE (2016)

5. Redmon, J., Farhadi, A.: YOLO9000: better, faster, stronger. In: IEEE Conference on Computer Vision and Pattern Recognition, pp. 6517–6525 (2017)

6. Redmon, J., Farhadi, A.: Yolov3: an incremental improvement. In: IEEE Conference on Computer Vision and Pattern Recognition. arXiv preprint arXiv:1804.02767 (2018)

7. Bochkovskiy, A., Wang, C.Y., Liao, H.Y.M.: YOLOv4: optimal speed and accuracy of object detection. In: IEEE conference on Computer Vision and Pattern Recognition. arXiv preprint arXiv:2004.10934 (2020)

8. Ali, S., Siddique, A., Ateş, H.F., Güntürk, B.K.: Improved YOLOv4 for aerial object detection. In: 2021 29th Signal Processing and Communications Applications Conference (SIU), pp. 1–4. IEEE (2021)

9. Liu, R., Yu, Z., Mo, D., Cai, Y.: An improved faster-RCNN algorithm for object detection in remote sensing images. In: 2020 39th Chinese Control Conference (CCC), pp. 7188–7192. IEEE (2020)

10. Wu, M.M., Zhang, Z.B., Song, Y.Z., Shu, Z.T., Li, B.Q.: Small object detection network based on adaptive feature enhancement. In: Progress in Laser and Optoelectronics, pp. 1–14 (2022). http://kns.cnki.net/kcms/detail/31.1690.tn.20220212.1752.026.html

11. Ye, K., et al.: Research on small target detection algorithm based on improved yolov3. In: 2020 5th International Conference on Mechanical, Control and Computer Engineering (ICMCCE), pp. 1467–1470. IEEE (2020)

12. Gongguo, Z., Junhao, W.: An improved small target detection method based on Yolo V3. In: 2021 International Conference on Electronics, Circuits and Information Engineering (ECIE), pp. 220–223. IEEE (2021)

13. Chen, J., Mai, H., Luo, L., Chen, X., Wu, K.: Effective feature fusion network in BIFPN for small object detection. In: 2021 IEEE International Conference on Image Processing (ICIP), pp. 699–703. IEEE (2021)

14. Feng, H., Huang, C.B., Wen, Y.Q.: Small object detection in remote sensing images based on improved YOLOv3. In: Computer Applications, pp. 1–11 (2022). http://kns.cnki.net/kcms/detail/51.1307.TP.20220120.0939.004.html

15. Zhu, X., Lyu, S., Wang, X., Zhao, Q.: TPH-YOLOv5: improved YOLOv5 based on transformer prediction head for object detection on drone-captured scenarios. In: Proceedings of the IEEE/CVF International Conference on Computer Vision, pp. 2778–2788. IEEE (2021)

16. Gu, Y., Wang, Q., Qin, X.: Real-time streaming perception system for autonomous driving. arXiv preprint arXiv:2107.14388 (2021)

17. Lin, T.Y., Dollár, P., Girshick, R., He, K., Hariharan, B., Belongie, S.: Feature pyramid networks for object detection. In: Proceedings of the IEEE Conference on Computer Vision and Pattern Recognition, pp. 2117–2125 (2017)

18. Liu, S., Qi, L., Qin, H., Shi, J., Jia, J.: Path aggregation network for instance segmentation. In: Proceedings of the IEEE Conference on Computer Vision and Pattern Recognition, pp. 8759–8768 (2018)

19. Ghiasi, G., Lin, T.Y., Le, Q.V.: NAS-FPN: learning scalable feature pyramid architecture for object detection. In: Proceedings of the IEEE/CVF Conference on Computer Vision and Pattern Recognition, pp. 7036–7045. IEEE (2019)

20. Liu, S., Huang, D., Wang, Y.: Learning spatial fusion for single-shot object detection. arXiv preprint arXiv:1911.09516 (2019)
21. Tan, M., Pang, R., Le, Q.V.: Efficientdet: scalable and efficient object detection. In: Proceedings of the IEEE/CVF Conference on Computer Vision and Pattern Recognition, pp. 10781–10790. IEEE (2020)
22. Woo, S., Park, J., Lee, J.-Y., Kweon, I.S.: CBAM: convolutional block attention module. In: Ferrari, V., Hebert, M., Sminchisescu, C., Weiss, Y. (eds.) ECCV 2018. LNCS, vol. 11211, pp. 3–19. Springer, Cham (2018). https://doi.org/10.1007/978-3-030-01234-2_1
23. Long, Y.C., Lei, R., Dong, Y., et al.: Optical remote sensing recognition of aircraft type based on YOLOv5 algorithm. J. Earth Inf. Sci. **24**(03), 572–582 (2022)
24. Long, Y., Gong, Y., Xiao, Z., Liu, Q.: Accurate object localization in remote sensing images based on convolutional neural networks. IEEE Trans. Geosci. Remote Sens. **55**(5), 2486–2498 (2017)
25. Su, H., Wei, S., Yan, M., Wang, C., Shi, J., Zhang, X.: Object detection and instance segmentation in remote sensing imagery based on precise mask R-CNN. In: IGARSS 2019–2019 IEEE International Geoscience and Remote Sensing Symposium, pp. 1454–1457. IEEE (2019)
26. Lu, X., Ji, J., Xing, Z., Miao, Q.: Attention and feature fusion SSD for remote sensing object detection. IEEE Trans. Instrum. Meas. **70**, 1–9 (2021)

Detection of Pin Defects in Transmission Lines Based on Dynamic Receptive Field

Zhenyu Zhang[1], Jianming Du[2(✉)], Shaowei Qian[2,3], and Chengjun Xie[2(✉)]

[1] Institutes of Physical Science and Information Technology, Anhui University, Hefei 230601, China

[2] Institutes of Intelligent Machines, Hefei Institute of Physical Science, Chinese Academy of Sciences, Hefei 230031, China
{djming,cjxie}@iim.ac.cn

[3] University of Science and Technology of China, Hefei 230026, China

Abstract. Pin plays a role in fixing components and stabilizing structures in transmission lines. At present, UAVs are introduced into the inspection of transmission lines. Due to the small size of the pins, which account for fewer than 0.04% of the pixels in the aerial image, their defects are difficult to be detected. At the same time, the complex background and different shooting angles are prone to cause the defect samples difficult to be identified, so the detection accuracy is not high and robust. Aiming at these problems, this paper proposes a detection method for pin defects in transmission lines based on the dynamic receptive field. In this method, a Dynamic Receptive Field (DRF) module is used to extract the contextual features of pin defects, which effectively fuses receptive fields of different sizes and in-channel information to improve detection accuracy. Second, a Spatial Activation Region Proposal Network (SARPN) is proposed to enhance the information acquisition of regions of interest in the proposal network. The experimental results show that the proposed method performs a noticeable effect on the two-stage object detection method, in which mAP is increased by 4.4% and recall is increased by 8.6% based on Cascade RCNN.

Keywords: Object detection · Dynamic receptive field · Spatial activation region proposal network · Transmission line inspection

1 Introduction

With the rapid development of unmanned aerial vehicle(UAV) aerial photography technology, transmission line images obtained through aerial photography can provide more and more comprehensive observation perspectives, efficiently capture the visual status of transmission lines, and have extremely high security. According to the Chinese national grid standard, the defects in the inspection of transmission lines mainly include tower defects, insulator defects and hardware defects. Pins are small in size and large in number, and are widely found in towers and connecting hardware. The pins are generally installed at the connection of various components of the transmission line to stabilize the structure. Due to the harsh environments and large forces, the pins are prone to fall off

S. Yu et al. (Eds.): PRCV 2022, LNCS 13537, pp. 389–399, 2022.
https://doi.org/10.1007/978-3-031-18916-6_32

and loose which is the critical defect, and it is easy to cause large-scale power outages in the power system and affect the safety of power transmission.

In recent years, with the development of convolutional neural networks, the use of deep learning for defect detection on transmission lines can make power transmission inspection more intelligent, and get rid of the drawbacks of the complex and labor-intensive manual inspections. In 2014, RCNN [1] introduced convolutional neural network into object detection for the first time, and then object detection developed into two classic methods: one-stage and two-stage. The one-stage method (YOLOs [5–8], SSD [9], RetinaNet [10], ATSS [11]) directly puts the image into the convolutional neural network, classifies and adjusts the object area through the CNN feature. Because of its superior speed, it can realize the function of real-time detection. The two-stage method (RCNN, Fast RCNN [2], Faster RCNN [3], Cascade RCNN [4]) first generates a series of candidate areas on the image. It then sends them to the subsequent convolution layer to classify and adjust the areas. Although this type of algorithm is relatively slow, it has higher accuracy.

Faster RCNN proposes a region proposal network (RPN) based on Fast R-CNN, which abandons the Selective Search method [12]. Cascade RCNN uses different IoU thresholds to divide positive and negative samples based on Faster RCNN, which greatly improves the detection effect. Due to their good detection effect, they have been applied to the detection of pin defects in transmission lines already. Wu et al. [13] first used transfer learning to build a defect detection model, and then used an improved Faster RCNN for pin defect detection. Zhang et al. [14] replaced VGG16 [15] backbone in the original Faster RCNN with resnet101, which improved the network's feature extraction for pin defects. He et al. [16] used bilinear interpolation to enhance the features of pin defects, which fused the global information of the network while maintaining high resolution. Zhao et al. [17] used a method of K-Means clustering to model the different shapes of the pins. Xiao et al. [18] proposed a cascaded detection network that first uses a shallow convolutional neural network to obtain regions of interest, and then uses a deep network to locate and classify these regions. Mei et al. [19] used an unsupervised learning method, which can use non-defective samples for model training, which alleviates the problem that defective samples are difficult to obtain in actual scenarios (Fig. 1).

Fig. 1. Pin defect sample.

Although these methods have improved the detection effect from the problems of lack of data and diverse sample shapes, they have not fundamentally solved the two key difficulties in pin defect detection on UAV images. (1) The pin defect scene of the transmission line is complex, and the change in the distance and height during the UAV shooting will cause the size of the pin defect to change. (2) As the depth of the network increases, the defect features will lose a lot of information, and the region of interest generated by the network will also be affected. Aiming at the two key issues, this paper proposes a Dynamic Receptive Field (DRF) module to extract the contextual features of pin defects, which effectively fuses receptive fields of different sizes and in-channel information to improve detection accuracy. Then a Spatial Activation Region Proposal Network (SARPN) is proposed to enhance the information acquisition of regions of interest in the proposal network.

The main contributions of this paper are as follows:

(1) A Dynamic Receptive Field (DRF) module is proposed to improve the feature pyramid, which extracts network features from multiple different receptive fields and fuses the information of each channel.
(2) A Spatially Activated Region Proposal Network (SARPN) is designed to improve the quality of regional features through further spatial activation.
(3) This method can be applied to a variety of two-stage object detection networks to effectively improve the detection accuracy of the network.

2 Materials and Methods

2.1 Materials

The dataset in this paper uses the UAV inspection images of the State Grid transmission line, with a total of 5000 pin defect pictures, and the picture resolution is 5472×3078. Data labeling is done in a semi-automatic way. We label a batch of data with labelImg manually at first. LabelImg is a visual image calibration software, the xml file it generates is in PASCAL VOC format [20]. We use a small part of the data to train a coarse detection model, and use it to detect unlabeled pictures to obtain the coarse label information to assist labelImg for the rest data. During the experiment, 4000 of them were set as the train set and 1000 as the test set.

2.2 Overall Structure

In this paper, the Dynamic Receptive Field (DRF) module is embedded in the feature pyramid network [21] of the basic network of object detection algorithms to further improve the network's extraction of feature information. Through the spatial activation of the region of interest, a Spatial Activation Region Proposal Network (SARPN) is proposed. Then the higher-quality region of interest is sent to the subsequent classification and regression network for the improvement of the recognition accuracy of the detectors. Figure 2 shows the overall process of detecting pin defects designed in this paper. DRF can be easily embedded after the fusion part of the upper and lower layers of the feature pyramid networks (FPN). SARPN is based on the original RPN network through the activation of spatial information, and this method of activating spatial information is efficient and requires marginal computational burden.

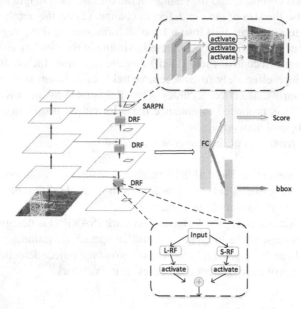

Fig. 2. Overall frame diagram, where *L-RF* and *S-RF* refer to large and small receptive fields respectively.

2.3 Dynamic Receptive Field

The receptive field refers to the area size of the input layer corresponding to an element in the output result of a certain layer in the convolutional neural network. The receptive fields corresponding to different convolution kernels are different. The larger the convolution kernel is, the larger the receptive field is.

During the inspection of transmission lines, the size of the pin defect will change greatly due to the difference in the shooting distance and angle of the UAV. Therefore, a dynamic receptive field feature extraction mechanism needs to be adopted to enable the network to adapt to the pin defect objects of different sizes. In addition, the lack of pins is more complicated than other pin defects, because the pins exist on various connecting hardware and components, and need to combine contextual semantic information. Therefore, this paper integrates the information between channels while designing the dynamic receptive field. By activating the information between each channel, it can better fuse the context to learn the missing features of pins in different scenarios.

Atrous convolution [22] is a method of injecting holes into the convolution layer to achieve the effect of different convolution kernel sizes. By setting a certain expansion coefficient, the number of intervals between the convolution kernels can be controlled. Under normal circumstances, the coefficient is 1. When the number of intervals is greater than 1, holes will be filled in the corresponding interval area. Therefore, it can expand the range of the convolution output without losing information, and has the effect of increasing the receptive field. The relationship between the output feature map size and the input feature map can be expressed by the following formula:

$$\text{output} = \frac{\text{input} + 2 * \text{padding} - \text{dilation} * (\text{kernel} - 1) - 1}{\text{stride}} + 1 \tag{1}$$

where *padding* is the filling coefficient, *dilation* is the expansion coefficient, *kernel* is the size of the convolution window, and stride is the step size.

As shown in Fig. 3, the DRF module in this paper is added after the upper and lower layers of the feature pyramid which has been fused, and it contains two branches. The atrous convolution control network uses different receptive fields. Each branch is fed back through the activation factors of global average pooling and global max pooling respectively. One of the branches first passes through a 3×3 convolution kernel, the number of input and output channels remains unchanged, and the size of the feature map is maintained through padding. Then after two-way processing, a $1 \times 1 \times c$ vector is generated for its global average pooling, which is used to describe the global features at a deep level and generates the activation factors of each dimension. On the other hand, the global maximum pooling is used to obtain deep spatial information to generate corresponding activation factors. Because the dimensions of the activation factors of the two ways are the same, they are directly added and fed back to each channel through the nonlinear activation functions relu and sigmoid.

The other branch is similar, and expects the expansion factor to 2. Therefore, through DRF, different receptive fields can be used to obtain deep-level information and be activated, so as to improve the effect of feature extraction. The DRF process can be represented by the following formula:

$$y = \text{relu}(\text{bn}(c_n(x))) \tag{2}$$

where c_n represents the convolutional layer, c_1 is a 3×3 convolution and c_2 is a 3×3 convolution with an expansion factor of 2.

$$A = f_2(\text{relu}(f_1(\text{avgpool}(y)))) \tag{3}$$

$$B = f_2(\text{relu}(f_1(\text{maxpool}(y)))) \tag{4}$$

where $f_1 \in R^{C/r \times C}$, $f_2 \in R^{C \times C/r}$ are fully connected layers.

$$f(x) = \sigma(A_1 + B_1) * y_1 + \sigma(A_2 + B_2) * y_2 \tag{5}$$

where *relu*, σ is the linear rectification function and the sigmoid function, A_1, B_1, y_1 and A_2, B_2, y_2 represent branches that pass through different convolutional layer and are activated respectively.

2.4 Spatial Activation Region Proposal Network

Most of the two-stage detection methods use the region proposal network (RPN). This network maps each feature point on the feature map generated by convolution back to

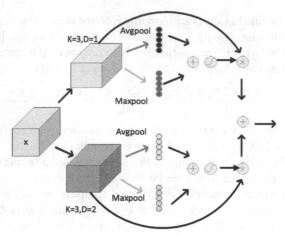

Fig. 3. DRF module, the X input is the feature map after the fusion of the shallow and deep layers of the feature pyramid, K is the size of the convolution kernel, and D is the expansion coefficient of the hole convolution.

the center of the receptive field of the original image as a reference point, and then selects K anchor boxes of different sizes and different aspect ratios around this reference point. Then all anchor boxes are subjected to softmax binary classification and bounding box regression respectively to generate $2K$ scores and $4K$ coordinate positions. The softmax classifier compares the overlapping area between the ground truth and the anchor of the training image. If the intersection ratio is greater than a certain threshold, it is set as a positive sample, and if it is less than a certain threshold, it is set as a negative sample. Then select a part of the region of interest to be cut out by ROI align for final classification and boundary regression.

These regions will be mapped to different levels of feature maps in the feature pyramid according to their size. The size of the pin defect is smaller, and a part will be cut out from the deep feature map. Due to the low resolution of the deep feature map, the classification effect is poor, which will affect the accuracy of defect recognition. Therefore, a spatial activation region proposal network as shown in Fig. 4 is designed to further activate the spatial information of the region of interest. SARPN consists of two branches placed after each ROI operation. One branch averages the pixel values of the corresponding points of the feature maps of all channels to obtain a feature map, and the global information of the feature layer is better obtained through the averaging process. The other branch takes the maximum pixel values of the corresponding points of the feature maps of all channels value to obtain another feature map, and the texture information of the feature layer can be better obtained by taking the maximum value. Then the two feature maps are spliced together, and activated by a 3×3 convolutional layer and a sigmoid nonlinear function to generate the heatmap which is fed back to the corresponding region of interest.

$$f(x) = \sigma\{c[\text{mean}(x) + \text{max}(x)]\} * x \tag{6}$$

where $c \in R^{1 \times 2}$, σ is the sigmoid activation function.

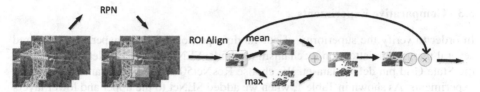

Fig. 4. Schematic diagram of SARPN.

3 Experiment

3.1 Experiment Setting

The experimental server has 8 NVIDIA Tesla P40s, and the single GPU memory is 24 GB. The deep learning framework is Pytorch, the SGD optimizer is used, the learning rate is set to 0.02, the batch_size is set to 8, a total of 24 epochs are trained, and the learning rate drop stage is set to [16, 22]. Multi-scale preprocessing is performed on the input image during training, and it is adjusted to $1333 \times 800, 2000 \times 1200$. All experiments are conducted on MMDetection [23], a deep learning object detection toolbox based on Pytorch.

3.2 Evaluation Metrics

This paper uses the precision rate, the average precision mAP and the recall rate as the indicators to measure the detection effect of the pin defect. The detector produces a series of predicted boxes, whose intersection with the ground truth can be calculated. They can be divided into true-positive samples (TP), true-negative samples (TP), false-negative samples (FN), false-positive samples (FP) by setting the IoU threshold. The precision and recall of each category can be calculated:

$$\text{precision} = \frac{TP}{TP + FP} \tag{7}$$

$$\text{recall} = \frac{TP}{TP + FN} \tag{8}$$

Setting different confidences will get different PR curves. In order to comprehensively measure the recognition effect of different confidences and multiple categories, this experiment adopts the average precision mAP:

$$mAP = \frac{1}{N_{cls}} \sum (\int_0^1 p_{cls}(r) dr) \tag{9}$$

where N_{cls} refers to the number of categories in the dataset, and p_{cls} is the PR curve of each category.

3.3 Comparative Experiments

In order to verify the superiority of our module proposed in this paper, we compared several mainstream attention mechanism methods: SENet [24], ECANet [25] based on the State Grid pin defect dataset. We choose ResNet50 as the basic framework for the experiments. As shown in Table 1, when we added SENet to the upper and lower layers of the feature pyramid of Cascade RCNN, the mAP decreased by 1.4% and the recall increased by 0.2% compared with the original algorithm. Similarly, we add ECANet, experiments show that mAP decreases by 0.4% and recall increases by 1.2%. In contrast, our method achieved a 4.4% mAP and an 8.6% recall improvement. Meanwhile, from the PR curve shown in Fig. 5, the performance of our method is better than others. We also verified the effectiveness of our work on the one-stage method. Because the one-stage method does not have an RPN network, we only test the effect of DRF. Comparing the above two attention mechanisms on the ATSS algorithm, our method works better.

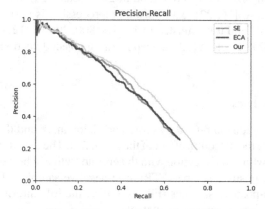

Fig. 5. PR curve on cascade RCNN.

3.4 Ablation Experiments

The above experiments show that our method works best on Cascade RCNN. In order to further verify the improvement effect of the method proposed in this paper, we do further ablation experiments on the basis of Cascade RCNN. Table 2 gives the specific experimental details. First, the DRF module was embedded in the feature pyramid network of the original algorithm, and the improvement effect was obvious. The mAP increased by 3.9% and the recall increased by 6.3%. Then we applied SARPN to the original algorithm, the recall improves by 3.6%. Finally, DRF and SARPN are added at the same time. The experiment shows that this combination greatly improves the detection effect, a 4.4% mAP improvement and an 8.6% recall improvement are obtained respectively (Fig. 6).

Table 1. Comparison experiments.

Method	AP	AP$_{50}$	AP$_{75}$	AR
CascadeRCNN	23.6	46.8	20.4	69.4
+ SENet	22.6	45.4	20.0	69.6
+ ECANet	23.0	46.4	19.4	68.2
+ Ours	**25.3**	**51.1**	**21.4**	**78.0**
FasterRCNN	22.3	44.7	20.4	66.3
+ SENet	21.7	44.3	17.9	67.4
+ ECANet	22.2	44.5	18.9	65.4
+ Ours	**23.2**	**46.3**	**20.6**	**69.7**
ATSS	22.1	45.6	18.0	77.2
+ SENet	21.5	44.5	17.6	77.4
+ ECANet	21.6	44.7	16.5	75.8
+ Ours	**22.4**	**46.2**	**19.1**	**82.1**

Table 2. Ablation experiments.

Method	AP	AP$_{50}$	AP$_{75}$	AR
CascadeRCNN	23.6	46.8	20.4	69.4
+ DRF	25.2	50.6	**21.9**	75.7
+ SARPN	23.2	47.0	18.7	**73.0**
+ DRF + SARPN	**25.3**	**51.1**	**21.4**	**78.0**

Fig. 6. The test results of pin defects on transmission lines.

4 Conclusion

Pin defect detection is a difficult task in transmission line inspection. The pin itself is small in size, and its shape features are not obvious, so it is not easy to identify. The scene of the transmission line is complex, and the pin defect exists on the tower, hardware and plate at the same time. Moreover, there are various types of components on the transmission line, such as insulators, suspension clips, shock-proof hammers, etc., which are easy to be blocked. In addition, UAVs are often used in line inspections at present. The disadvantage of aerial inspections is the transformation of visual information, and changes in distance and height will affect the quality of the pictures.

This paper makes a targeted study based on these detection problems. In view of the defect size change caused by UAV shooting, we added a DRF module to the feature pyramid, which allows the network to adaptively use different receptive fields. Due to the complexity of the pin defect scene, our proposed DRF module fully incorporates contextual information from multiple channels. Furthermore, we proposed SARPN further activates the spatial information of the region of interest, retaining more information for the final classification and regression of the two-stage detector.

Acknowledgments. This work was supported by Research on the new method and application of power grid equipment inspection and operation sensor control for major scientific and technological projects in Anhui Province (202203a05020023) and Hefei City's Key Common Technology R&D Project R&D and industrialization of key technologies for visual intelligence and edge computing for complex power scenarios (2021GJ020).

References

1. Girshick, R., Donahue, J., Darrell, T., Malik, J.: Rich feature hierarchies for accurate object detection and semantic segmentation. In: Proceedings of the IEEE Conference on Computer Vision and Pattern Recognition, pp. 580–587 (2014)
2. Girshick, R.: Fast r-cnn. In: Proceedings of the IEEE International Conference on Computer Vision, pp. 1440–1448 (2015)
3. Ren, S., He, K., Girshick, R., Sun, J.: Faster r-cnn: towards real-time object detection with region proposal networks. In: Proceedings o fthe Advances in Neural Information Processing Systems, 28 (2015)
4. Cai, Z., Vasconcelos, N.: Cascade r-cnn: delving into high quality object detection. In: Proceedings of the IEEE conference on computer vision and pattern recognition, pp. 6154–6162 (2018)
5. Redmon, J., Divvala, S., Girshick, R., Farhadi, A.: You only look once: unified, real-time object detection. In: Proceedings of the IEEE Conference on Computer Vision and Pattern Recognition, pp. 779–788 (2016)
6. Redmon, J., Farhadi, A.: YOLO9000: better, faster, stronger. In: Proceedings of the IEEE Conference on Computer Vision and Pattern Recognition, pp. 7263–7271 (2017)
7. Redmon, J., Farhadi, A.: Yolov3: An incremental improvement (2018). arXiv preprint arXiv: 1804.02767
8. Bochkovskiy, A., Wang, C.Y., Liao, H.Y.M.: Yolov4: Optimal speed and accuracy of object detection (2020). arXiv preprint arXiv:2004.10934

9. Liu, W., et al.: Ssd: Single shot multibox detector. In: Proceedings of the European Conference on Computer Vision, pp. 21–37 (2016)
10. Lin, T.Y., Goyal, P., Girshick, R., He, K., Dollár, P.: Focal loss for dense object detection. In: Proceedings of the IEEE International Conference on Computer Vision, pp. 2980–2988 (2017)
11. Zhang, S., Chi, C., Yao, Y., Lei, Z., Li, S.Z.: Bridging the gap between anchor-based and anchor-free detection via adaptive training sample selection. In: Proceedings of the IEEE Conference on Computer Vision and Pattern Recognition, pp. 9759–9768 (2020)
12. Uijlings, J.R., Van De Sande, K.E., Gevers, T., Smeulders, A.W.: Selective search for object recognition. Int. J. Comput. Vision **104**(2), 154–171 (2013)
13. Wu, J., et al.: Detection method based on improved faster R-CNN for pin defect in transmission lines. In: Proceedings of the E3S Web of Conferences, vol. 300 (2021)
14. Zhang, W., Gu, C., Li, Z., Sheng, G.: Image detection technology on pin defect to overhead power lines. In: Proceedings of the 2020 5th Asia Conference on Power and Electrical Engineering, pp. 229–233 (2020)
15. Simonyan, K., Zisserman, A.: Very deep convolutional networks for large-scale image recognition (2014). arXiv preprint arXiv:1409.1556
16. He, H., Li, Y., Yang, J., Wang, Z., Chen, B., Jiao, R.: Pin-missing defect recognition based on feature fusion and spatial attention mechanism. Energy Rep. **8**, 656–663 (2022)
17. Zhao, Z., Qi, H., Qi, Y., Zhang, K., Zhai, Y., Zhao, W.: Detection method based on automatic visual shape clustering for pin-missing defect in transmission lines. IEEE Trans. Instrum. Meas. **69**(9), 6080–6091 (2020)
18. Xiao, Y., Li, Z., Zhang, D., Teng, L.: Detection of pin defects in aerial images based on cascaded convolutional neural network. IEEE Access **9**, 73071–73082 (2021)
19. Mei, S., Yang, H., Yin, Z.: An unsupervised-learning-based approach for automated defect inspection on textured surfaces. IEEE Trans. Instrum. Meas. **67**(6), 1266–1277 (2018)
20. Everingham, M., Van Gool, L., Williams, C.K., Winn, J., Zisserman, A.: The pascal visual object classes (voc) challenge. Int. J. Comput. Vision **88**(2), 303–338 (2010)
21. Lin, T.Y., Dollár, P., Girshick, R., He, K., Hariharan, B., Belongie, S.: Feature pyramid networks for object detection. In: Proceedings of the IEEE Conference on Computer Vision and Pattern Recognition, pp. 2117–2125 (2017)
22. Yu, F., Koltun, V.: Multi-scale context aggregation by dilated convolutions (2015). arXiv preprint arXiv:1511.07122
23. Chen, K., et al.: MMDetection: open mmlab detection toolbox and benchmark (2019). arXiv preprint arXiv:1906.07155
24. Hu, J., Shen, L., Sun, G.: Squeeze-and-excitation networks. In: Proceedings of the IEEE conference on computer vision and pattern recognition, pp. 7132–7141 (2018)
25. Wang, Q., Wu, B., Zhu, P., Li, P., Hu, Q.: ECA-Net: efficient channel attention for deep convolutional neural networks. In: Proceedings of the IEEE Conference on Computer Vision and Pattern Recognition (2020)

Few-Shot Object Detection Based on Latent Knowledge Representation

Yifeng Cao[1,2,3], Lijuan Duan[1,2,3], Zhaoying Liu[1(✉)], Wenjian Wang[1,2,3], and Fangfang Liang[4,5]

[1] Faculty of Information Technology, Beijing University of Technology, Beijing 100124, China
{ljduan,zhaoying.liu}@bjut.edu.cn, {caoyifeng,wangwj}@emails.bjut.edu.cn
[2] Beijing Key Laboratory of Trusted Computing, Beijing 100124, China
[3] National Engineering Laboratory for Critical Technologies of Information Security Classified Protection, Beijing 100124, China
[4] Hebei Agricultural University, Baoding, China
[5] Hebei Key Laboratory of Agricultural Big Data, Baoding, China
liangfangfang@hebau.edu.cn

Abstract. Few-shot object detection (FSOD) aims to achieve excellent novel category object detection accuracy with few samples. Most existing researches address this problem by fine-tuning Faster R-CNN, where the model is first trained on the base class set with abundant samples, and then fine-tuned on the novel class set with scarce samples. But in the fine-tuning stage, the connection between the base class set and the novel class set is ignored, which makes it difficult to learn novel classes with scarce samples. To solve this issue, we propose a latent knowledge-based FSOD method, which aims to utilize latent knowledge to build connections between categories. Specifically, first we propose a latent knowledge classifier (LK-Classifier), which realizes object recognition by splitting features through latent knowledge. Then a guidance module is designed to constrain latent knowledge with semantic expression, so as to realize the bridge between base class set and novel class set through latent knowledge. Experimental results show that our method achieves promising results on the FSOD task on the PASCAL VOC and COCO datasets, especially when the number of samples is extremely scarce.

Keywords: Few-shot object detection · Latent knowledge · Semantic expression

1 Introduction

Deep learning has been widely used, and the performance has been greatly improved in various vision tasks, such as image classification [3,8], object detection [6,13,16–19]. However, these performance improvements all rely on a large

Supported by the National Natural Science Foundation of China (No. 62176009, No. 62106065, No. 62176010).

S. Yu et al. (Eds.): PRCV 2022, LNCS 13537, pp. 400–411, 2022.
https://doi.org/10.1007/978-3-031-18916-6_33

amount of samples and labeled information. The labeling process consumes a lot of manpower and material resources, and the lack of the number of samples will seriously limit the performance of deep learning in various vision tasks. And it is difficult to construct large-scale datasets in many real-world scenarios, such as rare cases and rare animals. Therefore, research on few-shot learning is imperative.

Recently, many researchers have devoted themselves to the study of FSOD [2,5,9,10,15,20,21], which aims to detect objects of this class through one or a few samples of this class. The early FSOD methods [22,24,26–28] introduced the meta-learning strategy to avoid the problem of data imbalance as much as possible. The recent two-stage fine-tuning method [15,19–21,30] in which the model is first trained on the base class set with a large number of samples, and then fine-tuned on the novel class set with a small number of samples, not only obtains a great improvement in accuracy, but also shows a huge potential. AGFL [31] believes that building the connection between the base classes set and the novel classes set is beneficial for few-shot image recognition, and uses the annotated attributes to build the connection (see the left of Fig. 1). However, labeling a set of attributes suitable for classification is extremely difficult in many cases.

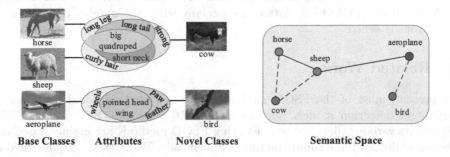

Base Classes   **Attributes**   **Novel Classes**   **Semantic Space**

Fig. 1. Different classes have different visual attributes and can be described by different combinations of visual attributes (for example, horse can be described by long legs, quadrupeds, long tail, long neck). Some attributes are shared, and the more similar classes share the more attributes. In addition, the visual attributes of the novel class can be described by the visual attributes of the base class (e.g., as a novel class, cow can be described by long tails, quadrupeds, short necks, no curly hair, no long legs, and no wing). The right panel shows the category distribution over the semantic space.

To overcome this difficulty, we propose a latent knowledge representation-based approach for FSOD without labeling its attributes separately. Our main point is that features can be described by latent knowledge, just as categories can be described by groups of attributes. Therefore, we first propose a latent knowledge classifier (LK-Classifier), which uses the latent knowledge extracted on the base class set to split the image features, and obtains the score of each latent knowledge for final classification. Meanwhile, to make our method more suitable for FSOD, we make similar classes have similar latent knowledge descriptions, and the more similar the classes, the more similar the latent knowledge descriptions. But only through visual space, the model cannot know which classes are similar and which are not, but the semantic space makes it possible (see the right of Fig. 1). Therefore, we introduce semantic expressions to constrain class prototypes, so that the similarity between the two class prototypes is consistent with the similarity of the corresponding semantic expression. In this way, when fine-tuning the model with novel class set, the semantic similarity between the novel class and the base class set can be used to obtain the latent knowledge that the novel class should have, providing more fine-tuning details for the model and making up for the huge negative impact caused by the scarcity of samples as much as possible.

The main contributions are summarized as follows:

- In the FSOD task without attribute annotation, we propose to associate the base class set with the novel class set using latent knowledge.
- We propose a latent knowledge classifier (LK-Classifier) and a guidance module based on semantic expression, it is beneficial to provide more detailed descriptions of novel classes to make up for the huge negative impact caused by the scarcity of samples of novel classes as much as possible.
- Our method achieves significant performance improvements in both PASCAL VOC [4] and COCO [12] datasets, especially when the number of samples is extremely scarce.

2   Related Work

At present, most of the FSOD methods are based on traditional deep learning target detection models, such as YOLO [16–18] series, SSD [13], R-CNN [7] and its variants [6,11,19], etc. Existing FSOD methods are mainly based on meta-learning and fine-tuning methods. Specifically, Wang et al. [22] designed a meta-learning framework to learn a novel class classifier using meta-knowledge learned from base classes with abundant samples. Meta R-CNN [26] combines Faster R-CNN with meta-learning for object detection. Later, the two-stage fine-tuning method TFA [21] based on the Faster R-CNN model has shown far superior performance and room for improvement over meta-learning based methods. MPSR [23] enriches the object scales in FSOD through a multi-scale sample refinement method to alleviate the inherent scale bias. SRR-FSD [30] proposes an object detection method based on semantic relational reasoning, which utilizes the invariance of semantic relations between novel classes and base classes to introduce explicit relational reasoning into the learning of new object detection. FSCE [20] shows through experiments that in FSOD, the error rate of classification is much higher than that of regressor, and introduced contrastive learning to facilitate object classification. DeFRCN [15] extends Faster RCNN with gradient decoupling layers for multi-stage decoupling and a prototype calibration module for multi-task decoupling, reaching new state-of-the-art on various benchmarks. Our method is also based on fine-tuning. But different from existing FSOD methods, we facilitate the classification of novel classes by building the relationship between base class set and novel class set.

3 Methodology

In this section, we first detail the setup for the FSOD problem. Then, we introduce our latent knowledge representation-based FSOD method, as shown in Fig. 2. Our method takes DeFRCN as the baseline. We design a latent knowledge classifier (LK-Classifier) to split and classify image features using latent knowledge. At the same time, in order to make similar classes have similar latent knowledge representations, we construct a guidance module.

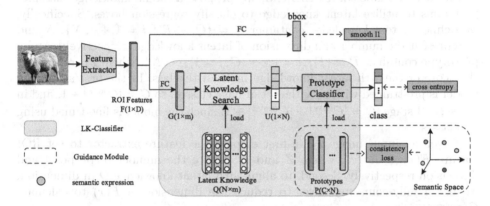

Fig. 2. Overview of our proposed method. 'FC' indicate fully-connected layer. 'Feature Extractor' consists of Backbone, Region-Proposal Network, ROI Pooling and RoI Feature Extractor.

3.1 Problem Setting

As in previous work [5,21,29,30], we use the standard problem setting for FSOD in our paper. Specifically, the training data set consists of a base class set $D^{base} = \{x_i^{base}, y_i^{base}\}$ with a large number of samples and a novel class set $D^{novel} = \{x_i^{novel}, y_i^{novel}\}$ with only a few samples, where x_i and y_i represent training samples and labels, respectively. The number of samples for each class in the novel class set is K, thus constructing the k-shot problem. The classes in the base class set are C^{base}, the classes in the novel class set are C^{novel}, and the classes in the two sets are disjoint, that is, $C^{base} \cap C^{novel} = \emptyset$. The training of the model is divided into two stages. In the first stage, only the base class set is used to train the model, and the model is a $\{|C^{base}| + 1\}$-way detector. In the second stage, the model is fine-tuned using both base class set and novel class set, at which time the model is expanded into a $\{|C^{base}| + |C^{novel}| + 1\}$-way detector. It is worth noting that when the model is fine-tuned in the second stage, the number of samples for each class in the base class set for training is the same as the number of samples for each novel class, which is k.

3.2   Latent Knowledge Classifier (LK-Classifier)

There are several problems with properties as one way of connecting the base set to the novel classes set. First, by manually annotating attributes, it is difficult to design a set of discriminative attributes for recognition tasks, because it is difficult to reflect all human-defined attributes through images, and it is difficult to judge whether the attributes that can be reflected are sufficient for recognition ability [25]. Second, attributes need to be marked manually, which consumes a lot of manpower and material resources.

We argue that there is latent knowledge in the feature space that can be used to split and classify features, just as attributes can split and classify classes in visual space, and the latent knowledge is learned autonomously and does not need to be labeled. To this end, we propose a latent knowledge classifier that aims to utilize latent knowledge to classify regression boxes. Specifically, we define a latent knowledge container $Q = \{Q_i \in R^m, i = 1, \cdots, N\}$, N and m represent the number and dimension of latent knowledge, respectively. And a prototype container $P = \{P_{ij}, i = 1, \cdots, C, j = 1, \cdots, N\}$, where P_{ij} represents the score of the j-th latent knowledge in the i-th class. In the first stage, the model is pre-trained with only the set of base classes, so $C = |C^{base}| + 1$, and in the second stage, $C = |C^{base}| + |C^{novel}| + 1$, since the model is fine-tuned using all classes.

Given an input image x, we first employ the feature extractor to get ROI feature $F(x) \in R^{Z \times D}$, where Z and D denote the number of proposal and dimension respectively. Second, to align with latent knowledge Q in dimension, we use a fully-connected layer to reduce the dimension of $F(x)$ to calculate $G(x) \in R^{Z \times m}$.

$$G(x)_i = W_c F(x)_i + b_c \tag{1}$$

where W_c and b_c are the parameters of the fully connected layer. Then, we conduct latent knowledge search on the feature $G(x)_i$ and split it by latent knowledge to obtain the relationship between it and each latent knowledge. Specifically, we use cosine similarity to obtain the similarity score $U_i = \{U_{i,1}, U_{i,2}, \cdots, U_{i,N}\}$ between $G(x)_i$ and each latent knowledge Q_j^T. $U_{i,j}$ denotes the score of $G(x)_i$ and Q_j^T.

$$U_{i,j} = \alpha \frac{G(x)_i Q_j^T}{\|G(x)_i\| \cdot \|Q_j^T\|} \tag{2}$$

Finally, we classify U_i by comprehensively considering the true probability distribution of all latent knowledge in each class and the actual probability distribution in U_i. Specifically, U_i and all class prototypes P^T are again subjected to cosine similarity judgment, and the final class probability is obtained after the score passes through a softmax layer. $S_{i,k}$ represents the probability that $G(x)_i$ is the k-th class.

$$S_{i,k} = softmax(\beta \frac{U_i P_k^T}{\|U_i\| \cdot \|P_k^T\|}) \tag{3}$$

α and β are scaling factors to enlarge the gradient, we set them both to 20 in the experiment.

3.3   Guidance Module

Our motivation is to build a bridge between the base class set and the novel class set through the latent knowledge, so that when the novel class arrive, the model can quickly obtain the latent knowledge representations that the novel classes should have, and fine-tune the model. Only through the above LK-Classifier can not achieve our purpose, because the model does not know the similarity between the various classes, it cannot make similar classes have similar latent knowledge representations. So we introduce a guidance module that makes the prototypes of the classes in P have a certain similarity(see Fig. 3).

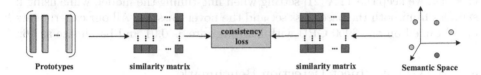

Fig. 3. Guidance module

First, we obtain semantic expressions $V \in R^{C \times m'}$ of all categories by using GloVe [14], where C and m' represent the number and dimension of semantic expressions respectively. Then, the similarity between each semantic expression and the similarity between each class prototype is calculated, and the normalization operation is performed. Finally, the KL-Divergence loss is employed to keep them consistent, so that the similarity between each class prototype is consistent with the similarity of the corresponding semantic expression. The consistency loss is formalized as:

$$L_{con} = \frac{1}{C} C \sum_{i=1}^{C} \sum_{j=1}^{C} I\{i \neq j\} \cdot v_{i,j} \log \frac{v_{i,j}}{p_{i,j}} \tag{4}$$

where $v_{i,j} = \frac{\exp(\tilde{V}_i \cdot \tilde{V}_j / \tau)}{\sum_{k=1}^{C} I\{i \neq j\} \exp(\tilde{V}_i \cdot \tilde{V}_k / \tau)}$, $p_{i,j} = \frac{\exp(\tilde{P}_i \cdot \tilde{P}_j / \tau)}{\sum_{k=1}^{C} I\{i \neq j\} \exp(\tilde{P}_i \cdot \tilde{P}_k / \tau)}$, τ is the hyper-parameter temperature,we set it as 0.05, $\tilde{V}_i = \frac{V_i}{\|V_i\|}$ and the same for $\tilde{P}_i$.

The total loss in training stage is:

$$L_{total} = L_{rpn} + L_{cls} + L_{reg} + L_{con} \tag{5}$$

where L_{rpn}, L_{cls} and L_{reg} represent the RPN loss, classification loss and regression loss in Faster R-CNN [19], respectively.

4   Experiments

In this section, we first describe the details in the experiments, and then perform extensive experiments on the benchmarks using PASCAL VOC [4] and COCO [12] dataset. For fairness, we strictly adhere to the construction and evaluation protocol for FSOD data. Finally, we provide ablation analysis and visualizations.

4.1   Implementation Details

Our method is based on DeFRCN [15], which uses Faster R-CNN [19] with Resnet-101, and strictly keeps the parameters of DeFRCN unchanged in all our experiments. We utilize the same data split as [21] to evaluate our method for fair comparison. When using the PASACL VOC and COCO datasets for evaluation, the latent knowledge is set to 64×256 and 128×256, namely $N = 64$, $m = 256$ and $N = 128$, $m = 256$, respectively. In particular, the number of categories in the PASACL VOC dataset are limited, so we use $v_{i,j} = \frac{\vec{V}_i \cdot \vec{V}_j}{\sum_{k=1}^{C} I\{i \neq j\} \vec{V}_i \cdot \vec{V}_k}$ in Eq. 4 to obtain the similarity between semantic expressions. To avoid forgetting the base class set, we keep the TFA [21] setting when fine-tuning the model, while using k samples from both the base class set and the novel class set. All our experiments are obtained on one 3090 GPU with learning rate as 0.01 and batch size as 16.

4.2   Few-Shot Object Detection Benchmarks

Results on PASCAL VOC. There are a total of 20 classes in the PASACL VOC dataset, which is divided into a base class set with 15 classes and a novel class set with 5 classes. We have three combinations of the base class set and the novel class set division, the same as the existing work. Each class in the base class set has a large number of samples, while each class in the novel class set has only k samples, in the experiment k=1, 2, 3, 5, 10, these k samples are in this class randomly selected from the sample. In the second stage, we extract k samples for each base class in the base class set, and fine-tune the model together with the novel class set. The experimental results are shown in Table 1.

As shown in Table 1, our experimental results show an improvement in accuracy when samples are scarce compared to existing works. This shows that the latent knowledge can improve FSOD by building a bridge between the base class set and the novel class set.

Results on COCO. For the COCO dataset, it contains a total of 80 categories. As in existing works, we randomly select 60 categories to form a base class set, and the remaining 20 categories form a novel class set. For the fine-tuning phase, we use k samples of all classes as the training set. Same as the baseline, we choose $k = 1, 2, 3, 5, 10, 30$ for comparative experiments. The experimental results are shown in Table 2.

The COCO dataset has many more categories than VOC dataset, but Table 2 proves that our method is still effective in improving the detection accuracy, and the smaller the number of samples, the more obvious the improvement effect.

Table 1. FSOD performance (novel AP50(%)) on three splits of PASCAL VOC dataset. *indicates that we directly run the released code to obtain the results.

Method/Shot	Novel Split 1					Novel Split 2					Novel Split 3				
	1	2	3	5	10	1	2	3	5	10	1	2	3	5	10
FSRW [9]	14.8	15.5	26.7	33.9	47.2	15.7	15.2	22.7	30.1	40.5	21.3	25.6	28.4	42.8	45.9
metaDet [22]	18.9	20.6	30.2	36.8	49.6	21.8	23.1	27.8	31.7	43.0	20.6	23.9	29.4	43.9	44.1
Meta R-CNN [26]	19.9	25.5	35.0	45.7	51.5	10.4	19.4	29.6	34.8	45.4	14.3	18.2	27.5	41.2	48.1
TFA w/fc [21]	36.8	29.1	43.6	55.7	57.0	18.2	29.0	33.4	35.5	39.0	27.7	33.6	42.5	48.7	50.2
TFA w/cos [21]	39.8	36.1	44.7	55.7	56.0	23.5	26.9	34.1	35.1	39.1	30.8	34.8	42.8	49.5	49.8
MPSR [23]	41.7	_	51.4	55.2	61.8	24.4	_	39.2	39.9	47.8	35.6	_	42.3	48.0	49.7
SRR-FSD [30]	47.8	50.5	51.3	55.2	56.8	32.5	35.3	39.1	40.8	43.8	40.1	41.5	44.3	46.9	46.4
FSCE [20]	44.2	43.8	51.4	61.9	63.4	27.3	29.5	43.5	44.2	50.2	37.2	41.9	47.5	54.6	58.5
FADI [1]	50.3	54.8	54.2	59.3	63.2	30.6	35.0	40.3	42.8	48.0	45.7	49.7	49.1	55.0	59.6
DeFRCN* [15]	55.3	58.5	63.6	**67.8**	66.6	34.6	41.5	48.5	53.5	**53.4**	52.4	56.2	55.8	**61.3**	**63.2**
Ours	**57.7**	**62.0**	**64.8**	66.5	**67.4**	**36.2**	**45.0**	**51.8**	**53.7**	52.3	51.8	55.7	**57.1**	61.1	62.0

Table 2. FSOD performance (novel AP(%)) on COCO dataset.

Method/Shot	Shot Number					
	1	2	3	5	10	30
FRCN-ft [26]	1.0	1.8	2.8	4.0	6.5	11.1
FSRW [9]	-	-	-	-	5.6	9.1
MetaDet [22]	-	-	-	-	7.1	11.3
Meta R-CNN [26]	-	-	-	-	8.7	12.4
TFA [21]	4.4	5.4	6.0	7.7	10.0	13.7
MPSR [23]	5.1	6.7	7.4	8.7	9.8	14.1
FSDetView [24]	4.5	6.6	7.2	10.7	12.5	14.7
DeFRCN* [15]	6.5	11.5	13.2	15.6	18.6	**22.2**
Ours	**8.5**	**12.3**	**14.2**	**15.7**	**18.8**	21.9

4.3 Ablation Analysis

In this section, we separately explore the influence of the guidance module and the number of latent knowledge on the experimental results through experiments. All ablation experiments in this section, like most existing works, are based on Novel Set 1 of PASCAL VOC.

The Effect of the Guidance Module. To make latent knowledge representations of similar classes have a certain similarity, we introduce a guidance module. We conduct ablation experiments to validate the effectiveness of the guidance module.

Table 3 shows the comparison results of the experiments. Taking 1-shot and 2-shot as an example, the accuracy is improved by 1.1% and 3.3% when using the guidance module compared to not using it. This shows that the guidance module is effective in improving the performance of the model.

Table 3. The effect of the guidance module.

Model\Shot	1	2	3	5	10
Baseline	55.3	58.5	63.6	**67.8**	66.6
Without guidance	56.6	58.7	63.7	67.0	66.5
Ours	**57.7**	**62.0**	**64.8**	66.5	**67.4**

The Number of Latent Knowledge. In our method, the number of latent knowledge is a very important hyperparameter. When the number is small, the latent knowledge will not be enough to describe the ROI features of all classes. In the case of large numbers, some latent knowledge may be similar and increase the computational cost.

Table 4. The effect of the number of latent knowledge. Only the number of latent knowledge is different here, other settings are exactly the same.

Number/Shot	1	2	3	5	10
48	57.6	61.0	63.6	**67.6**	65.3
56	56.6	59.3	62.5	66.4	65.2
64	**57.7**	**62.0**	**64.8**	66.5	**67.4**
72	56.2	59.8	62.0	66.0	65.2

Table 4 shows the impact of different numbers of latent knowledge on model performance. We can see that when the number of latent knowledge is 64, the overall accuracy is the best. In addition, when faced with a large-scale dataset with a large number of categories, it is necessary to increase the number of latent knowledge in a timely manner.

Fig. 4. Visualize our 1-shot object detection on the boat class on the COCO dataset as an example.

4.4 Visualization

As shown in Fig. 4, we use the COCO dataset 1-shot as an example to visualize the boat in the novel class set. In Fig. 5, we visualize the results by taking the 1-shot of the VOC dataset 1-split as an example. "motorbike", "bird", "cow", and "sofa" are categories in the novel class set, and the rest are in the base class set. We can see that our method can detect more novel classes of objects.

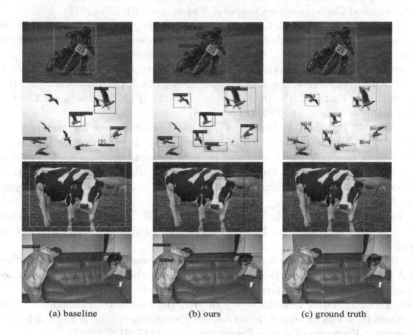

(a) baseline   (b) ours   (c) ground truth

Fig. 5. Visualization of baseline, ours and ground truth

5 Conclusion

In this paper, we propose a latent knowledge few-shot object detection model. Our motivation is to build a bridge between the base class set and the novel class set through the latent knowledge, thus, to add more details to the novel class set, and to make up for the negative impact of the scarcity of samples. To achieve it, we make similar classes have similar latent knowledge representations by introducing semantic expressions. When a novel class is encountered, the latent knowledge representations of the novel class can be quickly learned through the semantic expressions and base class set to provide more detailed descriptions of the novel class for the model. Experimental results show that our model has better performance compared to other networks, especially when the number of novel class samples is extremely scarce. We hope that our proposed method can be helpful for improving the accuracy of FSOD.

References

1. Cao, Y., et al.: Few-shot object detection via association and discrimination. In: Advances in Neural Information Processing Systems, vol. 34 (2021)
2. Chen, H., Wang, Y., Wang, G., Qiao, Y.: LSTD: a low-shot transfer detector for object detection. In: Proceedings of the AAAI Conference on Artificial Intelligence, vol. 32 (2018)
3. Dai, J., et al.: Deformable convolutional networks. In: Proceedings of the IEEE International Conference on Computer Vision, pp. 764–773 (2017)
4. Everingham, M., Van Gool, L., Williams, C.K., Winn, J., Zisserman, A.: The pascal visual object classes (VOC) challenge. Int. J. Comput. Vis. **88**(2), 303–338 (2010)
5. Fan, Q., Zhuo, W., Tang, C.-K., Tai, Y.-W.: Few-shot object detection with attention-RPN and multi-relation detector. In: Proceedings of the IEEE/CVF Conference on Computer Vision and Pattern Recognition, pp. 4013–4022 (2020)
6. Girshick, R.: Fast R-CNN. In: Proceedings of the IEEE International Conference on Computer Vision, pp. 1440–1448 (2015)
7. Girshick, R., Donahue, J., Darrell, T., Malik, J.: Rich feature hierarchies for accurate object detection and semantic segmentation. In: Proceedings of the IEEE Conference on Computer Vision and Pattern Recognition, pp. 580–587 (2014)
8. He, K., Zhang, X., Ren, S., Sun, J.: Deep residual learning for image recognition. In: Proceedings of the IEEE Conference on Computer Vision and Pattern Recognition, pp. 770–778 (2016)
9. Kang, B., Liu, Z., Wang, X., Yu, F. Feng, J., Darrell, T.: Few-shot object detection via feature reweighting. In: Proceedings of the IEEE/CVF International Conference on Computer Vision, pp. 8420–8429 (2019)
10. Karlinsky, L., et al.: Repmet: representative-based metric learning for classification and few-shot object detection. In: Proceedings of the IEEE/CVF Conference on Computer Vision and Pattern Recognition, pp. 5197–5206 (2019)
11. Lin, T.-Y., Dollár, P., Girshick, R., He, K., Hariharan, B., Belongie, S.: Feature pyramid networks for object detection. In: Proceedings of the IEEE Conference on Computer Vision and Pattern Recognition, pp. 2117–2125 (2017)
12. Lin, T.-Y., et al.: Microsoft COCO: common objects in context. In: Fleet, D., Pajdla, T., Schiele, B., Tuytelaars, T. (eds.) ECCV 2014. LNCS, vol. 8693, pp. 740–755. Springer, Cham (2014). https://doi.org/10.1007/978-3-319-10602-1_48
13. Liu, W., et al.: SSD: single shot MultiBox detector. In: Leibe, B., Matas, J., Sebe, N., Welling, M. (eds.) ECCV 2016. LNCS, vol. 9905, pp. 21–37. Springer, Cham (2016). https://doi.org/10.1007/978-3-319-46448-0_2
14. Pennington, J., Socher, R., Manning, C.D.: Glove: global vectors for word representation. In: Proceedings of the 2014 Conference on Empirical Methods in Natural Language Processing (EMNLP), pp. 1532–1543 (2014)
15. Qiao, L., Zhao, Y., Li, Z., Qiu, X., Wu, J., Zhang, C.: DEFRCN: decoupled faster R-CNN for few-shot object detection. In: Proceedings of the IEEE/CVF International Conference on Computer Vision, pp. 8681–8690 (2021)
16. Redmon, J., Divvala, S., Girshick, R., Farhadi, A.: You only look once: Unified, real-time object detection. In: Proceedings of the IEEE Conference on Computer Vision and Pattern Recognition, pp. 779–788 (2016)
17. Redmon, J., Farhadi, A.: Yolo9000: better, faster, stronger. In: Proceedings of the IEEE Conference on Computer Vision and Pattern Recognition, pp. 7263–7271 (2017)

18. Redmon, J., Farhadi, A.: Yolov3: an incremental improvement. arXiv preprint arXiv:1804.02767 (2018)
19. Ren, S., He, K., Girshick, R., Sun, J.: Faster R-CNN: towards real-time object detection with region proposal networks. In: Advances in Neural Information Processing Systems, vol. 28 (2015)
20. Sun, B., Li, B., Cai, S., Yuan, Y., Zhang, C.: FSCE: few-shot object detection via contrastive proposal encoding. In: Proceedings of the IEEE/CVF Conference on Computer Vision and Pattern Recognition, pp. 7352–7362 (2021)
21. Wang, X., Huang, T.E., Darrell, T., Gonzalez, J.E., Yu, F.: Frustratingly simple few-shot object detection. arXiv preprint arXiv:2003.06957 (2020)
22. Wang, Y.-X., Ramanan, D., Hebert, M.: Meta-learning to detect rare objects. In: Proceedings of the IEEE/CVF International Conference on Computer Vision, pp. 9925–9934 (2019)
23. Wu, J., Liu, S., Huang, D., Wang, Y.: Multi-scale positive sample refinement for few-shot object detection. In: Vedaldi, A., Bischof, H., Brox, T., Frahm, J.-M. (eds.) ECCV 2020. LNCS, vol. 12361, pp. 456–472. Springer, Cham (2020). https://doi.org/10.1007/978-3-030-58517-4_27
24. Xiao, Y., Marlet, R.: Few-shot object detection and viewpoint estimation for objects in the wild. In: Vedaldi, A., Bischof, H., Brox, T., Frahm, J.-M. (eds.) ECCV 2020. LNCS, vol. 12362, pp. 192–210. Springer, Cham (2020). https://doi.org/10.1007/978-3-030-58520-4_12
25. Xie, Y., He, X., Zhang, J., Luo, X.: Zero-shot recognition with latent visual attributes learning. Multimedia Tools Appl. **79**(37), 27321–27335 (2020)
26. Yan, X., Chen, Z., Xu, A., Wang, X., Liang, X., Lin, L.: Meta R-CNN: towards general solver for instance-level low-shot learning. In: Proceedings of the IEEE/CVF International Conference on Computer Vision, pp. 9577–9586 (2019)
27. Yang, Y., Wei, F., Shi, M., Li, G.: Restoring negative information in few-shot object detection. Adv. Neural. Inf. Process. Syst. **33**, 3521–3532 (2020)
28. Yang, Z., Wang, Y., Chen, X., Liu, J., Qiao, Y.: Context-transformer: tackling object confusion for few-shot detection. In: Proceedings of the AAAI Conference on Artificial Intelligence, vol. 34, pp. 12653–12660 (2020)
29. Zhang, W., Wang, Y.-X.: Hallucination improves few-shot object detection. In: Proceedings of the IEEE/CVF Conference on Computer Vision and Pattern Recognition, pp. 13008–13017 (2021)
30. Zhu, C., Chen, F., Ahmed, U., Shen, Z., Savvides, M.: Semantic relation reasoning for shot-stable few-shot object detection. In: Proceedings of the IEEE/CVF Conference on Computer Vision and Pattern Recognition, pp. 8782–8791 (2021)
31. Zhu, Y., Min, W., Jiang, S.: Attribute-guided feature learning for few-shot image recognition. IEEE Trans. Multimedia **23**, 1200–1209 (2020)

Identification of Bird's Nest Hazard Level of Transmission Line Based on Improved Yolov5 and Location Constraints

Yang Wu[✉], Qunsheng Zeng, Peng Li, Wenqi Huang, Lingyu Liang, and Jiajie Chen

Digital Grid Research Institute, China Southern Power Grid, Beijing, China
wuyang1@csg.cn

Abstract. Bird's nest is a common defect in transmission line, which seriously affects the safe and stable operation of the line. This paper presents a method of bird's nest hazard level identification based on improved yolov5 and location constraints, which solves the problem of bird's nest multiple identification and hazard level classification. We integrate GhostModule and ECA to design a lightweight attention mechanism convolution module (LAMCM). The original yolov5 is improved by using LAMCM and adding a prediction head, which improves the detection ability of small targets and alleviates the negative impact of scale violence. We only identify the bird's nest on the panorama of UAV patrol, and classify the hazard level of the bird's nest according to the location constraints of the bird's nest and insulator. Experiments on coco dataset and self built transmission line dataset (TL) show that our algorithm is superior to other commonly used algorithms. In particular, the recall rate of bird's nest hazard level identification has increased significantly. Compared with the original yolov5, the recall rate of the three levels of bird's nest improved by our proposed improved yolov5 is more than 3%.

Keywords: Bird's nest · Transmission line · Object detection · Attention mechanism

1 Introduction

In recent years, with the rapid development of power grid, overhead high-voltage lines are also increasing. As one of the important components of power system, high-voltage lines shoulder major tasks. In case of any problem, it may cause regional power failure, or endanger the safety of life and property. With the enhancement of people's awareness of environmental protection, the ecological environment is getting better and better, and the number of birds is also increasing. At the same time, there are also some problems. The activities of birds seriously affect the normal operation of transmission lines. The nesting behavior of birds will pollute the insulators in transmission lines, and also cause short circuit or tripping of lines. Therefore, in order to ensure the safe operation of the

S. Yu et al. (Eds.): PRCV 2022, LNCS 13537, pp. 412–425, 2022.
https://doi.org/10.1007/978-3-031-18916-6_34

transmission system, using UAV to patrol the transmission line and realize the accurate detection of bird's nest defects based on image is an urgent problem to be solved in intelligent power operation and maintenance. However, the complex background of patrol images, the change of light intensity, motion blur, target occlusion and scale change all bring great challenges to the detection.

Bird's nest recognition is a typical object detection problem. It needs to solve the location and category of defective targets in the patrol image, that is, to solve the problem of "what and where". Many researchers have carried out image-based bird's nest recognition research, which can be roughly divided into two categories: traditional image detection algorithm and deep learning image detection algorithm. Traditional target detection methods use artificially designed feature descriptors (such as SIFT, HOG, etc.) to extract the features of the image, and recognize the targets in the image through sliding window and classification model. The biggest disadvantage of this kind of methods is that the artificially designed feature descriptors have poor universality and poor robustness of the algorithm, which is not suitable for bird's nest detection in complex scenes. By learning a large number of training data, the deep learning target detection algorithm makes the deep convolution neural network have the ability to extract target features and automatically identify and mark bird's nest defects. The application of deep learning technology significantly improves the recognition effect and has good robustness.

The existing bird's nest recognition algorithms have the problem of multiple recognition of the same bird's nest. During patrol inspection, the UAV takes a panoramic image, a tower base image and multiple local images of a tower. The panoramic image is the complete transmission tower photographed by the UAV in the distance, and the local image is the detailed drawing of insulator, connecting hardware and other components photographed by the UAV in the near place. Because there are multiple local images, the scenes between the images may overlap, resulting in a bird's nest may appear in different local images at the same time. Figure 1 shows a local image of a tower at different angles. These images all contain the same bird's nest. Existing algorithms will detect bird's nest defects in all images, which will lead to the problem of multiple identification and repeated recording of defects in the same bird's nest. In addition, it is difficult to see the specific position of the bird's nest on the tower at a glance on the local images, and the position of the bird's nest cannot be accurately described during defect recording.

Fig. 1. The same nest photographed from different angles.

The existing identification algorithms do not classify the hazard level of bird's nest. In reality, most towers have birds nesting, and in order to protect birds, humans will specially place some mesh devices for birds to nest. Therefore, some non hazardous nests do not need to be handled in time, and some hazardous nests need to be handled immediately. The bird's nest above the insulator is considered to be a level I hazard, because feces and dripping water can easily lead to the decline of insulator insulation and affect the safe and stable operation of the line. The bird's nest on the cross arm and away from the insulator hanging point is considered to be a level II hazard. The bird's nest in the mesh device is considered to be a level III hazard, also known as artificial bird's nest. Level III hazards basically have no impact on the safe operation of transmission lines. Figure 2 shows bird nests with different hazard levels.

Fig. 2. From left to right, there are level I hazards, level II hazards and level III hazards.

In order to solve the problem of bird's nest multiple identification and hazard level division, this paper only focuses on the bird's nest in the panoramic image, and divides the hazard level of bird's nest by the position constraints of bird's nest and insulator string. In the panoramic image, the tower, insulator and other components are intact, and there is only one panoramic image for a tower. Due to the short shooting distance of local image, the shooting of insulator string is often incomplete, and the bird's nest and insulator generally do not exist at the same time in the local image. Therefore, the positional relationship between bird's nest and insulator string cannot be determined in the local image.

As mentioned above, we need to detect the tower, insulator and bird's nest in the panoramic image, which is a typical small target detection problem in the large-resolution image (the proportion of bird's nest in the image is about 1%). In addition, the scale size difference between the three types of targets is obvious, which brings many challenges to the detection. To solve the above problems, referring to the bneck module design in MobileNetv3 [1], we design a lightweight attention mechanism convolution module (LAMCM) integrating GhostModule [2] and ECA [3] to improve the feature extraction ability of the network. The original yolov5 is improved by using LAMCM and adding a prediction head, which improves the detection ability of small targets and alleviates the negative impact of scale violence. We further improve the detection ability of small targets by cut large image into small image and increasing the network input size. Experiments on coco dataset and self built transmission line dataset

(TL) show that our algorithm is superior to other commonly used algorithms. In particular, the recall rate of bird's nest hazard level identification has increased significantly. Compared with the original yolov5, the recall rate of the three levels of bird's nest improved by our proposed improved yolov5 is more than 3%.

We summarize our contributions as follows:

- We propose to identify the bird's nest hazard level only on the panoramic image, which solves the problem of bird's nest multiple identification and hazard level classification.
- Combining GhostModule and ECA, we designed a lightweight attention mechanism convolution module (LAMCM) to enhance the feature extraction ability of small targets.
- We use LAMCM and add a prediction head to improve the original yolov5, enhance the detection ability of small targets, and alleviate the negative impact of scale violence.

2 Related Work

2.1 Two-Stage Object Detection

Two-stage object detection consists of two steps: candidate regions proposal generation and label classification and location regression were performed on these candidate regions. Faster RCNN [4] used the region proposal network to find out the candidate regions of possible objects in the image, and then used two head networks to assign the correct category labels to these candidate regions and adjust the position of these candidate regions again. In [5], Dai et al. presented region-based fully convolutional networks for accurate and efficient object detection (R-FCN), R-FCN used position-sensitive score maps to address a dilemma between translation-invariance in image classification and translation-variance in object detection. Cascade RCNN [6] improves the quality of candidate frames generated by RPN in Faster RCNN, making the final target detection frame positioning more accurate. It consists of a series of detectors, each detector is trained based on positive and negative samples with different IOU thresholds. The later the detector, the greater the IOU threshold defining positive and negative samples, the output of the former detector is used as the input of the latter detector, so the detectors are trained stage by stage.

2.2 One-Stage Object Detection

Different from the two-stage object detection algorithm, the one-stage object detection completely eliminates proposal generation and directly regress and classify the anchors get the final bounding boxes. SSD [7] combines predictions from multiple feature maps with different resolutions to naturally handle objects of various sizes. In addition, it encapsulates all computation in a single network, making it easy to train. YOLO [8] predicts bounding boxes and class probabilities directly from full images, it is extremely fast. YOLO also predicts the bounding boxes and class probabilities directly from the full image, which is very fast. Later researchers continuously improved YOLO and proposed algorithms such as YOLOv3 [9], YOLOv4 [10], YOLOX [11] and Scaled-YOLOv4 [12]. RetinaNet [13] found that the main reason why the accuracy of the one-stage detectors is lower than that of the two-stage detectors is the extreme foreground-background class imbalance encountered during training, the paper introduces focal loss to address the class imbalance problem by reshaping the standard cross-entropy loss.

2.3   Anchor-Free Object Detection

Anchor-free object detection abandons anchors and transforms the object detection problem into key point and scale estimation. CornerNet [14] detect an object bounding box as a pair of keypoints, the top-left corner and the bottom-right corner, using a single convolution neural network. ExtremeNet [15] uses bottom-up approaches to detect four extreme points (top-most, leftmost, bottom-most, right-most) and one center point, and then group the five keypoints into a bounding box if they are geometrically aligned. Centernet [16] uses keypoint estimation to find the center point and regression width and height of the object bounding box. FoveaBox [17] predicts category-sensitive semantic maps for the object existing possibility, and produces category-agnostic bounding box for each position that potentially contains an object. RepPoints [18] represents the targets as a set of sample points useful for both localization and recognition, it learn to automatically arrange themselves in a manner that bounds the spatial extent of an object and indicates semantically significant local areas.

2.4   Identification of Bird's Nest

With the wide application of UAV in transmission line inspection, more and more researchers participate in image-based power grid defect recognition. Wang et al. [19] proposed a solution for identification of bird's nests on transmission lines based on feature identification, which locates the pole tower of transmission line by LSD line detection, Harris corner detection and morphological closing operation, and detects the bird's nests within the range of pole tower based on their shape and color features, in order to identify the bird's nests accurately. In [20], An improved Fast-RCNN algorithm is proposed to identify the defects of transmission equipment, the algorithm improves the feature extraction on transmission line targets and small target component defects. In [21], Li et al. proposed a deep learning-based birds' nests automatic detection framework-region of interest (ROI) mining faster region-based convolutional neural networks (RCNN). In [22], Lu et al. proposed a novel method of bird's nest images detection based on cascade classifier and combination features. In [23], Zhang et al. used RetinaNet model based on deep convolution neural network to automatically detect of bird's nest targets. In [24], Yang et al. proposed a bird's nest location recognition method based on YOLOv4-tiny.

3   Method

3.1   Lightweight Attention Mechanism Convolution Module (LAMCM)

GhostModule is a lightweight channel adjustment module proposed in Ghost-Net [2], the module passes 1×1 convolution and depth separable convolution are combined to realize the function of conventional 1×1 convolution. GhostModule can not only reduce the parameters of 1×1 convolution by half, but also increase the receptive field of the network and enhance the ability of feature extraction because of the introduction of 3×3 depth separable convolution. ECA is a channel attention module proposed in ECA-Net [3]. On the one-dimensional feature map obtained after global average pooling, ECA learns the weights of each channel through a one-dimensional convolution with shared weights. The size of the one-dimensional convolution kernel k represents the cross channel information interaction rate of the module, and k will be dynamically adjusted with the change of the number of channels. ECA solves the problem of information loss caused by the reduction of channel dimension of SE, and greatly reduces the amount of parameters. Referring to the bneck module design in MobileNetv3 [13], we design a lightweight attention mechanism convolution module (LAMCM) by integrating GhostModule and ECA, and its structure is shown in Fig. 3.

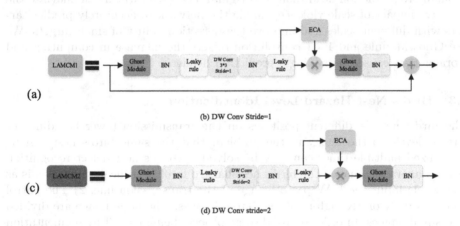

Fig. 3. Structure of LAMCM

Mobilenetv3 mainly uses 1×1 convolution to expand the number of channels. GhostModule is adopted in LAMCM, while ensuring a small number of network parameters, the combination of 3×3 depth separable convolution and 1×1 convolution can also obtain richer features and larger receptive fields than 1×1 convolution, which is of great benefit to the task of object detection. Compared with the SE module used by MobileNetv3, LAMCM adopts a more lightweight attention module ECA, which further reduces the number of network parameters and improves the performance of the network. LAMCM adds residual connection in the convolution block with stride = 1 to solve the problem of gradient disappearance of shallow network during network training.

3.2   Improved YOLOv5

In order to solve the problem of small target detection and large difference in the size of different types of objects under the complex background of transmission panoramic image, we propose an improved YOLOv5 algorithm based on YOLOv5l [25]. The network structure is shown in Fig. 4. The improved yolov5 includes three parts: Backbone, Neck and Prediction. The backbone network is composed of four modules: Focus, LAMCM2, CSP1_X, SPP and CSP2_X, which is mainly responsible for the extraction of image features and semantic information. The original Conv+BN+Leaky rule (CBL) in Focus, SPP, CSP1_X and CSP2_X is replaced with lightweight GhostModule+BN+Leaky rule (GBL), and the residual component in CSP1_X is replaced with LAMCM1, which can ensure that the backbone network has smaller network parameters and richer extracted features. Neck part adopts FPN and PAN for multi-scale feature fusion. The embedding of LAMCM1 and LAMCM2 further pays more attention to the channel features with large amount of information, so as to improve the efficiency of feature use. The prediction part adopts four prediction heads, which is one more prediction head than the original YOLOv5l, which can alleviate the negative impact of scale violence, enable the network to accurately predict targets with different scales and improve the detection ability of small targets. We use GhostModule and 1×1 convolution offsets the increase in computing and storage costs caused by adding a prediction header.

3.3   Bird's Nest Hazard Level Identification

The bird's nest at different positions on the transmission tower has different hazard levels to the line, and the problem that the same bird's nest can be recognized multiple times can only be solved by bird's nest defect recognition in the panoramic image. The bird's nest hazard level identification process is as follows: 1) input the UAV patrol image of the transmission line. 2) The patrol images are 4K or 8K high-resolution large images. The large image are divided into small images. In order to avoid some objects being cut off by segmentation (except towers), two adjacent small images need to be partially overlapped. This step can improve the detection rate of small objects, but it will increase the recognition time of a single image. This step is optional. 3) The improved yolov5 algorithm is used to detect seven kinds of objects: transmission tower, bird's nest, artificial bird's nest, horizontal glass insulator, vertical glass insulator, horizontal composite insulator and vertical composite insulator on large image and small images. There is basically no bird's nest above the horizontal glass insulator and the horizontal composite insulator. The coordinates of the detection objects on the small images are mapped to the high-resolution large image, and then the final detection results is obtained by NMS together with the detection results

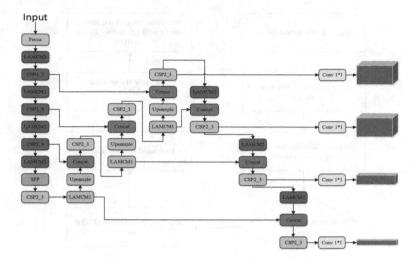

Fig. 4. The architecture of the improved YOLOv5

on the large image. 4) Judge whether there is tower in the detection results. If there is transmission tower, enter the next step. If there is no tower, exit directly. The image without tower is a local image, which avoids the hidden danger identification of bird's nest on the local image. 5) If the overlapping area between the bird's nest and the tower is equal to 0, the bird's nest is considered to be misidentified, and the misidentified bird's nest is deleted. 6) Expand the left and right frames and upper frames of vertical glass insulator and vertical composite insulator outward by half. 7) Calculate the overlap ratio R between the bird's nest and the extended vertical insulator. 8) The bird's nest is divided into hazard levels. If R is greater than 0, the bird's nest is a level I hazard. If R is equal to 0, the bird's nest is a level II hazard and the artificial bird's nest is a level III hazard (Fig. 5).

4 Experiments

We use COCO 2017 dataset and transmission line dataset to evaluate our proposed algorithm, which is the same or slightly improved compared with other common target detection algorithms.

4.1 Implementation Details

We implement our algorithm on Pytorch 1.8.0, All of our models use Tesla V100 for training and testing. We train the models for a total of 300 epochs, and the first 5 epochs are used for warm up. We use stochastic gradient descent (SGD) for training, and lr = 0.01 as the initial learning rate with the cosine lr schedule. The weight decay is 0.0005 and the SGD momentum is 0.937. The batch size is

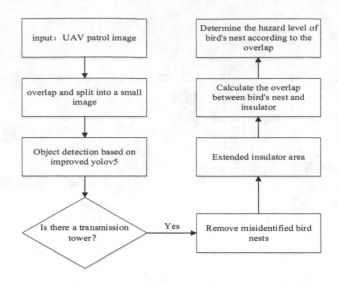

Fig. 5. Bird's nest hazard level identification flow chart.

128 by default to typical 8-GPU devices. On the coco datasets, the input image size of our model is 640, and the batch size is 128 on 8-GPU devices. On the transmission line UAV patrol datasets, the input image size of our model is 1280, and the batch size is 32 on 8-GPU devices.

4.2 Transmission Line Datasets(TL)

TL dataset is a data set established by ourselves, the pictures in the data set are all from the real images taken by the UAV when patrolling the transmission line. Table 1 lists the number of pictures and labels in the training set and test set. There are 3907 pictures in the training set and 850 pictures in the test set. We use labelme tool to label all pictures, the labeling information includes 8 types of labels, namely transmission tower (TT), vertical glass insulator (VGI), horizontal glass insulator (HGI), vertical composite insulator (VCI), horizontal composite insulator (HCI), bird's nest of level I hazard (I-H), bird's nest of level II hazard (II-H) and bird's nest of level III hazard (III-H).

4.3 Comparisons with the State-of-the-art on COCO Dataset

On the coco 2017 dataset, we use FPS, AP and to evaluate our algorithm and several algorithms commonly used in practical projects. In order to fairly compare with the original yolov5l, our improved yolov5 also adopts three prediction headers, and the input size is 640. It can be seen from Table 2 that the improved yolov5 algorithm has certain advantages in three indicators. Compared with the original yolov5l, our model AP is improved by 0.9 and FPS is improved by 6.6. It can be seen that the improved yolov5 proposed in this paper is effective.

Table 1. TL dataset.

Label category	Training set		Test set	
	Number of pictures	Number of labels	Number of pictures	Number of labels
TT	3907	4271	850	883
VGI		10824		697
HGI		8554		351
VCI		13767		1052
HCI		4173		169
I-H		496		182
II-H		2627		416
III-H		1463		375

Table 2. Comparison of the speed and accuracy of different object detectors on COCO 2017 test-dev.

Method	Size	FPS	AP(%)	AP_{50}
Faster-RCNN w/FPN [26]	1000 * 600	15.6	36.2	59.1
Cascade-RCNN [6]	1312 * 800	12.4	42.8	62.1
SSD512 [7]	512 * 512	28.0	28.8	48.5
YOLOv3+ASFF* [27]	608 * 608	45.5	42.4	63.0
FCOS [28]	1333 * 800	8.8	43.2	62.8
YOLOv4 [10]	608 * 608	62.0	43.5	65.7
YOLOv5l [25]	640 * 640	73.0	48.2	66.9
Improved YOLOv5(three prediction headers)	640 * 640	79.6	49.1	67.6

4.4 Comparisons with the State-of-the-Art on TL Dataset

All images in TL dataset are high-resolution large images. Training or prediction directly with the large images will lead to non convergence of the model and poor detection effect of small targets. During training, we use a 3200 × 3200 size window to randomly slide around the labeled objects to generate a small image. We can cut more small images for the categories with a small number in the training set to ensure sample balance. During the test, we use a 3200 × 3200 size window to slide on the large image to generate a small image. There is overlap between adjacent small images, and the overlapping pixels are 640. The model input size is 1280. In order to better detect targets with different scales, we add a prediction head to the model. By judging that the bird's nest does not fall in the tower detection box, we remove the wrongly identified bird's nest and reduce the wrong alarm. We use recall rate and accuracy rate to evaluate the performance of the original yolov5l and improved yolov5, as shown in Table 3.

If the IOU of the detection box by the algorithm and the manually labeled box is greater than 0.6, the recognition is correct. For fair comparison, the other settings of the two algorithms are the same except that there is one more prediction header in the improved yolov5. It can be seen from the table that the improved yolov5 algorithm in this paper has advantages in the recognition of all categories. In particular, the recall rate of small targets such as bird's nest has increased significantly. The recall rate of bird's nest with level I hazard has increased by 4.4%, that of bird's nest with level II hazard has increased by 3.4%, and that of bird's nest with level III hazard has increased by 4.8%.

Table 3. Performance comparison between original yolov5l and improved yolov5 on TL dataset.

Label category	YOLOv5l		Improved YOLOv5	
	Recall rate	Accuracy rate	Recall rate	Accuracy rate
TT	99.1%	98.5%	99.8%	99.3%
VGI	93.7%	94.3%	94.4%	95.3%
VGI	92.8%	91.1%	93.2%	91.9%
VCI	96.3%	98.5%	97.5%	98.8%
HCI	90.2%	96.9%	90.5%	97.5%
I-H	91.2%	93.3%	95.6%	94.1%
II-H	90.1%	89.7%	93.5%	90.9%
II-H	86.4%	94.7%	91.2%	96.3%

Figure 6 shows the identification results of some samples on the test set. Because the original image is a high-resolution image, the target is too small to display. The following figure shows enlarged screenshots. Blue is the tower detection box, orange is the insulator detection box, red is the bird's nest detection box with different hazard levels, and the text next to the box describes the defect category. It can be seen from the figure that the algorithm proposed in this paper can accurately locate the area of the tower and reduce the interference of background information. Our algorithm can also identify different types of insulators, which provides a basis for the hazard classification of bird's nest. The shape and size of the bird's nest in the figure are obviously different, and some bird's nests are blurred, but our algorithm can accurately identify the hazard level. Experiments show that the algorithm has strong applicability and high practical value.

Fig. 6. Identification results of some samples on the test set

4.5   Ablation Studies

we analyze importance of each proposed component on TL dataset. We only analyze the overall recall rate and accuracy rate of bird's nest hazard level, because the improvement of accuracy rate and recall rate of other categories is not very obvious, and the index of bird's nest hazard level is the focus of power inspectors. The impact of each component is listed in the Table 4. LAMCM represents a lightweight attention mechanism convolution module, APH represents adding a prediction header, and DELETE represents delete misidentification.

Table 4. Ablation study on the total recall and accuracy of bird's nest hazard level on TL dataset.

Methods	Recall rate	Accuracy rate
YOLOv5l	88.9%	90.4%
YOLOv5l+LAMCM	91.2%	90.9%
YOLOv5l+LAMCM+APH	93.0%	91.7%
YOLOv5l+LAMCM+APH+DELETE	93.0%	93.5%

5   Conclusion

In this paper, we propose a transmission line bird's nest hazard level identification method based on improved yolov5 and location constraints, which solves the problem of bird's nest multiple identification and hazard level classification. We propose a lightweight attention mechanism convolution module and add a prediction head to improve the original yolov5, which improves the detection ability of small targets and alleviates the negative impact of scale violence. Experiments on coco dataset and TL dataset established by ourselves show that the improved yolov5 proposed in this paper is better than the original yolov5, especially the recall rate of bird's nest hazard level identification is significantly improved (the recall rate is increased by more than 3%), which has high practical value.

References

1. Howard, A., et al.: Searching for mobilenetv3. In: Proceedings of the IEEE/CVF International Conference on Computer Vision, pp. 1314–1324 (2019)
2. Han, K., Wang, Y., Tian, Q., Guo, J., Xu, C., Xu, C.: Ghostnet: more features from cheap operations. In: Proceedings of the IEEE/CVF Conference on Computer Vision and Pattern Recognition, pp. 1580–1589 (2020)
3. Wang, Q., Wu, B., Zhu, P., Li, P., Zuo, W., Hu, Q.: Supplementary material for 'eca-net: efficient channel attention for deep convolutional neural networks. Technical report, Technical report
4. Ren, S., He, K., Girshick, R., Sun, J.: Faster R-CNN: towards real-time object detection with region proposal networks. In: Advances in Neural Information Processing Systems, vol. 28 (2015)
5. Dai, J., Li,Y., He, K., Sun, J.: R-FCN: object detection via region-based fully convolutional networks. In: Advances in Neural Information Processing Systems, vol. 29 (2016)
6. Cai, Z., Vasconcelos, N.: Cascade R-CNN: delving into high quality object detection. In: Proceedings of the IEEE Conference on Computer Vision and Pattern Recognition, pp. 6154–6162 (2018)
7. Liu, W., et al.: SSD: single shot MultiBox detector. In: Leibe, B., Matas, J., Sebe, N., Welling, M. (eds.) ECCV 2016. LNCS, vol. 9905, pp. 21–37. Springer, Cham (2016). https://doi.org/10.1007/978-3-319-46448-0_2
8. Redmon, J., Divvala, S., Girshick, R., Farhadi, A.: You only look once: unified, real-time object detection. In: Proceedings of the IEEE Conference on Computer Vision and Pattern Recognition, pp. 779–788 (2016)
9. Redmon, J., Farhadi, A.: Yolov3: an incremental improvement. arXiv preprint arXiv:1804.02767 (2018)
10. Bochkovskiy, A., Wang, C.-Y., Liao, H.-Y.M.: Yolov4: optimal speed and accuracy of object detection. arXiv preprint arXiv:2004.10934 (2020)
11. Ge, Z., Liu, S., Wang, F., Li, Z., Sun, J.: Yolox: exceeding yolo series in 2021. arXiv preprint arXiv:2107.08430 (2021)
12. Wang, C.-Y., Bochkovskiy, A., Liao, H.-Y.M.: Scaled-yolov4: scaling cross stage partial network. In: Proceedings of the IEEE/CVF Conference on Computer Vision and Pattern Recognition, pp. 13029–13038 (2021)
13. Lin, T.-Y., Goyal, P., Girshick, R., He, K., Dollár, P.: Focal loss for dense object detection. In: Proceedings of the IEEE International Conference on Computer Vision, pp. 2980–2988 (2017)
14. Law, H., Deng, J.: CornerNet: detecting objects as paired keypoints. In: Ferrari, V., Hebert, M., Sminchisescu, C., Weiss, Y. (eds.) Computer Vision – ECCV 2018. LNCS, vol. 11218, pp. 765–781. Springer, Cham (2018). https://doi.org/10.1007/978-3-030-01264-9_45
15. Zhou, X., Zhuo, J., Krahenbuhl, P.: Bottom-up object detection by grouping extreme and center points. In: Proceedings of the IEEE/CVF Conference on Computer Vision and Pattern Recognition, pp. 850–859 (2019)
16. Zhou, X., Wang, D., Krähenbühl, P.: Objects as points. arXiv preprint arXiv:1904.07850 (2019)
17. Kong, T., Sun, F., Liu, H., Jiang, Y., Li, L., Shi, J.: Foveabox: beyound anchor-based object detection. IEEE Trans. Image Process. **29**, 7389–7398 (2020)
18. Yang, Z., Liu, S., Hu, H., Wang, L., Lin, S.: Reppoints: point set representation for object detection. In: Proceedings of the IEEE/CVF International Conference on Computer Vision, pp. 9657–9666 (2019)

19. Wang, Q.: A solution for identification of bird's nests on transmission lines with UAV patrol. In: 2016 International Conference on Artificial Intelligence and Engineering Applications, pp. 202–206. Atlantis Press (2016)

20. Ni, H., Wang, M., Zhao, L.: An improved faster R-CNN for defect recognition of key components of transmission line. Math. Biosci. Eng. **18**(4), 4679–4695 (2021)

21. Li, J., Yan, D., Luan, K., Li, Z., Liang, H.: Deep learning-based bird's nest detection on transmission lines using UAV imagery. Appl. Sci. **10**(18), 6147 (2020)

22. Jianfeng, L., et al.: Detection of bird's nest in high power lines in the vicinity of remote campus based on combination features and cascade classifier. IEEE Access **6**, 39063–39071 (2018)

23. Hui, Z., Jian, Z., Yuran, C., Su, J., Di, W., Hao, D.: Intelligent bird's nest hazard detection of transmission line based on retinanet model. In: Journal of Physics: Conference Series, volume 2005, page 012235. IOP Publishing (2021)

24. Yang, Q., Zhang, Z., Yan, L., Wang, W., Zhang, Y., Zhang, C.: Lightweight bird's nest location recognition method based on yolov4-tiny. In: 2021 IEEE International Conference on Electrical Engineering and Mechatronics Technology (ICEEMT), pp. 402–405. IEEE (2021)

25. https://github.com/ultralytics/yolov5

26. Lin, T.-Y., Dollár, P., Girshick, R., He, K., Hariharan, B., Belongie, S.: Feature pyramid networks for object detection. In: Proceedings of the IEEE Conference on Computer Vision and Pattern Recognition, pp. 2117–2125 (2017)

27. Liu, S., Huang, D., Wang, Y.: Learning spatial fusion for single-shot object detection. arXiv preprint arXiv:1911.09516 (2019)

28. Tian, Z., Shen, C., Chen, H., He, T.: FCOS: fully convolutional one-stage object detection. In: Proceedings of the IEEE/CVF International Conference on Computer Vision, pp. 9627–9636 (2019)

Image Magnification Network for Vessel Segmentation in OCTA Images

Mingchao Li[1], Weiwei Zhang[2], and Qiang Chen[1]([✉])

[1] School of Computer Science and Engineering, Nanjing University of Science and Technology,
Nanjing 210094, China
Chen2qiang@njust.edu.cn
[2] Department of Ophthalmology, The First Affiliated Hospital with Nanjing Medical University,
Nanjing 210094, China

Abstract. Optical coherence tomography angiography (OCTA) is a novel non-invasive imaging modality that allows micron-level resolution to visualize the retinal microvasculature. The retinal vessel segmentation in OCTA images is still an open problem, and especially the thin and dense structure of the capillary plexus is an important challenge of this problem. In this work, we propose a novel image magnification network (IMN) for vessel segmentation in OCTA images. Contrary to the U-Net structure with a down-sampling encoder and up-sampling decoder, the proposed IMN adopts the design of up-sampling encoding and then down-sampling decoding. This design is to capture more low-level image details to reduce the omission of small structures. The experimental results on three open OCTA datasets show that the proposed IMN with an average dice score of 90.2% achieves the best performance in vessel segmentation of OCTA images. Besides, we also demonstrate the superior performance of IMN in cross-field image vessel segmentation and vessel skeleton extraction.

Keywords: OCTA · Image magnification network · Retina · Vessel segmentation

1 Introduction

Optical coherence tomography angiography (OCTA) is a relatively novel imaging modality for the micron-level imaging of the retinal microvasculature [1]. Compared to alternative angiographies, such as fluorescein angiography, it is fast, non-invasive and allows to provide angiographic images at different retinal depths. With these advantages, OCTA has been used to evaluate several ophthalmologic diseases, such as age-related macular degeneration (AMD) [2], diabetic retinopathy (DR) [3], artery and vein occlusions [4], and glaucoma [5], etc. A more recent study demonstrated that the morphological changes of microvascular calculated from OCTA images are related to Alzheimer's Disease and Mild Cognitive Impairment [6]. Thus, quantitative analysis of OCTA images is of great value for the diagnosis of the related diseases.

Quantitative phenotypes in OCTA image such as vessel density (VD) [7], vessel tortuosity (VT) [8], fractal dimension (FD) [9] rely on the segmented vessel masks.

© The Author(s), under exclusive license to Springer Nature Switzerland AG 2022
S. Yu et al. (Eds.): PRCV 2022, LNCS 13537, pp. 426–435, 2022.
https://doi.org/10.1007/978-3-031-18916-6_35

It is extremely time-consuming and laborious to draw these masks manually, so it is necessary to design automatic segmentation approaches for OCTA images. But there exist the following challenges (as shown in Fig. 1): (a) OCTA images contain a lot of high-value noise. (b) Some vascular signals are weak due to turbid refractive medium. (c) The capillary plexus is densely structured which is difficult to be identified. (d) The capillary plexus is very thin, most of which are only 1 pixel wide.

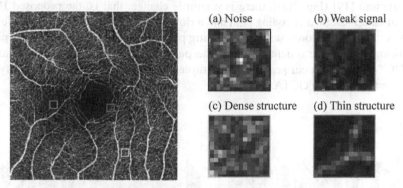

Fig. 1. An example of OCTA image projected within inner retina and its segmentation challenges.

Several approaches have been used for vessel segmentation in OCTA images, including threshold-based methods [10, 11], filter-based methods [12–16], and deep learning-based methods [17–22]. Threshold-based methods use global threshold or adaptive threshold to directly binarize OCTA images. The binary masks obtained by the threshold-based methods retain a lot of noise and many weak signal vessels are lost. Filter-based methods can suppress the noise in OCTA images to better visualize the microvasculature, but their quantitative performances are even worse than that of the threshold-based method as shown in Table 1. Besides, their performances are sensitive to the filter parameters. Deep learning-based methods have been used for vessel segmentation in OCTA images and obtained more excellent performance than filter-based methods. Mou et al. [18] introduced CS-Net, adding a spatial attention module and a channel attention module to the U-Net structure [19] to extract curvilinear structures from three biomedical imaging modalities including OCTA. Pissas et al. [20] recursively connected multiple U-Net to obtain refined predictions. More recently, Ma et al. [21] used two U-Net structures to segment pixel-level and centerline-level vessels and fuse them to obtain the final segmentation result.

The above deep learning-based methods use U-Net as the backbone. However, the U-Net structure focus on learning high-level features with limited low-level detail protection, which is easy to miss weak signal vessels and thin-and-small capillary. In this work, we propose an image magnification network (IMN), which adopts the design of up-sampling encoding and then down-sampling decoding. This design is to capture more image details and reduce the omission of thin-and-small structures. If U-Net is like a concave lens for observing global information, then IMN is like a convex lens for observing detailed information. The contribution can be summarized as: (1) IMN is a novel end-to-end structure, which has better detail protection performance than U-Net. (2)

Experimental results on three open datasets demonstrate that we achieve state-of-the-art vessel segmentation in OCTA images.

2 Network Architecture

The structure of our proposed IMN is illustrated in Fig. 2(b). Compared with the typical U-Net structure [19] (Fig. 2(a)), there is a simple change, that is, the proposed IMN consists of an up-sampled encoding path and a down-sampled decoding path, while the U-Net is composed of a down-sampled encoding path and an up-sampled decoding path. This structural difference is determined by the particularity of the vessel segmentation task in OCTA images. In our practice, this simple change is very useful for identifying thin-and-small vessels in OCTA images.

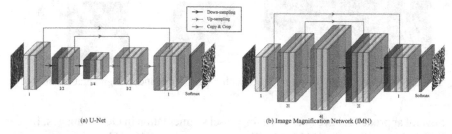

(a) U-Net   (b) Image Magnification Network (IMN)

Fig. 2. Architectures of the typical U-Net (a) and image magnification network (b).

Our key insight is using the up-sampling encoder to maintain image details. The down-sampling encoder in U-Net compresses the image to extract the high-level features, thereby identifying the specified structure in the complex content images. However, the content in the OCTA image is relatively simple, including only blood flow signal and noise signal. The high-level features extracted by the encoder in U-Net have a limited gain in vessel segmentation tasks. At the same time, the detailed information of the image will be weakened during the down-sampling operation and the convolution operation, resulting in incomplete segmentation of thin-and-small capillary structures (as shown in Fig. 3, yellow arrow). On the contrary, our proposed IMN contains an up-sampled encoding path and a down-sampled decoding path, which is to magnify the image details like using a magnifying glass, preventing the detailed information from being weakened and lost, thereby obtaining a more complete capillary structure.

In IMN, the encoding path consists of the repeated structure of two 3×3 convolution layers and one up-sampling layer. Each convolution operator follows a batch normal (BN) layer and a rectified linear unit (ReLU). Transposed convolution with the kernel of 2×2 and the stride of 2×2 is used for up-sampling. The decoding path contains the repeated structure of two 3×3 convolution layers same as the encoding path and follows by a 2×2 max-pooling layer for down-sampling. We use copy-and-crop operation as the connection method to connect the selected layers of the encoding path and the decoding path. The channel number of the convolutional layers is set to 256, and the 256 feature vectors are mapped to 2 (number of classes) feature maps through an additional convolutional layer. We use cross entropy as loss function to supervise network training. The implementation based on PyTorch framework is available at https://github.com/cha osallen/IMN_pytorch.

3 Datasets and Evaluation Metrics

We evaluated the proposed method on the three recently published OCTA datasets: an OCTA segmentation study[1] [23] (called OCTA-SS in this paper), OCTA-500[2] [24], and ROSE[3] [21]. OCTA-SS provides the most detailed vessel annotation, which is used for quantitative comparison and evaluation. Regrettably, it has not provided the complete field of view (FOV) images, only 55 slices of the region of interest were obtained from 3 mm × 3 mm FOV images of 11 participants with and without family history of dementia. OCTA-500 provides three-dimensional OCTA data of 500 eyes (Disease types include AMD, DR, choroidal neovascularization (CNV), etc.) with two FOV (6 mm × 6 mm, 3 mm × 3 mm) and complete projection images of different depths. We used OCTA-500 to evaluate the performance of the models trained by the OCTA-SS on the two complete FOV images. ROSE contains two sub-datasets, ROSE-1 and ROSE-2. In this paper, our experiments are performed on ROSE-1, which consists of a total of 117 OCTA images from 39 subjects with and without Alzheimer's disease. The ROSE dataset provides centerline-level vessel annotations, which are also used to explore the performance of the proposed method in vessel skeleton segmentation.

Four commonly used evaluation metrics for image segmentation are calculated: Dice coefficient (Dice), accuracy (Acc), recall (Rec), and precision (Pre). They are denoted as:

$$Dice = 2TP/(2TP + FP + FN) \tag{1}$$

$$Acc = (TP + TN)/(TP + TN + FP + FN) \tag{2}$$

$$Rec = TP/(TP + FN) \tag{3}$$

$$Pre = TP/(TP + FP) \tag{4}$$

where TP is true positive, FP is false positive, FN is false negative, TN is true negative.

To evaluate the global quality of vessel segmentation, we adopted the CAL metrics proposed in [25], which measures the connectivity, area and length of the segmentation result. Furthermore, to evaluate the integrity of the vascular skeleton, we designed a skeleton recall rate (S-Rec), which uses the method [26] to extract the vascular skeleton and follow Formula 3 to calculate the recall rate of the skeleton image as S-Rec. In addition, we also evaluated the inference time of each image to measure the running speed of the methods.

---

[1] https://datashare.ed.ac.uk/handle/10283/3528.

[2] https://ieee-dataport.org/open-access/octa-500.

[3] https://imed.nimte.ac.cn/dataofrose.html.

4   Experiments

The proposed IMN and the deep learning baselines we compared were implemented with PyTorch on 1 NVIDIA GeForce GTX 1080Ti GPU. We choose the Adam optimization with an initial learning rate of 0.0001, batch size of 1 and without weight decay. The threshold-based method and the filter-based based methods are run on the MATLAB platform, and all parameters are adjusted to the best performance through repeated experiments. In the OCTA-SS dataset, all images are cropped to 76×76. 30 images are used to train the model, and the remaining 25 images are used for testing and evaluation. ROSE dataset has a divided training set and a divided test set. The projection images in OCTA-500 are all regarded as the test set in this study.

4.1   Comparison with Other Methods

We compared the proposed method with several baseline methods in the OCTA-SS dataset, including threshold-based methods, filter-based methods, and deep learning-based methods. For the threshold-based method, we adopted an adaptive threshold method (AT) [27]. For filter-based methods, we selected three well-known filters for vessel segmentation: Frangi [12], SCIRD-TS [16], and Gabor [13]. The binary segmentation results are obtained from the filtered image by using the adaptive threshold [27]. The implementation of the above methods can be found in [23]. For deep learning-based methods, U-Net [19] is used as an important baseline, and we also designed a CNN with 7 convolutional layers without up-sampling and down-sampling processes. The comparison of CNN, U-Net and IMN can be regarded as an ablation study to explore the effect of sampling. Furthermore, two state-of-the-art methods for blood vessel segmentation, CS-Net [18] and DUNet [28] are also used for comparison.

Table 1. Performance of vessel segmentation methods on OCTA-SS dataset.

Method	Dice	Acc	Rec	Pre	CAL	S-Rec	Speed
AT [27]	0.8423	0.8879	0.9144	0.7922	0.7775	0.6699	0.006 s
Frangi [12]+AT	0.7967	0.8536	0.9237	0.7163	0.7100	0.6478	0.04 s
SCIRD-TS [16]+AT	0.7071	0.7704	0.8058	0.6446	0.6745	0.3912	0.14 s
Gabor [13]+AT	0.7688	0.8213	0.8643	0.7034	0.7609	0.5078	0.16 s
CNN	0.8943	0.9218	0.9197	0.8716	0.8991	0.7454	**0.003 s**
U-Net [19]	0.8958	0.9239	0.9105	**0.8830**	0.9038	0.7550	0.004 s
CS-Net [18]	0.8926	0.9213	0.9165	0.8711	0.8880	0.7563	0.004 s
DUNet [28]	0.8932	0.9224	0.9111	0.8776	0.8963	0.7528	0.05 s
IMN	**0.9019**	**0.9268**	**0.9270**	0.8794	**0.9075**	**0.7740**	0.03 s

The segmentation performances of all methods according to the evaluation metrics are shown in Table 1. Several important properties can be summarized as: (1) The quantitative results of filter-based methods are mostly lower than those of the threshold-based method, and much lower than that of deep learning-based methods. (2) Our proposed IMN reaches the best results in Dice, Acc, Rec, CAL, and S-Rec. (3) The S-Rec score of IMN is significantly higher than other deep learning methods, indicating that the vessel skeleton of the IMN segmentation results is the most complete. (4) In terms of running speed, all methods can process an image in less than 1 s, and IMN processes an image in 0.03 s, which is slower than U-Net and faster than filtering-based methods.

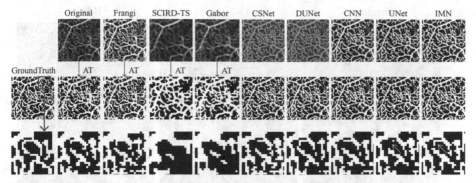

Fig. 3. Examples of vessel enhancement results (first row) and segmentation results (second row) between different methods. The third row shows the detailed segmentation results in the red box. (Color figure online)

Figure 3 shows the segmentation results of an example with different methods. Interestingly, although the quantitative results of the filter-based methods are worse than those of the threshold-based method, they have a better visualization of capillaries and have the effect of vessel enhancement. The deep learning-based methods have achieved the segmentation performance closest to the ground truth. In particular, the proposed IMN has a better segmentation performance on thin-and-small blood vessels than U-Net (in Fig. 3, yellow arrow), which hints at the reason for the highest S-Rec score of IMN.

By comparing CNN, U-Net and the proposed IMN in Table 1 and Fig. 3, we find that the performance of U-Net and CNN are close in this task, and the performance of IMN is better. It indicates that the down-sampled encoding path in the U-Net structure has limited use for vessel segmentation in OCTA images, while the up-sampled encoding path in IMN stores more detailed information to prevent the loss of thin-and-small vessel structures.

4.2 Performance on Cross-FOV Images

OCTA-SS only provides slice images cropped from 3 mm × 3 mm FOV images, which can only be used to observe the partial segmentation view. To explore the segmentation performance on the complete images and cross-FOV images, we run the trained model on the complete projection images with two FOV (6 mm × 6 mm, 3 mm × 3 mm) in the OCTA-500 dataset. Since the input size of the model is fixed, cropping and stitching are necessary. The final segmentation results are shown in Fig. 4.

We find that there is no obvious error in the segmentation of the complete image, which shows that the method of training partial slices is feasible in this task, and there is no need to label and train the entire image. Interestingly, the segmentation model trained on the 3 mm × 3 mm FOV images can also be used to segment the vessels of the 6 mm × 6 mm FOV images, which shows that the deep learning-based methods have good portability in cross-FOV.

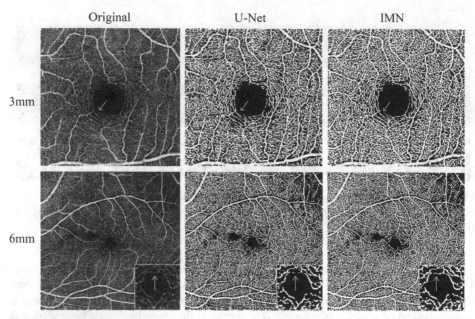

Fig. 4. The segmentation results on different FOV images by using U-Net and IMN. The first row is an example with 3 mm × 3 mm FOV. The second row is an example with 6 mm × 6 mm FOV. (Color figure online)

We compared the results of the proposed IMN and U-Net. The segmentation performance of IMN still maintains more vessel details, and the thin-and-small vessels are better segmented, as shown by the yellow arrows in Fig. 4. On the whole, the vessel segmentation results of IMN are more detailed and denser than U-Net, which once again proves the state-of-the-art performance of our proposed IMN.

4.3   Performance on Vessel Skeleton Segmentation

We have verified the excellent performance of IMN on the pixel-level vessel segmentation of OCTA images. Then, we explored vessel skeleton segmentation, which is one of the important research directions of vessel segmentation. The ROSE dataset contains the vessel skeleton labels as shown in Fig. 5(d). We trained U-Net and IMN models using these labels on the ROSE dataset, and the segmentation results are shown in Figs. 5(b)(c). The vessel skeleton segmentation of IMN is slightly more complete than that of U-Net

(Fig. 5, red arrows). However, most of the capillary network skeleton has not been segmented, and the results are still far from the ground truth. Therefore, it is not suitable to segment the vessel skeleton directly using U-Net or IMN.

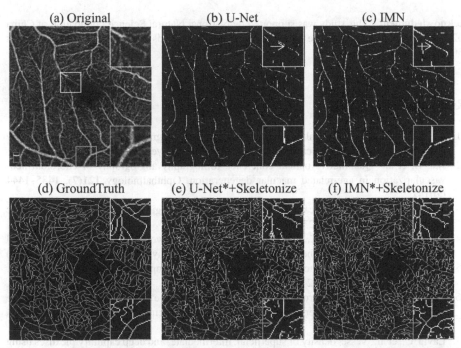

(a) Original	(b) U-Net	(c) IMN
(d) GroundTruth	(e) U-Net*+Skeletonize	(f) IMN*+Skeletonize

Fig. 5. An example of vessel skeleton segmentation on ROSE. The symbol * indicates the pixel-level segmentation model trained on OCTA-SS. (Color figure online)

We tried another vessel skeleton segmentation strategy. We first used the model trained on OCTA-SS to segment the pixel-level vessels on the OCTA images of ROSE, and then used the method [26] to extract the vessel skeleton. The experimental results are shown in Figs. 5(e)(f). This method achieves performance beyond the ground truth for manual labeling because more capillary skeletons are identified. Similarly, the vessel skeleton segmentation based on IMN has more vessel details than that based on U-Net (Fig. 5, yellow arrows). Therefore, instead of directly using the neural network to segment the vessel skeleton, we recommend segmenting the pixel-level blood vessels first and then skeletonizing.

5 Conclusion

In this paper, we developed a novel end-to-end framework named IMN for retinal vessel segmentation in OCTA images. It contains an up-sampled encoding path and a down-sampled decoding path. This design is to get better detail retention capabilities, thereby more accurately segmenting thin-and-small vessels. The experiments on three open datasets indicate that the proposed method achieves the state-of-the-art performance of vessel segmentation in OCTA images. We also found that the IMN model trained on one FOV image can be used for another FOV image, and its pixel-level vessel segmentation results can be used for the extraction of vessel skeletons.

Acknowledgment. This study was supported by National Natural Science Foundation of China (62172223, 61671242), and the Fundamental Research Funds for the Central Universities (30921013105).

References

1. Kashani, A.H., et al.: Optical coherence tomography angiography: a comprehensive review of current methods and clinical applications. Prog. Retin. Eye Res. **60**, 66–100 (2017)
2. Jia, Y., et al.: Quantitative optical coherence tomography angiography of choroidal neovascularization in age-related macular degeneration. Ophthalmology **121**(7), 1435–1444 (2014)
3. Hwang, T.S., et al.: Optical coherence tomography angiography features of diabetic retinopathy. Retina **35**(11), 2371–2376 (2015)
4. Rispoli, M., Savastano, M.C., Lumbroso, B.: Capillary network anomalies in branch retinal vein occlusion on optical coherence tomography angiography. Retina **35**, 2332–2338 (2015)
5. Jia, Y., et al.: Optical coherence tomography angiography of optic disc perfusion in glaucoma. Ophthalmology **121**(7), 1322–1332 (2014)
6. Yoon, S.P., et al.: Retinal microvascular and neurodegenerative changes in Alzheimer's disease and mild cognitive impairment compared with control participants. Ophthalmol. Retin. **3**(6), 489–499 (2019)
7. Lavia, C., et al.: Vessel density of superficial, intermediate, and deep capillary plexuses using optical coherence tomography angiography. Retina **39**, 247–258 (2019)
8. Lee, H., Lee, M., Chung, H., Kim, H.C.: Quantification of retinal vessel tortuosity in diabetic retinopathy using optical coherence tomography angiography. Retina **38**, 976–985 (2018)
9. Huang, P.W., Lee, C.H.: Automatic classification for pathological prostate images based on fractal analysis. IEEE Trans. Med. Imaging **28**(7), 1037–1050 (2009)
10. Gao, S.S., et al.: Compensation for reflectance variation in vessel density quantification by optical coherence tomography angiography. Invest. Ophthalmol. Vis. Sci. **57**, 4485–4492 (2016)
11. Nesper, P.L., et al.: Quantifying microvascular abnormalities with increasing severity of diabetic retinopathy using optical coherence tomography angiography. Invest. Ophthalmol. Vis. Sci. **58**, BIO307–BIO315 (2017)
12. Frangi, A.F., Niessen, W.J., Vincken, K.L., Viergever, M.A.: Multiscale vessel enhancement filtering. In: Wells, W.M., Colchester, A., Delp, S. (eds.) MICCAI 1998. LNCS, vol. 1496, pp. 130–137. Springer, Heidelberg (1998). https://doi.org/10.1007/BFb0056195
13. Soares, J.V.B., et al.: Retinal vessel segmentation using the 2-D Gabor Wavelet and supervised classification. IEEE Trans. Med. Imaging **25**(9), 1214–1222 (2006)
14. Breger, A., Goldbacn, F., Gerendas, B.S., Schmidt-Erfurth, U., Ehler, M.: Blood vessel segmentation in en-face OCTA images: a frequency based method. https://arxiv.org/pdf/2109.06116 (2021)
15. Li, A., You, J., Du, C., Pan, Y.: Automated segmentation and quantification of OCT angiography for tracking angiogenesis progression. Biomed. Opt. Express **8**(12), 5604–5616 (2017)

16. Annunziata, R., Trucco, E.: Accelerating convolutional sparse coding for curvilinear structures segmentation by refining SCIRD-TS filter banks. IEEE Trans. Med. Imaging **35**(11), 2381–2392 (2016)
17. Prentasic, P., et al.: Segmentation of the foveal microvasculature using deep learning networks. J. Biomed. Opt. **21**(7), 075008.1-075008.7 (2016)
18. Mou, L., et al.: CS-Net: channel and spatial attention network for curvilinear structure segmentation. In: Shen, D., et al. (eds.) MICCAI 2019. LNCS, vol. 11764, pp. 721–730. Springer, Cham (2019). https://doi.org/10.1007/978-3-030-32239-7_80
19. Ronneberger, O., Fischer, P., Brox, T.: U-Net: convolutional networks for biomedical image segmentation. In: Navab, N., Hornegger, J., Wells, W.M., Frangi, A.F. (eds.) MICCAI 2015. LNCS, vol. 9351, pp. 234–241. Springer, Cham (2015). https://doi.org/10.1007/978-3-319-24574-4_28
20. Pissas, T., et al.: Deep iterative vessel segmentation in OCT angiography. Biomed. Opt. Express **11**(5), 2490–2510 (2020)
21. Ma, Y., et al.: ROSE: a retinal OCT-angiography vessel segmentation dataset and new model. IEEE Trans. Med. Imaging **40**(3), 928–939 (2021)
22. Li, M., et al.: Image projection network: 3D to 2D image segmentation in OCTA images. IEEE Trans. Med. Imaging **39**(11), 3343–3354 (2020)
23. Giarratano, Y., et al.: Automated segmentation of optical coherence tomography angiography images: benchmark data and clinically relevant metrics. Transl. Vis. Sci. Technol. **9**(12), 1–10 (2020)
24. Li, M., et al.: IPN-V2 and OCTA-500: methodology and dataset for retinal image segmentation. arXiv:2012.07261 (2020)
25. Gegundez-Arias, M.E., et al.: A function for quality evaluation of retinal vessel segmentations. IEEE Trans. Med. Imaging **31**(2), 231–239 (2012)
26. Zhang, T.Y., Suen, C.Y.: A fast parallel algorithm for thinning digital patterns. Commun. ACM **27**(3), 236–239 (1984)
27. Bradley, D., Roth, G.: Adaptive thresholding using the integral image. Graph. Tools **12**, 13–21 (2007)
28. Jin, Q., et al.: DUNet: a deformable network for retinal vessel segmentation. Knowl. Based Syst. **178**, 149–162 (2019)

CFA-Net: Cross-Level Feature Fusion and Aggregation Network for Salient Object Detection

Jingyi Liu[1], Huiqi Li[2], Lin Li[3], Tao Zhou[4(✉)], and Chenglizhao Chen[5]

[1] Qingdao University of Science and Technology, Qingdao 266100, China
[2] Beijing Forestry University, Beijing 100091, China
[3] Ocean University of China, Qingdao 266100, China
[4] School of Computer Science and Engineering, Nanjing University of Science
and Technology, Nanjing 210094, China
taozhou.ai@gmail.com
[5] Qingdao University, Qingdao 266075, China

Abstract. Salient object detection (SOD) is a research hotspot yet challenging task in computer vision, aiming at locating the most visually distinctive objects in an image. Recently, several deep learning based SOD models have been developed and achieved promising performance. Due to the salient variations among different convolutional layers, it is still a challenge to fuse the multi-level features and obtain better prediction performance. In this paper, we propose a Cross-level Feature fusion and Aggregation Network (CFA-Net) for SOD, which effectively integrates cross-level features to boost salient object performance. Specifically, an Adjacent Fusion Module (AFM) is proposed to effectively integrate the location information from low-level features with the rich semantic information of high-level features. Then, a Cascaded Feature Aggregation Module (CFAM) is proposed to further process the fused feature map, which is conducive to avoiding the introduction of redundant information and makes the features of the fusion feature map more distinctive. Unlike existing decoders, CFAM is able to enhance its own scale information while collecting the multi-scale information provided by the encoder, while allowing adjacent scale features to gain. The Hybrid-loss is introduced to assign weights for different pixels, making the network that focuses on details and boundaries. Extensive experimental results on several public datasets show the effectiveness of the proposed CFA-Net over other state-of-the-art SOD methods.

1 Introduction

Salient object detection (SOD) targets finding the most important and conspicuous objects in an image [1]. Existing saliency detection models can be roughly divided into two types, *i.e.*, traditional features-based models and deep learning-based models. Although these traditional methods have a simple model structure, it is difficult to identify the salient object(s) in complex scenes. Currently, deep learning-based SOD methods have achieved promising performance.

S. Yu et al. (Eds.): PRCV 2022, LNCS 13537, pp. 436–448, 2022.
https://doi.org/10.1007/978-3-031-18916-6_36

The convolutional neural network (CNN) can learn effective feature representations from a large amount of training data, which captures high-level semantic information and low-level location spatial details from images [2]. Thus, how integrating the high-level and low-level features or multi-level features is critical for the SOD task. To achieve this, Zhang *et al.* [3] proposed an aggregating multi-level convolutional feature framework. Zhang *et al.* [4] proposed a progressive-attention guided recurrent network for SOD. Hu *et al.* [5] proposed a new recurrently aggregated deep feature framework for SOD, in which multi-level features are used to progressively refine each layer's features for capturing complementary information. Although great progress has been made at present, there are several challenges for SOD. First, CNN merges high-level features with low-level features, however, it will blur the originally clear features, thus making it impossible to fully utilize the localization information of low-level features and semantic information of high-level features. Secondly, most of the existing models rely on binary cross-entropy loss function (BCE) to treat each pixel equally, which causes the model result to be biased against the background pixel when the background information pixels far outnumber the salient object pixels.

To this end, we propose a novel Cross-level Feature Fusion and Aggregation Network (CFA-Net) for Salient Object Detection. First, an Adjacent Fusion Module (AFM) is proposed to integrate the high-level and low-level features and effectively complement each other's missing information while suppressing each other's background noises. Then, a Cascade Feature Aggregation Module (CFAM) is proposed to reduce the redundant information of the fused features across different levels and obtain more distinctive feature representations. Besides, a Hybrid-Loss [6] is introduced to measure the difference between the predicted and ground-truth maps. Extensive experimental results on benchmark datasets demonstrate that CFA-Net achieves highly competitive accuracy compared to other state-of-the-art methods. In summary, our main contributions are four-fold:

- We propose a novel SOD framework (termed CFA-Net), which can effectively integrate cross-level features to boost SOD performance.
- An Adjacent Fusion Module (AFM) is proposed to integrate the semantic information from high-level features with the location information from low-level features.
- A Cascaded Feature Aggregation Module (CFAM) is proposed to further process the fused feature representations, which is conducive to avoiding the introduction of redundant information.
- Extensive experimental results on benchmark datasets demonstrate the effectiveness of our CFA-Net over other state-of-the-art methods.

2   Related Work

Salient Object Detection. As one of the most important directions in the field of computer vision, the early SOD network is reliant mainly on the internal cues of the image, which causes most of these images to be concentrated on

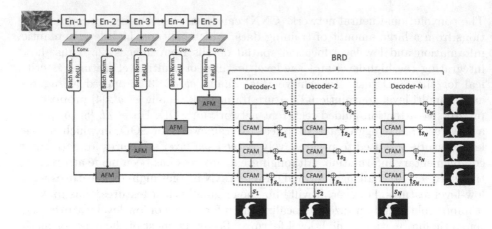

Fig. 1. The structure diagram of the proposed CFA-Net. Among them, AFM purposed to fuse high-level features and low-level features. CFAM aimed at strengthening the fusion of features in the feature map.

low-level features. As a result, the high-level features that are rich in semantic information get ignored. After extracting multi-level information from the original image, CNN merges the multi-level information to obtain the final salient feature figure, thus improving the results of salient object detection. Qin *et al.* [7] proposed a network called BASNet in 2019, the focus of which is placed on the edge information of the salient object. Based on the U-shaped structure in Pool-Net [8]. Liu *et al.* pinpoint the prominent objects of sharpening details. Xuebin Qin et al. designed the U2-net with a two-layer nested U-shaped structure. The RSU module in the network is capable to capture more semantic information on different scales. Mingming Cheng et al. designed a lightweight portrait segmentation model SINet [9], which consists of an information organization decoder and a spatial compression module. In addition, the excellent salient object detection network also includes: attention and boundary guided [10], STANet [11], TFCN [12] and CAGNet [13].

Multi-level/scale Fusion. Multi-level/scale fusion aims to fuse convolution layers of different levels with specific methods. Youwei Pang et al. proposed a network called MINet in 2020 [14], which applies a multi-scale fusion method to each decoder unit. Qin et al. proposed the Autofocus Layer [15], which can adaptively change the size of the receptive field to extract multi-scale features. Gu et al. proposed MRNet [16], which uses two parallel encoders to extract information at different scales and then uses a decoder to fuse them. Tokunaga et al. proposed the AWMF-CNN [17], which uses three parallel CNNs to extract information at different scales and uses a weighted concatenation to fuse the information. The network and method based on multi-level/scale fusion also includes: FuNNet [18], MSFNet [19], PANet [20], SP-Net [21], and so on.

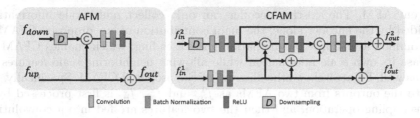

Fig. 2. Diagrams of the proposed AFM and CFAM modules.

3   Proposed Method

3.1   Overall Architecture

Figure 1 shows the overall architecture of the proposed CFA-Net, which is an encoding-decoding structure. Firstly, the pre-trained network ResNet-50 [22] is used to encode and extract image features. Then, the proposed AFM is applied to fuse features from different levels, which can effectively exploit multi-level information. Moreover, the fused features are fed into the proposed CFAM to obtain the aggregated features. Further, the BRD and the feedback model in the BRD are used to generate a feature map that propagates downwards. Finally, the multi-layer perceptual loss (*i.e.*, Hybrid-Loss [6]) is used to measure the predicted image of the model with the actual label image and to adjust the learning rate and weight parameters, thus further optimizing the convolutional neural network.

3.2   Adjacent Fusion Module

In the semantic segmentation model, high-level features are used to measure semantic similarity while low-level features are used to measure fine-grained similarity. Inspired by multiscale feature fusion operations, we propose an Adjacent Fusion Module (AFM) to filter and merge the high-level features and low-level features. Specifically, we denote the two adjacent features as f_{up} and f_{down} from different levels. Then, we combine the two features to obtain $f_{concat} = [f_{up}, f_{down}]$, and then the combined features are fed into a 3×3 convolution kernel followed batch normalization and a ReLU activation function. Finally, we obtain the fused features via a residual connection. The above process can be described as follows:

$$f_{\text{out}} = f_{\text{up}} + \mathcal{B}_{conv}\left(concat(\mathcal{D}\left(f_{\text{up}}\right), f_{\text{down}})\right), \quad (1)$$

where $\mathcal{B}_{conv}(\cdot)$ is a sequential operation that includes a 3×3 convolution followed by batch normalization and an activation function. $\mathcal{D}(\cdot)$ represents downsampling, and $concat(\cdot, \cdot)$ indicates the cross-channel concatenation.

3.3   Cascaded Feature Aggregation Module

To further exploit the correlations among multi-level features, we propose a Cascaded Feature Aggregation Module (CFAM) to integrate the outputs from different AFM. The existing decoder can only collect multi-scale information provided by the encoder alone, the main contribution of our proposed CFAM is the common attendance of summation and cascading, which enables CFAM to increase its own scale information while allowing neighboring scale features to gain as well. Figure 2 shows the diagram of the proposed CFAM. Specifically, we denote the outputs from two AFMs as f_{in}^1 and f_{in}^2. f_{in}^2 is first processed by a downsampling operation, and then the two features are fed into a convolution block (*i.e.*, a 3×3 convolution followed by batch normalization and a ReLU activation function), thus we can obtain:

$$
\begin{cases}
f_{conv}^1 = B_{conv}(f_{in}^1), \\
f_{conv}^2 = B_{conv}(\mathcal{D}(f_{in}^2)).
\end{cases}
\tag{2}
$$

Then, in order to obtain the complementary feature for the two levels, f_{conv}^1 and f_{conv}^2 are first cascaded, and then the fused feature is fed into a convolution block, which can be defined as follows:

$$
f_{concat} = \mathcal{B}_{conv}(concat(f_{conv}^1, f_{conv}^2)).
\tag{3}
$$

To preserve the original feature information, f_{conv}^1 and f_{conv}^2 are combined via an addition operation and then the combined features are cascaded with f_{com}, which can be represented as $concat(f_{conv}^1 + f_{conv}^2, f_{com})$. Furthermore, we can obtain the fused feature representation, *i.e.*, $f_{com} = \mathcal{B}_{conv}(concat(f_{conv}^1 + f_{conv}^2, f_{com}))$. Finally, the aggregated features for the two levels can be formulated as follows:

$$
\begin{cases}
f_{out}^1 = f_{com} + f_{conv}^1, \\
f_{out}^2 = f_{com} + f_{conv}^2.
\end{cases}
\tag{4}
$$

By using the proposed CFAM, we can first learn the fused feature representation for two different levels, which exploits more complementary information from cross-level features. More importantly, CFAM is able to enhance its own scale information while collecting the multi-scale information provided by multiple decoders.

3.4   Backward Recursive Decoder Module

Although CFAM is used to enhance the features of local images, whose refinement for multi-level features is not comprehensive. However, the obtained feature map contains more noise and obscures the original rich semantic information. To solve this problem, inspired by the F^{3}Net [23], a Backward Recursive Decoder (BRD) module based on CFAM is used.

As shown in Fig. 1, each BRD involves multiple CFAMs as well as an antegrade and retrograde process. The anterograde process aims to obtain CFAM aggregation from high-level to low-level. Monitored by the loss function, the retrograde process is purposed to down-sample the feature layer output from the top CFAM upward. The reverse output in the BRD is linked to the horizontal

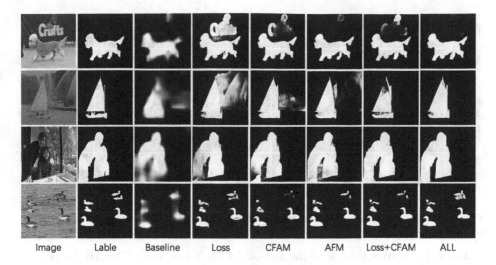

| Image | Lable | Baseline | Loss | CFAM | AFM | Loss+CFAM | ALL |

Fig. 3. Visual comparisons for validating the effectiveness of different key components in the proposed CFA-Net.

output of each CFAM, thus forming a decoding network capable to cooperate with each other. The decoding network improves clarity and accuracy for the global features of the feature image.

3.5 Loss Function

The weighted balance binary cross-entropy loss function [6], which adds a weight parameter to each category. That is to say, the positive sample (object) and negative sample (background) are weighted at the same time. It reduces not only the workload of calculation of the loss function but also the difference between the two types of data sets at the same time. In order to learn object segmentation in a wider range, the wIoU [24] loss function is introduced, which adds image pixel weights and background pixel weights to the IoU module. In the meantime, the intersection ratio is taken into account and the proportions of different categories are introduced. Besides, E-Loss [6] is used to capture global statistics and local pixel matching information. Finally, the overall loss of our proposed model is given as follows:

$$L^S_{Hybrid} = L^S_{wBCE} + L^S_{wIoU} + L^S_{E-loss}. \tag{5}$$

4 Experiments

4.1 Experimental Setup

Datasets. To evaluate the SOD performance, we conduct comparison experiments on five widely used public benchmark datasets, *i.e.*, **DUTS** [25], **ECSSD** [26], **PASCAL-S** [27], **HKU-IS** [28], and **DUT-OMRON** [29].

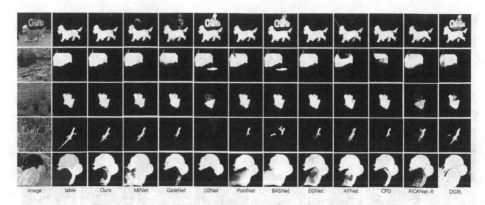

Fig. 4. Qualitative comparisons of the proposed CFA-Net and all comparison state-of-the-art SOD methods.

Table 1. Ablation studies for the proposed CFA-Net on the DUTS-TE dataset.

	Hybride Loss	CFAM	AFM	MAE	F_β	S_m	E_ϕ
No.1				0.069	0.766	0.820	0.827
No.2	√			0.040	0.863	0.880	0.913
No.3		√		0.038	0.867	0.884	0.917
No.4			√	0.038	0.866	0.884	**0.926**
No.5	√	√		0.039	0.866	0.882	0.917
No.6	√	√	√	**0.037**	**0.870**	**0.886**	0.921

Evaluation Metrics. To evaluate the proposed model and other state-of-the-art methods, we adopt four widely used evaluation metrics, *i.e.*, Mean Absolute Error (MAE) [30], F-measure (F_β) [31], Enhanced alignment measure (E-measure E_ϕ) [32], and structure measure (S-measure, S_m) [33].

Implementation Details. The ResNet-50 [22] network is applied to preprocess the DUTS-TR data set [25]. The Pytorch framework is adopted to implement our model, and Titan RTX3090Ti GPU is used to train our network. In the training stage, the DUTS-TR data set is first fed into our CFA-Net. After the completion of network training, a model of salient object detection will be constructed, and then the public data set will be fed into CFA-Net, which will be generated before the network test. We use the momentum SGD optimizer with a weight decay of 0.0005, The initial learning rate is set to 0.005 for the ResNet-50 backbone and 0.05 for the other parts.

4.2 Ablation Study

In this subsection, we provide comprehensive ablation studies on the DUTS-TR dataset to evaluate the effectiveness of each key component in the proposed CFA-

Net. Specifically, we investigate 1) the importance of AFM, 2) the effectiveness of CFAM, and 3) the effectiveness of Hybrid-Loss. During testing, challenging scenarios including background prominence, multiple targets, foregrounds, and backgrounds of great similarity were provided to our models to observe and record their performance under different conditions to demonstrate their effectiveness in responding to different situations.

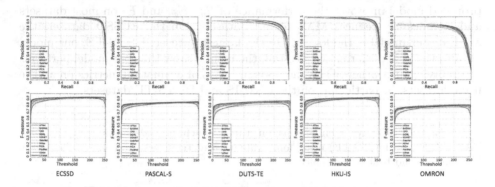

Fig. 5. Precision-recall curves and F-measures under different thresholds.

Effectiveness of Hybrid-Loss. The Hybrid Loss is composed of wBCE loss wIoU loss and E-Loss. This loss leads to an initial improvement in the performance of the network, with good performance in four metrics (as shown in the first row of Table 1). However, there is still the flaw of not accurately capturing the prominent objects in the case of prominent background objects (as shown in the first row of Fig. 4).

Effectiveness of AFM. To demonstrate the effectiveness of this module, we remove the hybrid loss and CFAM modules to test the AFM separately, and the results show that the AFM enables the network to improve its performance on all four evaluation metrics (as shown in Table 1) and further improved its ability to identify salient objects when background interference is strong (second row of Fig. 4) and also enhances the completeness of conspicuous object contour recognition (third row of Fig. 4).

Effectiveness of CFAM. The CFAM is used to adjust the number of channels of the feature maps generated by the previous module, and further feature fusion is performed on the adjusted feature maps based on this. To demonstrate the effectiveness of CFAM, we kept only this module for testing. Table 1) shows that the module led to a significant improvement in the network on the four evaluation metrics, and the results in Fig. 4) show that the use of this module led to a further improvement in the accuracy of significance detection, especially when the object and the background are in close proximity, allowing a more detailed treatment of the object contours (see the row of Fig. 4).

4.3 Comparison with State-of-the-arts

To comprehensively evaluate the performance of our CFA-Net, we compared it with 23 state-of-the-art SOD models. All the results are generated using the source codes and provided by the authors.

Quantitative Comparison. Table 2 shows the results of the proposed model and all comparison methods. From the results in Table 2, we can see that the proposed model improves the performance of S_m, E_ϕ, and F_β on most datasets and significantly reduces MAE for all datasets. On the ECSSD dataset, the MAE of our model is the lowest. On the largest dataset, DUTS-TE, our model obtains the best performance. Overall, the results show that our model performs favorably against other SOTA methods in terms of evaluation metrics on all the used datasets, in particular, on the HKU-IS and DUTS-TE datasets.

Table 2. Quantitative comparisons on three benchmark datasets (*i.e.*, ECSSD, PASCAL-S, and DUTS-TE) using four evaluation metrics. Red and Blue indicate the best and second best performance.

Model	ECSSD [26]				PASCAL-S [27]				DUTS-TE [25]			
	$M \downarrow$	$F_\beta \uparrow$	$S_m \uparrow$	$E_\phi \uparrow$	$M \downarrow$	$F_\beta \uparrow$	$S_m \uparrow$	$E_\phi \uparrow$	$M \downarrow$	$F_\beta \uparrow$	$S_m \uparrow$	$E_\phi \uparrow$
ELD[ICCV 16] [34]	.078	.849	.841	.882	.121	.734	.761	.803	.093	.738	.753	–
DCL[CVPR 16] [35]	.068	.882	.868	.881	.107	.787	.796	.814	.088	.742	.796	.774
SRM[ICCV 17] [36]	.054	.905	.895	.937	.084	.817	.834	.857	.059	.798	.836	.853
DSS[CVPR 17] [37]	.052	.906	.882	.918	.093	.805	.798	.850	.057	.825	.822	.885
Amulet[ECCV 17] [3]	.059	.915	.894	.912	.098	.837	.820	.831	.085	.778	.803	.803
RAS[ECCV 18] [38]	.056	.908	.893	.914	.101	.800	.799	.835	.059	.807	.839	.871
C2SNet[ECCV 18] [39]	.053	.911	.895	.915	.080	.777	.838	.850	.063	.809	.828	.847
DGRL[CVPR 18] [40]	.043	.921	.906	.917	.075	.844	.839	.836	.049	.828	.842	.863
ICNet [19] [41]	.041	.881	.918	.923	.071	.790	.850	.860	.048	.762	.865	.880
BANet [19] [42]	.041	.881	.918	.923	.070	.817	.853	.889	.040	.811	.879	.907
PiCANet-R[CVPR 19] [43]	.046	.935	.917	.913	.075	.843	.854	.870	.050	.860	.859	.862
CPD[CVPR 19] [44]	.037	.939	.918	.925	.071	.838	.848	.882	.043	.865	.858	.886
AFNet[CVPR 19] [45]	.042	.935	.914	.918	.070	.844	.850	.883	.046	.862	.861	.879
PoolNet[CVPR 19] [8]	.039	.944	.921	.924	.070	.846	.838	.880	.040	.882	.875	.886
BASNet[CVPR 19] [7]	.037	.942	.916	.921	.076	.840	.832	.879	.047	.860	.878	.844
EGNet[ICCV 19] [46]	.041	.936	.918	.943	.074	.841	.852	.881	.039	.866	.875	.907
TDBU[CVPR 19] [41]	.040	.926	–	.922	.072	.848	–	.852	.048	.836	–	.879
U^2-Net[PR 20] [47]	.041	.943	.918	.923	.074	.837	.844	.873	.054	.852	.847	.918
GateNet[ECCV 20] [48]	.040	.933	.920	.936	.069	.848	.857	.886	.040	.869	.885	.906
CSF+R[ECCV 20] [49]	.041	–	–	–	.073	–	–	–	.039	–	–	–
MINet[CVPR 20] [14]	.033	.938	.925	.950	.065	.846	.856	.896	.037	.865	.884	.917
SAMNet[TIP 21] [50]	.050	.915	.907	.916	.092	.807	.826	.838	.058	.812	.849	.859
ITSD+Bicon[Arxiv 21] [51]	.035	.920	–	.926	.064	.831	–	.857	.038	.838	–	.905
CFA-Net (Ours)	.033	.936	.923	.949	.064	.849	.859	.895	.037	.870	.886	.921

Qualitative Comparisons. To evaluate the proposed CFA-Net, we compare our method with some saliency maps produced by other methods in Fig. 3. Figure 3 shows a total of 13 images, including the original image and labels. From the results, it can be seen that our method performs better than other comparison methods for salient object detection. More importantly, our proposed method not only accurately captures salient objects but also effectively suppresses background noise.

Precision-Recall Curves. In addition to the numerical comparisons shown in Table 2, we also plot the precision-recall curves for the 11 state-of-the-art methods on the 5 datasets, as shown in Fig. 5. It can be seen that CFA-Net outperforms the other models in most cases when the thresholds are different.

Visual Comparison. Multiple images containing different scenarios from different datasets are selected for comparison with our images, which incorporate cases with prominent backgrounds, cluttered scenes, object occlusion, and cases

Table 3. Quantitative comparisons on two benchmark datasets (*i.e.*, HKU-IS and DUT-OMRON) using four evaluation metrics. Red and Blue indicate the best and second best performance.

Model	HKU-IS [28]				DUT-OMRON [29]			
	$M \downarrow$	$F_\beta \uparrow$	$S_m \uparrow$	$E_\phi \uparrow$	$M \downarrow$	$F_\beta \uparrow$	$S_m \uparrow$	$E_\phi \uparrow$
ELD$_{\text{ICCV 16}}$ [34]	.074	.739	.820	–	.092	.678	.750	.792
DCL$_{\text{CVPR 16}}$ [35]	.048	.885	.877	.902	.097	.739	.713	–
SRM$_{\text{ICCV 17}}$ [36]	.046	.893	.887	.866	.069	.725	.798	.808
DSS$_{\text{CVPR 17}}$ [37]	.041	.910	.879	.935	.063	.737	.790	.831
Amulet$_{\text{ECCV 17}}$ [3]	.052	.895	.883	.915	.098	.742	.780	.784
RAS$_{\text{ECCV 18}}$ [38]	.045	.913	.887	.931	.062	.753	.814	.843
C2SNet$_{\text{ECCV 18}}$ [39]	.046	.809	.828	.928	.072	.751	.798	.828
DGRL$_{\text{CVPR 18}}$ [40]	.036	.910	.905	.941	.062	.742	.814	.836
ICNet $_{19}$ [41]	.037	.858	.908	.943	.061	.730	.837	.859
BANet $_{19}$ [42]	.032	.887	.913	.955	.059	.736	.832	.865
PiCANet-R$_{\text{CVPR 19}}$ [43]	.043	.918	.904	.936	.605	.770	.832	.836
CPD$_{\text{CVPR 19}}$ [44]	.034	.911	.905	.938	.056	.754	.825	.847
AFNet$_{\text{CVPR 19}}$ [45]	.036	.923	.905	.942	.057	.759	.826	.846
PoolNet$_{\text{CVPR 19}}$ [8]	.032	.923	.917	.942	.056	.772	.836	.854
BASNet$_{\text{CVPR 19}}$ [7]	.032	.919	.909	.943	.056	.779	.836	.865
EGNet$_{\text{ICCV 19}}$ [46]	.031	.924	.918	.944	.052	.778	.818	.857
TDBU$_{\text{CVPR 19}}$ [41]	.038	.920	–	.942	.059	.780	–	.854
U^2-Net$_{\text{PR 20}}$ [47]	.031	.924	.916	.943	.054	.793	.847	.867
GateNet$_{\text{ECCV 20}}$ [48]	.033	.920	.915	.937	.055	.781	.837	.856
CSF+R$_{\text{ECCV 20}}$ [49]	.033	–	–	–	.055	–	–	–
MINet$_{\text{CVPR 20}}$ [14]	.029	.926	.919	.952	.056	.769	.833	.860
SAMNet$_{\text{TIP 21}}$ [50]	.045	.901	.898	.911	.065	.773	.830	.840
ITSD+Bicon$_{\text{Arxiv 21}}$ [51]	.029	.908	–	.952	.053	.774	–	.874
CFA-Net (Ours)	.028	.929	.920	.955	.054	.783	.838	.866

with extremely high similarity between the salient object and the background. It is worth mentioning that our proposed method not only produces a more accurate saliency map but also results in a higher contrast between the salient objects and the background, so it looks clearer.

5 Conclusion

In this paper, a novel CFA-Net is proposed for salient object detection. In the proposed model, an AFM is proposed to effectively integrate high-level and low-level features. To make the fused feature representation more accurate, we propose a CFAM to reduce the redundant information and obtain cross-level aggregated feature representations. Comprehensive experimental results on public saliency detection datasets demonstrate the effectiveness and robustness of the proposed CFA-Net. In addition, the ablation studies have shown the effectiveness of the key components in our CFA-Net.

References

1. Zhou, T., Fan, D.-P., Cheng, M.-M., Shen, J., Shao, L.: RGB-D salient object detection: a survey. Comput. Visual Media **7**(1), 37–69 (2021). https://doi.org/10.1007/s41095-020-0199-z
2. Ishikura, K., Kurita, N., Chandler, D.M., Ohashi, G.: Saliency detection based on multiscale extrema of local perceptual color differences. IEEE TIP **27**(2), 703–717 (2017)
3. Zhang, P., Wang, D., Lu, H., Wang, H., Ruan, X.: Amulet: aggregating multi-level convolutional features for salient object detection. In: ICCV, pp. 202–211 (2017)
4. Zhang, X., Wang, T., Qi, J., Lu, H., Wang, G.: Progressive attention guided recurrent network for salient object detection. In: CVPR, pp. 714–722 (2018)
5. Hu, X., Zhu, L., Qin, J., Fu, C.-W., Heng, P.-A.: Recurrently aggregating deep features for salient object detection. In: AAAI, vol. 32 (2018)
6. Fan, D.-P., Ji, G.-P., Qin, X., Cheng, M.-M.: Cognitive vision inspired object segmentation metric and loss function (2021)
7. Qin, X., Zhang, Z., Huang, C., Gao, C., Dehghan, M., Jagersand, M.: Basnet: boundary-aware salient object detection. In: CVPR, pp. 7479–7489 (2019)
8. Liu, J.-J., Hou, Q., Cheng, M.-M., Feng, J., Jiang, J.: A simple pooling-based design for real-time salient object detection. In: CVPR, pp. 3917–3926 (2019)
9. Fan, D.-P., Ji, G.-P., Sun, G., Cheng, M.-M., Shen, J., Shao, L.: Camouflaged object detection. In: CVPR, pp. 2777–2787 (2020)
10. Zhang, Q., Shi, Y., Zhang, X.: Attention and boundary guided salient object detection. Pattern Recogn. **107**, 107484 (2020)
11. Wang, G., Chen, C., Fan, D.-P., Hao, A., Qin, H.: From semantic categories to fixations: a novel weakly-supervised visual-auditory saliency detection approach. In: CVPR, pp. 15119–15128 (2021)
12. Zhang, P., Liu, W., Wang, D., Lei, Y., Wang, H., Lu, H.: Non-rigid object tracking via deep multi-scale spatial-temporal discriminative saliency maps. Pattern Recogn. **100**, 107130 (2020)

13. Mohammadi, S., Noori, M., Bahri, A., Majelan, S.G., Havaei, M.: Cagnet: content-aware guidance for salient object detection. Pattern Recogn. **103**, 107303 (2020)
14. Pang, Y., Zhao, X., Zhang, L., Lu, H.: Multi-scale interactive network for salient object detection. In: CVPR, pp. 9413–9422 (2020)
15. Qin, Y., et al.: Autofocus layer for semantic segmentation. In: Frangi, A.F., Schnabel, J.A., Davatzikos, C., Alberola-López, C., Fichtinger, G. (eds.) MICCAI 2018. LNCS, vol. 11072, pp. 603–611. Springer, Cham (2018). https://doi.org/10.1007/978-3-030-00931-1_69
16. Feng, G., Burlutskiy, N., Andersson, M., Wilén, L.: Multi-resolution networks for semantic segmentation in whole slide images
17. Tokunaga, H., Teramoto, Y., Yoshizawa, A., Bise, R.: Adaptive weighting multi-field-of-view CNN for semantic segmentation in pathology. In: CVPR, pp. 12597–12606 (2019)
18. Lyu, Y., Schiopu, I., Munteanu, A.: Multi-modal neural networks with multi-scale RGB-t fusion for semantic segmentation. Electron. Lett. **56**(18), 920–923 (2020)
19. Si, H., Zhang, Z., Lv, F., Yu, G., Lu, F.: Real-time semantic segmentation via multiply spatial fusion network
20. Liu, S., Qi, L., Qin, H., Shi, J., Jia, J.: Path aggregation network for instance segmentation. In: CVPR (2018)
21. Zhou, T., Fu, H., Chen, G., Zhou, Y., Fan, D.-P., Shao, L.: Specificity-preserving RGB-D saliency detection. In: ICCV (2021)
22. He, K., Zhang, X., Ren, S., Sun, J.: Deep residual learning for image recognition. In: CVPR, pp. 770–778 (2016)
23. Wei, J., Wang, S., Huang, Q.: F³net: fusion, feedback and focus for salient object detection. In: Proceedings of the AAAI Conference on Artificial Intelligence, vol. 34, pp. 12321–12328 (2020)
24. Everingham, M., Van Gool, L., Williams, C.K., Winn, J., Zisserman, A.: The pascal visual object classes (VOC) challenge. IJCV **88**(2), 303–338 (2010)
25. Wang, L., et al.: Learning to detect salient objects with image-level supervision. In: CVPR, pp. 136–145 (2017)
26. Xie, Y., Lu, H., Yang, M.-H.: Bayesian saliency via low and mid level cues. IEEE TIP **22**(5), 1689–1698 (2012)
27. Li, Y., Hou, X., Koch, C., Rehg, J.M., Yuille, A.L.: The secrets of salient object segmentation. In: CVPR, pp. 280–287 (2014)
28. Li, G., Yu, Y.: Visual saliency based on multiscale deep features. In: CVPR, pp. 5455–5463 (2015)
29. Yang, C., Zhang, L., Lu, H., Ruan, X., Yang, M.-H.: Saliency detection via graph-based manifold ranking. In: CVPR, pp. 3166–3173 (2013)
30. Perazzi, F., Krähenbühl, P., Pritch, Y., Hornung, A.: Saliency filters: contrast based filtering for salient region detection. In: 2012 CVPR, pp. 733–740. IEEE (2012)
31. Achanta, R., Hemami, S., Estrada, F., Susstrunk, S.: Frequency-tuned salient region detection. In: CVPR, pp. 1597–1604. IEEE (2009)
32. Fan, D.-P., Gong, C., Cao, Y., Ren, B., Cheng, M.-M., Borji, A.: Enhanced-alignment measure for binary foreground map evaluation. In: IJCAI (2018)
33. Fan, D.-P., Cheng, M.-M., Liu, Y., Li, T., Borji, A.: Structure-measure: a new way to evaluate foreground maps. In: ICCV, pp. 4548–4557 (2017)
34. Lee, G., Tai, Y.-W., Kim, J.: Deep saliency with encoded low level distance map and high level features. In: CVPR, pp. 660–668 (2016)
35. Li, G., Yu, Y.: Deep contrast learning for salient object detection. In: CVPR, pp. 478–487 (2016)

36. Wang, T., Borji, A., Zhang, L., Zhang, P., Lu, H.: A stagewise refinement model for detecting salient objects in images. In: ICCV, pp. 4019–4028 (2017)
37. Hou, Q., Cheng, M.-M., Hu, X., Borji, A., Tu, Z., Torr, P.H.: Deeply supervised salient object detection with short connections. In: CVPR, pp. 3203–3212 (2017)
38. Chen, S., Tan, X., Wang, B., Hu, X.: Reverse attention for salient object detection. In: Ferrari, V., Hebert, M., Sminchisescu, C., Weiss, Y. (eds.) ECCV 2018. LNCS, vol. 11213, pp. 236–252. Springer, Cham (2018). https://doi.org/10.1007/978-3-030-01240-3_15
39. Li, X., Yang, F., Cheng, H., Liu, W., Shen, D.: Contour knowledge transfer for salient object detection. In: Ferrari, V., Hebert, M., Sminchisescu, C., Weiss, Y. (eds.) ECCV 2018. LNCS, vol. 11219, pp. 370–385. Springer, Cham (2018). https://doi.org/10.1007/978-3-030-01267-0_22
40. Wang, T., Zhang, L., Wang, S., Lu, H., et al.: Detect globally, refine locally: a novel approach to saliency detection. In: CVPR, pp. 3127–3135 (2018)
41. Wang, W., Shen, J., Cheng, M.-M., Shao, L.: An iterative and cooperative top-down and bottom-up inference network for salient object detection. In: CVPR, pp. 5968–5977 (2019)
42. Su, J., Li, J., Zhang, Y., Xia, C., Tian, Y.: Selectivity or invariance: boundary-aware salient object detection. In: ICCV, pp. 3799–3808 (2019)
43. Liu, N., Han, J., Yang, M.-H.: Picanet: learning pixel-wise contextual attention for saliency detection. In: CVPR, pp. 3089–3098 (2018)
44. Wu, Z., Su, L., Huang, Q.: Cascaded partial decoder for fast and accurate salient object detection. In: CVPR, pp. 3907–3916 (2019)
45. Feng, M., Lu, H., Ding, E.: Attentive feedback network for boundary-aware salient object detection. In: CVPR, pp. 1623–1632 (2019)
46. Zhao, J.-X., Liu, J.-J., Fan, D.-P., Cao, Y., Yang, J., Cheng, M.-M.: Egnet: edge guidance network for salient object detection. In: ICCV, pp. 8779–8788 (2019)
47. Qin, X., Zhang, Z., Huang, C., Dehghan, M., Zaiane, O.R., Jagersand, M.: U2-net: going deeper with nested u-structure for salient object detection. Pattern Recogn. **106**, 107404 (2020)
48. Zhao, X., Pang, Y., Zhang, L., Lu, H., Zhang, L.: Suppress and balance: a simple gated network for salient object detection. In: Vedaldi, A., Bischof, H., Brox, T., Frahm, J.-M. (eds.) ECCV 2020. LNCS, vol. 12347, pp. 35–51. Springer, Cham (2020). https://doi.org/10.1007/978-3-030-58536-5_3
49. Gao, S.-H., Tan, Y.-Q., Cheng, M.-M., Lu, C., Chen, Y., Yan, S.: Highly efficient salient object detection with 100K parameters. In: Vedaldi, A., Bischof, H., Brox, T., Frahm, J.-M. (eds.) ECCV 2020. LNCS, vol. 12351, pp. 702–721. Springer, Cham (2020). https://doi.org/10.1007/978-3-030-58539-6_42
50. Liu, Y., Zhang, X.-Y., Bian, J.-W., Zhang, L., Cheng, M.-M.: Samnet: stereoscopically attentive multi-scale network for lightweight salient object detection. IEEE TIP **30**, 3804–3814 (2021)
51. Yang, Z., Soltanian-Zadeh, S., Farsiu, S.: Biconnet: an edge-preserved connectivity-based approach for salient object detection, arXiv preprint arXiv:2103.00334

Disentangled Feature Learning for Semi-supervised Person Re-identification

Jin Ding[1], Xue Zhou[1,2,3](✉), and Gehan Hao[1]

[1] School of Automation Engineering, University of Electronic Science and Technology of China (UESTC), Chengdu, China
zhouxue@uestc.edu.cn
[2] Shenzhen Institute for Advanced Study, UESTC, Shenzhen, China
[3] Intelligent Terminal Key Laboratory of SiChuan Province, Chengdu, China

Abstract. Semi-supervised learning has become more and more popular in person re-identification because acquiring annotations is time-consuming and cumbersome. In this paper, we design a Disentangled Feature Learning (DFL) model based on an encoder-decoder mode by making use of less labeled data together with lots of unlabeled data. Specifically, a pair of horizontally flipped images are fed into the encoder module to decompose identity and structure features. Then different decomposed features are combined to reconstruct images in the decoder module. Multi-view consistent constraints are proposed for the further learning of feature disentanglement in the image-view, feature-view and feature-vector-view, respectively. Moreover, we separate the identity encoders into a teacher encoder and a student encoder for the stability of training and better performance. Extensive experiments on four ReID datasets demonstrate the effectiveness of our DFL model in the low proportion of the labeled data.

Keywords: Person re-identification · Semi-supervised · Disentangled feature learning · Multi-view consistent constraints · Teacher-student model

1 Introduction

Person Re-Identification (ReID) is a sub-task of image retrieval, which aims to identify a target pedestrian from a large-scale gallery set captured by other non-overlapping cameras. With the striking success of Convolution Neural Network (CNN), most ReID works [2,11,14,19,26,29] based on the supervised learning have achieved satisfactory performance.

Although these supervised ReID models have been applied in the literature extensively, they can not meet the needs of the practical application. There are mainly two reasons. Firstly, these methods are prone to over-fitting a training set. Usually, most state-of-the-art ReID algorithms train CNN with all labeled training set which only contain the single scenario. Secondly, insufficient labeled

S. Yu et al. (Eds.): PRCV 2022, LNCS 13537, pp. 449–463, 2022.
https://doi.org/10.1007/978-3-031-18916-6_37

samples hamper the generalization of these supervised ReID models. Compared with other tasks with millions of data, most ReID datasets [10,17,23,27] only have thousands of persons with several images per person because obtaining labels is time-consuming and labour-intensive.

To tackle the above problems, some methods [6,15,16] based on labeled data use data augmentation to increase the diversity of pedestrian image patterns or generate more pedestrian images through Generative Adversarial Network (GAN). Due to the confusion in attributes caused by data augmentation and the difficulty of convergence by GAN, utilizing the unlabeled data in unsupervised [12,22,25] and semi-supervised [4,5,8,13,24] ways has attracted more attention. However, most unsupervised ReID models require extra annotations and are far from the supervised methods in terms of accuracy, while a semi-supervised way can achieve considerable improvement by leveraging a few labeled in conjunction with lots of unlabeled data.

In this paper, we design a Disentangled Feature Learning (DFL) model based on an encoder-decoder way for semi-supervised ReID, which mainly contains three parts. Firstly, we found that a pair of horizontally flipped images maintain a symmetrical distribution in structure without changing the identity information of pedestrians. Thus, we disentangle the pedestrian features into identity and structure features by simply taking the original image and its horizontally flipped image as inputs of the encoder module. Then different disentangled features are combined to reconstruct the images through the decoder module. Secondly, we integrate constraints of consistency within three views into our DFL model. Such constraints make the learning of disentangled features take place in the image-view, feature-view and feature-vector-view. Specifically, in the image-view, the output of the decoder must meet the self-construction for the original image and the swap-construction for its mirror image. Meanwhile, the invariance of identity and the symmetry of structure should be kept on in the feature-view. Besides, the constraint in the feature-vector-view will be adopted on the labeled data via the identity loss. Thirdly, to further improve the performance of the DFL model and the stability of training, we separate identity encoders into a student encoder and a teacher encoder. The weights of the teacher identity encoder are updated by the exponential moving average weights of the student ones.

By integrating multi-view consistent constraints and the teacher-student mode based identity encoders, our DFL model achieves great performance on four ReID datasets in the low proportion of the labeled data. In particular, our method significantly outperforms other state-of-the-art methods when the labeled data ratio is set to 1/6.

Our major work and contributions are summarized as follows:

(1) We introduce a Disentangled Feature Learning (DFL) model based on an encoder-decoder way for semi-supervised ReID. By taking a pair of horizontally flipped images as inputs, identity-aware and structure-aware features are disentangled without extra annotations.
(2) Multi-view consistent constraints are integrated into the DFL model, including the image-view, feature-view and feature-vector-view. The constraints in

the image-view and feature-view are free of labels, while the feature-vector-view constraint is only adopted for the labeled data.

(3) In order to achieve better performance and the stability of training, we separate the identity encoders into a student encoder and a teacher encoder. By averaging the weights of consecutive student identity encoder, the teacher identity encoder learns faster and converges to a better result.

2 Related Work

2.1 Semi-supervised ReID

As a learning method that falls between supervised and unsupervised learning, semi-supervised ReID method achieves remarkable success by making full use of labeled and unlabeled data. These methods can be categorized into three types: pseudo-label generation based methods [5,8,13,24], Generative Adversarial Network (GAN) based methods [4,6] and feature disentanglement based methods [11,15,16]. For examples, Huang et al. [8] introduced a virtual label called Multi-pseudo Regularized Label (MpRL). Ge et al. [6] designed a pose-guided Feature Distilling Generative Adversarial Network (FD-GAN) to learn pose-invariant features, but auxiliary pose information are required.

Feature disentanglement based methods aim at decomposing the highly coupled pedestrian features into some specific features, such as appearance feature and structure feature. Ma et al. [15] proposed a multi-branch model to disentangle the input into foreground, background and pose, but it is unable to train in an end-to-end way. Li et al. [11] presented a Pose Disentanglement and Adaptation Network (PDA-Net) to obtain the posture feature, which requires a pre-trained PAFs [1] network. These methods can be generalized as follows: 1) Auxiliary annotations are applied on the network as guidance to disentangle the features of pedestrians. 2) More pedestrian images are generated with extra complicated modules. Our DFL model achieves satisfactory results by taking a horizontally flipped images as inputs without introducing additional annotations or complicated modules.

2.2 Teacher-Student Model

Teacher-student model is widely used in the semi-supervised learning and knowledge distillation. This model often uses the consistent supervision between the teacher and the student networks' predictions. Samuli et al. [9] proposed π-Model, whose main idea is to use regularization methods such as data augmentation and dropout. Based on π-Model, Temporal Ensembling is proposed in the same article, which uses the Exponential Moving Average (EMA) method to ensemble the previous predictions of the student network. Rather than averaging the label predictions in [9], Tarvainen et al. [20] introduced Mean-Teacher method to average the weights of models and achieved online learning.

In our DFL model, inspired by the Mean-Teacher method, we separate the identity encoders into a student encoder and a teacher encoder for further improvement of performance and the stability of training.

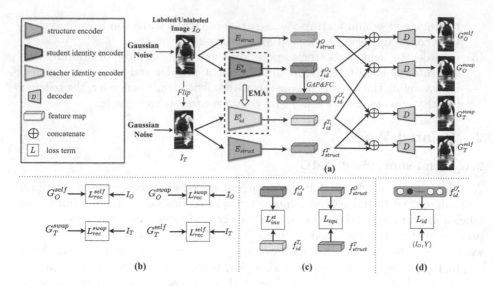

Fig. 1. A schematic overview of the DFL model. (a)The model is composed of encoders and decoders, where the structure encoders are weight-shared and the teacher identity encoder E_{id}^t is updated by an Exponential Moving Average (EMA) of the student identity encoder E_{id}^s. Multi-view constraints are implemented in modules: (b)image-view constraint (c)feature-view constraint and (d)feature-vector-view constraint. Note, the feature-vector-view constraint is only adopted for the labeled images.

3   Approach

3.1   Overall Framework

As shown in Fig. 1 (a), we take the original image I_O and its horizontal mirror image I_T as inputs. Besides, gaussian noise is involved in the both original image and horizontal mirror image for robustness. Based on an encoder-decoder way, the pedestrian features are disentangled into identity features and structure features in the encoder module. Then, these encoded features are combined to reconstruct the images through the decoder module. Note, the weights of the structure encoders are shared while the identity encoders are separated into a student identity encoder E_{id}^s and a teacher identity encoder E_{id}^t. The weights of the teacher encoder are updated by the Exponential Moving Average (EMA) of the student encoder's weights. With the help of the multi-view consistent constraints shown in Fig. 1(b) (c) and (d), our DFL model makes it more accessible to learn to disentangle the identity and structure features.

3.2   Disentangled Feature Learning

Considering the characteristic of the same pedestrian identity with various poses, we hope to guide the network to disentangle the highly coupled features into independent identity-aware features and structure-aware features. Inspired by

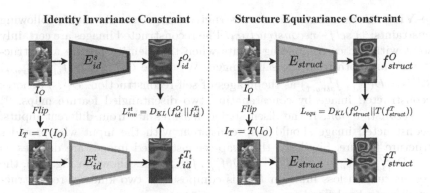

Fig. 2. Visualizations of consistent constraint in the feature view. Identity Invariance Constraint shows that the identity information will not be changed between the original image and its horizontal mirror version. Structure Equivariance Constraint shows the equivariance of two symmetrical images in the structure information. Grad-CAM [18] is adopted for feature maps visualization.

data augmentation, we found that simply horizontally flipping the original image can obtain a new mirror structural sample. A pair of images that have the same identity and the different structure can be built without extra modules.

Therefore, based on an encoder-decoder way, we design a DFL model which takes a pair of horizontally symmetric images as inputs, as shown in Fig. 1(a). DenseNet-121 [7] and five transposed convolutional layers are adopted as the backbones of the encoder (E) and decoder (D), respectively. Take the original image input I_O as an example. Firstly, in order to improve the robustness of the model, we apply gaussian noise on both I_O and its horizontal mirror image I_T. Then, we apply two encoders, termed as the student identity encoder E_{id}^s and the structure encoder E_{struct}, to obtain the identity feature map $f_{id}^{O_s}$ and the structure feature map f_{struct}^T, respectively. Similarly, the horizontal flipped image I_T is disentangled into $f_{id}^{T_t}$ and f_{struct}^T via the teacher identity encoder E_{id}^t and the structure encoder E_{struct}. Finally, two disentangled features with different semantics are concatenated in the channel dimension, leading to four different reconstructed images. The student identity encoder's parameters θ will be updated via back-propagation during the training while the teacher identity encoder's parameters θ' are computed as the exponential moving average of θ, which can be calculated as:

$$\theta_t' = \omega\theta_{t-1}' + (1-\omega)\theta_t, \tag{1}$$

where t is the training step and ω denotes a smoothing coefficient hyperparameter.

3.3 Multi-view Consistent Constraints

In order to disentangle semantic mixed features into independent features, we integrate consistent constraints in three views: image-view, feature-view and feature-vector-view, as shown in Fig. 1(a) (b) and (c).

Image-View Constraint. The reconstructed images should satisfy following two constraints: 1) $self-reconstruction$. The reconstructed images are certainly consistent with the corresponding inputs when the identity feature and structure feature are both from the same image. We define $G_O^{self} = D(f_{id}^{O_s}, f_{struct}^O)$ and $G_T^{self} = D(f_{id}^{T_t}, f_{struct}^T)$ as the images of self-reconstruction. $D(\cdot, \cdot)$ denotes the reconstructed image by concatenating two disentangled feature maps. 2) $swap-reconstruction$. If the disentangled features are from different inputs, the reconstructed image should keep consistent with the input who provides the structure feature. Similarly, the swap-reconstructed images are denotes as $G_O^{swap} = D(f_{id}^{T_t}, f_{struct}^O)$ and $G_T^{swap} = D(f_{id}^{O_s}, f_{struct}^T)$. As shown in Fig. 1(a), the final reconstruction loss function L_{rec} is composed of two kinds of reconstructions, which can be defined as:

$$L_{rec} = L_{rec}^{self} + L_{rec}^{swap}. \tag{2}$$

The first item L_{rec}^{self} follows the first constraint that each reconstruction is consistent with the corresponding input, i.e.,

$$L_{rec}^{self} = ||I_O - G_O^{self}||_2 + ||I_T - G_T^{self}||_2, \tag{3}$$

where $|| \cdot ||_2$ is the pixel-wise L_2 loss. Considering that the identity will not be changed after horizontally flipping the image, thus the reconstructed image depends on the structure-aware features, i.e.,

$$L_{rec}^{swap} = ||I_O - G_O^{swap}||_2 + ||I_T - G_T^{swap}||_2. \tag{4}$$

Feature-View Constraint. We introduce the feature-view constraint into our DFL model, as shown in Fig. 1(c). Four disentangled features are obtained after encoding the original image and its horizontal image. The two identity features should remain invariant due to the unchanged identity after horizontally flipping, meanwhile, the two structure features should satisfy mirror symmetry because of the equivariant transformation. Therefore, we design the identity invariance loss L_{inv} and structure equivariance loss L_{equ} in the feature-view as follows:

$$\begin{aligned} L_f &= L_{inv}^{st} + L_{equ} \\ &= D_{KL}(f_{id}^{O_s}||f_{id}^{T_t}) + D_{KL}(f_{struct}^O||T(f_{struct}^T)) \end{aligned} \tag{5}$$

where $D_{KL}(\cdot)$ is the Kullback-Leibler divergence distance and $T(\cdot)$ is a horizontally flipped transformation. It is worth noting that the distribution of these feature maps (i.e., $f_{id}^{O_s}$, $f_{id}^{T_t}$, f_{struct}^O, f_{struct}^T) is expected to meet the feature-view constraint in the channel dimension. Specifically, softmax is firstly applied on the channel dimension to restrict the element with a certain range. Then, element-wise KL divergence loss is computed between the two feature maps, i.e. ($f_{id}^{O_s}$ and $f_{id}^{T_t}$) or (f_{struct}^O and f_{struct}^T). An obvious illustration of this constraint is presented in Fig. 2. The left part of Fig. 2 displays the identity feature invariant constraint of the generated two identity feature maps $f_{id}^{O_s}$ and $f_{id}^{T_t}$, and the right part shows that the structure feature maps f_{struct}^O and f_{struct}^T should maintain horizontal symmetry.

Algorithm 1. Training algorithm for DFL model

Input: Train data I_O; Train data label Y (only for labeled data $B_S \in minibatch B$);
    Student identity encoder E_{id}^s; Teacher identity encoder E_{id}^t; Structure encoder
    E_{struct}; Decoder D; Parameter $\omega, \alpha, \beta, \gamma$.
Output: $E_{id}^s, E_{id}^t, E_{struct}, D$.
1: **Initialize** weights $\theta_{E_{id}^s}, \theta_{E_{id}^t}, \theta_{E_{struct}}, \theta_D$;
2: **for** n in epochs **do**
3:     **for** each minibatch B **do**
4:         $I_T = T(I_O)(I_O \in B)$;
5:         $f_{id}^{O_s}, f_{id}^{T_t} \leftarrow E_{id}^s(I_O), E_{id}^t(I_T)$;
6:         $f_{struct}^O, f_{struct}^T \leftarrow E_{struct}(I_O), E_{struct}(I_T)$;
7:         $G_O^{self}, G_T^{self} \leftarrow D(f_{id}^{O_s}, f_{struct}^O), D(f_{id}^{T_t}, f_{struct}^T)$;
8:         $G_O^{swap}, G_T^{swap} \leftarrow D(f_{id}^{T_t}, f_{struct}^O), D(f_{id}^{O_s}, f_{struct}^T)$;
9:         L_{rec}, L_f optimized with Eq. (2),(5);
10:        $L_U = \frac{1}{|B|} \sum_{I_O \in B}(\alpha L_f + \beta L_{rec})$;
11:        **if** I_O with label Y **then**
12:            $f_{id}^{O_s'} \leftarrow f_{id}^{O_s}$ after GAP&FC;
13:            L_{id} optimized with Eq. (6);
14:            $L_S = \frac{1}{|B_S|} \sum_{I_O \in B_S}(L_{id})$;
15:        **end if**
16:        $\theta_{E_{id}^s, E_{struct}, D} \xleftarrow{+} -\nabla_{\theta_{E_{id}^s, E_{struct}, D}}(\gamma L_U + L_S)$;
17:        $\theta_{E_{id}^t} \leftarrow \omega \theta_{E_{id}^t} + (1 - \omega)\theta_{E_{id}^s}$
18:     **end for**
19: **end for**

Feature-Vector-View Constraint. For the labeled inputs, we hope to adopt the identity label Y as a strong supervised signal that can guide to decompose identity and structure features. As shown in Fig. 1(d), $f_{id}^{O_s'}$ denotes the identity feature vector. It is generated by the disentangled feature map $f_{id}^{O_s}$ through GAP&FC operation. Cross-entropy function $CE(\cdot, \cdot)$ is used to design the identity loss, *i.e.*,

$$L_{id} = CE(f_{id}^{O_s'}, Y), \tag{6}$$

3.4 Semi-supervised Training and Testing

We introduce a DFL model for semi-supervised ReID by making full use of less labeled data together with lots of unlabeled data. During the training, for the unlabeled inputs, the image-view constraint and the feature-view constraint are applied on the reconstructed images and the disentangled features, respectively. We define the unsupervised training loss L_U as follows:

$$L_U = \frac{1}{|D|} \sum_{x \in D}(\alpha L_f + \beta L_{rec}), \tag{7}$$

where α and β are hyper-parameters. $|D|$ denotes the number of the samples containing both labeled and unlabeled data. As for the labeled inputs, the

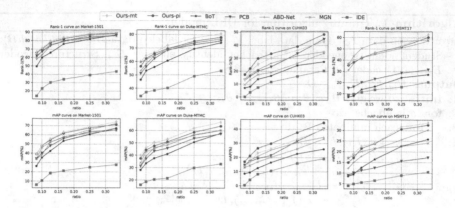

Fig. 3. Performance comparison of our proposed method with five state-of-the-art ReID methods on four ReID datasets when the labeled data ratio is set to 1/3, 1/4, 1/6, 1/8, 1/10 and 1/12.

feature-vector-view constraint is an add-on to boost the performance of the disentanglement. For the labeled data set D_s, we define the supervised training loss L_S as follows:

$$L_S = \frac{1}{|D_s|} \sum_{x \in D_s} (L_{id}),$$ (8)

The overall loss L_{total} can be defined as:

$$L_{total} = \gamma L_U + L_S,$$ (9)

where γ is the weight coefficient. In order to enhance the performance of our DFL model, we explore different types of γ in our experiments. Algorithm 1 summarizes the procedure of DFL model training with implementation details.

During the testing, the decoders will be discarded. Since the teacher identity encoder E_{id}^t gathers more identity-aware information by averaging the weights of consecutive student identity encoder E_{id}^s, it is applied to extract the identity features for query-gallery matching.

4 Experiments

4.1 Datasets and Implementation Details

Our proposed model is evaluated on four mainstream ReID datasets, consisting of Market-1501 [27], DukeMTMC-reID [17], CUHK03 [10] and MSMT17 [23]. Market-1501 is composed of 1501 identities of people captured from 6 different cameras. DukeMTMC-reID contains 36,411 images, belonging to 1,812 identities captured by 8 cameras. CUHK03 consists of 14,096 images of 1,467 identities from 6 camera views. MSMT17 has a great many images, which contains 4,101 identities with 126,441 images collected from 15 cameras. Cumulative matching characteristics (CMC) and mean average precision (mAP) are adopted as evaluation protocols.

Table 1. Comparison with five state-of-the-art ReID methods on four datasets when the labeled data ratio is set to 1/6. Our method shows great improvement of the performance.

Methods	Market-1501		DukeMTMC-reID		CUHK03		MSMT17	
	Rank-1	mAP	Rank-1	mAP	Rank-1	mAP	Rank-1	mAP
IDE [28]	30.4	18.5	40.1	21.5	11.7	10.5	13.7	6.4
MGN [21]	75.4	52.0	69.1	50.1	19.5	20.4	55.3	21.6
PCB [19]	74.1	48.2	68.4	45.8	23.2	21.4	23.2	12.4
BoT [14]	65.6	42.3	60.5	41.0	16.5	16.4	34.6	14.5
ABD-Net [2]	68.0	48.1	68.0	48.2	26.0	25.2	45.4	21.0
Ours-pi	77.8	54.5	69.0	50.5	**32.9**	**29.8**	44.5	**29.3**
Ours-mt	**80.1**	**55.9**	**72.5**	**53.8**	30.1	26.2	**46.9**	24.2

Implementation Details. Our DFL model is implemented on Pytorch. We refer to [14] and resize each input image to fixed 256×128. Notice that the encoders are based on the lightweight network DenseNet-121 pre-trained on ImageNet [3]. During the training, we only choose random erasing [30] for data augmentation. Each batch size is set to 96, incorporating the same number of labeled and unlabeled training samples with their horizontal flipped images. SGD is chosen to optimize our model with a momentum of 0.9. The initial learning rate is set to 0.01 in encoders and 0.1 in the decoder. We train our model for 90 epochs and decay the learning rates to its $0.1\times$ and $0.01\times$ after training for 70 and 80 epochs.

4.2 Comparison with State-of-the-Art Semi-supervised Methods

We evaluate our method on four datasets by setting labeled data ratio to 1/3, 1/4, 1/6, 1/8, 1/10 and 1/12. Take Market-1501 as an example, when the ratio is 1/3, 751 identities are randomly divided into 250 labeled identities and 501 unlabeled identities, and the identities in the two parts are mutually exclusive. We apply these six different ratios on five state-of-the-art ReID methods, including IDE [28], MGN [21], PCB [19], BoT [14], and ABD-Net [2]. Significantly, in order to verify the effectiveness of EMA, we design **Ours-pi** and **Ours-mt**. The former uses two identity encoders with shared weights while the latter separate the identity encoders into a student encoder and a teacher encoder.

As shown in Fig. 3, we observe that our method works better apparently with the lower proportion of the labeled data. For example, when the ratio is set to 1/12 in Market-1501, compared with IDE, BoT, MGN, PCB and ABD-Net, our method has got increase by 52.6%, 17.4%, 6.7%, 4.2%, 2.5% at Rank-1 score and 32.0%, 13.0%, 5.3%, 4.9%, 5.2% at mAP, respectively. Furthermore, we found that MGN has achieved better performance in MSMT17 under the ratio of 1/10, 1/8 and 1/6. The reason might be that the multi-branch granularity network has learned the fine-grained representations. However, among most of the results, our DFL model achieves the best performance on both Rank-1 score and mAP.

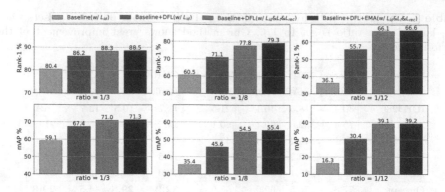

Fig. 4. Performance of each component in Market-1501 when the labeled data ratio is set to 1/3, 1/8 and 1/12. L_{id}, L_{rec} and L_f are consistent constraints in three views. **EMA** means Exponential Moving Average. With the combination of these parts, our method achieves best performance.

In particular, we show the representative results when the labeled data ratio is set to 1/6 in Table 1. We analyse that the reason for poor performance with IDE and BoT is the limitation of their global-based feature representation. For example, their Rank-1 scores are only 30.4% and 65.6% in Market-1501. Those fine-grained based methods perform better. For examples, MGN achieves 75.4% Rank-1 score and 52.0% mAP in Market-1501, which shows the effectiveness of the local feature representation. Moreover, ABD-Net has reached 26.0% Rank-1 score and 25.2% mAP in CUHK03 with the help of its attention-based architecture. Different from these methods, we only use the global feature representation with our feature disentanglement based model, leading to the best accuracy on the four ReID datasets.

4.3   Ablation Analysis

Effectiveness of Components. To better understand the contribution of the components of our model, we define four different models as follows:

Baseline(w/L_{id}). We create a baseline model that only uses one DenseNet-121 network and takes original images as inputs. For the sake of fairness, only the identity loss L_{id} is adopted in the baseline model.

Baseline+DFL(w/L_{id}). Two weight-shared identity encoders are added into the baseline without multi-view consistent constraints and the mean-teacher module. The inputs are a pair of horizontally flipped images.

Baseline+DFL(w/L_{id}&L_f&L_{rec}). Multi-view consistent constraints are added, including reconstruction loss L_{rec} (image-view), feature-view loss L_f and the identity loss L_{id} (feature-vector-view).

Baseline+DFL+EMA(w/L_{id}&L_f&L_{rec}). The two identity encoders are separated into a student encoder and a teacher encoder. Wherein the weights of the teacher encoder are from an EMA of the student version over epochs.

As shown in Fig. 4, we conduct comparisons under three different ratios. When the proportion of the labeled data is 1/3, the Rank-1 of the baseline is only 80.4%. Compared with the baseline, through incrementally applying DFL, multi-view consistent constraints and mean-teacher module, the Rank-1 accuracy increases by 5.8%, 7.9% and 8.1%, respectively. With the reduction of the ratio, the effectiveness of our proposed components becomes more obvious. For example, when the ratio is set to 1/12, 30.5% Rank-1 and 22.9% Rank-1 increases are shown on the final model compared with the baseline. The results demonstrate the advantages of combining these complementary components.

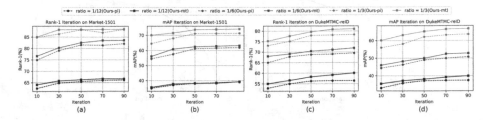

Fig. 5. Performance of **Ours-pi** and **Ours-mt** with different iteration numbers. (a) and (b) are experiments on Market-1501, the others are on DukeMTMC-reID. The lines of different colors represent different settings of ratio. The solid and dashed lines denote **Ours-mt** and **Ours-pi** models, respectively.

Exploration of Iteration. In order to explore the convergence of the training process, we compare the performance of **Ours-pi** and **Ours-mt** in Market-1501 and DukeMTMC-reID under three different ratios, as shown in Fig. 5. It shows that **Ours-mt** maintains more stability than **Ours-pi** during the training process and achieves better performance. The reason is that the teacher identity encoder in Ours-mt provides more complementary and independent predictions by integrating the past weights of the student version. What's more, according to comparing the slopes of Rank-1 and mAP curves under different ratios, we observe that the convergence is faster with the larger ratio, which shows the influence of the labeled data.

Experiments on Hyper-parameter. In Eq. (7) and Eq. (9), the parameters α, β and γ are set by an empirical search in Market-1501 when the labeled data ratio is set to 1/6. The hyper-parameter α is searched from $\{0, 0.1, 2, 5, 10\}$ and finally is set to 5. A large α is inclined to learn invariant identity features and equivariant structure features. Considering that the quality of the reconstructed images has a great impact on the learning of the network, β is searched from a smaller scope $\{0, 0.1, 0.2, 0.3, 0.4, 0.5\}$ and finally is set to 0.3. As for γ in

Eq. (9), we choose three different types to explore the optimal for our model, including constant, sigmoid ramp-up and linear ramp-up.

Constant. We conduct a search from $\{0, 0.001, 0.01, 0.1, 1\}$ and we found that 0.01 is the best one.

Sigmoid Ramp-up. The γ is replaced with a mapping function $\phi_s(\cdot)$ about iteration t as follow:

$$\phi_s(t) = \mu * e^{-5(1-\frac{t}{T})^2}, \tag{10}$$

where T denotes the total number of iterations and μ is a constant coefficient.

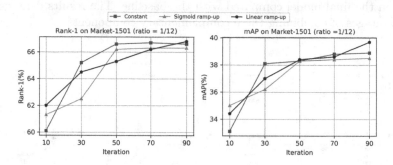

Fig. 6. Performance of **Ours-mt** with different types of weight coefficient γ in Market-1501 when the ratio is set to 1/12.

Linear Ramp-up. This type adopts different strategies in different iteration intervals as follow:

$$\phi_l(t) = \begin{cases} 0 & t < T_1 \\ \frac{t-T_1}{T_2-T_1}\mu & T_1 \leq t < T_2 \\ \mu & T_2 \leq t \end{cases} \tag{11}$$

where T_1 and T_2 represent the initial and the end of the iteration, respectively. We set $T_1 = 20$ and $T_2 = 70$ in the experiment and μ is set to 0.01.

Figure 6 shows the performance of Ours-mt in Market-1501 with different types of γ when the labeled data ratio is set to 1/12. An evident improvement of Rank-1 and mAP is observed at the beginning of the iteration when γ is set to a constant. However, the accuracy reaches the bottleneck at about the 50th iteration. We analyze that a large γ leads to more errors at the initial stage of training compared with the small γ in Eq. (10) and Eq. (11). With the small ratio of labeled data in the semi-supervised learning, the low accuracy at the beginning of the training will be amplified by a constant coefficient. Thus, we apply linear ramp-up in our experiments to avoid this situation.

5   Conclusion

In this paper, we propose a Disentangled Feature Learning (DFL) model based on an encoder-decoder way for semi-supervised person re-identification. The model is effective to alleviate the limitation of insufficient labeled samples by making full use of both labeled and unlabeled data. The multi-view consistent constraints are proposed to overcome the negative results performed by only image-view identity constraint in most normal ReID models. Furthermore, we separate the identity encoders of the DFL model into a student encoder and a teacher encoder, leading to faster feedback and better performance. The combinations of these components achieve best performance. Extensive experiments on four common ReID datasets have shown the effectiveness of our model.

Acknowledgment. This work was supported by the Natural Science Foundation of China (No.61972071, U20A20184), the Sichuan Science and Technology Program (2020YJ0036), the Research Program of Zhejiang Lab (2019KD0AB02), the 2019 Fundamental Research Funds for the Central Universities (ZYGX2019J068), and Grant SCITLAB-1005 of Intelligent Terminal Key Laboratory of SiChuan Province.

References

1. Cao, Z., Simon, T., Wei, S.E., Sheikh, Y.: Realtime multi-person 2d pose estimation using part affinity fields. In: Proceedings of the IEEE Conference on Computer Vision and Pattern Recognition, pp. 7291–7299 (2017)
2. Chen, T., et al.: Abd-net: attentive but diverse person re-identification. In: Proceedings of the IEEE/CVF International Conference on Computer Vision, pp. 8351–8361 (2019)
3. Deng, J., Dong, W., Socher, R., Li, L.J., Li, K., Fei-Fei, L.: Imagenet: a large-scale hierarchical image database. In: 2009 IEEE Conference on Computer Vision and Pattern Recognition, pp. 248–255. IEEE (2009)
4. Ding, G., Zhang, S., Khan, S., Tang, Z., Zhang, J., Porikli, F.: Feature affinity-based pseudo labeling for semi-supervised person re-identification. IEEE Trans. Multimedia **21**(11), 2891–2902 (2019)
5. Fan, H., Zheng, L., Yan, C., Yang, Y.: Unsupervised person re-identification: Clustering and fine-tuning. ACM Trans. Multimedia Comput. Commun. Appli. (TOMM) **14**(4), 1–18 (2018)
6. Ge, Y., et al.: Fd-gan: pose-guided feature distilling gan for robust person re-identification. arXiv preprint arXiv:1810.02936 (2018)
7. Huang, G., Liu, Z., Van Der Maaten, L., Weinberger, K.Q.: Densely connected convolutional networks. In: Proceedings of the IEEE Conference on Computer Vision and Pattern Recognition, pp. 4700–4708 (2017)
8. Huang, Y., Xu, J., Wu, Q., Zheng, Z., Zhang, Z., Zhang, J.: Multi-pseudo regularized label for generated data in person re-identification. IEEE Trans. Image Process. **28**(3), 1391–1403 (2018)
9. Laine, S., Aila, T.: Temporal ensembling for semi-supervised learning. arXiv preprint arXiv:1610.02242 (2016)
10. Li, W., Zhao, R., Xiao, T., Wang, X.: Deepreid: deep filter pairing neural network for person re-identification. In: Proceedings of the IEEE Conference on Computer Vision and Pattern Recognition, pp. 152–159 (2014)
11. Li, Y.J., Lin, C.S., Lin, Y.B., Wang, Y.C.F.: Cross-dataset person re-identification via unsupervised pose disentanglement and adaptation. In: Proceedings of the IEEE/CVF International Conference on Computer Vision, pp. 7919–7929 (2019)

12. Lin, Y., Dong, X., Zheng, L., Yan, Y., Yang, Y.: A bottom-up clustering approach to unsupervised person re-identification. In: Proceedings of the AAAI Conference on Artificial Intelligence. vol. 33, pp. 8738–8745 (2019)
13. Liu, Yu., Song, G., Shao, J., Jin, X., Wang, X.: Transductive centroid projection for semi-supervised large-scale recognition. In: Ferrari, V., Hebert, M., Sminchisescu, C., Weiss, Y. (eds.) ECCV 2018. LNCS, vol. 11209, pp. 72–89. Springer, Cham (2018). https://doi.org/10.1007/978-3-030-01228-1_5
14. Luo, H., Gu, Y., Liao, X., Lai, S., Jiang, W.: Bag of tricks and a strong baseline for deep person re-identification. In: Proceedings of the IEEE/CVF Conference on Computer Vision and Pattern Recognition Workshops (2019)
15. Ma, L., Sun, Q., Georgoulis, S., Van Gool, L., Schiele, B., Fritz, M.: Disentangled person image generation. In: Proceedings of the IEEE Conference on Computer Vision and Pattern Recognition, pp. 99–108 (2018)
16. Qian, X., et al.: Pose-normalized image generation for person re-identification. In: Ferrari, V., Hebert, M., Sminchisescu, C., Weiss, Y. (eds.) ECCV 2018. LNCS, vol. 11213, pp. 661–678. Springer, Cham (2018). https://doi.org/10.1007/978-3-030-01240-3_40
17. Ristani, E., Solera, F., Zou, R., Cucchiara, R., Tomasi, C.: Performance measures and a data set for multi-target, multi-camera tracking. In: Hua, G., Jégou, H. (eds.) ECCV 2016. LNCS, vol. 9914, pp. 17–35. Springer, Cham (2016). https://doi.org/10.1007/978-3-319-48881-3_2
18. Selvaraju, R.R., Cogswell, M., Das, A., Vedantam, R., Parikh, D., Batra, D.: Gradcam: Visual explanations from deep networks via gradient-based localization. In: Proceedings of the IEEE International Conference on Computer Vision, pp. 618–626 (2017)
19. Sun, Y., Zheng, L., Yang, Y., Tian, Q., Wang, S.: Beyond part models: Person retrieval with refined part pooling (and a strong convolutional baseline). In: Ferrari, V., Hebert, M., Sminchisescu, C., Weiss, Y. (eds.) ECCV 2018. LNCS, vol. 11208, pp. 501–518. Springer, Cham (2018). https://doi.org/10.1007/978-3-030-01225-0_30
20. Tarvainen, A., Valpola, H.: Mean teachers are better role models: Weight-averaged consistency targets improve semi-supervised deep learning results. arXiv preprint arXiv:1703.01780 (2017)
21. Wang, G., Yuan, Y., Chen, X., Li, J., Zhou, X.: Learning discriminative features with multiple granularities for person re-identification. In: Proceedings of the 26th ACM International Conference on Multimedia, pp. 274–282 (2018)
22. Wang, J., Zhu, X., Gong, S., Li, W.: Transferable joint attribute-identity deep learning for unsupervised person re-identification. In: Proceedings of the IEEE Conference on Computer Vision and Pattern Recognition, pp. 2275–2284 (2018)
23. Wei, L., Zhang, S., Gao, W., Tian, Q.: Person transfer gan to bridge domain gap for person re-identification. In: Proceedings of the IEEE Conference on Computer Vision and Pattern Recognition, pp. 79–88 (2018)
24. Xin, X., Wang, J., Xie, R., Zhou, S., Huang, W., Zheng, N.: Semi-supervised person re-identification using multi-view clustering. Pattern Recogn. 88, 285–297 (2019)
25. Yu, H.X., Zheng, W.S., Wu, A., Guo, X., Gong, S., Lai, J.H.: Unsupervised person re-identification by soft multilabel learning. In: Proceedings of the IEEE/CVF Conference on Computer Vision and Pattern Recognition, pp. 2148–2157 (2019)
26. Zhang, S., Zhang, Q., Wei, X., Zhang, Y., Xia, Y.: Person re-identification with triplet focal loss. IEEE Access 6, 78092–78099 (2018)

27. Zheng, L., Shen, L., Tian, L., Wang, S., Wang, J., Tian, Q.: Scalable person re-identification: A benchmark. In: Proceedings of the IEEE International Conference on Computer Vision, pp. 1116–1124 (2015)

28. Zheng, L., Yang, Y., Hauptmann, A.G.: Person re-identification: Past, present and future. arXiv preprint arXiv:1610.02984 (2016)

29. Zheng, Z., Yang, X., Yu, Z., Zheng, L., Yang, Y., Kautz, J.: Joint discriminative and generative learning for person re-identification. In: Proceedings of the IEEE/CVF Conference on Computer Vision and Pattern Recognition, pp. 2138–2147 (2019)

30. Zhong, Z., Zheng, L., Kang, G., Li, S., Yang, Y.: Random erasing data augmentation. In: Proceedings of the AAAI Conference on Artificial Intelligence, vol. 34, pp. 13001–13008 (2020)

Detection Beyond What and Where:
A Benchmark for Detecting Occlusion State

Liwei Qin[1], Hui Zhou[1], Zhongtian Wang[1], Jiaqi Deng[1], Yuanyuan Liao[1], and Shuiwang Li[1,2(✉)]

[1] Guilin University of Technology, Guilin, China
lishuiwang0721@163.com
[2] Guangxi Key Laboratory of Embedded Technology and Intelligent System, Guilin, China

Abstract. Object detection is a computer vision technique that provides the most fundamental information for computer vision applications: "What objects are where?", which has achieved significant progress thanks to the great success of deep learning in the past decade. With this kind of identification and localization, object detection is able to identify objects and track their precise locations in a scene. However, information beyond what and where is fairly desirable for more advanced applications, such as scene understanding, autonomous driving, and service robots, in which knowing the behavior or state or attribute of the objects is important. In this paper, we concern about the occlusion state of the target as well as its identification and localization, which is crucial for a service robot to keep track of a target or to grasp an object, for instance. We present a Dataset for Detecting Occlusion State of Objects (DDOSO). This benchmark aims to encourage research in developing novel and accurate methods for this challenging task. DDOSO contains 10 categories of bounding-box annotations collected from 6959 images. Based on this well-annotated dataset, we build baselines over two state-of-the-art algorithms. By releasing DDOSO, we expect to facilitate future researches on detecting the occlusion state of objects and draw more attention to object detection beyond what and where.

Keywords: Object detection · Occlusion state detection · Benchmark

1 Introduction

Object detection is a fundamental task in computer vision, aiming to localize and recognize the objects in prescribed images or videos. It is the basis of many other downstream computer vision tasks, e.g., object tracking, instance segmentation, image captioning, robotics, human-machine interaction and so forth. Object detection aims to develop computational models and techniques that provide one of the most basic pieces of information needed by computer vision applications: What objects are where? [33] Benefited from the application of deep neural networks, object detection has made great progress in recent years. However, knowing the information of identification and localization

Thanks to the support by Guangxi Science and Technology Base and Talent Special Project (No. Guike AD22035127).

(a) Example of conventional object detection.

(b) Example of detecting occlusion state of objects.

Fig. 1. While previous object detection has focused on the identification and localization of objects, we focused on information beyond that and concerned about the occlusion state of objects in addition, as shown in (a) and (b), respectively. Note the occlusion state of the objects (i.e., 'up', 'down', 'right' from left to right, respectively.) are marked in (b) additionally.

about the objects is not enough in more advanced computer vision tasks. For instance, the task of scene understanding needs to recognize the shape, attribute and state of an object in order to integrate meaningful information at multiple levels to extract semantic relationships, patterns and event about the scene [25]. The task of autonomous driving aims to design and construct a motor vehicle that is able to move autonomously without any driver supervision, in which the ability to identify potential dangerous situations and anomalies is very crucial to the driving safety which requires more information than the identification and localization of the objects [29]. Service robots have been widely applied to domestic, industrial and scientific applications, typically assisting human beings performing dirty, dull, distant, dangerous or repetitive jobs [22]. But knowing only what and where about the objects with which the robot is interacting cannot support a good interaction under many circumstances, since the right time and right place to conduct the interaction depend on more knowledge than what and where about the objects. For example, a static object is usually easier to deal with than it is falling or flying, in which the motion state of the object cannot be told by traditional objection detection. To draw attention to object detection beyond what and where for more advanced computer vision tasks, as an exploratory work, in this paper we concern about the occlusion state of the target as well as its identification and localization, which is crucial for a service robot to keep track of a target or to grasp an object. We also believe this task has potential impacts on computer vision to perceive, analyze, and interpret the visual scenes and may lead to new research areas. See Fig. 1 for an illustration of the difference between conventional object detection and the one concerned here. We present a Dataset for Detecting Occlusion State of Objects (DDOSO). This benchmark aims to encourage research in developing novel and accurate methods for this challenging task. DDOSO contains 10 categories of bounding-box annotations collected from 6959 images. Based on this well-annotated dataset, we build baselines over two state-of-the-art algorithms. By releasing DDOSO, we expect to facilitate future researches on detecting the occlusion state of objects and draw more attention to object detection beyond what and where.

1.1 Contribution

In this work, we make the first attempt to explore detection beyond what and where by introducing the DDOSO benchmark for detecting occlusion state of objects. DDOSO is made up of a diverse selection of 10 classes of generic objects, containing 6959 images annotated with axis-aligned bounding box, category, and the occlusion state of objects. See Fig. 2 for sample images in the DDOSO dataset. In addition, we develop two baseline detectors, i.e., OS-YOLOX and OS-YOLOF, for this proposed task based on two state-of-the-art detectors, i.e., YOLOX and YOLOF, in order to understand the performance of this task and provide comparisons for future research on DDOSO.

In summary, we have made the following contributions:

- We make the first attempt to explore detection beyond what and where, which, we believe, provides a fresh perspective for object detection and promotes more advanced applications.
- We propose DDOSO, which is the first benchmark dedicated to detect the occlusion state of objects, initiating a novel and challenging vision task.
- We develop two baseline detectors based on two state-of-the-art YOLO variants to encourage further research on DDOSO.

By releasing DDOSO, we hope to facilitate the further research and application of detecting the occlusion state of objects and attract more attention to detection beyond what and where.

2 Related Works

2.1 Datasets for Conventional Object Detection

Early detection algorithms and related datasets focused on face detection [13, 14] and the detection of pedestrians [2, 4]. The detection of basic object categories started from the pioneer PASCAL Visual Object Classes (VOC), which held challenges on object detection from 2005 to 2012 [5, 18]. The PASCAL VOC datasets and their evaluation metrics have been widely adopted in the computer vision community, in which the PASCAL VOC Challenge 2012 dataset contains 20 categories, 11,530 images, and 27,450 annotated bounding boxes. Afterwards, the ImageNet [3] dataset was released, which contains 200 classes in total and approximately 500, 000 annotated bounding boxesis and is an order of magnitude larger than PASCAL VOC. Later, MS COCO [18] was developed, which consists of 91 common object categories, more than 300K images, and 2.5 million labeled segmented objects. It has more instances and categories per image on average than PASCAL VOC and ImageNet. In addition to the above datasets for object detection, there are also other more specific datasets, e.g., for human running detection [15], road marking detection [21], object detection in agricultural contexts [30], and aerial object detection [24], etc.

Despite of the availability of the above benchmarks, they concern only about the identification and localization of the objects in the detection. However, information beyond what and where is fairly desirable for more advanced applications, such as scene understanding, autonomous driving, and service robots, in which knowing the behavior or state or attribute of the objects is important. Unfortunately, there were few or no attempt dedicated to this exploration. As an exploratory attempt, in this paper, we concern about the occlusion state of the target as well as its identification and localization, which is crucial for a service robot to keep track of a target or to grasp an object, for instance.

2.2 Deep Models for Conventional Object Detection

Dominating the recent progress in generic object detection are deep learning-based detectors [19], which can be divided into two types. One of them, following the traditional object detection pipeline, first generates region proposals and then classifies each proposal into different object categories. This type includes R-CNN [9], SPP-net [11], Fast R-CNN [8], Faster R-CNN [28], FPN [16] and Mask R-CNN [10], and etc. For instance, R-CNN is the pioneer using deep convolutional neural network (DCNN) instead of traditional methods for feature extraction on object detection task, with a workflow that involves first proposing a number of region of interest (ROI), then using CNN to extract features for the support vector machine (SVM) classifier. Faster R-CNN is a classic two-stage detector, in which both region proposal generation and objection detection tasks are all done by the same network, making the object detection much faster. The other type treats object detection as a regression or classification problem, and use a unified framework to directly obtain the final identification and localization [32], such as AttentionNet [31] G-CNN [23], YOLO [26], SSD [20], YOLOv2 [27], YOLOX [7], YOLOF [1], TOOD [6]. For instance, AttentionNet is an impressive end-to-end CNN architecture and adopts an iterative classification approach to handle object detection. G-CNN is a proposal-free iterative grid based object detector, which models object detection as finding a path from a fixed grid to boxes tightly surrounding the objects. YOLO considers object detection as a regression task concerning spatially separated bounding boxes and associated class probabilities, using a single neural network. It has dominated the object-detection field and become the most popular algorithm with many variants, because of its speed, accuracy, and learning ability. In this paper we exploit two latest variants of YOLO to build our baselines for detecting occlusion state of objects.

3 Benchmark for Detecting Occlusion State of Objects

We aim to construct a dedicated dataset for detecting the occlusion state of objects (DDOSO). When developing DDOSO, we cover a diverse selection of object categories and occlusion states, and provide manual annotations for each image as detailed later.

3.1 Image Collection

Defining the object categories is non-trivial in that whether fine-grained and object-part categories should be included is a mentally challenging exercise. Following the section principle of PASCAL VOC [5] and COCO [18] and taking into account the available objects at hand, we selected ten common objects in life for image collection. The list of

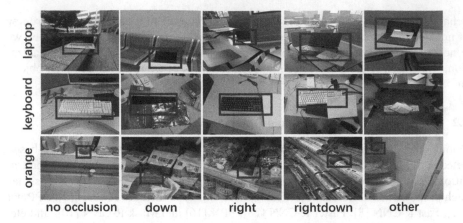

Fig. 2. Samples from 5 categories (i.e., laptop, keyboar, and orange from top to bottom) with 5 occlusion states (i.e., 'no occlusion', 'down', 'right', 'rightdown', and 'other' from left to right) of the objects in the DDOSO dataset. The objets are marked in red bounding boxes. (Color figure online)

object categories includes apple, bag, basketball, bowl, cup, hydrant, keyboard, laptop, mouse, and orange, which are all included in COCO dataset. The specificity of each object category can vary greatly, for example, a bowl could be a porcelain bowls or a iron bowl. Since iconic images may lack important contextual information and non-canonical viewpoint [18] and it is cumbersome to find images with diverse and well-defined occlusion states of objects on internet, we decide to take pictures using cameras equipped in cellphones (i.e., vivoS 7, realme q3 pro, Huawei enjoy 20). Occlusion sates are divided into top, bottom, left, right, top left, bottom left, top right, bottom right, no-occlusion, and other, taking into account how commonly they occur, their usefulness for practical applications, and their convenience to image collection. In our dataset, we ensure that each object category is captured in multiple scenes and is occluded by diverse things. See Fig. 2 for sample images of our dataset.

3.2 Annotation

In this section, we describe how to annotate the collected images. In the detection problem considered here, the image annotation includes the following attributes for every object in the target set of object categories:

- **Category:** one of: apple, bag, basketball, bowl, cup, hydrant, keyboard, laptop, mouse, and orange.
- **Bounding box:** an axis-aligned bounding box surrounding the extent of the object visible in the image.
- **Occlusion state:** one of: top, bottom, left, right, top left, bottom left, top right, bottom right, no-occlusion, and other.

Adhering to the annotation guidelines proposed in [5], we finish the annotation in three steps, i.e., manual annotation, visual inspection, and box refinement. In the first step,

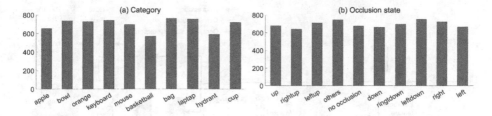

Fig. 3. (a) Number of images per category in DDOSO. (b) Number of images per occlusion state in DDOSO.

each image is labelled by an expert (i.e. a student engaged in object detection). Since annotation errors or inconsistencies are unavoidable in the first stage, a visual inspection is carried out by the verification team in the second stage to verify the annotations. If the validation team disagrees with the annotation unanimously, it will be sent back to the original annotator for refinement in the third step. This three-step strategy ensures high-quality annotation of objects in DDOSO. See Fig. 2 for examples of box annotations for DDOSO.

3.3 Dataset Statistics

Figure 3 summaries the statistics of the DDOSO dataset. Figure 3a shows the histogram of the number of images in the entire dataset for each category. The 'bag' category is the most frequent, with 764 images. Figure 3b shows the histogram of the number of occlusion states in the entire dataset. As can be seen, both the categories and the occlusion states distribute quite equally in DDOSO with the number of each state being about 700. To facilitate training and evaluation, the DDOSO dataset is divided into two main subsets: training data and test data. The ratio of training data to test data is 7:3.

4 Baseline Detectors for Detecting Occlusion State

To facilitate the development of detecting the occlusion state of objects, we present two baseline detectors based on two state-of-the-art YOLO variants, i.e., YOLOX [7] and YOLOF [1]. We introduce an additional head to predict the occlusion state of objects for each of them without changing their overall framework and dub the resulted detectors OS-YOLOX and OS-YOLOF, respectively. The details are described as follows.

4.1 OS-YOLOX

The network architecture of the proposed OS-YOLOX is showed in Fig. 4. The backbone of OS-YOLOX is comprised of the CSPDarknet and a spatial pyramid pooling (SPP) layer. The output features, i.e., C3, C4, and C5, have 128, 256, and 512 channels, respectively. These features are fed into the neck, which is made up of the PANet network to fuse local information in lower layers by bottom-up path augmentation. The head of the original YOLOX consists of two parallel task-specific heads: the classification head and the regression head. In OS-YOLOX, we propose in addition a prediction

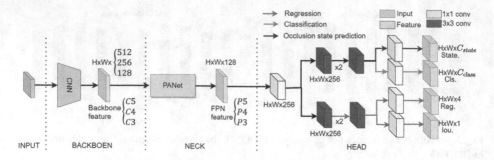

Fig. 4. An illustration of the proposed OS-YOLOX detector. The network structure is inherited from that of YOLOX [7]. The difference lies in the additional head for occlusion state prediction.

head to predict the occlusion state of the objects in parallel to the two heads for original tasks. The total loss for training OS-YOLOX is defined as follow,

$$L_{total} = L_{cls} + L_{reg} + L_{obj} + \lambda L_{state}, \tag{1}$$

where L_{cls}, L_{reg}, L_{obj}, and L_{state} are losses for the classification, regression, boxes' confidence, and prediction of occlusion state, respectively, λ is a constant to weight the loss for the occlusion state prediction head. The definitions of them are as follows,

$$
\begin{aligned}
L_{cls} &= \frac{-1}{N_{pos}} \sum_{n=1}^{N_{pos}} y_{cls}^n ln(\sigma(p_{cls}^n)), \quad L_{state} = \frac{-1}{N_{pos}} \sum_{n=1}^{N_{pos}} y_{state}^n ln(\sigma(p_{state}^n)) \\
L_{obj} &= \frac{-1}{N_{pos}} \sum_{n=1}^{N_{pos}} y_{obj}^n ln(\sigma(p_{obj}^n)), \quad L_{reg} = \frac{1}{N_{pos}} \sum_{n=1}^{N_{pos}} (1 - IOU(b_t^n, b_p^n))
\end{aligned} \tag{2}
$$

where $y_{cls}^n, y_{state}^n, y_{obj}^n$ are ground truth of classification, occlusion state and boxes (i.e. whether the box contain any object) and $p_{cls}^n, p_{state}^n, p_{obj}^n$ are the corresponding predictions. N_{pos} is the number of positive anchor, σ and $IOU(\cdot)$ denote the softmax activation and the IOU Loss function respectively, b_t^n and b_p^n denote the ground truth bbox and the prediction, respectively.

4.2   OS-YOLOF

The network architecture of the proposed OS-YOLOF is showed in Fig. 5. The backbone of OS-YOLOF is the Resnet50 [12]. The output feature of the backbone is denoted by C5, which has 2048 channels. These features are fed into the neck, which is made up of a dilated encoder. The head of the original YOLOF consists of two parallel task-specific heads: the classification head and the regression head. In OS-YOLOF, we propose in addition a prediction head to predict the occlusion state of the objects. The total loss for training OS-YOLOF is defined as follow,

$$L_{total} = L_{cls} + L_{reg} + \lambda L_{state}, \tag{3}$$

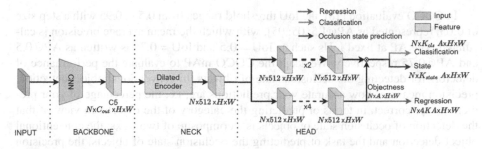

Fig. 5. An illustration of the proposed OS-YOLOF detector. The network structure is inherited from that of YOLOF [1]. The difference lies in the additional head for occlusion state prediction.

where L_{cls}, L_{reg}, L_{state} are losses for the classification, regression, occlusion state prediction, respectively, λ is a constant to weight the loss L_{state}. The definitions of these losses are as follows,

$$L_{cls} = \frac{1}{N_{pos}} \sum_{n=0}^{N_{pos}} FL(y_{cls}^n, p_{cls}^n \otimes p_{obj}^n), \quad L_{reg} = \frac{1}{N_{pos}} \sum_{n=0}^{N_{pos}} (smooth_{L_1}(b_t^n - b_p^n))$$

$$L_{state} = \frac{1}{N_{pos}} \sum_{n=0}^{N_{pos}} FL(y_{state}^n, p_{state}^n \otimes p_{obj}^n)$$

$$(4)$$

where y_{cls}^n, y_{state}^n are ground truth of classification and occlusion state, p_{cls}^n, p_{state}^n are the corresponding predictions. N_{pos} is the number of positive anchor, $FL(\cdot)$ and $smooth_{L1}$ denote the focal loss function [17] and the smooth L1 loss function, $\otimes$ denotes the dot product, b_t and b_p denote the ground truth bbox and the prediction, respectively.

5 Evaluation

5.1 Evaluation Metrics

Mean average precision (mAP) is a popular metric used to measure the performance of models doing object detection tasks. By definition, Average Precision (AP) calculates the average precision value for recall value over 0 to 1 (i.e., the area under precision/recall curve), and Recall is the True Positive Rate i.e. of all the actual positives, how many are True positives predictions. Precision is the positive prediction value i.e. of all the positive predictions, how many are True positives predictions. The mAP is the average of AP over all classes. The detailed computation of the precision and recall can refer to [5]. The intersection over union (IoU) is crucial in determining true positives and false positives, which are required to compute precision and recall. It is defines as the intersection between the predicted bbox and actual bbox divided by their union. A prediction is considered to be True Positive if IoU > threshold, and False Positive if IoU < threshold.

In COCO evaluation [18], the IoU threshold ranges from 0.5 to 0.95 with a step size of 0.05, represented as AP@[.5:.05:.95], with which the mean average precision is calculated. The AP at fixed IoUs such as IoU = 0.5 and IoU = 0.75 is written as AP@0.5 and AP@0.75 respectively. We adapt the COCO mAP to evaluate the performance of detectors for detecting the occlusion state of objects. In conventional object detection, precision measures how accurate your predictions are, i.e. the percentage of your predictions are correct, in terms of predicting the category of the objects. In view of that the detection of occlusion state of objects is a composite of two tasks: the conventional object detection and the task of predicting the occlusion state of objects, the precision metric for our task concerns about predicting both the category and the occlusion state of the objects simultaneously. To understand the performance of the sub-task of predicting the occlusion state of objects, we also concern about the precision of predicting the occlusion state of the objects. For convenience, we use AP_c, AP_s, and AP_{cs} to denote the precision metric for the prediction of the object's category, occlusion state, and the composite of the two, and by adding a prefix 'm' we mean the mean AP, e.g. mAP_c stands for the mean average precision of prediction of the object' s category.

5.2 Evaluation Results

Overall Performance. The proposed two baseline detectors, i.e., OS-YOLOX and OS-YOLOF, are extensively evaluated on DDOSO. The evaluation results are reported with the precision metrics AP_c, AP_s, and AP_{cs} as defined in Sect. 5.1. The results are shown in Table 1. As can be seen, OS-YOLOF is basically the best detector except that its AP_c@0.5 and mAP_c are slightly inferior to that of OS-YOLOX. For both detectors, the mean AP and the AP at fixed IoUs (i.e., 0.5 and 0.75) of the prediction of object's category is higher than the prediction of object's occlusion state. Specifically, the differences between mAP_c and mAP_s are all greater than 15%, with the biggest gap of 20.1% happening to the OS-YOLOX detector. It suggests that, disregarding localization, the detection of occlusion state of objects we concern here is more challenging than the conventional detection that concerns identification. This may attribute to the fact that conventional detection benefits very much from prior knowledge built up from large scale dataset for image classification, such as ImageNet and COCO [3,18], whereas, the information beyond what and where, such as the occlusion state of objects discussed here, is generally more task-specific and expects more availabe labeled data and more effective models for building prior knowledge. We believe our work will inspire more works on this problem.

Table 1. Comparsion of the APs of the proposed two baseline detectors, i.e., OS-YOLOF and OS-YOLOX, on the DDOSO dataset. Note that AP_c, AP_s, and AP_{cs} denote the precision metric for prediction of the object's category, occlusion state, and the composite of both.

	$\{AP_c, AP_s, AP_{cs}\}$@0.5	$\{AP_c, AP_s, AP_{cs}\}$@0.75	$\{mAP_c, mAP_s, mAP_{cs}\}$
OS-YOLOF	(0.952, **0.758, 0.880**)	(**0.904, 0.727, 0.857**)	(0.768, **0.618, 0.732**)
OS-YOLOX	(**0.964**, 0.706, 0.861)	(0.900, 0.669, 0.829)	(**0.770**, 0.569, 0.709)

Performance on per Category. We conduct performance evaluation on each category to further analyze and understand the performances of detecting the occlusion state of objects of the baseline detectors. The mAP_{cs} of the two detectors are shown in Table 2. As can be seen, the two detectors show the best performance on basketball and orange, with mAP_{cs} above 80%, and perform the worst on keyboard and hydrant, with mAP_{cs} almost below 60%. This may be on account of that basketball and orange are basically of round shape, with very high symmetry, but keyboard and hydrant have a bar shape in the mass. The high symmetry of the former poses smaller challenges to the detectors because of less intra-class variations. But keyboard may induce much complicated occlusion situations due to the large variation of its poses and hydrant is more likely to be occluded from bottom producing quite imbalanced occlusion states. This result implies that the performance of detecting the occlusion state of objects is in close connection to the category of the object itself.

Table 2. Comparsion of the mAP_c of the proposed two baseline detectors, i.e., OS-YOLOF and OS-YOLOX, on the DDOSO dataset. Note that mAP_{cs} denote the mean average precision for prediction of the composite of the object's category and its occlusion state.

	Apple	Bowl	Orange	Keyboard	Mouse	Basketball	Bag	Laptop	Hydrant	Cup
mAP_{cs}(**OS-YOLOF**)	0.761	0.763	0.828	0.567	0.646	**0.858**	0.721	0.773	0.607	0.744
mAP_{cs}(**OS-YOLOX**)	0.781	0.767	0.823	0.538	0.643	**0.855**	0.653	0.748	0.571	0.672

Fig. 6. Qualitative evaluation on 8 samples from DDOSO. The top and bottom row shows, respectively, examples that the proposed OS-YOLOF predicts correctly and wrongly the occlusion state of the objects. The objects are marked in red rectangles. (Color figure online)

Qualitative Evaluation. In Fig. 6, we show some qualitative detection results of the detector OS-YOLOF. As can be seen, in the top row the category and occlusion state of the apple, basketball, bowl, and laptop are all correctly predicted, whereas, in the bottom row the occlusion state of the mouse and keyboard are mistakenly predicted although the prediction of category is right. This conforms to the fact that keyboard and mouse may induce much complicated occlusion situations due to the large variation of its poses. It can be also seen that the occlusion state of the apple is incorrectly predicted under complex background. We will dedicate to these problems in our future work.

5.3   Ablation Study

Weighting the Loss of Predicting Occlusion State. To study the impact of the coefficient for weighting the loss of predicting occlusion state of objects, we evaluate OS-YOLOF on DDOSO with respect to the weighting coefficient, i.e., λ in Eq. (3), which ranges from 0.2 to 2.0 in step of 0.2. The the mean AP and the AP at fixed IoUs (i.e., 0.5 and 0.75) of OS-YOLOF are shown in Table 3. As can be seen, the best AP occurs within the range from 0.4 to 1.8 but OS-YOLOF cannot achieves simultaneously all the best APs at a fixed λ. An obvious conflict between AP_c and AP_s can be observed. By and large, AP_c decreases but AP_s increases as λ goes from 0.4 to 1.8, reaching their highest value at 0.4 and 1.8, respectively. A compromise is achieved at $\lambda = 1.0$, the default setting, where AP_{cs} reaches their highest value. For example, the highest mAP_c equal to 0.775 is at $\lambda = 0.4$, the highest mAP_s equal to 0.623 is at $\lambda = 1.8$, and the highest mAP_{cs} equal to 0.732 is at $\lambda = 1.0$. This suggests that detection beyond what and where is not so easily done since the balance between the identification and the beyond information, such as the occlusion state of objects concerned here, plays an important part in the composite task.

Table 3. Illustration of how the AP metrics of OS-YOLOF vary with respect to coefficient for weighting the loss of predicting occlusion state of objects on the DDOSO dataset.

λ	(AP_c, AP_s, AP_{cs})@0.5	(AP_c, AP_s, AP_{cs})@0.75	(mAP_c, mAP_s, mAP_{cs})
0.2	(0.955, 0.659, 0.835)	(0.901, 0.630, 0.806)	(0.772, 0.541, 0.696)
0.4	(**0.958**, 0.710, 0.856)	(**0.904**, 0.679, 0.833)	(**0.775**, 0.585, 0.717)
0.6	(0.952, 0.736, 0.867)	(0.894, 0.702, 0.838)	(0.769, 0.603, 0.723)
0.8	(0.954, 0.761, 0.875)	(0.900, **0.728**, 0.846)	(0.770, 0.621, 0.727)
1.0	(0.952, 0.758, **0.880**)	(**0.904**, 0.727, **0.857**)	(0.768, 0.618, **0.732**)
1.2	(0.949, 0.747, 0.869)	(0.897, 0.719, 0.844)	(0.765, 0.612, 0.721)
1.4	(0.951, 0.755, 0.877)	(0.903, 0.725, 0.853)	(0.768, 0.618, 0.729)
1.6	(0.942, 0.763, 0.878)	(0.887, 0.725, 0.846)	(0.752, 0.622, 0.725)
1.8	(0.943, **0.764**, 0.873)	(0.889, **0.728**, 0.839)	(0.757, **0.623**, 0.721)
2.0	(0.944, 0.760, 0.869)	(0.892, 0.726, 0.842)	(0.761, 0.622, 0.721)

6   Conclusions

In this paper, we study the detection beyond what and where by making the first attempt to explore detecting the occlusion state of objects, which is crucial for a service robot to keep track of a target or to grasp an object, for instance. We present the DDOSO dataset and two baseline detectors, i.e., OS-YOLOF and OS-YOLOX, based on two state-of-the-art YOLO variants to facilitate further study on the problem. We believe our work will draw more attention to object detection beyond what and where, which is fairly desirable for more advanced applications such as scene understanding, autonomous driving, and service robots, in which knowing the behavior or state or attribute of the objects is important.

References

1. Chen, Q., et al.: You only look one-level feature. In: 2021 CVPR, pp. 13034–13043 (2021)
2. Dalal, N., Triggs, B.: Histograms of oriented gradients for human detection. In: 2005 CVPR, vol. 1, pp. 886–893 (2005)
3. Deng, J., et al.: ImageNet: a large-scale hierarchical image database. In: 2009 CVPR (2009)
4. Dollár, P., Wojek, C., et al.: Pedestrian detection: an evaluation of the state of the art. IEEE Trans. Pattern Anal. Mach. Intell. **34**, 743–761 (2012)
5. Everingham, M., et al.: The pascal visual object classes (VOC) challenge. Int. J. Comput. Vision **88**, 303–338 (2009)
6. Feng, C., et al.: TOOD: task-aligned one-stage object detection. In: 2021 ICCV, pp. 3490–3499 (2021)
7. Ge, Z., et al.: YOLOX: exceeding yolo series in 2021. arXiv preprint arXiv:2107.08430 (2021)
8. Girshick, R.B.: Fast R-CNN. In: 2015 ICCV, pp. 1440–1448 (2015)
9. Girshick, R.B., et al.: Rich feature hierarchies for accurate object detection and semantic segmentation. In: 2014 CVPR, pp. 580–587 (2014)
10. He, K., et al.: Mask R-CNN. In: 2017 ICCV, pp. 2980–2988 (2017)
11. He, K., et al.: Spatial pyramid pooling in deep convolutional networks for visual recognition. IEEE Trans. Pattern Anal. Mach. Intell. **37**, 1904–1916 (2015)
12. He, K., et al.: Deep residual learning for image recognition. In: 2016 CVPR, pp. 770–778 (2016)
13. Hjelmås, E., Low, B.K.: Face detection: a survey. Comput. Vis. Image Underst. **83**, 236–274 (2001)
14. Huang, G.B., et al.: Labeled faces in the wild: a database for studying face recognition in unconstrained environments (2008)
15. Lao, S., et al.: Human running detection: benchmark and baseline. Comput. Vis. Image Underst. **153**, 143–150 (2016)
16. Lin, T.Y., et al.: Feature pyramid networks for object detection. In: 2017 CVPR, pp. 936–944 (2017)
17. Lin, T.Y., et al.: Focal loss for dense object detection. IEEE Trans. Pattern Anal. Mach. Intell. **42**, 318–327 (2020)
18. Lin, T.Y., et al.: Microsoft COCO: common objects in context. In: ECCV (2014)
19. Liu, L., et al.: Deep learning for generic object detection: a survey. Int. J. Comput. Vision **128**, 261–318 (2019)
20. Liu, W., et al.: SSD: Single shot multibox detector. In: ECCV (2016)
21. Liu, X., et al.: Benchmark for road marking detection: dataset specification and performance baseline. In: 2017 IEEE ITSC, pp. 1–6 (2017)
22. Lu, V.N., et al.: Service robots, customers and service employees: what can we learn from the academic literature and where are the gaps? J. Serv. Theor. Practic. **30**(3), 361–391 (2020)
23. Najibi, M., et al.: G-CNN: an iterative grid based object detector. In: 2016 CVPR, pp. 2369–2377 (2016)
24. Naudé, J.J., Joubert, D.: The aerial elephant dataset: a new public benchmark for aerial object detection. In: CVPR Workshops (2019)
25. Pawar, P., Devendran, V.: Scene understanding: a survey to see the world at a single glance. In: 2019 ICCT, pp. 182–186 (2019)
26. Redmon, J., et al.: You only look once: unified, real-time object detection. In: 2016 CVPR, pp. 779–788 (2016)
27. Redmon, J., Farhadi, A.: YOLO9000: better, faster, stronger. In: 2017 CVPR, pp. 6517–6525 (2017)

28. Ren, S., He, K., et al.: Faster R-CNN: towards real-time object detection with region proposal networks. IEEE Trans. Pattern Anal. Mach. Intell. **39**, 1137–1149 (2015)
29. Taeihagh, A., Lim, H.S.M.: Governing autonomous vehicles: emerging responses for safety, liability, privacy, cybersecurity, and industry risks. Transp. Rev. **39**, 103–128 (2018)
30. Wosner, O., et al.: Object detection in agricultural contexts: a multiple resolution benchmark and comparison to human. Comput. Electron. Agric. **189**, 106404 (2021)
31. Yoo, D., et al.: AttentionNet: aggregating weak directions for accurate object detection. In: 2015 ICCV, pp. 2659–2667 (2015)
32. Zhao, Z.Q., et al.: Object detection with deep learning: a review. IEEE Trans. Neural Netw. Learn. Syst. **30**, 3212–3232 (2019)
33. Zou, Z., et al.: Object detection in 20 years: a survey. arXiv arXiv:abs/1905.05055 (2019)

Weakly Supervised Object Localization with Noisy-Label Learning

Yuming Fan, Shikui Wei$^{(\boxtimes)}$, Chuangchuang Tan, Xiaotong Chen,
and Yao Zhao

Institute of Information Science, Beijing Jiaotong University, Beijing Key Laboratory
of Advanced Information Science and Network Technology, Beijing, China
20120300@bjtu.edu.cn

Abstract. A novel perspective for Weakly Supervised object localization is proposed in this paper. Most recent pseudo-label-based methods only consider how to get better pseudo-labels and do not consider how to apply these imperfect labels properly. We propose the Noisy-Label Learning on Weakly Supervised object localization (NL-WSOL) to improve localization performance by cleaning defective labels. First, we generate labels which more focused categories for images in the label generation stage. Then, we judge the quality of pseudo labels and enhance the labels with poor quality. Moreover, we introduce a composite loss function to guide the network training in the pseudo-label-based training phase. Our method achieves 97.39% localization performance on the CUB-200–2011 test set.

Keywords: Weakly supervised · Object localization · Noisy label

1 Introduction

Weakly supervised learning has made significant progress on many tasks. The existing approach have achieve remarkable result in object localization [4,31, 32,34], semantic segmentation [9,14,36], and object detection [1,8,20,23]. In this work, we mainly focus on Weakly Supervised Object Localization (WSOL) problem. WSOL only uses image-level annotations to learn object localization information.

Currently, most WSOL methods obtain the object location through convolutional classification networks. Zhou et al. revisited the classification networks and proposed a Class Activation Map (CAM) [34] to find the regions of the object by global average pooling (GAP) [10] layer. However, the CNN model only needs the most discriminative regions for image classification; therefore, CAM can usually locate only a small part of the object but not the whole area of the object. Early works propose many techniques to expend the activation map, such as erasing methods [4,12,31], spatial information methods [27,32],

S. Yu et al. (Eds.): PRCV 2022, LNCS 13537, pp. 477–489, 2022.
https://doi.org/10.1007/978-3-031-18916-6_39

etc. In particular, DGL [19] and SPOL [24] use the shallow features in the network to generate the localization result. Unlike the CAM-based approach, PSOL [30] proposed a new strategy for the WSOL problem; they divided the WSOL into two independent sub-tasks: localization and classification. They first generate pseudo-labels by classification network and then treat them as ground truth labels to train the localization network. However, previous work only considered how to generate better pseudo-labels but did not notice the effects of the imperfect label. We found that these labels usually contain a lot of noise information, which will misguide the network to the background information. In addition, although the activation map generated by the deep features only focuses on the most discriminative, they are generally strongly related to the target class. They thus do not contain false background information so that it can be used as auxiliary information for the shallow masks.

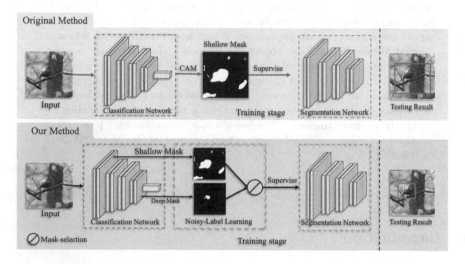

Fig. 1. Overview of our method. The shallow mask spreads its attention to the part of the branch of the tree, and the deep mask only focuses on the most discriminative regions of the bird. Neither can locate the whole object individually, but we utilize both simultaneously to generate localization results.

To tackle those mentioned weaknesses, we advocate a paradigm shift that transfers WSOL into the noise label selection problem. In this paper, we first use the CAM-based method to generate the pseudo labels, then train the localization network. In the pseudo-label generation stage, we use the shallow and deep features in the network to generate pseudo-labels, respectively. In the training phase, we judge the similarity between the background regions in pseudo labels and the input images, then regard the sample with high similarity as a low-quality pseudo label. For those lower-quality pseudo-labels, we design a loss function jointly guided by the pseudo-labels generated by two different features to ensure that the low-quality pseudo-labels will not misguide the network to the background regions.

Finally, we have achieved state-of-the-art performance on the ILSVRC [15] and CUB-200–2011 [22] datasets. To sum up, the main contributions of this article are as follows:

- We show that the Weakly Supervised Object Localization should be transferred to the noisy-based learning task. We propose NL-WSOL to solve the problems in previous two-stage WSOL methods.
- We introduce the idea of noisy labels into the WSOL task: we propose a label-based validation module for selecting low-quality pseudo-labels, which can be added to existing two-stage WSOL methods without adding new parameters.
- We propose a loss function that combines the deep and shallow features of the network, enabling full utilization of noisy pseudo-labels. Through mutual inhibition and adversarial learning of them, the network can explore more object regions and will not turn its attention to the background regions.
- We conduct extensive experiments to validate the effectiveness of our proposed method and demonstrate that our method achieves state-of-the-art results on two challenging WSOL datasets.

2   Related Work

2.1   One Stage WSOL Method

Class activation map (CAM) [34] introduce the global average pooling (GAP) layer to find the most exciting regions and generate a localization map. CAM can only locate part of the object regions, and the previous one-stage WSOL methods mainly focus on expanding the activation regions. For the most discriminative regions, a natural idea is erasing them and forcing the network to learn the other object regions. ACoL designed two parallel classifiers, one classifier is first used to erase the most discriminative regions, and the second classifier will be forced to learn the other object regions. ADL generates an erasing mask and introduces channel-wise attention to balancing the localization and classification tasks. EIL proposes a multi erasing module based on multiple loss functions, integrating adversarial erasing and discriminative regions extraction in a single propagation. SPG uses the attention-based method to distinguish the background and foreground regions and then uses the feature information of high-confidence areas to extend the activation map. SSAM/CCAM mining complementary spatial location information through two modules based on self-attention fusion. In addition, CutMix [29] and Has [17] use data augmentation to force the classification network to learn the entire region of the object. CCAM [28] fuses activation maps of multiple categories to suppress the impact of background regions on localization performance.

2.2 Two Stage WSOL Method

PSOL first proposed the pseudo-supervised object localization approach. They divided the WSOL task into two independent sub-tasks: class-agnostic object localization and object classification. To avoid the mutually negative effect between these tasks, PSOL predicts class labels for target images, then uses the class-agnostic method DDT [25] to generate pseudo masks, and finally introduces a regression network that trains by pseudo masks for localization. SLT-Net [6] proposes a class-tolerance classification module to improve the tolerance of misclassification between similar classes and thus mitigate the part domination problem, then train the regression network. SPOL [24] explores more object location information by fusing shallow and deep features in the classification network. At the same time, in the training stage using pseudo-labels, they use a combination of mask and segmentation network, which can guide the network better. SPA [13] utilizes the high-order self-correlation to extract the inherent structural information retained in the learned model and then aggregate them of multiple points for precise object localization. ORNet [26] first utilizes low-level features to generate activation maps with rich contextual information, then further proposes an evaluator driven by weighted entropy loss and attention-based erasing to evaluate the quality of activation maps, reduce the uncertainty of activations between objects and background substantially.

From the perspective of generating better pseudo-labels, the previous work has significantly improved the WSOL task, but they have some weaknesses in the use of pseudo-labels. Based on these works, this paper explores how to utilize these pseudo-labels properly and achieve better results.

3 Method

3.1 Overview

In the two-stage weakly supervised object localization method, previous works usually generate pseudo labels with a classification network, then use the pseudo label as supervision to train a class-agnostic segmentation model or a bounding box regressor.

However, these pseudo-labels may contain noisy information. For example, in a picture with a bird, the tree may be considered part of the foreground because they usually appear together, as shown in Fig. 1. Previous works usually directly treat these imperfect labels as correct labels for training. In this paper, we first propose a method to determine the quality of labels and then combine the deep and shallow features of the network to limit the wrong guidance in low-quality pseudo labels.

Figure 2 depicts the framework of the proposed approach, and the proposed NL-WSOL contains two stages. In the pseudo-label generation stage, we first input the image into the classification network and use the features of different layers to output the localization masks as pseudo-labels. In the training phase of the segmentation network, we first input the shallow mask into the network, judge its quality by an additional classifier (e.g., DenseNet161, EfficientNet-B7), and then use the deep mask to provide additional guidance for the shallow mask. Finally, we use the segmentation threshold to generate localization bounding boxes.

3.2   Stage1: Pseudo Mask Generation

In this stage, we generate two kinds of feature-generated activation maps by different layers. As shown in Fig. 2, in the pseudo-label generation stage, we first generate pseudo masks by class activation maps in the deep and shallow layers of the classification network, respectively. Deep features pay more attention to the most recognizable information of the object, they can make full use of the gradient of the classification network, but it is challenging to locate the entire object regions. Shallow features can spread attention to the whole areas of the object, but its gradient usually contains unavoidable noise Information.

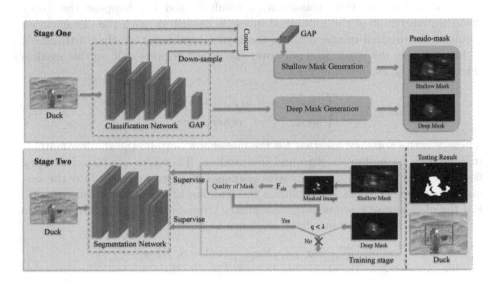

Fig. 2. The framework of our proposed methods. In the pseudo-label generation stage, we use the features of different layers in the network to generate shallow masks and deep masks, respectively; in the training stage of the localization network, we judge the quality of the shallow masks to decide whether to let the deep masks participate in training. λ is the threshold for judging the quality of the mask.

To combine the advantages of those features, we use the localization maps generated by these two different features to participate in the training so that the network focus on the whole object and reduces the influence of noise information. Given an input image as I, a classification network first uses it to generate the feature map F_2, F_3, F_4 in shallow layers. First, a GAP layer is used to extract class activation features, and then three 1×1 Conv layers transform the dimensions of the shallow features to the same shape. Then, we introduce channel-wise attention to generate attention vectors and finally up-sample the vectors to the same size. Fusing these vectors by dot product, we get the class activation map output by the shallow features $CAM_{shallow}$. In addition, we follow [34] to generate the class activation map output by the deep features CAM_{deep}, we feed the feature into a GAP layer and upsampling the output to the original image size. Considering the part where the activation scores over 0.5 as the object, we generate pseudo masks $mask_{shallow}$ and $mask_{deep}$ for the segmentation network.

3.3   Stage2: Training Segmentation Network

To define the quality of the pseudo shallow mask, we introduce a classifier F_{cls} to compare the class of images with and without masks, as shown in Fig 2. Given an input image as I and its pseudo shallow mask as M, we first generate an unmask-image I' by inverting the dot product of I and M, then a pretrained classifier is introduced to get their classification result C and C'. Suppose the Top-1 classification result of the unmasked image is consistent with the classification result of the original image, and the confidence level is higher than a threshold λ. In that case, the mask does not cover the object regions well, so this mask is relatively lousy, as shown in Eq. 1.

$$Quality(M) = \begin{cases} bad, & \lambda < S(F_{cls}(M')) \quad and \quad C == C' \\ good, & otherwise \end{cases} \tag{1}$$

where S is the Softmax function for the classifier's output, the shallow features may contain redundant background information. Therefore, we introduce deep features focus on most discriminative regions but more precisely into the second stage and let them jointly guide the training of the localization network. For the class-agnostic segmentation, a binary cross-entropy loss is introduced to supervise the segmentation model, as shown in Eq. 2.

$$L_{seg} = -\frac{\sum_{(i,j)} \omega_{i,j}[g_{i,j}\log_{(p_{i,j})} + (1 - g_{i,j})\log_{(1-p_{i,j})}]}{2a} \tag{2}$$

where p_{ij} and g_{ij} are the predicted probability and ground truth label at position (i,j), respectively.

As shown in Fig. 2, we compute the loss function separately for two different masks and introduce a coefficient γ to reduce the influence of deep features on the network. We set the coefficient as 0.2 in our experiment.

$$L = L_{shallow} + \gamma L_{deep} \tag{3}$$

Both of these losses are calculated by the cross-entropy function. By jointly guiding the network with two different masks, we can finally aggregate the gradients of the two masks toward the object regions and eventually generate a localization result that can cover the object regions without spreading its attention to the background regions.

Data: Image I, shallow pseudo mask M_S, deep pseudo mask M_D
Result: Training strategy for noisy labels
initialization a classification model;
while *Training stage* **do**
  multiple the input image I and mask M to get the unmasked image I';
  predict the classification result of them.;
  if *obtain same result* **then**
    | Regard this mask M_S as GT-label for training;
  else
    | Introduce deep mask M_D for training by composite loss function;
  end
end

Algorithm 1: Framework of our method

Finally, we generate class-agnostic masks for the dataset only with the image-level label, then use them for training a segmentation network. In the testing phase, the segmentation network generates segmentation masks for the images in the test set and obtains the predicted object bounding box. Refer to Algorithm 1 for more details.

Table 1. Localization performance on ILSVRC validation set

Dataset		ILSVRC		
BackBone	Method	Top1 Loc	Top5 Loc	GT-known Loc
VGG-GAP [16]	CAM [34]	42.80	54.86	59.00
VGG-GAP	ACoL [31]	45.83	59.43	62.96
VGG-GAP	ADL [4]	44.92	–	–
VGG-GAP	ORNet [26]	52.05	63.94	68.27
GoogLeNet	GC-Net [11]	49.06	58.09	–
InceptionV3 [18]	SPG [32]	48.60	60.00	64.69
InceptionV3	EIL [12]	49.5	–	–
InceptionV3	I2C [33]	53.10	64.10	68.50
InceptionV3	SLT-Net [6]	55.70	65.40	67.60
InceptionV3	PSOL [30]	54.82	63.25	65.21
Deit-S [21]	TS-CAM [5]	53.40	64.30	67.60
ResNet50 [7]	DGL [19]	53.41	62.69	66.52
ResNet50	DA-WSOL [35]	55.84	–	70.27
Resnet50	SPOL [24]	59.14	67.15	69.02
Resnet50	Ours (NL-WSOL)	**61.09**	**68.97**	**70.42**

Table 2. Localization performance on CUB-200–2011 test set

Dataset		CUB-200–2011		
BackBone	Method	Top1 Loc	Top5 Loc	GT-known Loc
VGG-GAP [16]	CAM [34]	36.13	–	–
VGG-GAP	ACoL [31]	45.92	56.51	62.96
VGG-GAP	ADL [4]	52.36	–	73.96
VGG-GAP	ORNet [26]	67.74	81.77	86.20
GoogLeNet	GC-Net [11]	58.58	71.10	75.30
InceptionV3 [18]	SPG [32]	46.64	57.72	–
InceptionV3	EIL [12]	57.46	–	–
InceptionV3	I2C [33]	65.99	68.34	72.60
InceptionV3	SLT-Net [6]	76.40	66.10	86.50
InceptionV3	PSOL [30]	65.51	83.44	–
Deit-S [21]	TS-CAM [5]	71.30	83.80	87.80
ResNet50 [7]	DGL [19]	60.82	70.50	74.65
ResNet50	DA-WSOL [35]	66.65	–	81.83
Resnet50	SPOL [24]	80.12	93.44	96.46
Resnet50	Ours (NL-WSOL)	**86.03**	**95.09**	**97.39**

4   Experiment

We evaluate the proposed method on the ILSVRC [15] and CUB-200–2011 [22] datasets. The ILSVRC dataset contains more than 1.2 million images with 1000 categories and only contains image-level labels for training and 50,000 images in the validation set, which come from 1000 classes. CUB-200–2011 includes images of 200 species of birds, consisting of 5994 images for training and 5794 images for testing.

When the IoU between the localization prediction result of the object and the ground truth reaches 0.5, we regard this case as correct localization. We use the three leading indicators to evaluate our proposed method:

- Top-1 localization error (Top1 Loc) means the localization and TOP-1 classification results are both correct.
- Top-5 localization error (Top5 Loc) means the localization and TOP-5 classification results are both correct.
- GT-K localization error (GT-Known Loc) means the localization result is correct given perfect classification.

4.1   Implementation Details

We use ResNet50 [7] as backbone network. In each experiment, we use the Google pre-trained model and fine-tune it. In the training phase, following previous works [4,31,32], we first resize the input image to 256 × 256 and randomly crop it to 224 × 224. On both two datasets, we train the classification network with the parameters suggested by [3]; we train ten epochs and keep the learning rate as 0.001 for the segmentation network. We set the threshold for generating bounding boxes in the testing phase to 0.8.

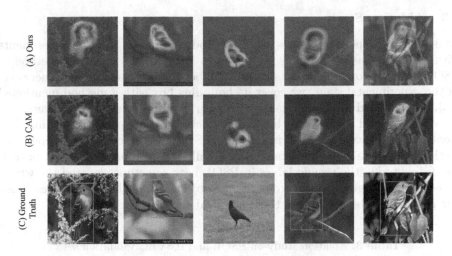

Fig. 3. Visual comparison. Example of localization maps produced during evaluating ResNet50 model with our method and original method. Compared with the original method, our proposed method locates the object regions more effectively and avoid learning background area.

4.2 Compare with State-of-the-Arts

Quantitative Comparison. We compare the proposed method with other state-of-the-art techniques on CUB-200–2011 test set and ILSVRC validation set in Tables 1 and 2. We achieve 70.42% on GT-Known Loc in ILSVRC dataset when using Resnet50 as the backbone. Our NL-WSOL surpass all the baseline method in Top1, Top5, and GT-Known localization accuracy, demonstrating that training with noisy labels is a significant problem. Our simple but effective approach does not require additional parameters or networks and outperforms all SOTA methods. Our method achieves the GT-Known error of 97.39% on the CUB dataset. Although the CUB dataset has a single category and is relatively simple, our approach can almost entirely correct locating objects lower than 3% error, demonstrating that the proposed method can achieve better localization performance on fine-grained images.

Visualization Comparison. The visualization results of the original strategy and our method show that the original strategy cannot correctly locate the whole object regions, as shown in Fig. 3. We consistently observe that our method outperforms the original method from these results. The localization map of the original method erroneously covers the background regions in the visualization results or only covers the most recognizable regions, which indicates that the pseudo-labels containing the wrong information cannot guide the network correctly.

4.3 Ablation Study

To demonstrate the effectiveness of our method, we conduct ablation experiments with PSOL [30] as the baseline, as shown in Table 3. The two-stage method of PSOL uses the bounding box as a pseudo-label to train the regression network. In the experimental stage, we cover its bounding box with a method mentioned in 3.3 and discard the pseudo-label with poor quality in the training stage.

When we used PSOL as the baseline, we achieved more performance improvements. We believe that this is because PSOL uses a category-independent method to generate pseudo-labels, which will contain more noise information. According to [2], the pseudo labels in PSOL have sometimes located the wrong object that is relevant to the ground truth object, such as birds and trees. Thus our method can better remove these noisy labels.

Table 3. Ablation study on PSOL and ILSVRC validation set

BackBone	Method	Top1 Loc	Top5 Loc	GT-K Loc
Resnet50	PSOL	53.98	63.08	65.44
Resnet50	PSOL+ours	55.17	64.32	67.12

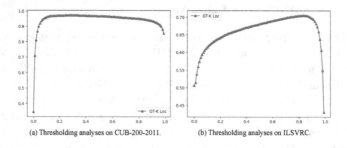

(a) Thresholding analyses on CUB-200-2011.   (b) Thresholding analyses on ILSVRC.

Fig. 4. Sensitive analyses of the localization map threshold procedure.

4.4 Threshold Sensitivity Analysis

In addition, Fig. 4 shows threshold sensitivity analysis on CUB-200–2011 and ILSVRC validation dataset. As seen, the performances of our method are stable when the threshold varies from 0.1 to 0.8. The problem of threshold instability has always been a weakness in previous works. According to [3], many classical

WSOL methods are unstable with the increase of the threshold, which means the localization map contains many uncertain pixels. In our method, jointly guiding the localization map with two different scale features can reduce the uncertainty of the object pixel and improve the robustness of our approach to the setting of the threshold.

5   Conclusion and Discussion

In this paper, we propose Noisy-Label learning on Weakly Supervised Object Localization (NL-WSOL). We consider the weakly supervised localization problem from a novel perspective of noisy labels and introduce deep and shallow features to co-supervise the network's training. Our approach can improve their performance by re-producing most of the current pseudo-label-based methods. The localization performance of our NL-WSOL achieves state-of-the-art performance on the ILSVRC and CUB datasets, which proves the effectiveness of our strategy. Our work suggests a novel perspective for weakly supervised object localization and semantic segmentation.

Acknowledgments. This work was supported in part by the National Key R&D Program of China (No. 2021ZD0112100), National NSF of China (No. 61972022, No. U1936212, No. 62120106009).

References

1. Bilen, H., Pedersoli, M., Tuytelaars, T.: Weakly supervised object detection with convex clustering. In: CVPR, pp. 1081–1089 (2015)
2. Chen, X., Ma, A.J., Guo, N., Chen, J.: Improving weakly supervised object localization by uncertainty estimation of pseudo supervision. In: ICME, pp. 1–6. IEEE (2021)
3. Choe, J., Oh, S.J., Lee, S., Chun, S., Akata, Z., Shim, H.: Evaluating weakly supervised object localization methods right. In: CVPR, pp. 3133–3142 (2020)
4. Choe, J., Shim, H.: Attention-based dropout layer for weakly supervised object localization. In: CVPR, pp. 2219–2228 (2019)
5. Gao, W., et al.: TS-CAM: token semantic coupled attention map for weakly supervised object localization. In: ICCV, pp. 2886–2895 (2021)
6. Guo, G., Han, J., Wan, F., Zhang, D.: Strengthen learning tolerance for weakly supervised object localization. In: CVPR, pp. 7403–7412 (2021)
7. He, K., Zhang, X., Ren, S., Sun, J.: Deep residual learning for image recognition. In: CVPR, pp. 770–778 (2016)
8. Inoue, N., Furuta, R., Yamasaki, T., Aizawa, K.: Cross-domain weakly-supervised object detection through progressive domain adaptation. In: CVPR, pp. 5001–5009 (2018)
9. Kervadec, H., Dolz, J., Tang, M., Granger, E., Boykov, Y., Ayed, I.B.: Constrained-CNN losses for weakly supervised segmentation. Med. Image Anal. **54**, 88–99 (2019)
10. Lin, M., Chen, Q., Yan, S.: Network in network. arXiv preprint arXiv:1312.4400 (2013)

11. Lu, W., Jia, X., Xie, W., Shen, L., Zhou, Y., Duan, J.: Geometry constrained weakly supervised object localization. In: Vedaldi, A., Bischof, H., Brox, T., Frahm, J.-M. (eds.) ECCV 2020. LNCS, vol. 12371, pp. 481–496. Springer, Cham (2020). https://doi.org/10.1007/978-3-030-58574-7_29
12. Mai, J., Yang, M., Luo, W.: Erasing integrated learning: a simple yet effective approach for weakly supervised object localization. In: CVPR, pp. 8766–8775 (2020)
13. Pan, X., et al.: Unveiling the potential of structure preserving for weakly supervised object localization. In: CVPR, pp. 11642–11651 (2021)
14. Pathak, D., Krahenbuhl, P., Darrell, T.: Constrained convolutional neural networks for weakly supervised segmentation. In: ICCV, pp. 1796–1804 (2015)
15. Russakovsky, O., et al.: ImageNet large scale visual recognition challenge. IJCV 115(3), 211–252 (2015)
16. Simonyan, K., Zisserman, A.: Very deep convolutional networks for large-scale image recognition. arXiv preprint arXiv:1409.1556 (2014)
17. Singh, K.K., Lee, Y.J.: Hide-and-seek: forcing a network to be meticulous for weakly-supervised object and action localization. In: ICCV, pp. 3544–3553. IEEE (2017)
18. Szegedy, C., Vanhoucke, V., Ioffe, S., Shlens, J., Wojna, Z.: Rethinking the inception architecture for computer vision. In: CVPR, pp. 2818–2826 (2016)
19. Tan, C., Gu, G., Ruan, T., Wei, S., Zhao, Y.: Dual-gradients localization framework for weakly supervised object localization. In: ACMMM, pp. 1976–1984 (2020)
20. Tang, P., et al.: PCL: proposal cluster learning for weakly supervised object detection. TPAMI 42(1), 176–191 (2018)
21. Touvron, H., Cord, M., Douze, M., Massa, F., Sablayrolles, A., Jégou, H.: Training data-efficient image transformers & distillation through attention. In: ICML, pp. 10347–10357. PMLR (2021)
22. Wah, C., Branson, S., Welinder, P., Perona, P., Belongie, S.: The caltech-UCSD birds-200-2011 dataset (2011)
23. Wan, F., Wei, P., Jiao, J., Han, Z., Ye, Q.: Min-entropy latent model for weakly supervised object detection. In: CVPR, pp. 1297–1306 (2018)
24. Wei, J., Wang, Q., Li, Z., Wang, S., Zhou, S.K., Cui, S.: Shallow feature matters for weakly supervised object localization. In: CVPR, pp. 5993–6001 (2021)
25. Wei, X.S., Zhang, C.L., Wu, J., Shen, C., Zhou, Z.H.: Unsupervised object discovery and co-localization by deep descriptor transformation. In: PR 88, 113–126 (2019)
26. Xie, J., Luo, C., Zhu, X., Jin, Z., Lu, W., Shen, L.: Online refinement of low-level feature based activation map for weakly supervised object localization. In: ICCV, pp. 132–141 (2021)
27. Xue, H., Liu, C., Wan, F., Jiao, J., Ji, X., Ye, Q.: DANet: divergent activation for weakly supervised object localization. In: ICCV, pp. 6589–6598 (2019)
28. Yang, S., Kim, Y., Kim, Y., Kim, C.: Combinational class activation maps for weakly supervised object localization. In: WACV, pp. 2941–2949 (2020)
29. Yun, S., Han, D., Oh, S.J., Chun, S., Choe, J., Yoo, Y.: CutMix: regularization strategy to train strong classifiers with localizable features. In: ICCV, pp. 6023–6032 (2019)
30. Zhang, C.L., Cao, Y.H., Wu, J.: Rethinking the route towards weakly supervised object localization. In: CVPR, pp. 13460–13469 (2020)
31. Zhang, X., Wei, Y., Feng, J., Yang, Y., Huang, T.S.: Adversarial complementary learning for weakly supervised object localization. In: CVPR, pp. 1325–1334 (2018)
32. Zhang, X., Wei, Y., Kang, G., Yang, Y., Huang, T.: Self-produced guidance for weakly-supervised object localization. In: ECCV, pp. 597–613 (2018)

33. Zhang, X., Wei, Y., Yang, Y.: Inter-image communication for weakly supervised localization. In: Vedaldi, A., Bischof, H., Brox, T., Frahm, J.-M. (eds.) ECCV 2020. LNCS, vol. 12364, pp. 271–287. Springer, Cham (2020). https://doi.org/10.1007/978-3-030-58529-7_17

34. Zhou, B., Khosla, A., Lapedriza, A., Oliva, A., Torralba, A.: Learning deep features for discriminative localization. In: CVPR, pp. 2921–2929 (2016)

35. Zhu, L., She, Q., Chen, Q., You, Y., Wang, B., Lu, Y.: Weakly supervised object localization as domain adaption. arXiv preprint arXiv:2203.01714 (2022)

36. Zhu, Y., Zhou, Y., Xu, H., Ye, Q., Doermann, D., Jiao, J.: Learning instance activation maps for weakly supervised instance segmentation. In: CVPR, pp. 3116–3125 (2019)

Enhanced Spatial Awareness for Deep Interactive Image Segmentation

Haochen Li[1], Jinlong Ni[1], Zhicheng Li[1], Yuxiang Qian[1], and Tao Wang[1,2]($\boxtimes$)

[1] School of Computer Science and Engineering, Nanjing University of Science and Technology, Nanjing 210094, China
wangtaoatnjust@163.com

[2] Jiangsu Key Laboratory of Spectral Imaging&Intelligent Sense, Nanjing University of Science and Technology, Nanjing 210094, China

Abstract. Existing deep interactive segmentation approaches can extract the desired object for the user based on simple click interaction. However, the first click provided by the user on the full image space domain is generally too local to capture the global target object, which causes them to rely on a large number of subsequent click corrections for satisfactory results. This paper explores how to strengthen the spatial awareness of user interaction especially after the first click input and increase the stability during the continuous iterative correction process. We first design an interactive cascaded localization strategy to determine the spatial range of the potential target, and then integrate this space-aware prior into a dual-stream network structure as a soft constraint for the segmentation. The above operation can increase the network's attention to the target of interest under very limited user interaction. A new training and inference strategy is also developed to completely adapt the benefit from the space-aware guidance. Furthermore, an object shape related loss is designed to better supervise the network based on user-provided prior guidance. Explicit subject, controllable correction and flexible interaction can help to significantly boost the interactive segmentation performance. The proposed method achieves state-of-the-art performance on several popular benchmarks.

Keywords: Interactive image segmentation · Spatial awareness · Multi task learning

1 Introduction

Deep learning has achieved great success in the field of computer vision, which has inspired researchers to expand tasks from image classification [1–3] to image semantic segmentation [4–7]. However, the algorithm performance of existing deep learning-based segmentation methods are inseparable from the support of large scale pixel-level image annotation. In general, data annotation is a very time-consuming and labor-intensive process, which severely limits the development of such methods.

© The Author(s), under exclusive license to Springer Nature Switzerland AG 2022
S. Yu et al. (Eds.): PRCV 2022, LNCS 13537, pp. 490–505, 2022.
https://doi.org/10.1007/978-3-031-18916-6_40

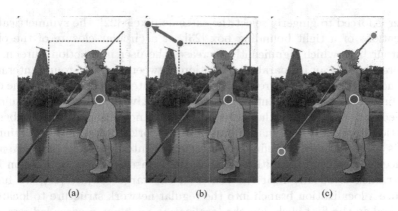

Fig. 1. User inputs of our method. (a) Our method will automatically predict the region of interest (ROI) according to the first click. (b) Our method allows users to modify ROI. (c) Our method also adopts addition positive or negative clicks for correction.

In terms of image annotation, compared with fully-automatic segmentation methods, interactive segmentation methods have the following advantages: first, the user is allowed to select any target of interest including unseen objects; second, in interactive mode the user can explicitly control the prediction and effectively correct inaccurate segmentation based on continuous user inputs. This paper mainly focuses on this semi-automatic approach for image segmentation and annotation.

In existing interactive approaches, user inputs can be generally represented by click points [8–10], bounding boxes [11,12] and scribbles [13,14]. Thanks to the powerful deep feature representation capability, click interaction has become the most used strategy in deep learning-based interactive segmentation approaches. Xu *et al.* [8] first propose a FCN-based model [4] for interactive segmentation task, and also introduce a click sampling strategy to simulate positive and negative clicks. Based on this framework, many extended works have been further developed in interaction characterization [15,16], training-evaluation strategy [17,18], network structure [19–21], etc. Though remarkable results have been produced by these deep interactive approaches, it is still hard for them to obtain satisfactory results based on one-round click interaction. Multiple rounds of click correction are still required for high-precision segmentation.

On the other hand, some extreme click-based interactive segmentation approaches have also been developed. Maninis *et al.* [22] take four extreme points of an object (top, bottom, left-most, right-most pixels) for interactive object extraction. Zhang *et al.* [23] porpose an inside-outside guidance approach with three points to advance the interactive annotation process. Dupont *et al.* [24] develop a novel interactive segmentation approach based on two unstructured contour clicks to reduce the number of clicks. Explicit click interaction enables these methods to have more stable segmentation performance. However, the user is forced to gingerly select the extreme pixels [22], the symmetrical corner locations of a tight bounding box [23], or a circular closure of the object on contour [24], which significantly increases the user interaction burden. Furthermore, there is an irreparable separation between the first-round interaction stage and the subsequent correction stage. After entering multiple extreme clicks in the first round, only one internal/external positive/negative click requires to be added each time during the correction phase. Inconsistent click number and interaction type per round may confuse the network during iterative training.

This paper focuses on refining the region of interest (ROI) as space-aware guidance to obtain better initial segmentation. Based on user interaction habit the first click is usually near the center of the target object [19], we further introduce a localization branch into the regular network structure to locate the ROI based on the first click. For the localization problem, a cascaded regression structure is proposed to make use of multiscale features. Another guidance map channel can be naturally generated to constrain the segmentation according to the prediction of the proposed localization branch. During iterative training, the segmentation prediction in each round can be always constrained by positive/negative clicks and the space-aware localization guidance. This consistent training strategy further improves the effect of modified clicks and avoids the confusion caused by different added click types. For the segmentation problem, an object shape prior-based loss function is designed to constrain the distribution of the network prediction. Correspondingly, during the inference stage we update the original iterative strategy to adapt the proposed segmentation model. As shown in Fig. 1, besides the segmentation correction, the user is also allowed to correct the localization result in our framework. The detailed contributions of this paper are summarized as follows:

- A dual-stream multi-task learning strategy is designed for deep interactive image segmentation.
- An interactive cascaded localization method is proposed to provide a space-aware guidance for the object of interest.
- A new training and inference strategy is proposed to better utilize the prior guidance with an object shape related loss.

2   Related Work

Classical Interactive Segmentation. In traditional methods, interactive segmentation is always solved as an energy optimization problem. Boykov and Jolly [13] propose a method to search a minimum cut on a specific s/t graph, which based on classical graph cut model. Rother *et al.* [11] extend graph cut by an iterative optimization and use Gaussian mixture model to substitute for statistical histogram. Grady *et al.* [25] design a model to calculate the probabilities of random walks from unlabeled pixels to labeled pixels. All these algorithms require substantial user interactions to obtain an accurate segmentation. In contrast, deep learning techniques have the capability to understand objectness and semantics, which makes it possible to obtain satisfactory segmentation results with only a few clicks.

Deep Interactive Segmentation. Neural networks have the ability to extract complex global and local features for sparser interactions such as simple clicks. Xu *et al.* [8] first use deep learning to solve interactive segmentation problems by guiding FCN [4] to utilize the distance maps encoded from the positive (foreground) and negative (background) clicks. Liew *et al.* [9] design a RIS-Net to refine the results by enlarging local context information with pairs of positive and negative clicks. Li *et al.* [10] propose a method to select the best from multiple candidate results with an extra trained model. Mahadevan *et al.* [17] propose a more reasonable iterative training strategy. Majumder and Yao [16] utilize superpixels as a particular guidance according to the clicks. Maninis *et al.* [22] use four extreme points of the object to construct a novel annotation method. Jang and Kim [20] design a backpropagating refinement scheme to redress the deviation between results and annotation. Sofiiuk *et al.* [21] propose shortening the inference time of [20] with auxiliary variables of intermediate characteristics. Lin *et al.* [19] design an attention module to utilizing the guidance information of the first click. Sofiiuk *et al.* [18] propose an iterative procedure and make a network aware of the last segmentation. Chen *et al.* [26] design a conditional diffusion network to optimize based on local and global similarity. Dupont *et al.* [24] develop another interactive pattern, which uses at least two unstructured contour clicks. A common limitation is that these methods are either difficult to achieve satisfactory results after first-round interaction, or adopt an abrupt interaction manner.

Semantic Segmentation. Many successful deep interactive segmentation methods are inseparable from semantic segmentation methods, such as FCN [4], DeepLab series [6,7,27,28] and so on. This does not mean that semantic segmentation methods can be directly applied in interactive segmentation area. Because the former only respond to predefined categories and cannot be further corrected in case of errors. In contrast, interactive segmentation can achieve satisfactory segmentation results for unseen classes according to the user inputs.

3 Method

3.1 Simulating User Interaction

Simulating user interactions is a key step in deep interactive segmentation methods. According to different user interaction intentions, we divide the entire interaction process into two categories: initial first click and subsequent correction clicks. The former interaction is used to explicitly select the object of interest, and the latter interaction is automatically adjusted according to the previous segmentation prediction.

Initializing Selection Click. It is obvious that the user is more accustomed to click near the center of an object [19] firstly. We choose the center point of an object as the initial selection click in this paper. $\mathcal{O}$ represents the collection of ground truth pixels of an object and $p \in \mathcal{O}$ represents a foreground pixel.

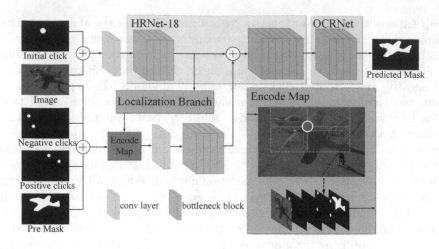

Fig. 2. The overall architecture of the proposed method. We utilize HRNet-18 [31] and OCRNet [32] as the basic segmentation network. The orange part represents the localization branch. 'Encode Map' represents the conversion from the predicted ROI of localization branch to a space-aware guidance map consistent with the user interaction. The green block represents the first stage of the backbone composed of four bottlenecks. (Color figure online)

If $dist\,(p,q)$ means the Euclidean distance between pixels p and q, its minimum distance $D_B(p)$ from the background can be calculated first:

$$D_B(p) = \min_{\forall q \in I, q \notin \mathcal{O}} dist\,(p,q) \tag{1}$$

Then, we define $\mathcal{G} = \{p | p \in \mathcal{O} \text{ and } D_B(p) \geq \alpha * max_{\forall q \in \mathcal{O}} D_B(q)\}$ as the internal region set of an object, where α is used for resizing $\mathcal{G}$ (default is 0.3). It can be seen that pixels in $\mathcal{G}$ maintain a distance from the boundary of an object. The distance $D_F(p)$ of pixel $p \in \mathcal{G}$ from the foreground can be defined as:

$$D_F(p) = \sum_{q \in \mathcal{O}} dist\,(p,q) \tag{2}$$

The initial selection click is determined as $p_c = \arg min_{p \in \mathcal{G}} D_F(p)$ during training.

Corrective Clicks. According to the prediction result in the last round, we can divide the current mispredicted area into two categories: the incorrect foreground set R_f and the incorrect background set R_b. We automatically determine the point $p_a = argmax_{\forall q \in max(R_f, R_b)} D_B(q)$ as the next input click which has the largest distance from the boundary in the maximum error area.

Click Encoding. In order to input clicks into the convolutional network, we need encode them first in the image space domain [8]. Refer to [29], we uniformly

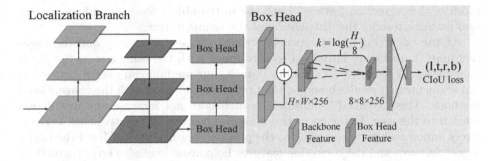

Fig. 3. Network architecture of localization branch. The green part represents the FPN-like [33] structure, and the resolution is halved layer by layer. The red area on the right shows the detailed structures of Box Head. The input features will pass through k convolution layers and maximum pooling layers, and finally output after the fully connected layer. (Color figure online)

encode all clicks into disk maps with a fixed radius in this paper. This strategy is computationally efficient compared with the Gaussian [30] or the Euclidean distances [8]. In order to distinguish clicks from the selection and correction stages, the radius of the first click is set to be twice that of subsequent clicks since the selection click focuses on the global object while correction clicks pay more attention to local details.

3.2 Network Architecture

Overall Network. We utilize the state-of-the-art semantic segmentation network HRNet-OCR [32] as our baseline. HRNet-18 [31] is selected as the backbone and OCRNet [32] is utilized as the segmentation head. Based on the first click interaction, a new task is derived in this paper by intelligently locating the specific ROI. An object localization branch is further embedded into the backbone after the first stage of HRNet-18 [31] in order to locate the ROI. These two tasks of localization and segmentation can be solved simultaneously in a unified framework.

According to different guidance types, we divide the information in the network into the initial object flow and the correction flow. As shown in Fig. 2, the initial object information refers to the user's first click, and the correction information consists of subsequent clicks and the previous segmentation results. The guidance map of the first click is concatenated with the original image, and together input into the first stage of the backbone for the initialization of object features. Based on the initialized features, the localization branch is utilized to predict the ROI to the user and generate a space-aware guidance map consistent with the correction maps. Then these prior information maps (localization map, correction maps and previous segmentation map) are fused together into the subsequent network structure composed of four serial bottlenecks [3] to produce the correction features. Both the initial object features and the correction features restrict the distribution of the segmentation.

At the beginning of the network, the last segmentation map and the negative map channels are initialized to zero maps with the same size as the input image. Benefit from the localization branch, our method can obtain better initial segmentation results based on the first click compared with the conventional methods. This extended localization branch does not increase any interaction burden to the user. In the correction phase, a positive or negative click is iteratively added each time according to the previous segmentation. Mixed the initial object features and the correction features help avoid excessive error correction. In general, the iterative point-by-point training strategy [17,37] is conducive to the stable learning of the network.

Localization Branch. For the input initial object features, we use a series of bottlenecks [3] to perform 2-fold and 4-fold downsampling operations to generate three-scale features as shown in Fig. 3. This structure has been used in ResNet [3] series networks, and proved to be able to successfully abstract the deep and bottom features. A cascade structure similar to FPN [33] is used to fuse the multi-scale features. A series of localization heads are designed to predict the ROI for each scale feature.

The localization head is composed of a series of 3×3 convolution layers and 2 times downsampling max-pooling layers. Figure 3(right) shows each scale feature will go through k maximum pooling layers until it is reduced to a size of 8×8. A 4D vector with (l, t, r, b) will be obtained at the end, where l, t, r and b are calculated as the distances from the first click position to the four sides of the predicted region. In addition, each layer features will integrate with the lower layer features, which is output before the second convolution of each head. In this bottom-up cascaded structure, the localization ability of high-level head will be strengthened because low-level feature contain more object details [34]

According to the first click position, we can simply get the bounding box coordinates for the target object. The median result of different scales is utilized as our final prediction. We generate disks [29] with a radius of 5 at four corner points of the predicted bounding box as the space-aware guidance map.

3.3   Training and Inference Scheme

Loss Function. For localization branch, we utilize the CIoU loss [35] which takes the aspect ratio into account to supervise the learning of parameters. At the end of HRNet-18 [31], the binary cross entropy is utilized as the auxiliary loss, and the normalized focal loss [36] is selected to supervise the OCRNet [32]. It is worth mentioning that we add a shape constraint loss ℓ_S at the end of the network to further control the distribution of the target object. First, according to the ground truth ROI, we divide the predicted mask and the ground truth mask into n blocks. $B_{pred,i}$ and $B_{gt,i}$ represent each divided block from the predicted and ground truth masks, respectively. We define a function $count(B, t)$

to count the number of pixels whose value is not lower than t in B. ℓ_S can be described as:

$$\ell_S(i) = \frac{|count\,(B_{pred,i}\,,\,0.5) - count\,(B_{gt,i}\,,0.5)\,|}{count\,(B_{gt,i}\,,0)} \qquad (3)$$

It should be noticed that the *sigmoid* activation for the predicted mask is required before calculating ℓ_S. In this paper, n is default as 16.

Training Scheme. Since the network needs to use the predicted ROI to generate the space-aware guidance map, we first train the localization branch separately to avoid error guidance. Then we train both branches at the same time, and mix the space-aware guidance map generated from the localization branch and the ground truth to improve the robustness of the network.

In order to cooperate with our corrective click sampling strategy, we adopt the scheme of iterative training [17,18,37] which has been proved effective in previous works. To reduce the expensive computational burden of the complete iterative training, for each batch we randomly select the number of iterations within the maximum number of iterations and switch the network to 'eval' mode before the last round. However, this training strategy needs to run more epochs to achieve the same effect as the fully iterative training.

Inference Scheme. Zoom-In technique [21] is quite simple and effective to improve the segmentation performance. Previous work [21] finds that a rough predicted mask can be achieved after first 1–3 clicks. Therefore, they can crop the image by a bounding box based on the predicted mask after the third click, and execute the interactive segmentation process only for this zoom-in area. Thanks to the proposed object localization branch, our method can produce better segmentation result after the first interaction, so we can implement zoom-in strategy after the first click. The bounding box can be generated after the first click segmentation, and then we extend it by 20% along sides in order to preserve more context and boundary details. The iterative segmentation correction will be carried out on a "new" image obtained by the clipping operation based on the bounding box. The proposed inference strategy allows the user to modify the predicted ROI before clipping. In the ROI modification phase, the bounding box of the predicted ROI will adjust the nearest point to the clicked position. Up to two clicks are required to adjust the entire bounding box. Our method has the advantage of starting zoom-in faster than the previous, and localization branch enables the network to obtain the region more accurately.

The backpropagating refinement scheme [20,21] of interactive segmentation can avoid the position of user comments being incorrectly marked in the results. In our inference scheme, we choose f-BRS-B [21] for backpropagating refinement.

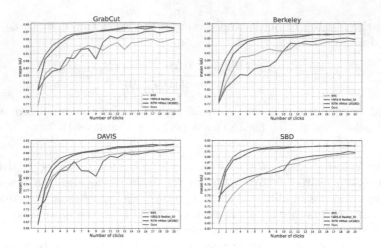

Fig. 4. The number of clicks vs. mean IoU (NoC-mIoU) curves of our method and others [18,20,21] on GrabCut, Berkeley, DAVIS and SBD datasets.

4 Experiments

4.1 Experiments Setting

Data Sets. We evaluate the performance of the proposed algorithm on four datasets, including GrabCut [11], Berkeley [38], DAVIS [39], and SBD [40]. The GrabCut dataset contains 50 images, and it is usually used to assess interactive segmentation models. The Berkeley dataset contains 200 training images and 100 test images. We select 100 object masks on 96 test images like other methods [38]. The DAVIS dataset is composed with 50 video sequences and we use their individual frames to evaluate interactive segmentation methods. 345 frames are sampled randomly as introduced in [20]. The SBD dataset is divided into a training set of 8,498 images and a validation set of 2,820 images. In the experiment, we use the training set to train the network. For performance evaluation, we use the validation set which contains 6671 instance-level object masks.

Implementation Details. We take HRNet-18 [31] pre-trained on ImageNet as the backbone for the proposed method. The training data will be randomly cropped, horizontally flipped, randomly rotated and scaled, and the size of 512×512 is used as the input of batch. The batch size is set to 8, and the initial learning rate is set to 5×10^{-5} for the backbone and 5×10^{-4} for localization branch and OCRNet [32]. On the SBD dataset, the network trained 120 epochs, excluding 80 epochs of additional training to localization branch. The maximum number of iterations is set to 3. We use Adam optimizer with $\beta_1 = 0.9$ and $\beta_2 = 0.999$ and stochastic gradient descent with 0.9 momentum, respectively. The proposed algorithm is implemented based on the PyTorch framework with single NVIDIA GTX 2080Ti GPU.

Table 1. Comparison of the mean NoC (mNoC) values on GrabCut, Berkeley, SBD and DAVIS datasets for DIOS [8], LD [9], RIS [10], CAG [16], BRS [20], f-BRS-B [21], CD-Net [26], FCA-Net [19], UCP-Net [24], RITM-H18 [18]. The best result is marked in bold.

Method	GrabCut		Berkeley		SBD		DAVIS	
	NoC@85	NoC@90	NoC@85	NoC@90	NoC@85	NoC@90	NoC@85	NoC@90
DIOS	5.08	6.04	–	8.65	9.22	12.80	9.03	12.58
LD	3.20	4.79	–	–	7.41	10.78	5.95	9.57
RIS	–	5.00	–	6.03	–	–	–	–
CAG	–	3.58	–	5.60	–	–	–	–
BRS	2.60	3.60	3.16	5.08	6.59	9.78	5.58	8.24
f-BRS-B	2.50	2.98	2.41	4.34	5.06	8.08	5.39	7.81
CD-Net	2.22	2.64	–	3.69	4.37	7.87	5.17	6.66
FAC-Net	–	2.08	–	3.92	–	–	–	7.57
UCP-Net	–	2.76	–	2.70	**2.73**	–	–	–
RITM-H18	1.76	2.04	2.69	3.22	3.39	5.43	4.94	6.71
Ours	**1.56**	**1.76**	**1.43**	**2.52**	2.75	**4.61**	**4.67**	**6.69**

Metric. We use the standard Number of Clicks (NoC) index [8] to evaluate the compared methods. NoC represents the number of clicks required to achieve a specific segmentation accuracy such as the commonly used intersection over union (IoU) metrics. Let NoC@85 and NoC@90 be the NoC values reaching 0.85 and 0.90 IoU accuracy, respectively. In order to simulate the user's correction interaction on the predicted ROI, we comprehensively consider three situations, i.e. no correction, one-click correction and two-click correction, at the same time for the evaluation. During the evaluation for each image, these three situations are adopted simultaneously, and the best among them will be counted to reduce unnecessary correction clicks.

4.2 Comparison to State-of-the-Art

As shown in Table 1, we evaluate NoC@85 and NoC@90 indexes on GrabCut, Berkeley, SBD and DAVIS datasets. For NoC@85, our method achieves the best performance on almost all datasets (except SBD). UCP-Net [24] requires the user to accurately click two points on the contour of an object in the first-round interaction. Comparatively, our method only requires the user to click near the center of the target, which is more in line with the user's habits. By comparison, our method does not have the user interaction burden it brings, but also achieves competitive results. For NoC@90, it can be seen that the proposed method achieves the best performance on all datasets. This means that even in complex scenes with occlusion, lighting and low contrast our method can still achieve high quality results (IoU greater than 0.9) with very limited user interaction. The excellent performance on multiple datasets also proves that the proposed method has greater robustness and generalization.

Fig. 5. Example results of the proposed method on the Berkeley dataset, where the green point represents the first click. (Color figure online)

Table 2. Analysis of results after the first click. We report the number of images that achieve 0.9 mIoU after the first click and the number of images that not reach 0.9 mIoU after 20 clicks. The best result is marked in bold.

Dataset	Method	#images = 1	#images ≥ 20
Berkeley	f-BRS [21]	20	**2**
	RITM [18]	26	3
	Ours	**55**	3
DAVIS	f-BRS [21]	87	78
	RITM [18]	69	**57**
	Ours	**101**	61
SBD	f-BRS [21]	1878	1466
	RITM [18]	1585	671
	Ours	**2384**	**437**

Figure 4 illustrates the mIoU curve of each method with the increasing number of clicks on GrabCut, Berkeley, DAVIS and SBD datasets. We can see that the mIoU value after the first click (beginning of the curve) of our method is much higher than other methods [18,20,21] on all datasets, which proves the effectiveness of the proposed localization branch. The localization stepfor the ROI is conducive to our method, which helps to quickly lock the main body of the target and obtain better results after the first click. Even in the correction stage, our method still has good stability after multiple iterations where mIoU improves gradually as the click increases. In our method, the roles of the corrective clicks can also be effectively constrained by the proposed space-aware guidance, which is difficult to radiate to the area outside the ROI. In this case, the situation that the mIoU value fluctuates violently with the increase of clicks can be effectively avoided. Compared with other methods, our method needs fewer clicks to obtain higher mIoU, which shows the superior performance of our method.

For the comparison of different methods, we count both the number of images that reach 0.9 mIoU after the first click and the number of images that not reach

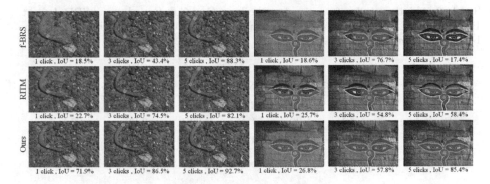

Fig. 6. Qualitative results of f-BRS [21], RITM [18] and the proposed method within five clicks on the Berkeley dataset, where the green points represent positive clicks and the red points represent negative clicks. In the third line, the red border represents the ROI predicted by localization branch, and the blue dot represents the user's correction for the ROI. (Color figure online)

0.9 IoU after 20 clicks. Table 2 shows the results on Berkeley, DAVIS and SBD datasets. In terms of one click input, it can be seen that our method is far more effective than others [18,21]. In our method, about one-third of the test images on DAVIS and SBD datasets obtain excellent segmentations (IoU greater than 0.9), and more than half of the images on Berkeley dataset also obtain high quality results after the first click. This observation shows that our method is likely to obtain satisfactory results with only one-click interaction without any additional correction. In terms of algorithm generalization, our method is comparable with other methods on Berkeley and DAVIS datasets, and even far ahead on SBD dataset. This shows that our method is equally reliable for difficult segmentation problems. In Fig. 5, we display some example results of our method after the first click interaction on Berkeley. It can be noticed that our click interaction strategy is clear and user-friendly, and high precision segmentation results are produced after the first click interaction.

In Fig. 6, we conduct qualitative comparison with f-BRS [21] and RITM [18] at different number of clicks. For the first test image, our method can extract the complete contour of the snake after the first click thanks to the proposed space-aware guidance. Comparatively, it is hard for other methods to obtain accurate results based on the first click. The second test image is utilized to evaluate the algorithm performance for unseen objects. From the first row, we can find that f-BRS [21] cannot effectively distinguish the target after five clicks. The same situation occurs in RITM [18] after the third click. By comparison, our inference strategy can effectively avoid the extreme correction situation. As shown by the blue dot, our method corrects the inaccurate space-aware guidance in the second click and reaches 0.85 IoU accuracy after five clicks. The stable convergence of our method mainly benefits from two aspects: first, space-aware guidance and corrective clicks influence each other and promote each other; second, the

Table 3. Ablation study of proposed methods on GrabCut, Berkeley and SBD dataset. BL: baseline; Loc: the localization branch; L: the object shape prior-based loss. The best result is marked in bold.

Method	GrabCut		Berkeley		SBD	
	NoC@85	NoC@90	NoC@85	NoC@90	NoC@85	NoC@90
BL	1.76	2.04	2.69	3.22	3.39	5.43
BL + Loc	**1.52**	1.80	1.45	2.61	3.00	4.89
BL + Loc + L	1.56	**1.76**	**1.43**	**2.52**	**2.75**	**4.61**

segmentation results can be effectively pulled by the initial object features and the correction features. The advantages of our method are demonstrated in the network structure and inference strategies.

4.3   Ablation Study

To further verify our contributions, we conduct ablation study on GrabCut, Berkeley and the validation set of SBD. The ablated results of the mean number of clicks (mNoC) are shown in Table 3. The baseline consists of HRNet-18 [31] as the backbone, OCRNet [32] as the segmentation head, and the input guidance map includes positive clicks, negative clicks and previous segmentation. Compared with the baseline, we can find that by adding localization branch, the performance is dramatically improved on each dataset. This improvement coincides with our original intention of localization branch. Localization branch, as an auxiliary branch of the network, brings two main improvements. First, predicted ROI helps network quickly identify the main body of interest to users. Second, the correction converges steadily as clicks increase, thanks to constraints of space-aware guidance and the dual-stream structure. Comparing 'BL+ Loc + L' with 'BL + Loc', we see that the loss proposed in this paper brings an effect improvement on almost all datasets (except GrabCut). Under the constraint of object shape, the loss makes the network consider the overall distribution of foreground pixels in inference.

5   Conclusion

In this paper, we explore how to increase the attention to the target of interest after the first click input. We propose an interactive cascaded localization strategy to determine the spatial range of the potential target. This space-aware prior information is integrated into the dual-stream network structure as a soft constraint of segmentation. Consistent with our network, we propose a series of sampling strategies, training and inference schemes and the object shape prior-based loss. The state-of-the-art performances over four datasets show the superiority of our method.

Acknowledgments. This work was supported in part by the National Natural Science Foundation of China under Grant 62172221, and in part by the Fundamental Research Funds for the Central Universities under Grant No. JSGP202204.

References

1. Simonyan, K., Zisserman, A.: Very deep convolutional networks for large-scale image recognition. arXiv preprint arXiv:1409.1556 (2014)
2. Szegedy, C., Liu, W., Jia, Y., Sermanet, P., Reed, S., Anguelov, D.: Going deeper with convolutions. In: Proceedings of the IEEE Conference on Computer Vision and Pattern Recognition, pp. 1–9 (2015)
3. He, K., Zhang, X., Ren, S., Sun, J.: Deep residual learning for image recognition. In: Proceedings of the IEEE Conference on Computer Vision and Pattern Recognition, pp. 770–778 (2016)
4. Long, J., Shelhamer, E., Darrell, T.: Fully convolutional networks for semantic segmentation. In: Proceedings of the IEEE Conference on Computer Vision and Pattern Recognition, pp. 3431–3440 (2015)
5. Zhao, H., Shi, J., Qi, X., Wang, X., Jia, J.: Pyramid scene parsing network. In: Proceedings of the IEEE Conference on Computer Vision and Pattern Recognition, pp. 2881–2890 (2017)
6. Chen, L.C., Papandreou, G., Kokkinos, I., Murphy, K., Yuille, A.L.: Deeplab: Semantic image segmentation with deep convolutional nets, atrous convolution, and fully connected CRFS. IEEE Trans. Pattern Analysis Mach. Intell. **40**(4), 834–848 (2018)
7. Chen, L.C., Zhu, Y., Papandreou, G., Schroff, F., Adam, H.: Encoder-decoder with atrous separable convolution for semantic image segmentation. In: Proceedings of the European Conference on Computer Vision (ECCV), pp. 801–818 (2018)
8. Xu, N., Price, B., Cohen, S., Yang, J., Huang, T. S.: Deep interactive object selection. In: Proceedings of the IEEE Conference on Computer Vision and Pattern Recognition, pp. 373–381 (2016)
9. Liew, J., Wei, Y., Xiong, W., Ong, S.H., Feng, J.: Regional interactive image segmentation networks. In: 2017 IEEE International Conference on Computer Vision (ICCV), pp. 2746–2754 (2017)
10. Li, Z., Chen, Q., Koltun, V.: Interactive image segmentation with latent diversity. In: Proceedings of the IEEE Conference on Computer Vision and Pattern Recognition, pp. 577–585 (2018)
11. Rother, C., Kolmogorov, V., Blake, A.: "GrabCut" interactive foreground extraction using iterated graph cuts. ACM Trans. Graph. **23**(3), 309–314 (2004)
12. Wu, J., Zhao, Y., Zhu, J. Y., Luo, S., Tu, Z.: Milcut: a sweeping line multiple instance learning paradigm for interactive image segmentation. In: Proceedings of the IEEE Conference on Computer Vision and Pattern Recognition, pp. 256–263 (2014)
13. Boykov, Y.Y., Jolly, M.P.: Interactive graph cuts for optimal boundary & region segmentation of objects in ND images. In: Proceedings Eighth IEEE International Conference on Computer Vision (ICCV 2001), vol. 1, pp. 105–112 (2001)
14. Bai, J., Wu, X.: Error-tolerant scribbles based interactive image segmentation. In: Proceedings of the IEEE Conference on Computer Vision and Pattern Recognition, pp. 392–399 (2014)
15. Forte, M., Price, B., Cohen, S., Xu, N., Pitié, F.: Getting to 99% accuracy in interactive segmentation. arXiv preprint arXiv:2003.07932 (2020)

16. Majumder, S., Yao, A.: Content-aware multi-level guidance for interactive instance segmentation. In: Proceedings of the IEEE/CVF Conference on Computer Vision and Pattern Recognition, pp. 11602–11611 (2019)
17. Mahadevan, S., Voigtlaender, P., Leibe, B.: Iteratively trained interactive segmentation. arXiv preprint arXiv:1805.04398 (2018)
18. Sofiiuk, K., Petrov, I.A., Konushin, A.: Reviving iterative training with mask guidance for interactive segmentation. arXiv preprint arXiv:2102.06583 (2021)
19. Lin, Z., Zhang, Z., Chen, L.Z., Cheng, M.M., Lu, S.P.: Interactive image segmentation with first click attention. In: Proceedings of the IEEE/CVF Conference on Computer Vision and Pattern Recognition, pp. 13339–13348 (2020)
20. Jang, W.D., Kim, C.S.: Interactive image segmentation via backpropagating refinement scheme. In: Proceedings of the IEEE/CVF Conference on Computer Vision and Pattern Recognition, pp. 5297–5306 (2019)
21. Sofiiuk, K., Petrov, I., Barinova, O., Konushin, A.: f-BRS: rethinking backpropagating refinement for interactive segmentation. In: Proceedings of the IEEE/CVF Conference on Computer Vision and Pattern Recognition, pp. 8623–8632 (2020)
22. Maninis, K.K., Caelles, S., Pont-Tuset, J., Van Gool, L.: Deep extreme cut: from extreme points to object segmentation. In: Proceedings of the IEEE Conference on Computer Vision and Pattern Recognition, pp. 616–625 (2018)
23. Zhang, S., Liew, J.H., Wei, Y., Wei, S., Zhao, Y.: Interactive object segmentation with inside-outside guidance. In: Proceedings of the IEEE/CVF Conference on Computer Vision and Pattern Recognition, pp. 12234–12244 (2020)
24. Dupont, C., Ouakrim, Y., Pham, Q.C.: UCP-net: unstructured contour points for instance segmentation. In: 2021 IEEE International Conference on Systems, Man, and Cybernetics (SMC), pp. 3373–3379 (2021)
25. Grady, L.: Random walks for image segmentation. IEEE Trans. Pattern Anal. Mach. Intell. **28**(11), 1768–1783 (2006)
26. Chen, X., Zhao, Z., Yu, F., Zhang, Y., Duan, M.: Conditional diffusion for interactive segmentation. In: Proceedings of the IEEE/CVF International Conference on Computer Vision, pp. 7345–7354 (2021)
27. Chen, L.C., Papandreou, G., Kokkinos, I., Murphy, K., Yuille, A.L.: Semantic image segmentation with deep convolutional nets and fully connected CRFS. arXiv preprint arXiv:1412.7062 (2014)
28. Chen, L.C., Papandreou, G., Schroff, F., Adam, H.: Rethinking atrous convolution for semantic image segmentation. arXiv preprint arXiv:1706.05587 (2017)
29. Benenson, R., Popov, S., Ferrari, V.: Large-scale interactive object segmentation with human annotators. In: Proceedings of the IEEE/CVF Conference on Computer Vision and Pattern Recognition, pp. 11700–11709 (2019)
30. Le, H., Mai, L., Price, B., Cohen, S., Jin, H., Liu, F.: Interactive boundary prediction for object selection. In: Proceedings of the European Conference on Computer Vision (ECCV), pp. 18–33 (2018)
31. Sun, K., Xiao, B., Liu, D., Wang, J.: Deep high-resolution representation learning for human pose estimation. In: Proceedings of the IEEE/CVF Conference on Computer Vision and Pattern Recognition, pp. 5693–5703 (2019)
32. Yuan, Y., Chen, X., Wang, J.: Object-contextual representations for semantic segmentation. In: European Conference on Computer Vision, pp. 173–190 (2020)
33. Lin, T.Y., Dollár, P., Girshick, R., He, K., Hariharan, B., Belongie, S.: Feature pyramid networks for object detection. In: Proceedings of the IEEE Conference on Computer Vision and Pattern Recognition, pp. 2117–2125 (2017)

34. Liu, S., Qi, L., Qin, H., Shi, J., Jia, J.: Path aggregation network for instance segmentation. In: Proceedings of the IEEE Conference on Computer Vision and Pattern Recognition, pp. 8759–8768 (2018)
35. Zheng, Z., Wang, P., Liu, W., Li, J., Ye, R., Ren, D.: Distance-IoU loss: faster and better learning for bounding box regression. Proc. AAAI Conf. Artif. Intell. **34**(07), 12993–13000 (2020)
36. Lin, T.Y., Goyal, P., Girshick, R., He, K., Dollár, P.: Focal loss for dense object detection. In: Proceedings of the IEEE International Conference on Computer Vision, pp. 2980–2988 (2017)
37. Kontogianni, T., Gygli, M., Uijlings, J., Ferrari, V.: Continuous adaptation for interactive object segmentation by learning from corrections. In: European Conference on Computer Vision, pp. 579–596 (2020)
38. McGuinness, K., O'Connor, N.E.: A comparative evaluation of interactive segmentation algorithms. Pattern Recogn. **43**(2), 434–444 (2010)
39. Perazzi, F., Pont-Tuset, J., McWilliams, B., Van Gool, L., Gross, M., Sorkine-Hornung, A.: A benchmark dataset and evaluation methodology for video object segmentation. In: Proceedings of the IEEE Conference on Computer Vision and Pattern Recognition, pp. 724–732 (2016)
40. Hariharan, B., Arbeláez, P., Bourdev, L., Maji, S., Malik, J.: Semantic contours from inverse detectors. In: 2011 International Conference on Computer Vision, pp. 991–998 (2011)

Anchor-Free Location Refinement Network for Small License Plate Detection

Zhen-Jia Li[1,2], Song-Lu Chen[1,2], Qi Liu[1,2], Feng Chen[2,3],
and Xu-Cheng Yin[1,2(✉)]

[1] School of Computer and Communication Engineering, University of Science and
Technology Beijing, Beijing, China
{zhenjiali,qiliu7}@xs.ustb.edu.cn, {songluchen,xuchengyin}@ustb.edu.cn
[2] USTB-EEasyTech Joint Lab of Artificial Intelligence, University of Science and
Technology Beijing, Beijing, China
[3] EEasy Technology Company Ltd., Zhuhai, China
cfeng@eeasytech.com

Abstract. In the road scenarios, small-sized license plates are challenging to detect due to their small area. The direct detection methods based on anchors are not experts in detecting small-sized license plates due to foreground-background class imbalance. In this work, we propose an anchor-free location refinement network to alleviate the imbalance problem. First, we adopt the anchor-free mechanism to increase the proportion of foreground samples. Second, we use a coarse-to-fine strategy to reduce the background noises. Specifically, the whole network is combined with a coarse detection module (CDM) and a location refinement module (LRM), where the anchor-free CDM can approximately locate the local region around the license plate, and LRM can get a more accurate location of the license plate in the local region. The whole network can be trained in an end-to-end manner. Moreover, the proposed network can detect multi-directional license plates by regressing the four corners of the license plate in LRM. Extensive experiments verify that our method outperforms the baseline model by 6% AP on the road license plate detection dataset and improves the recall of small-sized license plates by 7.5%, thus improving license plate recognition by 3.5%. Moreover, we improve the AP by 4.2% on the traffic sign dataset TT100K, verifying its generalization ability.

Keywords: License plate detection · Small-sized · Multi-directional

---

Z.-J. Li and S.-L. Chen—Equal contribution.

Supplementary Information The online version contains supplementary material available at https://doi.org/10.1007/978-3-031-18916-6_41.

1   Introduction

License plate detection (LPD) has attracted much attention with the rise of intelligent transportation systems and fully automated monitoring. However, LPD in road traffic scenarios is not satisfactory due to the complex changes in the environment. In particular, the small-sized license plate is challenging to detect due to occupying only a small area of the entire image.

The current methods can not effectively solve the problem of foreground-background class imbalance caused by small-sized license plates. There are some methods [1,2] to directly detect the license plate in the whole image (Fig. 1(a)). However, these direct LPD methods can be affected by extensive background noises, which will lead to low recall and false positives, such as regarding car lights as license plates. Moreover, these methods are based on anchors, which will exacerbate the class imbalance problem due to the unfriendly anchor matching mechanism. Many methods detect the vehicle first and then detect the license plate in the vehicle region [3–5] (Fig. 1(b)). These methods can reduce background interference by limiting the detection region inside the vehicle. However, when the vehicle detector can not work correctly due to occlusion or illumination change, the license plate will not be detected. Moreover, these methods can not correctly handle large vehicles, such as trucks and buses, because their license plates still occupy a tiny part of them. To solve this problem, [6] proposes to locate the vehicle head after getting the vehicle region and then detect the license plate in the vehicle head (Fig. 1(c)), where the vehicle head is defined as the smallest region comprising the car headlights and tires. However, this method

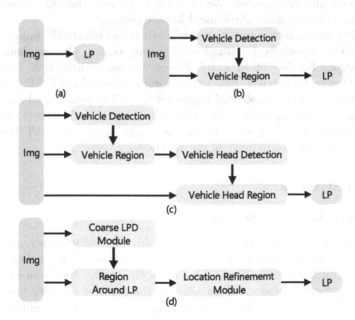

Fig. 1. (a) Direct license plate detection. (b) License plate detection with vehicle proposal. (c) License plate detection with vehicle head proposal. (d) Ours: anchor-free location refinement network.

requires time-consuming annotations of the vehicle and vehicle head and can not detect the license plate if the vehicle or vehicle head fails to be detected. Meanwhile, this method is complicated because of three separate detection networks, i.e., vehicle detection, vehicle head detection, and license plate detection.

In this work, we propose an anchor-free location refinement network for small-sized license plate detection (Fig. 1(d)). Our method combines the anchor-free mechanism and coarse-to-fine strategy to optimize the problem of foreground-background class imbalance. Moreover, the proposed network can be trained end-to-end, with no need for extra annotations of vehicle or vehicle head. Concretely, the whole network is formed by a coarse detection module (CDM) and a location refinement module (LRM), where CDM can approximately locate the license plate in the whole image. We adopt a modified anchor-free strategy in CDM to improve the detection recall, which can relieve the imbalance problem by increasing the number of positive samples matched to the small-sized license plate. The traditional anchor-free methods [7,8] consider the sample point as a positive sample if it falls into the ground-truth box, which will cause few sample points matched to small-sized objects. We allocate samples according to the distance between the sample point and the center of the object. Such an allocation strategy can regard more samples outside the license plate as positive samples, which can reduce the influence of the size of license plates. After that, we can simply get the local region around the license plate by enlarging the region that CDM proposes. LRM can refine the location of the license plate in the local region, which can relieve the imbalance problem by substantially reducing the background area. Moreover, the license plate is usually an arbitrary quadrilateral due to various shooting angles. We propose to regress the four corners of the license plate to locate multi-directional license plates.

Extensive experiments prove that our method can effectively improve license plate detection, especially for small-sized license plates. Our methods outperforms the strong baseline [3] by 4.26% F_1-score in multi-directional license plate detection. Our method outperforms the baseline model by 6% AP on the road license plate detection dataset and improves the AR of small-sized license plate by 7.5%, thus improving license plate recognition by 3.5%. Moreover, we outperforms the basline model by 4.2% AP on the traffic sign dataset TT100K, which verifies the generalization ability of our method.

2   Related Work

2.1   Generic Object Detection

Generic object detection methods can be roughly divided into anchor-based and anchor-free forms according to whether using the anchor. The anchor-based [9–15] methods fill the anchor boxes densely in the image and locate the object by regressing them. These methods allocate the positive samples based on the Intersection Over Union (IOU) between target boxes and pre-defined anchors. YOLO [16–18] and SSD [19] regress the objects based on the anchor directly. Faster-RCNN [9] uses an anchor-based network to propose candidate regions and then classifies these regions. However, the anchor-based methods are not friendly in detecting small-sized license plates because the IOU between the predefined anchor and the small-sized license plate is generally small, which leads to lacking positive samples assigned to the small-sized license plates. The anchor-free methods [7,8,20] remove the anchor box and directly predict the object box based on the point. CenterNet [7] uses Gaussian distribution to build the foreground map. FCOS [8] regards all the points inside target boxes as positive sample points and predict the offsets to the four sides of the bounding box. These methods assign sample points based on whether it falls into the ground-truth box, which is affected by the size of the object and not suitable for detecting small-sized license plates. CPN [21] applies the anchor-free network as the region proposal network. However, it adopts CornerNet [22] as the anchor-free module, which requires cumbersome post-processing procedures.

2.2   Direct License Plate Detection

[1] uses ROI-Align [23] to fuse the feature map of different layers and use the multi-scale features to regress the bounding box of the license plate. [24] proposes to detect the license plate using Faster-RCNN [9]. [25] addresses the challenge of LPD by using an automatic graph-cut-based segmentation approach. [2] uses YOLOv3 [16] for license plate detection in the entire image. [26] integrates multiple features to detect using Faster-RCNN [9]. [27] adopts SSD [19] to design two branches and uses high-level information to detect vehicles and locate license plates by low-level information. These direct detection methods ignore the foreground-background class imbalance caused by small-sized license plates, causing miss detection.

2.3   License Plate Detection with Vehicle Proposal

[28] uses EfficientDet [29] to detect the vehicle and then locate the license plate in the vehicle. [5] adopts YOLOv2 [17] to generate vehicle proposals and then dectect the license plate in the proposals. [3] uses SSD [19] to detect vehicles and uses the relationship between license plates and vehicles for license plate detection. [30] applies the Region Proposal Network (RPN) [10] to generate candidate vehicle proposals and then detects the license plate based on each proposal. The above methods can reduce background noises to improve small-sized license plate detection. However, these methods heavily rely on the accuracy of vehicle detection, and the license plate can not be detected if the vehicle fails to be detected. [31] adopts two branches that can simultaneously detect the license plate in the vehicle proposal and detect the license plate directly. However, this method has a cumbersome post-processing process and can not handle the license plate in large vehicles, such as trucks and buses. [6] locates the license plate in the vehicle head, which is detected in the vehicle region. However, this method requires extra annotations of the vehicle and vehicle head and is dependent on the performance of the pre-detection module.

3   Methodology

In this work, we propose an anchor-free location refinement network for small-sized license plate detection in a coarse-to-fine scheme. The overall architecture is illustrated in Fig. 2(a), mainly divided into coarse detection module and location refinement module. Coarse detection module (CDM) can approximately locate the local region around license plates in the whole image by a modified anchor-free strategy, and location refinement module (LRM) refines the license plate in the local region. In addition, we regress the four corner points based on the positive samples to locate the multi-directional license plates in LRM.

3.1   Coarse Detection Module

As shown in Fig. 2(a), coarse detection module (CDM) uses a one-stage detection network to predict the approximate location of the license plate. As shown in Fig. 2(b), we adopt a modified anchor-free strategy in the detection head to alleviate the problem of foreground-background class imbalance caused by small-sized license plates. Concretely, we allocate samples based on the relative distance between the center of the license plate and the sample points in the feature map, i.e., the three sample points closest to the center of license plates as positive samples. This way, we can allocate more positive samples to small-sized license

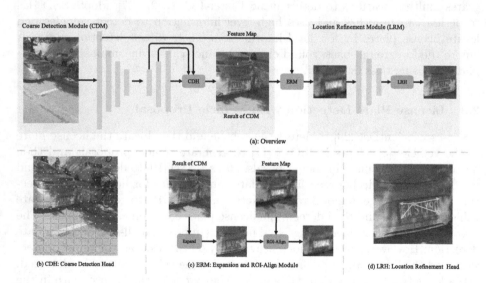

Fig. 2. (a) Overview of our method, including coarse detection module (CDM) and location refinement module (LRM). (b) We define the three sample points (red points) closest to the center of the license plate as positive samples and regress the approximate location of the license plate based on the positive samples. (c) We expand the region that CDM proposes and then use ROI-Align [23] to get the region features from the first layer of CDM. (d) We regress the four corner points of the license plate based on the positive sample point to detect the multi-directional license plate. (Color figure online)

plates than other methods [8, 16], thus reducing the influence of the size of license plates.

Network Output. CDM is based on YOLOv3 [16] for multi-scale detection using a multi-layer detection head. Let $F_m \in R^{H \times W \times (C+5)}$ be the feature map at layer m of the detection head. H and W denote the size of feature map, and C denotes the number of classes. Each sample point on the feature map F_m will predict a $(C + 5)$ dimension vector, and we use the vector to predict the license plate by the following formula.

$$B_x = 2 \times (\sigma(F_{(0)}) - 0.5) \quad B_y = 2 \times (\sigma(F_{(1)}) - 0.5) \tag{1}$$
$$B_w = \sigma(F_{(2)}) \times W/8 \qquad B_h = \sigma(F_{(3)}) \times H/8 \tag{2}$$
$$\mathbf{P} = \sigma(F_{(4)}) \qquad\qquad \mathbf{S} = \sigma(F_{(5:)}) \tag{3}$$

where (B_x, B_y) denotes the center of the bounding box, and (B_w, B_h) denotes the width and height of the bounding box. $\mathbf{P}$ denotes the foreground confidence, and $\mathbf{S}$ denotes the class score of the bounding box. σ denotes the sigmoid function to normalize the output.

Target Assignment. We assign the license plate to different layer of the coarse detection head (CDH) based on the width w and height h of the ground-truth bounding box. We firstly calculate the length of the longest side of the bounding box $max(w, h)$ divided by the size of the feature map $\mathbf{L}$. If a bounding box satisfies $max(w, h)/\mathbf{L} > m_j$ and $max(w, h)/\mathbf{L} < m_{j+1}$, this license plate will be assigned to the j-th level of CDH for detection. In this work, m is set as $[0, 0.25, 0.5, \infty]$.

Loss Function. We adopt CIOU loss [32] for bounding box regression and focal loss [33] for classification. We define the training loss of CDM as follows.

$$Loss_{CDM} = \frac{1}{N_{pos}} \sum_m \sum_{i,j} (L_{loc}(B_{(i,j)}, G_{(i,j)}) \times T_{(i,j)})$$
$$+ \lambda \sum_m L_{cls}(\mathbf{P}, T) + \beta \sum_m \sum_k L_{cls}(\mathbf{S}, C) \tag{4}$$

where N_{pos} denotes the number of positive samples. $B_{(i,j)}$ is the predicted bounding box, and $G_{(i,j)}$ is the ground-truth bounding box. $T_{(i,j)}$ being 1 if location (i,j) is a positive sample point and 0 otherwise. $\mathbf{P}$ and T denote the foreground confidence map and positive sample distribution map, respectively. $\mathbf{S}$ denote the classification score map of class k, C the denotes category distribution map of class k. The balance weight λ and β is set to 0.3 and 0.5 by default.

3.2 Expansion and ROI-Align Module

The expansion and ROI-Align module (ERM) is shown in Fig. 2(c). We first expand the approximate bounding box of the license plate detected by coarse detection module (CDM) to a square box. Concretely, we set the length of the expanded square box as twice the longest side of the box that CDM proposes, where the center of the bounding box is unchanged. By this way, the expanded region can cover the entire license plate and small background area. After that, we use ROI-Align [23] to extract the region features from the first layer of CDM, which can keep more visual information of the license plate and enable the entire network to be trained end-to-end. Since CDM can predict multiple regions that may contain license plates, we combine features of all the predicted regions for parallel computing to speed up the entire network.

3.3   Location Refinement Module

As shown in Fig. 2(d), we locate the multi-directional license plate by regressing the four corner points of the license plate based on the positive sample point. We adopt and modify ResNet18 [34] as the backbone network of location refinement module (LRM). First, we convert the features generated by ERM to 64 channels through 1×1 convolutional layer, which can fit the number of the input channel of ResNet18. Second, we remove the first convolutional layer of ResNet18 to reduce the down-sampling rate of LRM. In this way, we down-sample the feature map by 16 times and estimate the location of the license plate on a 2×2 feature map. The positive samples are assigned by the anchor-free mechanism same as CDM. However, we only set one positive sample for each license plate since the feature map is only 2×2. Formally, if a sample point is assigned to a target box G^*, the training regression targets can be formulated as follows.

$$G_{(x,k)} = G^*_{(x,k)} - p_x \qquad G_{(y,k)} = G^*_{(y,k)} - p_y \tag{5}$$

where k represents the upper-left corner, upper-right corner, lower-left corner, and lower-right corner of the quadrilateral box of the license plate, and (p_x, p_y) denotes the coordinate of the positive sample. $G^*_{(x,k)}$ and $G^*_{(y,k)}$ denote the ground-truth location of the k-th corner point.

Loss Function. The loss function of LRM is defined as follows.

$$Loss_{LRM} = \sum_{i,j} L_{loc}(G_{(i,j)}, B_{(i,j)}) \times T_{(i,j)} + \lambda L_{cls}(\mathbf{P}, T) \tag{6}$$

where L_{cls} is the focal loss [33] for classification, and L_{loc} denotes the smooth L1 loss [35] for corner regression. The balance weight λ is set to 0.3 by default. In addition, L_{loc} denotes CIOU [32] loss for bounding box regression if we experiment on the traffic sigh dataset TT100K to verify the generalization ability of the proposed method.

4   Experiments

4.1   Ablation Study

As shown in Table 1, we adopt anchor-based YOLOv3 [16] as the baseline model. CDM denotes our coarse detection module, and R-YOLO denotes adding our location refinement module (LRM) after the vanilla YOLOv3 [16].

Anchor Based/Free. Except for the anchor-free matching strategy, CDM is the same as the vanilla YOLOv3 [16]. We regard the three points closest to the center of license plates as positive samples, while YOLOv3 assigns samples based on the IOU. As shown in Table 1, CDM is better than YOLOv3 on all the test sets. Especially for $AP_{50:95}$, CDM can achieve a more significant improvement on both test sets.

Location Refinement Module. location refinement module (LRM) can refine the detection results that CDM predicts. After adding LRM to the vanilla YOLOv3 [16] and CDM, R-YOLO and our method can both improve AP50:95 on all the test sets, proving the effectiveness of our coarse-to-fine detection strategy. Our method achieves better performance than R-YOLO because CDM can achieve higher recall.

Input of LRM. After expansion and ROI-Align module (ERM), we can get many expanded regions that may contain the license plate. We compare the detection result that extract the region features from CDM or the original image. Table 2 shows that feature extraction from the first layer of CDM is better than others. It can also be seen from the figure that when the feature map sizes are consistent, deeper networks generally perform better, and larger feature map sizes can achieve higher detection performance than small-sized feature maps. Moreover, extracting region features from CDM can enable the entire network to be trained end-to-end, while cropping regions from the original image requires two separate networks.

Table 1. Ablation study

Method	TILT720		TILT1080		CCPD	
	AP_{50}	$AP_{50:95}$	AP_{50}	$AP_{50:95}$	AP_{50}	$AP_{50:95}$
YOLOv3 [16]	96.22	68.52	95.35	74.67	98.60	62.40
CDM	95.60	69.37	96.38	77.44	99.20	66.20
R-YOLO	97.08	72.41	97.78	79.64	99.10	64.60
Ours	**97.24**	**73.72**	**98.13**	**80.64**	**99.60**	**68.00**

Table 2. Input of LRM

Input	TILT720	TILT1080	Feature map size
Img	72.70%	79.28%	320
First Layer	**73.72%**	**80.64%**	320
Second Layer	72.68%	79.90%	160
Third Layer	72.68%	80.07%	160
Fourth Layer	70.13%	76.38%	80
Fifth Layer	71.45%	77.95%	80
Sixth Layer	64.68%	72.48%	40
Seventh Layer	66.78%	75.12%	40

4.2 Experiments of Horizontal Bounding Box

As shown in Table 3, we compare with methods [3,9,16,19,33,36] on TILT1080 to verify the detection capability on the horizontal bounding box. As can be seen, our method achieves the best $AP_{50:95}$, outperforming the method of late-set YOLO series YOLOv5 [36], anchor-free method FSAF [37], and two-stage detection method Faster-RCNN [9]. Our method can acquire a more significant performance gain than YOLOv5 [36] with a large IOU threshold, i.e., 6.78% AP_{75} vs. 1.98% AP_{50}, which proves our method can accurately detect the license plate.

4.3 Experiments of Small-Sized License Plate

Same as [31], we divide the test set into three levels according to the height of the license plates, i.e., small, medium, and large license plates. As shown in Table 4, we compare the average recall (AR) of the license plates of different size with the baseline model YOLOv3 [16] and Method [31]. For small-sized license plates, Our method achieves 20.12% improvement on the TILT1080 dataset and 7.5% improvement on the TILT720 dataset than baseline YOLOv3, and outperforming Method [31] by 13.35% on TILT1080 dataset, verifying the effectiveness of our method. For the medium-sized and large-sized license plates, our method slightly outperforms these two models because the license plates occupy a large area of the image.

Table 3. Experiments of horizontal bounding box

Method	AP_{50}	AP_{75}	$AP_{50:95}$
SSD [19]	89.80%	81.60%	56.10%
YOLOv3 [16]	95.35%	88.09%	74.67%
YOLOv5 [36]	96.15%	88.67%	75.88%
RetinaNet [33]	91.10%	81.20%	67.90%
FSAF [37]	89.70%	84.20%	68.30%
Faster-RCNN [9]	87.50%	81.60%	66.70%
Ours	**98.13%**	**95.45%**	**80.64%**

Table 4. Experiments of different object size

Dataset	Object Size	YOLOv3 [16]	Ours	Method [31]
TITL1080	Small	38.70%	**58.82%**	45.47%
	Medium	76.50%	**77.14%**	75.73%
	Large	**81.49%**	80.80%	79.26%
TILT720	Small	50.92%	**55.80%**	47.16%
	Medium	70.38%	**72.88%**	71.23%
	Large	72.50%	**80.00%**	72.17%

4.4 Experiments of Multi-directional License Plates

We compare with methods [3,38] on the test set of TILT720. As shown in Table 5, the method [38] directly detects the license plates using RetinaFace [11], which causes low recall with a large IOU threshold due to miss detection of small-sized license plates. The method [3] detects the license plates in the vehicle region detected by the SSD [19] and achieves a higher recall. However, this method fails to detect the license plate if the vehicle is not detected. Our method achieves the best F_1-score with different IOU thresholds, especially for the large IOU threshold 0.75. The results show our method can accurately detect the multi-directional license plate.

Table 5. Experiments of multi-directional license plate on TILT720

Method	IOU = 0.50			IOU = 0.75		
	P	R	F_1	P	R	F_1
Method [38]	**80.77%**	48.09%	60.28%	**69.87%**	41.60%	52.15%
Method [3]	73.28%	78.36%	75.73%	53.85%	53.45%	53.64%
Ours	71.76%	**87.04%**	**78.67%**	53.82%	**65.27%**	**58.90%**

4.5 License Plate Recognition

We compare with YOLOv3 [16] on TILT720 and TILT1080. We crop license plate from the original image based on the detected horizontal bounding box and input it to the recognition model [39], which is based on the 2D spatial attention for license plate recognition. As shown in Table 6, our method can improve the accuracy of recognition by 3.6% on TILT1080 and 3.65% on TILT720.

Table 6. License plate recognition

Method	TILT720	TILT1080
YOLOv3 [16]	35.25%	41.94%
Ours	**38.85%**	**45.57%**

4.6 Experiments on TT100k

To verify the generalization ability of our method for small-sized object detection, we test our method on TT100K. As shown in Table 7, CDM can improve 6.2% AR_{50} compared with the baseline model YOLOv3 [16] under the threshold of 0.5, which proves CDM can effetively detect small-sized objects due to its modified anchor-free matching strategy. Moreover, the entire method achieves 4.2% $AP_{50:95}$ improvement and 4.1% $AR_{50:95}$ than YOLOv3, which verifies the effectiveness for small-sized object detection and generalization ability of our method.

4.7   Runtime Analysis

We analyzed the running speed of our model, and the results are shown in the fifth column of Table 7, FPS represents the number of pictures that the model can detect per second. The results show that the running speed of our method is about 19 FPS slower than that of YOLOv3 [16], however, our method can still guarantee real-time and achieved a huge performance improvement.

Table 7. Detection results on TT100K and runtime analysis

Method	AP_{50}	$AP_{50:95}$	AR_{50}	$AR_{50:95}$	FPS
YOLOv3 [16]	63.3%	45.6%	68.5%	50.4%	68.43
CDM	67.1%	46.7%	74.7%	52.8%	67.37
Ours	**68.2%**	**49.8%**	**76.3%**	**55.5%**	49.20

4.8   Qualitative Results

As shown in the Figs. 3(a) and 3(b), our proposed method can detect small license plates on TILT1080 while the YOLOv3 [16] can not, corresponding to the results in Table 4. As shown in Fig. 3(c), our proposed method can accurately detect the four corner points of the license plate on TILT720.

(a) Horizontal results detected by YOLOv3[16]

(b) Horizontal results detected by our method

(c) Four corner points detected by our method

Fig. 3. Qualitative Results on TILT720 and TILT1080.

5 Conclusion

In this work, we improve small-sized license plate detection by a coarse-to-fine scheme. We adopt a modified anchor-free mechanism to improve the recall of small-sized license plates and optimize the detection precision by a location refinement module. Moreover, we regress the four corner points to locate the multi-directional license plate. Experiments show that our proposed method dramatically improves license plate detection and recognition. Moreover, the experiments on TT100K verifies the generalization ability of our method.

References

1. Xu, Z., et al.: Towards end-to-end license plate detection and recognition: a large dataset and baseline. In: Proceedings of the European Conference on Computer Vision, Munich, pp. 261–277 (2018)
2. Chou, J., Liu, C.: Automated sensing system for real-time recognition of trucks in river dredging areas using computer vision and convolutional deep learning. Sensors **21**(2), 555 (2021)
3. Chen, S., et al.: End-to-end trainable network for degraded license plate detection via vehicle-plate relation mining. Neurocomputing **446**, 1–10 (2021)
4. Silva, S.M., Jung, C.R.: License plate detection and recognition in unconstrained scenarios. In: Proceedings of the European Conference on Computer Vision, Munich, pp. 593–609 (2018)
5. Laroca, R., et al.: A robust real-time automatic license plate recognition based on the YOLO detector. In: International Joint Conference on Neural Networks, Rio de Janeiro, pp. 1–10 (2018)
6. Silva, S.M., Jung, C.R.: Real-time license plate detection and recognition using deep convolutional neural networks. J. Vis. Commun. Image Represent. **71**, 102773 (2020)
7. Zhou, X., Wang, D., Krähenbühl, P.: Objects as points. arXiv preprint arXiv:1904.07850 (2019)
8. Tian, Z., Shen, C., Chen, H., He, T.: FCOS: fully convolutional one-stage object detection. In: Proceedings of the IEEE International Conference on Computer Vision, Seoul, pp. 9626–9635 (2019)
9. Ren, S., He, K., Girshick, R.B., Sun, J.: Faster R-CNN: towards real-time object detection with region proposal networks. In: Annual Conference on Neural Information Processing Systems, Montreal, Quebec, pp. 91–99 (2015)
10. Girshick, R.B.: Fast R-CNN. In: Proceedings of the IEEE International Conference on Computer Vision, Santiago, pp. 1440–1448 (2015)
11. Deng, J., Guo, J., Ververas, E., Kotsia, I., Zafeiriou, S.: Retinaface: single-shot multi-level face localisation in the wild. In: Proceedings of the IEEE Conference on Computer Vision and Pattern Recognition, Seattle, pp. 5202–5211 (2020)
12. Fang, F., Xu, Q., Li, L., Gu, Y., Lim, J.: Detecting objects with high object region percentage. In: International Conference on Pattern Recognition, Virtual Event/Milan, pp. 7173–7180 (2020)
13. Deguerre, B, Chatelain, C., Gasso, G.: Object detection in the DCT domain: is luminance the solution? In: International Conference on Pattern Recognition, Virtual Event/Milan, pp. 2627–2634 (2020)

14. Gan, Y., Xu, W., Su, J.: SFPN: semantic feature pyramid network for object detection. In: International Conference on Pattern Recognition, Virtual Event/Milan, pp. 795–802 (2020)
15. Guo, T., Zhang, L., Ding, R., Yang, G.: Edd-net: an efficient defect detection network. In: International Conference on Pattern Recognition, Virtual Event/Milan, pp. 8899–8905 (2020)
16. Redmon, J., Farhadi, A.: Yolov3: an incremental improvement. arXiv preprint arXiv:1804.02767 (2018)
17. Redmon, J., Farhadi, A.: YOLO9000: better, faster, stronger. In: Proceedings of the IEEE Conference on Computer Vision and Pattern Recognition, Honolulu, pp. 6517–6525 (2017)
18. Bochkovskiy, A., Wang, C., Liao, H.M.: Yolov4: optimal speed and accuracy of object detection. arXiv preprint arXiv:2004.10934 (2020)
19. Liu, W., et al.: SSD: single shot multibox detector. In: Proceedings of the European Conference on Computer Vision, Amsterdam, pp. 21–37 (2016)
20. Redmon, J., Divvala, S.K., Girshick, R.B., Farhadi, A.: You only look once: unified, real-time object detection. In: Proceedings of the IEEE Conference on Computer Vision and Pattern Recognition, Las Vegas, pp. 779–788 (2016)
21. Duan, K., Xie, L., Qi, H., Bai, S., Huang, Q., Tian, Q.: Corner proposal network for anchor-free, two-stage object detection. In: Vedaldi, A., Bischof, H., Brox, T., Frahm, J.-M. (eds.) ECCV 2020. LNCS, vol. 12348, pp. 399–416. Springer, Cham (2020). https://doi.org/10.1007/978-3-030-58580-8_24
22. Law, H., Deng, J.: Cornernet: detecting objects as paired keypoints. In: Proceedings of the European Conference on Computer Vision, Munich. Lecture Notes in Computer Science, vol. 11218, pp. 765–781 (2018)
23. He, K., Gkioxari, G., Dollár, P., Girshick, R.B.: Mask R-CNN. IEEE Trans. Pattern Anal. Mach. Intell. **42**(2), 386–397 (2020)
24. Li, H., Wang, P., Shen, C.: Toward end-to-end car license plate detection and recognition with deep neural networks. IEEE Trans. Intell. Transp. Syst. **20**(3), 1126–1136 (2019)
25. Salau, A.O.: An effective graph-cut segmentation approach for license plate detection. In: Recent Trends in Image and Signal Processing in Computer Vision, p. 19 (2020)
26. Omar, N., Abdulazeez, A.M., Sengur, A., Al-Ali, S.G.S.: Fused faster RCNNs for efficient detection of the license plates. Indonesian J. Electric. Eng. Comput. Sci. **19**(2), 974–982 (2020)
27. Chen, S., Yang, C., Ma, J., Chen, F., Yin, X.: Simultaneous end-to-end vehicle and license plate detection with multi-branch attention neural network. IEEE Trans. Intell. Transp. Syst. **21**(9), 3686–3695 (2020)
28. He, M., Hao, P.: Robust automatic recognition of Chinese license plates in natural scenes. IEEE Access **8**, 173804–173814 (2020)
29. Tan, M., Pang, R., Le, Q.V.: Efficientdet: scalable and efficient object detection. In: Proceedings of the IEEE Conference on Computer Vision and Pattern Recognition, pp. 10778–10787 (2020)
30. Fu, Q., Shen, Y., Guo, Z.: License plate detection using deep cascaded convolutional neural networks in complex scenes. In: Proceedings of the International Conference on Neural Information Processing, Guangzhou, pp. 696–706 (2017)
31. Chen, S.-L., Liu, Q., Ma, J.-W., Yang, C.: Scale-invariant multidirectional license plate detection with the network combining indirect and direct branches. Sensors **21**(4), 1074 (2021)

32. Zheng, Z., Wang, P., Liu, W., Li, J., Ye, R., Ren, D.: Distance-iou loss: faster and better learning for bounding box regression. In: Conference on Artificial Intelligence, New York, pp. 12993–13000 (2020)
33. Lin, T., Goyal, P., Girshick, R.B., He, K., Dollár, P.: Focal loss for dense object detection. In: Proceedings of the IEEE International Conference on Computer Vision, Venice, pp. 2999–3007 (2017)
34. He, K., Zhang, X., Ren, S., Sun, J.: Deep residual learning for image recognition. In: Proceedings of the IEEE Conference on Computer Vision and Pattern Recognition, Las Vegas, pp. 770–778 (2016)
35. Madsen, K., Nielsen, H.B.: A finite smoothing algorithm for linear l_1 estimation. SIAM J. Optim. **3**(2), 223–235 (1993)
36. G.J., et al.: ultralytics/yolov5: v6.0 - YOLOv5n 'Nano' models, Roboflow integration, TensorFlow export, OpenCV DNN support (2021)
37. Zhu, C., He, Y., Savvides, M.: Feature selective anchor-free module for single-shot object detection. In: Proceedings of the IEEE Conference on Computer Vision and Pattern Recognition, Long Beach, pp. 840–849 (2019)
38. gm19900510. Pytorch retina license plate. https://github.com/gm19900510/Pytorch_Retina_License_Plate/ (2020)
39. Liu, Q., Chen, S., Li, Z., Yang, C., Chen, F., Yin, X.: Fast recognition for multidirectional and multi-type license plates with 2d spatial attention. In: International Conference on Document Analysis and Recognition, Lausanne, pp. 125–139 (2021)

Multi-view LiDAR Guided Monocular 3D Object Detection

Junjie Liu$^{(\boxtimes)}$ and Weiyu Yu

School of Electronic and Information Engineering,
South China University of Technology, Guangzhou 510641, China
ee_junjieliu@mail.scut.edu.cn, yuweiyu@scut.edu.cn

Abstract. Detecting 3D objects from monocular RGB images is an ill-posed task for lacking depth knowledge, and monocular-based 3D detection methods perform poorly compared with LiDAR-based 3D detection methods. Some bird's-eye-view-based monocular 3D detection methods transform front-view image feature maps into bird's-eye-view feature maps and then use LiDAR 3D detection heads to detect objects. These methods get relatively high performance. However, there is still a large gap between monocular and LiDAR bird's-eye-view feature maps. Based on the fact that LiDAR bird's-eye-view feature maps are marginally better than monocular, to bridge their gap and boost monocular 3D detection performance, on the one hand, we directly employ the bird's-eye-view features from LiDAR models to guide the training of monocular detection models; on the other hand, we employ the front-view features from LiDAR models to help the monocular image backbone embed depth cues into image feature maps. Experimental results show that our method significantly boosts monocular 3D object detection performance without introducing any extra cost in the inference phase.

Keywords: Monocular · 3D object detection · Autonomous driving · Knowledge distillation

1 Introduction

In the field of 3D object detection for autonomous driving, there is a strong presumption that the ground is flat and all objects are on the ground. As a result, unlike the 9 DoF pose estimation task [22, 26], 3D object detection for autonomous driving does not need to output the roll and pitch angles of objects' direction. It just needs to output a three-dimensional position, a three-dimensional size, and a yaw angle. As can be seen, only the direction prediction is one-dimensional and it's on a horizontal plane. Besides, predicting position in the z-axis is easier than the other two axes for its limited distribution area. In addition, the Euclidean distance under the bird's-eye-view (BEV) can be used to measure an accurate spatial position, while the Euclidean distance under the front view (FV) is difficult to convert to actual distance due to the perspective projection. For these reasons, many LiDAR-based 3D object detection methods [9, 28, 32] convert raw point clouds to

S. Yu et al. (Eds.): PRCV 2022, LNCS 13537, pp. 520–532, 2022.
https://doi.org/10.1007/978-3-031-18916-6_42

BEV, then detect 3D objects on BEV maps. The concept of detection in BEV can be used for monocular 3D object detection as well. Some monocular 3D detection works design view converters based on neural networks or geometric relations to transform monocular FV feature maps to BEV feature maps [8, 19, 20], and then detect 3D objects on BEV feature maps like LiDAR 3D detection models. Like most monocular detection methods, these view converters will explicitly or implicitly estimate scene depth. As we all know, RGB images do not directly contain depth information, but depth information can be roughly inferred from the global context knowledge of images. High-level image features have a large receptive field, so that global context information is introduced into each pixel on the feature maps, and depth is estimated by the position and relative relationship of objects on image planes. Hence, FV features are embedded with depth knowledge. By leveraging a solid depth aware image backbone, a high-performance monocular 3D detection model can be built [16]. Moreover, the fusion of BEV and FV features can achieve higher performance in 3D detection [3]. We can conclude that BEV features have accurate geometric cues, and FV features get depth cues encoded from images.

Although the BEV-based monocular 3D detection models and the LiDAR 3D detection models both detect objects on BEV feature maps, the performance gap between monocular and LiDAR models is significant. The main reason for this is that the monocular RGB image inputs lack exact spatial position information, preventing the monocular model from obtaining accurate BEV features with a robust representation of 3D geometry structures. Inspired by the knowledge distillation, we propose to imitate the BEV feature maps from LiDAR models to get better monocular BEV feature maps and boost monocular 3D detection performance. We leverage BEV feature maps from the LiDAR detection model to guide the training of the monocular detection model. As the primary cause of this gap is the lack of depth knowledge in monocular, and monocular depth perception is based on global context information from FV image feature maps. We also extend the idea of imitating LiDAR BEV features to FV image features to guide the monocular model's image encoder in extracting image features with powerful depth cues, which in turn helps the monocular model generate more accurate BEV feature maps. Overall, our proposed the BEV feature imitation and the FV feature imitation both aim to assist the monocular model in generating a more accurate BEV feature map, though the former does so directly and the latter indirectly. Some recent works [4, 7, 33] are similar to ours by utilizing a better domain knowledge to assist the training of image-based methods, and we exhibit their differences with ours in Fig. 1.

Our contributions can be summarized as follows: Firstly, we explain the significance of BEV and FV feature maps for monocular 3D object detection. Furthermore, we analyze the gap between the monocular and the LiDAR BEV features. Secondly, to improve monocular 3D detection performance by narrowing the gap between monocular and LiDAR BEV feature maps, we propose to utilize LiDAR detection model features to guide the training of monocular detection models from BEV and FV spaces. This approach may be applied to any

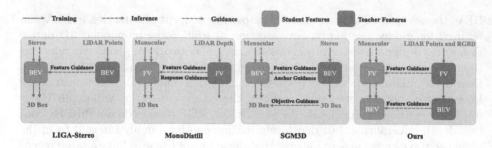

Fig. 1. Comparison of our method with LIGA-Stereo [7], MonoDistill [4], and SGM3D [33]. FV denotes features in front-view space; BEV denotes features in bird's-eye-view space. The primary differences are the input, the feature space where the guidance is implemented, and the way of the guidance.

BEV-based monocular detection method. It can achieve better accuracy with the same model structure. Thirdly, our proposed method improves AP by 2.38% on the KITTI 3D object detection dataset without introducing any extra cost in the inference phase.

2   Related Works

2.1   Point Cloud 3D Object Detection

Determining how to encode sparse point clouds is a critical aspect of the point cloud 3D object detection task. Mainstream methods can be roughly divided into the grid-based methods and the point-based methods according to the different ways of encoding point clouds, and grid-based methods are more relevant to our work. Grid-based methods project raw point clouds to BEV, and divide points into regular 3D grids, which could be processed by 3D convolution network or sparse 3D convolution network [28]. Furthermore, grids in height direction can be compressed to pillars when dividing grids [9] so that a simple 2D convolutional backbone can also be used to process the 2D BEV maps. Anchor-based [32] or achor-free [29] detection heads are utilized to predict the bounding box parameters from the BEV feature maps.

2.2   Monocular 3D Object Detection

Some works [11,15,24,31] leverage a 2D detection framework and some geometric constraints to perform 3D detection task. CenterNet [31] regards targets as points, locates the center of targets in a whole image, and then uses the context information brought by the convolution network to directly regression the 3D position and the pose of targets. MonoGRNet [18] employs instance depth estimation on 2D detection results and then regressions 3D bounding boxes. The above methods all detect 3D objects from FV. On the other hand, some methods generate 3D features from images then detect 3D objects from BEV feature maps, and we call them BEV-based methods. The pseudo LiDAR methods [25,30] use camera intrinsics and dense depth estimation on images to map each pixel to 3D space, which is called pseudo LiDAR; then LiDAR-based 3D detection methods can be used to pseudo LiDAR. In addition to lifting input data into 3D space, some works [17,20] transform 2D image features into 3D voxel features. OFT [20] and ImVoxelNet [21] obtain voxel features by projecting the preset voxel positions in 3D space into image planes through camera intrinsics. Lift-Splat-Shoot [17] divides the spatial depth into multiple bins and converts the depth estimation task into a multi-classification task. In this way, obtain the features of each depth bin by using the confidence of each bin as the weight of the current pixel feature. The bin features of all pixels form the frustum features in the camera coordinate, which can be transformed into voxel features. The Lift-Splat-Shoot method was initially applied to the BEV segmentation task, and it was soon used for monocular 3D detection [8,19].

Using Additional Information to Guide the Training Process. The models trained from a better domain can serve as the teacher network of the image-based 3D detection models [13], and transfer the learned spatial cues to the image-based methods with the knowledge distillation mechanism. MonoDistill [4] applies knowledge distillation to transfer the valuable cues from the LiDAR models to monocular models in FV space; the LiDAR teacher network is the same as the monocular, but the input is LiDAR depth maps. LIGA stereo [7] transforms stereo image features into 3D voxel features, and then uses LiDAR features to guide the stereo features learning from BEV space. SGM3D [33] utilizes powerful 3D features extracted from stereo images to guide the monocular detection model training in BEV.

3 Proposed Method

3.1 Network Structure

We propose a monocular 3D object detection method using LiDAR features to guide monocular feature learning from BEV and FV space. An overview of the framework is illustrated in Fig. 2. It consists of three main complements: a BEV-based monocular 3D object detection network, a LiDAR BEV teacher network that takes raw point clouds as input, and a LiDAR FV teacher network that takes RGBD images as input. Both the LiDAR BEV and FV teacher networks are used in the training stage to adapt monocular features to act as LiDAR features do, and they will be removed in the inference phase. The detailed network structure is introduced in the rest of this section.

Monocular Student Branch. A BEV-based monocular 3D detection model is required as our monocular baseline, which can generate both BEV and FV feature maps. The heart of the BEV-based monocular 3D detection models is

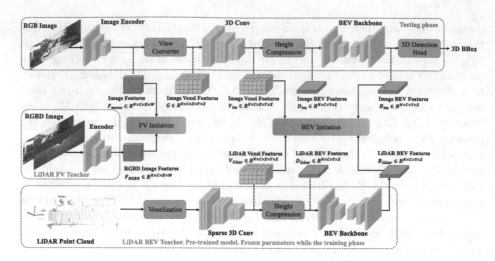

Fig. 2. Illustration of the proposed method. The top branch in the red dotted box is our monocular student network, and it's also our monocular detection baseline. The other two branches in the blue dotted boxes are the LiDAR teacher networks. We only depict the image encoder of the LiDAR FV teacher network because the remainder of its architecture is identical to that of the monocular student network. (Color figure online)

a view converter that can transform 2D image features into 3D BEV features. The view transform approach of CaDDN [19] is used as a view converter in our monocular model. Any other BEV-based monocular 3D detection methods [10,17,20,27] can also be used to replace in this part. We use the DORN [5] network as our depth aware image encoder to extract features from input images, then perform multi-classification on each pixel of the feature map to predict discrete depth distribution. Using the predicted depth distribution and camera intrinsics to translate the 2D image features to 3D voxel features. A 3D convolution network is applied to the 3D voxel features output by the view converter. Then the voxel features are compressed along the Z-axis and encoded to BEV feature maps through a BEV backbone. Finally, 3D detection results are output through a 3D detection head.

LiDAR BEV Teacher Branch. The input data of the LiDAR BEV Teacher network is raw LidAR points, which can be easily voxelized into 3D voxels. To generate BEV feature maps of LidAR data, any voxel-based LiDAR object detection methods [9,28,29] can be used as a LiDAR BEV teacher network. Here we utilize SECOND [28] as our LiDAR BEV teacher network to guide the monocular student network for its relatively straightforward structure and retention of 3D voxel features. This branch is pre-trained before being used as a tracher network, and the parameters will be frozen during the guidance, it only provides features as input. Note that the monocular student and the LiDAR

BEV teacher networks share the same architecture of their BEV backbone and detection head but different weights.

LiDAR FV Teacher Branch. To get the FV features of LiDAR data, it is better to directly use the input data from the FV space to extract the FV features. We project LiDAR points onto the RGB image plane using the calibration matrices, then preserve their coordinates on the image plane and points' depth. Since the LiDAR points is sparse, an interpolation algorithm is used to turn the sparse depth map into a dense depth map. We also concatenate the original RGB image with the depth map as the network's input in order to make the LiDAR FV features and image features more closer in modality. The LiDAR FV teacher network has the same structure as the monocular detection network except for the number of input channels. This branch is also pre-trained before using as a teacher network. We only need the feature maps with depth cues extracted by the image encoder when guiding the monocular detection network learning, so we just load the image encoder of this branch and fix its parameters.

3.2 BEV Feature Imitation

Depth distribution estimation from the monocular model cannot accurately capture spatial cues. Even if the depth prediction is accurate, the image-to-BEV transform still suffers from information loss due to the quantization of depth prediction in the monocular model. In contrast, our LiDAR BEV teacher model take raw point clouds as input and then encode 3D geometric information into high-level BEV feature representations, which can provide powerful and discriminative geometry-aware features [7]. As a result, there is still some misalignment between the monocular BEV features and the LiDAR BEV features. Inspired by LIGA [7], we enforce the monocular model to imitate BEV features of the LiDAR BEV teacher model to narrow the distances between them, and employ L2 regularization to calculate the feature similarity. The monocular and the LiDAR BEV features are of the same shape by some parameter settings. Due to the enormous modality gap between the features of these two modalities, We use a domain adaption network to adapt the monocular BEV features to the LiDAR BEV feature domain, and then optimize the similarity between the new monocular features and the LiDAR features. Since the background part occupies most of the BEV features, it will introduce additional noise, so we only focus on the foreground voxels. The BEV foreground mask is shown in Fig. 3. Following LIGA [7], we apply the guidance to both 3D voxel feature pairs (V_{im} and V_{lidar} in Fig. 2) and 2D BEV feature pairs (B_{im} and B_{lidar} in Fig. 2). Our BEV feature imitation loss is expressed as follows:

$$\mathcal{L}_{bev} = \frac{1}{N_{bevpos}} \parallel M_{bevfg} \cdot (F_{mbev} - F_{lbev}) \parallel_2^2 \tag{1}$$

where F_{mbev} and F_{lbev} stand for the 3D voxel features or the 2D BEV features of the monocular network and the LiDAR BEV teacher network, respectively. M_{bevfg} is the BEV foreground mask.

Fig. 3. The top two images are the scene image and point cloud data respectively. To better visualize the point cloud, image colours are added to the points to display. The bottom two images are the FV and BEV foreground masks, calculated by projecting 3D bounding boxes to the FV and BEV space.

3.3   FV Feature Imitation

In addition to directly bridging the gap between the monocular and the LiDAR BEV features, we can also reduce the gap between the monocular FV features and the LiDAR FV features, so that the monocular model can obtain better depth perception ability, which leads to more accurate BEV feature maps. We use the LiDAR FV teacher model to guide the monocular student model in learning how to encode FV features. The FV feature imitation is applied on the last layer features of the monocular image encoder and the RGBD image encoder (F_{mono} and F_{RGBD} in Fig. 2). The following describes the two FV feature imitation methods that we use.

Global-Level Imitation. Global knowledge can help the monocular model build a high-level understanding of FV images. Utilizing the method in MonoDistill [4], we train the monocular student model to imitate the affinity map of high-level FV features from the LiDAR FV teacher model. The affinity map can be calculated as follows:

$$A_{i,j} = \frac{F_i^T \times F_j}{\|F_i\|_2 \|F_j\|_2} \tag{2}$$

where F_i and F_j stand for pixel vectors of feature maps; i and j both belong to $[0, h \times w - 1]$, h and w are the height and width of the feature maps. As a result, the shape of the affinity map is $(h \times w) \times (h \times w)$. After calculating the student model feature affinity map A_m and the teacher model feature affinity map A_l, we employ L1 loss to enforce the student model to learn global depth cues from the teacher model. The loss function is formulated as follows:

$$\mathcal{L}_{fvg} = \frac{1}{(h \times w) \times (h \times w)} \|A_m - A_l\|_1 \tag{3}$$

Pixel-Level Imitation. We also apply the BEV feature imitation approach in Sect. 3.2 to FV feature imitation. L2 regularization is used to calculate the distance for each pixel pair composed of the student model FV features F_{mono} and the teacher model FV features F_{RGBD}, and then our network is trained to minimize that distance. We still only consider pixels in the foreground M_{fvfg}, and the FV foreground mask is shown in Fig. 3.

$$\mathcal{L}_{fvp} = \frac{1}{N_{fvpos}} \| M_{fvfg} \cdot (F_{mono} - F_{RGBD}) \|_2^2 \tag{4}$$

3.4 Total Loss Function

The total loss function consists of the monocular baseline loss and the three imitation losses that we propose. The monocular baseline loss $\mathcal{L}_{mono}$ is divided into 3D detection loss $\mathcal{L}_{det}$ and depth supervision loss $\mathcal{L}_{depth}$. $\mathcal{L}_{det}$ can be the same as the loss in PointPillars [9] or SECOND [28], and depth supervision loss $\mathcal{L}_{depth}$ following CaDDN [19]. For the BEV teacher model training, only $\mathcal{L}_{det}$ is adopted, and for the FV teacher model training, $\mathcal{L}_{mono}$ is adopted. All λ parameters represent hyper-parameters for balancing each loss.

$$\mathcal{L}_{mono} = \lambda_{det}\mathcal{L}_{det} + \lambda_{depth}\mathcal{L}_{depth} \tag{5}$$

$$\mathcal{L} = \mathcal{L}_{mono} + \lambda_{bev}\mathcal{L}_{bev} + \lambda_{fvg}\mathcal{L}_{fvg} + \lambda_{fvp}\mathcal{L}_{fvp} \tag{6}$$

4 Experiments

4.1 Datasets and Evaluation Metrics

We evaluate the proposed method on the KITTI [6] 3D object detection dataset which is a 3D object detection benchmark in autonomous driving. It consists of 7481 training images and 7518 testing images as well as the corresponding point clouds. The same as the previous works [9,28], we divide the training samples into a training set (3712 samples) and a validation set (3769 samples). We report our ablation studies on the validation set, and compare our method with others on the testing set. There are three classes in the KITTI dataset for 3D object detection, including car, cyclist, and pedestrian. Since most monocular 3D object detection works are only tested on the car category, we do the same. All targets are divided into three levels: easy, moderate, and hard. We mainly focus on the performance of the moderate level. Average precision (AP) is commonly used to measure the performance of 3D object detection, and we evaluate our approach on 3D results and BEV results using the $AP|_{R_{40}}$ as a metric instead of the KITTI's old metric $AP|_{R_{11}}$.

Fig. 4. Visualization of BEV features. At the top are the input images, and 3D ground-truth boxes are drawn in green. At the bottom are the BEV feature maps. The bottom left of each sample is the baseline feature map, and the bottom right of each sample is our LiDAR-guided model feature map. Yellow boxes in the BEV feature maps are the locations of some objects (not all objects); red boxes are some background. (Color figure online)

Table 1. The performances of the LiDAR teacher models and our baseline.

Model	$AP_{3D}@IOU = 0.7$			$AP_{BEV}@IOU = 0.7$		
	Easy	**Mod**	Hard	Easy	Mod	Hard
LiDAR BEV teacher model	89.73	**78.48**	76.13	92.14	87.37	85.29
LiDAR FV teacher model	73.94	**54.14**	47.79	87.09	68.33	61.88
Monocular baseline	21.10	**15.50**	13.14	30.57	22.50	19.68

4.2 Implementation Details

Our work is implemented on the OpenPCDet [1] code base. We train our networks using AdamW optimizer with a one-cycle learning rate schedule, and the initial learning rate is set to 0.001. We fix the batch size per GPU to 2 and train the networks for 80 epochs with 4 Nvidia Tesla V100 GPUs. We apply random flipping horizontally with a 50% probability to input images. Following the data augmentation strategy in BEVDet [8], We adopt data augmentation in BEV feature space. Monocular 3D voxel features are augmented by random rotation around z-axis in the angular range [-22.5, 22.5] and random scaling with a range of [0.95, 10.05]. For training the monocular detection network under the guidance of the LiDAR teacher networks, we apply an early stop policy: when the training reaches half of the total epoch, stop the guidance of the teacher networks and continue the training for the remaining half of the total epoch.

4.3 Experimental Results and Discussion

Baseline Results. We provide the results of our two LiDAR teacher models and the monocular baseline in Table 1. We can see that the two LiDAR teacher models' performance is significantly higher than that of the monocular baseline.

Table 2. Ablation studies on the KITTI validation set. BEV in the table stands for BEV feature imitation in Sect. 3.2. FV-Global and FV-Pixel denote FV global-level feature imitation and FV pixel-level feature imitation in Sect. 3.3, respectively.

Group	BEV	FV-Global	FV-Pixel	$AP_{3D}@IOU = 0.7$			$AP_{BEV}@IOU = 0.7$		
				Easy	Mod	Hard	Easy	Mod	Hard
a				21.10	**15.50**	13.14	30.57	22.50	19.68
b	✓			25.16	**17.57**	15.04	34.87	24.41	21.40
c		✓		22.56	**16.19**	14.27	31.53	22.95	20.78
d			✓	22.93	**16.06**	14.28	31.88	22.81	19.99
e		✓	✓	23.14	**16.34**	14.33	32.65	23.39	21.02
f	✓	✓	✓	25.58	**17.88**	15.29	34.06	24.66	21.63

The performance of the LiDAR BEV teacher model is higher than that of the LiDAR FV teacher model. It shows that the different ways of encoding the input data into BEV feature maps will cause a large gap in the final results. While both the two LiDAR teacher networks can generate BEV feature maps, we believe that BEV feature maps generated by the LiDAR BEV teacher are more accurate than those generated by the LiDAR FV teacher, and this is also the reason why we use the LiDAR raw points branch to be our BEV teacher model instead of the RGBD branch.

Ablation Studies. Table 2 shows the ablation study results of our proposed methods of the car category on the KITTI validation set. Compared with the baseline, our final method improves 4.48, 2.38, and 2.15 on the 3D AP of easy, moderate, and hard settings, respectively. Furthermore, it can be clearly seen that each strategy we use is helpful for performance improvement. It's worth noting that feature imitation in BEV space achieves higher gains than feature imitation in FV space. We believe the reason is that the FV feature maps are relatively advanced in the detection pipeline because our approach detects objects from BEV feature maps; in addition, we have added pixel-level depth supervision when training the network. So the improvement brought by the FV feature imitation is relatively tiny.

Results Visualization. In order to intuitively observe the changes of monocular BEV features after imitating LiDAR features, we visualize BEV features of the monocular detection network in Fig. 4. From the two visualized scenes, we can observe that the intensity in most of the background regions on the BEV feature maps has decrease after the guidance of LiDAR features. The decrease is noticeable when comparing the area in the red boxes of the LiDAR-guided features and baseline features. This can significantly reduce false detections. Comparing the foreground area of the baseline features and the LiDAR-guided features (The area inside the green boxes on the BEV feature maps), we can see that the BEV feature maps output by the LiDAR guided model is more geometrically accurate than the monocular baseline.

Table 3. Comparison with the state-of-the-art methods on the KITTI test set on car category with IOU thresh 0.7. Extra in the header represents extra data used when training the model.

Model	Published	Extra	$AP_{3D}@IOU = 0.7$			$AP_{BEV}@IOU = 0.7$		
			Easy	**Mod**	Hard	Easy	Mod	Hard
ImVoxelNet [21]	WACV2022	None	17.15	10.97	9.15	25.19	16.37	13.58
MonoDLE [14]	CVPR2021	None	17.23	12.26	10.29	24.79	18.89	16.00
MonoRUn [2]	CVPR2021	None	19.65	12.30	10.58	27.94	17.34	15.24
PCT [23]	NIPS2021	None	21.00	13.37	11.31	29.65	19.03	15.92
CaDDN [19]	CVPR2021	LiDAR	19.17	13.41	11.46	27.94	18.91	17.19
AutoShape [12]	ICCV2021	LiDAR	22.47	14.17	11.36	30.66	20.08	15.59
SGM3D [33]	Arxiv2022	Stereo	22.46	14.65	12.97	31.49	21.37	18.43
MonoDistill [4]	ICLR2022	LiDAR	22.97	16.03	13.60	31.87	22.59	19.72
Ours	–	LiDAR	**20.79**	**14.33**	**12.81**	**29.15**	**20.45**	**17.76**

Comparison with State-of-the-Art Methods. The comparison of our proposed approach with the other published monocular methods on the KITTI test is reported in Table 3. As the table shows, our method performs better than most recent works, and obtains improvements on the easy, moderate, and hard settings compared with CaDDN [19], which is similar to our baseline model in network structure. Our method achieves roughly comparable results with SGM3D [33] which is a latest work by using stereo detection models to guide monocular 3D object detection.

5   Conclusion

This paper proposed a novel 3D monocular detection approach using LiDAR detection models to guide monocular detection models from BEV and FV space. We utilize a voxel-based LiDAR 3D detection model as our LiDAR BEV teacher model, taking raw point clouds as input. On the other hand, we utilize a model with the same architecture as our monocular baseline model to be our FV LiDAR teacher model, but it takes RGBD images as input. Our proposed method improves 3D detection performance without modifying the monocular model structure or affecting the inference speed of the baseline. Our method achieves good performance on the KITTI validation and test set.

References

1. OpenPCDet. https://github.com/open-mmlab/OpenPCDet. Accessed 4 May 2022
2. Chen, H., Huang, Y., Tian, W., Gao, Z., Xiong, L.: MonoRUn: monocular 3D object detection by reconstruction and uncertainty propagation. In: Proceedings of the IEEE/CVF Conference on Computer Vision and Pattern Recognition, pp. 10379–10388 (2021)

3. Chen, X., Ma, H., Wan, J., Li, B., Xia, T.: Multi-view 3D object detection network for autonomous driving. In: Proceedings of the IEEE Conference on Computer Vision and Pattern Recognition, pp. 1907–1915 (2017)
4. Chong, Z., et al.: Monodistill: learning spatial features for monocular 3D object detection. arXiv preprint arXiv:2201.10830 (2022)
5. Fu, H., Gong, M., Wang, C., Batmanghelich, K., Tao, D.: Deep ordinal regression network for monocular depth estimation. In: Proceedings of the IEEE Conference on Computer Vision and Pattern Recognition, pp. 2002–2011 (2018)
6. Geiger, A., Lenz, P., Stiller, C., Urtasun, R.: Vision meets robotics: the Kitti dataset. Int. J. Robot. Res. **32**(11), 1231–1237 (2013)
7. Guo, X., Shi, S., Wang, X., Li, H.:LIGA-Stereo: learning lidar geometry aware representations for stereo-based 3D detector. In: Proceedings of the IEEE/CVF International Conference on Computer Vision, pp. 3153–3163 (2021)
8. Huang, J., Huang, G., Zhu, Z., Du, D.: Bevdet: high-performance multi-camera 3d object detection in bird-eye-view. arXiv preprint arXiv:2112.11790 (2021)
9. Lang, A.H., Vora, S., Caesar, H., Zhou, L., Yang, J., Beijbom, O.: Pointpillars: fast encoders for object detection from point clouds. In: Proceedings of the IEEE/CVF Conference on Computer Vision and Pattern Recognition, pp. 12697–12705 (2019)
10. Li, Z., et al.: BEVFormer: learning bird's-eye-view representation from multi-camera images via spatiotemporal transformers. arXiv preprint arXiv:2203.17270 (2022)
11. Liu, Z., Wu, Z., Tóth, R.: Smoke: single-stage monocular 3d object detection via keypoint estimation. In: Proceedings of the IEEE/CVF Conference on Computer Vision and Pattern Recognition Workshops, pp. 996–997 (2020)
12. Liu, Z., Zhou, D., Lu, F., Fang, J., Zhang, L.: Autoshape: real-time shape-aware monocular 3D object detection. In: Proceedings of the IEEE/CVF International Conference on Computer Vision, pp. 15641–15650 (2021)
13. Ma, X., Ouyang, W., Simonelli, A., Ricci, E.: 3D object detection from images for autonomous driving: a survey. arXiv preprint arXiv:2202.02980 (2022)
14. Ma, X., et al.: Delving into localization errors for monocular 3D object detection. In: Proceedings of the IEEE/CVF Conference on Computer Vision and Pattern Recognition, pp. 4721–4730 (2021)
15. Mousavian, A., Anguelov, D., Flynn, J., Kosecka, J.: 3D bounding box estimation using deep learning and geometry. In: Proceedings of the IEEE Conference on Computer Vision and Pattern Recognition, pp. 7074–7082 (2017)
16. Park, D., Ambrus, R., Guizilini, V., Li, J., Gaidon, A.: Is pseudo-lidar needed for monocular 3D object detection? In: Proceedings of the IEEE/CVF International Conference on Computer Vision, pp. 3142–3152 (2021)
17. Philion, J., Fidler, S.: Lift, splat, shoot: encoding images from arbitrary camera rigs by implicitly unprojecting to 3D. In: Vedaldi, A., Bischof, H., Brox, T., Frahm, J.-M. (eds.) ECCV 2020. LNCS, vol. 12359, pp. 194–210. Springer, Cham (2020). https://doi.org/10.1007/978-3-030-58568-6_12
18. Qin, Z., Wang, J., Lu, Y.: MonoGRNet: a geometric reasoning network for monocular 3d object localization. In: Proceedings of the AAAI Conference on Artificial Intelligence, vol. 33, pp. 8851–8858 (2019)
19. Reading, C., Harakeh, A., Chae, J., Waslander, S.L.: Categorical depth distribution network for monocular 3D object detection. In: Proceedings of the IEEE/CVF Conference on Computer Vision and Pattern Recognition, pp. 8555–8564 (2021)
20. Roddick, T., Kendall, A., Cipolla, R.: Orthographic feature transform for monocular 3D object detection. arXiv preprint arXiv:1811.08188 (2018)

21. Rukhovich, D., Vorontsova, A., Konushin, A.: ImVoxelNet: image to voxels projection for monocular and multi-view general-purpose 3d object detection. In: Proceedings of the IEEE/CVF Winter Conference on Applications of Computer Vision, pp. 2397–2406 (2022)
22. Wang, H., Sridhar, S., Huang, J., Valentin, J., Song, S., Guibas, L.J.: Normalized object coordinate space for category-level 6D object pose and size estimation. In: Proceedings of the IEEE/CVF Conference on Computer Vision and Pattern Recognition, pp. 2642–2651 (2019)
23. Wang, L., et al.: Progressive coordinate transforms for monocular 3D object detection. Adv. Neural Inf. Process. Syst. **34** (2021)
24. Wang, T., Zhu, X., Pang, J., Lin, D.: FCOS3D: fully convolutional one-stage monocular 3d object detection. In: Proceedings of the IEEE/CVF International Conference on Computer Vision, pp. 913–922 (2021)
25. Wang, Y., Chao, W.L., Garg, D., Hariharan, B., Campbell, M., Weinberger, K.Q.: Pseudo-lidar from visual depth estimation: bridging the gap in 3D object detection for autonomous driving. In: Proceedings of the IEEE/CVF Conference on Computer Vision and Pattern Recognition, pp. 8445–8453 (2019)
26. Weng, Y., et al.: CAPTRA: category-level pose tracking for rigid and articulated objects from point clouds. In: Proceedings of the IEEE/CVF International Conference on Computer Vision, pp. 13209–13218 (2021)
27. Xie, E., et al.: M^2bev: Multi-camera joint 3d detection and segmentation with unified birds-eye view representation. arXiv preprint arXiv:2204.05088 (2022)
28. Yan, Y., Mao, Y., Li, B.: Second: sparsely embedded convolutional detection. Sensors **18**(10), 3337 (2018)
29. Yin, T., Zhou, X., Krahenbuhl, P.: Center-based 3d object detection and tracking. In: Proceedings of the IEEE/CVF Conference on Computer Vision and Pattern Recognition, pp. 11784–11793 (2021)
30. You, Y., et al.: Pseudo-lidar++: accurate depth for 3d object detection in autonomous driving. arXiv preprint arXiv:1906.06310 (2019)
31. Zhou, X., Wang, D., Krähenbühl, P.: Objects as points. arXiv preprint arXiv:1904.07850 (2019)
32. Zhou, Y., Tuzel, O.: Voxelnet: end-to-end learning for point cloud based 3d object detection. In: Proceedings of the IEEE Conference on Computer Vision and Pattern Recognition, pp. 4490–4499 (2018)
33. Zhou, Z., et al.: SGM3D: stereo guided monocular 3d object detection. arXiv preprint arXiv:2112.01914 (2021)

Dual Attention-Guided Network for Anchor-Free Apple Instance Segmentation in Complex Environments

Yunshen Pei[1] , Yi Ding[2] , Xuesen Zhu[1] , Liuyang Yan[1] ,
and Keyang Cheng[1(✉)]

[1] School of Computer Science and Communication Engineering, Jiangsu University,
Zhenjiang 212013, China
kycheng@ujs.edu.cn
[2] School of Electronic Science and Engineering, Nanjing University,
Nanjing 210023, China
181180019@smail.nju.edu.cn

Abstract. Apple segmentation is an important part of the automatic picking system of apple plantation. However, due to the complexity of apple orchard environments, including light change, branch and leaf occlusion and fruit overlap, the segmentation accuracy of the existing methods is limited, which affects the large-scale application of the automatic picking system. To solve these problems, this paper proposes a new apple instance segmentation method based on a dual attention-guided network. Firstly, the image is preprocessed by the Image Correction Module (ICM) to improve the robustness of the network to the natural environment. Secondly, the Multi-Scale Enhanced Fusion Feature Pyramid Network (MSEF-FPN) is used as the feature extraction module to enhance the ability of image feature extraction, so as to reduce the interference of complex background on apple instance segmentation results without increasing the amount of calculation. Then, a new Dual Attention-Guided Mask (DAGM) branch is added to focus on the pixels of irregular occlusion and overlapping objects, and accurate pixel-level mask segmentation is carried out in the detection rectangular bounding box. Finally, this study carried out instance segmentation experiments on apples with different lighting conditions and different occlusion. The test results show that the model proposed in this paper has excellent detection accuracy, robustness and real-time, and has important reference value for solving the problem of accurate fruit recognition in complex environments.

Keywords: Apple segmentation · Complex environments · Feature extraction

1 Introduce

With the wide application of deep learning in the field of computer vision [1,2], increasingly researchers are engaged in intelligent agriculture-related work.

S. Yu et al. (Eds.): PRCV 2022, LNCS 13537, pp. 533–545, 2022.
https://doi.org/10.1007/978-3-031-18916-6_43

At present, practical problems in the agricultural production processes (such as pest prediction and monitoring, automatic harvest, etc.) have been solved by many network model methods. However, with the improvement in operating efficiency and upgrading of agricultural equipment, the requirements for real-time performance and accuracy of operating machines have also gradually increased [3–5], and the requirements for agricultural equipment vision system are also higher and higher [6,7]. In the complex orchard environment, the results of target fruit detection [8,9] and segmentation [10–12] limit the performance of the visual system. Such as apple density (Fig. 1)(a)), illumination angle change (Fig. 1)(b)), branch and leaf occlusion (Fig. 1)(c)) and overlapping apple (Fig. 1)(d)) will have a certain influence on target detection, which brings great difficulties and challenges to the accurate recognition of fruits.

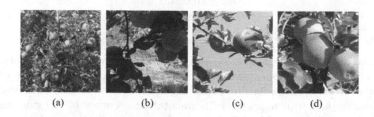

(a)   (b)   (c)   (d)

Fig. 1. Illustration of our framework. (a) Apple density; (b) illumination angle change; (c) branch and leaf occlusion; (d) overlapping apple

To address these deficiencies while considering the above factors, an effective and accurate Apple Instance Segmentation method based on a dual attention-guided network is proposed to improve the segmentation accuracy of apple in complex environments. More precisely, the main contributions of this paper are summarized as follows:

(1) Aiming at the problems of illumination, occlusion and overlap in a complex environments, an anchor-free apple instance segmentation method based on dual attention-guided.
(2) An adaptive Image Correction Module (ICM) is introduced to enhance the robustness of the image to natural illumination and contrast changes.
(3) The Multi-Scale Enhancement Fusion (MSEF) module is introduced into the feature pyramid network (FPN). Its purpose is to enhance the feature extraction ability of the image and reduce the interference of complex background to apple detection results without increasing the amount of calculation.
(4) To improve the segmentation accuracy of overlapping and occluding apples in complex environments, a new branch of Dual Attention-Guided Mask (DAGM) is added to deal with fruit occlusion and overlap.

2   Related Works

Traditional machine learning methods have made important contributions to fruit detection and segmentation [13–15]. A yield prediction strategy based on texture, fruit color and edge shape was proposed, and the recognition rate of green apples under natural light was close to 95% [16]. Tian used RGB spatial information to locate the center and radius of the apple, and combined with depth image information to match the target area [17]. These methods are not sufficient to identify overlapping or clustered fruits. To solve the above problems, a robust apple image segmentation algorithm based on a fuzzy reasoning system, which improves the generalization ability of segmentation [18]. However, due to the lack of in-depth analysis of image features, the above methods are usually poor in robustness and adaptability in complex environments with occlusion and overlapping.

With the rapid development of deep learning theory, an increasing number of deep learning methods have been proposed for agricultural fruit detection [19–24]. Liu used the improved single-stage detector Yolo-V3 to conduct tomato positioning detection in complex scenes [25]. Jia combined DenseNet and ResNet as the feature extraction backbone of the original model to improve the Mask R-CNN, greatly improving the identification accuracy of Apple in the overlapping and occlusion environments [4]. Compared with traditional visual methods, the accuracy and applicability of the recognition model based on deep learning have been greatly improved. However, these methods usually require many computing and storage resources, which will seriously affect the segmentation speed and operation stability of agricultural equipment in practical applications.

3   Methods

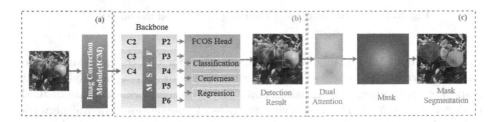

Fig. 2. Illustration of our framework. (a) Image Correction Module (ICM); (b) Anchor-free Detection Module; (c) Dual Attention-guided Mask (DAGM) Module

To improve the accuracy and efficiency of apple instance segmentation in complex environments, an accurate and efficient anchor-free apple instance segmentation method based on dual attention-guided network. The framework of our method is shown in Fig. 2, which includes three parts: (a) Image Correction Module (ICM); (b) Anchor-free Detection Module; (c) Dual Attention-guided Mask (DAGM) Module.

3.1   Image Correction Module (ICM)

To cope with the challenge of illumination change, ICM is used to transform images under different illuminations into similar illumination. The module follows IBNNet [26] and realizes image adaptive correction by constructing an encoding and decoding network (as shown in Fig. 3). First, the convolutional neural network is used to extract image features, and then deconvolution is used as a decoder for resampling to restore and correct the image with the same size as the input image. In the deconvolution process, network parameters are trained to ensure that the corrected images have similar illumination intensities.

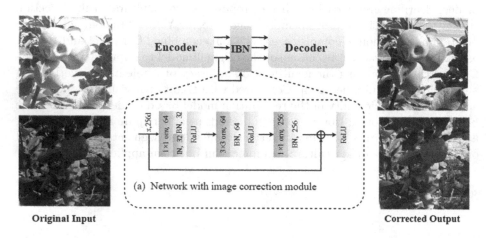

Original Input   Corrected Output

Fig. 3. Schematic diagram of the image correction module (ICM).

ICM is built on a trainable network, allowing for end-to-end training and adaptive correction of images rather than increasing or decreasing brightness at a specific rate during data enhancement. The basic network structure of ICM is shown in Fig. 3(a). The underlying features of convolutional neural network reflect the appearance features of objects, such as texture and color, while the high-level features reflect the semantic information of the target. Therefore, by adding image normalization in the lower layer of the network, the distribution of image data under different illumination can be adjusted to a similar area, increasing the adaptability of the network to illumination, and thus reducing the influence of illumination changes.

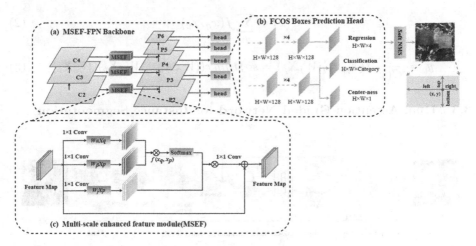

Fig. 4. Architecture of bounding box pre detection. (a) MSEF-FPN Backbone; (b) FCOS Boxes Prediction Head; (c) Multi-scale enhanced feature module (MSEF).

3.2 Feature Extraction MSFM-FPN Detection Network

Our model uses FCOS (shown in Fig. 4) as the basic detection model and improves it. The introduction of MSFM into the lateral connection in FPN solves some defects of FPN. For example, direct fusion of these features may be reduce the representation of multi-scale features due to the inconsistency of semantic information. In addition, in the process of picking, due to the interference of shooting distance, occlusion, or overlap, the proportion of the target in the image is insignificant. After the deep convolution operation on the image, the target feature map will be changed to a small extent, which greatly reduces the spatial information contained in the feature map, thus reducing the detection accuracy. Therefore, to gather multi-scale features and maintain a high-resolution representation in the process of convolution, MSFM is introduced at the lateral connection of FPN to improve the feature extraction capability of the image. Figure 4(c) shows the overall content of MSFM after improvement.

First, we use two weight transformations $W_\alpha X_q$ And $W_\beta X_p$ to reduce the number of channels and then reduce the amount of calculation. Multiply the two output matrices (where $W_\alpha X_q$ will be transposed), calculate the similarity, and then perform the softmax operation to obtain the position attention, that is, the normalized correlation between each pixel in the current feature map and all other position pixels. Finally, by multiplying with $W_j X_p$ matrix, the position attention mechanism is applied to the corresponding position of each feature graph of all channels. Restore the output channel through 1×1 convolution to ensure that the input and output scales are exactly the same. The corresponding nonlocal operations are shown in Eqs. (1), (2) and (3).

$$f(x_q, x_p) = e^{(W_\alpha X_q)^T (W_\beta X_p)} \tag{1}$$

$$C(x) = \sum_{\forall p} f(x_q, x_p) \tag{2}$$

$$y_q = \frac{1}{C(x)} f(x_q, x_p)(W_j X_p) = softmax((W_\alpha X_q)^T (W_\beta X_p)(W_j X_p)) \tag{3}$$

3.3   Dual Attention-Guided Netword for Instance Segmentation

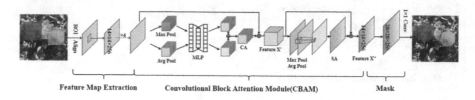

Feature Map Extraction   Convolutional Block Attention Module(CBAM)   Mask

Fig. 5. The architecture of DAGM.

Considering that fruits are located in complex environments, many interference factors greatly reduce the segmentation effect of the model. Therefore, we designed a Dual Attention-guided Mask module (DAGM), as shown in Fig. 5. Compared with the general segmentation framework, this method has obvious advantages in the segmentation of small objects with serious occlusion or overlap. At the front-end of the framework, the convolutional network is used for feature extraction, and at the back end, conditional/Markov random fields are used to optimize the front end output, and the segmentation results are obtained.

The DAGM branch applies the boundary box predicted by FCOS to further predict the segmentation mask of each region of interest (ROI). Firstly, the predicted ROI is distributed to different FPN feature layers according to the resolution, and ROI Align is used for feature alignment. This is similar to using the Mask R-CNN to predict the segmentaion mask. However, the relationship between the original image resolution and the ROI size must be considered in order to reasonably allocate the ROI to the feature layer of the corresponding resolution (considering the FPN multi-scale strategy). Secondly, after extracting the features in ROI with 14×14 resolution in ROI Align, these features are transmitted to Convolutional Block Attention (CBA) network. Specifically, the characteristics are divided into maximum pool and average pool to obtain two groups $1 \times 1 \times C$ characteristic matrix and transfer it to MLP, and then add the two output characteristic matrices to obtain the weight information Channel Attention (CA) of different channels. The calculation method is shown in Eq. (4). After CA is multiplied by the input characteristic matrix, the characteristic matrix combined with channel attention is obtained, as shown by Feature X' in Fig. 5. Then the feature matrix fused with channel attention is passed through $W \times H \times 1$, and condense the two feature maps in the depth direction, and then perform convolution operation to obtain spatial attention (SA) integrating spatial weight information. The calculation method is shown in Eq. (5).

In Eq. (5), $f^{7\times7}$ indicates that the size of the pooling kernel is 7×7. Finally, SA is multiplied by feature X' to obtain the feature map Refined Feature X", which combines channel andspatial attention information.

$$CA(X) = \Sigma(MLP(maxPool(X)) + MLP(avgPool(X))) \tag{4}$$

$$SA(X) = \sigma(f^{7\times7}([maxPool(X'); avgPool(X')])) \tag{5}$$

Then, the obtained enhanced spatial attention feature map is up sampled to generate a feature map with a resolution of 28×28. The 1×1 convolution kernel is used to generate the mask of instance segmentation.

3.4   The Loss Functions

The overall loss function L_{total} (as shown in Eq. (6)) of the model is composed of L_{cls}, L_{reg}, L_{center} and L_{mask}, where L_{cls} is the classification loss, L_{center} is the center-ness loss, L_{reg} is the box regression loss, and L_{mask} is the mask loss using the average binary crossentropy loss

$$L_{total} = \frac{1}{N_{pos}} \sum_{x,y} L_{cls}(p_{x,y}, p^*_{x,y}) + \frac{\lambda}{N_{pos}} \sum_{x,y} p^*_x L_{reg}(d_{x,y}, d^*_{x,y})$$
$$+ \frac{\beta}{N_{pos}} \sum_{x,y} p^*_{x,y} L_{center}(center_{x,y}, center^*_{x,y}) + L_{mask}(s_x, s^*_x) \tag{6}$$

In Eq. (6), $p_{x,y}$, $d_{x,y}$ and $center_{x,y}$ are the predicted values of classification branch, regression branch and centrality branch at the spatial position (x, y). $p^*_{x,y}$, $d^*_{x,y}$ and $center^*_{x,y}$ correspond to the training target at the spatial position (x, y). Among the three loss items, L_{reg} and L_{center} are only for positive samples, N_{pos} is the number of positive samples, and λ and β are the balance coefficients of each loss item.

The classification loss Lcls in Eq. (6) is shown in Eqs. (7) and (8):

$$L_{cls}(p_{x,y}, p^*_{x,y}) = -\alpha_t(1 - p^t_{x,y})^\gamma log(p^t_{x,y}) \tag{7}$$

$$p^t_{x,y} = \begin{cases} p_{x,y} & if \quad p^*_{x,y} = 1 \\ 1 - p_{x,y} & otherwise, \end{cases} \qquad \alpha_t = \begin{cases} \alpha & if \quad p^*_{x,y} = 1 \\ 1 - \alpha & otherwise \end{cases} \tag{8}$$

where α Responsible for balancing the importance between positive and negative samples, γ responsible for adjusting the rate of weight reduction of simple samples.

The regression loss L_{reg} in Eq. (6) is shown in Eq. (9):

$$L_{reg}(d_{x,y}, d^*_{x,y}) = -ln\frac{Intersection(d_{x,y}, d^*_{x,y})}{Union(d_{x,y}, d^*_{x,y})} \tag{9}$$

where $intersection(d_{x,y}, dx, y^*)$ and $Union(d_{x,y}, d^*_{x,y})$ are the intersection area and combined area between the prediction frame and the real frame respectively.

The center-ness loss L_{center} in Eq. (6) is shown in Eq. (10):

$$L_{center}(center_{x,y}, center^*_{x,y}) = -(center_{x,y}log(center^*_{x,y}) \\ +(1 - center_{x,y})log(1 - center^*_{x,y})) \tag{10}$$

The mask loss L_{mask} in Eq. (6) is shown in Eq. (11):

$$L_{mask} = \sum_x -[s^*_x log(s_x) + (1 - s^*_x)log(1 - s_x)] \tag{11}$$

where s_x is the probability that the x-th pixel belongs to the target pixel and s^*_x is the probability that the x-th pixel belongs to the real target pixel.

4   Experiment

4.1   Dataset and Evaluation Metrics

Apple Dataset Acquisition. In this paper, we choose the open dataset Fuji SFM dataset, and make appropriate modifications to the data set to cooperate with the experiment of this paper. We select 400 appropriate Apple images from 582 images (the resolution of each image is 5184 × 3456), then cut 15 images with the resolution of 1024 × 1024 from each image, and get 6000 images with the resolution of 1024 × 1024. Then select the appropriate 1400 images from the 6000 images as the final data set. Finally, in order to make the network model have high accuracy and robustness, we use the mainstream image annotation tool labelme to annotate and store the data set manually. Figure 1 shows some images in the dataset.

Evaluation Metrics. We follow the internationally unified measurement standards and use the AP (average precision), AP_{50} (AP for IoU threshold 50%) and AP_{75}(AP for IoU threshold 75%) to measure the quality of the model.

4.2   Implementation Details

In the training stage, we trained a total of 50 epochs with 200 steps each. And the initial learning rate is 0.01. The Network parameters are also optimized using adaptive moment estimation (Adam). The momentum, as well as decay weights, are 0.9 and 0.0001, respectively.

4.3   Comparative Experiments

In this study, apple fruits with different occlusion and different lighting conditions were detected on the computer workstation. The detection effects of Mask R-CNN, SOLO [27], PolarMask [28] and our method under the above conditions were compared, and the performance of the algorithm was evaluated with AP, AP_{50}, AP_{75}.

Comparison Experiment of Overlapping and Branch and Leaf Occlusion. In the natural environment, there will be overlapping fruits and fruits covered by branches and branches. The contour information of the fruit part is lost, which increases the difficulty of fruit detection. Therefore, this study tested the overlapping of fruits and different degrees of branch and stem shielding. The statistical results are shown in Fig. 6 and Table 1.

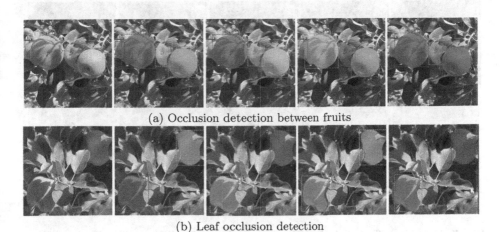

(a) Occlusion detection between fruits

(b) Leaf occlusion detection

Fig. 6. Detection effect of 4 algorithms on different occluded apples. (From left to right, there are pictures of the detection results of Original Image, our Model, Mask R-CNN, SOLO and Polar Mask)

Table 1. Experimental results of 4 algorithms for images with different occluded apples.

Occlusion category	Algorithm	AP	AP_{50}	AP_{75}
Apple overlap	Mask R-CNN	83.2	72.1	64.7
	SOLO	86.3	75.7	67.8
	PolarMask	86.8	75.5	68.2
	Ours	**88.1**	**77.2**	**69.3**
Leaf occlusion	Mask R-CNN	81.2	70.3	62.7
	SOLO	83.6	74.9	66.8
	PolarMask	84.8	74.7	64.2
	Ours	**85.1**	**76.8**	**68.6**

As can be seen from Table 1, in the apple overlapping scenario, the AP value of our algorithm is 4.9%, 5.1% and 4.6% higher than that of Mask R-CNN respectively. The AP value of the latter two algorithms in both cases is lower than that of the algorithm in this paper. From the comprehensive results, our algorithm can be competent in the detection of different occlusion and overlap.

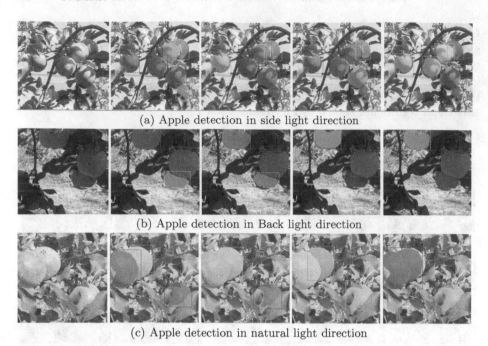

(a) Apple detection in side light direction

(b) Apple detection in Back light direction

(c) Apple detection in natural light direction

Fig. 7. Detection effect of 4 algorithms on apples under different illumination. (From left to right, there are pictures of the detection results of Original Image, our Model, Mask R-CNN, SOLO and Polar Mask)

Comparison Experiment with Different Light. Under the conditions of natural light, back light and side light, the fruit will be brighter or darker. And due to the great influence of dense apple samples, dense apple samples will not be considered when selecting images here.The statistical results are shown in Fig. 7 and Table 2.

As can be seen from Table 2, the AP value of the improved model in three different scenarios is higher than that of the other three algorithms. From different scenes, the four algorithms perform best in side light, while the model performs worst in backlight. Because the texture of the apple is clear under side light, the surface illumination intensity is uniform, and the backlight condition will cause some interference to the detection. Overall, our model can adapt to the influence of lighting conditions on apple surface color, texture features and contour, and can effectively detect apples in complex images.

4.4 Ablation Experiment

In this section, in order to clarify the impact of image correction module (ICM) and multi-scale enhaned fusion feature pyramid module (MSEF-FPN) on the performance of the model, ablation research is carried out, and the role of each module is analyzed in detail. We gradually introduced our module, tested the AP

Table 2. Experimental results of 4 algorithms for apples under different illumination.

Illumination angles	Algorithm	AP	AP_{50}	AP_{75}
Side light	Mask R-CNN	88.9	80.2	72.7
	SOLO	90.2	80.9	73.8
	PolarMask	89.8	80.4	73.5
	Ours	**91.8**	**82.3**	**75.6**
Back light	Mask R-CNN	85.3	78.1	69.3
	SOLO	88.6	79.4	71.8
	PolarMask	87.9	78.8	71.7
	Ours	**90.0**	**80.2**	**73.6**
Natural light	Mask R-CNN	86.8	79.6	71.8
	SOLO	88.9	80.6	72.3
	PolarMask	88.6	80.8	72.6
	Ours	**90.2**	**81.8**	**73.8**

value of each combined model, and obtained the experimental results shown in Table 3. The working mode of each module in the actual environment is discussed below.

As shown in Table 3, removing ICM will reduce the AP of the model by 1.3%. This shows that by adding the image correction module, the images under different lighting can be normalized to similar data distribution, which is equivalent to increasing the robustness of the model to complex environmental lighting. When MSEF-FPN is removed, the AP of the model decreases by 1.5%. This shows that adding MSEF-FPN can enhance the feature extraction ability of the image and reduce the interference of complex background to Apple detection results without increasing the amount of calculation.

Table 3. The results of Ablation experiments.

Method	ICM	MSEF-FPN	AP	AP_{50}	AP_{75}
Ours			85.3	80.1	74.0
Ours	✓		86.6	81.2	75.3
Ours		✓	86.8	82.0	76.0
Ours	✓	✓	**88.4**	**84.2**	**77.3**

5   Conclusion

In this paper, we propose a new instance segmentation method based on dual attention-guided network for Apple instance segmentation in complex environments, which solves the constraints of illumination, occlusion and overlapping changes in environments, so as to realize the visual guidance of automatic picking. The CNN model with an image correction module and a instance segmentation module is constructed to meet the challenges of illumination, occlusion and overlap in complex environments. Experimental results show that the proposed algorithm performs better performance than the previous algorithms in instance segmentation. This enables the model to be deployed on the apple picking robot detector for automatic Apple detection.

References

1. Saleem, M.H., Potgieter, J., Arif, K.M.: Automation in agriculture by machine and deep learning techniques: a review of recent developments. Precis. Agric. **22**(6), 2053–2091 (2021)
2. Maheswari, P., Raja, P., Apolo-Apolo, O.E., et al.: Intelligent fruit yield estimation for orchards using deep learning based semantic segmentation techniques-a review. Front. Plant Sci. **12**, 1247 (2021)
3. Bac, C.W., van Henten, E.J., Hemming, J., Edan, Y.: Harvesting robots for high-value crops: state-of-the-art review and challenges ahead. J. Field Rob. **31**(6), 888–911 (2014)
4. Jia, W., Tian, Y., Luo, R., Zhang, Z., Lian, J., Zheng, Y.: Detection and segmentation of overlapped fruits based on optimized mask R-CNN application in apple harvesting robot. Comput. Electron. Agric. **172**, 105380 (2020)
5. Jia, W., Wang, Z., Zhang, Z., Yang, X., Hou, S., Zheng, Y.: A fast and efficient green apple object detection model based on Foveabox. J. King Saud Univ. Comput. Inform. Sci. (2022)
6. Patrício, D.I., Rieder, R.: Computer vision and artificial intelligence in precision agriculture for grain crops: a systematic review. Comput. Electron. Agric. **153**, 69–81 (2018)
7. Chen, H., Sun, K., Tian, Z., et al.: BlendMask: top-down meets bottom-up for instance segmentation. In: Proceedings of the IEEE/CVF Conference on Computer Vision and Pattern Recognition, pp. 8573–8581 (2020)
8. Tang, Y., et al.: Recognition and localization methods for vision-based fruit picking robots: a review. Front. Plant Sci. **11** (2020)
9. Zhao, Z.-Q., Zheng, P., Xu, S.-T., Wu, X.: Object detection with deep learning: a review. IEEE Trans. Neural Netw. Learn. Syst. **30**(11), 3212–3232 (2019)
10. Wang, Z., Jia, W., Mou, S., et al.: KDC: a green apple segmentation method. Spectrosc. Spectral Anal. **41**(9), 2980–2988 (2021)
11. Vasconez, J.P., Delpiano, J., Vougioukas, S., Auat Cheein, F.: Comparison of convolutional neural networks in fruit detection and counting: a comprehensive evaluation. Comput. Electron. Agric. **173**, 105348 (2020)
12. Minaee, S., Boykov, Y.Y., Porikli, F., et al.: Image segmentation using deep learning: a survey. IEEE Trans. Pattern Anal. Mach. Intell. https://doi.org/10.1109/TPAMI.2021.3059968 (2021)
13. Lv, J., Wang, F., Xu, L., Ma, Z., Yang, B.: A segmentation method of bagged green apple image. Sci. Hortic. **246**, 411–417 (2019)
14. Sun, S., Jiang, M., He, D., Long, Y., Song, H.: Recognition of green apples in an orchard environment by combining the GrabCut model and Ncut algorithm. Biosyst. Eng. **187**, 201–213 (2019)

15. Ji, W., Gao, X., Xu, B.O., Chen, G.Y., Zhao, D.: Target recognition method of green pepper harvesting robot based on manifold ranking. Comput. Electron. Agric. **177**, 105663 (2020). https://doi.org/10.1016/j.compag.2020.105663
16. Linker, R., Cohen, O., Naor, A.: Determination of the number of green apples in RGB images recorded in orchards. Comput. Electron. Agric. **81**, 45–57 (2012)
17. Tian, Y., et al.: Fast recognition and location of target fruit based on depth information. IEEE Access **7**, 170553–170563 (2019)
18. Ahmad, M.T., Greenspan, M., Asif, M., et al.: Robust apple segmentation using fuzzy logic. In: 5th International Multi-Topic ICT Conference IEEE, pp. 1–5 (2018)
19. Bargoti, S., Underwood, J.P.: Image segmentation for fruit detection and yield estimation in apple orchards. J. Field Rob. **34**(6), 1039–1060 (2017)
20. Qi, C.R., Su, H., Mo, K., et al.: Pointnet: deep learning on point sets for 3d classification and segmentation. In: Proceedings of the IEEE Conference on Computer Vision and Pattern Recognition, pp. 652–660 (2017)
21. Sultana, F., Sufian, A., Dutta, P.: Evolution of image segmentation using deep convolutional neural network: a survey. Knowl. Based Syst. 106062 (2020)
22. Li, J., Liu, Z.M., Li, C., et al.: Improved artificial immune system algorithm for Type-2 fuzzy flexible job shop scheduling problem. IEEE Trans. Fuzzy Syst. (2020)
23. Jia, W., Zhang, Z., Shao, W., et al.: RS-Net: robust segmentation of green overlapped apples. Precis. Agric. (2021). https://doi.org/10.1007/s11119-021-09846-3
24. Anvari, F., Lakens, D.: Using anchor-based methods to determine the smallest effect size of interest. J. Exp. Soc. Psychol. **96**, 104159 (2021)
25. Liu, G., Nouaze, J.C., Touko Mbouembe, P.L., Kim, J.H.: YOLO-tomato: a robust algorithm for tomato detection based on YOLOv3. Sensors **20**(7), 2145 (2020). https://doi.org/10.3390/s20072145
26. Pan, X., Luo, P., Shi, J., Tang, X.: Two at once: enhancing learning and generalization capacities via ibn-net. In: Proceedings of the European Conference on Computer Vision (ECCV), pp. 464–479 (2018)
27. Wang, X., Kong, T., Shen, C., Jiang, Y., Li, L.: Solo: segmenting objects by locations. arXiv preprint arXiv:1912.04488 (2019)
28. Xie, E., et al.: Polarmask: single shot instance segmentation with polar representation. arXiv preprint arXiv:1909.13226 (2019)

Attention-Aware Feature Distillation for Object Detection in Decompressed Images

Bingqian Liu[1], Zhou Zheng[1], and Wenhao Mo[2]([✉])

[1] State Grid Fujian Electric Power Research Institute, Fuzhou, China
[2] China Electric Power Research Institute, Beijing, China
mowenhao@epri.sgcc.com.cn

Abstract. Recently, many object detection methods based on deep learning have achieved remarkable performance. Most of them are mainly trained on high-quality images. Due to the distribution difference between the high-quality training data and the data encountered during deployments, the performance of the detection model decreases rapidly on corrupted images (e.g., the decompressed images). In this paper, we propose an attention-aware feature distillation method to improve the performance of the detector on decompressed images. Conventional methods used l_2-norm as distillation loss that treats every region in feature maps equally. However, the features of different regions may have different importance for object detection. Therefore, we propose to learn an attention weight for feature distillation so that important regions in feature maps can be restored better. Extensive experimental results show that our attention-aware feature distillation method can lead to significant improvements in object detection for decompressed images.

Keywords: Decompressed image · Object detection · Feature distillation · Attention

1 Introduction

In recent years, the existing object detection methods [17,19,21,24] have achieved remarkable performance. But one fundamental weakness is their lack of robustness against input perturbations. Even minimal perturbations that are hardly noticeable for humans can derail the predictions of high-performance detectors. Recent benchmark research [15] on the robustness of object detection models have shown that the performance of a standard neural network model is sensitive to image quality. For instance, the mean Average Precision (mAP) of Faster-RCNN [21] drops by 18% under several common image corruptions [15].

This work was supported by the Science and Technology Project of State Grid Corporation of China: Research and Application of Key Technologies for Transformer Multimodal Information Fusion and Diagnostic Reasoning (5700-202121258A-0-0-00).

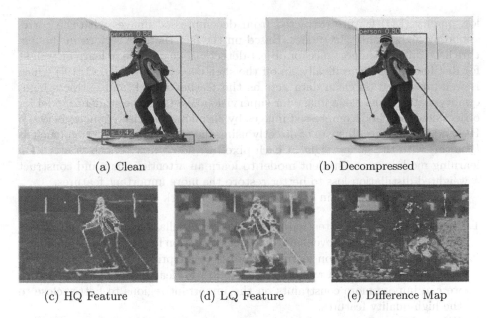

(a) Clean   (b) Decompressed

(c) HQ Feature   (d) LQ Feature   (e) Difference Map

Fig. 1. (a), (b): The detection results of an original clean image (left) and the corresponding decompressed image (right) by directly applying the detector [20] which is well-trained on high-quality data. (c), (d): The high-quality (HQ) feature and low-quality (LQ) feature are extracted from (a) and (b), respectively. (e): The difference map between (c) and (d), i.e., $|HQ - LQ|$. The result indicates that the degradation of each region in the feature map is different, so it has different importance in the process of feature distillation. **Best viewed in color.**

As shown in Fig. 1 (a) and (b), directly applying the detector which is well-trained on high-quality data to the decompressed image results in missed and false detections so that the performance declines.

To alleviate the aforementioned issues, several works on robust learning are proposed. A common strategy for corrupted image detection is to improve the robustness of feature extraction by data augmentation. AutoAugment [8] first used reinforcement learning to search for the optimal data augmentation strategy. Augmix [10] generated new training images by mixing multiple augmented ones. The recognition-friendly image restoration methods [14,23] proposed to first restore the image and then classify it. DDP [28] shown that degraded features extracted from corrupted images lead to significant decrease of classification performance. So an alternative solution is feature enhancement for degraded image recognition. For example, FSR [25] proposed to enhance the discriminatory power of a given representation in order to provide high recognition precision. However, none of these methods explicitly restore the important features for object detection.

In this paper, we prefer to tackle the aforementioned problem through an attention-aware feature distillation method. Our basic idea is to align the low-quality (LQ) feature extracted from decompressed images with the corresponding high-quality (HQ) ones. Based on the fact that the regions in the feature have different importance for object detection, we propose to learn an weight for distillation loss. Specifically, an off the shelf detector (e.g. YOLO [19]) which is well-pretrained on clean data acts as the teacher model, and extracts high-quality feature from clean image for supervision. We train the student model for object detection in decompressed images by shrinking the discrepancies between HQ and LQ features. Instead of directly using the common loss function (such as l_2-norm) with the same weight at each pixel, we add a new branch of attention learning module in the student model to learn an attention map and construct a weighted distillation loss to better restore the more important features.

To summarize, the main contributions of this work are in three folds:

1. We propose a novel attention-aware feature distillation method, which can lead to significant improvements on object detection for decompressed images.
2. We propose an attention learning module to adaptively learn the attention weights and construct a weighted l_2-norm loss for feature distillation. As such we can impose more constraints on the important regions to better close to the high-quality features.
3. We conduct sufficient experiments on popular benchmark datasets, and the results verify the superiority of our method.

2   Related Work

2.1   Image Compression

Image compression is a branch of data compression technology. Conventional hand-craft image compression methods, such as the JPEG [26], JPEG2000 [18] and BPG[1] rely on the manually designed modules. Specifically, these modules include intra prediction, discrete cosine transform or wavelet transform, quantization, and entropy encoder. They design multiple modes for each module and optimize the rate-distortion to determine the best mode.

Recently, image compression algorithms based on deep learning have been proposed continuously. [3,4] first proposed an end-to-end optimized image compression framework on convolutional neural networks (CNNs), and subsequently introduced the scale super a priori in [5], which improved the image encoding performance. This work surpassed the previous JPEG, BPG and other algorithms, and achieved excellent compression results. Therefore, the compression and decompression processes used in this paper are from [5].

2.2   Robust Object Detection

Despite the remarkable performance of object detection on high-quality images, detection under common corruptions (e.g., decompressed images) has received

---

[1] BPG (Better Portable Graphics) image format: https://bellard.org/bpg/.

relatively little attention so far. A commonly used method to improve the detection performance on degraded images is image enhancement first. [16] proposed a DCNNs-based method to improve the visual quality of rain and fog images. [1,2] proposed an algorithm to remove rain from the image as a preprocessing step and reported the subsequent increase in recognition accuracy. [7,29] introduced adversarial training to enhance the robustness of the object detection model against perturbations.

3   Proposed Method

In this section, we first briefly introduce the overall architecture of our method for object detection in decompressed images in Sect. 3.1. Then we elaborate on the proposed attention-aware feature distillation loss function and how to learn the attention map in Sect. 3.2. Finally, we describe the end-to-end training scheme of our method in Sect. 3.3.

3.1   Overall Architecture

The overall architecture of the proposed method is illustrated in Fig. 2. In our method, we employ YOLO [19] series single-stage detectors which are lightweight but have impressive performance in object detection. The student network has the same structure as the teacher but with decompressed images as input. As shown in Fig. 2, YOLOv3 [20] consists of two parts, the backbone network is used to extract features and the detection head for classification and bounding box regression. Under our experiment setting, the teacher network is well-pretrained on clean images, we fix the backbone network and remove the head during training since we only use the teacher's backbone to extract high-quality features. For the student model, both the backbone and head are preserved and we initialize it with the pretrained parameters for better convergence. Paired images, that is, high-quality images and the corresponding decompressed images, are input into the teacher and student network, respectively.

Subsequently, we use feature distillation to make the features extracted from decompressed images close to the high-quality ones. Conventional methods adopt the l_1 or l_2-norm for distillation, which treat every regions in the feature maps equally. However, in object detection, the importance of each region in features is different (e.g., the regions containing objects is obviously more important than the background). Based on this consideration, we propose an attention-aware feature distillation method by applying a learned attention map as the weight to the l_2-norm. Due to the different distillation weights for different regions, our method makes the degraded features extracted from decompressed images align with corresponding high-quality features better. In Sect. 3.2, We will describe the details of learning the attention map and apply it to distillation loss function. And it's worth noting that we jointly optimize the distillation and detection loss for training the student model.

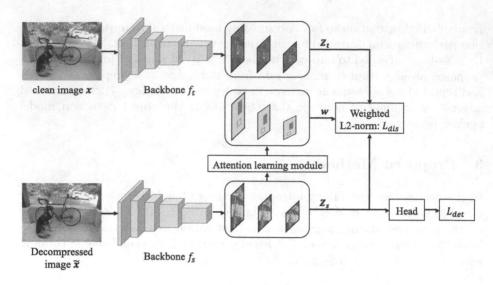

Fig. 2. The overall architecture of our proposed attention-aware feature distillation.

3.2   Attention-Aware Feature Distillation

In this section, We first introduce the problem formulation, then elaborate on the design of proposed attention-aware feature distillation, and finally present the attention learning module.

Problem Formulation. Hereafter, we use x and $\tilde{x}$ to denote the high-quality and decompressed images, z represent the corresponding extracted features. Then we have $z_t = f_t(x; \Theta_t), z_s = f_s(\tilde{x}; \Theta_s)$ where the subscripts t and s represent the teacher and student, f denotes the backbone network with parameter Θ. The goal of feature distillation is to optimize the student model by minimizing the discrepancy between z_t and z_s, that is,

$$\Theta_s = \arg\min_{\Theta_s} d(z_t, f_s(\tilde{x}; \Theta_s)), \tag{1}$$

where d is some distance (or divergence) metrics in the feature space.

Attention-Aware Feature Distillation. Several prior works [11,25,28] for distillation simply apply l_2-norm (i.e. *MSE* loss, $d(z_t, z_s) = ||z_t - z_s||_2^2$) to feature reconstruction from degraded observation. It treats different regions of feature maps equally. However, as described in [27], for the object detection task, different regions of a feature map are not of equal importance. Similarly, as shown in Fig. 1 (c), (d) and (e), we visualized the features and the result demonstrates that the difference map between high-quality feature and degraded one is diversified in spatial locations. Therefore, it is not suitable to regard the importance in each region as a constant.

Inspired by [6,12,27], we propose to learn an attention map/weight (denoted by w) that can represent the importance of different regions in the feature map and apply it to the distillation loss. Supposing that the importance is defined as the difference between z_s and z_t, that is, the greater the difference of a region in the feature (such as the edge and texture regions shown in Fig. 1) (e), the more important it is in the feature distillation process, and the larger the value of w should be. To achieve this goal, we add a branch which only work during training in the student model to learn the attention map w, and the proposed attention-aware feature distillation loss can be formulated as

$$L_{dis} = d(z_t, z_s) = \frac{||z_t - z_s||_2^2}{w + \epsilon} + R(w), \tag{2}$$

where w denotes the attention map with dimension $1 \times C \times H \times W$ of each input image, the later term refers to the regularization term due to the sparsity of difference map $|z_t - z_s|$. We empirically set $R(w) = ||w||_1$, and ϵ is usually taken as 1e-6.

Obviously, the value of the learned attention map w measures the difficulty/importance of feature reconstruction. If there exists a wide margin between z_t and z_s, the student network tends to learn a larger weight w to reduce the loss. In turn, once the w increases, the second term in the loss function will also increase, and the model will reduce the difference between z_t and z_s through optimization, which makes the student model pay more attention to the difficult/important regions in feature maps. Hence the student network can better enhance the features and improve the accuracy of detection under the guidance of the teacher network and the attention maps.

Attention Learning Module. As illustrated in Fig. 2, we add an attention learning module in the student network to obtain the attention maps from features. As shown in Fig. 3, this module consists of a transposed convolution layer for enlarging the feature maps, N residual blocks, and finally an activation ReLU layer and an average pooling layer used to keep the value $w >= 0$ and make the features back to the original resolution. N was empirically set to 3 in the experimental settings.

In our main experiments, we employ YOLO [19,20] as our detector. It uses three scales of features from the backbone network, which are input into the head network for classification and bounding box regression. Therefore, We add this module at all three locations and perform our proposed attention-aware feature distillation, respectively. The size of the learned attention map w is consistent with the corresponding feature. The l_2-norm and the reciprocal of w are dot multiplied to constitute the distillation loss function.

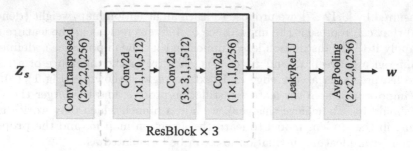

Fig. 3. The architecture of our attention learning module. The numbers in parentheses represent the kernel size, stride, padding, and output channels respectively.

3.3 Training Scheme

During training, only the parameters in the student detector are updated by back propagation. The clean image and the corresponding decompressed image are input into the teacher and student networks respectively. The teacher network extracts high-quality features from clean original images to provide a supervision for student model adaptation. We use the proposed attention-aware distillation loss to make features aggregate better even if they are extracted from two different distributions. Then the enhanced features are input into the head network to carry out the object detection and the detection label is used as another supervision item.

In summary, we optimize the whole student network by the jointly training loss which contains two parts: the attention-aware distillation loss and the detection loss,

$$L = L_{det} + \lambda \cdot L_{dis}. \tag{3}$$

Specifically, the first term L_{det} denotes the common used detection loss in YOLO, consists of classification and bounding box regression. L_{dis} represents the proposed attention-aware distillation loss which has been described in Eq. (2). λ is the weight balance parameter and is empirically set to 1. It is worth noting that, as described in Sect. 3.2, we do this distillation on the feature maps of three scales respectively, and L_{dis} is the total.

4   Experiments

Simulations and Dataset. Considering the promising performance of DCNNs-based image compression methods, in our experiments, we used the DCNNs-based method [5] to generate the simulated decompressed images from the clean ones in MS-COCO dataset [13]. The clean and corresponding decompressed images are input into the teacher and student detector respectively. To measure the performance of object detection, the mean Average Precision (mAP) [9] is a commonly used metric.

Training Setting. Considering the application scenario, we used the lightweight but high-accuracy single stage YOLOv3-tiny [20] and YOLOv5-small[2] model as our detector. We employed the model which is well-pretrained on clean images as teacher during training and fixed the parameters. The parameters in the student model were initialized by the pretrained one and kept updated. We used the proposed joint loss function described in Eq. (3) to train the student model and the hyperparameter λ was empirically set to 1. We adopted SGD [22] as the optimizer with momentum set to 0.937, weight-decay 5e-4 and initial learning rate 0.01. Our model was trained on $1 \times$ NVIDIA GeForce RTX 2080 Ti gpu for 300 epochs with batch size of 32 per iteration. The size of input images is 640×640

4.1 Ablation Study

In our experiments, we first conducted an ablation study to investigate the contribution of the proposed attention map for performance improvements. Specifically, we compared our method with the method which only use the common l_2-norm for distillation, that is, we removed the attention learning module and the weights w. Table 1 shows the mAP results of object detection in decompressed images. From it we can obtain that our proposed attention-aware feature distillation method has better performance than the common used l_2-norm.

Table 1. Ablation study on our method. "l_2-norm" denotes the common l_2-norm distillation loss without the attention weights. "weighted l_2-norm" means our proposed method which uses the learned attention maps as the weights for l_2-norm distillation loss. **The best mAP results are in bold.**

Method	l_2-norm	Weighted l_2-norm
YOLOv3-Tiny (mAP)	12.8	**15.6**
YOLOv5-Small (mAP)	27.1	**29.1**

4.2 Comparisons with Other Methods

Except the common used l_2-norm distillation, to demonstrate the effectiveness of our method on object detection in decompressed image, we have also compared our method with other common used methods such as training from scratch, fine-tuning and data augmentation training. Fine-tuning means we initialized the model with well-pretrained parameters on clean data and used the decompressed images to fine-tune the model. In contrast, training from scratch means we used the decompressed images to train the model with random initialized parameters. Data augmentation training means we used the decompressed images and augmented it (e.g., flip or add noise) to fine-tune the model. We have done the comparisons on YOLOv3-tiny and YOLOV5-small. The detection results are shown in Tables 2 and 3. These comparative experiments can prove the superiority of our method.

---

[2] https://github.com/ultralytics/yolov5.

Table 2. The YOLOv3-tiny detection results on simulated decompressed images in COCO [13]. "Training from Scratch" means we used the decompressed images to train the model with random initialized parameters. "Fine-Tuning" means we initialized the model with well-pretrained parameters and used the decompressed images to fine-tune the model. "AutoAugment" means we used the decompressed images and augmented it to fine-tune the model. "l_2-norm" means the common l_2-norm distillation method. It's worth noting that for the distillation method like "l_2-norm" and "Ours", training data contains pairs of images as described in Sect. 4. **The best results are in bold.**

Method	Training data	Testing data	mAP	mAP@0.5	mAP@0.75
YOLOv3-Tiny	COCO2017	COCO2017	17.3	37.3	15.4
YOLOv3-Tiny	COCO2017	COCO2017 Decompressed	10.7	24.5	9.1
Training from Scratch	COCO2017 Decompressed	COCO2017 Decompressed	12.8	27.1	11.3
Fine-Tuning	COCO2017 Decompressed	COCO2017 Decompressed	12.7	27.1	11.5
Fine-Tuning + AutoAugment [8]	COCO2017 Decompressed	COCO2017 Decompressed	13.0	27.8	11.8
l_2-norm	COCO2017 Pairs of Image	COCO2017 Decompressed	12.8	27.4	11.4
Ours	COCO2017 Pairs of Image	COCO2017 Decompressed	**15.6**	**31.2**	**14.2**

Table 3. The YOLOv5-small detection results on simulated decompressed images in COCO [13]. "Training from Scratch" means we used the decompressed images to train the model with random initialized parameters. "Fine-Tuning" means we initialized the model with well-pretrained parameters and used the decompressed images to fine-tune the model. "AutoAugment" means we used the decompressed images and augmented it to fine-tune the model. "l_2-norm" means the common l_2-norm distillation method. It's worth noting that for the distillation method like "l_2-norm" and "Ours", training data contains pairs of images as described in Sect. 4. **The best results are in bold.**

Method	Training data	Testing data	mAP	mAP@0.5	mAP@0.75
YOLOv5-Small	COCO2017	COCO2017	34.3	54.0	36.6
YOLOv5-Small	COCO2017	COCO2017 Decompressed	22.3	37.7	22.9
Training from Scratch	COCO2017 Decompressed	COCO2017 Decompressed	26.4	44.0	27.2
Fine-Tuning	COCO2017 Decompressed	COCO2017 Decompressed	26.3	44.2	27.1
Fine-Tuning + AutoAugment [8]	COCO2017 Decompressed	COCO2017 Decompressed	27.8	46.1	28.7
l_2-norm	COCO2017 Pairs of Image	COCO2017 Decompressed	27.1	45.2	27.9
Ours	COCO2017 Pairs of Image	COCO2017 Decompressed	**29.1**	**47.4**	**30.5**

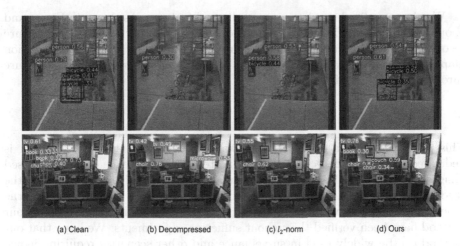

Fig. 4. The detection results for (a) clean images, (b) decompressed images, (c) l_2-norm distillation method on decompressed images and (d) our method. From this visualization we can obtain that our method has better object detection performance on decompressed images than the others. **Best viewed in color.**

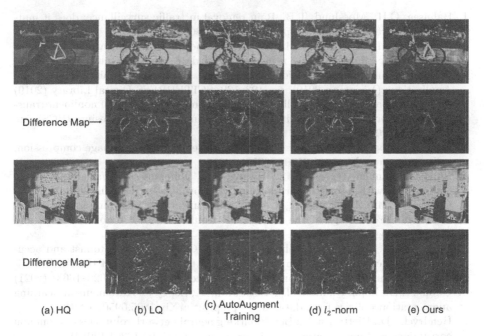

Fig. 5. The visualization of features extracted from two images. (a) High-quality (HQ) feature extracted from clean image. (b) Low-quality (LQ) feature. (c) Feature extracted from the detector after data augmentation training. (d) Feature restored from the model after l_2-norm distillation. (e) Feature restored from our method. The second and fourth row is the difference map between the high-quality (HQ) feature and the corresponding restored one. **Best viewed in color.**

We also visualized the detection results and features. As shown in Figs. 4 and 5, our method is superior to other methods in detection performance and feature recovery. This is because our method proposed the adaptive learned attention map and model can pay more attention to the important regions in the feature through weighted distillation loss.

5   Conclusion

This paper proposed a new attention-aware feature distillation method that is dedicated to making detectors perform better in the presence of decompressed images. Through the learned attention map and weighted distillation loss, the student model can better recover the degraded features so that improve the object detection performance in decompressed images. The advantages of our method have been verified throughout sufficient experiments. We hope that our method can be widely used in surveillance and other scenarios requiring image compression and object detection.

References

1. Bahnsen, C.H., Moeslund, T.B.: Rain removal in traffic surveillance: does it matter? IEEE Trans. Intell. Transp. Syst. **20**(8), 2802–2819 (2018)
2. Bahnsen, C.H., Vázquez, D., López, A.M., Moeslund, T.B.: Learning to remove rain in traffic surveillance by using synthetic data. In: 14th International Joint Conference on Computer Vision, Imaging and Computer Graphics Theory and Applications (Visigrapp 2019), pp. 123–130. SCITEPRESS Digital Library (2019)
3. Ballé, J., Laparra, V., Simoncelli, E.P.: End-to-end optimization of nonlinear transform codes for perceptual quality. In: 2016 Picture Coding Symposium (PCS), pp. 1–5. IEEE (2016)
4. Ballé, J., Laparra, V., Simoncelli, E.P.: End-to-end optimized image compression. arXiv preprint arXiv:1611.01704 (2016)
5. Ballé, J., Minnen, D., Singh, S., Hwang, S.J., Johnston, N.: Variational image compression with a scale hyperprior. arXiv preprint arXiv:1802.01436 (2018)
6. Chang, J., Lan, Z., Cheng, C., Wei, Y.: Data uncertainty learning in face recognition. In: Proceedings of the IEEE/CVF Conference on Computer Vision and Pattern Recognition, pp. 5710–5719 (2020)
7. Chen, X., Xie, C., Tan, M., Zhang, L., Hsieh, C.J., Gong, B.: Robust and accurate object detection via adversarial learning. In: Proceedings of the IEEE/CVF Conference on Computer Vision and Pattern Recognition, pp. 16622–16631 (2021)
8. Cubuk, E.D., Zoph, B., Mane, D., Vasudevan, V., Le, Q.V.: Autoaugment: learning augmentation policies from data. arXiv preprint arXiv:1805.09501 (2018)
9. Hendrycks, D., Dietterich, T.: Benchmarking neural network robustness to common corruptions and perturbations. arXiv preprint arXiv:1903.12261 (2019)
10. Hendrycks, D., Mu, N., Cubuk, E.D., Zoph, B., Gilmer, J., Lakshminarayanan, B.: Augmix: a simple data processing method to improve robustness and uncertainty. arXiv preprint arXiv:1912.02781 (2019)
11. Heo, B., Kim, J., Yun, S., Park, H., Kwak, N., Choi, J.Y.: A comprehensive overhaul of feature distillation. In: Proceedings of the IEEE/CVF International Conference on Computer Vision, pp. 1921–1930 (2019)

12. Lin, T.Y., Goyal, P., Girshick, R., He, K., Dollár, P.: Focal loss for dense object detection. In: Proceedings of the IEEE International Conference on Computer Vision, pp. 2980–2988 (2017)
13. Lin, T.-Y., et al.: Microsoft COCO: common objects in context. In: Fleet, D., Pajdla, T., Schiele, B., Tuytelaars, T. (eds.) ECCV 2014. LNCS, vol. 8693, pp. 740–755. Springer, Cham (2014). https://doi.org/10.1007/978-3-319-10602-1_48
14. Liu, D., Wen, B., Liu, X., Wang, Z., Huang, T.S.: When image denoising meets high-level vision tasks: a deep learning approach. arXiv preprint arXiv:1706.04284 (2017)
15. Michaelis, C., et al.: Benchmarking robustness in object detection: autonomous driving when winter is coming. arXiv preprint arXiv:1907.07484 (2019)
16. Mukherjee, J., Praveen, K., Madumbu, V.: Visual quality enhancement of images under adverse weather conditions. In: 2018 21st International Conference on Intelligent Transportation Systems (ITSC), pp. 3059–3066. IEEE (2018)
17. Qiao, S., Chen, L.C., Yuille, A.: Detectors: detecting objects with recursive feature pyramid and switchable atrous convolution. In: Proceedings of the IEEE/CVF Conference on Computer Vision and Pattern Recognition, pp. 10213–10224 (2021)
18. Rabbani, M., Joshi, R.: An overview of the jpeg 2000 still image compression standard. Signal Process. Image Commun. **17**(1), 3–48 (2002)
19. Redmon, J., Divvala, S., Girshick, R., Farhadi, A.: You only look once: unified, real-time object detection. In: Proceedings of the IEEE Conference on Computer Vision and Pattern Recognition, pp. 779–788 (2016)
20. Redmon, J., Farhadi, A.: Yolov3: an incremental improvement. arXiv preprint arXiv:1804.02767 (2018)
21. Ren, S., He, K., Girshick, R., Sun, J.: Faster r-CNN: towards real-time object detection with region proposal networks. Adv. Neural Inf. Process. Syst. **28**, 91–99 (2015)
22. Robbins, H., Monro, S.: A stochastic approximation method. In: The Annals of Mathematical Statistics, pp. 400–407 (1951)
23. Son, T., Kang, J., Kim, N., Cho, S., Kwak, S.: URIE: universal image enhancement for visual recognition in the wild. In: Vedaldi, A., Bischof, H., Brox, T., Frahm, J.-M. (eds.) ECCV 2020. LNCS, vol. 12354, pp. 749–765. Springer, Cham (2020). https://doi.org/10.1007/978-3-030-58545-7_43
24. Tan, M., Pang, R., Le, Q.V.: Efficientdet: Scalable and efficient object detection. In: Proceedings of the IEEE/CVF Conference on Computer Vision and Pattern Recognition, pp. 10781–10790 (2020)
25. Tan, W., Yan, B., Bare, B.: Feature super-resolution: make machine see more clearly. In: Proceedings of the IEEE Conference on Computer Vision and Pattern Recognition, pp. 3994–4002 (2018)
26. Wallace, G.K.: The jpeg still picture compression standard. IEEE Trans. Consum. Electron. **38**(1), xviii–xxxiv (1992)
27. Wang, T., Zhu, Y., Zhao, C., Zhao, X., Wang, J., Tang, M.: Attention-guided knowledge distillation for efficient single-stage detector. In: 2021 IEEE International Conference on Multimedia and Expo (ICME), pp. 1–6. IEEE (2021)
28. Wang, Y., Cao, Y., Zha, Z.J., Zhang, J., Xiong, Z.: Deep degradation prior for low-quality image classification. In: Proceedings of the IEEE/CVF Conference on Computer Vision and Pattern Recognition, pp. 11049–11058 (2020)
29. Zhang, H., Wang, J.: Towards adversarially robust object detection. In: Proceedings of the IEEE/CVF International Conference on Computer Vision, pp. 421–430 (2019)

Cross-Stage Class-Specific Attention for Image Semantic Segmentation

Zhengyi Shi[1], Li Sun[1,2]([✉]), and Qingli Li[1,2]

[1] Shanghai Key Laboratory of Multidimensional Information Processing,
Shanghai, China
[2] Key Laboratory of Advanced Theory and Application in Statistics and Data
Science, East China Normal University, Shanghai, China
sunli@ee.ecnu.com, qlli@cs.ecnu.edu.cn

Abstract. Recent backbones built on transformers capture the context within a significantly larger area than CNN, and greatly improve the performance on semantic segmentation. However, the fact, that the decoder utilizes features from different stages in the shallow layers, indicates that local context is still important. Instead of simply incorporating features from different stages, we propose a cross-stage class-specific attention mainly for transformer-based backbones. Specifically, given a coarse prediction, we first employ the final stage features to aggregate a class center within the whole image. Then high-resolution features from the earlier stage are used as queries to absorb the semantics from class centers. To eliminate the irrelevant classes within a local area, we build the context for each query position according to the classification score from coarse prediction, and remove the redundant classes. So only relevant classes provide keys and values in attention and participate the value routing. We validate the proposed scheme on different datasets including ADE20K, Pascal Context and COCO-Stuff, showing that the proposed model improves the performance compared with other works.

Keywords: Semantic segmentation · Vision transformer · Attention algorithm

1 Introduction

Semantic segmentation is one of the most widely used computer vision tasks, which aims to assign a category label to each pixel for an input image. In recent years, various studies based on Convolutional Neural Networks (CNNs) [1, 10, 42, 48] and Vision Transformers [30–32] have led to significant improvements in most segmentation benchmarks. Using features from different layers, the context representations and spatial details can be extracted and stored easily. However, it is still a challenge to design an efficient decoder and achieve better performance.

This work is supported by the Science and Technology Commission of Shanghai Municipality (No. 19511120800) and Natural Science Foundation of China (No. 61302125).

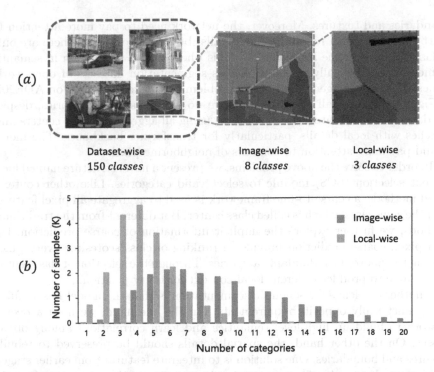

Fig. 1. Different context granularities. a) There are a huge number of categories in the dataset, but only a few of them appear in a specific image, even fewer within a local window. b) A statistic on ADE20K. The horizontal axis represents the number of categories, and the vertical axis tells how many samples belonging to the categories. We crop the images to 1/4 size of original to simulate the local details' reconstruction, which is shown in orange, while the image-wise statistic is shown in blue. (Color figure online)

One of the most effective approaches is exploiting representation by grouping pixels via contextual strategies [14,15,36,48,49]. ACFNet [36] aggregates all pixel features of the same category to calculate a class center, which describes the class-level representation of each category. OCRNet [15] further explores the relationship between categories and pixels. A context-based attention module is proposed to route pixel features by class centers. However, one eminent drawback of these relation context-based methods is that all the categories participate in the calculation even if some of them do not appear in the image. These redundant categories introduce a lot of noises, thereby reducing the performance of the network.

We argue here that it is not necessary for all categories to participate in the segmentation of a specific image, especially for the dataset with a huge number of categories. As is shown in Fig. 1 a), for a common image in ADE20K, there are only 8 classes appearing in a single image but 150 classes labeled in the entire dataset. This mismatch will be further deteriorated when predicting the boundaries and textures. Moreover, the network need to pay more attention to nearby features when rebuilding the details, but in our example, there are only 3 classes appear in the local window. This phenomenon is common in semantic segmentation, especially for multi classes segmentation datesets of open-world scenes. To prove the generality of the problem, we make a statistic on ADE20K in Fig. 1 b). Almost all the windows have no more than 10 categories, despite the dataset has 150 categories. Therefore, using all aggregated class centers mismatches with local details, particularly for transformer backbones. The model should pay more attention to contents of neighboring pixels.

In order to solve the above problems, we present a novel structure named local context selection (LCS) module to select valid categories. Like other context-based methods, a coarse-to-fine framework is used to aggregate all pixel features with the same class, which is called class center. But different from the traditional methods, we further explore the implicit information of coarse prediction. For each pixel, coarse prediction provides a ranking of class scores for every pixel, guiding to remove the redundant categories. Through the selection of class center, LCS is able to produce different local context for every position.

Another challenge for semantic segmentation is that the model has to fulfill two diametrically opposite requirements. On the one hand, we need a deeper network to build up high-level semantics and learn correlations among object classes. On the other hand, the spatial details should be preserved to rebuild textures and boundaries. One solution is to integrate features from earlier stages. Previous works [4, 5, 46, 47] choose to simply concatenate these features along the channels, which is inefficient because the high-level semantics are diluted by low-level features.

To deal with this situation, we propose a cross-stage attention (CSA) module to connect low-level features with its local context (the selected class centers) given by LCS. The idea is to use features in different stages as queries, and their local context as keys and values to complete normal attention calculation, so queries can be refined by the guidance of their context. Notice that for features in high resolutions, LCS assigns customized context to a window dynamically, and queries within it share the same context (keys and values). Moreover, since local context is constructed by the aggregated class centers, it represents high-level semantics and local details at the same time. Therefore, the cross-stage fusion resulted from CSA not only captures the representation of different scales, but also focuses on the class-specific local details. Only relevant categories participate in the attention calculation, which significantly improves the computational efficiency.

Combining all of these modules, we design a novel structure named Cross-stage Class Specific Network (CCSNet) to deal with the multi classes semantic segmentation task. We evaluate our CCSNet on various open-world datasets including ADE20K [38], PascalContext [39] and COCO-Stuff164k [40]. It achieves competitive performance comparing to mainstream semantic segmentation methods.

The contributions of this paper are three-fold:

- We present a local context selection (LCS) module to deal with the category mismatch between open-world segmentation dataset and specific image. It can select most likely categories for each location dynamically to reduce redundant noise and improve the performance.
- Cross stage attention (CSA) module is designed to capture the multi-scales representation extracted by feature pyramid. CSA assigns the local context to pixel features from different stages according to the spatial position. Therefore, features with the largest receptive field can guide representation reconstruction in different stages.
- Our CCSNet achieves the best performance on the benchmarks of ADE20K, PascalContext and COCO-Stuff164K. Under the same experimental environment conducted by MMsegmentation [41], our CCSNet outperforms the Swin-Transformer and SegFormer by 0.2%–1.0% in terms of mIoU.

2   Related Work

Coarse-to-Fine Frameworks. Coarse-to fine frameworks are widely used in computer vision tasks [33,34]. For semantic segmentation, PointRend [35] presents a strategy to pick the points of lower probability in coarse prediction. With the help of a well-trained MLP layer, these points are re-predicted for fine prediction. ACFNet [36] uses the coarse prediction map for computing class centers. It proposes a class attention block to adaptively combine class centers and features to get a more accurate result.

Similarly, we use coarse prediction to explore the distribution for each category. Moreover, we further explore the implicit information of coarse prediction. LCS module is proposed to select categories dynamically according to probability ranking, which can significantly improve the performance of the network.

Multi-scale Context. Incorporating multi-scale contextual features is an effective method in dense prediction tasks, which has been proven by a lot of studies [1–7]. PSPNet [1] exploits the capability of global context information by different-region-based context aggregation through pyramid pooling module. DeepLab families [2,8–10] use atrous convolution with different dilation rates to capture objects with different scales. Inspired by the feature pyramid structure in object detection [6,7,11], SemanticFPN [5] is proposed to fuse the representations from different stages.

Our CCSNet uses CSA module to capture multi-scale context. Different from the other multi-scale methods, we select the deepest features to refine local features from lower stages. This approach is able to retain more advanced semantic contexts while preserving detailed information.

Attention-Based Segmentation. There are two implementations when using attention module for segmentation. The first method attempts to extract the spatial dependencies from all of the pixels. NLNet [12] captures long-range contextual representations by calculating the similarity matrix. CCNet [13] replaces the common single densely-connected graph with two consecutive criss-cross modules, which can compute spatial attention effectively. The other method is channel-wise attention. DANet [14] uses channel attention module to explicitly model inter-dependencies between channels. OCRNet [15] uses object region representations to generate keys and values to explore the relationship between classes and channels. MaskFormer [51] uses a structure similar to DETR [26] to generate masks, and employs a classifier to predict categories for each mask.

Our approach also aggregates the pixel features with the same categories to participate in attention calculations. But the difference is that we choose the categories dynamically. Only the most likely classes are fed into the cross attention module, which makes the attention calculation more efficient.

Vision Transformers. Inspired by the successful achievements [16–18] in NLP, many researches [19–21] attempt to explore the potential of transformers in computer vision tasks. Vit [19] is the first to use pure transformers in image classification task. It employs a patch embedding layer to divide images and encode them to tokens. After that, a lot of studies have proven the effectiveness of transformer in other visual tasks including ReID [22,23] , GANs [24,25] , object detection [26–29] and semantic segmentation [30–32]. SETR [30] uses ViT [19] to extract semantic representations and a CNN-based decoder to predict final results. P2T [52] extracts features from different stages for downstream sense understanding tasks. Swin-Transformer [31] designs a novel backbone and employs UperNet [4] as a decoder head.

However, we notice that these CNN-based decoders don't perform well with transformers as backbone. One possible reason is CNN-based heads always try to expand the receptive field which is excessively emphasized by transformers. Our approach is aimed at intensifying local connections with the guidance of deepest features, which is helpful for transformers to reconstruct details.

3   Method

The overview architecture is shown in Fig. 2. Our model is built on a backbone with pyramid structure, extracting semantic representations from different scales. Guided by coarse prediction, the deeper features of low resolution are used to aggregate the class centers within the full image, and these centers form a global feature for each semantics. In order to avoid redundant irrelevant categories interfering the result, we propose a novel module named Local Context Selection (LCS) to remove less likely class centers according to the coarse prediction. For each location in the feature pyramid, we customize a unique local context based on the distribution of its category probabilities. After that, we use Cross Stage Attention (CSA) module to assign local context to features in different locations. All of them will be fed into a cross attention module to rebuild a new feature pyramid with richer semantic information. In the end, we use an MLP layer to get the final prediction result.

In this section, we take the backbone of SegFormer [32] as an example to introduce our structure details.

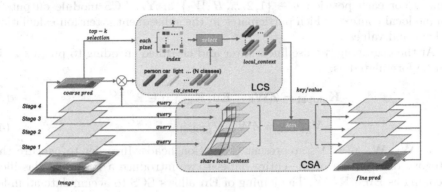

Fig. 2. An implementation of semantic segmentation based on CCSNet. First, we calculate the class center of this image using coarse prediction and deep feature. Then we adopt Local Context Selection (**LCS**) to pick the k classes with the most probabilities for each position from class center. After that, Cross Stage Attention (**CSA**) is used to capture the context information from different stages and locations. Finally, we employ a simple linear layer to fuse the features of different stages and get the final prediction results.

3.1 Class Center Calculation

Taking input Image $I \in \mathbb{R}^{H \times W \times 3}$, we use $\mathbf{F} = \{\mathbf{F_1}, \mathbf{F_2}, \mathbf{F_3}, \mathbf{F_4}\}$ to describe the outputs from each stages of the backbone. In our example, H_i, W_i describe the feature size of the i-th stage, which can be calculated by:

$$H_i = \frac{1}{2^{i+1}} H, \qquad W_i = \frac{1}{2^{i+1}} W \tag{1}$$

Supposing there are N classes to be segmented, we choose the third stage's feature and a classifier to obtain the coarse prediction $\mathbf{Y_c} \in \mathbb{R}^{H_3 W_3 \times N}$. Because the deep features of the network often have richer semantic context, we use $\mathbf{F_4} \in \mathbb{R}^{H_4 W_4 \times C_4}$ and $\mathbf{Y_c}$ to calculate class center $\mathbf{Z}$. This processing can be formulated as:

$$\mathbf{Z} = \sigma([\Phi(\mathbf{Y_c})]^T, \dim = -1)\mathbf{F_4} \tag{2}$$

where $\Phi(\cdot)$ is a bi-linear interpolation function. It downsamples $\mathbf{Y_c}$ to the same spatial size as $\mathbf{F_4}$. Then we get $\mathbf{Z} \in \mathbb{R}^{N \times C_4}$ to describe the overall presentation of different classes in this image.

After that, we use $\mathbf{Z}$ to generate keys and values to process queries, which are features from different stages.

3.2   Local Context Selection

As is shown in Fig. 3(Left), local context selection module takes $\mathbf{Z}$ and $\mathbf{Y_c}$ as inputs. For each position $p \in \{1, 2, ..., H_3 W_3\}$ in $\mathbf{Y_c}$, LCS module outputs a unique local context, which participates in the subsequent attention calculation as keys and values.

At the beginning, we use linear layer and classified encoding to process $\mathbf{Z}$. It can be formulated as:

$$\mathbf{K_{global}} = \mathbf{Z}\mathbf{W_k} + \mathbf{En}, \mathbf{K_{global}} \in \mathbb{R}^{N \times C} \tag{3}$$

$$\mathbf{V_{global}} = \mathbf{Z}\mathbf{W_v}, \mathbf{V_{global}} \in \mathbb{R}^{N \times C} \tag{4}$$

where $\mathbf{W_k}, \mathbf{W_v} \in \mathbb{R}^{C_4 \times C}$ represent projection heads. In order to capture the category distribution of the entire dataset, we introduce a learnable classified encoding as $\mathbf{En} \in \mathbb{R}^{N \times C}$. The joining of $\mathbf{En}$ allows LCS to accumulate an independent distribution during training phase. Since the $\mathbf{QKV}$ involved in attention algorithm are based on the information in the same image, $\mathbf{En}$ can provide category distribution of the whole dataset to help the inference.

Note that there are many categories do not appear in the image, but $\mathbf{K_{global}}$ and $\mathbf{V_{global}}$ still contain this redundant information. Figure 3(Left) shows how to remove them for a certain position p. For each pixel on $\mathbf{Y_c}$, we pick k categories with the most probabilities to generate index $\mathbf{I_p} \in \mathbb{R}^k$. Guiding by these indices, we select keys and values along the dimension of N, leaving only the k most likely classes. We use $\mathbf{K_L}^p \in \mathbb{R}^{k \times C}$ and $\mathbf{V_L}^p \in \mathbb{R}^{k \times C}$ to represent the local context selected from position p. The complete LCS module can be written as:

$$\mathbf{K_L} = \{\mathbf{K_L}^1, \mathbf{K_L}^2, ..., \mathbf{K_L}^{H_3 W_3}\}$$

$$\mathbf{K_L}^p = \text{Select}(\mathbf{K_{global}}, \mathbf{I}_p), p \in \{1, 2, ..., H_3 W_3\} \tag{5}$$

$$\mathbf{V_L} = \{\mathbf{V_L}^1, \mathbf{V_L}^2, ..., \mathbf{V_L}^{H_3 W_3}\}$$

$$\mathbf{V_L}^p = \text{Select}(\mathbf{V_{global}}, \mathbf{I}_p), p \in \{1, 2, ..., H_3 W_3\} \tag{6}$$

The advantages of LCS are two-fold. Note that the class center $\mathbf{Z}$ is based on the statistics of all categories in the whole dataset. But for a specific pixel, only a few categories are helpful for its classification. LCS removes redundant information and decreases computation costs of subsequent attention module to $(k/N)^2$. Moreover, LCS picks different local contexts for different positions, which can effectively enhance the local relevance of features.

3.3   Cross Stage Attention

The illustration of the proposed CSA module is shown in Fig. 3(Right). It takes $\mathbf{K_L}/\mathbf{V_L}$ as keys/values, and projects feature pyramid as queries. All of $\mathbf{QKV}$ are fed into a cross attention block to refine features from different stages. The main steps are as follows:

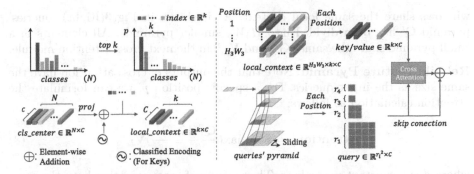

Fig. 3. The details of LCS module (Left) and CSA (Right). For LCS module, a specific pixel in coarse prediction provides a ranking of probabilities. Guiding by this ranking, LCS select the k categories from projected class center. A classified encoding is introduced to capture dataset distribution when generating keys. For CSA module, we slice the feature pyramid into windows of different sizes. Features from the same location at different stages share the same local context. Then we employ a cross attention block to calculate embeddings of different stages separately.

Project Queries. First, we project the feature pyramid to generate queries for cross attention. Using $\mathbf{W_Q} = \{\mathbf{W_Q}^1, \mathbf{W_Q}^2, \mathbf{W_Q}^3, \mathbf{W_Q}^4\}$ to represent the projection heads of each stages, queries can be written as: $\mathbf{Q} = \{\mathbf{Q}_1, \mathbf{Q}_2, \mathbf{Q}_3, \mathbf{Q}_4\}$, where each $\mathbf{Q}_i$ is defined as following:

$$\mathbf{Q}_i = \mathbf{F}_i \mathbf{W_Q}^i, \mathbf{Q}_i \in \mathbb{R}^{H_i W_i \times C} \tag{7}$$

Slice Queries. In LCS, we have allocated keys and values for $H_3 W_3$ positions. Next, we divide $\mathbf{Q}$ so that the $\mathbf{Q}_i$ of each stage is sliced to $H_3 W_3$ windows. Note that different stages have different $\mathbf{Q}_i$ sizes. A pixel of stage-3 corresponds to 16, 4, 1, 1/4 pixels on stage-1, stage-2, stage-3 and stage-4, respectively. In order to allow the division to proceed smoothly, we first upsample $\mathbf{Q}_4$ to the same size as $\mathbf{Q}_3$:

$$\mathbf{Q}_4' = \Psi(\mathbf{Q}_4)$$
$$\mathbf{Q}' = \{\mathbf{Q}_1, \mathbf{Q}_2, \mathbf{Q}_3, \mathbf{Q}_4'\}$$

where $\Psi(\cdot)$ means a bi-linear interpolate function. Then we slice each element in $\mathbf{Q}'$ regularly, so that each stage has $H_3 W_3$ windows. At this time, the window sizes of different stages are different. Assuming that the window size of the i-th stage is $r_i \times r_i$, we can get:

$$\mathbf{r} = \{r_1, r_2, r_3, r_4\} = \{4, 2, 1, 1\}$$

The query window at position p in the i-th stage can be written as $\mathbf{Q}_i^p \in \mathbb{R}^{r_i^2 \times C}$.

Share Local Context. For the windows at the same position from different stages, they correspond to the same area in ground truth. Therefore, we let these windows share the same local context. As is shown in Fig. 3(Right), queries' pyramid $\mathbf{Q}'$ has been divided into H_3W_3 smaller pyramids. All elements in a small pyramid share the same $\mathbf{K_L}^p$ and $\mathbf{V_L}^p$ in the next cross attention module.

Rebuild Feature Pyramid. Note that the outputs of cross attention have the same size as the input queries. For a specific position p, we can formulate the attention calculation as follows:

$$\text{Attention}_i^p = \text{Softmax}(\frac{\mathbf{Q}_i^p(\mathbf{K_L}^p)^T}{\sqrt{d}})\mathbf{V_L}^p \tag{8}$$

where d is a constant normalizer. The outputs of cross attention have the same size as the input queries, which means we can rebuild pyramid with the same size as $\mathbf{Q}'$ by the outputs from different stages and positions. A skip-connection is introduced after cross attention.

There are several benefits of CSA module. First, it makes good use of characteristics of feature pyramid and effectively combines the representation of different scales. Besides, CSA refines pixel features by the guidance of top layer which has the most abundant semantic context. Furthermore, because pixels in each region only focus on the same local context representation, it makes decoder pay more attention to the nearby pixels when rebuilding the boundaries and textures, which positively affects network performance.

4   Experiments

4.1   Experimental Settings

For fair comparisons, We use MMsegmentation [41] as our codebase, as which performs most mainstream semantic segmentation algorithm. All the models are trained on 4 RTX 3090 GPUs. We adopt polynomial decay policy to adjust learning rate dynamically. For experiments based on CNNs, we use SGD and set the base learning rate as 0.01. For vision transformers, we choose AdamW as the optimizer with the setting of base learning rate as 6e-5. We apply most widely used methods to augment data, including random scaling with ratio from 0.5 to 2.0, random flipping and random brightness jittering. There is no other additional data, except ImageNet-1K [37] for backbone's pretrain.

4.2   Results on ADE20K

As is shown in Table 1, we compare our approach with other mainstream semantic segmentation methods. During 160k iteration's training, we crop all the images to 512×512, and adopt the batch size as 16. The hyper-parameter k is set to 40 if not specifically stated. The results are evaluated on ADE20K val set. The statistics of **GFLOPs** and **Params** are calculated with the image size of (512, 512). **aAcc**, **mAcc** and **mIoU** are based on single-scale test. **MS/FP** means multi-scale and flip test.

Table 1. Comparison with other methods based on ADE20K dataset.

Method	Backbone	FLOPs	Params	aAcc	mAcc	mIoU	mIoU (MS/FP)
FCN [42]	ResNet101 [44]	275.69G	68.59M	79.52	49.62	39.91	41.40
UperNet [4]		257.37G	85.51M	81.03	54.75	43.82	44.85
CCNet [13]		278.37G	68.92M	81.02	53.75	43.71	45.04
PSP [1]		256.44G	68.07M	81.10	54.75	**44.39**	45.35
DNL [43]		277.84G	69.12M	81.30	54.42	44.25	**45.78**
Ours		**225.10G**	**51.24M**	81.48	54.82	44.36	45.40
FCN [45]	HR-W48 [45]	**95.13G**	**65.95M**	80.32	53.52	42.02	43.86
OCRNet [15]		164.79G	70.53M	80.90	**55.34**	43.25	**44.88**
Ours		101.96G	66.94M	**81.41**	55.01	**43.55**	**44.88**
UperNet [4]	Swin-B [31]	297.22G	121.28M	82.35	59.03	47.99	49.57
Ours		**127.71G**	**91.61M**	**82.53**	**60.09**	**48.20**	**49.78**
SegFormer [32]	MiT-B4 [32]	**95.73G**	**64.31M**	82.73	60.54	49.34	50.29
Ours		109.57G	67.76M	**83.41**	**61.87**	**50.43**	**51.18**

Table 2. Comparison with other methods using CNN-based decoder heads.

Head	Backbone	aAcc	mAcc	mIoU
Sem-FPN [5]	MiT-B1 [32]	79.06	51.85	40.81
PSP [1]		79.77	53.53	41.83
OCRNet [15]		79.27	53.55	41.13
UperNet [31]		79.95	53.08	41.80
SegFormer [32]		80.11	52.73	42.02
Ours		**80.36**	**54.88**	**43.09**

Compared with CNN-based models, we achieve a higher accuracy rate and mIoU with a lower complexity. In the case of using Resnet-101 [44] as backbone, our method greatly reduced computational cost (~17%) and model parameters (~15%). At the same time, we get a competitive result on accuracy and mIoU. While using HRNet-48 [45] as backbone, our algorithm has a best performance (43.55). It is +0.30 higher than OCRNet with 43.25 mIoU, which is the previous best context-based method.

We also adopt our approach with Vision Transformers. We chose Swin-Transformer and SegFormer as the comparison methods for our experiment. It can be seen that our structure is much more efficient than UperNet head in Swin-Transfomer. We only use 76% of the parameters and 43% of the calculations to achieve the same prediction results. The Table 1 also shows that our decoder head can greatly improve the performance with the backbone of MiT-B4 which is proposed in [32]. Compared to SegFormer's lightweight MLP decoder, our method has made a significant improvement of +1.09 in mIoU.

Because transformer has already expand the receptive field, the traditional CNN-based decode heads doesn't perform well with transformer backbone. On the contrary, our method still shows great advantages when compared with these approaches. Table 2 shows that our approach has the best compatibility with vision transformer.

Table 3. Comparison results on Pascal-Context and COCO-Stuff164K.

Method	Backbone	Pascal-context			COCO-Stuff164k		
		aAcc	mAcc	mIoU	aAcc	mAcc	mIoU
UperNet	Swin-B	76.75	62.18	51.49	71.21	58.76	45.74
Ours		**77.09**	**62.69**	**52.05**	**71.47**	**59.14**	**46.23**
SegFormer	MiT-B0	72.11	54.10	43.51	65.71	48.10	35.43
Ours		**72.62**	**54.37**	**43.85**	**66.39**	**49.63**	**36.89**
SegFormer	MiT-B4	77.93	64.86	53.61	71.41	59.18	46.22
Ours		**78.35**	**65.29**	**54.12**	**71.59**	**59.30**	**46.40**

Table 4. The change of model performances when k takes different values.

Selection of top-k	Backbone	aAcc	mAcc	mIoU
10	MiT-B1	79.94	53.10	42.41
20		80.33	54.21	42.77
40		**80.36**	**54.88**	**43.09**
150		80.15	53.16	42.70

4.3   Results on Pascal-Context and COCO-Stuff164K

In order to verify the performance of our CCSNet on other open-world datasets which have huge numbers of categories, we conducts some comparison experiments on Pascal-Context and COCO-Stuff164k. All the results are evaluated on val set with single-scale test.

The results in Table 3 prove that our approach achieves a better performance on both datasets. For Pascal-Context, our method outperforms the Swin-Transformer and SegFormer by 0.56 and 0.51 in terms of mIoU, separately. For COCO-Stuff, these improvements are coming to 0.49 and 0.18. We use MiT-B0 as the backbone to evaluate the performance on light-weight model. The result shows that we outperform the baseline by 0.34 and 1.47 on Pascal-Context and COCO-Stuff separately.

4.4   Ablation Studies

In this section, we conduct experiments to verify the effectiveness of our proposed modules. We choose ADE20K as dataset of our ablation studies, and all the models are trained using MiT as backbone if not specifically stated.

Choices of Hyper-parameter k. For each location, LCS module selects top-k categories to participate in subsequent calculations. In order to find out the regularity of performance changing with the value of k, we conduct an experiment on ADE20K whose result is shown in Table 4. In the early stage of the experiment, when other parameters of the network are fixed, the larger the value of k, the

Table 5. Performance comparison of CSA' projection heads under different settings.

Proj's position	Share weights	mIoU
After selection		42.10
	✓	42.33
Before selection		42.65
	✓	43.09

Table 6. Comparison of classified encoding with different top-k's selection.

top-k	Classified encoding	mIoU
20		42.60
	✓	42.77
40		42.83
	✓	43.09

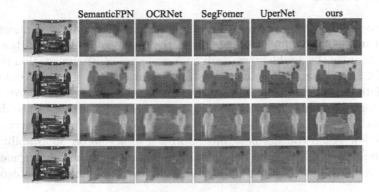

SemanticFPN   OCRNet   SegFomer   UperNet   ours

Fig. 4. The similarity visualization of features before fine segmentation.

better the network performance. But when k is set to 150, which means every categories are transmitted to the CSA as key and value, mIoU decreased by 0.39 compared to $k = 40$. One possible explanation is that too much category information increase the difficulty of network convergence. Redundant information adversely affects the network during the inference.

Effectiveness of CSA. In CSA module, features from different stages but same locations share the same key and value. To verify the effectiveness of CSA module, we compare the impact of different sharing mechanisms on network performance. We set $k = 40$ in these experiments. From Table 5 we found the best scheme is that the projection head of key/value is BEFORE top-k's selection, and they DO SHARE weights among different stages.

Effectiveness of Classified Encoding. After calculating the class centers of all categories, we introduce the classified encoding to tell the network which category it has selected. From another perspective, classified encoding accumulates class center information of different images during the training process. Table 6 shows that this mechanism can significantly improve the performance, especially at lower k values.

4.5 Visualization

To understand the role of LCS and CSA in inference, we select the feature map before fine segmentation to measure the cosine distance between a given pixel and other pixels in the same image. The visualization results are shown in Fig. 4. Comparing with other decoder heads, our CCSNet can not only effectively increase the distribution gap between the target object and others, but also produce clearer boundaries to help rebuilding details.

5 Conclusion

In this paper, we discuss a common phenomenon in semantic segmentation. For most images, the number of categories they have is far less than the entire dataset. To solve this problem, we design a novel semantic segmentation network named CCSNet based on the coarse-to-fine framework. It is able to select the appropriate semantic representations for each position dynamically according to the ranking of probability. Moreover, we optimize the structure of the decoder head, which makes the network focus on semantic context while preserving local relations. For vision transformers, our approach shows better adaptability than other complicated CNN-based decoders. Comparing with the existing methods, CCSNet achieves better results in datasets with a huge number of categories.

References

1. Zhao, H., Shi, J., Qi, X., Wang, X., Jia, J.: Pyramid scene parsing network. In: Proceedings of the IEEE Conference on Computer Vision and Pattern Recognition (CVPR) (2017)
2. Chen, L.-C., Zhu, Y., Papandreou, G., Schroff, F., Adam, H.: Encoder-decoder with atrous separable convolution for semantic image segmentation. In: Ferrari, V., Hebert, M., Sminchisescu, C., Weiss, Y. (eds.) ECCV 2018. LNCS, vol. 11211, pp. 833–851. Springer, Cham (2018). https://doi.org/10.1007/978-3-030-01234-2_49
3. Yang, M., Yu, K., Zhang, C., Li, Z., Yang, K.: Denseaspp for semantic segmentation in street scenes. In: Proceedings of the IEEE Conference on Computer Vision and Pattern Recognition (CVPR), pp. 3684–3692 (2018)
4. Xiao, T., Liu, Y., Zhou, B., Jiang, Y., Sun, J.: Unified perceptual parsing for scene understanding. In: Ferrari, V., Hebert, M., Sminchisescu, C., Weiss, Y. (eds.) ECCV 2018. LNCS, vol. 11209, pp. 432–448. Springer, Cham (2018). https://doi.org/10.1007/978-3-030-01228-1_26
5. Kirillov, A., Girshick, R., He, K., Dollar, P.: Panoptic feature pyramid networks. In: Proceedings of the IEEE/CVF Conference on Computer Vision and Pattern Recognition (CVPR) (2019)
6. Lin, T.Y., Dollár, P., Girshick, R., He, K., Hariharan, B., Belongie, S.: Feature pyramid networks for object detection. In: Proceedings of the IEEE Conference on Computer Vision and Pattern Recognition (CVPR), pp. 2117–2125 (2017)
7. Tian, Z., Shen, C., Chen, H., He, T.: FCOS: fully convolutional one-stage object detection. In: Proceedings of the IEEE/CVF International Conference on Computer Vision (ICCV) (2019)

8. Chen, L.-C., Papandreou, G., Kokkinos, I., Murphy, K., Yuille, A.L.: Semantic image segmentation with deep convolutional nets and fully connected CRFs. arXiv preprint arXiv:1412.7062 (2014)

9. Chen, L.-C., Papandreou, G., Kokkinos, I., Murphy, K., Yuille, A.L.: DeepLab: semantic image segmentation with deep convolutional nets, atrous convolution, and fully connected CRFs. IEEE Trans. Pattern Anal. Mach. Intell. **40**(4), 834–848 (2017)

10. Chen, L.-C., Papandreou, G., Schroff, F., Adam, H.: Rethinking atrous convolution for semantic image segmentation. arXiv preprint arXiv:1706.05587 (2017)

11. Lin, T.-Y., Goyal, P., Girshick, R., He, K., Dollár, P.: Focal loss for dense object detection. In: Proceedings of the IEEE International Conference on Computer Vision (ICCV), pp. 2980–2988 (2017)

12. Wang, X., Girshick, R., Gupta, A., He, K.: Non-local neural networks. In: Proceedings of the IEEE Conference on Computer Vision and Pattern Recognition (CVPR), pp. 7794–7803 (2018)

13. Huang, Z., Wang, X., Huang, L., Huang, C., Wei, Y., Liu, W.: CCNet: criss-cross attention for semantic segmentation. In: Proceedings of the IEEE/CVF International Conference on Computer Vision (ICCV), pp. 603–612 (2014)

14. Fu, J., Liu, J., Tian, H., Li, Y., Bao, Y., Fang, Z., Lu, H.: Dual attention network for scene segmentation. In: Proceedings of the IEEE/CVF Conference on Computer Vision and Pattern Recognition (CVPR), pp. 3146–3154 (2019)

15. Yuan, Y., Chen, X., Wang, J.: Object-contextual representations for semantic segmentation. In: Vedaldi, A., Bischof, H., Brox, T., Frahm, J.-M. (eds.) ECCV 2020. LNCS, vol. 12351, pp. 173–190. Springer, Cham (2020). https://doi.org/10.1007/978-3-030-58539-6_11

16. Vaswani, A., et al.: Attention is all you need. In: Advances in Neural Information Processing Systems, pp. 5998–6008 (2017)

17. Devlin, J., Chang, M.-W., Lee, K., Toutanova, K.: BERT: pre-training of deep bidirectional transformers for language understanding. arXiv preprint arXiv:1810.04805 (2018)

18. Raffel, C., et al.: Exploring the limits of transfer learning with a unified text-to-text transformer. arXiv preprint arXiv:1910.10683 (2019)

19. Dosovitskiy, A., et al.: An image is worth 16x16 words: transformers for image recognition at scale. arXiv preprint arXiv:2010.11929 (2020)

20. Touvron, H., Cord, M., Douze, M., Massa, F., Sablayrolles, A., Jégou, H.: Training data-efficient image transformers & distillation through attention. In: International Conference on Machine Learning, pp. 10347–10357. PMLR (2021)

21. Yuan, L., et al.: Tokens-to-token VIT: training vision transformers from scratch on imagenet. arXiv preprint arXiv:2101.11986 (2021)

22. He, S., Luo, H., Wang, P., Wang, F., Li, H., Jiang, W.: TransReID: transformer-based object re-identification. arXiv preprint arXiv:2102.04378 (2021)

23. Zhu, K., et al.: AAformer: auto-aligned transformer for person re-identification. arXiv preprint arXiv:2104.00921s (2021)

24. Lee, K., Chang, H., Jiang, L., Zhang, H., Tu, Z., Liu, C.: VitGAN: training GANs with vision transformers. arXiv preprint arXiv:2107.04589 (2021)

25. Jiang, Y., Chang, S., Wang, Z.: TransGAN: two transformers can make one strong GAN. arXiv preprint arXiv:2102.07074 (2021)

26. Carion, N., Massa, F., Synnaeve, G., Usunier, N., Kirillov, A., Zagoruyko, S.: End-to-end object detection with transformers. In: Vedaldi, A., Bischof, H., Brox, T., Frahm, J.-M. (eds.) ECCV 2020. LNCS, vol. 12346, pp. 213–229. Springer, Cham (2020). https://doi.org/10.1007/978-3-030-58452-8_13

27. Chu, X., et al.: Twins: revisiting the design of spatial attention in vision transformers. arXiv preprint arXiv:2104.13840 (2021)
28. Wang, W., et al.: Pyramid vision transformer: a versatile backbone for dense prediction without convolutions. arXiv preprint arXiv:2102.12122 (2021)
29. Wang, Y., Zhang, X., Yang, T., Sun, J.: Anchor DETR: query design for transformer-based detector. arXiv preprint arXiv:2109.07107 (2021)
30. Zheng, S., et al.: Rethinking semantic segmentation from a sequence-to-sequence perspective with transformers. In: Proceedings of the IEEE/CVF Conference on Computer Vision and Pattern Recognition (CVPR), pp. 6881–6890 (2021)
31. Liu, Z., et al.: Swin transformer: hierarchical vision transformer using shifted windows. In: Proceedings of the IEEE/CVF International Conference on Computer Vision (ICCV), pp. 10012–10022 (2021)
32. Xie, E., Wang, W., Yu, Z., Anandkumar, A., Alvarez, J.M., Luo, P.: SegFormer: simple and efficient design for semantic segmentation with transformers. In: Advances in Neural Information Processing Systems (2021)
33. Kuo, W., Angelova, A., Malik, J., Lin, T.-Y.: ShapeMask: learning to segment novel objects by refining shape priors. In: Proceedings of the IEEE/CVF International Conference on Computer Vision (ICCV) pp. 9207–9216 (2019)
34. Li, K., Hariharan, B., Malik, J.: Iterative instance segmentation. In: Proceedings of the IEEE Conference on Computer Vision and Pattern Recognition (CVPR), pp. 3659–3667 (2016)
35. Kirillov, A., Wu, Y., He, K., Girshick, R.: Pointrend: image segmentation as rendering. In: Proceedings of the IEEE/CVF Conference on Computer Vision and Pattern Recognition (CVPR), pp. 9799–9808 (2020)
36. Zhang, F., et al.: ACFNet: attentional class feature network for semantic segmentation. In: Proceedings of the IEEE/CVF International Conference on Computer Vision (ICCV), pp. 6798–6807 (2019)
37. Deng, J., Dong, W., Socher, R., Li, L.-J., Li, K., Fei-Fei, L.: ImageNet: a large-scale hierarchical image database. In: IEEE Conference on Computer Vision and Pattern Recognition (CVPR), pp. 248–255 (2009)
38. Zhou, B., Zhao, H., Puig, X., Fidler, S., Barriuso, A., Torralba, A.: Scene parsing through ade20k dataset. In: Proceedings of the IEEE Conference on Computer Vision and Pattern Recognition (CVPR), pp. 633–641 (2017)
39. Mottaghi, R., et al.: The role of context for object detection and semantic segmentation in the wild. In: Proceedings of the IEEE Conference on Computer Vision and Pattern Recognition (CVPR), pp. 891–898 (2014)
40. Caesar, H., Uijlings, J., Ferrari, V.: Coco-stuff: thing and stuff classes in contex. In: Proceedings of the IEEE Conference on Computer Vision and Pattern Recognition (CVPR), pp. 1209–1218 (2018)
41. MMSegmentation Contributors (2020). https://github.com/open-mmlab/mmsegmentation
42. Long, Shelhamer, J., Darrell, E., T.: Fully convolutional networks for semantic segmentation. In: Proceedings of the IEEE Conference on Computer Vision and Pattern Recognition (CVPR), pp. 3431–3440 (2015)
43. Yin, M., et al.: Disentangled non-local neural networks. In: Vedaldi, A., Bischof, H., Brox, T., Frahm, J.-M. (eds.) ECCV 2020. LNCS, vol. 12360, pp. 191–207. Springer, Cham (2020). https://doi.org/10.1007/978-3-030-58555-6_12
44. He, K., Zhang, X., Ren, S., Sun, J.: Deep residual learning for image recognition. In: Proceedings of the IEEE Conference on Computer Vision and Pattern Recognition (CVPR), pp. 770–778 (2016)

45. Sun, K., Xiao, B., Liu, D., Wang, J.: Deep high-resolution representation learning for human pose estimation. In: Proceedings of the IEEE/CVF Conference on Computer Vision and Pattern Recognition (CVPR), pp. 5693–5703 (2019)
46. Ronneberger, O., Fischer, P., Brox, T.: U-net: convolutional networks for biomedical image segmentation. In: International Conference on Medical Image Computing and Computer-Assisted Intervention, pp. 234–241 (2015)
47. Badrinarayanan, V., Kendall, A., Cipolla, R.: SegNet: a deep convolutional encoder-decoder architecture for image segmentation. IEEE Trans. Pattern Anal. Mach. Intell. **39**(12), 2481–2495 (2017)
48. Yuan, Y., Huang, L., Guo, J., Zhang, C., Chen, X., Wang, J.: OCnet: object context network for scene parsing. arXiv preprint arXiv:1809.00916 (2018)
49. Loshchilov, I., Hutter, F.: Fixing weight decay regularization in Adam (2018)
50. Cordts, M., et al.: The cityscapes dataset for semantic urban scene understanding. In: Proceedings of the IEEE/CVF Conference on Computer Vision and Pattern Recognition (CVPR) (2016)
51. Cheng, B., Schwing, A.G., Kirillov, A.: Per-pixel classification is not all you need for semantic segmentation. arXiv preprint arXiv:2107.06278 (2021)
52. Wu, Y.-H., et al.: P2T: pyramid pooling transformer for scene understanding. arXiv preprint arXiv:2106.12011 (2021)

Defect Detection for High Voltage Transmission Lines Based on Deep Learning

Zhiqiang Zheng[1], Mingyang Zhao[1], Xi Cheng[2], Zhi Weng[1(✉)], and Yu Wang[1]

[1] College of Electronic Information Engineering, Inner Mongolia University,
Hohhot 010021, China
wzhi@imu.edu.cn

[2] Ulanqab Power Supply Branch Company, Inner Mongolia Power (Group) Co., Ltd.,
Ulanqab 012000, China

Abstract. For UAV inspection of high-voltage transmission line defect detection, a cascading defect detection framework of component location and segmentation is proposed. This method solves the problem of time-consuming, laborious and inaccurate analysis of images by the naked eye of electrical personnel. Firstly, the YOLO v4 object location algorithm is used to locate the key components. Secondly, the localized key components are cropped, and then the images are reconstructed by SRGAN with super-resolution. Finally, the Mask-RCNN defect segmentation channel is designed. A feature reuse structure based on the ResNet-34 network is proposed to ensure accuracy while reducing the parameter redundancy. At the same time Point Set strong a priori anchor frame optimization mechanism approach is introduced, to achieve pin-missing and insulator self-shattering segmentation. The experimental results show that the mAP of the localization scheme is improved by up to 5.2% compared with other mainstream methods. The precision of the optimal defect segmentation scheme reaches 87.2%. The staff will be assisted by the proposed method which provides technical support for the intelligent level of the power system in this paper. It has important practical significance for the construction of smart grid.

Keywords: Defect detection · Object location · Instance segmentation · Deep learning

1 Introduction

With the rapid development of the national economy, the scale of the power grid is increasing, and people's living standards have undergone radical changes. As an important part of the electrical energy supply, the safety and stability of the connection fixture have high requirements [1]. The cotter pin, as a fastener attachment fixture, is exposed to wind, sun and rain for a long time and is prone to missing pins and other phenomena. Therefore, it need to regularly find its defects to reduce the safety risks. Currently, aerial inspection has become the mainstream way of power sector inspection [2]. In the past decade, the average number of high-voltage transmission lines above 220 kV has

© The Author(s), under exclusive license to Springer Nature Switzerland AG 2022
S. Yu et al. (Eds.): PRCV 2022, LNCS 13537, pp. 574–592, 2022.
https://doi.org/10.1007/978-3-031-18916-6_46

increased by 38,000 km [3]. However, a large number of inspection images or videos still need to be analyzed and investigated by the naked eye of staff, which is time-consuming and not very accurate. Therefore, an intelligent inspection image-based defect detection method for high-voltage transmission lines is urgently needed.

In recent years, deep learning has shown an explosive development in computing, from AlexNet [4] proposed by Hinton et al. then architectures such as VGG [5], ResNet [6], and MobileNet [7] were created. Deep learning has provided a multifaceted orientation to human intelligent life. It has been used in medical image recognition, autonomous driving, face recognition, and other fields to obtain fruitful results. The essential characteristic of deep learning to liberate human labor provides a solution for intelligent defect detection in high voltage transmission lines.

For high voltage transmission line defect detection, scholars have done a lot of work.

In 2011, Jiao Hong [8] proposed a method to improve the Hough transform by replacing the contour features of the generalized Hough transform with Harris corner point features, fast Fourier image index matching, and peak merging to achieve the study of identifying and locating the anti-shock hammer in inspection images.

In 2013, the literature [9] came out with adaptive fuzzy inference and discrete orthogonal S transform (DOST) methods to extract the position and state of insulators by boundary sensitivity of color features, k-mean clustering.

In 2014, the literature [10] proposed an improved balloon force snake method for edge detection, which enhanced the contour curvature control for anti-shock hammer detection by judging the boundary and enhancing the contour curvature by hessian matrix.

In 2016, the literature [11] came up with a deep convolution- al model for multi-level feature extraction and applied the support vector machine (SVM) approach for feature classification thus determining the state of the insulator.

In 2017, Yan et al. [12] proposed a linear fitting method to achieve effective detection of insulator strings by principal component analysis (PCA) and feature fusion based on histogram of directional gradients (HOG) and local binary patterns (LBP). Wang Sen. [13] proposed an AdaBoost based detection algorithm by Haar feature extraction analysis followed by feature classification thereby achieving the detection of anti-vibration hammer.

In 2018, Zhai et al. [14] achieved morphological processing of insulator defect locations by combining color and spatial features. Zhong, Junping et al. [15] proposed an improved deep convolutional neural network (CNN) and achieved effective SP automatic defect detection.

In 2019, the literature [16] implemented a YOLO model- based on insulator self-explosion detection method, which can effectively locate insulators and defects. The literature [17] came out with an improved Faster R-CNN insulator self-explosion detection model, which changed the traditional feature extraction network and achieved accurate localization without relying on a priori knowledge by soft non-maximal suppression. Miao et al. [18] proposed insulator detection technology based on deep learning, using a one-stage detector SSD pre-trained by COCO data set was fine-tuned and was able to locate ceramic and composite insulators very well. Ling et al. [19] implemented insulator self-detonation detection based on Faster R-CNN and U-net models.

In 2020, Xiantao *et al.* [20] proposed a convolutional neural network based on region suggestion network, while applying data enhancement such as affine transformation and Gaussian fuzzy to obtain better accuracy. Zhenbing Zhao et al. [21] proposed an automatic pin-defect detection model called automatic visual shape clustering network (AVSCNet). The model can effectively detect the missing pin defects of bolts in transmission lines and eliminate the non-uniform interference generated when mapping 3D bolt entities to 2D images. Wang Jian et al. [22] proposed a method for detecting split-pin defects in high-speed railroad conduit fastening devices with regard to their fault states, such as missing, loose, and improperly installed pins. The post-experimental results show that the proposed method has high accuracy in detecting split-pin defects and can ensure the stable operation of the catenary support device.

In 2021, Xiao, Yewei et al. [23] proposed a cascaded convolutional neural network-based target detection method that can accurately identify pin defects in aerial images, thus solving the engineering application problem of pin defect detection in power transmission lines.

In 2022, Zhongyun Liu et al. [24] proposed a method to detect critical targets and defects of high-voltage transmission lines based on deep learning object detection network, which can realize remote automatic detection of high-voltage transmission lines.

The above-mentioned defect detection for high-voltage transmission lines is focused on key components such as insulators, anti-vibration hammers, and pin-level defect detection. In their localization, the accuracy is not high and there is a problem of parameter redundancy and the algorithms for defect detection are incompatible with each other, making it impossible to detect two different types of defects at the same time.

The purpose of this paper is to explore a multi component generic and parallel defect detection algorithm. The main innovations are as follows.

1. For the problems of complex input background and many kinds of targets in aerial inspection images. A deep learning based on defect transmission line image detection system is proposed. The defect detection task is decomposed into two computer vision tasks. The first is key component detection. The second is super-resolution instance segmentation model.
2. In order to locate the critical components of high voltage transmission lines accurately and universally, YOLO v4 algorithm is used. Then the super-resolution generative adversarial network (SRGAN) is introduced to address the problem of blurring the localization crop map. Finally Mask RCNN algorithm is employed to quantitatively analyze the defect state, and to balance the defect detection accuracy and efficiency, ResNet-34 based feature reuse network and Point-Set anchor frame optimization mechanism are proposed.

2 Object and Methods

2.1 Defect Detection System

In the daily inspection of transmission lines, the UAV cruise is filmed to obtain high-definition images of transmission lines. The images are passed to the defect detection platform which judged by the naked eye of staff and recorded manually. The intelligent defect detection explored in this paper involves two key issues. The first step is to locate key components from the global image to obtain a cropped sub-image, thereby reducing redundant operations. The second step applies instance segmentation to achieve defective component status research and judgment. In this paper, the YOLO v4 object detection algorithm is used to locate the key components of high voltage transmission lines. The defect detection channel uses the localization information of the key component detection channel to crop the key component image, and the super-resolution algorithm SRGAN achieves super-resolution reconstruction to enrich the detailed features. The high voltage transmission line defect detection system is shown in Fig. 1.

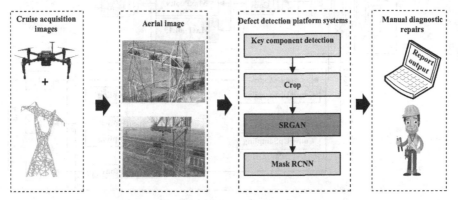

Fig. 1. High voltage transmission line defect detection system flow.

2.2   Key Component Location Stage

The backbone of yolov3 evolved from darknet-19 in the yolov2 period to darknet-53, deepening the number of network layers, and introducing the cross layer addition operation in RESNET to achieve the accuracy of resnet-152. In the prediction stage, FPN (feature pyramid network) uses three scale feature maps for reference. The small feature map provides semantic information, and the large feature map has more fine-grained information. Small feature maps are fused by up sampling and large-scale. Instead of using the soft Max loss function, we use the sigmod+cross entropy function, which can support multi label prediction.

YOLO v4 [20] was proposed by Alexey in 2020 based on YOLO v3, adding many training techniques to obtain excellent results with limited GPU resources. It uses the Mosaic data enhancement method. The method contains the classic flip, zoom, and color gamut distortion. The multiple image combinations (cutmix) and masking techniques such as randomly replacing regions, square clipping, and hiding regions are innovatively used in the method. Label Smoothing is introduced to reduce the occurrence of overfitting. Different from the regression optimization of YOLO v3, the aspect ratio of the prediction frame fitting the object frame is considered. That is the CIOU strategy, which makes the object frame regression more stable.

The network structure of YOLO v4 is shown as follows Fig. 2. The backbone feature extraction network CSPDarknet53 adopts the Mish activation function, and adds the cross stage partial network (CSPnet) to each of the five major residual blocks on the original Darknet53, which divides the feature map into two parts. One part is convolved and the other is combined with the previous convolved result, which solves the duplication problem of gradient information.

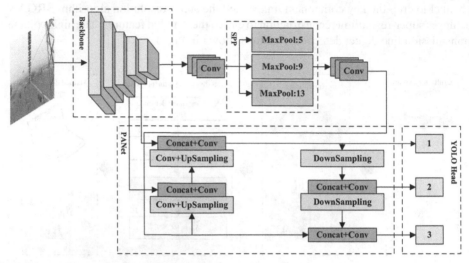

Fig. 2. YOLO v4 structure diagram.

For the feature pyramid module YOLO v4 not only uses the Spatial Pyramid Pooling(SPP) structure, but also introduces a new enhanced bottom-up path FPN structure, which can effectively improve the low-level information by stacking the feature maps of three different sizes, 8x, 16x and 32x, with multiple up and down sampling channels. Each stage takes the feature maps of the previous stage as input and processes them with convolution. Its output is added to the feature maps of the corresponding stage of the top-down pathway using lateral concatenation to provide information for the next segment. The final detection layer Head still inherits YOLO v3 and completes the anchoring in the feature map frame, generating a 5+C dimensional vector, where C denotes the total number of data categories and the 5-dimensional vector contains the border coordinates (4 values), and the border confidence (Confidence 1 value).

2.3 Defect Detection Stage

The defect detection channel takes the clipped connections detected by the YOLO v4 network as input. The effective pixel area after clipping is very small, so amplification of the image will result in blurred boundary lines. To address this problem, SRGAN network super-resolution reconstruction of cropped images is proposed, followed by instance segmentation, ResNet-34 feature structure reuse and point set optimization mechanisms.

2.3.1 Srgan

The SRGAN [21] network consists of a generative network and a discriminative network, both of which are played to obtain a Nash equilibrium. The backbone network in the generative network consists of 16 residual modules stacked iteratively. Each residual module is normalized by a primary convolution operation, after which it is activated using the Parametric ReLU function. Then the input is fed into the secondary convolution layer, and the output of the secondary convolution is also normalized by the BN layer. At the end of the network, two pixelshuffler up sampling is used to extend the size of the feature map to four times the input. Finally the generated super-resolution image is output via the 9 × 9 convolution layer, as shown in Fig. 3.

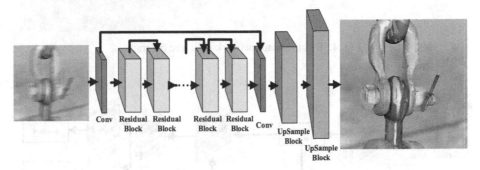

Fig. 3. Generator network structure diagram

The main structure of the discriminator network is based on the VGG network, whose input information is the real image. The high-resolution reconstructed image is generated by the generator network, and after the operation of 8 convolutional layers, it is input to the Dense fully connected layer with the channel number of 1024. Then it is activated by the Leaky ReLU function, and again input to the Dense fully connected layer with the channel number of one. Finally, it is activated by the sigmoid function and outputs the confidence value to determine whether the two images initially input to the network are the same one, as shown in Fig. 4.

2.3.2 Defect Detection Based on Mask RCNN

Mask RCNN [22] is able to achieve multi-scale small pixel object detection thanks to the architecture of the backbone feature extraction network ResNet-101 combined with the feature pyramid FPN, which combines multiple stages of top-down lateral connection fusion of features, preserving both the top-level semantic features and the low-level contour features.

The feature map obtained from the feature extraction module is fed into the region proposal network to obtain the possible regions of interest (ROI). To achieve smooth object contours, a ROI Align mechanism is invoked to make a pixel-by-pixel correspondence between the input image and the feature map output by the network. The last full convolutional network (FCN) branch predicts the corresponding object segmentation mask. Another parallel branch is used for object boundary regression and classification, and the network structure is shown in Fig. 5.

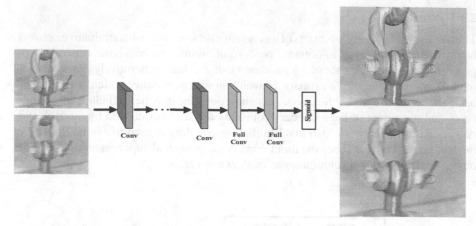

Fig. 4. Discriminator network structure diagram

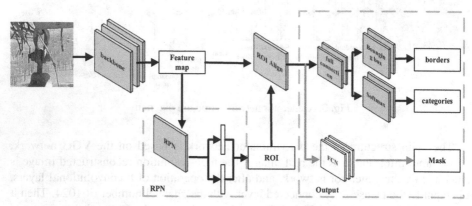

Fig. 5. Mask-RCNN structure diagram.

2.3.3   Improved Mask RCNN Algorithm

A)   *Improved feature extraction network based on ResNet*

For the analysis of the cropped image, the object to be segmented occupies the major pixels in the graph, and the morphology and difficulty of the segmented image are simpler compared to the common segmentation tasks. Both resnet-34 and resnet-101 have 5 convolutional groups, but the input channels of the resnet-34 network are 3, 64, 128, 256, 512, and the number of residual units in each convolutional group is 3, 4, 6, 3, and each residual unit has two 3 × 3 convolutional layers, which is the 34-layer network structure. However, each residual unit of the resnet-101 network has three 3 × 3 convolutional layers, so the workload of the resnet-101 network is quite huge. So Mask RCNN using ResNet-101 feature extraction backbone network will cause parameter redundancy to some extent. In order to improve the segmentation efficiency, feature reuse in the feature extraction network is proposed. This can effectively improve the segmentation efficiency of the model, and the feature processing in the deep layer of the network can draw on the information of the shallow features to improve the segmentation accuracy.

Based on the above considerations, ResNet-34 is used as the base feature network for optimization in this paper, and the feature reuse structure is designed based on DenseNet [23]. The overall structure is shown in Fig. 6.

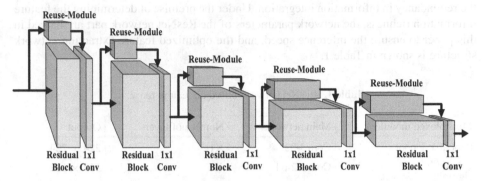

Fig. 6. Structure of feature extraction network.

The lower layer network structure follows the idea of ResNet-34, containing five residual blocks of different dimensions, with the addition of a 1×1 convolutional layer for transition integration of the multiplexed features. The upper layer network is stitched together by the multiplexed connection modules designed in this paper, and the structure of each module is shown at the top end of Fig. 7.

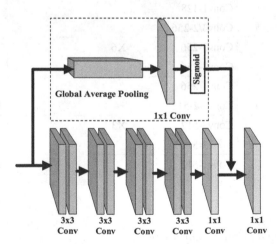

Fig. 7. Structure of the connection between the multiplexing module and the residual module.

The feature map is compressed to one-dimensional information via a Global Average Pooling layer, and the 1×1 convolutional layer is used to convolve the compressed channel information. While a sigmoid activation function is used to assign a value to each channel. The channel information map with entitled values is finally connected to the end of the ResNet residual module and integrated with the 1×1 convolutional layer for output.

The feature reuse module is not only able to transfer the upper layer feature map information to the next layer, but also to suppress useless channels by weighted assignment. And effectively enhance the object information volume channels, thus reducing the redundancy in information integration. Under the premise of determining the feature information richness, the network parameters of the ResNet network part are halved in this paper to ensure the inference speed, and the optimized feature extraction network structure is shown in Table 1.

Table 1. ResNet network based on feature reuse.

Multiplexed modules	Main network	Number of layers	Output
Global avg pool 1 ×1 conv sigmoid	Conv3-32	X1	224 × 224
	Conv3/2-64		112 × 112
Global avg pool 1 ×1 conv sigmoid	Conv3-64	X3	
	Conv3-64		
	Conv1-64		
	Conv3/2-128		56 × 56
Global avg pool 1 ×1 conv sigmoid	Conv3-128	X4	
	Conv3-128		
	Conv1-128		
	Conv3/2-256		28 × 28
Global avg pool 1 ×1 conv sigmoid	Conv3-256	X6	
	Conv3-256		
	Conv1-256		
	Conv3/2-512		14 × 14
Global avg pool 1 ×1 conv sigmoid	Conv3-512	X3	
	Conv3-512		
	Conv1-512		7 × 7

B) *Improved strong a priori anchor frame*

The effect of considering segmentation is not only related to the feature extraction network, but also the segmented. The candidate regions are closely related to the anchors that locate the object regions in the image. In order to improve the segmentation accuracy, to compensate for the missing region of the segmentation or divide the background region into segmentation regions, the Point-Set anchor frame optimization mechanism [30] is introduced, abandoning the traditional anchor frame to locate the object contour, and using point-set fitting to effectively improve the object a priori.

The Point-Set implementation principle is to represent the anchor box by an ordered set of points, which consists of two parts: the central anchor point and the boundary anchor point, with the boundary anchor point set initially taking the form of a rectangular box, as shown in Fig. 8.

The object to be segmented is assumed to be S, and the boundary information for its mask is represented by an ordered set of points $S = \{S_i\}_{i=1}^{n_s}$. The point set S_i represents the i point on the mask, corresponding to the i point on the anchor frame point set T. The original Mask RCNN algorithm is a regression fit to the dimensions of the anchor based on the centroid of the object, whereas the point set is a regression fit to the point set T to fit the mask point-set S, that is by calculating the offset of T from S. The offset is calculated by first identifying the points T^* corresponding to the anchor point-set and the mask boundary, after which the offset between the two is calculated $\Delta T = T^* - T$. The strategy for the correspondence between point set T and point-set S is chosen as follows, taking N points from the mask boundary as Ground Truth (the points taken belong to point set S) and connecting the neighboring points two by two. Find the nearest line segment to each point on the set T of anchor frame points. The point of vertical projection of a point on a line segment is the Ground Truth Point-T^*, then the final regression of the points on the point set T according to Ground Truth Point, Fig. 9 of the correspondence points is as follows.

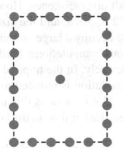

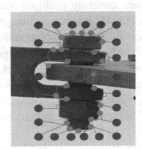

Fig. 8. Ordered set of anchor points   **Fig. 9.** Point set correspondence

In this paper, the anchor calculation in the original Mask RCNN is replaced with the Point-Set form, and the loss function calculation formula regarding the location information after the replacement as:

$$L = \frac{\lambda}{N_{pos}} \sum_{x,y} L_{reg}(t_{x,y}, t_{x,y}^*) \tag{1}$$

In the above equation, λ is the weight responsible for controlling the direct weight of location loss and classification loss; N_{pos} is the number of positive samples in the test set; L_{reg} is the L1 loss, $t_{x,y}$ is the points in the point set and $t_{x,y}^*$ is the regression object.

3   Results and Discussions

3.1   Experimental Environment

To ensure the relative fairness of the individual algorithm models tested in this paper, all experiments were conducted in the following hardware and software environments. As shown in Table 2.

Table 2.   Software and hardware operating environment

Hardware environment	Software environment
CPU central processing unit: i7 10700	IDE: PyCharm
GPU graphics processors: RTX 2080Ti	CUDA: 10.2
Memory: 32GB DDR4	CuDNN: 7.4.6
Operating systems: Win10	Frameworks: Pytorch & Tensorflow

3.2   Key Component Location Stage

3.2.1   Data Description

The dataset used in this paper is derived from images taken by UAVs inspecting transmission lines, covering multiple transmission lines with diverse scenes. However, the resolution of UAV inspection images is as high as 5472×3078, and the size of each image is about 7MB. The preservation of these data will occupy a large amount of storage space. The high- resolution images will cause a serious computational burden on the convolutional neural network object detection model severely. In the hope of retaining the essential characteristics of the sample, the image resolution is reduced to one-fifth of the original by down sampling, instead of cropping. Not only does this reduce the amount of storage space occupied, but also it saves a great deal of time in the later stages of the study.

As a data-driven supervised learning deep convolutional neural network algorithm, a large amount of data support is one of its advantages. Otherwise the network will produce overfitting or even fail to converge. For individually constructed datasets, the amount of data is generally not able to reach the huge scale of 10 million. To address the problem of data scarcity, the existing image processing is needed to augment the data volume and complete the data enhancement operation. In that way, it will effectively improving the performance of the network and strengthening the ability to prevent overfitting. In this paper, the data set was mainly flipped left and right, flipped up and down, rotated by 90° and rotated by 270°. The original 3,000 data were expanded to four times the original size by means of data augmentation, so that the overall number of data sets changed to 12,000. Among them, the training set is 9600, the verification set is 1200, and the test set is also 1200. This is shown in Fig. 10.

3.2.2 Experimental Results and Analysis

In this paper, YOLO v3, a typical representative of the YOLO series, SSD, which is also a single-stage detection network, and Faster RCNN, a typical two-stage detection network, were selected for multivariate comparison. Due to the large number of objects detected in this exercise, the comparison of detection accuracy for each class of object networks is shown in Table 3 below in order to provide a clearer reflection of the optimization effect.

Fig. 10. Sample chart

The Table 3 below shows that the accuracy of the YOLO v4 has improved significantly compared to the YOLO v3 in the categories of anti-shock hammers and connection fittings. Both the hammer and the connector are small objects, and the accuracy of these two categories is low compared to the results of the other categories. The other reason is due to the quality of the imaging, as the environment is usually unobstructed at high altitude and there is a large light ratio, the imaging appears to be vague and not easily detected. The other categories of detection objects are larger and easier to detect, and YOLO v4 has the highest detection accuracy from the comparison results.

Table 3. Detection accuracy for each type of object

Category	YOLO v4	YOLO v3	SSD	Faster RCNN
Hammer	86.4%	82.5%	80.8%	84.6%
Nest	87.9%	86.4%	83.5%	86.8%
Connector	85.1%	81.2%	79.3%	83.1%
Insulator	95.5%	94.5%	93.8%	95.5%
Tower	97.5%	97.8%	96.5%	98.1%
Sign	94.0%	92.4%	89.3%	91.2%

In this paper, the combined test metrics of the four structures are compared and the results are shown in Table 4 below. In the experiment, on the one hand, a high precision (Precision) and a relatively good recall (Recall) are desired. However, the two are mutually constrained, so the mean Average Precision (mAP), which represents the average of their reconciliation is used as the evaluation metric for model detection in this paper.

Table 4. Combined index test results

Models	mAP	Recall	Avg IoU	FPS
YOLO v4	92.4%	94.2%	85.3%	34
YOLO v3	89.1%	90.4%	81.4%	39
SSD	87.2%	88.7%	79.2%	30
Faster RCNN	89.9%	91.3%	87.8%	13

Analysis of the data in the table above shows that YOLO v4 has a significantly higher recall and average accuracy Average Intersection Over Union (Avg IoU). The more obvious comprehensive metric is Avg IoU, which mainly reflects the degree of overlap between the area of the prediction frame and the human-labelled object frame. The IoU of the RCNN is slightly higher than that of YOLO due to its two-stage detection mechanism and secondary fine-tuning of the area of the anchor. Although YOLO v4 is slightly inferior in terms of inference speed, its outstanding accuracy will serve as a shield for subsequent research in the field of electricity.

Figure 11 below shows a typical representation of an aerial inspection map, divided into four groups to demonstrate the visualization of the YOLO v4 network. Figure 11(a) shows the images taken by the drone from two angles, with the nest clearly visible in the upper image and the nest heavily obscured in the lower image. Figure 11(b) shows the difference in the number of key components, with only two key components in the upper panel compared to four times as many in the lower panel. In Fig. 11(c), the background of the lower panel contains distracting elements such as dwellings and trees, while the background of the upper panel is simple compared to the lower panel.

(a) Different camera angles, front shot vs. back shot

(b) Different types, less objects vs. more objects

(c) Different backgrounds, simple vs. complex backgrounds

Fig. 11. YOLO v4 key component inspection results

3.3 Defect Detection Stage

3.3.1 Data Description

The dataset used in this section is derived from (B) Key component positioning cut images. According to the official defect rate and the existing data set in this article, the representative selection includes the cut images of the insulator and pin area. The training samples of 3000 and a test samples of 600. The open source software Labelme was used to label the screws, cotter pins and insulator self-explosion areas, as shown in Fig. 12. An image data was produced in 3 steps, firstly establishing the json file, secondly extracting the file with 24 bit depth and finally converting the 8 bit masked image.

Fig. 12. Legend of labeling

3.3.2 Experimental Results And Analysis

In section II-C4 point-set anchors, there is no uniform regulation on the number of points to be taken from the anchor point set and the number of points to be taken from the object mask boundary point set. So in order to determine the appropriate number of points, this paper sets the point set as 20 points and increases by 8 points each time. The number of points in the point set is twice as many. The number of points in the point set is twice as many as the number of points in the point set. By setting different points for comparison, the number of points in the point set is chosen as the optimal value. The results of the comparison are shown in Table 5.

Table 5. Comparison of test results for different number of point sets

Methods	MIoU	mAP
Anchors	57.1%	73.8%
T = 20	52.4%	71.5%
T = 28	55.8%	72.8%
T = 36	58.5%	73.5%
T = 44	59.6%	74.2%
T = 52	60.3%	74.6%
T = 60	58.0%	73.1%

In this test, the IoU and mAP values were used as the evaluation indicators, and the data in Table 5 above were analyzed in conjunction with the results of the original Mask RCNN algorithm. From the above table, we can find that the number of points for Point-Set Anchors is set in an inverted U-shape structure, with the number of points being 20 and 28, the overall representation of the mask boundary is more rigid due to the smaller number of points, and the fitting effect is worse than before the optimization. As the number of points increases, the distance between points becomes shorter and the mask shape can be more accurately represented by line segments, which makes the regression of point-set anchors more effective. However, as the number of points increases, the boundary line segments of the mask become denser, and the points on point-set anchors may be mismatched, that is two points correspond to a line segment at the same time, which results in one less Ground Truth Point than expected and the regression effect becomes worse. The number of points in the point-set is set to 52.

After determining the number of Point-Set Anchors, the overall optimized Mask RCNN algorithm was tested in conjunction with the feature extraction network optimization in the first subsection, using the following test metrics: accuracy precision, recall, F1-score, mean intersection ratio MIoU, various object test accuracy AP values and mean accuracy mAP, and operational processing frame rate FPS. The test results are shown in Table 6 below.

Table 6. Comparison of splitting performance

	Models	Precision	Recall	F1-score	MIoU	FPS
1	Mask RCNN	77.3%	80.7%	79.0%	57.1%	2.7
2	Mask-New	80.8%	85.2%	82.9%	62.6%	4.8
3	SRGAN+Mask RCNN	80.5%	87.7%	85.4%	70.4%	2.2
4	SRGAN+Mask-New	87.2%	92.6%	90.8%	77.9%	3.8

A comparison of the results from groups 1, 3 and 2, 4 shows that the cut low-resolution images are better segmented by the SRGAN network in high resolution for the segmentation models. The significant increase in both accuracy and recall indicates that the models have higher confidence in the category determination and lower miss detection rates for small targets such as screws and cotter pins after HD processing. The increase in MIoU values by more than 10% after SRGAN super resolution reconstruction indicates that image sharpness has a greater impact on the model's boundary fit, with higher sharpness resulting in more accurate segmentation. The two sets of comparison tests were designed to optimize the feature extraction network and the anchors mechanism for Mask RCNN. Based on the comparison data in Table 5, the Point-Set anchor mechanism has been shown to improve the MIoU. Based on the comparison data in Table 6 for groups 1 and 2, the addition of the multiplexed module feature extraction network to the Point-Set Anchor has further improved the MIoU. It is indicates that the representation of the shallow network can also improve the model segmentation. The results show that the representational features of the shallow network can also improve the fit of the model to the target. The usefulness of the feature reuse module is also illustrated by the precision and recall values in the two comparison tests. Finally, this paper also compares the segmentation frame rates of the model. The test results show that the FPS of the ResNet34-based network is improved by more than 2 frames without SRGAN optimization, and by about 1 frame with SRGAN optimization, which also improves the overall usefulness of the algorithm.

The segmentation effects of the four groups of methods on the pin-missing detection and insulator self-explosion test sets are shown in Fig. 13. From the experimental results, the SRGAN+Mask-New proposed in this paper has a lower pin-missing detection rate and more well-defined boundaries than the other groups.

(a)original image   (b)Mask RCNN   (c)Mask-New (d)SRGAN+Mask RCNN (e) SRGAN+Mask-New

Fig. 13. Graph of test results for different algorithms

4 Conclusion

For high voltage transmission line defect detection, a hierarchical detection system with fusion of object localization and instance segmentation is proposed. In the detection stage, a multi-model comparison analysis is carried out, and YOLO v4 locates the key components of the inspection images with an accuracy of 92.4%, satisfying robustness and real-time performance. In the instance segmentation stage, SRGAN network was introduced for super-resolution reconstruction algorithm. Finally, Mask-RCNN algorithm was used to propose an optimized feature extraction network based on ResNet feature reuse, which effectively improved the efficiency of defect segmentation and introduced Point Set strong a priori anchor frame optimization mechanism. It improved the segmentation accuracy by 3.5 percentage points and achieved pixel segmentation for missing pins and self-detonation of insulators. This paper only considers two types of defects, and has not yet considered the determination of the defect degree level.

Declarations

Funding. This work was supported by the National Natural Science Foundation of China under Grant 61966026, and Natural Science Foundation of Inner Mongolia under 2020MS06015 and 2021MS06014.

Conflicts of Interests. The authors declare that they have no known competing financial interests or personal relationships that could have appeared to influence the work reported in this paper.

References

1. Zhou, M., Yan, J., Zhou, X.: Real-time online analysis of power grid. CSEE J. Power Energy Syst. **6**(1), 236–238 (2020)
2. Jenssen, R., Roverso, D.: Automatic autonomous vision-based power line inspection: a review of current status and the potential role of deep learning. Int. J. Electr. Power Energy Syst. **99**, 107–120 (2018)
3. Mai, G., et al.: LeapDetect: an agile platform for inspecting power transmission lines from drones. In: 2019 International Conference on Data Mining Workshops (ICDMW), pp. 1106–1109 (2019)
4. Krizhevsky, A., Sutskever, I.: ImageNet classification with deep convolutional neural networks. In: Advances in Neural Information Processing Systems 25, pp. 1097–1105 (2012)
5. Simonyan, K., Zisserman, A.: Very deep convolutional networks for large-scale image recognition. arXiv preprint arXiv:1409.1556 (2014)
6. He, K., Zhang, X., Ren, S., Sun, J.: Deep residual learning for image recognition. In: 2016 IEEE Conference on Computer Vision and Pattern Recognition (CVPR), pp. 770–778 (2016)
7. Howard, A.G., Zhu, M., Chen, B.: MobileNets: efficient convolutional neural networks for mobile vision applications. arXiv Preprint arXiv:1704.04861 (2017)
8. Jiao, H.: Identification and positioning of anti-vibration hammers in helicopter inspection of transmission line images, pp. 44–66. Dalian Maritime University (2011)
9. Reddy, M.J.B., Mohanta, D.K.: Condition monitoring of 11 kV distribution system insulators incorporating complex imagery using combined DOST-SVM approach. IEEE Trans. Dielectr. Electr. Insul. **20**(2), 664–674 (2013)
10. Haibin, W., Yanping, X., Weimin, F.: Damper detection in helicopter inspection of power transmission line. In: 2014 Fourth International Conference on Instrumentation and Measurement, Computer, Communication and Control, pp. 628–632 (2014)
11. Zhao, Z., Xu, G., Qi, Y.: Multi-patch deep features for power line insulator status classification from aerial images. In: Proceedings of 2016 International Joint Conference on Neural Networks, pp. 3187–3194 (2014)
12. Tiantian, Y., Guodong, Y., Junzhi, Y.: Feature fusion based insulator detection for aerial inspection. In: 2017 36th Chinese Control Conference, pp. 10972–10977 (2017)

13. Wang, S.: Research on anti-vibration hammer detection algorithm on transmission line images, pp. 33–51. Beijing Jiaotong University (2017)
14. Zhai, Y., Chen, R., Yang, Q.: Insulator fault detection based on spatial morphological features of aerial images. IEEE Access **6**, 35316–35326 (2018)
15. Zhong, J., Liu, Z., Han, Z., Han, Y., Zhang, W.: A CNN-based defect inspection method for catenary split pins in high-speed railway. IEEE Trans. Instrum. Meas. **68**(8), 2849–2860 (2018)
16. Adou, M.W., Xu, H., Chen, G.: Insulator faults detection based on deep learning. In: 2019 IEEE 13th International Conference on Anti-Counterfeiting, Security, and Identification, pp. 173–177 (2019)
17. Liao, G.P., Yang, G.J., Tong, W.T.: Study on power line insulator defect detection via improved faster region-based convolutional neural network. In: 2019 IEEE 7th International Conference on Computer Science and Network Technology, pp. 262–266, (2019)
18. Miao, X., Liu, X., Chen, J.: Insulator detection in aerial images for transmission line inspection using single shot multibox detector. IEEE Access **7**, 9945–9956 (2019)
19. Ling, Z., Zhang, D., Qiu, R.C.: An accurate and real-time method of self-blast glass insulator location based on faster R-CNN and U-Net with aerial images. CSEE J. Power Energy Syst. **5**(4), 474–482 (2019)
20. Tao, X., Zhang, D., Wang, Z.: Detection of power line insulator defects using aerial images analyzed with convolutional neural networks. IEEE Trans. Syst. Man Cybern. **50**(4), 1486–1498 (2020)
21. Zhao, Z., Qi, H., Qi, Y., Zhang, K., Zhai, Y., Zhao, W.: Detection method based on automatic visual shape clustering for pin-missing defect in transmission lines. IEEE Trans. Instrum. Meas. **69**(9), 6080–6091 (2020)
22. Wang, J., Luo, L., Ye, W., Zhu, S.: A defect-detection method of split pins in the catenary fastening devices of high-speed railway based on deep learning. IEEE Trans. Instrum. Meas. **69**(12), 9517–9525 (2020)
23. Xiao, Y., et al.: Detection of pin defects in aerial images based on cascaded convolutional neural network. IEEE Access **9**, 73071–73082 (2021)
24. Liu, Z., et al.: Key target and defect detection of high-voltage power transmission lines with deep learning. Int. J. Electr. Power Energy Syst. **142**, 108277 (2022)
25. Bochkovskiy, A., Wang, C.Y., Liao, H.: YOLOv4: optimal speed and accuracy of object detection. arXiv Preprint arXiv:2004.10934 (2020)
26. Ledig, C., Theis L., Huszar, F.: Photo-realistic single image super-resolution using a generative adversarial network. In: 2017 IEEE Conference on Computer Vision and Pattern Recognition, pp. 105–114 (2017)
27. Ledig, C., et al.: Photo-realistic single image super-resolution using a generative adversarial network. In: 2017 IEEE Conference on Computer Vision and Pattern Recognition (CVPR), pp. 105–114 (2017)
28. He K., Gkioxari, G., Dollár, P.: Mask R-CNN. In 2017 IEEE International Conference on Computer Vision, pp. 2980–2988 (2017)
29. Huang, G., Liu, Z., Van Der Maaten, L., Weinberger, K.Q.: Densely connected convolutional networks. In: 2017 IEEE Conference on Computer Vision and Pattern Recognition (CVPR), pp. 2261–2269 (2017)
30. Wei, F., Sun, X., Li, H., Wang, J., Lin, S.: Point-set anchors for object detection, instance segmentation and pose estimation. In: Vedaldi, A., Bischof, H., Brox, T., Frahm, J.-M. (eds.) ECCV 2020. LNCS, vol. 12355, pp. 527–544. Springer, Cham (2020). https://doi.org/10.1007/978-3-030-58607-2_31

ORION: Orientation-Sensitive Object Detection

Jingran Xia[1,2], Guowen Kuang[1](✉), Xu Wang[1], Zhibin Chen[2],
and Jinfeng Yang[1]

[1] Institute of Applied Artificial Intelligence of the Guangdong-Hong Kong-Macao
Greater Bay Area, Shenzhen Polytechnic, Shenzhen 518055, China
`gkuang@szpt.edu.cn`
[2] School of Electronics and Information Engineering, University of Science
and Technology Liaoning, Liaoning 114045, China
`zhibinchen1969@ustl.edu.cn`

Abstract. Object detection is of great importance to intelligent stock-breeding applications, but currently, basic tools like models and datasets are still in shortage in specific livestock breeding circumstances. In this paper, we build a cattle object detection dataset with real oriented bounding box (ROBB) annotation. In particular, this dataset is single-category, multiple-instance per frame, and has body-direction-aligned orientation and non-rigid targets. Benchmark models are investigated with our proposed orientation-sensitive IOU algorithm *COS-IOU* and angle-related loss *CosAngleLoss*. The combination of these two modules outperforms baseline IOU algorithms and MSE angle loss in a more strict angle-confined criterion. This work is a pioneering exploration in non-rigid oriented object detection with orientation in $[0, 2\pi)$, it will shed light on similar issues with single-category, non-rigid, oriented object detection in the stockbreeding and manufacturing industry. Code is available at https://github.com/guowenk/cattle-robb and the dataset will be released to the public later.

Keywords: Oriented object detection · Oriented bounding box · Orientation-sensitive detector

1 Introduction

Object detection is of great importance to intelligent stockbreeding. High-quality bounding boxes predicted from object detection models can be significantly beneficial to numerous downstream tasks, such as livestock tracking, activity monitoring, etc. Top-view surveillance images as shown in Fig. 1(a) and (b) are convenient for location analysis and livestock tracking. Detecting objects in top-view images is challenging since the objects normally have different textures and complex backgrounds. Moreover, the objects may be densely packed and arbitrarily oriented, which further increases detection difficulty. The horizontal

S. Yu et al. (Eds.): PRCV 2022, LNCS 13537, pp. 593–607, 2022.
https://doi.org/10.1007/978-3-031-18916-6_47

594   J. Xia et al.

bounding boxes (HBB) predicted by traditional object detection models may lead to severe overlap with adjacent bounding boxes in densely packed and oriented situations as illustrated in Fig. 1(c). Therefore, oriented bounding boxes (OBB) are preferred to capture object instances in top-view surveillance images (Fig. 1(d)).

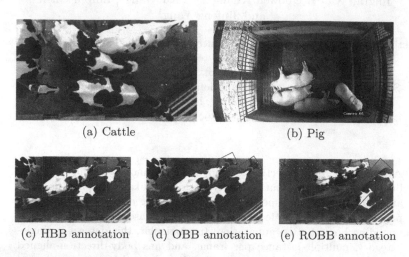

(a) Cattle   (b) Pig

(c) HBB annotation   (d) OBB annotation   (e) ROBB annotation

Fig. 1. (a) and (b) Top-view surveillance image of cattle and pig; (c) and (d) Cattle individuals are enclosed by HBB and OBB respectively. It is manifest that HBB annotation in (c) will generate huge overlap among boxes if cattle individuals are densely packed, while OBB annotation in (d) is precise and clear; (e) ROBB (real oriented bounding boxes) annotation of individual cattle, the orientation aligns with cattle body direction within $[0, 2\pi)$

Current oriented object detection datasets are mainly grouped into two categories: aerial images and scene text detection. Aerial images taken by satellite and Synthetic Aperture Radar (SAR) images are from bird's-eye view, e.g. DOTA [30], HRSC2016 [20], OHD-SJTU [34], SSDD+ [38], UCAS-AOD [44]. Scene text detection refers to detecting text regions in real life scene images, including dataset ICDAR2015 [22], ICDAR2017 [29], MSRA-TD500 [21], Total-Text [6], etc. These datasets use OBB or polygons to annotate objects, but the polygons are converted to minimum enclosing OBBs before fed into detection models. The OBB can be represented as $[x_c, y_c, w, h, \theta]$ while (x_c, y_c) is box centre and (w, h) is for width and height, θ refers to how much the rectangle rotates in range $(-\pi/2, 0]$, it can also be represented as four corner points $[x_1, y_1, x_2, y_2, x_3, y_3, x_4, y_4]$. Consequently, the orientation θ is just a parameter for oriented box definition instead of indicating the intrinsic orientation of the target object.

However, the livestock has intrinsic orientations in $[0, 2\pi)$, usually represented by head or body direction in stockbreeding circumstances. This intrinsic orientation is a very important indicator in developing intelligent stockbreeding downstream applications, such as body size estimation, and eating activity monitoring. Moreover, usually, only a single species is kept on one animal farm. Therefore, we build a single-category top-view cattle object detection dataset with real oriented bounding boxes (ROBB) annotation. The target cattle in this dataset are enclosed by rotated rectangles that align with cattle body direction in the range $[0, 2\pi)$ as shown in Fig. 1(e). Cattle individuals also have non-rigid body shapes which makes detection a further challenging task.

Current oriented object detection methods [7,31–33,39] are mainly extended from two-stage anchor-based horizontal detectors [11,12,28]. Hence these oriented detectors share the same drawbacks as horizontal ones, such as complex anchor box spreading and selecting strategy, and heavy computation. There are also single-stage oriented detectors [34–37,40], but the networks are heavily designed so it is difficult to balance the detection performance and processing speed. In this paper, we adopt the simple YOLOv1 [26] idea to build an oriented object detector based on our proposed orientation-sensitive IOU algorithm and loss function. We summarise our highlights and contributions as follows:

- We build a single-category multiple-instance cattle detection dataset Cattle-ROBB. The non-rigid cattle individuals are annotated by real oriented bounding boxes (ROBB) whose orientations are aligned with intrinsic cattle body direction and in the range $[0, 2\pi)$
- We propose an orientation-sensitive IOU algorithm and angle-related loss, and implement an oriented object detector by extending YOLOv1. This orientation-sensitive detector performs better in angle-confined criteria and meets real-time processing demand.

2 Related Work

2.1 Oriented Object Detection

Horizontal object detection methods detect axis-aligned HBB. Milestone models include single-stage YOLO [26], SSD [18], RetinaNet [17], CentreNet [42], Swin Transformer [19], and two-stage RCNN [12], Fast-RCNN [11], Faster-RCNN [28], Cascade-RCNN [4], etc. Oriented object detection methods can also be grouped into either single-stage or two-stage models. Current two-stage models are derived from horizontal RCNN model series. Specifically, in the first stage, anchor boxes are spread on feature maps densely. Then the detectors regress the differences between target box and anchor box parameters to generate region proposals. In the second stage, proposal feature maps are calculated from region proposals and feature maps by the ROI pooling layer, and they are eventually used for box parameter refining and object classification. Oriented detectors detect OBB where the additional parameter θ is learned either in the region proposal generating process [32,39] or in the ROI pooling process [7,15,33]. Single-stage oriented detectors are generally extended from key-point based HBB detectors [8,16,42,43]. For example, BBAVectors [36] derived from CentreNet [42] first detects the center key points and then regresses the box boundary-aware vectors based on the center point. R^3Det [35] derived from RetinaNet [17] designs a feature refinement module to solve feature misalignment and regresses box parameters progressively. DarkNet-RI [37] based on YOLOv3 [27] uses a pure classification approach and predicts pixel information directly instead of regressing box parameters. Generally, two-stage detectors have advantages in accuracy but suffer heavy computation issues.

2.2 Cattle Detection and Identification

Current works on cattle image processing include cattle identification, segmentation, and gait tracking. Cattle identification can be further divided into open-set or close-set problems. William Andrew proposed a deep metric learning method for open-set cattle identification [1]. First, the cattle ROI image is embedded to a latent space, then KNN is used for clustering and identification. Jing Gao also uses deep metric learning with triplet loss for ROI embedding and then Gaussian Mixture Model is applied for cattle clustering and identification [9]. A long-term recurrent convolutional network (LRCN) is usually adopted for close-set identification [2,3,23,24]. This method first extracts features with CNN in time-series images, and then feeds these time-series feature maps to LSTM for identification. Feature fusion model [14] is also utilised in close-set identification. Qiao uses Bonnet with data augmentation technique to do cattle segmentation [25]. Gardenier explores cattle gait tracking by keypoint detection based methods [10].

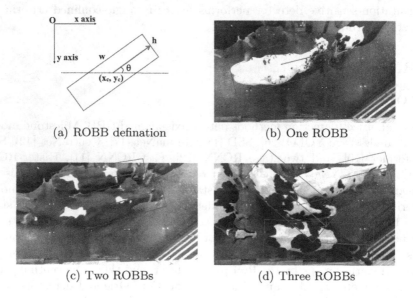

(a) ROBB defination   (b) One ROBB

(c) Two ROBBs   (d) Three ROBBs

Fig. 2. (a) ROBB definition adopted in Cattle-ROBB, (x_c, y_c) as centre point, w and h for along-body and cross-body dimension respectively, θ is rotation angle in range $[0, 2\pi)$ and counter-clockwise rotation makes positive θ starting from x-axis; (b) (c) and (d) depict images with one, two and three ROBBs cases respectively.

3 Cattle-ROBB Dataset

In this section, we first describe annotation rules and then present a thorough analysis of dataset details.

3.1 ROBB Annotation

We extend the Cows2021 dataset [9] by re-annotating entire cattle body with ROBB. In the Cows2021 dataset, only the cattle torso area is annotated without including the head and neck. The torso ROI is detected by oriented detectors and used for cattle identification. But the entire cattle body including head and neck is also important to many downstream intelligent stockbreeding tasks. For example, the entire body especially the head must be taken into consideration in eating and drinking behavior analysis. Only with entire body information can we empirically define cattle behaviors conveniently. Therefore we re-annotated images in the Cows2021 dataset by enclosing the entire cattle body with ROBB. We select 5587 images with at least one entire cattle body from total 10402 images in Cows2021. The original image is resolved at 1280×720, but for ROBB annotation the corner points of bounding boxes may locate outside the image if the cattle body is near the image boundary. So first the original image is padded to 1680×1120 with $(255, 255, 255)$, then open-source image-labeling tool roLabelImg[1] is utilized for raw annotation and finally, raw labels are processed by python scripts. The ROBB definition in Cattle-ROBB is illustrated in Fig. 2(a), (x_c, y_c) is centre point, w and h refers to along-body and cross-body dimension respectively, θ represents rotation angle in range $[0, 2\pi)$ and counter-clockwise rotation starting from x-axis makes positive θ. Figure 2(b)–(d) depicts one, two and three boxes in single image respectively.

3.2 Cattle-ROBB Analysis

Statistical information has been calculated on the Cattle-ROBB dataset, including the center point, orientation, w/h ratio, and box-number-per-image distributions.

Centre Point. The center point distribution is depicted in Fig. 3(a). Boxes are densely distributed on top part images because the region under surveillance is a corner on a walkway from top-left to top-right, hence the walking distance is shorter if cattle individuals pass this region through the top-part image area.

Orientation θ. Figure 3(b) shows orientation θ distribution, note that the y-axis is logarithmic and the x-axis is converted to degree. Orientations concentrate on a narrow range of $[0, \pm 50)$ degree approximately, which is also due to the left-to-right walking direction under the surveillance camera. But dataset users can

---

[1] https://github.com/cgvict/roLabelImg.

still apply data augmentation techniques like flipping and rotating to balance the orientation distribution.

w/h Ratio. w/h ratio is in a wide range from 1.0 to 4.0 and peaks at about 3.0 as shown in Fig. 3(c), which is consistent with our daily observation. Close inspections into samples near 1.0 show that cattle individuals turning their head backward will give a small w/h ratio. These samples enrich the non-rigid feature of cattle objects and increase detection difficulty.

Box-Number-Per-Image. Figure 3(d) shows that the majority of images contain just one ROBB, about 10% images have two ROBBs. 3 and 4-ROBB samples are less.

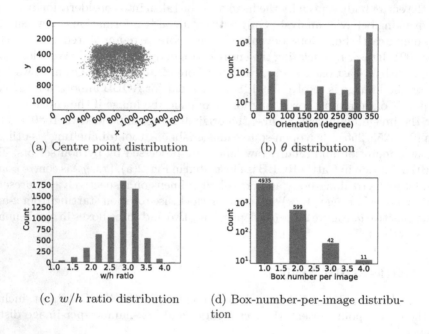

(a) Centre point distribution

(b) θ distribution

(c) w/h ratio distribution

(d) Box-number-per-image distribution

Fig. 3. Statistics on Cattle-ROBB dataset: (a) ROBB centre point distribution; (b) orientation θ distribution; (c) w/h ratio distribution and (d) box-number-per-image distribution

4 Method

We extend YOLOv1 to build baseline models. Later YOLO series models like YOLOv3 and YOLOv4 are stronger and have better performance on object detection tasks. YOLOv3 [27] is specifically designed for multi-scale object detections by adding a denser grid. But in Cattle-ROBB the scale of target objects does not vary much, therefore we apply the simple and elegant YOLOv1 idea for orientated object detection.

4.1   Architecture

Figure 4 shows overall architecture and workflow. The backbone is ResNet50 and there is (Conv: $3 \times 3 \times 32$, Maxpool: $2 \times 2 \div 2$) preceding ResNet50 and ((Conv: $1 \times 1 \times 256$, DilationConv: $3 \times 3 \times 256$, Conv: $1 \times 1 \times 256$)$\times 3$, Conv: $3 \times 3 \times 12$) after ResNet50. The input image is resized to 448×448 and the final output is $7 \times 7 \times 12$. YOLOv1 idea first draws $S \times S$ grid on images and then each grid cell is responsible to predict boxes whose centres locate in this grid cell. The detector totally predicts $S \times S \times B$ boxes where B represents the number of boxes a single grid cell predicts. In terms of our ROBB detector, we use $S = 7, B = 2$, and the final output ($7 \times 7 \times 12$) tensor is just corresponding to $7 \times 7 \times 2$ box parameters. Each grid cell predicts 2 boxes and each box has 5 relative location parameters $[x_r, y_r, w_r, h_r, \theta_r]$ and confidence C decoded from 6 tensor elements as illustrated in Fig. 4. Here the (x_r, y_r) represents the box centre relative to boundaries of the residing grid cell and (w_r, h_r) is also normalised by image width and height. θ_r is normalised to $[0, 1)$ as well. The relative box parameters are converted to absolute parameters in inference stage but keep relative when calculating loss function.

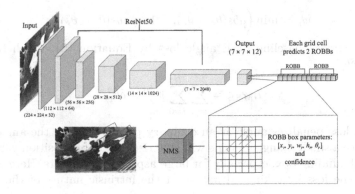

Fig. 4. The overall architecture of our proposed method. The backbone is ResNet50 [13] with additional CNN layers at both input and output sides. The input image is resized to 448×448 and the final output feature map is $7 \times 7 \times 12$ representing $7 \times 7 \times 2$ box proposals predicted by detector. These box proposals are selected by NMS for final prediction.

4.2   Loss Function

The loss of original YOLOv1 contains four parts: L_{noobj} for no-object loss, L_{obj} for contain-object loss, $L_{location}$ for location loss, and L_{cls} for classification loss. Here the detector performs no classification hence L_{cls} is omitted. Remaining 3 losses are defined as follows:

$$L_{noobj} = \lambda_{\text{noobj}} \sum_{i=0}^{S^2} \mathbb{1}_i^{\text{noobj}} \left(C_i - \hat{C}_i \right)^2 \tag{1}$$

$$L_{obj} = \sum_{i=0}^{S^2} \sum_{j=0}^{B} \mathbb{1}_{ij}^{obj} \left(C_i - \hat{C}_i \right)^2 \tag{2}$$

$$L_{location} = \lambda_{location} \sum_{i=0}^{S^2} \sum_{j=0}^{B} \mathbb{1}_{ij}^{obj} \left[(x_{ri} - \hat{x}_{ri})^2 + (y_{ri} - \hat{y}_{ri})^2 \right]$$

$$+ \lambda_{location} \sum_{i=0}^{S^2} \sum_{j=0}^{B} \mathbb{1}_{ij}^{obj} \left[\left(\sqrt{w_{ri}} - \sqrt{\hat{w}_{ri}} \right)^2 + \left(\sqrt{h_{ri}} - \sqrt{\hat{h}_{ri}} \right)^2 \right] \tag{3}$$

where $\mathbb{1}_i^{noobj}$ is an indicator function denoting if cell i does not contain object and $\mathbb{1}_{ij}^{obj}$ denotes that the jth bounding box predictor in cell i is responsible for that prediction. Variables without hat are predicted box parameters while with hat ones are encoded from ground truth. λ_{noobj} and $\lambda_{location}$ are weights to balance loss of each part.

In our ROBB detector, the most important angle loss is appended to $L_{location}$. The difference between predicted angle and ground truth angle is represented as Equation (4). It is in range $[0, \pi]$ because of periodicity hence the min operation is applied.

$$\delta\theta_r = \min \left(abs(\theta_r - \hat{\theta}_r), \quad 1. - abs(\theta_r - \hat{\theta}_r) \right) \tag{4}$$

First, we define a baseline MSE angle loss by Equation (5), which takes the square of $\delta\theta_r$.

$$L_{MSE} = \sum_{i=0}^{S^2} \sum_{j=0}^{B} \mathbb{1}_{ij}^{obj} \times \delta\theta_{ri}^2 \tag{5}$$

This MSE loss penalizes angle as an ordinary parameter, but the angle is very special since a small change in angle will give rise to notable position variation of the entire bounding box, especially for large aspect-ratio targets. Here we define another angle loss by taking advantage of the intrinsic nature of the angle as follows:

$$L_{cos} = \sum_{i=0}^{S^2} \sum_{j=0}^{B} \mathbb{1}_{ij}^{obj}(1. - \cos\left((\theta_{ri} - \hat{\theta}_{ri}) \times 2\pi \right)) \tag{6}$$

These two losses encourage θ_{ri} to step closer to $\hat{\theta}_{ri}$. L_{cos} and L_{MSE} is termed as $CosAngleLoss$ and $MSEAngleLoss$ respectively. The total loss is represented as $L_{total} = L_{noobj} + L_{obj} + L_{location}$ after appending angle loss to $L_{location}$. We will evaluate performance of two types of angle loss in next section.

4.3 IOU of ROBB

Many IOU calculation methods for orientated bounding boxes have been proposed, including differentiable 2D/3D IOU ($Diff\text{-}IOU$) algorithms [41], $P\text{-}IOU$ proposed by Chen [5] which is calculated through a pixel-wise manner, and

SkewIOU by Ma [21] which decomposes rectangles to triangles for IOU calculation.

In Cattle-ROBB the orientation angle is in range $[0, 2\pi)$. Suppose there are two ROBBs: BOX_1 and BOX_2 both with zero orientation angle, and the IOU between two boxes is $IOU_{original}$. If BOX_1 turns backward with new orientation π, the new IOU $IOU_{backward}$ remains unchanged for classical IOU calculation methods, but BOX_1 and BOX_2 make a worse match with opposite orientations. To overcome this issue we now propose $COS\text{-}IOU$ defined as follows:

$$COS\text{-}IOU = IOU_{MEHR} \times (1 + \cos(\theta - \hat{\theta})) \qquad (7)$$

where IOU_{MEHR} refers to IOU of Minimum Enclosing Horizontal Rectangle (MEHR) generated by oriented bounding boxes. The $COS\text{-}IOU$ is sensitive to rotation changes and penalises more on orientation misalignment. It calculates IOU as 0 in the opposite-orientation case hence pushes predicted orientations to ground truth. We will evaluate $COS\text{-}IOU$ with $Diff\text{-}IOU$ and $P\text{-}IOU$ in next section.

5 Experiments

5.1 Implementation Details

The input images are padded to 1680×1680 from 1680×1120 and then resized to 448×448 in the training and testing stage, producing an output tensor with resolution $7 \times 7 \times 12$. Our method is implemented with Pytorch and backbone weights are pre-trained on the ImageNet dataset. We use SGD optimiser with initial learning rate 1×10^{-3}, momentum 0.9 and decay 5×10^{-4}. The learning rate is further reduced to 1×10^{-4} and 1×10^{-5} at epoch 30 and 40 respectively. The network is trained 100 epochs on a single NVIDIA GTX 3080 GPU with batch size 8, during which best weights in validation performance are saved for a later testing stage.

5.2 Experimental Results

The detection results on different experimental setups are shown in Table 1, where AP is Average Precision and MAE refers to Mean Absolute Angle Error between predicted ROBBs and ground truth. AP shows overall precision with an IOU threshold of 0.5. Precisions are distributed in range $(83, 88)$ with highest precision 87.95 on $(Diff\text{-}IOU, MSEAngleLoss)$ and lowest value 83.89 on $(Diff\text{-}IOU, CosAngleLoss)$. MAE_{AP} shows the corresponding mean absolute angle error of each IOU-loss combination. Notably, MAE_{AP} of $CosAngleLoss$ are all less than values of $MSEAngleLoss$ by about 1 to 2° with the same IOU algorithm, which means models with $CosAngleLoss$ have better performance in terms of angle prediction.

Table 1. Detection results on Cattle-ROBB with different experimental setups, where AP is Average Precision and MAE refers to Mean Absolute Angle Error. AAP is angle-confined AP, which means angular condition is introduced to True Positive definition. Red and blue colour denotes highest and second highest precision.

IOU	Angle loss	AP	MAE_{AP}	AAP	MAE_{AAP}
$Diff\text{-}IOU$ [41]	$MSEAngleLoss$	87.95	9.40	51.29	4.56
$Diff\text{-}IOU$	$CosAngleLoss$	83.89	7.27	63.49	4.26
$P\text{-}IOU$ [5]	$MSEAngleLoss$	85.45	8.46	57.02	4.39
$P\text{-}IOU$	$CosAngleLoss$	87.71	7.99	59.42	4.16
$COS\text{-}IOU$	$MSEAngleLoss$	86.77	7.07	65.06	4.34
$COS\text{-}IOU$	$CosAngleLoss$	84.28	5.72	69.38	3.80

To further quantify the angle prediction performance of different IOU-loss combinations, a more strict matching criterion between predicted ROBB and ground-truth ROBB is introduced. In the AP evaluation matrix True Positive (TP) is triggered on condition that the IOU is less than the threshold (0.5). Now we introduce AAP which is angle-confined AP, under which condition the TP is only triggered once the IOU meets the threshold condition as well as the angle satisfies a particular requirement. In our AAP evaluation, we use an IOU threshold of 0.5 and an absolute angle error threshold of 10°. This also aligns with our original orientation detection purpose, paying more attention to angle. AAP in Table 1 shows that models with $CosAngleLoss$ have higher precisions than $MSEAngleLoss$ with the same IOU algorithm, and the highest precision 69.38 resides in $(COS\text{-}IOU, CosAngleLoss)$ regardless of ranking second-last in AP.

Distributions of absolute error in angle prediction are shown in Fig. 5. It is apparent that the angle errors in $(COS\text{-}IOU, CosAngleLoss)$ are more concentrated to 0, while $(Diff\text{-}IOU, MSEAngleLoss)$ errors spread over a wide range. The IOU score is further suppressed with misalignment between predicted angle and ground-truth angle in $COS\text{-}IOU$ algorithm, and $CosAngleLoss$ utilises intrinsic nature of angle to calculate angle-related loss. The experiment results demonstrate that the combination $(COS\text{-}IOU, CosAngleLoss)$ is more sensitive to orientation changes, therefore it is stronger in precise angle-prediction tasks.

Representative cattle ROBB detection results are presented in Fig. 6. Cattle individuals with different coat patterns, various gestures, and orientations are well localized by the $(COS\text{-}IOU, CosAngleLoss)$ model. Moreover, the processing speed achieves 39 FPS (Frame Per Second) with NVIDIA GTX 3080 GPU, which meets real-time processing needs.

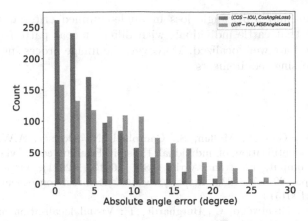

Fig. 5. Distributions of absolute error in angle prediction with setup (COS-IOU, $CosAngleLoss$) and ($Diff$-IOU, $MSEAngleLoss$)

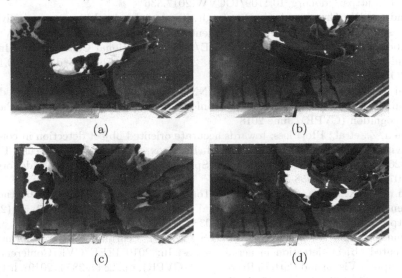

Fig. 6. Representative cattle ROBB detection results from IOU-loss combination of (COS-IOU, $CosAngleLoss$).

6 Conclusion

In this paper, we build a cattle object detection dataset Cattle-ROBB with real oriented bounding box annotation. ROBB means the annotated orientation aligns with intrinsic cattle body direction and is in the range $[0, 2\pi)$. This dataset is single-category, multiple-instance, and with non-rigid cattle targets. We propose an orientation-sensitive IOU algorithm COS-IOU and angle-related loss $CosAngleLoss$, and implement an oriented object detector by extending YOLOv1. The orientation-sensitive IOU and loss perform better than baseline

IOU algorithms and MSE angle loss in angle-confined criteria. Visualization results present that cattle individuals with different coat patterns in the complex background are well localized. Moreover, the image processing speed meets real-time processing requirements.

References

1. Andrew, W., Gao, J., Mullan, S., Campbell, N., Dowsey, A.W., Burghardt, T.: Visual identification of individual Holstein-Friesian cattle via deep metric learning. Comput. Electron. Agric. **185**, 106133 (2021). https://doi.org/10. 1016/j.compag.2021.106133, https://www.sciencedirect.com/science/article/pii/ S0168169921001514
2. Andrew, W., Greatwood, C., Burghardt, T.: Visual localisation and individual identification of Holstein Friesian cattle via deep learning. In: 2017 IEEE International Conference on Computer Vision Workshops (ICCVW), pp. 2850–2859 (2017). https://doi.org/10.1109/ICCVW.2017.336
3. Andrew, W., Greatwood, C., Burghardt, T.: Aerial animal biometrics: individual Friesian cattle recovery and visual identification via an autonomous UAV with onboard deep inference. In: 2019 IEEE/RSJ International Conference on Intelligent Robots and Systems (IROS), pp. 237–243 (2019). https://doi.org/10.1109/ IROS40897.2019.8968555
4. Cai, Z., Vasconcelos, N.: Cascade R-CNN: delving into high quality object detection. In: Proceedings of the IEEE Conference on Computer Vision and Pattern Recognition (CVPR), June 2018
5. Chen, Z., et al.: PIoU loss: towards accurate oriented object detection in complex environments. In: Vedaldi, A., Bischof, H., Brox, T., Frahm, J.-M. (eds.) ECCV 2020. LNCS, vol. 12350, pp. 195–211. Springer, Cham (2020). https://doi.org/10. 1007/978-3-030-58558-7_12
6. Ch'ng, C.-K., Chan, C.S., Liu, C.-L.: Total-text: toward orientation robustness in scene text detection. Int. J. Doc. Anal. Recogn. (IJDAR) **23**(1), 31–52 (2019). https://doi.org/10.1007/s10032-019-00334-z
7. Ding, J., Xue, N., Long, Y., Xia, G.S., Lu, Q.: Learning ROI transformer for oriented object detection in aerial images. In: 2019 IEEE/CVF Conference on Computer Vision and Pattern Recognition (CVPR), pp. 2844–2853 (2019). https:// doi.org/10.1109/CVPR.2019.00296
8. Duan, K., Bai, S., Xie, L., Qi, H., Huang, Q., Tian, Q.: CenterNet: keypoint triplets for object detection. In: 2019 IEEE/CVF International Conference on Computer Vision (ICCV), pp. 6568–6577 (2019). https://doi.org/10.1109/ICCV.2019.00667
9. Gao, J., Burghardt, T., Andrew, W., Dowsey, A.W., Campbell, N.W.: Towards self-supervision for video identification of individual Holstein-Friesian cattle: the cows2021 dataset (2021). https://doi.org/10.48550/ARXIV.2105.01938, https:// arxiv.org/abs/2105.01938
10. Gardenier, J., Underwood, J., Clark, C.: Object detection for cattle gait tracking. In: 2018 IEEE International Conference on Robotics and Automation (ICRA), pp. 2206–2213 (2018). https://doi.org/10.1109/ICRA.2018.8460523
11. Girshick, R.: Fast R-CNN. In: 2015 IEEE International Conference on Computer Vision (ICCV), pp. 1440–1448 (2015). https://doi.org/10.1109/ICCV.2015.169

12. Girshick, R., Donahue, J., Darrell, T., Malik, J.: Rich feature hierarchies for accurate object detection and semantic segmentation. In: 2014 IEEE Conference on Computer Vision and Pattern Recognition, pp. 580–587 (2014). https://doi.org/10.1109/CVPR.2014.81

13. He, K., Zhang, X., Ren, S., Sun, J.: Deep residual learning for image recognition. In: 2016 IEEE Conference on Computer Vision and Pattern Recognition (CVPR), pp. 770–778 (2016). https://doi.org/10.1109/CVPR.2016.90

14. Hu, H., et al.: Cow identification based on fusion of deep parts features. Biosyst. Eng. **192**, 245–256 (2020). https://doi.org/10.1016/j.biosystemseng.2020.02.001, https://www.sciencedirect.com/science/article/pii/S1537511020300416

15. Jiang, Y., et al.: R2CNN: rotational region CNN for orientation robust scene text detection (2017). https://doi.org/10.48550/ARXIV.1706.09579, https://arxiv.org/abs/1706.09579

16. Law, H., Deng, J.: CornerNet: detecting objects as paired keypoints. Int. J. Comput. Vision **128**(3), 642–656 (2019). https://doi.org/10.1007/s11263-019-01204-1

17. Lin, T., Goyal, P., Girshick, R., He, K., Dollar, P.: Focal loss for dense object detection. IEEE Trans. Pattern Anal. Mach. Intell. **42**(02), 318–327 (2020). https://doi.org/10.1109/TPAMI.2018.2858826

18. Liu, W., et al.: SSD: single shot multibox detector. In: Leibe, B., Matas, J., Sebe, N., Welling, M. (eds.) ECCV 2016. LNCS, vol. 9905, pp. 21–37. Springer, Cham (2016). https://doi.org/10.1007/978-3-319-46448-0_2

19. Liu, Z., et al.: Swin transformer: hierarchical vision transformer using shifted windows. In: Proceedings of the IEEE/CVF International Conference on Computer Vision (ICCV), pp. 10012–10022 (2021)

20. Liu, Z., Wang, H., Weng, L., Yang, Y.: Ship rotated bounding box space for ship extraction from high-resolution optical satellite images with complex backgrounds. IEEE Geosci. Remote Sens. Lett. **13**(8), 1074–1078 (2016). https://doi.org/10.1109/LGRS.2016.2565705

21. Ma, J., Shao, W., Ye, H., Wang, L., Wang, H., Zheng, Y., Xue, X.: Arbitrary-oriented scene text detection via rotation proposals. IEEE Trans. Multimedia **20**(11), 3111–3122 (2018). https://doi.org/10.1109/tmm.2018.2818020

22. Neumann, L., Matas, J.: Efficient scene text localization and recognition with local character refinement. In: 2015 13th International Conference on Document Analysis and Recognition (ICDAR), pp. 746–750 (2015). https://doi.org/10.1109/ICDAR.2015.7333861

23. Qiao, Y., Su, D., Kong, H., Sukkarieh, S., Lomax, S., Clark, C.: Individual cattle identification using a deep learning based framework. IFAC-PapersOnLine **52**(30), 318–323 (2019). https://doi.org/10.1016/j.ifacol.2019.12.558, https://www.sciencedirect.com/science/article/pii/S2405896319324772, 6th IFAC Conference on Sensing, Control and Automation Technologies for Agriculture AGRICONTROL 2019

24. Qiao, Y., Su, D., Kong, H., Sukkarieh, S., Lomax, S., Clark, C.: BiLSTM-based individual cattle identification for automated precision livestock farming. In: 2020 IEEE 16th International Conference on Automation Science and Engineering (CASE), pp. 967–972 (2020). https://doi.org/10.1109/CASE48305.2020.9217026

25. Qiao, Y., Su, D., Kong, H., Sukkarieh, S., Lomax, S., Clark, C.: Data augmentation for deep learning based cattle segmentation in precision livestock farming. In: 2020 IEEE 16th International Conference on Automation Science and Engineering (CASE), pp. 979–984 (2020). https://doi.org/10.1109/CASE48305.2020.9216758

26. Redmon, J., Divvala, S., Girshick, R., Farhadi, A.: You only look once: Unified, real-time object detection. In: 2016 IEEE Conference on Computer Vision and Pattern Recognition (CVPR), pp. 779–788 (2016). https://doi.org/10.1109/CVPR.2016.91
27. Redmon, J., Farhadi, A.: Yolov3: an incremental improvement (2018)
28. Ren, S., He, K., Girshick, R., Sun, J.: Faster R-CNN: towards real-time object detection with region proposal networks. IEEE Trans. Pattern Anal. Mach. Intell. **39**(6), 1137–1149 (2017). https://doi.org/10.1109/TPAMI.2016.2577031
29. Shi, B., et al.: ICDAR 2017 competition on reading Chinese text in the wild (RCTW-17). In: 2017 14th IAPR International Conference on Document Analysis and Recognition (ICDAR), vol. 01, pp. 1429–1434 (2017). https://doi.org/10.1109/ICDAR.2017.233
30. Xia, G.S., et al.: DOTA: a large-scale dataset for object detection in aerial images. In: 2018 IEEE/CVF Conference on Computer Vision and Pattern Recognition, pp. 3974–3983 (2018). https://doi.org/10.1109/CVPR.2018.00418
31. Xie, X., Cheng, G., Wang, J., Yao, X., Han, J.: Oriented R-CNN for object detection. In: 2021 IEEE/CVF International Conference on Computer Vision (ICCV), pp. 3500–3509 (2021). https://doi.org/10.1109/ICCV48922.2021.00350
32. Yang, X., et a.: Automatic ship detection in remote sensing images from google earth of complex scenes based on multiscale rotation dense feature pyramid networks. Remote Sens. **10**(1) (2018). https://doi.org/10.3390/rs10010132, https://www.mdpi.com/2072-4292/10/1/132
33. Yang, X., Sun, H., Sun, X., Yan, M., Guo, Z., Fu, K.: Position detection and direction prediction for arbitrary-oriented ships via multitask rotation region convolutional neural network. IEEE Access **6**, 50839–50849 (2018). https://doi.org/10.1109/ACCESS.2018.2869884
34. Yang, X., Yan, J.: On the arbitrary-oriented object detection: classification based approaches revisited. Int. J. Comput. Vision (3), 1–26 (2022). https://doi.org/10.1007/s11263-022-01593-w
35. Yang, X., Yan, J., Feng, Z., He, T.: R3DET: refined single-stage detector with feature refinement for rotating object. In: Proceedings of the AAAI Conference on Artificial Intelligence, vol. 35, no. 4, pp. 3163–3171, May 2021. https://ojs.aaai.org/index.php/AAAI/article/view/16426
36. Yi, J., Wu, P., Liu, B., Huang, Q., Qu, H., Metaxas, D.: Oriented object detection in aerial images with box boundary-aware vectors. In: 2021 IEEE Winter Conference on Applications of Computer Vision (WACV), pp. 2149–2158 (2021). https://doi.org/10.1109/WACV48630.2021.00220
37. Zand, M., Etemad, A., Greenspan, M.: Oriented bounding boxes for small and freely rotated objects. IEEE Trans. Geosci. Remote Sens. **60**, 1–15 (2022). https://doi.org/10.1109/TGRS.2021.3076050
38. Zhang, T., et al.: Sar ship detection dataset (SSDD): official release and comprehensive data analysis. Remote Sens. **13**(18) (2021). https://doi.org/10.3390/rs13183690
39. Zhang, Z., Guo, W., Zhu, S., Yu, W.: Toward arbitrary-oriented ship detection with rotated region proposal and discrimination networks. IEEE Geosci. Remote Sens. Lett. **15**(11), 1745–1749 (2018). https://doi.org/10.1109/LGRS.2018.2856921
40. Zhong, B., Ao, K.: Single-stage rotation-decoupled detector for oriented object. Remote Sens. **12**(19) (2020). https://doi.org/10.3390/rs12193262, https://www.mdpi.com/2072-4292/12/19/3262
41. Zhou, D., et al.: IOU loss for 2D/3D object detection. In: 2019 International Conference on 3D Vision (3DV), pp. 85–94 (2019). https://doi.org/10.1109/3DV.2019.00019

42. Zhou, X., Wang, D., Krähenbühl, P.: Objects as points (2019). https://doi.org/10.48550/ARXIV.1904.07850, https://arxiv.org/abs/1904.07850
43. Zhou, X., Zhuo, J., Krähenbühl, P.: Bottom-up object detection by grouping extreme and center points. In: 2019 IEEE/CVF Conference on Computer Vision and Pattern Recognition (CVPR), pp. 850–859 (2019). https://doi.org/10.1109/CVPR.2019.00094
44. Zhu, H., Chen, X., Dai, W., Fu, K., Ye, Q., Jiao, J.: Orientation robust object detection in aerial images using deep convolutional neural network. In: 2015 IEEE International Conference on Image Processing (ICIP), pp. 3735–3739 (2015). https://doi.org/10.1109/ICIP.2015.7351502

An Infrared Moving Small Object Detection Method Based on Trajectory Growth

Dilong Li[1,2], Shuixin Pan[1,2], Haopeng Wang[1,2], Yueqiang Zhang[1,2(✉)], Linyu Huang[1,2], Hongxi Guo[1,2], Xiaolin Liu[1,2], and Qifeng Yu[1,2]

[1] College of Physics and Optoelectronic Engineering, Shenzhen University, Shenzhen 518060, China
yueqiang.zhang@szu.edu.cn
[2] Institute of Intelligent Optical Measurement and Detection, Shenzhen University, Shenzhen 518060, China

Abstract. Aiming at the detection of infrared moving small objects for moving camera, an infrared moving small object detection method based on trajectory growth is proposed. In the first stage, the proposed method firstly estimates the homography between images by pairs of corresponding points obtained by pyramidal Lucas-Kanade optical flow method. Then the changed regions in the image are extracted by the three-frame difference method, and the optimized segmentation method is used to produce accurate extraction results. In the second stage, based on the assumption of short-time approximate uniform linear motion, the old trajectories are grown and the new trajectories are generated to reduce the interference of false alarm. Then, the final detection results are obtained by confirming the trajectories. Experiments on publicly available dataset show that the proposed method achieves F1 score higher than 0.91 on average, indicating it can accurately detect small objects in complex and even noisy background with low false alarm rate and high efficiency.

Keywords: Infrared small object · Object detection · Moving camera · Optimized segmentation · Trajectory growth

1 Introduction

Infrared imaging is widely used in long-distance detection. As one of the key technologies of infrared detection system, infrared small object detection is significant in the field of infrared detection [1]. On the one hand, small objects do not have concrete textures and shapes, so there is no useful texture and obvious feature information can be used. On the other hand, small objects are usually submerged in heavy background clutter and strong noise. Therefore, infrared small object detection is an extremely challenging task [2–4].

Existing methods of infrared small object detection can be categorized into detection based on single frame and detection based on sequential frames, respectively. The methods based on single frame mainly use the difference between the object and the background to detect infrared small objects. Among them, the classical methods are

S. Yu et al. (Eds.): PRCV 2022, LNCS 13537, pp. 608–620, 2022.
https://doi.org/10.1007/978-3-031-18916-6_48

based on filtering [5–7]. Bai et al. proposed a new top-hat operation, which considers neighborhood information more fully than the traditional top-hat operation [5]. Similar to [5], Deng et al. also used torus and circular structures for morphological filtering [6]. For each pixel, the local entropy is calculated, and the M estimator is used to obtain the filtering structure elements. Recently, a method based on frequency-domain filtering adaptively decomposes the input signal into multiple separated band-limited sub-signals to extract the objects [7]. In addition to filtering-based methods, there are also methods based on human visual system [2, 8, 9]. The LCM method proposed by Chen et al. uses local contrast saliency to enhance the objects and suppress the background clutter [8]. But it is not suitable for the detection of dark objects, and there is obvious block effect in the saliency map. After that, Han et al. improved the saliency calculation method of LCM, which can effectively avoid the block effect [9]. The sub-block mechanism is used to improve the efficiency of the algorithm, but it makes the detected object location inaccurate. In order to enhance the object more effectively, Wei et al. proposed a new local contrast saliency calculation method [2], which can detect both bright and dark objects. But it is not robust to heavy clutter. Recently, methods based on sparse representation have also received much attention [10]. These methods are mainly based on the sparseness of the object and the low rank of the background in infrared image to achieve the separation of the object and the background. The method proposed by Gao et al. divides the image into blocks by sliding window to enhance the correlation of the background [11]. It converts the detection of small objects into a recovery process of sparse components in the data matrix. The main disadvantage of it is the high computational cost. Recently, deep learning has achieved considerable success in many vision applications, and it has also been used in infrared small object detection. To highlight and preserve the small target features, Dai et al. exploited a bottom-up attentional modulation integrating the smaller scale subtle details of low-level features into high-level features of deeper layers [12]. Motivated by the fact that the infrared small objects are of unique distribution characteristics, Zhao et al. constructed a GAN (Generative Adversarial Network) model to automatically learn the features of objects and directly predict the intensity of objects [13]. The objects are recognized and reconstructed by the generator, built upon U-Net, according the data distribution. Such methods have difficulties in detecting infrared small objects under cluttered background.

When there is heavy background clutter in image, the methods based on single frame are usually not robust enough, resulting in false alarm. In contrast, the methods based on sequential frames can further utilize the temporal information between images [14–18], resulting in higher detection accuracy and robustness. Reed et al. applied the three-dimensional matched filter to the detection of small objects [14, 15]. This method combines the matched filtering in two-dimensional space and the accumulated energy in one-dimensional time to realize the detection of small objects. However, it requires priors on the gray distribution and motion information of the object, which is difficult to be satisfied in practical applications. In addition, there are also methods based on pipeline filtering [16–18]. This kind of methods are based on the detection result of a single frame, and confirms the object according to its motion continuity.

However, in complex scenes, especially ground scenes, there are a large number of strong edge regions and local bright regions in the image. Existing approaches are difficult to cope with such scenes. In addition, existing methods based on sequential frames are almost aimed at static camera and cannot be directly applied to moving camera. To solve the above problems, an infrared moving small object detection method based on trajectory growth is proposed in this paper. The contributions of this paper can be summarized as follows:

1) A candidate object extraction method based on three-frame difference method and optimized segmentation is proposed, which can effectively remove the background noise regions and obtain the complete regions of the candidate objects.
2) The proposed trajectory growth method is capable to effectively suppress noise and local bright regions in complex scenes with high detection accuracy.
3) The proposed method has low computational complexity and can work in real time even on the platform with low computational capability.

The rest of the paper is organized as follows: Sect. 2 provides a detailed description of the proposed method. Section 3 presents the experimental results on publicly available dataset to demonstrate the effectiveness of the proposed method. Finally, the conclusions are summarized in Sect. 4.

2 Proposed Method

The framework of the proposed method is shown in Fig. 1. It consists of two stages. In the first stage, candidate objects are extracted. Firstly, corresponding points are obtained by pyramidal Lucas-Kanade optical flow method [19]. And the homography between images is estimated by RANSAC [20]. After registration the changed regions in the image are extracted by the three-frame difference method, and the optimized segmentation method is used to produce accurate extraction results. In the second stage, based on the assumption of short-time approximate uniform linear motion, the old trajectories are grown and the new trajectories are generated to reduce the interference of false alarm. Then, the final detection results are obtained by confirming the trajectories according to the motion characteristics of the object.

2.1 Extraction of Candidate Objects

Registration. To address background motion caused by moving camera, image registration is required. In small object detection, the distance between the camera and the scene is far, and the imaging scene can be approximated as a plane. Therefore, homography is used for image registration in this paper.

$$\begin{bmatrix} x' \\ y' \\ 1 \end{bmatrix} = \mathbf{H} \begin{bmatrix} x \\ y \\ 1 \end{bmatrix} \tag{1}$$

In (1), $\mathbf{H}$ is the homography matrix from (x, y) to $\left(x', y'\right)$. It can be solved by a minimum of 4 pairs of corresponding points. Since the corresponding points may be selected by

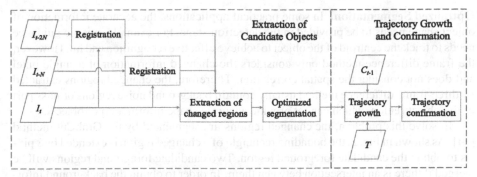

Fig. 1. The framework of the proposed method. I_{t-2N}, I_{t-N} and I_t are images at frame $t - 2N$, $t - N$ and t, respectively. C_{t-1} is the set of candidate objects at frame $t - 1$ and T is the set of trajectories.

mistake, the global motion may not be represented by the calculated homography matrix. The wrong estimation of **H** can be avoided by RANSAC method.

Some methods of features detection such as SIFT [21] and SURF [22] can be used to obtain pairs of corresponding points. But the pyramidal Lucas-Kanade optical flow method is of less computational complexity than the feature-based approach and usually provides satisfactory results. In this paper, Shi-Tomas corner detector [23] is used to provide initial key points for pyramidal Lucas-Kanade optical flow method. When pairs of corresponding points are obtained, the RANSAC method is used to estimate the homography matrix **H**. Therefore, image registration can be realized efficiently.

Extraction of Changed Regions. In order to extract candidate objects efficiently and robustly, the three-frame difference method is used to extract the changed regions in the image. Compared with the direct frame difference method, it can effectively avoid ghost effect. Due to the transitivity of homography, the homography matrix from frame $t - 2N$ to frame t can be obtained by:

$$\mathbf{H}_{t-2N}^t = \mathbf{H}_{t-N}^t \mathbf{H}_{t-2N}^{t-N} \qquad (2)$$

where $\mathbf{H}_{t-2N}^t$ is the homography matrix from frame $t - 2N$ to frame t, $\mathbf{H}_{t-N}^t$ is the homography matrix from frame $t - N$ to frame t, and $\mathbf{H}_{t-2N}^{t-N}$ is the homography matrix from frame $t - 2N$ to frame $t - N$.

According to the homography, I_{t-2N} and I_{t-N} are registered with I_t to obtain I_{t-2N}' and I_{t-N}', respectively. Then, the changed saliency map D_t can be obtained by

$$D_t = \min\left(\left|I_{t-2N}' - I_t\right|, \left|I_{t-N}' - I_t\right|\right) \qquad (3)$$

Once D_t is computed, the changed regions can be segmented by an adaptive thresholding method. Here, the threshold τ_D is determined by

$$\tau_D = \mu_D + k_D \sigma_D \qquad (4)$$

where k_D is a parameter, μ_D is the mean of D_t, and σ_D is the standard deviation of D_t. In our experiments, k_D is set to 9.

Optimized Segmentation. In some practical applications, the accurate information of object shape needs to be provided in the detection stage. For example, missile guidance needs to track the centroid of the object to achieve effective recognition and hit. However, the frame difference method only considers the changed information of a single pixel and does not consider the spatial correlation. Therefore, the changed regions extracted by three-frame difference method usually contain background noise regions or miss part of the object region, which cannot provide accurate shape information of objects.

To solve this problem, the changed regions are segmented by the GrabCut method [24]. As shown in Fig. 2, the bounding rectangle of a changed region is extended by s pixels to obtain the candidate foreground region. Two candidate foreground regions will be merged if there is an intersection between them. In order to obtain the background information, the candidate foreground region is extended by s pixels, in which the extended region is regarded as background. Once the candidate foreground and background are determined, the GrabCut method can be used to obtain accurate object segmentation results. For infrared small object detection, s is set to 3 in this paper.

After optimized segmentation, the background noise regions similar to their surrounding background will be regarded as background and be eliminated, while the changed regions not similar to their surrounding background will be retained and complete regions of the candidate objects will be generated.

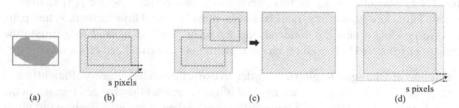

(a)   (b)   s pixels   (c)   (d)   s pixels

Fig. 2. Illustration of the optimized segmentation. (a) The changed region is marked in gray, and the green rectangle is its bounding rectangle; (b) The region marked by the solid blue line is the candidate foreground region; (c) Candidate foreground regions are merged; (d) The region marked by the solid yellow line is background. (Color figure online)

2.2 Trajectory Growth and Confirmation

In complex scenes, it is necessary to make full use of the motion information of the object to avoid the interference of local bright regions. Trajectory growth is to associate the candidate objects with the existing trajectories and generate new trajectories at the same time. In this paper, we assume that the real objects approximately satisfy uniform linear motion in a short time, and apply the loose constraint to the trajectory growth process.

Trajectory Growth. Before growing, the trajectories are aligned with the image coordinates according to the homography. At the same time, the trajectories are sorted to ensure that the newer trajectories can be prioritized for trajectory growth. In order to improve the detection efficiency, the length of the time window w is set to 50.

Let p_t^i denotes the predicted position of the ith trajectory at frame t, and based on the assumption of short-time approximate uniform linear motion, p_t^i can be obtained by

$$p_t^i = t_m^i + \frac{(t_n^i - t_m^i)}{(n - m)} \qquad (5)$$

where t_m^i represents the penultimate position of the ith trajectory and m represents the frame corresponding to t_m^i. t_n^i Represents the last position of the ith trajectory and n represents the frame corresponding to t_n^i.

Let L_t^{ij} denotes the distance between p_t^i and the jth candidate object and it can be mathematically expressed as:

$$L_t^{ij} = ||p_t^i - c_t^j||_2 \qquad (6)$$

where c_t^j represents the position of jth candidate object at frame t.

Then, the minimum of L_t^{ij} and the corresponding index of the candidate object can be obtained by

$$L_t^{ik} = \min_j L_t^{ij} \qquad (7)$$

$$k = \operatorname*{argmin}_j L_t^{ij} \qquad (8)$$

If L_t^{ik} is not greater than the trajectory growth threshold τ_L, c_t^k will be associated with the ith trajectory and labeled as difference result. After that, c_t^k will be removed from C_t. In this paper, τ_L is set to 5.

When the trajectory does not grow successfully, it is likely that the object is moving slowly and our extraction method cannot extract it successfully. In this case, the optimized segmentation method is used according to the last position of the trajectory.

For the ith candidate object at frame $t - 1$, denoted as c_{t-1}^i, and the jth candidate object at frame t, denoted as c_t^j, the distance between them can be calculated by

$$M_t^{ij} = ||c_{t-1}^i - c_t^j||_2 \qquad (9)$$

If M_t^{ij} is not greater than the velocity constraint threshold τ_M, a new trajectory will be generated by c_{t-1}^i and c_t^j. When all new trajectories are generated, the candidate objects participating in the generation will be removed from C_{t-1} and C_t. In this paper, τ_M is set to 10.

Trajectory Confirmation. The Trajectories need to be confirmed to get the final detection results. The trajectory length of real object should not be shorter than α, where α is the trajectory length threshold and set to 2 in this paper. At the same time, considering the real object will appear stably, the number of trajectory points belonging to the difference result should not be less than β:

$$\beta = \max(\tau_n, \text{floor}(\tau_r \times (t_{\text{back}} - t_{\text{front}}))) \qquad (10)$$

where τ_n and τ_r are parameters. t_{front} and t_{back} are the first and last moments of the trajectory, respectively. In this paper, τ_n is set to 5 and τ_r is set to 0.5.

3 Experiments

To demonstrate the effectiveness of the proposed method, some image sequences from a publicly available dataset [25] are used. This dataset captures varied scenarios under the background of both sky and ground. It includes 22 fixed-wing UAV object image sequences, 30 trajectories and 16177 frames in relation to 16944 objects. Each object corresponds to a label location in the image, and each image sequence corresponds to a label file, which can be used to evaluate the performance of detection method.

The most important metrics of evaluating the detection performance are Precision (Pr), Recall (Re) and F1-measure (F1). Pr and Re are measures of accurateness and completeness, respectively. F1 is a combination of Pr and Re. These metrics are defined as follows:

$$Pr = \frac{TP}{TP + FP} \tag{11}$$

$$Re = \frac{TP}{TP + FN} \tag{12}$$

$$F1 = \frac{2 \times Pr \times Re}{Pr + Re} \tag{13}$$

where TP, FP and FN are True Positive, False Positive and False Negative, respectively. In this paper, for infrared small object detection, the object is correctly detected if the detected location is within the three-pixel-neighborhood of the ground truth.

The proposed method is implemented by C++ on a PC with 8 GB RAM and 1.60-GHz Intel i5 CPU. The parameters used in the proposed method are set empirically and remain fixed in our experiments, as shown in Table 1.

Table 1. Parameters used in the experiments.

Parameter	N	k_D	w	τ_L	τ_M	α	τ_n	τ_r
Value	5	9	50	5	10	2	5	0.5

3.1 Effectiveness of the Optimized Segmentation

In order to verify the effectiveness of the optimized segmentation strategy, the detection performances on the changed regions extracted by the three-frame difference method with and without optimized segmentation are tested. Table 2 shows the detection performances with and without optimized segmentation and Fig. 3 illustrates a part of detection results.

Table 2. Detection performances with and without optimized segmentation.

Sequence	Without optimized segmentation			With optimized segmentation		
	Pr	Re	$F1$	Pr	Re	$F1$
data5	0.243	0.997	0.391	0.619	0.983	**0.760**
data6	0.142	0.997	0.249	0.542	0.910	**0.679**
data8	0.205	0.987	0.339	0.588	0.987	**0.737**
data11	0.139	0.997	0.244	0.320	0.909	**0.474**
data12	0.258	0.993	0.409	0.553	0.966	**0.703**
data13	0.133	0.954	0.233	0.244	0.894	**0.383**
data16	0.242	0.862	0.377	0.673	0.851	**0.752**
data17	0.032	0.853	0.062	0.268	0.761	**0.396**
data18	0.253	0.955	0.400	0.875	0.967	**0.919**
data21	0.063	0.896	0.118	0.196	0.810	**0.315**
data22	0.155	1.000	0.268	0.407	0.984	**0.576**
Average	0.170	0.954	0.281	0.480	0.911	**0.609**

(a)   (b)   (c)

Fig. 3. Detection results. (a) Images; (b) Detection results without optimized segmentation; (c) Detection results with optimized segmentation.

As shown in Table 2, although the detection results without optimized segmentation are of high Re, the Pr is much lower, resulting in a low F1 score, which indicates that the changed regions extracted by the three-frame difference method contain many background noise regions. With optimized segmentation, the Pr of detection results has been greatly improved, indicating that many background noise regions have been filtered out, and the segmented objects are closer to the real objects, thus obtaining higher F1 score. Although the optimized segmentation reduces the Re, it is acceptable compared with the substantial increase in Pr.

Table 3. Quantitative performance comparison.

Sequence	LCM			MPCM			With optimized segmentation		
	Pr	Re	F1	Pr	Re	F1	Pr	Re	F1
data5	0.347	0.738	0.472	0.138	0.856	0.237	0.619	0.983	**0.760**
data6	0.297	0.352	0.322	0.138	0.715	0.231	0.542	0.910	**0.679**
data8	0.466	0.905	0.615	0.126	0.753	0.216	0.588	0.987	**0.737**
data11	0.030	0.135	0.049	0.078	0.563	0.137	0.320	0.909	**0.474**
data12	0.208	0.552	0.302	0.124	0.857	0.216	0.553	0.966	**0.703**
data13	0.006	0.097	0.011	0.048	0.428	0.087	0.244	0.894	**0.383**
data16	0.419	0.990	0.588	0.263	0.998	0.417	0.673	0.851	**0.752**
data17	0.007	0.008	0.008	0.041	0.176	0.066	0.268	0.761	**0.396**
data18	0.481	0.814	0.605	0.149	1.000	0.259	0.875	0.967	**0.919**
data21	0.003	0.059	0.006	0.037	0.690	0.070	0.196	0.810	**0.315**
data22	0.336	0.763	0.467	0.106	0.912	0.191	0.407	0.984	**0.576**
Average	0.236	0.492	0.313	0.114	0.722	0.193	0.480	0.911	**0.609**

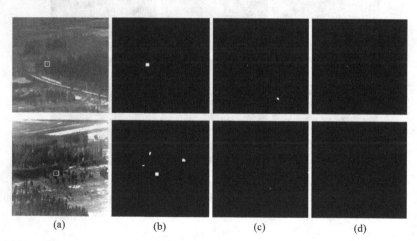

(a)   (b)   (c)   (d)

Fig. 4. Detection results. (a) Images; (b) Detection results of LCM; (c) Detection results of MPCM; (d) Detection results with optimized segmentation.

In addition, we also compare the optimized segmentation detection results with LCM [8] and MPCM [2]. Both LCM and MPCM are infrared small object detection methods based on visual saliency. For each sequence, LCM and MPCM are tested using the suggested range of parameters in the paper, and the results with the highest F1 score are selected for comparison. The quantitative performance comparison is shown in Table 3. As shown in Fig. 4, the infrared small object detection methods based on single frame are difficult to deal with complex scenes, and the Pr and Re are relatively low in most image sequences, indicating that these two methods are prone to missed detection and false alarm in complex scenes. In contrast, our optimized segmentation strategy has better performance.

3.2 Effectiveness of the Proposed Method

In complex scenes, it is difficult to eliminate local bright regions through optimized segmentation, resulting in false alarm. The trajectory growth strategy can make full use of the motion information of the object to eliminate false alarm and improve the detection performance. Table 4 shows the detection performance comparison between the method with optimized segmentation and the complete method. And the comparison results are shown in Fig. 5. The strategy based on trajectory growth is of robustness against the interference of local bright regions. And it can greatly improve the F1 score of detection.

Table 4. Comparison between method with optimized segmentation and complete method.

Sequence	With optimized segmentation			Our complete method		
	Pr	*Re*	*F*1	*Pr*	*Re*	*F*1
data5	0.619	0.983	0.760	0.972	0.969	**0.971**
data6	0.542	0.910	0.679	0.994	0.830	**0.905**
data8	0.588	0.987	0.737	0.901	0.910	**0.905**
data11	0.320	0.909	0.474	0.981	0.850	**0.911**
data12	0.553	0.966	0.703	0.943	0.963	**0.953**
data13	0.244	0.894	0.383	0.851	0.865	**0.858**
data16	0.673	0.851	0.752	0.880	0.837	**0.858**
data17	0.268	0.761	0.396	1.000	0.802	**0.890**
data18	0.875	0.967	0.919	1.000	0.933	**0.965**
data21	0.196	0.810	0.315	0.917	0.837	**0.875**
data22	0.407	0.984	0.576	0.996	0.967	**0.981**
Average	0.480	0.911	0.609	0.949	0.888	**0.916**

618 D. Li et al.

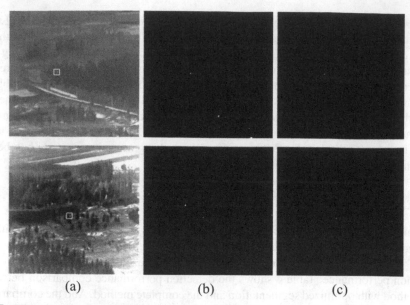

(a)   (b)   (c)

Fig. 5. Detection results. (a) Images; (b) Detection results with optimized segmentation; (c) Detection results of our complete method.

Table 5. Comparison between two versions of the proposed method.

Sequence	Our fast version				Our original version			
	Pr	*Re*	*F*1	fps	*Pr*	*Re*	*F*1	fps
data5	0.961	0.968	0.964	187	0.972	0.969	**0.971**	55
data6	0.972	0.810	0.884	168	0.994	0.830	**0.905**	62
data8	0.856	0.920	0.887	175	0.901	0.910	**0.905**	66
data11	0.987	0.842	0.909	147	0.981	0.850	**0.911**	55
data12	0.937	0.963	0.950	190	0.943	0.963	**0.953**	48
data13	0.885	0.866	**0.875**	147	0.851	0.865	0.858	51
data16	0.876	0.829	0.851	143	0.880	0.837	**0.858**	48
data17	0.973	0.812	0.885	81	1.000	0.802	**0.890**	41
data18	1.000	0.933	**0.965**	176	1.000	0.933	**0.965**	50
data21	0.927	0.824	0.873	104	0.917	0.837	**0.875**	44
data22	0.996	0.965	0.980	129	0.996	0.967	**0.981**	46
Average	0.943	0.885	0.911	150	0.949	0.888	**0.916**	51

In addition, in order to make the proposed method work on the platforms with low computational capability, we also design a fast version. In our original version, the computational effort is mainly focused on the image registration. Consequently, in the fast version, we use evenly set grid points instead of Shi-Tomas corners. In our experiments, 16×16 key points are selected with evenly distributed in each row and each column. Table 5 shows the comparison of the detection performance and running speed of the two versions of the proposed method. Compared with the original version, the overall F1 score of the fast version is slightly lower. This is because the uniformly set grid points will increase the image registration error, resulting in the reduction of detection performance. However, the overall performance of the fast version is still very close to the original version. At the same time, it runs much faster and can be better applied to the platforms with low computational capability.

4 Conclusions

In this paper, an infrared moving small object detection method based on optimized segmentation and trajectory growth for moving camera is proposed. Optimized segmentation is used for removing the background noise regions and obtain the complete regions of candidate objects when using three-frame difference method. And trajectory growth is proved to be of high effectiveness to suppress noise and local bright regions in complex/noisy scenes. Experiments on publicly available dataset show that the introducing of the proposed optimized segmentation and trajectory growth has greatly improved the performance of existing methods of infrared small object detection, achieving F1 score higher than 0.91 on average, and makes it possible to perform small object detection on the platform of moving camera. And experimental results demonstrate that the proposed method is of low computational complexity and high effectiveness.

Acknowledgement. This work is supported by the National Key Research and Development Program of China (No. 2019YFC1511102) and the National Natural Science Foundation of China (No. 12002215).

References

1. Srivastava, H.B., Kurnar, V., Verma, H.K., et al.: Image pre-processing algorithms for detection of small/point airborne targets. Def. Sci. J. **59**(2), 166–174 (2009)
2. Wei, Y., You, X., Li, H.: Multiscale patch-based contrast measure for small infrared target detection. Pattern Recogn. **58**, 216–226 (2016)
3. Hu, J., Yu, Y., Liu, F.: Small and dim target detection by background estimation. Infrared Phys. Technol. **73**, 141–148 (2015)
4. Qi, H., Mo, B., Liu, F., et al.: Small infrared target detection utilizing local region similarity difference map. Infrared Phys. Technol. **71**, 131–139 (2015)
5. Bai, X., Zhou, F.: Analysis of new top-hat transformation and the application for infrared dim small target detection. Pattern Recogn. **43**(6), 2145–2156 (2010)
6. Deng, L., Zhang, J., Xu, G., et al.: Infrared small target detection via adaptive M-estimator ring top-hat transformation. Pattern Recogn. **112**, 107729 (2021)
7. Wang, X., Peng, Z., Zhang, P., et al.: Infrared small target detection via nonnegativity-constrained variational mode decomposition. IEEE Geosci. Remote Sens. Lett. **14**(10), 1700–1704 (2017)

8. Chen, C.P., Li, H., Wei, Y., et al.: A local contrast method for small infrared target detection. IEEE Trans. Geosci. Remote Sens. **52**(1), 574–581 (2014)
9. Han, J., Ma, Y., Zhou, B., et al.: A robust infrared small target detection algorithm based on human visual system. IEEE Geosci. Remote Sens. Lett. **11**(12), 2168–2172 (2014)
10. Chen, Y., Nasrabadi, N.M., Tran, T.D.: Sparse representation for target detection in hyperspectral imagery. IEEE J. Sel. Top. Signal Process. **5**(3), 629–640 (2011)
11. Gao, C., Meng, D., Yang, Y., et al.: Infrared patch-image model for small target detection in a single image. IEEE Trans. Image Process. **22**(12), 4996–5009 (2013)
12. Dai, Y., Wu, Y., Zhou, F., et al.: Attentional local contrast networks for infrared small target detection. IEEE Trans. Geosci. Remote Sens. **59**(11), 9813–9824 (2021)
13. Zhao, B., Wang, C., Fu, Q., et al.: A novel pattern for infrared small target detection with generative adversarial network. IEEE Trans. Geosci. Remote Sens. **59**(5), 4481–4492 (2021)
14. Reed, I.S., Gagliardi, R.M., Shao, H.M.: Application of three-dimensional filtering to moving target detection. IEEE Trans. Aerosp. Electron. Syst. **19**(6), 898–905 (1983)
15. Reed, I.S., Gagliardi, R.M., Stotts, L.B.: Optical moving target detection with 3-D matched filtering. IEEE Trans. Aerosp. Electron. Syst. **24**(4), 327–336 (1988)
16. Wang, B., Xu, W., Zhao, M., et al.: Antivibration pipeline-filtering algorithm for maritime small target detection. Opt. Eng. **53**(11), 113109 (2014)
17. Wang, B., Dong, L., Zhao, M., et al.: A small dim infrared maritime target detection algorithm based on local peak detection and pipeline-filtering. In: 7th International Conference on Graphic and Image Processing (ICGIP), pp. 188–193 (2015)
18. Dong, L., Wang, B., Zhao, M., et al.: Robust infrared maritime target detection based on visual attention and spatiotemporal filtering. IEEE Trans. Geosci. Remote Sens. **55**(5), 3037–3050 (2017)
19. Tomasi, C.: Detection and tracking of point features. Tech. Rep. **91**(21), 9795–9802 (1991)
20. Fischler, M.A., Bolles, R.C.: Random sample consensus: a paradigm for model fitting with applications to image analysis and automated cartography. Commun. ACM **24**(6), 381–395 (1981)
21. Lowe, D.G.: Distinctive image features from scale-invariant keypoints. Int. J. Comput. Vision **60**(2), 91–110 (2004)
22. Bay, H., Tuytelaars, T., Van Gool, L.: SURF: speeded up robust features. In: Leonardis, A., Bischof, H., Pinz, A. (eds.) ECCV 2006. LNCS, vol. 3951, pp. 404–417. Springer, Heidelberg (2006). https://doi.org/10.1007/11744023_32
23. Shi, J.: Good features to track. In: 1994 Proceedings of IEEE Conference on Computer Vision and Pattern Recognition, Seattle, WA, USA, pp. 593–600. IEEE (1994)
24. Rother, C., Kolmogorov, V., Blake, A.: "GrabCut": interactive foreground extraction using iterated graph cuts. ACM Trans. Graph. **23**(3), 309–314 (2004)
25. Hui, B., Song, Z., Fan, H., et al.: A dataset for infrared detection and tracking of dim-small aircraft targets underground/air background. China Sci. Data **5**(3), 1–12 (2020)

Two-stage Object Tracking Based on Similarity Measurement for Fused Features of Positive and Negative Samples

Kai Huang[ID], Jun Chu[✉], and Peixuan Qin

Jiangxi Key Laboratory of Image Processing and Pattern Recognition,
Nanchang Hangkong University, Nanchang 330063, China
chuj@nchu.edu.cn, 1816085212011@nchu.edu.cn

Abstract. The tracking algorithm based on Siamese networks cannot change the corresponding templates according to appearance changes of targets. Therefore, taking convolution as a similarity measure finds it difficult to collect background information and discriminate background interferents similar to templates, showing poor tracking robustness. In view of this problem, a two-stage tracking algorithm based on the similarity measure for fused features of positive and negative samples is proposed. In accordance with positive and negative sample libraries established online, a discriminator based on measurement for fused features of positive and negative samples is learned to quadratically discriminate a candidate box of hard sample frames. The tracking accuracy and success rate of the algorithm in the OTB2015 benchmark dataset separately reach 92.4% and 70.7%. In the VOT2018 dataset, the algorithm improves the accuracy by nearly 0.2%, robustness by 4.0% and expected average overlap (EAO) by 2.0% compared with the benchmark network SiamRPN++. In terms of the LaSOT dataset, the algorithm is superior to all algorithms compared. Compared with the basic network, its success rate increases by nearly 3.0%, and the accuracy rises by more than 1.0%. Conclusions: The experimental results in the OTB2015, VOT2018 and LaSOT datasets show that the proposed method has a great improvement in the tracking success rate and robustness compared with algorithms based on Siamese networks and particularly, it performs excellently in the LaSOT dataset with a long sequence, occlusion and large appearance changes.

Keywords: Object tracking · Siamese network · Quality evaluation · Online update of sample library · Similarity measure

1 Introduction

Object tracking, as an important branch in the field of computer vision, can locate and track specific targets in video sequences, obtain their motion tra-

---

Supplementary Information The online version contains supplementary material available at https://doi.org/10.1007/978-3-031-18916-6_49.

jectories and understand behaviors of targets [1]. It plays an important role in aspects, such as unmanned driving, camera monitoring, unmanned aerial vehicle (UAV) search and augmented reality. The research on target tracking has developed rapidly, but its application in actual scenes still faces severe challenges, such as changes of shape, size and posture of targets as well as illumination, background change and occlusion, especially the interference of similar background in complex scenes.

The tracking algorithm based on Siamese networks is usually trained offline and only learns the template features of objects in the first frame. Therefore, a tracker is difficult to adapt to drastic changes in appearance of objects and is prone to failure in target tracking in complex scenes, especially when there are similar interferents. In order to solve this problem, the most direct solution is to update the tracker online [2,3]. This method [4] well solves the problem of template update, but it only focuses on the update of the appearance model of targets, not on the background information. In addition, the update process is an independent module, which is not embedded in the network and cannot benefit from joint training and cooperate closely with networks.

By using the target tracking algorithm based on Siamese networks, some researchers measured the similarity between the target template and candidate region through cross-correlation [2,5,6]. For most mainstream trackers, correlation plays a vital role in integrating templates or target information into a region of interest (ROI). However, the correlation is a linear matching process, which will lead to the loss of semantic information and easy to fall into local optimum. This limits the performance of trackers in capturing the complex nonlinear interaction between templates and ROIs. In order to improve the nonlinear representation ability of trackers, some effective structures and additional modules are introduced into the network in some trackers [7–10]. The current target tracking algorithm based on Siamese networks only learns template features of the object in the first frame and finds it difficult to adapt to interference of similar objects in complex scenes and changes of target appearance. Although an online update template is proposed in some algorithms, they pay too much attention to the update of the appearance model of targets while ignore the importance of background information to target update. Furthermore, the target tracking algorithm based on Siamese networks uses cross-correlation to measure the similarity between target templates and candidate regions. The cross-correlation is a linear matching process, which cannot correctly judge some hard samples with interferents and shows poor tracking robustness.

Aiming at the above problem, a two-stage target tracking algorithm based on the similarity measure for fused features of positive and negative samples is proposed. Based on the preliminary tracking with Siamese networks, a classifier trained in online positive and negative sample libraries is used for quadratic discrimination of candidate boxes in unreliably tracked video frames with interference of similar objects (referred to as hard sample frames in this research). In other words, the similarity between candidate features in hard samples and features of positive and negative samples in a sample pool is calculated to obtain the similarity score and the one with the highest score is the target. Dual-template update mechanisms are constructed by the established online sample library and the background information is increased by setting target and interferent templates. Moreover, the templates of positive and negative samples are updated online to improve the anti-interference ability of the tracking algorithm. The classifier trained by the positive and negative sample libraries is used to replace the simple similarity measure to improve the discrimination ability of the tracking algorithm.

The main contributions of this study are made as follows:

1. A tracking framework for quadratic discrimination of candidate boxes corresponding to multiple peaks in hard sample frames is proposed. In the quadratic discrimination, the similarity measure of fused positive and negative samples is used to replace the original similarity measure, namely convolution. The difference between the similarities of candidate boxes to target templates and to interferent templates is calculated and the candidate box with the largest difference is regarded as the target. In this case, the discrimination ability of the tracking algorithm is improved.
2. The positive and negative sample libraries are established. By taking eigenvectors of interferents in hard samples as negative samples and target features in different frames as positive samples, templates with different appearances and features of each interferent are obtained, which facilitates comparison of similarity of features of interferents and targets. Moreover, the templates of positive and negative samples are updated online, which improves the anti-interference ability of the tracking algorithm.
3. The proposed quadratic discrimination module is an independent structure and has strong portability.

2   Methods

This algorithm takes SiamRPN++ [7] as the network benchmark framework. After obtaining preliminary tracking results by SiamRPN++, a quadratic discrimination module for learning based on the similarity measure of positive and negative samples is added. Based on this, a two-stage tracking framework is constructed to eliminate interference of similar objects in complex scenes. The module includes discrimination of hard sample frames, construction of the positive and negative sample libraries and a quadratic discriminator based on feature fusion. The improved network framework is displayed in Fig. 1.

In the early stage of training, only SiamRPN++ is trained and then the discriminator is trained after the network is trained to be stable. During training, real boxes in different frames are selected as positive sample templates and the negative sample pool of the discriminator is empty in the early stage of training. The similarity of candidate boxes to positive samples is only calculated. In the later stage, more negative samples appear with the increase of hard samples.

In the early tracking stage, the negative sample library is empty and the samples are collected in the positive sample library when the response diagram of easy samples shows a single peak, to collect an appearance template of the target in a simple scene. Similarly, features of interferents are collected and put into a negative sample pool after discriminating hard sample frames. The update nodes of the sample templates are set to a fixed number of frames while the number of frames for easy samples and hard samples is verified through experiments.

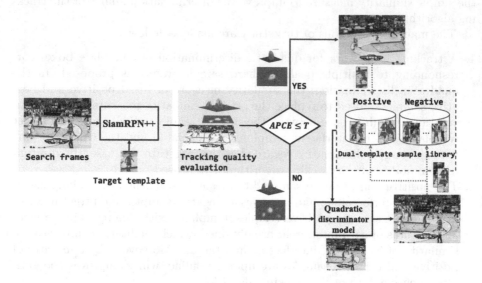

Fig. 1. Architecture of the tracking framework.

2.1 Discrimination of Hard Sample Frames Based on Tracking Quality Evaluation

For the target tracking algorithm based on Siamese networks, the classification confidence map will show multiple peaks when similar background interference appears in video frames or the target object is occluded. Therefore, whether the current frame is a hard sample frame can be determined by analyzing whether there are multiple peaks in the classification response diagram, that is, where there is interference of similar objects or target occlusion. If multiple peaks appear, the current frame is a hard sample frame. The candidate box corresponding to the peak is quadratically discriminated and the negative sample pool is updated. If there is a single peak in the response diagram, the frame is an easy sample frame and the positive sample pool is updated.

At present, there are two types of discrimination methods based on peaks in generative response diagrams, namely average peak-to-correlation energy (APCE) [11] and peak-to-sidelobe ratio (PSR) [1]. The PSR is calculated as follows:

$$P_t = \frac{max(f) - \mu}{\sigma}, \tag{1}$$

where, f represents the values of all pixels in the response diagram; μ, σ denote the mean value and variance of other peaks except for the highest peak in the response diagram, respectively. By comparing the mean values and standard deviations of the highest peak and other peaks in the response diagram, there is interferent when the values are slightly different.

The APCE can reflect the stability of peaks in the response diagram, which is mainly used to judge whether the tracking model is updated. It is expressed as follows:

$$A_t = \frac{|max(f) - min(f)|^2}{avg(\sum_{w,h} f_{w,h} - min(f))} \qquad (2)$$

where, $max(f)$ and $min(f)$ separately indicate the maximum and minimum values in the response diagram; w, h represent the pixels in the response diagram.

Based on the above formula, the APCE will suddenly decrease when the highest value is small and multiple peaks appear in the response diagram. Therefore, the APCE is selected as an index to judge multiple peaks in the response diagram. As the APCE is larger than the given threshold, there are multiple peaks in the response diagram.

The threshold of the APCE is obtained through experimental analysis. The experiment is conducted in different video sequences to compare response diagrams and APCEs of the same video sequence with no background noise and with interfering background noise. According to the experimental results, the thresholds APCEs in the VOT and OTB datasets are set as 43.8 and 36.25. The experimental results are shown in Sect. 1 of the supplementary materials.

After selecting hard samples based on the threshold of APCE, coordinates (w, h, c) of peaks in the response diagram are calculated. Different object boxes are selected by using Fast non-maximum suppression (NMS) and coordinates of $k(\leq 3)$ candidate boxes with the maximum response values are taken. According to coordinates of candidate boxes, offset in the corresponding regression response diagrams is obtained and the position of the candidate box of the candidate target in images is deduced based on offset. The eigenvectors of the candidate target in video frames in the search branch are extracted, encoded and marked with the number of frames. Finally, these eigenvectors are input into the discriminator to calculate similarity. For the remaining easy samples, whether their features corresponding to the target regression box are recorded in the positive sample pool is judged according to whether F_{max} reaches the historical average or not. If the maximum peak is larger than the average, the features are recorded in the pool; Otherwise, they are not.

2.2 Construction and Update of the Online Positive and Negative Sample Libraries

In traditional Siamese networks, the target in the first frame is used as the matched target template and the similarity between search features and template features in the subsequent frames is learned. As video frames move forward, the appearance, posture and even most forms of the target change. In the case, the template of the first frame cannot be used as the reference sample of subsequent frames, especially the application of the tracking algorithm in real scenes. This study designs a dual-template mode, that is, it increases the background information by setting the target and interferent templates and updates positive and negative samples online. The target and interferent templates are constructed by the established positive and negative sample libraries, so the positive and negative sample libraries are also collectively known as the dual-template library. The update conditions of the templates affect the purity of the sample pool and the update mode influences the speed of the algorithm. Therefore, the update timing and modes are mainly discussed in the following sections.

The samples are classified into easy and hard ones by evaluating the tracking quality, of which easy samples update the positive sample library by selecting target features, while hard samples update the negative sample library by selecting interferent features. This increases interfering background information while enriching the positive sample template and increases the diversity of the sample library when comparing discriminators in the later stage, so that there are two standards for comparing similarity of the target: similarity measures separately for positive and negative samples. Based on the two standards, the judgement for the target and interferent is more reliable. The supplementary materials are described in more detail in Sect. 2.

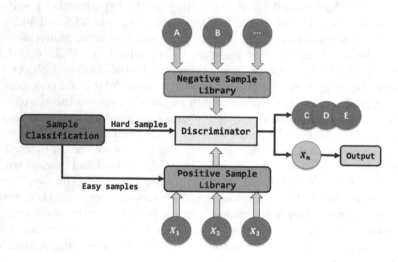

Fig. 2. Sample judgment and update mechanisms.

2.3 Quadratic Discrimination Based on Hard Samples

To learn a new similarity discriminator that can simultaneously compare templates of background information and foreground target information and enhance discrimination ability of the model, a discriminator for similarity between features of candidate boxes and positive and negative samples is proposed based on the idea of feature fusion. The framework of the discriminator is shown in Fig. 3. The target template and search regions are input into the convolutional neural networks (CNN) feature extractor and then their features are mapped and fused to form a long vector. Finally, the binary classification is performed by adding a fully-connected (FC) layer with the sigmoid function. The network is trained through cross-entropy loss. The supplementary materials are described in more detail in Sect. 3.

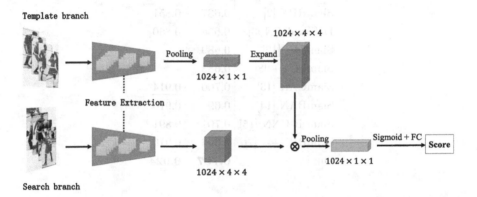

Fig. 3. Framework of the discriminator model.

3 Experimental Results

3.1 Experiment Environment

The proposed tracking scheme is evaluated in some general tracking datasets (VOT2018, OTB2015 and LaSOT), and an ablation experiment is carried out on parameter settings of different components. In the experiment, some of the latest mainstream tracking algorithms are selected for quantitative comparison with the algorithms proposed in this study, such as Siamese algorithms and ATOM [6]. Moreover, the visual results of qualitative analysis of some mainstream algorithms are present. Finally, different thresholds of APCE, the number of candidate boxes, update frequency of template library and effectiveness of threshold $\hat{f}_{max}$ are evaluated and the results are analyzed. The experiment is conducted in a computer with a 128 GB memory and 4 * 1080ti. The implementation details of the experiments are in Sect. 4, Subsect. 1 of the Supplementary Material.

3.2   Experimental Results

Results on OTB2015. The experimental results are displayed in Table 1. The proposed algorithm outperforms all other algorithms, and compared with the benchmark network framework, its success rate and accuracy improve by about 1.0%. Table 1 demonstrate comparison results of algorithms in the OTB dataset.

Table 1. Comparison results of the proposed algorithm with other algorithms in the OTB2015 dataset (The best results are bolded and the second-best results are marked with underlines).

Tracker	OTB2015	
	Success	Precision
SiamFC [5]	0.587	0.772
SiamRPN [2]	0.637	0.851
DaSiamRPN [3]	0.658	0.880
SiamDW [12]	0.689	-
SiamFC++ [8]	0.683	-
SiamCAR [13]	0.700	0.914
SiamBAN [14]	0.696	0.910
Siam R-CNN [15]	0.701	0.891
SiamRPN++ [7]	0.696	0.910
Ours	**0.707**	**0.924**

Results on VOT2018. Due to space limitations, the experimental results of the vot dataset are located in Sect. 4.3 of the Supplementary Material.

Results on LaSOT. Table 2 shows comparison results in the LaSOT dataset. The proposed algorithm is superior to all other algorithms, and compared with the basic network, its success rate increases by nearly 3.0%, and the accuracy rises by more than 1.0%. It is obvious that the proposed algorithm performs well in the LaSOT dataset with long sequences, occlusion and large changes in appearance, and the tracking performance is even superior to that of discriminant algorithm.

The discriminant tracking algorithm will fine tune the network online during tracking and updates according to the context information of images in the tracking process. The tracking effects on similar interferents are stronger than those of Siamese networks, but the tracking speed is lower than that of Siamese networks. The proposed algorithm has better performance in complex video sequences because quadratic discrimination is introduced and the similarity measure is constructed by the discriminator according to positive and negative samples.

Table 2. Comparison with some state-of-the-art trackers in the LaSOT dataset (The best results are written in bold and the second-best results are marked with underlines).

Tracker	LaSOT	
	Success	Precision
ECO [16]	0.324	0.338
SiamFC [5]	0.336	0.420
DSiam [17]	0.333	0.405
MDNet [18]	0.367	0.460
DaSiamRPN [3]	0.415	0.496
ATOM [6]	<u>0.515</u>	<u>0.576</u>
SiamRPN++ [7]	0.495	0.569
Ours	**0.522**	**0.581**

3.3 Analysis of Tracking Performances

Due to space limitations, tracking performance analysis is located in the supplementary materials Sect. 4.4.

3.4 Ablation Experiment

Comparison Between Single-Template and Multi-template Discriminators. The trackers are tested with single-template and multi-template discriminators in the VOT2018 dataset, and the experimental results are shown in Table 3. BaseLine is reproduction results of the benchmark network framework SiamRPN++. BL+Discrimination shows the structure of the discriminator obtained by adding the single-template mode to the benchmark network. BL+Discrimination+MT demonstrates the structure of the discriminator in which multi-template (MT) mode is added to the reference network. As shown in the table, if only the discriminator is added to perform quadratic discrimination on the single templates and candidate boxes, although it can play a certain role, the success rate of correcting the misjudged samples is very small and robustness is also improved slightly. Moreover, after introducing multi-template mechanisms for online update, the discriminator can effectively correct the frames in which the target is originally lost, and the robustness and EAO have been greatly improved.

Table 3. Performance of different template patterns in the VOT2018.

	Baseline	BL+Discrimination	BL+Discrimination+MT
Accuracy	0.600	0.602	**0.602**
Robust	0.234	0.228	**0.187**
EAO	0.377	0.379	**0.398**

Distribution Performance of Different Thresholds of APCE in Datasets. The screening mechanisms for hard samples proposed in this study need to discriminate multi-peak response diagram and use the APCE as the judgement index. Through the data analysis of peaks in the response diagram of easy samples and hard samples, three calculation methods for the threshold of APCE are finally selected: (**a**) calculating the median value of the averages of single-peak response diagram and multi-peak response diagram; (**b**) obtaining the confidence interval with the probability greater than 80% from the confidence interval of Gaussian distribution; (**c**) calculating the interval with the probability of Wilson confidence interval greater than 80%. The values obtained by these three methods are tested according to the data distribution of different datasets, and the results are shown in Tables 4 and 5.

The experiment shows that the median method has the best performance in the VOT dataset and the Wilson interval method performs best in the OTB dataset. The results have little difference, indicating that the value of the threshold has a little impact on the performance of the tracker. The specific analysis is shown as follows: the greater the threshold, a sample is more likely to be judged as hard sample, so the probability of quadratic discrimination is greater. The specific data distribution of different datasets needs to be further verified (which is at high labor and time costs). The method based on Gaussian distribution is less reliable for small sample data, so it has poor performance.

Table 4. Performance of different thresholds of APCE on data distribution in the VOT2018.

	a.(43.8)	b.(36.0)	c.(31.2)
Accuracy	**0.602**	0.602	0.601
Robust	**0.187**	0.193	0.190
EAO	**0.398**	0.399	0.396

Table 5. Performance of different thresholds of APCE on data distribution in the OTB2015.

	a.(28.8)	b.(31.9)	c.(36.2)
Accuracy	0.704	0.701	**0.707**
Precision	0.925	0.921	**0.924**

Effects of Different $\hat{f}_{max}$ on Tracking Performance. After screening hard samples, the remaining easy samples are screened according to the maximum average $\hat{f}_{max}$ of the response diagram and the samples with the highest response score are used as the positive sample templates and update into the template library. The sampling strategy for $\hat{f}_{max}$ and whether to use $\hat{f}_{max}$ to filter are tested and the results are demonstrated in Table 6.

Table 6. Performance of different $\hat{f}_{max}$ in data distribution in OTB datasets.

	a	b	c
Accuracy	0.702	0.706	**0.707**
Precision	0.922	0.924	**0.924**

4   Conclusions

Siamese networks are found to have some disadvantages, including lack of online fine tuning, poor discrimination ability for interferents, obsolete target templates and lack of background information for similarity learning. In view of this, the quadratic discrimination is conducted on hard samples by discriminating similarities of candidate boxes to different target templates and interferent templates by establishing the online template library. Based on this, the two-stage tracking algorithm for quadratic discrimination based on dual-template and candidate region of hard sample frames is proposed, so as to correct the wrong tracking that the similarity between the target and the template is smaller than the interferent. The online positive and negative sample libraries are built to improve the diversity of the samples and enhance the anti-interference ability of the tracker. Furthermore, the discriminator based on feature fusion is put forward. By calculating the similarity of features, the features of candidate boxes are compared with those of targets and interferents.

Acknowledgments. This research was funded by NSFC (No. 62162045, 61866028), Technology Innovation Guidance Program Project (No. 20212BDH81003) and Postgraduate Innovation Special Fund Project (No. YC2021133).

References

1. Bolme, D.S., Beveridge, J.R., Draper, B.A., Lui, Y.M.: Visual object tracking using adaptive correlation filters. In: 2010 IEEE Computer Society Conference on Computer Vision and Pattern Recognition, pp. 2544–2550. IEEE (2010)
2. Li, B., Yan, J., Wu, W., Zhu, Z., Hu, X.: High performance visual tracking with Siamese region proposal network. In: Proceedings of the IEEE Conference on Computer Vision and Pattern Recognition, pp. 8971–8980 (2018)
3. Zhu, Z., Wang, Q., Li, B., Wu, W., Yan, J., Hu, W.: Distractor-aware Siamese networks for visual object tracking. In: Ferrari, V., Hebert, M., Sminchisescu, C., Weiss, Y. (eds.) ECCV 2018. LNCS, vol. 11213, pp. 103–119. Springer, Cham (2018). https://doi.org/10.1007/978-3-030-01240-3_7
4. Zhang, L., Gonzalez-Garcia, A., Weijer, J.v.d., Danelljan, M., Khan, F.S.: Learning the model update for Siamese trackers. In: Proceedings of the IEEE/CVF International Conference on Computer Vision, pp. 4010–4019 (2019)
5. Bertinetto, L., Valmadre, J., Henriques, J.F., Vedaldi, A., Torr, P.H.S.: Fully-convolutional Siamese networks for object tracking. In: Hua, G., Jégou, H. (eds.) ECCV 2016. LNCS, vol. 9914, pp. 850–865. Springer, Cham (2016). https://doi.org/10.1007/978-3-319-48881-3_56

6. Danelljan, M., Bhat, G., Khan, F.S., Felsberg, M.: Atom: accurate tracking by overlap maximization. In: Proceedings of the IEEE/CVF Conference on Computer Vision and Pattern Recognition, pp. 4660–4669 (2019)

7. Li, B., Wu, W., Wang, Q., Zhang, F., Xing, J., Yan, J.: Siamrpn++: evolution of Siamese visual tracking with very deep networks. In: Proceedings of the IEEE/CVF Conference on Computer Vision and Pattern Recognition, pp. 4282–4291 (2019)

8. Xu, Y., Wang, Z., Li, Z., Yuan, Y., Yu, G.: Siamfc++: towards robust and accurate visual tracking with target estimation guidelines. In: Proceedings of the AAAI Conference on Artificial Intelligence, vol. 34, pp. 12549–12556 (2020)

9. Zhang, Z., Peng, H., Fu, J., Li, B., Hu, W.: Ocean: object-aware anchor-free tracking. In: Vedaldi, A., Bischof, H., Brox, T., Frahm, J.-M. (eds.) ECCV 2020. LNCS, vol. 12366, pp. 771–787. Springer, Cham (2020). https://doi.org/10.1007/978-3-030-58589-1_46

10. Chen, X., Yan, B., Zhu, J., Wang, D., Yang, X., Lu, H.: Transformer tracking. In: Proceedings of the IEEE/CVF Conference on Computer Vision and Pattern Recognition, pp. 8126–8135 (2021)

11. Wang, M., Liu, Y., Huang, Z.: Large margin object tracking with circulant feature maps. In: Proceedings of the IEEE Conference on Computer Vision and Pattern Recognition, pp. 4021–4029 (2017)

12. Zhang, Z., Peng, H.: Deeper and wider Siamese networks for real-time visual tracking. In: Proceedings of the IEEE/CVF Conference on Computer Vision and Pattern Recognition, pp. 4591–4600. IEEE (2019)

13. Guo, D., Wang, J., Cui, Y., Wang, Z., Chen, S.: SIAMcar: Siamese fully convolutional classification and regression for visual tracking. In: Proceedings of the IEEE/CVF Conference on Computer Vision and Pattern Recognition, pp. 6269–6277. IEEE (2020)

14. Chen, Z., Zhong, B., Li, G., Zhang, S., Ji, R.: Siamese box adaptive network for visual tracking. In: Proceedings of the IEEE/CVF Conference on Computer Vision and Pattern Recognition, pp. 6668–6677. IEEE (2020)

15. Voigtlaender, P., Luiten, J., Torr, P.H., Leibe, B.: SIAM R-CNN: visual tracking by re-detection. In: Proceedings of the IEEE/CVF Conference on Computer Vision and Pattern Recognition, pp. 6578–6588. IEEE (2020)

16. Danelljan, M., Bhat, G., Shahbaz Khan, F., Felsberg, M.: Eco: efficient convolution operators for tracking. In: Proceedings of the IEEE Conference on Computer Vision and Pattern Recognition, pp. 6638–6646. IEEE (2017)

17. Guo, Q., Feng, W., Zhou, C., Huang, R., Wan, L., Wang, S.: Learning dynamic Siamese network for visual object tracking. In: Proceedings of the IEEE International Conference on Computer Vision, pp. 1763–1771. IEEE (2017)

18. Nam, H., Han, B.: Learning multi-domain convolutional neural networks for visual tracking. In: Proceedings of the IEEE Conference on Computer Vision and Pattern Recognition, pp. 4293–4302. IEEE (2016)

PolyTracker: Progressive Contour Regression for Multiple Object Tracking and Segmentation

Sanjing Shen, Hao Feng, Wengang Zhou(✉), and Houqiang Li(✉)

University of Science and Technology of China, Hefei, China
{ssjxjx,fh1995}@mail.ustc.edu.cn, {zhwg,lihq}@ustc.edu.cn

Abstract. State-of-the-art multiple object tracking and segmentation methods predict a pixel-wise segmentation mask for each detected instance object. Such methods are sensitive to the inaccurate detection and suffer from heavy computational overhead. Besides, when associating pixel-wise masks, additional optical flow networks are required to assist in mask propagation. To relieve these three issues, we present PolyTracker, which adopts object contour, in the form of a vertex sequence along with the object silhouette, as an alternative representation of the pixel-wise segmentation mask. In the PolyTracker, we design an effective contour deformation module based on an iterative and progressive mechanism, which is robust to the inaccurate detection and has low model complexity. Furthermore, benefiting from the powerful contour deformation module, we design a novel data association method, which achieves effective contour propagation by fully mining contextual cues from contours. Since data association relies heavily on pedestrian appearance representation, we design a Reliable Pedestrian Information Aggregation (RPIA) module to fully exploit the discriminative re-identification feature. Extensive experiments demonstrate that our PolyTracker sets the promising records on the MOTS20 benchmark.

Keywords: Multiple object tracking and segmentation · Progressive mechanism · Contours regression

1 Introduction

Multi-object tracking (MOT) [22] is of fundamental importance in the field of smart security and autonomous driving. However, the results of MOT evaluations [7,9,12,13] show that the bounding box (bbox) level tracking performance is limited. Recently, multi-object tracking and segmentation (MOTS) [14] provides pixel-wise segmentation masks as an improved form to coarse bboxes, which locate objects more accurately. Since the pixel-wise segmentation masks accurately segment object boundaries in crowded scenes, MOTS largely eliminates the tracking failures caused by heavily overlapped objects in the same bbox. Therefore, these advantages of MOTS make it more potential than bbox-based methods and has gained more and more attention.

ⓒ The Author(s), under exclusive license to Springer Nature Switzerland AG 2022
S. Yu et al. (Eds.): PRCV 2022, LNCS 13537, pp. 633–645, 2022.
https://doi.org/10.1007/978-3-031-18916-6_50

The state-of-the-art MOTS methods [14,17–19] adopt pixel-wise segmentation masks. Typically, they first detect the instance objects and then estimate a pixel-wise segmentation mask within each bbox. However, such methods are sensitive to the inaccurate detection. The dense pixel-wise prediction also brings heavy computational overhead. Moreover, In the inference stage, mask-based IoU together with optical flow warping is a strong cue for associating pixel masks over time, which is proved in the method [14]. However, the extra optical flow network introduces additional training costs as well as model complexity.

To address the above issues, we consider designing an alternative representation of the pixel-wise segmentation mask. In this paper, we propose PolyTracker, which adopts the contour of object as an alternative representation scheme of the pixel-wise segmentation mask. The contour is in the form of a vertex sequence along with the object silhouette. Given a bbox of an instance object, PolyTracker first initializes it to an octagonal contour, then realizes effective automatic contour regression based on the iterative and progressive mechanism. Specifically, in each iteration, PolyTracker first builds the feature representation of the contour estimated at the previous iteration. Then, a recurrent update unit takes the feature as input and outputs the residual displacement to refine the coarse contour predicted at the previous iteration. Through the iterative refinements, even if the bbox of an instance object is inaccurate, the contour finally converges to a stable state tightly enclosing the object. Benefiting from the powerful contour regressor, we further propose a novel data association strategy that can directly implement contour propagation without the need for additional optical flow networks, which can reduce training costs as well as the model complexity.

The data association relies heavily on pedestrian appearance representation. To obtain discriminative appearance representation, we design a Reliable Pedestrian Information Aggregation (RPIA) module in the last iteration to fully exploit the discriminative re-identification feature of each pedestrian. Besides, we estimate the reliable score for the localized pedestrian contour, which effectively suppresses false positives and improves the accuracy of data association.

Our main contributions are summarized as follows:

- We firstly introduce the contour of object as an alternative representation scheme of the pixel-wise segmentation mask in the MOTS task. Our contour-based method realizes effective automatic contour regression based on the iterative and progressive mechanism.
- We propose a novel data association strategy, which is readily integrated into most existing contour-based instance segmentation methods and does not require additional optical flow networks for contour propagation.
- We propose a reliable pedestrian information aggregation module to fully exploit a discriminative re-identification feature of each pedestrian, which plays a very important role during data association.

2   Related Work

2.1   Contour-Based Instance Segmentation

Contour-based instance segmentation methods [8,10,15,16] aim to predict a sequence of vertices for object boundaries. PolarMask [15,16] models the contour by one center and rays emitted from the center to the contour in polar coordinate, which can only handle objects with convex shapes. Curve-GCN [8] regresses the coordinates of contour vertices in the Cartesian coordinate system. Curve-GCN adopts the traditional snake algorithm [6] to obtain an initial contour of each object, and then trains a neural network to regress the initial contour to match the object boundary. However, Curve-GCN does not support end-to-end training due to the need of an extra manual annotation of the object. DeepSnake [10] proposed a two-stage end-to-end pipeline for instance segmentation, which does not need an extra manual annotation of the object. DeepSnake divides the instance segmentation into two stages: initial contour proposal and contour deformation. However, in the initial contour proposal stage, DeepSnake still relies on the learning-based snake algorithm, which introduces extra training costs. Moreover, in the contour deformation stage, DeepSnake applies contour refinement by stacking the regression module. The times of contour deformation are limited, which restricts the performance upper bound.

2.2   Multiple Object Tracking and Segmentation

MOTS aims to track objects with pixel-wise instance masks, which is more robust to dense scenarios. TRCNN [14] and MOTSNet [11] add a re-identification branch on the MaskRCNN [4] method to extract discriminative re-identification feature of each object. In the inference stage, these methods abstract the tracking process as a bipartite matching problem. Then, they take the re-identification feature similarity of detections as the weight matrix of the bipartite graph. Finally, the Hungarian algorithm is adopted to solve the bipartite matching problem. PointTrack [18,19] breaks the compact image representation into 2D unordered point clouds to learn discriminative instance embeddings. Besides, different informative data modalities are converted into point-level representations to enrich point cloud features. STE [5] learns a spatio-temporal embedding integrating cues from appearance. Pixels with similar representations are considered as the same instances, and the average features belonging to the foreground pixels are considered as the representation of the instance. Besides, STE adopts a 3D causal convolutional network models motion, and a monocular self-supervised depth loss models geometry. Compared to the MaskRCNN-based methods, STE fully exploits the spatio-temporal context clues to extract more robust instance representations. CCP [17] exploits non-video frames into MOTS training and increases both the number of instances and the number of unique instance IDs by continuously copy-pasting instances to continuous frames, which is an effective data augmentation method in MOTS methods.

3   Method

In this section, we present PolyTracker, a novel framework for multiple object tracking and segmentation based on the iterative contour deformation mechanism and reliable pedestrian information aggregation mechanism. As shown in Fig. 1, PolyTracker is composed of a backbone network, a detection block, a segmentation block, and a reliable pedestrian information aggregation (RPIA) block. The segmentation block consists of an initial contour construction (ICC) module and an iterative contour deformation (ICD) module. Given an input frame, the detection block first detects objects and provides a bbox of each object. Then, in the segmentation block, the ICC module generates an octagon contour based on each bbox, which is fed into the ICD module as the initial contour. The ICD module progressively evolves it to match the object boundary by recurrently capturing the spatial context and updating the contour. Finally, the RPIA module generates the discriminative re-identification feature of each object with high contour confidence learned by the contour scoring mechanism.

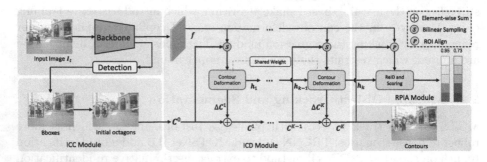

Fig. 1. An overview of PolyTracker framework. PolyTracker consists of a backbone network, a detection block, a segmentation block (containing ICC module and ICD module), and a reliable pedestrian information aggregation (RPIA) block. Given an input frame, the detection block first detects objects and provides a bbox of each object. Then, in the segmentation block, the ICC module generates an octagon contour $\mathbf{C}^0$ based on each bbox. The ICD module progressively evolves contour $\mathbf{C}^0$ to match the object boundary. Finally, the RPIA module generates the discriminative re-identification feature of each object with high contour confidence learned by the contour scoring mechanism.

3.1   Backbone and Detections

We apply DLA-34 [21] as our backbone and CenterNet [23] as our detector. Compared with standard architectures, DLA-34 adopts deeper aggregation to better fuse information across layers, which enriches the representation of each object. CenterNet is an anchor-free detector. CenterNet predicts the center, width, and height of the object respectively. CenterNet also predicts the center offset due to downsampling. In PolyTracker, since the ICD module iteratively refines the coarse contour, only coarse detections are needed. We only predict the center, width and height of each object.

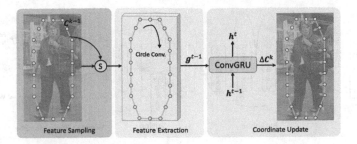

Fig. 2. An illustration of a single iteration in ICD module. "S" denotes vertex feature sampling based on bilinear interpolation.

3.2 Initial Contour Construction Module

The ICC module generates an initial contour based on each detected bbox. Following existing work [10], compared with a bbox, an octagon tends to enclose the object more tightly. Thus, we adopt octagons as the initial contour. Specifically, given a bbox, we first register the four center points of the top, left, bottom, and right edge of this box rectangle. Then, for each center point, a line is extended along the corresponding box edge in both directions by $\frac{1}{4}$ of the edge length. After that, the endpoints of the four line segments are connected to form an octagon. Finally, we obtain the initial contour $\mathbf{C}^0$ by uniformly sampling N vertices along the octagon, where $\mathbf{C}^0 = \{\mathbf{p}_1^0, \mathbf{p}_2^0, \cdots, \mathbf{p}_N^0\}$ and $\mathbf{p}_i^0 \in \mathbb{R}^2$ denotes the horizontal and vertical coordinates of the ith vertex.

During the training stage, the initial contour is constructed based on the ground truth bbox. In order to regress the contour from arbitrary cases in the inference stage, we augment the initial contour by randomly moving and scaling the ground truth bbox.

3.3 Iterative Contour Deformation Module

We introduce a ICD module to refine the coarse initial contour to a stable state tightly enclosing the object by an iterative and progressive mechanism. As shown in Fig. 2, we illustrate the contour update process at the tth iteration. Specifically, we first sample the vertex features $\mathbf{f}^{t-1} \in \mathbb{R}^{N \times D}$ from the feature map $\mathbf{F} \in \mathbb{R}^{\frac{H}{4} \times \frac{W}{4} \times D}$ based on the contour $\mathbf{C}^{t-1}$ predicted at the $t-1^{\text{th}}$ iteration by bilinear interpolation. Then, we construct the feature representation for the contour $\mathbf{C}^{t-1}$ by fusing the vertex features $\mathbf{f}^{t-1}$. Following [10], we adopt the circle-convolution to fuse the feature of the sequence. After that, we concatenate the output features $\mathbf{m}^{t-1} \in \mathbb{R}^{N \times D}$ and $\mathbf{C}^{t-1} \in \mathbb{R}^{N \times 2}$, obtaining the contour representation $\mathbf{g}^{t-1} \in \mathbb{R}^{N \times D_v}$, where $D_v = D + 2$. Finally, a recurrent GRU-based unit takes the input contour features $\mathbf{g}^{t-1} \in \mathbb{R}^{N \times D_v}$ as well as the hidden state $\mathbf{h}^{t-1} \in \mathbb{R}^{N \times D_v}$ as input and outputs the residual displacement $\Delta\mathbf{C}^t$ and the hidden state $\mathbf{h}^t \in \mathbb{R}^{N \times D_v}$. We use the residual displacement $\Delta\mathbf{C}^t$ to update the current contour prediction $\mathbf{C}^{t-1}$ as follows,

$$\mathbf{C}^t = \mathbf{C}^{t-1} + \Delta\mathbf{C}^t. \tag{1}$$

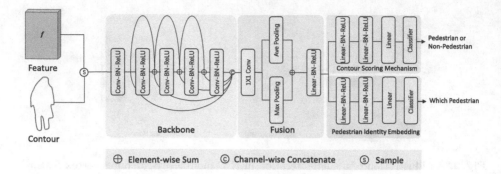

Fig. 3. Reliable pedestrian information aggregation mechanism.

3.4 Reliable Pedestrian Information Aggregation Module

The RPIA module aims to extract discriminative re-identification features of each object with high contour confidence. As shown in Fig. 3, we first sample the pedestrian re-identification feature $\mathbf{f}^{\text{reID}}$ on the feature map $\mathbf{f} \in \mathbb{R}^{\frac{H}{4} \times \frac{W}{4} \times D}$ based on the contour $\mathbf{C}^K$ predicted at the last iteration. Then, the re-identification features $\mathbf{f}^{\text{reID}}$ is fed to five Conv-BN-ReLU layers, and the output of the convolutional layer is element-wise added with the output of the previous convolutional layer starting from the second convolutional layer. All the outputs of the convolutional layers are concatnated to enrich the semantic information. Then, they are fed into a 1×1 convolutional layer to reduce dimensions. After that, the average pooling and the max pooling operation are utilized to generate feature vectors. We adopt a Linear-BN-ReLU operation to enhance the feature vectors. Finally, the feature vectors are fed into the contour scoring branch and the pedestrian identity embedding branch, respectively. The difference between two branches is that the final classifier of the contour score branch is a binary classifier, which is used to distinguish whether the object surrounded by the contour is a pedestrian or not, while the final classifier of the pedestrian identity embedding branch is a N-dimensional classifier, which is used to discriminate the identities of the pedestrians. N is the number of pedestrian identities in the training set.

The contour scoring branch requires positive samples and negative samples to train this network. Specifically, we consider the contours deformed by bboxes as positive samples. Furthermore, we exploit a shape-preserving negative sample mining technique to generate negative training samples. The negative sample mining technique first copies the contour of each pedestrian and randomly moves the duplicates on the image. Then, the overlaps between the generated contours and all positive contours are calculated. Finally, we choose the contour with the lowest interval of overlaps as the negative sample for each pedestrian.

3.5 Training Objectives

During the training stage, the overall architecture of the proposed PolyTracker is end-to-end optimized with the following training objectives:

$$\mathcal{L} = \mathcal{L}_{\text{det}} + \mathcal{L}_{\text{seg}} + \mathcal{L}_{\text{id}} + \mathcal{L}_{\text{s}}, \tag{2}$$

where $\mathcal{L}_{\text{det}}$ denotes the detection loss, $\mathcal{L}_{\text{seg}}$ denotes segmentation loss, $\mathcal{L}_{\text{id}}$ denotes the person re-identification loss in the RPIA module, and $\mathcal{L}_{\text{s}}$ denotes the contour scoring loss in the RPIA module. The instantiation of $\mathcal{L}_{\text{det}}$ depends on the object detector exploited in our framework.

$\mathcal{L}_{\text{seg}}$ is calculated by accumulating the loss over all T iterations:

$$\mathcal{L}_{\text{seg}} = \sum_{t=1}^{T} \lambda^{T-t} \mathcal{L}_{\text{R}}^{t}, \tag{3}$$

where $\mathcal{L}_{\text{R}}^{t}$ is the coordinate regression loss and λ is the temporal weighting factor. λ is always less than 1, which means the weight of the loss increases exponentially with the iteration.

The coordinate regression loss $\mathcal{L}_{\text{R}}^{t}$ is calculated by the smooth L_1 distance between the predicted contour $\mathbf{C}^t = \{\mathbf{p}_1^t, \mathbf{p}_2^t, \cdots, \mathbf{p}_N^t\}$ and the ground truth $\widetilde{\mathbf{C}}^t = \{\widetilde{\mathbf{p}}_1^t, \widetilde{\mathbf{p}}_2^t, \cdots, \widetilde{\mathbf{p}}_N^t\}$ as:

$$\mathcal{L}_{\text{R}}^{t} = \sum \text{smooth}_{L_1}(\mathbf{p}_n^t, \ \widetilde{\mathbf{p}}_n^t). \tag{4}$$

The re-identification loss $\mathcal{L}_{\text{id}}$ is calculated by the cross-entropy loss as:

$$\mathcal{L}_{\text{id}} = -\sum_{i=1}^{I} L_{\text{id}}(i) P_{\text{id}}(i), \tag{5}$$

where I is the number of pedestrian in the mini-batch, and $L_{\text{id}}(i)$ is the identify ground truth for i^{th} pedestrian. Note that the negative samples are not involved in the calculation.

The contour scoring loss is also calculated by the cross-entropy loss as:

$$\mathcal{L}_{\text{s}} = -\sum_{i=1}^{2I} L_{\text{s}}(i) P_{\text{s}}(i), \tag{6}$$

where $L_{\text{s}}(i)$ denotes the positive samples or negative samples for the ith pedestrian. Different from the re-identification loss, all positive samples and negative samples participate in the calculation of the contour scoring loss.

3.6   Data Association

The MOTS task can be divided into two phases: (1) segmenting object locations independently in each frame, and (2) associating corresponding segmentations frame by frame. The second phase is named data association.

Given a video, data association extracts the spatial and temporal positions of objects. The data association contains two steps. In the first step, we utilize the powerful ICD module to extend active tracks from frame $t-1$ to the current frame t. Specifically, the ICD module takes the feature map $\mathbf{F}$ of frame t and the contours in active tracks of frame $t - 1$ as input and outputs the contours in the current frame t, which denotes the new position of active tracks. Due to the high frame rates, the object has moved only slightly between frames. After the contour regression, we consider two cases for deleting a trajectory. In the first case, the new contour score of an object is below σ_s, which denotes the object is occluded by a non-object or leaves the frame. In the second case, the re-identification similarity of an object between frame $t - 1$ and frame t is below σ_{id}, which denotes the object occluded by another object. Finally, we delete the object contours from detections whose Intersection over Union (IoU) with any extended tracks is higher than the threshold σ_c.

In the second step, we adopt Hungarian algorithm to associate the remaining trajectory and object contours in frame t, which are both not associated in the first step. This stage obtains the visual similarity between the remaining trajectory and object contours. Then, the object are associated using the Hungarian matching algorithm. Finally, the remaining unmatched contours are initialized into new trajectories and the trajectories with accumulated unmatched s frames are deleted to indicate that the target disappears from the camera view.

4   Experiments

4.1   Dataset and Implementation Details

We evaluate our method on the MOTS20 dataset. MOTS20 focuses on pedestrians in crowded scenes and is very challenging due to many occlusion cases. The training set of the MOTS20 dataset consists of 4 video sequences with a total of 2862 frames, which have 228 different pedestrians and 26894 pixel-level segmentation masks. Among them, 3930 segmentation masks are manually labeled. The test set also consists of 4 video sequences. Since the ground truth of the test set is not publicly available, the tracking results should be submitted to the benchmark for evaluation. Due to the limited number of submissions, we divide the entire training set into two equal parts. In the ablation study, the first half is for training and the second half is for testing.

We apply CenterNet [23] as our detector and train the full model end-to-end for 160 epochs with 16 images per batch. The Adam optimizer is adopted and the learning rate starts from $1e^{-4}$ and drops by half at 80, 120, and 150 epochs, respectively. We set the vertex number $N = 128$ along a contour. The channel number of feature map $\mathbf{f}$ and contour feature $\mathbf{g}^{t-1}$ are set as $D = 64$ and $D_v = 66$, respectively. During the training stage, we set the iteration number T as 8. The iteration number during inference is the same as the setting in the training. For the training of the segmentation blcok, we use $\lambda = 0.85$ in Eq. (3). In the data association, the tracker can tolerate at most 20 consecutive disappearance of each track. We set the score of the reliable contours as $\sigma_s = 0.95$. The re-identification feature distance threshold is set to $\sigma_{id} = 0.20$. The IoU threshold of deleted object contours from detections is set to $\sigma_c = 0.50$.

Following [11,14], we adopt sMOTSA and IDF1 as the metrics. Since ID switches (IDS) varies with the instance segmentation results, we do not adopt IDS as metric. For example, more false negatives may lead to fewer IDS.

Table 1. Ablations of the ICC module on the MOTS20-val set.

Octagon	Bounding box	Data augmentation	sMOTSA	IDF1
	✓	✓	60.4	69.0
✓			59.2	68.1
✓		✓	**61.3**	**69.2**

Table 2. Ablations of the ICD module on the MOTS20-val set. Since the ICC module has no parameters, we only count the parameter numbers of the ICD module here.

ConvGRU	ConvLSTM	Shared weights	sMOTSA	IDF1	Para.
	✓	✓	60.6	69.0	1.92M
✓			60.7	68.9	15.0M
✓		✓	**61.3**	**69.2**	**1.88M**

4.2 Ablation Study

Initial Contour Construction Module. The default shape of the initial contour C^0 for PolyTracker is an octagon within the bbox. We then test another initial contour strategy by directly uniformly sampling N vertices along the bbox. As shown in Table 1, the performance is better using the octagon contour as the initial strategy, which can be ascribed to the fact that as an initial contour, an octagon can enclose the object more tightly than a rectangular.

We further verify the effectiveness of the proposed augmentation strategy for the initial octagon contour. As shown in Table 1, the performances are worse when we only construct the initial contour based on the ground truth bbox. The result demonstrates that the proposed augmentation strategy helps the learning for deforming the contours from various complex situations in the test stage.

Iterative Contour Deformation Module. In the ICD module, we adopt ConvGRU as the default update unit. We then try to replace ConvGRU with ConvLSTM, which is a modified version of standard LSTM. As shown in Table 2, ConvGRU is characterized by lower parameter numbers and higher performance.

The weights of the ICD module are shared as defaults across the total T iterations. We test the performance when using a distinctive set of weights in the ICD module. As shown in Table 2, when the weights are unshared, the performances are slightly worse while the parameters significantly increase.

In the following, we discuss the impact of the number of ICD module iterations on performance. As shown in Fig. 4, the main contour deformation lies in the top 3 iterations and the later iterations fine-tune the performance. In our final model, we set the iteration number $T = 8$ to stride a balance between the accuracy and the running efficiency.

Data Association. Following the existing work [2], for videos with a moving camera, we apply a straightforward camera motion compensation (CMC) by aligning frames via image registration using the Enhanced Correlation Coefficient (ECC) maximization [3]. As shown in Table 3, the result shows that the CMC plays an important role in performance enhancement.

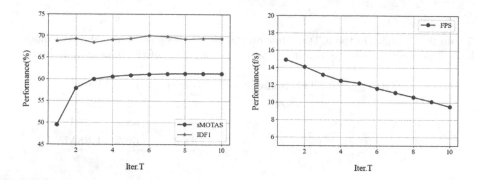

Fig. 4. Performance of the selected iterations during inference on the MOTS20-val set. Note that we only count the FPS of the iterative contour deformation module here.

Table 3. Ablations of data association on the MOTS20-val set. CMC denotes the camera motion compensation, CSM denotes Contour Scoring Mechanism, and RIE denotes Pedestrian Identity Embedding.

CMC	CSM	RIE	sMOTSA	IDF1
	✓	✓	58.2	67.1
✓			56.8	58.9
✓	✓		57.5	59.1
✓		✓	60.7	67.5
✓	✓	✓	**61.3**	**69.2**

The re-identification features of the pedestrians have a large impact on the data association. As shown in Table 3, the tracking performance can be greatly improved when using proposed RPIA module (containing CSM and RIE), especially the IDF1 performance is improved by 10.3%. In Table 3, we also discuss the impact of contour scoring mechanism and pedestrian identity embedding in the RPIA module. The result demonstrates that both modules can bring performance improvement.

4.3 Comparison with State-of-the-Art Methods

We compare our PolyTracker with other state-of-the-art methods on MOTS20 test sets. Since 5th BMTT MOTChallenge Workshop provides a strong public detection results generated by models pre-trained from extra datasets, some methods like REMOTS [20] reach very high performance. However, our PolyTracker is trained from scratch on MOTS20. For a fair comparison, we only compare PolyTracker with methods using private detections. As shown in Table 4, our PolyTracker achieves promising performances on the MOTS20 leaderboard.

Table 4. Performance comparison with existing state-of-the-art methods on the MOTS20 test set.

Methods	sMOTSA	IDF1
PointTrack++ [19]	62.3	64.8
CCP [17]	59.3	58.1
SORTS [1]	55.0	57.3
StructMOTS	55.0	64.0
UBVision	52.8	58.3
TrackRCNN [14]	40.3	42.4
PolyTracker	61.8	65.7

5 Conclusion

In this work, we present PolyTracker, an effective multiple object tracking and segmentation framework. In the training stage, it simultaneously introduces the iterative and progressive learning mechanism to obtain the contours tightly enclosing the objects. During inference, benefiting from the powerful contour regressor, PolyTracker does not require the extra optical flow network to propagate contours. Moreover, we design the reliable pedestrian information aggregation mechanism to mine reliable contours and extract discriminative re-identification features, which facilitates effective data association. Extensive experiments reveal the merits and superiority of our PolyTracker over the promising methods.

Aknowledgement. This work was supported by the National Natural Science Foundation of China under Contract 62021001.

References

1. Ahrnbom, M., Nilsson, M.G., Ardö, H.: Real-time and online segmentation multi-target tracking with track revival re-identification. In: VISIGRAPP, pp. 777–784 (2021)
2. Bergmann, P., Meinhardt, T., Leal-Taixe, L.: Tracking without bells and whistles. In: IEEE International Conference on Computer Vision (ICCV), pp. 941–951 (2019)

3. Evangelidis, G.D., Psarakis, E.Z.: Parametric image alignment using enhanced correlation coefficient maximization. IEEE Trans. Pattern Anal. Mach. Intell. (TPAMI) **30**(10), 1858–1865 (2008)
4. He, K., Gkioxari, G., Dollár, P., Girshick, R.: Mask R-CNN. In: IEEE International Conference on Computer Vision (ICCV), pp. 2961–2969 (2017)
5. Hu, A., Kendall, A., Cipolla, R.: Learning a spatio-temporal embedding for video instance segmentation. arXiv preprint arXiv:1912.08969 (2019)
6. Kass, M., Witkin, A., Terzopoulos, D.: Snakes: active contour models. Int. J. Comput. Vision (IJCV) **1**(4), 321–331 (1988)
7. Kim, C., Fuxin, L., Alotaibi, M., Rehg, J.M.: Discriminative appearance modeling with multi-track pooling for real-time multi-object tracking. In: IEEE Conference on Computer Vision and Pattern Recognition (CVPR), pp. 9553–9562 (2021)
8. Ling, H., Gao, J., Kar, A., Chen, W., Fidler, S.: Fast interactive object annotation with curve-GCN. In: IEEE Conference on Computer Vision and Pattern Recognition (CVPR), pp. 5257–5266 (2019)
9. Pang, J., et al.: Quasi-dense similarity learning for multiple object tracking. In: IEEE Conference on Computer Vision and Pattern Recognition (CVPR), pp. 164–173 (2021)
10. Peng, S., Jiang, W., Pi, H., Li, X., Bao, H., Zhou, X.: Deep snake for real-time instance segmentation. In: IEEE Conference on Computer Vision and Pattern Recognition (CVPR), pp. 8533–8542 (2020)
11. Porzi, L., Hofinger, M., Ruiz, I., Serrat, J., Bulo, S.R., Kontschieder, P.: Learning multi-object tracking and segmentation from automatic annotations. In: IEEE Conference on Computer Vision and Pattern Recognition (CVPR), pp. 6846–6855 (2020)
12. Saleh, F., Aliakbarian, S., Rezatofighi, H., Salzmann, M., Gould, S.: Probabilistic tracklet scoring and inpainting for multiple object tracking. In: IEEE Conference on Computer Vision and Pattern Recognition (CVPR), pp. 14329–14339 (2021)
13. Shuai, B., Berneshawi, A., Li, X., Modolo, D., Tighe, J.: SiamMOT: Siamese multi-object tracking. In: IEEE Conference on Computer Vision and Pattern Recognition (CVPR), pp. 12372–12382 (2021)
14. Voigtlaender, P., et al.: MOTS: multi-object tracking and segmentation. In: IEEE Conference on Computer Vision and Pattern Recognition (CVPR), pp. 7942–7951 (2019)
15. Xie, E., et al.: PolarMask: single shot instance segmentation with polar representation. In: IEEE Conference on Computer Vision and Pattern Recognition (CVPR), pp. 12193–12202 (2020)
16. Xie, E., Wang, W., Ding, M., Zhang, R., Luo, P.: PolarMask++: enhanced polar representation for single-shot instance segmentation and beyond. IEEE Trans. Pattern Anal. Mach. Intell. (TPAMI) **44**, 5385–5400 (2021)
17. Xu, Z., Meng, A., Shi, Z., Yang, W., Chen, Z., Huang, L.: Continuous copy-paste for one-stage multi-object tracking and segmentation. In: IEEE Conference on Computer Vision and Pattern Recognition (CVPR), pp. 15323–15332 (2021)
18. Xu, Z., et al.: Segment as points for efficient online multi-object tracking and segmentation. In: Vedaldi, A., Bischof, H., Brox, T., Frahm, J.-M. (eds.) ECCV 2020. LNCS, vol. 12346, pp. 264–281. Springer, Cham (2020). https://doi.org/10.1007/978-3-030-58452-8_16
19. Xu, Z., et al.: Pointtrack++ for effective online multi-object tracking and segmentation. arXiv preprint arXiv:2007.01549 (2020)
20. Yang, F., et al.: ReMOTS: self-supervised refining multi-object tracking and segmentation. arXiv preprint arXiv:2007.03200 (2020)

21. Yu, F., Wang, D., Shelhamer, E., Darrell, T.: Deep layer aggregation. In: IEEE Conference on Computer Vision and Pattern Recognition (CVPR), pp. 2403–2412 (2018)
22. Zhang, Y., Wang, C., Wang, X., Zeng, W., Liu, W.: FairMOT: on the fairness of detection and re-identification in multiple object tracking. Int. J. Comput. Vision (IJCV) **129**(11), 3069–3087 (2021)
23. Zhou, X., Wang, D., Krähenbühl, P.: Objects as points. arXiv preprint arXiv:1904.07850 (2019)

Dual-Branch Memory Network for Visual Object Tracking

Jingchao Wang[1,3] (ID), Huanlong Zhang[2], Jianwei Zhang[1,3(✉)], Mengen Miao[1,3], and Jiapeng Zhang[2]

[1] College of Software Engineering, Zhengzhou University of Light Industry, Zhengzhou 450000, China
[2] College of Electric and Information Engineering, Zhengzhou University of Light Industry, Zhengzhou 450000, China
[3] Henan Key Laboratory of Data Intelligence on Food Safety, Zhengzhou 450000, China
mailzjw@163.com

Abstract. In recent years, memory-based tracking has become the focus of visual object tracking due to its robustness toward objects with arbitrary forms. Although advanced memory networks have produced excellent results, balancing long-term and short-term memory remains a difficult problem in memory building. Therefore, we propose the dual-branch memory network (DualMN), which divided the memory-building task into long-term and short-term memory-building tasks, avoiding conflict between them skillfully. Specifically, the DualMN consists of a long-term memory branch and a short-term memory branch. The former is dedicated to learning the difference between the new target appearance and the surrounding environment. The latter focuses on learning the essential feature of the target to prevent the target drift. In the tracking process, the long-term memory branch and the short-term memory branch complement each other to achieve more accurate target positioning. Experiments results on OTB2015, NFS, UAV123, LaSOT, and TrackingNet benchmarks show that our DualMN achieves comparable performance to the advanced trackers.

Keywords: Computer vision · Visual objecting tracking · Memory network

1 Introduction

Object tracking is a basic task in computer vision and is widely applied in autonomous driving, video action recognition, and robot navigation [1]. Given a video and the region of interest, the target state should be predicted in subsequent frames. With the development of deep learning, visual object tracking research has also made great progress. However, it is still difficult to deal with various target changes and complex backgrounds in the sequence.

S. Yu et al. (Eds.): PRCV 2022, LNCS 13537, pp. 646–658, 2022.
https://doi.org/10.1007/978-3-031-18916-6_51

In recent years, most trackers solve the abovementioned problem through two methods, the first is to learn a more expressive feature embedding space and the second is to develop a more robust correlation operation. For the former, some advanced methods design deeper and wider network architectures for Siamese trackers [2,3], while providing deep analysis and ample evidence. To the latter, some trackers use graph attention [4], asymmetric convolution [5], or cross-attention [6] to replace the traditional cross-correlation to better capture correlation information. However, the available information in the first frame is limited after all. To achieve a more accurate tracking effect, it is not enough to rely on the above two methods.

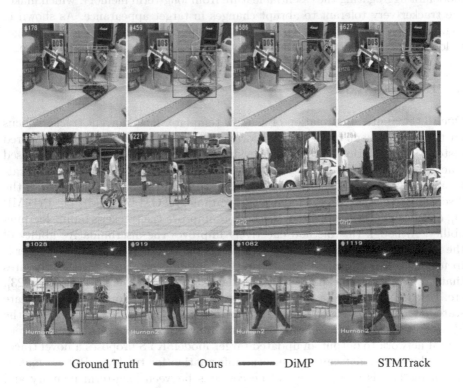

Ground Truth ───── Ours ───── DiMP ┄┄┄ STMTrack

Fig. 1. Visualized comparisons of our method with advanced trackers.

Recently, memory-based trackers [7–9] have attracted a lot of attention in visual object tracking due to their excellent robustness. Some trackers collect the latest tracking results to train the target model so that they can learn new target states to better locate targets in complex scenes. However, the newly collected samples are not as reliable as the template in the first frame, which can easily cause model pollution and overfitting. In general, it is the contradiction between long-term memory and short-term memory in memory construction. The former can make the tracker better deal with the violent deformation of the target, and prevent drifting. The latter enables the tracker to better distinguish between the target and the distractors and carry out the correct positioning in the complex environment. Currently, it is difficult for these trackers to balance short-term memory and long-term memory.

In this paper, inspired by MMLT [10], we proposed a dual-branch memory network (DualMN) based on the memory mechanism of humans. Which consists of a short-term memory branch and a long-term memory branch. The former is a discriminant model for learning the latest spatial relationship between the target and the background, which improves the discriminative ability of the tracker for differentiating the target from distractors. The latter is a generative model for aggregating the essential feature from long-term memory, which makes the tracker very tolerant to abrupt changes in target appearance. As shown in Fig. 1, compared with advanced trackers, our approach combines the advantages of long-term and short-term memory to achieve more advanced performance.

2   Related Work

Due to the limited information of a single template, most current trackers focus on the development of historical information. Any tracker that utilizes stored historical information to improve tracking can be regarded as a memory-based tracker. At present, memory-based trackers can be roughly divided into two categories. One is to use historical information to train the model and improve the discriminative ability of the model. For example, ATOM [7], DiMP [8], PrDiMP [9], and FCOT [20] use different methods to improve the tracker's online learning ability. Although this method effectively improves the discriminative ability of the model in complex scenarios, it also brings the risk of overfitting. The other is to use historical information to generate adaptable templates or other features that are useful for tracking, such as UpdateNet [21], SiamFC-lu [22], KYS [23], etc. UpdateNet utilizes a simple convolutional neural network to fuse template states at different stages to generate adaptive templates. SiamFC-lu uses the idea of meta-learning, using an online training set as input, using a recurrent neural network to output an updated target model. KYS proposes a novel tracking architecture that can utilize scene information for tracking. But no matter which method is used, there will be conflicts between long-term memory and short-term memory.

At present, there are many long-term tracking methods to achieve long-term tracking through combine local tracking and global detection. LTMU [28] proposes a new long-term tracking framework based on local search and re-detection, which achieves long-term stable tracking by combining multiple modules. Similar to CMT [29] and MUSTer [30]. Although these components solve the problem of local tracking which is difficult to relocate after losing the target, these complex components also impose a large burden on the performance of the tracker.

3   Proposed Approach

We proposed a dual-branch memory network for visual object tracking. The fundamental idea behind this network is that the long-term memory and the short-term memory in tracking tasks complement each other, and therefore should be jointly considered for robust visual object tracking.

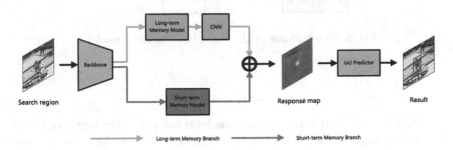

Fig. 2. An overview of dual-branch memory network.

As in most memory-based trackers, our tracker benefits from historical information. However, unlike existing memory networks, our approach can exploit memory in the short-term and long-term respectively. The structure of DualMN is shown in Fig. 2, which is derived from two main principles: (i) a discriminant model promoting short-term memory learning, and (ii) a generative model ensuring long-term memory retention. By such careful design, our approach can benefit from both long-term and short-term memory. Compared with existing memory-based trackers, it has better accuracy and robustness.

3.1   Short-Term Memory Branch

Inspired by DiMP [8], we treat the discriminant model as the short-term memory model (represented by f_s). The short-term memory building is shown in Fig. 3.

In the short-term memory branch, we use the lasted 50 frames (represented by S_{short}) to train the short-term memory model for learning the new target state and spatial relationship. In the first frame, we generate 30 initial training samples by data augmentation. Specifically, we use the ridge loss to train the model f_s. The loss function is formulated as:

$$\mathcal{L}(f_s) = \frac{1}{N} \sum_{(x_s, y) \in S_{short}} ||d(x_s * f_s, y)||^2 + \lambda ||f_s||^2 \qquad (1)$$

where $*$ denotes the convolution operator, N is the size of S_{short}, x_s is the feature extracted by the backbone, y is the classification label, and λ is the regularization factor. $d(\bar{y}, y)$ is a function to compute the difference at every position between the $\bar{y} = x_s * f_s$ and the classification label y. Then, employ the gradient of the loss ∇L to optimize the model using a step length α.

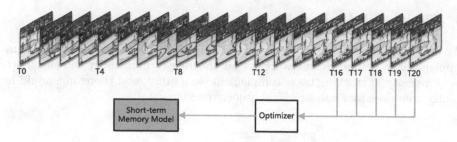

Fig. 3. The building of the short-term memory model.

$$f_s^{i+1} \leftarrow f_s^i - \alpha \nabla \mathcal{L} \left(f_s^i \right) \qquad (2)$$

In tracking, the short-term memory model is defined as the kernel of a convolutional layer to generate a response map $R_s \in \mathbb{R}^{1 \times H \times W}$ for locating the target. Which is defined as:

$$R_s = Q * f_s \qquad (3)$$

3.2   Long-Term Memory Branch

Inspired by STMTrack [11], we treat the generated model as the long-term memory model (represented by f_l). The long-term memory building is shown in Fig. 4.

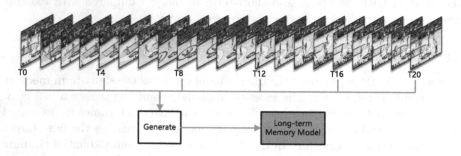

Fig. 4. The building of the long-term memory model.

In the long-term memory branch, the long-term memory model is consist of multiple features extracted by the backbone, which are connected in the spatial dimension. The historical frames (represented by S_{long}) that make up the model are uniformly sampled from the historical tracking results.

We first compute the similarities between each spatial pixel of the long-term memory model f_l and the search region feature Q extracted by backbone to obtain a similarity matrix $W \in \mathbb{R}^{THW \times HW}$, which is defined as:

$$w_{ij} = f_{lj} \cdot Q_i \tag{4}$$

where i is the index of each pixel on $Q \in \mathbb{R}^{C \times HW}$, the j is the index of each pixel on $f_l \in \mathbb{R}^{THW \times C}$. To balance the amount of memory information sent to the current frame, we employ the softmax function to normalize w_{ij}:

$$a_{ij} = \frac{\exp(w_{ij})}{\sum_{\forall k} \exp(w_{ik})} \tag{5}$$

The normalized similarity matrix is represented by A. In fact, a_{ij} represent how much attention the tracker should pay to the pixel i of the memory feature, according to the viewpoint of pixel j of the query feature. Then, we multiply f_l by A through treating A as a soft weight map and obtaining a feature map of the same size as Q. Although this method is good for calculating the similarity relationship between the target state at different times and the current search area, it cannot be used to locate the target, and it requires further processing to generate a response map. Therefore, We design a simple convolutional neural network(represented by θ) to decode the generated similarity relations after the long-term memory model. To avoid information loss during computation, we first concatenate it and the query feature along the channel dimension to generate the final synthetic feature z. The process is defined as:

$$z = concat \left(Q, (f_l)^T \otimes A \right) \tag{6}$$

where $\otimes$ donates the matrix multiplication. After that, we input z into θ. Specifically, θ contains three convolutional layers, which decoder the information of z to generate a response map $R_l \in \mathbb{R}^{1 \times H \times W}$ for locating the target.

3.3   Bounding Box Estimation

Different from RMIT [12] uses long-term memory as compensation for short-term memory through a residual framework, in this letter, long-term memory is as important as short-term. Therefore, we directly sum the response maps of the two branches as the final response map. The process is defined as:

$$R_{final} = R_S + R_L \tag{7}$$

After that, we utilize the IoU Predictor introduced in ATOM [7] to generate the accurate bounding box. It can use the rough target position generated by the short-term memory and the long-term memory branch, combined with the height and width of the target estimated in the previous frame, to generate multiple candidate boxes, and finally, output three bounding boxes with the highest IoU score. Then average the three bounding boxes to get the final tracking result.

4   Experiments

4.1   Implementation Details

In our experiment, we used a modified Swin-Transformer pretrained on ImageNet as the backbone of the memory network and use the activation outputs of stage2 and stage3 as the backbone feature. The training datasets include the COCO [13], LaSOT [19], GOT-10k [14], and TrackingNet [18] and we evaluate our tracker on OTB2015 [15], NFS [16], UAV123 [17], TrackingNet test set, and LaSOT test set. We implement the proposed approach on a PC with 4 GeForce RTX TITAN GPUs. The total sample pairs of each epoch are 26000. The learning rate is set to 2e-5 for the pretrained backbone weights, and 1e-3 for the rest. The learning rate decays by a factor of 0.2 every 15 epochs. We train the model for 50 epochs and spend about 22 h. Finally, the proposed DualMN run at 13 FPS on a single RTX-TITAN GPU.

4.2   Compare with State-of-the-Art Tracker

In visual object tracking, the performance of the tracker is usually evaluated using success, precision and normalized precision. The success is computed as the Intersection over Union (IoU) between tracking result and groundtruth bounding box. The precision is computed by comparing the distance between tracking result and ground-truth bounding box in pixels. And the normalization precision is computed by normalize the precision over the size of the ground truth bounding box. For details, please refer to Ref. [15] and Ref. [18].

OTB2015 is a widely used dataset that contains 100 short-term video sequences. DualMN is compared to others. The precision and success plots are shown in Fig. 5. Our DualMN has the highest Success rate of 70.4%. Compared to advanced memory-based trackers like KYS [23] and PrDiMP [9], our method improves the Success score by 0.9%. Although we are only third in accuracy, we are very close to the first.

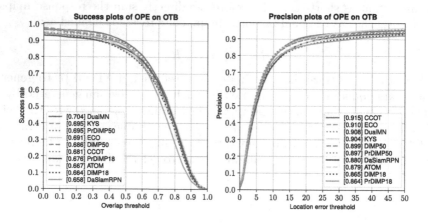

Fig. 5. Success and precision plots on the OTB2015 dataset.

UAV123 includes 123 aerial videos collected by the low-attitude UAV platform. We compare DualMN with advanced trackers on it. Table 1 shows the experimental results of success and precision. Our DualMN performs well, with the best success rate of 66.1% and the best precision rate of 86.2%. In precision, our DualMN outperforms ATOM [7] and DiMP [8] by 0.7% and 1.1%, respectively, demonstrating the effectiveness of combining long-term and short-term memory.

Table 1. Comparison with state-of-the-art on UAV123. The best two results are shown in red and blue fonts.

	SiamBAN [25]	SiamR-CNN [24]	SiamGAT [4]	ACM [5]	STMTrack [11]	DualMN
Success	63.1	64.9	64.6	64.8	64.3	66.1
Precision	83.3	83.4	84.3	–	–	86.2

NFS contains challenging videos with fast-moving objects. We evaluate our tracker on the 30fps version of the NFS. We compare DualMN with advanced trackers on it. Table 2 reports the experimental results in terms of Success score, and our DualMN achieves the best performance with the best success score of 65.2%.

Table 2. Comparison with state-of-the-art on NFS dataset in terms of overall success score. The best two results are shown in red and blue fonts.

ATOM [7]	DiMP [8]	SiamBAN [25]	PrDiMP [9]	SiamR-CNN [24]	KYS [23]	DualMN
59.0	62.0	59.4	63.5	63.9	63.5	65.2

LaSOT is a large-scale long-term dataset with high-quality annotations. Its testing set includes 280 challenging videos. Because the video time is longer than other datasets, there are more challenges in this dataset. We compare DualMN with advanced trackers on it. Figure 6 shows the success, precision, and normalized precision plots. The proposed DualMN achieves the best performance with a success score of 0.625, a precision score of 0.639, and a normalized precision score of 0.719. Compare with Siamese-based trackers, SiamGAT [4], SiamFC++ [26], and SiamRPN++ [2], our DualMN achieves performance gains of 8.6%, 8.2%, and 12.9%, respectively. This is mainly because Siamese-based trackers ignore the importance of memory. Compared with LTMU [28] and PrDiMP [9], the proposed approach achieves performance gains of 2.8% and 2.4% in success scores.

The attribute-based performance on the LaSOT test set is further analyzed in Fig. 7. Compared to state-of-the-art methods, our DualMN outperforms most of the challenges. New target appearances complicate accurately calculating target states in circumstances of deformation. Benefiting from long-term and short-term

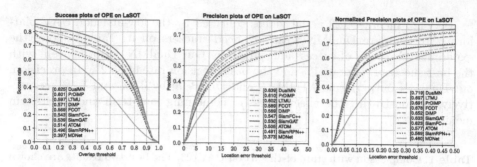

Fig. 6. Success, precision, and normalized precision plots on the LaSOT testing set.

memory, our tackers adapt well to changing target appearances, outperforming discriminative CNN-based trackers such as PrDiMP [9] and ATOM [7] that are dedicated to learning the new target appearance. The good results on this large-scale dataset demonstrate the stability potential of the method. Unfortunately, we did not achieve the best results in the perspective switching challenge, because the target shape before and after the perspective switching changed too much. For this challenge, the most efficient solution is global re-detection, like LTMU [28]. In future work, we will conduct further research on this issue.

TrackingNet is the largest signal object tracking dataset, the test set of it includes 511 videos. We compare our DualMN with advanced trackers on it. The comparison is shown in Table 3. The TrackingNet test set contains a large number of diverse tracking scenarios and allows for a more thorough assessment. Our DualMN achieves the best performance with a Success score 77.8%, a precision score 72.8%, and a Normalization Precision score 83.2%. Although the PrDiMP [9] obtains impressive performance with a Success score 75.8%, a precision score 70.4%, and a normalization precision score 81.6%, the proposed approach further improves the Success score by 2% and the normalized precision score by 1.6%, which demonstrates the effectiveness of the proposed dual-branch memory network. Compare with Siamese-based trackers such as SiamFC++ [26] and SiamRPN++ [2], our DualMN achieves performance gains of 2.4% and 3.8% in terms of Success, respectively.

4.3   Ablation Experiment

To verify the effectiveness of our proposed method, we conduct ablation experiments on the UAV123 dataset, and the results are shown in Table 4. By comparison, it can be found that building both a long-term memory model and a short-term memory model at the same time can effectively improve the performance of the tracker.

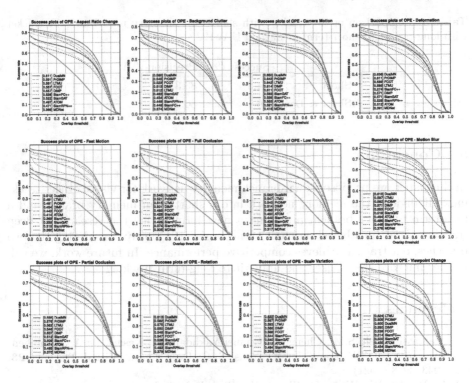

Fig. 7. Success plots over different attributes on the LaSOT test set.

Table 3. Comparison with state-of-the-art on TrackingNet test set. The best two results are shown in red and blue fonts

Trackers	Succ. (%)	Prec. (%)	Norm. Prec. (%)
UpdateNet [21]	67.7	62.5	75.2
ATOM [7]	70.3	64.8	77.1
SiamRPN++ [2]	74.0	69.4	80.0
DiMP [8]	74.0	68.7	80.1
PrDiMP [9]	75.8	70.4	81.6
SiamFC++ [26]	75.4	70.5	80.0
KYS [23]	74.0	68.8	80.0
STEM [27]	74.6	70.7	81.6
DualMN	77.8	72.8	83.2

Table 4. Comparison of the tracker with short-term memory model and the tracker with long-term and short-term models on UAV123

	Success (%)	Precision (%)
Short	64.3	83.3
Short & Long	66.1	86.2

5   Conclusion

In this paper, we propose a dual-branch memory network for visual object tracking. . It divided the memory network into a short-term memory branch and a long-term memory branch, providing a new formula for the research of deep tracking algorithms based on memory networks. By jointly considering the two branches, our tracker achieves competitive performance. In future work, we will further improve the tracker and apply it to long-term tracking.

References

1. Marvasti-Zadeh, S.M., Cheng, L., Ghanei-Yakhdan, H., Kasaei, S.: A comprehensive survey. IEEE Trans. Intell. Trans. Syst. Deep Learn. Visual Tracking **23**, 3943–3968 (2021)
2. Li, B., Wu, W., Wang, Q., Zhang, F., Xing, J., Yan, J.: Siamrpn++: evolution of siamese visual tracking with very deep networks. In: Proceedings of the IEEE/CVF Conference on Computer Vision and Pattern Recognition, pp. 4282–4291 (2019)
3. Zhang, Z., Peng, H.: Deeper and wider siamese networks for real-time visual tracking. In: Proceedings of the IEEE/CVF Conference on Computer Vision and Pattern Recognition, pp. 4591–4600 (2019)
4. Guo, D., Shao, Y., Cui, Y., Wang, Z., Zhang, L., Shen, C.: Graph attention tracking. In: Proceedings of the IEEE/CVF Conference on Computer Vision and Pattern Recognition, pp. 9543–9552 (2021)
5. Han, W., Dong, X., Khan, F.Z., Shao, L., Shen, J.: Learning to fuse asymmetric feature maps in siamese trackers. In: Proceedings of the IEEE/CVF Conference on Computer Vision and Pattern Recognition, pp. 16570–16580 (2021)
6. Chen, X., Yan, B., Zhu, J., Wang, D., Yang,X., Lu, H.: Transformer tracking. In: Proceedings of the IEEE/CVF Conference on Computer Vision and Pattern Recognition, pp. 8126–8135 (2021)
7. Danelljan, M., Bhat, G., Khan, F.S., Felsberg, M.: Atom: accurate tracking by overlap maximization. In: Proceedings of the IEEE/CVF Conference on Computer Vision and Pattern Recognition, pp. 4660–4669 (2019)
8. Bhat, G., Danelljan, M., Van Gool, L., Timofte, R.: Learning discriminative model prediction for tracking. In: Proceedings of the IEEE/CVF International Conference on Computer Vision, pp. 6182–6191 (2019)
9. Danelljan, M., Van Gool, L., Timofte, R.: Probabilistic regression for visual tracking. In: Proceedings of the IEEE/CVF conference on computer vision and pattern recognition, pp. 7183–7192 (2020)

10. Lee, H., Choi, S., Kim, C.: A memory model based on the siamese network for long-term tracking. In: Proceedings of the European Conference on Computer Vision (ECCV) Workshops (2018)

11. Fu, Z., Liu, Q., Fu, Z., Wang, Y.: Stmtrack: Template-free visual tracking with space-time memory networks. In: Proceedings of the IEEE/CVF Conference on Computer Vision and Pattern Recognition, pp. 13774–13783 (2021)

12. Zhang, H., Zhang, J., Nie, G., Hu, J., Chris Zhang, W.J.: Residual memory inference network for regression tracking with weighted gradient harmonized loss. Inf. Sci. **597**, 105–124 (2022)

13. Lin, T.-Y., et al.: Microsoft COCO: common objects in context. In: European Conference on Computer Vision, pp. 740–755 (2014)

14. Huang, L., Zhao, X., Huang, K.: Got-10k: a large high-diversity benchmark for generic object tracking in the wild. IEEE Trans. Pattern Anal. Mach. Intell. **43**(5), 1562–1577 (2019)

15. Wu, Y., Lim, J., Yang, M.-H.: Online object tracking: a benchmark. In: Proceedings of the IEEE Conference on Computer Vision and Pattern Recognition, pp. 2411–2418 (2013)

16. Galoogahi, H.K., Fagg, A., Huang, C., Ramanan, D., Lucey, S.: Need for speed: a benchmark for higher frame rate object tracking. In: Proceedings of the IEEE International Conference on Computer Vision, pp. 1125–1134 (2017)

17. Mueller, M., Smith, N., Ghanem, B.: A benchmark and simulator for UAV tracking. In: Leibe, B., Matas, J., Sebe, N., Welling, M. (eds.) ECCV 2016. LNCS, vol. 9905, pp. 445–461. Springer, Cham (2016). https://doi.org/10.1007/978-3-319-46448-0_27

18. Müller, M., Bibi, A., Giancola, S., Alsubaihi, S., Ghanem, B.: TrackingNet: a large-scale dataset and benchmark for object tracking in the wild. In: Ferrari, V., Hebert, M., Sminchisescu, C., Weiss, Y. (eds.) ECCV 2018. LNCS, vol. 11205, pp. 310–327. Springer, Cham (2018). https://doi.org/10.1007/978-3-030-01246-5_19

19. Fan, H.: Lasot: a high-quality benchmark for large-scale single object tracking. In: Proceedings of the IEEE/CVF Conference on Computer Vision and Pattern Recognition, pp. 5374–5383 (2019)

20. Cui, Y., Jiang, C., Wang, L., Wu, G.: Fully Convolutional Online Tracking. arXiv preprint arXiv:2004.07109 (2020)

21. Zhang, L., Gonzalez-Garcia, A., van de Weijer, J., Danelljan, M., Khan, F.S.: Learning the model update for Siamese trackers. In: Proceedings of the IEEE/CVF International Conference on Computer Vision, pp. 4010–4019 (2019)

22. Li, B., Xie, W., Zeng, W., Liu, W.: Learning to update for object tracking with recurrent meta-learner. IEEE Trans. Image Process. **28**(7), 3624–3635 (2019)

23. Bhat, G., Danelljan, M., Van Gool, L., Timofte, R.: Know your surroundings: exploiting scene information for object tracking. In: European Conference on Computer Vision, pp. 205–221 (2020)

24. Voigtlaender, P., Luiten, J., Torr, P.H.S., Leibe, B.: Siam R-CNN: visual tracking by re-detection. In: Proceedings of the IEEE/CVF Conference on Computer Vision and Pattern Recognition, pp. 6578–6588 (2020)

25. Chen, Z., Zhong, B., Li, G., Zhang, S., Ji, R.: Siamese box adaptive network for visual tracking. In: Proceedings of the IEEE/CVF Conference on Computer Vision and Pattern Recognition, pp. 6668–6677 (2020)

26. Yinda, X., Wang, Z., Li, Z., Yuan, Y., Gang, Yu.: SiamFC++: towards robust and accurate visual tracking with target estimation guidelines. In: Proceedings of the AAAI Conference on Artificial Intelligence, vol. 34(7), pp. 12549–12556 (2020)

27. Zhou, Z., Li, X., Zhang, T., Wang, H., He, Z.: Object tracking via spatial-temporal memory network. IEEE Trans. Circ. Syst. Video Technol. **32**(5), 2976–2989 (2021)
28. Dai, K., Zhang, Y., Wang, D., Li, J., Lu, H., Yang, X.: High-performance long-term tracking with meta-updater. In: Proceedings of the IEEE/CVF Conference on Computer Vision and Pattern Recognition (CVPR), pp. 6298–6307 (2020)
29. Nebehay, G., Pflugfelder, R.: Clustering of static-adaptive correspondences for deformable object tracking. In: Proceedings of the IEEE/CVF Conference on Computer Vision and Pattern Recognition (CVPR), pp. 2784–2791 (2015)
30. Hong, Z., Chen, Z., Wang, C., Mei, X., Prokhorov, D., Tao, D.: MUlti-store tracker (MUSTer): a cognitive psychology inspired approach to object tracking. In: Proceedings of the IEEE/CVF Conference on Computer Vision and Pattern Recognition (CVPR), pp. 749–758 (2015)

Instance-Wise Contrastive Learning for Multi-object Tracking

Qiyu Luo[ID] and Chunyan Xu[(✉)][ID]

School of Computer Science and Engineering, Nanjing University of Science and Technology, Nanjing 210094, China
{luoqiyu,cyx}@njust.edu.cn

Abstract. Multi-Object Tracking (MOT) is an important yet challenging problem in the field of computer vision. We observed that it is difficult for a single motion model to maintain the consistency of ID in complex scenes such as camera shake and pedestrian relative motion. Therefore, we propose an Instance-wise Contrastive Learning (ICL) method to jointly perform detection and embedding in a unified network. Specifically, to deal with the instance matching problem in the dynamic clutter situations, an instance-wise contrastive loss is introduced to make all the same instances to be near together, whereas all negatives are separated by a specified distance. Consequently, the semantic embedding space can be learned to not only help detect the moving objects but also contribute to the instance matching process. Furthermore, we adopt contextual information to perform the moving objects association along sequence frames. Comprehensive evaluations on three public tracking datasets (i.e., MOT16, MOT17, and MOT20) well demonstrate the superiority of our ICLTracker over other state-of-the-arts for the multi-object tracking task.

Keywords: Multi-object tracking · Instance-wise contrastive learning · Contextual information

1 Introduction

Multi-Object Tracking (MOT), which refers to locating multiple objects over time in a video sequence and correlating them frame by frame, is an important but challenging problem in the field of computer vision, and it serves several high-level applications, including traffic monitoring, autonomous driving, and intelligent security.

In recent years, benefiting from the rapid development of object detection, the field of multi-target tracking has made amazing progress. This dominant MOT framework divides MOT into joint detection and embedding (JDE) [28,34] and separate detection + embedding (SDE) [3,29] frameworks. The SDE first locates the target through the detection model, and then association model extracts embedding of the target. However, this method has high computational complexity. In order to solve this problem, several recent methods [28,34] unify the detector and the embedding model in one framework. Moreover, joint detection and embedding training achieves real-time performance while outperforming current state-of-the-art methods (SDE).

Due to the large number of occlusions between the objects in the pictures taken by the camera, the performance of the detector is greatly disturbed, and the detector will always fail when the objects are not visible. [24] proposes the concept of object permanence, once the target is identified, we can sense its physical presence and should be able to estimate the target's position under complete occlusion. Based on centerTrack [35], it extends two-frame input to multi-frame input, making it possible to the location and features of the current frame target are located through historical frame inference. However, [11,33] found that current tracking algorithms do not actually fully exploit the performance of the detector, and there are many false backgrounds, i.e. low-confidence objects, that are filtered out and not used for association with trajectories. OMC [11] proposes the One More Check mechanism to use the previous frame target embedding to search for targets on the current frame, trying to recover the targets that the detector mistakenly identified as the background. ByteTrack [33] associates trajectories with every detection box, outperforming state-of-the-art models using only a high-performance detector [4] and Kalman filtering. We found that although ByteTrack achieves surprising performance, it can only handle linear motion and cannot solve complex situations, especially severe camera shake, relative motion of pedestrians, cross motion, etc. Figure 1 show this problem.

Based on those observations, we propose an Instance-wise Contrastive Learning (ICL) method to learn high quality embedding in a unified network. In particular, recent methods[28,34] only use one positive sample per groundtruth for training, which is difficult to converge. In contrast to this, we dynamically select top-k positive samples for training to obtain more discriminative embedding. The heart of our methodology is to maintain a dictionary to store trajectory features. Thus, these encoded features can be reused without re-extracting features. Previous approaches use either memory banks [29] to store features from historical frames, or neural networks [5] to learn how to preserve old trajectory features. Compared to these methods, ours not only saves memory, but reduces the complexity of the model as well. Furthermore, we adopt contextual information to perform the moving objects association along sequence frames.

The main contributions of our work are as follows:

1. We propose ICLTracker, a unified framework for jointly learning detection and embedding. A lightweight embedding learning model effectively utilizes the historical trajectory features and enhances the ability to discriminate the same objects.
2. We use contextual information to combine feature embeddings and motion models for matching, thus achieving stronger robustness in complex scenarios.
3. Our method outperforms the state-of-the-art on the MOT benchmark. In particular, we achieve 63.7% HOTA and IDF1 of 78.3% on MOT17.

2 Related Work

Real-time Tracking. Due to the wide practical value of multi-object tracking, its real-time performance has also attracted much attention. SORT [3] simply uses the detector to get the target position, and then uses Kalman filter to predict the position of the target in the next frame, and uses iou as the cost matrix to associate, which achieves a high speed. Chained-Tracker [19] is the first to convert the data association problem into a pair-wise object detection problem. JDE [28] added a reid branch to YOLOV3 to extract target embeddings for data association, and proposed multi-task joint learning, using uncertainty to learn the weight of each loss. FairMOT [34] explores the fairness of detection and reid using a one-stage anchor-free detector. ByteTrack [33] recovers the ignored false background by a quadratic matching method, using only a high-performance detector yolox [4]. We are mainly base on ByteTrack, which achieves the state-of-the-art performance with a lightweight embedding head.

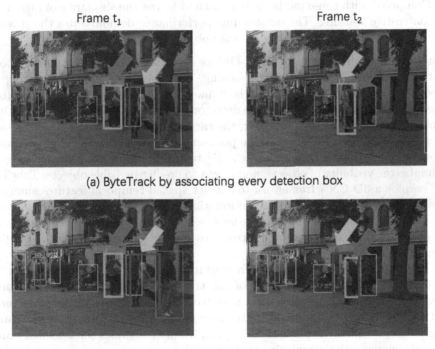

Frame t_1 Frame t_2

(a) ByteTrack by associating every detection box

(b) Ours by context information associating detection box

Fig. 1. Examples of matching in complex scenarios. The red arrow and the yellow arrow point to different people respectively, from frame t_1 to frame t_2. (a) shows the exchange of ids indicated by the yellow arrow and the red arrow when two targets overlap. (b) shows the tracklets obtained by our method, which combines feature embeddings and motion models for matching. (Color figure online)

Tracking with Apperence Feature. Usually the appearance features between different targets are strongly discriminative. In order to re-identify the target during tracking, some methods [1,9,10,16,21,22,29,31] independently use a reid model to extract target features or add an additional branch to learn appearance features for end-to-end training [13,28]. [8] propose to improve the predicted likelihood of such a classifier by augmenting its memory with appearance information about other tracks in the scene with multi-track pooling, leveraging the appearance information from the full set of tracks in the scene. TADAM [5] proposes a unified model with synergy of location prediction and id-embedding association. The attention module can make the prediction focus more on the target and less on the distractors, thereby extracting more reliable embeddings for association. CorrTracker [26] uses the local correlation network to model between the target and the surrounding environment and extends it to the temporal dimension, enhancing the feature representation. QDTrack [18] propose quasi-dense contrastive learning, which densely matches hundreds of regions of interest on a pair of images and learns the metric with contrastive loss.

Compared with these methods, our method learns the similarity of instances by contrastive learning. The outstanding performance demonstrates the success of contrastive similarity learning in multi-object tracking.

Tracking with Temporal Clues. Object detection is one of the most important components of multi-object tracking, and the bottleneck of tracking is affected by instance quality. Due to the influence of object occlusion and invisible objects, it is difficult for single-frame detectors to capture these objects, resulting in many missed detections. However, the target is permanent, and once the target is identified, we can estimate the position of the target with coherent visual information. [24] extends centerTrack [35] to frame inputs of arbitrary length, estimates the visibility of objects, and learns to predict invisible objects. TubeTK [17] employ a 3D CNN framework to extract spatial-temporal features simultaneously and these features capture information of motion tendencies. TransTrack [23] uses the transformer architecture for tracking, takes the features passed from the previous frame as queries and introduces a set of learnable queries to predict emerging targets.

The above methods use multi-frame input or additional modules such as GRU, LSTM to store the features of the trajectory, which increases the complexity of the model. We use a dictionary to store the features of the trajectory, and use the momentum method to dynamically update the features of the same target. Consistent throughout the life cycle, it only consumes some memory and does not increase the complexity of the model.

3   Method

We propose an instance-wise contrastive matching framework to jointly learn detection and embedding in a unified framework that can strengthen the discrimination of the same target and distinguish different targets bringing benefits to data association. Given as input a whole scene image, we first extract the features through the backbone to get the feature map, each grid predicts the bbox, and then selects the bbox of the positive sample through SimOTA [4]. These positive samples are extracted from multi-scale feature maps by roi-align and then fed into the embedding head to obtain L2-normalized 256-d features. And these bboxes have more accurate positions, which can extract discriminative embeddings. Finally, we adopt contextual information to data association. As shown in Fig. 2, this is the overall framework of the proposed method.

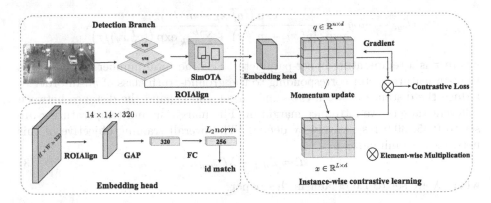

Fig. 2. Overview of the proposed ICL. We apply SimOTA that dynamically selects top-k positive samples for training to obtain more discriminative embedding, then uses momentum to update trajectory features.

3.1 Detection Branch

YOLOX [4] is an improvement of the YOLO series, switching to an anchor-free approach and implementing other advanced detection techniques, namely decoupled heads and leading label assignment strategy SimOTA[1], to achieve state-of-the-art results on a wide range of models. The backbone network adapts CSPDarknet [25] and an additional PAN [12] head. Decoupled head for locating and classifying objects of interest. The SimOTA label assignment strategy is to select the top-k with the smallest ground truth cost as the positive sample to calculate the loss. The loss function of the detection framework is:

$$\mathcal{L}_{det} = \mu * \mathcal{L}_{iou} + \mathcal{L}_{cls} + \mathcal{L}_{obj}, \tag{1}$$

where Intersection-over-Union(iou) loss $\mathcal{L}_{iou}$, classification loss $\mathcal{L}_{cls}$, object loss $\mathcal{L}_{obj}$ and the loss weight μ is set 5.0 as the original ByteTrack [33].

---

[1] SimOTA dynamically selects the top-k positive samples for each ground-truth.

3.2 Instance-Wise Contrastive Learning

As shown in Fig. 2, given a frame F for training, consider a set of trajectories $\{x_1, x_2, x_3, ..., x_L\}$ and a set of positive samples embedding $\{q_1, q_2, q_3, ..., q_n\}$ which was obtained by a lightweight identification network after SimOTA. When the similarity between the sample q_i and the trajectory x_k is greater, the more dissimilar to other trajectories, the lower the contrast loss value. Loss objective is to minimize the expected log-likelihood.

$$\mathcal{L}_{q_i} = -log \frac{\exp\left((q_i^T x_k - m)/\tau\right)}{\exp\left((q_i^T x_k - m)/\tau\right) + \sum_{j \neq k}^{L} \exp\left((q_i^T x_j)/\tau\right)}, \tag{2}$$

where τ is a temperature hyper-parameter, L is the total number of class, x_i is the i-th feature vector corresponding to the ground-truth class of y_i. In order to reduce the distance between the same target and expand the distance between different targets, we introduce margin m. The margin m and temperature τ are set to 0.35, 30.0 respectively by default. The overall training objective of this network is to minimize:

$$\mathcal{L} = \mathcal{L}_{det} + \lambda \mathcal{L}_{reid}, \tag{3}$$

where λ are set to 1.0 default in this paper.

Feature Aggregation Mechanism. It is unreliable to only use the features of the previous frame to correlate with the current frame, and the features obtained in some complex scenes such as severe occlusion are noisy. So the naive idea is to store the features. DeepSort [29] uses a memory bank to store features for ξ frames per trajectory, and ξ is a hyperparameter. Another mechanism is to use a neural network to learn features that need to be preserved from old trajectory features. TADAM [5] designs a discriminative memory aggregation module with convolutional gated recurrent unit (GRU) to decide whether the input is worth updating rather than naive accumulation that stores every input. In addition, the momentum update method we use was first proposed by [7]. This momentum update method is more memory-efficient and does not increase the complexity of the model.

The core of our method is to maintain a dictionary to store trajectory features. In this way, these encoded features can be reused without re-extracting features. The size L of the dictionary is equal to the number of ids in the dataset, denoted by $y \in \mathbb{R}^{L \times D}$, and the initial value is 0. Where D is the feature dimension. We expect that the feature embedding of each target will not vary greatly due to lighting, blurring, and other conditions during its lifetime. We use momentum updates to solve this problem. If the id of the track τ is i and matches the sample x, we update the i-th column of the dictionary by the following formula:

$$y_i = \delta y_i + (1 - \delta)x, \tag{4}$$

where δ is set to 0.9, and scale y_i to have unit L2-norm.

3.3   Data Association with Contextual Information

It is difficult to correlate objects across frames only by appearance features or motion models. For example, if different objects have similar body shapes, clothes, overlap, or occlusion, it is a tremendous challenge for feature embedding and it is difficult to distinguish them. In addition, if the camera sends violent jitters that cause too much displacement between objects in adjacent frames, detection of such anomalies is difficult for the movement model, which will increase the matching error rate. In the words, it is unreliable to rely on only one scheme, Our use of contextual information for matching can alleviate these problems.

We first calculate the similarity using detection boxes and trajectories with scores greater than the threshold t = 0.6 to obtain the cost matrix. A priori, we know that a person does not move very far in two consecutive frames, and that person motion is also directional. Based on this assumption, we set the value in the corresponding cost matrix to infinity for detections that are far away from the trajectory or strongly shifted in the direction of motion in the next frame.

4   Experiments

4.1   Setting

Experiments are evaluated on three popular MOT benchmarks. For a fair comparison, we also use the default training datasets as ByteTrack [33], including CrowdHuman, Cityperson, ETHZ, MOT16, MOT17, and MOT20. For all validation studies, we use the first half frames of each video in the training set of MOT17 for training and the second half for validation following [33]. We use Cityperson, ETHZ and the full of MOT17 as training set.

4.2   Metrics

We employ the CLEAR metrics [2], i.e., Multi-Object Tracking Accuracy (MOTA), IDF1, False Positives (FP), False Negatives (FN), Number of Identity Switches (IDs) [20], and HOTA [14] to evaluate tracking performance. As FN and FP are far more than IDs, MOTA focuses more on evaluate detection performance. On the contrary, IDF1 evaluates the ability of target recall and accuracy and focus more on the association performance. HOTA comprehensively reflects the ability of detection and correlation, and can better measure the overall performance of track.

4.3   Implementation Details

We build our tracker by integrating the proposed ICL network into ByteTrack [33]. The training process consists of two stages. First of all, we train it following the standard settings of ByteTrack. Specifically, the network is trained by an SGD optimizer with a weight decay of 5×10^{-4}, and momentum of 0.9 for 80 epochs on the combination of CrowdHuman, Cityperson, ETHZ, and MOT17. The batch size is 8, and the initial learning rate for each image is $\frac{1}{64} \times 10^{-3}$ with 1 epoch warm-up and cosine annealing schedule. In the second stage, we train the ICL module while fixing the basic network's parameters. The model is trained on 4 TITAN RTX GPU, and tracking time is measured with FP16-precision[15] and batch size of 1 on a single GPU.

4.4 Ablation Studies

To verify the effectiveness of our proposed method, we conduct analysis on the MOT17 validation set. The results of MOTA depend on FP, FN and IDs, focusing on the detection accuracy. IDF1 can measure the consistency of target matching well. There-

Table 1. Ablation studies on mot17 validation set. "M" stands for margin, "CM" for contextual information matching.

ICL	ICL + M	CM	IDF1↑	MOTA↑	FP↓	FN↓	IDs↓
–	–	–	79.1	76.6	**3372**	9096	163
✓	–	–	79.9	76.4	4180	**8374**	169
–	✓	–	80.1	76.6	3408	9065	150
–	✓	✓	**80.9**	**76.7**	3392	9011	**135**
			+1.8				

fore, we mainly concentrate on the improvement of IDF1. As shown in Table 1, when using the proposed ICL module to equip the baseline tracker, FN drops from 9096 to 8374, and IDF1 rises by 0.8 points. This shows that feature embedding can re-identify the failure of motion model matching. The purpose of the introduced margin is to reduce the intra-class distance and expand the inter-class distance. Table 1 shows that the IDs drop from 163 to 150, and IDF1 increased by 1.0, which shows that adding margin makes the feature embedding more discriminative. In the final data association stage, compared to the baseline tracker, the introduced contextual information matching further promotes the performance. i.e., IDF1 +1.8 points and IDs -28.

Inference Speed. In order to meet the real-time requirements, we test on a TITAN RTX GPU. Our method only uses a lightweight embedding head, which has little impact on the inference speed. Under the input size of 1440×800, the inference fps is 20.9.

4.5 Visualization Results

We show some visualization results of complex scenarios which ICLTrack is capable of dealing with in Fig. 3 (3) and (4). When the same target in consecutive frames has a large position shift, it is difficult to capture the occurrence of this state only by the motion model. Figure 3 (1) and (2) show this problem. When matching, either a different target is matched or the match fails, and the current detection is regarded as the newly appeared target. As we can see from these scenarios, ICLTrack not only reduces identity switch but also maintains identity persistence.

t-1

t

(1)   (2)   (3)   (4)

Fig. 3. Visualization of ByteTrack and ICLTrack. The red arrows indicate where the trajectory boxes are passed from frame t-1 to frame t. (1) and (2) show cases where ByteTrack fails to match in scenes with fast motion or camera shake. (3) and (4) show the results of ICLTrack. (Color figure online)

Table 2. Comparison of our method with state-of-the-arts methods under private detection protocol on the MOT benchmark. The best results of methods are marked in bold. The preformance is evaluated with the CLEAR and HOTA metrics. ↑/↓ indicate that higher/lower is better, respectively.

Tracker	MOTA↑	IDF1↑	HOTA↑	FP↓	FN↓	IDs↓	FPS↑
MOT16							
CTracker [19]	67.6	57.2	48.8	8934	48305	1121	6.8
TraDeS [30]	70.1	64.7	53.2	**8091**	45210	1144	15
FairMOT [34]	74.9	72.8	–	10163	34484	1074	**25.4**
CorrTracker [26]	76.6	74.3	61	10860	30756	979	14.8
ReMOT [32]	76.9	73.2	60.1	12278	29073	742	0.6
ICLTrack (ours)	**79.9**	**79.5**	**64.5**	11188	**24957**	**516**	20.9
MOT17							
CenterTrack [35]	67.8	64.7	52.2	**18498**	160332	30391	7.5
QuasiDense [18]	68.7	66.3	53.9	26589	146643	3378	20.3
MAT [6]	69.5	63.1	53.8	30660	138741	2844	9
FairMOT [34]	73.7	72.3	59.3	27507	117477	3303	25.9
PermaTrackPr [24]	73.8	68.9	55.5	28998	115104	3699	11.9
CorrTracker [26]	76.5	73.6	60.7	29808	99510	3369	15.6
ReMOT [32]	77	72	59.7	33204	93612	2853	1.8
ByteTrack [33]	80.3	77.3	63.1	25491	83721	2196	**29.6**
ICLTrack (ours)	**80.4**	**78.3**	**63.7**	26391	**83223**	**1578**	20.9
MOT20							
FairMOT [34]	61.8	67.3	54.6	103440	88901	5243	13.2
GSDT [27]	67.1	67.5	53.6	31913	135409	3131	0.9
SiamMOT [11]	70.7	67.8	–	**22689**	125039	–	6.7
ByteTrack [33]	**77.8**	75.2	61.3	26249	**87594**	1223	**17.5**
ICLTrack (ours)	77.6	**75.3**	**61.5**	24124	90802	**1186**	7.9

4.6   MOT Challenge Results

We compare with other state-of-the-art trackers on MOT16, MOT17, and MOT20 on private detection protocols, as shown in Table 2. Our method achieves new state-of-the-art IDF1 and HOTA on these two datasets. It surpassed the second place by a large margin (i.e. +6.4 IDF1 and +4.4 HOTA) at MOT16 benchmark and it outperforms recent state-of-the-art methods [33] (i.e. +1.0 IDF1 and 0.6 HOTA) at MOT17 benchmark. Our results are also competitive with the state-of-the-art methods on MOT20.

4.7   Tracklet Interpolation

Due to the limited field of view of the 2D image, some pedestrians are completely occluded, and it is almost impossible for the detector to detect them, resulting in missing trajectories. Linear interpolation is a very common method that can be used to fill trajectories.

Table 3. Comparing different time interval interpolations on mot17 validation set.

Interval	MOTA↑	IDF1↑	FP↓	FN↓	IDs↓
–	76.7	80.9	**3392**	9011	135
10	77.5	81.3	3688	8306	126
20	**78.5**	**81.8**	4050	7400	123
30	78.4	81.8	4376	7128	**121**
40	78.4	81.8	4467	**7037**	121
50	78.4	81.8	4467	7037	121

Suppose a trajectory T appears from the start frame t_s and disappears from the end frame t_e. This is its entire life cycle, but there may be a t-th frame in the middle that is not tracked. For better tracking performance, we need to pad the trajectory of frame t. The trajectory T is represented as $B_t \in \mathbb{R}^4$ by the coordinates of the upper left corner and the lower right corner in the box of each frame, and we set a threshold τ to represent the maximum time interval in which the trajectory can be inserted. Where τ is set to 20. Trajectory T missing at frame t can be computed as:

$$B_t = B_{t_s} + (B_{t_e} - B_{t_s})\frac{t - t_s}{t_e - t_s}. \tag{5}$$

5   Conclusions

We present an Instance-wise Contrastive Learning (ICL) method to jointly perform detection and embedding in a unified network and using contextual information combined with feature embeddings and motion models for matching during inference. Our method is robust to fast-moving, camera-shaking scenes thanks to the utilization of contextual information and the combination of feature embedding and motion models. There is still much to explore for the combination of feature embedding learning and motion model, and we expect our method can inspire MOT research.

References

1. Bergmann, P., Meinhardt, T., Leal-Taixe, L.: Tracking without bells and whistles. In: ICCV, pp. 941–951 (2019)
2. Bernardin, K., Stiefelhagen, R.: Evaluating multiple object tracking performance: the clear mot metrics. EURASIP J. Image Video Process. **2008**, 1–10 (2008)
3. Bewley, A., Ge, Z., Ott, L., Ramos, F., Upcroft, B.: Simple online and realtime tracking. In: ICIP, pp. 3464–3468. IEEE (2016)
4. Ge, Z., Liu, S., Wang, F., Li, Z., Sun, J.: Yolox: exceeding yolo series in 2021. arXiv preprint arXiv:2107.08430 (2021)
5. Guo, S., Wang, J., Wang, X., Tao, D.: Online multiple object tracking with cross-task synergy. In: CVPR, pp. 8136–8145 (2021)
6. Han, S., Huang, P., Wang, H., Yu, E., Liu, D., Pan, X.: Mat: motion-aware multi-object tracking. Neurocomputing **476**, 75–86 (2022)
7. He, K., Fan, H., Wu, Y., Xie, S., Girshick, R.: Momentum contrast for unsupervised visual representation learning. In: CVPR, pp. 9729–9738 (2020)
8. Kim, C., Fuxin, L., Alotaibi, M., Rehg, J.M.: Discriminative appearance modeling with multi-track pooling for real-time multi-object tracking. In: CVPR, pp. 9553–9562 (2021)
9. Kim, C., Li, F., Ciptadi, A., Rehg, J.M.: Multiple hypothesis tracking revisited. In: ICCV, pp. 4696–4704 (2015)
10. Leal-Taixé, L., Canton-Ferrer, C., Schindler, K.: Learning by tracking: Siamese cnn for robust target association. In: Proceedings of the IEEE Conference on Computer Vision and Pattern Recognition Workshops, pp. 33–40 (2016)
11. Liang, C., Zhang, Z., Zhou, X., Li, B., Lu, Y., Hu, W.: One more check: Making" fake background" be tracked again. arXiv preprint arXiv:2104.09441 (2021)
12. Liu, S., Qi, L., Qin, H., Shi, J., Jia, J.: Path aggregation network for instance segmentation. In: CVPR, pp. 8759–8768 (2018)
13. Lu, Z., Rathod, V., Votel, R., Huang, J.: Retinatrack: Online single stage joint detection and tracking. In: CVPR, pp. 14668–14678 (2020)
14. Luiten, J., et al.: Hota: A higher order metric for evaluating multi-object tracking. IJCV **129**(2), 548–578 (2021)
15. Micikevicius, P., et al.: Mixed precision training. arXiv preprint arXiv:1710.03740 (2017)
16. Milan, A., Rezatofighi, S.H., Dick, A., Reid, I., Schindler, K.: Online multi-target tracking using recurrent neural networks. In: Thirty-First AAAI Conference on Artificial Intelligence (2017)
17. Pang, B., Li, Y., Zhang, Y., Li, M., Lu, C.: Tubetk: Adopting tubes to track multi-object in a one-step training model. In: CVPR, pp. 6308–6318 (2020)
18. Pang, J., Qiu, L., Li, X., Chen, H., Li, Q., Darrell, T., Yu, F.: Quasi-dense similarity learning for multiple object tracking. In: CVPR, pp. 164–173 (2021)
19. Peng, J., et al.: Chained-tracker: Chaining paired attentive regression results for end-to-end joint multiple-object detection and tracking. In: Vedaldi, A., Bischof, H., Brox, T., Frahm, J.-M. (eds.) ECCV 2020. LNCS, vol. 12349, pp. 145–161. Springer, Cham (2020). https://doi.org/10.1007/978-3-030-58548-8_9
20. Ristani, E., Solera, F., Zou, R., Cucchiara, R., Tomasi, C.: Performance measures and a data set for multi-target, multi-camera tracking. In: Hua, G., Jégou, H. (eds.) ECCV 2016. LNCS, vol. 9914, pp. 17–35. Springer, Cham (2016). https://doi.org/10.1007/978-3-319-48881-3_2

21. Sadeghian, A., Alahi, A., Savarese, S.: Tracking the untrackable: Learning to track multiple cues with long-term dependencies. In: ICCV, pp. 300–311 (2017)
22. Son, J., Baek, M., Cho, M., Han, B.: Multi-object tracking with quadruplet convolutional neural networks. In: Proceedings of the IEEE Conference on Computer Vision and Pattern Recognition, pp. 5620–5629 (2017)
23. Sun, P., et al.: Transtrack: Multiple object tracking with transformer. arXiv preprint arXiv:2012.15460 (2020)
24. Tokmakov, P., Li, J., Burgard, W., Gaidon, A.: Learning to track with object permanence. In: ICCV, pp. 10860–10869 (2021)
25. Wang, C.Y., Liao, H.Y.M., Wu, Y.H., Chen, P.Y., Hsieh, J.W., Yeh, I.H.: Cspnet: A new backbone that can enhance learning capability of cnn. In: Proceedings of the IEEE/CVF Conference on Computer Vision and Pattern Recognition Workshops, pp. 390–391 (2020)
26. Wang, Q., Zheng, Y., Pan, P., Xu, Y.: Multiple object tracking with correlation learning. In: CVPR, pp. 3876–3886 (2021)
27. Wang, Y., Weng, X., Kitani, K.: Joint detection and multi-object tracking with graph neural networks. arXiv preprint arXiv:2006.13164 1(2) (2020)
28. Wang, Z., Zheng, L., Liu, Y., Li, Y., Wang, S.: Towards real-time multi-object tracking. In: Vedaldi, A., Bischof, H., Brox, T., Frahm, J.-M. (eds.) ECCV 2020. LNCS, vol. 12356, pp. 107–122. Springer, Cham (2020). https://doi.org/10.1007/978-3-030-58621-8_7
29. Wojke, N., Bewley, A., Paulus, D.: Simple online and realtime tracking with a deep association metric. In: ICIP, pp. 3645–3649. IEEE (2017)
30. Wu, J., Cao, J., Song, L., Wang, Y., Yang, M., Yuan, J.: Track to detect and segment: An online multi-object tracker. In: CVPR, pp. 12352–12361 (2021)
31. Yang, B., Nevatia, R.: An online learned crf model for multi-target tracking. In: CVPR, pp. 2034–2041. IEEE (2012)
32. Yang, F., Chang, X., Sakti, S., Wu, Y., Nakamura, S.: Remot: a model-agnostic refinement for multiple object tracking. Image Vis. Comput. **106**, 104091 (2021)
33. Zhang, Y., et al.: Bytetrack: Multi-object tracking by associating every detection box. arXiv preprint arXiv:2110.06864 (2021)
34. Zhang, Y., Wang, C., Wang, X., Zeng, W., Liu, W.: Fairmot: on the fairness of detection and re-identification in multiple object tracking. IJCV **129**(11), 3069–3087 (2021)
35. Zhou, X., Koltun, V., Krähenbühl, P.: Tracking objects as points. In: Vedaldi, A., Bischof, H., Brox, T., Frahm, J.-M. (eds.) ECCV 2020. LNCS, vol. 12349, pp. 474–490. Springer, Cham (2020). https://doi.org/10.1007/978-3-030-58548-8_28

Information Lossless Multi-modal Image Generation for RGB-T Tracking

Fan Li[1,2], Yufei Zha[2,3(✉)], Lichao Zhang[4], Peng Zhang[3], and Lang Chen[3]

[1] School of Cybersecurity, ASGO, Northwestern Polytechnical University,
Xi'an, China
leefan@mail.nwpu.edu.cn
[2] NingboInstitute of Northwestern Polytechnical University, Ningbo, China
zhayufei@126.com
[3] School of Computer Science, ASGO, Northwestern Polytechnical University,
Xi'an, China
zh0036ng@nwpu.edu.cn, transplus@mail.nwpu.edu.cn
[4] Aeronautics Engineering College, Air Force Engineering University, Xian, China

Abstract. Visible-Thermal infrared(RGB-T) multimodal target representation is a key issue affecting RGB-T tracking performance. It is difficult to train a RGB-T fusion tracker in an end-to-end way, due to the lack of annotated RGB-T image pairs as training data. To relieve above problems, we propose an information lossless RGB-T image pair generation method. We generate the TIR data from the massive RGB labeling data, and these aligned RGB-T data pair with labels are used for RGB-T fusion target tracking. Different from the traditional image modal conversion model, this paper uses a reversible neural network to realize the conversion of RGB modal to TIR modal images. The advantage of this method is that it can generate information lossless TIR modal data. Specifically, we design reversible modules and reversible operations for the RGB-T modal conversion task by exploiting the properties of reversible network structure. Then, it does not lose information and train on a large amount of aligned RGB-T data. Finally, the trained model is added to the RGB-T fusion tracking framework to generate paired RGB-T images end-to-end. We conduct adequate experiments on the VOT-RGBT2020 [14] and RGBT234 [16] datasets, the experimental results show that our method can obtain better RGB-T fusion features to represent the target. The performance on the VOT-RGBT2020 [14] and RGBT234 [16] datasets is 4.6% and 4.9% better than the baseline in EAO and Precision rate, respectively.

Keywords: Reversible network · RGB-T tracking · Data generation

1 Introduction

The unified multi-modal representation is a key issue for RGB-T tracking under various complex conditions. In the deep learning-based RGB-T tracking framework, large scale labeled RGB and TIR datasets are employed to train the network for representing the target of different modalities in an independent way.

S. Yu et al. (Eds.): PRCV 2022, LNCS 13537, pp. 671–683, 2022.
https://doi.org/10.1007/978-3-031-18916-6_53

Then the information complementarity between the RGB and TIR modalities to fuse and complement the information of the two modalities. Unlike the singe modal data(*e.g.* RGB images), the multi-modal data is difficult to acquire due to the expensive equipment and the hard acquisition manners. Furthermore, the different modal images are difficult to align due to the spatial location of the acquisition devices and the different resolutions of the RGB and TIR images.

Most RGB-T trackers focuses on the fusing the CNN features which are generated by the pre-trained model. Unlike the RGB modality has large-scale datasets and powerful pre-trained models, TIR data and pre-trained models is less. In existing trackers, off-the-shelf models trained on RGB modalities are used to extract CNN features from TIR images. Since the imaging mechanism of TIR is different from that of RGB images, this method ignores the properties of TIR itself.

A method that can fundamentally solve the problem of less TIR data is to use an image generation network to generate fake-TIR data. Recently, Zhang*et al.* [28] constructed a synthetic TIR dataset by employing pix2pix [12] to generate TIR images from RGB images for TIR tracking. We analyzed and compared the TIR images generated by the two commonly used image generation networks Pix2pix and Cyclegan, which are mentioned in its paper, as shown in Fig. 1 (b) and (c). It can be found that the image information is lost partly during training and generation due to the feedforward neural network. This degrades the discriminative ability of the extracted features for the TIR targets.

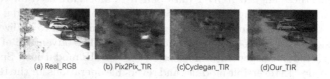

(a) Real_RGB   (b) Pix2Pix_TIR   (c)Cyclegan_TIR   (d)Our_TIR

Fig. 1. Real RGB image and images generated by pix2pix [31], cyclegan [12] and our proposed method.

The reversible network [7] is a reversible network composed of reversible modules and reversible operations. The network can use the reversibility of the network itself in terms of structure and operation to reversely restore the input without loss of information.

Based on the above reasons, we propose a Multi-Modal Image generation model for RGB-T tracking is designed. Using the characteristic of reversible network information without loss, fake-TIR images are generated end-to-end, and RGB-T data pairs are formed from RGB images, as shown in Fig. 1 (d), it can preserve more original image information. At the same time, the fake-TIR features generated by the data generation model are used to guide the training of RGB-T fusion tracking network. In summary, our contributions are as follows:

- Generating multi-modal image that can retain more original information by using the feature of reversible network without information loss. Since the fake-TIR image is obtained on the basis of the RGB image, the RGB and the fake-TIR image are completely aligned, which also solves the problem of the existing RGB-T data misalignment.

- We design a new RGB-T modal fusion tracking network training framework, which can obtain a better representation of TIR target depth features, and further obtain RGB-T fusion features.
- Using the generated RGB-T data pairs and fake-TIR features for the training of RGB-T fusion target trackers can improve the RGB-T tracking performance.

2   Related Work

This section mainly introduces the relevant theories of RGB-T fusion target tracking, image mode conversion and reversible network.

2.1   RGB-T Fusion Tracking

The key to the RGB-T fusion tracking is to design a reasonable fusion mechanism to reduce the redundant information of the two modalities, enhancing the complementarity between the modalities, and improving the multi-modal tracking performance. In recent years, there have been many RGBT fusion tracking algorithms based on different theories. Based on mean shift, Conaire et al. [2] fused the tracker tracking results for RGB modal images and the tracker tracking results for TIR modal images; Based on image sparse representation, Wu et al. [25] concat the sparse representation of RGB image and TIR image, and Li et al. [15] introduced a weighting mechanism to weighted fusion of the sparse representations of the two modalities.

2.2   Image Modal Conversion

The purpose of image modal conversion is to learn a network that can convert input modal images to specific modal images, such as converting RGB modal images to depth modal images. A basic algorithm is the Gan [11], which consist a generator and a discriminator, the generator generates fake images according to the task, and the discriminator calculates the similarity between the fake image and the real image. The Pix2pix [12] network improves the loss function of Gan [11]. The recent Cyclegan [31] network is designed with two generators and two discriminators, and the loss function is calculated in the forward and reverse directions to make the network generation better.

2.3   Reversible Network

A reversible network is a lossless network. The network consists of reversible operations and reversible modules. Through the reversibility of operations and modules, the output can be restored to the input without loss. The classical reversible network NICE [7] designs a reversible coupling layer based on the reversible module to realize the reversible transformation; RealNVP [8] generalizes the coupling layer of NICE.

3   Proposed Method

3.1   Methord Overview

In this section, we introduce our proposed RGB-T tracking framework. we propose a RGB-T image generation network based on a reversible network. The traditional image generation network will lose a lot of information of the original image while performing the image conversion task. The reversible image generation network proposed by us utilizes the characteristic of no loss of information in the reversible network, and reduces the loss of original image information while completing the task of converting RGB image to TIR image. Finally, during the tracking process, we use the RGB-T image generation network to generate TIR images end-to-end, and use its fake-TIR features to train the RGB-T fusion tracking network. The schematic diagram of the overall training framework is shown in Fig. 2.

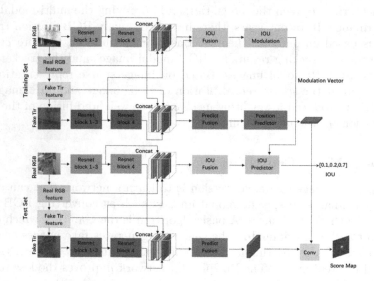

Fig. 2. Pipeline of our RGB-T fusion tracking network(Real RGB feature and Fake Tir feature are features generated by our proposed Image Generation network; Resnet block 1–4 represent the Resnet-50 feature extraction network; IOU Fusion and Predict Fusion modules are used to concat the features generated by our proposed Image Generation and feature extraction network; IOU Modulation and IOU Predictor modules are used to predit the bounding box of the target; Position Predictor is used to predict the posion of the target.) (Color figure online)

3.2   Baseline Tracker

Our goal is to train a better RGB-T tracking model with the generated TIR data. In this section, we will introduce the used benchmarks tracking framework DiMP [1], on which our tracking experiments are based. The benchmark tracking framework is mainly divided into three parts, feature extraction, target position prediction and target box prediction. our Baseline RGB-T fusion tracker mfDiMP [27] is also based on it.

Feature Extraction. The purpose of the feature extraction network is to extract effective target features to represent the target. In the Baseline Tracker, we use Resnet50 deep feature extraction network as the feature extraction network, the block4 output of the Resnet50 network is used for target position prediction, and the block3 and block4 outputs are used for target box prediction.

Target Position Prediction. The function of the target position prediction module is to train a model prediction network f, and convolve the output feature x of the Resnet50 block4 with the model prediction network f to obtain the position of the target to be tracked in the frame.

Target Box Prediction. The role of the target box prediction module is to calculate the size of the target regression box. It is mainly divided into two processes, the training process and the testing process. The training process is mainly to obtain the modulation vector through the training image and the real target box. Then in the testing process, the IOU score is calculated by using the modulation vector obtained in the training process, the test image and the candidate boxes, the candidate box with the largest IOU score is the final regression box.

3.3   GeneratING RGB-T Image

In this section, we introduce the designed reversible RGB-T image generation network and apply it to the conversion of RGB image to TIR image task. Next, we give a detailed introduction to the proposed reversible network-based RGB-TIR image generation network.

Reversible RGB-T Image Generation Network Framework. We add a reversible network on the basis of the cyclegan [31] network, and use the reversible network to convert the RGB image to the TIR image, In the RGB-T generation process, a reversible network is added, and the detailed information of the RGB image is preserved by using the reversible network structure and the characteristics of no information loss in operation, so that the information

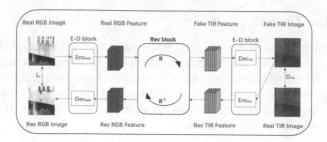

Fig. 3. Pipeline of our reversible RGB-T image generation network. (Color figure online)

loss of the final generated TIR image is as less as possible. Taking the input as a RGB image as an example, the model framework is shown in Fig. 3.

The input data of the training process is paired RGB and TIR image, taking RGB data as an example, the whole process is divided into two processes: forward generation and reverse recovery. The forward generation maps the RGB image to a high-dimensional feature space through the RGB Enc network, secondly, the RGB features are converted into fake-TIR features through the reversible feature transformation network R, and finally the fake-TIR features are converted into fake-TIR images through the TIR Dec network; Reverse recovery takes the generated fake-TIR image as input, firstly, the fake-TIR images are converted into TIR reconstruction features through the TIR Enc network, Secondly, the TIR reconstruction features are converted into RGB reconstruction features through the reverse operation R^{-1} of the reversible network, and finally the RGB reconstruction features are converted into RGB reconstruction images through the RGB Dec network.

Therefore, the RGB to TIR image generation task is performed at the feature level, which will retain more detailed information; In addition, using the characteristics of the reversible network that does not lose information, the transformed fake-TIR image can also retain more detailed information of the RGB image.

Reversible RGB-T Image Generation Network Analysis

E-D Block: E-D block is a dimension raising-dimension reduction network, which is used to convert low-dimensional image data to high-dimensional feature data and restore high-dimensional features to low-dimensional images; For image conversion tasks, performing image conversion tasks on high-dimensional feature spaces can obtain more representation information, which is also more conducive to network training; This module is not a reversible network, because for the task of converting RGB images to TIR images, the features of the two modalities are different, and the corresponding feature encoding and decoding methods are also different, if the feature extraction recovery network is designed as a reversible network, the network will diverge and cannot be trained.

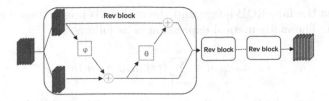

Fig. 4. Red represents RGB features, gray represents TIR features, φ, θ are reversible operations, and $+$ represents the addition of corresponding position elements. (Color figure online)

Rev Block: Rev block is a feature conversion network, which is used to convert RGB(TIR) high-dimensional features into TIR(RGB) high-dimensional features; This part of the network consists of reversible modules, and the network is completely reversible. The composition of the Rev block is shown in Fig. 4.

D_{RGB} , D_{TIR} block: D_{RGB} is a RGB discrimination network, which is used to calculate the similarity between the fake RGB image generated by the TIR image and the real RGB image. D_{TIR} is an TIR discrimination network, which is used to calculate the similarity between the fake TIR image generated from the RGB image and the real TIR image.

Loss Function: Before introducing the network loss function, we first introduce several image-level outputs. The loss functions are calculated on the basis of the following network outputs.

$$fake_{TIR} = Dec_{TIR}\left(R\left(Enc_{RGB}\left(I_{RGB}\right)\right)\right) \tag{1}$$

$$fake_{RGB} = Dec_{RGB}\left(R\left(Enc_{TIR}\left(I_{TIR}\right)\right)\right) \tag{2}$$

$$rec_{RGB} = Dec_{RGB}\left(R^{-1}\left(Enc_{TIR}\left(fake_{TIR}\right)\right)\right) \tag{3}$$

$$rec_{TIR} = Dec_{TIR}\left(R^{-1}\left(Enc_{RGB}\left(fake_{RGB}\right)\right)\right) \tag{4}$$

I_{RGB} is RGB image, I_{TIR} is TIR image, $fake_{TIR}$ indicates the fake-TIR image generated from RGB image, $fake_{RGB}$ indicates the fake RGB image generated from the TIR image, rec_{TIR} represents the fake-TIR image generated inversely from the fake-RGB image, rec_{RGB} represents the fake-RGB image generated inversely from the fake-TIR image. *Enc,Dec* are Dimension-raising and dimensionality-reducing operations in E-D block. R, R^{-1} are forward and reverse operations in the Rev block.

The network loss function consists of two parts: the cyclic loss function and the discriminative loss function. The cyclic loss function is used to update the generation network. Taking the RGB image as the input as an example, a fake-TIR image is generated from the input RGB image in the forward direction, and then the fake-TIR image is generated in the reverse direction, and the absolute error between the fake-RGB image and the real RGB image is used as the cycle loss function. The mathematical expression is as follows:

$$L_{cycle-RGB} = \sum_{i=1}^{n} |rec_{RGB} - I_{RGB}| \tag{5}$$

Similarly, the cyclic loss function when the input is an TIR image is:

$$L_{cycle-TIR} = \sum_{i=1}^{n} |rec_{TIR} - I_{TIR}| \tag{6}$$

The discriminative loss function is used to update the discriminative network, also taking the RGB image as the input as an example, the discriminant network uses the Euclidean distance between the generated fake-TIR image and the real label as the loss function to update the TIR discriminant network.

$$L_{disc-TIR} = \sum_{i=1}^{m} \sum_{j=1}^{n} \left(\theta \left(fake_{TIR} \right)_{ij} - \left(label_{TIR} \right)_{ij} \right) \tag{7}$$

When the input is TIR image, the RGB discrimination network is updated, and the discriminant loss function is:

$$L_{disc-RGB} = \sum_{i=1}^{m} \sum_{j=1}^{n} \left(\theta \left(fake_{RGB} \right)_{ij} - \left(label_{RGB} \right)_{ij} \right) \tag{8}$$

θ is the discriminant network parameter. The total network training loss function is:

$$L_{total} = L_{cycle-RGB} + L_{cycle-TIR} + L_{disc-RGB} + L_{disc-TIR} \tag{9}$$

4   Experiment

4.1   Implementation Details

In the training of the RGB-TIR image generation network, we select pairs of RGB-TIR data from several different RGBT tracking datasets, these datasets include the common RGBT234 [16] dataset, the VOT-RGBT2020 [14] dataset, and the recently released LasHeR [18] dataset. In the RGB-T fusion tracking, the trained RGB-TIR image generation is used to generate the TIR image from the input RGB image end-to-end.

We use two types of training datasets for the training of RGB-T modal fusion tracking network: real RGB-T paired data and generated paired RGB-T data. The real RGB-T data is the LASHER dataset, and the generated RGB-T data is generated end-to-end from RGB data.

Testing tools We use the official VOT [14] evaluation tool vot-toolkit to calculate the tracking average accuracy EAO, tracking success rate A and robustness R on the VOT-RGBT2020 dataset, and the RGBT234 [16] toolkit to analyze precision and success on the RGBT234 dataset.

4.2 Ablation Analysis

Analysis of Image Generation Quality. In order to verify that our method can retain more information of the original image while performing the RGB-TIR image generation task, we calculate the structural similarity between the generated TIR image and the original image and compare it with other image generation networks pix2pix, cyclegan, results are shown in table 1, and the images generated by the three networks are compared visually.

Table 1. Image quality of pix2pix, cyclegan and our method

	Pix2pix	Cyclegan	**Our**
PSNR	22.3	23.4	**24.5**
SSIM	0.712	0.723	**0.836**

The following Fig. 5 shows the fake-TIR images generated by pix2pix, cyclegan, and our reversible TIR image generation network.

Fig. 5. (a) is the original RGB image. (b) is the TIR image generated by pix2pix. (c) is the TIR image generated by cyclegan. (d) is the TIR image generated by our reversible RGB-T image generation network. (Color figure online)

According to comparing pix2pix, cyclegan, and the image similarity PSNR and structural similarity SSIM between the fake-TIR image generated by our method and the original image, and visualizing the fake-TIR image, we can find that our proposed RGB-T image generation network can preserve the structural information of the original image while completing the RGB to TIR image conversion task.

Analysis of RGB-T Tracking Results. In this section, we use the real RGB-T image pairs to train the network, the generated RGB-T image pairs to train the network, and the real RGB-T image pairs and the generated RGB-T image pairs to train the network together, The official VOT tool [14] is used to test its tracking indicators on the VOT-RGBT2020 [14] test dataset, respectively, in order to prove that adding the generated RGB-T image pairs can indeed improve the tracking success rate. The experimental results are shown in the following Table 2.

From the above experimental results, it can be found that the RGB-T dataset generated by the RGB-T image generation network can effectively improve the tracking accuracy.

4.3   State-of-the-Art Comparison

In this section, we compare our best result with the state-of-the-art TIR tracking algorithms on the VOT-RGBT2020 [14] dataset and the RGBT234 [16] dataset.

Table 2. Different mount of generated RGB-T image pairs result on VOT-RGBT2020 dataset.

	Baseline	Real	Generated	Real+HalfGenerate	**Real+AllGenerate**
EAO	0.380	0.398	0.407	0.418	**0.426**
A	0.638	0.603	0.638	0.632	**0.669**
R	0.793	0.768	0.799	0.801	**0.793**

Result on VOT-RGBT2020 Dataset. We compare our best result with the state-of-the-art RGB-T fusion tracking algorithms JMMAC [29], AMF [9], DFAT [14], SiamDW-T [30], mfDiMP [27], SNDCFT [14] and M2C2Frgbt [14] on the VOT-RGBT2020 dataset. Among these trackers, M2C2Frgbt, SNDCFT and DFAT are trackers used for VOT Challenge. As the results in Table 3, our perform the best on this dataset.

Table 3. Evaluation of our tracker with the state-of-art RGB-T trackers in terms of expected average overlap (EAO), accuracy values (A) and robustness values (R) on the VOT-RGBT2020 dataset.

	Our	JMMAC	AMF	DFAT	SiamDW-T	mfDiMP	SNDCFT	M2C2Frgbt
EAO	**0.426**	0.420	0.412	0.390	0.389	0.380	0.378	0.332
A	**0.669**	0.662	0.630	0.672	0.654	0.638	0.630	0.636
R	**0.793**	0.818	0.822	0.779	0.791	0.793	0.789	0.722

Result on RGBT234 Dataset. we compare our best results with the state-of-the-art RGB-TIR fusion tracking algorithms on the RGBT234 dataset. The following Table 4 and Fig. 6 shows the results.

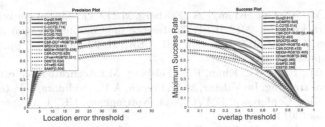

Fig. 6. Pression and Success plot mfDiMP [27], C-COT [6], SGT [28], ECO [3], SOWP+RGBT [13], SCR-DCF+RGBT [21], SRDCF [5], MEEM+RGBT [26], CSR-DCF [21], CFnet+RGBT [22], DSST [4], CFnet [22], SAMF [19] and our reversible TIR image generation network. mfDiMP is our baseline tracker, and the red line is our proposed method. (Color figure online)

Table 4. Evaluation of our tracker with the state-of-art trackers MANet[17], DAPNet [32], DAFNet [10], CMPP [23], APFNet [24] and DMCNet [20] in terms of Precision and Success rate on the RGBT234 dataset.

	MANet	DAPNet	DAFNet	CMPP	APFNet	DMCNet	**Our**
Precision	0.777	0.766	0.796	0.823	0.827	0.839	**0.846**
Success	0.539	0.537	0.544	0.575	0.579	0.593	**0.613**

5 Conclusion

In this paper, we propose an information lossless RGB-T pairwise image generation network for RGB-T fusion tracking. This method can generate TIR images and TIR features that can retain the original information on the existing large-scale RGB dataset end-to-end, and then use the generated RGB-T paired data to train the RGB-T fusion tracking network, at the same time, we use TIR features to supervise and optimize the details of the fused features to make the fused features better. The experimental results prove that our method can indeed solve the lack of TIR data fundamentally, and achieve the best results on some commonly used RGB-T datasets.

Acknowledgments. This work is supported in part by Natural Science Foundation of Ningbo (2021J049, 2021J048) and National Natural Science Foundation of China (U19B2037,62006245, 61971352,61862043).

References

1. Bhat, G., Danelljan, M., Gool, L.V., Timofte, R.: Learning discriminative model prediction for tracking. In: IEEE Conference on International Conference on Computer Vision (ICCV), pp. 6181–6190 (2019)
2. Conaire, C.Ó., O'Connor, N.E., Smeaton, A.F.: Thermo-visual feature fusion for object tracking using multiple spatiogram trackers. Mach. Vis. Appl. **19**(5–6), 483–494 (2008)

3. Danelljan, M., Bhat, G., Khan, F.S., Felsberg, M.: ECO: efficient convolution operators for tracking. In: 2017 IEEE Conference on Computer Vision and Pattern Recognition, CVPR 2017, Honolulu, HI, USA, 21–26 July 2017, pp. 6931–6939. IEEE Computer Society (2017)

4. Danelljan, M., Häger, G., Khan, F.S., Felsberg, M.: Accurate scale estimation for robust visual tracking. In: Valstar, M.F., French, A.P., Pridmore, T.P. (eds.) British Machine Vision Conference, BMVC 2014, Nottingham, UK, 1–5 September 2014. BMVA Press (2014)

5. Danelljan, M., Häger, G., Khan, F.S., Felsberg, M.: Learning spatially regularized correlation filters for visual tracking. CoRR abs/1608.05571 (2016)

6. Danelljan, M., Robinson, A., Shahbaz Khan, F., Felsberg, M.: Beyond correlation filters: learning continuous convolution operators for visual tracking. In: Leibe, B., Matas, J., Sebe, N., Welling, M. (eds.) ECCV 2016. LNCS, vol. 9909, pp. 472–488. Springer, Cham (2016). https://doi.org/10.1007/978-3-319-46454-1_29

7. Dinh, L., Krueger, D., Bengio, Y.: NICE: non-linear independent components estimation. In: 3rd International Conference on Learning Representations Workshope (ICLRW) (2015)

8. Dinh, L., Sohl-Dickstein, J., Bengio, S.: Density estimation using real NVP. In: 5th International Conference on Learning Representations (ICLR) (2017)

9. Kristan, M., et al.: The eighth visual object tracking VOT2020 challenge results. In: Bartoli, A., Fusiello, A. (eds.) ECCV 2020. LNCS, vol. 12539, pp. 547–601. Springer, Cham (2020). https://doi.org/10.1007/978-3-030-68238-5_39

10. Gao, Y., Li, C., Zhu, Y., Tang, J., He, T., Wang, F.: Deep adaptive fusion network for high performance RGBT tracking. In: 2019 IEEE/CVF International Conference on Computer Vision Workshops, ICCV Workshops 2019, Seoul, Korea (South), 27–28 October 2019, pp. 91–99. IEEE (2019)

11. Goodfellow, I.J., et al.: Generative adversarial networks. Commun. ACM **63**(11), 139–144 (2020)

12. Isola, P., Zhu, J., Zhou, T., Efros, A.A.: Image-to-image translation with conditional adversarial networks. In: IEEE Conference on Computer Vision and Pattern Recognition (CVPR), pp. 5967–5976 (2017)

13. Kim, H., Lee, D., Sim, J., Kim, C.: SOWP: spatially ordered and weighted patch descriptor for visual tracking. In: 2015 IEEE International Conference on Computer Vision, ICCV 2015, Santiago, Chile, 7–13 December 2015, pp. 3011–3019. IEEE Computer Society (2015)

14. Kristan, M., et al.: A novel performance evaluation methodology for single-target trackers. IEEE Trans. Pattern Anal. Mach. Intell. **38**(11), 2137–2155 (2016)

15. Li, C., Cheng, H., Hu, S., Liu, X., Tang, J., Lin, L.: Learning collaborative sparse representation for grayscale-thermal tracking. IEEE Trans. Image Process. **25**(12), 5743–5756 (2016)

16. Li, C., Liang, X., Lu, Y., Zhao, N., Tang, J.: RGB-T object tracking: benchmark and baseline. Pattern Recognit. **96**, 106977 (2019)

17. Li, C., Lu, A., Zheng, A., Tu, Z., Tang, J.: Multi-adapter RGBT tracking. In: 2019 IEEE/CVF International Conference on Computer Vision Workshops, ICCV Workshops 2019, Seoul, Korea (South), 27–28 October 2019, pp. 2262–2270. IEEE (2019)

18. Li, C., et al.: Lasher: a large-scale high-diversity benchmark for RGBT tracking. IEEE Trans. Image Process. **31**, 392–404 (2022)

19. Li, Y., Zhu, J.: A scale adaptive kernel correlation filter tracker with feature integration. In: Agapito, L., Bronstein, M.M., Rother, C. (eds.) ECCV 2014. LNCS, vol. 8926, pp. 254–265. Springer, Cham (2015). https://doi.org/10.1007/978-3-319-16181-5_18

20. Lu, A., Qian, C., Li, C., Tang, J., Wang, L.: Duality-gated mutual condition network for RGBT tracking. CoRR abs/2011.07188 (2020)

21. Lukezic, A., Vojír, T., Zajc, L.C., Matas, J., Kristan, M.: Discriminative correlation filter tracker with channel and spatial reliability. Int. J. Comput. Vis. **126**(7), 671–688 (2018)

22. Valmadre, J., Bertinetto, L., Henriques, J.F., Vedaldi, A., Torr, P.H.S.: End-to-end representation learning for correlation filter based tracking. In: 2017 IEEE Conference on Computer Vision and Pattern Recognition, CVPR 2017, Honolulu, HI, USA, 21–26 July 2017, pp. 5000–5008. IEEE Computer Society (2017)

23. Wang, C., Xu, C., Cui, Z., Zhou, L., Zhang, T., Zhang, X., Yang, J.: Cross-modal pattern-propagation for RGB-T tracking. In: 2020 IEEE/CVF Conference on Computer Vision and Pattern Recognition, CVPR 2020, Seattle, WA, USA, 13–19 June 2020, pp. 7062–7071. Computer Vision Foundation / IEEE (2020)

24. Wang, C., et al.: Attribute based progressive fusion network for rgbt tracking. In: AAAI (2022)

25. Wu, Y., Blasch, E., Chen, G., Bai, L., Ling, H.: Multiple source data fusion via sparse representation for robust visual tracking. In: Proceedings of the 14th International Conference on Information Fusion, FUSION 2011, Chicago, Illinois, USA, 5–8 July 2011, pp. 1–8. IEEE (2011)

26. Zhang, J., Ma, S., Sclaroff, S.: MEEM: robust tracking via multiple experts using entropy minimization. In: Fleet, D., Pajdla, T., Schiele, B., Tuytelaars, T. (eds.) ECCV 2014. LNCS, vol. 8694, pp. 188–203. Springer, Cham (2014). https://doi.org/10.1007/978-3-319-10599-4_13

27. Zhang, L., Danelljan, M., Gonzalez-Garcia, A., van de Weijer, J., Khan, F.S.: Multi-modal fusion for end-to-end RGB-T tracking. In: IEEE Conference on International Conference on Computer Vision WorkShope (ICCVW), pp. 2252–2261. IEEE (2019)

28. Zhang, L., Gonzalez-Garcia, A., van de Weijer, J., Danelljan, M., Khan, F.S.: Synthetic data generation for end-to-end thermal infrared tracking. IEEE Trans. Image Process. **28**(4), 1837–1850 (2019)

29. Zhang, P., Zhao, J., Bo, C., Wang, D., Lu, H., Yang, X.: Jointly modeling motion and appearance cues for robust RGB-T tracking. IEEE Trans. Image Process. **30**, 3335–3347 (2021)

30. Zhang, Z., Peng, H.: Deeper and wider siamese networks for real-time visual tracking. In: IEEE Conference on Computer Vision and Pattern Recognition (CVPR), pp. 4591–4600. Computer Vision Foundation/IEEE (2019)

31. Zhu, J., Park, T., Isola, P., Efros, A.A.: Unpaired image-to-image translation using cycle-consistent adversarial networks. In: IEEE Conference on International Conference on Computer Vision (ICCV), pp. 2242–2251 (2017)

32. Zhu, Y., Li, C., Luo, B., Tang, J., Wang, X.: Dense feature aggregation and pruning for RGBT tracking. In: Amsaleg, L., et al. (eds.) Proceedings of the 27th ACM International Conference on Multimedia, MM 2019, Nice, France, 21–25 October 2019, pp. 465–472. ACM (2019)

JFT: A Robust Visual Tracker Based on Jitter Factor and Global Registration

Haopeng Wang[1,2], Shuixing Pan[1,2], Dilong Li[1,2], Yueqiang Zhang[1,2(✉)],
Linyu Huang[1,2], Hongxi Guo[1,2], Xiaolin Liu[1,2], and Qifeng Yu[1,2]

[1] College of Physics and Optoelectronic Engineering, Shenzhen University,
Shenzhen 518060, China
yueqiang.zhang@szu.edu.cn
[2] Institute of Intelligent Optical Measurement and Detection, Shenzhen University,
Shenzhen 518060, China

Abstract. Visual object tracking is an important yet challenging task in computer vision, whose accuracy is highly subject to the problems of camera motion/shake and occlusion. In order to solve these two challenging problems and improve the tracking accuracy of real scenes, this paper proposed a robust visual object tracker based on Jitter Factor and global registration. The proposed tracker firstly extracts the histogram of oriented gradient (HOG) features and color features of the target object to train the correlation filter. When the response map is unreliable, the proposed tracker treats the tracking problems as a global background motion and target motion problem, and then evaluates the state (tracking or missing) of the target by using Jitter Factor. If the target is assumed to be missing, global image registration and correlated Kalman filter would be applied to correct and predict the corrected target position. Experimental results on RGB-T234 show that after introducing the proposed Jitter Factor and global image registration, the correlation-filter-based trackers gained a $\geq 2.2\%$ increase in precision rate.

Keywords: Visual object tracking · Jitter Factor · Correlated Kalman Filter

1 Introduction

Visual object tracking is an important and challenging branch in computer vision, which involves a wide range of applications in many fields such as security surveillance, broadcasting of sports events, autonomous driving, augmented reality [1–4], etc. Visual object tracking is to estimate the target location and its size based on the given initial frame, and its performance is largely subject to factors such as cluttered backgrounds, occlusions and camara motion.

In recent years, DCF (Discriminative Correlation Filter)-based tracking methods play an important role in visual object tracking [5–16]. DCF-based methods obtain training samples through cyclic shift to train a correlation filter, and converts the correlation operation in spatial domain into dot product operation in Fourier domain using FFT

S. Yu et al. (Eds.): PRCV 2022, LNCS 13537, pp. 684–693, 2022.
https://doi.org/10.1007/978-3-031-18916-6_54

(Fast Fourier Transform) to improve the efficiency of tracking. In 2010, Bolme et al. proposed the MOSSE (Minimum Output Sum of Squared Error [5]), which is one of the milestones of the correlation filter-based trackers. MOSSE performs tracking by optimizing the minimum square error function of the target appearance model. However, the tracking accuracy of MOSSE is not high enough in real scenes due to its using only grayscale features of the image. In 2014, Henriques et al. proposed KCF(Kernelized Correlation Filters [7]), which used the histogram of oriented gradient (HOG [17]) features of image and got better robustness with circular matrix and kernel function. KCF tracker is of less computational complexity while more training samples, thus it is of higher tracking accuracy. In 2015, Danelljan et al. proposed SRDCF (Spatially Regularized Discriminative Correlation Filters [11]), which reduced the problem of boundary effects by adding spatial regularization term, but simultaneously lower the efficiency of the tracker. In 2018, Li et al. proposed STRCF (Spatial-Temporal Regularized Correlation Filters [14]), which introduced the time constraints of the filter on the basis of SRDCF, and the final results were obtained via ADMM (Alternating Direction Method of Multipliers [18]), which further improved the accuracy and the efficiency of the tracker.

Although many excellent visual object trackers are successively proposed, none of them focus on the problem of camera motion/shake, which occurs frequently in practical applications. For example, when the target is about to exceed the field of view, it is necessary to move the camera to continue tracking. When the camera motion occurs, the image will become blurred, making the target difficult to recognize. Furthermore, when the camera moves drastically, the image coordinates of target also change drastically leading to failure of tracking. Therefore, this challenging yet significant problem ought to be solved.

In this paper, a robust visual object tracker based on Jitter Factor and correlated Kalman filter was proposed, which can adaptively evaluate the state (tracking or missing) of the target, and alleviate the effects of camera motion and occlusion by using Jitter Factor and correlated Kalman filter. To the best of our knowledge, it is the first time that Jitter Factor is proposed to alleviate the problems of camera motion/shake. Experiments on RGBT-234 show that the proposed tracker can effectively deal with the problems of camera motion and target occlusion, and is able to improve the performance of correlation filter-based trackers.

2 Proposed Approach

The proposed tracker consists of two parts. One is the process of prediction and the other one is the process of correction, as shown in Fig. 1.

2.1 Jitter Factor

Among the CF-based trackers, the response map is the basis to update the target position and judge whether the target tracking is reliable. When the peak of response map and modalities energy ratio of the tracker is lower than their respective historical average values, it means that the target is missing. In fact, camera motion and occlusion are

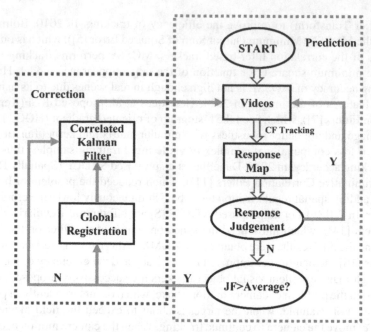

Fig. 1. Flowchart of the proposed tracker.

the main causes of tracking failure. For the target occlusion problem, Kalman filter is generally used for prediction, while camera motion still remains a challenging problem. When the camera moves slightly, the existing trackers would suffer from a low tracking accuracy, and probably do not work when drastic camera motion occurs due to the insufficiency of target features. To alleviate the effects of camera motion, Jitter Factor is proposed, which can be mathematically expressed as:

$$JF = \sum_{m=1}^{M} \sum_{n=1}^{N} O(I_{(m,n)}^{f} - I_{(m,n)}^{f-1})/MN \tag{1}$$

where I represents the M × N visible/infrared video image, f is the index of a certain frame, $O(\cdot)$ is the morphological opening operation, which is used to eliminate the effect of slight camera motion. The radius of structure element was set as four pixles. The Jitter Factor reveals the level of camera motion. When the Jitter Factor is abnormal, it is assumed that drastic camera motion or shake occurs, as shown in Fig. 2. Drastic camera shake occurred at frame I^{163} to I^{167}, causing the tracking failure of a woman's handbag, and the corresponding Jitter Factor was much larger than the average.

When the target is assumed to be missing and if the value of the Jitter Factor is much greater than the average, it can be determined camera motion is responsible for the failure of tracking, then the correction process (to introduce in the next section) will be implemented to correct the predictions.

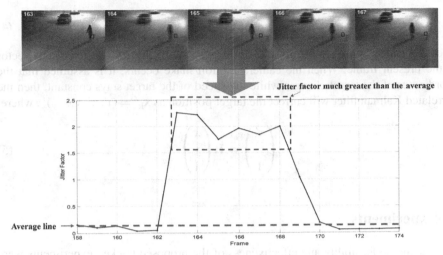

Fig. 2. Jitter Factor diagram

2.2 Background Motion and Correlated Kalman Filter

When the Jitter Factor of a certain frame is much greater than the average, the previous frame I_p would be recorded for correction, and the tracking task would be treated as a global compensation problem which can be divided into two parts. One is the movement of the background, and the other one is the movement of the target. The position offset of the target before and after the camera motion/shake can be mathematically expressed as:

$$\mathbf{offset} = (\mathbf{v^o} - \mathbf{v^b}) * T \tag{2}$$

where T is the continuous frames of the moving/shaking camera, $\mathbf{v_b}$ is the average speed of the camera movement in the image coordinates. $\mathbf{v_o}$ is the speed of the target movement, which can be predicted by Kalman filter under the premise that the target moves at a constant speed. When the camera stops moving/shaking, the frame I_q at that moment would be recorded. Due to the changes of viewing field of each frame in the process of camera motion/shake, the video frame would be blurred, making it difficult for the tracker to extract the target features. Fortunately, the frames before the camera motion/shake and after the changes of field of view are not affected, thus global registration of I_p and I_q can be implemented to correct the target position. The homography martrix H of I_p and I_q, which will be used lately, is obtained by ORB (Oriented Fast and Rotated Brief [19]).

In general, linear Kalman filter can be used to predict the target position of continuous tracking, but when the target position changes suddenly, it will lead to inaccurate prediction. To solve this problem, correlated Kalman filter is introduced. Given the prediction vector of the previous frame $\mathbf{x_{k-1}} = (x, y, v_x, v_y)^T$ and covariance matrix $\mathbf{P_{k-1}}$, the correlated Kalman filter predicts the position and speed of the target at the present frame:

$$\mathbf{x_k} = \mathbf{A}\mathbf{x_{k-1}} \tag{3}$$

$$P_k = AP_{k-1}A^T + Q \tag{4}$$

where P_k and x_k represent the updated covariance matrix and the predicted state vector of the present frame. When the camera motion/shake occurs, it is assumed that the coordinates of the target changes while the speed of the target stays constant, then the correlated Kalman filter will correct the target position as $x_k' = (x', y', v_x, v_y)^T$, where:

$$\begin{pmatrix} x' \\ y' \\ 1 \end{pmatrix} = H \begin{pmatrix} x \\ y \\ 1 \end{pmatrix} \tag{5}$$

3 Experiments

To validate the feasibility and effectiveness of the proposed tracker, experiments were carried out on a large benchmark dataset RGBT234(only visible part was used), which includes 234 visible-infrared video pairs, and all image frames are manually annotated.

The histogram of gradient orientation (HOG) [17] features, color space (Color Name, CN) [20] features and grayscale features were used for feature extraction. Experiments was carried out on the platform on MATLAB with 2.90GHz Intel Core i7–10700 CPU and 16GB RAM. STRCF was used as the benchmark algorithm and the comparisons between STRCF and STRCF-JFT (i.e., STRCF with Jitter Factor) are shown in Fig. 3. The top of Fig. 3 shows that STRCF failed to track the handbag in a woman while STRCF-JFT still worked when camera motion/shake occurred, and the bottom shows that STRCF-JFT was more robust than STRCF when occlusion occurred.

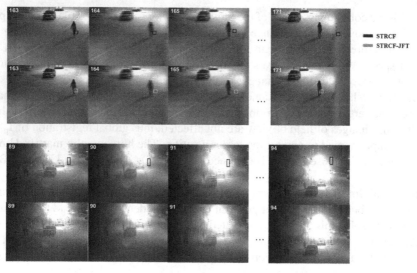

Fig. 3. Camera moving issue solving verification

Furthermore, a more challenging video was used to validate the proposed method, as shown in Fig. 4. The target (a child at the sidewalk) was occluded by streetlight in frame 226, and then there was a wide range of camera motion. The STRCF-JFT tracker firstly detect the unreliability of response map, and uses correlated Kalman Filter to predict the position of the target. When the camera moving occurred, STRCF-JFT tracker catch the abnormal Jitter Factor and apply global registration. Finally, the position of the target is corrected and our tracker continue accurate tracking.

Fig. 4. Experimental results on a challenging video.

To quantitatively validate the proposed tracking strategies (Jitter Factor and global registration), PR (Precision Rate) and SR (Success Rate) were calculated on the whole RGBT-234 dataset by using KCF-JFT, DSST-JFT, ASRCF-JFT, STRCF-JFT and their baseline trackers KCF, DSST [21], ASRCF [22] and STRCF, respectively. And the experimental results are shown in Table 1 and Fig. 5, showing that our proposed Jitter Factor and global registration can effectively improve the performance of CF-based trackers.

Table 1. Testing results on RGBT-234.

Trackers	PR/SR	Improvement
STRCF	0.685/0.498	+3.4%/+1.8%
STRCF-JFT	0.719/0.516	
ASRCF	0.651/0.468	+2.2%/+2.0%
ASRCF-JFT	0.673/0.488	
DSST	0.519/0.379	+3.3%/+2.0%
DSST-JFT	0.552/0.399	
KCF	0.423/0.282	+3.0%/+1.6%
KCF-JFT	0.453/0.298	

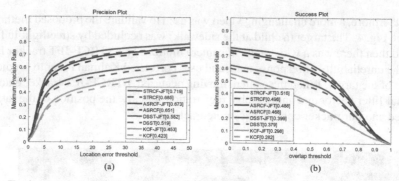

Fig. 5. Testing results on RGBT-234. (a) Relationship between location error threshold and PR; (b) Relationship between overlap threshold and SR.

Besides, the RGB-T234 dataset includes challenging object tracking issues including camera moving (CM), partial occlusion (PO) and heavy occlusion (HO), etc. The testing results of trackers in these 3 attributes are shown in Table 2, Table 3 and Table 4, respectively. Experimental results show that the JFT-based trackers can alleviate the issues of camera motion and target occlusion.

Table 2. Experimental results using videos of camera moving from RGBT-234.

Trackers	PR/SR(CM)	Improvement
STRCF	0.625/0.465	+3.5%/+2.5%
STRCF-JFT	0.660/0.490	
ASRCF	0.613/0.449	+5.3%/+4.4%
ASRCF-JFT	0.666/0.493	
DSST	0.391/0.296	+9.8%/+6.5%
DSST-JFT	0.489/0.361	
KCF	0.348/0.244	+7.8%/+4.2%
KCF-JFT	0.426/0.286	

Table 3. Experimental results using videos of heavy occlusion from RGBT-234.

Trackers	PR/SR(HO)	Improvement
STRCF	0.563/0.401	+3.9%/+2.0%
STRCF-JFT	0.602/0.421	
ASRCF	0.549/0.387	+4.8%/+4.2%
ASRCF-JFT	0.597/0.429	
DSST	0.401/0.289	+0.2%/+0.3%
DSST-JFT	0.403/0.292	
KCF	0.328/0.222	+1.6%/+0.9%
KCF-JFT	0.344/0.231	

Table 4. Experimental results using videos of partial occlusion from RGBT-234.

Trackers	PR/SR(PO)	Improvement
STRCF	0.731/0.532	+3.5%/+2.5%
STRCF-JFT	0.766/0.557	
ASRCF	0.667/0.477	+0.8%/+0.4%
ASRCF-JFT	0.675/0.481	
DSST	0.564/0.410	+6.4%/+3.9%
DSST-JFT	0.628/0.449	
KCF	0.468/0.306	+4.3%/+2.2%
KCF-JFT	0.511/0.328	

4 Conclusions

In this paper, a robust visual object tracker based on Jitter Factor and global registration was proposed. Jitter Factor is used to evaluate the level of camera motion/shake, and when it is much larger than the average, the global registration and correlated Kalman filter would be implemented to correct the target position, thereby improving the tracking accuracy. Experimental results on RGBT-234 verified that the PR and SR of CF-based trackers have increased after the implementation of Jitter Factor and global registration, and also proved that the proposed tracker is of robustness against camera motion/shake and occlusion.

Acknowledgements. This work was supported by the National Key Research and Development Program of China (No. 2019YFC1511102) and the National Natural Science Foundation of China (No. 12002215).

References

1. Yilmaz, A., Javed, O., Shah, M.: Object tracking: a survey. ACM Comput. Surv. **38**(4), 13 (2006)
2. Ali, A., et al.: Visual object tracking—classical and contemporary approaches. Front. Comput. Sci. **10**(1), 167–188 (2016). https://doi.org/10.1007/s11704-015-4246-3
3. Carreira-Perpián, M.: A review of mean-shift algorithms for clustering. Computer Science (2015)
4. Jia, X., Lu, H., Yang, M.H.: Visual tracking via adaptive structural local sparse appearance model. In: IEEE Conference on Computer Vision and Pattern Recognition. IEEE (2012)
5. Bolme, D.S., Beveridge, J.R., Draper, B.A., et al.: Visual object tracking using adaptive correlation filters. In: The Twenty-Third IEEE Conference on Computer Vision and Pattern Recognition, CVPR 2010, San Francisco, pp. 1822–1829. IEEE (2010)
6. Henriques, J.F., Caseiro, R., Martins, P., Batista, J.: Exploiting the circulant structure of tracking-by-detection with kernels. In: Fitzgibbon, A., Lazebnik, S., Perona, P., Sato, Y., Schmid, C. (eds.) ECCV 2012. LNCS, vol. 7575, pp. 702–715. Springer, Heidelberg (2012). https://doi.org/10.1007/978-3-642-33765-9_50
7. Henriques, J.F., Caseiro, R., Martins, P., et al.: High-speed tracking with kernelized correlation filters. IEEE Trans. Pattern Anal. Mach. Intell. **37**(3), 583–596 (2015)
8. Danelljan, M., Häger, G., Khan, F.S., et al.: Accurate scale estimation for robust visual tracking. In: British Machine Vision Conference (2014)
9. Danelljan, M., Häger, G., et al.: Discriminative scale space tracking. IEEE Trans. Pattern Anal. Mach. Intell. **39**(8), 1561–1575 (2017)
10. Li, Y., Zhu, J.: A scale adaptive kernel correlation filter tracker with feature integration. In: Agapito, L., Bronstein, M.M., Rother, C. (eds.) ECCV 2014. LNCS, vol. 8926, pp. 254–265. Springer, Cham (2015). https://doi.org/10.1007/978-3-319-16181-5_18
11. Danelljan, M., Hger, G., Khan, F.S., et al.: Learning spatially regularized correlation filters for visual tracking. In: Proceedings of the IEEE International Conference on Computer Vision, pp. 4310–4318 (2016)
12. Danelljan, M., Hager, G., Khan, F.S., et al.: Convolutional features for correlation filter based visual tracking. In: Proceedings of the IEEE International Conference on Computer Vision Workshops, pp. 58–66 (2015)
13. Chao, M., Huang, J.B., Yang, X., et al.: Hierarchical convolutional features for visual tracking. In: Proceedings of the IEEE International Conference on Computer Vision, pp. 3074–3082 (2016)
14. Li, F., Tian, C., Zuo, W., et al.: Learning spatial-temporal regularized correlation filters for visual tracking. In: Proceedings of the IEEE Conference on Computer Vision and Pattern Recognition, pp. 4904–4913 (2018)
15. Danelljan, M., Robinson, A., Shahbaz Khan, F., Felsberg, M.: Beyond correlation filters: learning continuous convolution operators for visual tracking. In: Leibe, B., Matas, J., Sebe, N., Welling, M. (eds.) ECCV 2016. LNCS, vol. 9909, pp. 472–488. Springer, Cham (2016). https://doi.org/10.1007/978-3-319-46454-1_29
16. Danelljan, M., Bhat, G., Khan, F.S., et al.: ECO: efficient convolution operators for tracking. In: Proceedings of the IEEE Conference on Computer Vision and Pattern Recognition, pp. 6638–6646 (2016)
17. Dalal, N., Triggs, B.: Histograms of oriented gradients for human detection. In: 2005 IEEE Computer Society Conference on Computer Vision and Pattern Recognition (CVPR 2005), vol. 1, pp. 886–893. IEEE (2005)
18. Boyd, S., Parikh, N., et al.: Distributed optimization and statistical learning via the alternating direction method of multipliers. Found. Trends Mach. Learn. **3**(1), 1–122 (2010)

19. Rublee, E., Rabaud, V., Konolige, K., Bradski, G.: ORB: an efficient alternative to SIFT or SURF. In: 2011 International Conference on Computer Vision, pp. 2564–2571. IEEE (2011)
20. Danelljan, M., Khan, F.S., Felsberg, M., et al.: Adaptive color attributes for real-time visual tracking. In: IEEE Conference on Computer Vision and Pattern Recognition. pp. 1090–1097. IEEE (2014)
21. Danelljan, M., et al.: Accurate scale estimation for robust visual tracking. In: British Machine Vision Conference, Nottingham (2014)
22. Dai, K., Wang, D., Lu, H., et al.: Visual tracking via adaptive spatially-regularized correlation filters. In: IEEE/CVF Conference on Computer Vision and Pattern Recognition (CVPR). IEEE (2019)

Caged Monkey Dataset: A New Benchmark for Caged Monkey Pose Estimation

Zheng Sun[1,2], Xiangyu Zhu[1,2], Zhen Lei[1,2], and Xibo Ma[1,2]

[1] CBSR & NLPR, Institute of Automation, Chinese Academy of Sciences,
Beijing 100190, China
[2] School of Artificial Intelligence, University of Chinese Academy of Sciences,
Beijing 100049, China
{zheng.sun,xiangyu.zhu,zlei,xibo.ma}@nlpr.ia.ac.cn

Abstract. Automatic monkey pose estimation is of great potential for quantitative behavior analysis of monkeys, which provides indispensable information for the studies of drug safety assessments and medical trials. With the development of deep learning, the performance of human pose estimation has been greatly improved, however, the study of monkey pose estimation is rare and the robustness of performance is unsatisfactory due to the lack of data and the variations of monkey poses. In this work, we propose a complete solution to address these problems in terms of data and methodology. For data, we collect a comprehensive Caged Monkey Dataset with 6021 samples, with labeled poses. For methodology, we propose a Mask Guided Attention Network (MGAN) to focus on the foreground target automatically so as to locate the occluded keypoints precisely and deal with the complex monkey postures. The proposed method is evaluated on the collected monkey dataset, achieving 79.2 Average Precision (AP), which is 6.1 improvement over the baseline method and is comparable with the state-of-the-art performance of human pose estimation. We hope our attempt on caged monkey pose estimation will serve as a regular configuration in drug safety assessments and medical trials in the future.

Keywords: Caged monkey dataset · Monkey pose estimation · Mask guided attention network · Drug safety assessments

1 Introduction

The application of computer methods in bioengineering has increased dramatically in recent years [1,13]. Meanwhile, in the field of drug safety assessments and medical trials, there are more and more requirements for automatic recognition of animal behaviors especially the primates [3,15]. As one of the most important

Supplementary Information The online version contains supplementary material available at https://doi.org/10.1007/978-3-031-18916-6_55.

animal models for humans, monkeys are widely used in the studies of drug safety assessments and medical trials [6,17]. Therefore, accurate quantification of caged monkey behavior becomes a primary goal in the medical domain.

Pose estimation, the task for prediction of anatomical keypoints in the images, is an efficient way to provides accurate posture information about the behavioral state. However, few scholars have paid attention to this field due to the lack of annotated pose data of caged monkeys. Therefore, the pose estimation of caged monkeys still needs further exploration. Although the adaptation of methods for human on animals has achieved progress like that on birds [2], horses [11], mice [25], etc., the estimation of monkey pose remains a tricky problem. The challenges are as following three folds: (i) The bushy fur of the monkey results in occlusion and similar appearances of keypoints, which obstruct the localization and classification of the keypoints. (ii) The monkey bodies are deformable with their four flexible limbs. Thus, their postures are more complex than those mammals like horses, or even human postures, which escalates the difficulty of monkey pose estimation. (iii) Monkeys have evolved to move swiftly, the keypoints are blurry in some collected images and videos. Recent works [2,7,12,15] in the field of animal pose estimation usually use pose predictors from the human domain for reference, which is more about the application of open-source approaches. So, there is a strong demand for the customized methods. Other attempts about general animal pose estimation [4,14] are made to solve the data shortage via transfer learning or domain adaptation. However, these paradigms may not work if there is a large gap between the source and target domain.

In order to address the aforementioned obstacles, contributions have been made to pose estimation of caged monkeys from data collection and method innovations. The collected dataset in this paper called Caged Monkey Dataset, which covers different categories, genders, and ages of monkeys to provide indispensable knowledge for neural network training. As shown in Fig. 1, all of the real-world images are directly collected from the daily lives of monkeys that are used for biological experiments. For the methods, an effective plug-in module called Mask Guided Attention Module (MGAM) is customized for our task. To capture the occluded, blurry keypoints and complex monkey postures, we propose MGAM that incorporates a vanilla RGB attention block and an extra mask recalibration block. The former prompts the model to focus on the foreground area of the image, and the latter learns the natural constraints contained in the monkey skeleton. When confronted with occluded, blurry keypoints and complex postures, the mask recalibration block is able to drive the model to locate and classify the keypoints by using the learned prior knowledge of the monkey skeleton. Furthermore, the recalibration process is achieved by a weighted summation between the RGB attention map and the mask attention map. The main contributions of this paper can be summarized as follows:

– We collect the extensive Caged Monkey Dataset that can be utilized to train and evaluate the designed method for caged monkey pose estimation. The scenarios for the dataset include one and five monkeys per cage;

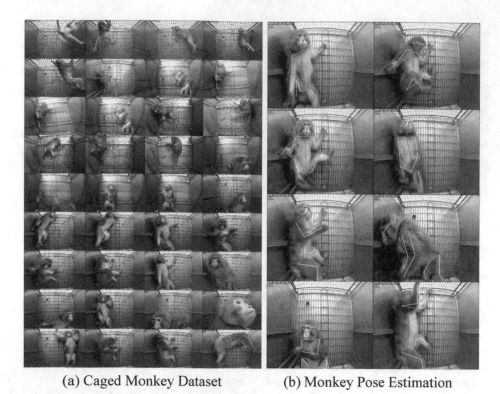

(a) Caged Monkey Dataset   (b) Monkey Pose Estimation

Fig. 1. Caged Monkey Dataset. (a) Image samples of the Caged Monkey Dataset. (b) Pose estimation results of the caged monkeys.

- We propose an effective attention mechanism called Mask Guided Attention Module to assist the model in focusing on the foreground monkeys, which is customized to handle the challenges in caged monkey pose estimation brought by occluded, blurry keypoints and complex postures;
- We analyze the differences between human and monkey pose estimation, and pioneer in investigating a complete solution to tackle the problems of pose estimation on caged monkeys. Our method achieves a significant improvement of 6.1 AP compared to its counterpart method SimpleBaseline-50 on Caged Monkey Dataset.

2   Related Works

Recently, some works [2, 4, 7, 11, 12, 14, 15, 22, 25] have started paying attention to the animal pose estimation, which is a promising field for medical trials. Zhou et al. [25] introduced a new challenging mouse dataset for pose estimation, and proposed a novel Graphical Model based Structured Context Enhancement Network (GM-SCENet) to model mouse behavior. Mu et al. [14] generated an ani-

Table 1. Statistics of the proposed Caged Monkey Dataset

Species	Age (years)	Gender	Image number	Total number
single rhesus macaque	1.5	Male	314	2481
	1.5	Female	290	
	3	Male	285	
	4.5	Female	307	
	5	Male	317	
	7	Female	252	
	14	Female	365	
	17	Male	351	
single crab-eating macaque	16	Male	269	514
	17	Female	245	
group rhesus macaques	3–4	Male&Female	3026	3026

mal dataset with 10+ different animal CAD models and proposed a consistency-constrained semi-supervised learning framework (CC-SSL) to train synthetic and real-world datasets jointly. However, this approach can't work if there is a large gap between the synthetic and real-world data. Mathis et al. [11] developed a novel horse dataset and achieved high accuracy with DeeperLabCut [12]. To take advantage of the general skeleton knowledge of animals and humans, cao et al. [4] did some researches on domain adaptation between human and four-legged mammals (i.e. dogs, cats, and horses), and they proposed a novel method called "weakly- and s emi-supervised cross-domain adaption" (WS-CDA) to extract cross-domain common features for animal pose estimation. The postures of horses or dogs are relatively fixed, not as arduous to deal with as the monkeys. In Negrete's research [15], the bottom-up method OpenPose [5] was utilized to estimate the postures of wild macaques, lacking scene adaptation innovation. OpenMonkeyStudio [3] focused on the 3D keypoints detection and the dataset lacked box, mask information of the target. In this work, we are dedicated to the caged monkeys that are often utilized in biological experiments rather than the wild macaques studied in Negrete's study [15] and single caged monkey in OpenMonkeyStudio [3]. We propose the real-world Caged Monkey Dataset to alleviate the data shortage in drug safety assessments. Besides, we propose a Mask Guided Attention Module to tackle the occluded, blurry keypoints and complex postures in monkey pose estimation.

3   Caged Monkey Dataset Collection

3.1   Raw Data Acquisition

The experimental monkeys are kept in iron cages for drug safety assessments. To capture the natural poses of caged monkeys, we customize tiny HD cameras to record the monkey's daily life and each cage is recorded for three days after the camera is installed. The entire data collection process included 35 monkeys in 15 cages, and we obsained more than 500 h videos finally.

After acquiring the video data, the discontinuous frames are extracted from monkey videos. During the annotating, eight volunteers are recruited to annotate the binary segmentation masks and coordinates of the 17 keypoints for each monkey. The skeleton of the rhesus is similar to that of the human, and the non-rigid tail has no impact on body posture, which is also intractable to define with keypoints. Thus, the keypoint settings are derived from the MS COCO [10] dataset, including eyes, nose, shoulders, elbows, wrists, hips, knees, and ankles. Considering the difficulty of keypoint labeling due to the bushy fur of the monkeys, all of the monkey images are cross-annotated to further ensure the reliability of the annotated labels. Each image will be labeled twice by different volunteers. If there exists a large deviation between the annotated results, the image will be labeled again.

3.2   Dataset Description

As illustrated in Table 1, we collect a comprehensive Caged Monkey Dataset that covers different categories, genders, and ages of monkeys. The dataset consists of 6021 caged monkey images in total, 5507 for rhesus macaques and 514 for crab-eating macaques. The rhesus macaque split is used for intraspecific training and evaluation. Single macaque means that there is only one monkey in the cage, and the group consists of five monkeys. The crab-eating macaque split is employed to further test the generalization ability of the trained model. Since the differences in appearance between the above two species monkey splits are non-negligible, the interspecific experiments on crab-eating macaque split are more challenging. More detailed information about dataset is provided in the supplementary material.

4   Methods

First, Random Background Augmentation (RBA) is designed to further improve the generalization ability of the model. Then, to tackle the difficulties brought by the occluded, blurry keypoints and the complex postures among the deformable bodies, we propose Mask Guided Attention Module (MGAM), which contains an RGB attention block and a mask attention block. The former is dedicated to helping the pose predictor focus on the related area nearby keypoints and the latter is utilized to guide the predictor to learn the physical constraints of the monkey skeleton. Finally, we give a concise description of the loss function and inference procedure.

4.1   Random Background Augmentation (RBA)

Under the principle of translation invariance, common data augmentations like global scaling, rotating, and flipping have been widely used and demonstrated their effectiveness in Human Pose Estimation. We establish a novel and effective augmentation method called Random Background Augmentation (RBA)

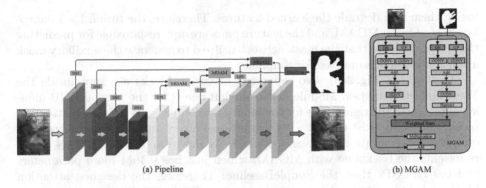

(a) Pipeline   (b) MGAM

Fig. 2. Mask Guided Attention Network. (a) The pipeline of the proposed approach. The green and red arrows denote the down-sampling and up-sampling processing, respectively. (b) The proposed Mask Guided Attention Module (MGAM). Note that the backbone network between the input images and attention blocks is omitted for simplicity. DS and UP denote features generated at specific down-sample and up-sample stages. (Color figure online)

to increase the diversity of the proposed dataset. In general, the RBA replaces the original background with randomly selected, randomly cropped, randomly scaled, and randomly rotated MS COCO dataset images. Note that the background dataset is not specified, it can be any source that contains a variety of images. More detailed information about RBA is provided in the supplementary material.

4.2 Mask Guided Attention Network (MGAN)

Based on the SimpleBaseline [21], we proposed Mask Guided Attention Network (MGAN) for the caged monkey scenario. As depicted in Fig. 2(a), the network generates intermediate features DS_1, DS_2, DS_3, DS_4 in down-sampling processing and UP_1, UP_2, UP_3 in up-sampling processing. The shallow features such as DS_1 and DS_2 retain higher spatial resolution while the deep features UP_1 and UP_2 contain rich semantic information. To integrate both the spatial context and the discriminative semantic information for pose estimation, there are several lateral connections between the intermediate features. The FPN [9] fusion structure and the pose-mask joint learning [20] is taken into consideration in the design of MGAN. Different from the FPN [9], we specially design Mask Guided Attention Module (MGAM) for the fusion of intermediate features instead of the simple convolution operation in FPN. Different from the joint learning method [20], the proposed MGAM utilize the mask attention heatmaps in the middle of the mask attention network, not the final segmentation results. What's more, the mask attention network is trained with binary segmentation image, to facilitate the predictor to locate the keypoints even under the absence of appearance information. We conjecture that the items in feature pairs $\{DS_i, UP_{4-i}\}$ differ greatly from each other, directly fusing them may degrade the learned features. Therefore, the fusion 1×1 convolution is added in MGAM, and the feature pairs are only responsible for predicting the attention. Note that the mask network utilized to generate the auxiliary mask attention features is omitted for simplicity.

As shown in Fig. 2(b), two separated attention blocks are kept inside the Mask Guided Attention Module, while the left one is for the normal RGB monkey images and the right one is for the binary mask images. Within each attention block, there only exist three 1×1 convolutional layers and other parameter-free operations like addition, relu, and sigmoid. As shown in Table 2, MGAN (ours) represents the backbone with MGAM, which just has 0.46M more parameters and 0.9 GFLOPs than the SimpleBaseline. Therefore, the designed attention block is light-weight and computation-saving, During training and inference, the RGB attention block takes the down-sample features DS_i and the counterpart up-sample features UP_{4-i} as the input to generate the spatial attention mask, aiming to locate the nearby area of keypoints and assist the predictor to learn discriminative and contextual information for keypoint classification and localization. For example, the texture and color of the monkey's eyes are quite different from other keypoints such as shoulders and elbows. The RGB attention block helps the predictor attend to the related area and learn useful clues to classify the keypoints.

In the actual scenario of monkey pose estimation, most of the keypoints (e.g., elbows and knees) are covered with thick fur and quite similar in appearance. Moreover, the occlusion exists widely in monkeys' daily complex postures and some keypoints are even blurry in the captured images due to their quick movements. In the above-mentioned situations, the appearance information is inaccessible and insufficient to locate the keypoints. To solve this problem, the mask attention block is designed to help the predictor learn the physical constraints of the monkey skeleton and locate joints in the limbs. Unlike the RGB attention block, the mask attention block focuses on the constraints between keypoints and monkey outlines, which is trained without appearance information. Therefore, the main goal of the mask attention block is to facilitate the predictor to locate the keypoints even under the absence of appearance information. To be specific, the mask attention block takes the features generated from the binary mask image and finally outputs the attention mask. Then the final attention map of MGAM is the weighted sum of the masks generated by the separated attention blocks. Afterward, the up-sampled features of the RGB image are multiplied with the final attention map. The whole process is described below:

$$UP_i' = MGAM(UP_i, DS_{4-i}, MaskAtt) \tag{1}$$

$$MGAM(x, y, z) = x + x * Att(x, y, z) \tag{2}$$

$$Att(x, y, z) = w_1 * z + w_2 * (Sigmoid[f_3(ReLU(f_1(x) + f_2(y)))]) \tag{3}$$

The $MaskAtt$ stands for the attention heatmaps from mask attention block. $Att(*)$ is the function that combines down-sample and up-sample features. f_i represent different linear operators, which are essentially convolution operations.

4.3   Training and Inference

Training Strategy. At the phase of training, we adopt a mask guided strategy to train the proposed MGAN. The mask attention block is trained first, then the parameters of the mask attention block are fixed during the training of the RGB attention block. In this way, the mask branch acts as a guide to help the RGB attention block to attend to the foreground area of the image.

Loss Function. Following the spirit of heatmap-based methods [19] in human pose estimation, the generation of the i_{th} ground truth heatmap is defined as Eq. 4.

$$H_{gt}^i(x, y) = \frac{1}{2\pi\sigma^2} exp(-\frac{(x - x_i)^2 + (y - y_i)^2}{2\sigma^2}) \qquad (4)$$

The (x, y) is the coordinates of the heatmap pixel. σ presents the spatial variance, which depends on the size of the output feature. x_i and y_i denote the ground truth coordinates of the i_{th} keypoint. The loss function is defined as the mean square error (MSE) between the ground truth heatmaps and the predicted heatmaps, which is formulated as Eq. 5.

$$Loss = \frac{1}{N} \sum_{i=1}^{N} ||H_p^i - H_{gt}^i||^2 \qquad (5)$$

The N is the number of keypoints, H_p^i and H_{gt}^i denote the predicted heatmap and ground truth heatmap of the i_{th} keypoint. The network is trained by minimizing the MSE loss in an end-to-end manner. During inference, locations with the maximal activation on the predicted heatmap are considered as the coordinates of keypoints in the heatmap space. By applying an inverse transformation relative to the data preprocessing stage, the coordinates are mapped back to the original image space as the final prediction.

5   Experimental Results

In this section, exhaustive experiments are conducted on the proposed Caged Monkey Dataset to verify the effectiveness of the designed methods.

5.1   Implementation Details

Dataset and Metric. We take the rhesus macaque split of the monkey dataset to train the pose network and validate the intraspecific accuracy. The crab-eating macaque split is used to validate the interspecific performance (training on rhesus macaque split while validating on crab-eating macaque split). The key rationale behind the split strategy is that individual monkey used for validation is unseen by the network during training.

Table 2. Quantitative results of methods on Caged Monkey Dataset (the bold font used to identify the best results). The final MGAN (ours) represents our proposed method.

Methods	Backbone	Params (M)	GFLOPs (G)	AP	AP.5	AP.75	AR	AR.5	AR.75
Intraspecific experiments									
LPN [24]	lpn50	2.91	1.08	62.3	97.0	66.3	67.4	97.6	73.0
4-Stage Hourglass [16]	hourglass	13.02	10.73	70.4	98.0	77.7	74.9	98.8	82.5
DarkPose [23]	hourglass	13.02	10.73	71.6	98.0	80.3	75.9	98.8	84.5
SimpleBaseline [21]	res50	34.0	8.99	73.1	98.9	82.4	77.4	99.2	86.5
DarkPose [23]	res50	34.0	8.99	73.5	97.9	85.9	77.7	98.8	88.1
HRNet [18]	w32	28.54	7.65	78.6	98.8	91.9	82.5	99.6	93.7
DarkPose [23]	w32	28.54	7.65	**79.5**	98.8	92.0	83.2	99.6	93.7
MGAN (ours)	res50	34.46	9.89	79.2	98.8	90.1	83.5	99.6	92.9
Interspecific Experiments									
LPN [24]	lpn50	2.91	1.08	26.0	68.3	16.0	32.5	73.9	25.7
4-Stage Hourglass [16]	hourglass	13.02	10.73	41.6	82.8	39.3	48.3	85.2	48.4
DarkPose [23]	hourglass	13.02	10.73	42.0	82.9	40.2	48.6	86.0	49.0
SimpleBaseline [21]	res50	34.0	8.99	50.2	91.5	48.1	55.7	92.8	56.4
DarkPose [23]	res50	34.0	8.99	51.0	90.3	50.4	56.4	91.8	58.9
HRNet [18]	w32	28.54	7.65	57.6	90.4	61.8	63.6	91.8	70.0
DarkPose [23]	w32	28.54	7.65	58.1	91.4	63.5	64.1	92.6	71.8
MGAN (ours)	res50	34.46	9.89	**59.1**	93.2	66.0	64.6	94.2	72.0

Following the MS COCO dataset, we use Object Keypoint Similarity (OKS) as the validation metric to indicate the similarity between the predicted and the ground truth monkey poses. The process is formulated in Eq. 6, where N denotes the number of keypoint categories, d_i represents the Euclidean distance between the i_{th} ground truth and predicted keypoint, s and k_i are object scale and deviation of the i_{th} keypoint respectively, $\delta(v_i > 0)$ is the visible function.

$$OKS = \frac{\sum_i^N exp(\frac{-d_i^2}{2s^2k_i^2})\delta(v_i > 0)}{\sum_i^N \delta(v_i > 0)} \tag{6}$$

Training. In this work, we adopt the simple and effective baseline method SimpleBaseline-50 [21] as our baseline network and the image input size is fixed as 256×192 unless commented. All of the pose networks are trained for 140 epochs in total and optimized by Adam optimizer. The mini-batch size is 16 and the initial learning rate is 1e-3, which drops by 10 at epoch 90 and epoch 120. The Mask R-CNN [8] is utilized to detect the bounding box and segmentation mask, which demonstrates 90 box AP and 86 segmentation AP on the validation dataset. Before being injected into the network, every original image goes through a series of augmentation operations, including scale ($\pm 30\%$), rotation ($\pm 40°$), flipping, and cropping like the original work [21]. With respect to MGAM, the weight of the RGB attention mask is empirically set as 0.9.

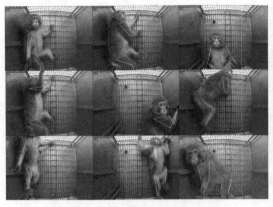 

(a) Intraspecific Experiments   (b) Interspecific Experiments

Fig. 3. Visualization results predicted by the proposed method in this work. (a) Visualization results of intraspecific experiments. (b) Visualization results of interspecific experiments.

5.2 Quantitative and Qualitative Results

As reported in Table 2, our method based on ResNet-50 outperforms SimpleBaseline-50 with a large margin of 6.1 AP in intraspecific experiments, 8.9 AP in interspecific experiments. Furthermore, the proposed MGAN are comparable with the HRNet-w32 and DarkPose methods in intraspecific experiments, which are superior pose detector and decode method in the field of human pose estimation. The reason for the lower AP of our method may be the use of a weaker backbone. The results of interspecific experiments show that the MGAN is more generalizable than the existing human pose estimation methods.

For qualitative evaluation, we draw the predicted monkey poses in Fig. 3. In intraspecific experiments, it can be seen that the predicted poses remain accurate in the occluded and complex scene. Especially when the monkey is on its side, the network cannot access the appearance features of the occluded keypoints, but the predictor still has the ability to infer credible locations of the keypoints. In interspecific experiments, our model is still robust for keypoint detection of blurry targets, which proves that our model can be generalized to different species.

Table 3. Ablation studies of the proposed RBA and MGAM, Exp-1 denotes the SimpleBaseline-50 model.

Exp-ID	RGB	MASK	RBA	AP
Exp-1				73.1
Exp-2	✓			75.7(+2.6)
Exp-3	✓	✓		76.5(+3.4)
Exp-4	✓		✓	78.1(+5.0)
Exp-5	✓	✓	✓	**79.2(+6.1)**

5.3   Ablation Study

To verify the effectiveness of each part of our proposed methods, ablation experiments have been conducted on the monkey dataset. Unless otherwise specified, the backbone networks in all experiments are still SimpleBaseline-50 and the input size is fixed as 256×192.

The Mask Guided Attention Module consists of an RGB attention block and a mask attention block. The results of Exp-2 reported in Table 3 show that the performance is improved by 2.6 AP with the help of RGB attention block. When collaborating with the full version of MGAM, the promotion of Exp-3 further increases to 3.4 AP compared to the baseline network. When the model is equipped with all components in Exp-5, including RBA and MGAM, the improvement comes to 6.1 AP finally.

6   Conclusion

In this paper, we build a comprehensive Caged Monkey Dataset and propose a novel augmentation strategy called Random Background Augmentation to alleviate the shortage of annotated monkey pose data. Based on the monkey dataset with great diversity, an efficient plug-in Mask Guided Attention Module is proposed to learn the natural constraints of the monkey skeleton, aiming to tackle the difficulties brought by the occluded, blurry keypoints and complex postures among deformable monkey bodies. The experiment results show that our proposed method significantly improves the performance in monkey pose estimation, which can be served as a very promising and practical monkey analysis tool in drug safety assessments and medical trials.

In caged monkey pose estimation, the process of data collection and labeling is very cumbersome. The transfer process of the pose knowledge in the virtual monkey data to the real scene will greatly reduce the costs. In fact, researchers have tried to use virtual data of animals for real-world animal pose estimation tasks, such as using semi-supervised learning and domain adaptation methods. Therefore, in the following research, realizing the knowledge transfer from virtual data to real scenes is an important research direction for the task of monkey pose estimation.

References

1. Acharya, U.R., Molinari, F., Sree, S.V., Chattopadhyay, S., Ng, K.H., Suri, J.S.: Automated diagnosis of epileptic EEG using entropies. Biomed. Signal Process. Control **7**(4), 401–408 (2012)
2. Badger, M., Wang, Y., Modh, A., Perkes, A., Kolotouros, N., Pfrommer, B.G., Schmidt, M.F., Daniilidis, K.: 3D bird reconstruction: a dataset, model, and shape recovery from a single view. In: Vedaldi, A., Bischof, H., Brox, T., Frahm, J.-M. (eds.) ECCV 2020. LNCS, vol. 12363, pp. 1–17. Springer, Cham (2020). https://doi.org/10.1007/978-3-030-58523-5_1
3. Bala, P.C., Eisenreich, B.R., Yoo, S.B.M., Hayden, B.Y., Park, H.S., Zimmermann, J.: Automated markerless pose estimation in freely moving macaques with open-monkeystudio. Nat. Commun. **11**(1), 1–12 (2020)
4. Cao, J., Tang, H., Fang, H.S., Shen, X., Lu, C., Tai, Y.W.: Cross-domain adaptation for animal pose estimation. In: Proceedings of the IEEE/CVF International Conference on Computer Vision, pp. 9498–9507 (2019)
5. Cao, Z., Simon, T., Wei, S.E., Sheikh, Y.: Realtime multi-person 2D pose estimation using part affinity fields. In: Proceedings of the IEEE Conference on Computer Vision and Pattern Recognition, pp. 7291–7299 (2017)
6. Ebeling, M., et al.: Genome-based analysis of the nonhuman primate macaca fascicularis as a model for drug safety assessment. Genome Res. **21**(10), 1746–1756 (2011)
7. Graving, J.M., et al.: Deepposekit, a software toolkit for fast and robust animal pose estimation using deep learning. Elife **8**, e47994 (2019)
8. He, K., Gkioxari, G., Dollár, P., Girshick, R.: Mask r-CNN. In: Proceedings of the IEEE international conference on computer vision, pp. 2961–2969 (2017)
9. Lin, T.Y., Dollár, P., Girshick, R., He, K., Hariharan, B., Belongie, S.: Feature pyramid networks for object detection. In: Proceedings of the IEEE Conference on Computer Vision and Pattern Recognition, pp. 2117–2125 (2017)
10. Lin, T.Y., Maire, M., Belongie, S., Hays, J., Perona, P., Ramanan, D., Dollár, P., Zitnick, C.L.: Microsoft coco: Common objects in context. In: European Conference on Computer Vision, pp. 740–755. Springer (2014)
11. Mathis, A., et al.: Pretraining boosts out-of-domain robustness for pose estimation. In: Proceedings of the IEEE/CVF Winter Conference on Applications of Computer Vision, pp. 1859–1868 (2021)
12. Mathis, A., et al.: Deeplabcut: markerless pose estimation of user-defined body parts with deep learning. Nat. Neurosci. **21**(9), 1281–1289 (2018)
13. Meiburger, K.M., Acharya, U.R., Molinari, F.: Automated localization and segmentation techniques for b-mode ultrasound images: a review. Comput. Biol. Med. **92**, 210–235 (2018)
14. Mu, J., Qiu, W., Hager, G.D., Yuille, A.L.: Learning from synthetic animals. In: Proceedings of the IEEE/CVF Conference on Computer Vision and Pattern Recognition, pp. 12386–12395 (2020)
15. Negrete, S.B., Labuguen, R., Matsumoto, J., Go, Y., Inoue, K.I., Shibata, T.: Multiple monkey pose estimation using openpose. bioRxiv (2021)
16. Newell, A., Yang, K., Deng, J.: Stacked Hourglass networks for human pose estimation. In: Leibe, B., Matas, J., Sebe, N., Welling, M. (eds.) ECCV 2016. LNCS, vol. 9912, pp. 483–499. Springer, Cham (2016). https://doi.org/10.1007/978-3-319-46484-8_29

17. Plagenhoef, M.R., Callahan, P.M., Beck, W.D., Blake, D.T., Terry, A.V., Jr.: Aged rhesus monkeys: cognitive performance categorizations and preclinical drug testing. Neuropharmacology **187**, 108489 (2021)
18. Sun, K., Xiao, B., Liu, D., Wang, J.: Deep high-resolution representation learning for human pose estimation. In: Proceedings of the IEEE/CVF Conference on Computer Vision and Pattern Recognition, pp. 5693–5703 (2019)
19. Tompson, J.J., Jain, A., LeCun, Y., Bregler, C.: Joint training of a convolutional network and a graphical model for human pose estimation. In: Advances in Neural Information Processing Systems, vol. 27 (2014)
20. Xia, F., Wang, P., Chen, X., Yuille, A.L.: Joint multi-person pose estimation and semantic part segmentation. In: Proceedings of the IEEE Conference on Computer Vision and Pattern Recognition, pp. 6769–6778 (2017)
21. Xiao, B., Wu, H., Wei, Y.: Simple baselines for human pose estimation and tracking. In: Proceedings of the European Conference on Computer Vision (ECCV), pp. 466–481 (2018)
22. Yu, H., Xu, Y., Zhang, J., Zhao, W., Guan, Z., Tao, D.: Ap-10k: A benchmark for animal pose estimation in the wild. arXiv preprint arXiv:2108.12617 (2021)
23. Zhang, F., Zhu, X., Dai, H., Ye, M., Zhu, C.: Distribution-aware coordinate representation for human pose estimation. In: Proceedings of the IEEE/CVF Conference on Computer Vision and Pattern Recognition, pp. 7093–7102 (2020)
24. Zhang, Z., Tang, J., Wu, G.: Simple and lightweight human pose estimation. arXiv preprint arXiv:1911.10346 (2019)
25. Zhou, F., et al.: Structured context enhancement network for mouse pose estimation. In: IEEE Transactions on Circuits and Systems for Video Technology (2021)

WTB-LLL: A Watercraft Tracking Benchmark Derived by Low-Light-Level Camera

Chongyi Ye[1,2] and Yuzhang Gu[1,2(✉)]

[1] Bionic Vision System Laboratory, State Key Laboratory of Transducer Technology, Shanghai Institute of Microsystem and Information Technology, Chinese Academy of Sciences, Shanghai 200050, China
{yechongyi,gyz}@mail.sim.ac.cn
[2] University of Chinese Academy of Sciences, Beijing 100049, China

Abstract. Object tracking under the low illumination condition draws insufficient attention so far. Low-light-level camera is a sophisticated sensor used for nighttime video surveillance. In this paper, we propose the first object tracking dataset derived by low-light-level camera, called Low-light-level Watercraft Tracking Benchmark (WTB-LLL). WTB-LLL consist of 57853 annotated frames with 7 challenge attributes. Since WTB-LLL is more challenging than common daytime benchmark, we extensively evaluate 14 state-of-the-art trackers and conduct two validation experiments to understand how the attributes of the dataset impact the trackers. We observed several instructive findings from the experiments. Briefly, Siamese trackers maintain the stablest performance when confronted with thermal noise. Reasonable assistance of transformer structure is helpful for the most severe challenge, background clutter, of WTB-LLL. However, the discriminative appearance modules are proved to be the best paradigms for our low-light-level dataset thanks to the powerful ability of feature representation and the strong discriminative capacity obtained by the online learning process. By proposing WTB-LLL, we expect to introduce a new prospect for low illumination object tracking and facilitate future research.

Keywords: Object tracking · Low-light-level camera · Benchmark · Dataset

1 Introduction

Object tracking has experienced an explosion due to the rapid development of deep learning over the past few years. Trackers utilize context information of video sequences to model appearance and motion information of target object and thus to estimate state and location of the object of interest [22].

Supplementary Information The online version contains supplementary material available at https://doi.org/10.1007/978-3-031-18916-6_56.

Object tracking plays an important role in real-world systems, especially in vedio surveillance [22]. For example, video surveillance system is applicable to many law enforcement scenarios of water areas, such as cracking down on illegal sand mining in waterway, anti-overloading and forewarning dangerous navigation behaviors of ship and combating prohibited fishing. The introduction of object tracking algorithm is conducive to constructing intellectualized surveillance system, which is in favour of promoting the development of water area monitoring and law enforcement.

However, despite the rapid development of general tracking algorithms used in scenes with favorable illumination, there are few schemes suitable for visual tracking in the low-illumination environment required in security surveillance. Specifically, in low-light conditions, pictures taken by normal cameras are terrible so that tracking algorithms need to be supplemented with additional image-enhancer to catch the target [38,39]. Besides, infrared thermal imaging is the general scheme of video surveillance under low light conditions. However, active infrared thermal imaging can be anti-detected easily, while passive infrared thermal images lack detailed information about target objects and exist many shortcomings like thermal crossover and low resolution [33]. For the above two scheme are hardly ideal, it is valuable to explore potentially methodology for low-illumination.

In contrast, low-light-level camera is a superior type of low-illumination imaging sensor, which has gradually entered the civilian field in recent years. Low-light camera can utilizes the weak light reflected by the objects of interest, and employs the principle of photoelectric effect and the method of photoelectronic imaging to enhance the image [31], so as to achieve extraordinary imaging effect in low illumination environment, which owns the characteristics of strong concealment so that it is suitable for the monitoring needs of law enforcement and campaign against crime at night.

Benchmark plays an indispensable role in the evolution of object tracking algorithms, for the reason of providing performance measurement approach to guide the improvement of trackers. At present, there are many benchmarks such as OTB [36] and VOT [13] in general tracking field. In recent years, the proposal of benchmarks like PTB-TIR [24] promotes the research of infrared pedestrian tracker. However, there is no public dataset, derived from low-light-level camera, can be used for tracking task so far, which limits the possibility and richness of feasible tracking algorithm in low illumination. To this end, we derive a low-light-level tracking datasets for monitoring navigation behavior of ship in low light circumstances. The dataset includes 57853 frames of low-light-level images with manual annotations in order to fairly evaluate object tracking algorithms. The video sequences consist the dataset are captured from locations nearby the main stream of the Yangtze River and the lakes along the river. It provides clear video sequence information under tough conditions, including tracking in extremely dark and in long distance. Our dataset makes up for the lack of diversity of low illumination tracking datasets and reveals a potential better choice for low illumination tracking applications.

Besides, low-light-level video sequences present some specific attributes, such as monochrome figures and limited dynamic range, which affect the performance of existing trackers trained by well-lit RGB images. In order to understand how general tracking algorithms perform on WTB-LLL and to provide comparisons for future research, we extensively evaluate 14 state-of-the-art trackers which proposed very recently, covering not only two currently dominating paradigms: Siamese networks [5,11,12,35,40] and discriminative appearance modules [2,3,8,28] but also the latest transformer-assisted tracking framework [4,34,37]. We conduct in-depth analysis on the overall evaluation results to discuss applicability of different tracking paradigms. The ability of trackers to handle different challenges is evaluated on attribute subsets. In addition, we implement validation experiments to explore the significance of two conceded improvement aspects relevant to WTB-LLL. The release of the WTB-LLL dataset is being prepared and will be available soon.

Our contributions can be summarized as follows:

1. We propose WTB-LLL benchmark dataset consisted of 57853 frames of annotated low-light-level images. To the best of knowledge, it is the first benchmark dataset derived by low-light-level camera, which reveals a potentially superior choice for low illumination tracking.
2. We conduct comprehensive evaluation experiments with 14 state-of-the-art trackers on our benchmark and further validation experiments are carried out to inspire future research.

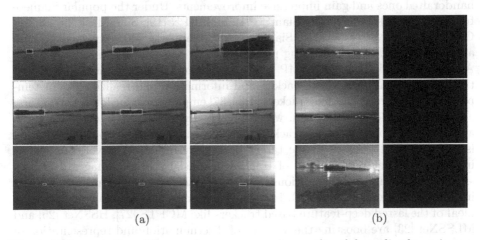

(a)   (b)

Fig. 1. (a)Presentation of 3 example sequences and groundtruth bounding boxes in our novel WTB-LLL. (b) Comparison of images captured by low-light-level camera(first column) in WTB-LLL and images captured by cellphone cameras from the same location at the same time.

2   Related Work

Object Tracking Benchmark. Object tracking benchmarks provide abundant data and reliable evaluation criteria, which is of crucial significance in promoting the development of tracking algorithms. A multitude of benchmarks like OTB [36], VOT [13], LaSOT [10], GOT-10k [15], TrackingNet [30], Nfs [16], OxUvA [32], UAV123 [29] can perform impartial evaluations of trackers in daytime scenes with favorable illumination. On the contrary, there are only a small amount of benchmarks, both in thermal infrared tracking field and nighttime tracking based on common RGB camera, suitable for visual tracking tasks under low illumination circumstances. In term of thermal infrared tracking, VOT-T2016 [17] and LSOTB-TIR [26] are developed for general object tracking, while PTB-TIR [24] is specific for pedestrian tracking. With respect to nighttime tracking dataset, UAV135 [21] and DarkTrack2021 [38] are specific for dark unmanned aerial vehicle (UAV) tracking, containing video sequences all shot by ordinary RGB camera from UAV perspective. So far, to our knowledge, there is no benchmark for object tracking task derived from low-light-level camera which is appropriate to low illumination scenarios. Now that using benchmarks to evaluate the performance of trackers can guide the improvement of the object tracking algorithm, we believe that the lack of benchmarks is one of the reasons that restricts the development of research on low illumination tracking method.

Object Tracking Algorithm. Briefly speaking, correlation filter-based tracking algorithms like C-COT [9] and ASRCF [6] utilize deep features to replace handcrafted ones and gain impressive improvements. Under the popular Siamese framework, trackers including SiamFC [1], SiamRPN [19], SiamMask [35], Siam-CAR [12], SiamRPN++ [18], SiamBAN [5], SiamAttn [40] etc. have concise architecture and show promising performance. Along another line trackers like ATOM [7], DiMP [2] and PrDiMP [8] are discriminative appearance model based trackers that can incorporate background information and realize efficient template update. Recently, some trackers [4, 34, 37] employ the transformer structure, aiming to pursue breakthrough, which reveals a new trend. Unfortunately, the above trackers only focus on tracking in daytime where illumination condition is adequate and features of the target object are intact. However, our experiments show that performance of trackers trained by bright images decreases significantly in dim light conditions (We provide the comparison results in Fig. 1 in the Supplementary Material). In terms of thermal infrared tracking, the core ideal of the lasted deep-feature based trackers like MCFTS [27], HSSNet [25] and MLSSNet [23] are boosting the abilities of discrimination and representation of features and making use of fine-grained level to cope with the particularity of thermal infrared images. In addition, Darklighter [39], ADTrack [20] and SCT [38] all integrate low-light enhancer before the tracking component to enhance the quality of RGB dark images so that the performance of algorithms can be improved. In general, the general trackers forms the foundation for the above specific tracking algorithms.

3 Proposed Benchmark

We aim to construct a dedicated low-light-level tracking benchmark of watercraft (WTB-LLL) for water area monitoring and law enforcement. In Sect. 3.1, we introduce the dataset for details. Later, we present the evaluation methodology for the trackers in Sect. 3.2.

3.1 Dataset

Characteristic. We collected videos from diversity of scenarios, including locks, docks and patrol vessels of the main and tributaries of the Yangtze River, covering different types of ships such as freighters, fishing boats, speedboats and cruise ships, etc. Considering the slow speed of the ship, we appropriately sample the video sequence based on the original video to increase the difficulty of tracking. After sorting out and screening effective fragments, irrelevant fragments were deleted. WTB-LLL consists of 38 sequences with a total of 57853 annotated frames eventually. The specific statistics are summarized in Table 1.

Table 1. Statistics of WTB-LLL

Characteristic	Statistic
Number of videos	38
Avg. duration	60s+
Total frames	57853
Original frame rate	25fps
Max frames	2880
Avg. frames	1522
Min frames	392
Number of att.	7

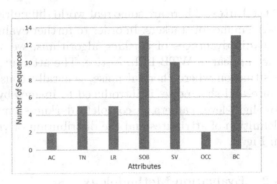

Fig. 2. Attributes distribution of WTB-LLL

Annotation. We provide fine annotation for each frame of the video sequences. The Github open source labeling tool Darklabel is adopted to edit an rectangle bounding box as the tightest one to fit the target object. We record the left corner point, width, and height of the bounding box which are formatted into a groundtruth text file to represent the location and size of target object later on. The annotation tool generates bounding box semi-automatically using embedded tracker to track object. To gain accurate and smooth bounding boxes for every video frames we refine the boxes every ten frames approximately by hand and adjust them timely when errors occurred. After the initial annotation work is completed, we perform two rounds of frame-by-frame checks to ensure high-quality of annotations.

Table 2. Descriptions of 7 different attributes in WTB-LLL.

Attributes	Description
SV	Scale variation - the ratios of the groundtruth bounding box in the first frame and current frame is outside the range [1/2, 2].
SOB	Similar Object - existing objects of similar shape or same type near the target.
LR	Low Resolution - the number of pixels inside the bounding box is no more than 400 pixels in at least one frame.
OCC	Occlusion - the target is partially or fully occluded
AC	Appearance Change - the appearance of the target object changes or viewpoint affects target appearance significantly during tracking.
BC	Background Clutter - the background has the similar appearance or texture as the target.
TN	Thermal Noise - the thermal noise introduced by the high gain amplifier circuit in the extreme dark environment.

Attributes. There are some real-world difficulties and challenges that can affect performance of trackers. In order to further evaluate and analyze the advantages and disadvantages of tracking algorithms, we summarize the seven attributes that appear in WTB-LLL. Notice, The attribute of Thermal Noise defines such a situation where thermal noise, generally consisted of a mixture of Gaussian noise and shot noise, is introduced to images by high-gain amplifier circuits of low-light-level camera in complete darkness environments.Table 2. Depicts the definition of attributes and the distribution of videos in each attribute is shown in Fig. 2.

3.2   Evaluation Methodology

We use Center Location Error (CLE) and Overlap Ratio (OR) as the base metrics for they are widely used as evaluation criteria in object tracking [36]. Specifically, CLE is the Euclidean distance between the center of the tracking result and the ground-truth bounding box. OR measures the overlap rate between the ground-truth bounding box and the predicted one. Base on these two metrics, we calculate precision, normalized precision, and success under One Pass Evaluation (OPE) to measure the performance of a tracker.

Precision Precision plot portrays the percentage of frames whose CLE is within the given threshold. Use the percentage of the frame whose CLE is within a given threshold (commonly 20 pixels) as the representative precision score.

Normalized precision Following LaSOT [10], normalize the precision to eliminate the influence of different scales of images and targets.

Success The success plot depicts the ratios of frames whose OR is larger than the given threshold at the thresholds varying from 0 to 1. The area under the curve (AUC) of each success plot is exploited as success score to rank trackers.

Speed We adopt the average frames per second (FPS) of a tracker on the dataset to measure the speed performance.

4 Experiments

In this section, we discuss the implementation of large-scale fair evaluation experiments on the proposed benchmark. First, an overall performance evaluation of the latest proposed 14 state-of-the-art trackers is reported in Sect. 4.1. Second, we give qualitatively analysis for the performance of these trackers on the attribute subset in Sect. 4.2. Third, validation experiments are presented in Sect. 4.3. We run all the trackers on the same PCs with a GTX TITAN X GPU.

Table 3. Comparison of performance of 14 state-of-art trackers on WTB-LLL. We rank these trackers according to their success score.

Tracker	Success(AUC)	Precision	Norm. Precision	Speed (fps)	Venue
PrDiMP	59.66	74.12	75.12	29.4	CVPR 2020
KeepTrack	58.43	73.18	72.71	13.9	ICCV 2021
TrDiMP	57.37	72.98	71.71	17.1	CVPR 2021
SiamAttn	57.10	70.39	67.99	17.8	CVPR 2020
DiMP50	56.70	71.50	68.61	35.1	CVPR 2019
KYS	56.60	71.88	69.03	19.3	ECCV 2020
TrSiam	56.53	72.96	69.13	17.6	CVPR 2021
SiamCAR	55.09	70.24	64.52	23.4	CVPR 2020
SiamBAN	53.65	68.37	63.33	24.4	CVPR 2020
TransT	52.64	69.13	66.22	26.7	CVPR 2021
Stark	52.63	64.75	63.13	30.5	ICCV 2021
SiamGAT	52.60	68.34	66.45	39.1	CVPR 2021
DiMP18	51.17	62.75	62.16	40.0	CVPR 2019
SiamMask	51.15	66.95	63.95	53.8	CVPR 2019

4.1 Overall Performance Evaluation

Evaluated Trackers. We evaluate 14 state-of-the-art trackers on WTB-LLL and provide basis for future comparison. Most of the evaluated trackers fall into two currently dominating paradigms: Siamese networks and discriminative appearance modules [28]. Furthermore, we notice that the transformer structure has been introduced into visual tracking algorithms recently. In order to explore this new research trend, we included trackers employing transformer architecture in our evaluation experiments. Specifically, we evaluated five Siamese trackers consisting of SiamCAR [12], SiamBAN [5], SiamAttn [40], SiamGAT [11], SiamMask [35]; Five discriminative appearance model based trackers including PrDiMP [8], DiMP50 [2], DiMP18 [2], KeepTrack [28], KYS [3]; Four transformer-assisted trackers comprising with TrDiMP [34], TrSiam [34], TransT [4] and Stark [37]. For all of the above trackers, we use the original parameters of them without changing the official configuration for evaluation.

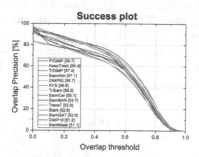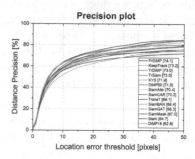

Fig. 3. The overall performance of the trackers on WTB-LLL using OPE success and precision plots.

Performance and Qualitative Analysis. As shown in the Fig. 3, PrDiMP [8], a discriminative appearance model based tracker employing the probabilistic bounding-box regression, performs best among all trackers with an success score of 59.66 and an precision score of 74.12. KeepTrack [28] achieves the second place in both success and precision score, using SuperDiMP [8] as the basic network and developing a target candidate association network. The third-ranked tracking algorithm is TrDiMP [34] which integrate transformer architecture to DCF pipeline reasonably, with a score of 72.98 in precision, which is only 0.2 points lower than KeepTrack [28]. Next up is SiamAttn [40] which gains 57.10 success score and shows more powerful performance than other Siamese trackers in our evaluation.

By observing the overall results, we notice that the discriminative appearance model based trackers generally show superior performance compared with Siamese trackers on our WTB-LLL benchmark. Considering the relatively low dynamic range of the low-ligth-level camera as well as the lack of color information, it is more difficult to distinguish foreground from background in our low-ligth-level images in WTB-LLL than ordinary well-lit RGB images. We consider that the trackers [8,28] can all integrate background information when learning the target classifier online, which provides more powerful capability to distinguish the foreground from the surrounding background. Therefore, they are more conducive to low-light-level sequence tracking than Siamese-based tracking algorithms. Meanwhile, we find that not all transformer-assisted tracking framework present favourable performance, so we believe that it is necessary to further explore the optimal approach to leverage the advantage of transformer architecture for tracking.

4.2   Attribute-Based Evaluation

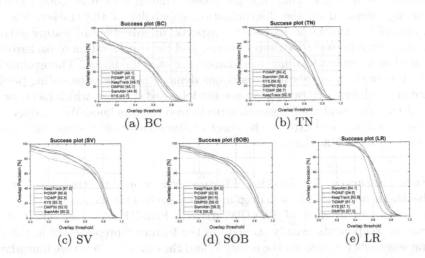

(a) BC   (b) TN

(c) SV   (d) SOB   (e) LR

Fig. 4. Success plots for OPE on five attribute subsets. The corresponding challenges are: (a) Background Clutter. (b) Thermal Noise. (c) Scale variation. (d) Similar Object. (e) Low Resolution.

In order to further analyze and understand the performance of different trackers, we evaluated the above tracking algorithms on the five attribute subsets. Figure 4 portrays the success plot for the top 6 trackers ranked by overall success score. We show the rest results in the supplementary material. We obverse that the ranking of these trackers is different between different attribute subsets, suggesting that it can be challenging for an algorithm to deal with all the challenges. Specifically, KeepTrack [28] achieves the best result on the challenge of scale variation(SV) and similar object(SOB), outperforming the second best PrDiMP [8] by 1.6% and 1.7% in terms of success scores respectively, whereas it performs worst of the six trackers on thermal noise subsets(TN), with success scores of 52.3 only. By contrast, although the performance of SiamAttn [40] is not favorable on SV subsets and SOB subsets since it lacks online learning process and the effectiveness of implicit template updates is limited, it gains the highest success score on low resolution(LR) subsets and maintains stable performance under the interference of thermal noise(TN). In addition, there is a remarkable phenomenon that the performance of all trackers is significantly degraded on background clutter subsets which turns out to be the severe challenge of WTB-LLL. TrDiMP [34] takes first place in this attribute. Accordingly, we suggest that appropriate leverage of transformer structure to encode and propagate spatio-temporal context can be inspiring.

4.3 Validation Experiments

Intuitively, the feature loss of low-light-level images may impair the performance of tracking algorithms, while the prominent challenge of background clutter places high demand on the discrimination capability of the tracker. We are reminded of two current focus research aspects: improvement of feature extractor to acquire representative deep features, and the consideration of background information in online learning to enhance the discrimination. The evaluation results presented in the above two sections demonstrate the outstanding performance of the discriminative appearance model based trackers, which incorporate both of the aforementioned research aspects into the pipelines. We conduct validation experiments to explore the effect of the above two mechanisms on our low-light-level tracking dataset.

Feature Extractor. The function of feature extraction of the tracker is done by the backbone networks. Modern deep networks like ResNet have been introduced after the earliest attempt of SiamDW [41] and SiamRPN++ [18]. The feature extraction components usually strengthen the feature representation in the following ways: one is to deepen the network, and the other is to leverage multi-layer features. In order to understand the impact of these two approaches, we take Dimp18 and DiMP50 [2], employing ResNet18 and ResNet50 [14] as backbone respectively, for verification experiments. Then, for both trackers, we experiment with mechanism of layer-wise feature aggregation and structures using single-layer features. The results are shown in Table 4. We can see that the success scores of both trackers has dropped. And there is an interesting phenomenon, rather than using a shallower network, the absence of multi-layer features causes more decline. Accordingly, We believe that fusing information from early layer used to assist localization with high-level features rich in semantic information is essential for maintaining the performance of trackers on WTB-LLL.

Table 4. Success of the trackers. The item 'Multi-layer' denotes the uses features from Layer2 and Layer3 of the backbone for tracking and 'Single' means that only features from Layer3 are used.

Tracker	Multi-layer	Single
DiMP50	56.7	49.2
DiMP18	51.2	44.4

Table 5. Success of the trackers. The item 'Keep' denotes that The target classifier keep online learning throughout the tracking process and 'Cease' means that online learning of classifier ceases after the initial stage.

Tracker	Keep	Cease
DiMP50	56.7	46.3
PrDiMP	59.6	45.5

Online Learning Classifier. DiMP [2] and PrDiMP [8] employ online learning target classifier, which renders the capacity to integrate background information and thus contribute to the favourable discrimination of trackers. In this verification experiment, We only keep the online learning procedure of classifier in the initial stage and cease the subsequent update mechanism, thereby incapacitating the online learning classifier. The results in Table 5 show that performances of both trackers decline significantly, after suspending the online learning procedure. So, it is reasonable to believe that learning a powerful target classifier online is beneficial to promoting the discrimination ability of tracking algorithms on the low-light-level sequences. In conclusion, these two mechanisms are indispensable for low-light-level tracking, especially the Integration of background information when learning the target classifier online, which induces the strong discrimination capacity for trackers.

5   Conclusion

In this paper we introduce the application of low-light-level camera into the filed of low illumination tracking, which can be used for nighttime video surveillance. In particular, we propose WTB-LLL with fully annotated sequences, which is the first object tracking benchmark derived by low-light-level camera. We implement comprehensive evaluation experiments for 14 state-of-the-art trackers with in-depth analysis and find out several inspiring observation. To sum up, Siamese trackers sustain the stablest performance under the interference of thermal noise, while Trackers benefit from assistance of appropriate transformer structure when coping with the most severe challenge of background clutter. However, the best approach for low-light-level tracking is revealed to be the discriminative appearance modules based trackers. Moreover, the validation experiments prove that not only powerful capability of feature representation but also strong discrimination acquired from online learning procedure are desirable for tracking algorithms so as to confront with information descent in WTB-LLL. In the future, we are going to extend the dataset and explore more challenge factors in low-light-level tracking. We believe that the benchmark, evaluation and validation experiment will motivate the new prospect for low illumination object tracking research and prompt related applications.

Acknowledgments. This work was supported by National Science and Technology Major Project from Minister of Science and Technology, China(2018AAA0103100). This work was also supported by Shanghai Municipal Science and Technology Major Project (ZHANGJIANG LAB) under Grant 2018SHZDZX01.

References

1. Bertinetto, L., Valmadre, J., Henriques, J.F., Vedaldi, A., Torr, P.H.S.: Fully-convolutional siamese networks for object tracking. In: Hua, G., Jégou, H. (eds.) ECCV 2016. LNCS, vol. 9914, pp. 850–865. Springer, Cham (2016). https://doi.org/10.1007/978-3-319-48881-3_56

2. Bhat, G., Danelljan, M., Gool, L.V., Timofte, R.: Learning discriminative model prediction for tracking. In: Proceedings of the IEEE/CVF International Conference on Computer vision, pp. 6182–6191 (2019)
3. Bhat, G., Danelljan, M., Van Gool, L., Timofte, R.: Know your surroundings: exploiting scene information for object tracking. In: Vedaldi, A., Bischof, H., Brox, T., Frahm, J.-M. (eds.) ECCV 2020. LNCS, vol. 12368, pp. 205–221. Springer, Cham (2020). https://doi.org/10.1007/978-3-030-58592-1_13
4. Chen, X., Yan, B., Zhu, J., Wang, D., Yang, X., Lu, H.: Transformer tracking. In: Proceedings of the IEEE/CVF Conference on Computer Vision and Pattern Recognition, pp. 8126–8135 (2021)
5. Chen, Z., Zhong, B., Li, G., Zhang, S., Ji, R.: Siamese box adaptive network for visual tracking. In: Proceedings of the IEEE/CVF conference on computer vision and pattern recognition, pp. 6668–6677 (2020)
6. Dai, K., Wang, D., Lu, H., Sun, C., Li, J.: Visual tracking via adaptive spatially-regularized correlation filters. In: Proceedings of the IEEE/CVF Conference on Computer Vision and Pattern Recognition, pp. 4670–4679 (2019)
7. Danelljan, M., Bhat, G., Khan, F.S., Felsberg, M.: Atom: Accurate tracking by overlap maximization. In: Proceedings of the IEEE/CVF Conference on Computer Vision and Pattern Recognition, pp. 4660–4669 (2019)
8. Danelljan, M., Gool, L.V., Timofte, R.: Probabilistic regression for visual tracking. In: Proceedings of the IEEE/CVF conference on computer vision and pattern recognition, pp. 7183–7192 (2020)
9. Danelljan, M., Robinson, A., Shahbaz Khan, F., Felsberg, M.: Beyond correlation filters: learning continuous convolution operators for visual tracking. In: Leibe, B., Matas, J., Sebe, N., Welling, M. (eds.) ECCV 2016. LNCS, vol. 9909, pp. 472–488. Springer, Cham (2016). https://doi.org/10.1007/978-3-319-46454-1_29
10. Fan, H., et al.: LaSOT: A high-quality benchmark for large-scale single object tracking. In: Proceedings of the IEEE/CVF Conference on Computer Vision and Pattern Recognition, pp. 5374–5383 (2019)
11. Guo, D., Shao, Y., Cui, Y., Wang, Z., Zhang, L., Shen, C.: Graph attention tracking. In: Proceedings of the IEEE/CVF Conference on Computer Vision and Pattern Recognition, pp. 9543–9552 (2021)
12. Guo, D., Wang, J., Cui, Y., Wang, Z., Chen, S.: SiamCar: Siamese fully convolutional classification and regression for visual tracking. In: Proceedings of the IEEE/CVF Conference on Computer Vision and Pattern Recognition, pp. 6269–6277 (2020)
13. Hadfield, S., Lebeda, K., Bowden, R.: The visual object tracking vot2014 challenge results. In: European Conference on Computer Vision (ECCV) Visual Object Tracking Challenge Workshop. University of Surrey (2014)
14. He, K., Zhang, X., Ren, S., Sun, J.: Deep residual learning for image recognition. In: Proceedings of the IEEE Conference on Computer Vision and Pattern Recognition, pp. 770–778 (2016)
15. Huang, L., Zhao, X., Huang, K.: Got-10k: a large high-diversity benchmark for generic object tracking in the wild. IEEE Trans. Pattern Anal. Mach. Intell. **43**(5), 1562–1577 (2019)
16. Kiani Galoogahi, H., Fagg, A., Huang, C., Ramanan, D., Lucey, S.: Need for speed: A benchmark for higher frame rate object tracking. In: Proceedings of the IEEE International Conference on Computer Vision, pp. 1125–1134 (2017)
17. Lebeda, K., Hadfield, S., Bowden, R., et al.: The thermal infrared visual object tracking VOT-TIR2016 challenge result. In: Proceedings, European Conference on Computer Vision (ECCV) workshops. University of Surrey (2016)

18. Li, B., Wu, W., Wang, Q., Zhang, F., Xing, J., Yan, J.: SiamRPN++: Evolution of siamese visual tracking with very deep networks. In: Proceedings of the IEEE/CVF Conference on Computer Vision and Pattern Recognition, pp. 4282–4291 (2019)
19. Li, B., Yan, J., Wu, W., Zhu, Z., Hu, X.: High performance visual tracking with siamese region proposal network. In: Proceedings of the IEEE Conference on Computer Vision and Pattern Recognition, pp. 8971–8980 (2018)
20. Li, B., Fu, C., Ding, F., Ye, J., Lin, F.: Adtrack: Target-aware dual filter learning for real-time anti-dark UAV tracking. In: 2021 IEEE International Conference on Robotics and Automation (ICRA), pp. 496–502. IEEE (2021)
21. Li, B., Fu, C., Ding, F., Ye, J., Lin, F.: All-day object tracking for unmanned aerial vehicle. IEEE Transactions on Mobile Computing (2022)
22. Li, Q., et al.: Survey of visual object tracking algorithms based on deep learning. J. Image. Graph. **24**(12), 2057–2080 (2019)
23. Li, X., Liu, Q., Fan, N., He, Z., Wang, H.: Hierarchical spatial-aware siamese network for thermal infrared object tracking. Knowledge-Based Syst. **166**, 71–81 (2019)
24. Liu, Q., He, Z., Li, X., Zheng, Y.: PTB-TIR: a thermal infrared pedestrian tracking benchmark. IEEE Trans. Multimedia **22**(3), 666–675 (2019)
25. Liu, Q., Li, X., He, Z., Fan, N., Yuan, D., Wang, H.: Learning deep multi-level similarity for thermal infrared object tracking. IEEE Trans. Multimedia **23**, 2114–2126 (2020)
26. Liu, Q., et al.: LSOTB-TIR: A large-scale high-diversity thermal infrared object tracking benchmark. In: Proceedings of the 28th ACM International Conference on Multimedia. pp. 3847–3856 (2020)
27. Liu, Q., Lu, X., He, Z., Zhang, C., Chen, W.S.: Deep convolutional neural networks for thermal infrared object tracking. Knowledge-Based Syst. **134**, 189–198 (2017)
28. Mayer, C., Danelljan, M., Paudel, D.P., Van Gool, L.: Learning target candidate association to keep track of what not to track. In: Proceedings of the IEEE/CVF International Conference on Computer Vision, pp. 13444–13454 (2021)
29. Mueller, M., Smith, N., Ghanem, B.: A benchmark and simulator for UAV tracking. In: Leibe, B., Matas, J., Sebe, N., Welling, M. (eds.) ECCV 2016. LNCS, vol. 9905, pp. 445–461. Springer, Cham (2016). https://doi.org/10.1007/978-3-319-46448-0_27
30. Muller, M., Bibi, A., Giancola, S., Alsubaihi, S., Ghanem, B.: TrackingNet: A large-scale dataset and benchmark for object tracking in the wild. In: Proceedings of the European Conference on Computer Vision (ECCV), pp. 300–317 (2018)
31. Shiming, X., Xuewu, F., Na, H., Zhe, B., et al.: Review on low light level remote sensing imaging technology (2018)
32. Valmadre, J., et al.: Long-term tracking in the wild: A benchmark. In: Proceedings of the European conference on computer vision (ECCV), pp. 670–685 (2018)
33. Walia, G.S., Kapoor, R.: Recent advances on multicue object tracking: a survey. Artif. Intell. Rev. **46**(1), 1–39 (2016). https://doi.org/10.1007/s10462-015-9454-6
34. Wang, N., Zhou, W., Wang, J., Li, H.: Transformer meets tracker: Exploiting temporal context for robust visual tracking. In: Proceedings of the IEEE/CVF Conference on Computer Vision and Pattern Recognition, pp. 1571–1580 (2021)
35. Wang, Q., Zhang, L., Bertinetto, L., Hu, W., Torr, P.H.: Fast online object tracking and segmentation: A unifying approach. In: Proceedings of the IEEE/CVF conference on Computer Vision and Pattern Recognition, pp. 1328–1338 (2019)
36. Wu, Y., Lim, J., Yang, M.: Object tracking benchmark. IEEE Trans. Pattern Anal. Mach. Intell. **37**(9), 1834–1848 (2015)

37. Yan, B., Peng, H., Fu, J., Wang, D., Lu, H.: Learning spatio-temporal transformer for visual tracking. In: Proceedings of the IEEE/CVF International Conference on Computer Vision, pp. 10448–10457 (2021)
38. Ye, J., Fu, C., Cao, Z., An, S., Zheng, G., Li, B.: Tracker meets night: a transformer enhancer for UAV tracking. IEEE Robot. Autom. Lett. **7**(2), 3866–3873 (2022)
39. Ye, J., Fu, C., Zheng, G., Cao, Z., Li, B.: Darklighter: Light up the darkness for uav tracking. In: 2021 IEEE/RSJ International Conference on Intelligent Robots and Systems (IROS), pp. 3079–3085. IEEE (2021)
40. Yu, Y., Xiong, Y., Huang, W., Scott, M.R.: Deformable siamese attention networks for visual object tracking. In: Proceedings of the IEEE/CVF Conference on Computer Vision and Pattern Recognition, pp. 6728–6737 (2020)
41. Zhang, Z., Peng, H.: Deeper and wider siamese networks for real-time visual tracking. In: Proceedings of the IEEE/CVF Conference on Computer Vision and Pattern Recognition, pp. 4591–4600 (2019)

Dualray: Dual-View X-ray Security Inspection Benchmark and Fusion Detection Framework

Modi Wu[1,2], Feifan Yi[1], Haigang Zhang[1(✉)], Xinyu Ouyang[2], and Jinfeng Yang[1]

[1] Institute of Applied Artificial Intelligence of the Guangdong-Hong Kong-Macao Greater Bay Area, Shenzhen Polytechnic, Shenzhen 518055, Guangdong, China
{feifanyi,jfyang}@szpt.edu.cn, zhg2018@sina.com
[2] School of Electronic and Information Engineering, University of Science and Technology Liaoning, Anshan 114045, Liaoning, China

Abstract. Prohibited item detection in X-ray security inspection images using computer vision technology is a challenging task in real world scenarios due to various factors, include occlusion and unfriendly imaging viewing angle. Intelligent analysis of multi-view X-ray security inspection images is a relatively direct and targeted solution. However, there is currently no published multi-view X-ray security inspection image dataset. In this paper, we construct a dual-view X-ray security inspection dataset, named Dualray, based on real acquisition method. Dualray dataset consists of 4371 pairs of images with 6 categories of prohibited items, and each pair of instances is imaged from horizontal and vertical viewing angles. We have annotated each sample with the categories of prohibited item and the location represented by bounding box. In addition, a dual-view prohibited item feature fusion and detection framework in X-ray images is proposed, where the two input channels are applied and divided into primary and secondary channels, and the features of the secondary channel are used to enhance the features of the primary channel through the feature fusion model. Spatial attention and channel attention are employed to achieve efficient feature screening. We conduct some experiments to verify the effectiveness of the proposed dual-view prohibited item detection framework in X-ray images. The Dualray dataset and dual-view object detection code are available at https://github.com/zhg-SZPT/Dualray.

Keywords: Multi-view object detection · Security inspection · X-ray image benchmark · Feature fusion

1 Introduction

Using computer vision technology to realize the intelligent analysis of prohibited items in X-ray images is an important measure to promote the development of intelligent security inspection [2]. Under normal circumstances, security inspectors hope to obtain the category and location of prohibited items at the same time,

S. Yu et al. (Eds.): PRCV 2022, LNCS 13537, pp. 721–734, 2022.
https://doi.org/10.1007/978-3-031-18916-6_57

so as to facilitate subsequent risk removal operations [3]. Due to the transmission imaging mode of X-ray, the security inspection images have some unique characteristics, which increases the difficulty of object detection of prohibited items.

- There is a wide variety of prohibited items. Typically, there is a limited number of objects that are deemed contraband. However, dismantling parts of the prohibited items are still forbidden.
- Objects take on different shapes. The appearance of the same object is different. Knives are very common prohibited items, and their shapes are varied.
- Objects are gathered in packages, cluttered and obscured from each other. It is a very common situation that objects are cluttered. Due to the transmission of X-rays, it causes occlusion between objects.
- The prohibited items show multi-scale feature. There are size differences between items. For small size objects, it is prone to miss detection.
- Relatively extreme imaging perspectives will greatly increase the difficulty of feature extraction. The random placement of objects in the luggage increases the randomness of the imaging angle. In extreme cases, both humans and computers have difficulty in distinguishing the prohibited items in compressed and distorted images. Figure 1 shows X-ray imaging of the same object at both vertical and horizontal viewing angles. Some prohibited items made of metal material are reflected as blue lines under the X-ray imaging irradiated at a parallel angle to them. In this case, it is very unfavorable for object detection.

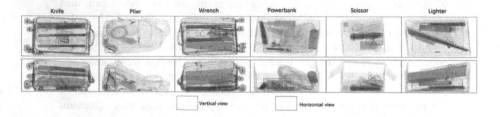

Fig. 1. X-ray imaging effects of different viewing angles.

The richness and variety of object types and shapes can be addressed by enhancing training datasets, while powerful feature extraction networks can deal with the object occlusion problem [15]. In contrast, it is difficult to achieve object detection in X-ray images under extreme imaging viewing angles through computer vision technology [6]. As shows in Fig. 1, the prohibited items in X-ray images can be displayed more completely and clearly through imaging from another auxiliary perspective, which motivates us to carry out research on intelligent analysis of multi-view X-ray security inspection images.

Multi-view object detection is not a new research direction. In the field of autonomous driving, we can integrate LIDAR point cloud and RGB images for better object detection or semantic segmentation [10]. For pedestrian recognition, Multi-view imaging can get rid of the occlusion phenomenon without doubt, and improve the detection accuracy through information complementation [9]. For the intelligent analysis of X-ray images, the research on multi-view prohibited items detection has not been fully carried out. One of the most important reasons is that there is currently no public multi-view X-ray security inspection image benchmark that meets the requirements of deep learning training, which motivates our research.

In this paper, we have constructed the first dual-view X-ray security inspection benchmark, named Dualray, which contains 4371 pairs of images with 6 categories of prohibited items. A security inspection device equipped with horizontal and vertical dual-view imaging modes is used to collect images. We have annotated the category and location (Bounding box) of the prohibited item in each pair of images. We believe that such dataset can improve the research on prohibited items detection in multi-view X-ray images. In addition, a dual-view feature fusion and object detection framework based on YOLOv4 backbone [8] is proposed, which is suitable to deal with Dualray datasets. The model adopts a dual-stream channel, in which the secondary channel is used for feature enhancement in the primary channel based on attention mechanism. The main contributions of this paper are summarized as follows:

- The first dual-view X-ray security inspection benchmark involving six categories of prohibited items is constructed and published.
- A dual-view object detection network for X-ray image analysis is proposed, where attention mechanism is applied for feature filtering to ensure effective feature alignment and information enhancement.
- Numerous experiments are conducted on Dualray dataset to demonstrate the effectiveness of the proposed approach.

2 Related Work

2.1 X-ray Security Inspection Benchmarks

Deep learning technologies represented by convolutional neural networks [13] rely on rich and diverse data. The intelligent analysis of X-ray security inspection images belongs to the object detection task in computer vision. The deep learning model needs to obtain not only the categories of prohibited items, but also the location information. In recent years, the publication of various security inspection benchmarks has promoted the application of deep learning technology in the intelligent analysis of X-ray security inspection images.

GDXray [1] is a relatively early security inspection image dataset that includes three types of prohibited items (gun, shuriken and razor blade). It is worth noting that the instances in the GDXray dataset are grayscale images, which is different from the imaging modes of the security inspection equipments currently used. Dbf6 and Dbf3 [3] are two relatively similar datasets, where the number in the name indicates the number of categories of prohibited items in X-ray images. The Dbf6 dataset contains 11,627 images, while the Dbf3 dataset contains 7,603 images. These images all contain prohibited items and are annotated by categories and locations in the form of bounding boxes. Liu et al. [15] published a dataset containing 32, 253 X-ray images with 12, 683 images containing prohibited items. In the strict sense, this dataset is not rigorous for the research on the detection of prohibited items in security inspection images, because some categories of items (such as mobile phones, umbrellas, computers, and keys) it contains are not prohibited items. The SIXray dataset [20] is currently the largest X-ray security inspection image dataset. It contains 1,059,231 Xray images, in which 8,929 instances are with prohibited items annotated with bounding boxes. OPIxray [26] and PIDray [25] are both security inspection image datasets in real scenes, and they are mainly used to develop the deep learning models against the effects of occlusion and complex background interference.

Table 1 shows the statistics of public datasets. The currently published datasets are all single-view imaging, which is unfavorable for promoting the intelligent analysis of multi-view security inspection images. In this paper, we publish the Dualray dataset of X-ray security inspection collected from two perspectives, which contains 4371 pairs of images with 6 categories of prohibited items. More information can be referred in Sect. 3.

Table 1. Statistics of X-ray Security Inspection Datasets. C, B, and M represent the classification, bounding box, and mask respectively.

Dataset	Year	Classes	Images		Annotations	Availability
			Total	Prohibited		
GDXray	2015	3	8,150	8,150	C+B	Yes
Dbf6	2017	6	11,627	11,627	C+B	No
Dbf3	2018	3	7,603	7,603	C+B	No
[15]	2019	6	32, 253	12, 683	C+B	No
SIXray	2019	6	1,059,231	8,929	C+B	Yes
OPIXray	2020	5	8,885	8,885	C+B	Yes
PIDray	2021	12	47,677	47,677	C+B+M	Yes
Dualray	2022	6	4,371×2	4,371×2	C+B	Yes

2.2 Prohibited Items Detection in X-ray Images

The intelligent analysis of X-ray security inspection images has attracted enthusiastic research in industry and academia, where the traditional machine learning approaches are widely applied. It is the most common processing method to manually extract X-ray image features based on prior knowledge and imaging characteristics and set up a classifier to complete the target recognition task. Some representative work can be referred in [22] and [19]. Traditional methods are poor in robustness and weak in generalization performance, unable to cope with complex security inspection operating environments. For security inspections that require higher detection accuracy, traditional image processing methods are not suitable.

Deep learning technology based CNN (Convolutional Neural Networks) model has demonstrated strong performance in the intelligent analysis of X-ray security inspection images with its powerful feature expression capabilities, where the research interest can be divided into classification, detection and segmentation. For the research on the classification of prohibited items, the related work focuses more on solving key problems such as small objects, unbalanced samples, and mutual occlusion [19]. From an application point of view, object detection and segmentation are essential to the promotion of intelligent security checking. Popular object detection algorithms YOLO [18], RCNN [2], Faster RCNN [4], R-FCN [11], F-RCNN [24], SSD [16] have been applied in security inspection image analysis tasks. With the in-depth understanding of security inspection issues, the semantic segmentation of prohibited items has gradually attracted attention. Semantic segmentation can obtain the pixel-level classification of X-ray images, and learn the attributes, positions and outlines of prohibited items. Some work can be referred in [5, 7].

Limited by the impact of datasets, there are few studies on intelligent analysis of multi-view X-ray security inspection images. [12] systematically analyze the appearance variations of objects in X-ray images from inspection systems, and proposed a novel multi-view detection approach that combines single-view detection from multiple views and takes advantage of the mutual reinforcement of geometrically consistent hypotheses. [23] developed a CNN-based object detection approach for multi-view X-ray image data, which is based on Faster R-CNN framework with modified pooling layer. However, due to the limitation of datasets, these works do not deal well with feature alignment and information fusion of X-ray images collected from different perspectives.

3   Dualray Dataset

3.1   Data Collection and Annotation

We use a dual-view X-ray security inspection machine for data collection. As shown in Fig. 2, the dual-view X-ray security inspection equipment can emit X-rays from both horizontal and vertical directions at the same time, and form transmission imaging with two mutually perpendicular viewing angles. The built-in program in the security inspection machine can automatically segment the X-ray image and obtain two images at the same time. Six categories of prohibited items (Knife, Plier, Wrench, Scissor, Lighter, Powerbank) with different sizes are taken into consideration. Two images collection ways are carried out. We place the security inspection machine in public places, and with the consent of pedestrians, the prohibited items are placed in their packages for inspection. In addition, some commonly used daily necessaries are prepared for random combination with various prohibited items, and then manually sent into the security inspection equipment.

We invited 10 volunteers for the annotation task of categories and locations of prohibited items. Location annotations are displayed in bounding boxes. The volunteers are divided into 5 groups, and 2 members of each group performed the same annotation work. The annotation result will be retained only when the category annotation results are the same and the location annotations satisfy a predetermined similarity in the same group.

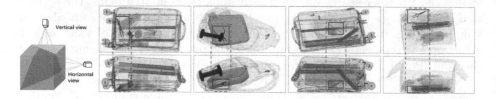

Fig. 2. Prohibited pictures from different views.

3.2   Statistics

In tatal, we collect 4371 pairs of images from two imaging views. The specific statistics are shown in Table 2. All images are stored in *.jpg* format. The size of each image varies depending on the size of the object being inspected. The average vertical view image resolution is 540×340, while The average resolution of the horizontal view image is 600×250. Each image contains only one complete package and each package contains one prohibited item. Figure 3 shows the visual statistics of Dualray dataset. The number of images containing different prohibited item is basically relatively balanced. The number of image samples containing "Lighter" is the least, and the ones with "Wrench" are the most. The proportion of images containing different prohibited item is as follows:

$$\text{Knife : Lighter : Plier : Powerbank : Scissor : Wrench} = 22{:}7{:}13{:}14{:}21{:}23 \quad (1)$$

Table 2. Statistics of Dualray dataset.

Views	Categories						Total
	Knife	Lighter	Plier	Powerbank	Scissor	Wrench	
Vertical	981	310	556	622	898	1004	4371
Horizontal	981	310	556	622	898	1004	4371
Total	1962	620	1112	1244	1796	2008	8742

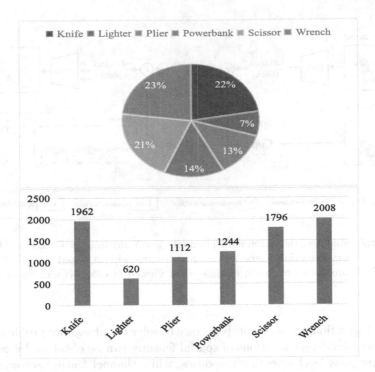

Fig. 3. Statistics of Dualray dataset.

4   Dual-View Fusion and Detection Network

In this section, we propose a dual-view fusion and object detection framework for the Dualray dataset. Figure 4 presents the overall network architecture. The prohibited item detection model in dual-view X-ray security inspection images is shown in the upper left corner, while The lower right corner is the specific feature fusion module. The prohibited items detection network is based on the YOLOv4 backbone [8] and takes dual-stream channels as input. We name the two channels the primary channel (up) and the secondary channel (down) respectively. The construction goal of our network is to ensure that the secondary channel features assist the primary channel to complete the object detection task by designing an appropriate Feature Fusion Module (FFM). Two key issues need to be addressed in FFM:

1) How to implement spatial feature screening? The feature extraction of the secondary channel should enhance the target area and suppress the non-target area. For a certain feature of the secondary channel, it is necessary to calculate the feature contribution distribution of the spatial dimension.

2) How to implement channel feature screening? In CNN feature extraction, different channels extract different visual features. It is very important to realize the effective selection of feature channels for enhancing the targeted features.

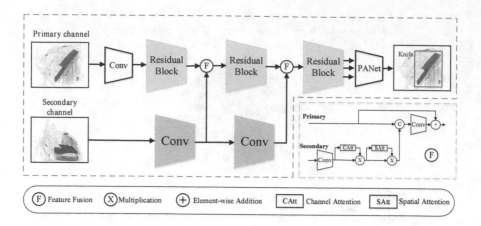

Fig. 4. Prohibited item detection model in dual-view X-ray images. Green box: Feature fusion and object detection framework with two-stream input based on YoloV4 architecture; Pink box: Feature fusion module. Best viewed in color. (Color figure online)

Visual attention is a very suitable choice to solve the above two problems. The importance of different locations of spatial features can be obtained by computing feature pixel-level attention responses, while channel feature screening can be achieved by assigning trainable weights to different feature channels. CBAM attention module consists of spatial attention and channel attention [27], which has the ability to achieve targeted feature screening. YOLOv4 applies CSPDarknet53 as the backbone network, and we take features fusion for the dual-view inputs after the first two residual blocks.

Assuming that x_1 and x_2 are the inputs of the primary channel and the secondary channel respectively, the channel and spatial attention feature extraction will be carried out in the secondary channel in turn. Then the output x'_2 of the secondary channel after attention operation can be obtained as

$$x'_2 = \text{SAtt}\left(\text{CAtt}\left(\text{Conv}\left(x_2\right)\right)\right) \tag{2}$$

where $\text{CAtt}\left(\cdot\right)$ and $\text{SAtt}\left(\cdot\right)$ are the channel and spatial attention functions respectively; $\text{Conv}\left(\cdot\right)$ is the convolution operation.

Then we use concatenation to couple the dual channel features together and perform subsequent convolution operations. In order to ensure the dominant position of the primary channel features and emphasize the auxiliary role of the secondary channel features, the residual operation is implemented, that is

$$x'_1 = \text{Conv}\left(C\left(x_1, x'_2\right)\right) + x_1 \tag{3}$$

where $C\left(x_1, x'_2\right)$ is the concatenation operation.

Figure 5 shows the attention modules, which will be described in detail below.

Channel Attention. Channel attention aims to automatically select the contribution weights of different channels to target features. We transform the input features into vector representations through average pooling and max pooling. Different from the operation in [27], the 1×1 convolution kernels are applied to resize the feature vector dimension. Then *Sigmoid* activation function normalizes the channel attention. The output of channel attention can be obtained as

$$A_c(F) = \sigma\left(f^{1\times1}\left(AvgPool_s(F)\right) + f^{1\times1}\left(MaxPool_s(F)\right)\right)$$
$$F' = F \odot A_c(F) \tag{4}$$

where F' and F are the output and input respectively; $AvgPool_s(\cdot)$ and $MaxPool_s(\cdot)$ are the average pooling and max pooling operations on spatial dimensions; σ denotes the *Sigmoid* function and $f^{1\times1}$ represents the convolution operation with the filter size of 1×1; $\odot$ is the dot multiply operation.

Spatial Attention. Spatial attention calculates the contribution weights of pixel-level features on the same feature channel from another perspective. For the output of channel attention F', the average pooling and max pooling are performed on the channel dimension. Then we use a convolution kernel with size of 7×7 to achieve channel dimensionality reduction. Similarly, *Sigmoid* activation function is applied to normalize the spatial attention. Such that

$$A_p(F) = \sigma\left(f^{7\times7}\left(AvgPool_c(F')\right) + f^{7\times7}\left(MaxPool_c(F')\right)\right)$$
$$F'' = F' \odot A_p(F) \tag{5}$$

where F'' is the final output of channel and spatial attentions; $AvgPool_c(\cdot)$ and $MaxPool_c(\cdot)$ are channel-wise average pooling and max pooling operations; $f^{7\times7}$ represents the convolution operation with the filter size of 7×7.

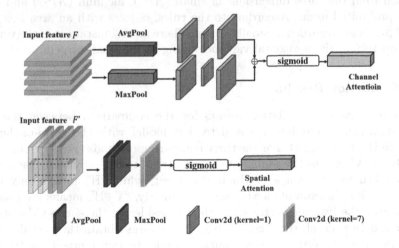

Fig. 5. Channel and spatial attention modules.

5   Experiment Results

In this section, we conduct several simulation experiments. On the one hand, the rationality of Dualray dataset is verified; on the other hand, we demonstrate the effectiveness of the proposed dual-view fusion and object detection method through comparative and ablation experiments.

5.1   Implementation Details

We use YOLOv4 [8] with Pytorch architecture as the base model to implement our model, and the experiments are executed on a computer with a NVIDIA DGX A100 SXM4 40G GPU. The image size is set to 416 × 416. The initial learning rate is 0.001. The stochastic gradient descent algorithm with a weight decay of 0.0005 is applied. The batch size of training phrase is set to 8. Because our model uses two images at the simultaneous detection, we do not use any data augmentation methods to extend or modify the original image in order to ensure the consistency of the images. Unless otherwise specified, all other parameters involved in the experiments are kept consistent.

The famous object detection frameworks, such as Faster R-CNN [21], SSD [17], and YOLOv4 are applied to test our Dualray dataset and take comparison experiments. For fair comparison, all models are trained on the same training set and evaluated on the same test set. We use COCO AP [14] as the evaluate metrics. Different from the VOC metrics, the COCO AP metrics does not use a fixed IoU (Intersection over Union) threshold to calculate the detection precision. It employs 100 IoU thresholds between 0.50 and 0.95. In particular, the AP score is the mean of all 100 IoU thresholds and all six categories of prohibited items detection results. In addition, COCO AP metrics calculate the detection precision from the three dimensions of small (AP_S), medium (AP_M) and large (AP_L) prohibited items. According to the rules, objects with an area less than $32 * 32$ pixels are regarded as small targets. There are 5% instances in the vertical view and 10% in the horizontal view belonging to the small targets.

5.2   Evaluation Results

Table 3 presents the simulation results for the comparison between the proposed dual-view prohibited items detection model with the state-of-the-arts using the Dualray dataset. For the three comparing methods (Faster r-cnn, SSD, YOLOv4), "V" means the simulation results are obtained only using the images from vertical viewing angle in Dualray dataset, while "H" means only using the images from horizontal viewing angle. Similarly, "V+H" means merging the images from the two perspectives together. Considering the single-view prohibited item detection, all three comparison frameworks obtain the best detection precision based on vertical viewing images, while the image quality of the horizontal viewing angle is poor, and the object detection models obtain the worst precision. Our proposed dual-view prohibited item detection model obtains the best detection precision. Notably, our model performs poorly (AP_s) for the detection of prohibited items with small size (Lighter). The number of images with the prohibited item "Lighter" is relatively small. In addition, the size of "Lighter" is too small, which is the main reason for the failure of our model.

Table 3. Comparison results between our proposed object detection model with the state-of-the-arts using Dualray dataset. "V" represents the vertical viewing angle; "H" represents the horizontal viewing angle; Best results in bold.

Method	Image view	AP_{50}	AP_{75}	AP	AP_S	AP_M	AP_L
Faster r-cnn	V	90.2%	66.6%	56.4%	20.0%	51.7%	55.9%
	H	78.2%	48.5%	45.0%	5.1%	38.4%	48.9%
	V+H	82.6%	51.1%	48.0%	12.5%	41.1%	51.0%
SSD	V	91.5%	68.5%	60.2%	33.7%	53.0%	64.6%
	H	90.1%	64.1%	57.5%	34.8%	50.6%	62.4%
	V+H	90.1%	64.4%	57.8%	35.6%	50.9%	62.8%
YoloV4	V	96.9%	77.7%	65.5%	15.0%	**61.9%**	66.7%
	H	91.1%	57.6%	53.7%	**45.1%**	52.3%	55.2%
	V+H	95.4%	71.4%	61.7%	25.5%	57.9%	63.4%
Ours	V+H	**97.2%**	**79.0%**	**65.8%**	5.0%	**61.9%**	**67.0%**

Table 4. Simulation results of various types of prohibited items detection. (score threshold $= 0.5$, $\beta = 1$)

Class	Precision	AP	Recall	F1-Measure
Knife	82.89%	75.56%	66.6%	0.82
Lighter	75.86%	60.12%	48.5%	0.72
Plier	88.66%	82.44%	51.1%	0.88
Powerbank	89.78%	86.11%	68.5%	0.89
Scissor	87.57%	85.69%	64.1%	0.88
Wrench	93.58%	90.81%	64.4%	0.94

Specifically, Table 4 shows the detection results of six types of prohibited items in X-ray images using the proposed dual-view detection model, where it shows the highest detection precision for "Wrench". We think the main reason is that the wrench has relatively obvious features and large size. The precision and recall rates for the detection of "Lighter" are relatively low, which is consistent with the results above.

Figure 6 shows the visualize comparison results, where we can see that the proposed dual-view prohibited item detection framework obtains the most satisfied results, especially for the less friendly visual imaging conditions. The images from the two perspectives achieve information complementarity, which maximizes the enhancement of object features, and in turn leads to satisfactory object detection results.

In the proposed object detection model, we combine the spatial and channel attention mechanisms for targeted selection of secondary channel features. The ablation experiments are carried out to verify the role of attention, and the simulation results are presented in Table 5. After the attention mechanism is removed, the detection precision decreases to varying degrees. Detection of small objects still attracts our attention. Under the premise of no attention, the detection accuracy of "Lighter" is improved. We believe that perhaps the feature filtering of attention further weakens the small target features.

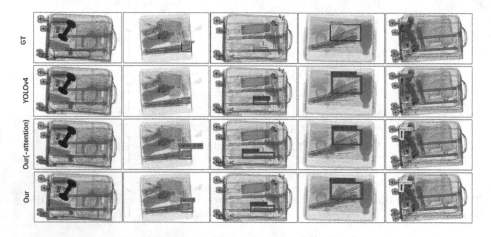

Fig. 6. Visualize comparison results

Table 5. Ablation experiment results

Method	AP_{50}	AP_{75}	AP	AP_S	AP_M	AP_L
-S	69.8%	78.3%	65.3%	20.3%	61.5%	65.0%
-C	96.9%	78.2%	65.1%	20.5%	61.5%	64.8
-SC	96.6%	78.0%	64.9%	20.0%	61.0%	63.9%
Ours	97.2%	79.0%	65.8%	5.0%	61.9%	67.0%

6   Conclusion

This paper focuses on the intelligent analysis of multi-view X-ray security inspection images, and builds and publishes the first dual-view X-ray security inspection benchmark, named Dualray, which consists of 4371 pairs of images with six categories of prohibited items (Knife, Lighter, Plier, Powerbank, Scissor,

Wrench). In addition, we propose a feature fusion and object detection framework for the dual-view prohibited item detection in X-ray images. The detection model applies YOLOv4 as the backbone, except that the dual stream input channel is applied. The spatial and channel attentions are combined to filter the secondary channel features in order to enhance the object features of the primary channel in a targeted manner. Some experiments including the ablation test are carried out to verify the effectiveness of the proposed dual-view prohibited item detection model. In addition, some deficiencies of the model are also revealed. For the detection of objects with small size, our model does not perform well, and the adopted attention mechanism even weakens the small object features. In future work, we will continue to conduct in-depth research on fusion and detection model for multi-view X-ray images.

Acknowledgments. This work was supported in part by Shenzhen Science and Technology Program (No. RCBS20200714114940262), and in part by General Higher Education Project of Guangdong Provincial Education Department (No. 2020ZDZX3082), and in part by Stable Supporting Programme for Universities of Shenzhen (No. 20200825181232001).

References

1. GDXray: the database of X-ray images for nondestructive testing. J. Nondestr. Eval. **34**(4), 1–12 (2015)
2. Akcay, S., Breckon, T.P.: An evaluation of region based object detection strategies within X-ray baggage security imagery. In: 2017 IEEE International Conference on Image Processing (ICIP) (2017)
3. Akcay, S., Kundegorski, M.E., Willcocks, C.G., Breckon, T.P.: Using deep convolutional neural network architectures for object classification and detection within x-ray baggage security imagery. IEEE Trans. Inf. Forensics Secur. **13**, 2203–2215 (2018)
4. An, C.A., Yu, Z.B., Sz, C., Lz, D., Li, Z.A.: Detecting prohibited objects with physical size constraint from cluttered x-ray baggage images (2021)
5. An, J., Zhang, H., Zhu, Y., Yang, J.: Semantic segmentation for prohibited items in baggage inspection. In: International Conference on Intelligent Science and Big Data Engineering (2019)
6. Baqué, P., Fleuret, F., Fua, P.: Deep occlusion reasoning for multi-camera multi-target detection. In: Proceedings of the IEEE International Conference on Computer Vision, pp. 271–279 (2017)
7. Bhowmik, N., Gaus, Y., Akcay, S., Barker, J.W., Breckon, T.P.: On the impact of object and sub-component level segmentation strategies for supervised anomaly detection within x-ray security imagery (2019)
8. Bochkovskiy, A., Wang, C.Y., Liao, H.Y.M.: YOLOv4: optimal speed and accuracy of object detection. arXiv preprint arXiv:2004.10934 (2020)
9. Chavdarova, T., Fleuret, F.: Deep multi-camera people detection. In: 2017 16th IEEE International Conference on Machine Learning and Applications (ICMLA), pp. 848–853. IEEE (2017)
10. Chen, X., Ma, H., Wan, J., Li, B., Xia, T.: Multi-view 3D object detection network for autonomous driving. In: Proceedings of the IEEE conference on Computer Vision and Pattern Recognition, pp. 1907–1915 (2017)

11. Dai, J., Li, Y., He, K., Sun, J.: R-FCN: object detection via region-based fully convolutional networks. Adv. Neural Inf. Process. Syst. **29** (2016)
12. Franzel, T., Schmidt, U., Roth, S.: Object detection in multi-view X-Ray images. In: Pinz, A., Pock, T., Bischof, H., Leberl, F. (eds.) DAGM/OAGM 2012. LNCS, vol. 7476, pp. 144–154. Springer, Heidelberg (2012). https://doi.org/10.1007/978-3-642-32717-9_15
13. Lecun, Y., Bengio, Y., Hinton, G.: Deep learning. Nature **521**(7553), 436 (2015)
14. Lin, T.-Y., et al.: Microsoft COCO: common objects in context. In: Fleet, D., Pajdla, T., Schiele, B., Tuytelaars, T. (eds.) ECCV 2014. LNCS, vol. 8693, pp. 740–755. Springer, Cham (2014). https://doi.org/10.1007/978-3-319-10602-1_48
15. Liu, J., Leng, J., Liu, Y.: Deep convolutional neural network based object detector for x-ray baggage security imagery. In: ICTAI 2019 (2019)
16. Liu, J., Leng, X., Liu, Y.: Deep convolutional neural network based object detector for X-ray baggage security imagery. In: 2019 IEEE 31st International Conference on Tools with Artificial Intelligence (ICTAI), pp. 1757–1761. IEEE (2019)
17. Liu, W., et al.: SSD: single shot MultiBox detector. In: Leibe, B., Matas, J., Sebe, N., Welling, M. (eds.) ECCV 2016. LNCS, vol. 9905, pp. 21–37. Springer, Cham (2016). https://doi.org/10.1007/978-3-319-46448-0_2
18. Liu, Z., Li, J., Yuan, S., Zhang, D.: Detection and recognition of security detection object based on YOLO9000. In: 2018 5th International Conference on Systems and Informatics (ICSAI) (2018)
19. Mery, D.: Computer vision for x-ray testing. Springer International Publishing (2015). https://doi.org/10.1007/978-3-319-20747-6
20. Miao, C., et al.: SIXray: a large-scale security inspection X-ray benchmark for prohibited item discovery in overlapping images. In: 2019 IEEE/CVF Conference on Computer Vision and Pattern Recognition (CVPR) (2019)
21. Ren, S., He, K., Girshick, R., Sun, J.: Faster R-CNN: towards real-time object detection with region proposal networks. IEEE Trans. Pattern Anal. Mach. Intell. **39**(6), 1137–1149 (2017)
22. Rogers, T.W., Jaccard, N., Morton, E.J., Griffin, L.D.: Automated X-ray image analysis for cargo security: critical review and future promise. J. Xray Sci. Technol. **25**(1), 33 (2017)
23. Steitz, J.M.O., Saeedan, F., Roth, S.: Multi-view X-ray R-CNN. Springer, Cham (2018). https://doi.org/10.1007/978-3-030-12939-2_12
24. Sterchi, Y., Hättenschwiler, N., Michel, S., Schwaninger, A.: Relevance of visual inspection strategy and knowledge about everyday objects for X-ray baggage screening. In: 2017 International Carnahan Conference on Security Technology (ICCST), pp. 1–6. IEEE (2017)
25. Tao, R., et al.: Towards real-world X-ray security inspection: a high-quality benchmark and lateral inhibition module for prohibited items detection. In: Proceedings of the IEEE/CVF International Conference on Computer Vision, pp. 10923–10932 (2021)
26. Wei, Y., Tao, R., Wu, Z., Ma, Y., Zhang, L., Liu, X.: Occluded prohibited items detection: an X-ray security inspection benchmark and de-occlusion attention module. CoRR abs/2004.08656 (2020). arxiv:2004.08656
27. Woo, S., Park, J., Lee, J.Y., Kweon, I.S.: CBAM: convolutional block attention module. In: Proceedings of the European Conference on Computer Vision (ECCV), pp. 3–19 (2018)

Author Index

Printed in the United States
by Baker & Taylor Publisher Services